D1756862

IUS COMMUNE CASEBOOKS
FOR THE COMMON LAW OF EURO

CASES, MATERIALS AND TEXT ON JUDICIAL REVIEW OF ADMINISTRATIVE ACTION

This casebook studies the law governing judicial review of administrative action. It examines the foundations and the organisation of judicial review, the types of administrative action, and corresponding kinds of review and access to court. Significant attention is also devoted to the conduct of the court proceedings, the grounds for review, and the standard of review and the remedies available in judicial review cases.

The relevant rules and case law of Germany, England and Wales, France and the Netherlands are analysed and compared. The similarities and differences between the legal systems are highlighted. The impact of the jurisprudence of the European Court of Human Rights is considered, as well as the influence of EU legislative initiatives and the case law of the Court of Justice of the European Union, in the legal systems examined. Furthermore, the system of judicial review of administrative action before the European courts is studied and compared to that of the national legal systems.

During the last decade, the growing influence of EU law on national procedural law has been increasingly recognised. However, the way in which national systems of judicial review address the requirements imposed by EU law differs substantially. The casebook compares the primary sources (legislation, case law etc) of the legal systems covered, and explores their differences and similarities: this examination reveals to what extent a *ius commune* of judicial review of administrative action is developing.

WITHDRAWN

19 FEB 2025

York St John University
3 8025 00639248 7

IUS COMMUNE CASEBOOKS FOR THE COMMON LAW OF EUROPE

Steering Committee

W van Gerven (Chair)†, Professor Emeritus at the University of Leuven and at Maastricht University, former Advocate General at the CJEU
The Rt Hon Lord Bingham of Cornhill†, Senior Law Lord
X Blanc-Jouvan, Professor Emeritus at the University of Paris I
The Rt Hon H Danelius, former Justice of the Supreme Court of Sweden
R Errera, Conseiller d'État honoraire, Paris
T Koopmans†, former Judge of the CJEU
H Kötz, former Director Max Planck Institute for Comparative and International Private Law and Professor at the University of Hamburg
F Jacobs, Professor at King's College London, President of the European Law Institute, former Advocate General at the CJEU
J Schwarze, Professor at the University of Freiburg
M Faure, Professor at Maastricht University and at Erasmus University Rotterdam
B de Witte, Professor at Maastricht University
D Droshout, Research Coordinator, University of Leuven and Maastricht University

Management Committee

W Devroe, University of Leuven and Maastricht University
J van Erp, Maastricht University
P Larouche (Chair), Tilburg University
J Smits, Maastricht University
S Stijns, University of Leuven
J Wouters, University of Leuven

Cases, Materials and Text on Judicial Review of Administrative Action

Edited by
Chris Backes
and
Mariolina Eliantonio

YORK ST. JOHN
LIBRARY & INFORMATION
SERVICES

•HART•
OXFORD • LONDON • NEW YORK • NEW DELHI • SYDNEY

HART PUBLISHING

Bloomsbury Publishing Plc

Kemp House, Chawley Park, Cumnor Hill, Oxford, OX2 9PH, UK

HART PUBLISHING, the Hart/Stag logo, BLOOMSBURY and the Diana logo are trademarks of Bloomsbury Publishing Plc

First published in Great Britain 2019

Copyright © The editors severally 2019

The editors have asserted their right under the Copyright, Designs and Patents Act 1988 to be identified as Authors of this work.

All rights reserved. No part of this publication may be reproduced or transmitted in any form or by any means, electronic or mechanical, including photocopying, recording, or any information storage or retrieval system, without prior permission in writing from the publishers.

While every care has been taken to ensure the accuracy of this work, no responsibility for loss or damage occasioned to any person acting or refraining from action as a result of any statement in it can be accepted by the authors, editors or publishers.

All UK Government legislation and other public sector information used in the work is Crown Copyright ©. All House of Lords and House of Commons information used in the work is Parliamentary Copyright ©. This information is reused under the terms of the Open Government Licence v3.0 (http://www.nationalarchives.gov.uk/doc/open-government-licence/version/3) except where otherwise stated.

All Eur-lex material used in the work is © European Union, http://eur-lex.europa.eu/, 1998–2019.

A catalogue record for this book is available from the British Library.

Library of Congress Cataloging-in-Publication data

Names: Backes, Chr., editor. | Eliantonio, Mariolina, 1978- editor.

Title: Cases, materials and text on judicial review of administrative action / edited by Chris Backes, Mariolina Eliantonio.

Description: Oxford, UK ; Chicago, Illinois : Hart Publishing, 2019. | Series: Ius commune casebooks for the common law of Europe | Includes bibliographical references and index.

Identifiers: LCCN 2018061339 (print) | LCCN 2019000535 (ebook) | ISBN 9781509921485 (EPub) | ISBN 9781509921478 (paperback)

Subjects: LCSH: Judicial review of administrative acts—Europe, Western. | BISAC: LAW / Administrative Law & Regulatory Practice. | LCGFT: Casebooks (Law)

Classification: LCC KJC5647 (ebook) | LCC KJC5647 .C37 2019 (print) | DDC 347.4/012—dc23

LC record available at https://lccn.loc.gov/2018061339

ISBN: PB: 978-1-50992-147-8
ePDF: 978-1-50992-149-2
ePub: 978-1-50992-148-5

Typeset by Compuscript Ltd, Shannon
Printed and bound in Great Britain by CPI Group (UK) Ltd, Croydon CR0 4YY

MIX
Paper from responsible sources
FSC® C013604

To find out more about our authors and books visit www.hartpublishing.co.uk. Here you will find extracts, author information, details of forthcoming events and the option to sign up for our newsletters.

ACKNOWLEDGEMENTS

Preparing this casebook proved to be a rewarding, yet challenging task. Many have contributed to the preparation and publication of this work. This book is the result of real teamwork, although one or more authors are responsible for the separate chapters. All chapters have been discussed at length during various group meetings in Brussels, Hamburg and Maastricht. Besides the editors and chapter authors, Astrid Epiney (University of Fribourg), Martina Künnecke (McClean) (University of Hull), Timothée Paris (Conseil d'État, Paris) and René Seerden (Maastricht University) participated in earlier stages of the project. Both the editors and authors are very grateful for the sage advice of Jean Bernard Auby (SciencesPo, Paris) and Jacques Ziller (University of Pavia). They participated in almost all group meetings and discussions on the correct understanding of the respective legal orders and the comparative conclusions to be drawn and commented on many drafts at various stages of the process. In a certain phase of the project, Gordon Anthony (Queens University Belfast) also provided valuable advice for the team. Dimitri Droshout, the living memory of the casebook-series and Ius Commune Casebook Project research coordinator, made us familiar with the structure and peculiarities of writing a casebook and guided us through the specific method of preparing a casebook.

We owe a special debt of gratitude to Mike Varney who kindly agreed to proofread all chapters of the casebook. Over the years of working on the manuscript, we have been helped by many student assistants, in particular Florence Eicher, Eva Lütkemeyer and Sofie Oosterhuis. They provided us with invaluable editorial support and helped us with the translations of the excerpts.

This work has been made possible thanks to financial support from the European Commission (under a Jean Monnet Project action). Without this support, the various group meetings in Brussels, Hamburg and Maastricht would not have been possible and the launching conference where the results of this project were presented to the public could not have taken place. Diana Schabregs (Maastricht University) managed the financial part of the project perfectly.

Last, but not least many thanks are due to Linda Staniford and her colleagues from Hart Publishing for their tremendous support and patience in dealing with a long and difficult manuscript and making a beautiful book.

CONTENTS

LIST OF CONTRIBUTORS

Chris Backes studied law, political science and Dutch philology in Freiburg, Münster and Nijmegen. In 1995, he became Professor of International and European Environmental Law at Tilburg University and in 1998 Professor of Environmental Law at Utrecht University. From 2007 until 2016 he worked as Professor of Constitutional and Administrative Law at Maastricht University, where he did research in European, comparative and Dutch administrative law. Since 2016 he has been Professor of Environmental and Planning Law at the Utrecht Centre for Water, Oceans and Sustainability Law (UCWOSL).

Emilie Chevalier is an Associate Professor in European and Public law and vice-dean of the Law and Economics Faculty of Limoges. She obtained a PhD from the University of Limoges in 2010, after an LL.M in International, European and Comparative Law from Maastricht University (2004). Her PhD concerns the principle of good administration and European Union law (published by Bruylant-Larcier, 2014). She has extensive teaching experience in the field of European and administrative law and supervised several master theses in this field. Her fields of research are European administrative law, administrative procedural rights, European environmental law and the procedural enforcement of European law at national level.

Mariolina Eliantonio is Professor of European and Comparative Administrative Law and Procedure at Maastricht University. She carries out research on the enforcement of European law before national and European courts. She specifically investigates the concept and implications of the system of shared administration, especially from a judicial protection perspective, and she examines the role of courts in the new modes of governance (such as soft law and co-regulation) and the future of the system of judicial accountability in the European integration process. She teaches courses in European and comparative administrative law.

Franziska Grashof studied European and comparative law at Maastricht University, spent a semester at the Université de Bordeaux, and studied German law at the Universität zu Köln. In her doctoral thesis on the principle of national procedural autonomy, she examined differences in national administrative litigation rules in the European Union. She worked as a teacher of European and comparative administrative law at Maastricht University.

Anika Klafki studied law at Bucerius Law School in Hamburg and the University of Queensland. After her legal clerkship in Hamburg, Istanbul, and Marseille, she wrote her doctoral thesis "Risiko und Recht. Risiken und Katastrophen im Spannungsfeld von Effektivität, demokratischer Legitimation und rechtsstaatlichen Grundsätzen am Beispiel von Pandemien" about risk regulation at the chair of public law, administrative sciences and comparative law of Hermann Pünder at Bucerius Law School. Since 2016 she has been working on her habilitation project concerning participation of non-state actors in administrative planning procedures.

Thomas Perroud first read economics, history and political sciences at HEC and SciencesPo before studying law at Panthéon-Sorbonne University. He obtained a PhD in public law from this University as well as an MPhil and a PhD from the University of Warwick. He has been professor of public law since 2014. He was appointed at Aix Marseille University and is now professor at Panthéon-Assas University.

Hermann Pünder holds the chair of Public Law, Science of Public Administration and Comparative Law at Bucerius Law School in Hamburg. After studies of law and political sciences at the Universities of Freiburg, Geneva and Münster (doctorate and Habilitation), at the Faculté Internationale de Droit Comparé in Strasbourg, and at the University of Iowa (LL.M), Pünder worked in Münster as chief executive officer of the Freiherr-vom-Stein-Institut and of the Centre of External Economic Law. He lectured at the Chinese Academy of Social Sciences (2005, 2006), was a fellow at the University of Oxford (2007, 2009), guest professor at the University Catolica Argentina (2009), research professor at Stanford Law School (2012) and taught at Bilgi University in Istanbul (2013, 2016).

Mike Varney studied Law at the University of Hull, obtaining an LL.B with first class Honours in 2000 and subsequently a PhD degree in 2005. In 2003 he was appointed to a lectureship in law at the University of Hull and has taught there ever since, becoming a Senior Lecturer in 2015. Mike undertakes research in constitutional, administrative and EU law and has also published on issues relating to data protection, freedom of information and company law.

Rob Widdershoven studied law at Utrecht University. In 1997 he became Professor of European Administrative Law at Utrecht University. His research focuses on the influence of European law on national administrative (procedural) law, law enforcement and state liability. He is a member of the Montaigne Institute for Rule of Law and Administration of Justice. In 2013 he was appointed as the first Advocate General of Administrative Law of the Netherlands. In this capacity he is a part-time member of the Dutch Council of State, the Central Appellate Court and the High Administrative Court of Trade and Industry.

TABLE OF CASE LAW

EUROPEAN COURT OF HUMAN RIGHTS

COURT OF JUSTICE OF THE EUROPEAN UNION

ENGLAND AND WALES

FRANCE

GERMANY

NETHERLANDS

TABLE OF LEGISLATION

UNITED NATIONS

COUNCIL OF EUROPE

EUROPEAN UNION

GERMANY

FRANCE

NETHERLANDS

ENGLAND AND WALES

TABLE OF TERMINOLOGY

FRANCE

Term	Translation
Abrogation	Withdrawal
Acte réglementaire	Regulatory act
Annulation pour excès de pouvoir	Annulment
Appel	Appeal on points of fact and law
Arrêté	Administrative decision adopted by either a minister or a local administrative authority
Assemblée du contentieux	Assembly (in the Council of State, top panel, pronouncing on the most important cases)
Assemblée nationale	National assembly
Autorisation de plaider	Permission to plead
Autorité de la concurrence	Competition authority
Autorité de régulation des activités ferroviaires et routières	Rail and road activities authority
Autorité des marchés financiers	Financial markets authority
Autorité préfectorale	Prefect
Avocat au Conseil d'État et à la Cour de cassation	Attorney to the Council of State and to the Court of Cassation
Caractère d'un règlement	Regulatory nature
Cassation	Appeal on points of law
Circulaire	Circular
Code de justice administrative	Code of Administrative Justice
Code de la construction et de l'habitation	Construction and Housing Code
Code de l'entrée et du séjour des étrangers et du droit d'asile (CESEDA)	Code of Entry and Residence of Foreigners and of Asylum Law
Code de l'urbanisme	Planning Code
Code des relations entre le public et l'administration	Code of Relations between Administration and Members of the Public

Term	Translation
Code des tribunaux administratifs et des cours administratives d'appel	Code of the Administrative Courts of First Instance and the Administrative Courts of Appeal
Code du commerce	Commercial Code
Code du sport	Sports Code
Code général des collectivités territoriales	General Code of Local and Regional Authorities
Code monétaire et financier	Monetary and Financial Code
Code pénal	Criminal Code
Collectivité territoriale	Local or regional authority
Commission d'accès aux documents administratifs	Commission for access to administrative documents
Commission de régulation de l'énergie	Energy authority
Communauté urbaine	Urban community
Conseil d'État	Council of State
Conseil supérieur de la magistrature	Supreme Judicial Council
Contentieux de l'annulation	Annulment litigation
Contentieux de pleine juridiction	Full jurisdiction litigation
Contrat administratif	Administrative law contract
Contrôle bilan côuts-avantages	Cost-benefit analysis
Contrôle maximum	Intense scrutiny
Contrôle minimum	Limited review
Cour de cassation	Court of Cassation
Cour administrative d'appel	Administrative Court of Appeal
Cour Nationale du Droit d'Asile	National Court on Asylum Law
Décision individuelle	Decision directed towards one or several determined addressees
Décision particulière/décision d'espèce	Decision addressed to undetermined addressees regulating a concrete case
Décision préalable	Preliminary binding decision
Décision réglementaire	Regulatory decision
Déclaration des droits de l'homme et du citoyen	Declaration of the Rights of Man and of the Citizen

Term	Translation
Décret	Decree
Dénaturation des faits	Error in the assessment of the facts
Département	Department
Détournement de pouvoir	Misuse of power
Domaine privé	Public property subject to private law
Domaine public	Public property subject to public law
Droit administratif	Administrative law
Ecole Nationale d'Administration	National School of Administration
Égalité	Equality
Égalité devant les charges publiques	Equality in suffering public burdens
Emprise irrégulière	Violation of property right
Erreur dans la qualification juridique des faits	Error in the legal assessment of facts
Erreur de droit	Error of law
Erreur de fait	Error of fact
Erreur manifeste d'appréciation	Manifest error of assessment
Établissement public	Public corporation
Exception d'illégalité	Indirect review
Excès de pouvoir	Illegality (literally: misuse of powers)
Faute lourde	Serious fault
Faute simple	Fault
Formalités accessoires	Non-essential formalities
Formalités substantielles	Essential formalities
Garde des sceaux	Minister of Justice
Groupement d'intérêt public	Public–private joint venture
Incompétence	Lack of competence
Inexactitude matérielle des faits	Error in the establishment of facts
Intérêt à agir	Interest in taking legal action/standing
Juge de l'excès de pouvoir	Judge entrusted with legality control
Juge des référés	Interim relief judge
Juge du fond	Court hearing the substance of the case
Juridiction de plein contentieux	Full jurisdiction control

Term	Translation
Juridiction judiciaire	Ordinary court
Illégalité externe	Lack of competence, or formal and procedural defects (literally: external illegality)
Illégalité interne	Violation of the law or misuse of power (literally: internal illegality)
Ligne directrice	Guideline
Loi du 24 mai 1872 relative au Tribunal des conflits	Act on the Court of Jurisdictional Disputes
Loi organique n° 2011-333 du 29 mars 2011 relative au Défenseur des droits	Organic law concerning the Defender of Rights
Mémoire	Written pleading
Motivation	Reasons giving
Moyens d'ordre public	Grounds of public order
Ordonnance	Ordinance
Ordre judiciaire	Ordinary branch of courts
Pouvoir d'appréciation	Discretion of the judge
Pouvoir réglementaire autonome	Autonomous governmental regulatory power
Pouvoir réglementaire d'application des lois	Law-implementing governmental regulatory power
Prérogatives de puissance publique	Prerogatives of public power
Président du Sénat	President of the Senate
Procédure contradictoire	Adversarial proceedings
Qualification juridique des faits	Legal assessment of the facts
Qualité pour agir	Legal capacity to take legal action/standing
Rapporteur	Judge-rapporteur
Rapporteur public	Public rapporteur (formerly: Commissaire du gouvernement)
Recours administratifs préalables obligatoires	Mandatory intra-administrative objection procedure
Recours de pleine juridiction	Full jurisdiction remedy

Term	Translation
Recours gracieux/hiérarchique	Intra-administrative objection procedure addressed to the decision-maker/to a superior authority
Recours pour excès de pouvoir	Action for annulment
Référé-liberté	Fundamental rights interim remedy
Référé-mesure utile	Useful measure interim remedy
Référé suspension	Suspension
Réglementation	Regulation
Requête introductive d'instance	Application commencing legal proceedings
Section du contentieux	Judicial Division of the Council of State
Service public	Public service
Services publics administratifs	Administrative public services
Services publics industriels et commerciaux	Industrial and commercial public services
Silence vaut acceptation	Administrative silence amounts to acceptance of a request
Silence vaut rejet	Administrative silence amounts to rejection of a request
Tribunal administratif	Administrative Court of First Instance
Tribunal des conflits	Court of Jurisdictional Disputes
Vice de forme ou de procédure	Procedural or formal irregularity
Violation de la loi	Violation of the law

GERMANY

Term	Translation
Abgabeordnung	Fiscal Code
Adressatenbezogene Allgemeinverfügung	General administrative act directed at a determined or determinable group of people
Adressatentheorie	Theory that addressees of an onerous administrative act are prima facie attributed with *locus standi*
Allgemein anerkannte Beurteilungsmaßstäbe	Generally accepted evaluation standards
(Allgemeine) Leistungsklage	(General) action for performance

Term	Translation
Allgemeine Rechtsprinzipien	General principles of law
Allgemeinverfügung	General administrative act
Altruistische Verbandsklage	General interest collective action
Amtshaftung	Public liability
Amtspflichtverletzung	Breach of official duties
Anfechtungsklage	Action for annulment of an administrative act
Angemessenheit	Proportionality *stricto sensu*
Antrag	Application
Auffangstreitwert	Residual value in the claim
Aufhebung	Annulment
Aufopferung	Sacrificial encroachment
Aufopferungsanspruch	Claim for compensation for sacrificial encroachment
Auslegung	Legal interpretation
Außenwirkung	External legal consequences
Baugenehmigung	Building permit
Baugesetzbuch	Federal Building Code
Bauordnungsrecht	Building and construction law
Beauftragter für den Haushalt	Budget officer
Bebauugsplan	Development plan
Behörde	Administrative authority
Beliehene	Private bodies vested with public authority
Benutzungsregelnde Allgemeinverfügungen	General administrative act relating to the use of a public good
Berichterstatter	Judge-rapporteur
Berufung	Appeal on grounds of fact and law
Beschluss	Order
Beschwerde	Complaint
Besonderes Gewaltverhältnis	Special relationship of subordination
Bestechlichkeit	Corruption
Beteiligtenfähigkeit/ Beteiligungsfähigkeit	Capacity to take part in the proceedings
Beurteilungsspielraum	Margin of interpretation

Term	Translation
Bundesagentur für Arbeit	Federal Labour Office
Bundesarbeitsgericht	Federal Labour Court
Bundesfinanzhof	Federal Fiscal Court
Bundesgerichtshof	Federal Court of Justice
Bundesimmissionsschutzgesetz	Federal Emission Control Act
Bundeskriminalamtgesetz	Federal Criminal Police Office Act
Bundessozialgericht	Federal Social Court
Bundesverfassungsgerichtsgesetz	Federal Constitutional Court Act
Bundesversorgungsgesetz	Federal Law on Pensions
Bundesverwaltungsgericht	Federal Administrative Court
Bürgerbeaugtragte	Ombudsmen
Datenschutzbeauftragte	Ombudsman for data protection
Echte Rückwirkung	Real retroactivity
Egoistische Verbandsklage	Group interest collective action
Einführungsgesetz zum Gerichtsverfassungsgesetz	Introductory Act to the Court Constitution Act
Einleitung zum preußischen Allgemeinen Landrecht	Introduction to the Prussian General Land Law
Einstweilige Verfügung	Interim injunction
Einzelfall	Individual case
Enteignender Eingriff	Expropriatory encroachment
Enteignung	Expropriation
Entscheidung	Decision
Erforderlichkeit	Necessity
Ermessen	Discretion
Ermessensdefizit	Unreasonable way of exercising discretion
Ermessensfehler	Error in exercising discretion
Ermessensfehlerfreie Entscheidung	Discretionary decision
Ermessensfehlgebrauch	Abuse of discretion
Ermessensnichtgebrauch	Failure to use discretion
Ermessensreduzierung auf Null	Discretion reduced to zero
Ermessensüberschreitung	Excess of discretion

Term	Translation
Feststellungsinteresse	Interest in a declaratory judgment
Feststellungsklage	Action for declaration
Finanzgerichte	Fiscal Courts
Finanzgerichtsordnung	Fiscal Court Procedure Act
Formelle Rechtswidrigkeit	Unlawfulness in terms of competence, procedure or form
Gebietskörperschaften	Territorial public bodies
Geeignetheit	Suitability
Gemeinde	Municipality
Gemeinsamer Senat der obersten Gerichtshöfe der Bundes	Joint Senate of the Highest Courts of the Federation
Genehmigungsfiktion	Deemed approval
Gerichtsbescheid	Summary judgment
Gerichtskostengesetz	Court Fees Act
Gerichtsverfassungsgesetz	Court Constitution Act
Geschäftsfähigkeit (§ 104 BGB)	Legal capacity
Gesetzeskraft	Force of law
Gesetzlicher Richter	Judge foreseen by law
Gestaltungsklage	Action for modification of a right or legal relationship
Gleichstellungsbeauftragter	Ombudsperson for gender equality
Glaubhaftmachung	Prima facie evidence
Großer Senat	Grand Senate
Grundgesetz	Basic Law
Grundrechtsschutz durch Verfahren	Protection of fundamental rights through procedure
Grundsatz der Mündlichkeit	Principle of oral proceedings
Grundsatz der Unmittelbarkeit	Principle of direct evidence
Grundsatz der völkerrechtskonformen Auslegung	Legal interpretation in accordance with international law
Handlungsformenlehre	Doctrine of administrative actions
Höchstgericht	Highest Court
Horizontale Drittwirkung	Horizontal direct effect

Term	Translation
Individualrechtsschutz	Judicial protection of individual rights
Inhalt, Zweck und Ausmaß	Content, purpose and extent
Inzidentkontrolle	Incidental control
Klage	Action
Klagebefugnis	*Locus standi*
Körperschaften	Public bodies
Land/Länder	State/states
Landesgesetz	State statute
Landesrecht	State law
Landessozialgerichte	Higher Social Courts
Landesverwaltungsverfahrensgesetz	Administrative Procedure Act of a state
Landwirtschaftskammer	Chamber of Agriculture
Leistung	Performance
Letzte Tatsacheninstanz	Final instance ruling on facts
Materielle Rechtswidrigkeit	Unlawfulness in terms of substance
Nachfrist	Period of grace
Negative Konkurrentenklage	Action against a benefit granted to a competitor
Nichtigkeit	Voidness *ab initio*
Nichtigkeitsklage	Declaration of voidness
Normenkontrollantrag	Action to review by-laws and executive regulations
Normenkontrollverfahren	Procedure to review by-laws and executive regulations
Normkonkretisierende Verwaltungsvorschriften	Administrative directions concretising legal provisions
Oberverwaltungsgericht	Higher Administrative Court
Öffentliche Sicherheit und Ordnung	Public safety and order
Ordentliche Gerichte	Ordinary courts of law
Ordentliche Gerichtsbarkeit	Ordinary court branch (civil and criminal courts)

Term	Translation
Ordnungsgeld	Coercive fine
Öffentlich-rechtlicher Vertrag	Public law contract
Paulskirchenverfassung	Constitution of St Paul's Church
Preußisches Oberverwaltungsgericht	Prussian Higher Administrative Court
Prozessfähigkeit (§ 62 VwGO)	Capacity to effect procedural acts
Realakt	Factual action
Rechtsbeugung	Perverting the course of justice for the benefit or detriment of one party
Rechtsfähigkeit (§1 BGB)	Legal personality
Rechtsfortbildung	Judicial law-making
Rechtsreflex	Accidental effect on the right of a third party
Rechtsschutzauftrag	Legal protection mandate
Rechtsperson, juristische Person	Legal person
Rechtsstaatsprinzip	Rule of law principle
Rechtsträger	Legal entity
Rechtsverordnung	Executive regulation
Regelung	Regulation
Restitutionsklage	Action for retrial of the case
Revision	Appeal on points of law
Revisionsverfahren	Appeal procedure on points of law
Rücknahme	Revocation
Rundfunkanstalten	Public broadcasting corporations
Sachbezogene Allgemeinverfügung	General administrative act relating to a public good
Sachverständiger	Expert
Sachverständiger Zeuge	Expert witness
Satzung	By-law
Schlichtes Verwaltungshandeln	Factual action
Schutznorm	Norm aiming to protect rights of individuals
Schutznormerfordernis	Necessity of a norm aiming to protect rights of individuals
Schutznormtheorie	Protection of rights doctrine

Term	Translation
Sofortige Beschwerde	Immediate complaint
Sofortige Vollziehung	Immediate execution
Sonderopfer	Special sacrifice
Sozialgerichte	Social courts
Sozialgerichtsgesetz	Social Courts Act
Streitwert	Value of the dispute
Subjektives öffentliches Recht	Subjective public right
Substanzverletzung	Violation of the essence of a right
Teleologische Reduktion	Teleological reduction
Tun, Dulden, Unterlassen	Action, tolerance or omission
Umweltrechtsbehelfsgesetz	Environmental Remedies Act
Unbestimmte Rechtsbegriffe	Undefined legal terms
Unechte Rückwirkung	Apparent retroactivity
Untersuchungsgrundsatz	Inquisitorial principle
Unmittelbare Horizontalwirkung	Direct horizontal effect between individuals
Unterlassungsklage	Action for omission
Untersuchungsgrundsatz	Inquisitorial principle
Urkundsbeamter der Geschäftsstelle	Clerk of the registry
Vergleich	Settlement
Verhältnismäßigkeitsgrundsatz	Proportionality principle
Verpflichtungsklage	Action seeking the issuance of an administrative act
Versäumnisurteil	Judgment by default
Verwaltungsakt	Administrative act
Verwaltungsgericht	Administrative Court of First Instance
Verwaltungsgerichtshof	Higher Administrative Court
Verwaltungsgerichtsordnung	Administrative Court Procedure Act
Verwaltungsverfahrensgesetz	Administrative Procedure Act
Verwaltungsvorschrift	Administrative direction
Verwirkung	Pre-effect
Vorsitzender (Richter)	Presiding judge
Weisung	Instruction

Term	Translation
Widerruf	Withdrawal
Widerspruch	Intra-administrative objection
Widerspruchsbescheid	Decision on the objection
Widerspruchsverfahren	Intra-administrative objection procedure
Zivilprozessordnung	Code of Civil Procedure

THE NETHERLANDS

Term	Translation
Aanpassingswetgeving	Adaptation laws
Aanvraag	Request
Administratief beroep	Appeal to a higher administrative authority
Advocaat Generaal	Advocate General
Afdeling bestuursrechtspraak Raad van State	Judicial Division of the Council of State
Afdeling geschillen van Bestuur Raad van State	Administrative Disputes Division of the Council of State
Afdeling rechtspraak Raad van State	Jurisdiction Division of the Council of State
Algemene belangen	General interests
Algemene maatregel van bestuur	Executive Regulation
Algemeen verbindend voorschrift (AVV)	General binding regulation
Algemene Wet Bestuursrecht	General Administrative Law Act
Behoorlijkheid	Properness
Beleidsovereenkomst	Policy contract
Beleidsregel	Policy rule
Beleidsruimte	Discretion
Bemiddeling	Mediation
Beoordelingsruimte	Margin of interpretation
Beroep	Judicial review
Beroep instellen bij een administratieve rechter	To file a claim for judicial review
Beschikking	Single-case decision

Term	Translation
Beslissing	Decision
Besluit	Decision as defined in Article 1:3 AWB
Besluit van algemene strekking (BAS)	Decision of general scope
Bestuursrechter	Administrative judge
Bevoegdheden-overeenkomst	Competence contract
Bevoegdheid	Competence
Bevoegdheidsregeling bestuursrechtspraak	Competence Regulation Administrative Jurisdiction
Bezwaar	Objection
Burgemeester en Wethouders	Mayor and Aldermen
Centrale Raad van Beroep	Central Appellate Court
Collectieve belangen	Collective interests
College van Beroep voor het Bedrijfsleven	High Administrative Court for Trade and Industry
Commissie Rechtseenheid	Committee for Legal Unity
Commissie voor de verzoekschriften	Committee of Petitions
Concretiserende BAS	Concretising decision of general scope
Connexiteitseis	Connectivity requirement
Crisis- en Herstelwet	Crisis and Recovery Act
Exceptieve toetsing	Incidental review
Feitelijke handeling	Factual action
Gedeputeerde Staten	Provincial Executive
Gemeenteraad	Municipal Council
Gerechtshoven	Ordinary courts of appeal
Grondwet	Constitution
Grote Kamer	Grand Chamber
Hoge Raad	Supreme Court
Interventie	Intervention
Klacht	Complaint
Nieuwe zaaksbehandeling	New case approach
Onbehoorlijkheid	Improperness
Procesbelang	Procedural interest

Term	Translation
Publiekrechtelijke rechtshandelingen	Action governed by public law
Raad van State	Council of State
Rechtbank, sector bestuursrecht	Administrative division of the district court
Rechter-plaatsvervanger	Alternate-judge
Rechtsgevolgen	Legal consequences
Regeling rechtstreeks beroep	Regulation on direct appeal
Relativiteitsvereiste	Relativity requirement
Richtlijn	Guidance
Stichting Advisering Bestuursrechtspraak	Foundation of Independent Court Experts in Environmental and Planning Law
Hoge Raad	Supreme Court
Tussenuitspraak	Interlocutory judgment
Tweede Kamer van de Staten Generaal	Second Chamber of the Parliament
Uitgebreid onderzoek	Thorough investigation
Uniforme openbare voorbereidingsprocedure	Uniform public preparatory procedure
Voorzieningenrechter	Judge in interlocutory proceedings/interim relief judge
Wet algemene bepalingen omgevingsrecht	General Provisions of Environmental Law Act
Wetboek burgerlijke rechtsvordering	Civil Procedure Code
Wet Nationale Ombudsman	National Ombudsman Act
Wet rechtspositie rechterlijke ambtenaren	Act on the Legal Status of Judicial Civil Servants
Wet op de Raad van State	Act on the Council of State
Wet op de Rechterlijke Organisatie	Organisation of the Courts Act

INTRODUCTION

Chris Backes and Mariolina Eliantonio

1. AIMS AND APPROACH OF THE CASEBOOK

Administrative law, and within this branch of law, the law concerning judicial review of administrative action, has traditionally (and certainly until the second half of the twentieth century) been regarded as a product of the national history and tradition of a state, and hence as an area in which there was little room for convergence.[1]

It is therefore not surprising that, apart from notable early exceptions,[2] there are not very many comprehensive comparative works on administrative law[3] (and judicial review in particular)[4] and the question whether a *ius commune* of administrative law or of judicial review is developing has not been intensively dealt with in legal scholarship.[5]

[1] In the context of a study on the influence of French administrative law on the development of German law, Scheuner wrote in 1963 that administrative law belongs to those areas of law 'in which the national characteristics of the people and the State are revealed most starkly', see U Scheuner, 'Der Einfluss des französischen Verwaltungsrecht auf die deutsche Rechtsentwicklung' (1963) Die Öffentliche Verwaltung 714. See, however, the view of Otto Meyer, who is considered the father of modern German administrative law, who, albeit on a very general level, stated that 'le droit administratif ... a pour base certains principes généraux qui sont partout les memes' (administrative law is based on principles which are everywhere the same): O Mayer, *Le droit administratif allemand* (Paris, Giard et Brière, 1905) 3.

[2] L von Stein, *Handbuch der Verwaltungslehre und des Verwaltungsrechts mit Vergleichung von Frankreich, England und Deutschland* (Stuttgart, Cotta, 1870); FJ Goodnow, *Comparative Administrative Law. An Analysis of the Administrative Systems National and Local of the United States, England, France and Germany* (New York, Knickerbocker, 1903). See more recently HB Jacobini, *An Introduction to Comparative Administrative Law* (New York, Oceana Publications, 1991); A Piras (ed), *Administrative Law: The Problem of Justice* (Milan, Giuffré, 1991); MD Alberti, *Diritto amministrativo comparato. Trasformazioni dei sistemi amministrativi in Francia, Gran Bretagna, Stati Uniti, Italia*, Bologna, il Mulino, 1992. Each volume concentrates on the administrative law of two or three legal systems.

[3] There is, however, a large amount of comparative literature on specific aspects of administrative law or judicial review. For example: M Ruffert (ed), *The Transformation of Administrative Law in Europe* (Munich, Sellier, 2006); C Forsyth, M Elliot, S Jhaveri, M Ramsden and A Scully-Hill (eds), *Effective Judicial Protection* (Oxford, Oxford University Press, 2010); S Rose-Ackerman and P Lindseth (eds), *Comparative Administrative Law*, 2nd edn (Cheltenham, Edward Elgar, 2017); JS Bell, 'Comparative Administrative Law' in M Reimann and R Zimmermann (eds), *The Oxford Handbook of Comparative Law* (Oxford, Oxford University Press, 2006); J-B Auby and T Perroud, *Droit comparé de la procédure administrative [Comparative Law of Administrative Procedure]* (Brussels, Bruylant, 2016); S Ranchordás and B de Waard (eds), *The Judge and the Proportionate Use of Discretion: A Comparative Study* (Abingdon, Routledge, 2016).

[4] For an exception, see JM Auby and M Fromont, *Les recours contre les actes administratifs dans les pays de la Communauté économique européenne* (Paris, Dalloz, 1971).

[5] See, however, the extensive work of J Schwarze, *European Administrative Law*, revised 1st edn (London, Sweet & Maxwell, 2006); J Schwarze, *Administrative Law under European Influence: On the Convergence of the Administrative Laws of the EU Member States* (Baden Baden, Nomos, 1996). See also M Eliantonio, *Europeanisation of Administrative Justice? The Influence of the ECJ's Case Law in Italy, Germany and England* (Groningen, Europa Law Publishing, 2008); JH Jans, S Prechal and RJGM Widdershoven (eds), *Europeanisation of Public Law*, 2nd edn (Groningen, Europa Law Publishing, 2015). T von Danwitz, *Europäisches*

Often, as has been stated also with reference to many comparative works in private law, the exercise is more a 'juxtaposition' than a comparison.[6] As with many endeavours before, the only recent work which describes the administrative law of some legal orders in a rather comprehensive way[7] is organised through country reports and adds to the national reports only relatively limited comparative remarks.[8]

Cases, Materials and Text on Judicial Review of Administrative Action aims to partially fill this gap by applying a different approach.[9] By adopting a functional comparative approach and presenting and comparing cases and other materials, its aim is to examine different areas of judicial review in various legal systems, in order to identify commonalities and differences amongst the systems, to analyse the impact of EU law on judicial review, to explore whether there are tendencies of convergence, and to discuss whether and to what extent a *ius commune* might be developing in this field. This functional method makes it possible to search for similarities and differences in dealing with comparable situations.

Furthermore, the case-based and therefore bottom-up approach which is chosen in this casebook makes it possible to uncover common general principles that are already present in the living law, rather than a top-down approach followed by other complementary projects, which endeavour to formulate (new) rules and model principles.

The casebook comprises case law and other materials (legislative materials, international materials and excerpts from books or articles, as appropriate) on the EU legal system, as well as the legal systems of France, Germany, the Netherlands, and England and Wales. Those materials relate, insofar as possible, to similar problems or situations in the various legal systems under study. The materials are accompanied by short introductory and explanatory notes to place them into context. For all the important elements of judicial review, the case law and relevant materials are presented as excerpts and subsequently compared. The excerpts have been chosen on the basis of three criteria: either because they explain the traditional way in which a legal system approaches a certain issue of judicial review; because they explain patterns of deviations from the standard or traditional approach; or because they explain how the standard or traditional approach has been modified under the influence of the EU legal system. At the end of each section,

Verwaltungsrecht (Berlin, Springer, 2008) provides an overview of the administrative law of six EU countries, followed by a comparative section on the implications of the different traditions and convergences for the development of EU administrative law. Probably the first to study the comparative method used by the CJEU and the development of a convergence process is J Rivero, 'Vers un droit commun européen: nouvelles perspectives en droit administratif' in M Cappelletti (ed), *Nouvelles perspectives du droit commun de l'Europe* (Berlin, De Gruyter, 1978) 389.

[6] G della Cananea, 'The "Common Core" of Administrative Laws in Europe: A Research Agenda' (30 January 2018), available at https://ssrn.com/abstract=3169163, 12 ff.

[7] RJGH Seerden, *Comparative Administrative Law: Administrative Law of the European Union, its Member States and the United States*, 4th edn (Antwerp, Intersentia, 2018).

[8] ibid, 417–38.

[9] See also the call for a new 'Research Agenda' by della Cananea, who argues that 'what is required is an approach to the study of public law that goes beyond the more "static" comparison between the principles and institutions of two or more legal systems and, of course, beyond what is suggested by the law in the books. What is needed is an empirical understanding of how those principles and institutions live in and shape the legal reality of European legal systems and an adequate understanding of the interplay between the various legal formants': della Cananea (n 6 above) 17–18.

a comparative overview ties together the materials and puts the emphasis, where possible, on the influence of EU law (or the ECHR) on the legal systems examined and any convergence trends identified.

The casebook focuses on the concepts, principles and functioning of the law in practice as opposed to mere 'rules', and thus attempts to examine the various legal national laws in their application in practice. The casebook demonstrates how questions and problems in administrative law can be solved in similar or different ways, as well as how and to what extent the national systems of judicial review have adapted to the European requirements, and to what extent they have converged under the European influence. The casebook thus shows the actual application of the national rules and actual influence of European law in real cases, not merely from a theoretical point of view. This makes it easier to position the concepts and instruments of the different legal orders, and to understand which solutions were chosen in a given legal order, and why. The casebook may also, perhaps, ultimately contribute to a more uniform interpretation and application of European law by inspiring courts and legislators about how to implement and apply EU law requirements.

2. LIKELY USERS OF THE CASEBOOK

This Ius Commune Casebook can be used for teaching purposes in many countries. Although it directly deals with five legal orders (the EU, Germany, France, England and Wales, and the Netherlands), it can be used in comparative administrative law courses throughout Europe. By comparing the legal concepts and legal cultures of four EU Member States[10] and the EU, students get a clear picture of what questions are to be answered when dealing with judicial review in administrative law cases, and of the variety of concepts and answers to these questions.

The Ius Commune Casebooks are suitable not only for educational, but also for research and reference purposes. They may furthermore be useful for members of the judiciary, particularly in the EU courts. This casebook also hopes to serve as a source of inspiration for attorneys at law, civil servants or in-house legal counsellors who wish to study how other national legal systems or the EU legal order respond to questions with which they find themselves confronted.

3. SCOPE OF THE CASEBOOK AND SOME REMARKS ON TERMINOLOGY

The casebook deals with judicial review of administrative action. This applies to the exclusion of a number of related aspects. First of all, the casebook does not touch upon

[10] Please note that, for the UK, this book concentrates on the legal system of England and Wales. Where appropriate, the UK is addressed as a whole. If four Member States are mentioned, reference is made to the legal system of England and Wales as part of the UK.

constitutional review, hence the review of laws against the respective constitutions and the conflicts between different constitutional subjects, such as governments and parliaments, or federal and regional authorities. Administrative law is understood as the law governing the relations between public authorities (the administration) and private parties. This book does not concern all aspects administrative law, but, rather, concentrates on the judicial review of the administrative action.

The book covers five legal orders: the legal order of the EU and the national laws of Germany, France, the Netherlands and England and Wales. The German and French administrative laws are both continental law systems; however, they have very different roots and approaches to administrative justice. Both systems have inspired the administrative law in other legal orders and on the EU level. The law of England and Wales, as an example of a common law system, is, at least at first sight and as a point of departure, fundamentally different from the three continental legal orders and is therefore essential in such a comparative exercise. Schwarze argued that, regarding what he calls 'administrative law protection', three 'systems' should be distinguished within Europe: the British, the French and the German.[11] The Dutch legal system is of special interest for its 'hybridity', as it has traditionally had many similarities to the French law, but has taken much inspiration from German law during the last decades.

The EU level is studied first, as a separate legal order. Most of EU law can be characterised as being administrative law.[12] In the casebook, the system of judicial review of administrative action of EU institutions is examined. As a consequence, infringement procedures and preliminary question procedures before the CJEU are not dealt with. They do not concern the possibilities of private parties to lodge judicial review claims against actions of EU institutions.

The EU level is also examined from the perspective of its influence on the national systems of administrative justice. In this context, the requirements applicable to judicial review and stemming from the treaties, secondary EU law and the case law of the CJEU have been examined. These requirements influence the national rules on judicial review of administrative action, at least as far as cases with EU law implications are dealt with on the national level. This influence, together with the influence of international law, such as the law of the Council of Europe or the Aarhus Convention, is discussed within the analyses of the respective national systems. An important question in this context is whether the EU law requirements have brought about a process of convergence of the national systems and can be seen as a driver of the emergence of a form of *ius commune* in the field of judicial review.

In comparative exercises, terminology always plays an important role. Translating national legal terms and concepts into English comes with a great danger of causing misunderstandings. The casebook tries to limit these risks in two ways. First, all original sources of law, such as case law and legislation, were studied, and only subsequently translated. Secondly, whenever the authors thought that this would be desirable, the English translation of a certain term is followed by the same term in the original language

[11] J Schwarze, *European Administrative Law* (n 5 above), 98.

[12] See eg P Craig, *EU Administrative Law*, 2nd edn (Oxford, Oxford University Press, 2012); A Turk, *Judicial Review in EU Law* (Cheltenham, Edward Elgar, 2010).

(in brackets and in italics). Legal terms which were deemed essential to understand the respective system are listed in a Table of Terminology to facilitate the user.

European Case Law Identifier numbers have been added to all case law in legal orders (the EU, the Netherlands), where the use of common European labelling is already accepted and broadly applied in practice. In the other legal orders, other, more traditional and country-specific, ways of identifying court decisions have been used.

Finally, it should be noted that, whenever 'he' and 'his' are used, the terms should be understood as 'he or she' and 'his or her', respectively.

4. SOME READING INSTRUCTIONS

The book is structured in 11 chapters, each dealing with a different aspect of judicial review of administrative action. After an introduction to the different historical roots and developments of the legal system, Chapter 2 gives an overview on the organisational structure of judicial review in administrative matters. This is followed, in Chapter 3, by an analysis of the types of administrative action and the corresponding kinds of review. Chapter 4 concentrates on access to the court. Chapter 5–7 deal with court proceedings, whereby the conduct of the proceedings (Chapter 5), the grounds and scope of review (Chapter 6) and the remedies (Chapter 7) are distinguished. The possibilities and peculiarities of appeal are studied in Chapter 8. Chapter 9 provides an overview on the differences and similarities in the structure and style of judgments. Chapters 10 and 11 deal with two special issues, namely non-judicial redress mechanisms (Chapter 10) and the topic of liability claims (Chapter 11).

Comparison of the different topics and approaches is possible, and comparative remarks are made within each of these topics and chapters and for many subsections and questions. However, the different chapters and questions within chapters may not be assessed in isolation. Aspects such as access to court, the grounds of review and the range of remedies are interrelated. To just mention two examples: the answer to the question of which remedies can be sought has consequences for the grounds of review. The question of whether access to court is broad may have consequences for the intensity of review and the conduct of proceedings. Therefore, specific questions and solutions cannot be solely discussed in an isolated way, apart from the respective system of judicial review in total. Where this would seemed to be desirable, the authors have addressed such connections in their comparative remarks and overviews. As in other casebooks, however, the editors have refrained from adding a final chapter with comprehensive comparative conclusions on the systems of judicial review as such and in total. Such general comparative conclusions would either be rather superficial or would require repeating much of what was said in the comparative sections of the respective chapters.

CHAPTER 1
CONSTITUTIONAL STRUCTURE AND BASIC CHARACTERISTICS OF THE LEGAL SYSTEMS EXAMINED (CONCERNING JUDICIAL REVIEW)

Thomas Perroud

1.1 INTRODUCTION

The main purpose of judicial review is to settle disputes between individuals and public authorities, hence it is a method of control of administrative action. In this sense, judicial review is as old as the state itself. However, judicial review as it is known today is a historical construct. That is why the main purpose of this chapter is to explain the development of judicial review into its present shape.

The first part of the chapter will present the historical evolution of judicial review in the legal systems studied in this book. This evolution was slow, and took different forms in different countries. It is possible to discern two separate periods – roughly, before and after the Second World War. These periods correspond to the strengthening of democracy, the development of the welfare state and the rise of litigation that it entailed. In the second part of the chapter, several basic elements of the structures of judicial review in the legal systems studied in this book will be analysed: the sources of law, the constitutional guarantees and the basis of judicial review. These elements will help the reader understand several key characteristics of the legal systems of judicial review studied in this book.

1.2 BRIEF HISTORICAL INTRODUCTION

1.2.A ADMINISTRATIVE JUSTICE BEFORE THE SECOND WORLD WAR

1.2.A.1 FRANCE

A de Tocqueville, Ancien Regime and the French Revolution[1] **1.1 (FR)**

No European country's ordinary courts of law were less dependent on government than France; but hardly any countries made more use of extraordinary courts either.

These two things were more closely related than might be imagined. Since the king could do nothing about the careers of judges, neither dismiss them, nor transfer them to other posts, nor even, in most cases, promote them, since, in short, he had no hold over them either through ambition or fear, he soon felt irritated by their independence. This had led him, here more than anywhere, to withhold information from them about matters which directly involved his own power and to create for his own special use, alongside the ordinary courts, a kind of more independent tribunal which would display to his subjects some semblance of justice without making them fearful about the reality.

In areas such as certain parts of Germany, where the ordinary courts had never been so independent of government as the French courts of that period, similar precautions were not taken and administrative justice never existed. The ruler was sufficiently in control over judges never to need special commissioners.

If we read carefully the royal edicts and decrees published in the last century of the monarchy along with the decrees from the Royal Council of the same period, we will find few in which the government, having issued a regulation, has omitted to state that the challenges which might arise, and the lawsuits resulting from them, would be brought exclusively before the Intendants[2] and the Council. 'His Majesty furthermore commands that all challenges arising from the implementation of this decree, its circumstances and dependent clauses, shall be brought before the Intendant to be adjudicated by him except in the case of an appeal to the council. We forbid our ordinary courts and tribunals to take note of them'. That was the usual formula of words.

...

From that time on, the majority of legal disputes about tax collection were exclusively the domain of the Intendant and the Council. The same can be said for anything connected with the regulation of traffic, with public transport, with highways, river navigation, etc. In general terms, all lawsuits which involved public authorities were siphoned off to government courts.

...

Modern legal experts reassure us, with respect to administrative law, that great progress has been achieved since the Revolution: 'Formerly, judicial and government powers were confused,' they say. 'We have untangled them since then and returned each to its proper sphere.'

[1] A de Tocqueville, *Ancien Regime and the Revolution* (London, Penguin Classics, 2008) 155.

[2] The intendants used to represent the king in the provinces.

Edit de Saint-Germain-en-Laye of 21 February 1641[3] **1.2 (FR)**

(1) On the basis of our knowledge, full power and royal authority, we hereby declare that our court in Paris, and all our other courts, have been established only to render justice to our subjects; we hereby explicitly prohibit them from hearing not only disputes similar to those which are hereby presented but also in general all those disputes which may concern the state, the administration and the government, which we reserve for our sole person and our successor kings ....

Loi du 16 et 24 et août 1790 sur l'organisation judiciaire[4] **1.3 (FR)**

Article 13 Judicial functions are separate and shall always remain separate from administrative functions. It shall be a criminal offence for the judges of the ordinary courts to interfere in any manner with the operation of administrative bodies, nor shall they call the administrators to account to them in respect of the exercise of their duties.

H McCleave Cake, The French Conseil d'État – An Essay on Administrative Jurisprudence[5] **1.4 (FR)**

Separation of powers in France means independence of the executive from both the legislative and judicial branches of government. From its inception the Conseil d'État has served as an arm of the executive, functioning initially as an informal body charged with planning and advising the head of state and 'of resolving the difficulties which arise in the administrative field'. By early decree administrative advisors were protected against judicial interference, and gradually their advisory work was overshadowed by judicial functions performed in hearing disputes and resolving complaints brought to the head of state. From the beginning the Conseil was divided into five sections, four dealing with administrative and one with quasi-judicial business. The present distinction was drawn in 1806 with the formal creation of the Commission du Contentieux. Important ordinances in the year 1831 marked the complete separation of administrative and judicial duties within the Conseil, which fully recognized the judicial character of its contentious proceedings and provided that the latter include public hearings of a contradictory nature in subsequent adjudication of administrative disputes. By the same laws the office of Commissaire du Government was created, a position to assume great significance as its holders quickly came to represent the interest of the general public instead of the executive branch of government. In 1849 the group within the Conseil charged with primarily judicial responsibilities was renamed the Section du Contentieux, by which title it is known today. By decree-law of May 24, 1872 the Conseil d'État was recognized as a fully independent tribunal; by express authority its decisions were given the power of judgments.

[3] *Edit qui défend aux parlements et autres cours de justice de prendre à l'avenir connaissance des affaires d'état et d'administration, et qui supprime plusieurs charges de conseillers au parlement de Paris* (Saint-Germain-en-Laye, February 1641). F-A Isambert et al, *Recueil général des anciennes lois françaises, depuis l'an 420 jusqu'à la Révolution de 1789* (1829) XVI 529.

[4] L Rondonneau, *Collection générale des lois, décrets, arrêtés* (Paris, Rondonneau et Dècle, 1817) vol 1, 434.

[5] H McCleave Cake, 'The French Conseil d'État – An Essay on Administrative Jurisprudence Administrative' (1972) 24 *Administrative Law Review* 315, 318–19.

...

By the *Cadot* decision of 3 December 1889 the Conseil established its competence as a court of general jurisdiction (*juge de droit commun*) in the field of administrative law, holding that it had power to review all administrative acts in the absence of specific statutory grants. Thus by the end of the nineteenth century the Section du Contentieux of the Conseil d'État was ready to meet the demands of the twentieth.

Loi du 24 mai 1872 portant réorganisation du Conseil d'État **1.5 (FR)**

Article 9 The Council of State (Conseil d'État) adjudicates ... on actions for the annulment (*annulation pour excès de pouvoir*) of the acts of the various administrative authorities.

Conseil d'État, 13 December 1889[6] **1.6 (FR)**

Cadot v Minister of the Interior

JURISDICTION OF ADMINISTRATIVE COURTS

Cadot

Administrative disputes must be settled by the administrative courts.

Facts: Mr Cadot was employed by the city of Marseille and fired. The municipal council suppressed his function by a decision, the grounds of which contained comments that Mr Cadot deemed detrimental to his professional reputation. He sued the city and asked the Minister of the Interior for damages. The Minister refused to hear the challenge, hence Mr Cadot challenged the refusal before the Conseil d'État. No statute attributed the competence to hear such disputes to the Conseil d'État. On the contrary, the legislative framework provided that challenges against administrative decisions were to be heard by the competent minister. However, the Conseil d'État accepted to hear the case, without further explaining its reasons.

Held: The Council of State considered itself competent to hear the challenges against administrative decisions.

Judgment: Considering that, from the refusal of the mayor and of the municipal council to award damages to Mr Cadot, a controversy arose between the parties, which the Conseil d'État was competent to hear. ...

Note

The *Ancien Régime* (the period prior to the Revolution beginning in 1789) in France is characterised by the settlement of disputes by a separate set of courts under the control of the king. The French Revolutionaries followed the same trend. They adopted the Law of 16 and 24 August 1790 on judicial organisation establishing the principle of separation between administrative and judicial authorities, prohibiting any court from interfering with the functioning of administrative authorities. In order to avoid the interference of the judiciary with the administrative action, Napoleon formally instituted the Council of State as a separate and independent entity in 1799, and as a councillor to advise the government on draft legislation and governmental acts.

[6] No 66145.

This system suffered from two deficiencies: first, despite the existence of a separate court, the vast majority of administrative disputes were in fact decided within the administration itself; and second, as the Council of State did not have a final say on the disputes brought before it, the head of state could always overturn its decisions. With the law of 24 May 1872, the Council of State became the final court in administrative disputes, and on 13 December 1889 (with the *Cadot* case) the Council of State held that all administrative disputes should be adjudicated by administrative courts. At this stage, the modern physiognomy of the French administrative justice system was set.

1.2.A.2 GERMANY

FJ Goodnow, Comparative Administrative Law – An Analysis of the Administrative Systems, National and Local, of the United States, England, France and Germany[7] **1.7 (DE)**

1. *From 1806 to the formation of the empire*. When the old German kingdom and Holy Roman Empire was broken up in 1806 the administrative jurisdiction of the royal-imperial courts was completely destroyed and individuals were left at the mercy of the separate states which then came into being. The imperial administrative jurisdiction over the acts of the officers of the most important members of the empire was not very great as a result of the *privilegium de non appellando* which was possessed by most of them and in accordance with which appeals to the imperial courts against the acts of officers in these sections were not allowed. The separate German states were very generally guided in their regulation of the relations of the courts and the administration by the new principle of the separation of powers which had been so fully developed by the French revolution. This had for its corollary, it will be remembered, the complete independence of the administration over the courts, which were to be confined to the decisions of private and criminal law cases. That is all complaints against the action of the administration, so far as they did not come within the domain of the private or the criminal law, were in Germany as in France to be decided by the administration itself; and perfect freedom of appeal from the decisions of the subordinate authorities to the higher authorities was provided. This condition of things did not, however, lead at first to great arbitrariness of action on the part of the administration. For the administrative authorities in their higher instances were so organized as to ensure to the individual almost the same guaranties of impartial action as were to be found in the courts. They were organized for the most part as boards whose members had tenure similar to that of the judges, i.e. practically during good behaviour. When, however, the absolute monarchy was changed into the constitutional monarchy as a result of the revolution of 1848, all this was changed. The highest administrative authorities, the ministers, became partisans rather than the representatives of an impartial crown. The administrative organization became more single-headed in form and was more completely subordinated to the ministers. The administration thus became an instrument which might be made use of by the political party which happened to be

[7] FJ Goodnow, *Comparative Administrative Law – An Analysis of the Administrative Systems, National and Local, of the United States, England, France and Germany* (New York, JP Putnam's Sons, 2011) 240 ff.

in power in the legislature to further its own ends; and as all of the great political parties were essentially social parties, the danger became very great of the partisan application of the administrative law in the interest of some particular social class. In Prussia this was actually the case during the reactionary period from 1850–60. The conservative party which was the landholding interest, i.e. the nobility, got control of the administration and prostituted it in the interest of their own social class and to the detriment of other social classes. German publicists saw that change had to be made, and that some judicial control over the administration had to be provided. The great question was how this judicial control should be formed. Should it be given to the ordinary courts or should special courts following the model of the French courts be formed, which by this time had shown themselves to be efficient protectors of individual rights? Prussia, where the condition of things was the worst, was the first to answer this question and answered it by granting in 1861 to the ordinary courts a control over certain administrative acts connected with tax administration. It is, however, to be noticed that a Prussian ordinance of as early a date as 1808 and another of May 11, 1842, had taken steps in this direction by permitting appeal to the courts in the case of police orders on the ground that they were absolutely contrary to law. Further, in case the law recognized an obligation on the part of the government to indemnify an individual for an invasion of his property rights, the courts were permitted to decide as to the necessity and the amount of the indemnity. At about the same time Baden declared in favour of special administrative courts. The progress of the reform in Prussia, however, was interrupted by the serious internal and external questions which presented themselves for solution and it was not until after the wars with Austria and France had been fought that the question was taken up again. It is therefore with the formation of the empire that the problem was definitely solved.

2. *Since the formation of the empire*. As a result of imperial legislation the following is the condition of things: the imperial law organizing the courts maintains in theory the independence of the administration in its former extent, but it and other laws have given to the courts in a few special instances control over the administration, while as a result of the general principle of German law which is in many cases formally expressed in the imperial statutes, the courts control all private legal acts of the administration, i.e. when acting as *fiscus* it makes contracts or commits torts. Other imperial laws have also provided in special instances for special administrative courts. The imperial legislation, however, leaves everything else to be regulated by the legislation of the separate members of the empire, simply providing that questions of competence between the administration and the courts shall be decided by a body in which the courts shall have a fair representation.

Note

The history of German administrative law also shows that administrative justice was first discharged by the rulers themselves. They adjudicated on the disputes that their actions created. German administrative law dates back to the seventeenth century, when sovereigns managed to free themselves from the ties of the outdated law of the 'estates' (*Stände*).[8] This development was based on the so-called *ius eminem*,

[8] For details, see H Pünder and A Klafki, 'Administrative Law in Germany' in R Seerden (ed), *Administrative Law of the European Union, its Member States and the United States*, 4th edn (Antwerp, Intersentia, 2018) 50–55.

which gave the ruler the right to interfere with the duly acquired rights (*iura quaesita*) of the subjects. There was no independent judicial authority. Acting in a judicial capacity was a part (often the most important part) of regional sovereignty; the duty was discharged by the ruler himself, or delegated by him to dependent jurists (*Kameraljustiz*). The administration was thus controlled to a certain extent, but there was no legal protection against the ruler himself. As a result, jurists developed the so-called 'fiscal theory', according to which the subjects had to tolerate the ruler's interference but were compensated for it.

Administrative law in the modern sense of the term developed when constitutions came into force in the nineteenth century. Interference with liberty and property then was only possible if it was based on a statute (so-called 'legal reservation'). The state was supposed to restrict itself to warding off danger to public safety and order (*öffentliche Sicherheit und Ordnung*). This was the time of the minimal state, or night-watchman state, where disputes were limited because state interference with rights was itself limited. Moreover, a state that was based on the rule of law required a separation of powers, including an independent judiciary. The structure of these powers was disputed. Many were of the opinion that the 'ordinary' courts of law (*ordentliche Gerichte*) should not only settle legal disputes between citizens, but, as in England, should also control the administrative action.[9] In the end, the idea prevailed that the ordinary courts should restrict themselves to dealing with private law disputes, and that there would have to be separate administrative courts in charge of controlling state administration in support of the 'common good'.[10] This was in line with the credo of liberalism, according to which the state was to be distinguished from society. Gradually, first instance and higher administrative courts developed in the German states. A key institution was the Prussian Higher Administrative Court (Preußisches Obverwaltungsgericht), which enforced the restriction of police powers and developed the principle of proportionality.[11]

However, until 1848, remedies in case of violation of rights were limited to actions for damages, and there was no clear division of competences between ordinary and administrative courts. In 1871, with the formation of Bismarck's Reich and the strengthening of centralisation, administrative courts at the lower and intermediate levels were created in several parts of the German Empire. At the same time, judicial review was limited to an exhaustive catalogue of specific actions and to situations in which individual rights were allegedly infringed, as opposed to an objective control of legality. Claimants had to show that they were infringed in their subjective public rights (*subjektive öffentliche Rechte*).

Finally, there was no judicial protection for those citizens who, either voluntarily or by virtue of the law, were subject to a special relationship of subordination

[9] O Bähr, *Der Rechtsstaat: eine publicistische Skizze* (Kassel, GH Wigand, 1864) 45 ff.

[10] This idea was fought for above all by R von Gneist, *Der Rechtsstaat und die Verwaltungsgerichte in Deutschland*, 3rd edn (Darmstadt, J Springer, 1879) 110 ff.

[11] See Higher Administrative Court of Prussia (Preußisches Oberverwaltungsgericht), PrOVGE 13, 426 ff; 38, 421 ff; 51, 284 ff; O Bühler, *Die subjektiven öffentlichen Rechte und ihr Schutz in der deutschen Verwaltungsrechtsprechung* (Berlin, Kohlhammer, 1914) 197 ff.

(*besonderes Gewaltverhältnis*) within the administration. Such a special relationship of subordination was assumed with regard to civil servants, soldiers, pupils and prison inmates.[12] During the time of the Weimar Republic, any attempts to strengthen the administrative control failed in the absence of a common position on judicial review. Judicial protection against public power became virtually impossible during the Third Reich until the entry into force of the Basic Law in 1949.

1.2.A.3 THE NETHERLANDS

J Schwarze, European Administrative Law[13] **1.8 (NL)**

(1) Both the system of administrative law and the legal protection against the administration in the Netherlands have been exposed to a great number of foreign influences in the course of their varied history. To this day, the Dutch system reveals traces of English law, and – increasingly of late – of the French and German systems.

As early as the mid-nineteenth century, a clear distinction was established between private law and public law. In its capacity as fiscal authority, the State acted through private law procedures, whereas it exercised public law powers when acting as the public authority. Legal protection against the administration could be sought before the ordinary courts, which had jurisdiction for all matters involving property rights or claims for the repayment of debts. For the rest, complaints could be addressed to superior organs of the executive, in particular to the Crown, which adjudicated after having heard the opinion of the Raad van State (the Dutch Council of State). As a result of the increase in state intervention at the end of the nineteenth century, it was not long before the available legal protection was deemed unsatisfactory. For the purpose of obtaining compensation on grounds of unlawful intervention by the administration, private law was, at the turn of the century, considered to constitute the normally applicable body of rules, which also applied to the public authorities. Specific administrative law provisions were complementary by nature and constituted the exception.

The change from a liberal state based on the rule of law to a welfare state saw the development of new instruments for the provision of services and for planning purposes, which could not be satisfactorily accommodated by either private law theory or traditional administrative law theory, which was geared to the individual administrative act. As a result of this development, the notion of administrative law as a complementary and exceptional body of rules increasingly lost ground to that of an independent system of administrative law, which also covered the field of the provision of services, which occupied an intermediate position between state intervention and the law of contracts.

[12] For a discussion of the concept of special relationships of subordination, which prevailed until the twentieth century, see H Krüger, 'Das besondere Gewaltverhältnis' (1957) 15 *Veröffentlichungen der Vereinigung der Deutschen Staatsrechtslehrer* 109; CH Ule, 'Das besondere Gewaltverhältnis' (1957) 15 *Veröffentlichungen der Vereinigung der Deutschen Staatsrechtslehrer* 133.

[13] J Schwarze, *European Administrative Law* (London, Sweet & Maxwell, 1992) 187–88.

Note

Van der Hoeven has demonstrated that, in the Netherlands, administrative law had already been developed in medieval times.[14] In the eighteenth and nineteenth centuries, some acts and regulations of provinces, municipalities and water boards provided for a right of intra-administrative objection procedure against decisions of public authorities. Therefore, similar to the position in France and Germany, complaints against actions of the administration were to be decided by the administration itself, sometimes even in two instances (eg objection to the provincial executive and higher objection to the Crown).

In the middle of the nineteenth century, the emerging discussion over whether the judiciary or the Crown should decide on disputes between the administrative authorities and citizens was decided in favour of the latter.[15] One of these types of intra-administrative review was the appeal to the Crown. Since the Act on the Council of State (Wet op de Raad van State) came into force in 1861, a decision of the Crown was prepared by the Administrative Disputes Division of the Council of State (Afdeling Geschillen van Bestuur Raad van State), often called *Afdeling contentieux*, following its French counterpart. Although the decision was ultimately taken by the Crown which, in fact, meant by a minister, and therefore not by an impartial and independent body, the procedure was quite similar to the procedure before an administrative court, and the advice of the Council of State was followed by the Crown in the majority of its decisions.[16] The most significant difference between this kind of intra-administrative objection procedure and judicial review by courts was, however, that the authorities could review not only the legality of the decision, but also its merits. Furthermore, the authority could replace the original decision with one of its own.

The necessity of an administrative court, separate from the ordinary courts, had been discussed since the end of the nineteenth century.[17] However, the discussion did not lead to a change in legislation. Therefore, no independent general administrative courts were created during the nineteenth century or the first part of the twentieth century. Since the beginning of the twentieth century, several specialised administrative courts have been established.[18] An important example is the Central Appellate Court (Centrale Raad van Beroep), established in 1902, which is still the last instance court on social security decisions.

In the Dutch system, the civil courts recognised the right of access to an independent and impartial judicial body in the case of administrative disputes at the beginning

[14] J van der Hoeven, *De drie dimensies van het bestuursrecht*, VAR-reeks 100 (Alphen aan den Rijn, Tjeenk Willink, 1989) 70.

[15] ibid.

[16] M Schreuder-Vlasblom, *Rechtsbescherming en bestuurlijke voorprocedure*, 6th edn (Deventer, Wolters Kluwer, 2017) 26.

[17] More especially after the amendment of the constitution in 1887; see further van der Hoeven (n 14 above) 107 ff.

[18] See further RGJM Widdershoven, *Gespecialiseerde rechtsgangen in het administratieve recht* (Alphen aan de Rijn, Tjeenk Willink, 1989).

of the twentieth century. Since the landmark case of *Guldemond/Noordwijkerhout* (1915), the civil judge deems himself competent if someone claims that a public authority acted unlawfully against him, even if such a claim is rooted in public law.[19] The case can be explained by the fact that the legislator failed to create general administrative courts, competent in all administrative matters.

1.2.A.4 ENGLAND AND WALES

The jurisdiction of England and Wales demonstrates some significant differences to the systems that have previously been discussed. It has no written constitution and also relies on one set of courts to adjudicate on all disputes, whether public or private. In common law systems, there are no separate administrative courts, which may be explained by the absence of a clear substantive distinction between matters regarded as public law and those regarded as private law. Thus, the English approach to judicial review is based on the seeking of remedies for alleged unlawful action, mainly through claims based on what were known as the prerogative writs.[20] Since the thirteenth century, the writ system has been a procedure of channelling individual complaints into a pre-existing system of orders of the monarch directed to the person who had injured the individual. The writ originated in a personal request by an individual to the king to remedy a wrong suffered by another individual. They were sealed governmental documents by which the king conveyed notifications or orders. These forms of personal requests developed into a set of standardised writs. Aggrieved subjects had to try and fit their complaints into one of the existing writs and submit them through the Lord Chancellor to the king. Over time, claims were no longer submitted to the monarch for resolution, but were instead brought before the courts. The prerogative writs developed complex procedural requirements and each was limited in the sense that it could apply only to certain types of unlawful action. Some elements of this remedial system have survived until today; for example, though renamed, the prerogative remedies remain in place and such remedies are still granted by the courts.[21] In addition to the prerogative writs, it was and still is also possible for claimants to seek private law remedies in the form of declarations and injunctions.[22] Since the procedural reforms of 1977, ultimately reflected in the Senior Courts Act 1981, claimants are no longer so rigidly bound by the need to fit their claims to the circumstances previously required by the prerogative writs, and there is now no need to launch separate

[19] See below excerpt 1.23, section 1.4.C.

[20] The prerogative writs were those of certiorari, mandamus, prohibition and habeas corpus. Certiorari instructs the person or body whose decision is challenged to deliver the record of the decision to the Office of the Queen's Bench Division to be quashed. Mandamus is designed to enforce the performance by governmental bodies of their duties owed to the public. Prohibition orders a body to refrain from illegal action. The writs of habeas corpus were designed to order the appearance of a person before one of the King's courts to attend judicial proceedings.

[21] The prerogative writs have been renamed as a 'quashing order' (certiorari), a 'prohibiting order' (prohibition) and a 'mandatory order' (mandamus). These are all still claimed from the courts and are the predominant methods through which remedies are granted for unlawful administrative action.

[22] See Chapter 7, sections 7.3.B.1 and 7.4.A.1.

forms of proceedings in circumstances where claimants might seek both a prerogative and a private law remedy.[23]

Another important point for the development of English administrative law was the impact of the so-called bills, which were dealt with in the Star Chamber. These bills were requested by people to the king and his council, the Chancellor and Parliament by subjects who needed some form of advice or help. Many of the bills were converted into writs or legislation, or direct intervention by the king. The so-called conciliar courts, which, unlike the common law courts, did not use writs, began to accept these bills and to issue orders. A new institution, the Star Chamber, gradually filled the gap left by the common law courts and the courts of equity. The Star Chamber dealt particularly with cases concerning the state, but also had jurisdiction in private law disputes and cases of religious deviation. This early form of administrative court was given additional powers in the Star Chamber Statute in 1487. It imposed a strict control over the organs of local government and the exercise of judicial and administrative functions. The Star Chamber applied the common law, but followed different procedures for obtaining confessions, such as the rack or other torture. As a consequence of major criticism of the procedures and involvement in ecclesiastical decisions, the Star Chamber was eventually abolished during the struggles over constitutional reform of the seventeenth century.

The Star Chamber left an indelible mark upon English legal culture against the creation of special courts. The idea of the rule of law, so deeply entrenched in this culture, entails that everyone should be judged by the same independent courts using the same law. This explains the first rejection of administrative law, expressed by Dicey in his *Introduction to the Law of the Constitution*.

AV Dicey, Introduction to the Law of the Constitution[24] **1.9 (EW)**

[The] 'rule of law' then, which forms a fundamental principle of the constitution, has three meanings, or may be regarded from three different points of view.

It means, in the first place, the absolute supremacy or predominance of regular law as opposed to the influence of arbitrary power, and excludes the existence of arbitrariness, of prerogative, or even of wide discretionary authority on the part of the government. Englishmen are ruled by the law, and by the law alone; a man may with us be punished for a breach of law, but he can be punished for nothing else.

It means, again, equality before the law, or the equal subjection of all classes to the ordinary law of the land administered by the ordinary Law Courts; the 'rule of law' in this sense excludes the idea of any exemption of officials or others from the duty of obedience to the law which governs other citizens or from the jurisdiction of the ordinary tribunals; there can be with us nothing really corresponding to the 'administrative law' (*droit administratif*) or the 'administrative tribunals' (*tribunaux administratif*) of France. The notion which lies at the bottom of the 'administrative law' known to foreign countries is, that affairs or disputes in which the government or its servants are concerned are beyond

[23] For an account of the reforms of the late 1970s and the impact upon the remedial system in England and Wales, see HWR Wade and CF Forsyth, *Administrative Law*, 11th edn (Oxford, Oxford University Press, 2014) chs 15, 16 and 18; D Feldman (ed), *English Public Law* (Oxford, Oxford University Press, 2009) ch 18.

[24] AV Dicey, *Introduction to the Law of the Constitution*, 6th edn (London, Macmillan, 1902) 198–99.

the sphere of the civil Courts and must be dealt with by special and more or less official bodies. This idea is utterly unknown to the law of England, and indeed is fundamentally inconsistent with our traditions and customs.

The 'rule of law', lastly, may be used as a formula for expressing the fact that with us the law of the constitution, the rules which in foreign countries naturally form part of a constitutional code, are not the source but the consequence of the rights of individuals, as defined and enforced by the Courts …

AV Dicey, Introduction to the Law of the Constitution[25] **1.10 (EW)**

Chapter 12, Rule of Law contrasted with Droit *administratif*

It has been already pointed out that in many countries, and especially in France, servants of the State are in their official capacity to a great extent protected from the ordinary law of the land, exempted from the jurisdiction of the ordinary tribunals, and subject to official law, administered by official bodies. This scheme of so-called administrative law is opposed to all English ideas, and by way of contrast admirably illustrates the full meaning of that rule of law which is an essential characteristic of our Constitution. A student therefore will do well to try and understand the general characteristics of that administrative law which under one name or another prevails in most continental States, and this end is most easily attained by a survey (which for our present purpose must be a cursory one) of the nature and principles of the system known to Frenchmen as *droit administratif*.

Note

For a common lawyer in the nineteenth century, the idea that a separate court should judge administrative action under a separate system of law was repugnant. However, Dicey's account was, to a large extent, incorrect. The absence of a body of administrative law, in the field of torts, for instance, meant that individuals in fact had no remedy against administrative wrongdoing: only since 1947, after the enactment of the Crown Proceedings Act, could public officials be held liable in tort for negligent exercise of public powers in their official capacity. Before then, they were immune from suit.

1.2.B AFTER THE SECOND WORLD WAR AND THE WELFARE STATE

In many countries, administrative law adopted its modern form after the Second World War. Democracy and the rule of law finally triumphed and citizens obtained legal protection from state interference. Also, in light of the development of the welfare state, instances of state interventions in the lives of individuals increased. This led to dramatic changes in the administrative laws of Germany, the Netherlands and of England and Wales. Most importantly, in all legal systems judicial review was developed progressively by courts. France will not be examined in this section as this evolution took place as a result of the *Cadot* case in 1889.[26]

[25] ibid 322–23.
[26] See excerpt 1.6 above.

1.2.B.1 GERMANY

Grundgesetz **1.11 (DE)**

Article 1 (3) The following basic rights shall bind the legislature, the executive and the judiciary as directly applicable law.

Article 19 (4) Should any person's rights be a violated by public authority, he shall have recourse to the courts. If no other jurisdiction has been established, recourse shall be to the ordinary courts. ...

Article 34 If any person, in the exercise of a public office entrusted to him, violates his official duty to a third party, liability shall rest in principle with the state or public body that employs him. In the event of intentional wrongdoing or gross negligence, the right of recourse against the individual officer shall be preserved. Access to ordinary courts shall not be precluded for claims for compensation or recourse.

Note

The establishment of a constitutional state in Germany after the Second World War led to the recognition of judicial review in the Basic Law. From this time onwards, administrative law in Germany has been regarded as 'specified constitutional law' (*konkretisiertes Verfassungsrecht*).[27] Article 19 of the Basic Law on the one hand guarantees the fundamental right to judicial review, and on the other hand warrants a complete control of the administrative action by the courts.[28]

1.2.B.2 THE NETHERLANDS

European Court of Human Rights, 23 October 1985[29] **1.12 (COE)**

Benthem v the Netherlands

ACCESS TO AN INDEPENDENT AND IMPARTIAL TRIBUNAL

Benthem

The Dutch system of appeal to the Crown is in violation of Article 6 of the European Convention on Human Rights.

Facts: The college of mayor and aldermen of the municipality of Weststellingerwerf had granted an environmental permit to Benthem for the operation of an LPG station in the municipality. The permit was contested by the Regional Health Inspector before the Crown. At that time, the Crown decided such disputes in final instance, after having been advised by the Administrative Disputes Division of the Council of State (Afdeling Geschillen van Bestuur Raad van State). This advice had no binding force, although in practice it was followed

[27] F Werner, 'Verwaltungsrecht als konkretisiertes Verfassungsrecht' (1959) *Deutsches Verwaltungsblatt* 527.
[28] BVerfGE 15, 275, 282; BVerfGE 61, 82, 110; BVerfGE 78, 214, 226.
[29] ECLI:CE:ECHR:1985:1023JUD000884880.

in a great majority of cases. In the case of Benthem, the Administrative Disputes Division was of the opinion that the permit was unlawfully granted to Benthem and advised the Crown to refuse Benthem's request. This advice was followed by the Crown. Benthem filed a complaint before the European Court of Human Rights, claiming that the Netherlands had violated Article 6(1) of the European Convention on Human Rights (ECHR), because his case was not decided by an independent and impartial tribunal.

Held: The Netherlands was found to be in violation of Article 6(1) ECHR.

Judgment: 37. In order to determine whether the proceedings complained of were in conformity with Article 6 para. 1, two institutions fall to be considered, namely the Administrative Litigation Division of the Council of State and the Crown.

...

40. ... It is true that, in order to decide whether the Convention rights have been infringed, one must frequently look beyond the appearances and the language used and concentrate on the realities of the situation. However, a power of decision is inherent in the very notion of 'tribunal' within the meaning of the Convention. Yet the Division renders only advice. Admittedly, that advice is – as happened on the present occasion – followed in the great majority of cases, but this is only a practice of no binding force, from which the Crown can depart at any moment. The proceedings before the Administrative Litigation Division of the Council of State thus do not provide the 'determination by a tribunal of the matter in dispute' which is required by Article 6 para. 1.

...

43. It is true that the Crown, unlike the Administrative Litigation Division, is empowered to determine the dispute, but the Convention requires more than this: by the word 'tribunal', it denotes 'bodies which exhibit ... common fundamental features' of which the most important are independence and impartiality and 'the guarantees of judicial procedure'. The Court refers on this point to its established case law, and notably to its *De Wilde, Ooms and Versyp* judgment of 18 June 1971 (Series A no. 12, p. 41, para. 78).

However, the Royal Decree by which the Crown, as head of the executive, renders its decision constituted, from a formal point of view, an administrative act and it emanated from a Minister who was responsible to the Parliament thereof. Moreover, the Minister was the hierarchical superior of the Regional Health Inspector, who had lodged the appeal, and of the Ministry's Director General, who had submitted the technical report to the Division. Finally, the Royal Decree was not susceptible to review by a judicial body as required by Article 6 para 1. ....

44. There was accordingly a violation of Article 6 para. 1.

Note

Until 1976, some disputes between citizens and administrative authorities in the Netherlands were decided in final instance by specialised administrative courts, amongst which were the Central Appellate Court (Centrale Raad van Beroep), competent in social security and civil servants' disputes and the High Administrative Court for Trade and Industry (College van Beroep voor het Bedrijfsleven), competent in specific economic law disputes. Other disputes, eg in the area of environmental law, were decided by way of an intra-administrative objection procedure, with an appeal to the Crown in final instance. In this procedure, the Crown was advised by the Administrative Disputes Division of the Council of State (Afdeling Geschillen van

Bestuur Raad van State). The advice had no binding force, although it was in practice followed by the Crown in the great majority of cases. In other administrative disputes, there was no possibility of judicial review before a specialised court or of access to an objection procedure, and judicial protection was provided by the civil courts. This possibility was generally considered to be unattractive, as procedures before the civil courts were quite expensive and civil procedural law was not entirely appropriate for deciding administrative law disputes. Civil courts did not, for instance, avail themselves of the power to annul unlawful decisions.

To remedy this gap, a complementary facility of judicial review before an administrative court was introduced in 1976. Under it, citizens, having sufficient interest, could contest administrative decisions before the Jurisdiction Division of the Council of State (Afdeling rechtspraak Raad van State) if 'no other facility of judicial protection' was available. Judicial review by specialised administrative courts, as mentioned above, and also appeal to the Crown were regarded to be such 'other facility of judicial protection'. Therefore, in important areas of administrative law, such as environmental law, the only existing remedy against administrative decisions was still the appeal to the Crown. In 1985, the European Court of Human Rights ruled, in the case of *Benthem v the Netherlands*, that the Crown did not qualify as an independent and impartial judicial body, as required by Article 6(1) ECHR. As decisions of the Crown were not susceptible to review by a judicial body that met the requirements of Article 6 ECHR either, the Netherlands was in violation of the right of access to a court, guaranteed by Article 6 ECHR.

As a first reaction to *Benthem*, the Supreme Court decided that the appeal to the Crown was no longer considered to have sufficient procedural safeguards, so that parties concerned could contest the decision of the Crown before the civil courts.[30] As a result, Crown decisions, as well as those that were consistent with the advice of the Administrative Disputes Division of the Council of State, could be contested in three instances (district court, court of appeal, Supreme Court) and could possibly be overruled. To put an end to this situation, in 1988 the legislator opted for a new approach by replacing the appeal to the Crown by the possibility of judicial review before the Administrative Disputes Division of the Council of State.

Finally, the structure of judicial review as it stands today was shaped by a reform of 1994, by the introduction of the General Administrative Law Act (Algemene Wet Bestuursrecht).[31] In this reform, the two divisions of the Council of State – the Administrative Disputes Division and the Jurisdiction Division – were merged into the new Judicial Division of the Council of State (Afdeling Bestuursrechtspraak Raad van State), which was designated as appellate court by default in all administrative disputes. Since 1994, the administrative divisions of the district courts have also functioned as general administrative courts of first instance.

[30] ECLI:NL:HR:1986:AC2772.

[31] For more details of the current situations, see Chapter 2, section 2.2.A.3.

1.2.B.3 ENGLAND AND WALES

Since the Second World War, administrative law and particularly judicial review in England and Wales has been the subject of considerable development. The law relating to judicial review remains predominantly in case law, although statute has intervened in some areas.[32] The Crown Proceedings Act of 1947 ended Crown immunity and rendered it possible for the Crown to be liable for torts committed by civil servants. Prior to the enactment of the 1947 Act, the Crown was immune from civil proceedings.

As far as procedure is concerned, the process of application for judicial review was regulated in the late 1970s by Order 53,[33] and these reforms were soon afterwards given a clear statutory endorsement by the Senior Courts Act 1981. Order 53 has since been repealed, and further reform of the procedure for bringing a judicial review claim was brought about by part 54 of the Civil Procedure Rules in 1998.[34] Alongside these changes, there has been a degree of institutional reorganisation within the court system. Although the court system in England and Wales adopts a common law approach to the settlement of administrative disputes and there is a unitary court system, a degree of specialisation has occurred. In October 2000, a part of the Queen's Bench Division of the High Court was named the Administrative Court.

Another important reform was made in the early twenty-first century. Although judicial review has existed in England and Wales for many hundreds of years, compared with the other national jurisdictions under examination, relatively few cases have come before the courts. The majority of cases where there was a grievance about the actions of public bodies were settled by tribunals, which enjoyed varying degrees of independence from the administration, although they were often considered to be executive rather than judicial bodies.[35] Such tribunals were generally only available where a right of appeal had been created in legislation by Parliament, although there were some instances of them being created through the exercise of executive discretion.[36]

It has been noted above that in all of the legal systems examined, the history of administrative law is that of a progressive separation between administration and administrative justice. At first, administrative disputes were managed by the administration. The UK is no exception to this. To continental lawyers and scholars, the name 'tribunal' is misleading, for tribunals were administrative bodies in charge of settling disputes inside the administration.[37] Sir Andrew Leggatt was appointed to review the system in the year 2000 and concluded: 'We do not believe that the current arrangements meet what the modern user needs and expects from an appeal system running in parallel to

[32] Examples include the statutory regulation of access to judicial review, most recently in the Senior Courts Act 1981, and also the development of the protection of human rights through the domestic implementation of the major rights contained in the ECHR by the Human Rights Act 1998.

[33] Rules of the Supreme Court (Revision) SI 1965/1776, Order 53.

[34] Civil Procedure Rules SI 1998/3132 (as amended).

[35] See Chapter 2, section 2.2.B.1 (ii).

[36] For an interesting analysis of the role of tribunals in the legal system in England and Wales and the historical development of their position, see P Cane, *Controlling Administrative Power: An Historical Perspective* (Cambridge, Cambridge University Press, 2016) chs 5 and 8.

[37] For an analysis of the independence of tribunals in England and Wales and the developments in this regard see P Cane, *Administrative Tribunals and Adjudication* (Oxford, Hart Publishing, 2010) 108–10.

the courts'.[38] This led to two important developments, the first being the extension of the guarantee contained in section 3 of the Constitutional Reform Act 2005 of judicial independence to the tribunals and tribunal judiciary by section 1 of the Tribunals, Courts and Enforcement Act 2007. The second significant development is that the Tribunals, Courts and Enforcement Act 2007 seeks to dissolve a significant number of existing tribunals and pull them together into a more coherent and organised system. The provisions in the 2007 Act transfer the jurisdictions of many tribunals dealing with areas where there are a significant number of administrative disputes into a two-tier structure: a First-tier Tribunal and an Upper Tribunal. Through this reform, many administrative disputes are now settled through a tribunal system, including both first-instance and appellate decision-making. The new tribunal system can be considered an independent and impartial body, outside the administration and much more closely integrated with the court system and the system of judicial decision-making that this implies.

However, the reform did not lead to the creation of a separate body of administrative courts, on the French model, because the final appeal – on points of law – from the Upper Tribunal lies still with the Court of Appeal. The UK is still a monist country, with a single set of courts to adjudicate on administrative disputes.[39]

1.2.B.4 THE EUROPEAN UNION

J Schwarze, European Administrative Law[40] **1.13 (EU)**

The European Community as a Community of Administrative Law

Administrative law as a field of law and a scientific discipline has in the past been almost entirely limited to the intellectual confines of the exclusively domestic administrative legal order, taken as a closed system and source of knowledge. The truth of this basic contention is in no way impugned by the fact that Otto Mayer, generally regarded as the father of modern German administrative law, had already produced a book on French Administrative Law even before he wrote his *Deutsches Verwaltungsrecht* or that he made use of French models for the development of the German doctrine of administrative law. Indeed, the principles of French administrative law, in the development and determination of which the Conseil d'État has played a crucial role, have exercised a significant influence on systems of administrative law throughout Europe.

Nevertheless, administrative law has emerged only reluctantly and under pressure from comparative law from the Cocoon of its national isolation. A perspective which truly stretches beyond and across frontiers was achieved only after the foundation of the European Community.

On the one hand, European Community law itself is primarily made up of rules of administrative law, drawn in particular from the area of law governing the management of the economy. To that extent, the European Community, already described by the European Court of Justice as a community based on law, could more precisely be termed a community based on administrative law.

[38] Sir A Leggatt, *Tribunals for Users: One System, One Service* (London, The Stationery Office, 2001) para 1.4.

[39] For more on this point, see Chapter 2, section 2.2.B.1.

[40] J Schwarze, *European Administrative Law* (London, Sweet & Maxwell, 1992) 3–4.

On the other hand, the need for a cross-cultural perspective and the search for similarities and differences in the resolution of administrative law problems within the European legal system is not the result simply of a thirst for knowledge on a theoretical level on the part of modern comparative law, but also and above all the product of practical necessity. As a continuously evolving legal order, European Community law is particularly dependent upon appropriate supplementation and growth. Of course, there are a number of essential principles such as the duty to state reasons (Article 190 EEC [296 TFEU]) or the grounds for review drawn from French law and incorporated in the judicial review provisions (Article 33 ECSC; Article 173 EEC [230 TFEU]), which are set out in the Treaties themselves. A number of rules of administrative law of notable scope have also been written into secondary sources of law in some fields of Community policy.

However, by far the greatest number of legal principles governing administrative activity recognised today in Community law originate in the creative law-making and decision-making process of the European Court of Justice. As is characteristic of the development of national administrative law systems, administrative law in the European Community has expanded primarily through judicial decisions.

H Hofmann, G Rowe, A Türk, Administrative Law and Policy of the European Union[41] **1.14 (EU)**

The first steps towards European integration in the 1950s were characterised by the pooling of certain regulatory powers concerning specific sectors of industry. The six founding Member States of the European Coal and Steel Community (ECSC) set up in 1951 a joint organisation with a distinctively administrative character. They delegated clearly circumscribed regulatory powers in a limited policy area to an organizational structure having a strong technocratic executive, the High Authority, empowered to make delegated (administrative) rules and take single-case decisions. The simultaneously established European Court of Justice (ECJ), located then in Villa Pescatore in Luxembourg, established a case law perceiving the ECSC as being of a distinctively administrative nature. It addressed the then unfamiliar legal problems which emerged mainly through the lens of the administrative law traditions common to the six founding Member States. These judgments laid down a number of the foundations of the administrative law systems of the later European Communities.

Note

The EU was born as a supranational system of administrative law. The evolution of European administrative law and judicial review at the EU level has been shaped by the changing nature of EU law and the expansion of the policy fields which fall within the competence of the EU.

[41] HCH Hofmann, GC Rowe and AH Türk, *Administrative Law and Policy of the European Union* (Oxford, Oxford University Press, 2011) 6.

R Barents, EU Procedural Law and Effective Legal Protection[42] **1.15 (EU)**

A remarkable feature of EU procedural law is its rather homogeneous nature. Direct actions are all dealt with according to the same procedure, without differences on account of the subject matter of the action (annulment, failure to act, damages), the nature of the contested act (regulation, directive, etc.), the forms of order sought, or the parties involved (Member States, institutions, individuals). For example, there is no difference between the procedure in the case of an action brought by an individual applicant against an act of an institution or agency of the Union and a 'constitutional' dispute between the European Parliament and the Council on the proper choice of the legal basis of a legislative measure. This feature confirms that to a large extent the function of the Union judicature is to settle disputes relating to the implementation of primary and secondary Union law by institutions as well as the Member States. The common feature of direct actions and preliminary ruling procedures is the similarity of their subject matter. In the majority of cases, the dispute concerns the 'administration' of Union law at the national or at the European level through measures of general application or individual decisions. The homogeneous nature of EU procedural law is also reflected in the enumeration of the grounds for annulment in Article 263 TFEU [Treaty on the Functioning of the European Union], in which no difference is made between Member States, institutions or private applicants or as to the form of the acts whose annulment may be sought.

Notes

(1) To the extent that the European courts settle disputes between EU institutions and natural and legal persons in annulment actions, actions for failure to act and actions for liability, their main task is the review of the administrative action.[43]

(2) The European Court of Justice was established in 1952 as an institution of the European Coal and Steel Community.[44] It was the only court in charge of controlling the correct application and interpretation of EEC and subsequently EC law by the European institutions. However, the caseload of the court had become unmanageable as the years went on. That is why, in 1988, the Court of First Instance (later renamed General Court) was established.[45] In a progressive fashion, it received additional competences to hear cases brought by natural and legal persons against unlawful acts or failure to act by the EU institutions. Decisions of the General Court can be contested before the Court of Justice (Article 256 TFEU). In addition, the Treaty on European Union (TEU) and the Treaty on the Functioning of the European Union (TFEU) mention the possibility of creating 'specialised courts' (Article 257 TFEU). Upon this basis

[42] R Barents, 'EU Procedural Law and Effective Legal Protection' (2014) 51 Common Market Law Review 1437, 1439.

[43] See Chapter 2, section 2.2.B.2.

[44] D Tamm, 'The History of the Court of Justice of the European Union Since its Origin' in Court of Justice of the European Union, *The Court of Justice and the Construction of Europe: Analyses and Perspectives on Sixty Years of Case-Law* (The Hague, Asser Press, 2013) 9–35.

[45] See E Van Ginderachter 'Le Tribunal de première instance des Communautés européennes – un nouveau-né prodige?' (1989) *Cahiers de droit européen* 62.

and in order to relieve the workload of the General Court, the Civil Service Tribunal was established in 2004. As a consequence of the reform of the General Court, which took effect in September 2016, the Civil Service Tribunal has stopped operating and has been absorbed into the General Court.[46] In the future, new specialised courts may be created in order to exercise judicial competence in certain specific areas.

(3) In the EU legal system, there is no conceptual separation between ordinary and administrative courts: there is only one court system, the Court of Justice of the European Union (CJEU), which consists of the Court of Justice and the General Court.[47]

1.2.C COMPARATIVE REMARKS

This brief historical introduction shows a common trend: in the legal systems covered by this book, administrative disputes have been largely extracted from the administration and given to courts. This can be understood as an expression of the *nemo judex in causa sua* rule: the administration cannot be a judge in its own claim. It also shows the influence of the idea of separation of powers: the judicial function should be kept separate from the administrative function. Some remnants of the old system still exist in several of the systems under study: the very existence of a Council of State and comparable bodies in many countries is interpreted as a privilege given to the administration that wants to be judged in its own court.

However, despite this common point, a major difference exists between monist countries, where ordinary courts deal with administrative disputes (England and Wales), and dualist countries, which created a separate branch of courts to adjudicate on these issues (France, Germany, the Netherlands). In dualist systems that follow the French model of the Council of State (France and, to a certain extent, the Netherlands), this body was developed inside the administration itself by creating an independent court. The Conseil d'État and the Raad van State are therefore remnants of the fact that previously disputes were indeed resolved inside the administration. However, the distinction between monist and dualist countries should not be overexaggerated. As was seen in the English system, administrative disputes were in fact mostly resolved within the administration, by the tribunal system. It is only recently that a part of this tribunal system was brought into the court system by the Tribunals, Courts and Enforcement Act 2007.

As mentioned above, the EU is in a different position, in that there are no separate civil courts but only one court system, which has a peculiar nature and is not readily comparable to that of the national legal systems.

[46] Regulation 2015/2422 of the European Parliament and of the Council amending Protocol No 3 on the Statute of the Court of Justice of the European Union (Euratom) [2015] OJ L341/14.

[47] For more on this point, see Chapter 2, section 2.2.B.2.

1.3 SOURCES OF LAW

Comparative law scholarship usually divides legal families into at least two main groups,[48] as far as sources of law are concerned: continental law on the one hand, attached to written law and codes, and the common law on the other hand, attached to case law. Comparative law scholarship therefore contrasts common law countries, such as the UK, and civil law countries, such as France, Germany and the Netherlands. Studying the sources of law, one should find this contrast between, say, France and the UK. In the field of public law, considering the respective roles of written and unwritten law, matters are more complicated.

The developments examined in this section will be quite general, for it is difficult to assess clearly the respective roles written and unwritten law play in a legal system today. Therefore, the argument will be illustrated using as a point of comparison an important piece of legislation in administrative law, namely the law concerning administrative procedure. In many countries, codes were written containing the details of administrative procedure, ie the procedure to administrative decision-making. Whether procedural principles are written in a statute or regulated by the judge is helpful in understanding the role of sources of law in the field of administrative law.

1.3.A GERMANY

The German legal system is characterised by statutory law. Judges base their decisions on statutory law and, in general, judges decide the cases by deriving solutions from the provisions of the legal codes. However, this does not exclude the consideration of general principles of law (*allgemeine Rechtsprinzipien*).

In contrast to the UK system,[49] Germany has no strict system of binding precedent. Instead, judgments of German courts ordinarily have effect *inter partes*. Nonetheless, the judgments of higher courts are usually followed by the lower courts. Thus, even though there is no system of binding precedent, in Germany the higher court decisions are also very influential.[50] Landmark decisions of the federal courts have an especially strong influence on the development of the law. Specifically, some of the judgments of the Federal Constitutional Court have the force of law (*Gesetzeskraft*) according to §31(2) of the Federal Constitutional Court Act (Bundesverfassungsgerichtsgesetz). The findings of the Federal Constitutional Court are binding upon Federal and Land constitutional organs as well as on all courts and authorities according to §31(1) of the Bundesverfassungsgerichtsgesetz. Another distinct feature of German jurisprudence is that the judges

[48] R David, C Jauffret-Spinosi and M Goré, *Les grands systèmes de droit contemporains*, 12th edn (Paris, Dalloz, 2016); HP Glenn, 'Comparative Legal Families and Comparative Legal Traditions' in M Reimann and R Zimmermann (eds), *The Oxford Handbook of Comparative Law* (Oxford, Oxford University Press, 2016).

[49] See below section 1.3.C.

[50] For details, see Chapter 9, section 9.4.

give special importance to academic writing. Court decisions often cite various pieces of literature in their reasoning.[51]

The administrative procedure is codified in the Federal Administrative Procedure Act (Verwaltungsverfahrensgesetz, VwVfG) and the Administrative Procedure Acts of the states (Landesverwaltungsverfahrensgesetz).[52] The Administrative Procedure Acts of the states and the Federal Administrative Procedure Act are essentially identical in wording. In order to have a consistent administrative procedure throughout Germany, the states copied the Federal Act. In the Administrative Procedure Act, the administrative procedure is stipulated in detail. For example §35 VwVfG defines the German concept of the so-called 'administrative act' (*Verwaltungsakt*).[53] It also regulates the right to a hearing before the adoption of a burdensome administrative act (§28 VwVfG) and the duty to give reasons (§39 VwVfG). The procedural rules applicable in the administrative law disputes in front of the administrative courts are also codified, namely in the Administrative Court Procedure Act (Verwaltungsgerichtsordnung).

1.3.B FRANCE

France is a civil law country. Therefore, in principle, the sources of administrative law should be, as in Germany, mainly statutory. Judges in France are supposed to base their decisions on statutes and codes. These decisions are legally binding only on the parties involved in the case and not on future decisions of the courts.

Contrary to these assumptions, French administrative law has for a long time been a judge-made law. Indeed, due to the lack of statutory law guiding the administrative action, most principles and rules at the basis of French administrative law were set out by the case law of the Council of State. This is the case, for example, with the main rules and principles governing judicial review of administrative decisions,[54] as well as with the specific tort law rules applicable to administrative bodies and civil servants,[55] or the specific rules regarding the functioning of public contracts.[56] This does not mean, obviously, that judicial review was only judge-made: important statutes in the field of public procurement, for instance, have existed since the nineteenth century.[57]

During the last decades of the twentieth century, numerous statutes were adopted in various fields of administrative law, complementing judge-made law. It is important to underline that the statutes adopted in those fields sometimes confined themselves to codifying the principles formerly set out by the case law of the Council of State and

[51] For details, see Chapter 9, section 9.4.B.2.
[52] For a comparative analysis of the German administrative procedure, see H Pünder, 'German administrative procedure in a comparative perspective: Observations on the path to a transnational ius commune proceduralis in administrative law' (2013) 11 *International Journal of Constitutional Law* 940–961.
[53] For details, see Chapter 3, section 3.2.A.1.
[54] See Chapter 6, section 6.5.
[55] See Chapter 11.
[56] See Chapter 3, section 3.5.C.
[57] L Richer, *Droit des contrats administratifs*, 9th edn (Issy-les-Moulineaux, Lextenso, 2016) 312.

sometimes developed new principles (such as in the case of requiring the giving of reasons when a request for access to documents is refused). Today, many parts of French administrative law are codified, meaning that the laws, governmental acts or judicial principles governing a field of administrative law are grouped in a single book. The movement of codification began at the end of the twentieth and beginning of the twenty-first centuries. Today, for example, the laws on public property,[58] public procurement,[59] local government[60] and urbanism[61] are codified, in the sense that one can find all rules regulating such fields in a single act.

The last important code to be drafted was the Code of relations between administration and members of the public (Code des relations entre le public et l'administration). Before, in France, the general law on administrative procedure was made of jurisprudential and statutory provisions. The Code of relations between administration and members of the public only entered into force on 1 January 2016. Also, the procedure before administrative courts was codified in 2001 in the Code of Administrative Justice (Code de justice administrative).

Thus, the specific construction of French administrative law also resulted in a system where case law is very important, but where statutory law plays an increasingly significant role.

1.3.C ENGLAND AND WALES

In the legal system of England and Wales, case law has been an important method through which legal principles have been developed in both public and private law.

The sources of law are primary legislation, secondary legislation and case law. In the realm of general administrative law, there has been relatively little legislative intervention. The Human Rights Act 1998 and European Communities Act 1972 have evidently had considerable influence on judicial review. Parliament has also sought to regulate access to judicial review in terms of time limits and standing in the Senior Courts Act 1981. The process of judicial review is further regulated by the Civil Procedure Rules 1998, a piece of secondary legislation.

However, the principle of legality is predominantly judge-made through case law, with little being drawn from legislation. Such fundamental principles as the law on the rationality (such as the 'unreasonableness' test) and proportionality of administrative decisions, the *audi alteram partem* and *nemo iudex in causa sua* principles, and the principle of legitimate expectations are all derived from the decisions of the courts, rather than from any legislative source.[62] The Human Rights Act 1998 has no doubt had considerable

[58] See Code général de la propriété des personnes publiques (General Code on the Property of Public Entities).

[59] See Code des marchés publics (Public Procurement Code).

[60] See Code général des collectivités territoriales (Local Authorities Code).

[61] See Code de l'urbanisme (Planning Code).

[62] For a detailed exposition of these issues, see Chapter 6, sections 6.3.B.3, 6.5.A.5 and 6.5.B.4.

impact on some of these principles, as has EU law, but they are still developed by the courts.[63] In conclusion, case law is the predominant source, with relatively few statutory sources of general application.

As an example of the force of case law as a source of administrative law in England and Wales, administrative procedure is very interesting, for England and Wales is the only legal system (among the legal systems examined in this book) without a code of administrative procedure. This is not to say that there is no process for the regulation of administrative procedure, but such procedures tend to be regulated either by administrative rule-making or by individual pieces of legislation that empower action in specific policy fields and by the overarching principle of the rule of law, with its principles extracted from the case law.[64]

1.3.D THE NETHERLANDS

Dutch administrative law is a continental legal system where written and codified law plays an important role. The importance of case law must be put in perspective against the other systems under study. In the Netherlands, case law plays a less significant role than in England and Wales. At the same time, in comparison with Germany, administrative law rules are less codified and case law appears to be more important. In addition to this, unwritten principles play a very significant role in the Dutch system, especially the principles of good administration. An example of the importance of the general principles of good administration is as follows: although the Dutch Constitution identifies the principle of equality in Article 1, in administrative law cases, the administration and citizens usually apply and rely on the unwritten principle of equality, being one of the principles of good administration.[65] Therefore, they prefer using the principle of good administration instead of their written constitutional rights and norms.

Until 1994, there were a large number of acts regulating administrative procedure, access to the court and court procedures. All of these regulations differed in detail, often without any valid reason. On 1 January 1994, the General Administrative Law Act (Algemene Wet Bestuursrecht, AWB) came into force – or, at least, the main parts of the act. In the following years, the AWB has been extended and parts have been substantially revised on a number of occasions.[66] The AWB contains some general rules on public administration (chapter 2), rules on decision-making (chapters 3 and 4), enforcement measures (chapter 5), objection and judicial review procedures (chapters 6–8), complaint procedures (chapter 9) and provisions on the allocation of administrative powers to administrative authorities (chapter 10). Many rules, including all of the rules relating

[63] See, eg P Birkinshaw, *European Public Law*, 2nd edn (Alphen aan den Rijn, Kluwer, 2014) ch 8.

[64] See, eg A Tomkins, 'The Struggle to Delimit Executive Power in Britain' in A Tomkins and P Craig (eds), *The Executive and Public Law: Power and Accountability in Comparative Perspective* (Oxford, Oxford University Press, 2005) 16–51.

[65] For more on this point, see Chapter 6, section 6.5.C.3.

[66] The most recent substantial revision came into force on 1 January 2013 and concerned parts of the rules on administrative court procedures, Wet aanpassingen bestuursprocesrecht, Stb 2012, 682.

to objection and judicial review procedures, are meant to be exhaustive in the sense that the legislator should not deviate from them in other statutory acts. To prevent differences and inconsistencies between exhaustive AWB provisions and other statutory acts, all other acts have been adapted to the AWB provisions in so-called adaptation laws (*aanpassingswetgeving*). Other rules, however, are meant to function as a default option (deviation for valid reasons in other acts is possible) or to function only as a safety net that applies only if there is no other special rule in other legislation. The introduction of the AWB has not only harmonised and simplified administrative law to a large extent, but also pushed the development of administrative law forward to a higher level in general.

1.3.E THE EUROPEAN UNION

P Craig, Administrative Law[67] **1.16 (EU)**

The sources of EU administrative law are eclectic. They are to be found primarily in the Treaty, EU legislation, the case law of the EU courts, and decisions made by the European Ombudsman. The administrative law of the Member States has moreover been influential in shaping the EU regime. The more particular role played by each will become apparent in this chapter and those that follow. It may nonetheless be helpful at this juncture to exemplify their respective contributions.

The Treaty contains articles that deal with principles, both procedural and substantive, which are directly relevant for judicial review. The following are simply examples. Thus Article 296 TFEU establishes a duty to give reasons that applies to all legal acts, whether legislative, delegated, or implementing. The reasons must refer to any proposals, initiatives, recommendations, requests, or opinions required by the Treaties. It is noteworthy that Article 296 imposes a duty to give reasons not only for administrative decisions, but also for legislative norms. Article 15 TFEU deals with access to information. It provides for a right of access to documents of the Union's institutions, bodies, offices, and agencies, whatever their medium, subject to certain principles and conditions. Non-discrimination provides an example of a substantive principle within the Treaty that is of direct relevance for judicial review. Thus Article 18 TFEU contains a general proscription of discrimination on the grounds of nationality, and this is also to be found in the specific Treaty articles dealing with free movement of workers, freedom of establishment, and the provision of services. Non-discrimination on the grounds of gender is dealt with by Article 157 TFEU. There are also provisions dealing with non-discrimination as between producers or consumers in the field of agriculture, Article 40(2) TFEU, and specific provisions such as Article 110 TFEU prohibiting discriminatory taxation.

EU legislation made pursuant to the Treaty may also deal with the principles of judicial review. This legislation may flesh out a principle contained in a Treaty article. This was the case in relation to the legislation adopted pursuant to Article 15 TFEU, dealing with access to information. EU legislation may also establish a code of administrative procedure for a particular area.

The EU courts have, however, made the major contribution to the development of administrative law principles. They have read principles such as proportionality,

[67] P Craig, *Administrative Law* (Oxford, Oxford University Press, 2012) 246.

fundamental rights, legal certainty, legitimate expectations, equality, and procedural justice into the Treaty, and used them as the foundation for judicial review under Article 263 or 267 TFEU.

Notes

(1) As far as judicial review is concerned, the Treaties contain provisions on the number of judges, the available remedies for Member States, institutions and private parties, and the fundamental characteristics of EU judicial proceedings.

(2) The procedure before the European Court of Justice and the General Court is furthermore governed by the Statute of the Court of Justice. Its provisions have the same force as treaty articles. The Statute, provided in Protocol No 3 of the TFEU, is framework legislation for the proceedings before the EU courts. Furthermore, the Rules of Procedure of the Court of Justice[68] and General Court[69] complete the procedural framework applicable in the proceedings before the European courts.

(3) In the EU legal system, sources are mixed, but, as the excerpt above shows, judge-made law plays a very important part.

(4) It is to be noted that administrative procedure is not yet codified, although there are pushes by academics, the European Ombudsman and the European Parliament to draft a law to regulate the topic.[70]

1.3.F COMPARATIVE REMARKS

In the legal systems examined, the sources of law in administrative matters are mixed, but everywhere the courts play a very important role. If one were to design a scale of sources, Germany, where statutes are a primary source in judicial review, would be at one end and at the other end would be France and England and Wales, as countries where courts play a key role in designing judicial review. The Netherlands would be somewhere in the middle, as would the EU.

Legal systems are, however, changing and this is reflected in the law of administrative procedure. France has joined the group of countries having a law regulating the topic. Only England and Wales and the EU, of the legal systems covered, still do not, which does not mean that the procedure is completely judge-made, but it does mean that

[68] Rules of Procedure of the Court of Justice of 25 September 2012 [2012] OJ L265/1, as amended on 18 June 2013 [2013] OJ L173/65 and on 19 July 2016 [2016] OJ L217/69.

[69] Rules of Procedure of the Court of First Instance of 30 May 1991 [1991] OJ L136/1 with further amendments.

[70] See the Research Network on EU Administrative Law (ReNEUAL) project on administrative procedure. ReNEUAL is a network scholars from all over Europe. For further details, see www.reneual.eu. ReNEUAL has developed 'Draft Model Rules on EU Administrative Procedures', available at www.reneual.eu/index.php/projects-and-publications/reneual-1-0. The European Parliament voted for a Proposal for a regulation of the European Parliament and of the Council on the Administrative Procedure of the European Union's institutions, bodies, offices and agencies: www.europarl.europa.eu/meetdocs/2014_2019/plmrep/COMMITTEES/JURI/DV/2016/01-28/1081253EN.pdf.

general principles of law (which are mostly judge-made) play a prominent role. In the EU, as mentioned above, there is a movement towards codifying administrative procedure.

1.4 CONSTITUTIONAL GUARANTEES

The study of constitutional guarantees implies providing an answer to two broad questions. The first question is whether the right to judicial review of administrative action is guaranteed by constitutional norms or whether it finds its basis only in statutory law or case law. The second question is whether the administrative court system itself is constitutionally protected. Are there any constitutional norms for the division of power between administrative and other (ordinary) courts or is this only a question of mere statutory law? The two questions are intertwined and are therefore dealt with within one section.

1.4.A GERMANY

Grundgesetz **1.17 (DE)**

Article 19 (4) Should any person's rights be violated by a public authority, he shall have recourse to the courts. If no other jurisdiction has been established, recourse shall be to the ordinary courts. ...

Notes

(1) The Basic Law guarantees a fundamental right to judicial review in Article 19(4) and a right to be heard in Article 103(1). Article 19(4) of the Basic Law requires that judicial protection against public power[71] is as comprehensive as possible and efficient without leaving jurisdictional gaps (*möglichst lückenlos, umfassend und effektiv*).[72] The constitutional right of effective judicial protection enshrined in Article 19(4) of the Basic Law is a fundamental pillar of the German *Rechtsstaatsprinzip* (rule of law principle).

(2) The courts and legal scholars have come to the conclusion that Article 19(4) of the Basic Law warrants a complete control of the administrative action.[73] The guarantee of access to the courts, however, requires that the plaintiff alleges a violation of a subjective right (*subjektives Recht*), as the German administrative law focuses on the protection of individual rights.

[71] Understood as the exercise of public power, not economic activities carried out by the administration.

[72] BVerfGE, 8, 274, 326; BVerfGE 84, 34, 49. F Hufen, *Verwaltungsprozesrecht*, 9th edn (Munich, Beck, 2013) 9. For historical reasons, namely mistrust towards the administrative judiciary, Art 14(3), Art 19(4) sentence 2 and Art 34 Basic Law assign certain disputes relating to state liability and expropriation to ordinary courts.

[73] BVerfGE 15, 275, 282; BVerfGE 61, 82, 110; BVerfGE 78, 214, 226. For a brief English overview of the consequences of Art 19 (IV) GG, see F Erath, 'Scope of Judicial Review in German Administrative Law' (1997) 8 Stellenbosh Law Review 193, 197.

(3) Even though Article 19(4) of the Basic Law guarantees judicial access, it grants judicial recourse only to the extent provided for by the respective implementing procedural law in force,[74] which must not, however, render access to administrative courts unreasonably difficult or impossible.[75]

Grundgesetz **1.18 (DE)**

Article 95 (1) The Federation shall establish the Federal Court of Justice, the Federal Administrative Court, the Federal Finance Court, the Federal Labour Court and the Federal Social Court as supreme courts of ordinary, administrative, financial, labour and social jurisdiction.

Note

The court structure of Germany is laid out in Articles 92–96 of the Basic Law and characterised by decentralisation and specialisation. Article 95(1) establishes five branches of the judiciary, namely ordinary, labour, administrative, social and financial jurisdiction. Article 95(1) of the Basic Law thereby includes an institutional guarantee for administrative jurisdiction. Each of the branches of jurisdiction is crowned with an apex court at the federal level and one or more levels below at state level. Furthermore, every state has a state Constitutional Court and there is a Federal Constitutional Court. This structure provides the constitutional guarantee for the administrative courts in Germany.

1.4.B FRANCE

Conseil d'État, 17 February 1950[76] **1.19 (FR)**

Minister of Agriculture v Lamotte

JUDICIAL REVIEW OF ADMINISTRATIVE DECISIONS

Dame Lamotte

There is a general principle of law according to which any administrative decision may be subject to judicial review.

Facts: A statute of 17 August 1940 had given the prefects the power to grant uncultivated and abandoned pieces of land to third persons. On that basis, the lands owned by Ms Lamotte had been granted on three separate occasions to someone else (Mr Testa). On each occasion, the Council of State quashed the decision of the prefect on the ground that the designated pieces of land were not abandoned and uncultivated. The prefect took a fourth decision, which should have been considered lawful by the administrative courts because, in the

[74] BVerfGE 10, 264, 267.

[75] BVerfGE 49, 329, 341; BVerfGE 80, 244, 250. According to BVerwGE 100, 262, however, judicial protection is only guaranteed according to the system of enumerated actions. This is questioned by Hufen (n 73 above) 9–10. According to Hufen, there has to be an action available against any form of interference of the administration with individual rights.

[76] No 86949.

meantime, statutory provisions had been adopted stating that 'adoption of the grant decision may not be the object of any review, administrative or judicial'.

Held: The Council of State annulled the decision.

Judgment: Considering that Article 4(2) of the said Act of 23 May 1943 establishes these terms: 'The making of the grant decision may not be the object of any review, administrative or judicial'; that, if this provision, to the extent that its nullity has not been established under the Ordinance of 9 August 1944 on the re-establishment of republican legality, has the effect of removing the right of review which Article 29 of the Act of 19 February 1942 had made available to the owner to challenge the validity of the grant decision before the Prefecture Council, it has not removed the right to have the adoption of the grant decision reviewed before the Council of State on the issue of lack of powers, a ground of review available against any act of the executive even in the absence of a statutory text, and one whose purpose is, in conformity with the general principles of law, to ensure respect for legality; that it follows from this that, on the one hand, the Minister of Agriculture is entitled to request the annulment of the decision cited above of the Lyon Prefecture council dated 4 October 1946; but, on the other hand, that it is for the Council of State, as the judge entrusted with legality control (*juge de l'excès de pouvoir*), to decide on Ms Lamotte's claim for the annulment of the decision of the prefect of Ain of 10 August 1944.

Note

In this case, the Council of State held that it follows from the general principles of French law that any administrative decision must be reviewable before the administrative courts. Hence, while there is no constitutionally enshrined right to judicial review, this right has been recognised by the case law of the Council of State.

Conseil Constitutionnel, 22 July 1980[77] **1.20 (FR)**

INDEPENDENCE OF ADMINISTRATIVE COURTS

Law validating administrative acts

The independence of the administrative courts is guaranteed by the Constitution.

Facts: This was the first case in which the Constitutional Council was requested directly to examine a law validating administrative acts, ie a law that restored an administrative act previously annulled. In 1977, a central joint technical committee of teaching staff subject to the regulations governing university teachers was established by a decree. However, the Council of State quashed the decree. Therefore, all the individual or general decisions adopted on the basis of this text were threatened. A validating bill consisting of a single article was then proposed: 'Orders adopted following consultation of the joint technical committee … established by order N°77-679 of 29 June 1977 and all measures, whether in the form of regulations or not, adopted on the basis of those orders are validated.' The law was referred to the Constitutional Council. The applicants claimed a breach of the principle of separation of powers and failure to observe the distribution of legislative and regulatory powers.

Held: The application was dismissed and the law validating administrative acts was declared compatible with the Constitution.

[77] 80–119 DC.

Judgment: 6. Considering that it follows from the provisions of Article 64 of the Constitution regarding the judicial authority and of the fundamental principles recognized by the laws of the Republic regarding, according to the law of 24 May 1872, the administrative the courts, that the independence of courts is guaranteed as well as the specific nature of their duties which may not be encroached upon neither by the legislator nor by the Government; that, as such, it belongs neither to the legislature nor to the Government to control the decisions of the courts, to address injunctions to the courts and to substitute themselves to the decision of disputes of their competence. …

Conseil Constitutionnel, 23 January 1987[78] **1.21 (FR)**

JURISDICTION OF ADMINISTRATIVE COURTS

Conseil de la concurrence

Administrative courts are competent to review decisions taken by authorities in the exercise of prerogatives of public power.

Facts: The French Parliament had decided to confer the jurisdiction to review the decisions of the Conseil de la concurrence (now Autorité de la concurrence, Competition Authority, ie the body responsible to adjudicate on competition law issues) to the ordinary courts.

Held: The Council declared the transfer of jurisdiction lawful but found the law invalid on the ground that (in the absence of any provision for a stay of execution) it infringed the rights of the defence, a principle of constitutional rank.

Judgment: 15. Considering that the provisions of Articles 10 and 13 of the law of 16 and 24 August 1790 and the decree of 16 fructidor year III which have laid down the principle of the separation between administrative and judicial authorities in a general manner do not in themselves have constitutional value; considering that, nevertheless, in conformity with the French conception of the separation of powers, amongst the 'fundamental principles recognized by the Republic', there is the principle according to which, with the exception of matters reserved by their nature to the ordinary courts, jurisdiction concerning the annulment or amendment of the decisions taken, in the exercise of prerogatives of public power, by the authorities exercising the executive power, their agents, the regional authorities of the Republic or the public bodies placed under their authority or under their control belongs to the administrative courts; …

Note

The French Constitution of 4 October 1958 does not expressly mention the existence or the jurisdiction of administrative courts, because these institutions predate the drafting of the Constitution that takes them for granted. However, the French Constitutional Council ruled that the independence of the administrative courts is guaranteed by the Constitution in two decisions: 80–119 DC of 22 July 1980 and 86–224 DC of 23 January 1987. In these decisions, the Constitutional Council proclaimed not only the independence of administrative courts, but also their exclusive competence to annul fully or in part decisions taken by the administration.

[78] 86–224 DC.

1.4.C THE NETHERLANDS

Grondwet **1.22 (NL)**

Article 112 (1) The adjudication of disputes involving rights under civil law and debts is attributed to the judiciary.

(2) The competence to adjudicate disputes which do not arise from civil law legal relations may be attributed by Act of Parliament either to the judiciary or to courts that do not form part of the judiciary. The method of dealing with such cases and the consequences of decisions shall be regulated by Act of Parliament.

Article 115 Appeal to a higher administrative authority shall be possible in the case of the disputes referred to in Article 112(2).

Article 117 Members of the judiciary responsible for the administration of justice ... shall be appointed for life by Royal Decree.

Article 121 Except where deviations are laid down in a statute, court hearings are open to the public and the judgments include the grounds on which they are based. The judgments are delivered in open court.

Notes

(1) The Dutch Constitution does not contain significant guidance or guarantees to ensure the right of access to a court in administrative matters, or on the existence of specific administrative courts or the institutional and procedural guarantees applicable to such courts. The administrative court system is not protected in the constitution.

(2) The right of access to a court, however, is guaranteed by means of a combination of Article 112(1) of the Constitution, as it has been interpreted by the Dutch Supreme Court in the landmark case of *Guldemond/Noordwijkerhout*, along with Article 6 ECHR, which is directly applicable in the Netherlands on the ground of Articles 93 and 94 of the Constitution. As regards specific institutional and procedural guarantees, Article 6 ECHR is of even more importance.

Hoge Raad, 31 December 1915[79] **1.23 (NL)**

Guldemond v Municipality of Noordwijkerhout

COMPETENCE OF THE ORDINARY COURTS TO DECIDE ALL CASES CONCERNING CIVIL RIGHTS

Guldemond/Noordwijkerhout

It is not the public or private law nature of the dispute, but the right which is to be protected that determines the exclusive competence of the judiciary.

Facts: Guldemond owned a piece of land in Noordwijkerhout. On his land, he had dug a canal, which crossed (and hence cut) a footpath. Therefore the path could no longer be used. The municipality of Noordwijkerhout

[79] ECLI:NL:HR:1915:AG1773.

wanted to fill in parts of the canal and reinstall the footpath. To prevent this from happening, Guldemond commenced proceedings before the ordinary courts. In these proceedings, the municipality argued that the civil court was not competent to adjudicate the case as the action of the municipality constituted the exercise of a public task to guarantee that public roads can be used. The dispute ultimately came before the Supreme Court.

Held: The Dutch Supreme Court held that ordinary courts are exclusively competent to decide on administrative matters provided that the right that the claimant seeks to assert can be characterised as a civil right.

Judgment: Considering that Article 165 of the Constitution of 1815, in order to break away from the French administration system, in which the administration claims jurisdiction over all disputes in which the interests of the State come into conflict with the interests of specified individuals, determines the following principle: 'All disputes regarding property or rights arising therefrom, concerning financial claims and civil rights belong exclusively to the sphere of the judiciary' – and that as a consequence of this constitutional precept, Article 2 of the Organisation of the Courts Act (Wet op de Rechterlijke Organisatie) of 18 April 1827 was adopted;

Considering that it cannot be assumed that the aforementioned constitutional article intended to make a clear distinction between private and public law disputes; as such, a distinction was essentially unknown in 1815, but, as appears from the words 'exclusively', the idea was to restrict the power of the administration, and to place the rights referred to in that article unconditionally under the supervision of the judiciary;

Considering that it is therefore not the public or private law nature of the dispute, but the right which is to be protected that determines the exclusive competence of the judiciary, as is further evidenced by the French text of this constitutional article: '*Les contestations qui ont pour objet la propriéte ou les droits qui en dérivent etc.*';

Considering that Article 2 of the Organisation of the Courts Act should have the same meaning ….

Considering that from the foregoing it can be derived that, also according to Article 2 of the Organisation of the Courts Act, the exclusive competence of the judiciary is dependent on the object of the dispute, i.e. of the right which the claimant demands to be protected, and not on the nature of the right on which the defendant has based his defense.

… That thus, as Guldemond claims to hold a right to a quiet and peaceful enjoyment of the canal which he owns, and as the municipality of Noordwijkerhout renders the exercise of this right extremely difficult or even impossible, there is certainly a dispute as referred to in Article 2 of the Organisation of the Courts Act;

…

Considering that property is a civil right, so that the judiciary is exclusively competent to hear the case and to rule on it;

Notes

(1) Article 112(1) of the Dutch Constitution – which is in substance identical to Article 165 of the former Constitution and the former Article 2 of the Organisation of the Courts Act (Wet op de Rechterlijke Organisatie), interpreted in *Guldemond/Noordwijkerhout* – stipulates that the judiciary is competent in disputes about civil rights and obligations. According to Article 112(2) of the Constitution, the competence to decide disputes which do not arise from a civil law relationship (ie administrative law disputes) may be attributed by Act of Parliament to the judiciary, to a court

which is not part of the judiciary or – according to Article 115 of the Constitution – to a higher administrative authority. Thus, the Constitution does not contain any hard rules as regards the existence of administrative courts separate from the ordinary judiciary. As a result, it does not guarantee the existence of the administrative courts.

(2) For the current picture of judicial review in administrative law matters, the case of *Guldemond/Noordwijkerhout* is still essential. In this case, the Supreme Court decided in favour of a wide interpretation of the notion 'disputes about property or rights arising therefrom, about financial claims and about civil rights', a notion that, according to Article 165 of the old Constitution, is decisive for the exclusive competence of the judiciary. This wide interpretation also applies to the (in substance identical) notion of 'disputes involving rights under civil law' contained in Article 112 of the current Constitution. According to this interpretation, the judiciary is competent whenever a claimant demands that a civil right should be protected and also if the possible violation of the civil right is committed by an administrative authority exercising a public law task. Within the structure of the judiciary, this competence is exercised by the ordinary courts. As a result, the ordinary courts are always competent to decide in administrative law disputes whenever an individual 'frames' a violation of the public law rules by an administrative authority in terms of a violation of a civil right. As every violation by an authority can be labelled either as an infringement of property right or as a tort, the ordinary courts are therefore always competent to decide in administrative law matters. Thus, since 1915, the right of access to a court in administrative law disputes seems to be constitutionally guaranteed on the basis of a wide interpretation of Article 112 of the current Constitution (Article 165 of the old Constitution). The wide interpretation of Article 165 of the old Constitution by the Supreme Court in *Guldemond/Noordwijkerhout* can be explained by the fact that, at the time of the judgment, there was no (other) possibility of judicial review against most administrative action. In the following years, however, the legislator increasingly established specialised administrative courts and other means of legal protection in specific areas of law. In reaction to this development, the Supreme Court upheld its line of case law in which it maintained its competence in administrative law disputes in principle, but declared that claims against the administrative action are inadmissible if and to the extent that such action could be contested through a form of judicial protection offering 'sufficient procedural safeguards' ('*een met voldoende waarborgen omgeven administratieve rechtsgang*').[80]

1.4.D THE EUROPEAN UNION

Treaty on European Union **1.24 (EU)**

Article 19 (1) … Member States shall provide remedies sufficient to ensure effective legal protection in the fields covered by Union law.

[80] Hoge Raad, 25 November 1977, ECLI:NL:HR:1977:AC6111, NJ 1978, 255.

Charter of Fundamental Rights of the European Union **1.25 (EU)**

Article 47 Everyone whose rights and freedoms guaranteed by the law of the Union are violated has the right to an effective remedy before a tribunal in compliance with the conditions laid down in this Article.

Everyone is entitled to a fair and public hearing within a reasonable time by an independent and impartial tribunal previously established by law. Everyone shall have the possibility of being advised, defended and represented.

Legal aid shall be made available to those who lack sufficient resources in so far as such aid is necessary to ensure effective access to justice.

Note

A constitutional guarantee of the right of judicial review in all areas of European law can be found in the Treaties. Articles 19 and 47 can be regarded as a codification of the principle of effective judicial protection before a court.[81] These provisions are especially relevant for the intense doctrinal and jurisprudential debate concerning access to court.[82]

Treaty on European Union **1.26 (EU)**

Article 13 (1) The Union shall have an institutional framework which shall aim to promote its values, advance its objectives, serve its interests, those of its citizens and those of the Member States, and ensure the consistency, effectiveness and continuity of its policies and actions.

The Union's institutions shall be:

...

– the Court of Justice of the European Union,

...

Article 19 (1) The Court of Justice of the European Union shall include the Court of Justice, the General Court and specialised courts. It shall ensure that in the interpretation and application of the Treaties the law is observed. ...

Note

Similar to the German legal system, the jurisdiction of the CJEU is constitutionally guaranteed. The TFEU contains further rules detailing the jurisdiction of the Court of Justice, the types of proceedings which may be brought before the European courts, and the method of appointment of the judges and Advocates General.[83]

[81] This principle was first mentioned by the Court of Justice in the *Heylens* case (Case C-222/86 *Unectef v Georges Heylens and others* ECLI:EU:C:1987:442) and has been reiterated since then on many occasions (see, eg Case C-432/05 *Unibet (London) Ltd and Unibet (International) Ltd v Justitiekanslern* ECLI:EU:C:2007:163).

[82] See Chapter 4, section 4.4.B.5.

[83] See Section 5, ch 1, title 1, pt 6 of the TFEU.

1.4.E ENGLAND AND WALES

Foreign Compensation Act 1950[84] **1.27 (EW)**

Section 4 (4) The determination by the commission of any application made to them under this Act shall not be called in question in any court of law.

House of Lords, 17 December 1968[85] **1.28 (EW)**

Anisminic v Foreign Compensation Commission

EFFECTIVENESS OF OUSTER CLAUSES; NULLITIES

Anisminic

'Ouster' or preclusion clauses will not generally be effective where a decision of a public authority is unlawful and thus ultra vires and void – a 'nullity'.

Facts: Anisminic was a British company operating in Egypt at the time of the Suez crisis. Its property was sequestrated by a decision of the Egyptian government, which in 1957 sold the property to an Egyptian organisation under the terms of the sequestration order. The UK government brought about a compensation scheme for those who faced sequestration of their property as a result of the Suez crisis and the Foreign Compensation Commission held that Anisminic was not entitled to compensation under the provisions of the compensation scheme. When Anisminic brought a claim for judicial review, the Foreign Compensation Commission sought to rely on the preclusion clause in Section 4(4) of the Foreign Compensation Act 1950.

Held: The 'ouster' or preclusion clause did not serve to protect unlawful decisions from judicial review as such decisions were *ultra vires* and thus a 'nullity'.

Judgment: Lord Reid: The next argument was that, by reason of the provisions of section 4 (4) of the 1950 Act, the courts are precluded from considering whether the respondent's determination was a nullity, and therefore it must be treated as valid whether or not an inquiry would disclose that it was a nullity. Section 4 (4) states these terms:

'The determination by the commission of any application made to them under this Act shall not be called in question in any court of law.'

The respondent maintains that these are plain words only capable of having one meaning. Here is a determination which is apparently valid: there is nothing on the face of the document to cast any doubt on its validity. If it is a nullity, that could only be established by raising some kind of proceedings in court. But that would be calling the determination in question, and that is expressly prohibited by the statute. The appellants maintain that that is not the meaning of the words of this provision. They say that 'determination' means a real determination and does not include an apparent or purported determination which in the eyes of the law has no existence because it is a nullity. Or, putting it in another way, if you seek to show that a determination is a nullity you are not questioning the purported determination; you are maintaining that it does not exist as a determination. It is one thing to question a determination which does exist: it is quite another thing to say that there is nothing to be questioned.

[84] Chapter 12, 12 July 1950. Note that this section of the Act is no longer in force, but is included to provide an illustration of the issue in the *Anisminic* case.

[85] [1969] 2 AC 147 (HL).

Let me illustrate the matter by supposing a simple case. A statute provides that a certain order may be made by a person who holds a specified qualification or appointment, and it contains a provision, similar to section 4 (4), that such an order made by such a person shall not be called in question in any court of law. A person aggrieved by an order alleges that it is a forgery or that the person who made the order did not hold that qualification or appointment. Does such a provision require the court to treat that order as a valid order? It is a well established principle that a provision ousting the ordinary jurisdiction of the court must be construed strictly – meaning, I think, that, if such a provision is reasonably capable of having two meanings, that meaning shall be taken which preserves the ordinary jurisdiction of the court.

Statutory provisions which seek to limit the ordinary jurisdiction of the court have a long history. No case has been cited in which any other form of words limiting the jurisdiction of the court has been held to protect a nullity. If the draftsman or Parliament had intended to introduce a new kind of ouster clause so as to prevent any inquiry even as to whether the document relied on was a forgery, I would have expected to find something much more specific than the bald statement that a determination shall not be called in question in any court of law. Undoubtedly such a provision protects every determination which is not a nullity. But I do not think that it is necessary or even reasonable to construe the word 'determination' as including everything which purports to be a determination but which is in fact no determination at all. And there are no degrees of nullity. There are a number of reasons why the law will hold a purported decision to be a nullity. I do not see how it could be said that such a provision protects some kinds of nullity but not others: if that were intended it would be easy to say so.

Note

In the UK's unwritten constitution, there is an absence of any express constitutional guarantee of access to judicial review proceedings. Parliament may seek to include 'ouster clauses', limiting or removing the ability of the courts to engage in judicial review of particular decisions, although the courts have always sought to read such clauses restrictively, and since the decision in *Anisminic*, most 'ouster' clauses have had limited effect.

Regulation of Investigatory Powers Act 2000, Chapter 23 **1.29 (EW)**

Section 65 (1) There shall, for the purpose of exercising the jurisdiction conferred on them by this section, be a tribunal consisting of such number of members as Her Majesty may by Letters Patent appoint.

(2) The jurisdiction of the Tribunal shall be–

(a) to be the only appropriate tribunal for the purposes of section 7 of the Human Rights Act 1998 in relation to any proceedings under subsection (1)(a) of that section (proceedings for actions incompatible with Convention rights) which fall within subsection (3) of this section;

...

(3) Proceedings fall within this subsection if–

(a) they are proceedings against any of the intelligence services

...

Supreme Court, 9 December 2009[86] **1.30 (EW)**

R (A) v Director of Establishments of the Security Service

OUSTER CLAUSES; EFFECTIVENESS; LEGALITY

Security Service

Preclusion clauses can be effective at removing the jurisdiction of the court to undertake judicial review in certain circumstances, particularly where alternative means of redress exist.

Facts: A former agent of the security service wished to publish a book about his work and needed the permission of the Director of Establishments of the Security Service in order to do so. The Director refused permission. The former agent sought judicial review of this decision, arguing that the denial of permission was a breach of his rights under the ECHR. The Security Service claimed that the court had no jurisdiction to hear the case as Parliament had excluded the jurisdiction of the court in judicial review and created the Investigatory Powers Tribunal to provide redress in cases such as the one before the court.

Held: Section 65 of the Regulation of Investigatory Powers Act 2000 precluded the jurisdiction of the courts in judicial review.

Judgment: Lord Brown JSC: 21. A and JUSTICE argue that to construe section 65 as conferring exclusive jurisdiction on the IPT constitutes an ouster of the ordinary jurisdiction of the courts and is constitutionally objectionable on that ground. They pray in aid two decisions of high authority: *Pyx Granite Co Ltd v Ministry of Housing and Local Government [1960] AC 260* and *Anisminic Ltd v Foreign Compensation Commission [1969] 2 AC 147*. To my mind, however, the argument is unsustainable. In the first place, it is evident, as the majority of the Court of Appeal pointed out, that the relevant provisions of RIPA, HRA and the CPR all came into force at the same time as part of a single legislative scheme. With effect from 2 October 2000 section 7(1)(a) HRA jurisdiction came into existence (i) in respect of section 65(3) proceedings in the IPT pursuant to section 65(2)(a), and (ii) in respect of any other section 7(1)(a) HRA proceedings in the courts pursuant to section 7(9) and CPR r 7.11. True it is, as Rix LJ observed, that CPR r 7.11(2) does not explicitly recognise the exception to its apparent width represented by section 65(2)(a). But that is not to say that section 65(2)(a) ousts some pre-existing right.

22. This case, in short, falls within the principle recognised by the *House of Lords in Barraclough v Brown [1897] AC 615* – where, as Lord Watson said, at p 622: 'The right and the remedy are given uno flatu, and the one cannot be dissociated from the other' – rather than the principle for which *Pyx Granite* stands, at p 286: 'It is a principle not by any means to be whittled down that the subject's recourse to Her Majesty's courts for the determination of his rights is not to be excluded except by clear words.' Distinguishing *Barraclough v Brown*, Viscount Simonds pointed out that the statute there in question could be construed as merely providing an alternative means of determining whether or not the company had a pre-existing common law right to develop their land; it did not take away 'the inalienable remedy … to seek redress in [the courts]'. Before 2 October 2000 there was, of course, no pre-existing common law or statutory right to bring a claim based on an asserted breach of the Convention. Section 65(2)(a) takes away no 'inalienable remedy'.

23. Nor does *Anisminic* assist A. The ouster clause there under consideration purported to remove any judicial supervision of a determination by an inferior tribunal as to its

[86] [2009] UKSC 12, [2010] 2 AC 1.

own jurisdiction. Section 65(2)(a) does no such thing. Parliament has not ousted judicial scrutiny of the acts of the intelligence services; it has simply allocated that scrutiny (as to section 7(1)(a) HRA proceedings) to the IPT. Furthermore, as Laws LJ observed, ante, p 13, para 22: 'statutory measures which confide the jurisdiction to a judicial body of like standing and authority to that of the High Court, but which operates subject to special procedures apt for the subject matter in hand, may well be constitutionally inoffensive. The IPT ... offers ... no cause for concern on this score.' True it is that section 67(8) of RIPA constitutes an ouster (and, indeed, unlike that in *Anisminic*, an unambiguous ouster) of any jurisdiction of the courts over the IPT. But that is not the provision in question here and in any event, as A recognises, there is no constitutional (or article 6) requirement for any right of appeal from an appropriate tribunal.

24. The position here is analogous to that in *Farley v Secretary of State for Work and Pensions (No 2) [2006] 1 WLR 1817* where the statutory provision in question provided that, on an application by the Secretary of State for a liability order in respect of a person liable to pay child support, 'the court ... shall not question the maintenance assessment under which the payments of child support maintenance fall to be made'. Lord Nicholls of Birkenhead, with whom the other members of the committee agreed, observed, at para 18: 'The need for a strict approach to the interpretation of an ouster provision ... was famously confirmed in the leading case of Anisminic ... This strict approach, however, is not appropriate if an effective means of challenging the validity of a maintenance assessment is provided elsewhere. Then section 33(4) is not an ouster provision. Rather, it is part of a statutory scheme which allocates jurisdiction to determine the validity of an assessment and decide whether the defendant is a 'liable person' to a court other than the magistrates' court.'

Note

As illustrated by the excerpt above, it is possible for Parliament to exclude the jurisdiction of the courts to engage in judicial review in respect of particular issues or areas of administrative activity. However, it is notable in the excerpt above that the Supreme Court accepted the ouster clause at least in part because Parliament had not sought to remove any prospect of redress from the individual but had sought to provide an alternative forum from which redress could be sought.

Court of Appeal (Civil Division), 16 March 1976[87] **1.31 (EW)**

R v Secretary of State for the Environment, ex parte Ostler

EFFECTIVENESS OF LIMITATION CLAUSES

Ostler

Clauses which seek to limit, rather than to exclude, access to judicial review will generally be effective.

Facts: A corn merchant launched judicial review proceedings against an order made to compulsorily purchase his premises pursuant to a road development scheme. Mr Otler did not make his claim within 6 weeks,

[87] [1977] QB 122 (CA).

as required by the relevant provisions of the Highways Act 1959. Mr Ostler sought to argue that the requirement imposed on his claim was an 'ouster' clause and should be limited accordingly, due to the decision in *Anisminic*. The Divisional Court found in Mr Ostler's favour.

Held: The appeal was allowed. The provision in the Highways Act 1959 reducing the time limit for claims to 6 weeks was considered a limitation clause rather than an ouster clause and served an important public policy goal.

Judgment: Lord Denning MR: In these circumstances, I think that *Smith v. East Elloe Rural District Council* must still be regarded as good and binding on this court. It is readily to be distinguished from the *Anisminic* case [1969] 2 A.C. 147. The points of difference are these:

First, in the *Anisminic* case the Act ousted the jurisdiction of the court altogether. It precluded the court from entertaining any complaint at any time about the determination. Whereas in the East Elloe case the statutory provision has given the court jurisdiction to inquire into complaints so long as the applicant comes within six weeks. The provision is more in the nature of a limitation period than of a complete ouster. That distinction is drawn by Professor Wade, *Administrative Law*, 3rd ed. (1971), pp. 152–153, and by the late Professor S. A. de Smith in the latest edition of *Halsbury's Laws of England*, 4th ed., vol. 1 (1973), para. 22, note 14.

Second, in the *Anisminic* case, the House was considering a determination by a truly judicial body, the Foreign Compensation Tribunal, whereas in the *East Elloe* case the House was considering an order which was very much in the nature of an administrative decision. That is a distinction which Lord Reid himself drew in *Ridge v. Baldwin* [1964] A.C. 40, 72. There is a great difference between the two. In making a judicial decision, the tribunal considers the rights of the parties without regard to the public interest. But in an administrative decision (such as a compulsory purchase order) the public interest plays an important part. The question is, to what extent are private interests to be subordinated to the public interest.

Third, in the *Anisminic* case the House had to consider the actual determination of the tribunal, whereas in the *Smith v. East Elloe* case the House had to consider the validity of the process by which the decision was reached.

So *Smith v. East Elloe Rural District Council* [1956] A.C. 736 must still be regarded as the law in regard to this provision we have to consider here. I would add this: if this order were to be upset for want of good faith or for lack of natural justice, it would not to my mind be a nullity or void from the beginning. It would only be voidable, and as such, if it should be challenged promptly before much has been done under it, as Lord Radcliffe put it forcibly in *Smith v. East Elloe Rural District Council* [1956] A.C. 736, 769–770:

'But this argument is in reality a play on the meaning of the word nullity. An order,' – and he is speaking of an order such as we have got here – 'even if not made in good faith, is still an act capable of legal consequences. It bears no brand of invalidity upon its forehead. Unless the necessary proceedings are taken at law to establish the cause of invalidity and to get it quashed or otherwise upset, it will remain as effective for its ostensible purpose as the most impeccable of orders, and that brings us back to the question that determines this case: Has Parliament allowed the necessary proceedings to be taken?'

The answer which he gave was 'No'. That answer binds us in this court today.

Since the *Anisminic* case the court has considered the position in *Routh v. Reading Corporation*, December 2, 1970, Bar Library Transcript No. 472 of 1970. Salmon L.J., supported by Karminski and Cairns L.JJ., held that *Smith v. East Elloe Rural District Council* was of good authority, even after the *Anisminic* case. In Scotland, too, it has been applied, in *Hamilton v. Secretary of State for Scotland*, 1972 S.L.T. 233.

Looking at it broadly, it seems to me that the policy underlying the statute is that when a compulsory purchase order has been made, then if it has been wrongly obtained or made, a person aggrieved should have a remedy. But he must come promptly. He must come within six weeks. If he does so, the court can and will entertain his complaint. But if the six weeks expire without any application being made, the court cannot entertain it afterwards. The reason is because, as soon as that time has elapsed, the authority will take steps to acquire property, demolish it and so forth. The public interest demands that they should be safe in doing so. Take this very case. The inquiry was held in 1973. The orders made early in 1974. Much work has already been done under them. It would be contrary to the public interest that the demolition should be held up or delayed by further evidence or inquiries. I think we are bound by *Smith v. East Elloe Rural District Council* [1956] A.C. 736 to hold that Mr. Ostler is barred by the statute from now questioning these orders. He ought to be stopped at this moment. I would allow the appeal accordingly.

Note

Although the operation of ouster clauses has been limited by the decision in *Anisminic*, it remains possible for Parliament to enact legislation that limits access to judicial review through the imposition of time limits that are stricter than the norm, or limiting standing only to those affected by certain decisions.[88]

1.4.F COMPARATIVE REMARKS

This section examined two questions: do citizens have a right to judicial review which is constitutionally guaranteed? And is the administrative court system constitutionally protected? A right to judicial protection against the administrative action is guaranteed in all legal systems dealt with in this book (albeit not necessarily in the Constitution), except England and Wales. This may be due to the absence of a written constitution and the strong emphasis on the principle of parliamentary supremacy in England and Wales. This principle is a constitutional law concept and holds that the legislative body has absolute sovereignty, and is supreme over all other government institutions, including executive and judicial bodies. It therefore also allows the Parliament to introduce ouster clauses or (other) procedural rules which limit the possibilities to ask for judicial review. However, judges have tried to limit the consequences of such statutes.

The differences between the legal systems regarding the question whether the existence of the administrative courts is constitutionally guaranteed are more substantial. This is the case in Germany and the EU, but not in the Netherlands, France and England and Wales. In the Netherlands, the ECHR played a key role in the establishment of separate courts in administrative law matters.

[88] An example can be found in ss 287–88 of the Town and Country Planning Act 1990, which limits the standing to challenge certain planning decisions only to 'persons aggrieved' (ie directly affected) by the planning decision concerned. See also Chapter 4, section 4.8.B.1 (iii).

1.5 THE BASIS OF JUDICIAL REVIEW: OBJECTIVE VERSUS SUBJECTIVE MODELS

Although no system under study here is completely subjective or objective, a division may be made between systems where judicial review will lie only where a subjective right has been breached (whose aim is mainly to protect individuals) and systems that are aimed at protecting legality.

R Barents, EU Procedural Law and Effective Legal Protection[89] **1.32 (EU)**

According to the objective conception, the main function of legality review is to guarantee the respect of the law by the administration. By ensuring the observance of the law, legality review by the courts serves the general interest. What matters in this approach is in particular whether the administration has complied with its obligations under public law. As a consequence, in principle, the rights of the individual are derived from the legal obligations of the administration. Accordingly, it is not for an individual to bring an action in order to protect the general interest, which explains that a private action is admissible only if the applicant demonstrates that he or she has a personal interest. The action is well-founded if the applicant demonstrates that the contested act is vitiated by an objective illegality, for example, incompetence of its author, abuse of power or procedural defects. The fact that the courts exercise limited control, mainly regarding the facts and their legal qualification, in order not to substitute the executive's appreciation with their own assessments also fits into the objective conception of legality review. The intensity of legality review is usually more limited than that in the subjective approach. In the objective conception, moreover, particular attention is given to legal certainty. In general, the role of the courts is more passive in the sense that they only examine the pleas in fact and in law invoked by the applicant. Usually, if the action is well founded, the court must annul the act in question since it conflicts with the general interest. Whether this result constitutes an appropriate solution for the applicant is, in principle, not relevant since it is not the task of the courts to establish a new legal relationship between the administration and the plaintiff. Following an annulment, it is for the administration to adopt a new act or to take any other measure necessary to remedy the illegality. Generally speaking, in this approach effective legal protection of the applicant does not constitute the raison d'être of procedural law. What matters particularly is the enforcement of the law as it stands (including general principles of law), as a consequence of which the annulment of an act is first of all intended to remedy an infringement by the administration. Accordingly, in the objective approach, legal protection is more the result and less the aim of the proceedings. …

In the subjective conception of legality review, the principal aim of the proceedings is to safeguard individual rights against any infringement by the administration. Contrary to the objective approach, the obligations of the administration are, as a starting point, determined by the subjective rights of the individual. As far as the admissibility of the action is concerned it is, in principle, sufficient that the individual claims the infringement of a subjective right. As to the substance of the action, the courts examine first of all whether this right has been infringed in any manner. In principle, review by the courts

[89] Barents (n 42 above) 1445–46.

is more extensive, in particular with respect to the establishment and the qualification of the facts. In the subjective conception, the principle of protection of legitimate expectations is of considerable importance. In general, the courts play a more active role in the solution of the dispute in the sense that they examine all the relevant elements in order to rule on the claimed infringement of subjective rights. Accordingly, legality review is more intensive than in the objective approach. Apart from annulment of the act, the courts may, under certain conditions, also reform an act or give an injunction.

It is obvious that the two conceptions reflect theoretical models. In practice, each system of legality review demonstrates features of both conceptions, although to a different extent. Although in most European countries administrative law was initially conceived as a means of objective legality control, in modern times a general tendency towards individual legal protection can be seen, in particular under the influence of fundamental rights.

Note

A system of judicial review is based on an objective (*objectif*) basis, where the main question the court has to answer is whether the decision challenged is lawful or not and its main power is to quash that decision. Usually, in these systems, standing will be generous. Conversely, systems based on a subjective (*subjectif*) basis are those where the first question the court has to answer is whether a subjective right has been violated. Accordingly, the powers of the judge here will be wider in order to restore the previous situation or to compensate damage. Today, no legal system can be said to be purely objective or subjective. This, however, does not make the classification impossible.

1.5.A GERMANY

Grundgesetz **1.33 (DE)**

Article 19 (4) Should any person's rights be violated by a public authority, he shall have recourse to the courts. If no other jurisdiction has been established, recourse shall be to the ordinary courts. The second sentence of paragraph (2) of Article 10 shall not be affected by this Article.

Verwaltungsgerichtsordnung **1.34 (DE)**

§42 (2) Unless otherwise provided by law, the action shall only be admissible if the plaintiff claims that his rights have been violated by an administrative act or its refusal or omission.

Verwaltungsverfahrensgesetz **1.35 (DE)**

§46 Application for annulment of an administrative act which is not invalid under §44 cannot be made solely on the ground that the act came into being through the infringement of regulations governing procedure, form or local competence, where it is evident that the infringement has not influenced the decision on the substance.

Notes

(1) The German judicial review system is focused on the protection of individual rights.[90] Thus, the admissibility of a court action always requires the allegation of the violation of a subjective public right (*subjektives öffentliches Recht*), ie a right accorded to the individual by virtue of legislative choice or administrative decision. A special 'protection of rights doctrine' (*Schutznormtheorie*)[91] has been developed in German administrative law to establish whether the alleged infringed law grants an actionable individual public right or solely protects a 'general public interest'.

(2) In addition, German administrative law is characterised by the predominance of substantive law over procedural law. The administrative procedure has an 'auxiliary function' (*dienende Funktion*), being, in principle, only relevant in administrative court proceedings when it influences the outcome of the substantial administrative decision.[92] Thus, administrative decisions are generally not annulled because of procedural flaws which did not affect the content.[93]

1.5.B THE NETHERLANDS

Algemene Wet Bestuursrecht **1.36 (NL)**

Article 8:69 (1) The administrative judge shall give judgment on the basis of the act introducing the claim, the documents lodged, the proceedings during the preliminary investigations and the investigations in court.

(2) The administrative judge shall supplement the legal grounds of his own motion.

(3) The administrative judge may supplement the facts of his own motion.

Article 8:69a The administrative judge does not annul a decision on the ground that it is incompatible with a written or unwritten legal rule or a general legal principle if this rule or this principle evidently does not protect the interest of the one invoking it.

Explanatory memorandum to the Algemene Wet Bestuursrecht[94] **1.37 (NL)**

In the first place, the objectives of administrative procedural law are of relevance. In line with the developments outlined, we [the Ministers of Justice and the Interior, responsible for the AWB] opt in favour of the function of protecting individual rights as the primary function of administrative procedural law. ... This implies that the characteristics of the

[90] For an in-depth analysis of this characteristic of German judicial review of administrative action, see B Wegener, 'Subjective Public Rights' in H Pünder and C Waldhoff (eds), *Debates in German Public Law* (Oxford, Hart Publishing, 2014) 219–37.

[91] For more on this point, see Chapter 4, section 4.4.B.1.

[92] For details, see Chapter 6, section 6.6.

[93] For details, see Chapter 6, section 6.6. See also H Pünder, 'German Administrative Procedure in a Comparative Perspective: Observations on the Path to a Transnational Ius Commune Proceduralis in Administrative Law' (2013) 11 *International Journal of Constitutional Law* 940; H Pünder and A Klafki, 'Administrative Law in Germany' in Seerden (n 8 above) 49–106.

[94] PG Awb II, 174–75.

existing rules of administrative procedural law, which only serve the realisation of the aim to maintain the objective legal order, do not appear again in the new General Administrative Law Act (Algemene Wet Bestuursrecht) …

An important consequence is that the administrative judge is in principle bound to the scope of the dispute as it has been presented to him by the person filing the act introducing the claim and by the possible third parties. Going beyond this scope is, in the light of the judicial protection function of the administrative dispute and the existence of a legal relation between the parties, neither necessary nor desirable. Thus, the administrative judge should not rule beyond the scope of the dispute as presented – he should not rule *ultra petita*. This rule has been laid down in Article 8:69(1) AWB.

A second connected consequence, flowing from Article 8:69(1) AWB as well, is that the possibility of *reformatio in peius* in the strict sense will disappear.

L van den Berge, The Relation Turn in Dutch Administrative Law[95] **1.38 (NL)**

The need for a fundamental re-examination of continental administrative law's theoretical fundaments clearly emerges from recent developments in Dutch administrative law as a case in point. Responding to its changing socio-cultural and institutional context, the system of Dutch administrative law underwent some significant changes, slowly but surely drifting away from its classical orientation on the lawful division of goods and services amongst all members of society towards dispute settlement and the protection of individual rights as its primary aims. Originally directed at safeguarding the abstract legal order against unlawful infringements, judicial review of government action traditionally followed the logic of the 'recours objectif', typically directed at safeguarding the 'légalité abstraite' of government decisions erga omnes. Driven by the centrifugal forces of the ongoing 'horizontalization' and 'fragmentation' of the public sphere, the General Administrative Law Act (GALA) of 1994 replaced legality erga omnes with the 'recours subjectif' as its main orientation, geared towards the 'protection des droit individuels des particuliers', rather than towards abstract legality. Notwithstanding some significant modifications, however, the GALA left administrative law's underlying structure untouched, adhering to the ex tunc legality test of government decisions as its unaltered 'objective' skeleton. In this way, Dutch administrative law has developed into a 'bipolar' and thus rather incoherent and unstable system.

Note

Before 1994, the procedural law applicable before the administrative courts – and also before the appeal to the Crown – had strong elements of *recours objectif*.[96] The primary aim of the system was not to solve a conflict between a claimant and the administration or to protect individual rights, but to review the legality of a certain decision. In order to maintain the objective legal order, the courts were allowed, and sometimes obliged, to rule beyond an applicant's claim (*ultra petita*), even if this would place the claimant in a less favourable position (*reformatio in peius*).

[95] L van den Berge, 'The Relation Turn in Dutch Administrative Law' (2017) 13 *Utrecht Law Review* 99.
[96] See also section 1.2.A.3 above.

Since the entry into force of the Algemene Wet Bestuursrecht (AWB) in 1994, the system has changed; a change which is inspired by German law. The preparatory materials for the AWB explicitly state that, under the new AWB regime, maintaining the objective legal order is no longer a primary objective of administrative procedural law. Instead, the main aim is currently the legal protection of individual rights. As a result of this shift to a more 'subjective' model, the courts are no longer allowed to act *ultra petita*. Moreover, the *reformatio in peius* has been excluded.

A further element of the evolution to a more subjective model is the so-called 'relativity requirement' (*relativiteitsbeginsel*). According to Article 8:69a AWB, which was introduced in January 2013, an applicant can only rely on norms which aim to protect his or her interest. The introduction of the relativity requirement was to some extent inspired by the German *Schutznormtheorie.*[97]

In principle, however, the courts can still only annul a single-case decision (Articles 8:1 and 8:72(1) AWB) with an effect *erga omnes*. The judge cannot decide about other (factual) acts of the administration, nor can he forbid or order the administrative body to do or omit something. This does not fit very well with a *recours subjectif* and may still be seen as a consequence of the fact that the system started as a (mainly) *recours objectif* system.

To sum up, the Dutch system of judicial review originated in a mainly *recours objectif* model, but since 1994 has gradually shifted towards a more *recours subjectif* model. The current system still combines subjective and objective elements, but the ongoing trend is clearly towards *recours subjectif.*

1.5.C FRANCE

E Laferrière, Traité de la juridiction administrative et des recours contentieux[98] **1.39 (FR)**

The powers of administrative courts do not have the same nature and the same extent in all matters. They are, as the case may be, powers of full jurisdiction (*pouvoirs de pleine juridiction*), involving the exercise of full control of the dispute on points of law and of fact; or the powers of annulment limited to the power to annul unlawful administrative acts, without the administrative court having the power to amend them and to substitute its own decision for that of the authority.

Full jurisdiction litigation (*Contentieux de pleine juridiction*) – This first branch of administrative litigation comprises numerous categories of cases in which the administrative court exercises the broadest powers. In this form of litigation, the court may decide on points of law and of fact, it rules on disputes between the administration and its opponents as the ordinary courts between two private parties; it amends the decisions taken by the administration, not only when they are illegal, but also when they are incorrect on

[97] See further Chapter 4, section 4.4.G.

[98] E Laferrière, *Traité de la juridiction administrative et des recours contentieux* (Paris, Berger-Levrault, 1887) vol 1, 15 ff.

the merits; it replaces them with new decisions; it declares the existence of obligations and imposes pecuniary penalties. …

Annulment litigation (*Contentieux de l'annulation*) – The acts and decisions of the administration having the character of acts of command and public power give rise to this type of litigation. They cannot be amended by the administrative courts; they can only be annulled, and only on grounds of illegality, not as a result of factual error. The only action which may be brought against acts of this nature is the action for annulment which is called *recours pour excès de pouvoir*. …

Code de justice administrative **1.40 (FR)**

Article L911-1 When a court decision necessarily requires a legal entity governed by public law or an entity governed by private law charged with the management of a public service to adopt an enforcement measure for a specific purpose, the said court, having heard submissions to this effect, will order the said measure, in the same decision, and, where appropriate, will specify a time limit within which the decision must be enforced.

Article L911-2 When a court decision necessarily requires a legal entity governed by public law or an entity governed by private law charged with the management of a public service to take a decision again after a new investigation, the said court, having heard submissions to this effect, will order, in the same decision, that the new decision be taken within a specific time limit.

Notes

(1) Since the beginning of the nineteenth century, the French system of administrative justice has been both objective and subjective. If one looks at the action for annulment (*recours pour excès de pouvoir*), the French model of judicial review is highly objective, in the sense that the question the court is asked is only a question of legality. No questions of subjective rights are debated before French administrative courts in the action for annulment. As the purpose of this challenge is to uphold legality, standing is very generous. Of course, an individual must have standing to challenge the decision, which means that he must be concerned by the decision, but no breach of a subjective right is needed.[99] The action for annulment was described as a claim of general interest,[100] its purpose being to prevent the administration from acting illegally; it is an 'instrument accessible to everyone at the service of the ignored legality'.[101]

(2) The subjective dimension of the French system of administrative justice is shown in the 'full jurisdiction remedy' (*recours de pleine juridiction*). The aim of the full jurisdiction remedy is not ensuring legality as such, but safeguarding the legal rights of the individual. The powers of the court in the full jurisdiction remedy include

[99] See further Chapter 4, section 4.4.B.3.

[100] See R Chapus, *Droit administratif general*, 9th edn (Montchrétien, Domat, 2001) 202.

[101] This observation was made by the Commissaire du gouvernement Pichat on the *Lafarge* case of 8 March 1912 (No 42612) (*un instrument mis à la portée de tous au service de la légalité méconnue*).

not only the annulment of the decision, but also the correction and substitution of the challenged decision, and, if relevant, the award of a sum of money.[102]

(3) One of the contemporary evolutions of the action for annulment in France is to integrate more and more aspects deriving from the *recours subjectif* model in the *recours pour excès de pouvoir*. The most important development in this respect was the law of 8 February 1995, whereby powers to issue injunctions were given to the administrative courts.[103] The *recours pour excès de pouvoir* can therefore be considered as an action aimed not only at quashing an illegal decision, but nowadays also at upholding citizens' rights.[104]

1.5.D THE EUROPEAN UNION

R Barents, EU Procedural Law and Effective Legal Protection[105] **1.41 (EU)**

The system of legal remedies as this was laid down in the ECSC Treaty and subsequently in the EEC Treaty (later re-named the EC Treaty), and found its origin in French administrative law. This field of law, the roots of which date back to the beginning of the nineteenth century, was particularly influenced by the concept of the '*recours objectif*', according to which administrative procedural law was principally aimed at the enforcement of substantive law. This background explains the fact that the review of legality in the framework of an action for annulment has a limited character in the sense that the performance of the administration is only reviewed in the light of the four grounds mentioned in Article 33(1) ECSC and, at present, in Article 263(2) TFEU, as well as the obligation for the courts to annul the contested act if the action is well founded. Any other decision is excluded. The conception of objective legality review is also reflected in the drafting of Article 31 ECSC on the CJ's mandate which, at present, is laid down in identical terms in Article 19(1) TEU. What matters, according to this provision, is that the Union judicature ensures the observance of 'the law'. In the Statute and the Rules of Procedure this conception is expressed by the system of '*moyens de fait et de droit*'. As will be set out below, this system, also taken over from French administrative law, constitutes the hard core of the proceedings before the Union Courts. …

In the course of time the conception of the '*recours objectif*' has been abandoned. The CJ has consistently interpreted its mandate in the perspective of effective legal protection, in particular regarding access to justice, both at the level of the Union and at the national level. The right to an effective remedy has become the leading principle for the interpretation of the provisions of the Treaties on direct actions and the function of national courts to guarantee the full effect of Union law in the Member States. One of the consequences of this development is that the practical significance of the four grounds for annulment mentioned in Article 263(2) TFEU has diminished. What matters is whether there is an infringement of 'the law' in a broad sense (written and unwritten). Another consequence is that for an act to be challengeable within the meaning of this provision only

[102] On this distinction, see Chapter VII, section 7.2.A.4.

[103] See further Chapter 7, section 7.3.A.3 (ii).

[104] B Pacteau, 'Du recours pour excès de pouvoir au recours de pleine juridiction?' (1999) 52 *La revue administrative* 51.

[105] Barents (n 42 above) 1447–48.

its substance is relevant, i.e. whether the act produces legal effects capable of modifying the legal position of the applicant. At present, as far as access to court is concerned, the only significant trace in Union law of the conception of objective legality control is the admissibility conditions for actions for annulment brought by private applications (Art. 263(4) TFEU), the practical result of which is that review of the effects of measures of general application on subjective rights is almost excluded.

Treaty on the Functioning of the European Union **1.42 (EU)**

Article 264 If the action is well founded, the Court of Justice of the European Union shall declare the act concerned to be void.

However, the Court shall, if it considers this necessary, state which of the effects of the act which it has declared void shall be considered as definitive.

Note

If one looks at the administrative court functions of the European courts in annulment actions, it seems at first sight that the prevalent conception is that of *recours objectif*. This is best exemplified with regard to the remedies, and the fact that the basic remedy is that of annulment of an unlawful administrative decision. Furthermore, the strict system of pleas and the prohibition of *ultra petita* and *ex officio* review also reflect a vision of *recours objectif*.[106]

Court of First Instance, 9 August 1995[107] **1.43 (EU)**

Greenpeace and others v Commission

STANDING; ENVIRONMENTAL ASSOCIATIONS; INDIVIDUAL CONCERN

Greenpeace

The interpretation of 'individual concern' established in the Plaumann *case remains applicable whatever the nature, economic or otherwise, of those of the applicants' interests which are affected.*

Facts: Several applicants, including the environmental organisation Greenpeace, brought an action to annul a Commission decision which granted financial assistance from the European Regional Development Fund to the Kingdom of Spain for the construction of two power stations on Gran Canaria and Tenerife.

Held: The court dismissed the application as inadmissible.

Judgment: 49 Before considering whether the conditions laid down in that line of authority are met in the present instance, it is appropriate to examine first the merits of the applicants' argument that when determining the admissibility of their action the Court should free itself from the restrictions those authorities impose, which are that third-party applicants must establish that they are affected by the contested measure in the same

[106] See further on these points Chapter 5, sections 5.4.C. and 5.4.D.

[107] ECLI: ECLI:EU:T:1995:147.

way as the addressee of the decision, and concentrate rather on the sole fact that they have suffered or potentially will suffer detriment or loss from the harmful environmental effects arising out of unlawful conduct on the part of the Community institutions. As noted above (see paragraphs 30 and 32), the applicants stress here that their interests affected by the contested decision are not economic, as has been the case in almost all the judgments delivered in relation to Article 173 of the Treaty, but of a quite different kind, relating to environmental and health protection.

50 The Court observes that whilst the abovementioned line of authority comprises judgments given mostly in cases concerning, in principle, economic interests, it is none the less true that the essential criterion applied in those judgments – in substance, a combination of circumstances sufficient for the third-party applicant to be able to claim that he is affected by the contested decision in a manner which differentiates him from all other persons – remains applicable whatever the nature, economic or otherwise, of those of the applicants' interests which are affected. …

60 The three applicant associations, Greenpeace, TEA and CIC, claim that they represent the general interest, in the matter of environmental protection, of people residing on Gran Canaria and Tenerife and that their members are affected by the contested decision; they do not, however, adduce any special circumstances to demonstrate the individual interest of their members as opposed to any other person residing in those areas. The possible effect on the legal position of the members of the applicant associations cannot, therefore, be any different from that alleged here by the applicants who are private individuals. Consequently, in so far as the applicants in the present case who are private individuals cannot, as the Court has held (see paragraph 58 above), be considered to be individually concerned by the contested decision, nor can the members of the applicant associations, as local residents of Gran Canaria and Tenerife.

Note

Viewed from the perspective of access to courts, the EU displays some features of a *recours subjectif* legal system. This is particularly visible in the European courts' approach to standing,[108] which is focused on the legal position of the individual (in the form of the criterion of 'individual concern'). While this criterion does not as such require the infringement of subjective rights (which is typical of the *recours subjectif* legal systems), the interpretation given by the Court of Justice to the concept of individual concern almost amounts to the same threshold, thereby excluding any possibility of litigating for the restoration of objective legality, as the excerpt above shows.

1.5.E ENGLAND AND WALES

The English system is very much based on a *recours objectif* model. The role of the court is to determine whether the action of the public authority challenged in the claim is lawful or unlawful. In this sense, the question is an objective one: has the public authority acted beyond its powers?

[108] See further on this Chapter 4, section 4.4.B.5.

High Court (Queen's Bench Division), 18 April 1997[109] **1.44 (EW)**

R v Somerset County Council, ex parte Dixon

NATURE OF PUBLIC LAW DISPUTES

Dixon

Public law disputes are predominantly focused on questions of the legality of the action of a public body, rather than about infringements of rights.

Facts: Dixon claimed judicial review of Somerset county council's decision to grant conditional planning permission to a quarry in the area where he lived. The council sought to argue that Dixon should not be permitted to claim as he was not a relevant landowner, so his rights would not be affected by the decision and he did not have an interest in the issue at hand.

Held: The court held that the claimant could proceed with the judicial review claim, but the substantive claim was not successful.

Judgment: Sedley J: Public law is not at base about rights, even though abuses of power may and often do invade private rights; it is about wrongs – that is to say misuses of public power; and the courts have always been alive to the fact that a person or organisation with no particular stake in the issue or the outcome may, without in any sense being a mere meddler, wish and be well placed to call the attention of the court to an apparent misuse of public power. If an arguable case of such misuse can be made out on an application for leave, the court's only concern is to ensure that it is not being done for an ill motive. It is if, on a substantive hearing, the abuse of power is made out that everything relevant to the applicant's standing will be weighed up, whether with regard to the grant or simply to the form of relief.

1.5.F COMPARATIVE REMARKS

The basis of judicial review is different between the legal systems studied. If one takes as a point of comparison the action for annulment, then France and Germany represent opposing models. In France, the court will only examine the legality of a decision, and no breach of a subjective right is required because the aim of judicial review is not to protect rights but to uphold legality. Other than in cases brought under the Human Rights Act 1998, England and Wales adopts the same approach as France: the court's mission is to police the boundaries of administrative action and ensure that the administration does not act ultra vires: as Sedley J clearly states in the *Dixon* case: 'Public law is not at base about rights, even though abuses of power may and often do invade private rights; it is about wrongs – that is to say misuses of public power.'

On the other hand, judicial review in Germany aims to protect rights. This is shown not only by the standing rules which are centred around the infringement of subjective rights, but also by the ancillary function of rules concerning procedures.

The EU seems to adhere to the German model in that, at least in the interpretation of standing adopted by the Court of Justice, it establishes a system which is aimed at

[109] [1998] Env LR 111 (QB).

protecting the legal sphere of the individual rather than the objective legality, while, if one looks at the main remedy, namely annulment, it seems like the system is modelled around the French tradition. One could therefore argue that, while traditionally starting from a *recours objectif* model, the EU has evolved, under the pressure of the case law of the CJEU, towards displaying some features of *recours subjectif*.

The Netherlands also seem to be in a mixed situation: the system started from an objective system and evolved towards a subjective one. Now, the law seems to bend strongly towards a subjective model (even if some remnants of the old system are still present): Article 8:69a AWB shows that the primary aim of judicial review is to protect citizens' rights. As a consequence, an applicant can only rely on norms which aim to protect his interests; this last aspect is completely antithetical to the spirit of objective models, whose goal is to uphold legality and not citizens' interests.

FURTHER READING

Barents, B, 'EU Procedural Law and Effective Legal Protection' (2014) 51 *Common Market Law Review* 1437.

van den Berge, L, 'The Relation Turn in Dutch Administrative Law' (2017) 13 *Utrecht Law Review* 99.

Cassese, C, von Bogdandy, A and Huber, P, *The Max Planck Handbooks in European Public Law, Vol. I: The Administrative State* (Oxford, Oxford University Press, 2017).

van der Hoeven, P, *De drie dimensies van het bestuursrecht, VAR-reeks 100* (Alphen aan den Rijn, Tjeenk Willink, 1989).

Massot, J, 'The Powers and Duties of the French Administrative Judge' in S Rose-Ackerman and P Lindseth (eds), *Comparative Administrative Law*, 2nd edn (Cheltenham, Edward Elgar, 2017) 435–45.

Singh, MP, *German Administrative Law in Common Law Perspective* (Springer, Berlin, 2001).

Prechal, S and Heukels, T, 'Algemene beginselen in het Nederlands en het Europees recht: rechtsvergelijking en interactie' (1986) 34 *SEW Tijdschrift voor Europees en economisch recht* 287.

Schwarze, J, *European Administrative Law* (London, Sweet & Maxwell, 1992).

Sordi, B, '*Révolution*, Rechtsstaat and the Rule of Law: Historical Reflections on the Emergence and Development of Administrative Law' in S Rose-Ackerman and P Lindseth (eds), *Comparative Administrative Law*, 2nd edn (Cheltenham, Edward Elgar, 2017) 23–37.

CHAPTER 2
ORGANISATION OF JUDICIAL REVIEW IN ADMINISTRATIVE MATTERS AND INTRA-ADMINISTRATIVE OBJECTION PROCEDURE

Mariolina Eliantonio

2.1 INTRODUCTION

This chapter deals with the way in which judicial review is organised in the legal systems examined. Several historical, cultural and also practical factors have influenced the way in which the legal systems have organised their structures for judicial review.

First of all, organising judicial review concerns the question of separation between administrative and ordinary courts. Some systems adopt a unified court structure, whereas others establish a clear distinction between ordinary courts and administrative courts. A second important question concerning the organisation of judicial review concerns the criteria on the basis of which the jurisdiction of the administrative courts is allocated. Furthermore, organising judicial review requires a determination of the court structure and especially how many court layers are foreseen for administrative disputes, as well as whether specialised courts exist or can be created. Finally, the organisation of judicial review is linked to the existence of a mandatory or voluntary system of intra-administrative objection procedure.

2.2 MONISM AND DUALISM: THE SEPARATION BETWEEN ADMINISTRATIVE COURTS AND ORDINARY COURTS

Legal systems can be roughly subdivided into monistic and dualistic with regard to court structure in administrative matters, depending on whether administrative courts are separate from ordinary courts.

The most important argument in favour of a dualistic system is that proceedings against administrative authorities are different from those between private parties and therefore require a different type of courts and procedural framework.

2.2.A DUALISTIC SYSTEMS: FRANCE, GERMANY AND THE NETHERLANDS

2.2.A.1 FRANCE

Code de justice administrative **2.1 (FR)**

Article L311-1 The administrative tribunals are, in first instance, judges of general jurisdiction in administrative disputes, save for the competences that the object of the dispute or the interest of a proper administration of justice require to be attributed to another body of administrative jurisdiction.

Article L211-1 The Administrative Courts of First Instance are, in first instance and without prejudice to the competences attributed to other bodies of administrative jurisdiction, judges of general jurisdiction in administrative disputes.

Article L211-2 The Administrative Courts of Appeal hear cases adjudicated in first instance by the Administrative Courts of First Instance, subject to the powers awarded to the Council of State (Conseil d'État) in its capacity as an appeal court and those stipulated in Articles L552-1 and L552-2.

Article L821-1 Decisions rendered by the Administrative Courts of Appeal and, in general, all decisions rendered at the last instance by the administrative courts can be brought before the Council of State (Conseil d'État) by way of cassation proceedings.

Notes

(1) Within the separate administrative judicial branch there are 42 Administrative Courts of First Instance (tribunaux administratifs) dealing with all cases concerning

administrative law. Appeals against rulings of the Administrative Courts of First Instance may be lodged with one of the eight Administrative Courts of Appeal (cours administratives d'appel). At the top of the French three-level administrative judicial branch is the Council of State (Conseil d'État), which is the highest administrative court. The Council of State can also be the first and final instance court in some cases: for example, jurisdiction over the decrees of the Prime Minister and the President of the Republic or over the actions of most regulatory bodies (such as in the field of energy or telecommunications) belongs to the Council of State, and its decisions are final.[1]

(2) Administrative proceedings before an Administrative Court of First Instance are in principle conducted by trial chambers consisting of three judges.[2] Apart from the president of the chamber, there is one judge-rapporteur and another judge. Nevertheless, many cases are in fact dealt with by a single judge, either because the case is simple or does not need to be decided in substance.[3] In this case, the procedure is similar to the one applied to cases heard by several judges, and a ruling is adopted.[4] In the Administrative Courts of Appeal, in principle, a panel of five judges is usual; however, in certain circumstances, a single judge may rule on the case. Proceedings can also be conducted by a panel made of several chambers or in plenary sessions.[5] The trial chambers of the Council of State may be composed of three, nine, 15 or 17 judges, comprising one president, senior associates and one judge-rapporteur.[6] The Assemblée du contentieux of the Council of State, which deals only with important cases, consists of 17 judges, coming both from the litigation and the advisory sections of the Council of State.[7] In order to comply with requirements of Article 6 of the European Convention on Human Rights and the *Procola* ruling of the European Court of Human Rights (ECtHR),[8] it is foreseen that the members of the Council of State cannot take part in the decision of claims directed against measures which have been subject to the advice of the Council of State if they have taken part in the drafting of that advice.[9]

(3) French administrative courts also have a so-called public rapporteur (*rapporteur public*), which is comparable to what in other legal orders would be referred to as Advocate General.[10] Although the public rapporteur is an ordinary member of the

[1] Code de justice administrative, Art R311-1 provides for the list of the cases heard in first and last instance by the Council of State.
[2] Code de justice administrative, Art R222-18.
[3] See the cases mentioned in Art R222-1 of the Code de justice administrative. The provision foresees this possibility for the Administrative Courts of First Instance and the Administrative Courts of Appeal.
[4] Code de justice administrative, Art R222-13.
[5] Code de justice administrative, Art R222-25.
[6] Code de justice administrative, Art L122-1. For more details, see Code de justice administrative, Arts R122-11 to R122-20.
[7] Code de justice administrative, Art R122-20.
[8] ECtHR, *Procola v Luxembourg*, ECLI:CE:ECHR:1995:0928JUD001457089.
[9] Code de justice administrative, Art R122-21-1, as introduced by Décret n° 2008-225 du 6 mars 2008 relatif à l'organisation et au fonctionnement du Conseil d'État.
[10] For more on this, see J Bell, 'From "Government Commissioner" to "Public Reporter": A Transformation in French Administrative Court Procedure?' (2010) 16 *European Public Law* 533.

court, he does not undertake adjudicative tasks. The public rapporteur merely gives his assessment of a case at hand and formulates what he thinks is the best possible outcome. The public rapporteur is present in the oral hearings and presents his conclusions orally. In compliance with the ECtHR's case law, the public rapporteur does not take part in the deliberation of the decision with the other judges of the panel.[11] Before the Council of State, however, the public rapporteur is present in the deliberation, except if one of the parties is opposed to his presence.[12] However, he does not have the right to intervene in the process.

2.2.A.2 GERMANY

Verwaltungsgerichtsordnung **2.2 (DE)**

§40 (1) Recourse to the administrative courts shall be available in all public law disputes of a non-constitutional nature insofar as the disputes are not explicitly allocated to another court by a federal statute. Public law disputes in the field of state law (*Landesrecht*) may also be assigned to another court by a state statute (*Landesgesetz*).

(2) Recourse shall be available to the ordinary courts for property claims from sacrifice for the public good and from bailment by public authorities, as well as for compensation claims arising from the violation of public law obligations which are not based on a public law contract; this shall not apply to disputes regarding the existence and amount of a compensation claim in the context of Article 14(1) no 2 of the Basic Law (Grundgesetz). The special provisions of civil service law, as well as those on legal recourse to compensate for property disadvantages arising out of the withdrawal of unlawful administrative acts, shall remain unaffected.

§45 The Administrative Court of First Instance decides in first instance on all disputes for which the administrative legal recourse is available.

§46 The Higher Administrative Court decides on the legal remedy

1. of appeal on points of fact and law (*Berufung*) against judgments of the Administrative Court of First Instance,

2. of complaint (*Beschwerde*) against other decisions of the Administrative Court of First Instance and …

§49 The Federal Administrative Court decides on the legal remedy

1. of appeal on points of law (*Revision*) against judgments of the Higher Administrative Court under §132,

2. of appeal on points of law (*Revision*) against judgments of the Administrative Court of First Instance under §§134 and 135,

3. of complaint (*Beschwerde*) under §§99(2) and 133(1) of this Act as well as under §17a(4) no 4 of the Court Constitution Act (Gerichtsverfassungsgesetz).

[11] Code de justice administrative, Art R732-2. See also J Bell, 'Rapport: France: The Role of the Commissaire du Gouvernement and the European Convention on Human Rights' (2003) 9 *European Public Law* 309.

[12] Code de justice administrative, Art R733-3: 'Unless the parties request the contrary, the public rapporteur is present during the deliberation. He does not take part in it.'

Notes

(1) A separate administrative judicial branch is constitutionally guaranteed in Germany.[13] It consists of a three-level system[14] with 52 Administrative Courts of First Instance (Verwaltungsgerichte), one Higher Administrative Court (Oberverwaltungsgericht or Verwaltungsgerichtshof) in each of the 16 federal states and the Federal Administrative Court (Bundesverwaltungsgericht) as the administrative court of last instance.[15] Apart from having appeal functions, the Higher Administrative Courts have jurisdiction in first instance concerning (the review of) the legality of certain legal acts[16] and in cases of specific administrative law fields.[17] In general, the Federal Administrative Court constitutes the third and final level of judicial review. The Federal Administrative Court can also serve as court of first and final instance in the specific cases mentioned in §50 of the Verwaltungsgerichtsordnung (VwGO).

(2) Furthermore, there is the Federal Constitutional Court (Bundesverfassungsgericht), which is particularly influential for the administrative courts in Germany. Where the claimant alleges that his fundamental rights have been violated by public authorities and the violation has not been remedied by the administrative courts, he may take recourse to the Federal Constitutional Court.[18]

(3) On the level of the Administrative Courts of First Instance, one professional judge presides over the proceedings if the case at hand does not show any particular factual or legal difficulties and is not of fundamental importance.[19] Where this is the case, a trial chamber consists of three professional judges and two honorary judges.[20] These honorary judges assist the professional judges on matters of fact, whereas the professional judges are concerned with the actual resolution of the case at hand. The Higher Administrative Courts generally have so-called 'senates' of three professional judges. State legislation may prescribe that the senates have five members, two of whom may be honorary judges.[21] The Federal Administrative Court consists of different senates as well.[22] Each senate is usually composed of five professional judges. A Grand Senate (*Großer Senat*) of 11 judges exists as well, consisting of the President of the Federal Administrative Court and one judge of the ten present senates. The Grand Senate is competent when a senate wishes to derogate from a judgment of another senate. A further distinction is to be made vis-à-vis the judge-rapporteur (*Berichterstatter*), who is mentioned in §82(2) VwGO, whose tasks include the

[13] Grundgesetz, Art 95. See further Chapter 1, section 1.4.A.
[14] §2 VwGO.
[15] There are special provisions for the fiscal jurisdiction. It only consists of a two-level system. There are fiscal courts on state level (Finanzgerichte) and one Federal Fiscal Court (Bundesfinanzhof) on the Federal level.
[16] §47 VwGO.
[17] §48 VwGO.
[18] Grundgesetz, Art 93(1) no 4a.
[19] §6 VwGO.
[20] §5(3) VwGO.
[21] §9(2)(3) VwGO.
[22] §10 VwGO.

drafting of the decisions, the correspondence with the parties and taking part in the taking of evidence (§96(2) VwGO)).

(4) There is no such institution comparable to an advocate general in the German administrative legal system.

2.2.A.3 THE NETHERLANDS

Algemene Wet Bestuursrecht **2.3 (NL)**

Article 8:1 A party concerned may bring a claim for judicial review (*beroep*) against a decision before the administrative judge.

Article 8:6 (1) A claim for judicial review (*beroep*) may be lodged with the district court, unless, pursuant to Chapter 2 of the Specification of Jurisdiction of Administrative Courts (*Bevoegdheidsregeling bestuursrechtspraak*) or another legal provision, another administrative judge is competent.

Article 8:105 An appeal can be lodged before the Judicial Division of the Council of State unless, pursuant to Chapter 4 of the Specification of Jurisdiction of Administrative Courts or another legal provision, another appellate court is competent.

Notes

(1) In the Netherlands, a claim for judicial review (*beroep*) has to be brought before the administrative division of the district court.[23] Therefore, one might at first sight qualify the Netherlands as a monistic system. However, that would not reflect the reality: within the district court, the administrative division is independent from the other divisions and the proceedings follow their own set of procedural rules,[24] which is different from the procedural law for civil law cases and criminal law cases. Therefore, content-wise, the Dutch system has to be characterised as dualistic.

(2) Appeals against rulings of district courts can be lodged before one of the appellate courts, the competence of which depends on the subject matter of the dispute. Here, the dualistic character of the Dutch system is more obvious than at first instance. With the exception of tax law cases, all appellate courts are separate administrative courts. The Judicial Division of the Council of State (Afdeling bestuursrechtspraak Raad van State) is the main administrative court of appeal, with residual competence vis-à-vis the other courts of appeal, in accordance with Article 8:105 AWB. The Central Appellate Court (Centrale Raad van Beroep) is the competent court in cases

[23] R Seerden and D Wenders, 'Administrative Law in the Netherlands' in R Seerden (ed), *Comparative Administrative Law*, 4th edn (Antwerp, Intersentia, 2017) 141 ff.

[24] Which can be found primarily in the Algemene Wet Bestuursrecht.

regarding social security and civil servants.[25] The High Administrative Court for Trade and Industry (College van Beroep voor het Bedrijfsleven) rules on disputes in the area of social-economic administrative law as well as on appeals for specific laws, such as the Competition Act (Mededingingswet) and the Telecommunications Act (Telecommunicatiewet).[26] Apart from these three main specialised courts, the ordinary courts of appeal are the appellate courts, and the Supreme Court (Hoge Raad) is the court of cassation in administrative matters related to tax law decisions.[27] The above-mentioned specialised appellate courts also have jurisdiction in first instance in several administrative disputes. They are the 'other administrative judges' described in Article 8:6 of the Algemene Wet Bestuursrecht (AWB), excluding the district court as the default competent court in first instance. Chapter 2 of Annex 2 of the AWB describes when one of the three specialised appellate courts is competent in first instance.[28]

(3) In principle, administrative cases are decided by a chamber with a single judge.[29] If that single judge does not deem it appropriate to deal with the case alone, the case is transferred to a chamber of three judges.[30] There are no laymen in the chambers.[31] The same applies for the Judicial Division of the Council of State. In the district courts, the High Administrative Court for Trade and Industry and the Central Appellate Court, alternate judges are a well-known phenomenon. Each chamber of three judges may be composed of two 'full' or ordinary judges and one alternate judge. All judges and alternate judges are responsible for adjudicating cases; the concept of a judge-rapporteur does not exist in the administrative court system of the Netherlands.

(4) Since January 2013, there has been the possibility for every appellate court to refer a case to the Grand Chamber (Grote Kamer) if this seems to be necessary for the aim of the further development of law or legal unity (Article 8:10a AWB). According to Article 8.10a(4) AWB, the Grand Chamber consists of five judges, who belong to different courts. The Grand Chamber can, and often does, ask for an opinion from the Advocate General (Advocaat Generaal).

(5) The Advocate General is a new phenomenon in Dutch administrative law. According to Article 8:12a AWB, the Advocate General is required to be a member of one of the highest courts, but may pursue a different main profession outside the judiciary.[32] Therefore, he has a position 'above' the respective highest courts, but

[25] Arts 9 and 10 of chapter 4 of Annex 2 AWB (*Hoger beroep bij de Centrale Raad van Beroep*).

[26] Art 11 of chapter 4 of Annex 2 AWB (*Hoger beroep bij het College van Beroep voor het Bedrijfsleven*).

[27] Wet op de Rechterlijke Organisatie (Organisation of the Courts Act), Art 60(1). See further Art 28 of the Algemene wet inzake rijksbelastingen (General Act on State Taxes).

[28] Arts 2, 3 and 4 of chapter 2 of Annex 2 AWB (*Beroep in eerste aanleg bij een bijzondere bestuursrechter*).

[29] Wet op de Rechterlijke Organisatie, Art 43 in conjunction with Art 8:10 (1) AWB.

[30] Art 8:10(2) AWB in conjunction with Art 6(2) of the Wet op de Rechterlijke Organisatie.

[31] Art 6(2) AWB in conjunction with Art 1(1)(c) of the Wet op de Rechterlijke Organisatie.

[32] In practice, there are two Advocates General; one is a member of the Council of State, the other is a member of the Supreme Court. One of the Advocates General is one of the authors of this book.

fulfils the legal requirement of Article 8:12a AWB to be 'a member of the respective court'. The Advocate General can be asked to deliver a 'conclusion' if questions of legal unity between the highest courts or questions on the further development of law arise. After having provided his conclusion, the Advocate General does not take part in the proceedings. In part, the function of the Dutch Advocate General is similar to the Advocate General in the EU legal system.[33] He undertakes a thorough analysis of the case, akin to an academic analysis. However, as the Advocate General is supposed to be asked about legal questions which have not yet been decided and are relevant for the jurisdiction of more than one highest administrative court, his function is special and more limited than in the EU legal system. The Advocate General does not usually participate in the oral proceedings.

2.2.B MONISTIC SYSTEMS: ENGLAND AND WALES AND THE EUROPEAN UNION

2.2.B.1 ENGLAND AND WALES

2.2.B.1 (i) Judicial Review

England and Wales have a unified court structure and do not have a separate system of administrative courts. Although there is a division of the Queen's Bench Division of the High Court known as the Administrative Court, all judicial review cases (ie cases seeking public law remedies and thus dealt with in accordance with Part 54 of the Civil Procedure Rules and the associated Practice Directions) are heard within the unified court structure, which comprises the Queen's Bench Division of the High Court, the Civil Division of the Court of Appeal and the Supreme Court.

It is usual for judges to sit alone in the High Court (Queen's Bench Division).[34] In the Court of Appeal, the court will comprise three judges[35] and in the Supreme Court the panels are usually composed of five judges,[36] although in some cases the court will

[33] See section II.B.2 below.

[34] Senior Courts Act 1981, s 19(3).

[35] For the Court of Appeal, it is usual practice for the judges to sit to hear appeals (but not applications for permission to appeal, which are normally heard by one judge) in banks of three. The rule in s 54(2) of the Senior Courts Act 1981 states that the Court of Appeal is validly constituted when it hears cases with one or more judges – the panel of three convention arises because it is usual for more than one judge to hear an appeal and if they sat in panels of an even number they would likely fall foul of the provisions of s 54(5) of the Senior Courts Act 1981 on occasion because if the Court was divided evenly on an outcome to the appeal, either party could require another hearing.

[36] The Constitutional Reform Act 2005, s 42 requires that the Supreme Court is only competent to hear proceedings when it consists of an uneven number of judges and any panel must consist of at least three judges, though the usual practice of the Court is for appeals to be heard by panels of five. The criteria used to determine when panels of more than five judges will hear an appeal can be found at www.supremecourt.uk/procedures/panel-numbers-criteria.html.

sit in panels of seven,[37] or occasionally even of nine,[38] where the case is of particular importance or the issue is particularly controversial. It is always necessary for the appellate courts to sit in panels with an odd number of judges, as dissenting judgments are permitted.

There is no institution comparable to an Advocate General in the English legal system.

2.2.B.1 (ii) Tribunals

Tribunals, Courts and Enforcement Act 2007 **2.4 (EW)**

Chapter 2

First-tier Tribunal and Upper Tribunal
Establishment

3 The First-tier Tribunal and the Upper Tribunal

(1) There is to be a tribunal, known as the First-tier Tribunal, for the purpose of exercising the functions conferred on it under or by virtue of this Act or any other Act.

(2) There is to be a tribunal, known as the Upper Tribunal, for the purpose of exercising the functions conferred on it under or by virtue of this Act or any other Act.

(3) Each of the First-tier Tribunal, and the Upper Tribunal, is to consist of its judges and other members.

(4) The Senior President of Tribunals is to preside over both of the First-tier Tribunal and the Upper Tribunal.

(5) The Upper Tribunal is to be a superior court of record.

Note

In addition to the court system, in England and Wales there is a set of 'First-tier' Tribunals with jurisdiction to hear cases arising from specific administrative areas (eg tax, state benefits, certain housing matters, immigration etc),[39] with a possibility to appeal the decision of First-tier Tribunals to an Upper Tribunal. The tribunal system in England and Wales developed over time and originally had the character of an intra-administrative objection procedure, with the tribunals being staffed by civil servants. The tribunals were created to deal with the large number of grievances arising from certain areas of public administration, including allocation of state benefits, taxation, and immigration and asylum. Over time, there have been efforts to imbue tribunals

[37] *Smith and Ors v Ministry of Defence* [2013] UKSC 41, [2014] AC 52.

[38] See, eg *R (on the application of Jackson) v Attorney General* [2005] UKHL 56, [2006] 1 AC 262. Note that this is a House of Lords case, but the Supreme Court has continued the practice. See *Al-Rawi v Security Service* [2011] UKSC 34, [2012] 1 AC 531.

[39] There are presently seven Chambers: General Regulatory; Social Entitlement; Health, Education and Social Care; Tax; War and Armed Forces Compensation; Asylum and Immigration; and Property. The General Regulatory Chamber deals with the most diverse array of cases, including appeals relating to transport, charity and estate agents. For full details of the jurisdiction of the First-Tier Tribunal, see www.gov.uk/government/organisations/hm-courts-and-tribunals-service/about.

with a clearer, more court-like structure. These efforts commenced with the Franks Report,[40] leading to the Tribunals and Inquiries Act 1958, most recently re-enacted in 1992. The other significant effort at reform of the tribunals commenced with the Leggatt Report[41] and culminated with the Tribunals, Courts and Enforcement Act 2007, which created the structure of tribunals outlined here and sought to ensure the independence of the tribunal judiciary.[42]

2.2.B.2 THE EUROPEAN UNION

Treaty on the European Union **2.5 (EU)**

Article 19 (1) The Court of Justice of the European Union shall include the Court of Justice, the General Court and specialised courts. It shall ensure that in the interpretation and application of the Treaties the law is observed.

Treaty on the Functioning of the European Union **2.6 (EU)**

Article 256 (1) The General Court shall have jurisdiction to hear and determine at first instance actions or proceedings referred to in Articles 263, 265, 268, 270 and 272, with the exception of those assigned to a specialised court set up under Article 257 and those reserved in the Statute for the Court of Justice. The Statute may provide for the General Court to have jurisdiction for other classes of action or proceeding.

Decisions given by the General Court under this paragraph may be subject to a right of appeal to the Court of Justice on points of law only, under the conditions and within the limits laid down by the Statute.

(2) The General Court shall have jurisdiction to hear and determine actions or proceedings brought against decisions of the specialised courts.

Decisions given by the General Court under this paragraph may exceptionally be subject to review by the Court of Justice, under the conditions and within the limits laid down by the Statute, where there is a serious risk of the unity or consistency of Union law being affected.

(3) The General Court shall have jurisdiction to hear and determine questions referred for a preliminary ruling under Article 267, in specific areas laid down by the Statute.

Where the General Court considers that the case requires a decision of principle likely to affect the unity or consistency of Union law, it may refer the case to the Court of Justice for a ruling.

[40] Franks Committee, *The Report of the Committee on Administrative Tribunals and Enquiries* (Cmnd 218, 1957).

[41] Sir Andrew Leggatt, *Tribunals for Users: One System, One Service – Report of the Review of Tribunals by Sir Andrew Leggatt* (London, Department for Constitutional Affairs, 2001).

[42] For a more detailed discussion of the reform of the tribunals in England and Wales, see Peter Cane, *Administrative Tribunals and Adjudication* (Oxford, Hart Publishing, 2009); R Carnwath, 'Tribunal Justice – A New Start' (2009) *Public Law* 48.

Decisions given by the General Court on questions referred for a preliminary ruling may exceptionally be subject to review by the Court of Justice, under the conditions and within the limits laid down by the Statute, where there is a serious risk of the unity or consistency of Union law being affected.

Notes

(1) In the EU legal system, the judicial powers are exercised by a body referred to as the Court of Justice of the European Union (CJEU). This institution consists at present of two courts – the Court of Justice and the General Court. As a consequence of the reform of the General Court, which took effect as of September 2016, the Civil Service Tribunal has stopped operating and has been absorbed into the General Court.[43] In the future, new specialised courts may be created in accordance with the procedure set up in Article 257 of the Treaty on the Functioning of the European Union (TFEU), in order to exercise judicial competence in certain specific areas. The most important cases in which the General Court has jurisdiction concern actions for annulment under Article 263 TFEU and actions for failure to act under Article 265 TFEU brought by natural or legal persons (for example, a case brought by a company against a Commission decision imposing a fine on that company); actions seeking compensation for damage caused by the institutions or the bodies, offices or agencies of the European Union or their staff under Articles 268 and 270 TFEU; and actions based on contracts made by the European Union which expressly give jurisdiction to the General Court under Article 272 TFEU. The decisions of the General Court may, within two months, be subject to an appeal before the Court of Justice limited to points of law.

(2) Apart from appeal functions against rulings of the General Court, the Court of Justice has jurisdiction in first and last instance in proceedings against the EU institutions for annulment and for failure to act when they are brought by a Member State or an EU institution.[44]

(3) In the EU legal system, there is no conceptual separation between ordinary and administrative courts: there is only one court system, the CJEU.

(4) The General Court sits in chambers of three or five judges,[45] although a single judge may also decide in certain cases,[46] and whenever the legal difficulty or the importance of the case or special circumstances so justify, a case may be referred to the General Court sitting in plenary session, to the Grand Chamber or to a Chamber composed of a different number of judges.[47] The Court of Justice also has chambers

[43] Regulation EU 2015/2422 of the European Parliament and of the Council amending Protocol No 3 on the Statute of the Court of Justice of the European Union (Euratom) [2015] OJ L341/14.

[44] Note that rules concerning preliminary questions and infringement proceedings will not be further analysed in this book. See Introduction.

[45] Rules of Procedure of the General Court, Art 11(1).

[46] Rules of Procedure of the General Court, Art 11(1).

[47] Rules of Procedure of the General Court, Art 14.

of three or five judges,[48] each consisting of the president of the chamber, a judge-rapporteur and one or three judge(s).[49] The Grand Chamber holds 15 judges.[50] The Grand Chamber is formed by the president and vice-president of the Court of Justice, a judge-rapporteur, three presidents of chambers of five judges and the amount of judges required to reach 15.[51] In limited situations, the Court shall adjudicate a case as full Court.[52] The judge-rapporteur is responsible for drafting the preliminary report, which includes a recommendation for the chamber to which the case should be assigned.[53] Whether a case is assigned to a chamber of three or five judges, or to the Grand Chamber, depends on the complexity and significance of that case. In principle cases are assigned to chambers of three or five judges, unless the case is of such difficulty or importance that it needs to be dealt with by the Grand Chamber.[54] If a Member State or an institution of the European Union requests so, the case is assigned to the Grand Chamber.[55]

(5) In a similar manner to the French legal system, the judges of the Court of Justice are assisted by 11 Advocates General who are responsible for presenting a legal opinion on the cases assigned to them. In the EU legal order, the Advocate General is not part of the chamber determining the case, but participates in the oral proceedings and may question the parties. The Advocate General then delivers his opinion in public on the legal questions of the case, based on a thorough analysis akin to an academic discussion, and suggests how the court should decide. The opinion is always published separately and in full. In the General Court there are no Advocates General, but the judges themselves may be called upon to perform the task of Advocate General.

2.2.C COMPARATIVE REMARKS

The organisation of judicial review varies quite significantly between the legal systems analysed. The most important difference lies in the contrast between monistic systems (England and Wales and the European Union), where there are no separate administrative courts, and dualistic systems (Germany, France and the Netherlands), where a clear distinction exists between ordinary and administrative courts. England and Wales is also peculiar in this respect because of the existence of the so-called Tribunals. Beyond these macro-differences in the organisation of judicial review, legal systems also differ on

[48] Statute of the Court of Justice of the European Union, Art 16(1); Rules of Procedure of the Court of Justice, Art 11.
[49] Rules of Procedure of the Court of Justice, Art 28.
[50] Statute of the Court of Justice of the European Union, Art 16(2).
[51] Rules of Procedure of the Court of Justice, Art 27.
[52] These are mentioned in Art 16(4) and (5) of the Statute of the Court of Justice of the European Union.
[53] Rules of Procedure of the Court of Justice, Art 59.
[54] Rules of Procedure of the Court of Justice, Art 60(1).
[55] Statute of the Court of Justice of the European Union, Art 16(3).

the micro-level, in that some legal systems use the institution of an Advocate General (France, the Netherlands and the European Union), whereas others do not (Germany and England and Wales). On the same micro-level, however, there are also some similarities, in that all legal systems strive, for purposes of efficiency, to assign cases to small chambers of one or three judges, with larger compositions (up to the full court) reserved only for important or difficult cases.

2.3 THE LAYERS OF COURTS IN ADMINISTRATIVE MATTERS

All legal systems provide for the general possibility of appealing rulings delivered by the courts of first instance to higher courts in the hierarchy. The number of layers of courts varies, however, as does their competence to fully review the ruling of the lower court both in law and in fact, or to only exercise a review in law.[56] Furthermore, a system of permission or leave to appeal may be required. This system has the function of filtering appeals, thereby ensuring that only 'meritorious' cases are reviewed by higher courts.

2.3.A THREE LAYERS OF COURTS: GERMANY, FRANCE, AND ENGLAND AND WALES

2.3.A.1 GERMANY

Verwaltungsgerichtsordnung **2.7 (DE)**

§2 Courts of administrative jurisdiction are, in the states (Länder) the Administrative Courts of First Instance and one Higher Administrative Court (Oberverwaltungsgericht) (in each state), in the Federation the Federal Administrative Court (Bundesverwaltungsgericht) with its seat in Leipzig.

§124 (1) The parties involved shall be entitled to an appeal on points of fact and law (*Berufung*) against final judgments, including the partial judgments in accordance with §110, and against interim judgments in accordance with §§109 and 111, if such appeal is admitted by the Administrative Court of First Instance or the Higher Administrative Court.

(2) The appeal on points of fact and law shall only be admitted

1. if serious doubts exist as to the correctness of the judgment,
2. if the case has special factual or legal difficulties,
3. if the case is of fundamental significance,
4. if the judgment deviates from a ruling of the Higher Administrative Court, of the Federal Administrative Court, of the Joint Senate of the Highest Courts of the Federation or of the Federal Constitutional Court, and is based on this deviation, or
5. if a procedural shortcoming subject to the judgment of the Higher Administrative Court on points of fact and law is alleged which may have influenced the merits of the decision.

[56] See further Chapter 8, sections 8.2 and 8.4.

§132 (1) Those concerned shall have recourse to an appeal on points of law (*Revision*) to the Federal Administrative Court against the judgments of the Higher Administrative Court (§49 no 1), and against orders (*Beschlüsse*) in accordance with §47(5), first sentence, if the Higher Administrative Court, or the Federal Administrative Court in response to a complaint against non-admission, has admitted it.

(2) The appeal on points of law shall only be admitted if

1. the legal case is of fundamental significance,

2. the judgment deviates from a ruling of the Federal Administrative Court, of the Joint Senate of the Highest Courts of the Federation or of the Federal Constitutional Court and is based on this deviation, or

3. a procedural flaw is alleged which may have influenced the merits of the decision.

Notes

(1) Article 19(4) of the Basic Law does not guarantee legal protection through several levels of courts.[57] Nonetheless, §2 VwGO establishes a three-tier court system.

(2) Both *Berufung* (ie an appeal on points of fact and law) and *Revision* (ie an appeal on points of law) require special leave by the court that issued the challenged judgment or the court to which the (higher) appeal is brought.[58]

2.3.A.2 FRANCE

Code de justice administrative **2.8 (FR)**

Article L211-2 The Administrative Courts of Appeal hear cases adjudicated in first instance by the Administrative Courts of First Instance, subject to the powers awarded to the Council of State (Conseil d'État) in its capacity as an appeal court and those stipulated in Articles L552-1 and L552-2.

Article L111-1 The Council of State is the highest administrative court. It rules, without further possibility of appeal, on appeals on points of law (*cassation*) lodged against judgments rendered at the last instance by the various administrative courts and on cases of which it is seized as a court of first instance or as an appeal court.

Article L821-1 The rulings issued by the Administrative Courts of Appeal and, in general, all the decisions issued in last resort by the administrative courts can be brought before the Council of State (Conseil d'État) by way of cassation proceedings.

Note

In French law, the word '*appel*' has a precise meaning: it means a new trial where the questions of law and of fact raised at first instance may be considered again. In contrast, '*cassation*' means, in principle, that only points of law are reviewed.[59] Leave or permission is not required.

[57] BVerfGE 4, 74, 95; 92, 365, 410.
[58] See further Chapter 8, section 8.3.A.2.
[59] For more details on the appeal procedure, see Chapter 8, section 8.4.A.

2.3.A.3 ENGLAND AND WALES

2.3.A.3 (i) Judicial Review

Senior Courts Act 1981 **2.9 (EW)**

Section 16 (1) Subject as otherwise provided by this or any other Act … the Court of Appeal shall have jurisdiction to hear and determine appeals from any judgment or order of the High Court.

Constitutional Reform Act 2005 **2.10 (EW)**

Section 40 (1) The Supreme Court is a superior court of record.[60]

(2) An appeal lies to the Court from any order or judgment of the Court of Appeal in England and Wales in civil proceedings.

Notes

(1) Judicial review in England and Wales is a two-stage procedure – the claimant must first seek permission from the High Court (Queen's Bench Division) to bring a claim for judicial review, then, if permission is granted, the court will hear the substantive judicial review claim at a later date. If permission is refused, it is possible to appeal to the Court of Appeal against the refusal of permission. Appeals from decisions of the High Court (Queen's Bench Division) in judicial review cases are ordinarily to be made to the Court of Appeal, either with permission from the High Court (Queen's Bench Division), or with permission granted by the Court of Appeal.[61] This process is governed by Part 52 of the Civil Procedure Rules (CPR) and, in particular, Rule 52.15 CPR on judicial review appeals. The appeal process itself is, again, a two-stage process, as appellants must first seek permission to appeal, which will either be granted by the High Court (Queen's Bench Division) or, if refused,[62] may be sought from the Court of Appeal.[63] In exceptional circumstances, a High Court (Queen's Bench Division) judge might grant a certificate which permits a 'leapfrog' appeal direct to the Supreme Court.[64] In practice, these certificates are seldom granted,[65]

[60] In the law of England and Wales, a superior court is a court which cannot face judicial review proceedings questioning its jurisdiction to hear a particular case or make a particular order. A court of record is a court which must keep records of the proceedings before it. These archived records are treated as being determinative of the proceedings and decisions made in the case. For a more detailed account of the historical development of these terms, see Lord Mackay of Clashfern, *Halsbury's Laws*, 5th edn (London, LexisNexis, 2010) vol 24, paras 618 and 619.

[61] Senior Courts Act 1981, s 16(1) and Civil Procedure Rules, s 52.3, which outlines the process of seeking permission to appeal.

[62] This is not provided for in the Civil Procedure Rules, but was accepted in *R (Plowman) v Secretary of State for Foreign and Commonwealth Affairs* [2001] EWHC (Admin) 617.

[63] See s 52.15(1) CPR.

[64] See the provisions of Part II of the Administration of Justice Act 1969 for details of the process.

[65] For a recent example of such a 'leapfrog' appeal, see *R (on the application of Miller) v Secretary of State for Exiting the European Union* [2017] UKSC 5, [2018] AC 61.

and even where the certificate is granted, the Supreme Court might still refuse permission to appeal directly. If the Supreme Court refuses to hear an appeal in a case where a certificate is granted, this does not necessarily preclude the potential for an appeal to the Court of Appeal.[66] Appeals from the Court of Appeal should be made to the Supreme Court. In order to make an appeal to the Supreme Court, permission is required. Permission to appeal might be granted by the Court of Appeal, or a petition might be made to the Supreme Court for leave to appeal.[67]

(2) There is no hard and fast rule about what is subject to appeal in English law. There is no doubt that full review of both findings of fact and points of law is possible, although the general practice is that the appellate courts will generally leave findings of fact made by lower courts in place, because hearings in the Court of Appeal and Supreme Court do not hear witnesses and do not generally permit the introduction of new evidence.[68]

2.3.A.3 (ii) Tribunals

Tribunals, Courts and Enforcement Act 2007 **2.11 (EW)**

Section 11 Right to appeal to Upper Tribunal

(1) For the purposes of subsection (2), the reference to a right of appeal is to a right to appeal to the Upper Tribunal on any point of law arising from a decision made by the First-tier Tribunal other than an excluded decision.

Notes

(1) If an individual wishes to appeal the decision of a First-tier Tribunal, there are a number of possible options. First, he may ask the First-tier Tribunal itself to review its decision.[69] Alternatively, he may seek to appeal to the Upper Tribunal. Should an appeal to the Upper Tribunal be sought, permission must be obtained either from the First-tier Tribunal or from the Upper Tribunal.[70] Appeals to the Upper Tribunal are available only on points of law, and not on issues of fact.[71]

[66] See *R (Jones) v Ceredigion CC (Permission to Appeal)* [2005] EWCA Civ 986, [2005] 1 WLR 3626.

[67] The requirement of permission to appeal was introduced by s 1 of the Administration of Justice (Appeals) Act 1934. The requirement of permission is now to be found in s 40(6) of the Constitutional Reform Act 2005. Should the appellant need to seek permission from the Supreme Court, the process is governed by Part II of SI 2009/1603 The Supreme Court Rules 2009.

[68] For more details on the appeal procedure, see Chapter 8, section 8.4.D.

[69] Tribunals, Courts and Enforcement Act 2007, s 9(2)(b). By virtue of s 9(2)(a), the tribunal might also review its decision on its own initiative. In its review, the Tribunal might correct accidental errors in the decision or its record, amend its reasoning for the decision or set its decision aside. See s 9(4). In accordance with s 9(5), should the tribunal set its decision aside, it must either decide the matter afresh or refer the matter to the Upper Tribunal for a decision.

[70] Tribunals, Courts and Enforcement Act 2007, s 11(4).

[71] Tribunals, Courts and Enforcement Act 2007, s 11(1).

(2) Appeals from the Upper Tribunal to the Court of Appeal follow a similar format – the Upper Tribunal might review its own decision,[72] or it is possible to appeal an Upper Tribunal decision to the Court of Appeal on a point of law.[73] In order for such an appeal to proceed, it is necessary for permission to appeal to be granted either by the Upper Tribunal itself or the Court of Appeal.[74] Further appeal may be possible to the Supreme Court on the same basis as described above for judicial review claims. This mechanism creates a four-layer system.

(3) The Upper Tribunal may also engage in judicial review in cases that are transferred to it from the High Court (Queen's Bench Division).[75] The precise scope and extent of the Upper Tribunal's judicial review jurisdiction is not entirely clear, but the Senior President of the Tribunals has suggested that he believes that transfers will be confined, at least in the early stages, to categories which have a direct link with subjects already within the scope of the Upper Tribunal's appellate jurisdiction.[76]

(4) Where statute sets out a right of appeal to a Tribunal, it will frequently outline whether appeal is available only in relation to points of law or whether appeal is possible in relation to matters both of fact and law.

2.3.B TWO LAYERS OF COURTS: THE NETHERLANDS AND THE EUROPEAN UNION

2.3.B.1 THE NETHERLANDS

Algemene Wet Bestuursrecht **2.12 (NL)**

Article 8:104 (1) A party concerned and the administrative authority are entitled to lodge an appeal against:

a. a judgment of the district court within the meaning of Article 8:66(1) or Article 8:67(1),

b. a judgment of the interim relief judge of the district court, within the meaning of Article 8:86(1),

c. a judgment of the district court on a request within the meaning of Article 8:88(1).

[72] Tribunals, Courts and Enforcement Act 2007, s 10(2)(b). By virtue of s 10(2)(a), the Upper Tribunal might also review its decision on its own initiative. In its review, the Upper Tribunal might correct accidental errors in the decision or its record, amend its reasoning for the decision or set its decision aside. See s 10(4). In accordance with s 10(5), should the Upper Tribunal set its decision aside, it must decide the matter afresh. There is no potential for it to refer the matter to a court above, unlike the position for the First-Tier Tribunal.

[73] Tribunals, Courts and Enforcement Act 2007, s 13(1).

[74] Tribunals, Courts and Enforcement Act 2007, s 13(4). By virtue of s 13(5), an application for permission to appeal may only be made to the Court of Appeal if the applicant has requested permission to appeal from the Upper Tribunal and has been refused.

[75] The Upper Tribunal's judicial review jurisdiction is granted by ss 15–21 of the Tribunals, Courts and Enforcement Act 2007.

[76] R Carnwath, 'Tribunal Justice – A New Start' (2009) *Public Law* 48, 56.

Article 8:105 An appeal can be lodged before the Judicial Division of the Council of State unless, pursuant to Chapter 4 of the Specification of Jurisdiction of Administrative Courts or another legal provision, another appellate court is competent.

Notes

(1) In the Netherlands, all appellate courts consider all factual and legal aspects of the case, within the limits of the scope of the case.[77] Leave or permission is not required.

(2) Things are different with regard to cassation in tax law cases. The tax law divisions of the ordinary district courts are competent to rule on tax law disputes. Full appeal against a judgment of the district court on factual and legal aspects is possible before the Court of Appeal. An appeal from the Court of Appeal to the Supreme Court is possible only on points of law.[78]

2.3.B.2 THE EUROPEAN UNION

Statute of the Court of Justice of the European Union **2.13 (EU)**

Article 58 An appeal to the Court of Justice shall be limited to points of law. It shall lie on the grounds of lack of competence of the General Court, a breach of procedure before it which adversely affects the interests of the appellant as well as the infringement of Union law by the General Court.

No appeal shall lie regarding only the amount of the costs or the party ordered to pay them.

Treaty on the Functioning of the European Union **2.14 (EU)**

Article 256 (1) The General Court shall have jurisdiction to hear and determine at first instance actions or proceedings referred to in Articles 263, 265, 268, 270 and 272, with the exception of those assigned to a specialised court set up under Article 257 and those reserved in the Statute for the Court of Justice. The Statute may provide for the General Court to have jurisdiction for other classes of action or proceeding.

Decisions given by the General Court under this paragraph may be subject to a right of appeal to the Court of Justice on points of law only, under the conditions and within the limits laid down by the Statute.

[77] Art 8:69 AWB. What 'within the limits of the scope of the case' means is discussed further in Chapter 5, section 5.6.C.

[78] Wetboek van Burgerlijke Rechtsvordering (Civil Procedure Code), Art 419(3) states that the Supreme Court is bound by the judgment of the Court of Appeal regarding the facts of the case.

Notes

(1) Appeal against decisions of the General Court lies with the Court of Justice and it is limited to points of law only. Leave or permission is not required. The Court of Justice has clearly stated that parties are not entitled on appeal to contest the factual findings of the General Court,[79] or to offer to adduce evidence of fact which was not found by the General Court.[80]

(2) There is no appeal procedure to the European courts from Member States' courts.

2.3.C COMPARATIVE REMARKS

Some legal systems (England and Wales, Germany and France) organise judicial review in three layers of courts, with the consequence that there are potentially two layers of appeal proceedings. The England and Wales system is peculiar in this respect in that some claims may originate from a Tribunal, with the consequence that in these cases there is potentially a four-layer system. Other systems (the Netherlands and the European Union) only provide two layers of courts, with only one layer of appeal, although clear differences exist between the Dutch system and the EU system, in that the Dutch system provides for several different appeal courts in administrative matters which are competent in accordance with the subject matter. The legal systems also differ in their requirements of a system of permission or leave: while this is not required in France, the Netherlands and the EU, it does exist in a similar fashion both in Germany and in England and Wales. The different functions of appeal and the scope of review of each of the courts which are competent in appellate proceedings will be further explored in Chapter 8.

2.4 STATUS AND EMPLOYMENT OF ADMINISTRATIVE JUDGES

2.4.A SYSTEMS WITH POLITICAL APPOINTMENT OF JUDGES: THE EUROPEAN UNION

Treaty on the Functioning of the European Union **2.15 (EU)**

Article 253 The Judges and Advocates-General of the Court of Justice shall be chosen from persons whose independence is beyond doubt and who possess the qualifications required for appointment to the highest judicial offices in their respective countries or

[79] Eg C-62/94 P *Turner v Commission* ECLI:EU:C:1995:327, para 25; C-1/98 P *British Steel v Commission* ECLI:EU:C:2000:644, para 53.

[80] C-320/92 P *Finsider v Commission* ECLI:EU:C:1994:414, para 28.

who are jurisconsults of recognised competence; they shall be appointed by common accord of the governments of the Member States for a term of six years, after consultation of the panel provided for in Article 255.

Every three years there shall be a partial replacement of the Judges and Advocates-General, in accordance with the conditions laid down in the Statute of the Court of Justice of the European Union.

Article 254 The members of the General Court shall be chosen from persons whose independence is beyond doubt and who possess the ability required for appointment to high judicial office. They shall be appointed by common accord of the governments of the Member States for a term of six years, after consultation of the panel provided for in Article 255. The membership shall be partially renewed every three years. Retiring members shall be eligible for reappointment.

Article 255 A panel shall be set up in order to give an opinion on candidates' suitability to perform the duties of Judge and Advocate-General of the Court of Justice and the General Court before the governments of the Member States make the appointments referred to in Articles 253 and 254.

The panel shall comprise seven persons chosen from among former members of the Court of Justice and the General Court, members of national supreme courts and lawyers of recognised competence, one of whom shall be proposed by the European Parliament. The Council shall adopt a decision establishing the panel's operating rules and a decision appointing its members. It shall act on the initiative of the President of the Court of Justice.

Note

Article 255 TFEU has been introduced by the Treaty of Lisbon, with the aim of rendering the process of appointment of European judges more transparent.[81]

2.4.B SYSTEMS WITH A SYSTEM OF ADMINISTRATIVE RECRUITMENT

2.4.B.1 GERMANY

In Germany, professional judges complete legal education that is compulsory for every law student, including two state examinations and a two-year apprenticeship (*Referendariat*).[82] In contrast to the common law system, judges follow a different career path to that pursued by attorneys. It is not necessary for professional judges to

[81] For more on this point, see T Dumbrovský, B Petkova and M van der Sluis, 'Judicial Appointments: The Article 255 TFEU Advisory Panel and Selection Procedures in the Member States' (2014) 51 *Common Market Law Review* 455.

[82] For a good overview of the German system of legal education, see M Stürner, 'The Internationalisation of Legal Education in Germany' in M Schmidt-Kessel (ed), *German National Reports on the 19th International Congress of Comparative Law* (Tübingen, Mohr Siebeck, 2014) 135–48.

have practised as an attorney beforehand.[83] As a general rule, professional judges are appointed for life until retirement age. They cannot be discharged, dismissed, retired or transferred from office against their will except for severe violations of the law according to a strict procedure laid down in §30 and following of the German Judiciary Act (Deutsches Richtergesetz).

Article 97 of the Basic Law declares that the judges are independent and bound by the law. This principle is also laid down in the German Judiciary Act and the Administrative Court Procedure Act (Verwaltungsgerichtsordnung), and applies equally to professional and honorary judges. However, the courts themselves are administrative bodies subordinate to the respective department of justice. With regard to the courts that are administered by the states (Administrative Courts of First Instance and Higher Administrative Courts), the department of justice of the state is responsible for the employment of judges. The employment of judges at state level is regulated by state laws. In some states, certain parliamentary bodies, the Judges Election Committees (*Richterwahlausschuss*), are involved in the investiture of the judges. The judges sitting in the federal courts are chosen jointly by the competent federal Minister and a committee for the selection of judges consisting of the competent state ministers and an equal number of members elected by the Bundestag (Article 95(2) of the Basic Law). Public hearings or discussions about the suitability of candidates are very unusual.

2.4.B.2 THE NETHERLANDS

According to Article 5 of the Act on the Legal Status of Judicial Civil Servants (Wet rechtspositie rechterlijke ambtenaren), to become a judge one has to successfully have passed both a bachelor of law and a master of law degree at a Dutch university.[84] After having passed these exams and after having worked as a lawyer for a certain time, one has to be selected to become a judge in apprenticeship.

Depending on the length and type of work experience, candidates have to successfully complete a specialised four-year training course or a more limited training which lasts between 18 months and three years.[85] Most judges are appointed for life and may not have another job. However, there are some important exceptions. Nearly all courts have 'alternate judges' (*rechter-plaatsvervanger*). These are lawyers who have a different main job, eg they work at a university, or are solicitors or barristers (in a different district), and join the court occasionally (ie several times a year).

2.4.B.3 FRANCE

Administrative judges in France may be recruited in two ways. The first requires a prospective judge to follow the two-year curriculum of the National School of Administration

[83] N Foster and S Sule, *German Legal System and Laws*, 3rd edn (Oxford, Oxford University Press, 2002) 89.

[84] The Act of the Legal Status of Judicial Civil Servants, Art 5 mentions some exceptions to this rule that do not play any role in practice.

[85] The details for the procedure are contained in the Executive Regulation concerning the training of judges and public prosecutors (*Besluit opleiding rechters en officieren van justitie*).

(École Nationale d'Administration). Entering this school requires passing a high-level exam. The second way consists of passing a high-level exam organised by the Council of State specifically dedicated to the recruitment of administrative judges.[86]

Judges working in administrative courts in France are appointed for life. The appointment is formally made by the President of the Republic. However, the principle of separation of powers does not leave him any discretionary power as regards this appointment: only the persons having passed the exam and fulfilling the conditions required by the statutes may be appointed.

During their careers, both ordinary and administrative judges may, at their request, be placed on secondment positions in state agencies or public bodies for a specific period of time (subject to certain conditions to ensure that the principles of impartiality and independence of the judiciary are not violated).

The members of the Council of State are recruited by competitive examination or by external appointment.[87] Each year, five positions of auditor (*auditeur*) are made available to the top graduates of the National School of Administration. After four years, an *auditeur* is promoted to master of petitions (*maître des requêtes*), and after 12 years, to Councillor of State (*Conseiller d'État*). Promotion is based exclusively on seniority, which assures independence and impartiality in the promotion of members. Recruitment by external appointment accounts for one out of four *maîtres des requêtes* and one out of three *Conseillers d'État*. A number of external appointments are reserved for members of the Administrative Court of First Instance and the Administrative Courts of Appeal upon the nomination of the Vice-President of the Council of State. Members are appointed to serve in the litigation department, and/or in an advisory department. Certain members choose to work outside the Council of State, for example by assisting the President of the Republic, the Prime Minister or other members of the cabinet. They may also be seconded to key posts in the French administration. Members also have the option of taking leave of absence in order to work in the private sector for a limited period of time.

Judges of the Administrative Courts of First Instance, the Courts of Appeal and the Council of State are not permitted to have other jobs.

2.4.B.4 ENGLAND AND WALES

The requirements for judicial office are set out in the Senior Courts Act 1981 and the Constitutional Reform Act 2005. Section 10 of the Senior Courts Act 1981 requires that no one shall be appointed to judicial office in the High Court (Queen's Bench Division) or Court of Appeal unless they meet the 'judicial appointment eligibility condition', provided for in the Tribunals, Courts and Enforcement Act 2007.[88] The basic requirement is

[86] The details are contained in Arts L233-1 to L233-6 of the Code de justice administrative.

[87] The details are contained in Arts L133-1 to L133-7 of the Code de justice administrative.

[88] Note that for Supreme Court Justices, there are additional requirements: the applicant must have held high judicial office (usually in the High Court (Queen's Bench Division) or the Court of Appeal, or their Scottish or Northern Irish equivalents) for two years and have satisfied the judicial appointment eligibility condition for 15 years.

that an applicant must be a qualified solicitor or barrister[89] for at least seven continuous years and must also have 'gained experience of law' for the relevant seven-year period. It is notable that the 2007 Act creates a broad definition of legal experience, to include not only practising the law, but also acting as an arbitrator, offering legal advice outside of legal practice or working, for example, as a legal academic.[90] In the past, it was usual for judges to be appointed from the Bar – solicitors were seldom appointed, particularly at the higher levels of judicial office. This is becoming less the case, and the Supreme Court has had a Justice who worked as a solicitor[91] and the President of the Supreme Court who took up office in 2017 was a distinguished legal academic prior to taking up judicial office.[92]

Appointment to judicial office is undertaken on the basis of merit and good character, with some additional encouragement of judicial diversity.[93] Selection is undertaken by independent panels made up of some members of the judiciary and some lay members. Since the Constitutional Reform Act 2005, there has been an effort to reduce the influence of the executive in selections for judicial office.[94]

Once appointed, judges remain in office until they choose to retire or they reach the maximum age when retirement is mandated, which is presently 70 years.[95]

2.4.C COMPARATIVE REMARKS

The EU is the only legal system which follows a more 'political' way of appointing judges. In all other legal systems, the appointment is based on the successful passing of various types of examinations. Amongst this second category of legal systems, one can detect a peculiarity in England and Wales and the Netherlands, where it is usually imperative for judges to have practised as a lawyer outside the judicial branch – in the other legal systems, this is not required.

2.5 THE JURISDICTION OF THE ADMINISTRATIVE COURTS

The extent of the jurisdiction of the administrative courts differs between the legal systems examined. Jurisdiction will be the broadest if a legal system provides that virtually all acts and actions of the public authorities will be subject to the jurisdiction of the administrative courts; a more restrictive criterion might provide that administrative courts can exercise jurisdiction over the actions of the public authorities only if there is a sufficient public law connection to these actions. An even more restrictive criterion

89 See ss 50–51 of the Tribunals, Courts and Enforcement Act 2007.
90 See ss 50–52 of the Tribunals, Courts and Enforcement Act 2007.
91 Lawrence Collins JSC (now retired).
92 Lady Hale PSC.
93 See ss 63–64 of the Constitutional Reform Act 2005.
94 For an analysis of some of these reforms, see G Gee and others, *The Politics of Judicial Independence in the UK's Changing Constitution* (Cambridge, Cambridge University Press, 2015).
95 See s 26 of the Judicial Pensions and Retirement Act 1993.

might limit jurisdiction of the administrative courts to unilateral or single-case decisions of the public authorities. Furthermore, all systems need to foresee mechanisms to solve the conflicts of jurisdiction between administrative and ordinary courts.

The EU Treaties do not provide for any requirements concerning the allocation of jurisdiction at Member State level in cases falling within the scope of application of EU law. The Court of Justice of the European Union has stated that the EU is as such neutral towards the allocation of jurisdiction at Member State level, provided that the principle of effective judicial protection is guaranteed.[96]

2.5.A CRITERIA TO ALLOCATE JURISDICTION

2.5.A.1 JURISDICTION LIMITED TO UNILATERAL MEASURES: THE NETHERLANDS

Algemene Wet Bestuursrecht **2.16 (NL)**

Article 8:1 A party concerned may bring a claim for judicial review (*beroep*) against a decision before the administrative judge.

Article 8:3 (1) A claim for judicial review (*beroep*) may not be lodged against a decision:

(a) containing a general binding regulation or a policy rule

(b) repealing or laying down the entry into force of a general binding regulation or a policy rule

(c) approving a decision containing a general binding regulation or a policy rule or repealing or laying down the entry into force of a general binding regulation or a policy rule.

Notes

(1) In the Dutch legal system, only single-case decisions[97] and so-called 'concretising decisions of general scope'[98] may be directly[99] challenged before administrative courts. This also includes the refusal to issue a single-case decision and the failure to take a single-case decision within a reasonable time, because the legal system equates them to decisions.[100]

(2) Administrative courts also have jurisdiction to hear claims concerning damages caused by single-case decisions. Until 2013, such cases could only be decided in connection with the annulment of a single-case decision resulting in damage. Since 1 February 2013, the administrative courts can hear claims concerning damages

[96] Case 13/68 *SpA Salgoil v Italian Ministry of Foreign Trade* ECLI:EU:C:1968:54.

[97] For an examination of the concept of a single-case decision in the Dutch administrative legal system, see Chapter 3, section 3.2.A.2.

[98] For an examination of the concept of a concretising decision of general scope in the Dutch administrative legal system, see Chapter 3, section 3.3.A.1. (iii).

[99] On the possibility of indirect control of legality, see Chapter 7, section 7.7.E.

[100] Art 1:3(2) AWB on the refusal to issue a single-case decision and Art 6:2 AWB on failure to take a single-case decision.

arising from unlawful single-case decisions in a freestanding action.[101] This enlargement of the jurisdiction of the administrative courts may be regarded as a small revolution for the Dutch legal system. For the first time, administrative courts can hear cases that do not concern a single-case decision or the refusal or failure to take a single-case decision.

(3) The limited jurisdiction of the administrative courts is supplemented by the general jurisdiction of the ordinary courts.[102] The ordinary courts are competent to determine any claim of a private party against a decision of general application or any factual action of the administration.[103] However, such claims are not admissible if a more specialised form of judicial protection exists, which offers 'sufficient procedural safeguards'.[104] Thus, on the basis of Article 112 of the Grondwet (Dutch Constitution), the ordinary courts are competent in all disputes of administrative law and function as a safety net if a specialised (ie administrative) court does not exist.

2.5.A.2 JURISDICTION INCLUDING UNILATERAL MEASURES AND CONTRACTS: GERMANY

Verwaltungsgerichtsordnung **2.17 (DE)**

§40 (1) Recourse to the administrative courts shall be available in all public law disputes of a non-constitutional nature insofar as the disputes are not explicitly allocated to another court by a federal statute. Public law disputes in the field of state law (*Landesrecht*) may also be assigned to another court by a state statute (*Landesgesetz*).

Note

In the German legal system, a number of public law disputes are expressly assigned to another jurisdiction: matters expressly excluded from the general administrative jurisdiction are matters assigned to the Social Courts (Sozialgerichte),[105] matters assigned to the Fiscal Courts (Finanzgerichte),[106] matters relating to the Administrative Act of the Judiciary (Justizverwaltungsakte) which are assigned to the ordinary courts,[107] matters assigned to the disciplinary courts[108] and the administration of the church in certain matters.

[101] See further Title 8.4 AWB and Chapter 11, section 11.2.B.2.

[102] See the case of the Dutch Supreme Court, *Guldemond/Noordwijkerhout* ECLI:NL:HR:1915:AG1773; see also Chapter 1, excerpt 1.23.

[103] On the concept of decision of general scope and factual action in the Netherlands, see Chapter 3, sections 3.3.A.1 (iii), 3.3.B.2 (ii) and 3.4.B.1.

[104] ECLI:NL:HR:1977:AC6111.

[105] Sozialgerichtsgesetz (Social Courts Act), §1.

[106] Finanzgerichtsordnung (Fiscal Court Procedure Act), §32.

[107] See Einführungsgesetz zum Gerichtsverfassungsgesetz (Introductory Act to the Court Constitution Act), §23. More references to the ordinary courts can be found, for example, with regard to state liability law, in Grundgesetz, Art 34, sentence 3.

[108] (1991) NJW 1579.

Joint Senate of the Highest Courts of the Federation, 29 October 1987[109] 2.18 (DE)

PUBLIC LAW DISPUTE; DEFINITION

Whether a lawsuit constitutes a public or a private law dispute is to be determined by the nature of the legal relationship on which the claim is based.

Facts: The claimant was a health insurance fund. It provided, amongst other things, used wheelchairs to its customers. The respondent was responsible for the orthopaedics technology in the claimant's district. The respondent requested the claimant to no longer provide its customers with used wheelchairs. Subsequently, the claimant filed a suit before the Social Court (Sozialgericht) and asked for a declaration that it would continue to be authorised to provide wheelchairs to be used by customers which it had received back from other customers or their entitled relatives. The Social Court found in favour of the claimant; the Higher Social Court (Landessozialgericht) rejected the appeal. The Federal Social Court (Bundessozialgericht), which was to decide on the appeal of the respondent, considered itself to have jurisdiction on the matter. However, it considered itself to be hindered in taking such a decision in light of the jurisprudence of the Federal Court of Justice (Bundesgerichtshof). Therefore, it asked the Joint Senate of the Highest Courts of the Federation whether legal disputes between the health insurance providers on the one hand and service providers or their associations on the other were subject to the jurisdiction of the social courts.

Held: The relation between insurance providers and service providers was held to have a private law nature. Thus, the ordinary courts were considered to have jurisdiction.

Judgment: Whether a lawsuit constitutes a public or a private law dispute is to be determined with regard to the nature of the legal relationship on which the claim is based, if, as in this case, an explicit statutory allocation is missing … . That generally depends on – as the Joint Senate of the Highest Courts of the Federation ruled in its order of 10 April 1986 – whether the parties to the lawsuit are in a hierarchical relationship where one is subordinate to the other and whether the public authority applies the public law provisions that are specifically assigned to it, or rather applies the civil law provisions applying to everybody.

Note

The public law nature of a dispute is not dependent upon the unilateral or consensual nature of the measure, but on the public law nature of the dispute.[110] Therefore, disputes relating to unilateral measures, public law contracts (*öffentlich-rechtliche Verträge*)[111] and compensation for loss of property due to the withdrawal of unlawful administrative acts, even if they involve compensation for the wrongs of the administration, lie within the jurisdiction of the administrative courts.[112]

[109] (1987) NJW 2295.

[110] See further H Pünder and A Klafki, 'Administrative Law in Germany' in R Seerden (ed), *Administrative Law of the European Union, its Member States and the United States*, 4th edn (Antwerp, Intersentia, 2018) 61–62.

[111] For a definition of the concept of 'public law contract' in the German legal system, see Chapter 3, section 3.5.A.

[112] For more on liability issues, see Chapter 11, section 11.2.B.1.

Verwaltungsgerichtsordnung **2.19 (DE)**

§40 (2) Recourse shall be available to the ordinary courts for property claims from sacrifice for the public good and from bailment by public authorities, as well as for compensation claims arising from the violation of public law obligations which are not based on a public law contract; this shall not apply to disputes regarding the existence and amount of a compensation claim in the context of Article 14(1) no 2 of the Basic Law (Grundgesetz). The special provisions of civil service law, as well as those on legal recourse to compensate for property disadvantages arising out of the withdrawal of unlawful administrative acts, shall remain unaffected.

Note

On the basis of this provision, most tort claims brought against the administration lie within the jurisdiction of civil courts.

2.5.A.3 JURISDICTION INCLUDING UNILATERAL MEASURES AND TORTS: ENGLAND AND WALES AND THE EUROPEAN UNION

2.5.A.3 (i) England and Wales

Halsbury's Laws of England[113] **2.20 (EW)**

General Principles: The courts have an inherent jurisdiction to review the exercise by public bodies or officers of statutory powers impinging on legally recognised interests. Powers must be exercised fairly, and must not be exceeded or abused. Moreover, the repository of a statutory power or duty will be required genuinely to discharge its functions when the occasion for their performance has arisen.

The superior courts have a somewhat similar inherent jurisdiction over inferior courts and tribunals. If such a body has exceeded or acted without jurisdiction, or has failed to act fairly or in accordance with the rules of natural justice, or if it has committed an error of law in reaching a decision, its decision may be set aside. Alternatively, a tribunal may be prohibited from violating the conditions precedent to a valid adjudication before it has made a final determination. A tribunal wrongfully refusing to carry out its duty to hear and determine a matter within its jurisdiction may be ordered to act according to law.

The courts also have an inherent jurisdiction to review those exercises of Crown prerogative which are justiciable. The Crown prerogative must be exercised fairly and the prerogative must not be exceeded or abused.

Note

In the English legal system, common law courts are considered to have 'inherent jurisdiction' to exercise judicial control over the activities of the public authorities.

[113] Lord Mackay of Clashfern (n 60 above) para 601.

Hence, questions of how to allocate jurisdiction are not posed in these terms. The more relevant question is who and what is amenable to judicial review, ie the specific procedure governed by Part 54 CPR and the associated Practice Directions.

Civil Procedure Rules **2.21 (EW)**

Rule 54.1 (2) In this Section –
(a) a 'claim for judicial review' means a claim to review the lawfulness of –
(i) an enactment; or
(ii) a decision, action or failure to act in relation to the exercise of a public function.

Note

What a 'decision in relation to the exercise of a public law function' is was clarified in the *Datafin* case.

Court of Appeal (Civil Division), 5 December 1986[114] **2.22 (EW)**

R v Panel on Takeovers and Mergers, ex parte Datafin

AVAILABILITY OF JUDICIAL REVIEW; JURISDICTION

Datafin

If a body is exercising public law functions or if the exercise of its functions has public law consequences, it is possible to bring the body within the reach of judicial review.

Facts: Datafin complained that a competitor company in a takeover bid had breached the City Code on Takeovers and Mergers, a claim that was rejected by the Panel on Takeovers and Mergers, a self-regulatory body which derived its powers from the rules of the London Stock Exchange (a private company). Datafin claimed judicial review of the Panel's rejection of its complaint, seeking a quashing order to quash the Panel's rejection of its complaint and a mandatory order requiring the Panel to reconsider the complaint.

Held: The claim was heard and the remedies sought were granted.

Judgment: Lloyd LJ: I do not agree that the source of the power is the sole test whether a body is subject to judicial review … Of course the source of the power will often, perhaps usually, be decisive. If the source of power is a statute, or subordinate legislation under a statute, then clearly the body in question will be subject to judicial review. If, at the other end of the scale, the source of power is contractual, as in the case of private arbitration, then clearly the arbitrator is not subject to judicial review.

But in between these extremes there is an area in which it is helpful to look not just at the source of the power but at the nature of the power. If the body in question is exercising public law functions, or if the exercise of its functions has public law consequences, then that may be sufficient to bring the body within the reach of judicial review.

[114] [1987] QB 815 (CA).

Note

The *Datafin* case established that the decisions of a private body exercising public functions may be amenable to judicial review. Before *Datafin*, it was generally held that only bodies established by statute were so amenable, while private bodies could only be sued for their actions in private law.

S Bailey, Judicial Review of Contracting Decisions[115] **2.23 (EW)**

The extent to which judicial review is available as a remedy in respect of the contracting decisions of public authorities has caused difficulty for as long as judicial review has existed in anything like its modern form. It forms part of a wider set of issues concerning the proper scope of judicial review proceedings. … The case law tends to support the proposition that for contracting decisions taken in the exercise of statutory powers to be subject to judicial review, there must be some specific public law element beyond the mere fact that the body is exercising a statutory power to contract. It has been argued by others, for some time, that this adds an unnecessary and undesirable complication.

Most of the cases concerning contracting in the exercise of a statutory power say that for the decision in question to be amenable to judicial review, there must be a 'sufficient public law element' beyond the statutory background. The voluminous case law on this topic demonstrates a number of problems. First, this is a test that is inherently unclear. It has led to the waste of much litigation time as the authorities do not, and indeed cannot, provide sufficient guidance. Time spent on the amenability case law is likely to be better spent in considering the case law on the scope of the particular public law grounds raised on the facts of the case. It is unsuitable as a test that enables permission to claim judicial review to be refused straightforwardly in unmeritorious cases. Secondly, some of the distinctions drawn seem arbitrary and unconvincing. For example, it makes little sense to make amenability turn on whether a decision is to sell, or not to sell land; or whether an activity takes place on land owned by a public authority to which the public have access; or on the importance of the activity; or on whether a decision involves the invocation of a 'policy'. Thirdly, some of the cases focus narrowly on the decision in the abstract without considering the nature of the challenge. Fourthly, the uncertainty of the test has led some courts to take an excessively narrow view of the amenability of judicial review. It has been accepted that judicial review is available where the ground of challenge is based on some specific statutory provision, and it seems to be accepted that it would be available in cases of fraud, corruption, bad faith or malice. However, there has been hesitancy over the application of general public law standards concerning considerations, rationality and fairness. … It is submitted that this hesitancy at the amenability stage is misplaced. Each of these standards is sufficiently flexible to protect the legitimate interests of public authorities. Time would be better spent on the substantive case law on these matters than on a debate on amenability. Proper attention would then be placed, as appropriate, to the dimension of the public interest in the decision-making process in question.

[115] S Bailey, 'Judicial Review of Contracting Decisions' (2007) *Public Law* 444.

Note

Because of the need to prove a 'sufficient public law element', most contractual matters are not subject to judicial review in England and Wales. The nature of the 'sufficient public law element' required to render contractual matters subject to judicial review remains unclear in the case law and there is very little treatment of this issue by the courts. Examples of a 'sufficient public law element' include situations where a contracting decision was contrary to a published policy and frustrated a legitimate expectation engendered in the claimant,[116] or, where a contracting decision is taken under a statutory power, the contract relates to public land and the authority has the power to make by-laws in relation to the activity in addition to controls exerted via contract.[117]

Civil Procedure Rules **2.24 (EW)**

Rule 54.3 (2) A claim for judicial review may include a claim for damages, restitution or the recovery of a sum due but may not seek such a remedy alone.

Senior Courts Act 1981 **2.25 (EW)**

Section 31 (4) On an application for judicial review the High Court may award to the applicant damages, restitution or the recovery of a sum due if–

(a) the application includes a claim for such an award arising from any matter to which the application relates; and

(b) the court is satisfied that such an award would have been made if the claim had been made in an action begun by the applicant at the time of making the application.

Note

In judicial review proceedings, the court can only award damages, restitution or recovery of a sum due if the claim is brought in combination with a public law remedy[118] and if the claimant can demonstrate that a private law claim against a public authority for such a remedy would have been successful.[119]

2.5.A.3 (ii) The European Union

Treaty on the Functioning of the European Union **2.26 (EU)**

Article 263 (1) The Court of Justice of the European Union shall review the legality of legislative acts, of acts of the Council, of the Commission and of the European Central

116 *R v Barnet London Borough Council, ex parte Pardes House School Ltd* [1989] COD 512 (DC).
117 *R (Agnello) v Hounslow London Borough Council* [2003] EWHC 3112 (Admin).
118 See Chapter 7, section 7.2.A.2 for an explanation of the concept of public law remedies.
119 See further Chapter 11, section 11.2.A.

Bank, other than recommendations and opinions, and of acts of the European Parliament and of the European Council intended to produce legal effects vis-à-vis third parties. It shall also review the legality of acts of bodies, offices or agencies of the Union intended to produce legal effects vis-à-vis third parties.

Article 265 Should the European Parliament, the European Council, the Council, the Commission or the European Central Bank, in infringement of the Treaties, fail to act, the Member States and the other institutions of the Union may bring an action before the Court of Justice of the European Union to have the infringement established. This Article shall apply, under the same conditions, to bodies, offices and agencies of the Union which fail to act.

Article 268 The Court of Justice of the European Union shall have jurisdiction in disputes relating to compensation for damage provided for in the second and third paragraphs of Article 340.

Note

The EU courts have jurisdiction to review unilateral measures (including omissions) and torts in relation to the activities of the European institutions.

Treaty on the Functioning of the European Union **2.27 (EU)**

Article 272 The Court of Justice of the European Union shall have jurisdiction to give judgment pursuant to any arbitration clause contained in a contract concluded by or on behalf of the Union, whether that contract be governed by public or private law.

Article 274 Save where jurisdiction is conferred on the Court of Justice of the European Union by the Treaties, disputes to which the Union is a party shall not on that ground be excluded from the jurisdiction of the courts or tribunals of the Member States.

Note

Jurisdiction to determine disputes arising out of contracts lies by default with national courts (Article 274 TFEU). However, it is possible to insert a so-called 'arbitration clause' in the contract, which, under Article 272 TFEU, establishes the jurisdiction of the European courts on the contract.[120]

2.5.A.4 JURISDICTION INCLUDING UNILATERAL MEASURES, CONTRACTS AND TORTS: FRANCE

The question that is central to the allocation of jurisdiction of administrative courts in France is which administrative activities qualify as 'public service' (*service public*).

120 See further Chapter 3, section 3.5.E on contracts in the EU legal system.

G Bermann and E Picard, Introduction to French Law[121] **2.28 (FR)**

The notion of public service can therefore be defined as follows: A public service is an activity of general interest performed or provided for by a public body making use, if necessary, of some public law prerogatives. But each term of this definition requires further definition: What is the 'general interest'? What is a 'public person'? What are 'public prerogatives'? We may assume that 'performed' means that the public body itself provides the service, whereas 'provides for' suggests the public body does not itself supply the service, but rather entrusts it to some other entity (a private entity, a natural person, or even another public entity) to perform that service in its place. Of course, the public body must still ensure that the other entity performs the activity in accordance with the public interest. In order to do that, the public body must be able to exert sufficient power or control over the other entity. This is something that private law, grounded on the principle of equality between persons, does not allow.

It follows from this definition that private parties may well perform public services, and this, the Conseil d'État case law was willing to accept. The Conseil d'État even admitted that private persons could perform administrative public services (Conseil d'État, *Assemblée*, 13 May 1938, *Caisse primaire Aide et protection*). During the Second World War, the Conseil d'État finally recognized, albeit in a very different political context which heavily favoured corporatist ideas, that private person could even take unilateral administrative acts (Conseil d'État, *Assemblée*, 31 July 1942, *Montpeurt*).

Note

As a starting point, in the French legal system, whenever there is a 'public service', administrative courts are competent. The notion of 'public service' has thus become a core notion in order to qualify administrative acts or actions and consequently to determine the jurisdiction of administrative courts with respect to unilateral measures, contracts and torts.

Conseil d'État, 28 June 1963[122] **2.29 (FR)**

Narcy v Minister of Finances, Economic Affairs and Planning

JURISDICTION; PUBLIC SERVICE; ACTIVITY CARRIED OUT BY A PRIVATE BODY

Narcy

An activity carried out by a private body can also be qualified as a public service.

Facts: Mr Narcy, employed by a private body, challenged an implicit decision of the Minister of Finances, Economic Affairs and Planning that refused to award him a salary for his status as reserve officer, in addition to his current salary.

Held: Since the body that employed Mr Narcy was responsible for discharging a public service, the relevant administrative rules had to be applied and jurisdiction for this case was held to belong to the administrative courts.

[121] G Bermann and E Picard, *Introduction to French Law* (The Hague, Kluwer Law International, 2008) 65.
[122] N° 72002.

Judgment: Considering that it results from the case file that, since its creation, the functioning of the technical centre of the foundry industries has always been managed for more than half by compulsory contributions and that, notably, the percentage of said contributions to the resources of the centre increased in 1957 and 1958 to 95% and 97% respectively;

Considering that in accordance with Article 1 of the law of 22 July 1948, the competent ministers are authorised to create in every business activity, when required by the general interest, organs of public utility called industrial technical centres with the aims, in the terms of Article 2 of the law, 'to promote technical progress, to participate in the improvement of performance and to guarantee the quality of the industry'; considering that, in order to enable them to perform the mission of general interest with which they have thus been entrusted and to guarantee to the administration a right to scrutinize the modalities of the accomplishment of this mission, the legislator has granted to the industrial technical centres certain prerogatives of public power and has subjected them to various controls of the supervisory authority; considering that, in particular, it follows from the terms of the same Article 1 of the aforementioned law that only one industrial technical centre can be created in the activities sector; considering that each centre is granted the right to levy compulsory contributions from the members of the profession; considering that the ministers entrusted with the regulation of the technical industrial centres proceed to the appointment of members of their board of directors and control their activity by means of a governmental commission which holds a suspensory veto right; considering that, by adopting these provisions, notwithstanding the fact that the trade unions which are most representative of the employers, the white collars and the blue collars are closely associated in the creation and the functioning of the industrial technical centres, the legislator has decided, without at the same time removing their characteristic of a private body, to entrust those centres with the management of a true public service.

Note

In order to qualify an activity as a 'public service', especially in the case where the activity is carried out by a private body, the courts usually refer to a set of criteria, such as the general interest dimension of the activity, the control exercised by the administration, the financing system and the monopolistic position of the body.

Tribunal des conflits, 22 January 1921[123] **2.30 (FR)**

Société commerciale de l'ouest africain

JURISDICTION; CONTRACTS; PUBLIC SERVICE

Société commerciale de l'ouest africain 'Bac d'Eloka'

In case of liability arising from a contract, administrative courts have jurisdiction only where the contract relates to an 'administrative public service'.

Facts: The company Société commerciale de l'ouest africain was the owner of a car which was badly damaged in a ferry accident involving a ferry directly operated by the Colony of Ivory Coast (the public body

[123] N° 00706.

responsible for the management of the former French colony of Ivory Coast). The company claimed compensation for the damage before the ordinary courts. The lieutenant governor of the Colony of Ivory Coast raised a point on the jurisdiction of the court and the matter was referred to the Court of Jurisdictional Disputes (Tribunal des conflits).

Held: The jurisdiction for this case was held not to belong to the administrative courts.

Judgment: Considering that, firstly, the Eloka ferry is not a public work; secondly, by performing, in return for remuneration, the operations of ferrying pedestrians and cars from one shore to another of the lagoon, the Colony of Ivory Coast operates a transport service under the same conditions as an ordinary industrial operator; considering that, therefore, in the absence of a particular text allocating jurisdiction to the administrative courts, it is the ordinary courts' sole responsibility to hear and deal with the damaging consequences of the accident invoked, whether its cause was, as alleged by Société commerciale de l'ouest africain, a fault committed in the operation of the ferry or its poor maintenance. Considering that if, therefore, in view of the objection to jurisdiction addressed by the lieutenant governor, the president of the court was wrong not to limit himself to ruling on the objection to jurisdiction, but, in the same order appointed an expert contrary to Articles 7 and 8 of the Order of 1 June 1828, he was correct in ruling that he was competent to hear the dispute.

Note

As a result of this judgment, public services are divided into so-called 'administrative public services' (*services publics administratifs*), which are generally subject to the jurisdiction of the administrative courts, and 'industrial and commercial public services' (*services publics industriels et commerciaux*), which are generally subject to the jurisdiction of civil courts.

Conseil Constitutionnel, 23 January 1987[124] **2.31 (FR)**

JURISDICTION; DEROGATION FROM PUBLIC SERVICE; PREROGATIVES OF PUBLIC POWER; UNILATERAL MEASURES

Conseil de la concurrence

Unilateral measures adopted by an administrative authority in the exercise of its public law powers lie within the jurisdiction of the administrative courts.

Facts: The French Parliament had decided to confer the jurisdiction to review the decisions of the Conseil de la concurrence (now Autorité de la concurrence, Competition Authority, i.e. the body responsible to adjudicate on competition law issues) to the ordinary courts.

Held: The Council declared the transfer of jurisdiction lawful but found the law invalid on the ground that (in the absence of any provision for a stay of execution) it infringed the rights of defence, a principle of constitutional rank.

Judgment: 15. Considering that the provisions of Articles 10 and 13 of the law of 16 and 24 August 1790 and the decree of 16 fructidor year III which have laid down the principle

[124] N° 86-224 DC.

of the separation between administrative and judicial authorities in a general manner do not in themselves have constitutional value; considering that, nevertheless, in conformity with the French conception of the separation of powers, amongst the 'fundamental principles recognized by the Republic', there is the principle according to which, with the exception of matters reserved by their nature to the ordinary courts, jurisdiction concerning the annulment or amendment of the decisions taken, in the exercise of prerogatives of public power, by the authorities exercising the executive power, their agents, the regional authorities of the Republic or the public bodies placed under their authority or under their control belongs to the administrative courts;

16. Considering, however, that in the implementation of this principle, when the application of a specific law or a regulation might generate several claims which would be split, according the usual rules on jurisdiction, between the administrative courts and the ordinary courts, it is permissible for the legislator, in the interest of the good administration of justice, to allocate the jurisdiction to the jurisdictional order mainly concerned.

Notes

(1) This ruling shows that, apart from the public service criterion, a second criterion to establish the jurisdiction of administrative courts is that of the use of prerogatives of public power (*prérogatives de puissance publique*).

(2) This ruling also established that unilateral measures of the administration fall within the jurisdiction of the administrative courts if they enforce (or are the expression of the use of) prerogatives of public power.

(3) This ruling finally shows that in some situations derogating from the *service public* criterion, or the *prerogatives de puissance publique* criterion, a statutory provision may also vest either ordinary courts or administrative courts with the power of adjudicating on certain cases. For example, because of a 1987 statute,[125] decisions of the Competition Authority (Autorité de la Concurrence) must be challenged before ordinary courts, even though this body is an administrative body, whose decisions would normally fall under the jurisdiction of the administrative courts.

Conseil d'État, 20 April 1956[126] **2.32 (FR)**

Époux Bertin v Minister for Veterans Affairs and Victims of War

CONTRACTS; PUBLIC SERVICE

Époux Bertin

A contract that confers the execution of a public service on a private party is an administrative law contract.

Facts: The Bertin couple had agreed, by virtue of a contract concluded orally, to feed some Soviet citizens housed in the Repatriation Centre of Meaux, in exchange for a lump sum of 30F per person per day. The Bertin couple subsequently argued that an addendum had been made to the initial contract, as a consequence of

[125] Loi n° 87-499 du 6 juillet 1987, JORF du 7 juillet 1987, 7391.

[126] N° 98637.

which the Repatriation Centre had agreed to pay a supplementary fee of 7.50F in exchange for the provision of new foodstuffs. The Centre refused to pay the supplementary fee and was taken to court by the claimants.

Held: The Council of State considered the contract to be an administrative law contract. It held that the jurisdiction belonged to the administrative courts.

Judgment: Considering that it appears that, by an oral contract concluded by the administration on 24 November 1944, the couple had committed, for a lump sum of 30 francs per person per day, to provide food to the Soviet nationals hosted in the Repatriation Centre of Meaux while waiting for their return to Russia; considering that the said contract has the object to confer on the concerned individuals, in this regard, the execution of the public service of ensuring the repatriation of the refugees of foreign nationality which were on French territory; considering that this circumstance itself is sufficient to conclude that this contract has the characteristics of an administrative law contract (*contrat administratif*); considering that therefore, without there being the need to see whether said contract contains clauses which derogate from ordinary law, since the dispute concerns the existence of an engagement complementary to this contract, on the basis of which the administration has allegedly allotted an additional bonus of 7.50 francs per person per day to the Bertin couple in exchange for new types of food, the jurisdiction belongs to the administrative courts …

Tribunal des conflits, 13 October 2014[127] **2.33 (FR)**

SA AXA France IARD v Mutuelle Assurance des Instituteurs de France (MAIF)

CONTRACTS; PUBLIC POWER PREROGATIVES

SA AXA France IARD

A contract falls within the jurisdiction of the administrative courts if it contains clauses which vest the administration with special prerogatives for the enforcement of the contract.

Facts: The city of Joinville-le-Pont concluded a contract with an association whereby the city rented some facilities to the association for the purposes of rowing. A fire destroyed the building. The insurer of the city sued the insurer of the association for reimbursement of the damages caused by the fire.

Held: The contract was considered a private law contract. The jurisdiction was held not to belong to the administrative courts.

Judgment: Considering that, in third instance, the disputed contract does not include any clause which, notably because of the prerogatives recognised to the contracting public person in the execution of the contract, requires in the general interest that the special regime of administrative law contracts (*contrats administratifs*) be followed. …

Ordonnance n° 2015-899 du 23 juillet 2015 relative aux marchés publics[128] **2.34 (FR)**

Article 3 Public procurement contracts falling within the scope of the present ordinance (*ordonnance*) concluded by legal persons of public law are administrative law contracts (*contrats administratifs*).

[127] N° C3963.
[128] JORF n° 0169, 24 July 2015, 12602.

Note

In the case of contractual relations, the administrative courts have jurisdiction when a contract is qualified as an 'administrative law contract'. The case of *Époux Bertin* established that when a contract is concluded for the performance of a public service, the contract is to be qualified as an 'administrative law contract'. In recent cases, the scope of 'public service' has been broadened. Today, it encompasses both cases where, through a contract, an individual is in charge of the performance of a public service and cases where the individual merely participates in the performance of a public service (without being the main person responsible for the public service).[129] Secondly, a contract can be qualified as an 'administrative law contract' if some of its provisions vest the administration with prerogatives of public power for the purposes of promoting the general interest which derogate from the generally applicable rules of law regulating private parties (eg the power to terminate the contract unilaterally). The *AXA* case from 2014 forms part of a series of judgments rendered by French courts since the beginning of the twentieth century on the identification of contractual clauses which are the expression of prerogatives of public power.[130] In that case, there were no such provisions, hence the contract was qualified as a private law contract. Furthermore, the law itself may specify that the contract is an 'administrative law contract'. By way of example, public procurement contracts are qualified by the law as 'administrative law contracts' by Article 3 of Ordinance n° 2015-899 of 23 July 2015.

Tribunal des conflicts, 8 February 1873[131] **2.35 (FR)**

Blanco v Prefect of Gironde

JURISDICTION; DAMAGES; PUBLIC SERVICE

Blanco

The state is responsible before the administrative courts if it caused damage in the performance of a public service.

Facts: Mr Blanco's daughter (Agnes) was run over by a wagon that was being pushed by employees of a tobacco manufactory in Bordeaux (which, at that time, was an organ of the State). Mr Blanco applied to the civil court in Bordeaux in order to get compensation for the damage suffered by his daughter. The prefect of Gironde contested the jurisdiction of the civil court to deal with the matter on the ground that the manufactory was an emanation of the State and argued therefore that the matter should be dealt with by the Council of State (which was at that time the only administrative court).

Held: The jurisdiction for the case was held to belong to the administrative courts.

Judgment: Considering that the responsibility of the state, being neither general nor absolute, is subject to special rules which vary depending on the needs of the public service and the need to reconcile the rights of the state with the rights of private persons;

[129] Tribunal de conflits, 21 May 2007, *SA CODIAM*, N° C3609.
[130] Council d'État, 31 July 1912, *Société des granits porphyroïdes des Vosges*, N° 30701.
[131] N° 00012.

considering that accordingly, under the laws cited above, the jurisdiction to rule on these matters is vested exclusively in the administrative courts. …

Notes

(1) With regard to tort claims, the *Blanco* case established that there is a responsibility of the state for the damages caused when carrying out a public service, and torts committed by public authorities in the exercise of a public service fall within the jurisdiction of administrative courts.

(2) Furthermore, administrative courts are always competent to hear tort claims arising from unlawful unilateral measures.

Conseil d'État, 19 October 1956[132] **2.36 (FR)**

Société Le Béton v Conseil de Préfecture de la Seine

JURISDICTION; PUBLIC PROPERTY

Société Le Béton

Decisions concerning public property that belongs to a public body, that is open to the public and that is adapted to facilitate public access fall within the jurisdiction of the administrative courts.

Facts: The company Le Béton concluded a contract with a public body, the Office national de la Navigation, regarding the lease of land located in a port. The company had to pay a penalty with regard to the enforcement of the contract. It challenged the decision.

Held: Since the land, which is the object of the lease contract, is part of public property subject to public law (*domaine public*), the case was considered to fall within the jurisdiction of the administrative courts.

Judgment: Considering, on the other hand, that it results from the provisions of the decree of 4 February 1932 and of the requirements specifications annexed to it, notably those aforementioned, that, under the regime of this decree, the part of the land that forms the 'industrial' harbour constitutes one of the elements of the overall organisation forming the harbour of Bonneuil-sur-Marne; considering that it is, thus, as any other parts of this harbour, operated for the purpose of public utility which has determined the concession to the National Office of Navigation of the entirety of these lands and by reason of which they have been incorporated, as a result of this concession, in the public property subject to public law (*domaine public*) belonging to the State.

Considering that the circumstance that, differently from the other land which has been adapted in view of a common use by the users of this harbour, the land concerned is the object of a contract for private use, to the benefit of private individuals or the company exercising purely private activities, cannot lead to the consequence that the land concerned is removed from the regime of the public property placed under public law, since it is in its nature to contribute to the functioning of the entirety of the port only under this form and that it results, on the other hand, from the case file that this land has formed the object of installations aimed at making them fit for this usage through their junction to the waterways, railways or highways whose development and connection constitute the port; …

[132] N° 20180.

Note

In case of property claims of the administration, the administrative courts have jurisdiction if the case is linked with public property that is placed subject to public law (*domaine public* as opposed to *domaine privé*, ie the part of public properties subject to private law). Such a qualification is given either by statute (in limited cases) or by case law. The case *Société Le Béton* established that decisions concerning public property that belongs to a public body, that is open to the public and that is adapted to this end fall under the jurisdiction of the administrative courts.

2.5.B MEANS AND PROCEDURES TO SOLVE THE CONFLICTS OF JURISDICTION

All legal systems provide for solutions for situations in which the wrong judicial avenue is chosen, or two courts or no court declare themselves as having jurisdiction on a certain matter. As a general principle, these jurisdictional conflicts can be resolved either by the courts concerned or by another court which is specifically constituted for these purposes.

2.5.B.1 SYSTEMS WITHOUT A SPECIAL COURT FOR JURISDICTIONAL CONFLICTS

2.5.B.1 (i) England and Wales

In England and Wales, given the monistic structure of the legal system, the issue of jurisdictional conflicts is not posed in terms of conflicts between administrative courts and other courts (as there is only one unified court structure), but rather in terms of use of the judicial review procedure.[133]

House of Lords, 25 November 1982[134] **2.37 (EW)**

O'Reilly v Mackman

PROCEDURAL EXCLUSIVITY; ABUSE OF PROCESS

O'Reilly

It is not permissible to bring an action in private law if judicial review is available to an applicant.

Facts: O'Reilly and other former prisoners issued proceedings against the Board of Visitors (a disciplinary body) of Hull Prison by issuing writs (a private law action) seeking a declaration that the Board of Visitors had acted contrary to natural justice.

Held: The claim was considered inadmissible.

133 See above section 2.2.B.1 on jurisdiction in England.
134 [1983] 2 AC 237 (HL).

Judgment: Lord Diplock: Now that those disadvantages to applicants have been removed and all remedies for infringements of rights protected by public law can be obtained upon an application for judicial review, as can also remedies for infringements of rights under private law if such infringements should also be involved, it would in my view as a general rule be contrary to public policy, and as such an abuse of the process of the court, to permit a person seeking to establish that a decision of a public authority infringed rights to which he was entitled to protection under public law to proceed by way of an ordinary action and by this means to evade the provisions of Order 53 for the protection of such authorities.

Notes

(1) Prior to 1977, administrative law in England and Wales did not draw a clear distinction between public law and private law, and the claimant issued a writ to commence a case against a public authority whether seeking a 'public law remedy' or a 'private law remedy'.[135] Certain of the 'prerogative' (ie public law) remedies, could only be sought from the courts to offer redress against public authorities, but the process for commencing all claims was, in essence, the same. In 1977, a new procedure was created which endeavoured to channel all public law claims through a particular procedure. This situation is presently maintained by Part 54 CPR, with Rules 54.2 and 54.3 seeking to confine claims for judicial review to the procedure contained in Part 54. In this case, the House of Lords held that it was not possible for the claimants to proceed under the private law (writ) procedure that would have been used prior to the introduction of the reforms in 1977 and that any claim where the claimants were seeking a public law remedy against a public authority should be brought using the judicial review procedure, with the attendant procedural restrictions and limitations that the procedure brings.

(2) As the years have passed, the courts have become more flexible, occasionally permitting claimants to proceed in private law (eg in an action for breach of contract) where there were also 'public law' matters to be determined.[136] Furthermore, the court has the power to order the transfer between procedures under Part 30 CPR.

2.5.B.1 (ii) The European Union

Like England and Wales, the EU legal system is also a monist system, hence there are no conflicts of jurisdiction between administrative and ordinary courts. However, there may be conflicts between the two EU courts (ie the General Court and the Court of Justice). Furthermore, considering that national and European administrative authorities often cooperate in the implementation of EU law, there may be conflicts of jurisdiction between the national and the European courts.

[135] See further Chapter 7, section 7.2.A.2.

[136] See, eg *Roy v Kensington and Chelsea Family Practitioner Committee* [1992] 1 AC 624, which established that a doctor could bring a claim for breach of contract to seek payment for providing public healthcare services even though the preliminary issue in the case was one of whether the public authority had acted lawfully (in a public law sense) in exercising a statutory power to deny payment.

Statute of the Court of Justice of the European Union **2.38 (EU)**

Article 54 Where an application or other procedural document addressed to the General Court is lodged by mistake with the Registrar of the Court of Justice, it shall be transmitted immediately by that Registrar to the Registrar of the General Court; likewise, where an application or other procedural document addressed to the Court of Justice is lodged by mistake with the Registrar of the General Court, it shall be transmitted immediately by that Registrar to the Registrar of the Court of Justice.

Where the General Court finds that it does not have jurisdiction to hear and determine an action in respect of which the Court of Justice has jurisdiction, it shall refer that action to the Court of Justice; likewise, where the Court of Justice finds that an action falls within the jurisdiction of the General Court, it shall refer that action to the General Court, whereupon that Court may not decline jurisdiction.

Note

A case can be brought before the Court of Justice[137] or the General Court[138] by submitting an application to the Registrar.

Case 314/85, 22 October 1987[139] **2.39 (EU)**

Foto-Frost v Hauptzollamt Lübeck-Ost

JURISDICTION OF EUROPEAN COURTS; JURISDICTION OF NATIONAL COURTS; EU MEASURES

Foto-Frost

National courts do not have the power to declare EU measures unlawful.

Facts: The Finanzgericht (Fiscal Court) Hamburg referred to the Court of Justice a preliminary ruling concerning, amongst other matters, the interpretation of Article 177 of the EEC Treaty (currently Article 267 TFEU). The case concerned the recovery of duties related to Foto-Frost's importation into the Federal Republic of Germany of prismatic binoculars originating in the German Democratic Republic for the purposes of releasing them for sale. The applicant questioned the validity of the Commission measure on the basis of which the German customs authorities had asked for the recovery of certain import duties. The national court therefore referred to the Court of Justice a question concerning the possibility for a national court to declare EU measures unlawful.

Held: National courts do not have the power to declare EU measures unlawful.

Judgment: 12. Article 177 confers on the Court jurisdiction to give preliminary rulings on the interpretation of the Treaty and of acts of the Community institutions and on the validity of such acts. The second paragraph of that article provides that national courts may refer such questions to the Court and the third paragraph of that article

[137] Statute of the Court of Justice of the European Union, Art 21(1).
[138] Statute of the Court of Justice of the European Union, Art 53 in conjunction with Art 21(1).
[139] ECLI:EU:C:1987:452.

puts them under an obligation to do so where there is no judicial remedy under national law against their decisions.

13. In enabling national courts, against those decisions where there is a judicial remedy under national law, to refer to the Court for a preliminary ruling questions on interpretation or validity, Article 177 did not settle the question whether those courts themselves may declare that acts of Community institutions are invalid.

14. Those courts may consider the validity of a Community act and, if they consider that the grounds put forward before them by the parties in support of invalidity are unfounded, they may reject them, concluding that the measure is completely valid. By taking that action they are not calling into question the existence of the Community measure.

15. On the other hand, those courts do not have the power to declare acts of the Community institutions invalid. As the Court emphasized in the judgement of 13 May 1981 in Case 66/80 *International Chemical Corporation v Amministrazione delle Finanze* [1981] ECR 1191, the main purpose of the powers accorded to the Court by Article 177 is to ensure that Community law is applied uniformly by national courts. That requirement of uniformity is particularly imperative when the validity of a Community act is in question. Divergences between courts in the Member States as to the validity of Community acts would be liable to place in jeopardy the very unity of the Community legal order and detract from the fundamental requirement of legal certainty.

16. The same conclusion is dictated by consideration of the necessary coherence of the system of judicial protection established by the Treaty. In that regard it must be observed that requests for preliminary rulings, like actions for annulment, constitute means for reviewing the legality of acts of the Community institutions. As the Court pointed out in its judgement of 23 April 1986 in Case 294/83 *Parti écologiste 'les Verts' v European Parliament* [1986] ECR 1339, 'in Articles 173 and 184, on the one hand, and in Article 177, on the other, the Treaty established a complete system of legal remedies and procedures designed to permit the Court of Justice to review the legality of measures adopted by the institutions'.

17. Since Article 173 gives the Court exclusive jurisdiction to declare void an act of a Community institution, the coherence of the system requires that where the validity of a Community act is challenged before a national court the power to declare the act invalid must also be reserved to the Court of Justice.

Case C-97/91, 3 December 1992[140] **2.40 (EU)**

Oleificio Borelli Spa v Commission

JURISDICTION OF EUROPEAN COURTS; JURISDICTION OF NATIONAL COURTS; NATIONAL MEASURES

Oleificio Borelli

The European courts do not have jurisdiction to rule upon the lawfulness of national measures, but national courts should ensure that these measures are reviewable, in order to avoid a situation where an applicant is deprived of judicial protection.

Facts: Oleificio Borelli SpA brought an action for annulment against a Commission decision in which the Commission informed the applicant that it was unable to grant aid from the European Agricultural Guidance

[140] ECLI:EU:C:1992:491.

and Guarantee Fund. The applicant had submitted to the Commission, through the Italian Government, an application for the construction of an oil mill. The Italian authorities had informed the Commission that the Regional Council of Liguria had issued an unfavourable opinion in respect of that application for aid submitted by the applicant, and, on the basis of this opinion, the Commission issued an unfavourable decision.

Held: The action for annulment was rejected.

Judgment: It should be pointed out that in an action brought under Article 173 of the Treaty the Court has no jurisdiction to rule on the lawfulness of a measure adopted by a national authority … . Accordingly, it is for the national courts, where appropriate after obtaining a preliminary ruling from the Court, to rule on the lawfulness of the national measure at issue on the same terms on which they review any definitive measure adopted by the same national authority which is capable of adversely affecting third parties and, consequently, to regard an action brought for that purpose as admissible even if the domestic rules of procedure do not provide for this in such a case.

Note

These two cases depict two examples of 'shared administration', ie a situation in which both national and European authorities are involved in the same decision-making process aimed at the implementation of EU law. In cases of 'shared administration', there is no mechanism in the Treaties to solve the jurisdictional conflict. However, the case law of the Court of Justice basically established that national courts have to adjudicate on national measures and EU courts on EU measures. Furthermore, in *Oleificio Borelli*, the European Court of Justice also ruled that national courts cannot decline jurisdiction to rule on national administrative measures, even with regard to measures that, according to the domestic procedural rules, would not be reviewable.[141] Of course, when claims are brought against measures which are a preparatory step in the decision-making process, even if the correct (national or EU) judicial instance is seized, the claim might be inadmissible for lack of standing, as preparatory measures might be considered unable to produce a change in the applicant's legal sphere.[142]

2.5.B.1 (iii) Germany

Gerichtsverfassungsgesetz **2.41 (DE)**

§17a (1) If a court has declared with final and binding effect that the recourse taken to it is admissible, other courts shall be bound by this decision.

(2) If the recourse taken is inadmissible, the court shall declare this *proprio motu* after hearing the parties and shall at the same time refer the legal dispute to the competent court of admissible recourse. If several courts are competent, the dispute shall be referred

[141] For more on these situations, see M Eliantonio, 'Judicial Review in an Integrated Administration: The Case of "Composite Procedures"' (2014) 7 *Review of European Administrative Law* 65.

[142] On standing requirements, see Chapter 4, section 4.4.

to the court to be selected by the plaintiff or applicant or, if no selection is made, to the court designated by the referring court. The decision shall be binding upon the court to which the dispute has been referred in respect of the admissibility of the recourse.

(3) If the recourse taken is admissible, the court may give a preliminary decision to this effect. It must give a preliminary decision if a party challenges the admissibility of the recourse.

(4) The decision referred to in sections 2 and 3 may be given without an oral hearing, and must be motivated. The immediate complaint (*sofortige Beschwerde*) shall be available against the decision pursuant to the provisions of the respective applicable code of procedure. The participants shall only be entitled to lodge a complaint against a decision of a higher regional court at the highest federal court if this has been admitted in the decision. The complaint must be admitted if the legal issue concerned is of fundamental importance or if the court deviates from a decision of one of the highest federal courts or from a decision of the Joint Senate of the Highest Courts of the Federation (Gemeinsamer Senat der obersten Gerichtshöfe des Bundes). The highest federal court shall be bound by the admission of the complaint.

(5) The court that rules on an appellate remedy against a decision by the court seized of the case shall not review whether the recourse taken was admissible.

Notes

(1) In cases where the competent court cannot be determined without doubt, §17a of the Court Constitution Act (Gerichtsverfassungsgesetz) gives the court seized of the action the autonomy to either establish its jurisdiction for the case or refer it to another court. This decision is binding on the parties and the court to which the matter is referred. Thereby, it is guaranteed that the claimant's action proceeds in a timely manner without lengthy disputes with regard to court competence. The courts normally determines questions of competence without an oral hearing on the basis of the statement of claim.

(2) To preserve the uniformity of decisions by the federal courts, there exists a Joint Senate of the Highest Courts of the Federation (Gemeinsamer Senat der Obersten Bundesgerichte). If one federal court (eg the Federal Court of Justice) intends to deviate on a point of law from the decision of another federal court (eg the Federal Social Court), the Joint Senate decides on this point of law.[143] Therefore, conflicts of jurisdiction that occur between two court branches (eg between ordinary courts and administrative courts) may be resolved when they reach the highest instance.

2.5.B.1 (iv) The Netherlands

Algemene Wet Bestuursrecht **2.42 (NL)**

Article 8:71 If a claim may be brought only before the civil courts, this shall be stated in the judgment. The civil courts are bound by this decision.

[143] See §2 of the Act on the preservation of the uniformity of decisions by the Supreme Courts of the Federation (Gesetz zur Wahrung der Einheitlichkeit der Rechtsprechung der obersten Gerichtshöfe des Bundes).

Note

If an administrative court is of the opinion that there is no administrative jurisdiction, for instance, because the contested measure does not qualify as a decision as defined in Article 1:3 AWB (*besluit*), the claim has to be declared inadmissible. In this judgment, the court declares that the claim must be brought before the ordinary courts (Article 8:71 AWB). The ordinary court will have to accept this ruling and declare itself competent. A reverse provision is applicable if an ordinary court is of the opinion that the claim should have been brought to the administrative court, can be found in Article 70 of Civil Procedure Code (Wetboek burgerlijke rechtsvordering). Because of these two provisions, negative competence conflicts cannot occur and lengthy procedures about competence issues are avoided.

2.5.B.2 SYSTEMS WITH A SPECIAL COURT FOR JURISDICTIONAL CONFLICTS: FRANCE

Loi du 24 mai 1872 relative au Tribunal des conflits **2.43 (FR)**

Article 1 The conflicts of attribution between administrative and ordinary courts are settled by a Court of Jurisdictional Disputes (Tribunal des conflits) composed of an equal number of members of the Council of State (Conseil d'État) and the Court of Cassation (Cour de Cassation).

Article 12 The Court of Jurisdictional Disputes regulates the conflict of attribution between the two judicial branches, in the situations provided for by decree of the Council of State:

1 When the representative of the state in the department (départment) or the local authorities (collectivité) has raised the conflict in the situation provided for in Article 13;

2 When the courts of both branches have respectively declared themselves incompetent to rule on a dispute with the same subject matter;

3 When a court of either branch has referred to it the question of competence raised in a dispute.

Article 13 When the representative of the state in the départment or collectivité believes that the acceptance of a dispute or of a preliminary question brought before a court of the ordinary branch raises a question concerning the competence of the administrative jurisdiction, he can, even if the administration is not party to the dispute, ask the seized court to waive its competence.

Article 15 The Court of Jurisdictional Disputes can be seized of final decisions delivered by the administrative and ordinary courts in instances initiated before both judicial branches regarding disputes concerning the same subject matter, when they create a situation that leads to a denial of justice.

On the disputes that are thus referred to it, the Court of Jurisdictional Disputes rules on the merits, having regard to all the parties to the dispute. Its decisions are not subject to any appeal.

Décret n° 2015-233 du 27 février 2015 relatif au Tribunal des conflits et aux questions préjudicielles 2.44 (FR)

Article 32 Where an ordinary or administrative court has, by a decision which is no longer subject to appeal, declined the jurisdiction of the order to which it belongs on the ground that the dispute does not fall within the jurisdiction of its order, any court of the other order, seized of the same dispute, if it considers that the dispute belongs to the jurisdiction of the court originally seized, must, by reasoned decision which is not subject to any appeal even in cassation, refer the question of jurisdiction over the matter to the Court of Jurisdictional Disputes. Proceedings must be stayed untl the Court of Jurisdictional Disputes reaches a decision.

Article 34 If the Court of Jurisdictional Disputes considers that the referring court does not have jurisdiction to hear the action giving rise to the reference, it shall declare, with the exception of the order for reference, all the judgments and procedural acts to which that action gave rise before the court which pronounced the referral null and void. This also applies to judgments and procedural acts before any other courts of the same order. If it considers that the court of the other order has wrongly rendered a judgment of lack of competence on the action between the same parties, the Court of Jurisdictional Disputes declares null and void the judgment of the court which wrongly declined jurisdiction and refers the examination of the dispute or exception to that court.

Article 35 When a court is seized of a dispute which involves a question of jurisdiction raising serious difficulties and involving the separation of the orders of jurisdiction, it may, through a reasoned decision which is not subject to appeal, refer the matter to the Court of Jurisdictional Disputes for a decision on this question of jurisdiction. The court seized shall transmit its decision and the pleadings or submissions of the parties to the Court of Jurisdictional Disputes. The proceedings shall be suspended until the decision of the Court of Jurisdictional Disputes.

Article 37 Where the courts of each of the two orders have irrevocably declared themselves to be incompetent on the same matter, without the court reaching the most recent decision on the matter having referred the dispute to the Court of Jurisdictional Disputes, the interested parties may refer a dispute to it for the purpose of designation of the competent court. The application shall set out the details of the facts and the law as well as the subject-matter of the dispute and shall be accompanied by copies of the decisions taken.

Note

Several instances of conflict may happen:

(1) Positive conflicts: when the administration is made to appear before an ordinary court and challenges the jurisdiction of this court to hear the question, the prefect can ask the Court of Jurisdictional Disputes to solve the issue (Article 12, first option and Article 13 of the Loi du 24 mai 1872 relative au Tribunal des conflits (Act on the Court of Jurisdictional Disputes)).

(2) Negative conflicts: when the courts of the two orders have declared themselves not to have jurisdiction, any party can refer the matter to the Court of Jurisdictional

Disputes (Article 12, second option of the Loi du 24 mai 1872 relative au Tribunal des conflits and Article 37 of Décret n° 2015-233 du 27 février 2015 relatif au Tribunal des conflits et aux questions préjudicielles (Decree Concerning the Court of Jurisdictional Disputes and preliminary questions)).

(3) Conflicts after a referral: if a court from one order (administrative or ordinary) has decided that it does not have jurisdiction and the decision is final, while a court from another order is about to decide that the matter should have been dealt with by the first court, the second court cannot take a decision declining jurisdiction; it has instead to refer the matter to the Court of Jurisdictional Disputes (Article 12, third option and Articles 32 and 34 of Décret n° 2015-233 du 27 février 2015 relatif au Tribunal des conflits et aux questions préjudicielles). Another situation of referral takes place when a court of one order is about to take a decision concerning its jurisdiction which may endanger the boundaries of the jurisdiction between ordinary and administrative courts (Article 35 of Décret n° 2015-233 du 27 février 2015 relatif au Tribunal des conflits et aux questions préjudicielles).

The Court of Jurisdictional Disputes can also be called to adjudicate on conflicting decisions made by courts of both orders on the same subject matter. In this specific case, the Court of Jurisdictional Disputes rules on the merits of the case (Article 15 of the Loi du 24 mai 1872 relative au Tribunal des conflits).

2.5.C COMPARATIVE REMARKS

The extent of the jurisdiction of the administrative courts (or the extent of the judicial review procedure in England and Wales) varies quite significantly in the legal systems under examination.[144]

One can see at the two extremes the Dutch approach, which grounds jurisdiction on, as a starting point, unilateral administrative measures only, and the French approach, which considers almost all conflicts in which administrative authorities are involved (including unilateral measures, contracts and torts) as falling within the jurisdiction of the administrative courts. Similar to the Dutch legal system, the English legal system excludes most contracts from the remit of the judicial review procedure and includes damages only in a limited way when these are pursued through judicial review proceedings, ie only if they are asked for in combination with a public law remedy. Somewhere in between is the German legal system, which uses the criterion of 'public law dispute', thereby also including public law contracts,[145] though mostly excluding tort claims.

[144] For comparative overviews of this issue, see N Verheij, 'Relatief onaantastbaar', available at http://digitalarchive.maastrichtuniversity.nl/fedora/get/guid:158b5442-77a8-40bb-a04d-7946a6caf4d5/ASSET1; AJ Bok, *Rechtsbescherming in Frankrijk en Duitsland* (Deventer, Kluwer, 1992); CW Backes, *Suum Cuique? Enkele opmerkingen over de rechtsmachtverdeling tussen bestuursrechter en burgerlijke rechter* (The Hague, BJU Press, 2009).

[145] For an explanation of the German concept of 'public law contract', see Chapter 2, section 2.5.A.

The European Union constitutes a *sui generis* system of allocation of jurisdiction not only because of its monist nature, but also because of the need to delimit the jurisdiction of the European courts from that of the national courts.

In terms of jurisdictional conflicts, the analysed legal systems mostly opt for a system whereby the seized courts decide themselves whether they have jurisdiction on a certain matter, and provide for mechanisms to ensure that no other court will declare itself as having jurisdiction. France, instead, has a specific judicial body in place to resolve jurisdictional conflicts.

2.6 EXISTENCE OF (THE POSSIBILITY TO CREATE) SPECIALISED COURTS

Specialised courts in administrative matters are mostly created in certain subject matters that may be considered more 'technical', such as tax law. Specialised courts thus ensure that cases are tried by judges with expert knowledge in a certain subject matter, but they also add to the complexity of the system because more sets of courts exist, thereby augmenting the likelihood of jurisdictional conflicts. The questions examined in this section are whether the legal systems in question provide for the possibility to create specialised courts, and, where this is possible, whether these courts exist.

2.6.A THE EUROPEAN UNION

Treaty on the Functioning of the European Union **2.45 (EU)**

Article 257 The European Parliament and the Council, acting in accordance with the ordinary legislative procedure, may establish specialised courts attached to the General Court to hear and determine at first instance certain classes of action or proceeding brought in specific areas. The European Parliament and the Council shall act by means of regulations either on a proposal from the Commission after consultation of the Court of Justice or at the request of the Court of Justice after consultation of the Commission.

The regulation establishing a specialised court shall lay down the rules on the organisation of the court and the extent of the jurisdiction conferred upon it.

Decisions given by specialised courts may be subject to a right of appeal on points of law only or, when provided for in the regulation establishing the specialised court, a right of appeal also on matters of fact, before the General Court.

Notes

(1) The TFEU allows for the possibility to create specialised courts. However, none are operational at the moment. The only specialised court to exist within the EU legal system was the Civil Service Tribunal. As a consequence of the reform of the General Court, which took effect in September 2016, the Civil Service Tribunal ceased operations and was absorbed into the General Court.[146]

[146] Regulation 2015/2422 (n 43 above).

(2) An intergovernmental treaty on a Unified Patent Court[147] was signed by 25 EU Member States (all except for Croatia, Poland and Spain) in February 2013, but has not yet been ratified by enough states for the court to operate. It is possible that more specialised courts could be set up by way of an intergovernmental treaty.

2.6.B THE NETHERLANDS

Before 1994, several specialised administrative courts existed in the Netherlands, which were only competent in a very limited area of law.[148] For example, in social security law, there were several courts throughout the country in first instance and a second instance Central Appellate Court. In other areas, such as planning law and environmental law, there was only one first and last instance court: the Council of State. This fragmentation was considered to be unacceptable. In 1992 and 1994, the first steps towards a fundamental reform became effective. Almost all first instance judicial review bodies were abolished and the (administrative divisions of the) district courts became the competent courts in administrative matters. In a further step, the appellate courts should have been reformed and unified. This has not been realised. This explains the somewhat peculiar situation that exists at present, in which there are no specialised administrative courts of first instance in the judicial branch of the Netherlands. However, there are several specialised appellate courts.[149] The civil courts are, moreover, competent in appeals and cassation procedures relating to tax law, so it can also be said that a 'special' court deals with these issues.

2.6.C GERMANY

Sozialgerichtsgesetz **2.46 (DE)**

§51 (1) The courts of social jurisdiction rule on matters concerning disputes relating to public law

1. in matters of statutory pensions, including the agricultural pension scheme,

2. in matters of statutory health insurance, social care insurance and private care insurance (eleventh book on social law), also if third parties are affected; this does not apply to disputes in matters falling under §110 of the fifth book on social law due to termination of supply contracts which apply for university clinics or 'plan hospitals' (*Plankrankenhäuser*) (§108 No 1 and 2 of the fifth book on social law),

3. in matters of statutory accident insurance with the exception of disputes concerning the monitoring of measures of the providers of statutory accident insurance aiming at prevention of accidents,

4. in matters of employment promotion, including other tasks of the Federal Labour Office (Bundesagentur für Arbeit),

4a. in matters of basic income for job-seekers,

[147] Agreement on a Unified Patent Court 2013/C 175/01 OJ C175/01.

[148] See further RJGM Widdershoven, *Gespecialiseerde rechtsgangen in het administratieve recht* (Zwolle, Tjeenk Willink, 1989).

[149] For more details, see section 2.3.B.1 above.

5. in other matters of social security,

6. in matters of social compensation law, with the exception of disputes falling under §25 in conjunction with §27 of the Federal Act on Pensions (Bundesversorgungsgesetz), also as far as other laws provide for the respective application of those provisions,

6a. in matters of social welfare and the law on the support of asylum seekers,

7. for the diagnosis of disabilities and their extent, as well as further sanitary characteristics also concerning the issuance, extension, justification and seizure of identification cards under §69 of the ninth book on social law,

8. which occur because of the Expenditure Compensation Act (Aufwendungsausgleichsgesetz),

9. (repealed)

10. for which the recourse of law to those courts is opened.

Finanzgerichtsordnung **2.47 (DE)**

§33 (1) The fiscal legal recourse is available

1. in disputes concerning public law about tax matters, as far as the taxes are subject to federal law and are administered by federal tax authorities or tax authorities of the federal states,

2. in disputes concerning public law about the execution of administrative acts in matters other than those qualified as number 1, as far as the administrative acts are to be executed by the federal fiscal tax or the state tax authority in accordance with the provisions of the Fiscal Code (Abgabeordnung),

3. in disputes concerning public law and professional disputes about matters which are regulated through the first part, the second and sixth section of the second part and the first section of the third part of the Fiscal Code,

4. in disputes concerning public law other than those identified in numbers 1–3 above, as far as this is established for the fiscal recourse by federal law or state law.

(2) Tax matters under this law are all provisions concerning the administration of taxes, including tax refunds, or the application of the provisions relating to taxes and matters connected to the tax authorities, including measures of the federal tax authorities for the compliance with the prohibitions and limits to the movement of goods over the border; the tax matters are of equal rank as the matters of the administration of the fiscal monopoly.

Note

The only specialised courts dealing with certain fields of administrative law in Germany are tax courts and social courts.

2.6.D FRANCE

Cour Nationale du Droit d'Asile (CNDA): Compétences de la CNDA[150] **2.48 (FR)**

The National Court on Asylum Law (Cour Nationale du Droit d'Asile), which is competent to hear claims concerning asylum applications, is a specialised administrative court ruling

[150] Available at www.cnda.fr/La-CNDA/Competences-de-la-CNDA.

in first and last instance on the claims brought against the decisions of the French office for the protection of refugees and stateless persons (Office Français de Protection des Réfugiés et Apatrides – OFPRA).

This court is placed under the control on points of law of the Council of State and its jurisdiction is national. It exercises full jurisdiction control (*juridiction de plein contentieux*), as recognised by the Council of State in its decision of *Aldana Barrena* of 8 January 1982.

This means that the asylum court cannot only annul the decisions taken by the Director General of the OFPRA, but it can also substitute its decisions for those of the authority by ruling on the applicant's right to qualify as a refugee ...

Note

In France, specialised courts deal with, amongst others, disputes relating to refugees and disciplinary sanctions applied to doctors, architects, midwives and accountants.

2.6.E COMPARATIVE REMARKS

Two issues for comparison arise with regard to the theme of specialised administrative courts. The first is whether it is possible to create such courts in the first place. All systems provide for this possibility. The second issue is whether, in those legal systems where it is possible to have specialised courts, they actually do exist. None of the legal systems examined make a wide use of specialised courts in administrative matters, but specialised courts do exist in France and Germany, and, in second instance, also in the Netherlands. However, while in Germany the only specialised courts are in tax and social security matters, in France there are many more types of specialised administrative courts. In England and Wales, if one excludes the phenomenon of Tribunals (which cannot be assimilated to courts),[151] there are no specialised courts engaging in judicial review.

2.7 NECESSARY OR FACULTATIVE CHARACTER OF INTRA-ADMINISTRATIVE OBJECTION PROCEDURE

The system of intra-administrative objection procedure in general refers to the mechanism whereby a person is required or allowed to go back to the administrative authorities to ask for a reconsideration of an administrative measure. The aim of this system is, above all, efficiency, because it gives the administrative authorities the chance to reconsider their decisions and amend them if necessary, thereby reducing the courts' workload and minimising the time frame for the conclusion of disputes between citizens and

[151] See section 2.2.B.1 (ii) above.

the authorities. Furthermore, objection procedures are cheaper than judicial proceedings and often allow the authorities to fully review their decisions, while judicial review is in principle limited to a review of legality. However, the intra-administrative objection procedure can conversely also be seen as a 'waste of time' for the citizen: how likely is it that the authorities will admit their mistake and change their minds? The intra-administrative objection procedure can, from this perspective, be seen as a 'hurdle' to be surmounted between the citizen and the courts.

On the basis of the principle of national procedural autonomy, Member States are free to set up intra-administrative objection procedures: the Court of Justice has held that the existence of such procedures is not itself a violation of the principle of effective judicial protection, provided that the practical arrangements for the exercise of such possibilities do not disproportionately affect the right to an effective remedy.[152]

2.7.A SYSTEMS WITH NO GENERAL SYSTEM OF INTRA-ADMINISTRATIVE OBJECTION PROCEDURE

2.7.A.1 THE EUROPEAN UNION

Regulation (EC) No 1367/2006 of the European Parliament and of the Council of 6 September 2006 on the application of the provisions of the Aarhus Convention on Access to Justice in Environmental Matters to Community institutions and bodies[153] **2.49 (EU)**

Article 10
Request for internal review of administrative acts

1. Any non-governmental organisation which meets the criteria set out in Article 11 is entitled to make a request for internal review to the Community institution or body that has adopted an administrative act under environmental law or, in case of an alleged administrative omission, should have adopted such an act.

Such a request must be made in writing and within a time limit not exceeding six weeks after the administrative act was adopted, notified or published, whichever is the latest, or, in the case of an alleged omission, six weeks after the date when the administrative act was required. The request shall state the grounds for the review.

2. The Community institution or body referred to in paragraph 1 shall consider any such request, unless it is clearly unsubstantiated. The Community institution or body shall state its reasons in a written reply as soon as possible, but no later than 12 weeks after receipt of the request.

Article 12
Proceedings before the Court of Justice

1. The non-governmental organisation which made the request for internal review pursuant to Article 10 may institute proceedings before the Court of Justice in accordance with the relevant provisions of the Treaty.

[152] Case C-73/16 *Peter Puškár v Finančné riaditeľstvo Slovenskej republiky and Kriminálny úrad finančnej správy* ECLI:EU:C:2017:725.
[153] [2006] OJ 264/13.

Notes

(1) This Regulation implemented the requirements of the Aarhus Convention[154] into the EU legal systems as far as the EU institutions are concerned.

(2) In the EU legal system, secondary law may set up review procedures which resemble the system of intra-administrative objection procedure. The excerpt above provides one example of this system, because it set up an 'internal review' procedure for acts of the European institutions in environmental matters. Procedures which may be assimilated to an objection procedure are also often set up with respect to decisions of the European agencies through the creation of independent commissions instituted within the agencies themselves. Exhausting the 'objection procedure' is often a requirement for subsequent access to court.[155]

2.7.A.2 ENGLAND AND WALES

While a general system of formal intra-administrative objection procedure (in the sense of the possibility or the obligation for an individual to go back to the administrative authorities before going to court) does not exist in the English legal system, it is a general expectation that public authorities will have a complaints or grievance procedure (which in the English system is generally referred to as 'administrative appeal') that should be pursued before bringing a claim for judicial review. In a number of cases, the courts have held that claimants for judicial review must have exhausted all available routes of administrative appeal.[156] These methods of administrative appeal are not uniform or mandated in law in the vast majority of cases.

In some fields of decision-making, such as in social security and benefits claims, there is a formal and mandated system of intra-administrative objection procedure known as the 'mandatory reconsideration procedure'.[157] This procedure applies to the vast majority of social benefits decisions made by the Department of Work and Pensions. Where the mandatory reconsideration procedure applies, it is not possible for a claimant to make an appeal to the Social Entitlement Chamber of the First-tier Tribunal unless they can supply a decision from the mandatory reconsideration procedure to the Tribunal.[158]

[154] Available at www.unece.org/env/pp/treatytext.html.

[155] On this topic, see B Marchetti (ed), *Administrative Remedies in the European Union. The Emergence of a quasi-Judicial Administration* (Turin, Giappichelli, 2017).

[156] *R (On the Application of Cowl) v Plymouth City Council* [2001] EWCA Civ 1935, [2002] 1 WLR 803. See also *R v Falmouth and Truro Port HA, ex parte South West Water Ltd.* [2001] QB 445 (QB), where the High Court (Queen's Bench Division) held that in circumstances where a statutory appeal mechanism existed, it would not permit the company concerned to proceed with a claim for judicial review.

[157] For more on this point, see Social Security Advisory Committee Decision Making and Mandatory Reconsideration (Occasional Paper No 18, Social Security Advisory Committee, 2016), available at www.gov.uk/government/uploads/system/uploads/attachment_data/file/538836/decision-making-and-mandatory-reconsideration-ssac-op18.pdf.

[158] See Rule 22(2)(d)(i) of SI 2006/2685, the Tribunal Procedure (First-tier Tribunal) (Social Entitlement Chamber) Rules 2008 (as amended).

2.7.B SYSTEMS WITH A GENERAL SYSTEM OF INTRA-ADMINISTRATIVE OBJECTION PROCEDURE

2.7.B.1 SYSTEM WITH A COMPULSORY SYSTEM OF INTRA-ADMINISTRATIVE OBJECTION PROCEDURE

2.7.B.1 (i) Germany

Verwaltungsgerichtsordnung **2.50 (DE)**

§68 (1) Before an action for annulment (*Anfechtungsklage*) is lodged, the lawfulness and expedience of the administrative act must be reviewed in pre-trial proceedings. Such a review is not required if a statute so provides, or if

1. the administrative act has been issued by a supreme federal authority or by a supreme state authority, unless a statute prescribes the review, or

2. the remedial notice or the decision on an objection contains a grievance for the first time.

(2) Section 1 shall apply mutatis mutandis to the action seeking the issuance of an administrative act (*Verpflichtungsklage*) if the request to carry out the administrative act has been rejected.

§70 (1) The objection shall be lodged in writing within one month of notification of the administrative act to the aggrieved party, in writing or for the record of the authority which has carried out the administrative act. The deadline shall also be deemed to have been adhered to with the filing of an objection with the authority which has to issue the ruling on an objection.

§73 (1) Where the authority does not provide redress for the objection, a decision on the objection is handed down. The latter is issued by:

1. The next higher authority, unless another higher authority is designated by statute,
2. The authority which has issued the administrative act, in case the next higher authority is a supreme federal or supreme state authority,
3. The self-administration authority in matters of self-administration, unless a statute provides otherwise.

By way of derogation from the second sentence, no 1, a statute may provide that the authority that has issued the administrative act is also competent to decide on the objection.

...

(3) The decision on the objection must be motivated, must contain information on legal remedies, and must be served. Service is effected *ex officio* in accordance with the provisions of the Act on Service in Administrative Procedures (Verwaltungszustellungsgesetz). The decision on the objection also determines who bears the costs.

§75 If, with regard to an objection or an application for the issuance of an administrative act the merits, have not been decided upon within a suitable period without sufficient reason, the action shall be admissible by way of derogation from §68. The action may not be lodged prior to the expiry of three months after the lodging of the objection or since the filing of the application to carry out the administrative act, unless a shorter period is required because of the special circumstances of the case. If an adequate reason why the objection has not yet been ruled on applies, or the requested administrative act has not yet been carried out, the court shall suspend the proceedings until the expiry of a deadline it has set, which can be extended. If the objection is admitted within the deadline set by the court or the administrative act is carried out within this deadline, the main case shall be declared to have been settled.

Notes

(1) The requirement of the exhaustion of the intra-administrative objection procedure (*Widerspruchsverfahren*) only applies to actions for annulment (*Anfechtungsklage*) and actions for seeking the issuance of an administrative act (*Verpflichtungsklage*) and not to other actions.[159]

(2) The intra-administrative objection (*Widerspruch*) must be filed with the same authority that issued the decision within one month after the decision has been notified (§70 VwGO). If the administrative act fails to mention the legal remedy and the time limit of the intra-administrative objection procedure, the objection can be filed within one year.[160]

(3) Filing an objection generally has a suspensive effect, ie, in principle, the administrative act must not be executed during the objection procedure.[161]

(4) The admissibility of the objection requires that the applicant claim that the administrative act infringes his subjective public rights.[162] This means that the rules on standing relating to the court actions apply also in the context of the objection procedure, albeit extending to a legality and suitability check.[163]

(5) If the authority before which the objection was brought rejects the objection, it must pass the matter to a higher administrative body (§73 VwGO), which decides upon the case by issuing a decision on the objection (*Widerspruchsbescheid*). If the objection is considered grounded, the authority before which the objection was brought issues a decision on the objection.

(6) The question of whether the authority may also change the original administrative act to the detriment of the complainant within the intra-administrative objection procedure (*reformatio in peius*) is disputed. The prevailing opinion of courts and scholars answers this question in the affirmative.[164]

159 See Chapter 7, sections 7.2.A.1 and 7.3.B.2 for these actions in the German legal system.

160 §70 VwGO in conjunction with §58(2) VwGO. §60 VwGO governs the restoration of *status quo ante*.

161 §80(1) VwGO. Exceptions to that principle can be found in §80(2) VwGO. See further Chapter 7, section 7.8.B.

162 BVerwG 65, 313, 318.

163 §42(2) VwGO by analogy. See F Hufen, *Verwaltungsprozessrecht*, 10th edn (Munich, CH Beck, 2016) 65 ff.

164 For a discussion see Hufen (n 163 above) 129.

2.7.B.1 (ii) The Netherlands

In the Netherlands, two different kinds of intra-administrative objection procedures are known.[165] The most common and 'default' procedure is the objection procedure (*bezwaar*) that is set out in Article 7:1 AWB. In a few cases, however, an 'administrative appeal' (*administratief beroep*) (Division 7.3 AWB) may be lodged instead of the objection procedure.

Algemene Wet Bestuursrecht **2.51 (NL)**

Article 1:5 (1) 'Making an objection' means making use of a statutorily conferred power to seek redress against a decision from the administrative authority which took the decision.

(2) 'Lodging an administrative appeal' means making use of a statutorily conferred power to seek redress against a decision from an administrative authority other than the one which made the decision.

Note

The important difference between an objection procedure and an administrative appeal is that the administrative authority which took the contested decision also decides on the objection, whilst in an administrative appeal another, often higher, administrative authority decides.

Algemene Wet Bestuursrecht **2.52 (NL)**

Article 7:1 (1) The person who has been given the right to bring a claim for judicial review (*beroep*) before an administrative judge must, before bringing this claim, file an objection, unless:

a. the decision has been taken on an objection or an administrative appeal,

b. the decision is subject to approval,

c. the decision contains the approval of another decision or the denial of such approval,

d. the decision has been prepared in accordance with Division 3.4;

e. the decision has been taken on the basis of a judgment in which the court, in application of Article 8:72(4)(a), had determined that Division 3.4 is disapplied wholly or in part;

f. the claim is directed against the failure to take a decision in due time;

g. the decision has been taken on the basis of a rule as referred to in the Regulation on Direct Appeal (*Regeling rechtstreeks beroep*) belonging to this Act or if the decision is otherwise described in that Regulation.

(2) Against the decision on the objection a claim for judicial review may be brought in accordance with the rules that apply to bringing a claim against the decision against which the objection has been filed.

[165] For more on this, see Seerden and Wenders (n 23 above) 145 ff.

Article 7:1a (1) In the letter of objection, the complainant may request the administrative authority to agree to an immediate claim for judicial review (*beroep*) before the administrative judge, by way of derogation from Article 7:1.

(2) The administrative authority in any event rejects the request, if another letter of objection against the decision has been submitted in which an identical request is missing, unless that other letter of objection is evidently inadmissible.

(3) The administrative authority may agree to the request if the matter is suitable for this.

(4) The administrative authority decides on the request as soon as possible. A decision to agree is taken as soon as it may reasonably be assumed that no new letters of objection will be submitted. Articles 4:7 and 4:8 do not apply.

(5) If the administrative authority agrees with the request, it forwards the letter of objection, after the date of receipt has been noted on it, without delay to the competent judge.

(6) A letter of objection received after the agreement is forwarded to the competent judge without delay as well. If this letter of objection does not contain a request in the meaning of section 1, then by way of derogation from Article 8:41(1), no registration fee is levied.

Notes

(1) According to Article 7:1 AWB, the objection procedure (*bezwaar*) is the default option. In order for a claim for judicial review before a court to be admissible, the objection procedure has to be followed as a preliminary step. Article 7:1 mentions some exceptions from this general rule. The alternative, administrative appeal, is only applicable if specific statutory acts require so. There are only a few examples of administrative appeals. Hence, there is no general rule on the applicability of administrative appeal that is comparable to Article 7:1 AWB.

(2) No objection procedure is required when challenging a decision resulting from an objection procedure or an administrative appeal (Article 7:1(1)(a) AWB). Furthermore, a claim for judicial review before a court is open directly when the disputed decision has to be approved by a different authority than the authority issuing the decision (Article 7:1(1)(b) AWB) or is the approval of a decision of a different authority (Article 7:1(1)(c) AWB). An intra-administrative objection procedure is not required in this case because the approval of another public authority already entails a review of the decision. Another important exception in practice involves decisions that result from the so-called 'uniform public preparatory procedure' (*uniforme openbare voorbereidingsprocedure*, Division 3.4 AWB). This specific procedure guarantees the possibility for everyone to state his opinion regarding a (draft) decision. Because of this *ex ante* public consultation, the intra-administrative objection procedure would only repeat and delay the (already extensive) decision-making process (Article 7:1(1)(d) and (e) AWB). Logically, an intra-administrative objection procedure is not necessary if the administrative authority has not yet adopted a decision and the fact that it did not decide on time is contested (Article 7:1(1)(f) AWB). For certain specific administrative acts, no intra-administrative objection procedure is available. The types of decisions

falling under this category are mentioned in Annex 1 to the AWB (Article 7:1(1)(g) AWB). Finally, the intra-administrative objection procedure can be skipped if the claimant has requested this and the authority permits the action to progress to court (Article 7:1a AWB). However, if more than one party has objected to the same decision and not all parties have sought to progress immediately to court, the authority must reject the request to leapfrog the objection procedure. This is logical, because the same decision cannot be dealt with in an objection procedure and in judicial review at the same time.

(3) The authority must make a decision within six weeks from the day after which the period to lodge an objection has passed (Article 7:10(1) AWB).[166] If it does not react within this time, the non-decision is equated with a decision (Article 6:2 AWB) against which the citizen can bring legal proceedings.[167]

(4) The objection procedure can be followed only by those who have standing in the case (Article 7:1 AWB), that is, by 'anyone concerned' (Article 8:1 AWB). Therefore, individuals have to prove a sufficient interest (Article 1:2 AWB).

(5) In the objection procedure, the authority which took the original decision re-examines the decision fully and *ex nunc*, but in general the objection procedure cannot lead to a worse outcome for the claimant compared with the original contested decision (*reformatio in peius*).[168] However, the case law is not consistent on this.[169]

2.7.B.2 SYSTEM WITH AN OPTIONAL SYSTEM OF INTRA-ADMINISTRATIVE OBJECTION PROCEDURE: FRANCE

Conseil d'État, 6 January 1995[170] **2.53 (FR)**

Assemblée territoriale de la Polynésie française v Haut-commissaire de la République en Polynésie française

OBJECTION PROCEDURE; TIME LIMIT

Assemblée territoriale de la Polynésie française

An objection procedure may be brought within the same time limit as an action for annulment.

Facts: The claimant, the prefect of the French Republic (Haut Commissaire de la République), challenged the decision of the territorial assembly of Polynésie Française to impose a five-year residence condition in order to access the territorial civil service. The Administrative Court of First Instance of Papeete quashed the decision.

Held: The Council of State upheld the first instance judgment.

166 The period is 12 weeks if the authority is assisted by an advisory committee.
167 On the effects of silence, see further Chapter 3, section 3.6.B.2.
168 For example, ECLI:NL:CRVB:2011:BQ5018.
169 For example, ECLI:NL:CRVB:2003:AI0054.
170 N° 152654.

Judgment: Except in the case where legislative or regulatory provisions created special procedures, every administrative decision can be the object, within the foreseen time limit of an action for annulment (*recours pour excés de pouvoirs*), of a *recours gracieux* (intra-administrative objection procedure addressed to the decision maker) or a *recours hiérarchique* (intra-administrative objection procedure addressed to a superior authority) which interrupts the running of this time limit.

Code des relations entre le public et l'administration **2.54 (FR)**

Article L411-2 Every administrative decision can be the object, within the time limit imposed for the introduction of an action for annulment, of a *recours gracieux* (intra-administrative objection procedure addressed to the decision-maker) or a *recours hiérarchique* (intra-administrative objection procedure addressed to a superior authority) which interrupts the running of this time limit.

When a *recours gracieux* or a *recours hiérarchique* is introduced within the time limit foreseen for an action for annulment, the time limit for the action for annulment, extended by virtue of the commencement of those administrative appeal procedures (*recours administratifs*), does not recommence to run in regard to the initial decision until both procedures are concluded.

Code de justice administrative **2.55 (FR)**

Article R421-1 A claim against a decision must be brought before the court within two months of the notification or publication of the contested decision.

Notes

(1) There is no specified time for the administration to respond to the objection. However, two months' silence on the part of the administration generally creates a decision that can be challenged before the administrative courts.[171]

(2) If the individual is the addressee of the contested decision, he will be entitled to bring an objection procedure. If this is not the case, he or she will have to prove to have a sufficient interest in the procedure.[172]

Code des relations entre le public et l'administration **2.56 (FR)**

Article L411-4 The administration decides on the objection concerning a decision establishing rights on the basis of the situation of fact and law at the date of the decision. In case of an objection lodged against a decision which does not establish rights, the administration decides on the situation of fact and law at the date on which the objection is decided.

[171] On the effects of silence, see further Chapter 3, section 3.6.B.1.

[172] On standing before French administrative courts, see Chapter 4, section 4.4.B.3.

Note

The decision of the authorities is fully reconsidered at the objection procedure stage, including its merits. The decision on the objection procedure may result in a worse outcome for the applicant.

Code de l'entrée et du séjour des étrangers et du droit d'asile **2.57 (FR)**

Article D211-5 A commission under the jurisdiction of the Minister of Foreign Affairs and the Minister of Immigration is responsible for examining objections against visa refusal decisions taken by diplomatic or consular authorities. The referral to this commission is a compulsory prerequisite for the admissibility of an action for annulment.

Note

The nature of the objection procedure in France is predominantly facultative; however, regarding certain administrative decisions, an intra-administrative objection procedure must be pursued in advance of a claim being brought to court.

2.7.C RECENT TRENDS ON THE COMPULSORY NATURE OF THE OBJECTION PROCEDURE

Recently, the categorisations made above have been somewhat strained by the introduction of legislative reforms inverting the national trends on the compulsory or optional nature of the intra-administrative objection procedure.

In Germany, where the intra-administrative objection procedure has traditionally had a compulsory nature, in some of the states,[173] such as Bavaria and North Rhine-Westphalia, the procedure has been abandoned or limited to special fields of administrative law because it was considered ineffective and too time consuming.[174] Conversely, in France, the trend seems to point towards making the objection procedure compulsory in more and more cases, with so-called *recours administratifs préalables obligatoires* (mandatory intra-administrative objection procedures),[175] although this still constitutes the exception to the main rule on the voluntary nature of the objection procedure.

Les recours administratifs préalables obligatoires[176] **2.58 (FR)**

A procedure which is often efficient

The mandatory intra-administrative objection procedure delivers numerous advantages. First, for the citizen, it constitutes a means that is simple, inexpensive and quick

[173] Note that the law on administrative procedure falls within the competence of the states.

[174] For details, see D Ehlers and F Schoch (eds), *Rechtsschutz im Öffentlichen Recht* (Berlin, De Gruyter, 2009) §20, para 93.

[175] The procedure of the compulsory intra-administrative objection procedure is regulated in Arts L-412-3 to L412-8 of the Code des relations entre le public et l'administration.

[176] Les recours administratifs préalables obligatoires, *Les Etudes du Conseil d'Etat*, La Documentation française, 2009.

to obtain a different decision with reasonable chances of success or, at least, to offer a better explanation for it. Thereafter, for the administration, the procedure allows the effective review of its decisions, the correction of possible flaws and the harmonisation of its practices for a better understanding of citizens' grievances. Finally, the mandatory intra-administrative objection procedure enhances the potential for the prevention and reduction of judicial disputes. It is thus in the interests of citizens, the administration and the courts that in the present study, the development of this alternative dispute settlement mechanism is envisaged.

Proposals of extension

On the basis of these principles, the study of the Council of State opens, with practical ambitions, concrete perspectives for the extension of the mandatory intra-administrative objection procedure in the four big domains which represent around a third of the disputes pending before the Administrative Courts of First Instance.

2.7.D COMPARATIVE REMARKS

The legal system of the EU is the only system of the countries under examination where no general system of intra-administrative objection procedure exists. Of the legal systems with a general system of intra-administrative objection procedure, some legal systems also give a compulsory nature to the objection procedure. In Germany and the Netherlands, claimants are generally required to exhaust the objection procedure before being allowed to bring a claim to court. In England and Wales, claimants are required to exhaust all non-judicial avenues available before being able to bring a claim for judicial review. The only exception in the group of legal systems with a general system of intra-administrative objection procedure is France, where, unlike in England and Wales, the Netherlands and Germany, the objection procedure generally has an optional character.

FURTHER READING

van den Berge, L, 'Rethinking the Public–Private Law Divide in the Age of Governmentality and Network Governance. A Comparative Analysis of French, English and Dutch Law' (2018) 5 *European Journal of Comparative Law and Governance* 119.

della Cananea, G, '"Public Law Disputes" in a Unified Europe' (2015) 7 *Italian Journal of Public Law* 102.

Dragos, D and Neamtu, B (eds), *Alternative Dispute Resolution in European Administrative Law* (Heidelberg, Springer, 2014).

Freedland, MR and Auby, J-B (eds), *The Public Law/Private Law Divide. Une entente assez cordiale?* (Oxford, Hart Publishing, 2006).

Jurgens, GTJM and van Ommeren, F, 'The Public–Private Divide in English and Dutch law, a Multifunctional and Context-Dependent Divide' (2012) 71 *Cambridge Law Journal* 172.

Marchetti, B (ed), *Administrative Remedies in the European Union. The Emergence of a quasi-Judicial Administration* (Turin, Giappichelli, 2017).

VAR-Commissie Rechtsbescherming, *De toekomst van de rechtsbescherming tegen de overheid, VAR Vereniging voor Bestuursrecht* (The Hague, Boom Juridische Uitgevers, 2004).

CHAPTER 3
TYPES OF ADMINISTRATIVE ACTION AND CORRESPONDING REVIEW

Mariolina Eliantonio and Franziska Grashof

3.1 INTRODUCTION

The central question of this chapter is which type of administrative action corresponds to which type of review proceedings before the administrative courts. This question presupposes that a legal system differentiates between several types of administrative action and types of review proceedings, and that there is a certain 'correspondence' between them. However, it should be noted from the outset that the legal concept of a strict correspondence between a certain classification of administrative action and different review proceedings is not shared by all legal systems. Instead, a highly differentiated 'doctrine of administrative action' (*Handlungsformenlehre*) is only found in some legal systems, whereas such a doctrine is hardly known to other legal systems.

This chapter will first provide an overview of the relative importance of a classification of administrative action and corresponding review proceedings in the different legal systems under consideration. Secondly, the chapter will examine several forms of administrative action and the corresponding review proceedings.

3.1.A REVIEW PROCEEDINGS DEPENDENT ON THE CLASSIFICATION OF ADMINISTRATIVE ACTION

3.1.A.1 THE NETHERLANDS

In the Netherlands, a distinction is made between administrative actions that intend to deliver legal consequences and actions that do not intend to deliver legal consequences (*rechtsgevolgen*). Whereas decisions governed by public law (*publiekrechtelijke rechtshandelingen*) intend to deliver legal consequences, simple action (*feitelijke handelingen*) is not directed at delivering legal consequences.

Algemene Wet Bestuursrecht **3.1 (NL)**

Article 1:3 (1) The meaning of a decision (*besluit*) is: a written decision by an administrative authority containing a legal act under public law.

Note

The definition of a decision (*besluit*) is very broad: it comprises single-case decisions (*beschikkingen*) and decisions of general scope (*besluiten van algemene strekking*). The precise conditions that need to be fulfilled so that a certain type of action is a *besluit* will be explained in the relevant sections of this chapter.

Algemene Wet Bestuursrecht **3.2 (NL)**

Article 8:1 A party concerned may bring a claim for judicial review (*beroep*) against a decision before the administrative judge.

Article 8:3 (1) A claim for judicial review (*beroep*) may not be lodged against a decision:

(a) containing a general binding regulation or a policy rule

(b) repealing or laying down the entry into force of a general binding regulation or a policy rule

(c) approving a decision containing a general binding regulation or a policy rule or repealing or laying down the entry into force of a general binding regulation or a policy rule.

Notes

(1) Access to administrative courts is only possible if a claimant seeks to challenge a decision (Article 8:1 of the Algemene Wet Bestuursrecht (AWB)), which does not concern a general binding regulation or a policy rule (Article 8:3 AWB).

Therefore, only single-case decisions (*beschikking*) or decisions which concretise decisions of general scope (*concretiserende besluiten van algemene strekking*) can be challenged. Any other action of organs under public law and other bodies empowered to exercise public functions (Article 1:1 AWB) may be challenged indirectly before the administrative courts[1] or must be challenged before the civil courts. Hence, in the Netherlands, the classification of the forms administrative action and, more precisely, the classification of an action as a single-case decision, is relevant for the purpose of determining whether or not an administrative court can review an action.

(2) In the Netherlands, there is only one type of review proceedings before the administrative courts. This is the *beroep*, which is usually translated as 'judicial review'.

3.1.A.2 FRANCE

G Dupuis, Définition de l'acte unilatéral[2] **3.3 (FR)**

The unilateral act is a decision whose legal force is independent of the consent of its addressees. In other terms (as simple as possible), the unilateral act attributes rights and obligations to citizens, independently from their consent. ... It is essential to understand that the unilateral act is the juridical expression of a power.

Note

In France, the demarcation line between different types of administrative action is between unilateral and bilateral measures, hence between administrative decisions and contracts. There are three categories of administrative decisions, depending on whether the addressees are defined or not. First, there are decisions addressed to defined persons, which can be decisions directed towards one addressee or decisions directed towards several addressees (*décision individuelle*). Secondly, there are regulatory decisions (*décision réglementaire*), which are decisions regulating abstract situations and an undefined number of addressees. In addition to these two categories, there is a third type of decision, which is directed at an undefined number of addressees in a concrete case (*décision particulière/decision d'espèce*). The precise conditions that need to be fulfilled so that a certain type of action is a '*décision*' will be explained in the relevant sections of this chapter. Unlike the German and Dutch legal systems, these concepts do not have a statutory definition.

[1] See Chapter 7, section 7.7.E.

[2] G Dupuis, 'Définition de l'acte unilatéral' in C Eisenmann and M Waline (eds), *Recueil d'études en hommage à Charles Eisenmann* (Paris, Éditions Cujas, 1975) 205–06.

Conseil d'État, 17 February 1950[3] **3.4 (FR)**

Minister for Agriculture v Lamotte

JUDICIAL REVIEW OF ADMINISTRATIVE DECISIONS

Dame Lamotte

There is a general principle of law according to which any administrative decision may be subject to judicial review.

Facts: A statute of 17 August 1940 had given the prefects the power to grant uncultivated and abandoned pieces of land to third persons. On that basis, the lands owned by Ms Lamotte had been granted on three separate occasions to someone else (Mr Testa). On each occasion, the Council of State quashed the decision of the prefect on the ground that the designated pieces of land were not abandoned and uncultivated. The prefect took a fourth decision, which should have been considered lawful by the administrative courts because, in the meantime, statutory provisions had been adopted stating that 'adoption of the grant decision may not be the object of any review, administrative or judicial'.

Held: The Council of State annulled the decision.

Judgment: Considering that Article 4(2) of the said Act of 23 May 1943 establishes these terms: 'The making of the grant decision may not be the object of any review, administrative or judicial'; that, if this provision, to the extent that its nullity has not been established under the Ordinance of 9 August 1944 on the re-establishment of republican legality, has the effect of removing the right of review which Article 29 of the Act of 19 February 1942 had made available to the owner to challenge the validity of the grant decision before the Prefecture Council, it has not removed the right to have the adoption of the grant decision reviewed before the Council of State on the issue of lack of powers, a ground of review available against any act of the executive even in the absence of a statutory text, and one whose purpose is, in conformity with the general principles of law, to ensure respect for legality; that it follows from this that, on the one hand, the Minister of Agriculture is entitled to request the annulment of the decision cited above of the Lyon Prefecture council dated 4 October 1946; but, on the other hand, that it is for the Council of State, as the judge entrusted with legality control (*juge de l'excès de pouvoir*), to decide on Ms Lamotte's claim for the annulment of the decision of the prefect of Ain of 10 August 1944.

Notes

(1) In this case, the Council of State held that it follows from the general principles of French law that any administrative decision must be reviewable before the administrative courts. The applicable 'type' of review procedure is the action for annulment (*recours pour excès de pouvoir*), which is considered to be the default action before the administrative courts (*recours de droit commun*). Hence, in France, the classification of a certain form of action as a decision (*décision*) is important for the question of the applicable review procedure.

[3] N° 86949.

(2) Contracts concluded by the administration and relating to prerogatives of public power or the performance of public services are also subject to review by the administrative courts, together with the contracts assigned by law to the jurisdiction of administrative courts.[4] In cases relating to these contracts, the action for annulment (*recours pour excès de pouvoir*) is not applicable. Instead, an action concerning the contractual relations between an individual and the administration and an action for liability can be brought to the administrative courts in a 'full jurisdiction remedy' (*recours de pleine juridiction*).

3.1.A.3 GERMANY

German law distinguishes between different types of administrative action, namely single-case decisions (*Verwaltungsakt*, §35(1) of the Verwaltungsverfahrensgesetz (VwVfG)), general administrative acts (*Allgemeinverfügung*, §35(2) VwVfG), factual action without immediate legal effects, which is called *Realakt*, public law contracts (*öffentlich-rechtlicher Vertrag*, §54 ff VwVfG), by-laws (*Satzung*), executive regulations (*Rechtsverordnung*) and administrative directions (*Verwaltungsvorschrift*).[5]

The starting point for an analysis of the judicial procedure applicable to the different forms of administrative action is the German Basic Law.

Grundgesetz **3.5 (DE)**

Article 19 (4) Should any person's rights be violated by a public authority, he shall have recourse to the courts.

Note

The constitutional guarantee of access to courts means that *any type of action* of the administration that possibly infringes individual rights (*subjektiv öffentliches Recht*) must be reviewable before the courts. Whether or not an administrative court is competent to hear the claim concerning a particular administrative action is determined according to the so-called 'general clause' of the Administrative Court Procedure Act (Verwaltungsgerichtsordnung (VwGO), §40).[6] This provision states that in principle all administrative action is reviewable in the administrative courts. The Administrative Court Procedure Act provides for different types of review procedures. For each type of administrative action or inaction, a (specific) corresponding type of review procedure is applicable. The specific types of action and corresponding review procedures will be examined in the course of this chapter.

[4] See below, section 3.5.C.

[5] For a more detailed description of administrative forms of action, see B Remmert, '§17. Handlungsformen der Verwaltung' in D Ehlers and H Pünder (eds), *Allgemeines Verwaltungsrecht*, 15th edn (Munich, CH Beck, 2016) §17. See also H Pünder and A Klafki, 'Administrative Law in Germany' in R Seerden (ed), *Administrative Law of the European Union, its Member States and the United States*, 4th edn (Antwerp, Intersentia, 2018) 67 ff.

[6] Further on this point, see Chapter 2, section 2.5.A.2.

3.1.A.4 THE EUROPEAN UNION

Treaty on the Functioning of the European Union **3.6 (EU)**

Article 288 To exercise the Union's competences, the institutions shall adopt regulations, directives, decisions, recommendations and opinions.

A regulation shall have general application. It shall be binding in its entirety and directly applicable in all Member States.

A directive shall be binding, as to the result to be achieved, upon each Member State to which it is addressed, but shall leave to the national authorities the choice of form and methods.

A decision shall be binding in its entirety. A decision which specifies those to whom it is addressed shall be binding only on them.

Recommendations and opinions shall have no binding force.

Note

Article 288 of the Treaty on the Functioning of the European Union (TFEU) sets out the different forms of action available to the European institutions. Next to these types of action, the institutions can adopt so-called *sui generis* measures (such as guidance documents, resolutions), as well as factual action, and can conclude contracts.

Treaty on the Functioning of the European Union **3.7 (EU)**

Article 289 (1) The ordinary legislative procedure shall consist in the joint adoption by the European Parliament and the Council of a regulation, directive or decision on a proposal from the Commission.

This procedure is defined in Article 294.

(2) In the specific cases provided for by the Treaties, the adoption of a regulation, directive or decision by the European Parliament with the participation of the Council, or by the latter with the participation of the European Parliament, shall constitute a special legislative procedure.

(3) Legal acts adopted by legislative procedure shall constitute legislative acts.

(4) In the specific cases provided for by the Treaties, legislative acts may be adopted on the initiative of a group of Member States or of the European Parliament, on a recommendation from the European Central Bank or at the request of the Court of Justice or the European Investment Bank.

Article 290 (1) A legislative act may delegate to the Commission the power to adopt non-legislative acts of general application to supplement or amend certain non-essential elements of the legislative act.

The objectives, content, scope and duration of the delegation of power shall be explicitly defined in the legislative acts. The essential elements of an area shall be reserved for the legislative act and accordingly shall not be the subject of a delegation of power.

(2) Legislative acts shall explicitly lay down the conditions to which the delegation is subject; these conditions may be as follows:

(a) the European Parliament or the Council may decide to revoke the delegation;

(b) the delegated act may enter into force only if no objection has been expressed by the European Parliament or the Council within a period set by the legislative act.

For the purposes of (a) and (b), the European Parliament shall act by a majority of its component members, and the Council by a qualified majority.

(3) The adjective 'delegated' shall be inserted in the title of delegated acts.

Article 291 (1) Member States shall adopt all measures of national law necessary to implement legally binding Union acts.

(2) Where uniform conditions for implementing legally binding Union acts are needed, those acts shall confer implementing powers on the Commission, or, in duly justified specific cases and in the cases provided for in Articles 24 and 26 of the Treaty on European Union, on the Council.

(3) For the purposes of paragraph 2, the European Parliament and the Council, acting by means of regulations in accordance with the ordinary legislative procedure, shall lay down in advance the rules and general principles concerning mechanisms for control by Member States of the Commission's exercise of implementing powers.

(4) The word 'implementing' shall be inserted in the title of implementing acts.

Note

In the EU legal order, unilateral measures can have a legislative or non-legislative nature, in accordance with the procedure through which they have been adopted. This distinction is not directly linked to the type of measure which can be adopted. This means that there can be decisions adopted through a legislative procedure[7] and regulations adopted through a non-legislative procedure.[8] The focus of this chapter shall be on non-legislative measures, as these qualify as 'administrative action'.

Case 294/83, 23 April 1986[9] **3.8 (EU)**

Parti écologiste 'Les Verts' v European Parliament

JUDICIAL REVIEW; COMPLETE SYSTEM OF REMEDIES

Les Verts

The EU legal order establishes a complete system of remedies which allows action taken by the EU institutions to be reviewed by the Court of Justice.

Facts: The Green Party had challenged the political party funding scheme of the European Parliament. The party claimed the system was unfair in distribution against newer parties. The question was, however, whether it was possible to bring an action for annulment against a measure adopted by the European Parliament, because, at that time, the relevant provisions did not include the Parliament as an institution against whose measures an action for annulment could be brought.

Held: The Court of Justice considered the action admissible and upheld the claim.

[7] eg Decision 1082/2013/EU of the European Parliament and of the Council of 22 October 2013 on serious cross-border threats to health [2013] OJ L293/1.

[8] eg Commission Delegated Regulation (EU) 1059/2010 of 28 September 2010 supplementing Directive 2010/30/EU of the European Parliament and of the Council with regard to energy labelling of household dishwashers [2010] OJ L314/1.

[9] ECLI:EU:C:1986:166.

Judgment: It must first be emphasized in this regard that the European Economic Community is a community based on the rule of law, inasmuch as neither its Member States nor its institutions can avoid a review of the question whether the measures adopted by them are in conformity with the basic constitutional Charter, the Treaty. In particular, in Articles 173 [Article 263 TFEU] and 184, on the one hand, and in Article 177 [Article 267 TFEU], on the other, the Treaty established a complete system of legal remedies and procedures designed to permit the Court of Justice to review the legality of measures adopted by the institutions. Natural and legal persons are thus protected against the application to them of general measures which they cannot contest directly before the court by reason of the special conditions of admissibility laid down in the second paragraph of article 173 of the Treaty [Article 263 TFEU]. Where the Community institutions are responsible for the administrative implementation of such measures, natural or legal persons may bring a direct action before the court against implementing measures which are addressed to them or which are of direct and individual concern to them and, in support of such an action, plead the illegality of the general measure on which they are based. Where implementation is a matter for the national authorities, such persons may plead the invalidity of general measures before the national courts and cause the latter to request the court of justice for a preliminary ruling.

Notes

(1) This case establishes that any action (legislative or non-legislative) of the EU institutions is in principle reviewable by the Court of Justice, either directly in an action for annulment in accordance with Article 263 TFEU or indirectly through a preliminary question of validity pursuant to Article 267 TFEU.

(2) Inaction can be challenged in an action for failure to act on the basis of Article 265 TFEU.

3.1.B REVIEW PROCEEDINGS INDEPENDENT OF A CLASSIFICATION OF ADMINISTRATIVE ACTION: ENGLAND AND WALES

P Cane, Administrative Law[10] **3.9 (EW)**

The Distinction between Decisions and Acts

Both decisions and acts can be invalid in a public law sense, and in this respect there is no particular reason to distinguish between them. But the distinction between acting and deciding to act can be important from the point of view of available remedies. If an authority has decided to perform an act which is allegedly illegal but has not yet done it then, of course, the applicant will want to challenge the decision to act and to obtain an order instructing the authority not to carry out its decision. If the authority has decided not to perform some duty the applicant will often be satisfied with an order requiring it to act. If the authority has already acted and the act can be easily undone, the applicant can challenge the decision to act and seek an order requiring the authority to undo its action.

[10] P Cane, *Administrative Law*, 2nd edn (Oxford, Oxford University Press, 1992) 23 ff.

Note

In England and Wales, there is no legal doctrine on 'administrative action' comparable to the German *Handlungsformenlehre*.[11] Hence, in English administrative law, the question of whether a measure qualifies as a decision or not, which has been central in the other legal systems described so far, is of limited relevance. Instead, the central question is whether a certain remedy can be obtained against the administration, hence whether, at the end of review proceedings, a decision can, for example, be quashed or an injunction obtained.[12] Thus, the central question of English law is whether or not the relevant administrative action is amenable to judicial review.

Civil Procedure Rules **3.10 (EW)**

Rule 54.1. (2) In this Section

(a) a 'claim for judicial review' means a claim to review the lawfulness of

(i) an enactment; or

(ii) a decision, action or failure to act in relation to the exercise of a public function.

Note

The Civil Procedure Rules (CPR) define what a 'claim for judicial review' is, setting out what might be reviewed in a broad sense. In general, the courts will look for a 'decision' of a public authority to review: a communication to the subject of the action,[13] or maybe more general – the publication of guidance,[14] issuance of regulations,[15] the development of policies[16] and the giving of directions[17] may all constitute reviewable acts. Similarly, in some cases, the expression of an opinion[18] (ie not a formal decision) by a decision-maker may serve as a reviewable act. A failure to act may also bring the possibility of judicial review.[19] The concepts of 'decision' and 'action' are generally construed broadly by the courts.

[11] G Kleve and B Schirmer, 'England und Wales' in JP Schneider (ed), *Verwaltungsrecht in Europa* 1 (Göttingen, V&R Unipress, 2007) 96.

[12] On remedies in the English legal system, see Chapter 7.

[13] See, eg *R v Oldham MBC, ex parte Garlick* [1993] AC 509 (HL); *R (Yogathas) v Secretary of State for the Home Department* [2002] UKHL 36, [2003] 1 AC 920 (where the 'decisions' were communicated by letter to the claimant). It is possible for other forms of communication to constitute a reviewable act: *R v Secretary of State for Trade and Industry, ex p Lonrho* [1989] 1 WLR 525 (HL) (communication of decision via press releases); *Council of Civil Service Unions v Minister for the Civil Service* [1985] AC 374 (HL) (decision announced to Parliament in the House of Commons).

[14] *R (Axon) v Secretary of State for the Health* [2006] EWHC 37 (Admin), [2006] QB 539. This applies even to 'non-statutory guidance' (ie guidance not required to be produced by legislation): *R v Securities and Investments Board, ex p Independent Financial Advisers Association* [1995] 2 BCLC 76 (DC).

[15] *R (C) v Secretary of State for Justice* [2008] EWCA Civ 882, [2009] QB 657.

[16] *R (Faarah) v Southwark LBC* [2008] EWCA Civ 807, [2009] HLR 12; *R v Secretary of State for the Home Department, ex p Daly* [2001] UKHL 26, [2001] 2 AC 532.

[17] *R (Quark Fishing Ltd) v Secretary of State for Foreign and Commonwealth Affairs* [2002] EWCA Civ 1409.

[18] *R v Worthing BC, ex p Burch* (1985) 50 P&CR 53 (QB) (Secretary of State gave an opinion as to the kind of planning consent that might be granted in a particular case).

[19] *R v Secretary of State for the Home Department, ex p Fire Brigades' Union* [1995] 2 AC 513 (HL) (failure to use powers to bring a scheme created by secondary legislation into force); *R (Green) v Police Complaints Authority* [2004] UKHL 6, [2004] 1 WLR 725 (failure to disclose requested material).

Civil Procedure Rules **3.11 (EW)**

Rule 54.2 The judicial review procedure must be used in a claim for judicial review where the claimant is seeking –

(a) a mandatory order;
(b) a prohibiting order;
(c) a quashing order; or
(d) an injunction under section 30 of the Supreme Court Act 1981 (restraining a person from acting in any office in which he is not entitled to act).

Rule 54.3 (1) The judicial review procedure may be used in a claim for judicial review where the claimant is seeking –

(a) a declaration; or
(b) an injunction.

(2) A claim for judicial review may include a claim for damages, restitution or the recovery of a sum due but may not seek such a remedy alone.

Note

Even though in the English legal system there is no connection between a specific type of administrative action and the corresponding review procedure, it should be noted that, within the judicial review procedure, different types of remedies can be distinguished, which are set out in parts 54.2 and 54.3 CPR.[20]

3.1.C COMPARATIVE REMARKS

This section has shown that the legal systems under consideration differ as to the questions whether and to what extent judicial review procedures are dependent on the classification of types of administrative action. In the Netherlands, the 'correspondence' between the classification and review procedures can be considered to be strongest, since it is only possible to directly access an administrative court (in accordance with Articles 8:1 and 8:3 AWB) if an administrative action qualifies as a single-case decision (*beschikking*) or a decision which concretises a decision of general scope (*concretiserende BAS*).

In France, the 'correspondence' between the classification of administrative action and review procedures is also strong. Traditionally, there have been two 'types' of review proceedings, the action for annulment (*recours pour excès de pouvoir*) and the 'full jurisdiction remedy' (*recours de pleine juridiction*), although it should be stressed that this distinction is no longer very clear-cut, since judges have also been able to issue injunctions in annulment actions since 1995.[21] An action for annulment (*recours pour*

[20] See further Chapter 7.

[21] Law No 95-125 of 8 February 1995 concerning the organisation of courts and concerning civil, criminal and administrative procedure (Loi No 95-125 du 8 février 1995 relative à l'organisation des juridictions et à la procédure civile, pénale et administrative). See further Chapter 7, section 7.3.A.3 (ii).

excès de pouvoir) can only be instituted against administrative decisions (*décisions*). Certain other types of administrative action, like contracts, are challengeable in the *recours de pleine juridiction*.

In Germany, there is also a strict correspondence between different types of administrative action and different review procedures. However, contrary to the Netherlands, an administrative action does not need to qualify as a decision for the purpose of triggering a review procedure before the administrative courts. Instead, in principle, all types of administrative action with external effects are reviewable in the administrative courts (see Article 19(4) of the Grundgesetz and the first sentence of §40(1) VwGO). In Germany, there is a very elaborate and detailed doctrine on how to classify certain types of administrative action (*Handlungsformenlehre*). Each type of action corresponds to a specific review procedure, with different rules and requirements.

In contrast to these continental legal systems, the common law system of England and Wales does not provide for a doctrine on the classification of administrative action, and the procedure of 'judicial review' is independent of a strict classification of administrative action. The courts of England exercise judicial review with regard to enactments, decisions, action or failure to act (in accordance with Part 54(2) CPR), but these categories are not as precisely defined as on the continent. As a result, in England, the review of administrative action in judicial review is not excluded simply on the ground that an action does not qualify as a decision.

The European Union adopted a system which is influenced by the continental tradition of different types of action and corresponding review proceedings although no European 'doctrine of administrative action' can be identified yet.

3.2 SINGLE-CASE DECISIONS

All legal systems empower the administration to issue measures which are directed to one or more defined addressees. However, depending on the legal system, there are – in addition to the requirement of a defined addressee – other criteria that need to be fulfilled, in order for the action in question to qualify as a single-case decision which can be challenged before the administrative courts. This section first presents the legal systems that have a clear definition of single-case decisions and compares them with systems that have a more open concept of single-case decisions. Moreover, in all legal systems, the corresponding review procedures to challenge single-case decisions will be described.

3.2.A SYSTEMS WITH A DEFINITION OF SINGLE-CASE DECISIONS

3.2.A.1. GERMANY: *VERWALTUNGSAKT*

Verwaltungsverfahrensgesetz **3.12 (DE)**

§35 An administrative act shall be any order, decision or other sovereign measure taken by an authority to regulate an individual case in the sphere of public law and intended to have a direct external legal effect.

Note

§35 VwVfG provides for the definition of a core concept of German administrative law, the administrative act (*Verwaltungsakt*).[22] The first sentence of this section lists several criteria that must be fulfilled cumulatively for an administrative measure to qualify as an administrative act.

First, the measure must be an 'order, decision or other sovereign measure', which means that a public body has to act unilaterally, making use of powers under public law. This type of action is contrasted with bilateral action, meaning the conclusion of a (public law) contract.

Next, the measure must be taken by a public authority, as opposed to a measure being taken by private actors. According to §1(4) VwVfG, any entity which fulfils tasks of public administration constitutes a public authority. It should be noted that, in certain cases, private companies can fall under the definition of §35(1) VwVfG if they carry out administrative tasks but act autonomously to a certain extent (*Beliehene*).[23]

Moreover, the measure must contain a 'regulation', meaning that the measure constitutes, alters, abrogates or determines rights and duties. Hence, the measure must have legal consequences, as opposed to factual action (*Realakt*).[24]

Furthermore, the measure must concern an 'individual case' (*Einzelfall*), which means that it addresses only one specific addressee or a narrowly defined small group of addressees. This criterion distinguishes the administrative act from general and abstract measures, such as executive regulations.[25]

In addition to that, the administrative measure must relate to the sphere of public law. This means that the power to act is derived from provisions of public law.[26]

Finally, the measure must have a direct external effect or external legal consequences (*Außenwirkung*). This means that the measure must produce legal effects outside the administration. It is important to note that these effects must be intended and not merely coincidental. Measures which only regulate the internal organisation of the administration or which are only taken in order to prepare an administrative act do not qualify as an administrative act in the sense of §35 VwVfG.

It should be noted that an administrative act can be taken either in writing or orally (§37(2) VwVfG).

Verwaltungsgerichtsordnung **3.13 (DE)**

§42 (1) By legal action, the annulment (*Aufhebung*) of an administrative act (action for annulment (*Anfechtungsklage*)) as well as the order to issue a refused or omitted

[22] For a brief overview of the German *Verwaltungsakt*, see N Foster and S Sule (eds), *German Legal System and Laws*, 3rd edn (Oxford, Oxford University Press, 2002) 259. For a more detailed examination, see M Ruffert, in Ehlers and Pünder (n 5 above) §21.

[23] H Schmitz, in P Stelkens, HJ Bonk and M Sachs (eds), *Verwaltungsverfahrensgesetz: VwVfG* (Munich, CH Beck, 2014) §1, 246.

[24] See below, section 3.4.A.

[25] See below, section 3.3.B.2 (i).

[26] Granting a building permit is a measure in the sphere of public law, but the purchase of materials for the administration does not fall under the definition of §35 VwVfG.

administrative act (action seeking the issuance of an administrative act (*Verpflichtungsklage*)) may be requested.

Note

§42(1) VwGO provides for two different types of judicial review that concern administrative acts as defined in §35 VwVfG. First, a claimant can file an action for annulment of an administrative act (*Anfechtungsklage*) if he is challenging a burdensome administrative act. Secondly, a claimant can file an action seeking the issuance of an administrative act (*Verpflichtungsklage*) if he is challenging the refusal or omission to issue an administrative act. Both types of review require, in principle, that an intra-administrative objection procedure (*Widerspruchsverfahren*) has been completed beforehand and that in this procedure the problem was not resolved (§68 VwGO).[27] Moreover, both actions are dependent on the possibility that a subjective right of the claimant is infringed (§42(2) VwGO).[28]

3.2.A.2 THE NETHERLANDS: *BESCHIKKING*

Algemene Wet Bestuursrecht **3.14 (NL)**

Article 1:3 (1) The meaning of a decision (*besluit*) is: a written decision by an administrative authority containing a legal act under public law.

(2) The meaning of a single-case decision (*beschikking*) is: a decision which is not of a general scope, including the rejection of a request for such a decision.

(3) The meaning of a request is: the request by a party concerned to take a decision.

Notes

(1) Article 1:3(1) AWB lists several criteria that must be fulfilled for a measure to qualify as a decision (*besluit*) in the Netherlands.

First, the measure must be issued in writing. An oral measure cannot constitute a decision in the Netherlands.

Next, the measure must be taken by a public authority, as defined in Article 1:1 AWB, which comprises organs under public law and other bodies empowered to exercise public functions, which also may be private persons (comparable to the German concept of *Beliehene*).

Moreover, the measure must regulate a situation (ie it must contain a legal act). Hence, it must intend to deliver legal consequences. In this context, it should be noted that the explicit refusal, based on substantive grounds, of a 'request' (*aanvraag*) for a decision by a party concerned does not produce any legal changes, but such a refusal

[27] See further Chapter 2, section 2.7.B.1 (i).
[28] See further Chapter 4, section 4.4.B.1.

is a decision in the sense of Article 1:3(2) AWB. The regulation criterion excludes factual action from the scope of Article 1:3 AWB.

Finally, the measure must be taken 'under public law', which means that the administrative body must act on the basis of a certain competence (*bevoegdheid*) under public law.

(2) Article 1:3(2) AWB provides for the definition of a single-case decision (*beschikking*). These types of decisions are distinct from decisions of general scope.

(3) According to Article 1:3(2) AWB, refusals to issue a single-case decision are also single-case decisions.

(4) According to Article 8:1 AWB, single-case decisions (including the refusal to issue a single-case decision) can be challenged in the administrative court (through the action called *beroep*).

3.2.A.3 FRANCE: *DECISION INDIVIDUELLE*

D Truchet, Droit administratif[29] **3.15 (FR)**

The *décision individuelle* is a unilateral administrative act with named addressees: it addresses one or more named persons. It can be taken by an authority which has regulatory powers as well as by an authority which does not, provided that one or the other is competent to adopt the act. The list of authors of non-regulatory acts is therefore larger than the one of authors of regulatory acts. The *décision individuelle* is more precise and less general than the regulatory decision (*décision reglementaire*). It leads the administrative process to its conclusion, individually designating the holders of rights and obligations established by legislation and regulation: through this act, one moves from the anonymity of the recipients to their personal designation.

Note

Under French law, the concept of *décision individuelle* means that there must be a unilateral sovereign measure, taken by a public authority, to regulate a specific case and addressed to one addressee. A *décision individuelle* can also be addressed towards several identified addressees. Furthermore, it should be also noted that so-called *arrêtés* can exceptionally qualify as a single-case decision, if, for example, someone is appointed to a specific position.[30] If a claimant wants to challenge a *décision individuelle*, the corresponding type of procedure is the action for annulment (*recours pour excès de pouvoir*). This is the essence of the case of *Dame Lamotte*.[31] If a claimant asks the administration to take an administrative decision but the administration refuses to do so, the refusal will amount to a decision, which can be challenged in the court through an action for annulment.

[29] D Truchet, *Droit administratif* (Paris, Presses Universitaires de France, 2008) 230–31.
[30] On the concept of *arrêtés*, see below, section 3.3.B.1 (ii).
[31] See above, section 3.1.A.2, excerpt 3.4.

3.2.B SYSTEMS WITH AN OPEN CONCEPT OF SINGLE-CASE DECISIONS

3.2.B.1 ENGLAND AND WALES

There is no clear overarching legislative definition of an administrative decision targeted at one identified addressee in English law, but many statutes empower decision-makers to make single-case decisions, and these decisions will then be subject to judicial review.

Supreme Court, 27 November 2013[32] **3.16 (EW)**

Zoumbas v Secretary of State for the Home Department

JUDICIAL REVIEW; SINGLE-CASE DECISIONS

Zoumbas

Single-case decisions are generally subject to judicial review.

Facts: Z was a citizen of the Republic of Congo and arrived in the UK by virtue of a French passport that did not belong to him. While in the UK, Z had two children with his wife. Z claimed leave to remain in the UK based on Article 8 of the European Convention on Human Rights (ECHR) due to his family connection. He also claimed that the Secretary of State should permit him to remain in the UK because this would be in the best interests of his children and that the primacy of the interests of his children was secured by Section 55 of the Borders, Citizenship and Immigration Act 2009. The Secretary of State ultimately rejected Z's claim for leave to remain and sought to have him removed from the UK and returned to the Republic of Congo.

Held: The appeal was dismissed.

Judgment: This is the judgment of the court. The appellant, Mr Zoumbas, challenges a decision by the Secretary of State for the Home Department dated 4 October 2011 that he did not qualify for asylum or humanitarian protection and that his further representations were not a fresh human rights claim under paragraph 353 of the Immigration Rules. He challenged the Secretary of State's decision for the manner in which she dealt with the best interests of his children in the light of the decision of this court in *ZH (Tanzania) v Secretary of State for the Home Department* [2011] 2 AC 166. He was unsuccessful in his judicial review application before both the Lord Ordinary, Lady Clark of Calton, and an Extra Division of the Inner House of the Court of Session.

The judicial review application and this appeal are concerned only with the fifth of the questions which Lord Bingham of Cornhill set out in para 17 of his speech in *R (Razgar) v Secretary of State for the Home Department* [2004] 2 AC 368. That is, in this case, whether the interference with the family life of Mr Zoumbas' family unit by his removal to the Republic of Congo was proportionate to the legitimate public end which the Secretary of State sought to achieve.

[32] [2013] UKSC 74, [2013] 1 WLR 3690.

Note

This case illustrates the trite point of law that, in the English legal system, it is possible to challenge a decision or action that targets one or more addressees, including measures containing refusals.

3.2.B.2 THE EUROPEAN UNION

Treaty on the Functioning of the European Union **3.17 (EU)**

Article 288 (4) A decision shall be binding in its entirety. A decision which specifies those to whom it is addressed shall be binding only on them.

Note

In the European Union, a single-case decision is qualified as a 'decision' in the sense of Article 288(4) TFEU. The definition of a decision in the TFEU provides for two elements: the measure must be binding and it must be addressed towards a defined addressee.[33] However, not all 'decisions' in the sense of Article 288(4) TFEU qualify as single-case decisions, as they can also qualify as a general act.[34]

Treaty on the Functioning of the European Union **3.18 (EU)**

Article 263 (1) The Court of Justice of the European Union shall review the legality of legislative acts, of acts of the Council, of the Commission and of the European Central Bank, other than recommendations and opinions, and of acts of the European Parliament and of the European Council intended to produce legal effects vis-à-vis third parties. It shall also review the legality of acts of bodies, offices or agencies of the Union intended to produce legal effects vis-à-vis third parties. …

(4) Any natural or legal person may, under the conditions laid down in the first and second paragraphs, institute proceedings against an act addressed to that person or which is of direct and individual concern to them, and against a regulatory act which is of direct concern to them and does not entail implementing measures.

Note

Single-case decisions taken by the EU institutions can be challenged via an action for annulment provided for in Article 263 TFEU. In order to compel the EU institutions to issue a decision, the action for failure to act should instead be used (Article 265 TFEU).[35]

[33] M Vogt, *Die Entscheidung als Handlungsform des Europäischen Gemeinschaftsrechts* (Tübingen, Mohr Siebeck, 2005) 20.

[34] See below, section 3.3.A.2.

[35] See below, section 3.6.A.3.

Case 182/80, 4 March 1982[36] **3.19 (EU)**

Gauff v Commission

REVIEWABLE ACT; ACTION FOR ANNULMENT

Gauff

A letter by which an EU institution concludes the decision-making process cannot be considered to 'produce legal effects' for the purposes of an annulment action.

Facts: On 25 August 1980, Gauff Ingenieure GmbH & Co lodged an action for annulment before the Court of Justice seeking the annulment of the decision contained in a letter of 20 June 1980 addressed to it by the Commission, according to which it was not eligible to participate in invitations to tender or mutual agreement contracts concerning public service contracts financed by the European Development Fund.

Held: The Court dismissed the claim.

Judgment: In the absence of the exercise, upon the conclusion of an internal procedure laid down by law, of a power provided for by law which is intended to produce legal effects of such a nature as to affect adversely the interests of the applicant by modifying its legal position, the letter of 20 June 1980 may not be validly considered as a decision within the meaning of the second paragraph of article 173 of the EEC Treaty [Article 263 TFEU] and accordingly cannot give rise to a review by means of the proceedings under that provision.

Note

In order to be reviewable, decisions must be able to produce legal effects on the claimant's legal position.

Case C-141/02 P, 22 February 2005[37] **3.20 (EU)**

Commission v Max.mobil

REVIEWABLE ACT; ACTION FOR ANNULMENT

Max.mobil

A refusal by an EU institution to comply with a request by an individual to start an investigation for the violation of EU competition law cannot be challenged in an action for annulment.

Facts: The Max.mobil company entered the Austrian market as the second GSM operator in October 1996. At that time, the Austrian postal and telegraph administration already held a statutory monopoly over the telephony sector, which had been assigned to Mobilkom on 1 June 1996. On 14 October 1997, Max.mobil submitted a complaint against the Republic of Austria to the Commission, stating that certain provisions of EU competition law had been breached by means of the fact that fee payment advantages were solely granted to Mobilkom. On 11 December 1998, the Commission informed Max.mobil, by way of the letter which formed the subject matter of the dispute before the Court of First Instance, that it was rejecting in part its complaint

[36] ECLI:EU:C:1982:78.
[37] ECLI:EU:C:2005:98.

of 14 October 1997. On 22 February 1999, Max.mobil brought an action before the Court of First Instance in which it sought partial annulment of the rejection.

Held: The Court of Justice set aside the judgment of the Court of First Instance and dismissed the claim.

Judgment: Individuals may, in certain circumstances, be entitled to bring an action for annulment against a decision which the Commission addresses to a Member State on the basis of Article 90(3) of the Treaty if the conditions laid down in the fourth paragraph of Article 173 of the EC Treaty (now, following amendment, the fourth paragraph of Article 230 EC) are satisfied.

It follows, however, from the wording of Article 90(3) of the Treaty and from the scheme of that article as a whole that the Commission is not obliged to bring proceedings within the terms of those provisions, as individuals cannot require the Commission to take a position in a specific sense.

The fact that Max.mobil has a direct and individual interest in annulment of the Commission's decision to refuse to act on its complaint is not such as to confer on it a right to challenge that decision. The letter by which the Commission informed Max.mobil that it was not intending to bring proceedings against the Republic of Austria cannot be regarded as producing binding legal effects, with the result that it is not a challengeable measure that is capable of being the subject of an action for annulment.

Note

A refusal by an EU institution to comply with a request will not always be challengeable in an action for annulment. The test used by the court is whether the act (which the institution refused to adopt) would itself be reviewable.[38]

Treaty on the Functioning of the European Union **3.21 (EU)**

Article 267 The Court of Justice of the European Union shall have jurisdiction to give preliminary rulings concerning:

(a) the interpretation of the Treaties;

(b) the validity and interpretation of acts of the institutions, bodies, offices or agencies of the Union;

Case C-322/88, 13 December 1989[39] **3.22 (EU)**

Salvatore Grimaldi v Fonds des maladies professionnelles

REVIEWABLE ACT; PRELIMINARY QUESTION OF VALIDITY

Grimaldi

In a preliminary question of validity, the Court of Justice can review the validity of any act of the EU institutions.

Facts: Salvatore Grimaldi, a migrant worker of Italian nationality, worked in Belgium from 1953 to 1980. He requested the Fonds des maladies professionnelles (Occupational Diseases Fund) to recognise that

[38] Case T-396/03 *Arizona Chemical and others v Commission* ECLI:EU:T:2005:406, para 64.
[39] ECLI:EU:C:1989:646.

Dupuytren's contracture, from which Grimaldi suffered, be considered as an occupational disease. The Fund refused to classify this as an occupational disease on the sole ground that it did not appear in the Belgian schedule of occupational diseases. Mr Grimaldi brought an action against this measure of denial before the Labour Court. However, the court decided to stay the proceedings and refer a question to the Court of Justice for a preliminary ruling.

Held: The Commission Recommendation of 23 July 1962 on the Adoption of the European Schedule of Industrial Diseases and the Commission Recommendation 66/462 on the Conditions for Granting Compensation to Persons Suffering from Occupational Diseases cannot in themselves confer rights on individuals which can be invoked before national courts.

Judgment: It is sufficient to state in that respect that, unlike Article 173 of the EEC Treaty [Article 263 TFEU], which excludes review by the Court of acts in the nature of recommendations, Article 177 [Article 267 TFEU] confers on the Court jurisdiction to give a preliminary ruling on the validity and interpretation of all acts of the institutions of the Community without exception.

Notes

(1) EU single-case decisions may not only be challenged directly through an action for annulment, but also indirectly through a preliminary question of validity.

(2) The range of reviewable acts in a preliminary question of validity is wider than in an action for annulment.

3.2.C COMPARATIVE REMARKS

The legal systems differ as to the concrete criteria that must be fulfilled so that an action directed at a (defined number of) addressee(s) classifies as a decision that can be reviewed. In Germany, the Netherlands and France, the single-case decision is a clearly defined concept, which entails that the administrative action must aim at the unilateral regulation of the legal sphere of the addressee(s). Moreover, in Germany and in the Netherlands, the single-case decision must have an external effect, to the exclusion of purely internal measures. In France, the distinctive element is whether or not an act produces 'legal consequences', meaning that some single-case decisions are considered to have an internal effect. Contrary to these three continental legal systems, the English and EU concept of a single-case decision is rather openly construed. In all legal systems under consideration, single-case decisions can be challenged before the administrative courts.

3.3 GENERAL ACTS

Next to single-case decisions, administrative authorities are empowered to issue measures which are not addressed to a specific addressee.

Some legal systems subdivide this category of general acts into administrative action which regulates a defined situation (ie general action in concrete cases), and general action which regulates an undefined number of situations (ie general action in 'abstract' cases), while other legal systems do not know such categorisation. This section will first compare the legal systems with regard to the existence of a separate category of 'general action in concrete cases' and assess the possibility of review proceedings of this category of administrative action.[40] Secondly, it will provide an overview of the concept of 'general action in "abstract" cases' and the respective review possibilities.[41]

3.3.A GENERAL ACTION IN CONCRETE CASES

Some legal systems provide for a separate category of administrative action that concerns an undefined number of addressees (general) in a defined case (concrete). This section will describe this category in Germany, the Netherlands and France, including the respective review proceedings,[42] and compare these systems to the English and EU legal systems.[43]

3.3.A.1 SYSTEMS WITH A SEPARATE CATEGORY OF ADMINISTRATIVE ACTION

3.3.A.1 (i) Germany: *Allgemeinverfügung*

As explained previously,[44] the administrative act as defined in §35(1) VwVfG relates to a defined (number of) addressee(s).

Verwaltungsverfahrensgesetz **3.23 (DE)**

§35 (2) A general administrative act (*Allgemeinverfügung*) shall be an administrative act directed at a group of people defined or definable on the basis of general characteristics or relating to the public law aspect of a good or its use by the public at large.

Notes

(1) This sentence provides for the definition of a general administrative act (*Allgemeinverfügung*). It is a special form of administrative act, which means that all the requirements of §35(1) VwVfG apply, with the only exception being the 'individual case' (*Einzelfall*) requirement. The general administrative act does not concern a clearly defined addressee or addressees in a concrete case, but an undefined number of addressees in a concrete case. §35(2) VwVfG names three different cases of general administrative acts. First, this section refers to 'general administrative acts directed at a defined or definable group of people' (*adressatenbezogene Allgemeinverfügung*).

[40] See below, section 3.3.A.
[41] See below, section 3.3.B.
[42] See below, section 3.3.A.1.
[43] See below, section 3.3.B.2.
[44] See above, section 3.2.A.1.

At the moment at which the general administrative act is issued, the addressees are not yet defined, but they are definable on the basis of objective common characteristics. For example, if the competent authority prohibits a public demonstration, this measure qualifies as a general administrative act, since at the moment of taking the decision the addressees are not defined. Next, §35(2) VwVfG names 'general administrative acts relating to a public good' (*sachbezogene Allgemeinverfügung*). This type of general administrative act is used to declare that a good becomes a public good, that it ceases to be a public good or that the characteristics of a good as a public good change. For example, a measure declaring that a certain street is a public good is qualified as a general administrative act. Finally, §35(2) VwVfG names 'general administrative acts relating to the use of a public good' (*benutzungsregelnde Allgemeinverfügungen*). This type of general administrative act regulates the modalities of use of a certain public good. For example, the 'regulations' concerning the use of a public museum or a public library are general administrative acts.

(2) The corresponding types of actions are the same as described with respect to a single-case decision (*Verwaltungsakt*). This means that a claimant can either bring an action for annulment against a general administrative act in accordance with the first alternative of §42(1)VwGO or he can bring an action seeking the issuance of a general administrative act in accordance with the second alternative of §42(1) VwGO.

3.3.A.1 (ii) France: *Décision Particulière/Décision d'Espèce*

R Chapus, Droit administratif général[45] **3.24 (FR)**

Les décisions d'espèce

Decisions which have not attracted attention for a long time contain norms which are neither individual nor general. This means that, with those decisions, one is faced with some ambiguity. Not surprisingly, this ambiguity manifests itself in its legal regime. On one hand, these decisions share the regime of the *décisions individuelles*: notably because of their (in principle) temporary character, with the exception of their illegality and of the lack of jurisdiction of the Council of State to rule in first instance on the claims brought against them, even if they are issued by a minister. On the other hand, they share the regime of regulatory acts: they are subject to an obligation of publication, at least in general, rather than notification; they do not confer rights; they are not subject to the requirement of a motivation as established by the law of 11 July 1979; to this, the lack of jurisdiction of the ordinary courts to interpret their provisions is added. In positive terms, one cannot better present those decisions than as enacting certain standards (*normes d'espèce*) concerning a particular situation or a particular circumstance. This is the case, for example in case of a decree convening electors for the purpose of a specific election, or pronouncing the dissolution of a municipal council – as well as decisions (*arrêtés*) on the opening of a competition or fixing dates of tests, …

[45] R Chapus, *Droit administratif général 1*, 15th edn (Nanterre, Monchrestien, 2001) 516–17.

Note

Decisions which are addressed to undefined addressees and which regulate a concrete case are called *décisions particulières* or *decisions d'espèce*. They can be challenged in an action for annulment (*recours pour excès de pouvoir*) before the administrative courts.

3.3.A.1 (iii) The Netherlands: *Concretiserende BAS*

In the Netherlands, decisions which are not single-case decisions are qualified as 'decisions of general scope' (*besluiten van algemene strekking*). *Besluiten van algemene strekking* are subdivided into general binding regulations (*algemeen verbindend voorschrift*) and other decisions of general scope. One sub-category of these 'other decisions of general scope' are the so-called 'concretising decisions of general scope' (*concretiserende besluiten van algemene strekking*).

Concretising decisions of general scope are decisions which concretise the applicability of general binding regulations in respect of time, place or object. They are therefore general measures with undefined addressees regulating concrete cases. An example is the decision to designate a certain area as a nature conservation area. This decision concretises general binding regulations which apply to nature conservation areas in general. The legal consequence of the concretising decision is that the general binding regulation which, for example, prohibits hunting or the destruction of certain plants applies to the area which is designated as a nature conservation area. Another example is the decision to install a traffic sign at a particular place, as this decision concretises the general binding regulation concerning the traffic rules in force in the area where the sign is installed.

Raad van State, 16 January 2008[46] **3.25 (NL)**

Municipal Council of Skarsterlân v Appellant

JUDICIAL REVIEW; CONCRETISING DECISIONS OF GENERAL SCOPE

Gemeente Skarsterlân

Concretising decisions of general scope may be subject to judicial review before the administrative courts.

Facts: On 21 December 2005, the municipal council of Skarsterlân established a list of second homes in the municipality. The list was based on a general binding municipality regulation, the Housing Regulation Skarsterlân. The list designated which homes did not, as an exception to the general rule laid down in the Housing Regulation, need permission for suspending the function of a home as a permanent residence. The reason for designating a house on the list was that it was already used as a second home – and already

[46] ECLI:NL:RVS:2008:BC2100.

had a non-permanent destination – before the date of entry of the Regulation. The claimant filed an intra-administrative objection against the list to the Council, as his home was not included on the list. The objection was declared inadmissible because the Council was of the opinion that the list qualified as a general binding regulation which could not be subject to judicial review. The district court annulled this decision, stating that the list could be challenged in judicial review because it qualified as a concretising decision of general scope. The Council appealed against this ruling before the Council of State.

Held: The decision was considered to be subject to judicial review before the administrative courts.

Judgment: Pursuant to Article 2.2 of the Housing Regulation Skarsterlân 2005 (hereafter: the regulation) it is prohibited, for a living space as designated in Section 2.1 to be withdrawn as destination for permanent residence in whole or in part without a withdrawal permit.

Pursuant to Article 4.1, first paragraph, the duty to have a withdrawal permit, prescribed by Article 2.2, does not apply where, on the date of entry into force of the regulation, the home was already used for non-permanent residence and was included in the 'Skarsterlân Second Homes List as of 7 July 2005' ...

The district court correctly held that the list is not a general binding regulation. The individual, personal and concrete naming of the homes which enjoy acquired rights does not establish a general binding regulation. A decision which specifies the place, time or object to which a general binding regulation is applicable, cannot itself be a generally binding regulation because it does not involve the settting of any independent standards.

The district court has rightly concluded that the decision of the Council to declare the objection inadmissible is unlawful. The appeal is not founded.

Note

This judgment provides for an example of the judicial review of a concretising decision of general scope (*concretiserende besluiten van algemene strekking*). In this case, the concretising decision specifies the applicability of a general binding regulation in relation to an object and a person, namely the home of the claimant. Unlike the general binding regulation itself, which cannot be challenged directly before the administrative courts (Article 8:3(1)(a) AWB),[47] the concretising decision can be reviewed by the administrative courts though the procedure of *beroep* (judicial review).

3.3.A.2 SYSTEMS WITHOUT A SEPARATE CATEGORY OF ADMINISTRATIVE ACTION: ENGLAND AND THE EUROPEAN UNION

Since, in England, there is no strict categorisation of administrative action, there is no separate category comparable to the type of administrative action discussed in this section.

In the European Union, general action in concrete cases can take the form of decisions or regulations in the sense of Article 288 TFEU. There is no explicit differentiation of general action regulating concrete cases and general action regulating abstract cases. An example of a measure of general action regulating a concrete case is a marketing

[47] See below, section 3.3.B.2 (ii).

authorisation concerning a specific genetically modified organism.[48] This is because the measure has effects for all those who want to market that specific product.

3.3.B GENERAL ACTION IN ABSTRACT CASES

Next to administrative action addressed to undefined addressees (general) and regulating defined cases (concrete), all legal systems provide for administrative action that is addressed to undefined addressees (general) and regulates an undefined number of cases (abstract). This type of action is legislation in substance; however, formally, it is adopted by the administration. The legal systems under consideration differ as to the extent to which they allow a direct review of general action in abstract cases. Whereas in England, France and the European Union it is in principle possible to directly challenge this type of action in the administrative courts (although it may in practice be difficult to do so),[49] such review is in general not possible in Germany or the Netherlands.[50]

3.3.B.1 SYSTEMS WITH POSSIBILITY OF DIRECT REVIEW BY ADMINISTRATIVE COURTS

3.3.B.1 (i) England and Wales

In England, forms of general administrative action are statutory instruments (SIs) and by-laws, which can be challenged in judicial review.

Statutory Instruments Act 1946 **3.26 (EW)**

Section 1 Definition of 'Statutory Instrument'

Whereby this Act or any Act passed after the commencement of this Act power to make, confirm or approve orders, rules, regulations or other subordinate legislation is conferred on His Majesty in Council or on any Minister of the Crown then, if the power is expressed –

(a) in the case of a power conferred on His Majesty, to be exercisable by Order in Council;

(b) in the case of a power conferred on a Minister of the Crown, to be exercisable by statutory instrument,

any document by which that power is exercised shall be known as a 'statutory instrument' and the provisions of this Act shall apply thereto accordingly.

Note

According to the definition provided for in the Statutory Instruments Act, the legislator can confer rule-making power to the king or queen or to ministers in an

[48] Commission Implementing Decision 2015/684 of 24 April 2015 authorising the placing on the market of genetically modified maize NK603 (MON-ØØ6Ø3–6) and renewing the existing maize NK603 (MON-ØØ6Ø3–6) products, pursuant to Regulation (EC)1829/2003 of the European Parliament and of the Council [2015] OJ L122/6.

[49] See below, section 3.3.B.1.

[50] See below, section 3.3.B.2.

enabling act. SIs are pieces of secondary legislation, and are used to amend, update or enforce primary legislation.[51]

Local Government Act 1972 **3.27 (EW)**

Section 235 Power of councils to make by-laws for good rule and government and suppression of nuisances

(1) The council of a district, the council of a principal area in Wales and the council of a London borough may make by-laws for the good rule and government of the whole or any part of the district or principal area or borough, as the case may be, and for the prevention and suppression of nuisances therein.

(2) The confirming authority in relation to by-laws made under this section shall be the Secretary of State.

(3) By-laws shall not be made under this section for any purpose as respects any area if provision for that purpose as respects that area is made by, or is or may be made under, any other enactment.

Note

This section of the Local Government Act serves as an example for the power of local councils to adopt by-laws, which are applicable in a specific area. However, these pieces of subordinate legislation are subject to approval ('confirmation') by the Secretary of State.

Court of Appeal (Civil Division), 28 July 2008[52] **3.28 (EW)**

R (on the application of C) v Secretary of State for Justice

JUDICIAL REVIEW; STATUTORY INSTRUMENTS

C

Courts can review the lawfulness of SIs.

Facts: The Secretary of State created an SI, the Secure Training Centre (Amendment) Rules 2007, SI 2007/1709, which permitted the use of physical restraint in a greater number of circumstances in secure training centres (units for adolescents, mainly aged between 12 and 16, who have been sentenced to prison terms). The claimants argued that the SI was unlawful on a number of grounds, including that the changes may constitute an infringement of Articles 3 and 8 ECHR and that there had been a failure to consult relevant parties when the new rules were created.

Held: The Court of Appeal held that the SI was not lawful and quashed it accordingly.

[51] See further in a comparative perspective, H Pünder, 'Democratic Legitimation of Delegated Legislation – a Comparative View on the American, British and German Law' (2009) 58 *International Law Review Quarterly* 353, 360.

[52] Above n 15.

Judgment: Lady Hale: At its para 48 the Divisional Court cited, and apparently were much influenced by, some observations of Webster J in *R v Secretary of State for Social Services ex parte the AMA* [1986] 1 All ER 164, 83 LGR 796, [1986] 1 WLR 1 at p 15. This passage was strongly relied on by the Secretary of State before us. It reads: '… it is not necessarily to be regarded as the normal practice, where delegated legislation is held to be ultra vires, to revoke the instrument, but … the inclination would be the other way, in the absence of special circumstances making it desirable to revoke that instrument … in principle, I treat the matter as one of pure discretion.'

It has proved difficult to find other authority on the specific point. Webster J's dictum does not seem to be discussed, much less adopted, in any of the standard works on administrative law, and for my part I would not wish to endorse it. As with any administrative decision, the court has discretion to withhold relief if there are pressing reasons for not disturbing the status quo. It is, however, wrong to think that delegated legislation has some specially protected position in that respect. If anything, the imperative that public life should be conducted lawfully suggests that it is more important to correct unlawful legislation, that until quashed is universally binding and used by the public as a guide to conduct, than it is to correct a single decision, that affects only a limited range of people.

Note

SIs can be challenged on a wide variety of grounds. This case serves to illustrate the court's willingness to review SIs and deprive them of their effects where they are considered unlawful.

House of Lords, 2 April 1998[53] **3.29 (EW)**

Boddington v British Transport Police

JUDICIAL REVIEW; BY-LAWS

Boddington

By-laws can be challenged in judicial review.

Facts: B was convicted of the offence of smoking a cigarette in a railway carriage where smoking was prohibited, contrary to By-law 20 of the British Railways Board's By-laws 1965, which in turn were created under statutory authority in section 67(1) of the Transport Act 1962. B challenged the validity of the by-law, arguing that the by-law itself was ultra vires. The divisional court identified the question to what extent subordinate legislation can be challenged by defendants subject to criminal charges laid under that subordinate legislation.

Held: B could challenge the by-law through an indirect challenge. The by-law was not considered to be invalid.

[53] [1999] 2 AC 143 (HL).

Judgment: Lord Irvine of Lairg LC: … [w]here subordinate legislation (e.g. statutory instruments or by-laws) is promulgated which is of a general character in the sense that it is directed to the world at large, the first time an individual may be affected by that legislation is when he is charged with an offence under it: so also where a general provision is brought into effect by an administrative act, as in this case. A smoker might have made his first journey on the line on the same train as Mr Boddington; have found that there was no carriage free of no smoking signs and have chosen to exercise what he believed to be his right to smoke on the train. Such an individual would have had no sensible opportunity to challenge the validity of the posting of the no smoking signs throughout the train until he was charged, as Mr Boddington was, under by-law 20. In my judgment in such a case the strong presumption must be that Parliament did not intend to deprive the smoker of an opportunity to defend himself in the criminal proceedings by asserting the alleged unlawfulness of the decision to post no smoking notices throughout the train. I can see nothing in s 67 of the Transport Act 1962 or the by-laws which could displace that presumption. It is clear from *Wandsworth London BC v Winder* and *R v Wicks* [1997] 2 All ER 801 at 815, [1998] AC 92 at 116 per Lord Hoffmann that the development of a statutorily based procedure for judicial review proceedings does not of itself displace the presumption.

Accordingly, I consider that the Divisional Court was wrong in the present case in ruling that Mr Boddington was not entitled to raise the legality of the decision to post no smoking notices throughout the train, as a possible defence to the charge against him.

Lord Nicholls of Birkenhead noted in *R v Wicks* [1997] 2 All ER 801 at 806, [1998] AC 92 at 106–107 that there may be cases where proceedings in the Divisional Court are more suitable and convenient for challenging a by-law or administrative decision made under it than by way of defence in criminal proceedings in the magistrates' court or the Crown Court. Nonetheless, Lord Nicholls ([1997] 2 All ER 801 at 805, [1998] AC 92 at 106) held that 'the proper starting point' must be a presumption that 'an accused should be able to challenge, on any ground, the lawfulness of an order the breach of which constitutes his alleged criminal offence'. No doubt the factors listed by Lord Nicholls may, where the statutory context permits, be taken into account when construing any particular statute to determine Parliament's intention, but they will not usually be sufficient in themselves to support a construction of a statute which would preclude the right of a defendant to raise the legality of a by-law or administrative action taken under it as a defence in other proceedings. This is because of the strength of the presumption against a construction which would prevent an individual being able to vindicate his rights in court proceedings in which he is involved. Nor do I think it right to belittle magistrates' courts: they sometimes have to decide very difficult legal questions and generally have the assistance of a legally qualified clerk to give them guidance on the law. For example, when the Human Rights Bill now before Parliament passes into law, the magistrates' courts will have to determine difficult questions of law arising from the European Convention on Human Rights. In my judgment only the clear language of a statute could take away the right of a defendant in criminal proceedings to challenge the lawfulness of a by-law or administrative decision where his prosecution is premised on its validity. Is Mr Boddington's defence made out?

The burden was on Mr Boddington to establish, on a balance of probabilities, that the decision of Network South Central to post no smoking notices in all the carriages of its trains was unlawful.

Note

This case illustrates that it will usually be possible to challenge by-laws, particularly where they create the potential for criminal liability, either directly through a claim for judicial review or, more often, through an indirect challenge when facing a sanction under the by-law.[54]

3.3.B.1 (ii) France

R Chapus, Droit administratif général[55] **3.30 (FR)**

... (t)his distinction between decisions according to whether they do or do not have a regulatory character is of a fundamental nature. With the numerous interests attached to them, the regime of administrative decisions is, as will be seen, differentiated in many respects according to their regulatory or non-regulatory character, both as far as the substantive rules and the process of litigation are concerned. The distinction has more or less absolute implications on what concerns, notably: the procedure of adoption of the decisions, the obligation to give reasons, the regime of their entry into force, the regime of their withdrawal; the determination also impacts the regime of the time limit for actions for annulment, the possibility of an indirect challenge and the jurisdiction in first instance. Regulatory decisions can be distinguished from decisions which, considered globally, do not have the features of a regulatory decision. It is possible to further distinguish those decisions according to whether they are *décisions individuelles* or decisions which I will call *décisions d'espèce* ...

Note

Under French law, decisions which do not have a defined addressee and which regulate 'abstract' cases are said to have a 'regulatory nature' (*caractère d'un règlement*). There are different forms of general administrative action regulating 'abstract' cases, namely *décrets*, *ordonnances* and *arrêtés*, all of which are generally challengeable (although often indirectly) before the administrative courts.[56]

Constitution de la République française **3.31 (FR)**

Article 37 Matters other than those falling under the scope of statute (*loi*) are of regulatory nature (*réglementaire*).

Texts of statutory form enacted with regard to these matters may be modified by decree issued after an opinion by the Council of State. Of these texts, those enacted after the entry into force of the present Constitution may not be modified by decree except if the Constitutional Council has declared that they are of a regulatory nature pursuant to the foregoing section.

54 See Chapter 7, section 7.7.A.
55 Chapus (n 45 above) 514.
56 See Chapter 7, section 7.7.B.

Note

In the French legal system, a regulatory act (*acte réglementaire*) can take the form of a decree, made by the President or the Prime Minister when making use of their public powers. Most of the decrees issued by the Prime Minister are made in order to implement statutes adopted in parliament (*pouvoir réglementaire d'application des lois*). However, the Prime Minister can also adopt regulatory acts in other cases that do not implement laws (*pouvoir réglementaire autonome*). Whether this is possible is determined by Articles 34 and 37 of the Constitution. Article 34 provides for a list of subject matters which can only be regulated by law. 'Autonomous' regulatory acts can only be made with regard to issues not covered by the list.

Constitution de la République française **3.32 (FR)**

Article 38 The Government may, in order to implement its programme, request the Parliament to authorise, for a limited period of time, the taking of measures by ordinances (*ordonnances*) which ordinarily fall under the scope of a statute.

Ordinances are issued in the Council of Ministers after an opinion by the Council of State. They enter into force upon their publication but become ineffective if the government bill for their ratification is not submitted to Parliament before the date set by the enabling statute. They may only be ratified in an explicit manner.

Upon the expiry of the period of time referred to in the first section of the present Article, ordinances may not be modified except by statute in matters falling under the scope of statute.

Notes

(1) Article 38 of the French Constitution provides that the legislator is entitled to empower the administration to adopt ordinances.

(2) An *arrêté* is an administrative decision adopted by either a minister or a local administrative authority (such as the prefect or the mayor). It is adopted either to implement a decree or to regulate public order. However, it should be noted that *arrêtés* can also be adopted with regard to a defined number of addressees, hence in such cases qualifying as single-case decisions.[57]

Conseil d'État, 6 December 1907[58] **3.33 (FR)**

Compagnie des chemins de fer de l'est v Minister for Public Works

JUDICIAL REVIEW; GENERAL ADMINISTRATIVE ACTION

Compagnie des chemins de fer de l'est

General acts regulating abstract cases are subject to the jurisdiction of the administrative courts.

[57] See above, section 3.3.A.3.

[58] N° 04244 04245 04246 04247 04248 04249.

Facts: A railway company (Compagnie des chemins de fer de l'est) sought the annulment of a decree of 1 March 1901, adopted by the President of the Republic on the basis of the laws of 11 June 1843 (Article 9) and 15 July 1845 (Article 21), prescribing the steps required to ensure the good order, security, maintenance, functioning and development of the railways. The company claimed that the decree had gone beyond the powers delegated to the government by the statutes. The Minister for Public Works, as a defendant, argued that the decree could not be challenged before the Council of State as it was a regulation of public administration made within the powers delegated to the executive branch by the parliament.

Held: The Council of State confirmed the legality of the decree.

Judgment: Considering that, under Article 9 of the law of 24 May 1872, the acts of the various administrative authorities may be annulled; considering that, although it is true that the acts of the Head of State in regulating the public administration pursuant to powers delegated to the Government by the legislature have as full an authority in the particular case as the powers so delegated, in as much as they emanate from an administrative authority, they remain subject to the control envisaged by Article 9 of the law already cited; considering that therefore it is appropriate for the Council of State, in its litigation jurisdiction, to check whether the measures issued by the public administration fall within the powers conferred on it ...

Note

With this judgment, the Council of State ruled that administrative courts have the jurisdiction to exercise judicial review over general action which regulates 'abstract' cases (decrees (*décrets*) and administrative decisions (*arrêtés*)). The court held that as long as these rules emanate from an administrative body, such general measures – just like any other – are subject to judicial review.

Conseil Constitutionnel, 8 August 1985[59] **3.34 (FR)**

JUDICIAL REVIEW; ORDONNANCES

Loi sur l'évolution de la Nouvelle-Calédonie

Delegated legislation is subject to the jurisdiction of administrative courts as long as it has not been ratified by a law of the parliament.

Facts: A law amending the status of New Caledonia was adopted by the parliament. It delegated to the government the possibility to adapt and modify the status of the territory of New Caledonia, by using ordinances (*ordonnances*). The claimants argued that such an option prevented the enforcement of the right to an effective judicial protection on the ground that they could not lodge an action before the Constitutional Council against ordinances.

Held: The Council of State considered the law constitutional because the reviewability of the ordinances was ensured after they have been adopted as a law.

Judgment: Considering that, if, in accordance with this provision, the control of constitutionality exercised by the Constitutional Council can only concern statutes (*lois*), not ordinances as laid down in Article 38 of the Constitution, ordinances are nevertheless

[59] N° 85–196 DC.

subject to the control of legality (*excès de pouvoir*) by a court; considering that ultimately, by fixing on 1 December 1985 the fixed time period allotted to the government for the submission of the law on the ratification of ordinances, the legislator has exercised, without distorting it, the power which has been conferred upon it by Article 38 of the Constitution. …

Note

Ordinances (*ordonnances*) have to be turned into legislation after a certain period of time by means of the adoption of a law of ratification. After the ratification, there is no possibility to challenge the law before the administrative courts.

3.3.B.1 (iii) The European Union

Treaty on the Functioning of the European Union **3.35 (EU)**

Article 288 A regulation shall have general application. It shall be binding in its entirety and directly applicable in all Member States.

A directive shall be binding, as to the result to be achieved, upon each Member State to which it is addressed, but shall leave to the national authorities the choice of form and methods.

A decision shall be binding in its entirety. A decision which specifies those to whom it is addressed shall be binding only on them.

Notes

(1) In the EU legal order, general administrative action regulating 'abstract' cases can be carried out through the use of regulations, decisions and directives. Directives mostly have a legislative character as they are adopted by the Council and the European Parliament. However, directives can also be of non-legislative nature, and thus qualify as general measures regulating 'abstract' cases. It is therefore possible for the EU to carry out administrative action regulating 'abstract' cases through the use of delegated decisions, regulations and directives that need to respect the conditions set out in Article 290 TFEU and implementing decisions, regulations and directives that need to respect the conditions set out in Article 291 TFEU.[60]

(2) From the wording of Article 263 TFEU, acts of general nature can, in principle, be subject matter of actions for annulment. As far as annulment actions brought by natural and legal persons are concerned, however, challenges against general measures will most likely fail at the admissibility stage because of the hurdle posed by the

60 For an overview of the limits and requirements of this form of administrative action, see H Hoffmann, G Rowe and A Türk, *Administrative Law and Policy of the European Union* (Oxford, Oxford University Press, 2011) ch 15.

Court of Justice of the European Union (CJEU) in its interpretation of 'individual concern', one of the standing requirements provided by Article 263(5) TFEU. On the other hand, after the reforms brought by the Lisbon Treaty, challenges against general acts of a non-legislative nature are likely to have more chance of success as the requirement to prove individual concern has been removed if these acts do not entail implementing measures.[61] When a direct action is not possible, general measures can be challenged indirectly.[62]

(3) These limitations of admissibility do not apply to preliminary rulings under Article 267 TFEU, which can be regarded as an indirect way to challenge general measures that could not be subject to an action for annulment.

3.3.B.2 SYSTEMS WITH LIMITED DIRECT REVIEW BY ADMINISTRATIVE COURTS

3.3.B.2 (i) Germany

In the German legal system, general measures regulating abstract cases are executive regulations (*Rechtsverordnungen*) and by-laws (*Satzungen*).

Grundgesetz **3.36 (DE)**

Article 80 (1) The Federal Government, a Federal Minister or the state governments may be authorised by a law to issue executive regulations (*Rechtsverordnungen*). The content, purpose and scope of the authority conferred shall be specified in the law. Each executive regulation shall contain a statement of its legal basis. If the law provides that such authority may be further delegated, such subdelegation shall be effected by statutory instrument ...

Note

This article of the German Constitution provides for the conditions for the adoption of executive regulations (*Rechtsverordnungen*). It should be noted that, on the level of states (*Länder*), many state constitutions provide for a similar rule.[63] An executive regulation can only be issued where a law explicitly empowers the administration to adopt such a measure.[64] Hence, the basic content, purpose and extent (*Inhalt, Zweck und Ausmaß*) for adopting an executive regulation must be determined by law. Moreover, it is important to note that essential (*wesentlich*) issues have to be regulated by law and cannot be delegated to the administration.

[61] On this point see Chapter 4, section 4.4.B.5.
[62] See Chapter 7, section 7.7.C.
[63] eg Constitution of North-Rhine-Westphalia, Art 70; Constitution of Bavaria, Art 55(2).
[64] Pünder (n 51) 356 ff.

D Ehlers, §2 Rechtsquellen und Rechtsnormen der Verwaltung[65] **3.37 (DE)**

By-Laws (*Satzungen*) (1) *Term and Function.* In the present context, the term of by-laws (*Satzungen*) only refers to those legal norms which are issued by means of the self-government (*Selbstverwaltung*) of administrative bodies under public law for the purpose of the unilateral sovereign regulation of their affairs. The Federal Constitutional Court (Bundesverfassungsgericht) understands by-laws (*Satzungen)* as legal norms which are issued by a juridical person of public law (*juristische Person des öffentlichen Rechts)* belonging to the state, within the limits of the autonomy with which it was vested by law, having effects for those persons which belong to and are subjected to this juridical person of public law. Usually, by-laws (*Satzungen*) are adopted by bodies of public law (which are organised according to their members), namely the municipalities and the associations of municipalities (Art 28(2) Basic Law) or by the so-called functional bodies of self-government. … By-laws (*Satzungen*) are distinct from parliamentary laws since they usually have a reduced number of addressees and they are content-wise less important (*Bedeutungsgehalt*) than laws, and especially, because the competent body for the adoption of the rule (*Normgeber*) is different from parliament.

As to the content, the power to adopt by-laws (*Satzungsbefugnis*) concerns the (legally determined) remit and field of competence of the juridical person. As to the personal scope of application, it concerns the body of self-administration itself or the person which uses the institutions of the body of self-administration. On the basis of statutory norms, by-laws can also determine, under certain circumstances, the relations to other persons. By-laws can be directed at the arrangement of the external relations as well as at the internal organisational setting. …

(2) *Relation to statutes and the legislator*. Just like executive regulations (*Verordnungen*), by-laws (*Satzungen*) also constitute legal norms derived from hierarchically superior rules. The power to adopt by-laws can only be derived directly from constitutional law (Articles 28(2) and 87(2) of the Basic Law) or from statutory law …

(4) *Procedure for the adoption of by-laws.* The procedure for the adoption of by-laws is mostly regulated in the legislation in detail. By-laws often need an approval (*Genehmigung*) and must – as any other rules with external effect – be publicly promulgated, whereby a publication in the official journal, a newspaper or the tables of announcement (*Bekanntmachungstafeln*) suffices.

Note

By-laws are adopted by public bodies (*Körperschaften*), which are vested by law with a certain degree of autonomy. By-laws are applicable to the persons that belong to this public body. For example, according to the principle of local self-government enshrined in Article 28(2) of the Grundgesetz, municipalities possess such a degree of autonomy, which means that they can adopt by-laws. Other public authorities that are vested with the power to adopt by-laws include public broadcasting agencies (*Rundfunkanstalten*) and public universities.

[65] D Ehlers, in Ehlers and Pünder (n 5 above) §2, 58.

Verwaltungsgerichtsordnung **3.38 (DE)**

§47 (1) The Higher Administrative Court shall adjudicate on application within the boundaries of its jurisdiction on the validity of

1. by-laws issued under the provisions of the Federal Building Code (Baugesetzbuch) and executive regulations issued on the basis of §246(2) of the Federal Building Code,

2. other legal provisions ranking below state legislation, to the extent that this is provided in state law.

(2) Applications may be made by any natural person or administrative authority claiming to have been aggrieved by the legal provision or its application, or that he will be aggrieved within the foreseeable future, or by any public authority within one year of announcement of the legal provision. It shall be directed against the corporation, institution or foundation which issued the legal provision. The Higher Administrative Court may grant to the state and other corporate bodies under public law whose competence is touched by the legal provision an opportunity to be heard on the matter within a specified period of time. §65(1) and (4), and §66 shall apply mutatis mutandis. …

(3) The Higher Administrative Court shall not examine the compatibility of a legal provision with state law where it is provided in law that the legal provision is subject to review exclusively by the constitutional court of a state.

(4) Where proceedings to review the validity of a legal provision are pending at a constitutional court, the Higher Administrative Court may order the suspension of the proceedings until such time as the case has been concluded by the constitutional court.

(5) The Higher Administrative Court shall adjudicate by handing down a judgment or, if it does not consider oral proceedings to be necessary, it shall hand down an order. Should the Higher Administrative Court come to the conclusion that the legal provision is invalid, it shall declare it to be null and void; in this case, the ruling shall be binding erga omnes, and the respondent shall be required to publish the ruling in exactly the same manner as the legal provision would be required to be made public. §183 shall apply mutatis mutandis in respect of the effect of the decision.

(6) On application, the court may issue a temporary injunction where this is urgently required in order to avert serious disadvantages or for other compelling reasons.

Notes

(1) Executive regulations (*Rechtsverordnungen*) and by-laws (*Satzungen*) cannot be challenged by means of an action for annulment (*Anfechtungsklage*). For the purpose of reviewing this type of administrative action before the administrative courts, the special procedure set out in §47 VwGO may be applicable under limited circumstances. This provision incorporates the possibility of an action by which the control of certain general measures regulating abstract cases can be obtained (*Normenkontrollverfahren*). The scope of application of §47 VwGO is, however, limited. This type of action can (only) be instituted where a claimant wants to challenge a by-law or executive regulation adopted under the Baugesetzbuch[66] (§47(1), no 1).

[66] Baugesetzbuch (BauGB) BGBl I, 2414.

This statute governs zoning plans. Moreover, each of the German states can determine by state law that certain general measures regulating abstract cases others than those mentioned in no 1 be reviewable before the courts (§47(1), no 2). For example, in North-Rhine Westphalia, there is no state law on § 47(1), no 2, so no abstract and general measure is challengeable under this provision. However, this is different in Bavaria. Article 5 of the Bavarian Act on the Application of the Administrative Court Procedure Act (Gesetz zur Ausführung der Verwaltungsgerichtsordnung, AGVwGO Bay) expressly refers to §47 VwGO; hence, it is, in principle, possible to review abstract and general measures in this state.

(2) For any other measure qualifying as a general measure regulating abstract cases, a direct challenge in the administrative courts is not possible. However, it is possible to ask for an indirect review of such measures if, on the basis of this measure, an administrative act was taken against which a claimant brings an action to the courts.[67]

3.3.B.2 (ii) The Netherlands

As explained above,[68] decisions of general scope (*besluiten van algemene strekking*) are subdivided into general binding regulations (*algemeen verbindend voorschrift*) and other decisions of general scope. Except for the 'concretising decisions of general scope' (*concretiserende besluiten van algemene strekking*), all other *besluiten van algemene strekking* in the Dutch legal system qualify as general measures regulating 'abstract cases', because they are addressed to an undefined number of addressees in an undefined number of cases.

Hoge Raad, 10 June 1919[69] **3.39 (NL)**

AO v The State

GENERAL BINDING REGULATION; QUALIFICATION

Cultivation Regulation

*The term 'law (*wet*) in the sense of Article 99 RO' is to be understood as also referring to general binding regulations which have external effects.*

Facts: A farmer had grown certain kinds of crops on his land without having permission from the mayor and aldermen of the municipality. This permission was necessary according to the law. For that reason, he was punished and had to pay a fine of 2,500 guilders. The farmer started a lawsuit against this fine. In the proceedings before the Supreme Court, the issue arose whether the Supreme Court could deal with the

[67] See further on this point Chapter 7, section 7.7.D.
[68] See above, section 3.3.A.1 (iii).
[69] (1919) NJ 647.

question of whether the legal basis, a ministerial rule based on an article of a statutory act, was valid. According to Article 99 of the Wet rechterlijke organisatie (Judicial Organisation Act), the Supreme Court can only scrutinise 'law'. Therefore, the question was how the term 'law' is defined.

Held: Ministerial rules, based on statutory provisions, can be qualified as law. The judgment of the district court, upholding the fine, was quashed, but the fine was nevertheless upheld for a different reason.

Judgment: It holds that, in the first place, the question arises whether the alleged infringement of the decision of the minister (*ministeriële beschikking*) can be reviewed in cassation; it holds in this regard, that the term 'law (*wet*) in the sense of Article 99 RO' is to be understood as also referring to general binding regulations, which have external effects, meaning that they are addressed to everyone, and which are taken by a public body (*openbaar gezag*), that derives this power from a 'law' in the sense of a regulation by the legislator (*wetgevende macht*), that where the order of the minister in question fulfils these criteria, the Supreme Court can also review this grievance.

Note

This judgment offers some guidance as to the applicable criteria to qualify a public law action as a general binding regulation. The action has to be a measure with external effect, issued by a public authority, which has derived the power to adopt an *algemeen verbindend voorschrift* from a law enacted by the legislator. The adjective 'general' refers to time, place, persons and actions or occurrences which have legal consequences. Often, the action or occurrence will be repeated several times.

Algemene Wet Bestuursrecht **3.40 (NL)**

Article 1:3 (4) The meaning of 'policy rule' is: a general rule established by decision, not being a general binding regulation (*AVV*), concerning the weighing of interest, the establishment of facts or the interpretation of legal rules in the exercise of a power of an administrative authority.

Article 4:84 The administrative authority acts in accordance with the policy rule, unless, due to special circumstances, this would affect one or more interested parties disproportionately in relation to the objectives of the policy rule.

Notes

(1) The definition in Article 1:3(4) AWB enumerates three types of policy rules. Policy rules 'concerning the weighing of interests' deal with the application of rules that vest the public authority with discretionary powers. Policy rules concerning the 'establishment of facts' prescribe, for example, how the quality of the air or of water is to be measured. Finally, an example of a policy rule concerning the interpretation of a legal rule is a rule which lays down criteria for the interpretation of the term

'special circumstances', which might be decisive for the granting of, for example, a social security benefit.

(2) Policy rules are decisions of general scope; however, they are not fully binding. According to Article 4:84 AWB, in special circumstances, the authorities may be obliged not to apply policy rules.

(3) Since the AWB came into force in 1994, it has been accepted that policy rules may determine the legal position of individuals, so that they actually have external effects. This is different from the German categorisation of *Verwaltungsvorschriften* (administrative directions).[70]

Algemene Wet Bestuursrecht **3.41 (NL)**

Article 8:3 (1) A claim for judicial review (*beroep*) may not be lodged against a decision:

(a) containing a general binding regulation or a policy rule

....

Note

As a general rule, access to administrative courts is in principle only available in order to challenge single-case decisions or decisions which concretise decisions of general scope (*concretiserende BAS*) (Articles 8:1, 8:3 and 1:3 AWB). As far as general acts regulating 'abstract' cases are concerned, Article 8:3 AWB provides that it is in principle not possible to challenge general binding regulations and policy rules (Article 8:3(1)(a)).[71] However, it is possible that general binding regulations and policy rules are reviewed indirectly (through the procedure called *exceptieve toetsing*) in an action against a single-case decision.[72]

3.3.C COMPARATIVE REMARKS

This section has demonstrated that some legal systems subdivide 'general acts' into acts which regulate a concrete case and acts which regulate an undefined number of cases, ie they regulate 'abstract' cases. The legal system of Germany provides for a category of general measures regulating concrete cases (*Allgemeinverfügungen*), which is comparable to the classifications undertaken in the Netherlands (*concretiserende besluiten van algemene strekking*) and France (*décision d'espèce*). This type of administrative action is

[70] See below section 3.7.B.2.

[71] Note that there are exceptions to this rule: any action (not necessarily a decision) against a civil servant can be challenged in the administrative court (Art 8:2(1) AWB).

[72] See further on this point Chapter 7, section 7.7.E.

directly reviewable in the administrative courts in all three legal systems. In England and Wales and the European Union, such a categorisation is not, as such, known; however, judicial review is possible in both legal systems.

As regards administrative action that is neither addressed towards defined addressees nor concerned with concrete cases (ie general measures regulating 'abstract' cases), the legal systems under consideration differ as regards their possibility of direct review in the administrative courts. In England, France and the European Union, it is generally open to applicants to challenge these general acts before the administrative courts, although this might not always possible in practice. Contrary to this, in Germany and the Netherlands, the potential to review general acts regulating 'abstract' cases is somewhat limited.

3.4 FACTUAL ACTION (*REALAKT*)

The term '*Realakt*' is taken from the German legal system and refers to administrative action that does not 'regulate' something, meaning that it is not intended to produce legal consequences. In the German legal system, this category of administrative action is considered different from that of 'internal measures', since action that does not produce any legal consequences can still have (factual) external effects.

This section will provide for an overview of systems which have a separate category of '*Realakt*' and the respective possibility of review proceedings.[73] This will then be compared with legal systems in which the '*Realakt*' is not a separate category of administrative action and with the different classifications undertaken in these legal systems.[74]

3.4.A SEPARATE TYPE OF ACTION REVIEWABLE BY ADMINISTRATIVE COURTS: THE GERMAN *REALAKT*

H Maurer, Allgemeines Verwaltungsrecht[75] **3.42 (DE)**

1. Real acts (*Realakte*) (factual acts (*Tathandlungen*), simple administrative act (*schlichtes Verwaltungshandeln*)) are those administrative measures which are *not* directed to have legal consequences, but have *factual consequences*.

Thereby, they are differentiated from legal acts of the administration (administrative act (*Verwaltungsakt*), public law contract (*öffentlich-rechtlicher Vertrag*),[76] executive

[73] See below, sections 3.4.A and 3.4.B.

[74] See below, section 3.4.C.

[75] H Maurer, *Allgemeines Verwaltungsrecht*, 18th edn (Munich, CH Beck, 2011) §15, 1 ff.

[76] Note that the original text mentions the word *Verwaltungsvertrag*, which, translated literally, would mean 'administrative law contract'. For the purposes of this book, the terms 'public law contract' (*öffentlich-rechtlicher Vertrag*) and 'administrative law contract' should be taken as having the same meaning.

regulation (*Rechtsverordnung*) and by-law (*Satzung*)). The terms *Realakt* or administrative real act (*Verwaltungsrealakt*) emphasise the demarcation from the administrative act (*Verwaltungsakt*)...

Thereby, however, it is important to consider that the real act does not only lack the regulatory nature which otherwise is a typical feature of administrative acts, but that it is also not restricted to individual cases and does not have to be adopted unilaterally....

2. Administrative practice knows numerous very different real acts. In the literature, occasionally a distinction is made between declarations of knowledge (information, warnings, reports, speeches and the like) and actual performance (disbursement of a sum of money, driving a company car, execution of a protective vaccination, cleansing of a street, construction of an administrative building, maintenance of a school, etc). This differentiation is typologically correct but does not have any further legal consequences.

Verwaltungsgerichtsordnung **3.43 (DE)**

§43 (1) By legal action, the declaration of the existence or non-existence of a legal relationship or of the voidness *ab initio* (*Nichtigkeit*) of an administrative act may be requested if the claimant has a legitimate interest in a speedy declaration (action for declaration) (*Feststellungsklage*).

(2) The declaration may not be requested as far as the claimant is able or could have been able to pursue his rights by an action for modification (*Gestaltungsklage*) or by an action for performance (*Leistungsklage*). This does not apply where a declaration of the invalidity of a void act is requested.

§111 (1) If, in an action for performance, a claim is contentious in terms of its reason and amount, the court may rule in advance on the reason by means of an interim judgment.

§113 (4) If a performance (*Leistung*) may be demanded in addition to the annulment of an administrative act, a sentence to effect the action shall also be permissible in the same proceedings.

Note

Factual action cannot be challenged through an action for annulment, since this type of action is only applicable with regard to administrative acts. Instead, the review of factual action or inaction can be requested in an action for performance (*Leistungsklage*). With the general action for performance, a claimant can request the administration to act, tolerate or omit to do something (*Tun, Dulden, Unterlassen*). This type of administrative review proceeding is not explicitly regulated in the Administrative Court Procedure Act, but it is implied in several provisions of this statute (§43(1) and (2), §111(1) and §113(4) VwGO). As a subsidiary remedy, it is possible to request from the court the declaration that a certain legal relationship existed or did not exist (§43(1) VwGO).

3.4.B SEPARATE TYPE OF ACTION NOT REVIEWABLE BY ADMINISTRATIVE COURTS

3.4.B.1 THE NETHERLANDS

Raad van State, 15 February 2012[77] **3.44 (NL)**

Mayor and Aldermen of Woudrichem v Claimant

FACTUAL ACTION; JUDICIAL REVIEW

Lay-by Woudrichem

Factual action cannot be contested before the administrative courts.

Facts: By letter of 22 February 2010, the mayor and aldermen of Woudrichem informed the public of the decision of the council of Woudrichem to construct a parking lay-by at a certain location and provided the financial details of the construction. The district court declared the objection filed against the information by the claimant inadmissible, as the decision did not result in legal consequences and could not be qualified as a decision as defined in Article 1:3 AWB (*besluit*). The claimant appealed against the judgment before the Council of State.

Held: The letter containing the information was not considered to result in legal consequences and thus was considered not capable of being contested before the administrative courts.

Judgment: The plea of the claimant failed. The letter of 22 February 2010 announced the decision of the mayor and aldermen to construct a lay-by. This announcement does not qualify as decision as defined in Article 1:3 AWB, as it does not entail any legal consequences. Such consequences will only come into being if the mayor and aldermen take one or more decisions regarding traffic. Insofar, the claim was not well-founded.

Notes

(1) In the Netherlands, factual administrative action cannot be challenged before the administrative courts and must be challenged before the civil courts instead. In the case law, the expression 'factual action' is never used, but the court states that a certain measure 'does not entail any legal consequences', which means that it is a factual action.

(2) Examples of factual administrative action are cases concerning the factual action of executing a decision, such as the removal of a building which was built unlawfully, or the monitoring acts undertaken by inspectors, such as the exercise by an inspector of his power to enter a place or to request information.[78] All examples of the German *Realakt*[79] would also qualify as factual action in the Netherlands.

[77] ECLI:NL:RVS:2012:BV5106.

[78] See eg ECLI:NL:CBB:1998:ZF3595.

[79] See above, section 3.4.A, excerpt 3.42.

3.4.B.2 THE EUROPEAN UNION

In the EU legal order, a category of 'factual action' is also recognised. This is a form of action which is not 'intended to produce legal effects' for the purposes of Article 263(4) TFEU. This form of factual action can consist of the transfer of information, the publication of information or public statements.

Case T-193/04, 4 October 2006[80] **3.45 (EU)**

Tillack v Commission

EXCHANGE OF INFORMATION; FACTUAL ACTION; ACTION FOR ANNULMENT; INADMISSIBILITY

Tillack

An exchange of information, constituting a mere factual conduct, cannot be the subject matter of an action for annulment. It can, however, be challenged through a preliminary question of validity.

Facts: The German journalist Tillack published articles in the magazine *Stern* on 28 February and 7 March 2002 in which he referred to irregularities within EU institutions, which were based on, inter alia, a confidential European Anti-Fraud Office (OLAF) note. In order to identify the Community officials who unlawfully disclosed their documents, OLAF opened an internal investigation. In 2004, the claimant brought an action to challenge the seizure of documents and personal belongings obtained during the search at his home and office. Subsequently, the claimant requested the annulment of the act by which OLAF submitted information regarding suspicions of breach of professional secrecy and bribery, and damages in compensation for the non-material injury resulting from the publication of press releases by OLAF.

Held: The claim was dismissed.

Judgment: In the present case, the action for annulment is brought against the act by which OLAF, on the basis of Article 10(2) of Regulation No 1073/1999, forwarded the German and Belgium judicial authorities information concerning suspicions of breach of professional secrecy and bribery involving the applicant.

According to settled case-law, measures the legal effects of which are binding on and capable of affecting the interests of the applicant by bringing about a distinct change in his legal position are acts or decisions which may be the subject of an action for annulment in terms of Article 230 EC (Case 60/81 *IBM v Commission* [1981] ECR 2639, paragraph 9, and Case T-309/03 *Camós Grau v Commission* [2006] ECR II-0000, paragraph 47).

However, in the present case, the contested act does not bring about a distinct change in the applicant's legal position .... Finally, the argument alleging the lack of effective judicial protection is irrelevant. That argument is not, in itself, sufficient to justify the admissibility of an action. In addition, the applicant also had the opportunity to request the national courts, which have no jurisdiction themselves to declare that the act by which OLAF forwarded information to the Belgian judicial authorities is invalid, to make a preliminary reference to the Court of Justice in that regard.

[80] ECLI:EU:T:2006:292.

Note

The court argued that the lack of possibility of a direct challenge of factual action could be compensated by a reference for preliminary ruling.

3.4.C NO SEPARATE TYPE OF ACTION AND THE QUESTION OF REVIEWABILITY

3.4.C.1 FRANCE

N Marsch, Frankreich[81] **3.46 (FR)**

Factual administrative action is neither the subject of procedural regulations, nor literature. Even if it can be the trigger of claims for state liability, the object of the litigation in court is still the administrative decision rejecting the request for damages.

Notes

(1) In the French legal system, there is no conceptualisation of factual action comparable to the German legal system. As a general rule, only decisions can be challenged before the administrative courts by means of the action for annulment (*recours pour excès de pouvoir*). However, the concept of an administrative decision is rather broad. Since there is no general requirement on the form of a decision, administrative action can be qualified as a decision, even though, on the surface, it appears to be 'speech' or 'words'.

(2) In a comparative perspective, all the examples described in the excerpt from *Maurer* in Germany[82] (information, warning, reporting, expert opinion, payment of money, travel by official vehicle, giving protective vaccinations, cleaning of roads, construction of building, construction and maintenance of transport routes) cannot be challenged in an action for annulment before the French courts. The only thing that can be challenged in an action for annulment is the decision related to these actions – for example, the municipal deliberation stating that someone will receive money.

(3) It should be noted that, in France, a distinction is made between administrative action that produces legal consequences and action that does not have legal consequences. However, this differentiation refers to the question of whether or not something is purely an internal measure.[83]

[81] N Marsch, 'Frankreich' in JP Schneider (ed), *Verwaltungsrecht in Europa* 2 (Göttingen, V&R Unipress, 2009) 103.

[82] See above, section 3.4.A, excerpt 3.42.

[83] See below, section 3.7.B.1.

3.4.C.2 ENGLAND AND WALES

G Kleve and B Schirmer, England und Wales[84] **3.47 (EW)**

As simple and informal, factual administrative action, 'advice' and 'guidance' should be considered. Next to this, 'recommendations' should be mentioned. The status and the legal force of, for example, a recommendation depend on the context of the facts and the concrete circumstances of each single case.

Note

A separate concept of '*Realakt*' is unknown to the English legal system, given that there is no clear legal definition of an administrative act. However, the courts are willing to review many forms of administrative action, including advice or opinions offered by public authorities,[85] official guidance[86] and directions.[87] A warning given by a state authority will be based on some statutory provisions or decisions, which are challengeable.[88]

3.4.D COMPARATIVE REMARKS

The German concept of factual action (*Realakt*) is comparable to the Dutch concept of factual action, which does not produce legal consequences. What is different between the two legal systems is that, in Germany, the corresponding type of review procedure is the general action to perform or to omit to perform an action. In the Netherlands, it is not possible to review action without legal consequences in administrative courts, since this action does not qualify as a *besluit* (in accordance with Article 1:3 AWB). Similarly, in the European Union, factual conduct cannot be the subject matter of an action for annulment, but it can be challenged indirectly in a preliminary question of validity.

In France, action that does not produce legal consequences is considered to be 'soft law' or internal action, which is not challengeable before the French administrative courts. As such, in France, there is no doctrinal category of factual action. Comparable to France, the concept of factual action (*Realakt*) is not known as such in England, and

[84] Kleve and Schirmer (n 11 above) 100.

[85] See eg *Burch* (above n 18), where the Secretary of State offered an opinion on the likelihood of planning permission being granted.

[86] See eg *R (A) v Secretary of State for Health* [2008] EWHC 855 (Admin), [2008] HRLR 29; *R (Burke) v General Medical Council* [2005] EWCA Civ 1003, [2006] QB 273.

[87] *Quark Fishing* (n 17 above).

[88] *R (P) v General Dental Council* [2016] EWHC 3181 (Admin), [2017] 4 WLR 14; *R (Davies) v Financial Services Authority* [2003] EWCA Civ 1128, [2004] 1 WLR 185.

examples of action without direct legal consequences resemble the category of 'internal' measures.[89] These remain, however, subject to the jurisdiction of the courts exercising judicial review.

3.5 CONTRACTS

In addition to unilateral actions, ie actions which are undertaken without the consent of the addressee, administrative authorities in all legal systems are able to enter into bilateral, ie contractual, relationships. The primary question that arises in this regard is whether these bilateral measures are reviewable before the administrative courts or whether it is the ordinary courts that are competent.[90] Next, where a legal system allocates conflicts arising out of contracts to administrative courts, the question is whether a specific type of review procedure is applicable. In this context, the crucial question that arises is whether or not (and how) a legal system distinguishes between contracts with a public law element and private law contracts concluded by the administration. Since, in this regard, the legal systems adopt very different approaches, they shall be dealt with separately. An issue that will not be further elaborated on in this section are rules of public procurement. In practice, this body of rules establishes a specific regime that may modify the rules of general administrative law on contracts. It should be noted, however, that EU legislation on public procurement has led to considerable harmonisation in the Member States.[91]

3.5.A GERMANY

A contract is a bilateral measure, so that this type of action cannot qualify as an administrative act in the sense of §35(1) VwVfG. In Germany, a distinction is made between 'private law contracts' and 'public law contracts'. Whether a bilateral measure is qualified as a private or a public law contract depends on the subject matter of the contract. It must be determined whether the contract creates, modifies or annuls a legal relationship in the private or in the public sphere.[92]

The two different types of contracts are governed by different rules and conflicts are settled in different courts. An example of a private law contract is the purchase of goods or services by the administration. Private law contracts concluded by the administration are based on the idea of an equal footing of the contracting parties. In these cases, the

[89] See below, section 3.7.

[90] On this point, see Chapter 2, section 2.5.

[91] Directive 2007/66/EC of the European Parliament and of the Council of 11 December 2007 amending Council Directives 89/665/EEC and 92/13/EEC with regard to improving the effectiveness of review procedures concerning the award of public contracts OJ L335/31; C Bovis, *Research Handbook on EU Public Procurement Law* (Cheltenham, Edward Elgar, 2016).

[92] For further details, see §§54 ff VwVfG; M Singh, *German Administrative Law in Common Law Perspective*, 2nd edn (Berlin, Springer, 2001) 94 ff; Maurer (n 75 above) §14, 1 ff. See also BVerwGE 23, 213; BVerwG NJW 1976, 2360. The BGH used to be more inclined to assume a civil law contract, but has come closer to the stance of the BVerwG: see, eg BGHZ 56, 365, 367 ff.

rules of the German Civil Code are applicable and the disputes are decided before the ordinary courts.

In contrast to private law contracts, public law contracts (*öffentlich-rechtlicher Vertrag*) are governed by the rules of the Administrative Procedure Act.[93]

Verwaltungsverfahrensgesetz **3.48 (DE)**

§54 A legal relationship under public law may be constituted, amended or annulled by contract (public law contract) insofar as this is not contrary to a legal provision. In particular, the authority may, instead of issuing an administrative act, conclude an agreement under public law with the person to whom it would otherwise direct the administrative act.

§57 A public law contract must be in written form except where another form is prescribed by law.

Notes

(1) §54 VwVfG enumerates three main requirements that must be fulfilled for a contract to qualify as a public law contract (*öffentlich-rechtlicher Vertrag*). First, there needs to be a contract, meaning that the rules on the conclusion of contracts are in principle applicable.[94] Secondly, the contract needs to regulate a relationship in the area of public law, otherwise the contract is governed by private law. Thirdly, the contract needs to constitute, amend or annul a legal relationship.

(2) There are two different types of public law contracts, namely subordinate and coordinate contracts. As far as the former type of contract is concerned, the contracting parties are not on an equal footing; it is a contract between an administrative authority and an individual. A coordinate contract is a contract in which the parties are on an equal footing.

Verwaltungsgerichtsordnung **3.49 (DE)**

§40 (2) Recourse shall be available to the ordinary courts for property claims from sacrifice for the public good and from bailment by public authorities, as well as for compensation claims arising from the violation of public law obligations which are not based on a public law contract; this shall not apply to disputes regarding the existence and amount of a compensation claim in the context of Article 14(1) no 2 of the Basic Law (*Grundgesetz*)....

Note

Claims seeking to enforce a public law contract must be brought before the administrative courts. The question of which type of judicial action is applicable depends on the concrete aim of the respective dispute.[95] If the claimant wants to achieve

[93] See §§54 ff VwVfG.
[94] See also §62 VwVfG.
[95] HJ Bonk and W Neumann, in Stelkens et al (n 23 above) §54, 206.

the performance of a simple action, the action for performance will be applicable. If the claimant holds that the contract is invalid, he may file an action for declaration (§43 VwGO).

3.5.B THE NETHERLANDS

In the Netherlands, contracts do not qualify as decisions as defined in Article 1:3 AWB (*besluit*), since they do not entail legal consequences of a public law nature. However, since public-law entities (eg the state, provinces and municipalities) enjoy legal personality, they are entitled to conclude contracts with private parties or with other public-law entities.

In the Dutch system of contracts concluded by public law entities, a distinction can be made between 'normal contracts', 'policy contracts' (*beleidsovereenkomsten*) and so-called 'competence contracts' (*bevoegdheden-overeenkomsten*).

An example of a 'normal contract' is an agreement with an energy company on the supply of gas or electricity to the public-law entity. 'Normal contracts' are in principle regulated by private law. The same approach is adopted in relation to 'policy contracts'. Policy contracts are concluded by the administration to achieve a certain aim which in principle could have been achieved through a public law action. An example would be the sale of a piece of land by a municipality under the condition that the buyer sells the houses built on the plot only to people who are already registered to live in the municipality.

So-called 'competence contracts' are contracts in which the administration binds itself through a contract to exercise or not exercise a public law competence. In other words, the administration makes the exercise of a competence the subject matter of a contract. This type of contract is often concerned with area development projects in which the private party intends to invest. In the contract, the private party's promise to invest is concretised and, in return, the public-law entity promises to (make an effort to) provide for the necessary public law permits and other decisions. For example, the public-law entity can make an agreement relating to its competence to grant a building or an environmental permit, or to its competence to establish a spatial plan.[96]

Algemene Wet Bestuursrecht **3.50 (NL)**

Article 8:3 (2) A claim for judicial review (*beroep*) may not be lodged against a decision for the preparation of a legal act under private law.

Note

According to this article, decisions that are taken in preparation of a contract, such as the decision of a city council to conclude a contract with a certain party,

[96] FJ van Ommeren, 'De bevoegdhedenovereenkomst in de AWB en de verhouding met het BW' in T Barkhuysen, W den Ouden and JEM Polak (eds), *Bestuursrecht harmoniseren: 15 jaar AWB* (The Hague, Boom Juridische Uitgevers, 2010) 717–35.

cannot be challenged before the administrative courts. More generally, contracts, including 'competence contracts', are as such not reviewable before the administrative courts.

Hoge Raad, 8 July 2011[97] **3.51 (NL)**

ETAM v Municipality of Zoetermeer

DIVISION OF JURISDICTION BETWEEN THE ADMINISTRATIVE AND ORDINARY COURTS IN CASES CONCERNING (THE NON-OBSERVANCE OF) COMPETENCE CONTRACTS

ETAM

Claims concerning the observance of a contractual obligation to take a decision belong to the jurisdiction of the administrative courts, while claims concerning compensation for damage belong to the jurisdiction of the ordinary courts.

Facts: ETAM and the municipality of Zoetermeer concluded a contract according to which the municipality of Zoetermeer sold a piece of land to ETAM, who wanted to build a factory outlet and several offices on it, and the municipality would make every effort to establish a new development plan[98] that facilitated the construction of these buildings. In due course, the municipality of Zoetermeer established the plan. However, according to ETAM, the content of the plan was in breach of the contract, as it did not allow for the construction of all the buildings included in the contract. ETAM claimed compensation for the damage thereby suffered before the civil courts. In the end, the case was brought before the Supreme Court.

Held: The claim was dismissed.

Judgment: If a contracting party in a contract with a municipality seeks the observance of a contractual obligation to take a decision, it should commence proceedings before the administrative court. ... Concerning a claim for damages on the ground of non-observance of the contract, the civil court is the competent court.

Note

This judgment demonstrates that the administrative courts may have to rule on issues relating to the implementation of a 'competence contract', namely if the administrative authority does not take a decision which it should have taken according to the contract. In the case of *ETAM*, the company should have brought an action against the spatial plan before the administrative court. Hence, in order to enforce a public-law element of the contract, the private party has to start proceedings before the administrative court, and not the ordinary courts.

[97] ECLI:NL:HR:2011:BP3057.

[98] 'Plans' are not a distinct legal category. They may contain policy rules, single-case decisions or nothing legally relevant at all. Some plans, especially municipal zoning plans, are, as far as judicial review is concerned, treated as single-case decisions. Hence, judicial review (*beroep*) against such plans is possible before the administrative court.

3.5.C FRANCE

In France, contracts concluded by the administration are subdivided into 'administrative law contracts' and 'private law contracts'.[99]

Public bodies can conclude both, but a specific regime only applies to the first category. Whether or not a contract is classified as an 'administrative law contract' (*contract administratif*) is a matter which, in France, is closely linked to the jurisdiction of the administrative courts, because only the latter have jurisdiction with regard to administrative law contracts.[100] Some administrative law contracts are defined by legislation, others by criteria established in case law.

Conseil d'État, 20 April 1956[101] **3.52 (FR)**

Époux Bertin v Minister for Veterans Affairs and Victims of War

CONTRACTS; PUBLIC SERVICE

Époux Bertin

A contract that confers the execution of a public service on a private party is an administrative law contract.

Facts: The Bertin couple had agreed, by virtue of a contract concluded orally, to feed some Soviet citizens housed in the Repatriation Centre of Meaux, in exchange for a lump sum of 30F per person per day. The Bertin couple subsequently argued that an addendum had been made to the initial contract, as a consequence of which the Repatriation Centre had agreed to pay a supplementary fee of 7.50F in exchange for the provision of new foodstuffs. The Centre refused to pay the supplementary fee and was taken to court by the claimants.

Held: The Council of State considered the contract to be an administrative law contract. It held that the jurisdiction belonged to the administrative courts.

Judgment: Considering that it appears that, by an oral contract concluded by the administration on 24 November 1944, the couple had committed, for a lump sum of 30 francs per person per day, to provide food to the Soviet nationals hosted in the Repatriation Centre of Meaux while waiting for their return to Russia; considering that the said contract has the object to confer on the concerned individuals, in this regard, the execution of the public service of ensuring the repatriation of the refugees of foreign nationality which were on French territory; considering that this circumstance itself is sufficient to conclude that this contract has the characteristics of an administrative law contract (*contrat administratif*); considering that therefore, without there being the need to see whether said contract contains clauses which derogate from ordinary law, since the dispute concerns the existence of an engagement complementary to this contract, on the basis of which the administration has allegedly allotted an additional bonus of 7.50 francs per person

[99] For an overview of administrative contracts in France, see J-B Auby, L Cluzel-Metayer and L Xenou, *Administrative Law of the European Union, its Member States and the United States*, 4th edn (Antwerp, Intersentia, 2018) 19–21.

[100] See Chapter 2, section 2.5.A.4.

[101] N° 98637.

per day to the Bertin couple in exchange for new types of food, the jurisdiction belongs to the administrative courts...

Tribunal des Conflits, 13 October 2014[102] **3.53 (FR)**

SA AXA France IARD v Mutuelle Assurance des Instituteurs de France (MAIF)

CONTRACTS; PUBLIC POWER PREROGATIVES

SA AXA France IARD

A contract falls within the jurisdiction of the administrative courts if it contains clauses which vest the administration with special prerogatives for the enforcement of the contract.

Facts: The city of Joinville-le-Pont concluded a contract with an association whereby the city rented some facilities to the association for the purposes of rowing. A fire destroyed the building. The insurer of the city sued the insurer of the association for reimbursement of the damages caused by the fire.

Held: The contract was considered a private law contract. The jurisdiction was held not to belong to the administrative courts.

Judgment: Considering that, in third instance, the disputed contract does not include any clause which, notably because of the prerogatives recognised to the contracting public person in the execution of the contract, requires in the general interest that the special regime of administrative law contracts (*contrats administratifs*) be followed.

Ordonnance n° 2015-899 du 23 juillet 2015 relative aux marchés publics[103] **3.54 (FR)**

Article 3 Public procurement contracts falling within the scope of the present ordinance (*ordonnance*) concluded by legal persons of public law are administrative law contracts (*contrats administratifs*).

Notes

(1) The case of *Epoux Bertin* established that, when a contract is concluded for the performance of a public service, the contract is to be classified as an 'administrative law contract'. In recent cases, the scope of 'public service' has been broadened. Today, it encompasses both those cases where, through a contract, an individual is in charge of the performance of a public service and those cases where the individual merely participates in the performance of a public service (without bearing the main responsibility for delivering the public service).[104]

Secondly, a contract can be qualified as an 'administrative law contract' if some of its provisions vest the administration with prerogatives of public power for the purposes of promoting the general interest, which derogate from the generally applicable

[102] N° C3963.
[103] JORF N° 0169, 24 July 2015, 12602.
[104] Tribunal des Conflits, 21 May 2007, *SA CODIAM*, N° C3609.

rules of law regulating private parties (eg the power to terminate the contract unilaterally). The *AXA France* case from 2014 forms part of a series of judgments rendered by French courts since the beginning of the twentieth century on the identification of contractual clauses which are the expression of prerogatives of public power.[105] In the case, there were no such provisions, hence the contract was qualified as a private law contract.

Furthermore, the law itself may specify if the contract is an 'administrative law contract'. By way of example, public procurement contracts are qualified by the law as 'administrative law contracts' by Article 3 of Ordinance n° 2015-899 of 23 July 2015.

(2) 'Administrative law contracts' are reviewable in the 'full jurisdiction remedy' (*recours de pleine juridiction*) for both contracting parties and third parties.[106] However, as regards third parties, the remedies in the 'full jurisdiction remedy' (*recours de pleine juridiction*) are limited: they can only ask for the termination of the contract and they can only challenge the most severe irregularities, which affect the general interest.[107]

3.5.D ENGLAND AND WALES

In England and Wales, there is no categorical distinction between public law contracts and private law contracts. The question of whether or not a contract can be subject to judicial review and whether public law remedies[108] can be sought in relation to contracts made by public bodies will depend on the characterisation of the contract and the nature of the dispute. If the contract is of what the courts would describe as a purely 'private law' nature (ie contracts for the purchase of office equipment or employment contracts), then it will not be possible for a claimant to seek judicial review and public law remedies.[109] Some contractual disputes contain a 'public law element'. Examples of a 'sufficient public law element' include situations where a contracting decision was contrary to a published policy, frustrating a legitimate expectation engendered in the claimant,[110] or, where a contracting decision is taken under a statutory power, the contract relates to public land and the authority has the power to make by-laws in relation to the activity in addition to controls exerted via contract.[111] For those disputes, it may be possible to seek public law remedies during a private law action[112] (ie not commenced under the procedure under Part 54 of the Civil Procedure Rules) or to seek judicial review.[113]

[105] Conseil d'État, 31 July 1912, *Société des granits porphyroïdes des Vosges*, N° 30701.
[106] Conseil d'État, 4 April 2014, *Département de Tarn-et-Garonne*, N° 358994.
[107] Conseil d'État, 30 June 2017, *Société France-Manche*, N° 398445.
[108] See further Chapter 7, section 7.2.A.2.
[109] *R v East Berkshire Health Authority, ex parte Walsh* [1985] QB 152 (CA).
[110] *R v Barnet London Borough Council, ex parte Pardes House School Ltd* [1989] COD 512 (QB).
[111] *R (Agnello) v Hounslow London Borough Council* [2003] EWHC 3112 (Admin), [2004] BLGR 536.
[112] *Roy v Kensington and Chelsea Family Practitioner Committee* [1992] 1 AC 624 (HL).
[113] *R v British Coal Board, ex parte Vardy* [1993] ICR 720 (DC). See also *Clark v University of Lincolnshire and Humberside* [2000] 1 WLR 1988 (CA), where the Court of Appeal allowed the claimant to proceed in a judicial review claim in relation to a dispute between a student and her university which was essentially contractual because otherwise the student would have had no route to achieve a possible remedy.

House of Lords, 6 February 1992[114] **3.55 (EW)**

Roy v Kensington and Chelsea Family Practitioner Committee

PRIVATE LAW PROCEEDINGS; ABUSE OF PROCESS

Roy

It is not an abuse of process to commence a private law action in a case which may also require the determination of some issues of public law.

Facts: R was a doctor who ran a general practice. As part of the service he offered, he saw National Health Service (NHS) patients registered with his practice. Doctors who saw patients for the NHS were entitled to payment accordingly, provided that they met the requirements imposed on doctors providing NHS services. The Kensington and Chelsea Family Practitioner Committee (FPC) determined that Dr Roy had not devoted sufficient time to seeing NHS patients and thus made a deduction from his basic allowance that would normally have been payable under the Statement of Fees and Allowances published under Regulation 24 of the National Health Service (General Medical and Pharmaceutical Services) Regulations 1974. Dr Roy brought a claim for breach of contract and the FPC sought to defend itself by seeking a striking out of Dr Roy's claim as an abuse of process, arguing that the claim concerned a public law decision that he had not devoted adequate time to his NHS services under Regulation 24 of the National Health Service (General Medical and Pharmaceutical Services) Regulations 1974. The judge at first instance struck out the claim as an abuse of process. The Court of Appeal allowed an appeal and permitted the claim to proceed.

Held: The House of Lords upheld the judgment of the Court of Appeal. It was considered legitimate to proceed with a private law action.

Judgment: Lord Lowry: The judge, however, held that, even if the doctor's rights to full payments under the scheme were contractually based, the committee's duty was a public law duty and could be challenged only on judicial review. Mr. Collins admitted that, if the doctor had a contractual right, he could (subject always to paragraph 80.1) vindicate it by action. But, my Lords, I go further: if Dr. Roy has any kind of private law right, even though not contractual, he can sue for its alleged breach.

In this case it has been suggested that Dr. Roy could have gone by judicial review, because there is no issue of fact, but that would not always hold good in a similar type of case. And I do not forget that he might have been faced with the argument which succeeded in *Ex parte Walsh*. In any event, a successful application by judicial review could not lead directly, as it would in an action, to an order for payment of the full basic practice allowance. Other proceedings would be needed.

An important point is that the court clearly has jurisdiction to entertain the doctor's action. Furthermore, even if one accepts the full rigour of *O'Reilly v. Mackman*, there is ample room to hold that this case comes within the exceptions allowed for by Lord Diplock. It is concerned with a private law right; it involves a question which could in some circumstances give rise to a dispute of fact and one object of the plaintiff is to obtain an order for the payment (not by way of damages) of an ascertained or ascertainable sum of money. If it is wrong to allow such a claim to be litigated by action, what is to be said of other disputed claims for remuneration? I think it is right to consider the whole

[114] [1992] 1 AC 624.

spectrum of claims which a doctor might make against the committee. The existence of any dispute as to entitlement means that he will be alleging a breach of his private law rights through a failure by the committee to perform their public duty. If the committee's argument prevails, the doctor must in all these cases go by judicial review, even when the facts are not clear. I scarcely think that this can be the right answer....

The judgments to which I have referred effectively dispose of an argument pressed by the committee that Dr. Roy had no right to be paid a basic practice allowance until the committee had carried out their public duty of forming an opinion under paragraph 12.1(b), with the supposed consequence that, until that had happened, the doctor had no private law right which he could enforce. The answer is that Dr. Roy had a right to a fair and legally correct consideration of his claim. Failing that, his private law right has been infringed and he can sue the committee.

Mr. Collins sought to equate the committee's task under paragraph 12.1(b) with the council's duty in phase 1 of *Cocks v. Thanet District Council* and the committee's duty to pay with the council's duty in phase 2. For an answer to that argument I refer to the judgments in the Court of Appeal and would also point out that Mr. Cocks was simply a homeless member of the public in phase 1, whereas Dr. Roy had already an established relationship with the committee when his claim under paragraph 12.1 fell to be considered.

Dr. Roy's printed case contained detailed arguments in favour of a contract between him and the committee, but before your Lordships Mr. Lightman simply argued that the doctor had a private law right, whether contractual or statutory. With regard to *O'Reilly v. Mackman* [1983] 2 A.C. 237 he argued in the alternative. The 'broad approach' was that the rule in *O'Reilly v. Mackman* did not apply generally against bringing actions to vindicate private rights in all circumstances in which those actions involved a challenge to a public law act or decision, but that it merely required the aggrieved person to proceed by judicial review only when private law rights were not at stake. The 'narrow approach' assumed that the rule applied generally to all proceedings in which public law acts or decisions were challenged, subject to some exceptions when private law rights were involved. There was no need in *O'Reilly v. Mackman* to choose between these approaches, but it seems clear that Lord Diplock considered himself to be stating a general rule with exceptions. For my part, I much prefer the broad approach, which is both traditionally orthodox and consistent with the Pyx Granite principle [1960] A.C. 260, 286, as applied in *Davy v. Spelthorne Borough Council* [1984] A.C. 262, 274 and in *Wandsworth London Borough Council v. Winder* [1985] A.C. 461, 510. It would also, if adopted, have the practical merit of getting rid of a procedural minefield.

In conclusion, my Lords, it seems to me that, unless the procedure adopted by the moving party is ill suited to dispose of the question at issue, there is much to be said in favour of the proposition that a court having jurisdiction ought to let a case be heard rather than entertain a debate concerning the form of the proceedings.

Note

This case illustrates the developing flexibility of approach of the courts towards the 'public/private divide' created in the process for claiming judicial review and illustrates that it is possible in some circumstances for claimants to commence proceedings in private law (such as in this case for breach of contract) even when the courts will be required to engage in aspects of judicial review in order to decide the case.

3.5.E THE EUROPEAN UNION

A Glaser, Die Entwicklung des europäischen Rechts aus der Perspektive der Handlungsformenlehre[115] **3.56 (EU)**

Primary law does not expressly provide for a contractual public law form of action.

In particular, it does not appear in the context of the enumerations of legal acts under Article 288 TFEU. This provision, however, is only exhaustive as regards to the adoption of unilateral legal acts. It follows from Article 340(1) TFEU that the Union can bind itself contractually and be held liable accordingly. Thereby, the rule of law must be observed and the procedural guarantees which are connected to the adoption of legal acts under Article 288 TFEU must not be circumvented through the choice of the contractual form. Moreover, through the recognition of the jurisdiction of the Court of Justice of the European Union on the ground that an agreement on an arbitration clause was concluded, Article 272 TFEU recognizes implicitly that the Union can conclude public law as well as private law contracts. Thus, primary law does not follow the equally conceivable premise that contracts are always of a private law nature, but differentiates explicitly between public law and private law contracts.

Note

The European Union can conclude both private and public law contracts. However, this distinction is based on national law criteria; EU rules on contracts concluded by the EU institutions do not contain a distinction between private and public law contracts.[116] Agreements may be concluded between the European Union and the Member States, or between the European Union and private parties or international organisations. They may be governed by EU law or the law of a Member State.[117] Normally, contracts concluded by the EU institutions contain a clause stipulating that EU law is applicable, complemented, where necessary, by national law.[118]

[115] A Glaser, *Die Entwicklung des europäischen Rechts aus der Perspektive der Handlungsformenlehre* (Tübingen, Mohr Siebeck, 2013) 395.

[116] N Athanasiadou, *Der Verwaltungsvertrag im EU-Recht* (Tübingen, Mohr Siebeck, 2017) 57.

[117] For more on contracts concluded by the EU, see Hofmann et al (n 60 above) ch 19; H Hofmann, 'Agreements in EU Law' (2006) 31 *European Law Review* 800; D Ritleng 'Les contracts de l'administration communautaire' in JB Auby and J Dutheil de la Rochère (eds), *Droit Administratif Européen* (Brussels, Bruylant, 2007) 147–70.

[118] Further on this, see Athanasiadou (n 116 above) 83.

Case T-186/96, 3 October 1997[119] **3.57 (EU)**

Mutual Aid Administration Services NV v Commission

CONTRACTS; ACTION FOR ANNULMENT; INADMISSIBILITY

Mutual Aid Administration Services

A contractual claim cannot be the subject matter of an action for annulment.

Facts: On 22 February 1996, the Commission decided to confer a contract for the supply of fruit juice and fruit jams under the tendering procedure to the Italian undertaking Trento Frutta. The Mutual Aid Administration Services NV (MAAS) was responsible for the transport of all the lots of fruit juice, fruit jams and common wheat flour. Trento Frutta informed MAAS that the pallets should not be stacked on more than two levels. At the time the goods were loaded onto the vessel, there was no other option than to load the pallets of fruit juice and jams on three levels. MAAS subsequently informed the Commission that the goods had been damaged as a result of inappropriate packing and asked the Commission to pay the full transport costs, which should include the additional costs incurred as a result of chartering a third ship to be able to store the cargo on two levels. The Commission refused to pay parts of those costs.

Held: The Court of First Instance declared the claim manifestly inadmissible.

Judgment: It follows that, with regard to the successful tenderer, the contested refusal to pay is not one of the unilateral decisions referred to by Article 189 of the Treaty, which the Commission must adopt under the conditions laid down by the Treaty.

In respect of the successful tenderer, that refusal cannot therefore constitute an act against which an action for annulment may be brought in accordance with Article 173 of the Treaty. Accordingly, insofar as the present action relates to such a refusal, it is, in any event, manifestly inadmissible.

Note

Although not directly derived from the wording of Article 263 TFEU, this ruling makes clear that contracts concluded by the EU cannot be the subject matter of an action for annulment.

Treaty on the Functioning of the European Union **3.58 (EU)**

Article 272 The Court of Justice of the European Union shall have jurisdiction to give judgment pursuant to any arbitration clause contained in a contract concluded by or on behalf of the Union, whether that contract be governed by public or private law.

Article 274 Save where jurisdiction is conferred on the Court of Justice of the European Union by the Treaties, disputes to which the Union is a party shall not on that ground be excluded from the jurisdiction of the courts or tribunals of the Member States.

[119] ECLI:EU:T:1997:149.

Note

Jurisdiction for determining disputes arising out of contracts lies by default with national courts (Article 274 TFEU). However, it is possible to insert a so-called 'arbitration clause' into the contract, which, under Article 272 TFEU, establishes the jurisdiction of the CJEU on the contract. However, the expression 'arbitration clause' is misleading since, when the CJEU is competent to decide on contracts concluded by the EU, they are not acting as arbitrators but as 'real' courts whose judgments can be directly enforced.[120] The Treaty does not specify any requirement for the wording of arbitration clauses, so any wording which demonstrates that the parties intend to remove any dispute between them from the jurisdiction of national courts will suffice.[121] In cases in which an 'arbitration clause' is contained in the contract, the extent of jurisdiction of the CJEU emerges from the clause itself, which means that only claims and pleas arising from the contract or directly connected to the contract may be ruled upon by the Court.[122]

3.5.F COMPARATIVE REMARKS

This section has shown that all legal systems know a distinction between purely private law contracts and contracts with a public law element. However, the concrete scope of the concept 'public law contract' differs. Also, there are differences as regards the question of which courts will be competent to rule on contracts concluded by the administration and what type of review procedure is applicable. In Germany and the Netherlands, most contracts (and certainly all of the types of contracts which the administration may conclude in France) fall outside the jurisdiction of the administrative courts. This is different in France, where administrative law contracts come within the jurisdiction of the administrative courts. Furthermore, while, in the Netherlands and Germany, it is possible to contract out public law powers (through the public law contract in Germany and the competence or policy contract in the Netherlands), this is not possible in the other legal systems. Private law contracts in Germany and the Netherlands thus encompass what in France are both private law and administrative law contracts.

3.6 SILENCE AND FAILURE TO ACT

Administrative authorities may not react to claimants' requests. The question which arises in all legal systems is how this 'administrative silence' may be challenged in court. The next question is whether it is possible, in cases in which the administration is obliged to act by statute, to compel the administration to act in case of inaction.

[120] K Lenaerts and others, *Procedural Law of the European Union*, 2nd edn (London, Sweet & Maxwell, 2014) 689.

[121] Case C-294/02 *Commission v AMI Semiconductor Belgium and others* ECLI:EU:C:2005:172, para 50.

[122] Case 426/85 *Commission v Zoubek* ECLI:EU:C:1986:501, para 11; Case C-337/96 *Commission v IRACO* ECLI:EU:C:1998:582.

3.6.A DIRECT CHALLENGE OF FAILURE TO ACT IN ADMINISTRATIVE COURTS

3.6.A.1 GERMANY

Verwaltungsgerichtsordnung **3.59 (DE)**

§42 (1) By legal action, the annulment (*Aufhebung*) of an administrative act (action for annulment (*Anfechtungsklage*)) as well as the order to issue a refused or omitted administrative act (action seeking the issuance of an administrative act (*Verpflichtungsklage*)) may be requested.

§75 If, with regard to an objection or an application for the issuance of an administrative act, the merits have not been decided upon within a suitable period without sufficient reason, the action shall be admissible by way of derogation from §68. The action may not be lodged prior to the expiry of three months after the lodging of the objection or the filing of the application to carry out the administrative act, unless a shorter period is required because of special circumstances of the case. If an adequate reason why the objection has not yet been ruled on applies, or the requested administrative act has not yet been carried out, the court shall suspend the proceedings until the expiry of a deadline it has set, which can be extended. If the objection is admitted within the deadline set by the court or the administrative act carried out within this deadline, the main case shall be declared to have been settled.

Note

If a claimant seeks an administrative act but the administrative authority fails to adopt the requested administrative act within a reasonable period of time, the claimant can bring an action seeking the issuance of an administrative act (*Verpflichtungsklage*) (§42(1) VwGO). According to §75 VwGO, the obligatory intra-administrative objection procedure is not required.

Verwaltungsverfahrensgesetz **3.60 (DE)**

§42a (1) Upon expiry of a specified decision-making period, an approval that has been applied for shall be deemed granted (*Genehmigungsfiktion*) if this is stipulated by law and if the application is sufficiently clearly defined in content. The provisions concerning the validity of administrative acts and the proceedings for legal remedy shall apply *mutatis mutandis*.

(2) The decision-making period pursuant to section 1 first sentence shall be three months unless otherwise stipulated by law. The period starts upon reception of the complete application documents. It may be extended once by a reasonable period of time if this is warranted by the complexity of the matter. Any such extension of the decision-making period shall be justified and communicated in good time.

(3) Upon request, the fact that the approval is deemed granted (*Genehmigungsfiktion*) shall be confirmed in writing to the person to whom the administrative act would have had to be notified pursuant to §41(1).

Note

The rule on the deemed approval (*Genehmigungsfiktion*) for applications of a permit is applicable whenever a statute provides for this. If a public authority remains silent for three months after a citizen has requested the adoption of a permit, such as a building permit, §42a VwVfG provides a deemed approval with the same legal consequences as if the administration had granted an actual permit. This means, inter alia, that the permit can be challenged in an administrative court in an action for annulment (*Anfechtungsklage*).

3.6.A.2 ENGLAND AND WALES

Civil Procedure Rules **3.61 (EW)**

Rule 54.1 (2) In this Section
(a) a 'claim for judicial review' means a claim to review the lawfulness of…
(ii) a decision, action or failure to act in relation to the exercise of a public function.

Note

As a starting point, Part 54.1 CPR stipulates that a claim for judicial review also concerns omissions.

Court of Appeal (Civil Division), 5 April 1995[123] **3.62 (EW)**

R v Secretary of State for the Home Department, ex p Fire Brigades' Union

SILENCE TREATED AS A DECISION

FBU

Inaction of the administration can be considered as a decision not to act which is reviewable in judicial review.

Facts: The claimants comprised a number of trade unions and other bodies and the Trades Union Congress. They claimed to have one feature in common: that their members, in the course of their working duties, were liable to be the victims of criminally caused personal injuries. They sought to challenge two decisions of the Secretary of State for the Home Department and requested a declaration that the Secretary of State, by failing or refusing to bring into force part of an act, had acted unlawfully in breach of his duty under that act.

Held: The Secretary of State was not under a duty to bring the relevant provisions of the act into force, but it was unlawful to state that the provisions would never be brought into force and it was also unlawful to use the prerogative power to introduce a scheme contrary to that provided for in the statute.

Judgment: Sir Thomas Bingham M.R.: The applicants submitted that the effect of this subsection was to confer on the Secretary of State a discretion as to *when* the relevant

[123] [1995] 2 WLR 1 (CA).

sections should be brought into force but none as to *whether* the sections should be brought into force. They recognised that the Secretary of State could, for good reason, delay the coming into force of the sections. But they did not accept that he could, for no reason or bad reason, delay the implementation of the sections. If he determined not to bring the sections into force he should seek their repeal. So long as the sections remained on the statute book he was under a duty to bring them into force as soon as he properly judged it appropriate to do so.

In the result, I reject the Secretary of State's contention that he was subject to no legal duty of any kind in relation to implementation of these provisions. But I reject the applicants' invitation to hold that the Secretary of State lacked any good grounds for failing to exercise the power which section 171(1) conferred. Between 1987–88 and 1993-94 the cost of the non-statutory scheme nearly trebled and the cost of administration rose significantly. These facts alone provided reasons for delay. I am unwilling to declare that in failing or refusing to bring the provisions into force the Secretary of State acted unlawfully in breach of his duty under the Act of 1988. On this issue I arrive at the same conclusion as the Divisional Court, although by a different route.

Note

This case illustrates that 'administrative silence' can be considered a decision that is reviewable in judicial review. However, it should be stressed that in England it is in general possible to directly challenge the administrative silence before the courts, even though, in this case, silence was considered to be a decision.

3.6.A.3 THE EUROPEAN UNION

Case C-123/03 P, 9 December 2004[124] **3.63 (EU)**

Commission v Greencore

SILENCE; IMPLIED REFUSAL; ACTION FOR ANNULMENT

Greencore

Silence on the part of an EU institution cannot be equated with an implicit decision of refusal against which an action for annulment may be brought.

Facts: On 14 May 1997, the Commission imposed a fine of 8,800,000 ECU relating to a proceeding pursuant to Article 86 of the EC Treaty (currently Article 102 TFEU) on a subsidiary of Greencore (Irish Sugar). Irish Sugar brought an action before the Court of First Instance seeking annulment of that decision before the fine was paid by Irish Sugar on 22 August 1997. However, the fine was merely reduced to ECU 7,883,326 and the remainder of the action was dismissed by the Court of First Instance. In October 1999, an official of the Commission contacted Irish Sugar's lawyer in order to prepare reimbursement of the part of the fine that had been annulled. Subsequently, the Commission transferred the sum of €914,647 to Irish Sugar's account

[124] ECLI:EU:C:2004:783.

without paying any interest. Therefore, Greencore brought an action against the Commission ordering it to pay the interest. The Court of First Instance held that the Commission was obliged to repay the principal amount of the sum and the default interest on that sum. At the same time, the Commission raised an objection of inadmissibility and asked the Court to dismiss Greencore's action as manifestly inadmissible. In particular, the Commission argued that Greencore ought, in accordance with the procedure for failure to act laid down in Article 256 TFEU, to have first called upon the institution to act within a reasonable period.

Held: The Court of Justice set aside the order of the Court of First Instance.

Judgment: It is next appropriate to observe that, as a rule, mere silence on the part of an institution cannot be placed on the same footing as an implied refusal, except where that result is expressly provided for by a provision of Community law. While not excluding that in certain particular circumstances that principle may not be applicable, so that an institution's silence or inaction may exceptionally be considered to constitute an implied refusal, the Court considers that in the circumstances of the present case the Commission's paying of the principal sum only without explicitly taking a position on the request for payment of interest does not amount to an implied decision rejecting that request. Indeed, in this case, such exceptional circumstances have not been invoked and have not arisen.

Note

In the EU legal order, silence on the part of the EU institutions when a request is made is generally not equated with an implied refusal, hence it cannot be the subject matter of an action for annulment unless the transformation of silence into an implied refusal is expressly provided in EU legislation.

Treaty on the Functioning of the European Union **3.64 (EU)**

Article 265 Should the European Parliament, the European Council, the Council, the Commission or the European Central Bank, in infringement of the Treaties, fail to act, the Member States and the other institutions of the Union may bring an action before the Court of Justice of the European Union to have the infringement established. This Article shall apply, under the same conditions, to bodies, offices and agencies of the Union which fail to act.

The action shall be admissible only if the institution, body, office or agency concerned has first been called upon to act. If, within two months of being so called upon, the institution, body, office or agency concerned has not defined its position, the action may be brought within a further period of two months.

Any natural or legal person may, under the conditions laid down in the preceding paragraphs, complain to the Court that an institution, body, office or agency of the Union has failed to address to that person any act other than a recommendation or an opinion.

Notes

(1) The fact that silence is not treated as a decision does not mean that there is no judicial protection against such silence. Instead, an action for failure to act under Article 265 TFEU may be brought. The subject matter of an action for failure to act is

a determination as to whether an omission to issue a decision was unlawful. In order for the action to be admissible, some preliminary steps need to be taken.

(2) First, an action for failure to act will be admissible only if the institution concerned has first been called upon to act. The case law has clarified that the claimant's request must be specific in that it must be clear what decision the institution should have taken.[125] There is no time limit within which the request must be made. The Court of Justice has held, however, that the claimant may not delay the exercise of his rights indefinitely.[126] If, within two months of this request, the institution concerned has not defined its position, the action may be brought.

(3) Certainly, it can be considered that, by complying with the request, the institution will have defined its position. The Court of Justice has clarified that the same can be considered when the institution adopted a decision different from that which the claimant requested.[127]

(4) If an action for failure to act is brought by a national or legal person, it will only be admissible if it concerns an EU institution's failure to adopt a binding act.[128] If, in contrast, the action for failure to act is brought by an institution or a Member State, this limitation does not apply.[129]

(5) The case law is consistent in that a failure to take a decision is unlawful only if the institution was under a duty to act, which can be derived from a provision of primary or secondary EU law.[130]

3.6.B NEED FOR A FICTIONAL DECISION OR SILENCE EQUATED TO A DECISION

3.6.B.1 FRANCE

In France, there are two possible legal consequences resulting from 'administrative silence': either the acceptance of a request or the rejection of a request.

Code des relations entre le public et l'administration **3.65 (FR)**

Article L231-1 Failure on the part of the administration to respond to a request will be treated as a decision of approval once two months from the date of the request have elapsed.

[125] Case 25/85 *Nuovo Campsider v Commission* ECLI:EU:C:1986:195, para 8.
[126] Case 59/70 *Netherlands v Commission* ECLI:EU:C:1971:77, para 19.
[127] Joined Cases 166 and 220/86 *Irish Cement Ltd v Commission* ECLI:EU:C:1988:549, para 17.
[128] Art 265 TFEU mentions 'any act other than a recommendation or an opinion'.
[129] For example, an action may be brought against the Commission if it fails to submit a proposal for a legislative measure to the Council relating to a matter on which the EU is under an obligation to legislate. See eg Case 13/83 *European Parliament v Council* ECLI:EU:C:1985:220.
[130] Case C-141/02 P *Commission v T-Mobile Austria* ECLI:EU:C:2005:98; Case T-277/94 *AITEC v Commission* ECLI:EU:T:1996:66.

Notes

(1) This rule stipulates the general principle of 'administrative silence amounts to acceptance of a request' (*silence vaut acceptation*). Accordingly, the silence of the competent administrative authority on a request made by any person is transformed into an administrative decision of approval. This rule is applicable in more than 1500 cases specifically regulated by numerous statutes.[131] However, it should be noted that this rule was only introduced in 2013. Before then, the general rule was the opposite, namely that silence amounts to rejection.

(2) In contrast to the legal consequence that silence transforms into acceptance, there is also the option that 'silence amounts to rejection of a request' (*silence vaut rejet*).[132] Whether this rule is applicable is determined by statute.

(3) After two months, a claimant can bring an action for annulment (*recours pour excès de pouvoir*) against the implicit decision of acceptance or of rejection.

3.6.B.2 THE NETHERLANDS

In the Netherlands, failure to take a decision on the part of the authority can also have two consequences.

Algemene Wet Bestuursrecht **3.66 (NL)**

Article 6:2 For the purposes of the legal rules regarding objections and judicial review, the following are equated with a decision (*besluit*):

...

b. the failure to take a decision in due time.

Article 4:13 (1) A single-case decision must be issued within the time limit provided for by a legal rule or, in the absence of such a time limit, within a reasonable time after the receipt of the request.

(2) The reasonable time mention in section 1 has in any event expired where the administrative authority has, within eight weeks after the receipt of the request, neither issued a single-case decision...

Note

Article 6:2 AWB provides that, when applying the rules on the intra-administrative objection procedure (*bezwaar*) and judicial review (*beroep*), failure to take a decision in due time shall be equated with a decision. Hence, in this case, no decision is taken. However, to enable claimants and third parties to object and bring an action to court, undue delay to decide is equated with a decision. What constitutes an undue delay can be deduced from Article 4:13 AWB.

[131] www.legifrance.gouv.fr/Droit-francais/Silence-vaut-accord-SVA.
[132] www.legifrance.gouv.fr/Droit-francais/Silence-vaut-accord-SVA/Silence-vaut-rejet-SVR.

Algemene Wet Bestuursrecht **3.67 (NL)**

Artcle 4:20b (1) When a request to issue a single-case decision is not answered in due time, the requested single-case decision shall be deemed as having been granted.

(2) The granting of the decision by law shall be regarded as a single-case decision.

(3) In derogation from Article 3:40, the single-case decision shall enter into force on the third day following the expiry of the term which the administration was given to take the decision.

Note

In specific cases provided for in legislation, it is possible that failure to adopt a decision in due time is deemed to be a single-case decision granting the request. An example of this situation can be found in the environmental permit foreseen by the Environmental Licensing General Provisions Act (Wet algemene bepalingen omgevingsrecht – Wabo).

3.6.C COMPARATIVE REMARKS

This section has shown that there are two different solutions for how 'administrative silence' can be interpreted before the administrative courts, which are linked to the question of whether or not access to a judicial review procedure is made dependent on the existence of a 'decision'.

In Germany, England and the European Union, there is no need to have a decision for the purpose of accessing administrative courts. In Germany, silence on the part of the administration can be challenged through an action seeking the issuance of an administrative act. Comparable to this, in the European Union, Article 265 TFEU provides for a separate procedure in which a failure to act can be challenged. In England, 'omissions' are expressly mentioned in the Civil Procedure Rules as being reviewable in judicial review.

In contrast to this, in France and in the Netherlands, a decision is a prerequisite for an action for annulment (*recours pour excès de pouvoir*) or judicial review (*beroep*), respectively. It should be noted again that, in these two legal systems, the concept of decision is rather broad. However, 'administrative silence' is clearly not covered. Hence, in order to ask for the review of a failure to act, in France a fictional decision of approval or rejection is created that will be subject to review in the administrative courts. In the Netherlands, the silence is equated with a decision, so that the silence can be challenged before the administrative courts.

3.7 INTERNAL MEASURES

The term 'internal measures' refers to a category of administrative action which does not, in principle, have external effects. Depending on the legal system, this can include, inter alia, administrative action which determines the organisational structure of an administrative body and which allocates specific tasks to specific units. Moreover, it can concern administrative action which guides civil servants in interpreting the terminology used in a statute for the purpose of applying it to a specific case, or which guides civil servants in exercising discretion. This section will contrast the English legal system, which provides for a general review possibility of 'internal measures', to the other legal systems, which only provide for limited review proceedings.

3.7.A GENERAL REVIEW BY ADMINISTRATIVE COURTS: ENGLAND AND WALES

In England, there is no strict classification of administrative action as 'internal action'. The determination of the organisational structure of an administrative body or the allocation of tasks will usually be laid down in primary or secondary legislation. However, this type of action can also be taken as a 'decision', which can be challenge-able in the courts.[133] Documents guiding the interpretation of terms used in legislation or on the exercise of discretion are called 'guidance' or 'policy', and are reviewable before the administrative courts.

Court of Appeal (Civil Division), 20 February 2002[134] **3.68 (EW)**

Lindsay v Commissioners for Customs and Excise

JUDICIAL REVIEW; POLICIES

Lindsay

Courts may exercise judicial review of policies.

Facts: Mr Lindsay took a trip to France in his car in order to purchase items, including cigarettes and tobacco. He was stopped by a customs official, who found that he was carrying an amount of tobacco beyond that which might be expected for personal use and thus advised him that he should have paid duty on his purchases. Mr Lindsay advised the customs official that he had purchased some of the tobacco for family members using money that they had given to him. The customs official determined that Mr Lindsay had breached the relevant customs legislation through failure to pay duty and thus decided to seize both the goods and the vehicle in which they were transported. This decision was taken pursuant to a policy adopted by the Commissioners of Customs and Excise which defined the approach to be adopted to seizure of goods and vehicles, and which did not draw a clear distinction between commercial smuggling and importation of goods for family and friends.

Held: The policy adopted by the Commissioners for Customs and Excise and the action taken under it were considered unlawful, as the seizure of the vehicle in a case like Lindsay's, which involved bringing in goods for social distribution to family and friends, was disproportionate under Article 1 of the First Protocol ECHR.

Judgment: Lord Phillips MR: The Commissioners' Policy: We asked to see the document in which the policy was originally promulgated. It was in the form of a circular letter (a DCL)

[133] For the English concept of 'decision', see above, section 3.2.B.1.

[134] [2002] EWCA Civ 267, [2002] 1 WLR 1766.

dated 13 July 2000 to various Customs Officers, including Review Officers. I shall read a few extracts from this document:

'1. The Government's intention to tackle tobacco smuggling announced on 22 March by the Paymaster General included not only a £209 million investment in Customs but also a commitment to ensure that those caught would face the most severe penalties and sanctions available.

2. One of the most direct ways to strike at the smugglers' activities is by seizing the vehicles they use to smuggle in their contraband. As the Paymaster General has said, we are determined to ensure that this sanction is as tough as it can be. The more effective this sanction is, the more we will hit the smugglers in the pocket and reduce the profitability of their illegal trade.

3. We are now in the process of applying the toughest possible sanctions in terms of our vehicle seizure policy. We are tackling the different components involved – e.g. privately owned cars and light goods vehicles, hire or lease vehicles and commercial tractors and trailers – in separate, but coherent, bite-size chunks....

Revised Policy – "No Second Chances"

8. With immediate effect, our headline policy will be that any car or light goods vehicle (other than rented) used for smuggling or for transporting smuggled or diverted excise goods within the UK will be seized and not restored. Restoration will be very much the exception, not the rule, irrespective of whether it is the first time the smuggler has been caught. This policy is to be applied vigorously both at the ports and at all inland locations where it can be proved that a vehicle was used to transport goods which are liable to seizure...

12. It is important for seizing officers to bear in mind the issues of proportionality and human rights (ECHR) when considering whether restoration is appropriate. It is not intended that restoration will be an option in any other circumstances.'...

Conclusions

55. Broadly speaking, the aim of the Commissioners' policy is the prevention of the evasion of excise duty that is imposed in accordance with European Community law. That is a legitimate aim under Article 1 of the First Protocol to the Convention. The issue is whether the policy is liable to result in the imposition of a penalty in the individual case that is disproportionate having regard to that legitimate aim. More specifically, did it have that effect in the case of Mr Lindsay?...

64. The Commissioners' policy does not, however, draw a distinction between the commercial smuggler and the driver importing goods for social distribution to family or friends in circumstances where there is no attempt to make a profit. Of course even in such a case the scale of importation, or other circumstances, may be such as to justify forfeiture of the car. But where the importation is not for the purpose of making a profit, I consider that the principle of proportionality requires that each case should be considered on its particular facts, which will include the scale of importation, whether it is a 'first offence', whether there was an attempt at concealment or dissimulation, the value of the vehicle and the degree of hardship that will be caused by forfeiture. There is open to the Commissioners a wide range of lesser sanctions that will enable them to impose a sanction that is proportionate where forfeiture of the vehicle is not justified.

65. I do not think that it would be impractical to distinguish between the truly commercial smuggler and others. The current regulations shift the burden to the driver of showing that he does not hold the goods 'for commercial purposes' when these exceed the quantity in the Schedule. In a case such as the present the driver importing for family or friends should be in a position to demonstrate that that is the case if called upon to do

so (see the comments of Lord Woolf CJ in *Goldsmith v Custom and Excise Commissioners* [2001] 1 WLR 1673 at pp 1679–70).

66. Unfortunately, in the present case and, I suspect, in others, the Customs Officers have drawn no distinction between the true commercial smuggler and the driver importing goods for family and friends. Because of the confusion to which I referred at the outset, the cars of both have been treated as subject to almost automatic forfeiture. Review Officer Florence appears to have understood that the Commissioner's policy rendered it irrelevant whether or not Mr Lindsay's story was true and equally irrelevant the value of his car and the effect that its deprivation would have on him. I believe that she correctly interpreted the policy.

Note

This case illustrates that, in England, courts will exercise judicial review with regard to policies.

High Court (Queen's Bench Division), 26 May 1999[135] **3.69 (EW)**

R (Pfizer) v Secretary of State for Health

JUDICIAL REVIEW; GUIDANCE

Pfizer

Courts may exercise judicial review of guidance.

Facts: Pfizer created a new drug with the trade name of Viagra for the treatment of erectile dysfunction in men. The Secretary of State feared that demand for the drug on the National Health Service would be great and would lead to a significant drain on resources. As such, Circular No 1998/158 dated 16 September 1998 was produced, discouraging doctors from prescribing the drug other than in exceptional circumstances.

Held: The court held that the circular was unlawful as it was in breach of EU law and was also unlawful in domestic law terms as it conflicted with the overarching duties incumbent on doctors.

Judgment: Collins J: Advice or guidance promulgated by a public authority may be the subject of judicial review if it contains an error of law. This is particularly so if it is likely to be acted upon by those it addresses: see *Gillick v. West Norfolk Area Health Authority* [1986] AC 112 at p.193G-H per Lord Bridge of Harwich. In *R v. Worthing B.C. ex p. Burch* (1985) 50 P &CR 53, Mann J granted judicial review of an opinion of the Secretary of State for the Environment given under a planning circular. The circular set out a procedure whereby the Minister could be asked to give an opinion whether or not he would have granted planning permission to resolve an issue between an applicant and the LPA in respect of what could be done on Government land which was being disposed of. The Secretary of State argued that the opinion was to be regarded only as a material consideration because it was not and did not purport to be binding. It was only advice. Mann, J said this: 'In my judgment, it is quite unreal to suppose that a local planning authority

135 [1999] 3 CMLR 875 (QB).

would do otherwise then accept the opinion as decisive. ... So, in practice, I am quite satisfied that the procedure that is envisaged by the circular does constrain the local authority and does, accordingly, preclude local people from having a chance of making a representation.'

All this, which I have summarised very briefly, enables Mr. Pannick to submit that the purpose and effect of the circular was indeed to deter G.P.s from carrying out their statutory duties under their Terms of Service. He submitted that Paragraph 43 imposed a duty on a G.P. to prescribe a drug if he was satisfied the patient had a clinical need for it. Paragraph 43 in my judgment does not impose a duty to prescribe a drug. It is dealing with the mechanism to enable a patient to receive a drug if the doctor decides that that drug should be used to treat the patient. The doctor's duty is contained in Paragraph 12(1), which really does no more than set out his professional obligations as a doctor and itself reflects the obligations referred to in Regulation 3(1). The doctor must give such treatment as he, exercising the professional judgment to be expected from an average G.P., considers necessary and appropriate. Miss Baxendale submits that 'appropriate' qualifies 'necessary' so that, if a G.P. considers a particular treatment to be necessary, he must go on to consider whether it is also appropriate. In reaching his final decision, he should have regard to the advice from SMAC and may therefore decide that the treatment is not appropriate. I find this suggested construction impossible. If a G.P. decides that a particular treatment is necessary, it must inevitably be appropriate. If it were not appropriate, a G.P. could not rationally decide that it was necessary. 'Appropriate' in Paragraph 12(1) is included so that G.P.s will provide services which go beyond those that are needed by their patients. Such services could include, for example, advice on various medical matters or family planning. Some treatment may be considered appropriate but not necessary. No doubt, if a G.P. in exercising his professional judgment decided that a particular treatment was not appropriate, he would conclude that that treatment was not necessary.

The very fact that the advice in the circular comes from SMAC is likely to make G.P.s respect it the more and thus to follow it. Mr. Pannick has attacked the reasons given for imparting it, castigating them as irrational. I do not think that attack succeeds. I should hesitate long before branding the views on medical matters of eminent practitioners to be irrational. In any event, whether the reasons be good or bad cannot affect the lawfulness of the circular if its purpose and effect is to cause G.P.s to act contrary to their professional obligations and contrary to their duty as reflected in Paragraph 12(1).

In September 1998 the B.M.A. issued its own guidance on the circular. This included the advice that from a legal standpoint G.P.s could prescribe Viagra since it had not been blacklisted. Miss Baxendale relied on this to make the point that the medical profession could have been in no doubt that the circular was only advisory and could not and did not require G.P.s not to prescribe Viagra. But the B.M.A.'s advice continued that G.P.s should adhere to SMAC's advice ('as a body representing the medical profession') which was contained in the circular. Thus the B.M.A.'s advice does not serve to diminish the effect of the circular and, as it seems to me, the problem with the circular is that the advice was given in a manner which meant that G.P.s would inevitably regard it as overriding their professional judgement. Mr. Pannick accepted that advice could be given in strong terms to deter the prescribing of Viagra, but it must make clear that the G.P.s' clinical judgment is supreme. In essence, the advice should have been reasoned, at least so that G.P.s knew why they should only prescribe Viagra sparingly. To state in bald terms that Viagra should not be prescribed save in (undefined) exceptional circumstances is tantamount to telling the recipients of the advice to follow it. They cannot know how their professional judgment should be influenced by the advice. In my judgment, the evidence confirms that this was and was intended to be acted upon by G.P.s independently of whether in their professional judgment a patient needed treatment for ED and so should have the better such treatment available, namely Viagra. Thus I am satisfied that the circular was and is unlawful in terms of domestic law.

Note

This excerpt illustrates that, in England, courts will exercise judicial review with regard to guidance.

3.7.B LIMITED REVIEW BY ADMINISTRATIVE COURTS

3.7.B.1 FRANCE

In France, there are two types of internal measures, circulars (*circulaires*) and guidelines (*lignes directrices*). Circulars contain instructions and recommendations provided by higher civil servants to lower civil servants. They determine how certain legislative provisions should be interpreted, how to approach a certain issue and which time limits have to be observed. Guidelines provide for internal rules on the exercise of discretion so as to guarantee a coherent application of the law.

Conseil d'État, 18 December 2002[136] **3.70 (FR)**

Duvignères v Minister of Justice

JUDICIAL REVIEW; *CIRCULAIRES*

Ms Duvignères

Under certain circumstances, it is possible to review a circulaire.

Facts: Ms Duvignères requested of the Ministry of Justice the withdrawal (*abrogation*) of the decree of 19 December 1991 and the circular (*circulaire*) of 26 March 1997, since both did not exclude housing assistance as a criterion for determining whether an individual is entitled to apply for legal aid. With a decision of the Ministry of Justice of 23 February 2001, the request to withdraw the decree and the circular was rejected.

Held: The Council of State annulled the decision of the Minister of Justice, rejecting the request to partially withdraw the decree and the circular.

Judgment: Considering that the interpretation that the administrative authority gives to the laws and regulations that it is responsible for, through the application, in particular, of circulars or instructions, may not be referred to the administrative courts since, being devoid of a mandatory nature, it may not, regardless of its basis, adversely affect a person's interests; considering that, however, the mandatory provisions of general nature

[136] N° 233618.

of a circular or an instruction must be regarded as adversely affecting a person's interests, as is the refusal to withdraw them; considering that a claim brought against them should be allowed if these provisions lay down, if the texts remain silent in this regard, a new rule vitiated by lack of competence or if, even though they have been taken with competence, it is correctly argued that they are unlawful for other reasons; considering that the same is true if it is argued correctly that the interpretation that they require to be adopted, either misinterprets the meaning and scope of legislative or regulatory provisions that it intended clarify, or reiterates a rule contrary to a higher legal norm. …

Note

As a general rule, administrative action which does not qualify as a decision cannot be challenged in an action for annulment. As such, circulars (*circulaires*) and guidelines (*lignes directrices*) do not qualify as decisions. However, this excerpt shows that where a *circulaire* shows a mandatory character, it can be reviewed before the administrative court. In order to determine whether or not a circular is exceptionally reviewable before the administrative courts, a distinction must therefore be made between circulars which have no mandatory content (*circulaires dénuées de caractère impératif*) and circulars with mandatory content (*circulaires impératives/circulaires à caractère réglementaire*). The latter category of administrative action may adversely affect the interests of individuals, so that it can in fact have external effects. Substantively, this type of administrative action is a regulatory act (*acte réglementaire*), which is challengeable in the administrative courts. The same line of reasoning applies to guidelines (*lignes directrices*).

Conseil d'État, 7 February 1936[137] **3.71 (FR)**

Jamart v Minister for Pensions

JUDICIAL REVIEW; MEASURE RELATED TO THE ORGANISATION OF THE SERVICE

Jamart

'Mesures d'organisation du service' *may be challenged in an action for annulment.*

Facts: The Minister for Pensions refused Mr Jamart access to a public medical centre, the place where he worked. The decision was challenged.

Held: The Council of State annulled the decision.

Judgment: Considering that if, even in the case where no legislative provision confers regulatory power to the ministers, they can, as any head of department, take the measures necessary for the good functioning of the administration placed under their authority, and they can, notably, to the extent required by the service, prohibit access to the concerned premises to those persons whose presence would potentially disturb the

[137] N° 43321.

regular functioning of the said service, they could not, however, except under exceptional circumstances, issue an individual decision prohibiting access to those persons which are supposed to enter the concerned premised to exercise their profession....

Note

In France, rules which determine the organisational structure of an administrative body, which are based on the autonomous regulatory power awarded to ministers and whose scope is limited to this purpose are called *mesures d'organisation du service.* These types of measures will usually qualify as decisions and can be challenged in the administrative courts, provided that the claimant has standing, meaning that the interests of the civil servant must be affected.[138]

Conseil d'État, 17 February 1995[139] **3.72 (FR)**

Marie v Director of the Prison of Fleury-Merogis

JUDICIAL REVIEW; MESURES D'ORDRE INTÉRIEUR

Marie

'Mesures d'ordre intérieur' *may be challenged in an action for annulment.*

Facts: The director of a prison imposed on Mr Marie, who was detained in the prison, a conditional sanction of placement in a punishment cell for eight days, on the grounds that he wrote a letter to complain about the medical service of the prison.

Held: The Council of State annulled the decision.

Judgment: Considering that according to the wording of Art. D. 167 of the Code of Criminal Procedure: 'The punishment of a prison cell consists in its placement of the prisoner in a cell equipped for this purpose and which he must occupy alone; its duration cannot exceed forty-five days...'; considering that, Art. D. 167 of the same code provides that 'The placement in the cell as punishment caused during the entire duration of the punishment includes the deprivation of access to the canteen and of visits. It also includes restrictions to the correspondence other than family correspondence...'; considering that in accordance with Art. 721 of the same code, reduced sentences can be accorded to the convicted prisoner during the enforcement of the custodial sentences 'if the prisoners have given sufficient proof of good conduct' and that the reduction granted can be taken back 'in case of bad conduct of the prisoner in detention'; considering that, with regard to the nature and the gravity of this measure, the custodial punishment constitutes a decision which can fall within the jurisdiction of the administrative courts.

Considering that in the terms of Art. D. 262 of the Code of Criminal Procedure, 'the detainees can, at any point in time, address letters to the French administrative and

[138] On standing, see Chapter 4, section 4.4.B.3.
[139] N° 97754.

judicial authorities .... The detainees which would use this possibility which is thereby accorded to them either to bring foward insults, threats or slanderous imputations, or to reiterate unjustified complaints which have already been the object of a decision of a rejection, shall incur a disciplinary sanction without prejudice to a possible criminal sanction'; considering that, to impose on Mr Marie ... a sanction of eight days, with a conditional sentence, in a punishment cell, the director of the Fleury-Mérogis detention centre has based his decision on the letter of 4 June 1987, addressed from the detainee to the head of the general inspection service of social affairs to complain about the functioning of the medical service of the establishment, which was an unjustified complaint; considering that it does not appear from the dossier, and that it is besides not alleged, that this complaint, even if unjustified, has followed previous complaints which have been object of a decision of rejection; considering that, if the Minister of Justice supports that this reclamation contained slanderous imputations, such grief does not appear in the grounds of the challenged decision and moreover, if the letter of Mr Marie ... put forwards points of criticisms within barely measured terms, it contains no outrage, no threats, no imputation which could be qualified as slanderous; considering that, therefore, by taking the challenged decision, the director of the detention centre whose decision has been implicitly confirmed by the regional director of prison services, has based himself on facts which are not of a nature to justify a sanction; considering that, following this and without there having been need to examine the other grounds of the request, the claim of Mr Marie ... for the annulment of those decisions is well founded.

Note

Under French law, measures the object of which is to ensure public order and discipline in the functioning of a service, for both public agents and users of the service, are referred to as *mesures d'ordre intérieur*. They are mainly applicable to the army, prisons and schools. In the past, due to their limited external effects, these measures could not be challenged in an action for annulment. However, under the influence of ECHR, and especially Articles 6 and 13 thereof, the *mesures d'ordre intérieur* are, since the *Marie* case, considered as reviewable if they affect the situation of the individual, for example, in case of a possible breach of a fundamental right.

3.7.B.2 GERMANY

Measures which do not produce immediate external effects cannot qualify as administrative acts in the sense of §35 VwVfG. A type of administrative action which generally lacks external effect is administrative directions (*Verwaltungsvorschriften*). This form of administrative action qualifies as general action regulating 'abstract' cases. Administrative directions are usually given by higher administrative authorities and are directed towards lower administrative authorities. They can either contain stipulations concerning the organisation of administrative organs or provide for specifications on administrative decision-making processes (ie how to interpret a certain rule or how to exercise administrative discretion).

It should be noted that some administrative directions concretise legal provisions (*normkonkretisierende Verwaltungsvorschriften*), which is often the case in environmental law (eg TA Luft[140] and TA Lärm)[141]. These concretising provisions usually have an external effect. At first sight, the German terminology employed seems to be comparable to the Dutch *concretiserende besluiten van algemene strekking*.[142] However, it should be noted that the Dutch category aims to concretise general administrative action regulating 'abstract' cases, so that they apply in a concrete case. Contrary to this, the German 'concretising provisions' still constitute general action regulating 'abstract' cases. Comparable to the German administrative directions concretising legal provisions (*normkonkretisierende Verwaltungsvorschriften*) are the Dutch policy rules (*beleidsregels*) aimed at providing guidance for the interpretation of terms (Article 1:3(4) AWB).

Another type of German administrative action which generally lacks external effect is *Weisungen* (instructions), with which a superior official instructs a subordinate official or a subordinate public authority in how to exercise certain tasks. Instructions 'regulate' cases, which means that they have legal effects, but they do not have external effects.

Bundesverwaltungsgericht, 2 November 1993[143] **3.73 (DE)**

ADMINISTRATIVE DIRECTIONS; PROCEDURE TO REVIEW BY-LAWS AND EXECUTIVE REGULATIONS

An administrative direction can be challenged by means of §47 VwGO before the administrative courts if it produces external effects.

Facts: The standard rates for the social benefit payment were regulated in an administrative direction. The plaintiff alleged that the rates were too low.

Held: The Federal Administrative Court held that the administrative direction was reviewable following the procedure to review by-laws and executive regulations (*Normenkontrollverfahren*).

Judgment: The referring court is correct in stating that administrative directions are not legal provisions in the sense of §47(1) no 2 VwGO if they only bind and govern the conduct of subordinate administrative authorities. In these cases the provisions lack the characteristic external legal effect of a legal rule. It can be left open whether the distinction between executive regulations (having external legal effects) (*Rechtsverordnungen*) and administrative directions (having internal legal effects) (*Verwaltungsvorschriften*) shall be maintained. Even if this understanding – as the referring court holds – underlies §47(1) no 2 VwGO, this does not preclude but rather suggests that the term 'legal provision' in §47(1) no 2 VwGO also includes administrative directions which exceptionally have external legal effects…

[140] Technische Anleitung zur Reinhaltung der Luft, 24.07.2002, GMBl 511.
[141] Technische Anleitung zum Schutz gegen Lärm, 26.08.1998, GMBl 503.
[142] See above, section 3.3.A.1 (iii).
[143] BVerwGE 94, 335.

Note

As a general rule, administrative directions (*Verwaltungsvorschriften*) cannot be challenged before the administrative courts. In principle, this type of administrative action cannot qualify as a 'legal rule' under §47(1), no 2 VwGO.[144] However, as far as the states (*Länder*) have made use of the possibility of §47(1), no 2 VwGO to grant access to courts with regard to abstract general measures,[145] the question arises whether administrative directions can also, under certain circumstances, qualify as 'legal rule'. According to the Federal Administrative Court, that is the case if these directions exceptionally create external effects due to administrative practice in relation to individuals. In such exceptional cases, these directions can be challenged by way of analogical application of §47 VwGO. For example, if the administrative direction regulates how to grant a certain social benefit, individuals might have a right to the benefit based on the administrative direction and the right to equal treatment (provided in Article 3(1) of the Grundgesetz). This forms the basis for the possibility of judicial review.

3.7.B.3 THE NETHERLANDS

Algemene Wet Bestuursrecht **3.74 (NL)**

Article 1:3 (1) The meaning of a decision (*besluit*) is: a written decision by an administrative authority containing a legal act under public law.

Note

A decision as defined in Article 1:3(1) AWB (*besluit*) always creates legal consequences with an external effect. This means that decisions (*beslissingen*) which do not have any external effect cannot qualify as decisions as defined in Article 1:3(1) AWB. Consequently, they cannot be challenged before the administrative courts. However, it should be noted that, when compared with the German system, this type of administrative action is more narrowly defined, since in the Netherlands policy rules (*beleidsregels*) are considered to have external effect and are considered to be decisions as defined in Article 1:3 AWB (Article 1:3(4) AWB).

Legislative Records to the AWB[146] **3.75 (NL)**

Decisions (*beslissingen*) of a organ which have a purely internal character, such as the determination of priority treatment of a certain case, directions on drawing up certain files or similar examples, are no decisions (*besluiten*) in the sense of this law.

[144] P Unruh, in M Fehling, B Kastner and R Störmer (eds), *Verwaltungsrecht*, 4th edn (Baden-Baden, Nomos, 2016) §47 VwGO, 41.

[145] See above, section 3.3.B.2 (i).

[146] TK (1988–1989) 21 221, nr 3, 38–39, PG AWB I, 38.

Note

In the Netherlands, administrative action which determines the organisational structure of an administrative body and which allocates specific tasks to specific units is a purely internal measure with no external effects, so that no review before the administrative courts (or before the civil courts) is possible. In general terms, administrative action which guides civil servants in interpreting the terminology used in a specific statute will qualify as guidance (*richtlijn*), which has no external effects and which will not be challengeable in the administrative courts. However, if an administrative authority publishes a guidance document which defines how it wants to apply the provision in question in the future, then this is a policy rule (*beleidsregel*),[147] which qualifies as a decision as defined in Article 1:3 AWB. This cannot be challenged directly (pursuant to Article 8:3(1)(a)), but can be reviewed indirectly (through *exceptieve toetsing*) before the administrative courts.[148]

3.7.B.4 THE EUROPEAN UNION

In the EU legal system, there are various types of measures which are intended to have primarily internal effects. Through these measures, the EU administration can be informed about how to interpret a certain provision of EU law or how to exercise its discretion. This kind of action comes in many forms, such as guidelines, notices, communications and declarations.[149]

Internal instructions and guidelines have in general not been held capable of producing legal effects, hence judicial review in actions for annulment has been considered unavailable.[150]

Case C-189/02 P, 28 June 2005[151] **3.76 (EU)**

Dansk Rørindustri and others v Commission

GUIDANCE DOCUMENTS; ACTION FOR ANNULMENT

Dansk Rørindustri

Actions for annulment against guidance documents are admissible if the document produces external effects.

Facts: The claimants were companies producing pre-insulated pipes for the heating sector. On 21 October 1998, the Commission adopted a decision stating that those undertakings had been involved in a series of

[147] See above, section 3.3.B.II (ii).

[148] See further Chapter 7, section 7.7.E.

[149] For an overview, see Hofmann et al (n 60 above) ch 16.

[150] Case 151/88 *Italy v Commission* ECLI:EU:C:1989:201; Case C-308/95 *Netherlands v Commission* ECLI:EU:C:1999:477, paras 27–29; Case C-163/06 P *Finland v Commission* ECLI:EU:C:2007:371, paras 40–41.

[151] ECLI:EU:C:2005:408.

agreements and concerted practices in breach of EU competition law and imposed fines on them. The fines were calculated by the Commission on the basis of the 'Guidelines on the method of setting fines imposed pursuant to Article 15(2) of Regulation No 17 and Article 65 of the ECSC Treaty'. Eight of the ten undertakings fined by this decision brought actions for annulment of that decision in whole or in part, and for an annulment of or a reduction in the fine imposed on them. Their action was partly based on a challenge of the validity of the underlying guidelines and their application.

Held: The Court of Justice dismissed the appeal.

Judgment: The Court has already held, in a judgment concerning internal measures adopted by the administration, that although those measures may not be regarded as rules of law which the administration is always bound to observe, they nevertheless form rules of practice from which the administration may not depart in an individual case without giving reasons that are compatible with the principle of equal treatment. Such measures therefore constitute a general act and the officials and other staff concerned may invoke their illegality in support of an action against the individual measures taken on the basis of the measures (see Case C-171/00 P *Libéros v Commission* [2002] ECR I-451, paragraph 35).

That case-law applies a fortiori to rules of conduct designed to produce external effects, as is the case of the Guidelines, which are aimed at traders.

In adopting such rules of conduct and announcing by publishing them that they will henceforth apply to the cases to which they relate, the institution in question imposes a limit on the exercise of its discretion and cannot depart from those rules under pain of being found, where appropriate, to be in breach of the general principles of law, such as equal treatment or the protection of legitimate expectations. It cannot therefore be precluded that, on certain conditions and depending on their content, such rules of conduct, which are of general application, may produce legal effects.

Note

This excerpt shows that judicial review of internal measures has been considered possible when the Court of Justice has determined that the guideline concerned produces external legal effects.

3.7.C COMPARATIVE REMARKS

All legal systems under consideration classify certain types of administrative action as internal measures, although in England this is not an express categorisation.

In Germany, administrative directions (*Verwaltungsvorschriften*) and instructions (*Weisungen*) are internal measures which, in principle, cannot be challenged directly in the administrative courts. In the Netherlands, the only types of action that are considered to be internal are *beslissingen*. Policy rules (*beleidregels*) are nowadays considered to have external effects and qualify as decisions as defined in Article 1:3 AWB (*besluit*). This does not, however, mean that they are directly challengeable before the administrative courts. Thus, the category of 'internal measures' in the Netherlands has a smaller scope of application than the category of internal measures in Germany. In France, internal measures are measures that do not produce external legal consequences, and, as in

Germany, in principle, they cannot be challenged before the administrative courts. Comparable to the national legal systems, internal measures can also only be reviewed by the courts in the EU legal system if they produce external legal effects.

FURTHER READING

Athanasiadou, N, *Der Verwaltungsvertrag im EU-Recht* (Tübingen, Mohr Siebeck, 2017).

Glaser, A, *Die Entwicklung des Europäischen Rechts aus der Perspektive der Handlungsformenlehre* (Tübingen, Mohr Siebeck, 2013).

Jansen, O, 'Silence of the Administration: General Comments and Dutch Law' in JB Auby (ed), *Droit comparé de la procédure administrative/Comparative Law of Administrative Procedure* (Brussels, Bruylant, 2016) 623–46.

Noguellou, R and Stelkens, U, *Droit comparé des contrats publics* (Brussels, Bruylant, 2010).

Pünder, H, 'Democratic Legitimation of Delegated Legislation – a Comparative View on the American, British and German Law' (2009) 58 *International Law Review Quarterly* 353.

CHAPTER 4
ACCESS TO COURT

Chris Backes

4.1 INTRODUCTION

A sufficiently broad access to courts or other independent and impartial bodies is one of the essential elements to guaranteeing effective judicial protection.

Access to court comprises all elements which are decisive for the question whether one can take part in judicial proceedings, such as the capacity to institute proceedings, the duty to have legal representation, standing requirements, costs and a number of other aspects. This chapter analyses, from a comparative perspective, all these aspects of access to court as well as the influence of European and international law on these issues.

4.1.A DOMESTIC GUARANTEES FOR ACCESS TO COURT

Rules on access to court can be contained in a variety of documents. As far as the European Union is concerned, the rules are found, to a considerable extent, in the Treaty on the Functioning of the European Union (TFEU) itself. In most national legal systems, rules on access to court are laid down in statutory law or are developed in case law. In some legal systems, the constitution provides an explicit legal basis for a right of access to courts. This is the case, for example, in Germany (Article 19(4) of the Grundgesetz) or in the Netherlands (Article 112(1) of the Grondwet), as it was interpreted by the Dutch Supreme Court (Hoge Raad) in the landmark case of *Guldemond/Noordwijkerhout*.[1] In France, the Council of State (Conseil d'État) recognised the right of access to court, as in the *Dame Lamotte* case,[2] and decided that, by virtue of a general principle of French law, any administrative decision may be subject to judicial review.[3] Moreover, the Constitutional Council considered access to court to be a fundamental right, based on Article 16 of the Declaration of Rights of the Man and of the Citizen of 1789 (Déclaration des droits de l'homme et du citoyen), even if access was not explicitly provided in any constitutional provision. In the European legal system, Article 19 of the Treaty on European Union (TEU) and Article 47 of the EU Charter of Fundamental Rights can be regarded as codifications of the principle of 'effective judicial protection before a court' and therefore guarantee access to a court. In England and Wales access to court is not guaranteed in constitutional norms, but only in statutory law.[4] If the rules are to be found in treaties or constitutions, changing them is more difficult and the rules become less flexible.

4.1.B REQUIREMENTS OF ACCESS TO COURT STEMMING FROM INTERNATIONAL LAW

There are some sources of international law which also compel the parties of the respective treaties to ensure access to court within the scope of the treaties. The most important

[1] See further Chapter 1, excerpt 1.23.
[2] Conseil d'État, 17 February 1950, N° 86949.
[3] See further Chapter 3, section 4.1.A.2.
[4] See further Chapter 1, section 1.4.

provision is Article 6 of the European Convention on Human Rights (ECHR), to which all legal systems discussed in this book are bound.[5]

European Convention on Human Rights **4.1 (COE)**

Article 6 (1) 1n the determination of his civil rights and obligations or of any criminal charge against him, everyone is entitled to a fair and public hearing within a reasonable time by an independent and impartial tribunal established by law. Judgment shall be pronounced publicly but the press and public may be excluded from all or part of the trial in the interests of morals, public order or national security in a democratic society, where the interests of juveniles or the protection of the private life of the parties so require, or to the extent strictly necessary in the opinion of the court in special circumstances where publicity would prejudice the interests of justice.

...

(3) Everyone charged with a criminal offence has the following minimum rights:

(a) to be informed promptly, in a language which he understands and in detail, of the nature and cause of the accusation against him;

(b) to have adequate time and facilities for the preparation of his defence;

(c) to defend himself in person or through legal assistance of his own choosing or, if he has not sufficient means to pay for legal assistance, to be given it free when the interests of justice so require;

(d) to examine or have examined witnesses against him and to obtain the attendance and examination of witnesses on his behalf under the same conditions as witnesses against him;

(e) to have the free assistance of an interpreter if he cannot understand or speak the language used in court.

Notes

(1) Whilst the letter of Article 6(1) ECHR does not immediately indicate so, this provision has a fundamental influence on the availability and conditions of access to court in many administrative law cases. For example, all administrative action restricting property rights determine 'civil rights' in the sense of Article 6(1) ECHR and therefore fall within the scope of its guarantee of access to an independent and impartial judge. As most permits and other similar administrative decisions fall within the broad interpretation of 'possession' by the European Court of Human Rights, such decisions also fall within the scope of Article 6 (1) ECHR.[6] This provision and the case law based thereon not only guarantee access, but also set further criteria for the quality of access to justice, such as the requirement of timeliness.

(2) Article 6(3) ECHR applies primarily to criminal law cases. However, as administrative sanctions, especially administrative fines, can also be qualified as 'criminal

[5] Germany, France, the UK and the Netherlands are party to the ECHR; the European Union is bound through Art 6 TEU.

[6] See, eg *Tre Traktorer Aktiebolag v Sweden* ECLI:CE:ECHR:1989:0707JUD001087384; *Pine Valley Developments Ltd v Ireland* ECLI:CE:ECHR:1991:1129JUD001274287.

charge' under certain circumstances,[7] this provision also influences access to justice in national legal systems in some administrative law cases.

UNECE Convention on Access to Information, Public Participation in Decision-making and Access to Justice in Environmental Matters (Aarhus Convention) **4.2 (UN)**

Article 9 (1) Each Party shall, within the framework of its national legislation, ensure that any person who considers that his or her request for information under article 4 has been ignored, wrongfully refused, whether in part or in full, inadequately answered, or otherwise not dealt with in accordance with the provisions of that article, has access to a review procedure before a court of law or another independent and impartial body established by law.

In the circumstances where a Party provides for such a review by a court of law, it shall ensure that such a person also has access to an expeditious procedure established by law that is free of charge or inexpensive for reconsideration by a public authority or review by an independent and impartial body other than a court of law. Final decisions under this paragraph 1 shall be binding on the public authority holding the information. Reasons shall be stated in writing, at least where access to information is refused under this paragraph.

(2) Each Party shall, within the framework of its national legislation, ensure that members of the public concerned

(a) Having a sufficient interest or, alternatively,

(b) Maintaining impairment of a right, where the administrative procedural law of a Party requires this as a precondition,

have access to a review procedure before a court of law and/or another independent and impartial body established by law, to challenge the substantive and procedural legality of any decision, act or omission subject to the provisions of article 6 and, where so provided for under national law and without prejudice to paragraph 3 below, of other relevant provisions of this Convention.

What constitutes a sufficient interest and impairment of a right shall be determined in accordance with the requirements of national law and consistently with the objective of giving the public concerned wide access to justice within the scope of this Convention. To this end, the interest of any non-governmental organization meeting the requirements referred to in article 2, paragraph 5, shall be deemed sufficient for the purpose of subparagraph (a) above. Such organizations shall also be deemed to have rights capable of being impaired for the purpose of subparagraph (b) above.

(3) In addition and without prejudice to the review procedures referred to in paragraphs 1 and 2 above, each Party shall ensure that, where they meet the criteria, if any, laid down in its national law, members of the public have access to administrative or judicial procedures to challenge acts and omissions by private persons and public authorities which contravene provisions of its national law relating to the environment.

(4) In addition and without prejudice to paragraph 1 above, the procedures referred to in paragraphs 1, 2 and 3 above shall provide adequate and effective remedies, including injunctive relief as appropriate, and be fair, equitable, timely and not prohibitively expensive. Decisions under this article shall be given or recorded in writing. Decisions of courts, and whenever possible of other bodies, shall be publicly accessible.

(5) In order to further the effectiveness of the provisions of this article, each Party shall ensure that information is provided to the public on access to administrative and judicial

[7] See *Öztürk v Germany* ECLI:CE:ECHR:1984:1023JUD000854479.

review procedures and shall consider the establishment of appropriate assistance mechanisms to remove or reduce financial and other barriers to access to justice.

Note

In addition to Article 6 ECHR, there are some other international treaties, with a more limited and special scope, which set conditions for access to justice within the scope of the treaty. The most well known example is the 'third pillar' of the UNECE Convention on Access to Information, Public Participation in Decision-making and Access to Justice in Environmental Matters (the 'Aarhus Convention'), which applies only to environmental decision-making.

4.2 CAPACITY TO INSTITUTE PROCEEDINGS

The question of who has legal capacity is determined by national law. In most legal systems, natural persons who are 18 years or older and legal persons generally have legal capacity and hence are able to institute proceedings.[8] The issue becomes more diverse and disputed in respect of persons who do not have legal capacity. These may be natural persons under the age of 18 or entities without legal personality. Should these groups of claimants be admitted at court and, if so, under what circumstances?

4.2.A PRAGMATIC APPROACH

4.2.A.1 THE EUROPEAN UNION

Case 175/73, 8 October 1974[9] **4.3 (EU)**

Union Syndicale – Amalgamated European Public Service Union – Brussels, Denise Massa and Roswitha Kortner v Council

CAPACITY TO INSTITUTE PROCEEDINGS

Union Syndicale

The capacity to institute proceedings is recognised according to whether a person or entity is in a position to act as a 'responsible body' in legal matters.

Facts: The European Commission decided to arrange for a deduction to be made from the salaries of officials and other servants who took part in a strike. The Amalgamated European Public Service Union brought an action for annulment against this decision. The Commission raised a plea of inadmissibility.

Held: Although the claimant had the capacity to institute proceedings, the application was ultimately dismissed as inadmissible.

Judgment: 10 The applicant union is an association organizing a substantial number of officials and servants of the Community institutions and component bodies established in Brussels and there is no reason to doubt its representative character.

8 See, eg §104, 106 Bürgerliches Gesetzbuch; Art. 1:234 Burgerlijk Wetboek.

9 ECLI:EU:C:1974:95.

11 Under its rules, its constitutional structure is such as to endow it with the necessary independence to act as a responsible body in legal matters.

12 The Community institutions officially recognize it as a negotiating body on questions involving the collective interests of the staff.

13 It is therefore impossible to deny the applicant union's capacity to institute proceedings.

Note

The EU system takes a pragmatic approach. On a case-by-case basis, it is decided whether a person or entity is in a position to act as a 'responsible body' in legal matters. Entities without legal personality may, on this basis, be admitted to bring actions before the EU courts.

4.2.A.2 THE NETHERLANDS

Raad van State, 24 August 2011[10] **4.4 (NL)**

Stichting in oprichting Zorg om Duizel and X v Municipality of Eersel

CAPACITY TO INSTITUTE PROCEEDINGS; TRUST IN THE MAKING

Stichting in oprichting Zorg om Duizel

The ability to act as a 'person concerned' in the sense of Article 1:2(1) Algemene Wet Bestuursrecht (AWB) is not reserved to natural and legal persons, but may also include other entities identifiable in legal relations.

Facts: A claim against a land use plan was brought by a trust in the making which had not yet obtained legal personality.

Held: Although the claimant had the capacity to institute proceedings, the claim was ultimately declared inadmissible.

Judgment: 2.3 The ability to act as a 'person concerned' in the sense of Article 1:2(1) AWB is not reserved to natural and legal persons. Other entities may also be regarded as a 'person concerned'. Taking the wording of 'the one who' defined in Article 1:2(1) AWB into account, such entities have to be identifiable in legal relations.

As it was obvious in this case by whom and with which aim Zorg om Duizel would be established and who would be part of the board of this entity, the requirement of identifiability is, to the opinion of the Judicial Division, fulfilled.

[10] ECLI:NL:RVS:2011:BR5686.

Note

Similar to the approach in the EU legal system, Dutch courts do not require legal personality for a claimant to have capacity to institute proceedings. Natural persons who do not have legal capacity may have access to court if they are expected to be able to look after their own interests. Other entities without legal personality may also have access to court, as the excerpt above demonstrates.

4.2.A.3 ENGLAND AND WALES

High Court (Queen's Bench Division), 30 November 1999[11] **4.5 (EW)**

R v Ministry of Agriculture Fisheries & Food, ex parte British Pig Industry Support Group and Meryl Suzanne Ward

CAPACITY TO INSTITUTE PROCEEDINGS; LEGAL PERSONALITY

British Pig Industry Support Group

Legal personality is not required to start judicial review proceedings.

Facts: A group claimed judicial review of what they felt to be a discriminatory policy of the central government which had granted greater financial aid to the sheep and cattle farming industry than it had to those who farmed pigs.

Held: The application for judicial review was dismissed.

Judgment: Richards J.: I do not think that there is any overriding requirement for an applicant for judicial review to have legal personality, but it is important in such a case that adequate provision should be made for the protection of the respondent in costs.

Note

In England and Wales, the approach is also relatively flexible, and decisions are taken on a case-by-case basis. Legal capacity is not required. If for example a child or other natural parties without full legal capacity want to act in court, courts make use of the powers in Part 21 of the Civil Procedure Rules (CPR) and usually, but not always, appoint a 'litigation friend'. With regard to unincorporated associations lacking legal personality, the case law of the courts of England and Wales has not in the past always been consistent; sometimes their claims were declared admissible, and sometimes they were not.[12] The more recent case law, such as the case outlined above, has moved towards a pragmatic question: can it be assured that someone can be held liable for the costs of the other party if the association loses the case?

[11] [2000] Eu LR 724 (QB).

[12] See, eg *R* v *North Western Traffic Commissioners, ex parte Brake* [1996] COD 248 (QB).

4.2.A.4 FRANCE

Conseil d'État, 10 June 1959[13] **4.6 (FR)**

Dame Poujol v Prefect of Gironde

CAPACITY TO INSTITUTE PROCEEDINGS; MENTALLY ILL PERSON

Dame Poujol

A mentally ill person has the capacity to institute proceedings personally to challenge the decision ordering her detention in a psychiatric hospital.

Facts: A person wishing to challenge before the Council of State the decision to detain her in a psychiatric hospital was denied access to court because she was not represented by a legal guardian, which was required under civil law.

Held: Whereas the court considered that Mrs Pujol could be granted access to court without being represented by a guardian, the court confirmed the legality of the decision of the prefect ordering her detention in a psychiatric hospital.

Judgment: Considering, on the other hand, that if, pursuant to Article 33 of the law of 30 June 1838, the Administrative Court of First Instance, upon request of the provisional administrator [person responsible for the affairs of the claimant during her detention] or by decision of the public prosecutor (procureur de la République), must designate a special representative in order to represent before the court every individual not having been deprived of his legal capacity and having been placed in a hospital for mentally ill people, who would be engaged in a legal dispute at the time of the placement in the hospital or against which an action would be initiated subsequently and if, according to the same provision, the court can, in case of urgency, designate itself a representative in order to introduce, on behalf of the aforementioned individuals, an action, this provision is not applicable when the action is introduced against the decision ordering to detain the individual concerned;

Considering that such action, which involves the fundamental principle of individual freedom, would – in the absence of an express legislative provision in that sense – be restricted at the expense of the individual who is affected by a measure of confinement and intends to invoke its illegality in order to have this measure declared void and regain the liberty of which he claims to have been deprived under irregular conditions; considering that it results therefrom that the inmate is qualified to personally introduce an action for annulment (*recours pours excès de pouvoir*) against the decision of the prefect ordering his placement in a psychiatric establishment …

Note

In France, the requirements for the capacity to bring an action for annulment are quite minimal. The Council of State in general follows the rules of the Code civil on legal capacity. Persons without legal capacity can only institute proceedings if they are

[13] N° 42760.

represented by a legal guardian. However, as *Dame Poujol* shows, a person deprived of legal capacity may act on his own in order to challenge the decision which deprived him of legal capacity.

Conseil d'État, 21 December 1906[14] **4.7 (FR)**

Syndicat des propriétaires du quartier Croix-de-Seguey-Tivoli v Prefect of Gironde

CAPACITY TO INSTITUTE PROCEEDINGS; LEGAL PERSON

Syndicat des propriétaires du quartier Croix-de-Seguey-Tivoli

An association constituted in compliance with the relevant legal requirements to defend the interests of a certain geographical area has the capacity to institute proceedings.

Facts: A tramway company in Bordeaux decided to close the route it had been operating towards an area of the city named Croix-de-Seguey-Tivoli. An association, constituted for the defence of the interests of that area, asked the prefect to order the company to fulfil the requirements of the contract (related to the provision of the public service of transportation on the route) concluded between the city and the company. It challenged the refusal of the prefect before the Council of State.

Held: The action of the association was considered admissible. However, the action was rejected since the decision of the prefect was considered as providing sufficient reasons.

Judgment: On the inadmissibility of the claimant's claim due to the fact it would not be considered as an association capable to bring legal action; considering that the union of owners and taxpayers of the district Croix-de-Seguey-Tivoli (syndicat des propriétaires et contribuables du quartier de la Croix-de-Seguey-Tivoli) is constituted with the purpose to defend the interests of this area, to promote all improvements of the roadway, sanitation and embellishment; considering that those matters can justify the establishment of an association in line with the wording of Article 1 of the law of 1 July 1901; considering also that the claimant association which has complied with the requirements of Article 5 and following of the law of 1 July 1901, has the capacity to institute proceedings …

Note

Under French law, groups can go to the administrative courts only if they have legal personality. The only exception to this general rule is for associations, which can bring an action for annulment (*recours pour excès de pouvoir*) even if the association has only recently been established and has not yet achieved legal personality. Hence, French law seems to be somewhat stricter than, for example, Dutch law, as legal personality is generally required. On the other hand, as will be seen hereafter, it is more lenient than German law, as exceptions are made to this rule in case law.

[14] N° 19167.

4.2.B FORMAL APPROACH: GERMANY

Verwaltungsgerichtsordnung **4.8 (DE)**

§61 The following shall be able to take part in the proceedings
1. natural persons and legal persons,
2. associations insofar as they can be entitled to a right,
3. authorities insofar as state law thus provides.

§62 (1) The following shall be able to undertake procedural acts
1. persons who are capable of contracting in accordance with civil law,
2. persons who are restricted in their legal capacity in accordance with civil law insofar as they are recognised by provisions of civil or public law as being capable of entering into a valid contract in relation to the subject-matter of the proceedings.

Note

The German system differentiates between the capacity to take part in the proceedings (eg as a claimant or defendant or only as a co-summoned person) (*Beteiligtenfähigkeit*) and the capacity to undertake procedural acts (eg to file a claim, lodge a statement, etc) (*Prozessfähigkeit*). According to §61 of the Verwaltungsgerichtsordnung (VwGO), all natural persons, legal persons and associations are able to take part in proceedings. That means that an infant can also formally be a claimant or a defendant in court proceedings. In order to effect procedural acts, however, according to §62 VwGO, a person who is capable of contracting according to civil law is needed. This means that legal personality is not required to take part in the proceedings, but it is a requirement in order to be able to effect procedural acts.

4.2.C COMPARATIVE REMARKS

As a general rule, everyone who has legal capacity can bring a claim to and act in court. This point of departure is not explicitly mentioned and not much discussed in the legal systems under study. Nevertheless, a more formal and strict approach (Germany) and a more lenient and pragmatic approach (the EU, England and Wales, the Netherlands, France) can be identified with regard to natural persons without legal capacity and legal persons without legal personality.

4.3 DUTY TO HAVE LEGAL REPRESENTATION

Legal systems can require claimants to be represented by a lawyer when bringing a case to court. In general terms, there are two reasons for such a rule. First, a lawyer may be required to ensure a certain quality of discussion before the court. Secondly, legal representation may be required to protect private parties against the legal power of the public authorities and to strive for a certain balance of powers in the court proceedings.

4.3.A NO LEGAL REPRESENTATION REQUIRED BEFORE ADMINISTRATIVE COURTS

4.3.A.1 THE NETHERLANDS

In the Netherlands, the rules on the requirement of legal representation vary considerably. There is no such requirement before the administrative courts, either in first instance or in appeal. The rationale for the adoption of this approach is the underlying assumption that the court itself would, to a certain extent, be able to compensate an inequality of arms, if necessary. However, it is questionable whether this is (still) true, as the procedural law has become more adversarial and the active role of the judge has decreased.[15] If a civil court hears disputes regarding administrative issues,[16] the position is different. At civil courts, representation by a qualified lawyer is required in most cases, according to Article 79 of the Code of Civil Procedure (Wetboek burgerlijke rechtsvordering).

4.3.A.2 ENGLAND AND WALES

In England and Wales, legal representation is not required before courts which hear judicial review claims, including the Supreme Court, and is not generally expected before tribunals. It is possible for those who appear in person without legal representation to have someone to assist them in the proceedings.[17]

4.3.B NO NEED FOR LEGAL REPRESENTATION ONLY BEFORE FIRST INSTANCE COURTS: GERMANY

Verwaltungsgerichtsordnung **4.9 (DE)**

§67 (1) Those concerned may themselves pursue the dispute before the Administrative Court of First Instance.

(2) Those concerned may seek representation as a proxy-holder by an attorney or a law teacher at a state or state-recognised institution of higher education of a Member State of the European Union, of another Contracting Party to the Agreement on the European Economic Area or Switzerland who has qualification for judicial office. ...

(3) ...

(4) Those concerned must be represented before the Federal Administrative Court and the Higher Administrative Court by an authorised legal representative, apart from in legal aid proceedings. This shall also apply to procedural acts by means of which proceedings are initiated before the Federal Administrative Court or a Higher Administrative Court.

[15] For more detail, see Chapter 5, section 5.3.B.1.

[16] These can be cases of claims for damages against the administrative authorities (see Chapter 11, section 11.2.B.2) or cases concerning factual conduct and some administrative action of general scope (see Chapter 3, sections 3.3.B.2 (ii) and 3.4.B.1).

[17] The most famous case here is *McKenzie v McKenzie* [1970] 3 WLR 472 (QB). This case suggested that in order for there to be a degree of equality between the parties where one party did not have legal representation, it would be necessary for the court to allow an assistant to be present (now known as 'a McKenzie friend').

Note

In Germany, the need to be represented by a lawyer mainly depends on the question of whether the case is pending before an Administrative Court of First Instance, a Higher Administrative Court or the Federal Administrative Court. No representation is required for cases which are dealt with by the Administrative Courts of First Instance, pursuant to §67(1) VwGO. On the contrary, according to §67(4) VwGO, legal representation is required in proceedings before the Higher Administrative Courts and the Federal Administrative Court.

4.3.C NEED FOR LEGAL REPRESENTATION DEPENDING ON INSTANCE AND ON KIND OF PROCEDURE: FRANCE

In France, a lawyer is not compulsory for an action for annulment (*recours pour excès de pouvoir*) at the Administrative Court of First Instance.

Code de justice administrative **4.10 (FR)**

Article R431-2 In order to be admissible, applications and pleadings must be presented either by a lawyer, or by a lawyer authorised to appear before the Council of State and the Court of Cassation, when the submissions relating to the application seek the payment of a sum of money, the discharge or reduction of sums requested from the claimant, or the settlement of a dispute that has arisen from a contract.

Note

In an action on the ground of liability or concerning the duties deriving from a contract, namely a 'full jurisdiction remedy' (*recours de pleine juridiction*), unlike the action for annulment (*recours pour excès de pouvoir*), legal representation is always needed. Article R431-2 of the Code de justice administrative only applies to courts which act as courts of first instance. The need for legal representation before the Administrative Courts of Appeal is governed by Article R811-7 of the Code de justice administrative, and the need for legal representation in appeal or higher appeal before the Council of State is governed by Article R432-1 of the Code de justice administrative.

Code de justice administrative **4.11 (FR)**

Article R811-7 Subject to the provisions of Article L774-8, in order to be admissible, applications and pleadings filed before the Administrative Court of Appeal must be submitted by one of the agents mentioned in Article R431-2.

When the notification of the decision submitted to the Administrative Court of Appeal does not contain the reference provided for under the second section of Article R751-5, the claimant is invited by the court to rectify his application according to the conditions set out in Article R612-1.

Application seeking the enforcement of a decision rendered by an Administrative Court of Appeal or a judgment rendered by an Administrative Court of First Instance located in the judicial district of the court of appeal and appealed before that court, may also be brought without the intervention of a lawyer.

Article R432-1 In order to be admissible, applications and the pleadings of the parties must be presented by a lawyer authorized to appear before the Council of State (Conseil d'État). …

Note

In proceedings before the Administrative Courts of Appeal, a lawyer is required in case of action for annulment, except when an application is lodged before the Administrative Court of Appeal in the first instance.[18] In addition, a specialised lawyer is required in proceedings before the Council of State. These are lawyers registered on a specific list, kept by the Ministry of Justice. If the Council of State has jurisdiction in both the first and final instance, no lawyer is required.

4.3.D LEGAL REPRESENTATION ALWAYS REQUIRED: THE EUROPEAN UNION

Statute of the Court of Justice of the European Union **4.12 (EU)**

Article 19 The Member States and the institutions of the Union shall be represented before the Court of Justice by an agent appointed for each case; the agent may be assisted by an adviser or by a lawyer.

…

Other parties must be represented by a lawyer.

Note

According to Article 19 of the Statute of the CJEU, legal representation is required in all procedures before the European courts except where the procedure is a request for legal aid.[19]

4.3.E COMPARATIVE REMARKS

The main reason for requiring legal representation in the French, German and EU legal systems seems to be the aim of ensuring a certain legal quality of the proceedings in court, which presumably facilitates a better administration of justice. The strictest requirements are in place before the European courts.

18 Code de justice administrative, Art R431-11.

19 Another exception is the preliminary ruling procedure, for which legal representation is required only if the procedural rules of the Member States' courts require such representation.

4.4 STANDING

4.4.A INTRODUCTION

In both EU and national law, the requirements for standing are a tool to regulate access to court and are frequently the subject of vigorous debate.[20] All legal systems apply rules and principles which determine the standing requirements in general. In addition to the general rules, more specific rules are imposed in some areas of law, such as environmental law, or with regard to particular kinds of actions.

Whether a claimant has standing is usually checked at the admissibility stage of a claim, hence without dealing with the merits of the case. However, there may be exceptions to this in some legal systems.

House of Lords, 9 April 1981[21] **4.13 (EW)**

R v Inland Revenue Commissioners, ex parte National Federation of Self Employed and Small Businesses Ltd

STANDING; SUFFICIENT INTEREST; CONTROL AT PERMISSION STAGE

National Federation of Small Businesses

Courts may need to consider the question of standing in the full legal and factual context of a case, rather than as a preliminary matter to be assessed at the permission stage.

Facts: Upon discovering that a large number of workers in the newspaper printing industry (known as the 'Fleet Street Casuals') had been involved in tax evasion for a number of years, the Inland Revenue Commissioners determined that they would introduce a special scheme whereby if the workers concerned identified themselves they would not face liability for the full amount of unpaid tax. The claimant was a representative federation that wished to challenge the lawfulness of the Inland Revenue's approach.

Held: In light of the overall merits of the case, the claimant did not have standing to challenge the lawfulness of the Inland Revenue's approach.

Judgment: ... Lord Diplock: The procedure under the new Order 53 involves two stages: (1) the application for leave to apply for judicial review, and (2) if leave is granted, the hearing of the application itself. The former, or 'threshold', stage is regulated by rule 3. The application for leave to apply for judicial review is made initially ex pane, but may be adjourned for the persons or bodies against whom relief is sought to be represented. This did not happen in the instant case. Rule 3(5) specifically requires the court to consider at this stage whether 'it considers that "the applicant has a sufficient interest in the matter" to which the application "relates"'. So this is a 'threshold' question in the sense that the

[20] For a comparative overview see, eg M Eliantonio, CW Backes, CH Rhee, TNBM Spronken and A Berlee, *Standing Up for Your Right(s) in Europe – a Comparative Study on Legal Standing (Locus Standi) before the EU and Member States' Courts* (Antwerp, Intersentia, 2013); also available at www.europarl.europa.eu/committees/en/studiesdownload.html?languageDocument=EN&file=75651.

[21] [1982] AC 617 (HL).

court must direct its mind to it and form a prima facie view about it upon the material that is available at the first stage. The prima facie view so formed, if favourable to the applicant, may alter on further consideration in the light of further evidence than may be before the court at the second stage, the hearing of the application for judicial review itself.

...

My Lords, at the threshold stage, for the Federation to make out a prima facie case of reasonable suspicion that the Board in showing a discriminatory leniency to a substantial class of taxpayers had done so for ulterior reasons extraneous to good management, and thereby deprived the national exchequer of considerable sums of money, constituted what was in my view reason enough for the Divisional Court to consider that the Federation or, for that matter, any taxpayer, had a sufficient interest to apply to have the question whether the Board was acting ultra vires reviewed by the court. The whole purpose of requiring that leave should first be obtained to make the application for judicial review would be defeated if the court were to go into the matter in any depth at that stage. If, on a quick perusal of the material then available, the court thinks that it discloses what might on further consideration turn out to be an arguable case in favour of granting to the applicant the relief claimed, it ought, in the exercise of a judicial discretion, to give him leave to apply for that relief. The discretion that the court is exercising at this stage is not the same as that which it is called upon to exercise when all the evidence is in and the matter has been fully argued at the hearing of the application.

Lord Wilberforce: ... I think that it is unfortunate that this course has been taken. There may be simple cases in which it can be seen at the earliest stage that the person applying for judicial review has no interest at all, or no sufficient interest to support the application: then it would be quite correct at the threshold to refuse him leave to apply. The right to do so is an important safeguard against the courts being flooded and public bodies harassed by irresponsible applications. But in other cases, this will not be so. In these it will be necessary to consider the powers or the duties in law of those against whom the relief is asked, the position of the applicant in relation to those powers or duties, and to the breach of those said to have been committed. In other words, the question of sufficient interest cannot, in such cases, be considered in the abstract, or as an isolated point: it must be taken together with the legal and factual context. The rule requires sufficient interest in the matter to which the application relates. This, in the present case, necessarily involves the whole question of the duties of the Inland Revenue and the breaches or failure of those duties of which the respondents complain.

...

Note

In the *National Federation of Small Businesses* case, Lord Wilberforce noted that it would not always be appropriate to make a determination over the issue of standing before the substantive merits of the case are considered. Courts in England and Wales sometimes feel the need to look at the substance of the claim in order to determine whether the claimant has a sufficient interest and hence *locus standi* for the purposes of obtaining one or other remedy.

Raad van State, 12 November 2014[22]

4.14 (NL)

Stichting Pietengilde and others v Mayor of Amsterdam

STANDING; GENERAL SOCIETAL INTERESTS

Zwarte Piet

Courts can take the general societal interest of the case into account when they determine the of a Santa Claus event which was planned for admissibility of a claim.

Facts: In his decision of 13 August 2013, the mayor of Amsterdam gave permission for the yearly parade of a Sinterklaas event which was planned for 17 November 2013. Twenty-one claimants sought the annulment of this decision. The district court of Amsterdam upheld some of these claims and annulled the permit. The Mayor and the Stichting Pietengilde lodged an appeal against this judgment.

Held: Both the appeals of the mayor of Amsterdam and of the Stichting Pietengilde were upheld. The judgment of the district court of Amsterdam was quashed. The decision of the mayor of Amsterdam was also quashed.

Judgment: 5. The Division firstly must consider, partly on its own motion, the question of whether the Stichting Pietengilde and others constitute parties concerned to the dispute at hand as defined in Article 1:2 AWB, and also if the district court has correctly deemed the claimants in the proceedings to be parties concerned.

In the opinion of the Division, questions can be raised about Stichting Pietengilde being a party concerned because the Stichting Pietengilde was established only on 30 July 2014 and therefore after the mayor took his decision on 30 October 2013 and after the district court rendered its judgment. There are also doubts whether the claimants [claimant sub 2D], [claimant sub 2B], [claimant sub 2E], [claimant sub 2C] and [claimant sub 2A], who together with Stichting Pietengilde jointly lodged a claim for judicial review, qualify as parties concerned. Even though they have stated that they acted as the figure of 'Black Pete' (Zwarte Piet) and they intend to continue doing so, this fact in itself does not necessarily mean that they have a sufficiently objective, actual, personal and subjective interest which can be sufficiently distinguished from the public at large that wants the character of 'Black Pete' to survive and wishes to permit individuals to appear as this character.

Furthermore, the Division finds it doubtful whether the claimants [claimant sub 3A], [claimant sub 3B], [claimant sub 3C], [person A], [person B], [person C] and [person D], whose claims were considered admissible by the district court, qualify as parties concerned now that it is at first sight not obvious that they can be sufficiently distinguished from others who are of the opinion that 'Black Pete' should not be part of the Sinterklaas parade.

In this case, however, the following circumstances altogether have led to the Division's decision to scrutinize the lawfulness of the permit for the Sinterklaas parade of 2013 in Amsterdam. Firstly, the Division identifies a public and legal interest that surpasses the case at hand, including the interest of an unambiguous interpretation of the law by the courts and public authorities. This interest is served by giving the answer of the highest administrative court to the main question at hand within a short time frame.

[22] ECLI:NL:RVS:2014:4117; see also Y Schuurmans, *Van bestuursrechtelijke detailhandel naar maakindustrie* (inaugural thesis, Leiden University, 2015).

This question is whether the mayor, when applying his legal powers, vested on him in order to ensure public order, may take into account the content of the utterances and the possible violations of human rights of other persons, which may come along with these utterances. The answer to this main question is not only of importance for the mayor of Amsterdam, but for all other mayors who are awaiting a judgment of the highest administrative court on this issue.

Notes

(1) In this exceptional case, a strict application of the Dutch rules on standing would have led to the conclusion that the claim would be considered inadmissible. However, not only the claimants themselves, but also almost all other municipalities were awaiting a decision of the highest administrative court on this question. Furthermore, the same question would have been raised by the Sinterklaas march a year later. At that time, the claimants would have had standing. Therefore, the court decided to hear and rule on the case because of the public interest of the case, despite the fact that the claimants had no standing.

(2) A somewhat similar construction has been used in a French case, where permission to plead (*autorisation de plaider*) was granted by the administrative court.[23] However, this type of possibility occurs only very rarely. In the *Commune de Menton* case, a local authority had neglected to introduce an action in order to protect its own material interests. Subsequently, a local taxpayer was authorised by the Administrative Court of First Instance to bring proceedings in place of the failing local authority and to challenge an act, but at his own expense and risk. The individual was considered to be acting on behalf of the administrative authority.[24]

(3) In England and Wales, such constructions to circumvent standing rules in very special cases are not needed. The standing criteria are flexible, allowing convenient solutions for 'special' cases or cases that raise matters of 'public interest'.[25]

4.4.B GENERAL RULES ON STANDING

All legal systems under examination provide for some general rules on standing, which may be modified or may be derogated from in specific areas of law or in relation to certain types of actions. When dealing with standing requirements, one must keep in mind that similar types of actions – for example, the action for annulment of an administrative measure – may nevertheless have a different scope. In France, for example, the action for annulment can relate to single-case decisions or measures of general scope. In Germany, however, this is not the case, although annulment of measures of general scope can, in some cases, be sought in a special type of action (§47 VwGO). In the Netherlands, administrative courts deal mostly with single-case decisions; actions against most decisions

[23] See Code de justice administrative, Art L212-2.
[24] Conseil d'Ètat, 4 July 2012, *Commune de Menton*, N° 356130.
[25] An example may be *R v Secretary of State for Foreign and Commonwealth Affairs ex parte World Development Movement Ltd* [1995] 1 WLR 386 (HL).

of general scope must be brought before the civil courts.[26] These differences in scope must be taken into account when comparing the general rules for standing in actions for annulment. The general rules for standing broadly follow two different approaches: the right-based approach and the interest-based approach.

4.4.B.1 RIGHT-BASED APPROACH: GERMANY

Verwaltungsgerichtsordnung **4.15 (DE)**

§42 (2) Unless otherwise provided by law, the action shall only be admissible if the plaintiff claims that his rights have been violated by an administrative act or its refusal or omission.

Grundgesetz **4.16 (DE)**

Article 19 (4) Should any person's rights be violated by public authority, he shall have recourse to the courts. If no other jurisdiction has been established, recourse shall be to the ordinary courts.

Notes

(1) There are a few legal systems within the EU which grant standing before the (administrative) courts only if the claimant can argue that the contested act infringes his rights derived from public law. In addition to Germany, Austria also follows this approach. This approach to judicial review also underlies Article 19(4) of the Grundgesetz. The subjective public right (*subjektives öffentliches Recht*) can be described as the cornerstone of the German system of administrative judicial review.[27] As a general rule, the enforcement of rights of others or an *actio popularis* are not permissible.[28]

(2) Addressees of an onerous administrative act are prima facie attributed with *locus standi*, as onerous administrative acts limit the individual's liberty according to Article 2(1) of the Grundgesetz (*Adressatentheorie*).[29] Also, non-addressees of an administrative act may be entitled to bring an action for annulment if they establish that the administrative act at issue is likely to infringe their subjective public rights.[30] For example, where a neighbour is given permission to build on his land by an administrative act, this can constitute a violation of the rights of the owner of the adjoining property.

[26] See further Chapter 3.

[27] For an in-depth discussion of the German model of administrative legal redress with regard to European developments see B Wegener, 'Conceptualizing Administrative Law – Legal Protection v Regulatory Approach' in H Pünder and C Waldhoff (eds), *Debates in German Public Law* (Oxford, Hart Publishing, 2014) 219–24.

[28] In this regard, see BVerwGE, 17, 87, 91; BVerfGE 19, 269, 271; BVerfGE 36, 192, 199.

[29] BVerfGE 6, 32, 36; BVerfGE 9, 83, 88.

[30] The infringed subjective public right can result from a non-constitutional provision or constitutional provisions in conjunction with other norms. See BVerwGE 39, 235; BVerfGE 20, 150; BVerfGE 33, 303; BVerwGE 39, 235; BVerfGE 20, 150.

(3) The right infringed must be a legal right or a legally protected interest.[31] A possibly violated subjective public right is to be distinguished from the mere accidental effect on the right of the non-addressee (*Rechtsreflex*).

(4) The plaintiff must invoke a right attributed to him and not a mere right of the general public or of others. Non-governmental organisations (NGOs) and associations which seek to represent the interests of their members (*egoistische Verbandsklage*) or the interests of the general public (*altruistische Verbandsklage*) are not generally granted standing.[32]

O Bühler, Die subjektiven öffentlichen Rechte und ihr Schutz in der deutschen Verwaltungsrechtsprechung[33] **4.17 (DE)**

A statute only creates subjective public rights for persons if 1. the statute is of binding nature, ie the administration has no discretion as to its application, 2. the statute is adopted in favour of certain persons or groups of persons, to meet their individual interests and not only in the public interest, and if the statute is 3. adopted in the interest of the person with the effect that the person can refer to the law and request a certain behaviour of the public authority.

Note

In order to establish whether a provision intends to confer a subjective public right on the claimant, a specific test, the *Schutznormtheorie*, which was developed by Bühler, is applied. Pursuant to this theory, subjective public rights can only be established by norms which do not merely serve to protect the general public, but at least, in some way, intend to protect the individual as well. If the law at issue, by contrast, aims only to serve public interests, it provides no subjective public right to individuals. The purpose of the law is to be determined by means of common methods of legal interpretation.[34] A provision, thus, provides subjective public rights if it intends to confer subjective rights to a specified category of persons, which can be distinguished from the general public.[35] Other than in the historic conception of Bühler, today, legal norms which grant discretion to the administration may also provide subjective public rights.

[31] See BVerwG 16,187.

[32] Standing for NGOs and associations will be dealt with below in section 4.4.D.1 (ii).

[33] O Bühler, *Die subjektiven öffentlichen Rechte und ihr Schutz in der deutschen Verwaltungsrechtsprechung* (Stuttgart, Kohlhammer, 1914), 224.

[34] BverwG 19 September 1986, DVBl 1987, 476, 477.

[35] BVerwGE 94, 151, 158; BVerwGE 52, 122, 126; BVerwGE 67, 334, 338; BVerwG, DVBl 1981, 928; BVerwG, DVBl 2005, 702.

Bundesverfassungsgericht, 16 January 1957[36] **4.18 (DE)**

PROVISIONS CONFERRING SUBJECTIVE RIGHTS; IDENTIFICATION

Anyone may claim that his basic right contained in Article 2(1) of the Basic Law has been infringed.

Facts: The claimant publicly criticised and fought against the politics of the federal government in an aggressive way. The competent authority therefore refused to issue an extension of the validity of his passport.

Held: The constitutional complaint against the refusal of the extension of the validity of the passport was found admissible but was ultimately dismissed.

Judgment: 16 Apart from the freedom of action provided by Article 2(1) Basic Law, the Basic Law provides specific provisions for freedoms concerning specific spheres of life, which can – in light of the lessons from history – be particularly seriously affected by the public authorities. …

Anyone can claim, by means of a constitutional complaint, that a law which limits his freedom of action is unconstitutional because it infringes (formal or substantial) provisions of the constitution; thus, he may claim that his basic right contained in Article 2(1) Basic Law has been infringed.

Notes

(1) In the absence of a subjective public right granted by statutory law, standing can further be derived from fundamental rights.[37] In such cases, it must be determined whether the claimant falls under the scope *ratione personae* of the fundamental right, whether the fundamental right is applicable *ratione materiae* and whether there is a likelihood of a violation. The most important fundamental rights invoked before administrative courts are the right to property (Article 14 of the Basic Law),[38] the right to inviolability of the person, especially in the context of environmental law claims (Article 2(2), sentence 1 of the Basic Law),[39] the right to free development of personality (Articles 1(1) and 2(1) of the Basic Law) and the right to equal treatment (Article 3 of the Basic Law). It is recognised that standing can be derived from the likelihood that the ECHR is violated,[40] even though the ECHR enjoys a rank inferior to constitutional law.[41]

[36] BVerGE 6, 32.

[37] This follows from Grundgesetz, Arts 1(3) and 19(4).

[38] Standing was accepted in cases of direct and deliberate restriction of the right to property, in particular by means of expropriation, BVerwGE 32, 173, 178 (settled case law). In most cases, however, there will be non-constitutional provisions, such as the Baugesetzbuch, specifying the scope of the right to property and its limits, see, eg BVerwGE 89, 69, 78; BVerwG, NVwZ 1995, 1200; BVerwG, NVwZ 1998, 842.

[39] See BVerwGE 54, 211, 222; BVerwGE 56, 54, 78; BVerwG, NVwZ 1997, 161.

[40] eg OVG Münster NVwZ 1997, 512.

[41] See T Masuch, 'Zur fallübergreifenden Bindungswirkung von Urteilen des EGMR' (2000) *Neue Zeitschrift für Verwaltungsrecht* 1266.

(2) Particularly in situations in which a person wishes to file an action against a benefit granted to a competitor (*negative Konkurrentenklage*), the distinction between a right that has possibly been violated and the mere possibility that exploitation of an opportunity may reap economic benefits prove highly difficult and complex.[42]

4.4.B.2 INTEREST-BASED APPROACH: ENGLAND AND WALES

Senior Courts Act 1981 **4.19 (EW)**

Section 31(3) No application for judicial review shall be made unless the leave of the High Court has been obtained in accordance with rules of court; and the court shall not grant leave to make such an application unless it considers that the applicant has a sufficient interest in the matter to which the application relates.

House of Lords, 9 April 1981[43] **4.20 (EW)**

R v Inland Revenue Commissioners, ex parte National Federation of Self Employed and Small Businesses Ltd

CRITERIA FOR STANDING

National Federation of Small Businesses

Standing is granted where this is necessary to vindicate the rule of law and prevent unlawful action.

Facts: Upon discovering that a large number of workers in the newspaper printing industry (known as the 'Fleet Street Casuals') had been involved in tax evasion for a number of years, the Inland Revenue Commissioners determined that they would introduce a special scheme whereby if the workers concerned identified themselves they would not face liability for the full amount of unpaid tax. The Divisional Court held that the Federation did not have standing to bring the claim; the Court of Appeal allowed an appeal and permitted the claim to proceed.

Held: The appeal from the Court of Appeal was allowed but the Federation's claim for judicial review was rejected.

Judgment: Lord Diplock: It would, in my view, be a grave lacuna in our system of public law if a pressure group, like the Federation, or even a single public-spirited taxpayer, were prevented by outdated technical rules of locus standi from bringing the matter to the

[42] Restrictions of free competition (by granting state subsidies to a competitor) can be invoked on the basis of Grundgesetz, Arts 2(1) and 3(1). See, eg BVerwGE 30, 191, 197 (action brought against a state subsidy that is directly beneficial to the competitor). Standing was rejected in cases in which the admission of a competitor to the market was challenged, BVerwGE 16, 187; see further P Huber, *Die Konkurrentenklage im Verwaltungsrecht* (Tübingen, Mohr Siebeck, 1991). Further controversial cases relating to standing include the standing of tenants of property and the distinction from the standing of the owners themselves, see, eg BVerwG, NVwZ, 1983, 672; BVerwG, DÖV 1984, 37; BVerfGE 89, 1, 6; BVerwG, NVwZ 1998, 956. Similar problems include the standing of a co-owner, see, eg BVerwG, NJW 1998, 954.

[43] [1982] AC 617 (HL).

attention of the court to vindicate the rule of law and get the unlawful conduct stopped. The Attorney-General, although he occasional applies for prerogative orders against public authorities that do not form part of central government, in practice never does so against government departments.

It is not, in my view, a sufficient answer to say that judicial review of the actions of officers or departments of central government is unnecessary because they are accountable to Parliament for the way in which they carry out their functions. They are accountable to Parliament for what they do so far as regards efficiency and policy, and of that Parliament is the only judge; they are responsible to a court of justice for the lawfulness of what they do, and of that the court is the only judge.

I would allow this appeal upon the ground upon which, in my view, the Divisional Court should have dismissed it when the application came to be heard, instead of singling out the lack of a sufficient interest on the part of the Federation, viz. that the Federation completely failed to show any conduct by the Board that was ultra vires or unlawful.

Notes

(1) In England and Wales, claimants in judicial review have to demonstrate 'sufficient' interest; however, the decision whether someone has a sufficient interest does not follow strict rules, but is made on a case-by-case basis. The *National Federation of Small Businesses* case illustrates that the question of standing is sometimes determined in the context of the merits of the substantive legal arguments brought forward in the case. Standing is often granted in order to allow a claimant to prevent unlawful conduct and does not adhere firmly to the requirement for a claimant to demonstrate a strong personal, direct interest in the matter to which the application relates.[44]

(2) It is sufficient for the interest in the case to be 'moral' in the sense that proceedings can be brought in relation to interests that support religious or ethical views. For example, a claimant acting on behalf of the Society for the Protection of Unborn Children had standing to challenge the licensing of the emergency contraceptive pill for prescription.[45] There are also cases where those who seek to challenge general public acts, such as the UK's transfer of funds to the EU in line with its obligations under EU law, have been granted standing to do so given their status as taxpayers.[46]

(3) The courts have not generally explored the question of whether the decision complained about is of direct interest to the claimant, although in some circumstances the courts have held that competitors may have standing to bring judicial review claims against decisions to grant planning permission to competitors.[47] Similarly, it has been held that a homeless person resident in a particular area for a considerable

[44] See, eg the broad ability of associations and NGOs to bring claims in English law as discussed below in section 4.4.D.2 (iii).

[45] *R (John Smeaton on Behalf of Society for the Protection of Unborn Children) v The Secretary of State for Health* [2002] EWHC 610 (Admin), [2002] 2 FLR 146.

[46] *R v HM Treasury, ex parte Smedley* [1985] QB 657 (QB).

[47] See, eg *R (on the application of Noble Organisation Ltd) v Thanet DC* [2005] EWCA Civ 782, [2006] Env LR 8.

length of time had standing to bring a judicial review claim against a permit granted to a cement works permitting it to burn an experimental type of fuel.[48] These interests could be argued to be relatively indirect and, in the latter case, perhaps not of great significance, given that no property interests were affected, but the courts still permitted these claims to proceed.

4.4.B.3 INTEREST-BASED APPROACH: FRANCE

Conseil d'État, 29 March 1901[49] **4.21 (FR)**

Casanova v Municipality of Olmeto

STANDING; SUFFICIENT INTEREST

Casanova

Taxpayers of a city have standing to challenge a decision of the city council which has consequences on the city budget.

Facts: On 4 November 1897, the municipal council of Olmeto voted to pay an amount of 2000F to a doctor who would provide free medical care to the inhabitants of the city. Taxpayers from Olmeto brought an action for annulment against this decision.

Held: The action was declared admissible and the decision was annulled.

Judgment: On the inadmissibility of the claim due to the lack of interest of the claimants other than Mr X ..., doctor in Olmeto; considering that the challenged measure has as its subject matter the imposition of an expense on the budget of the municipality of Olmeto; considering that the claimants are taxpayers of this municipality, and have an interest in having this measure be declared null and void and that they are, consequently, interested parties in the sense of Article 65 of the aforementioned law of 5 April 1884 ....

Notes

(1) In France, an interest-based approach applies with regard to the action for annulment (*recours pour excès de pouvoir*). The threshold requirement to prove standing in this action is an 'interest in taking legal action' (*intérêt à agir*) and the courts are very flexible with regard to standing. As the *Casanova* case shows, all local taxpayers can challenge any local decision that affects the budget and users of public services can challenge decisions which have an effect on the operation of these services.[50]

[48] *R (on the application of Edwards) v Environment Agency (No.1)* [2004] EWHC 736 (Admin), [2004] Env LR 43.

[49] N° 94580.

[50] Conseil d'État, 21 December 1906, *Syndicat des propriétaires et contribuables du quartier Croix de Séguey-Tivoli*, N°19167.

On a local level, this becomes something close to an *actio popularis*. However, the national taxpayer (paying towards the state budget) has no standing to challenge tax decisions.[51]

(2) As regards the kind of interest to be proven, even moral or ideological interests can be deemed to be sufficient.[52] This is the case, for example, if one challenges the decision to close a church for religious reasons[53] or if one challenges a decision which may harm one's reputation.[54] However, the interest must be sufficient, meaning that the decision affects the claimant's situation in a significant manner. Often, this element is missing in the case of 'purely personal emotions'. For example, the irritation of a policeman caused by a decision authorising constables to wear regular clothing is not sufficient to grant him standing.[55]

(3) One question to be considered when assessing the *intérêt à agir* is whether the link between the decision or rule at stake and the possibly affected interest is 'direct' enough. This is always the case if the contested act was directed at the claimant. However, in France, courts have also been willing to allow claimants to bring actions for annulment in circumstances where the impact on such interests has been indirect. An example of this is where a claimant considers that his business rivals have been treated by public authorities more favourably than himself.[56]

(4) Apart from being 'direct', the claimant's interest must also be 'actual'. The mere possibility that an interest of the claimant might be affected by the challenged decision or act is not sufficient.

(5) Finally, the claimant's interest must be 'certain'. Courts are not very strict in applying this criterion. An interest has been considered to exist even where the claimant's legal sphere would only potentially be affected by the decision.[57] In the *Abisset* case, the claim of a member of a camping association to challenge a decision prohibiting camping in a certain area was declared admissible even if the claimant had never camped. The claimant's interest was nevertheless considered 'certain' on the sole basis of the fact that, should he have wanted to camp, the claimant might have liked to camp in the area concerned.

(6) The notion of *intérêt à agir* and its characteristics are not enshrined in legislation but are entirely the product of case law.

[51] Conseil d'État, 23 November 1988, *Dumont*, N° 94282.

[52] The person residing in a city may challenge the decision changing the name of the city (Conseil d'État, 4 April 1997, *Marchal*, N° 177987). However, an architect had no interest to challenge a building permit which would have as its consequence the destruction of the square of Strasbourg railway station which he had worked on some years before (Conseil d'État, 27 October 2006, *Mme Marie-Dominique C et al*, N° 286569). In addition, applicants, who presented themselves as residing in Alsace and having secular convictions, had no interest to challenge a decision related to the regime applicable to Catholics, Protestants and Jews in the departments of Bas-Rhin, Haut-Rhin and Moselle (Conseil d'État, 17 May 2002, *Hofmann*, N° 231905).

[53] Conseil d'État, 8 February 1908, *Abbé Deliard*, N° 30383.

[54] Conseil d'État, 21 May 1948, *Clausi*, N° 372112.

[55] Conseil d'État, 13 January 1993, *Syndicat national autonome des policiers en civil*, N°10423.

[56] This is especially the case when an action for annulment is brought against a contract by a third party, see Conseil d'État, 4 April 2014, *Département de Tarn-et-Garonne*, N° 358994.

[57] Conseil d'État, 14 February 1958, *Abisset*, N° 7715.

4.4.B.4 INTEREST-BASED APPROACH: THE NETHERLANDS

Algemene Wet Bestuursrecht **4.22 (NL)**

Article 1:2 (1) Party concerned means: the person whose interest is directly affected by a decision.

(2) As regards administrative authorities, the interests entrusted to them are considered their own interests.

(3) As regards legal persons, their interests are considered to include the general and collective interests which they particularly promote by virtue of their objectives as shown by their factual activities.

Notes

(1) In Dutch law, the general requirements for standing seem to be structured in more detail and at the same time seem to be applied in a stricter fashion than in England and Wales and France. In case law, the courts have distinguished five criteria which must be met to qualify as a 'party concerned' and hence to have *locus standi*:

(a) the 'personal' interest of the claimant has to be concerned;
(b) the interest has to be one which can be determined 'objectively';
(c) the interest has to be 'actual';
(d) the claimant has to be concerned 'personally'; and
(e) the claimant has to be concerned 'directly'.[58]

(2) The requirement that the interest has to be 'personal' means that nobody can institute proceedings to protect the interests of others, unless acting as an attorney. In that case, the person for whom the attorney acts must have a personal interest. However, associations which act for the collective interests of a certain group are not excluded by this requirement. The third section of Article 1:2 AWB provides a separate legal basis for the standing of such groups.[59]

(3) The second criterion entails that purely subjective interests, such as personal emotions, which cannot be objectified, are not sufficient to be relied on before the administrative courts.

(4) Furthermore, the interest must not only be fictional or prospective, but must be 'actual'. As seen above, the French courts may apply this criterion more leniently in some cases.[60]

(5) The most discussed and most problematic criterion probably is that an applicant has to be concerned 'personally' (see criterion (d) above). This criterion implies that claimants must distinguish themselves from the general public.

[58] Regarding these five criteria, see W Konijnenbelt and RM van Male, *Hoofdstukken van Bestuursrecht*, 16th edn (Alphen an den Rijn, Kluwer, 2014), 67 ff.

[59] Standing of associations is examined in section 4.4.D.2 (ii) below.

[60] See section 4.4.B.3.

Raad van State, 13 February 2008[61] **4.23 (NL)**

Belangenvereniging Amstelwijck and others (b, c) v Mayor and Aldermen of Dordrecht

STANDING; NOTION OF 'PERSONALLY CONCERNED'; SIGHT CRITERION

Belangenvereniging Amstelwijck

A claimant who cannot see a planned mosque from his property and is not living on one of the access roads to the mosque is not personally concerned in such a way that sufficiently distinguishes him from others. The possibility that the air quality in the area might be influenced by the additional traffic to the mosque does not qualify as a personal interest.

Facts: A local action group brought a claim for judicial review (*beroep*) against the building permit for a mosque. The permit was granted by permitting a derogation from the urban land use plan. One of the arguments was that the mosque would generate additional traffic. The district court declared the claim to be inadmissible. The action group appealed against this judgment.

Held: The claim was declared inadmissible.

Judgment: The court was correct to apply as a decisive criterion for the question of who should be considered as 'party concerned' within the meaning of Article 1:2(1) AWB, the question of whether the claimant resides in the vicinity with a view of the building plot. The permit was given with regard to this plot. Contrary to the argument of the association and others, reliance on the degradation of air quality does not make them a 'party concerned' within the meaning of Article 1:2(1) AWB. In the present case, the residence of [claimant c] is more than 300 metres away from the plot and the claimant can hardly or perhaps even not see the planned mosque. Furthermore, he does not live at the entrance to the mosque or on any of the other access roads. Therefore, the court correctly held that the claimant cannot be considered to be a concerned party because of the possible increase of traffic and possible decrease in air quality as a consequence of building the mosque. The above considerations lead to the conclusion that the court rightly held that there is no evidence that the claimant is personally concerned by the decision in such a way that sufficiently distinguishes him from other residents and that his claim was rightly declared inadmissible.

Note

In general, the criterion of personal interest seems to be applied in a substantially stricter manner than, for example, in France. Dutch courts would not grant standing to someone who challenges a decision of his local government which affects him only to the extent that it has financial consequences for which he could have to pay.

[61] ECLI:NL:RVS:2008:BC4233.

Raad van State, 9 November 2009[62] **4.24 (NL)**

Jumbo Supermarkten BV and others v Mayor and Aldermen of 's Hertogenbosch

STANDING; DIRECT INTEREST

Jumbo

A person who did not apply for a building permit, but had the intention to use the prospective building, does not have a direct interest in bringing a claim against the refusal of the building permit.

Facts: The application for a building permit was refused. Jumbo BV, a supermarket chain which wanted to run a supermarket in the building for which a building permit was requested, filed a claim for judicial review (*beroep*) against the decision to refuse the permit.

Held: The claim was declared inadmissible.

Judgment: Jumbo B.V. wishes to make use of the building, but did not itself apply for the building permit. The decision only has indirect legal effects on Jumbo B.V. *via* the civil law relation of Jumbo B.V. with the owner of the plot of land subject to the application for the building permit. Hence, Jumbo B.V. has only an indirect, parallel interest. The district court was correct in declaring that the claim of Jumbo B.V. not admissible.

Notes

(1) This case shows that the criterion of 'direct' interest may be interpreted restrictively. For example, tenants and other users have not been deemed to be directly concerned regarding a decision to designate a building as a heritage building.[63]

(2) This strict interpretation of the notion of 'direct' interest has sometimes been nuanced in case law. Not only the owner of a shop, but also the business which had rented the shop have been deemed to be directly concerned regarding a decision concerning a parking restriction in front of the shop.[64] Furthermore, claimants who have an indirect interest, which is opposite to that of the person who is directly concerned, can qualify as being 'directly concerned'. Hence, a tenant who rents a flat can bring a claim against a decision issued on request of the owner of the flat (therefore his contractual partner) which would allow the owner to demolish the building.[65]

62 ECLI:NL:RVS:2009:BR4305.

63 ABRvS 2 February 2011, ECLI:NL:RVS:2011:BP2774.

64 ECLI:NL:RVS:2005:AU2619.

65 ECLI:NL:RVS:2005:AS2173. A similar case in the UK would be *R (Sargeant) v Essex County Council* [2009] EWHC 2232 (Admin).

4.4.B.5 INTEREST-BASED, BUT RESTRICTIVE APPROACH: THE EUROPEAN UNION

4.4.B.5 (i) Introduction

Treaty on the Functioning of the European Union **4.25 (EU)**

Article 263 (1) The Court of Justice of the European Union shall review the legality of legislative acts, of acts of the Council, of the Commission and of the European Central Bank, other than recommendations and opinions, and of acts of the European Parliament and of the European Council intended to produce legal effects vis-à-vis third parties. It shall also review the legality of acts of bodies, offices or agencies of the Union intended to produce legal effects vis-à-vis third parties.

(2) It shall for this purpose have jurisdiction in actions brought by a Member State, the European Parliament, the Council or the Commission on grounds of lack of competence, infringement of an essential procedural requirement, infringement of the Treaties or of any rule of law relating to their application, or misuse of powers.

(3) The Court shall have jurisdiction under the same conditions in actions brought by the Court of Auditors, by the European Central Bank and by the Committee of the Regions for the purpose of protecting their prerogatives.

(4) Any natural or legal person may, under the conditions laid down in the first and second paragraphs, institute proceedings against an act addressed to that person or which is of direct and individual concern to them, and against a regulatory act which is of direct concern to them and does not entail implementing measures.

Notes

(1) Article 263 TFEU, which governs the action for annulment, distinguishes between three types of claimants: the 'privileged applicants' (Member States, the Commission, the Council and the European Parliament), 'semi-privileged applicants' (the European Central Bank, the Committee of the Regions and the Court of Auditors) and 'non-privileged applicants' (natural and legal persons). This distinction is significant, because applicants with different status must meet different requirements in order to gain standing under the annulment procedure. Hence, while privileged applicants have direct and unrestricted *locus standi* and semi-privileged applicants have standing to challenge measures affecting their prerogatives, natural and legal persons have only limited access to the EU courts.

(2) As can be seen from the text of Article 263(4) TFEU, actions of individuals against measures of EU institutions are also governed by an interest-based approach. Furthermore, some of the requirements of the national general standing rules discussed above can also clearly and explicitly be found in Article 263(4) TFEU, namely the conditions of 'direct concern' and of 'individual concern'. What cannot be seen from the wording of Article 263(4) TFEU is the very restrictive interpretation of these criteria by the CJEU, particularly when compared with the approach of national courts.

4.4.B.5 (ii) Direct Concern

Case 41-44/70, 13 May 1971[66] **4.26 (EU)**

International Fruit Company and Others v Commission

STANDING; DIRECT CONCERN

International Fruit Company

The criterion of direct concern requires that the challenged measure must not leave any discretion to those entrusted with implementing it.

Facts: On the basis of a regulation on the import of fruit from third countries, the Commission denied several applications for licences to import dessert apples from third countries. These refusals were notified to the claimants through the Dutch International Fruit Company. The claimants sought the annulment of this Commission decision.

Held: The actions for annulment were declared admissible but unfounded.

Judgment: 25 Article 1(2) of Regulation no 459/70, by providing that 'the member states shall in accordance with the conditions laid down in article 2, issue the licence to any interested party applying for it', makes it clear that the national authorities do not enjoy any discretion in the matter of the issue of licences and the conditions on which applications by the parties concerned should be granted.

…

27 In these circumstances as far as the interested parties are concerned, the issue of or refusal to issue the import licences must be bound up with this decision.

28 The measure whereby the commission decides on the issues of the import licences thus directly affects the legal position of the parties concerned.

Note

The Court of Justice of the European Union (CJEU) has consistently held that a measure is of direct concern only if it affects the claimant's legal position directly and it leaves no discretion to the addressees of the measure. In other words, a direct link between the challenged measure and the loss or damage that the claimant has suffered must be established.[67] Moreover, the implementation must be automatic and result from EU rules without the application of other intermediate rules. If the measure leaves national authorities of the Member States a degree of discretion as to how the measure should be implemented, the claimant will not be considered to be directly concerned.[68]

[66] ECLI:EU:C:1971:53.

[67] See also Case 207/86 *Asociación Profesional de Empresarios de Pesca Comunitarios (Apesco) v Commission* ECLI:EU:C:1988:200, para 12; Case C-417/04 P *Regione Siciliana v Commission* ECLI:EU:C:2006:282.

[68] See, eg Case 69/69 *SA Alcan Aluminium Raeren and others v Commission* ECLI:EU:C:1970:53; Case 222/83 *Municipality of Differdange and Others v Commission* ECLI:EU:C:1984:266.

4.4.B.5 (iii) Individual Concern

Case 25/62, 15 July 1963[69] **4.27 (EU)**

Plaumann & Co v Commission

STANDING; INDIVIDUAL CONCERN

Plaumann

In order to be individually concerned, a claimant has to be affected by reason of certain attributes which are peculiar to him.

Facts: In 1961, the Federal Republic of Germany requested an authorisation from the Commission to suspend the collection of customs duties set out in the Common Customs Tariff on the import of clementines from third countries. The Commission refused the German government's request. Plaumann & Co, which was an importer of clementines, brought an action for annulment against this decision.

Held: The action for annulment was declared inadmissible.

Judgment: Persons other than those to whom a decision is addressed may only claim to be individually concerned if that decision affects them by reason of certain attributes which are peculiar to them or by reason of circumstances in which they are differentiated from all other persons and by virtue of these factors distinguishes them individually just as in the case of the person addressed. In the present case, the applicant is affected by the disputed decision as an importer of clementines, that is to say, by reason of a commercial activity which may at any time be practised by any person and is not therefore such as to distinguish the applicant in relation to the contested decision as in the case of the addressee.

Notes

(1) As a result of the doctrine developed in the *Plaumann* case, individual concern cannot be established when the claimant operates a trade which could be engaged in by any other person at any time. In particular, the claimant has to demonstrate, according to the case law developed by the CJEU, that, at the time when the decision was adopted, he belonged to a so-called 'closed class', which is affected differently by the EU measure than all other persons.[70] This means that, in order to have standing, it is not sufficient simply to be affected directly by a measure of an EU institution. If this measure affects not only a very limited number of persons, but potentially a large number of persons, no member of this group is regarded as being individually concerned and hence no one has standing, no matter how significant the interests affected may be or even if individual rights are infringed.

(2) The *Plaumann* test has been challenged from within the EU courts due to its restrictive nature. The question of the appropriateness of the CJEU's approach was called into question by Advocate General Jacobs in the *Union de Pequeños Agricultores*

[69] ECLI:EU:C:1963:17.

[70] eg Joined Cases 106 and 107/63 *Alfred Toepfer and Getreide-Import Gesellschaft v Commission* ECLI:EU:C:1965:65.

(*UPA*) case[71] and by the then Court of First Instance (CFI) in the *Jégo-Quéré* case.[72] In the *UPA* case and in the appeal brought by the Commission against the judgment of the CFI in the *Jégo-Quéré* case,[73] the European Court of Justice issued a judgment in favour of maintaining the traditional interpretation of the 'individual concern' test. According to the European Court of Justice, if the 'individual concern' test needed to be reformed, such reform had to come from Treaty revision rather than from judicial decision-making.[74]

(3) A reform came with the Treaty of Lisbon and led to the current formulation of Article 263(4) TFEU. The Treaty of Lisbon modified the standing requirements for non-privileged applicants by dispensing with the need to show individual concern in relation to a regulatory act that does not entail implementing measures.

4.4.B.5 (iv) 'Complete' System of Remedies?

The CJEU has justified this restrictive approach to the standing of private applicants in annulment actions by referring to the idea of a 'complete system of remedies' created by the European Treaties (now the TEU and the TFEU) on several occasions. In the court's view, this system is complete because an EU measure may be challenged either through a direct action under Article 263 TFEU or through the preliminary ruling procedure pursuant to Article 267 TFEU. Hence, according to the CJEU, a restrictive interpretation of 'individual concern' does not create a gap in judicial protection because individuals have the option to bring actions against the national implementation of EU measures before the national courts, which creates the obligation, pursuant to Article 267 TFEU and the CJEU's ruling in *Foto-Frost*,[75] to refer the questions of validity of EU measures to the CJEU. However, this view may be questioned.

Case C-50/00, 21 February 2002[76] **4.28 (EU)**

Unión de Pequeños Agricultores v Council of the European Union

STANDING; INDIVIDUAL CONCERN; WIDENING OF CRITERION

Unión de Pequeños Agricultores (UPA)

The principle of effective judicial protection may not be satisfied if judicial review is only possible through the preliminary reference procedure.

Facts: The Unión de Pequeños Agricultores (UPA) was an association of Spanish farmers which brought an action to annul a regulation which amended the common organisation of the olive oil market. This action was

[71] Opinion of Advocate General Jacobs in Case C-50/00 P *Unión de Pequeños Agricultores v Council of the European Union* ECLI:EU:C:2002:197. See below excerpt 4.28.
[72] Case T-177/01 *Jégo-Quéré & Cie SA v Commission* ECLI:EU:T:2002:112.
[73] Case C-263/02 *P Commission v Jégo-Quéré & Cie SA* ECLI:EU:C:2004:210.
[74] ECLI:EU:C:2002:462, paras 44–45.
[75] Case 314/85 *Foto-Frost v Hauptzollamt Lübeck-Ost* ECLI:EU:C:1987:452.
[76] Case C-50/00 P *Unión de Pequeños Agricultores v Council of the European Union* ECLI:EU:C:2002:197.

declared to be inadmissible by the CFI as UPA was not considered to be 'individually concerned' by the provisions of the regulation. UPA appealed against the CFI's ruling.

Opinion: 41 It may be recalled, first of all, that the national courts are not competent to declare measures of Community law invalid. In a case concerning the validity of a Community measure, the competence of the national court is limited to assessing whether the applicant's arguments raise sufficient doubts about the validity of the impugned measure to justify a request for a preliminary ruling from the Court of Justice. It seems to me, therefore, artificial to argue that the national courts are the correct forum for such cases ....

42 Second, the principle of effective judicial protection requires that applicants have access to a court which is competent to grant remedies capable of protecting them against the effects of unlawful measures. Access to the Court of Justice via Article 234 EC is, however, not a remedy available to individual applicants as a matter of right. National courts may refuse to refer questions, and although courts of last instance are obliged to refer under the third paragraph of Article 234 EC, appeals within the national judicial systems are liable to entail long delays which may themselves be incompatible with the principle of effective judicial protection and with the need for legal certainty. National courts – even at the highest level – might also err in their preliminary assessment of the validity of general Community measures and decline to refer questions of validity to the Court of Justice on that basis. Moreover, where a reference is made, it is in principle for the national court to formulate the questions to be answered by the Court of Justice. Individual applicants might thus find their claims redefined by the questions referred. Questions formulated by national courts might, for example, limit the range of Community measures which an applicant has sought to challenge or the grounds of invalidity on which he has sought to rely ...

43 Third, it may be difficult, and in some cases perhaps impossible, for individual applicants to challenge Community measures which – as appears to be the case for the contested regulation – do not require any acts of implementation by national authorities. In that situation, there may be no measure which is capable of forming the basis of an action before national courts. The fact that an individual affected by a Community measure might, in some instances, be able to bring the validity of a Community measure before the national courts by violating the rules laid down by the measures and rely on the invalidity of those rules as a defence in criminal or civil proceedings directed against him does not offer the individual an adequate means of judicial protection. Individuals clearly cannot be required to breach the law in order to gain access to justice.

Notes

(1) For the reasons highlighted by Advocate General Jacobs in the *UPA* case, an indirect challenge of EU measures at the national level may not be regarded as an adequate substitute for a direct action before the European judicature, and may result

in the denial of any remedy or any effective remedy. In its judgment of 25 July 2002, the European Court of Justice finally refused to adopt this point of view and to amend the *Plaumann* interpretation of individual concern.[77]

(2) The problems linked to a possible denial of justice are exacerbated by the situation created by the CJEU's ruling in *Textilwerke Deggendorf v Germany*,[78] where the Court held that litigants are precluded from bringing Article 267 TFEU validity proceedings before national courts if 'without any doubt' they would have been entitled to bring an annulment action within the two-month deadline provided in Article 263(5) TFEU. However, it is not always an easy task to assess whether the claimant falls within a 'closed class', entitled to standing before the General Court. This means that it may not be a simple choice for claimants to determine whether they are amongst the group bound to seek an annulment remedy or whether they should instead seize the national courts.

(3) As mentioned above,[79] the Treaty of Lisbon removed the need for claimants to prove individual concern if the challenge is directed against a regulatory act which does not entail implementing measures. However, this change only partially resolves the issues highlighted by Advocate General Jacobs. The notion of 'regulatory act' is not contained in the Treaties and has been interpreted by the Court of Justice as a non-legislative act of general application.[80] As a consequence of this definition, a claimant such as UPA would still face great difficulties in exercising its right to an effective legal remedy, since it would not be challenging a 'regulatory act' (it challenged a Council Regulation, hence a legislative act under Article 289 TFEU) and would thus still need to demonstrate individual concern – the lack of which was the very reason why it was not granted standing. This situation would consequently lead to a complete lack of remedy since there would not be any national measure which UPA could have challenged. Therefore, the preliminary ruling procedure would not have been open to the claimant.

(4) Furthermore, the problems highlighted by the Advocate General in the *UPA* case remain. The question whether the alternative route of challenge of EU measures via the preliminary reference procedure effectively guarantees the right to access to justice of individuals will continue to be posed with the new formulation of Article 263(4) TFEU, since the problems of the use of the preliminary reference procedure highlighted by Advocate General Jacobs remain unresolved. The same can be argued with regard to the choice imposed by the Court to litigants through its *Textilwerke Deggendorf* ruling.

[77] Case C-50/00 P *Unión de Pequeños Agricultores v Council of the European Union* ECLI:EU:C:2002:462.

[78] Case C-188/92 *TWD Textilwerke Deggendorf GmbH v Bundesrepublik Deutschland* ECLI:EU:C:1994:90.

[79] See above note (3) under excerpt 4.27.

[80] Case C-583/11 P *Inuit Tapiriit Kanatami and Others v European Parliament and Council of the European Union* ECLI:EU:C:2013:625.

4.4.B.6 COMPARATIVE REMARKS

Most EU countries do not require claimants to rely on a subjective right derived from public law, but grant standing as long as one can demonstrate a sufficient interest. In general, this means that the hurdle of standing in these countries is significantly lower than in countries with a right-based approach. In all legal systems, addressees of a decision always have standing. In a comparative perspective, the general criteria for granting *locus standi* in France, England and Wales and the Netherlands are quite similar, though they use different wording. The issue of whether someone has standing regarding a decision benefiting a competitor is discussed in France as a question of 'direct' concern, whilst in the Netherlands the discussion in such cases touches the question whether the claimant is 'personally' concerned. Overall, English and French judges seem to apply these criteria in a more lenient way than their counterparts in the Netherlands. In the EU legal system, an interest-based approach is also applied. However, the CJEU interprets Article 263 TFEU, and more specifically, the need to be directly and individually concerned, much more narrowly than national courts interpret similar requirements in the national legal systems. As a consequence, standing before the EU courts for natural and legal persons is very limited compared with in national legal systems. From the perspective of the need for an effective remedy, one can argue that this constraint is only partly 'compensated' by the existence of the preliminary reference procedure.

4.4.C DIFFERENT RULES AND APPROACHES ON STANDING IN SPECIAL AREAS OF LAW

In the previous section, the general rules on standing in the four legal systems discussed have been examined, as well as the rules on standing applicable to private applicants before the EU courts. In certain areas of the law, these general rules may be specified, or even modified or applied, differently. In the following, some examples from different legal systems are described.

4.4.C.1 STANDING IN ENGLISH HUMAN RIGHTS CASES

Human Rights Act 1998 **4.29 (EW)**

Section 7 (1) A person who claims that a public authority has acted (or proposes to act) in a way which is made unlawful by section 6(1) may–

(a) bring proceedings against the authority under this Act in the appropriate court or tribunal, or

(b) rely on the Convention right or rights concerned in any legal proceedings,

but only if he is (or would be) a victim of the unlawful act.

(2) In subsection (1)(a) 'appropriate court or tribunal' means such court or tribunal as may be determined in accordance with rules; and proceedings against an authority include a counterclaim or similar proceeding.

(3) If the proceedings are brought on an application for judicial review, the applicant is to be taken to have a sufficient interest in relation to the unlawful act only if he is, or would be, a victim of that act.

...

(7) For the purposes of this section, a person is a victim of an unlawful act only if he would be a victim for the purposes of Article 34 of the Convention if proceedings were brought in the European Court of Human Rights in respect of that act.

House of Lords, 26 June 2003[81] **4.30 (EW)**

R v Her Majesty's Attorney General, ex parte Rusbridger and another

STANDING; HUMAN RIGHTS ACT; VICTIM TEST

Rusbridger

In order to bring a claim under the Human Rights Act 1998, the alleged infringement of the ECHR right must be actual rather than putative.

Facts: Alan Rusbridger, who was editor of a major national newspaper, brought a claim seeking a declaration that section 3 of the Treason Act 1848 was contrary to Article 10 ECHR and also that the Attorney General's refusal to give an assurance that no prosecution under section 3 of the Act would take place was unlawful and contrary to section 6 of the Human Rights Act 1998 as the refusal was contrary to Article 10 ECHR. Section 3 of the Treason Act 1848 is drafted in broad terms and seeks to make any action seeking to damage or remove the monarchy in the UK a criminal offence. Rusbridger's newspaper advocated, and continues to advocate, a peaceful campaign for the abolition of the monarchy.

Held: The appeal against the decision of the Court of Appeal which granted a declaration of incompatibility was allowed.

Judgment: Lord Rodger of Earlsferry: 54 Unlike, I suspect, the vast majority of the population, the claimants have actually heard of section 3 of the 1848 Act and know what it says. But they also know that they will not be prosecuted for publishing their articles and so, as rational individuals, they are not adversely affected by the mere existence of section 3. In the Court of Appeal Schiemann LJ, giving a twist to the Duke of Wellington's famous challenge, described the claimants' attitude in this way, at para 21:

'We do not understand the claimants to suggest that the uncertainty of our law as to treason has affected their decision to publish in the past or is likely to in the future. Their stance is that of the Duke of Wellington: publish and be damned. Nor is there any evidence to suggest that the existence of the 1848 Act causes them to sleep in their beds less soundly.'

In other words, neither any decision that the claimants take in their professional lives nor their general well-being is adversely affected by the existence of section 3 of the 1848 Act. In argument on their behalf Mr Robertson QC accepted this but – with understandable diffidence – suggested that section 3 might have subconsciously affected them in deciding on the tone of the articles. But for section 3, they might not, for instance, have

[81] [2003] UKHL 38, [2004] 1 AC 357.

proposed that a referendum should be held before any change to a republic. Nothing supports that implausible suggestion. Section 3 has no 'chilling effect' on the claimants' freedom of expression.

Note

In England and Wales, standing is more limited when claims are brought under the Human Rights Act 1998 than when they are brought under the standard procedure for judicial review claims. Section 7(1) of the Act provides that only 'victims' of an infringement of ECHR rights may bring legal proceedings under the Act, and section 7(7) then defines a 'victim' as being anyone who qualifies as a victim under Article 34 of the Convention. The *Rusbridger* case illustrates a further limitation, in the sense that the breach of the Convention right must be actual and not simply potential. The 'victim' test under section 7 of the Human Rights Act has been subject to some criticism.[82] In part, this is because the test is more restrictive than the ordinary rules of standing, and also because the Act does not clarify which standing rules ought to apply where a claim for judicial review involves not only a challenge to the infringement of Convention rights, but also other grounds of judicial review. Furthermore, it is not entirely clear whether the Human Rights Act is intended to create an exclusive procedure for the protection of human rights issues. The common law protected individuals from infringements of Convention rights in some cases prior to the Human Rights Act coming into force, so should individuals be able to rely on common law protection? If so, this protection would be available under the usual rules of standing, permitting claimants to circumvent section 7 of the Human Rights Act. This issue does not yet appear to have been considered by the courts.

4.4.C.2 STANDING IN PLANNING AND ENVIRONMENTAL LAW

4.4.C.2 (i) England and Wales

Town and Country Planning Act 1990 **4.31 (EW)**

Section 287 (1) This section applies to–

(a) a simplified planning zone scheme or an alteration of such a scheme;

(b) an order under section 247, 248, 249, 251, 257, 258 or 277,

and anything falling within paragraphs (a) and (b) is referred to in this section as a relevant document.

[82] See, eg M Supperstone and J Coppel 'Judicial Review after the Human Rights Act' (1999) 3 *European Human Rights Law Review* 301; D Wolfe and K Steyn 'Judicial Review and the Human Rights Act: Some Practical Considerations' (1999) 6 *European Human Rights Law Review* 614; N Garnham 'A Sufficient Victim? Standing and the Human Rights Act 1998' (1999) 4 *Judicial Review* 39.

(2) A person aggrieved by a relevant document may make an application to the High Court on the ground that–

(a) it is not within the appropriate power, or

(b) a procedural requirement has not been complied with.

...

Section 288 (1) If any person–

(a) is aggrieved by any order to which this section applies and wishes to question the validity of that order on the grounds–

(i) that the order is not within the powers of this Act, or

(ii) that any of the relevant requirements have not been complied with in relation to that order; or

(b) is aggrieved by any action on the part of the Secretary of State [or the Welsh Ministers] to which this section applies and wishes to question the validity of that action on the grounds–

(i) that the action is not within the powers of this Act, or

(ii) that any of the relevant requirements have not been complied with in relation to that action, he may make an application to the High Court under this section.

Note

The provisions of the Town and Country Planning Act set out above change the usual conditions upon which planning decisions can be challenged. The standing test covers 'persons aggrieved' rather than those with 'sufficient interest', as is otherwise usual in judicial review cases. This test permits property owners and others whose property is impacted by planning decisions to bring claims. The scope of the term 'persons aggrieved' has been interpreted in the *Bowen* case, which is dealt with in section 4.7.B.1 (iii) below.[83]

4.4.C.2 (ii) France

Code de l'urbanisme **4.32 (FR)**

Article L600-1-2 An action for annulment brought by a person other than the State, local authorities or their groupings or an association is only admissible against a permit to build, to demolish or to develop, if the building, the development, or the workings would be of such nature as to directly affect the conditions of the occupation, use or enjoyment of the property held or which is occupied regularly or which benefits from a sale commitment, rental agreement or a preliminary contract as mentioned in Article L261-15 of the Construction and Housing Code (*Code de la construction et de l'habitation*).

[83] Additional elaboration of the requirements can be found in the judgment of the Court of Appeal in *Ashton v Secretary of State for Communities and Local Government* [2010] EWCA Civ 600, [2011] 1 P & CR 5.

Conseil d'État, 10 February 2016[84] **4.33 (FR)**

Mmes C and D v Mayor of Marseille

STANDING; NEED TO BE 'DIRECTLY AFFECTED' BY PLANNING AUTHORISATIONS

Mmes C et D

In order for an action to challenge a building permit to be admissible, a neighbour has to demonstrate that he is directly affected and must provide specific evidence to this end.

Facts: The mayor of Marseille awarded a building permit, which was challenged by the claimant. The action was declared inadmissible by the Administrative Court of First Instance of Marseille. Since there is no right to appeal before the Administrative Court of Appeal when challenging a building permit, Mrs C and D challenged the ruling directly before the Council of State through an appeal on points of law (*cassation*).

Held: The action was declared inadmissible, since the claimant did not bring sufficient evidence of the harm caused by the permit.

Judgment: 3. Considering that, according to Article L600-1-2 of the Planning Code: 'An action for annulment brought by a person other than the State, local authorities or their groupings or an association, is only admissible against a permit to build, to demolish or to develop, if the building, the development or the workings would be of such nature as to directly affect the conditions of the occupation, use or enjoyment of the property held or which is occupied regularly or for which it benefits from a sale commitment, rental agreement or a preliminary contract as mentioned in Article L261-15 of the Construction and Housing Code'; that it follows from these provisions that it rests with each claimant, who brings an action for annulment (*recours pour excès de pouvoir*) before the administrative court seeking the annulment of a construction, demolition or development permit, to specify the infringement he invokes to justify an interest that gives him standing to take legal action, by presenting all elements in a manner that is sufficiently precise and substantiated to establish that this infringement has the potential to directly affect the conditions of occupation, use and enjoyment of his or her property;

4. Considering that the documents and contracts provided by the author of the action must show clearly in what respect the conditions of occupation, use and enjoyment of his property are potentially directly affected by the challenged project; that it appears from the documents of the file submitted to the court that, in order to justify their interest in taking legal action, the claimants rely only on their capacity as 'owners of immovable goods and direct neighbours to the plot on which the disputed constructions would be built'; that, furthermore, the documents they have provided in support of their request establish only that their plots are, on the one hand, adjacent to and, on the other, within sight of the contested project; that, the summary site plan of the plots of land which they have provided only entailed the indication: 'southern glazed facade which will have views'; that having been invited by the registry of the Administrative Court of First Instance, by letter of 28 August 2014, to provide the specifications that are necessary for the assessment of the direct infringement of their conditions of the use of their occupation or enjoyment of their property brought about by the contested project, they only provided, on or after 5 September, the copy of their certificates of ownership as well as the cadastral

[84] N° 387507.

plan which had already been provided; that, under these conditions, the president of the second chamber of the Administrative Court of First Instance of Marseille has carried out a correct legal assessment of the facts when ruling that the claimants lacked interest in taking legal action against the contested construction permit; ...

Note

As can be seen from Article L600-1-2 of the Planning Code, also in France the rules on standing in planning law are more restrictive than the general rules. In order to demonstrate that there is a direct interest to challenge the decision, the fact of being a neighbour is not sufficient: the claimant has to show that the decision would affect the enjoyment of his property.

Code de l'urbanisme **4.34 (FR)**

Article L600-1-1 An action brought by an association against a decision related to land use is only admissible if the statute of the association has been registered at the prefecture at least one year before the application for the decision was announced in the town hall.

Note

Specific conditions also apply to associations in order to limit the possibility for review of planning law decisions to avoid the multiplication of actions and the consequent possible delays to the management of a project, especially when the claims are brought by associations created solely to challenge a specific project and not to promote a more general interest.

4.4.C.2 (iii) The Netherlands

In the Netherlands, the general criterion of being 'personally concerned' is further specified in planning law. A building permit can be challenged only by persons living within a short distance to the building or who can see the permitted building from their property, as already demonstrated in the case of *Belangenvereniging Amstelwijck*, which was considered in section 4.4.B.4 above.[85]

4.4.C.2 (iv) Germany

In Germany, the requirement to claim the violation of a subjective right derived from public law (*Schutznormtheorie*) applies to all areas of law. However, the question whether or not a certain legal provision provides a subjective right depends on the peculiarities

[85] ECLI:NL:RVS:2008:BC4233.

of specific areas of law. For example, certain provisions of building and construction law (*Bauordnungsrecht*) confer subjective rights upon neighbours. By contrast, provisions of building planning law (*Bauplanungsrecht*) are not usually intended to confer subjective rights upon individuals.[86] Furthermore, §5(1) of the Federal Emission Control Act (Bundesimmissionsschutzgesetz) explicitly mentions 'neighbours' and thereby provides subjective public rights to owners of property that is affected by emissions.[87]

According to the courts, environmental rules are aimed at protecting the public rather than individuals.[88] Procedural provisions may confer standing under limited circumstances, provided that they protect the procedural rights of the persons participating in the procedure.[89]

4.4.C.3 APPLICATION OF THE *PLAUMANN* CRITERION IN DIFFERENT AREAS

Differentiation between certain areas of law can also be found with regard to the *Plaumann* criterion for standing before the EU courts. In certain policy fields, the CJEU has adopted a more liberal approach to the test of individual concern. In particular, in the fields of anti-dumping,[90] state aid[91] and competition investigations,[92] the CJEU has held that claimants were individually concerned as a result of their participation in the procedure leading to the adoption of the contested EU measure. The 'orthodox' application of the *Plaumann* doctrine would have led, in these cases, to the dismissal of the claim because the measure affected only members of an 'open' category of potential claimants.

Case T-585/93, 9 August 1995[93] **4.35 (EU)**

Greenpeace v Commission

STANDING; APPLICATION OF *PLAUMANN* CRITERIA IN ENVIRONMENTAL LAW CASES

Greenpeace

In order to be granted standing, (environmental) associations must demonstrate an individual interest on the part of their members as opposed to any other person residing in the areas affected by the challenged decision.

Facts: Several claimants, including the environmental organisation Greenpeace, brought an action to annul a Commission decision which granted financial assistance from the European Regional Development Fund to the Kingdom of Spain for the construction of two power stations on the islands of Gran Canaria and Tenerife.

[86] BVerwG, NVwZ 1996, 170. However, some provisions, such as §34(2) of the Building Code, provide subjective rights, as they address a specific group of persons, see BVerwGE 94, 151.

[87] BVerwG, NVwZ, 1997, 161.

[88] See, eg BVerwGE 128, 358 (*Mühlenberger Loch*).

[89] BVerwGE 87, 62, 69. The likelihood of a violation of a right depends on whether, at the same time, there is a possible violation in substance, see BVerwGE 61, 256; BVerwGE 88, 286; BVerwG, NVwZ, 1999, 876; critical on this, F Hufen, *Verwaltungsprozessrecht*, 9th edn (Munich, CH Beck, 2013) 259.

[90] Case 264/82 *Timex Corporation v Council and Commission* ECLI:EU:C:1985:119, paras 14–15.

[91] Case C-169/84 *Société CdF Chimie azote et fertilisants SA and Société chimique de la Grande Paroisse SA v Commission* ECLI:EU:C:1986:42.

[92] Case C-75/84 *Metro SB-Großmärkte GmbH & Co. KG v Commission* ECLI:EU:C:1986:399.

[93] ECLI:EU:T:1995:147.

Held: The court declared the claim inadmissible.

Judgment: 60 The three applicant associations, Greenpeace, TEA and CIC, claim that they represent the general interest, in the matter of environmental protection, of people residing on Gran Canaria and Tenerife and that their members are affected by the contested decision; they do not, however, adduce any special circumstances to demonstrate the individual interest of their members as opposed to any other person residing in those areas. The possible effect on the legal position of the members of the applicant associations cannot, therefore, be any different from that alleged here by the applicants who are private individuals. Consequently, in so far as the applicants in the present case who are private individuals cannot, as the Court has held (see paragraph 58 above), be considered to be individually concerned by the contested decision, nor can the members of the applicant associations, as local residents of Gran Canaria and Tenerife.

Note

The strict application of the requirement of the *Plaumann* interpretation of the notion of 'individual concern' to the environmental field has led to the outcome that environmental claims will hardly ever be admissible.

4.4.D STANDING OF NGOs AND OTHER GROUPS

Two kinds of interest groups regularly seek judicial protection before the courts. A group may advocate for the common interest of the members of the group. Dutch law calls these interests 'collective interests' (*collective belangen*). German lawyers call this form of action an 'group interest collective action' (*egoistische Verbandsklage*). However, a group can also advocate for the general public interest, hence in Dutch for '*algemene belangen*', or in German bring an 'general interest collective action' (*altruistische Verbandsklage*). The rules on standing for interest groups often differ from those applicable to individual claims. However, they have all been subject to a strong harmonising influence brought about by the EU and, in particular, the EU transposition of the Aarhus Convention in the field of environmental law.[94]

4.4.D.1 LEGAL SYSTEMS WITH NO OR VERY LIMITED ACCESS FOR NGOs AND OTHER GROUPS

4.4.D.1 (i) The European Union

There are no special rules on the standing of NGOs and other groups before EU courts, hence the usual requirements of 'individual' and 'direct' concern contained in Article 263 TFEU apply to claims brought by interest groups.

[94] The influence of EU law and the Aarhus Convention on the rules on standing is examined below in section 4.4.E.

Case C-321/95, 2 April 1998[95] **4.36 (EU)**

Greenpeace v Commission

STANDING; INDIVIDUAL CONCERN; NGO; ENVIRONMENTAL POLICY

Greenpeace

In order to be granted standing in an annulment action, an environmental association must prove to be individually and directly concerned.

Facts: Several claimants, including the environmental organisation Greenpeace, brought an action to annul a Commission decision which granted financial assistance from the European Regional Development Fund to the Kingdom of Spain for the construction of two power stations on the islands of Gran Canaria and Tenerife. The Court of First Instance had declared the claim inadmissible. Greenpeace appealed against this order before the European Court of Justice.

Held: The appeal was dismissed.

Judgment: 17. In their appeal the appellants submit that, in determining whether they were individually concerned by the contested decision within the meaning of Article 173 of the Treaty, the Court of First Instance erred in its interpretation and application of that provision and that, by applying the case-law developed by the Court of Justice in relation to economic issues and economic rights, according to which an individual must belong to a 'closed class' in order to be individually concerned by a Community act, the Court of First Instance failed to take account of the nature and specific character of the environmental interests underpinning their action.

18. In particular, the appellants argue, first, that the approach adopted by the Court of First Instance creates a legal vacuum in ensuring compliance with Community environmental legislation, since in this area the interests are, by their very nature, common and shared, and the rights relating to those interests are liable to be held by a potentially large number of individuals so that there could never be a closed class of applicants satisfying the criteria adopted by the Court of First Instance.

19. Nor can that legal vacuum be filled by the possibility of bringing proceedings before the national courts. According to the appellants, such proceedings have in fact been brought in the present case, but they concern the Spanish authorities' failure to comply with their obligations under Council Directive 85/337/EEC, and not the legality of the Commission measure, that is to say the lawfulness under Community law of the Commission's disbursement of structural funds on the ground that that disbursement is in violation of an obligation for protecting the environment.

…

27. The interpretation of the fourth paragraph of Article 173 of the Treaty that the Court of First Instance applied in concluding that the appellants did not have *locus standi* is consonant with the settled case-law of the Court of Justice.

28. As far as natural persons are concerned, it follows from the case-law, cited at both paragraph 48 of the contested order and at paragraph 7 of this judgment, that where, as in the present case, the specific situation of the applicant was not taken into

[95] ECLI:EU:C:1998:153.

consideration in the adoption of the act, which concerns him in a general and abstract fashion and, in fact, like any other person in the same situation, the applicant is not individually concerned by the act.

29. The same applies to associations which claim to have *locus standi* on the basis of the fact that the persons whom they represent are individually concerned by the contested decision. For the reasons given in the preceding paragraph, that is not the case.

30. In appraising the appellants' arguments purporting to demonstrate that the case-law of the Court of Justice, as applied by the Court of First Instance, takes no account of the nature and specific characteristics of the environmental interests underpinning their action, it should be emphasised that it is the decision to build the two power stations in question which is liable to affect the environmental rights arising under Directive 85/337 that the appellants seek to invoke.

31. In those circumstances, the contested decision, which concerns the Community financing of those power stations, can affect those rights only indirectly.

Notes

(1) The question of whether associations could be regarded as individually concerned has frequently arisen before the CJEU. It appears from the case law that actions brought by associations are only admissible in three cases:[96]

(a) when a legal provision grants procedural rights to these associations;[97]
(b) where every single member of the association would be directly and individually concerned;[98] or
(c) where the association's interests, and especially its position as a negotiator, are affected by the measure.[99]

These requirements have made it almost impossible for associations to succeed in showing individual concern, given that the cases under (a) are rare and the cases under (b) are as difficult (if not harder) to be successful as cases concerning individuals under the strict interpretation of the *Plaumann* formula. Successful cases under (c) are also uncommon, since the CJEU has held that the test to be met is that the position of the association as negotiator is clearly defined and must be related to the

[96] Case C-321/95 P *Stichting Greenpeace Council (Greenpeace International) and Others v Commission* ECLI:EU:C:1998:153; Case T-122/96 *Federazione nazionale del commercio oleario (Federolio) v Commission* ECLI:EU:T:1997:142.

[97] Case 191/82 *EEC Seed Crushers' and Oil Processors' Federation (FEDIOL) v Commission* ECLI:EU:C:1983:259; Case T-12/93 *Comité Central d'Entreprise de la Société Anonyme Vittel and Comité d'Etablissement de Pierval and Fédération Générale Agroalimentaire v Commission* ECLI:EU:T:1995:78.

[98] Joined Cases T-447/93, T-448/93 and T-449/93 *Associazione Italiana Tecnico Economica del Cemento and British Cement Association and Blue Circle Industries plc and Castle Cement Ltd and The Rugby Goup plc and Titan Cement Company SA v Commission* ECLI:EU:T:1995:130; Case T-380/94 *Association internationale des utilisateurs de fils de filaments artificiels et synthétiques et de soie naturelle (AIUFFASS) and Apparel, Knitting & Textiles Alliance (AKT) v Commission* ECLI:EU:T:1996:195; Case T-229/02 *Osman Ocalan acting on behalf of Kurdistan Workers' Party (PKK) v Council of the European Union* ECLI:EU:T:2008:8.

[99] Joined Cases 67/85 R, 68/85 R and 70/85 R *Kwekerij Gebroeders van der Kooy BV and others v Commission* ECLI:EU:C:1988:38; Case T-84/01 *Association contre l'horaire d'été (ACHE) v Council of the European Union and European Parliament* ECLI:EU:T:2002:5.

subject matter of the contested act, and that that position must have been affected by the adoption of the contested act.[100] The fact that an association has communicated information to an EU institution or has tried to influence the position adopted by the national authorities in the EU legislative procedure has been regarded as insufficient in itself to show that the act adopted affects an association in its position as a negotiator.[101]

(2) As the *Greenpeace* case shows, specifically in the field of environmental law, where often no individual claimant is entitled to bring a claim, the restrictive interpretation of the notion of individual concern to claims brought for the collective interest of its members or for the general interest significantly restricts the access to the European courts.[102]

4.4.D.1 (ii) Germany

As a general rule, in German law, both kinds of group actions are not possible. As noted above,[103] the general approach is that standing is only granted if the plaintiff can invoke a right attributed to him by law. A mere right of the general public or of others is not sufficient. As a consequence, standing of NGOs and associations which want to represent the interest of their members (*egoistische Verbandsklage*) or the interests of the general public (*altruistische Verbandsklage*) is not generally provided for.[104] Thus, unless corporate bodies, such as NGOs, can claim that their own individual rights are affected by the administrative action, they have no access to the courts due to a lack of standing. A mere infringement of rights of their members does not entitle an association to have access to court. In fact, each individual member must file a claim in his or her own name. An association would have to demonstrate a direct financial loss or damage to its own property to gain standing. However, exceptions have been made to that general rule in particular fields of law, such as environmental law, mostly because of the influence of EU law and the Aarhus Convention.[105]

[100] Case C-106/98 P *Comité d'entreprise de la Société française de production, Syndicat national de radiodiffusion et de télévision CGT (SNRT-CGT), Syndicat unifié de radio et de télévision CFDT (SURT-CFDT), Syndicat national Force ouvrière de radiodiffusion et de télévision and Syndicat national de l'encadrement audiovisuel CFE-CGC (SNEA-CFE-CGC) v Commission* ECLI:EU:C:2000:277, para 45.

[101] Case T-391/02 *Bundesverband der Nahrungsmittel- und Speiseresteverwertung eV and Josef Kloh v European Parliament and Council of the European Union* ECLI:EU:T:2004:138; Case T-264/03 *Jürgen Schmoldt and Others v Commission* ECLI:EU:T:2004:157.

[102] eg Case T-585/93 *Stichting Greenpeace Council (Greenpeace International) and Others v Commission* ECLI:EU:T:1995:147; Joined Cases T-236/04 and T-241/04 *European Environmental Bureau (EEB) and Stichting Natuur en Milieu v Commission* ECLI:EU:T:2005:426; Case C-355/08 P *WWF-UK v Council of the European Union* ECLI:EU:C:2009:286.

[103] See section 4.4.B.1.

[104] ibid.

[105] See, eg §61 ff of the Federal Nature Protection Act (Bundesnaturschutzgesetz) and §2 of the Environmental Remedies Act (Umweltrechtsbehelfsgesetz). For further examples, see BVerwG, NVwZ, 1991, 162; BVerwGE 87, 62, 69; BVerwG, NVwZ 2007, 576; BVerwG, NVwZ 2006, 817. See further below, section 4.4.E.

4.4.D.2 LEGAL SYSTEMS WITH BROAD ACCESS FOR NGOs AND OTHER GROUPS

4.4.D.2 (i) France

In France, associations can bring a *recours pour excès de pouvoir* (action for annulment) as soon as they have been created.

Conseil d'État, 13 January 1975[106] **4.37 (FR)**

Da Silva et CFDT v Minister for Home Affairs and Minister for Work, Employment and Population

ACTION FOR ANNULMENT; STANDING; ASSOCIATIONS

Da Silva et CFDT

A trade union has standing to challenge measures which affect the collective interests of its members.

Facts: A trade union (Confédération française démocratique du travail – CFDT) introduced an action to challenge measures adopted by the Minister for Home Affairs and the Minister for Work, Employment and Population relating to the conditions applicable to the establishment of foreign workers. Mr Da Silva, a Portuguese national, introduced an action against the same measures. The two actions were joined in one ruling before the Council of State.

Held: The actions of Mr Da Silva and the CFDT were declared admissible. The Council of State partially annulled the measures on the ground of lack of competence.

Judgment: on the interest in taking legal action (intéret à agir) of Mr x … Da Silva and of the French Democratic Confederation of Labour (CFDT): considering, on the one hand, that Mr x … Da Silva is a worker of Portuguese nationality employed in France; that the circulars contested concern the situation of foreign workers in France and do not exclude from their scope of application Portuguese nationals, that, since Mr x … Da Silva is currently holding a working card and a residence card both valid for several years, the contested circulars are to be likely contested at the eventual renewal of the former; considering, on the other hand, that the French Democratic Confederation of Labour has as its purpose to defend the material and moral interests of both French and foreign workers; considering that it follows from the foregoing that the Minister for Home Affairs and the Minister for Labour, Employment and Population are not right in arguing that Mr x … Da Silva and the French Democratic Confederation of Labour do not have a sufficient interest in seeking the annulment of the contested circulars …

Note

Actions brought to protect collective group interests are possible in the French legal system, for example, in case of actions of trade unions, but only insofar as these associations either have received an explicit mandate from those whom they seek to represent or they challenge a decision affecting collective interests, namely the

[106] N° 90193, 90194, 91288.

interests promoted by the association,[107] which are distinct from (the sum of) all the individual interests of its members.[108] Consequently, a group can only challenge individual decisions addressed to one of their members if this decision also concerns the collective interests of the group, as following from the statutory aims of the group.[109]

Code de l'environnement **4.38 (FR)**

Article L142-1 Every association whose purpose is the protection of nature and the environment can bring claims before the administrative courts for any grievance related to this field.

Every association dealing with the protection of the environment approved under Article L141-1 as well as the departmental federations of approved fishing and water protection associations and approved associations of professional fishermen are to be treated as having an interest in taking legal action (intéret à agir) against any administrative decision which is directly related to their aim and their statutory activities and having harmful effects on the environment on the entire or part of the territory for which they have been approved, if the decision was adopted after the date of their approval.

Note

There is a specific legal regime regarding environmental NGOs. According to the law of 10 July 1976,[110] approved environmental NGOs benefit from a presumption of standing when bringing an action for annulment. This presumption is interpreted widely, as long as the action for annulment is brought against a decision having a direct link with their interests and statutory activities. The challenged decision must furthermore have harmful effects on the territory for which the environmental NGO is approved. This may be local, regional or national.

4.4.D.2 (ii) The Netherlands

Algemene Wet Bestuursrecht **4.39 (NL)**

Article 1:2 …

(3) As regards legal persons, their interests are considered to include the general and collective interests which they particularly promote by virtue of their objectives as shown by their factual activities.

Note

In the Netherlands, legal entities which advocate a collective or general interest have standing before administrative courts on the basis of Article 1:2(3) AWB.

[107] Conseil d'État, 1 June 1979, *Association Défense et Promotion des langues de France*, N° 06410, 06411, 06412.
[108] Conseil d'État, 28 December 1906, *Syndicat des patrons-coiffeurs de Limoges*, N° 25521.
[109] Conseil d'État, 3 April 1987, *Ligue Languedoc-Roussillon de course d'orientation*, N° 80239.
[110] Loi n° 76-629 du 10 juillet 1976 relative à la protection de la nature.

Environmental groups and local action groups are well-known examples of such entities acting in favour of a general interest. Article 1:2(3) AWB provides that the collective or general interests which a legal entity strives to protect according to (a) its statute and (b) its factual activities are deemed to be the personal interests of such an entity. In practice, all kinds of (collective and general) interest groups are accepted as parties before the administrative courts.

Raad van State, 1 October 2008[111] **4.40 (NL)**

Stichting Openbare Ruimte v Provincial Executive Gelderland

STANDING; ASSOCIATIONS; TIGHTENING OF TEST

Stichting Openbare Ruimte

The sole action of opposing decisions does not generally qualify as activity as defined by Article 1:2(3) AWB.

Facts: An environmental group challenged a permit for an enlargement of a pig farm close to an area falling within the scope of the Natura 2000 network established by the Habitats Directive 92/43/EEC.

Held: The claim was declared inadmissible.

Judgment: 2.2 According to Article 2(1) of its statutes, the association aims to strive to create a sustainable and healthy environment for all living beings on a local, regional and global scale. More concretely this means:

— to pursue a healthy and sustainable environment for human beings, animals and plants, including artificial and natural environment;
— to pursue good spatial development for human beings, animals and plants. This also includes the promotion of appropriate biotopes of flora and fauna and care for nature and the landscape appropriate to local conditions. …

2.3 Concerning the question whether an association qualifies as 'a party concerned' in the sense of Article 1:2(3) AWB, it is decisive whether the association, according to its statutes and its factual activities, has a particular role in looking after a collective or general interest which is directly affected by the decision which is challenged …

According to the statutes, the aims of the association are too broad to be sufficiently special for the court to be able to rule that the interests of the association are directly affected by the decision.

Furthermore, it appears that the association does not do anything which could qualify as a factual activity in the meaning of Article 1:2(3) AWB and which demonstrates that the association has a particular role in protecting the general interests which are influenced by the disputed decision ….

As the court considers, the sole action of bringing legal proceedings to oppose decisions does generally not qualify as factual activity in the sense of Article 1:2(3) AWB.

[111] ECLI:NL:RVS:2008:BF3911.

Note

Until 2008, some NGOs specialised in instituting intra-administrative objection procedures and legal proceedings, often with a high success rate. In the *Stichting Openbare Ruimte* case, the Council of State adopted a more restrictive interpretation of Article 1:2(3) AWB and strengthened the requirement that an entity must advocate something by undertaking 'factual' activities.[112] Moreover, as the excerpt demonstrates, associations whose aims are so broad that they will be concerned by almost all decisions with any effect on the environment at some place in the world will not be granted standing. However, associations such as Greenpeace or the WWF, which also campaign for a relatively broad range of environmental issues over a wide geographical area, are accepted. Political parties, or local divisions thereof, are not accepted as entities acting in favour of a (certain) general interest as the scope of their activities is too broad and general.[113] Article 1:2(3) AWB provides standing only for groups which advocate for 'a certain' aspect of general interest, such as healthy living conditions in a certain area or the protection of the natural environment. Furthermore, they are deemed to act in the political, not the legal, arena.

4.4.D.2 (iii) England and Wales

Courts in England and Wales have been willing to permit groups to bring claims for judicial review. Groups such as Greenpeace have brought claims relatively often, with the most famous case being when they were permitted to proceed in a challenge to the licence to operate granted to part of the Sellafield nuclear reprocessing plant in Cumbria.

High Court (Queen's Bench Division), 29 September 1993[114] **4.41 (EW)**

R v Inspectorate of Pollution, ex parte Greenpeace Ltd (No 2)

STANDING; ASSOCIATIONS

Greenpeace

NGOs with a strong reputation and evidence of activities in the area of the challenged action are likely to have standing.

Facts: British Nuclear Fuels Limited had applied to the Inspectorate of Pollution for the extension of licences granted to it in relation to the operation of a nuclear reprocessing plant. Greenpeace brought a claim for judicial review, arguing that the grant was unlawful because the variation to the licence was not justified and there had not been adequate consultation in respect of the decision. The Inspectorate of Pollution argued that Greenpeace lacked standing to bring the claim.

Held: It was held that Greenpeace had standing to bring the claim, but that its claim would not be successful as none of the grounds of the claim were accepted.

[112] ECLI:NL:RVS:2008:BF3911.
[113] ECLI:NL:RVS:1997:ZF2789.
[114] [1994] 2 CMLR 548 (QB).

Judgment: Otton J: Greenpeace International has also been accredited with consultative status with the United Nations Economic and Social Council (including United Nations General Assembly). It has accreditation status with the UN Conference on Environment and Development. They have observer status or right to attend meetings of 17 named bodies including Parcom (Paris Convention for the Prevention of Marine Pollution from Land Based Sources). BNFL rightly acknowledge the national and international standing of Greenpeace and its integrity. So must I. I have not the slightest reservation that Greenpeace is an entirely responsible and respected body with a genuine concern for the environment. That concern naturally leads to a bona fide interest in the activities carried on by BNFL at Sellafield and in particular the discharge and disposal of radioactive waste from their premises and to which the respondents' decision to vary relates. The fact that 400,000 supporters in the United Kingdom carries less weight than the fact that 2,500 of them come from the Cumbria region. I would be ignoring the blindingly obvious if I were to disregard the fact that those persons are inevitably concerned about (and have a genuine perception that there is) a danger to their health and safety from any additional discharge of radioactive waste even from testing. I have no doubt that the issues raised by this application are serious and worthy of determination by this court.

It seems to me that if I were to deny standing to Greenpeace, those they represent might not have an effective way to bring the issues before the court. There would have to be an application either by an individual employee of BNFL or a near neighbour. In this case it is unlikely that either would be able to command the expertise which is at the disposal of Greenpeace. Consequently, a less well-informed challenge might be mounted which would stretch unnecessarily the court's resources and which would not afford the court the assistance it requires in order to do justice between the parties. Further, if the unsuccessful applicant had the benefit of legal aid it might leave the respondents and BNFL without an effective remedy in costs. Alternatively, the individual (or Greenpeace) might seek to persuade H.M. Attorney-General to commence a relator action which (as a matter of policy or practice) he may be reluctant to undertake against a government department (see the learned commentary by Schiemann J. on '*Locus Standi*' in [1990] P.L. 342). Neither of these courses of action would have the advantage of an application by Greenpeace, who, with its particular experience in environmental matters, its access to experts in the relevant realms of science and technology (not to mention the law) is able to mount a carefully selected, focused, relevant and well-argued challenge. It is not without significance that in this case the form 86 contains six grounds of challenge, but by the time it came to the substantive hearing before me, the Greenpeace 'team' (if I can call them that) had been able to evaluate the respondents' and BNFL's evidence and were able to jettison four grounds and concentrate on two. This responsible approach undoubtedly had the advantage of sparing scarce court resources, ensuring an expedited substantive hearing and an early result (which it transpires is helpful to the respondents and to BNFL). This line of reasoning has some support from the approach to be found in a line of cases in the Supreme Court of Canada. See *Thorson v. Att.-Gen. Canada* [1975] 1 S.C.R. 138, *McNeill v. Nova Scotia Board of Census* [1976] 2 S.C.R. 265, *Borowski v. Minister of Justice of Canada* [1981] 2 S.C.R. 575, *Finlay v. Minister of Finance of Canada* [1986] 2 S.C.R. 60. See in particular the judgment of Le Dain J. in *Finlay v. Ministry of Finance of Canada* [1986] 2 S.C.R. 60. See also the helpful and imaginative commentary of the authors Goudie and Supperstone in *Judicial Review* pp. 335–336 and 338–340.

I also take into account the nature of the relief sought. In the 'Fleet Street Casuals' case the House of Lords expressed the view that if mandamus were sought that would be a reason to decline jurisdiction. Here, the primary relief sought is certiorari (less stringent) and, if granted, the question of an injunction to stop the testing pending determination of the main applications would still be in the discretion of the court. I also take into account the fact that Greenpeace has been treated as one of the consultees during the consultation process and that they were invited (albeit with other non-consultees) to comment on the 'minded to vary' letter.

It follows that I reject the argument that Greenpeace is a 'mere' or 'meddlesome busybody.' I regard the applicants as eminently respectable and responsible and their genuine interest in the issues raised is sufficient for them to be granted *locus standi*.

I should add that Lord Roskill in 'Fleet Street Casuals' at p. 695A–B approved the commentary to Order 53 of the Supreme Court Practice that the question of whether the applicant has a sufficient interest appears to be:

'A mixed question of fact and law; a question of fact and degree and the relationship and the applicant and the matter to which the application relates, having regard to all the circumstances of the case.'

Thus it must not be assumed that Greenpeace (or any other interest group) will automatically be afforded standing in any subsequent application for judicial review in whatever field it (and its members) may have an interest. This will have to be a matter to be considered on a case by case basis at the leave stage and if the threshold is crossed again at the substantive hearing as a matter of discretion.

In exercising my discretion I would grant Greenpeace standing in this case. ...

High Court (Queen's Bench Division), 10 November 1994[115] **4.42 (EW)**

R v Secretary of State for Foreign and Commonwealth Affairs, ex parte World Development Movement Ltd

STANDING; ASSOCIATIONS

World Development Movement

The importance of vindicating the rule of law, the importance of the issue raised, the likely absence of any other responsible challenger, the nature of the breach of duty against which relief is sought and the prominent role of the applicants and their activities with regard to the subject discussed are all factors to take into account when deciding whether an interest group has standing.

Facts: The World Development Movement challenged the legality of a decision by the Secretary of State to grant foreign aid for the development of the Pergau Dam in Malaysia. The Secretary of State, acting under the Overseas Development and Co-operation Act 1980, made the decision to grant the aid despite receiving strong advice that the economic case for building the dam was not a strong one. A significant factor in his decision to grant the aid was the desire to secure political and commercial links with Malaysia for UK firms.

Held: The association was granted standing and the decision was quashed.

Judgment: Rose L.J.: I turn now to the issues earlier identified. As to standing, the Supreme Court Act 1981, section 31(3) provides:

'No application for judicial review shall be made unless the leave of the High Court has been obtained in accordance with rules of court; and the court shall not grant leave to

[115] [1995] 1 WLR 386 (CA).

make such an application unless it considers that the applicant has a sufficient interest in the matter to which the application relates.'

Rules of the Supreme Court, Ord. 53 r 3(7) provides:

'The Court shall not grant leave unless it considers that the applicant has a sufficient interest in the matter to which the application relates.'

The affidavit of Mr Jackson, the Applicants' Campaign Coordinator, describes the Applicant company. It is a non-partisan pressure group, over 20 years old and limited by guarantee. It has an associated charity which receives financial support from all the main United Kingdom development charities, the churches, the European Community and a range of other trusts. About 60 per cent of its total income comes from members and supporters. The Council of the Applicants has cross political party membership, and, indeed, historically, a Member of Parliament from each of the three main political parties has sat on the Council. There are 7,000 full voting members throughout the United Kingdom with a total supporter base of some 13,000. There are 200 local groups whose supporters actively campaign through letter writing, lobbying and other democratic means to improve the quantity and quality of British aid to other countries. It conducts research and analysis in relation to aid. It is a founder member of the Independent Group on British Aid, which brings academics and campaigners together. It has pressed the British Government, the European Union, the banks and other businesses for better trade access for developing countries. It is in regular contact with the ODA and has regular meetings with the Minister of that department, and it makes written and oral submissions to a range of Select Committees in both Houses of Parliament. It has run all party campaigns against aid cuts in 1987 and 1992.

Internationally, it has official consultative status with UNESCO and has promoted international conferences. It has brought together development groups within the OECD. It tends to attract citizens of the United Kingdom concerned about the role of the United Kingdom Government in relation to the development of countries abroad and the relief of poverty abroad.

Its supporters have a direct interest in ensuring that funds furnished by the United Kingdom are used for genuine purposes, and it seeks to ensure that disbursement of aid budgets is made where that aid is most needed. It seeks, by this application, to represent the interests of people in developing countries who might benefit from funds which otherwise might go elsewhere. If the Applicants have no standing, it is said that no person or body would ensure that powers under the 1980 Act are exercised lawfully.

The applicant referred the court to a number of authorities: *R v Inland Revenue Commissioners, ex parte National Federation of Self Employed and Small Businesses Ltd* [1982] AC 617; in particular the speech of Lord Wilberforce at page 630E and the speech of Lord Diplock at 644E G, where there appears this passage:

'It would, in my view, be a grave lacuna in our system of public law if a pressure group, like the federation, or even a public spirited taxpayer, were prevented by outdated technical rules of locus standi from bringing the matter to the attention of the court to vindicate the rule of law and get the unlawful conduct stopped. The Attorney General, although he occasionally applies for prerogative orders against public authorities that do not form part of central government, in practice never does so against government departments. It is not, in my view, a sufficient 'answer to say that judicial review of the actions of officers or departments of central government is unnecessary because they are accountable to Parliament for the way in which they accountable to Parliament for the way in which they carry out their functions. They are accountable to Parliament for what they do so far as regards efficiency and policy, and of that Parliament is the only judge; they are responsible to a court of justice for the lawfulness of what they do, and of that the court is the only judge.'

...

Leaving merits aside for a moment, there seem to me to be a number of factors of significance in the present case: the importance of vindicating the rule of law, as Lord Diplock emphasised at 644E; the importance of the issue raised, as in *ex parte Child Poverty Action Group and Others*; the likely absence of any other responsible challenger, as in *ex parte Child Poverty Action Group and Others* and *ex parte Greenpeace Ltd*; the nature of the breach of duty against which relief is sought (See per Lord Wilberforce at 630D in *ex parte National Federation of the Self Employed and Small Businesses Ltd*); and the prominent role of these Applicants in giving advice, guidance and assistance with regard to aid (See *ex parte Child Poverty Action Group and Others* at 1048J). All, in my judgement, point, in the present case, to the conclusion that the Applicants here do have a sufficient interest in the matter to which the application relates within section 31(3) of the Supreme Court Act and Ord. 53 r.3(7).

Note

The standing requirements for interest groups and NGOs in English law are liberal. If a group has a substantial reputation in respect of the issues to which the claim relates and also raises awareness and takes steps to protect the interests of those who might be impacted by particular state activities, then this will create a strong prima facie case that the group should have standing. This will be augmented if it can also be demonstrated that, in the absence of a claim by the interest group, there will be no other claimant in a position to challenge the alleged unlawful act. As emphasised in both the *Greenpeace* and *World Development Movement* excerpts, the grant of standing in a particular case may also turn on the strength of the case that is being pursued.

Court of Appeal (Civil Division), 23 June 2006[116] **4.43 (EW)**

R (Countryside Alliance) v Attorney General

STANDING; ASSOCIATIONS; HUMAN RIGHTS ACT; VICTIM TEST

Countryside Alliance

Groups can pass the 'victim test' that is required in cases falling under the Human Rights Act.

Facts: This case concerned a number of complex challenges to the legality of the Hunting Act 2004, which banned hunting with hounds other than in very limited and closely regulated circumstances. The claimants

[116] [2006] EWCA Civ 817, [2007] QB 305.

(who were all involved in hunting) sought judicial review of the legality of the provisions of the Act both under the Human Rights Act 1998, as they claimed that the Act infringed Articles 8, 11 and 14 and Article 1 of Protocol 1 ECHR, and also under EU law.

Held: The group was granted standing. However, no breach of Article 11 or 14 ECHR was found, and insofar as there was a breach of Article 1 of the Protocol 1 ECHR, that breach was justified. As such, the claimants were unsuccessful.

Judgment: Lord Clarke M.R.: 65. In that context section 7(7) provides that for the purposes of section 7, a person is a victim of an unlawful act only if he would be a victim for the purposes of article 34 of the Convention if proceedings were brought in the European Court of Human Rights. By that article that court may receive applications from any person, non-governmental organisation or group of individuals claiming to be the victim of a violation by one of the High Contracting Parties of the rights set forth in the Convention or the protocols thereto. Strasbourg case law treats a person as a victim within the meaning of article 34 if they run the risk of being directly affected by a law or other act of state interference which violates their Convention rights (see *Marckx v Belgium* (1979) 2 EHRR 330; *Institut de Prêtres Français v Turkey* 92-A DR 15 (1998) Appl. No. 26308/95). In the present proceedings, there has been no suggestion that the Appellants do not have standing to seek the proposed declaration, and at the centre of their concern is the fear that the Hunting Act creates the risk of violating their Convention rights.

Note

In cases falling under the Human Rights Act, the standing test is that of a 'victim' of a human rights violation. The excerpt above shows that standing of groups has been accepted, although it is often not obvious that a group is a 'victim' of a violation of a human right.

4.4.E THE INFLUENCE OF INTERNATIONAL LAW ON STANDING CRITERIA IN ENVIRONMENTAL LAW CASES

4.4.E.1 THE INFLUENCE OF ARTICLE 9(2) OF THE AARHUS CONVENTION ON STANDING BEFORE NATIONAL COURTS

UNECE Convention on Access to Information, Public Participation in Decision-making and Access to Justice in Environmental Matters (Aarhus Convention) **4.44 (UN)**

Article 9 (1) …

(2) Each Party shall, within the framework of its national legislation, ensure that members of the public concerned

(a) Having a sufficient interest or, alternatively,

(b) Maintaining impairment of a right, where the administrative procedural law of a Party requires this as a precondition, have access to a review procedure before a court of law and/or another independent and impartial body established by law, to challenge the substantive and procedural legality of any decision, act or omission subject to the provisions of article 6 and, where so provided for under national law and without prejudice to paragraph 3 below, of other relevant provisions of this Convention.

What constitutes a sufficient interest and impairment of a right shall be determined in accordance with the requirements of national law and consistently with the objective of giving the public concerned wide access to justice within the scope of this Convention. To this end, the interest of any non-governmental organization meeting the requirements referred to in article 2, paragraph 5, shall be deemed sufficient for the purpose of subparagraph (a) above. Such organizations shall also be deemed to have rights capable of being impaired for the purpose of subparagraph (b) above.

...

(4) In addition and without prejudice to paragraph 1 above, the procedures referred to in paragraphs 1, 2 and 3 above shall provide adequate and effective remedies, including injunctive relief as appropriate, and be fair, equitable, timely and not prohibitively expensive. Decisions under this article shall be given or recorded in writing. Decisions of courts, and whenever possible of other bodies, shall be publicly accessible.

(5) In order to further the effectiveness of the provisions of this article, each Party shall ensure that information is provided to the public on access to administrative and judicial review procedures and shall consider the establishment of appropriate assistance mechanisms to remove or reduce financial and other barriers to access to justice.

Directive 2011/92/EU on the assessment of the effects of certain public and private projects on the environment[117] *(former Article 10a, Directive 85/337/EEC)*[118] **4.45 (EU)**

Article 11 (1) Member States shall ensure that, in accordance with the relevant national legal system, members of the public concerned:

(a) having a sufficient interest, or alternatively;

(b) maintaining the impairment of a right, where administrative procedural law of a Member State requires this as a precondition;

have access to a review procedure before a court of law or another independent and impartial body established by law to challenge the substantive or procedural legality of decisions, acts or omissions subject to the public participation provisions of this Directive.

(2) Member States shall determine at what stage the decisions, acts or omissions may be challenged.

(3) What constitutes a sufficient interest and impairment of a right shall be determined by the Member States, consistently with the objective of giving the public concerned wide access to justice. To that end, the interest of any non-governmental organisation meeting the requirements referred to in Article 1(2) shall be deemed sufficient for the purpose of point (a) of paragraph 1 of this Article. Such organisations shall also be

[117] Directive 2011/92/EU of the European Parliament and of the Council of 13 December 2011 on the assessment of the effects of certain public and private projects on the environment [2012] OJ L26/1.

[118] Council Directive of 27 June 1985 on the assessment of the effects of certain public and private projects on the environment [1985] OJ L175/40.

deemed to have rights capable of being impaired for the purpose of point (b) of paragraph 1 of this Article.

(4) The provisions of this Article shall not exclude the possibility of a preliminary review procedure before an administrative authority and shall not affect the requirement of exhaustion of administrative review procedures prior to recourse to judicial review procedures, where such a requirement exists under national law.

Any such procedure shall be fair, equitable, timely and not prohibitively expensive.

(5) In order to further the effectiveness of the provisions of this Article, Member States shall ensure that practical information is made available to the public on access to administrative and judicial review procedures.

Notes

(1) All EU Member States and the EU itself are parties to the Aarhus Convention. The requirements of the Aarhus Convention have partly been transposed into secondary EU law. In particular, the EU has adopted Directive 2003/35/EC[119] in order to implement Article 9(2) of the Aarhus Convention with regard to measures taken by authorities of the Member States in the area of the EU directives on environmental impact assessments and industrial emissions. To this end, Article 10a was added to Directive 85/337/EEC (the so-called Environmental Impact Assessment Directive), which now has become Article 11 of Directive 2011/92/EU,[120] and the almost identical Article 25 was introduced in Directive 2010/75/EU[121] (the so-called Industrial Emissions Directive). Article 9(2) of the Aarhus Convention mainly relates to the areas of environmental law covered by these Directives, but its scope is broader. Besides the activities listed in Annex I of the Convention – and which are covered by Directive 2003/35/EC, Article 9(2) relates to all other activities 'which may have a significant effect on the environment'. The parties to the Convention have to determine which activities may have significant effects on the environment and hence fall within the scope of Article 9(2). Amongst these are, in any case, all activities for which, because they may have significant effects on a Natura 2000 area, require an appropriate assessment as defined in Article 6(3) of the Habitats Directive (Directive 92/43/EC).[122]

(2) The Convention and the implementing EU law leave room for different national concepts and allow both right-based systems (Germany) and interest-based systems (eg France, the Netherlands),[123] as the wording of both Article 9(2) of the Aarhus Convention and Article 11(1) of Directive 2011/92/EC makes clear.

[119] Directive 2003/35/EC of the European Parliament and of the Council of 26 May 2003 providing for public participation in respect of the drawing up of certain plans and programmes relating to the environment [2003] OJ L156/17.

[120] Directive 2011/92/EU of the European Parliament and of the Council of 13 December 2011 on the assessment of the effects of certain public and private projects on the environment [2012] OJ L26/1.

[121] Directive 2010/75/EU of the European Parliament and of the Council of 24 November 2010 on industrial emissions (integrated pollution prevention and control) [2010] OJ L334/17.

[122] Council Directive 92/43/EEC of 21 May 1992 on the conservation of natural habitats and of wild fauna and flora [1992] OJ L 206/7. This was established by the Court of Justice in Case C-243/15 *Lesoochranárske zoskupenie VLK v Obvodný úrad Trenčín* ECLI:EU:C:2016:838.

[123] See above sections 4.4.B.1 and 4.4.B.2.

Case C-115/09, 12 May 2011[124] **4.46 (EU)**

Bund für Umwelt und Naturschutz Deutschland (Bund), Landesverband Nordrhein-Westfalen eV v Bezirksregierung Arnsberg

STANDING; ENVIRONMENTAL ASSOCIATIONS; NATIONAL COURTS; EU LAW REQUIREMENTS

Trianel

Whichever option a Member State chooses for the admissibility of an action, environmental protection organisations are entitled to have access to a review procedure to challenge the substantive or procedural legality of decisions, acts or omissions covered by Article 10a of Directive 85/337/EEC.

Facts: Trianel – the intervener in the main proceedings – intended to construct and operate a coal-fired power station in Lünen and obtained a permit to this end. Bund initiated proceedings for the annulment of this permit. According to the applicable standing requirements, an action challenging an administrative measure would have been admissible only if the rule which had allegedly been breached intended to confer rights. On this basis, the referring court found that an environmental protection organisation was not entitled to rely on infringement of the law for the protection of water and nature or on the precautionary principle because these provisions primarily concern the general public and are not intended to confer individual rights. Since it considered that such a restriction on access to justice could nevertheless undermine the effectiveness of Directive 85/337/EEC, the referring court asked the Court of Justice whether the action brought by Bund ought to be allowed on the basis of Article 10a of that directive.

Held: 1. Article 10a of Directive 85/337/EEC precludes legislation which does not permit NGOs promoting environmental protection, as referred to in Article 1(2) of that directive, to rely before the courts, in an action contesting a decision authorising projects 'likely to have significant effects on the environment', on the infringement of a rule flowing from the environment law of the European Union and intended to protect the environment, on the ground that that rule protects only the interests of the general public and not the interests of individuals.

2. Such an NGO can derive, from the last sentence of the third paragraph of Article 10a of Directive 85/337, the right to rely before the courts on the infringement of the rules of national law flowing from Article 6 of Directive 92/43/EC of 21 May 1992 on the conservation of natural habitats and of wild fauna and flora even where, on the ground that the rules relied on protect only the interests of the general public and not the interests of individuals, national procedural law does not permit this.

Judgment: 38 With regard to the conditions for the admissibility of such actions, Article 10a of Directive 85/337 provides for two possibilities: the admissibility of an action may be conditional on 'a sufficient interest in bringing the action' or on the applicant alleging 'the impairment of a right', depending on which of those conditions is adopted in the national legislation.

39 The first sentence of the third paragraph of Article 10a of Directive 85/337 further states that what constitutes a sufficient interest and impairment of a right is to be determined by the Member States consistently with the objective of giving the public concerned 'wide access to justice'.

40 With regard to actions brought by environmental protection organisations, the second and third sentences of the third paragraph of Article 10a of Directive 85/337 add that, to that end, such organisations must be regarded as having either a sufficient

[124] ECLI:EU:C:2011:289.

interest or rights which may be impaired, depending on which of those conditions for admissibility is adopted in the national legislation.

41 Those various provisions must be interpreted in the light of, and having regard to, the objectives of the Aarhus Convention, with which – as is stated in recital 5 to Directive 2003/35 – EU law should be 'properly aligned'.

42 It follows that, whichever option a Member State chooses for the admissibility of an action, environmental protection organisations are entitled, pursuant to Article 10a of Directive 85/337, to have access to a review procedure before a court of law or another independent and impartial body established by law, to challenge the substantive or procedural legality of decisions, acts or omissions covered by that article.

43 Lastly, it should also be recalled that where, in the absence of EU rules governing the matter, it is for the legal system of each Member State to designate the courts and tribunals having jurisdiction and to lay down the detailed procedural rules governing actions for safeguarding rights which individuals derive from EU law, those detailed rules must not be less favourable than those governing similar domestic actions (principle of equivalence) and must not make it in practice impossible or excessively difficult to exercise rights conferred by EU law (principle of effectiveness).

44 Thus, although it is for the Member States to determine, when their legal system so requires and within the limits laid down in Article 10a of Directive 85/337, what rights can give rise, when infringed, to an action concerning the environment, they cannot, when making that determination, deprive environmental protection organisations which fulfil the conditions laid down in Article 1(2) of that directive of the opportunity of playing the role granted to them both by Directive 85/337 and by the Aarhus Convention.

Note

Regardless of whether a right-based or an interest-based system is chosen, the Aarhus Convention requires that Member States must comply with the overarching aim of ensuring broad access to justice. NGOs must have access to justice to challenge decisions covered by Article 9(2) of the Aarhus Convention. The application of national rules and requirements may thus not result in excluding NGOs from access to justice.[125]

Umweltrechtsbehelfsgesetz **4.47 (DE)**

§2 (1) A domestic or foreign association which is recognized according to §3 can, without alleging the infringement of its own right, file judicial remedies pursuant the Administrative Court Procedure Act against a decision taken in accordance with §1(1) sentence 1 or its omission, if the association

1. claims that the decision or its omission infringes provisions that protect the environment and can be relevant for the decision,

2. claims that it is affected in its statutory mandate of the promotion of the aims of environmental protection by the decision taken in accordance with §1(1) or its omission and

[125] See, eg Case C-263/08 *Djurgården-Lilla Väans Miljöskyddsförening* ECLI:EU:C:2009:631.

3. was entitled to participation in a procedure according to §1(1) and presented its concerns or was unlawfully not granted the opportunity to participate.

Notes

(1) In response to the *Trianel* judgment, Germany has amended its Environmental Remedies Act (Umweltrechtsbehelfsgesetz),[126] which regulates access to court in environmental law cases in such a way that NGOs can also gain standing before the administrative courts when they allege the violation of a norm of environmental law which only protects the public interest.

(2) The Aarhus Convention relates only to environmental decision-making. As a consequence, some legal systems, such as Germany, have chosen to adapt their rules on standing only with regard to environmental law cases (through the Umweltrechtsbehelfsgesetz). Hence, standing requirements in these cases differ from and are broader than the general rules. In other countries, such as France, England and Wales and the Netherlands, the requirements of the Aarhus Convention do not differ from the general rules on access to justice, and Article 9(2) of the Aarhus Convention has not led to changes in legislation. In these countries, the influence of Article 9(2) of the Aarhus Convention and the relevant implementing EU law (Directive 2003/35/EC) is also limited due to the extensive conception of standing and the possibility for a group or an association to challenge a decision before the administrative court.

4.4.E.2 THE INFLUENCE OF ARTICLE 9(3) OF THE AARHUS CONVENTION ON STANDING BEFORE THE NATIONAL COURTS

UNECE Convention on Access to Information, Public Participation in Decision-making and Access to Justice in Environmental Matters (Aarhus Convention) **4.48 (UN)**

Article 9 (3) In addition and without prejudice to the review procedures referred to in paragraphs 1 and 2 above, each Party shall ensure that, where they meet the criteria, if any, laid down in its national law, members of the public have access to administrative or judicial procedures to challenge acts and omissions by private persons and public authorities which contravene provisions of its national law relating to the environment.

Note

Article 9(3) of the Aarhus Convention, which applies to a much broader area of environmental decisions than Article 9(2), has not been implemented into EU law. However, this provision also influences the interpretation and application of standing criteria in environmental law cases in the Member States.[127]

[126] Gesetz zur Änderung des Umweltrechtsbehelfgesetzes v. 21.01.2013 BGBl I S 95.

[127] See further UNECE, *The Aarhus Convention: An Implementation Guide*, 2nd edn (2014) 190 ff.

Case C-240/09, 8 March 2011[128] **4.49 (EU)**

Lesoochranárske zoskupenie VLK v Ministerstvo životného prostredia Slovenskej republiky

DUTY OF INTERPRETATION OF NATIONAL RULES ON STANDING IN CONFORMITY WITH INTERNATIONAL LAW

Lesoochranárske zoskupenie, or Slovac Brown Bear

In order to ensure effective judicial protection in the fields covered by EU environmental law, national law has to be interpreted in a way which, to the fullest extent possible, is consistent with the objectives laid down in Article 9(3) of the Aarhus Convention.

Facts: Lesoochranáske zoskupenie VLK ('zoskupenie'), an association established in accordance with Slovak law whose objective is the protection of the environment, requested to be heard as a 'party' to the administrative proceedings relating to the grant of derogations to the system of protection for protected species, such as the brown bear. The request was denied and, based on Slovak law, the standing of 'zoskupenie' to challenge this decision was denied. The national court asked the Court of Justice whether Article 9(3) of the Aarhus Convention has direct effect and whether individuals, in particular environmental protection associations, can rely on this provision before the national courts. It also asked whether individuals, where they wish to challenge a decision to derogate from a system of environmental protection, may derive a right to bring proceedings under EU law from this provision.

Held: Article 9(3) of the Aarhus Convention does not have direct effect in EU law. It is, however, for national courts to interpret, to the fullest extent possible, the procedural rules relating to the conditions to be met in order to bring administrative or judicial proceedings in accordance with the objectives of Article 9(3) and the objective of effective judicial protection of the rights conferred by European Union law, in order to enable an environmental protection organisation, such as Lesoochranárske zoskupenie, to challenge before a court a decision taken following administrative proceedings liable to be contrary to EU environmental law.

Judgment: 28 ... The referring court asks essentially whether individuals, and in particular environmental protection associations, where they wish to challenge a decision to derogate from a system of environmental protection, ... may derive a right to bring proceedings under EU law, having regard, in particular, to the provisions of Article 9(3) of the Aarhus Convention on direct effect, to which its questions relate ....

45 It must be held that the provisions of Article 9(3) of the Aarhus Convention do not contain any clear and precise obligation capable of directly regulating the legal position of individuals. Since only members of the public who meet the criteria, if any, laid down by national law are entitled to exercise the rights provided for in Article 9(3), that provision is subject, in its implementation or effects, to the adoption of a subsequent measure.

46 However, it must be observed that those provisions, although drafted in broad terms, are intended to ensure effective environmental protection.

47 In the absence of EU rules governing the matter, it is for the domestic legal system of each Member State to lay down the detailed procedural rules governing actions for safeguarding rights which individuals derive from EU law. ...

[128] ECLI:EU:C:2011:125.

48 On that basis, as is apparent from well-established case-law, the detailed procedural rules governing actions for safeguarding an individual's rights under EU law must be no less favourable than those governing similar domestic actions (principle of equivalence) and must not make it in practice impossible or excessively difficult to exercise rights conferred by EU law (principle of effectiveness) (Impact, paragraph 46 and the case-law cited).

49 Therefore, if the effective protection of EU environmental law is not to be undermined, it is inconceivable that Article 9(3) of the Aarhus Convention be interpreted in such a way as to make it in practice impossible or excessively difficult to exercise rights conferred by EU law.

50 It follows that, in so far as concerns a species protected by EU law, and in particular the Habitats Directive, it is for the national court, in order to ensure effective judicial protection in the fields covered by EU environmental law, to interpret its national law in a way which, to the fullest extent possible, is consistent with the objectives laid down in Article 9(3) of the Aarhus Convention.

Note

On the one hand, the CJEU decided that Article 9(3) of the Aarhus Convention is not unconditional, but instead leaves significant discretion to the Member States, hence it does not have direct effect before national courts. On the other hand, the Court stressed that the laws of the Member States should be interpreted, as far as possible, in order to ensure that Article 9(3) of the Aarhus Convention is complied with – more precisely, in order to ensure that NGOs have access in the cases falling under the scope of this provision. Legal scholars debate the precise meaning of this wording. Some argue that national courts have to ensure access to courts for NGOs within the scope of Article 9(3) of the Aarhus Convention anyway, and national law has to be interpreted in such a way that it is possible for environmental organisations to challenge in court administrative decisions that conflict with EU environmental law.[129] Others suggest that the duty stemming from Article 9(3) of the Aarhus Convention to ensure standing for NGOs is not unconditional but is limited to all cases where national law leaves any room for interpretation, 'to the fullest extent possible', to reach that outcome.[130] However, the law of some Member States does not leave any potential for such an interpretation, and in these cases standing for environmental associations would therefore not be granted. This seems to be the case in, for example, Germany and Austria.

[129] See, eg J Ebbesson, 'Access to Justice at a National Level. Impact of the Aarhus Convention and European Union Law' in M Pallemaerts (ed), *The Aarhus Convention at Ten. Interactions and Tensions between Conventional International Law and EU Environmental Law* (Groningen, Europa Law Publishing 2011) 245; J Jans and H Vedder, *European Environmental Law after Lisbon*, 4th edn (Groningen, Europa Law Publishing, 2012) 237.

[130] See, eg CW Backes and M Eliantonio, 'Access to Courts for Environmental NGOs at the European and National Level: Improvements and Room for Improvement since Maastricht?' in M de Visser and AP van der Mei (eds), *The Treaty on European Union 1993–2013: Reflections from Maastricht* (Cambridge, Intersentia, 2013) 557, 575.

Conseil d'État, 23 October 2015[131] **4.50 (FR)**

Janin v Minister of Ecology, Sustainable Development and Energy

STANDING; INDIVIDUALS; ENVIRONMENTAL MATTERS; AARHUS CONVENTION

Janin

An individual cannot rely on Article 9(3) of the Aarhus Convention to get standing to challenge a regulatory decision dealing with environmental matters.

Facts: The claimant, who is an academic specialised in environmental law and a member of an environmental association, challenged a decision (*arrêté*), adopted by the Minister of Environment, relating to the listing, methods and periods for the destruction of animal species considered to be a pest.

Held: The action was considered inadmissible due to the lack of a personal, direct and certain interest.

Judgment: Considering that, to justify his interest in taking legal action (intéret à agir), Mr A … provides, firstly, his interest in wildlife and its preservation, which is conveyed by the publication of numerous articles in specialized journals, his commitment over many years as a founding member or executive director of an association protecting the environment and that he has taken part in the procedure of public participation, enforced in compliance with Article L120-1 of the Environmental Code, related to the draft of the challenged decision (*arrêté*); considering that, however, those circumstances would not in themselves have been regarded as conferring him a direct and certain personal interest in the annulment of the challenged decision; considering that Mr A … asserts, secondly, that Article 7 of the Charter of Environment provides for the right of every person to participate in the decision-making concerning matters which impact the environment; considering that, however, contrary to what is alleged, those provisions do not have the aim, or the effect of modifying the conditions of assessment by the administrative court of the interest which allows to bring an action against decisions which have an impact on the environment; considering also that the stipulations of Article 9 of the Convention of Aarhus have, in any event, neither the aim, nor the effect to grant every person the right to challenge against any decision which has an impact on the environment. …

Note

The excerpt shows that individuals cannot invoke Article 9 of the Aarhus Convention to claim standing in environmental matters in cases where the individual cannot prove the existence of an individual interest but only of a collective interest, such as the protection of the environment or wildlife. According to the Council of State, compliance with Article 9 of the Aarhus Convention does not require the court to interpret the French rules on standing more extensively.

[131] N° 392550.

4.4.E.3 THE INFLUENCE OF ARTICLE 9 OF THE AARHUS CONVENTION ON STANDING BEFORE THE EU COURTS

In order to apply the provisions of the Aarhus Convention to European institutions and bodies, the European Community adopted Regulation 1367/2006/EC (the Aarhus Regulation).[132] Specifically with regard to access to courts for NGOs, the Regulation allows those organisations which fulfil certain requirements contained in Article 11 of the Regulation to institute proceedings before the European courts against the acts of EU institutions and the decisions of EU bodies. However, it expressly states, in Article 12(1), that NGOs may do so only 'in accordance with the relevant provisions of the EC Treaty', namely Article 263 TFEU. As seen, Article 263(4) TFEU as interpreted by the *Plaumann* doctrine of CJEU excludes standing of interest groups and individuals against environmental decisions of EU bodies in most cases.[133]

Findings and Recommendations of the Aarhus Compliance Committee with regard to Communication ACCC/C/2008/32 (Part II) concerning compliance by the European Union Adopted by the Compliance Committee on 17 March 2017[134] **4.51 (UN)**

Facts: In December 2008, Client Earth, a non-governmental organisation, submitted a communication to the Aarhus Compliance Committee arguing that the EU failed to comply with its obligations under Articles 3(1) and 9(3)–(5) of the Aarhus Convention.

Held: The Committee found that the party concerned failed to comply with Article 9(3) and (4) of the Aarhus Convention.

Findings: 122. The Committee recalls its findings on Part I of the communication, namely that if the jurisprudence of the EU Courts on access to justice were to continue, unless fully compensated for by adequate administrative review procedures, the Party concerned would fail to comply with article 9, paragraphs 3 and 4, of the Convention (para. 94, findings on Part I). Having considered the main jurisprudence of the EU Courts since Part I, the Committee finds there has been no new direction in the jurisprudence of the EU Courts that will ensure compliance with the Convention and that the Aarhus Regulation does not correct or compensate for the failings in the jurisprudence (paras. 81 and 121 above).

123. Accordingly, the Committee finds that the Party concerned fails to comply with article 9, paragraphs 3 and 4, of the Convention with regard to access to justice by members of the public because neither the Aarhus Regulation, nor the jurisprudence of the CJEU implements or complies with the obligations arising under those paragraphs.

[132] Regulation (EC) No 1367/2006 of the European Parliament and of the Council of 6 September 2006 on the application of the provisions of the Aarhus Convention on Access to Information, Public Participation in Decision-making and Access to Justice in Environmental Matters to Community institutions and bodies [2006] OJ L264.

[133] See above sections 4.4.B.5 and 4.4.D.1 (i).

[134] On the basis of Art 15 of the Aarhus Convention, the parties have established a Compliance Committee. Not only the parties, but also 'members of the public' may submit cases concerning a party's compliance. The Committee may also investigate on its own initiative. After a thorough communication with the respective party on the findings on a certain case, the Committee may submit its findings to the Conference of the Parties (CoP), which can then take a decision on the compliance of the party at stake. See further www.unece.org/env/pp/cc.html.

Note

In order to bring the EU into compliance with Article 9 of the Aarhus Convention, it would be possible to change the interpretation of the notion of 'individual concern' contained in the *Plaumann* case. However, as the CJEU has argued that the *Plaumann* doctrine follows from Article 263 TFEU and that therefore a change of its case law would infringe primary law,[135] either the Court has to develop this case law or the treaty itself will have to be changed to bring the EU into compliance with the Aarhus Convention. Such a change would remove the tension between Article 263 TFEU and the EU principle of effective judicial protection.

4.4.E.4 COMPARATIVE REMARKS

International law can have an influence on the criteria imposed for access to courts, especially on standing, in both the EU and the Member States' legal systems. The most obvious and far-reaching example is the Aarhus Convention, which deals with environmental matters. Article 9 of the Aarhus Convention comprises requirements for access to justice. This article explicitly leaves room to implement these requirements into different concepts of standing. It therefore does not imply a choice between right-based and interest-based systems.

The influence of the Aarhus Convention on the legal systems under discussion is significant, but different. Article 9(2) of the Aarhus Convention has partly been transposed into EU directives which, in turn, have been transposed into the law of the Member States. In the case of Germany, compliance with these requirements occurred only after several judgments of the CJEU, and Germany has chosen to differentiate between general standing criteria and standing criteria that only apply within the scope of the EU directives implementing Article 9(2) of the Aarhus Convention. Other legal systems did not need to (substantially) adapt their application of the existing (general) rules on standing to the requirements of Article 9 of the Aarhus Convention and therefore do not differentiate between general standing criteria and standing criteria applicable to (some categories of) environmental law cases.

Article 9(3) of the Aarhus Convention is not transposed at EU level. As this provision leaves a considerable amount of discretion to the parties, it has not been considered as having a direct effect. However, as the CJEU emphasised, the standing requirements should be interpreted insofar as possible in accordance with this provision. The rules on standing in some legal systems leave room for an interpretation that ensures compliance with Article 9(3) of the Aarhus Convention. However, other legal systems, for example, the German rules on standing, do not provide much room for an interpretation that conforms with international law.

135 *Unión de Pequeños Agricultores* (n 77 above) especially para 45.

4.4.F DIFFERENT RULES AND APPROACHES WITH REGARD TO DIFFERENT KINDS OF ACTIONS

In some of the legal systems studied, the standing rules depend on the kind of action and the type of remedy the claimant seeks. The chapter has, up to this point, covered mainly the action of annulment of an administrative act, especially single-case decisions. However, many legal systems provide for slight variations of standing rules in other actions.[136] Standing in actions for damages is not usually a subject of controversy, as the plaintiff logically will claim a violation of his own rights. Hence, actions for damages are always, and in all legal systems, right-based actions. If the claimant alleges that he suffered any damage, the requirement of standing is fulfilled.

4.4.F.1 COMPARABLE CRITERIA FOR OTHER KINDS OF ACTIONS

4.4.F.1 (i) The European Union and the Action for Failure to Act

Treaty of the Functioning of the European Union **4.52 (EU)**

Article 265 (1) Should the European Parliament, the European Council, the Council, the Commission or the European Central Bank, in infringement of the Treaties, fail to act, the Member States and the other institutions of the Union may bring an action before the Court of Justice of the European Union to have the infringement established. …

(2) The action shall be admissible only if the institution, body, office or agency concerned has first been called upon to act. If, within two months of being so called upon, the institution, body, office or agency concerned has not defined its position, the action may be brought within a further period of two months.

(3) Any natural or legal person may, under the conditions laid down in the preceding paragraphs, complain to the Court that an institution, body, office or agency of the Union has failed to address to that person any act other than a recommendation or an opinion. Any natural or legal person may, under the conditions laid down in the first and second paragraphs, institute proceedings against an act addressed to that person or which is of direct and individual concern to them, and against a regulatory act which is of direct concern to them and does not entail implementing measures.

Note

The EU courts have taken Article 265 TFEU to mean that an action brought by a natural or legal person can only be admissible if it relates to failure to adopt an act which has a direct influence on that person's legal position.[137] Consequently, actions for failure to adopt measures of general application have consistently been held to

[136] On the remedies available in the various legal systems, see Chapter 7.

[137] Case 6/70 *Gilberto Borromeo Arese and others v Commission* ECLI:EU:C:1970:75; Case 15/70 *Amedeo Chevalley v Commission* ECLI:EU:C:1970:95; Case C-371/89 *Maria-Theresia Emrich v Commission* ECLI:EU:C:1990:158, para 6; Case T-5/94 *J v Commission* ECLI:EU:T:1994:58, para 16.

be inadmissible.[138] In spite of the more stringent wording of Article 265(3) TFEU in comparison with Article 263(4), the CJEU has held that the two provisions prescribe one and the same method of recourse.[139] Consequently, according to the CJEU, the scope of the action for failure to act is not confined to the defendant institution's failure to adopt a particular measure addressed to the claimant. This means that it is possible, in principle, to challenge a failure to adopt a measure of general application, but the requirements of individual and direct concern will have to be met.[140]

4.4.F.1 (ii) Germany

In Germany, the general rule of §42(2) VwGO applies explicitly not only to the action for annulment (*Anfechtungsklage*), but also to the action seeking the issuance of an administrative act (*Verpflichtungsklage*). Settled case law furthermore applies this provision to other types of judicial actions with no specific rules regarding *locus standi* (*Klagebefugnis*).[141] Hence, the same standing rules apply by analogy to the general action for performance (*allgemeine Leistungsklage*) and to the action for declaration (*Feststellungsklage*). However, apart from standing according to §42(2), §43(1) VwGO prescribes that actions for declarations also require a legitimate individual interest in a prompt declaration of the court (*Feststellungsinteresse*). This special requirement, though, is a fairly low threshold. Any non-material, economic or legal interest can constitute such an interest.[142]

4.4.F.1 (iii) England and Wales

Judicial review in England and Wales does not draw distinctions between separate kinds of actions. There are different kinds of remedies which are available to claimants, all of which can be sought, either separately or in combination, through the claim for review procedure.[143] The criteria for standing in judicial review cases do not depend on the remedy which is requested. Section 31(3) of the Senior Courts Act 1981 applies whenever judicial review is claimed, no matter which remedy is sought.

[138] Case 15/71 *C Mackprang jr v Commission* ECLI:EU:C:1971:98, para 4; Case 134/73 *Holtz & Willemsen GmbH v Council of the European Communities* ECLI:EU:C:1974:1, para 5.

[139] Case C-68/95 *T Port GmbH & Co KG v Bundesanstalt für Landwirtschaft und Ernährung* ECLI:EU:C:1996:452, para 59; Case T-17/96 *Télévision française 1 SA (TF1) v Commission* ECLI:EU:T:1999:119, para 27; Case T-103/99 *Associazione delle cantine sociali venete v European Ombudsman and European Parliament* ECLI:EU:T:2000:135.

[140] See, eg Case 247/87 *Star Fruit Company SA v Commission* ECLI:EU:C:1989:58, para 13; Case C-107/91 *ENU v Commission* ECLI:EU:C:1993:56.

[141] C Sennekamp, in M Fehling, B Kastner and R Störmer (eds), *Verwaltungsrecht*, 4th edn (Baden-Baden, Nomos, 2016) §42 VwGO, para 44.

[142] D Ehlers, in D Ehlers and F Schoch (eds), *Rechtsschutz im Öffentlichen Recht* (Berlin, De Gruyter, 2009) §25, para 42.

[143] For more detail, see Chapter 7, section 7.2.A.2.

4.4.F.2 DIFFERENT CRITERIA FOR OTHER KINDS OF ACTIONS THAN THE ACTION FOR ANNULMENT

4.4.F.2 (i) France

Unlike the action for annulment (*recours pour excès de pouvoir*), where the standing threshold is that of *intérêt à agir* (interest in taking legal action), in liability actions and actions concerning the duties deriving from a contract (which in France are brought through a 'full jurisdiction remedy' – *recours de pleine juridiction*), different standing rules are prescribed.[144] As this kind of action concerns the subjective rights of the claimants, it is logical that someone who wants to start such an action has to claim that one of his rights is infringed by the respondent.

4.4.F.2 (ii) The Netherlands

In Dutch law, almost all actions against public authorities which do not concern the annulment of a single-case decision have to be brought to a ordinary court (or, more precisely, the civil division of the district court).[145] That may concern an action against measures of general scope or actions against the factual conduct of administrative authorities.[146] In all these cases, the claimant will have to claim the infringement of an own right. However, this threshold of standing is usually very low.

As noted in Chapter 2[147] and further dealt with in Chapter 11,[148] as of late, under certain conditions, the administrative courts can also hear actions concerning liability for unlawful action of administrative authorities. In these cases, administrative courts, like civil courts, grant standing if the plaintiff claims an infringement of an individual right, which, as noted above, is not usually a controversial issue.

4.4.G COMPARATIVE REMARKS

In comparing the standing requirements, significant differences appear between the generally quite lenient interest-based approaches in France, England and Wales and the Netherlands and the more restrictive right-based approach in Germany. As regards standing of non-privileged applicants before the EU courts, the EU legal system is an example of a very restrictive interest-based legal system. It is remarkable that the CJEU has rejected all proposals to adapt its case law on standing for non-privileged applicants[149] before EU courts in order to better comply with its own principle of effective judicial protection and, in the area of environmental law, with the Aarhus Convention.

[144] For an explanation of this remedy in the French legal system, see Chapter 7, section 7.2.A.4.

[145] See Chapter 2, section 2.5.A.1 and Chapter 3.

[146] For an explanation of the types of measures of general scope and the concept of factual conduct in the Netherlands, see Chapter 3, sections 3.3.B.2 (ii) and 3.4.B.1.

[147] Chapter 2, section 2.5.A.1.

[148] Chapter 11, section 11.2.B.2.

[149] For the difference between privileged and non-privileged applicants, see section 4.4.B.5 (i) above.

English and French laws on standing have stayed more or less unchanged. There has not been a significant influence of EU law, or any other reasons for convergence with other EU legal systems. In contrast, over the last decade, there has been a substantial convergence between German and Dutch law, at least in some areas of law. In Germany, several changes to the right-based approach in the direction of a more interest-based approach had to be made in the field of environmental law to comply with the Aarhus Convention and EU law. Some debate has developed over whether this will lead to more general changes in the future. However, no general transformation of the right-based approach is in sight in Germany.[150] On the other hand, the Dutch courts have tightened the standing rules by interpreting them more restrictively on some issues.[151]

Algemene Wet Bestuursrecht **4.53 (NL)**

Article 8:69a The administrative judge does not annul a decision on the ground that it is incompatible with a written or unwritten legal rule or a general legal principle if this rule or this principle evidently does not protect the interest of the one invoking it.

Note

Besides the convergence brought about by case law, the Dutch legislator introduced the so-called 'relativity requirement' (*relativiteitsvereiste*), which does not concern standing, but limits the power of the court to annul a decision if it is found to be illegal. As Article 8:69a AWB prescribes, a court may not annul a decision when this decision infringes a public law provision which is evidently not meant to protect the interests of the claimant. Although important differences remain, since the Dutch relativity principle is less strict than §42(2) VwGO overall, this principle is quite similar to the German *Schutznormtheorie* and was inspired by German law.[152] As in German law, the Dutch AWB excludes claims of individuals who have an individual interest in the contested decision but who cannot claim that a legal norm which aims to protect their interest is infringed. This, however, is achieved using different methods – the criteria of standing in Germany and the grounds for review in the Netherlands – as the 'relativity requirement' limits the grounds on which a court reviews a decision.[153]

[150] For a discussion, see F Schoch, 'Die Europäisierung des Verwaltungsprozessrechts' in E Schmidt-Aßmann and D Sellner (eds), *FG 50 Jahre Bundesverwaltungsgericht* (Cologne, Carl Heymanns, 2003) 507; T Wiedmann and M Gebauer, *Verwaltungsprozessrecht unter europäischem Einfluss* (Munich, CH Beck, 2003) 105 ff, 133; M Ruffert, 'Dogmatik und Praxis des subjektiv-öffentlichen Rechts unter dem Einfluss des Gemeinschaftsrechts' (1998) *Deutsches Verwaltungsblatt* 69; T van Danwitz, 'Zur Grundlegung einer Theorie der subjektiv-öffentlichen Gemeinschaftsrechts' (1996) *Die Öffentliche Verwaltung* 481; B Wegener, *Rechte des Einzelnen – Die Interessentenklage im Europäischen Umweltrecht*' (Baden-Baden, Nomos, 1998) 172.

[151] See section 4.4.D.2 (ii) above.

[152] See also R Seerden and D Wenders, 'Administrative Law in the Netherlands' in R Seerden (ed), *Administrative Law of the European Union, its Member States and the United States*, 4th edn (Antwerp, Intersentia, 2018) 154.

[153] See also Chapter 6, section 6.2.B.2.

4.5 PUBLIC BODIES AS CLAIMANTS

In most legal systems, the question of whether a public body can institute proceedings is dealt with as a question of standing. However, it also touches on some aspects of the capacity of public bodies to act as parties of a proceeding.[154]

4.5.A FRANCE

If an administrative authority wants to challenge a decision, it can do so. As regards the capacity to act before a court, the rules applicable to a public body do not depart from the ones applicable to legal persons in general:[155] only public bodies provided with legal personality have the capacity to bring a claim. The state, local and regional authorities, public corporations (*établissement public*), overseas territories and public–private joint ventures (*groupement d'intérêt public*) all have legal personality.

Conseil d'État, 6 October 1976[156] **4.54 (FR)**

Law Faculty of Jean Moulin University v Minister of National Education

STANDING; PUBLIC BODY WITHOUT LEGAL PERSONALITY

Faculté de droit de l'Université Jean Moulin

Given that it has no legal personality distinct from the university, the Faculty of Law is not entitled to challenge an administrative decision.

Facts: The Ministry of Education allocated a position to the Foreign Languages Department of the University Jean Moulin Lyon-III. The Dean of the Faculty of Law challenged this decision.

Held: The action of the dean was declared inadmissible.

Judgment: Considering that the teaching and research unit of the 'Faculty of Law' of the University Jean Moulin Lyon-III does not have the quality of a public body of scientific and cultural nature under the conditions determined by Article 4 of the Law providing guidance on academic education of 12 November 1968 as amended by the Law of 12 July 1971; considering, therefore, that the Secretary of State for universities has a legitimate basis to claim that the aforementioned application of the teaching and research unit of the 'Faculty of Law' of the University Jean Moulin Lyon-III presented under the name of its Dean, who was not entitled to act, is not admissible. …

Code général des collectivités territoriales **4.55 (FR)**

Article L3132-1 Within two months following their transmission, the representative of the State in the department defers to the Administrative Court of First Instance those acts mentioned in Article L3131-2 which he deems to be illegal.

[154] See section 4.2 above.
[155] See section 4.2.A.4 above.
[156] N° 98179.

Notes

(1) The rules with regard to standing of public bodies differ from the general rules. Some administrative bodies do not have to prove standing. This is the case for the prefect. Article 72 of the Constitution vests the prefect with a special power to defend national interests, and Article L3131-1 of the General Code of Local and Regional Authorities (Code general des collectivités territoriales) gives him a special power to bring actions for annulment (*recours pour excès de pouvoir*). Since the process of decentralisation at the beginning of the 1980s, leading to more autonomy of local and regional authorities (municipalities and regions), the prefects (who are the local representatives of the central state) are no longer entitled to review or modify administrative decisions taken by authorities themselves. In order to ensure legality and the general interest of the state, the prefects have nevertheless retained the power to assess the legality (but not the appropriateness) of the most important decisions taken by the local and regional authorities and, in the event that they consider those decisions illegal, to refer the decisions to the administrative courts in an action for annulment. Such action works in almost exactly the same way as the normal action for annulment, the only difference being the fact that the prefect has a special *locus standi* derived from those statutory provisions (which he would not normally have). This 'special treatment' can be explained by the specific history of France, which has a (compared with most other countries) quite heavily centralised architecture of administrative powers.

(2) Furthermore, the French Ombudsman, the Defender of Rights (Défenseur des droits), may be invited by courts, either *ex officio* or at the request of a party, to intervene in an ongoing judicial procedure. He may also do so on his own initiative.[157] In that case, he has a legal right to be heard by the court.[158] Furthermore, the Defender of Rights has the right to claim for interim relief before the administrative courts.[159]

4.5.B ENGLAND AND WALES

Local Government Act 1972 **4.56 (EW)**

Section 222 Power of local authorities to prosecute or defend legal proceedings.

(1) Where a local authority considers it expedient for the promotion or protection of the interests of the inhabitants of their area–

(a) they may prosecute or defend or appear in any legal proceedings and, in the case of civil proceedings, may institute them in their own name, and

[157] Loi organique n° 2011–333 du 29 mars 2011 relative au Défenseur des droits, Art 33. See further Chapter 10.

[158] Conseil d'État, 11 April 2012, *GISTI et FAPIL*, N° 322326.

[159] Code de justice administrative, Arts R557-1 and R557-2.

(b) they may, in their own name, make representations in the interests of the inhabitants at any public inquiry held by or on behalf of any Minister or public body under any enactment.

Note

The Crown in England and Wales (hence the central government) has the power to commence proceedings as a matter of prerogative. Other public bodies only have standing if an act explicitly empowers them to bring legal proceedings. For example, all local authorities have the capacity, granted by section 222 of the Local Government Act 1972, to institute legal proceedings, including judicial review claims. The same may be true for many other public bodies, but it is not possible where the empowering legislation that creates the body does not grant capacity to do so. As emanations of the state, it is not ordinarily possible for public authorities to commence legal proceedings under the Human Rights Act 1998, but section 30 of the Equality Act 2006 empowers the Equality and Human Rights Commission to commence judicial review proceedings in order to prevent breaches of Convention rights in cases where it determines this to be appropriate.

4.5.C GERMANY

The rules on standing of public bodies in Germany differ somewhat from those applicable in the other legal systems because of the right-based approach to standing in Germany.[160] Legal persons of public law have standing provided that they can allege that their rights have been infringed. However, public bodies cannot rely on fundamental rights, as these are not generally conferred on public bodies. An exception to the general rule applies to municipalities, which can derive standing from their right to self-government, laid down in Article 28(2) of the Grundgesetz against the respective state.

Verwaltungsgerichtshof Baden-Württemberg, 11 May 2016[161] **4.57 (DE)**

STANDING; UNIVERSITY

A university can invoke Article 5 of the Basic Law and, on the basis of this right, can be granted standing.

Facts: The claimant, a public university, challenged a planning approval (*Planfeststellungsbeschluss*) for tramway lines on the university estate, because the noise of the tramway would affect teaching and research. The defendant, the state of Baden-Wuerttemberg, argued that the university had no standing to bring such a claim.

Held: The planning approval was annulled.

[160] See section 4.4.B.1 above.
[161] ECLI:DE:VGHBW:2016:0511.5S1443.14.0A.

Judgment: The claimant has standing (§42(2) VwGO) .... The claimant is an organization under public law which can rely on the basic rights stemming from Article 5(3) first sentence of the Grundgesetz. It sufficiently asserted, notwithstanding the fact that at the same time it is an institution of the *Land*, to be infringed in its right to a fair consideration of their own legitimate interests in the weighing process. ... Its interest that its actual research institutions and the areas where they can expand, located in the 'University' area of the 'New University Area' construction plan will not suffer from detrimental effects from being exposed to the planned project – such as vibrations and electromagnetic fields – which would be harmful to the research activities, qualifies as an interest worthy of protection. Ultimately, this follows from Article 5(3), first sentence of the Grundgesetz, which directly relates to public institutions, serving scientific and/or research purposes .... The scope of protection of the Grundgesetz does not only encompass (direct) interference in organisational structures, but it is also affected if, as is considered in this case, the protected activity is (directly) factually hindered. Article 5(3) first sentence of the Grundgesetz implies the responsibility of the state to advocate freedom in science and research and obliges the state to positively direct its conduct towards this end, meaning protecting against the undermining of this guarantee of freedom and promoting it ...

Note

The question of whether public law entities such as municipalities or regional authorities can invoke the protection of fundamental rights is highly controversial. In certain cases where public authorities work in a relatively autonomous field of law, such as churches, universities (as shown in the excerpt above) or publicly financed radio stations, the Federal Constitutional Court has answered this question in the affirmative. Generally, however, public law entities do not possess public law rights that are different from the rights of the general public or their members and therefore, in general, do not have standing.

4.5.D THE NETHERLANDS

Algemene Wet Bestuursrecht **4.58 (NL)**

Article 1:2 ...

(2) As regards administrative authorities, the interests entrusted to them are considered to be their own interests.

Notes

(1) As a point of departure, Article 1:2(2) AWB provides that administrative authorities have standing if they advocate an interest which concerns their public tasks. A purely factual interest is not sufficient. Hence, public authorities qualify as a party concerned only if the decision relates to the competences they have and to the tasks they have to fulfil. One of the consequences of this rule is that advisory bodies normally cannot challenge decisions because they do not have any decision-making

competences (other than advising).[162] An authority with competences to supervise another authority cannot bring an action against the supervised authority if it omitted to use its supervisory powers.[163]

(2) Article 1.4 of the Crisis and Recovery Act (Crisis- en herstelwet), a piece of Dutch legislation which had the aim of shortening administrative decision-making and judicial proceedings to foster economic growth, forbids municipalities and provinces to bring claims against decisions of the central government taken on the basis of this Act. The reason (officially) given for this provision is that public authorities should resolve their disputes outside, rather than inside, the court. However, this policy is not (yet) consistently applied in the Crisis and Recovery Act: according to Article 1.4 of the Act, the central government may still, if it qualifies as a party concerned, bring a claim against a decision of the lower public bodies, and municipalities may still bring claims against a decision of the provinces.

4.5.E THE EUROPEAN UNION

Treaty on the Functioning of the European Union **4.59 (EU)**

Article 263 (1) The Court of Justice of the European Union shall review the legality of legislative acts, of acts of the Council, of the Commission and of the European Central Bank, other than recommendations and opinions, and of acts of the European Parliament and of the European Council intended to produce legal effects vis-à-vis third parties. It shall also review the legality of acts of bodies, offices or agencies of the Union intended to produce legal effects vis-à-vis third parties.

(2) It shall for this purpose have jurisdiction in actions brought by a Member State, the European Parliament, the Council or the Commission on grounds of lack of competence, infringement of an essential procedural requirement, infringement of the Treaties or of any rule of law relating to their application, or misuse of powers.

(3) The Court shall have jurisdiction under the same conditions in actions brought by the Court of Auditors, by the European Central Bank and by the Committee of the Regions for the purpose of protecting their prerogatives.

(4) Any natural or legal person may, under the conditions laid down in the first and second paragraphs, institute proceedings against an act addressed to that person or which is of direct and individual concern to them, and against a regulatory act which is of direct concern to them and does not entail implementing measures.

Notes

(1) The public bodies mentioned in Article 263(2) TFEU can bring an action for annulment before the CJEU without the need to prove any standing requirement. For this reason, they are called 'privileged applicants'.[164]

[162] ECLI:NL:RVS:1997:ZF2912.
[163] ECLI:NL:RVS:2004:AO8488.
[164] It is to be noted that, on the basis of Art 263 TFEU, the European Council cannot apply for an action of annulment, although its acts may be challenged.

(2) The European Central Bank, the Committee of the Regions and the Court of Auditors are considered 'semi-privileged applicants' because they can only obtain standing for protection of their prerogatives.

(3) Regional and devolved authorities are not equated to Member States and are therefore not privileged applicants. They are only allowed to bring actions for annulment to the EU courts if they have legal personality under national law and may therefore be regarded as legal persons for the purposes of Article 263(4).[165] As a non-privileged applicant, whenever a measure is not addressed to a particular region or devolved authority, such an entity must fulfil the admissibility requirements of individual and direct concern within the meaning of the case law.[166]

4.5.F COMPARATIVE REMARKS

The rules on standing of public bodies and authorities appear to differ significantly across the legal systems. Germany, for example, applies the general rules on standing. As a consequence, German public bodies only have standing if they can claim that a subjective public right of the body could be infringed. In France, the general rules on capacity to institute proceedings and standing are also applied. However, unlike in Germany, this leads to relatively broad possibilities for French public bodies to start judicial review proceedings. Moreover, prefects generally have standing to challenge the most important decisions taken by local and regional authorities. Here, one can clearly see an element of supervision via court procedures which is missing in the other legal systems.

Different again from the approaches in Germany and France, in the Netherlands, Article 1:2(2) AWB determines that public authorities have standing only insofar as their public tasks are concerned. Hence, a special rule, rather than the application of the general rules, guarantees the standing of public authorities. This results in broad possibilities to bring cases before the administrative courts, which is ultimately comparable to France. In England and Wales, standing of public authorities is not ensured and is not determined by the application of the general rules. Public authorities other than the Crown can only start judicial review proceedings if legislation explicitly empowers them to do so. This is obviously a more limited approach than in the other legal systems.

The concept of privileged applicants that is applied in the EU is similar to the approach taken in French law. The general rules apply, but some public parties have privileged standing. The result, however, is different from France. As the general rules on standing in the EU are far more restrictive than in France, the standing of public entities such as regional authorities, except for the privileged applicants (that is, the Member States in their entirety), is also more limited.

[165] See, eg Case 222/83 *Municipality of Differdange and Others v Commission* ECLI:EU:C:1984:266, para 9; Case C-417/04 P *Regione Siciliana v Commission* ECLI:EU:C:2006:282.

[166] See sections 4.4.B.5 (ii) and 4.4.B.5 (iii) above. For more on this point, see K Lenaerts and N Cambien, 'Regions and the European Courts: Giving Shape of the Regional Dimension of Member States' (2010) 10 *European Law Review*, 622.

In England and Wales, the ability of administrative bodies to start judicial review proceedings is mainly discussed as a question of legal capacity. In some other legal systems, like Germany and France, questions of legal capacity of certain public law entities also play a certain role. This point is less relevant in the Netherlands and the EU.

4.6 THIRD-PARTY INTERVENTION

In interest-based systems of access to court, the assumption is that rules concerning the intervention of third parties do not differ much from the standing rules of the main parties to proceedings. In right-based systems, however, the situation may be different, as the intervention of a third party does not in principle serve the purpose of enforcing the individual rights of the third parties concerned. In this section, the focus of the analysis is on who can be an intervener and what rights an intervener has.

4.6.A LEGAL SYSTEMS WHERE STANDING RULES AND PROCEDURAL RIGHTS OF INTERVENERS DO NOT SUBSTANTIALLY DIFFER FROM THOSE OF THE MAIN PARTIES

4.6.A.1 THE NETHERLANDS

Algemene Wet Bestuursrecht **4.60 (NL)**

Article 8:26 (1) Until the end of the hearing, the administrative judge may allow parties concerned to join as parties to the proceedings on his own initiative, at the request of the parties or at their own request.

(2) If the administrative judge suspects that there are unknown parties concerned, he may announce in the Government Gazette that a case is pending before the court. The announcement may also be made by other means in addition to the announcement in the Government Gazette.

Notes

(1) Third parties do not differ from the 'main parties'. Both have to qualify as 'parties concerned' in the sense of Article 1:2 AWB. Hence, all the criteria of Article 1:2 AWB must be met.[167] An important limitation, which often excludes third parties, are the preclusion rules which will be dealt with in section 4.8 below. For example, third parties who want to join someone else's claim for judicial review (*beroep*) but did not participate in the intra-administrative objection procedure (*bezwaar*) even though they could have done so, may be excluded from intervention.[168]

(2) On its own initiative or at the request of one of the main parties, or at the request of the potential interveners themselves the court may invite other parties to join as a

[167] See section 4.4.B.4 above.

[168] On the intra-administrative objection procedure in the Netherlands, see Chapter 2, section 2.7.B.1 (ii).

third party. However, the court cannot *order* third parties to join. As there are no specific provisions regarding the procedural rights and duties of third parties, once they have access, they are treated no differently from the main parties.

4.6.A.2 ENGLAND AND WALES

Civil Procedure Rules **4.61 (EW)**

Rule 54.17 (1) Any person may apply for permission–
(a) to file evidence; or
(b) make representations at the hearing of the judicial review.

Notes

(1) As in the Netherlands, in England and Wales, the rules for admitting interventions of third parties do not differ significantly from the standing rules for the main parties. Both have to prove to have an interest in the case. The courts have generally been open to interventions from interested parties[169] and there is very little case law that considers the precise scope of a third party's ability to intervene. In some cases, the courts have adjourned judicial review cases in order for interested parties to be given the opportunity to intervene.[170]

(2) If third parties are granted access, their procedural rights are dependent on the scope of the permission that is granted. They may file any evidence that the court allows and make such representations as the court permits.

High Court (Queen's Bench Division), 27 May 2010[171] **4.62 (EW)**

R (Air Transport Association of America Inc) v Secretary of State for Energy and Climate Change

THIRD-PARTY INTERVENTION; STANDING

Air Transport Association of America

Interventions by groups, bodies or individuals may be allowed because of the particular knowledge and expertise they have in the area at issue.

Facts: The claimant claimed that the Aviation Greenhouse Gas Emissions Trading Scheme Regulations 2009 were unlawful, although the challenge really concerned questions of the lawfulness of the European Directive which the UK secondary legislation was seeking to implement. The main issue in this case, which arose before

[169] For some guidance, see *Re Northern Ireland Human Rights Commission* [2002] UKHL 25, [2002] HRLR 35. Here, the House of Lords made it clear that it expected interveners to make very focused submissions that do not duplicate points made by the main parties.

[170] *R (Howard League for Penal Reform) v Secretary of State for the Home Department* [2002] EWHC 1750 (Admin).

[171] [2010] EWHC 1554 (Admin).

a referral to the CJEU was to be made, concerned whether a number of parties, including the International Air Transport Association and a group of environmental pressure groups, could intervene in the case under Rule 54.17 CPR.

Held: The court held that the parties could intervene, although considered the potential impact of this on the proceedings before the CJEU.

Judgment: Ouseley J: 7 The three applicant interveners apply under 54.17. Although it might very well be the case that at least the airline members of IATA and NACC might qualify as interested parties for the purposes of 54.7, I do not need to consider that further because the applications are made under 54.17.

8 It has been the practice of this court for a number of years, well established and beneficial, to allow interventions by groups or bodies, or individuals who have particular knowledge and expertise in the area, whether in terms of the effect which the action at issue may have upon them and their interests, or by virtue of the work which they carry out or through close study of the law, practice and problems in an area, or because of the campaigning experience and knowledge which their activities have brought.

9 There is no doubt that each of the bodies who apply to participate come well within those categories. The legislation at issue affects the application of emissions trading to airlines on international journeys to and from the non-EU Member States and by companies in other countries where there are other international agreements of relevance.

10 The membership of IATA covers 230 airlines providing international air services throughout the world. Over 180 of its member airlines provide services to and from the EU Member States and I accept are directly affected by the Directive and many of those are directly affected by the operation of the implementing regulation. The role of IATA is well-known as a representative body before courts, regulatory bodies and it has observer status on the International Civil Aviation Organisation.

11 The submissions and experience that it would bring to a debate about the lawfulness of the domestic regulation and hence its role in relation to the implementing Directive is clear; it would bring value and perspective to the argument in a way that the claimants alone will be less able to do, although the matter at issue will be closely related to the arguments of the claimant. …

13 So far as the five environmental organisations are concerned, it is clear not merely do they have a long-standing interest in the most general sense in emissions standards and trading but they have had specific experience in the negotiation of relevant international treaties and will be able to provide submissions on the background to relevant treaties and to the Directive which is of particular assistance.

14 If this were proceeding as a wholly domestic case, those are the decisions I would have made and the reasons for them. It is, in my judgement, for this court to decide who should be interveners before it, but bearing in mind, as Mr Anderson rightly says I should, the resource and time problems of the European Court of Justice and not wishing to overburden them or add any delay, I make the order that these be joined as interveners subject to IATA and NACC acting as one.

Note

As the judgment above demonstrates, overall, the courts' approach to third-party intervention is very open. However, the High Court also held that a national association of tobacco growers did not have the right to intervene in a case concerning a domestic challenge to the EU Directive on Tobacco Marketing as it held that the intervention would have no practical value in the drafting of the reference to the CJEU. This demonstrates that the courts will impose some limitation on the right of third parties to intervene where it is deemed that there is no practical benefit from allowing such an intervention.[172]

4.6.B LEGAL SYSTEMS WHERE STANDING RULES APPLICABLE TO INTERVENERS ARE SIMILAR BUT THE PROCEDURAL RIGHTS ARE MORE LIMITED THAN THOSE OF THE MAIN PARTIES: FRANCE

In a similar way to England and Wales, the French approach to third-party intervention is that interventions are admissible if the party has a 'sufficient interest' to intervene. Therefore, the rules for intervention do not differ significantly from those applicable in the Netherlands and England and Wales. The intervener has to prove an interest to intervene and not to act, which may mean an (even) more lenient application of the interest criterion applicable to standing. What differs in France, however, are the rights and function interveners have in the proceedings.

Conseil d'État, 25 July 2013[173] **4.63 (FR)**

OPFRA v National Asylum Court

THIRD-PARTY INTERVENTION; SUFFICIENT INTEREST

OFPRA

Third-party interveners have to demonstrate a sufficient interest with regard to the nature and object of the dispute to be admissible to intervene in the course of the proceedings.

Facts: Mrs A, a Nigerian national, was denied the status of refugee by the National Court on Asylum Law. She argued that she would be exposed to threats and violence if she returned to Nigeria. The French office for the protection of refugees and stateless persons (OFPRA) challenged this decision before the Council of State. Two NGOs, whose mission is to assist persons who claim refugee status, requested to intervene in the proceedings.

Held: The intervention of the NGOs was admitted. The decision of the National Asylum Court was annulled.

Judgment: 1. Considering that any person who demonstrates a sufficient interest with regard to the nature and to the object of the dispute may lodge an intervention before the court, when adjudicating on the substance or on points of law; that such an intervention, which is of an incidental nature, does not, however, have the effect of conferring on its author the quality of a party to the proceedings and cannot, therefore, confer upon him a right of access to the files of the proceedings; that furthermore, in accordance with

[172] *R (on the application of British American Tobacco UK Ltd) v Secretary of State for Health* [2014] EWHC 3515 (Admin).

[173] N° 350661.

a general rule of procedure from which Article R623-1 of the Code of Administrative Justice is inspired, the ruling the case cannot be delayed by an intervention; that, in the case at hand, the *Cimade* and the association called *'Les amis du bus des femmes'* show, by their statutory object and their action, an interest which allows them to intervene before the asylum court; that their interventions must, consequently, be admitted. …

Note

The requirement that a third party concerned should have an interest to obtain the status of intervener is interpreted very leniently, even more leniently than the *locus standi* requested to lodge the main action. The third party needs to prove 'a sufficient interest with regard to the nature and object of the litigation'. For example, as shown in the *OPFRA* case, an association whose purpose is to 'defend the interests of suffering or oppressed people and to fight for their rights' and an association with the purposes of fighting against human trafficking and helping prostitutes were considered to have a sufficient interest as third-party interveners before the administrative court in procedures concerning asylum. A company was also admitted to intervene in a procedure challenging a sanction adopted by the data protection authority, since its name was mentioned in the sanctioning decision.[174]

Code de justice administrative **4.64 (FR)**

Article R632-1 The intervention is lodged by specific pleadings. When the intervention is brought by a person specified in the first paragraph of Article R414-1, it is submitted according to the conditions provided by this article and by Article R414-3.

The president of the court formation, or, at the Council of State, the president of the chamber in charge of the investigation, orders, if there is a reason for it, that the application for intervention shall be sent to the parties and sets the deadline for response. Nevertheless, the examination of the case may not be delayed by the intervention.

Notes

(1) The third party who is admitted as an intervener has to submit pleadings that are distinct from those of the parties. The intervention is not limited by any time limit, as long as the claim is still pending. It can be presented for the first time before the Administrative Court of First Instance, the Administrative Court of Appeal or the Council of State. The court is free to decide whether it will give the opportunity to the parties to respond to the points raised by the intervener; however, the proceedings cannot be delayed by an intervention.

(2) Third parties are not granted the same rights as the main parties. They do not have access to the file of the case (apart from the submissions produced by other

[174] Conseil d'État, 11 March 2015, *Société Total raffinage marketing*, N° 368748.

parties which are communicated to them by the court) and they are not entitled to appeal against the decision of the court, since this right is only open to the parties of a proceedings before the Administrative Court of First Instance. In addition, while they can submit a pleading, the claims of the interveners are limited to those made by the parties, otherwise their intervention would be qualified as an application and its admissibility would be assessed according to the standing requirements. Finally, the third party cannot claim for the reimbursement of costs of the procedure incurred as a result of the intervention.

(3) A forced intervention is possible. A third party is then involved in a pending case due to the link he has with it, upon the request of one of the main parties. In this case, the third party is considered as a main party to the proceedings. It can present its own pleadings along with its autonomous claims. This mechanism is only used in litigation relating to pecuniary matters, mainly in liability cases. For example, when it appears that a public body, whose liability was initially claimed, is not solely responsible for the damage, another public body that has contributed to the damage can be required to intervene and becomes a party in the proceedings.

4.6.C LEGAL SYSTEMS WHERE STANDING RULES APPLICABLE TO INVERVENERS DIFFER FROM THOSE OF THE MAIN PARTIES BUT PROCEDURAL RIGHTS ARE SIMILAR

4.6.C.1 THE EUROPEAN UNION

Statute of the Court of Justice of the European Union **4.65 (EU)**

Article 40 (1) Member States and institutions of the Union may intervene in cases before the Court of Justice.

(2) The same right shall be open to the bodies, offices and agencies of the Union and to any other person which can establish an interest in the result of a case submitted to the Court. Natural or legal persons shall not intervene in cases between Member States, between institutions of the Union or between Member States and institutions of the Union.

...

(4) An application to intervene shall be limited to supporting the form of order sought by one of the parties.

Notes

(1) Intervention of third parties before the European courts is always a right, but never an obligation. Interveners are not parties themselves and therefore their submissions must be limited to supporting the form of order sought by one of the parties.

This also means that interveners must accept the case as they find it at the time of the intervention.[175]

(2) According to Article 40 of the Statute of the Court of Justice, Member States and EU institutions are 'privileged interveners' in the sense that they can intervene in any case submitted to the European courts. Natural and legal persons must instead establish an interest in the result of the case. This interest will be established if the intervener's legal or economic position might be affected directly by the decision to be taken by the European courts.[176] In cases between the institutions of the EU, between Member States (which are very rare) or between the institutions and the Member States, natural and legal persons cannot intervene at all. As far as associations are concerned, it is settled case law that intervention is permissible if the outcome of the dispute is liable to affect the collective interests defended by the associations as evidenced by their statutes.[177] Hence, the threshold to intervene as a third party in pending proceedings is lower than the standing requirements for the main party, who has to be individually concerned, a requirement that has been interpreted strictly by the CJEU in the *Plaumann* case.[178]

(3) Interveners (whether privileged or not) are free, within the form of order sought, to bring forward their own arguments independently of the main parties. However, they cannot raise an objection of inadmissibility that has not been raised by the main party,[179] and are bound by any acts which may have been carried out in the course of the proceedings before they intervened. For the remainder of the proceedings, the interveners have the same procedural rights as the main parties.

4.6.C.2 GERMANY

The differences between the standing requirements of a claimant and the criteria for allowing a third-party intervention are probably most obvious in a right-based system, such as the German system.

Verwaltungsgerichtsordnung **4.66 (DE)**

§65 (1) As long as the proceedings have not yet been concluded in a final and non-appealable way or are pending at a higher instance, the court, may summon, *ex officio* or on request, those whose legal interests are affected by the ruling.

[175] Rules of Procedure of the European Court of Justice, Art 129(3); Rules of Procedure of the General Court, Art 116(3).

[176] eg Case T-210/01 *General Electric v Commission* ECLI:EU:C:2005/456, where the Court of Justice recognised that competitors of undertakings which had brought an action for annulment against a Commission decision declaring a merger incompatible with the common market had an interest in intervening in support of the Commission.

[177] Case T-253/03 *Akzo Nobel v Commission* ECLI:EU:T:2007:58, para 21 and the case law quoted.

[178] See section 4.4.B.5 (iii) above.

[179] Case C-313/90 *CIRFS v Commission* ECLI:EU:C:1993:111.

(2) If third parties are involved in the contentious legal relationship in such a way that the ruling can only be imposed on them uniformly, they shall be subpoenaed (necessary subpoena, *notwendige Beiladung*).

(3) If the subpoena of more than fifty persons is considered in accordance with section 2, the court may, by issuing an order, impose that only those persons who so apply within a certain period are subpoenaed. The order shall be not be contestable. The order shall be announced in the Federal Gazette. It must furthermore be published in newspapers that are disseminated in the area in which the ruling is likely to exert an impact ....

The court should, also without a request to this end, subpoena persons who are discernibly particularly affected by the ruling. ....

§66 Within the application of one of the main parties, those who are subject to the subpoena may independently bring forward all means of attack and defence as well as effectively undertake all procedural acts. Only a party subject to a necessary subpoena may lodge motions which deviate from those lodged by the main parties (*abweichende Sachanträge*).

Notes

(1) Third parties do not need to claim that the contested decision infringes their rights derived from public law. As the function of an intervention by a third party is different from the function of the main parties, the rules on admissibility are not right-based, but interest-based. Third parties can be permitted or may be summoned to join the proceedings. According to §65(1) VwGO, third-party interventions may take place as long as the proceedings have not yet been concluded in a final and non-appealable way, or are still pending at a higher instance. The court may invite to join *ex officio* or on request those third parties whose legal interests are affected by the ruling. If third parties are involved in the contentious legal relationship in such a way that the ruling can only be imposed on them uniformly, they shall all be subpoenaed (necessary subpoena). That is the case, for example, where a neighbour files an action to annul an administrative act which grants a building permit. In that case, the builder who is the addressee of the administrative act must be subpoenaed by the court.

(2) According to §66 VwGO, the subpoenaed parties generally have the same rights as the other parties. They may bring forward all means of attack and defence, and may act independently in terms of procedure. Thus, they may, for example, provide or request further evidence. However, only parties subject to a necessary subpoena may file procedural motions which deviate from the ones filed by the main parties. Thus, only the party subject to the necessary subpoena may broaden or limit the subject matter of the action.[180]

[180] See W Porz, in M Fehling, B Kastner and R Störmer (eds), *Verwaltungsrecht*, 4th edn (Munich, CH Beck, 2016) §66 VwGO, para 6.

4.6.D COMPARATIVE REMARKS

In most legal systems, the possibility to intervene as a third party is a right, not an obligation. However, 'necessary subpoenas' exist in German law and, in certain cases, in French law too. In such a case, the court orders a third party to join the proceedings.

In interest-based systems of access to court, such as France, England and Wales and the Netherlands, rules on standing of interveners do not differ significantly, if at all, from the standing rules of the main parties to the proceedings. This is different with regard to the EU and Germany. As the function of standing criteria for interveners is different from the function of standing criteria for the main parties in Germany, this legal system also allows interveners if they show sufficient interest. They do not have to claim that a subjective right is infringed. The rules for standing of interveners in the EU depend on the identity of the intervener, but are generally more lenient than the standing rules for the main applicant.

Regarding the procedural rights of third parties, two models can be identified: either the third party in general is treated as the 'first and second party' (the main parties) and has the roughly the same rights as the claimant and the defendant, as is the case in the Netherlands, Germany, the EU and England and Wales, or the third party has a more limited function and more limited rights, as is the case in France.

4.7 TIME LIMITS

4.7.A INTRODUCTION

All legal systems provide for time limits within which individuals are entitled to challenge the administrative action. Time limits reflect the need to ensure legal certainty and at the same time the effectiveness and efficiency of administrative decision-making. Usually, time limits are norms of public order. The authority which issued the decision cannot extend or otherwise prescribe a different time limit if the legal provision does not explicitly provide for such a power. If it does so, the court has to apply the statutory time limit *ex officio*.

A general rule in all legal systems studied is that decisions become final when time limits have run out and they are not challenged in time. The decision is no longer vulnerable to a direct action. The interest of legal certainty, especially the interest of the beneficiary of the decision, prevails. However, in some situations the weighing of interests may be different. For example, decisions of general scope may be subject to indirect control, regardless of the expiry of the time limits, in the context of an action directed against an 'implementing' single-case decision. The French call this '*exception d'illégalité*', the Dutch '*exceptieve toetsing*' and the Germans '*Inzidentkontrolle*'. In England and Wales, this is described as 'collateral challenge'. The same mechanism exists in the EU legal system, and is referred to as the 'plea of illegality'.[181]

[181] For more on this, see Chapter 7, section 7.7.

In this section, first time limits in actions for annulment of a single-case decision will be discussed, then time limits in cases of administrative silence or failure to act will be examined.[182] Finally, time limits in other cases will be presented.

In cases with an EU law dimension, any time limit imposed by national law must comply with the principles of equivalence, effectiveness and effective judicial protection. In the 1970s, the European Court of Justice developed its jurisprudence on effectiveness in the *Rewe* judgment, which dealt with time limits in German law.

Case 33/76, 16 December 1976[183] **4.67 (EU)**

Rewe Zentralfinanz v Commission

EFFECTIVE JUDICIAL PROTECTION; TIME LIMITS

Rewe

It is for the domestic legal system of each Member State to designate the courts having jurisdiction and to determine the procedural conditions governing actions intended to ensure the protection of the rights which citizens derive from EU law. Such conditions cannot be less favourable than those relating to similar actions of a domestic nature (equivalence) and may not render it impossible in practice to exercise the rights which the national courts are obliged to protect (effectiveness). Provided that these conditions are respected, time limits for bringing a claim to court are an application of the fundamental principle of legal certainty and they do not infringe EU law.

Facts: Rewe-Zentralfinanz AG paid charges for phyto-sanitary inspection in respect of the import of French apples which were found to be equivalent to customs duties. In 1973, the company applied to the Chamber of Agriculture (Landwirtschaftskammer) of Saarland to annul the decisions imposing the charges and to refund the amounts paid including interest. This claim was declared inadmissible on the ground that it was out of time under §58 of the Code of Administrative Court Procedure (VwGO). The Federal Administrative Court, acting in third and final instance, referred some questions to the European Court of Justice. One of these questions concerned the legality of the time limit contained in §58 of the Code of Administrative Court Procedure.

Held: A citizen who contests before a national court a decision of a national authority on the ground that it is incompatible with EU law may be confronted with the defence that limitation periods laid down by national law have expired, if the procedural conditions governing the action are not less favourable than those relating to similar actions of a domestic nature.

Judgment: 5 Applying the principle of cooperation laid down in Article 5 of the Treaty, it is the national courts which are entrusted with ensuring the legal protection which citizens derive from the direct effect of the provisions of Community law.

Accordingly, in the absence of Community rules on this subject, it is for the domestic legal system of each Member State to designate the courts having jurisdiction and to determine the procedural conditions governing actions at law intended to ensure the protection of the rights which citizens have from the direct effect of Community law, it being understood that such conditions cannot be less favourable than those relating to similar actions of a domestic nature.

[182] See on silence of administrative authorities, Chapter 3, section 3.7.
[183] ECLI:EU:C:1976:188.

Where necessary, Articles 100 to 102 and 235 of the Treaty enable appropriate measures to be taken to remedy differences between the provisions laid down by law, regulation or administrative action in Member States if they are likely to distort or harm the functioning of the Common Market. In the absence of such measures of harmonization the right conferred by Community law must be exercised before the national courts in accordance with the conditions laid down by national rules.

The position would be different only if the conditions and time-limits made it impossible in practice to exercise the rights which the national courts are obliged to protect. This is not the case where reasonable periods of limitation of actions are fixed.

The laying down of such time-limits with regard to actions of a fiscal nature is an application of the fundamental principle of legal certainty protecting both the tax-payer and the administration concerned.

6 The answer to be given to the first question is therefore that in the present state of Community law there is nothing to prevent a citizen who contests before a national court a decision of a national authority on the ground that it is incompatible with Community law from being confronted with the defence that limitation periods laid down by national law have expired, it being understood that the procedural conditions governing the action may not be less favourable than those relating to similar actions of a domestic nature.

Note

In this judgment, the European Court of Justice developed what was later called 'the principle of effectiveness'.[184] It is within the autonomy of the Member States to draft national procedural rules as long as these rules meet two criteria:

(a) The conditions for actions intended to ensure the protection of the rights which citizens derive from EU law may not be less favourable than those relating to similar actions of a domestic nature (principle of equivalence).
(b) National procedural rules may not make it impossible in practice to exercise the rights derived from EU law which the national courts are obliged to protect (principle of effectiveness).

Rules on time limits, as any other national procedural rule, must respect these requirements.[185]

4.7.B TIME LIMITS FOR ACTIONS FOR ANNULMENT OF A SINGLE-CASE DECISION

In order to illustrate the differences between the general rules on time limits with regard to actions for annulment of a single-case decision in the various legal systems, this section will take one legal system as an example and compare the others with it.

[184] See S Prechal and R Widdershoven, 'Redefining the Relationship between "Rewe-effectiveness" and Effective Judicial Protection' (2011) 4 *Review of European Administrative Law* 31.

[185] For more on the case law of the Court of Justice on time limits, see R Ortlep and RJGM Widdershoven, 'Judicial Protection' in JH Jans, S Prechal and RJGM Widdershoven (eds), *Europeanisation of Public Law*, 2nd edn (Europa Law Publishing, Groningen, 2015) 383 ff.

4.7.B.1 GERMANY

Verwaltungsgerichtsordnung **4.68 (DE)**

§70 (1) The objection shall be lodged in writing within one month of notification of the administrative act to the aggrieved party, in writing or for the record of the authority which has carried out the administrative act. The deadline shall also be deemed to have been adhered to with the filing of an objection with the authority which has to issue the ruling on an objection.

(2) §§58 and 60(1) to 4, shall apply mutatis mutandis.

§74 (1) The action for annulment (*Anfechtungsklage*) must be lodged within one month of service of the decision on the objection. If in accordance with §68 a decision on an intra-administrative objection is not required, the action must be lodged within one month of the notification of the administrative act.

§58 (1) The time period for an action for annulment or an other legal remedy commences only once the party involved has been informed in writing or in electronic form of the availability of a legal remedy, of the administrative authority or the court from which such a remedy can be sought, the address at which the action is to be lodged and the deadline to be observed.

(2) If the information has not been provided or has been provided incorrectly, the lodging of a legal remedy is allowed within one year of service, publication or notification, unless the lodging was impossible prior to expiry of the year period as a result of *force majeure*, or a written or electronic notification took place according to which a legal remedy was not available. §60(2) applies mutatis mutandis to the case of *force majeure*.

§60 (1) If someone was unable, without fault, to observe a statutory deadline, he shall be granted *restitutio in integrum* on request.

(2) The request must be made within two weeks of the disappearance of the impediment; if the deadline for the period granted to substantiate the appeal on points of fact and law (*Berufung*), the application to admit the appeal on points of fact and law, the appeal on points of law (*Revision*), the complaint against non-admission (*Nichtzulassungsbeschwerde*) or the complaint has passed, the time period is one month. …

(3) One year after the expiry of the unobserved time limit, the application becomes inadmissible unless filing the application prior to expiry of the year period was impossible as a result of *force majeure*.

Notes

(1) Before any action for annulment (*Anfechtungsklage*) can be filed, the claimant must have filed an intra-administrative objection (*Widerspruch*) within one month of the administrative act giving rise to the grievance being notified to him or the requested administrative act being denied (§70 VwGO).[186] The statutory period to file the objection is extended to one year if the administrative authority has failed to give the citizen the correct instructions about the legal remedies available (§58(2) VwGO).

[186] On the intra-administrative objection procedure, see Chapter 2, section 2.6.

(2) After the intra-administrative objection procedure, an action for annulment must be lodged within one month of the notification of the decision on the objection (§74VwGO). If, in accordance with §68 VwGO, an intra-administrative objection procedure is not required, the action must be lodged within one month of notification of the administrative act. The time limit for lodging an objection or starting a court action only commences if the claimant has been informed in writing or in electronic form of the judicial remedy, the court before which the action is to be lodged, the seat and the deadline to be adhered to (§58(1) VwGO). If the information has not been provided or has been incorrectly provided, the lodging of the claim is permissible within one year (§58(2) VwGO). The one-year limit does not apply if the applicant is prevented from filing an action because of *force majeure*, or there was a written or electronic notification that an action was not possible or that no legal remedy was available.

(3) Delay in filing an action may be condoned by the court pursuant to §60 VwGO if no fault of the plaintiff prevented him from approaching the court within the prescribed time limit. In that case, he must file the action along with an application for condonation of delay (*Antrag auf Wiedereinsetzung in den vorigen Stand*) within two weeks of the removal of the hindrance. The decision to condone the delay is final, but a refusal to condone the delay is subject to appeal on grounds of fact and law or appeal on grounds of law,[187] depending on whether such appeals are possible in the main proceedings.

4.7.B.2 THE NETHERLANDS

Algemene Wet Bestuursrecht **4.69 (NL)**

Article 6:7 The time limit for submitting a letter of objection or for filing a claim for judicial review shall be six weeks.

Note

The general time limit for intra-administrative objection procedures and claims for judicial review (*beroep*) is six weeks.[188]

Algemene Wet Bestuursrecht **4.70 (NL)**

Article 6:11 If an intra-administrative objection or a claim for judicial review is lodged after the expiry of the term, the claim shall not be declared inadmissible by reason of delay if it cannot reasonably be assumed that the claimant was at fault.

[187] See on these concepts Chapter 8, section 8.2.C.1.

[188] For example, a shorter period determined in a specific act concerns claims against decisions based on the Aliens Act, which can be brought within four weeks, and in some special cases only within one week, of the notification of the decision to the applicant (Aliens Act, Art 69).

Raad van State, 8 May 2001[189] **4.71 (NL)**

JMA Hormes v Mayor and Aldermen of Wijchen

JUDICIAL REVIEW; TIME LIMITS; EXCUSE FOR EXCEEDANCE OF A TIME LIMIT

Huisboot Wijchen

The fact that a decision does not contain the required notification of the rights for bringing a claim for judicial review does not excuse a failure to observe the time limit, unless there are special circumstances.

Facts: In their decision dated 2 February 1998, the mayor and aldermen of Wijchen refused to grant permission to berth the appellant's houseboat at the place he requested. In their decision of 9 September 1999, they declared inadmissible the intra-administrative objection of the appellant against this decision, which was lodged on 24 May 1999. The claimant brought a claim for judicial review against the decision on the objection.

Held: The claim was declared inadmissible.

Judgment: 2.2 It is not disputed that the objection of the claimant has not been lodged within the legal time limit of six weeks and that therefore the time limit is exceeded.

2.3 It is further not disputed that the contested decision of 2 February 1998 did not contain a notification of the rights for bringing a claim for judicial review as required by Article 3:45 AWB.

...

The Judicial Division of the Council of State considers that in such cases the exceedance of the time limit, as a point of departure, cannot be excused, unless there are special circumstances.

Notes

(1) Similar to the German situation, an action against a single-case decision submitted after the end of the time limit shall not be ruled inadmissible because the time limit was exceeded if it 'cannot reasonably be assumed that the claimant was at fault' (Article 6:11 AWB). Courts apply this provision strictly because of its importance in serving public order.

(2) As the excerpt above shows, if the authority did not, as required, announce how and until when a decision can be challenged, this does not automatically justify a failure to observe the time limit. In fact, in the Dutch legal system, until recently, it has been unusual for such an omission to justify the exeedance of the time limit. As a consequence, the Dutch approach towards exceedance of time limits has been stricter than the German approach based on §58 VwGO. However, more recently, the Dutch case law has aligned with the German approach, and delay due to failure to properly communicate the information on the legal remedies will not lead to the inadmissibility

[189] ECLI:NL:RVS:2001:AB1706.

of the claim if the applicant is not represented in the legal proceedings by a lawyer and the applicant is not involved on a regular basis in a procedure.[190,191]

4.7.B.3 FRANCE

Code de justice administrative **4.72 (FR)**

Article R421-1 A claim against a decision must be brought before the court within two months of the notification or publication of the contested decision.

Note

In France, the period to bring an action for annulment (*recours pour excès de pouvoir*) is even longer than in the Netherlands and more than twice as long as in Germany: two months, starting on the day after the publication or notification of the contested measure. Sometimes the time limit is different because of special statutory provisions: for example, decisions concerning the grant of environmental permits can be challenged within one year by residents of the area and associations.[192]

Code des relations entre le public et l'administration **4.73 (FR)**

Article L411-2 Every administrative decision can be the object, within the time limit imposed for the introduction of an action for annulment, of a *recours gracieux* (intra-administrative objection procedure addressed to the decision-maker) or a *recours hiérarchique* (intra-administrative objection procedure addressed to a superior authority) which interrupts the running of this time limit.

When a *recours gracieux* or a *recours hiérarchique* is introduced within the time limit foreseen for an action for annulment, the time limit for the action for annulment, extended by virtue of the commencement of those administrative appeal procedures (*recours administratifs*), does not recommence to run in regard to the initial decision until both procedures are concluded.

Note

In France, the time limit can be extended by challenging the decision before the administration itself (through a *recours gracieux* or a *recours hierarchique*).[193] If one does so within the two-month limit, one may still bring the case to court within two months of the decision on the objection procedure.

[190] ECLI:NL:RVS:2011:BT2131; ECLI:NL:CRVB:2011:BR0151.
[191] ECLI:NL:CRVB:2007:BB9715.
[192] Code de l'Environnement, Art R514-3-1.
[193] Chapter 2, section 2.7.B.2.

Code de justice administrative **4.74 (FR)**

Article R421-5 Deadlines for claims against administrative decisions are enforceable only provided that they are mentioned, together with the remedies available, in the notification of the decision.

Notes

(1) Public authorities are under an obligation to provide the information concerning the available remedies and the time limits to challenge an individual decision when they notify it provides notification of a decision to its addressee. A consequence of the absence of such information is that the time limit can be set aside, meaning that the decision becomes challengeable without time limits. The same approach is adopted when the notification of the decision has not been delivered at all or has been provided incorrectly. However, if the addressee acts in such way that it can be demonstrated that he is aware of the existence of the act (*théorie de la connaissance acquise*) (for example, by introducing an objection against the decision before the administrative authority), this exception does not apply, and the decision cannot be challenged after the expiry of the two-month time limit. Furthermore, in order to safeguard legal certainty, the Council of State has limited the possibility to challenge an individual decision indefinitely in case of a flaw in the notification, holding that after a reasonable time it would not be possible to introduce an action. Generally, one year is to be regarded as reasonable.[194]

(2) Under French law, the notion of excusable delay does not exist. If the application does not fall within the scope of the law on failure of notification or inadequacy of notification, or of cases where the time limit can be extended, the failure to comply with the time limit requirement leads to the inadmissibility of the action, which cannot be repaired before the court.

4.7.B.4 THE EUROPEAN UNION

Treaty of the Functioning of the European Union **4.75 (EU)**

Article 263 (6) The proceedings provided for in this Article shall be instituted within two months of the publication of the measure, or of its notification to the plaintiff, or, in the absence thereof, of the day on which it came to the knowledge of the latter, as the case may be.

Statute of the Court of Justice of the European Union **4.76 (EU)**

Article 45 …

No right shall be prejudiced in consequence of the expiry of a time limit if the party concerned proves the existence of unforeseeable circumstances or of *force majeure*.

[194] Conseil d'État, 13 July 2016, *M. Czabaj*, N° 387763.

Notes

(1) In actions for annulment before the EU courts, the time limit is two months, as in the French legal system. The moment at which the time starts running (publication, notification, knowledge of the applicant) depends on the type of measure which is at stake.

(2) The case law of the European courts is consistent in holding that the rule contained in Article 263(6) is a matter of public policy and may not be derogated from either by the agreement of the parties or by the courts themselves, since it was established to maintain legal certainty and avoid discriminatory treatment.[195]

(3) However, the time limit might be derogated from in cases of unforeseeable circumstances or *force majeure*. According to the Court of Justice, 'in the context of the European Union's rules on time-limits for instituting proceedings, the concept of excusable error justifying a derogation from those rules can concern only exceptional circumstances in which, in particular, the conduct of the institution concerned has been, either alone or to a decisive extent, such as to give rise to a pardonable confusion in the mind of the party acting in good faith and displaying all the diligence required of a normally well-informed person'.[196]

4.7.B.5 ENGLAND AND WALES

Civil Procedure Rules **4.77 (EW)**

Rule 54.5 (1) The claim form must be filed–

(a) promptly; and

(b) in any event not later than 3 months after the grounds to make the claim first arose.

(2) The time limits in this rule may not be extended by agreement between the parties.

(3) This rule does not apply when any other enactment specifies a shorter time limit for making the claim for judicial review.

(4) Paragraph (1) does not apply in the cases specified in paragraphs (5) and (6).

(5) Where the application for judicial review relates to a decision made by the Secretary of State or local planning authority under the planning acts, the claim form must be filed not later than six weeks after the grounds to make the claim first arose.

(6) Where the application for judicial review relates to a decision governed by the Public Contracts Regulations 2015, the claim form must be filed within the time within which an economic operator would have been required by regulation 92 of those Regulations (and disregarding the rest of that regulation) to start any proceedings under those Regulations in respect of that decision.

[195] Case 152/85 *Misset v Council* ECLI:EU:C:1987:10, para 11; Case C-246/95 *Myrianne Coen v Belgian State* ECLI:EU:C:1997:33, para 21.

[196] Case C-73/10 P *Internationale Fruchtimport Gesellschaft Weichert GmbH & Co KG v Commission* ECLI:EU:C:2010:684, para 42.

Notes

(1) A somewhat peculiar approach can be found in England and Wales. On the one hand, Rule 54.5 CPR provides the longest general time limit of all legal systems covered in this book. The usual time limit for the bringing of claims for judicial review is three months from the date of the decision or action that is the subject of the challenge. On the other hand, a court may refuse to hear a claim that was brought within the three-month time limit because it was brought with undue delay – and hence not 'promptly'.

(2) In some areas, Rule 54.5 CPR provides for fixed maximum periods to bring a claim. English law considers these to be 'time limited ouster clauses'.[197] Many statutes, particularly in the area of planning law, compulsory purchase of land and the development of public utilities infrastructure, impose a time limit of six weeks, after which statute purports to prohibit claims for judicial review. In the case of the Inquiries Act 2005, a judicial review claim against decisions of a minister or panel member of an inquiry must lodged within 14 days. The present situation is that the courts treat such timelimited ouster clauses as an acceptable use of legislative power to provide certainty in certain spheres, particularly in planning and public procurement.[198]

High Court (Queen's Bench Division), 16 December 2003[199] **4.78 (EW)**

R v Hounslow London Borough Council, ex parte A1 Veg Ltd

JUDICIAL REVIEW; TIME LIMITS; PROMPTNESS

A1 Veg

The 'utmost promptitude' is required where third parties are or will probably be affected by the delay in pursing an application for judicial review.

Facts: The Hounslow London Borough Council owned a large indoor market in which the claimants were tenants. The Council decided to build a new market which was smaller than the old market, so it brought about a selection process to choose traders who would have the opportunity to trade in the new market. The claimants were not successful in securing a place, so they brought a judicial review claim, arguing that the allocation process was unlawful for a number of reasons. However, they brought the claim on the last day of the three-month period foreseen for a claim for judicial review.

Held: The claim was permitted, with the court rejecting the argument in this particular case that the claim was not prompt.

Judgment: Silber J.: 40. Thus, the requirement for a claimant to issue proceedings 'promptly' remains. Mr. Fordham agreed with me that a useful starting point is that when judicial review claims are brought within the prescribed three month period, there is a rebuttable presumption that they have been brought promptly, but Mr. Fordham

[197] In more detail, see *R v Secretary of State for the Environment, ex parte Ostler* [1977] QB 122 (CA), discussed in Chapter 1, section 1.4.E.

[198] *Ostler* (ibid).

[199] [2003] EWHC 3112 (Admin), [2004] BLGR 536.

contends that the presumption can be rebutted in the present case. In order to show why the claimants in the present applications did not act promptly and permission should not be granted, Mr. Fordham relies on what he considers to be the comparable position considered by the Court of Appeal in *R v. Independent Television Commission ex parte TVNI Limited* (1991) [1996] JR 60 ('the ITC case'), in which it refused to grant permission to an unsuccessful applicant to pursue a judicial review application to challenge the granting of a Television Channel Licence. Lord Donaldson MR explained that 'in these matters, people must act with the utmost promptitude because so many third parties are affected by the decision and are entitled to act on it unless they have clear and prompt notice that the decision is challenged' [at page 61]. In other words, his decision was based on the fact that the 'utmost promptitude' is required where third parties are or will probably be affected by the delay in pursing an application for judicial review.

Note

The possibility to refuse hearing a claim that was not brought promptly provides the judge with more discretion than his counterparts in other legal systems have.

Case C-406/08, 28 January 2010[200] **4.79 (EU)**

Uniplex v NHS Business Services Authority

JUDICIAL REVIEW; TIME LIMITS; PROMPTNESS; PRINCIPLE OF EFFECTIVENESS

Uniplex

The criterion provided in English law according to which claims must be brought 'promptly' is in violation of the principle of effectiveness.

Facts: Uniplex took part in a public procurement procedure. However, its tender was not awarded. After some further discussions with the authority which took the decision to not award the tender, Uniplex filed a claim against the decision. The High Court sought guidance on how it should interpret the requirement for judicial review proceedings to be brought promptly.

Held: Article 1(1) of Directive 89/665 precludes a national provision, which allows a national court to dismiss, as being out of time, proceedings seeking to have an infringement of the public procurement rules established or to obtain damages for the infringement of those rules on the basis of the criterion, appraised in a discretionary manner, that such proceedings must be brought promptly.

Judgment: 41 A national provision such as Regulation 47(7)(b) of the 2006 Regulations, under which proceedings must not be brought 'unless … those proceedings are brought promptly and in any event within three months', gives rise to uncertainty. The possibility cannot be ruled out that such a provision empowers national courts to dismiss an action as being out of time even before the expiry of the three-month period if those courts take the view that the application was not made 'promptly' within the terms of that provision.

42 As the Advocate General observed in point 69 of her Opinion, a limitation period, the duration of which is placed at the discretion of the competent court, is not

[200] ECLI:EU:C:2010:45.

predictable in its effects. Consequently, a national provision providing for such a period does not ensure effective transposition of Directive 89/665.

43 It follows that the answer to the first part of the second question is that Article 1(1) of Directive 89/665 precludes a national provision, such as that at issue in the main proceedings, which allows a national court to dismiss, as being out of time, proceedings seeking to have an infringement of the public procurement rules established or to obtain damages for the infringement of those rules on the basis of the criterion, appraised in a discretionary manner, that such proceedings must be brought promptly.

Note

Answering the questions of the High Court, the CJEU emphasised that national law transposing EU law provisions must be sufficiently precise, clear and foreseeable to enable individuals to ascertain their rights and obligations. A discretionary power of a court to refuse a claim that was not brought promptly does not correspond with these requirements. In order to comply with the *Uniplex* ruling, English law had to be adapted. One issue to be tackled was whether this duty applies only to public procurement law or, rather, to all falling within the scope of application of EU law. In August 2015, the Department of Justice proposed a change to the time limits for bringing judicial review and launched a public consultation on this issue.[201] English law has now been adapted, solely in the realm of public procurement cases, to address the issues raised in *Uniplex*. Rule 54.5(6) CPR now requires that any challenge brought by an economic operator (within the definition of European public procurement law) via judicial review must be brought within the time limits imposed on other challenges by Regulation 92 of the Public Contracts Regulations 2015. Under these Regulations, 'proceedings must be started within 30 days beginning with the date when the economic operator first knew or ought to have known that grounds for starting the proceedings had arisen'. However, for all other parties, outside the scope of public procurement law, nothing has changed and the requirement to bring a claim 'promptly' remains.

Senior Courts Act 1981 **4.80 (EW)**

Section 31(6) Where the High Court considers that there has been undue delay in making an application for judicial review, the court may refuse to grant

(a) leave for the making of the application; or

(b) any relief sought on the application,

if it considers that the granting of the relief sought would be likely to cause substantial hardship to, or substantially prejudice the rights of, any person or would be detrimental to good administration.

[201] See www.gov.uk/government/uploads/system/uploads/attachment_data/file/78919/Uniplex_consultation_response_18-Aug-2011.pdf.

Notes

(1) Section 31(6) of the Senior Courts Act 1981 provides a specific discretion for the courts to refuse to grant leave to make the application (where the application is for permission to proceed), or to grant relief even where the claim is brought within the three-month period, where a claimant is thought to have delayed excessively in bringing a claim. The *Swale BC*[202] case is an example of the exercise of this discretion – the court held that there was a breach of the principle of legitimate expectations, but refused a remedy given the lack of promptness in bringing the claim. Similarly, the Court of Appeal in *Walters*[203] held that there had been a defect in the consultation procedure leading to a new policy on the provision of public housing, but refused a remedy given that the claimant had waited until the final day of the three-month period before issuing proceedings. In general, the court will be more likely to withhold a remedy if it is presented with evidence that there will be prejudice to third parties,[204] or to the efficiency and effectiveness of public administration,[205] should the remedy be granted.

(2) It has not yet been considered, either in the courts of England and Wales or in the EU courts, whether the potential to refuse a remedy because the claim was not brought promptly would be, in circumstances where EU law is involved, in accordance with the principles of effectiveness and effective judicial protection. It could be argued that the arguments which plead against the promptness requirement to deny leave also forbid the use of promptness as a criterion to refuse remedies.

House of Lords, 17 May 1990[206] **4.81 (EW)**

R v Dairy Produce Quota Tribunal for England and Wales, ex parte Caswell

JUDICIAL REVIEW; TIME LIMITS; EXCEEDANCE; EXCUSE

Caswell

Delay in bringing a claim beyond the time limit cannot be excused if this would cause detriment to good administration.

Facts: The Caswell family sold milk to the UK Milk Marketing Board, which purchased milk on the basis of a quota system allocated under the relevant provisions of EC law. The Dairy Produce Quota Tribunal

[202] *R v Swale Borough Council, ex parte Royal Society for the Protection of Birds* [1991] 1 PLR 6 (QB).

[203] *R v Secretary of State for the Environment, Transport and the Regions, ex p Walters* (1998) 30 HLR 328 (CA).

[204] *Swale Borough Council* (n 198).

[205] See, eg *R v Newbury DC, ex parte Chieveley Parish Council* (1998) 10 Admin LR 676 (CA), where the court held that delay in challenging a planning decision for a major project would constitute such administrative inconvenience. It is notable that in many cases, particularly where the rights of individuals are at stake, the courts will wish to see evidence of the administrative inconvenience that a grant of remedy will cause. See, eg *R v Secretary of State for the Home Department, ex parte Oyeleye (Florence Jumoke)* [1994] Imm AR 268, where the court found that no satisfactory evidence had been presented.

[206] [1990] 2 AC 738 (HL).

(an appellate tribunal) was created to deal with cases where farmers were dissatisfied with the level of quota awarded in their case. The family was dissatisfied with the decision of the Tribunal. They received the decision of the Tribunal in 1995, but did not seek legal advice or seek to challenge the decision until they read about the potential to claim judicial review in a case such as theirs in a farming publication in 1997.

Held: Permission to proceed was not granted.

Judgment: Lord Goff of Chieveley: First, when section 31(6) and (7) refer to 'an application for judicial review,' those words must be read as referring, where appropriate, to an application for leave to apply for judicial review. Next, as I read rule 4(1), the effect of the rule is to limit the time within which an application for leave to apply for judicial review may be made in accordance with its terms, i.e. promptly and in any event within three month. The court has however power to grant leave to apply despite the fact that an application is late, if it considers that there is good reason to exercise that power; this it does by extending the period.

It follows that, when an application for leave to apply is not made promptly and in any event within three month, the court may refuse leave on the ground of delay unless it considers that there is good reason for extending the period; but, even if it considers that there is such good reason, it may still refuse leave … if in its opinion the granting of the relief sought would be likely to cause hardship or prejudice (as specified in section 31(6)) or would be detrimental to good administration.

…

Consideration was given to the possibility of other producers seeking judicial review of adverse decisions of D.P.Q.T. if the appellants' application for substantive relief was successful …. a small but administratively substantial number of milk producers could be encouraged to make applications for judicial review relying on the same point as the appellants, or a variation of it; and that could mean re-opening the quota for the year 1984–85, and for each succeeding year. Further allocations of quota could only be made at the expense of all other producers whose quotas would have to be reduced accordingly.

…

The judge's conclusion, on the evidence before him, that there was likely to be a very real problem in relation to a number of cases, was a finding of fact with which I can see no reason to interfere. Once that conclusion was reached, it seems to me inevitable that to grant the relief sought in the present case would cause detriment to good administration …

Notes

(1) As in the other legal systems dealt with above, courts in England and Wales also have to decide whether a claimant who exceeded a time limit had a good reason to do so. Different from eg Germany, there are no written rules on this question.

(2) The court has discretion to decide, taking all circumstances of the case into account, whether to admit a claim brought after the expiry of the time limit. In general, the courts have taken a relatively strict approach. In the *Caswell* case, the House of Lords held that there were strong policy reasons, in terms of the efficiency and effectiveness of public administration, and also of legal certainty, in adhering strictly

to the three-month time limit. In *Moses*,[207] there was clear evidence that the claimant knew of a planning application for the extension of an airport runway and that permission was likely to be granted for more than a year before a claim for judicial review was made. The Court of Appeal held that the fact that the claimant was unaware that permission had finally been granted did not justify an extension of the time limit, not least because the claimant could have easily discovered that the permission had been granted earlier if he had enquired.

(3) A particular issue that arises in England and Wales and that has been a challenge for the courts is the extent to which they will be willing to extend a time limit where a claimant has pursued other means of redress, such as complaints mechanisms or administrative appeals.[208] The issue here is that those who pursue appeals or other means of redress may not receive a new 'decision' that can be challenged on completion of the alternative redress mechanism. In general, the courts have been willing to extend time limits in such cases, particularly where the claimant can demonstrate that the steps taken were reasonable. In *Jackson*,[209] the Court of Appeal held that a claimant's endeavour to ask the Secretary of State to intervene in a planning dispute, and then to seek legal aid to assist with a judicial review claim once the Secretary of State had refused, were reasonable steps to have taken which justified extension of the time limit. Similarly, in *Greenwich Properties*,[210] the claimant pursued an administrative appeal before launching a claim for judicial review, and the court deemed that the pursuit of appeal was a reasonable step (even though the appeal was unsuccessful as the relevant tribunal held that it did not have jurisdiction to hear the appeal) and thus permitted the claimants to proceed.

4.7.C TIME LIMITS IN CASE OF SILENCE OF THE ADMINISTRATION

4.7.C.1 GERMANY

Verwaltungsgerichtsordnung **4.82 (DE)**

§75 If, with regard to an objection or an application for the issuance of an administrative act, the merits have not been decided upon within a suitable period without sufficient reason, the action shall be admissible in derogation from §68. The action may not be lodged prior to the expiry of three months after the lodging of the objection or the filing of the application to carry out the administrative act, unless a shorter period is required because of the special circumstances of the case. …

[207] *R v North West Leicestershire District Council and another, ex parte Moses (No 2)* (2000) JPL 1287 (CA).
[208] See Chapter 2, section 2.7.A.2.
[209] *R v Stratford upon Avon District Council, ex parte Jackson* [1985] 1 WLR 1319 (CA).
[210] *R (on the application of Greenwich Property Ltd) v Customs and Excise Commissioners* [2001] EWHC Admin 230, [2001] STC 618.

Notes

(1) If the administrative authority does not react to an objection or an application to carry out an administrative act, the claimant can file a court action within three months after he has lodged his request. In such cases, there is no need to file an intra-administrative objection procedure.[211]

(2) There is no time limit for filing such an action, either according to the Administrative Court Procedure Act or developed in case law. If an action is filed more than one year after the claimant has lodged his request, the court may decide that the right to file an action has been forfeited.[212]

4.7.C.2 THE NETHERLANDS

Algemene Wet Bestuursrecht **4.83 (NL)**

Article 4:13 (1) A single-case decision shall be issued within the time limit prescribed by any general binding regulation, or, in the absence of such a time limit, within a reasonable time after the receipt of the request.

(2) The reasonable time referred to in section 1 has in any event expired if the administrative authority has, within eight weeks after receiving the request, neither issued a decision, nor given a notice as referred to in Article 4:14(3).

Article 6:12 (1) If the objection or claim for judicial review is directed against failure to take a decision as defined in Article 1:3 AWB in due time or against failure to announce a decision which was created by operation of law in due time, it shall not be subject to any time limit.

(2) A notice of objection or a claim for judicial review may be submitted when:

a. the administrative authority fails to take a decision in due time or fails to announce of a decision which has been issued by operation of law and

b. two weeks have passed after the day on which the party concerned has notified the administrative authority that it is in default.

(3) If the party concerned cannot reasonably be expected to notify the administrative authority of its default, the claim for judicial review may be brought as soon as the administrative authority is in default taking a decision in due time.

(4) The objection or claim for judicial review shall be ruled inadmissible if the notice of objection or claim for judicial review is submitted unreasonably late.

Article 4:17 (1) If a decision on request is not given in time, the administrative authority shall be liable for a penalty to the applicant for each day that it is in default, subject to a maximum of 42 days. …

(2) The penalty payment is €20 per day for the first fourteen days, €30 per day for the next fourteen days and €40 per day for the remaining days.

(3) The penalty payment is due as of two weeks after the day on which the period for issuing the decision expires and the administrative authority has received a written notice of the applicant.

[211] See further Chapter 2, section 2.6.A.1.

[212] FO Kopp and WR Schenke, *VwGO Kommentar*, 15th edn (Munich, Beck, 2018) § 76, Nr 2.

Notes

(1) There is no general time limit in the Netherlands within which a decision on request has to be taken. If specific legal provisions do not determine a specific time limit, a 'reasonable' period has to be offered. This period is of a maximum eight weeks.

(2) If the authority fails to take a decision in due time, the applicant has to notify the authority that it is in default (Article 6:12(2) AWB). After two weeks have elapsed following the submission of the notification, a claim for judicial review can be filed. Article 6:12 AWB has to be read in conjunction with Article 4:17 AWB. This latter provision empowers the applicant to give the authority a written notice of default (Article 4:17(3) AWB). Such a notice can be sent immediately after the period for issuing the decision has elapsed. Once two weeks have elapsed from the day on which the applicant has notified the administrative authority that it is in default, the authority will automatically owe a penalty to the applicant of up to a maximum of €1,260 (Article 4:17(1) and (2) AWB). The possibility of this penalty does not change the rules on time limits for filing a claim for judicial review.

(3) According to Article 7:1(1)(f) AWB, in cases of failure to take a decision in due time, the applicant is not required to first bring an intra-administrative objection procedure before filing a claim for judicial review.

(4) There is no time limit for bringing a claim for judicial review in cases of failure to take a decision in due time, other than that the claim must not be submitted unreasonably late (Article 6:12(4) AWB).

4.7.C.3 FRANCE

With regard to failure to act, there are no special time limits. As was mentioned in Chapter 3,[213] after two months of silence, failure to act leads to either an implicit positive or an implicit negative decision. Once a period of two months has elapsed following the applicant's request to the administration seeking a decision, a claimant can bring an action for annulment (*recours pour excès de pouvoir*), in accordance with the general rules on time limits. Therefore, a claim against the implicit decision can usually be brought within two months after the implicit decision is (deemed to have been) taken, which means four months after the applicant's request.

4.7.C.4 THE EUROPEAN UNION

Treaty of the Functioning of the European Union **4.84 (EU)**

Article 265 (1) Should the European Parliament, the European Council, the Council, the Commission or the European Central Bank, in infringement of the Treaties, fail to act, the Member States and the other institutions of the Union may bring an action before the

[213] Chapter 3, section 3.6.B.1.

Court of Justice of the European Union to have the infringement established. This Article shall apply, under the same conditions, to bodies, offices and agencies of the Union which fail to act.

(2) The action shall be admissible only if the institution, body, office or agency concerned has first been called upon to act. If, within two months of being so called upon, the institution, body, office or agency concerned has not defined its position, the action may be brought within a further period of two months.

Note

The time limit for an action for failure to act in the European Union is the same as for an action for annulment: two months. However, the moment at which the time starts running is different. The silence of the EU authorities can be challenged in an action for failure to act only after the EU authorities have been 'called upon' to act. The concerned authority has two months to define its position from the moment at which it has been called upon to act by an individual. If the authority does not act within those two months, the applicant has a two further months to bring a court action under Article 265 TFEU.

4.7.C.5 ENGLAND AND WALES

There are no specific legislative provisions governing the time limit for a failure to act in England and Wales, and this issue does not seem to have been subject to treatment in the case law. It is likely that any claim for failure to act would be subject to the same principles as outlined above in section 4.7.B.5 in the sense that a claimant would need to be able to demonstrate that he had acted without 'undue delay' in bringing a claim. The courts have generally taken the approach that the time limit begins to run once a 'juristic act', such as a decision being issued or an action being taken, occurs.[214] In cases of silence, the challenge arises because such a juristic act has not occurred. It may be that in such cases the courts might seek to adopt an approach similar to that in the European Union as outlined above – where a claimant has sought a decision or action from a public authority, perhaps by writing to it or perhaps by issuing a letter before claim for judicial review, the courts may treat the three-month time limit as starting to run from the date on which the public authority receives the demand from the claimant, or perhaps from a reasonable period after such a demand has been received by the public authority.

4.7.D TIME LIMITS WHERE REMEDIES OTHER THAN ANNULMENT ARE SOUGHT

Alongside actions brought for the annulment of single-case decisions and actions brought against administrative silence, legal systems may provide for other types of

[214] See *R (on the Application of Burkett) v Hammersmith and Fulham London Borough Council (No 1)* [2002] UKHL 23, [2002] 1 WLR 1593 at [42]–[43] (Lord Steyn).

action to challenge the administrative action.[215] The rules on time limits may differ in these other types of action.

4.7.D.1 GERMANY

Verwaltungsgerichtsordnung **4.85 (DE)**

§74 (2) Section 1 shall apply mutatis mutandis to the action for seeking the issuance of an administrative act if the application to carry out the administrative act has been rejected.

Notes

(1) Under German law, the rules on time limits for actions seeking the issuance of an administrative act (*Verpflichtungsklage*) are the same as for actions for annulment (*Anfechtungsklage*) if the authority refused to issue the decision the claimant applied for. All the material covered in section 4.7.B.1 above therefore also applies to the *Verpflichtungsklage*. However, the time limits for other actions differ.

(2) No time limit is applicable to the action for performance (*Leistungsklage*). Their filing is subject to the general principles of forfeiture (*Verwirkung*). As a general rule, forfeiture requires a behaviour of the citizen that creates the expectation that he will not file a court action (*Umstandmoment*) and the lapse of a considerable time period (one year) (*Zeitmoment*). For example, a neighbour cannot file an action for demolition because a neighbouring house is too close to his property if he agreed to the building plan of the house beforehand and did not raise any objections during the building of the house and for a considerable time afterwards.[216]

(3) Similarly, no time limit, except for forfeiture, applies to the action for declaration (*Feststellungsklage*). As the action for declaration is subsidiary to the other court actions, the time limit of the action for annulment (*Anfechtungsklage*) and of the action for seeking the issuance of an administrative act (*Verpflichtungsklage*) cannot be circumvented by filing an action for declaration after the lapse of the time limit of the action for annulment or of the action for seeking the issuance of an administrative act.

(4) Finally, the procedure to review by-laws and executive regulations according to §47 VwGO (*Normenkontrollverfahren*) has to be filed within two years after the publication of the act in question.[217]

4.7.D.2 FRANCE

Specific time limits apply with regard to the 'full jurisdiction remedy' (*recours de pleine juridiction*). The time limits differ depending on the subject matter of the action (contract, tort, tax law and so on).

[215] See Chapters 3 and 7.
[216] See BVerwG, ZfBR 2001, 143.
[217] §47(2), first sentence VwGO.

In tort cases, no time limit is applicable for an individual to claim for compensation. However, once the claimant has started the proceedings by requesting a 'preliminary binding decision' (*décision préalable*), which is a compulsory requirement before going to court in order to claim for compensation, the time limit of two months is applicable to challenge the preliminary binding decision.[218]

If the *recours de pleine juridiction* concerns duties stemming from a contract, an action by a third party must be brought within the two-month time limit, commencing from the public notification of the challenged contract.[219]

4.7.D.3 THE EUROPEAN UNION

Statute of the Court of Justice of the European Union **4.86 (EU)**

Article 46 Proceedings against the Union in matters arising from non-contractual liability shall be barred after a period of five years from the occurrence of the event giving rise thereto. The period of limitation shall be interrupted if proceedings are instituted before the Court of Justice or if prior to such proceedings an application is made by the aggrieved party to the relevant institution of the Union. In the latter event the proceedings must be instituted within the period of two months provided for in Article 263 of the Treaty on the Functioning of the European Union; the provisions of the second paragraph of Article 265 of the Treaty on the Functioning of the European Union shall apply where appropriate.

Note

The time limit for an action for damages is different to that applicable to actions for annulment and actions for failure to act. An action for damages becomes time-barred, according to Article 46 of the Statute of the Court of Justice, after five years have elapsed from the occurrence of the 'event giving rise thereto'. This last phrase has been interpreted as meaning that the limitation period starts running from the point at which the claimant is able to identify all of the elements required for the case, ie the existence of an allegedly unlawful conduct on the part of the institutions, the alleged damage created and the causal link between the conduct and the damage.[220]

4.7.D.4 ENGLAND AND WALES AND THE NETHERLANDS

In England and Wales and in the Netherlands, the issue of time limits in types of action other than actions to annul single-case decisions does not play a (substantial) role. In England and Wales, there are no different 'types of action'. Although there are different

[218] Code de justice administrative, Art R 421-1.
[219] Tribunal administratif de Montpellier, 20 April 2017, *M. X*, N° 1506220.
[220] Case T-332/99 *Jerstaedt v Council and Commission* ECLI:EU:T:2001:218, para 40.

remedies,[221] there are no rules linking different time limits to a certain remedy: regardless of the type of remedy, the applicable procedure is always the one set in Part 54 CPR. Where claimants seek damages in private law, the limitation periods in the Limitation Act 1980 apply. These are three years where the claim relates to personal injury[222] and six years in relation to all other matters.[223]

In the Netherlands, most claims other than claims for judicial review (*beroep*) have to be brought as tort law actions before the civil courts. In (Dutch) tort law, no time limits except prescription apply. The same is true for actions for actions for damages brought before the administrative courts (Article 8:88 AWB).[224] According to Article 8:93 AWB in conjunction with Article 3:310 of the Civil Code, such claims must be brought within five years after the damage and the perpetrator is known or 20 years after the incident which caused the damage occurred.

4.7.E COMPARATIVE REMARKS

The rules on time limits differ significantly. For example, the time limit to bring a court action for annulment is between one month (Germany) and three months (England and Wales). All legal systems provide for possibilities to extend or ignore the time limits under certain circumstances if they were exceeded through no fault of the claimant. However, the details of these rules differ significantly. In France, for example, the only acceptable reason to deviate from the time limits is when the information provided to the claimants on what the time limits are is omitted or erroneous. One peculiarity of the English legal system is the requirement of 'promptness' in addition to the time limit.

The case law of the CJEU has had a clear harmonising effect in this area of law. The rules on time limits in England and Wales have had to be amended under the influence of the CJEU's case law. However, this harmonising effect is limited. The government has not changed the time limit as such, which is by far the longest when compared with the other legal systems.

4.8 PRECLUSION

4.8.A INTRODUCTION: PRECLUSION AS A CONSEQUENCE OF GENERAL RULES OF DUE PROCESS

Efficiency of administrative procedures and of court procedures may give rise to the exclusion of certain legal arguments, grounds for review or facts from the court proceedings if they were brought forward at a very late stage. All courts in the legal systems under study apply some kind of general rule of due process. Three examples are provided.

221 See further Chapter 7.
222 Limitation Act 1980, s 11.
223 Limitation Act 1980, ss 2 (torts) and 5 (contracts).
224 For more detail, see Chapter 11, section 11.2.B.2.

Verwaltungsgerichtsordnung **4.87 (DE)**

§87b (1) The presiding judge or the reporting judge may set the claimant a deadline to state the facts, if the claimant considers to be aggrieved by the consideration or non-consideration of certain facts in the administrative procedure. The deadline set in accordance with the first sentence may be combined with the deadline set in accordance with §82(2), second sentence.

(2) The presiding judge or the reporting judge can instruct a party concerned, setting a deadline, with regard to certain events

1. to state facts or designate items of evidence,
2. to submit certificates or other movables and to transmit electronic documents insofar as the party concerned is obliged to do so.

(3) The court may reject declarations and items of evidence which are not submitted until after expiry of the deadline set in accordance with sections 1 and 2 and rule without any further investigations if

1. in the freely-formed conviction of the court its admission would delay the conclusion of the dispute, and
2. the party concerned does not provide sufficient excuses for the lateness of the submission, and
3. the party concerned has been notified of the consequences of missing the deadline.

Any excuse relied upon to justify late submission shall be substantiated at the request of the court. The first sentence shall not apply if the facts are readily available to the court without the cooperation of the party concerned.

Note

In Germany, the general rule of due process, prohibiting the bringing forward of information or arguments at a very late stage, is laid down in §87(b) VwGO, which leaves some flexibility to the court to set a concrete date by when a claimant is to state that the authority did not consider certain facts or, to the contrary, did consider facts which it should not have considered. According to §87(b) VwGO, the court may preclude certain declarations and evidence if they are presented after such a deadline.

Algemene Wet Bestuursrecht **4.88 (NL)**

Article 8:45 (1) The administrative judge may request the parties and anyone else to provide written information and submit documents in their possession within such time limit as it may set.

(2) Administrative authorities shall comply with a request as referred to in section 1 even if they are not a party to the action. …

(3) Employers of parties shall comply with a request as referred to in section 1 even if they are not a party to the action. …

Article 8:58 (1) The parties may submit additional documents until ten days before the hearing.

(2) The attention of the parties shall be drawn to this right in the invitation referred to in Article 8:56.

Note

The Dutch law, which is quite similar, but less detailed, than the German law, also has written rules about deadlines until which submissions can be made and evidence can be brought forward. New facts and evidence are generally precluded if they are brought forward less than ten days before the hearing.

Conseil d'État, 20 February 1953[225] **4.89 (FR)**

Société Intercopie v Commission nationale des accidents du travail

PRECLUSION; NEW GROUNDS

Intercopie

Once the time limit of action has expired, the applicant cannot raise new arguments belonging to a different category of grounds.

Facts: The National Commission on Industrial Accidents adopted a decision which had rejected the complaint brought by the company Intercopie, which challenged the contribution rate imposed on it. Intercopie introduced an action for annulment against the decision of refusal of the Commission before the Council of State.

Held: The action was considered inadmissible.

Judgment: Considering that the company Intercopie, in its preliminary request and explanatory statement, limited itself to invoking the alleged irregularity of the composition of the National Commission; that if it challenged, in its statement of reply, the legality of the way in which the rules contained in the decision of 2 April 1948 have been applied, these claims, based on a distinct legal ground, constitute a new request; that the statement of reply in question was registered to the secretariat of the Litigation Section of the Council of State on 3 December 1951, that is to say after the expiry of the deadline to challenge the contested decision, which was notified to the company on 26 June 1950; that, henceforth, the new request contained in this statement was submitted late and is therefore not admissible; …

Notes

(1) In the French legal system, as a rule, an applicant can raise any grounds for review of a decision until the expiry of the time limit for court action, even after the application has been lodged. However, once the time limit has expired, such

[225] N° 9772.

possibility is strictly limited. At that point, the applicant can raise new arguments only if they are related to the same 'category' of grounds (external illegality or internal illegality).[226] For example, if the applicant challenged a decision because of the lack of competence of the authority having adopted the decision, he can still, once the time limit has expired, raise a new issue related to formal or procedural illegality, since all these grounds belong to the 'category' of grounds of external illegality. Conversely, the applicant cannot raise a new ground concerning the violation of a constitutional norm, which is a type of ground (violation of the law) belonging to internal illegality. The possibility to add new grounds belonging to the same 'category' expires with the closing of the preparation stage.

(2) From 1 January 2017, following an amendment to the Code of Administrative Justice,[227] it is possible for the President of the Chamber in charge of the preparation of the case to adopt an ordinance while the preparation stage is still ongoing and set a date after which the parties will not be allowed to raise new grounds (even within the same 'category' of grounds).[228]

4.8.B PRECLUSION CLAUSES

Besides these general rules of due process, which prohibit presenting documents and making submissions unduly late, preclusion clauses are used also to exclude grounds of review or evidence because the claimant did not bring these grounds or items of evidence during the decision-making process or to exclude a person who did not participate in the decision-making process in the first place. To this end, most legal systems apply preclusion clauses that are either generally applicable or apply in certain areas of law.

4.8.B.1 LEGAL SYSTEMS PROVIDING FOR PRECLUSION CLAUSES

4.8.B.1 (i) Germany

Umweltrechtsbehelfsgesetz **4.90 (DE)**

§7 ...

(3) If an association within the meaning of §4(3), first sentence, No. 2, in a proceeding under §1(1), first sentence, No. 4, has had the opportunity to provide comments, it shall, in the proceedings under section 2, be prevented from raising all submissions it has not made or has not made in a timely manner, according to the applicable legislation, but could have made in the proceedings under §1(1), first sentence, No. 4.

[226] See Chapter 6, section 6.2.A.1.

[227] Décret n° 2016-1480 du 2 novembre 2016 portant modification du code de justice administrative (partie réglementaire) (JORF n° 0257 du 4 novembre 2016).

[228] Art R611-1-7 of the Code of Administrative Justice.

Notes

(1) Claims may be excluded if they could have been brought forward at an earlier stage, such as during the decision-making proceedings or in an intra-administrative objection procedure.[229] An example of this mechanism is contained in §7(3) of the Environmental Remedies Act (Umweltrechtsbehelfsgesetz). This section concerns the environmental impact assessment (EIA) procedure for plans and programmes (§1(1), first sentence, No 4 of the Environmental Appeals Act). If an association had the opportunity to make certain submissions during this EIA procedure but did not (timely) make use of the opportunity, it cannot bring forward those arguments in the judicial procedure.

(2) In Germany, these kinds of preclusion clauses were quite common, mainly in those fields of administrative law where administrative planning occurs, such as physical planning law and environmental law. The idea was that, as the planning procedure is comprehensive and time consuming, and fosters citizens' participation by granting rights to a hearing, preclusion clauses aim to protect the efficiency of this procedure and the validity of the plan.[230] However, some of these preclusion clauses have been abolished as a consequence of the case law of the CJEU on the Aarhus Convention and the EU directives transposing the provisions of the Aarhus Convention.[231]

4.8.B.1 (ii) The Netherlands

Algemene Wet Bestuursrecht **4.91 (NL)**

Article 6:13 No claim for judicial review before the administrative judge may be filed by a party concerned if he may reasonably be considered to be at fault in not delivering an opinion as defined in Article 3:15, in not having objected or not having lodged an administrative appeal.

Notes

(1) In the Netherlands, a general preclusion clause is laid down in Article 6:13 AWB. In short, it determines that claims for judicial review are excluded if the claimant could have brought forward his arguments at an earlier stage. There are different kinds of procedures providing the possibility to be heard.

[229] See further Chapter 2, section 2.7.B.1 (ii).

[230] See, eg BVerwG, NVwZ 1997, 171; BVerwG, NVwZ 1999, 70.

[231] See, eg Art 5 of the Act amending the Environmental Remedies Act (Umweltrechtsbehelfsanpassungsgesetz), BGBl I S 1298, which led to the repeal of §47(2a) VwGO in reaction to the Court of Justice's Case C-137/14. This judgment will be discussed below in section 4.8.C.

If the comprehensive 'uniform public preparatory procedure' (*uniforme openbare voorbereidingsprocedure*, division 3.4 AWB) is applicable, 'anyone concerned' may deliver an opinion, according to Article 3:15 AWB.[232] In a similar fashion, the intra-administrative objection procedure and the possibility of appeal to a higher administrative authority,[233] if applicable, offer opportunities to bring forward arguments and objections before the decision-making process of the administration is finalised.

If the claimant could reasonably have been expected to use one of these possibilities and has not done so, judicial review is not possible. According to Article 6:24 AWB, Article 6:13 AWB is also applicable in the relation between first-instance proceedings and appeal.

However, apart from the uniform public preparatory procedure, there is no general preclusion rule requiring participation in decision-making procedures. If the 'uniform public preparatory procedure' does not apply, there is no preclusion if one did not participate in the preparation of a decision.

(2) A further consequence of Article 6:13 AWB is that if one did not bring a claim for judicial review against a decision on an objection, and this decision is annulled (in reaction to someone else's claim for judicial review), one cannot lodge a claim for judicial review against the new decision taken after the annulment of the earlier decision.[234]

(3) Article 6:13 AWB is also applied with regard to legal persons and their members. If, for example, (only) an association objected to a decision, the individual members of the association cannot lodge a claim against the decision on the objection. If a claimant, eg an NGO, is founded after the objection period has passed, it cannot lodge a claim for judicial review.

Logically, Article 6:13 AWB does not make a claim inadmissible if a claimant who did not object to the initial decision is affected (more) negatively by the decision on the objection of another claimant. In such situations, it cannot be said that the claimant was reasonably at fault in not objecting against the primary decision, because he had no reason to do so, as the disadvantages for the claimant were caused only by the decision on the objection of another claimant.

(4) If Article 6:13 AWB applies, claimants are not only precluded if they did not participate in the decision-making procedure at all, but are also precluded insofar as they did not participate. That means that they cannot object to a 'part' of a decision which they did not comment on in the decision-making procedure. The question which arises is what is to be regarded as a 'part' of a decision. This question is of special relevance in environmental law cases.

232 Kamerstukken II, 2003/2004, 29 421, nr 3, p. 7 ff. ABRvS 16 May 2012, ECLI:NL:RVS:2012:BW5950. This is, with valid arguments, criticised by scholars such as M Schreuder-Vlasblom, *Rechtsbescherming en bestuurlijke voorprocedure* 6th edn (Kluwer, Deventer 2017) 404 ff.

233 See Chapter 2, section 2.7.B.1 (ii).

234 ECLI:NL:RVS:2007:BA9815.

Raad van State, 9 November 2011[235] **4.92 (NL)**

X and Milieuvereniging Land van Cuijk v Mayor and Aldermen of Boxmeer

PRECLUSION CLAUSES; 'PART' OF A DECISION

Milieuvereniging Land van Cuijk

Decisions on the different categories of environmental impacts contained in a decision on an environmental permit are, for the purposes of the application of Article 6:13 AWB, not to be treated as separate parts of the decision.

Facts: The applicant was granted a permit for a horse breeding farm. The municipality (the defendant) claimed that the arguments of the applicant (an NGO) concerning the application of the best available techniques were not brought forward in the decision-making process.

Held: The claim was declared admissible in all parts but was rejected as unfounded.

Judgment: 2.4.1. An environmental permit as referred to in Articles 2.1 and 2.2 of the Environmental Licensing General Provisions Act (Wet algemene bepalingen omgevingsrecht) involves implementing a project that can consist of several activities. It is reasonable for the purposes of Article 6:13 AWB that each of the permissions referred to in Articles 2.1 and 2.2 of the Wabo, which are included in an environmental permit, qualifies as a separate part of the decision. …

2.4.2. The Judicial Division decides, … that the decisions on the different categories of environmental impacts contained in a decision on an environmental permit are, for the purposes of the application of Article 6:13 AWB, not to be treated as separate parts of the decision.

Notes

(1) In environmental law cases, all different kinds of environmental effects of a decision are qualified as separate parts of the decision. Dutch law provides for an environmental permit which covers environmental law in a narrow sense, water quality and quantity, physical planning, nature conservation and similar aspects. These different aspects of the physical environment, which are all regulated according to separate decision-making rules and criteria, can be seen as separate parts of a decision. If one commented only on the building permit aspects of a decision, one cannot object to the effects on flora and fauna aspects of the same decision later on.[236] However, within, for example, the environmental aspects of a decision in a narrow sense, comments on eg noise are not excluded because in an earlier phase only comments on air quality issues had been brought forward. Prior to 2011, the case law was stricter. If one had only commented about the effect of a permit for an industrial installation on the air

[235] ECLI:NL:RVS:2011:BP7155.
[236] ECLI:NL:RVS:2011:BP7161.

quality, one was not allowed to object to the increase in noise later.[237] This strict line has been abandoned, as the excerpt demonstrates.

(2) In areas other than environmental law (in a broad sense), the courts are more lenient and usually do not subdivide a decision into several parts.[238] Hence, an objection or claim for judicial review can be based on grounds which have not been brought forward in the decision-making phase or the objection phase as long as the principle of due process is not infringed.[239]

Crisis- en herstelwet **4.93 (NL)**

Article 1:6a After the period to lodge a claim for judicial review has passed, new grounds can no longer be brought forward.

Note

In the area of (mainly) environmental and planning law, Article 1.6a of the Crisis and Recovery Act (Crisis- en herstelwet) strengthened the rules on preclusion. Generally, it is possible to object or lodge a claim for judicial review by delivering a notice of objection to the administrative authority or claim for judicial review to the court in time and to substantiate the reasons for the objection or claim later on, within the limits of due process. However, Article 1.6a of the Crisis- en herstelwet requires that all grounds for an objection or a claim for judicial review be submitted within the time limit for the objection or for lodging the claim. Once the time limit has passed, an objection or claim for judicial review cannot be further substantiated with new grounds. The Council of State has decided that this strict preclusion clause does not infringe Article 6 ECHR or the EU principles of effectiveness and effective judicial protection.[240]

4.8.B.1 (iii) England and Wales

In England and Wales, clauses which seek to preclude access to judicial review in the manner envisaged in this section are infrequent. However, some examples can be found in the domain of planning law.

Town and Country Planning Act 1990 **4.94 (EW)**

Section 287 (1) This section applies to–

(a) a simplified planning zone scheme or an alteration of such a scheme;

[237] ECLI:NL:RVS:2006:AZ1288.
[238] ECLI:NL:RVS:2007:BB2930.
[239] ECLI:NL:RVS:2006:AZ4818.
[240] ECLI:NL:RVS:2010:BO4248.

(b) an order under section 247, 248, 249, 251, 257, 258 or 277,

and anything falling within paragraphs (a) and (b) is referred to in this section as a relevant document.

(2) A person aggrieved by a relevant document may make an application to the High Court on the ground that–

(a) it is not within the appropriate power, or

(b) a procedural requirement has not been complied with.

...

Section 288 (1) If any person–

(a) is aggrieved by any order to which this section applies and wishes to question the validity of that order on the grounds–

(i) that the order is not within the powers of this Act, or

(ii) that any of the relevant requirements have not been complied with in relation to that order; or

(b) is aggrieved by any action on the part of the Secretary of State [or the Welsh Ministers] to which this section applies and wishes to question the validity of that action on the grounds–

(i) that the action is not within the powers of this Act, or

(ii) that any of the relevant requirements have not been complied with in relation to that action,

he may make an application to the High Court under this section.

High Court (Queen's Bench Division), 20 July 2009[241] **4.95 (EW)**

Bowen v Bristol City Council

PRECLUSION CLAUSES; DEFINITION OF 'PERSON AGGRIEVED'

Bowen

In order to be classified as a 'person aggrieved' for the purposes of challengeing a planning decision, a claimant must be able to demonstrate substantial involvement in the planning process.

Facts: Bowen was employed by the Bristol City Council as an arboricultural officer. He recommended that the Council should not make tree-preservation orders to protect trees in a particular area of local woodland and attended a meeting of the Council committee considering whether to make an order, where he informed them of his recommendation. However, Bowen did not enter an objection to the Council's proposed decision as a private individual and did not participate any further in the process leading to the making of the order. Bowen then brought proceedings to challenge the making of the order and the Council sought to defend the claim on the basis that Bowen was not a 'person aggrieved' for the purposes of section 288 of the Town and Country Planning Act 1990.

Held: Bowen was considered not to be a 'person aggrieved' for the purposes of the Town and Country Planning Act 1990 because he had not filed an objection as a private individual, had no interest in the land that was affected and did not live in the vicinity of the land affected.

241 [2009] EWHC 1747.

Judgment: Wyn-Williams J: 6. Section 288(1) of the 1990 Act permits a person to make an application to quash an order such as a Tree Preservation Order if he is a person who 'is aggrieved' by the Order. The Act contains no further elucidation of the phrase 'is aggrieved' but, not surprisingly, the phrase has been the subject of debate in the Courts. The most recent authoritative exposition of whether or not a person 'is aggrieved' within section 288 of the 1990 Act is to be found in the decision of the Court of Appeal in *Eco-Energy(GB) Limited v First Secretary of State and others* [2004] EWCA Civ 1566. During the course of his judgement, with which the other members of the Court expressly agreed, Buxton LJ defined the persons having the right to bring a claim under section 288 of the 1990 Act in the following terms:-

'7. The First question that arises is: who indeed can apply to the court under section 288? The judge considered, and there is before us, the case of *Times Investment Ltd v Secretary of State for the Environment* [1991] PLR 67. In my judgement, the upshot of that authority (which of course is binding on us) is that persons aggrieved under section 288 are either (1) the appellant in the planning process, or (2) someone who took a sufficiently active role in the planning process that is to say, probably a substantial objector, not just somebody who objected and did no more about it or (3) someone who has a relevant interest in the land. ...'

...

9. There seems little doubt that substantial local interest was generated by the alleged tree felling activities and whether or not any Tree Preservation Order was justified in respect of some or all of the trees in Grove Wood. At a meeting of the Planning Committee on 17 September 2008 a discussion took place about whether or not a Tree Preservation Order should be made. The Claimant attended that meeting since, at that stage, he was the case officer dealing with the issue. At the meeting on 17 September 2008 the Planning Committee resolved that a full report should be brought to its next meeting setting out the merits and disadvantages of imposing a Tree Preservation Order over Grove Wood. Following that meeting the Claimant's Line Manager, Mr Richard Charles Ennion, took over as the officer providing advice to the Committee.

10. As is clear from the documentation which the Claimant has submitted in this case he feels passionately that a Woodland Tree Preservation Order over the whole of the wood was completely unjustified. As I understand it he has made that view known with vigour to his employers, the Defendant. It does not seem to me to be necessary to recite in this judgement the steps which the Claimant has taken internally to make his view known about (a) the merits, in planning terms, of the making of a Tree Preservation Order and (b) the legality of the Defendant's actions.

11. The Claimant accepts that he did not register an objection, as a private individual, to the making of the Tree Preservation Order when notice was given that objections should be made on 12 November 2008. He has not registered an objection in a private capacity at any stage prior to the resolution passed by the sub-committee on 1 April 2009. As a matter of fact, of course, it is correct to record he began these proceedings before notification had been given giving effect to the resolution of 1 April 2009.

12. The Claimant has no conceivable interest (legal or equitable) in the land upon which the wood lies. He does not live in the immediate vicinity of the wood.

13. On the basis of these facts I simply do not see how the Claimant can bring himself within the category of persons identified by Buxton LJ in Eco-Energy. He is not the Appellant in a planning process. He has no relevant interest in the land in question. He is someone who took an active role in the planning process in the sense that he was

an employee of the decision maker and, in the course of his employment, he exercised delegated powers and provided advice to his employers. In my judgment, however, he was not a person who took a sufficiently active role in the planning process in the sense that Buxton LJ used in Eco-Energy. It seems clear to me as the Learned Lord Justice had in mind a person who had been a substantial objector to the proposed and actual decision but who was unconnected with the actual decision-making process. In my judgment he did not intend that his phrase 'someone who took a sufficiently active role in the planning process' should extend to an employee of the decision maker who has participated in the decision-making process and disagrees with the decision ultimately reached. In my judgment that is so even when that employee wishes to allege illegality against his employers (as he must do for a claim to succeed under section 288 of the 1990 Act). In my judgment to interpret section 288 of the 1990 Act so as to permit challenges by persons in the Claimant's position would be to widen the category of persons permitted to make such challenges far beyond that which was intended by the legislature as interpreted by the Higher Courts. Mrs. Townsend submits that where a Claimant wishes to question the validity of a Tree Preservation Order he requires an interest in the outcome which can objectively be recognised as such. I am satisfied that the Claimant has no such interest in this case. Accordingly, I conclude that that the Claimant is not a person who is entitled to bring a claim under section 288 of 1990 Act so as to seek to quash the Woodland Tree Preservation Order made in respect of Grove Wood.

Note

As already dealt with in section 4.4.C.2, the provisions of the Town and Country Planning Act change the usual standing conditions upon which planning decisions can be challenged. The standing test mentioned in these provisions covers 'persons aggrieved' rather than the 'sufficient interest' test that is usual in judicial review cases. This test has been interpreted in the *Bowen* case. The court held that property owners and others whose property is impacted by planning decisions may bring claims under the Town and Country Planning Act.[242] Others are permitted to bring claims under these provisions only if they have been actively involved with the planning process leading to the challenged decision. With regard to this last group of claimants, these provisions, and the interpretation of 'persons aggrieved' by the courts, function as preclusion clauses.

4.8.B.1 (iv) The European Union

Rules of Procedure of the General Court **4.96 (EU)**

Article 188 Subject-matter of the proceedings before the General Court

The pleadings lodged by the parties in proceedings before the General Court may not change the subject-matter of the proceedings before the Board of Appeal.

[242] See section 4.4.C.2 above.

Case T-413/17, 19 June 2018[243] **4.97 (EU)**

Karl Storz GmbH & CO KG v European Union Intellectual Property Office

PRECLUSION CLAUSES; INTRA-ADMINISTRATIVE OBJECTION PROCEDURE

Storz

An applicant may not bring different arguments at the judicial stage from those submitted during the intra-administrative objection procedure.

Facts: The applicant had filed with the European Union Intellectual Property Office (EUIPO) an application for extension of a trademark registration. The EUIPO rejected the application. The applicant subsequently brought an intra-administrative objection procedure before the Board of Appeal of the EUIPO, which dismissed the applicant's objection. The applicant subsequently brought proceedings before the General Court.

Held: The decision of the Board of Appeal was annulled.

Judgment: 17 EUIPO maintains that the annexes referred to in paragraph 16 above, four pieces of evidence relating to the description of specific goods covered by the sign at issue, are inadmissible, since they were not presented during the administrative proceedings.

18 That plea of inadmissibility is well founded, as, according to case-law, the purpose of bringing an action before the Court is the review of the legality of the decisions of the Boards of Appeal for the purposes of Article 65 of Regulation No 207/2009 (now Article 72 of Regulation 2017/1001) and that, in proceedings for annulment, the legality of the contested measure must be assessed on the basis of the elements of fact and of law existing at the time when the measure was adopted. It is therefore not the Court's function to re-evaluate the factual circumstances in the light of evidence adduced for the first time before it. To admit such evidence would be contrary to Article 188 of the Rules of Procedure of the General Court, which states that the parties' pleadings may not change the subject matter of the proceedings before the Board of Appeal (see judgment of 30 September 2016, *Alpex Pharma v EUIPO – Astex Pharmaceuticals (ASTEX)*, T-355/15, not published, EU:T:2016:591, paragraph 15 and the case-law cited).

Note

In the EU, some preclusion clauses exist. One example regards the proceedings concerning intellectual property rights. In *Storz*, the General Court interpreted Article 188 of the Rules of Procedure of the General Court and the phrase 'subject matter' restrictively, by holding that an applicant cannot bring forward elements of facts and of law which have not been presented during the intra-administrative objection stage.[244]

243 ECLI:EU:T:2018:356.

244 See also Case C-38/09 P *Schräder v Community Plant Variety Office (CPVO)* ECLI:EU:C:2010:196, para 76.

4.8.B.2 LEGAL SYSTEMS WITHOUT PRECLUSION CLAUSES: FRANCE

Conseil d'État, 21 March 2007[245] **4.98 (FR)**

Garnier v Minister of Defence

PRECLUSION CLAUSES; INTRA-ADMINISTRATIVE OBJECTION PROCEDURE

Garnier

An applicant may bring different arguments at the judicial stage from those submitted during the intra-administrative stage.

Facts: The Minister of Defence had adopted a decision setting up the list of the eligible candidates to be admitted to a military division. Mr Garnier, who was not on this list, challenged the decision by introducing an intra-administrative objection before the Minister of Defence. The latter rejected it. Mr Garnier challenged the rejection decision before the Council of State.

Held: An applicant may bring different arguments at the judicial stage of proceedings from those submitted at the intra-administrative stage of proceedings.

Judgment: Considering that the submission of a mandatory intra-administrative appeal to the administrative authority prior to any referral to the court has allows the competent authority to be aware of the necessity of establishing in a definite manner the position of the administration; that consequently the decision taken following the intra-administrative appeal necessarily replaces the original decision; that it alone can be brought to the courts to check its legality; that if the purpose of the exercise of such an intra-administrative appeal is to enable the administrative authority, within the limits of its powers, to remedy the unlawfulness of which the initial decision could be tainted without waiting for the intervention of the court, the decision taken on the intra-administrative appeal itself still remains subject to the principle of legality; that the applicant who intends to contest this decision can raise before the court, until the completion of the examination phase, any new legal grounds, even if they were not raised during the intra-administrative appeal against the initial decision, since those grounds relate to the same claim of which the administrative authority was seized; ...

Notes

(1) The *Garnier* case brought about a change in the case law. In the past, an applicant was not allowed to raise grounds before the court which had not previously been brought forward during the intra-administrative objection stage. Since the *Garnier* case, an applicant is permitted to raise grounds for the first time at the judicial stage, when submitting his file and until the end of the preparation stage.

(2) In France, there are no rules according to which an applicant is excluded from lodging an action because he did not participate in the decision-making process.

[245] N° 284586.

4.8.C INFLUENCE OF EUROPEAN LAW

Case C-137/14, 15 October 2015[246] **4.99 (EU)**

Commission v Germany

PRECLUSION CLAUSES; EU LAW

Commission v Germany

German preclusion clauses applicable in the field of environmental law are in violation of EU law and cannot be justified by considerations of compliance with the principles of legal certainty and efficiency of judicial procedures.

Facts: The Commission stated that Germany violated Article 11 of Directive 2011/92/EU of the European Parliament and of the Council of 13 December 2011 on the assessment of the effects of certain public and private projects of the environment and Article 25 of Directive 2010/75/EU of the European Parliament and of the Council of 24 November 2010 on industrial emissions.

Held: Germany failed to fulfil its obligations under Article 11 of Directive 2011/92/EU and Article 25 of Directive 2010/75/EU.

Judgment: Arguments of the parties: 68 The Commission is of the opinion that the restriction, in accordance with Paragraph 2(3) of the UmwRG [Umweltrechtbehelfsgesetz] and Paragraph 73(4) and (6) of the VwVfG [Verwaltungsverfahrensgesetz], of the objections which may be raised in legal proceedings to those which were previously made in the administrative procedure runs counter to Article 11 of Directive 2011/92 and Article 25 of Directive 2010/75.

69 That institution argues that such a restriction constitutes a disproportionate obstacle to the right of the public concerned to challenge the legality of administrative decisions in the areas covered by those directives. The national legislation providing for that restriction accordingly runs counter to the principle of access to justice and restricts the effective legal protection of that public. The EU legal order does not allow the admissibility of pleas raised during legal proceedings to be made subject to the fact that they were previously raised in the administrative procedure.

...

75 Paragraph 2(3) of the UmwRG and Paragraph 73(4) and (6) of the VwVfG restrict the pleas in law which may be raised by a claimant in support of legal proceedings against an administrative decision falling within the scope of Article 11 of Directive 2011/92 and Article 25 of Directive 2010/75 to objections made during the administrative procedure.

76 In that regard, although, indeed, neither Article 11(4) of Directive 2011/92 nor Article 25(4) of Directive 2010/75 excludes an action before an administrative authority preceding the legal proceedings and does not prevent national law from requiring the claimant to exhaust all administrative review procedures before being authorised to bring legal proceedings, those provisions of EU law do not, however, allow restrictions on the pleas in law which may be raised in support of legal proceedings.

77 The Court has previously held that Article 11(1) of Directive 2011/92, pursuant to which the decisions, acts or omissions covered by that article must be subject to a

[246] ECLI:EU:C:2015:683.

review procedure before a court of law or another independent and impartial body established by law to challenge their substantive or procedural legality, lays down no restriction whatsoever on the pleas which may be relied on in support of such a review (see, to that effect, judgment in *Bund für Umwelt und Naturschutz Deutschland, Landesverband Nordrhein-Westfalen*, C-115/09, EU:C:2011:289, paragraph 37). That consideration meets the objective pursued by that provision of ensuring broad access to justice in the area of environmental protection.

78 Paragraph 2(3) of the UmwRG and Paragraph 73(4) of the VwVfG lay down specific conditions restricting the review by the courts which are not provided for in either Article 11 of Directive 2011/92 or Article 25 of Directive 2010/75.

79 Such a restriction laid on the claimant as to the nature of the pleas in law which he is permitted to raise before the court reviewing the legality of the administrative decision which concerns him cannot be justified by considerations of compliance with the principle of legal certainty. It is in no way established that a full review by the courts of the merits of that decision would undermine that principle.

80 As regards the argument concerning the efficiency of administrative procedures, although it is true that the fact of raising a plea in law for the first time in legal proceedings may, in certain cases, hinder the smooth running of that procedure, it is sufficient to recall that the very objective pursued by Article 11 of Directive 2011/92 and Article 25 of Directive 2010/75 is not only to ensure that the litigant has the broadest possible access to review by the courts but also to ensure that that review covers both the substantive and procedural legality of the contested decision in its entirety.

81 None the less, the national legislature may lay down specific procedural rules, such as the inadmissibility of an argument submitted abusively or in bad faith, which constitute appropriate mechanisms for ensuring the efficiency of the legal proceedings.

82 It follows that the third complaint raised by the Commission in support of its action is well founded.

Notes

(1) In this judgment, the European Court of Justice ruled that the preclusion clauses laid down in the German §2(3) of the German Environmental Remedies Act (Umweltrechtbehelfsgesetz) and §73(4) of the Administrative Procedure Act (Verwaltungsverfahrensgesetz) do not comply with the provisions of the EU directives transposing Article 9(2) of the Aarhus Convention. In response to this ruling, the Act amending the Environmental Remedies Act (Umweltrechtsbehelfsanpassungsgesetz) came into force.[247]

(2) One should note that the Commission had argued that the preclusion clauses would also infringe the principle of effective judicial protection and 'the principle of access to justice'.[248] If that argument had been upheld, such clauses would be excluded generally, hence even outside the scope of Article 9(2) of the Aarhus Convention and the corresponding EU directives. However, the court based its judgment only on the content of Article 11 of Directive 2011/92 and Article 25 of

[247] BGBl I S 1298.

[248] See para 69 of the judgment, not added in the excerpt.

Directive 2010/75, which are the provisions transposing Article 9(2) of the Aarhus Convention. Although the argument of the European Commission was not explicitly rejected, it must, at least for the time being, be considered that the use of such preclusion clauses is forbidden by international and European law only within the scope of Article 9(2) of the Aarhus Convention.

4.8.D COMPARATIVE REMARKS

As far as court procedures are concerned, most legal systems use some kind of general procedural norm of due process. Parties must have adequate time to examine the submissions of the other party and to react to each other's arguments and items of evidence. Hence, in most legal systems, there is some rule or judicial practice prescribing a cut-off date prior to the hearing of the case after which parties may not submit new material.

In addition, some legal systems use stricter preclusion clauses, which exclude judicial review partly or completely. These apply in cases where the claimant could have made representations against the contested decision during the decision-making procedure or in an intra-administrative objection procedure but failed to do so without good reason. The legal systems compared in this book differ significantly with regard to such clauses. None of the countries exclude judicial review entirely in all cases in which someone did not participate in the decision-making phase. However, in the Netherlands, preclusion clauses are applicable if the decision is prepared using the so-called 'uniform public preparatory procedure', which includes an announcement of the proposed project to the general public and the opportunity for them to react to the proposal (Article 6:13 AWB). Furthermore, Dutch law provides for another rule, which excludes the possibility to bring forward new grounds of review after the deadline provided for a claim before the administrative courts (Article 1.6a of the Crisis and Recovery Act). This latter provision is applicable only in certain cases, mainly in the area of planning and environmental law. Similarly, the General Court (of the European Union) has ruled that, in proceedings concerning intellectual property rights, applicants are not allowed to bring forward new evidence that was not brought forward in the intra-administrative objection stage which took place prior to the court proceedings. Since the *Garnier* ruling, French law no longer recognises such preclusion clauses.

General preclusion clauses are also unknown in England and Wales. In planning law, however, the courts have interpreted the definition of the 'person aggrieved' concept, which is a different requirement for standing than the general-interest criterion, in such a way that persons who do not have a conceivable interest (legal or equitable) in the land affected and do not live in the immediate vicinity are only regarded as a 'person aggrieved' if they participated substantially in the planning process. In substance, this is a kind of preclusion clause.

International and European law, particularly Article 9(2) of the Aarhus Convention, limit the potential for preclusion clauses, as was made clear in a judgment of the Court of Justice against Germany in 2015. It is still an open question whether and to what extent preclusion clauses are in accordance with the principle of effective judicial protection, insofar as the case has an EU law dimension.

All in all, it can be observed that the most important area for the application of preclusion clauses is planning and environmental law.

4.9 COURT FEES AND OTHER COSTS

Legal systems may provide for broad access to justice insofar as standing is concerned. However, if court procedures are too expensive, many potential claimants will refrain from bringing claims to court. Before administrative courts, costs mainly consist of court fees and the costs for legal representation, if required. However, if a claimant loses the case, he may risk having to pay the costs of the other parties. Risks for other costs (hereafter called cost-risks) are often much higher and more prohibitive than court fees and fees for legal representation.

4.9.A COURT FEES

4.9.A.1 LEGAL SYSTEMS WITHOUT COURT FEES

4.9.A.1 (i) France

In France, bringing a case to the administrative court does not in general involve any fee.

4.9.A.1 (ii) The European Union

Rules of Procedure of the Court of Justice of the European Union **4.100 (EU)**

Article 143 Proceedings before the Court shall be free of charge, except that:

(a) where a party has caused the Court to incur avoidable costs the Court may, after hearing the Advocate General, order that party to refund them;

(b) where copying or translation work is carried out at the request of a party, the cost shall, in so far as the Registrar considers it excessive, be paid for by that party on the Registry's scale of charges referred to in Article 22.

Note

Similar to France, the EU courts generally do not charge any fees.

4.9.A.2 LEGAL SYSTEMS WITH COURT FEES IN THE FORM OF FIXED AMOUNTS

4.9.A.2 (i) England and Wales

The court fees for commencing judicial review proceedings in England and Wales have seen substantial increases in recent years. The fee for lodging a claim is £154, with a further £770 to be paid for an application for permission to proceed.[249] If permission is refused on the papers and an oral permission hearing is sought, a further fee of £385 is required, although the £770 fee for permission to proceed is reduced to £385 in such cases. If permission is granted and a full hearing in pursuit of remedy is then held, a further fee of £528 is required.[250]

4.9.A.2 (ii) The Netherlands

The court fees in the Netherlands are relatively limited. Natural persons have to pay a court fee of €165 for starting a procedure before an administrative court at first instance.[251] There are some exceptions. For certain categories of decisions, mentioned in Annex 3 of the AWB, the court fee is only €45. These exceptions mainly concern proceedings about social security benefits.

Legal persons have to pay €328. At second instance, the amounts are the same. If one seeks interim relief, this is treated as an additional procedure. Hence another €165 (or €328 or €45 in first instance and the same amount in second instance) must be paid. The amount of court fees is automatically adapted to inflation on 1 January every year, according to Article 11:2(1) AWB.

On a number of occasions, claimants have argued that these court fees hinder access to justice and constitute an infringement of Article 6 ECHR and the right to effective judicial review. The Dutch courts have rejected this plea more than once.[252]

4.9.A.3 LEGAL SYSTEMS WITH COURT FEES IN THE FORM OF RELATIVE AMOUNTS: GERMANY

In Germany, the rules on costs differ somewhat from the Dutch and English approach, as there are no fixed court fees, but the fee depends on the economic value of the claim (*Streitwert*). The costs of proceedings include the court costs (fees and expenses) and the expenditure incurred into by those concerned which necessary to properly pursue or defend their rights, including the costs of the intra-administrative objection procedure. The value of the claim is determined by the courts. If there are no concrete indications relating to the economic value of the claim, the court will normally set it at €5,000 (*Auffangstreitwert*), pursuant to §52(2) of the Court Fees Act (Gerichtskostengesetz).[253] The court fees for such a court action in front of a lower administrative court would then amount to €438 if normal court proceedings took place. In appeals, court fees amount to €584 if the value of the case (*Streitwert*) does not exceed €5,000.

Hence, court fees may ultimately be more or less comparable with those in the Netherlands, at least in cases with a comparable low value. However, the court fees rise in cases with a higher value, and are then significantly higher than in all of the other legal systems compared.

[249] An outline of the requirements of permission to proceed can be found in Chapter 7, section 7.2.C.
[250] HM Courts and Tribunals Service, *EX50A – Court Fees* (24 July 2018).
[251] Executive Order on Administrative Law Costs (Besluit proceskosten bestuursrecht).
[252] eg ECLI:NL:CRVB:2015:2079; ECLI:NL:RVS:2000:AP5413.
[253] Gerichtskostengesetz vom 5 Mai 2004, BGBl 2004 I, 718.

4.9.A.4 COMPARATIVE REMARKS

In some legal systems, in general, no court fees have to be paid (France and the EU). In the other legal systems examined, court fees are at a more or less comparable, quite limited level, although they have risen significantly in England and Wales. The only exception may be Germany in cases with a high economic value. In such cases, court fees rise significantly.

4.9.B COST-RISKS

Much more problematic in practice and more diverse are the cost-risks that a claimant faces.

4.9.B.1 LEGAL SYSTEMS WHICH APPLY THE 'LOSER PAYS' PRINCIPLE

4.9.B.1 (i) The European Union

Rules of Procedure of the Court of Justice of the European Union **4.101 (EU)**

Article 138 (1) The unsuccessful party shall be ordered to pay the costs if they have been applied for in the successful party's pleadings.

(2) Where there is more than one unsuccessful party the Court shall decide how the costs are to be shared.

(3) Where each party succeeds on some and fails on other heads, the parties shall bear their own costs. However, if it appears justified in the circumstances of the case, the Court may order that one party, in addition to bearing its own costs, pay a proportion of the costs of the other party.

Note

In principle, the unsuccessful party bears all costs of the procedure before the European courts, ie the costs of the other party as well as its own costs, unless special rules or exceptions apply.[254] However, the court may decide to derogate from this general rule in two circumstances: when there are no clear winners and losers, and in the event of 'exceptional circumstances'. In such cases, the court may decide to either divide the costs or rule that each party bears its own costs.

4.9.B.1 (ii) France

Code de justice administrative **4.102 (FR)**

Article L761-1 In all courts, the judge orders the party that is bound to pay the costs or, failing that, the losing party, to pay the other party the sum that he determines, by virtue

[254] Ie, those set in Art 141 of the Rules of Procedure of the European Court of Justice and Art 87(5) of the Rules of Procedure of the General Court on discontinuance and withdrawal.

of the expenses incurred that are not included in the costs. The judge takes account of the needs of equity or of the economic situation of the losing party. He may, also *ex officio*, for reasons that derive from the same considerations, find that there are no grounds to make such an order.

Note

In France, the 'loser pays' principle is applied as a default rule. Hence, the party who loses the case has to pay all the costs of the winning party. However, French courts may rule that, on the ground of equity, costs will not (fully) be charged to the losing party.

4.9.B.1 (iii) Germany

Verwaltungsgerichtsordnung **4.103 (DE)**

§154 (1) The losing party shall pay the costs of the proceedings.

(2) The costs of an appeal lodged unsuccessfully shall be imposed on the party who lodged the appeal.

(3) Costs may only be imposed on the subpoenaed party if he lodged motions or appeals; §155(4) shall remain unaffected.

Note

The default rule in Germany is the same as in France: the losing party pays the costs of the proceedings. However, there are particular fields of administrative law, such as asylum law and educational support law, where no costs are levied.

4.9.B.1 (iv) England and Wales

The 'loser pays' principle also applies in England and Wales. The costs which the losing party has to pay may be quite high. The Jackson Report, a recent report by a judge from the Court of Appeal into the costs regime,[255] suggested that typical legal costs for a paper application for judicial review were between £3,000 and £5,000, with a further £10,000–15,000 in costs for each side if permission is granted and the case proceeds to a full hearing.[256] There have even been cases where costs have exceeded £50,000 or £100,000.[257] However, courts have, under certain circumstances, the discretion to limit the costs which have to be paid by the losing party.

[255] www.judiciary.gov.uk/wp-content/uploads/JCO/Documents/Reports/jackson-final-report-140110.pdf.

[256] R Jackson, *LJ Review of Civil Litigation Costs: Preliminary Report* (London, TSO, 2009) ch 35, para 2.7.

[257] This can be seen, eg from the *Edwards* case, Case C-260/11, dealt with in section 4.9.C below, where the costs were £88,100.

Civil Procedure Rules **4.104 (EW)**

Rule 44.2 (1) The court has discretion as to–

(a) whether costs are payable by one party to another;

(b) the amount of those costs; and

(c) when they are to be paid.

(2) If the court decides to make an order about costs–

(a) the general rule is that the unsuccessful party will be ordered to pay the costs of the successful party; but

(b) the court may make a different order.

Notes

(1) In administrative law cases, the courts have been clear that the general rule will ordinarily be applied. This situation has led to criticism of the present costs rules, not least because there is a disincentive for individuals to bring judicial review claims on public interest grounds, or where the frontiers of administrative law are being tested.[258]

(2) A Costs Capping Order (CCO; known until 2017 as a Protective Costs Order, or PCO) is a regime which seeks to limit the liability of unsuccessful claimants where judicial review claims are brought in the public interest. It is usual for the CCO to be awarded only in the first-instance proceedings, although it is possible for appellants to seek a further order for any appeals that might be brought from the appellate court. CCOs can be very important in environmental cases.

Court of Appeal (Civil Division), 1 March 2005[259] **4.105 (EW)**

R (Corner House Research) v Secretary of State for Trade and Industry

COST-RISK; PROTECTIVE COSTS ORDERS / COST CAPPING ORDERS

Corner House Research

A Protective Costs Order (now Costs Capping Order) should only be granted in accordance with the criteria outlined in this decision and, in particular, only where the claimant can demonstrate that the claim seeks to serve a broader public interest alongside his individual interest.

Facts: The claimants were a specialist interest group with an interest in reducing the incidence of bribery and corruption in international trade. They wished to claim judicial review of the failure of the Export Credit

[258] See, eg M Fordham and J Boyd, 'Rethinking Costs in Judicial Review' (2009) 14 *Judicial Review* 306.
[259] [2005] EWCA Civ 192.

Guarantee Department of the Department of Trade and Industry to consult Corner House Research when carrying out a detailed consultation on the measures appropriate to prevent bribery and corruption in international trade and argued that there had been a serious breach of basic public law standards of fairness and of the department's own published consultation policy. The judge at first instance refused a PCO to facilitate the claim for judicial review on the basis that the public interest in the case was not sufficiently great and the claim was not likely to succeed.

Held: A Protective Cost Order was ordered.

Judgment: … It commonly happens when a court has to take an important decision at an early stage of proceedings that it must do no more than conclude that the applicant's case has a real (as opposed to a fanciful) prospect of success, or that its case is 'properly arguable'. To place the threshold any higher is to invite heavy and time-consuming ancillary litigation of the type that disfigured the conduct of civil litigation 25 years ago. We realise that in CPR Part 54 the rule-maker prescribed no explicit criterion for the grant of permission to apply for judicial review, but we consider that no PCO should be granted unless the judge considers that the application for judicial review has a real prospect of success and that it is in the public interest to make the order.

74. We would therefore restate the governing principles in these terms:

1. A protective costs order may be made at any stage of the proceedings, on such conditions as the court thinks fit, provided that the court is satisfied that:

i) The issues raised are of general public importance;

ii) The public interest requires that those issues should be resolved;

iii) The applicant has no private interest in the outcome of the case;

iv) Having regard to the financial resources of the applicant and the respondent(s) and to the amount of costs that are likely to be involved it is fair and just to make the order;

v) If the order is not made the applicant will probably discontinue the proceedings and will be acting reasonably in so doing.

2. If those acting for the applicant are doing so pro bono this will be likely to enhance the merits of the application for a PCO.

3. It is for the court, in its discretion, to decide whether it is fair and just to make the order in the light of the considerations set out above.

75. A PCO can take a number of different forms and the choice of the form of the order is an important aspect of the discretion exercised by the judge

…

We would rephrase that guidance in these terms in the present context:

i) When making any PCO where the applicant is seeking an order for costs in its favour if it wins, the court should prescribe by way of a capping order a total amount of the recoverable costs which will be inclusive, so far as a CFA-funded party is concerned, of any additional liability;

ii) The purpose of the PCO will be to limit or extinguish the liability of the applicant if it loses, and as a balancing factor the liability of the defendant for the applicant's costs if the defendant loses will thus be restricted to a reasonably modest amount. The applicant should expect the capping order to restrict it to solicitors' fees and a fee for a single advocate of junior counsel status that are no more than modest.

iii) The overriding purpose of exercising this jurisdiction is to enable the applicant to present its case to the court with a reasonably competent advocate without being exposed to such serious financial risks that would deter it from advancing a case of general public importance at all, where the court considers that it is in the public interest that an order should be made. The beneficiary of a PCO must not expect the capping order that will accompany the PCO to permit anything other than modest representation, and must arrange its legal representation (when its lawyers are not willing to act pro bono) accordingly.

...

Note

CCOs (formerly PCOs) are available only in cases where the claim is brought in order to vindicate public (rather than private) interests, and are granted in judicial review cases in accordance with the principles in *Corner House Research*.

The huge cost-risks for claimants in England and Wales and the uncertain and limited possibilities to claim a PCO led to the preliminary questions of the Supreme Court of the UK in a case falling under the Aarhus Convention.[260] Furthermore, the European Commission started an infringement procedure which led to a ruling by the European Court of Justice.[261]

4.9.B.2 LEGAL SYSTEMS WHICH APPLY THE PRINCIPLE OF ONE-WAY COST SHIFTING: THE NETHERLANDS

Algemene Wet Bestuursrecht **4.106 (NL)**

Article 8:74 (1) If the administrative judge rules the claim to be well-founded, the judgment shall also order the administrative authority to reimburse the claimant the registry fee paid by him.

(2) In other cases, the judgment may order that the administrative authority shall reimburse all or part of the registry fee.

Article 8:75 (1) The administrative judge shall have exclusive jurisdiction to order a party to pay the costs which another party has reasonably incurred in connection with the judicial review proceedings before the administrative judge. ... A natural person may be ordered to pay costs only in case of a manifestly unreasonable use of the right of judicial review. ...

Notes

(1) In the Netherlands, rules with regard to the cost-risks of proceedings before administrative courts differ from the approach adopted in the other systems that have

[260] Case C-260/11 *The Queen, on the application of David Edwards and Lilian Pallikaropoulos v Environment Agency and Others* ECLI:EU:C:2013:221; see further section 4.9.C below.

[261] Case C-530/11 *Commission v UK* ECLI:EU:C:2014:67.

been analysed so far. If a claimant is at least partly successful in the case, the losing authority must compensate his court fees (Article 8:74(1) AWB) and all costs a 'party has reasonably incurred in connection with the judicial review proceedings', hence the costs of legal assistance and other experts (Article 8:75(1) AWB). Fixed costs rates are applied to the costs of legal assistance and other experts, which do not usually cover all the actual costs. The amount of money paid depends on how the proceedings in the concrete case developed. Certain 'points' are calculated each step of the procedure. In an average case, 2 × €490 (1 point for the written part of the procedure and 1 point for attending the court session) is paid. Other costs that may have to be paid in a case that is well founded are reasonable costs for travelling, experts and unpaid leave.

Claimants who lose the case do not have to pay the costs (either the court fees or the costs of legal representation or experts) of the public authority. Hence, Dutch law applies the principle of one-way cost shifting. Therefore, the cost-risks in procedures in Dutch administrative courts are very low. However, one-way cost shifting does not apply if the court rules that the claimant has clearly misused his procedural rights.

(2) One has to bear in mind that judicial review in the Netherlands is not possible against all acts of the administration, but in most circumstances is available only against single-case decisions.[262] Review of all other forms of administrative action is possible by bringing a claim to the civil division of the district court. The court fees before the civil division of the district courts are significantly higher; in most cases, one has to be represented by a legal professional[263] and, according to Article 237 Code of Civil Procedure (Wetboek van Burgerlijke Rechtsvordering), there is no rule of one-way cost shifting (hence the 'loser pays' principle fully applies). Therefore, judicial protection is far more costly in cases where the administrative courts cannot be seized.

4.9.C INFLUENCE OF INTERNATIONAL AND EUROPEAN LAW

UNECE Convention on Access to Information, Public Participation in Decision-making and Access to Justice in Environmental Matters (Aarhus Convention) **4.107 (UN)**

Article 9 …

(4) In addition and without prejudice to paragraph 1 above, the procedures referred to in paragraphs 1, 2 and 3 above shall provide adequate and effective remedies, including injunctive relief as appropriate, and be fair, equitable, timely and not prohibitively expensive. Decisions under this article shall be given or recorded in writing. Decisions of courts, and whenever possible of other bodies, shall be publicly accessible.

262 See further Chapter 3, section 3.1.A (i).

263 Wetboek van Burgerlijke Rechtsvordering, Art 79.

Case C-260/11, 11 April 2013[264] **4.108 (EU)**

David Edwards and Lilian Pallikaropoulos v Environment Agency and Others

COSTS OF PROCEEDINGS; ENVIRONMENTAL LAW; ARTICLE 9(4) AARHUS CONVENTION

Edwards

An assessment of whether the costs are prohibitively expensive must not be carried out solely on the basis of the financial situation of the person concerned, but must also be based on an objective analysis of the amount of the costs involved.

Facts: Mr Edwards and Ms Pallikaropoulos objected against a decision of the Environment Agency which had issued a permit for the operation of a cement works in Rugby relying, in particular, on the fact that the project had not been the subject of an environmental impact assessment. The House of Lords ordered Ms Pallikaropoulos, whose appeal had been dismissed as unfounded, to pay the costs of the opposing parties, the amount of which, in the event of disagreement between the parties, was to be fixed by the Clerk of the Parliaments.

The respondents submitted two bills for recoverable costs in the amounts of £55,810 and £32,290. The Supreme Court asked a number of questions, mainly about how to examine whether the cost of the litigation is or is not 'prohibitively expensive' within the meaning of Article 9(4) of the Aarhus Convention.

Held: The requirement that judicial proceedings should not be prohibitively expensive means that the persons covered by those provisions should not be prevented from seeking review by the courts by reason of the financial burden that might arise as a result. Where a national court is called upon to make an order for costs against a member of the public who is an unsuccessful claimant in an environmental dispute or to state its views on a possible capping of the costs for which the unsuccessful party may be liable, it must satisfy itself that that requirement has been complied with, taking into account both the interest of the person wishing to defend his rights and the public interest in the protection of the environment.

The national court cannot act solely on the basis of that claimant's financial situation but must also carry out an objective analysis of the amount of the costs. It may also take into account the situation of the parties concerned, whether the claimant has a reasonable prospect of success, the importance of what is at stake for the claimant and for the protection of the environment, the complexity of the relevant law and procedure, the potentially frivolous nature of the claim at its various stages, and the existence of a national legal aid scheme or a costs protection regime.

That assessment cannot be conducted according to different criteria depending on whether it is carried out at the conclusion of first-instance proceedings, an appeal or a second appeal.

Judgment: Lord Carnwath JSC: 25 As the Court has already held, it should be recalled, first of all, that the requirement, under the fifth paragraph of Article 10a of Directive 85/337 and the fifth paragraph of Article 15a of Directive 96/61, that judicial proceedings should not be prohibitively expensive does not prevent the national courts from making an order for costs (see, to that effect, Case C-427/07 *Commission v Ireland* [2009] ECR I-6277, paragraph 92).

26 That follows expressly from the Aarhus Convention, with which European Union law must be 'properly aligned', as is evident from recital 5 in the preamble to Directive 2003/35, which amended Directives 85/337 and 96/61, since Article 3(8) of that Convention states that the powers of national courts to award reasonable costs in judicial proceedings are not to be affected.

[264] ECLI:EU:C:2013:221.

27 Next, it must be pointed out that the requirement that litigation should not be prohibitively expensive concerns all the costs arising from participation in the judicial proceedings (see, to that effect, *Commission v Ireland*, paragraph 92).

28 The prohibitive nature of costs must therefore be assessed as a whole, taking into account all the costs borne by the party concerned. …

33 Moreover, the requirement that the cost should be 'not prohibitively expensive' pertains, in environmental matters, to the observance of the right to an effective remedy enshrined in Article 47 of the Charter of Fundamental Rights of the European Union, and to the principle of effectiveness, in accordance with which detailed procedural rules governing actions for safeguarding an individual's rights under European Union law must not make it in practice impossible or excessively difficult to exercise rights conferred by European Union law (see, inter alia, Case C-240/09 *Lesoochranárske zoskupenie VLK* [2011] ECR-1255, paragraph 48) ….

35 It follows from the foregoing that the requirement, under the fifth paragraph of Article 10a of Directive 85/337 and the fifth paragraph of Article 15a of Directive 96/61, that judicial proceedings should not be prohibitively expensive means that the persons covered by those provisions should not be prevented from seeking, or pursuing a claim for, a review by the courts that falls within the scope of those articles by reason of the financial burden that might arise as a result. Where a national court is called upon to make an order for costs against a member of the public who is an unsuccessful claimant in an environmental dispute or, more generally, where it is required – as courts in the United Kingdom may be – to state its views, at an earlier stage of the proceedings, on a possible capping of the costs for which the unsuccessful party may be liable, it must satisfy itself that that requirement has been complied with, taking into account both the interest of the person wishing to defend his rights and the public interest in the protection of the environment. …

38 It follows that, as regards the methods likely to secure the objective of ensuring effective judicial protection without excessive cost in the field of environmental law, account must be taken of all the relevant provisions of national law and, in particular, of any national legal aid scheme as well as of any costs protection regime, such as that referred to in paragraph 16 of the present judgment. Significant differences between national laws in that area do have to be taken into account. ….

40 That assessment cannot, therefore, be carried out solely on the basis of the financial situation of the person concerned but must also be based on an objective analysis of the amount of the costs, particularly since, as has been stated in paragraph 32 of the present judgment, members of the public and associations are naturally required to play an active role in defending the environment. To that extent, the cost of proceedings must not appear, in certain cases, to be objectively unreasonable. Thus, the cost of proceedings must neither exceed the financial resources of the person concerned nor appear, in any event, to be objectively unreasonable.

41 As regards the analysis of the financial situation of the person concerned, the assessment which must be carried out by the national court cannot be based exclusively on the estimated financial resources of an 'average' applicant, since such information may have little connection with the situation of the person concerned.

42 The court may also take into account the situation of the parties concerned, whether the claimant has a reasonable prospect of success, the importance of what is at stake for the claimant and for the protection of the environment, the complexity of the relevant law and procedure and the potentially frivolous nature of the claim at its various stages (see, by analogy, Case C-279/09 DEB [2010] ECR I-13849, paragraph 61).

43 It must also be stated that the fact, put forward by the Supreme Court of the United Kingdom, that the claimant has not been deterred, in practice, from asserting his or her claim is not in itself sufficient to establish that the proceedings are not, as far as that claimant is concerned, prohibitively expensive for the purpose (as set out above) of Directives 85/337 and 96/61.

44 Lastly, as regards the question whether the assessment as to whether or not the costs are prohibitively expensive ought to differ according to whether the national court is deciding on costs at the conclusion of first-instance proceedings, an appeal or a second appeal, an issue which was also raised by the referring court, no such distinction is envisaged in Directives 85/337 and 96/61, nor, moreover, would such an interpretation be likely to comply fully with the objective of the European Union legislature, which is to ensure wide access to justice and to contribute to the improvement of environmental protection.

45 The requirement that judicial proceedings should not be prohibitively expensive cannot, therefore, be assessed differently by a national court depending on whether it is adjudicating at the conclusion of first-instance proceedings, an appeal or a second appeal.

Notes

(1) In the *Edwards* case, the CJEU developed a series of criteria to decide whether the costs for judicial review are prohibitively expensive. Less than a year after *Edwards*, the Court of Justice also decided that the English rules on allocating costs infringe Articles 3(7) and 4(4) of Directive 2003/35, which transposes the requirements of Article 9(4) of the Aarhus Convention into EU law. The main argument of the court in this case was that the UK rules do 'not ensure the claimant reasonable predictability as regards both whether the costs of the judicial proceedings in which he becomes involved are payable by him and their amount'.[265]

(2) Also, the Aarhus Convention Compliance Committee has decided in several cases that the cost orders imposed on claimants before UK courts were prohibitively high and therefore infringed Article 9(4) of the Aarhus Convention.[266] It was also decided that the rules determining the allocation of costs of procedures between the parties infringed the Convention.[267]

(3) It should be noted that the *Edwards* judgment was not only based on the Aarhus Convention itself and the EU law transposing these requirements. The court, especially in para 33, expressly referred also to Article 47 of the Charter of Fundamental Rights, and to the principles of effective judicial protection and effectiveness. Therefore, one can argue that at least some of the elements of the court's decision set out the outer limits for national cost schemes in general, not only in the area of environmental protection.

[265] Case C-530/11 *Commission v UK* ECLI:EU:C:2014:67, para 58.

[266] ACCC/C/2008/23 United Kingdom (available at www.unece.org/env/pp/compliance/Compliancecommittee/23TableUK.html) and ACCC/C/2008/27 United Kingdom (available at www.unece.org/env/pp/compliance/Compliancecommittee/27TableUK.html).

[267] ACCC/C/2008/23 United Kingdom (available at www.unece.org/env/pp/compliance/Compliancecommittee/23TableUK.html).

(4) As a consequence of the need to ensure compliance with the rulings of the Court of Justice and the findings of the Compliance Committee, the legal regime of costs in environmental matters in England and Wales has changed. In Aarhus Convention cases, courts may not order costs beyond those permitted by section VII of the Practice Direction accompanying Part 45 CPR. The sums are relatively low when seen from an English perspective – claimants who launch a claim as an individual (so not as a representative of a company or other legal person) face an award of costs capped at £5,000, whereas all other claimants have costs capped at £10,000. Defendants in Aarhus Convention claims have their costs liability capped at £35,000.

4.9.D COMPARATIVE REMARKS

The rules on cost-risks for judicial proceedings before the administrative courts differ substantially between the legal systems examined. Except in the Netherlands, all legal systems usually or always apply the rule that the loser pays all costs, such as the fees for the lawyers and the costs of the experts. In all legal systems, the courts can deviate from this default rule if the circumstances of the case require a different approach to be adopted. In some legal systems, some of these costs are limited by using standard rates, eg for lawyers. However, the total sum of these costs can be quite high. To limit the cost risks and to ensure the right of effective judicial protection, judges in England and Wales may, under certain circumstances, decide to issue Costs Capping Orders.

To meet the requirements of the Aarhus Convention, cost-risks in cases falling within the scope of the Convention have been limited in England and Wales. It may be concluded that the case law of the CJEU has, at least to some extent, had a harmonising effect with regard to this topic. It remains to be seen whether the rules on costs and cost-risks of other legal systems will also have to be adapted.

4.10 LEGAL AID

All national legal systems, as well as the procedural rules applicable before the EU courts, provide the possibility to grant legal aid to those who otherwise would not be able to participate in court proceedings.

4.10.A GERMANY

Verwaltungsgerichtsordnung **4.109 (DE)**

§165 (1) The provisions of the Code of Civil Procedure on legal aid, as well as §569(3) No. 2 the Code of Civil Procedure shall apply mutatis mutandis.

Zivilprozessordnung **4.110 (DE)**

§114 (1) Any party who, due to his personal and economic circumstances, is unable to pay the costs of litigation, or is able to pay them only in part or only as instalments, will be granted assistance with the court costs upon filing a corresponding application, provided that the action he intends to bring or his defence against an action that has been brought against him has sufficient prospects of success and does not seem frivolous. ...

Note

According to §165(1) VwGO, legal aid in administrative court proceedings is provided to the same extent as in civil law procedures. Pursuant to §114 of the Code of Civil Procedure (Zivilprozessordnung), parties who, due to their personal and economic circumstances, are unable to pay the costs of litigation, or are able to pay them only in part or only as instalments, will be granted assistance with court costs upon filing a corresponding application, provided that the action they intend to bring or their defence against an action that has been brought against them has sufficient prospects of success and does not seem frivolous. The application for approval of assistance with court costs is to be submitted to the court hearing the case.[268] The application is to summarise the case and to cite the evidence. With the application, the party is to include a declaration describing his personal and economic circumstances (family circumstances, profession, assets, income and financial obligations), and is to attach the corresponding proof of the same.[269] General amounts do not apply as the legal aid is dependent on the amount in dispute. Legal aid is only granted if neither the income (§115(1) of the Zivilprozessordnung) nor the deployable assets (§115(3)) of the claimant are sufficient to meet the costs of the proceedings. Thus, if the amount in dispute is low (eg €400) and the proceedings thus only costs €422, legal aid will be very exceptional. If the amount in dispute amounts to €1,000,000, the costs will amount to €44,100, and even middle-class claimants can obtain legal aid.[270]

4.10.B FRANCE

In France, full legal aid is granted for those without dependants with a monthly income under €1,000 (€1,360 with two dependants). If the income of such a person is between €1,001 and €1,182 (€1,361 and €1,542 with two dependants), the aid will be 55%, and

[268] It may be recorded with the registry for the files of the court (Zivilprozessordnung, §117(1)).

[269] The declaration and the proof may be made accessible to the opponent in the proceedings only upon the party having consented to this being done, unless the opponent is entitled, vis-à-vis the claimant, to be informed of the claimant's earnings and assets pursuant to the stipulations of civil law. Prior to his declaration being forwarded to the opponent, the claimant is to be given the opportunity to state his position. The claimant is to be informed of the fact that the declaration has been forwarded (Zivilprozessordnung, §117(2)).

[270] On the costs of proceedings, see www.anwalt-seiten.de/Prozesskostenrechner.php.

if the income is between €1,183 and €1,500 (€1,543 and €1,860 with two dependants), legal aid will cover only 25% of the costs. No legal aid will be granted for single persons earning more than €1,500 per month (€1,860 with two dependants).[271]

4.10.C THE NETHERLANDS

In the Netherlands, claimants who may ask for legal aid usually have to pay a (small) part of the costs. Any single person who earns up to €18,400 (€25,600 for a married couple) has to pay €196. The maximum income a single person might receive before a request for legal aid is precluded is currently €26,000 (€36,800 for a married couple).[272] Hence, the legal aid scheme seems to be partly more generous in the Netherlands than in France (as people with higher incomes will get aid), but also partly stricter (as aid to cover full costs is never given).

4.10.D ENGLAND AND WALES

In England and Wales, legal advice and, if necessary, help by a professional Bar-registered lawyer are made available by two parties: the so-called Legal Services Counters acts as what is commonly known as the 'front office' (primary help), whereas private lawyers and mediators provide legal aid in more complicated or time-consuming matters (secondary help). The legal aid system, therefore, is a mixed model, consisting of public first-line and private second-line help. Civil Legal Aid is available in judicial review cases, subject to a test for eligibility (based on the financial means of the claimant[273] and the merits of the claim)[274] and subject to a number of significant exclusions.[275] An example for these exclusions is that people are generally excluded if they have £8,000 or more in savings that are readily accessible or if they own their own home (which is treated as capital). The most notable exception in provisions for legal aid for judicial review claims is that 'public interest' claims are not generally supported. Paragraph 19(3) of schedule 1 of the Legal Aid, Sentencing and Punishment of Offenders Act provides that support will not be provided where 'services provided to an individual in relation to judicial review … [do] not have the potential to produce a benefit for the individual, a member of the individual's family or the environment'. There are also a number of exclusions where legal aid is being sought in immigration or asylum cases. The overall thrust of government policy in the area of legal aid is to reduce costs to the exchequer.

[271] www.service-public.fr/particuliers/vosdroits/F18074.

[272] www.rvr.org/nieuws/2015/december/inkomen-vermogen-en-eigen-bijdrage-2016.html.

[273] The requirements set a maximum level of earnings and a maximum level of assets which, if exceeded, preclude access to civil legal aid.

[274] See the Civil Legal Aid (Merits Criteria) Regulations 2013 (SI 2013/104).

[275] See the Legal Aid, Sentencing and Punishment of Offenders Act 2012, sch 1, para 19(1). Claims for a writ of habeas corpus may be supported under para 20, claims for 'abuse of position or powers by a public authority' (predominantly claims in tort for damages) may be supported under para 21 and claims for breach of Convention rights (tort or damages claims – other claims would fall under judicial review) may be supported under para 22.

4.10.E THE EUROPEAN UNION

Rules of Procedure of the General Court **4.111 (EU)**

Article 94 (1) In order to ensure effective access to justice, legal aid shall be granted for proceedings before the General Court in accordance with the following rules.

Legal aid shall cover, in whole or in part, the costs involved in legal assistance and representation by a lawyer in proceedings before the General Court. The cashier of the General Court shall be responsible for those costs.

(2) Any natural person who, because of his economic situation, is wholly or partly unable to meet the costs referred to in paragraph 1 shall be entitled to legal aid.

The economic situation shall be assessed, taking into account objective factors such as income, capital and the family situation.

(3) Legal aid shall be refused if the action in respect of which the application is made appears to be manifestly inadmissible or manifestly unfounded.

Notes

(1) Before the General Court, only natural persons (ie to the exclusion of legal persons) may apply for legal aid for the costs involved in legal assistance and representation by a lawyer.

(2) Legal aid is of more limited importance before the General Court and the European Court of Justice than in proceedings before national courts.[276] Before the European Court of Justice, legal aid plays a rather minor role, being relevant only in appeals proceedings against judgments of the General Court and, marginally, in preliminary ruling proceedings since, in the other cases in which natural and legal persons are involved, the competent court is the General Court.

4.10.F COMPARATIVE REMARKS

In some legal systems, such as Germany and England and Wales, the decision over whether legal aid will be granted depends to some extent, or to an important extent such as (in England and Wales),[277] on the prospects of success of the case. The same is true in the EU legal system; a request for legal aid before the General Court will not be considered if the claim is manifestly inadmissible or unfounded.[278] In other legal systems, such as France or the Netherlands, this is not the case, at least not in general. As may be expected, rules about legal aid differ in detail and are sometimes complex. In England

[276] B Wägenbaur, *Court of Justice of the EU* (Munich, CH Beck, 2013) 766.

[277] See s 11 of the Legal Aid, Sentencing and Punishment of Offenders Act 2012; see also the more detailed framework in regs 4 and 5 of the Civil Legal Aid (Merits Criteria) Regulations SI 2013/104.

[278] Rules of Procedure of the General Court, Art 94(3). See Case T-30/96 *Gomes de Sa Pereira v Council* ECLI:EU:T:1996:107.

and Wales, many exclusion clauses apply which seem to limit the availability of legal aid more than in the other legal systems under discussion.

FURTHER READING

Auby, JB, 'About Europeanization of Domestic Judicial Review' (2014) 7 *Review of European Administrative Law* 19.

Desrameaux, A, 'L'intérêt donnant qualité pour agir en justice. D'une règle du contentieux administratif à l'esprit du droit administratif français' in V Donier and B Lapérou-Schneider (eds), *L'accès au juge – Recherches sur l'effectivité d'un droit* (Brussels, Bruylant, 2013) 319–38.

Ebbesson, J, *Access to Justice in Environmental Matters in the EU* (Alphen aan de Rijn, Kluwer, 2002).

Eliantonio, M, Backes, CW, Rhee, CH, van Spronken, TNBM, and Berlee, A, *Standing Up for Your Right(s) in Europe – a Comparative Study on Legal Standing (Locus Standi) before the EU and Member States' Courts* (Antwerp, Intersentia, 2013); also available at www.europarl.europa.eu/committees/en/studiesdownload.html?languageDocument=EN&file=75651.

de Graaf, KJ and Marseille, AT, 'Final Dispute Resolution by Dutch Administrative Courts: Slippery Slope and Efficient Remedy' in S Comtois and KJ de Graaf (eds), *On Judicial and Quasi-Judicial Independence* (Governance & Recht, No 7) (The Hague, Eleven International Publishing, 2013) 205–18.

de Graaf, KJ and Marseille, AT, 'On Administrative Adjudication, Administrative Justice and Public Trust: Analyzing Developments on Access to Justice in Dutch Administrative Law and its Application in Practise' in S Comtois and KJ de Graaf (eds), *On Lawmaking and Public Trust* (Governance & Recht, No 14). (The Hague, Eleven International Publishing, 2016) 103–20.

Robbe, J and Willemsen, PA, 'The Influence of Union Law on National Standing Requirements in France, the Netherlands and Germany' in DC Dragos, F Lafarge and PA Willemsen (eds), *Proceedings of the EGPA Study Group Law and Public Administration* (Bucharest, Editura Economica, 2012) 62–78.

Wegener, B, 'Subjective Public Rights – Historical Roots and Requisite Adjustments to the Confines of Legal Protection' in H Pünder and Ch Waldhoff (eds), *Debates in German Public Law* (Oxford, Hart Publishing, 2014) 219–38.

CHAPTER 5
CONDUCT OF COURT PROCEEDINGS

Mike Varney

5.1 INTRODUCTION

The consideration of procedural steps for the conduct of court proceedings is crucial, given that the procedural requirements will govern the ability of the individual to bring a claim before and to obtain a remedy from the courts. It was noted earlier in this book that there are distinctions to be drawn between systems that adopt a dualistic approach, with separate systems of administrative courts, and systems with a monistic approach, where unified courts hear both public and private law claims.[1] All systems adopt specialised procedures for administrative law claims when contrasted with other legal proceedings. In the case of the Court of Justice of the European Union (CJEU), there is no specific procedural route for judicial review applications. However, given that any such claims before the General Court and Court of Justice will be direct actions, one might argue that the procedure for direct actions serves in the same way as the specialised procedures in place in other jurisdictions in many respects. These procedures generally acknowledge the fundamental differences that exist between proceedings brought against public authorities in an administrative law claim and disputes between private parties in private law disputes.[2]

Procedural rules may be designed to serve a number of objectives. They may be imposed in part to manage the caseload of courts and to try and promote efficiency in the use of judicial resources. They may also sometimes be used to limit access to judicial remedies. The conduct of the court proceedings will be crucial to the fair hearing of the case, and there is a considerable amount of case law before the European Court of Human Rights on the application of Article 6 of the Convention to administrative proceedings. The Council of Europe Committee of Ministers has also undertaken work on judicial review proceedings, and a number of the principles drawn from its recommendations are pertinent to the subject matter of this chapter.

This chapter will start by looking at the steps of the proceedings in judicial review claims, before examining the approach of the courts to hearing evidence in judicial review cases. Once these general issues have been examined, the chapter will focus on specific elements of the proceedings. There will be an examination of the approach to the hearing of experts and amici curiae (friends of the court). The chapter will then consider the general power of courts to decide issues *ultra petita* (ie beyond the requests of the parties) and also the power of the court to act *ex officio* in order to gather evidence and raise legal issues that have not otherwise been raised by the parties. The approach of the courts to the equality of the parties will also be examined, as this is an important aspect of all judicial proceedings and has been impacted by principles of EU law and Article 6 of the European Convention on Human Rights (ECHR).

At the outset, it is important to emphasise that EU law and the approach of the European Court of Human Rights is based on the procedural autonomy of the Member States, provided that the principles of equivalence and effectiveness are satisfied in EU law and that the requirements of Article 6 ECHR are met by the procedural rules in place in each state under the ECHR.

[1] See Chapter 2, section 2.2.

[2] Some authors writing on the English legal system have expressed doubt that a specialised system of procedures and remedies for public law disputes are necessary. See D Oliver, 'Public Law Procedures and Remedies – Do We Need Them?' (2002) *Public Law* 91.

Case 33/76, 16 December 1976[3] **5.1 (EU)**

Rewe Zentralfinanz v Commission

EFFECTIVE JUDICIAL PROTECTION; TIME LIMITS

Rewe

It is for the domestic legal system of each Member State to designate the courts having jurisdiction and to determine the procedural conditions governing actions intended to ensure the protection of the rights which citizens derive from EU law. Such conditions cannot be less favourable than those relating to similar actions of a domestic nature (equivalence) and may not render it impossible in practice to exercise the rights which the national courts are obliged to protect (effectiveness).

Facts: Rewe-Zentral AG paid charges for phyto-sanitary inspection in respect of the import of French apples which were found to be equivalent to customs duties. In 1973, the company applied to the Chamber of Agriculture (Landwirtschaftskammer) of Saarland to annul the decisions imposing the charges and to refund the amounts paid, including interest. This claim was declared inadmissible on the ground that it was out of time under §58 of the Code of Administrative Court Procedure. The Federal Administrative Court, acting in third and final instance, referred some questions to the European Court of Justice. One of these questions concerned the legality of the time limit in §58 of the Code of Administrative Court Procedure.

Held: In the present state of Community law, there is nothing to prevent a citizen who contests before a national court a decision of a national authority on the ground that it is incompatible with Community law from being confronted with the defence that limitation periods laid down by national law have expired, it being understood that the procedural conditions governing the action may not be less favourable than those relating to similar actions of a domestic nature.

Judgment: Applying the principle of cooperation laid down in Article 5 of the Treaty, it is the national courts which are entrusted with ensuring the legal protection which citizens derive from the direct effect of the provisions of Community law.

Accordingly, in the absence of Community rules on this subject, it is for the domestic legal system of each Member State to designate the courts having jurisdiction and to determine the procedural conditions governing actions at law intended to ensure the protection of the rights which citizens have from the direct effect of Community law, it being understood that such conditions cannot be less favourable than those relating to similar actions of a domestic nature.

Where necessary, Articles 100 to 102 and 235 of the Treaty enable appropriate measures to be taken to remedy differences between the provisions laid down by law, regulation or administrative action in Member States if they are likely to distort or harm the functioning of the Common Market. In the absence of such measures of harmonization the right conferred by Community law must be exercised before the national courts in accordance with the conditions laid down by national rules.

The position would be different only if the conditions and time-limits made it impossible in practice to exercise the rights which the national courts are obliged to protect. This is not the case where reasonable periods of limitation of actions are fixed.

The laying down of such time-limits with regard to actions of a fiscal nature is an application of the fundamental principle of legal certainty protecting both the tax-payer and the administration concerned.

[3] ECLI:EU:C:1976:188.

Notes

(1) In this judgment, the European Court of Justice developed what later was called 'the principle of effectiveness'.[4] It is within the autonomy of the Member States to adopt national procedural rules as long as these rules meet two criteria:

(a) The conditions for actions intended to ensure the protection of the rights which citizens derive from EU law may not be less favourable than those relating to similar actions of a domestic nature (principle of equivalence).

(b) National procedural rules may not make it impossible or excessively difficult in practice to exercise the rights derived from EU law which the national courts are obliged to protect (principle of effectiveness).

(2) As such, some significant differences between the approaches of the various Member States are likely to be identified, even if there is a degree of harmonisation brought about through the decisions of the CJEU,[5] EU secondary law rules[6] and the approach of the European Court of Human Rights (ECtHR) to Article 6 ECHR[7] in such procedural matters. Throughout this chapter, one aspect of the analysis will be to consider whether it is possible to identify a growing harmonisation of procedural rules through a process of Europeanisation.

(3) When examining the approach of EU law, this chapter will consider only direct actions brought by claimants against a named defendant and will not consider preliminary ruling procedures dealing with questions of law referred by national courts. The reason for this is that only direct actions are directly analogous to judicial review proceedings in Member States, so serve most appropriately as points of comparison and analysis.

Council of Europe, Recommendation Rec(2004)20
of the Committee of Ministers to Member States
on Judicial Review of Administrative Acts **5.2 (COE)**

The Committee of Ministers, under the terms of Article 15 b of the Statute of the Council of Europe,

...

Recommends that the governments of member states apply, in their national legal system and in practice, the principles set out below:

[4] See, eg S Prechal and R Widdershoven, 'Redefining the Relationship between "Rewe-effectiveness" and Effective Judicial Protection' (2011) 4 *Review of European Administrative Law* 31.

[5] For an examination of the impact of EU law on national procedural autonomy, see D-U Galetta, *Procedural Autonomy of EU Member States: Paradise Lost?* (Berlin, Springer, 2010).

[6] On this issue, see the contributions to the special issue on proceduralisation of EU law in (2015) 8 *Review of European Administrative Law*.

[7] For an examination of the impact of the ECHR on administrative procedural law, see, eg European Court of Human Rights, *Guide to Article 6 of the European Convention on Human Rights: Right to a Fair Trial (Civil Limb)* (Strasbourg, Council of Europe, 2017); some discussion of the systems where administrative procedure is codified and the impact of Art 6 ECHR can also be found in the contributions to J-B Auby (ed), *Codification of Administrative Procedure* (Paris, Bruylant, 2014).

A. Definitions

For the purposes of this Recommendation,

1. By 'administrative acts' are meant:

legal acts – both individual and normative – and physical acts of the administration taken in the exercise of public authority which may affect the rights or interests of natural or legal persons;

situations of refusal to act or an omission to do so in cases where the administrative authority is under an obligation to implement a procedure following a request.

2. By 'judicial review' is meant the examination and determination by a tribunal of the lawfulness of an administrative act and the adoption of appropriate measures, with the exception of review by a constitutional court.

B. Principles

…

3. An independent and impartial tribunal

Judicial review should be conducted by a tribunal established by law whose independence and impartiality are guaranteed in accordance with the terms of Recommendation No. R (94) 12.

The tribunal may be an administrative tribunal or part of the ordinary court system.

4. The right to a fair hearing

The time within which the tribunal takes its decision should be reasonable in the light of the complexity of each case and of the procedural steps or postponements attributable to the parties, while respecting the adversary principle.

There should be equality of arms between the parties to the proceedings. Each party should be given an opportunity to present his or her case without being placed at a disadvantage.

Unless national law provides for exceptions in important cases, the administrative authority should make available to the tribunal the documents and information relevant to the case.

The proceedings should be adversarial in nature. All evidence admitted by the tribunal should in principle be made available to the parties with a view to adversarial argument.

The tribunal should be in a position to examine all of the legal and factual issues relevant to the case presented by the parties.

The proceedings should be public, other than in exceptional circumstances.

Judgment should be pronounced in public.

…

5.2 STEPS OF THE PROCEEDINGS

The steps of the proceedings are important because they govern the way in which the case is to be heard by the court and through which a decision will ultimately be adopted. The steps are thus intrinsic to the right to a fair trial, and each legal system has its own nuances in the way that cases must be brought and heard. The steps of the proceedings are, as will be seen, often linked to the approach of the judicial system to the hearing of administrative law cases. At the outset, a distinction that might be made between the systems under examination is that the majority of them deal with administrative proceedings as 'single-stage' proceedings, ie when a claim is submitted to the court there is the potential for the court to dispose of the case with a single hearing. The system in England and Wales is distinct because judicial review proceedings have two stages, the first where the claimant seeks permission to bring the claim and the second (in cases where permission is granted) where the claim is heard.

5.2.A SINGLE-STAGE PROCEEDINGS IN DUALISTIC COURT SYSTEMS

In all three systems, there are specific rules of procedure for administrative law courts which differ from those which apply to courts dealing with private law matters. There is generally a desire to ensure that proceedings are open, fair and transparent, with an opportunity for the parties to be heard. There is some difference over whether the proceedings are predominantly written, as in France,[8] or have written and oral components, as in the Netherlands[9] and Germany.[10]

5.2.A.1 SUMMARY PROCEEDINGS

Summary proceedings are a way in which courts can deal rapidly with cases that do not require a full hearing by nature of their merits or admissibility, or because the court lacks the jurisdiction to hear the case.

5.2.A.1 (i) France

Code de justice administrative **5.3 (FR)**

Article R222-1 The Presidents of the Administrative Courts of First Instance and the Administrative Courts of Appeal, the first Vice-presidents of Administrative Courts of First Instance and Administrative Courts of Appeal, the Vice-president of the Administrative Court of First Instance of Paris, the Presidents of the court formation of the Administrative Courts of First Instance and Administrative Courts of Appeal and the judges who have a seniority of a minimum of two years and have attained at least the rank of first councillor,[11] designated for that purpose by the president of their court, may, by ordinance:

1. Take formal note of withdrawals;
2. Dismiss applications that are clearly not within the jurisdiction of the administrative courts;
3. Find that there are no grounds to rule on an application;
4. Dismiss applications that are clearly inadmissible, in situations where the court is not bound to invite the authority that has adopted the act to correct them or if they have not been corrected on the expiry of the time limit set in a request to this end;

[8] This is a practice in the French administrative courts, rather than being mandated by law. See the website of the Conseil d'État at www.conseil-etat.fr/Conseil-d-Etat/Demarches-Procedures/L-examen-des-requetes-et-l-audience/Quelle-est-la-procedure-devant-le-juge-administratif for an example of the practice.

[9] See Arts 8:42 and 8:43 AWB for details of the initial stage of written proceedings in the Netherlands.

[10] See §84 VwGO, where, even in the case of summary decisions disposed of purely on written documents, parties have a right to request a court hearing if no route of appeal is available.

[11] This term refers to a rank attributed to Council of State judges according to the stage of their career in the court.

5. Rule on applications that do not pose any questions to judge on other than the penalty provided for in Article L761-1 or the burden of the costs;

6. Rule on applications that form part of a series which, without calling for new evaluation or legal assessment of the facts, pose the seized court questions, to be judged in law, that are identical to those that the court has already decided on by an identical decision that has the authority of a final court decision, or identical to questions decided on by an identical decision of the Council of State ruling on the questions at stake or dealt with by an opinion rendered by the Council of State according to Article L113-1 and, concerning the Administrative Court of First Instance, identical to questions that have been decided on by an identical judgment that has the authority of a final court decision by the Administrative Court of Appeal with jurisdiction over the case.

7. Dismiss, after the expiry of the appeal period or, when notice has been given of an additional statement, after that statement has been submitted, applications that only present arguments based on lack of jurisdiction, or formal and procedural defects that are clearly unfounded; inadmissible arguments; arguments that are ineffective because they will not led to the annulment of the act; or arguments that are only accompanied by facts that are clearly unable to support them or that are clearly not accompanied by details by which to assess the merits.

The Presidents of the Administrative Courts of Appeal, the first Vice-presidents of the Administrative Courts of Appeal and the Presidents of the court formation of the Administrative Courts of Appeal may also, by ordinance, dismiss submissions seeking to have the enforcement of a court decision which is subject to appeal suspended, appeals against ordinances made in accordance with points 1 to 5 of this Article as well as, after the expiry of the appeal period or, when notice has been given of an additional statement, after that statement has been submitted, appeals which are manifestly unfounded. They may also annul any ordinance made in accordance with points 1 to 5 of this Article, provided that they settle the merits of the case by applying one of these provisions.

Note

The power to make 'ordinances' allows a single judge to terminate a case that is unmeritorious, or precluded from proceeding due to one of the reasons outlined above, by delivering a short ruling. Where there are a number of cases based that raise questions which are identical to those decided upon in another case that has already been decided, the judge also has the power to determine these later cases through the adoption of an ordinance. Pursuant to the second section of Article R222-1 (No 7) of the Code de justice administrative, it is possible to appeal the adoption of an ordinance.

5.2.A.1 (ii) Germany

Verwaltungsgerichtsordnung **5.4 (DE)**

§84 (1) The court may rule by means of a summary decision (*Gerichtsbescheid*) without an oral hearing if the case does not show any particular factual or legal difficulties and the facts have been clarified. Those concerned shall be heard in advance. The provisions regarding judgments shall apply mutatis mutandis.

(2) Within one month of service of the summary decision, those concerned may

1. submit an appeal on grounds of fact and law if it has been admitted (§124a),

2. apply for admission of the appeal on grounds of fact and law or an oral hearing; if use is made of one of these remedies, an oral hearing shall take place,

3. submit an appeal on points of law if it has been admitted,

4. submit a complaint against non-admission (*Nichtzulassungsbeschwerde*) or request an oral hearing if the appeal on points of law has not been admitted; if use is made of one of these remedies, an oral hearing shall take place,

5. request an oral hearing if an appeal is not available.

(3) The summary decision shall have the effect of a judgment; if an oral hearing is requested in good time, the summary decision shall be deemed not to have been issued.

(4) If an oral hearing is requested, the court may in the judgment refrain from a further rendering of the facts and of the reasoning for the decision insofar as it concurs with the reasoning contained in the summary decision and establishes this in its decision.

Notes

(1) If the case does not show any particular factual or legal difficulties and the facts have been clarified, the court may rule by means of a summary decision (*Gerichtsbescheid*). Those concerned shall be heard in advance of such a decision being taken. The provisions regarding judgments apply mutatis mutandis, meaning that the court must still produce a judgment.

(2) Within one month of service of the summary decision, any of the parties to the action may file an appeal if an appeal is available or may apply for a hearing before the court if no appeal is available. Unless an appeal or application for a court hearing is made, the summary decision has the effect of a final judgment. However, it is argued that §84 of the Verwaltungsgerichtsordnung (VwGO) is problematic in terms of its compliance with Article 6(1) ECHR, which guarantees every person the right to an oral hearing.[12]

5.2.A.1 (iii) The Netherands

Algemene Wet Bestuursrecht **5.5 (NL)**

Article 8:54 (1) Until the parties have been invited to appear at a hearing of the court, the court may close the investigations if it is not necessary to continue the investigations because:

(a) the court lacks jurisdiction;

(b) the claim for judicial review is manifestly inadmissible;

(c) the claim for judicial review is manifestly unfounded, or

(d) the claim for judicial review is manifestly well-founded.

[12] See T Dünchheim, *Verwaltungsprozessrecht unter europäischem Einfluss* (Munich, CH Beck, 2003) 207 ff, concerning the reform of §84 VwGO that now allows the claimant to request an oral hearing, but still raises questions relating to the compatibility with Art 6(1) ECHR.

(2) When judgment is given after application of section 1, the attention of the parties shall be drawn to Article 8:55(1).

Article 8:55 (1) A party concerned and the defendant may oppose the judgment (*verzet doen*) referred to in Article 8:54(2), before the court.

Notes

(1) If the court lacks jurisdiction or if the claim for judicial review is manifestly inadmissible or manifestly well-founded or unfounded, the court can close the preliminary investigations and decide the case accordingly without having an oral hearing. In practice, this possibility is applied mainly in cases where the court lacks jurisdiction or where the claim for judicial review is manifestly inadmissible.

(2) A judgment in such a summary procedure may be opposed by an interested party before the court itself. In this so-called opposition procedure (*verzet*), this party may ask to be given an opportunity to be heard, in which case a hearing will generally take place. If the opposition is well-founded, the case will be continued with the ordinary procedure.[13] If the opposition is unfounded or inadmissible, this judgment is final. There is no possibility to appeal against it before a higher court.

5.2.A.1 (iv) Comparative Remarks

In each of the jurisdictions under examination, the summary procedure dispenses with the need for an oral hearing unless one is requested by one of the parties to the proceedings. In France, the court has the power to dismiss inadmissible claims without the need for a hearing. In Germany and the Netherlands, the court may also dispose of cases that are manifestly well founded in favour of the claimant, although in the Netherlands this is not a frequent practice. These processes clearly have considerable importance, as they allow for the rapid conclusion of cases which are well founded and also for the dismissal of cases where it is clear that they cannot proceed further, whether because they are not well founded, because the court lacks jurisdiction or because the case is plainly inadmissible. In Germany, there is presently some debate over whether the use of such summary proceedings is compatible with Article 6 ECHR in light of the possible lack of an oral hearing.

5.2.A.2 FULL PROCEEDINGS

In France, Germany and the Netherlands, cases that cannot be determined through the summary procedure are considered through the procedure for ordinary claims. The steps of the process are prescribed in law and are considered below.

[13] See section 5.2.A.2 (iii) below.

5.2.A.2 (i) France

Code de justice administrative **5.6 (FR)**

Article R611-1 The application and statements of the case, and the documents submitted by the parties, are filed with or sent to the court registry.

The application, any additional statement of which notice is given in the application and the first statement of case of the respondent are sent to the parties with the attachments under the conditions laid down in Articles R611-3, R611-5 and R611-6.

The statements in reply, any other statements of case and case materials are sent if they contain new information.

Article R611-3 The decisions taken during the preparatory phase are notified to the parties, at the same time as the copies, produced in compliance with Articles R411-3 ff and Article R412-2, of the applications, statements of case and documents filed with the court registry. The notice may be given in the form of ordinary letters.

However, the application, applications for rectification, formal notices, closure orders, decisions to resort to one of the preparatory steps provided for in Articles R621-1 to R626-3, and the information provided for in Article R611-7, are notified by means of letters signed for on delivery or any other means that can certify the date of receipt.

Notifications of applications and statements of case must mention that, if the time limit for submitting a document in accordance with Article R611-10 or Article R611-17 is not complied with, the preparatory stage may be closed under the conditions laid down in Articles R613-1 and R613-2 without any formal notice.

Article R611-9 Immediately after the application initiating proceedings has been registered at the court registry, the president of the Administrative Court of First Instance or, in Paris, the President of the Chamber to which the application has been transmitted appoints a judge-rapporteur (*juge rapporteur*).

A case may only be removed from a designated judge-rapporteur (*rapporteur désigné*) at his request and with the consent of the President of the Administrative Court of First Instance, or by decision of the President of the Administrative Court of First Instance.

Article R611-10 Under the authority of the President of the Chamber to which he belongs and with the assistance of the registrar of that chamber, the designated judge-rapporteur (*rapporteur désigné*) sets the time period to be granted to the parties to submit their statements, taking the circumstances of the case into account. He may ask the parties for all case materials or documents that are helpful to solve the dispute, to be submitted to the adversarial procedure.

The President of the court formation may delegate the powers that are vested upon him under Articles R611-7, R611-7-1, R611-8-1, R611-8-5, R611-11, R612-3, R612-5, R613-1, R613-1-1 and R613-4 to the reporting judge.

Article R611-11 When it is justified by the circumstances of the case, the President of the court formation may, as soon as the application has been registered, use the power provided for in Article R613-1(1) to set the date on which the investigation of the case of the case will be closed. When the ordinance is notified to the parties, they are informed of the date set for the hearing. This information does not replace the notice provided for in Article R711-2.

Article R611-11-1 When the case is ready for judgment, the parties may be informed of the date on which, or the period in which, the court envisages holding the hearing. This notice will specify the date from which the investigation of the case of the case may be closed under the conditions laid down in Article R613-1, final section, and in Article R613-2, final section. This does not replace the notice provided for in Article R711-2.

...

Article R611-13 When, after having been considered by the judge-rapporteur, the case is ready for the hearing, the case file is sent to the public rapporteur (*rapporteur public*). ...

Article R711-2 All the parties are informed, by means of a notice sent by registered letter signed for on delivery, or through the administrative channel mentioned in Article R611-4, of the day on which the case will be heard.

The notice of the hearing reproduces the provisions of Articles R731-3 and R732-1-1. It also specifies how the parties or their representatives may be informed of the content of the legal opinion of the public rapporteur (*rapporteur public*), in accordance with Article R711-3(1), or, if the case is covered by Article R732-1-1, of the decision taken on the exemption from the submission of the legal opinion of the public rapporteur (*rapporteur public*), in accordance with article R711-3(2).

Notice is given at least seven days before the hearing. However, in case of urgency, this time limit may be reduced to two days by an expedited decision of the President of the court formation with this decision being mentioned in the notice of the hearing. ...

Article R711-3 If the case is to be judged after the public rapporteur (*rapporteur public*) has delivered his legal opinion, the parties or their representatives are informed, before the hearing is held, of the content of this opinion for the case concerned.

When the case is liable to be exempted from the submission of a legal opinion of the public rapporteur (*rapporteur public*), in accordance with Article R732-1-1, the parties or their representatives are informed, before the hearing is held, whether the public rapporteur (*rapporteur public*) will deliver a legal opinion or not and, if he is not exempted from that, of the content of this opinion. ...

Article R732-1 After the report which is drawn up on each case by a member of the court formation or by the judge mentioned in Article R222-13, the public rapporteur (*rapporteur public*) delivers his opinion when prescribed by the provisions of this code. The parties may make observations, either in person, or through a lawyer authorized to plead before the Council of State and to the Court of Appeal, or through a lawyer, make observations in support of their written submissions.

When the public rapporteur (*rapporteur public*) does not deliver an opinion, especially under Article R732-1-1, the president will allow the parties the opportunity to make comments.

The court formation can also hear the officials from the competent administration or call on them, before [the court formation], to provide explanations.

Before the Administrative Court of First Instance, the President of the court formation may, during the hearing and in exceptional cases, seek clarifications from any person present at the hearing whom any of the parties would like to be heard.

Article R732-2 The decision is deliberated in the absence of the parties and of the public rapporteur (*rapporteur public*).

Notes

(1) *Preliminary steps:* In France, the applicant commences proceedings by submitting a written document outlining the basis of the claim.[14] This must be communicated in the French language and be signed by the claimant or the claimant's lawyer.[15] The claim must include the name and address of the parties and a copy of the administrative act that is to be challenged. The claim should be brought within two months of the date of notification of the administrative decision, other than in exceptional circumstances.[16]

The registrar of the court, under the supervision of the president of the court formation (ie the head of the chamber to which the case is affected), considers whether the main conditions of admissibility are fulfilled (eg whether the time limit is complied with, whether there is legal representation when compulsory and whether the formal aspects of the claim meet the requirements of the law).[17] In some cases, the registrar may ask the applicant to rectify the claim – due to lack of signature, for example. If the case is inadmissible, it will be rejected by a simple ordinance of the court signed by the head of the chamber.[18]

Admissible cases are assigned to a designated judge-rapporteur (*rapporteur désigné*).[19] The claim submitted by the applicant (and the evidence accompanying it) is sent to the defendant (the administrative body having taken the challenged decision), who will be asked to respond to it within a given time limit.[20] The response submitted by the defendant is communicated by the court to the plaintiff. Other submissions made by the parties are communicated to the other party only if the designated judge-rapporteur considers that the claim brings in new elements.[21] During this adversarial phase, the designated judge-rapporteur may also require documents (eg written evidence) from the party likely to possess such documents.[22] Should this request not be fulfilled, the judge may conclude that the facts alleged by the other party are established. The designated judge-rapporteur may also inform the parties that, when this is the case, *ex officio* pleas will be raised and give them the opportunity to submit statements on them.[23] There is no potential for proceedings to be paused in order to heal or repair procedural or other flaws.

(2) *Oral hearing:* Once the case is ready to be determined, the judge-rapporteur and the president of the court formation (who will both sit on the judging panel) separately analyse the case and come to a decision regarding the disposal of the case,

[14] Code de justice administrative, Art R611-1.
[15] The requirement for the claimant or lawyer to sign is found in Code de justice administrative, Art R611-2.
[16] For a discussion of the approach to time limits in France, see Chapter 4, section 4.7.B.3.
[17] Code de justice administrative, Art R222-1 empowers presidents to do this, but in practice this is frequently done by the registrar under the supervision of the president.
[18] Code de justice administrative, Art R222-1.
[19] Code de justice administrative, Art R611-9.
[20] Code de justice administrative, Art R611-1.
[21] ibid.
[22] Code de justice administrative, Art R611-10.
[23] Code de justice administrative, Art R611-7.

through the analysis of facts, legal provisions, case law, etc. The case is then transmitted to the public rapporteur (*rapporteur public*), who will also analyse the case and independently make his decision about the solution he would give in the case. During the public hearing, the public rapporteur (who does not sit on the panel) publicly and independently gives his opinion on the questions raised by the different cases and how they might best be resolved.[24] The parties or their representatives may also present observations (as the proceedings are mainly written, the public hearing is usually rather short, the parties being invited not to repeat the elements they have submitted to the court in their submissions, but rather to focus on the central issues of the case).[25] Each case is deliberated on after the public hearing by the judge-rapporteur, the head of the chamber and another judge, the three of them composing the ordinary judging panel.

5.2.A.2 (ii) Germany

Verwaltungsgerichtsordnung **5.7 (DE)**

§81 (1) The action shall be lodged with the court in writing. It may also be lodged at the administrative court for the record of the clerk of the registry.

(2) Duplicates for the other parties concerned should be enclosed with the action and all written statements subject to the provisions of §55a(5), third sentence.

§82 (1) The action must designate the plaintiff, the defendant and the subject matter of what is at stake in the action. It should contain a specific motion. The facts and evidence serving as reasoning should be stated; the original or a duplicate of the challenged act and the decision on the objection should be enclosed.

(2) If the action does not meet these requirements, the presiding judge or the competent professional judge (judge-rapporteur) in accordance with §21g of the Courts Constitution Act (Gerichtsverfassungsgesetz) shall call on the plaintiff to provide the required supplement within a specific period. He may set a final deadline to the plaintiff for the supplement if one of the requirements named in section 1, first sentence, is not met.

...

§85 The presiding judge shall order the action to be served on the defendant. At the same time as service, the defendant shall be called upon to make a written statement; §81(1), second sentence, shall apply mutatis mutandis. A deadline may be set for this.

§86 (1) The court shall investigate the facts *ex officio*; those concerned shall be consulted in doing so. It shall not be bound to the submissions and to the motions for the taking of evidence of those concerned.

(2) A motion for the taking of evidence made in the oral hearing may only be rejected by a court order, which shall be reasoned.

[24] Code de justice administrative, Art L7.

[25] Code de justice administrative, Art R732-1 deals with the ability of the parties to make oral observations, but the practice is to expect a focus on the central issues of the case.

(3) The presiding judge shall endeavour to ensure that formal errors are remedied, unclear requests explained, pertinent motions made, deficient factual information supplemented, as well as all declarations submitted which are material to the establishment and assessment of the facts.

(4) Those concerned shall submit written statements to prepare the oral hearing. The presiding judge can call on them to do so, setting a deadline. The written statements shall be communicated to those concerned *ex officio*.

(5) The originals or duplicates of the certificates or electronic documents to which reference is made shall be enclosed in full or in part with the written statements. If the certificates or electronic documents are already known to the opponent or are very extensive, the precise designation shall be sufficient, coupled with the offer to grant inspection in the court.

§87 (1) The presiding judge or the judge-rapporteur shall, prior to the oral hearing, issue all orders that are necessary to deal with the dispute, where possible, in one oral hearing. He may in particular

1. summon those concerned to discuss the facts and the dispute and to reach an amicable settlement of the dispute and accept a settlement;
2. instruct those concerned to supplement or explain their prepared written statements, submit certificates, transmit electronic documents and submit other objects for deposit with the court, in particular set a deadline to explain certain points that are in need of clarification;
3. obtain information;
4. order the submission of certificates or the transmission of electronic documents;
5. order the personal appearance of those concerned; …
6. summon witnesses and experts to the oral hearing.

(2) Those concerned shall be informed of each order.

(3) The president or the judge-rapporteur may take individual items of evidence. This may only take place insofar as it is expedient to simplify the hearing before the court and it can be presumed from the outset that the court is able to appreciate the result of the evidence properly, even without obtaining a direct impression of the course of the taking of evidence. …

§90 (1) The matter at dispute shall become pending by the action being lodged. …

§101 (1) The court shall rule on the basis of an oral hearing unless otherwise provided.

(2) The court may rule without an oral hearing with the consent of those concerned.

(3) Rulings of the court which are not judgments may be handed down without an oral hearing unless provided otherwise. …

§103 (1) The presiding judge shall open and chair the oral hearing.

(2) Once the case has been called, the presiding judge or the judge-rapporteur shall present the essential content of the files.

(3) In response to this, those concerned shall be afforded the opportunity to speak in order to make and reason their motions.

§104 (1) The presiding judge shall discuss the dispute with those concerned in factual and legal terms.

(2) The presiding judge shall on request afford each member of the court the opportunity to ask questions. If a question is objected to, the court shall decide.

(3) After the dispute has been discussed, the presiding judge shall declare the oral hearing to be closed. The court may decide on the reopening.

Notes

(1) *Preliminary steps:* If the action is not disposed of by summary decision,[26] after the reply has been received, the court examines the subject matter of the dispute in the presence of the parties without being bound by their pleadings or offer of evidence.[27] For oral proceedings, the parties should submit written briefs, for which the court may set a time limit. Pursuant to §87(1) VwGO, the presiding judge or the judge to whom the matter is assigned (the judge-rapporteur, or *Berichterstatter*) shall issue all orders prior to the oral hearing necessary to deal with the dispute in one oral hearing where possible. He may summon those concerned to discuss the facts and the dispute, to reach an amicable settlement of the dispute and to accept that settlement. He may also instruct those concerned to supplement or explain their prepared written statements, submit certificates, transmit electronic documents and submit other objects for deposit with the court, and in particular set a deadline to explain certain points that are in need of clarification. The presiding judge or judge-rapporteur may also obtain information, order the submission of certificates, the transmission of electronic documents or the personal appearance of those concerned, or summon witnesses and experts to the oral hearing *ex officio*. The court is thus required to facilitate and speed up the proceedings (*Konzentrationsmaxime*).

(2) *Oral hearing:* As soon as the date for the oral proceedings is fixed, the parties are informed of it. This must be at least two weeks in advance.[28] The notice informs the parties that if they do not appear on the date fixed for proceedings, the court may proceed and decide the matter in their absence and without their participation.[29] According to §101 VwGO, the court rules on the basis of an oral hearing unless otherwise provided. However, pursuant to §101(2) VwGO, the court may rule without an oral hearing with the consent of those concerned.[30]

The procedural steps of an oral hearing are outlined in §§103 and 104 VwGO. The presiding judge opens the oral proceedings on the assigned day in the presence of his colleagues on the panel by announcing the name of the parties to the action.[31]

[26] §85 VwGO.

[27] §86(1) VwGO.

[28] §102(1) VwGO. At the Federal Administrative Court, notice must be given no less than four weeks, between the date of service and the date of the hearing.

[29] §102(2) VwGO. There is no judgment by default (*Versäumnisurteil*) in the administrative court proceedings.

[30] The dispensation with the need for oral proceedings is problematic in the light of Art 6 ECHR, which guarantees the right to a hearing. See further, W Roth, 'Der Anspruch auf öffentliche Verhandlung nach Art 6 1 EMRK im verwaltungsgerichtlichen Rechtsmittelverfahren' (1998) *Europäische Grundrechte-Zeitschrift* 495.

[31] BVerfGE 42, 364, 369 (the calling of the case must take place in the court room and the waiting area); BVerwG NVwZ 1989, 857 (the court must not open the oral hearing if participants of the proceedings are only slightly late or even present in the building of the court but uninformed of the start of the oral proceedings).

Once the case has been called, the presiding judge or the judge-rapporteur shall present the essential content of the files. In response to this, the parties are given the opportunity to speak in order to make and reason their applications. The presiding judge chairs the oral proceedings and discusses the subject matter of the dispute with the parties on facts as well as on law. He also asks his fellow judges to raise any questions. If a question is objected to by the parties, the court decides on the admissibility of the question. After the discussion and questions, the presiding judge declares the oral proceedings closed.[32] The court records of the oral hearing are made in accordance with §159 and subsequent provisions of the Code of Civil Procedure.[33] Where nothing is stated to the contrary, the decision on an action is given in the form of a reasoned judgment.[34]

5.2.A.2 (iii) The Netherlands

Algemene Wet Bestuursrecht **5.8 (NL)**

Article 8:41a The administrative judge should decide a conflict which has been brought before him in a definitive manner as far as possible.

Article 8:42 (1) Within four weeks of the date on which the notice of the claim is sent to the administrative authority, the latter shall send the documents relating to the case to the court and lodge a defence.

(2) The administrative judge may extend the period referred to in section 1.

Article 8:43 (1) The administrative judge may give the person who has lodged the claim the opportunity to submit a written reply. In that case, the administrative authority shall be given the opportunity to submit a written rejoinder. The administrative judge shall fix the periods for reply and rejoinder.

(2) The administrative judge shall give parties other than those referred to in section 1 the opportunity at least once to state their views on the case in writing. He shall fix a period for this purpose.

Article 8:44 (1) The administrative judge may summon parties to appear in person or represented by an agent either to provide information or otherwise. If not all parties are summoned, the parties not summoned shall be given the opportunity to attend the hearing and give their views on the case.

(2) A record of the information provided shall be prepared by the registrar.

...

Article 8:45 (1) The administrative judge may request the parties and other persons to provide written information and lodge documents in their possession within a period to be specified by it.

(2) Administrative authorities are obliged to comply with a request as referred to in section 1 even if they are not party to the action. Article 8:29 shall apply mutatis mutandis.

...

32 Nonetheless, the court may decide on reopening the oral hearing (§104(3), second sentence VwGO).
33 §105 VwGO.
34 §§107–13 VwGO.

Article 8:46 (1) The administrative judge may summon witnesses.

(2) The administrative judge shall inform the parties at least one week in advance of the names and addresses of the witnesses, the place and time at which they will be heard and the facts to which the hearing will relate.

...

Article 8:51a (1) The administrative judge may grant the administrative authority the opportunity to repair or have repaired a flaw in the contested decision. The preceding sentence shall not apply if concerned persons who are not parties to the proceedings may thereby be disproportionately disadvantaged.

(2) The administrative judge shall determine the time limit within which the administrative authority may repair the flaw. He may extend this time limit.

Article 8:51b (1) As soon as possible, the administrative authority informs the judge of whether it will use the opportunity to repair or have the flaw repaired.

(2) If the administrative authority uses the opportunity to repair the flaw, it shall inform the judge as soon as possible in writing of the way in which the flaw has been repaired.

(3) Parties may, within four weeks after the information referred to in section 2 has been sent to them, submit their views in writing about the way in which the flaw has been repaired. The judge may extend this time limit.

Article 8:51c The administrative judge shall inform the parties of how the proceedings will continue within four weeks after:

a. the administrative authority informed it that it does not want to make use of the opportunity to repair the flaw;
b. the period referred to in Article 8:51a(2) has passed and the flaw has not been repaired;
c. it has received the views of the parties;
d. the period referred to in Article 8:51b(3) has passed and the flaw has not been repaired.

Article 8:51d If the administrative court decides as a last instance court, it may order the administrative authority to repair or have the flaw repaired. ...

Article 8:56 After the end of the preliminary examination the parties shall be invited at least three weeks in advance to appear at a session of the court at a time and place specified in the invitation.

Article 8:57 (1) If the parties have consented to this, the administrative judge may determine that there will not be an investigation in court. In such a case the administrative judge shall end the investigation.

(2) If the claim already has been dealt with orally and the administrative judge has applied Article 8:51a(2), he may decide without further oral investigations if:

a. the administrative authority has informed the court that it does not want to make use of the opportunity to repair the flaw;
b. the period as mentioned in Article 8:51a(2) has passed and the flaw has not been repaired;
c. he has received the views of the parties; or
d. the period as mentioned in Article 8:51b(3) has passed and no views have been received, except where parties would be thereby disadvantaged.

(3) If the administrative judge determines that the case can be decided without the further investigation, he closes the investigations.

Article 8:58 (1) The parties may submit additional documents up to ten days before the hearing.

(2) The attention of the parties shall be drawn to this right in the invitation referred to in Article 8:56.

Article 8:59 The administrative judge may summon a party either to appear in person or to appear either in person or represented by an agent, either for the purpose of giving information or otherwise. …

Article 8:65 (1) The administrative judge shall close the investigations in court if he considers that they have been completed.

(2) Before the investigations in court end, the parties shall be entitled to speak for the last time.

(3) As soon as the investigations in court have ended, the president shall announce when the judgment will be issued.

Notes

(1) *Preliminary investigation*: After a claim for judicial review is brought before the administrative judge, the preliminary investigation phase of the procedure begins. The administrative judge seeks a response from the administrative authority within four weeks and orders the authority to submit all documents which are relevant for the case. The administrative judge may give the claimant the opportunity to submit a written reply to the response of the administrative authority, in which case the administrative authority shall be given the opportunity to submit a written rejoinder. The administrative judge shall give parties other than the claimant and the authority (eg an interested party such as the holder of the contested permit) the opportunity on at least one occasion to state their views on the case in writing. The administrative judge, or an expert whom the administrative judge asks to do so, can carry out an investigation at the location where the dispute has arisen. The administrative judge may also summon the parties to appear in person either for the purpose of giving information or otherwise. The administrative judge may use this power in order to encourage the parties to agree on a settlement. Until a few years ago, this power was used only infrequently.

The most frequent method of proceeding is for the administrative judge to request the claimant and respondent, plus any other interested parties, to provide written information and to send in documents in their possession to the court. In cases with an obvious outcome, the summary procedure outlined above will be followed.[35]

(2) *Oral hearing:* When the administrative judge has prepared the case sufficiently, he will invite the parties for the public hearing. This is the end of the preliminary

[35] See section 5.2.A.1 (iii) above.

inquiry phase. A public hearing is required in all cases, except those which fall under the summary proceedings.[36] A hearing is not required if the parties agree that a hearing is not necessary.

Parties may submit new documents to the court up to ten days before the hearing takes place. This period is designed to ensure that parties can sufficiently prepare their pleas for the oral hearing. Therefore, the administrative judge may impose a time limit longer than ten days if the documents sent to the court are voluminous or complex. If the parties submit a document less than ten days prior to the hearing, the judge has discretion to determine whether the document nevertheless can be taken into account without infringing the principle of due process. Even documents which are provided at the hearing may be taken into account if it is considered appropriate to do so.

A party is not normally obliged to appear at the hearing, although a failure to attend may result in a procedural disadvantage for such a party. The administrative judge may summon a party to appear in person, or to appear in person or be represented by a legal representative. The power to require the attendance of parties is not often used. In this oral phase, the administrative judge may, on its own motion, summon witnesses and appoint experts and interpreters.[37] The administrative judge may adjourn the hearing for a certain period of time in order to resume the preliminary inquiry.[38]

The administrative loop (*bestuurlijke lus*) (Articles 8:51a ff of the Algemene Wet Bestuursrecht (AWB)) provides an important instrument in practice as it offers the potential to heal certain procedural defects in the decision-making phase, to provide a better basis for the decision or even to replace the contested decision with a new one, having weighed the interests again. This practice was already applied by the courts before 2013 (when it was called the 'unofficial administrative loop'), but a statutory 'loop' was included in the AWB in 2013. Since that time, the courts have applied this instrument very frequently. By doing so, the parties, particularly the authority, can react to what is discussed during the hearing so far. In many cases, this offers an efficient way to repair flaws in the decision-making procedure or in the content of the decision and hence to solve the case without the need to annul the contested decision. Therefore, the administrative loop is an important instrument to bring the dispute to a definite end, an obligation that is imposed on the administrative judge in Article 8:41a AWB.[39]

Before the hearing is closed, the parties shall have the right to speak for a final time. If, at the hearing or after the hearing is closed, it becomes obvious that there are still doubts and further investigations are necessary, the judge has the power to reopen the investigations phase.

[36] See Art 8:54 AWB.
[37] Art 8:60 AWB.
[38] Art 8:64 AWB.
[39] For the legal remedies available to the Dutch courts to provide a final settlement of disputes, see Chapter 7, sections 7.2 and 7.3.

Unless judgment is given orally immediately after the hearing, the administrative judge will give its judgment in writing within six weeks after closing the hearing. In special circumstances, the administrative judge may extend this time limit for a further six weeks.[40] There is no legal consequence if this time limit for releasing the judgment is exceeded. This occasionally happens in complex cases.

(3) *New case approach:* Since 2013, many courts have chosen to apply the so-called 'new case approach' (*nieuwe zaaksbehandeling*).[41] This approach serves two aims. First, to speed up the proceedings and to decide the case finally and definitely insofar as this is possible. The latter is a statutory duty for the courts.[42] The second aim is to address the 'real' conflict between the parties, and to try to find a way to solve it. In this respect, it is of importance that in many cases the conflict between a citizen and the authorities goes beyond the decision contested in the concrete case and is also concerned with, for example, the way the authorities have treated the citizen or whether his interests were taken seriously. In order to address the wider conflict, and possibly solve it, the oral hearing is scheduled as soon as possible, as otherwise the relationship between the authorities and the individual will deteriorate further. In practice, the hearing now takes place within 13 weeks after the case has been submitted to the court.[43] Before the introduction of the 'new case approach', the hearing was generally scheduled 10 months to 1 year after the case was brought to the court. At the hearing, the administrative judge actively investigates what the 'real' conflict is and may suggest alternative ways to solve it, eg by agreeing on a settlement or by submitting the conflict to mediation. If the parties are not willing to pursue these alternatives, the administrative judge will clarify what the parties may expect of the formal route. In this regard, the administrative judge will inform the parties what the decisive legal questions are and, if possible, what its preliminary legal opinion is about the outcome of the case. Parties may also be informed of issues which still have to be proven, in order to change the preliminary legal opinion of the court. After the hearing, the case is closed, awaiting the possible reactions of the parties. Depending on those, the administrative judge will either reopen the case or come to a final judgment.

(4) *Fast track:* There is a fast-track procedure, which the administrative judge can apply on its own motion or on the request of one of the parties, if the case is 'urgent'.[44] The administrative judge may then reduce the time limits and may wholly or partly exclude the application of the requirements in Articles 8:43(2) and 8:47(3) AWB.

[40] Art 8:66 AWB.

[41] For more information on the 'new case approach', see A Verburg and B Schueler, 'Procedural Justice in Dutch Administrative Court Proceedings' (2014) 10 *Utrecht Law Review* 56.

[42] Art 8:41a AWB.

[43] This period of 13 weeks cannot be found in the AWB or elsewhere in the statutes.

[44] Art 8:52 AWB.

5.2.B SINGLE-STAGE PROCEEDINGS IN A MONISTIC COURT SYSTEM: THE EUROPEAN UNION

5.2.B.1 SUMMARY PROCEEDINGS

It is possible for both the Court of Justice and the General Court to deliver summary judgments without pursuing the full procedure for hearings in some circumstances. This process serves the same objectives as in the legal systems outlined above.

Rules of Procedure of the Court of Justice **5.9 (EU)**

Article 53 Procedures for dealing with cases

...

(2) Where it is clear that the Court has no jurisdiction to hear and determine a case or where a request or an application is manifestly inadmissible, the Court may, after hearing the Advocate General, at any time decide to give a decision by reasoned order without taking further steps in the proceedings.

Note

The Court of Justice can issue a reasoned order at any stage of the proceedings before it in order to dispose of cases where an application is manifestly inadmissible. It is generally the case that the defendant in a case will raise a preliminary objection,[45] arguing the manifest inadmissibility of the case. The Court may then decide to allow an oral hearing on the issue of manifest inadmissibility or, in cases where the case is clearly inadmissible, may dispose of the case via a reasoned order without an oral hearing taking place.[46] The General Court may also determine that a case is manifestly inadmissible in a similar fashion[47] and has an additional power to determine that a case before it manifestly lacks foundation in law, although it may only do so if there is no aspect of the proceedings where the outcome turns on an assessment of the facts of the case.[48]

[45] Under the provisions of Art 151 of the Rules of Procedure of the Court of Justice.

[46] See, eg Case C-224/03 *Italy v Commission* ECLI:EU:C:2003:658.

[47] Rules of Procedure of the General Court, Art 111.

[48] ibid. For a detailed treatment of the power of the General Court, see K Lenaerts, A Maselis and K Gutman, *EU Procedural Law*, 2nd edn (Oxford, Oxford University Press, 2014) paras 23.40 and 25.45.

5.2.B.2 FULL PROCEEDINGS

Statute of the Court of Justice of the European Union **5.10 (EU)**

Article 20 The procedure before the Court of Justice shall consist of two parts: written and oral.

The written procedure shall consist of the communication to the parties and to the institutions of the Union whose decisions are in dispute, of applications, statements of case, defences and observations, and of replies, if any, as well as of all papers and documents in support or of certified copies of them.

Communications shall be made by the Registrar in the order and within the time laid down in the Rules of Procedure.

The oral procedure shall consist of the reading of the report presented by a Judge acting as Rapporteur, the hearing by the Court of agents, advisers and lawyers and of the submissions of the Advocate-General, as well as the hearing, if any, of witnesses and experts.

Where it considers that the case raises no new point of law, the Court may decide, after hearing the Advocate-General, that the case shall be determined without a submission from the Advocate- General.

Article 21 A case shall be brought before the Court of Justice by a written application addressed to the Registrar. The application shall contain the applicant's name and permanent address and the description of the signatory, the name of the party or names of the parties against whom the application is made, the subject-matter of the dispute, the form of order sought and a brief statement of the pleas in law on which the application is based.

The application shall be accompanied, where appropriate, by the measure the annulment of which is sought or, in the circumstances referred to in Article 265 of the Treaty on the Functioning of the European Union, by documentary evidence of the date on which an institution was, in accordance with those Articles, requested to act. If the documents are not submitted with the application, the Registrar shall ask the party concerned to produce them within a reasonable period, but in that event the rights of the party shall not lapse even if such documents are produced after the time limit for bringing proceedings.

...

Article 23 In the cases governed by Article 267 of the Treaty on the Functioning of the European Union, the decision of the court or tribunal of a Member State which suspends its proceedings and refers a case to the Court of Justice shall be notified to the Court by the court or tribunal concerned. The decision shall then be notified by the Registrar of the Court to the parties, to the Member States and to the Commission, and to the institution, body, office or agency of the Union which adopted the act the validity or interpretation of which is in dispute.

Within two months of this notification, the parties, the Member States, the Commission and, where appropriate, the institution, body, office or agency which adopted the act the validity or interpretation of which is in dispute, shall be entitled to submit statements of case or written observations to the Court.

In the cases governed by Article 267 of the Treaty on the Functioning of the European Union, the decision of the national court or tribunal shall, moreover, be notified by the Registrar of the Court to the States, other than the Member States, which are parties to the Agreement on the European Economic Area and also to the EFTA Surveillance Authority referred to in that Agreement which may, within two months of notification, where one of the fields of application of that Agreement is concerned, submit statements of case or written observations to the Court.

Where an agreement relating to a specific subject matter, concluded by the Council and one or more non-member States, provides that those States are to be entitled to submit statements of case or written observations where a court or tribunal of a Member State refers to the Court of Justice for a preliminary ruling a question falling within the scope of the agreement, the decision of the national court or tribunal containing that question shall also be notified to the non-member States concerned. Within two months from such notification, those States may lodge at the Court statements of case or written observations.

...

Article 36 Judgments shall state the reasons on which they are based. They shall contain the names of the Judges who took part in the deliberations.

Rules of Procedure of the Court of Justice **5.11 (EU)**

Article 61 Measures of organisation prescribed by the Court

(1) In addition to the measures which may be prescribed in accordance with Article 24 of the Statute, the Court may invite the parties or the interested persons referred to in Article 23 of the Statute to answer certain questions in writing, within the time-limit laid down by the Court, or at the hearing. The written replies shall be communicated to the other parties or the interested persons referred to in Article 23 of the Statute.

(2) Where a hearing is organised, the Court shall, in so far as possible, invite the participants in that hearing to concentrate in their oral pleadings on one or more specified issues.

...

Article 63 Decision on measures of inquiry

(1) The Court shall decide in its general meeting whether a measure of inquiry is necessary.

(2) Where the case has already been assigned to a formation of the Court, the decision shall be taken by that formation.

Article 64 Determination of measures of inquiry

(1) The Court, after hearing the Advocate General, shall prescribe the measures of inquiry that it considers appropriate by means of an order setting out the facts to be proved.

(2) Without prejudice to Articles 24 and 25 of the Statute, the following measures of inquiry may be adopted:

(a) the personal appearance of the parties;

(b) a request for information and production of documents;

(c) oral testimony;

(d) the commissioning of an expert's report;

(e) an inspection of the place or thing in question.

(3) Evidence may be submitted in rebuttal and previous evidence may be amplified.

...

Article 76 Hearing

(1) Any reasoned requests for a hearing shall be submitted within three weeks after service on the parties or the interested persons referred to in Article 23 of the Statute of notification of the close of the written part of the procedure. That time-limit may be extended by the President.

(2) On a proposal from the Judge-Rapporteur and after hearing the Advocate General, the Court may decide not to hold a hearing if it considers, on reading the written pleadings or observations lodged during the written part of the procedure, that it has sufficient information to give a ruling.

(3) The preceding section shall not apply where a request for a hearing, stating reasons, has been submitted by an interested person referred to in Article 23 of the Statute who did not participate in the written part of the procedure.

...

Article 133 Decision relating to the expedited procedure

(1) At the request of the applicant or the defendant, the President of the Court may, where the nature of the case requires that it be dealt with within a short time, after hearing the other party, the Judge-Rapporteur and the Advocate General, decide that a case is to be determined pursuant to an expedited procedure derogating from the provisions of these Rules.

(2) The request for a case to be determined pursuant to an expedited procedure must be made by a separate document submitted at the same time as the application initiating proceedings or the defence, as the case may be, is lodged.

(3) Exceptionally the President may also take such a decision of his own motion, after hearing the parties, the Judge-Rapporteur and the Advocate General.

Article 134 Written part of the procedure

(1) Under the expedited procedure, the application initiating proceedings and the defence may be supplemented by a reply and a rejoinder only if the President, after hearing the Judge-Rapporteur and the Advocate General, considers this to be necessary.

(2) An intervener may submit a statement in intervention only if the President, after hearing the Judge-Rapporteur and the Advocate General, considers this to be necessary.

Article 135 Oral part of the procedure

(1) Once the defence has been submitted or, if the decision to determine the case pursuant to an expedited procedure is not made until after that pleading has been lodged, once that decision has been taken, the President shall fix a date for the hearing, which shall be communicated forthwith to the parties. He may postpone the date of the hearing where it is necessary to undertake measures of inquiry or where measures of organisation of procedure so require.

(2) Without prejudice to Articles 127 and 128, a party may supplement his arguments and produce or offer evidence during the oral part of the procedure. The party must, however, give reasons for the delay in producing such further arguments or evidence.

Notes

(1) *Preliminary steps:* The written procedure has the purpose of defining the subject matter of the action and to put before the Court of Justice and the General Court all the grounds of the dispute between the parties.

A case is brought before the Court of Justice or the General Court by addressing an application to the Registrar.[49] At that point, the case becomes pending before the Court of Justice or the General Court, and the Registrar serves the application on the defendant[50] and ensures that notice is given in the Official Journal of the European Union of the date of registration of the application initiating proceedings, the name of the parties, the form of order sought by the applicant, and a summary of the pleas in law and of the main supporting arguments.[51]

The defendant has two months following service upon it of the application in which to lodge a defence.[52] The president of the Court of Justice or the General Court, as the case may be, may decide to extend this time limit upon a reasoned request by the defendant, although this extension might be granted only in exceptional circumstances.[53]

After the defence has been lodged, the applicant may supplement his application by lodging a reply within a time limit prescribed by the president of the court. The defendant may then lodge a rejoinder on the same terms.[54] If the party allows the relevant period to expire without lodging such a pleading or if it waives its right to do so, the proceedings continue.[55]

After the rejoinder has been lodged or the parties have refrained from lodging a reply or a rejoinder,[56] the written procedure comes to an end and the president fixes a date on which the judge-rapporteur is to present the preliminary report to the Court of Justice or the General Court.[57]

If, despite the fact that the application was duly served on the defendant, the latter fails to lodge a defence in the proper form within the prescribed time limit, the applicant may apply for an order to be granted. In this situation, the Court of Justice or

[49] Statute of the Court of Justice, Art 21(1). For the content of the application, see Art 21(1) of the Statute of the Court of Justice, Art 120 of the Rules of Procedure of the Court of Justice and Art 44 of the Rules of Procedure of the General Court. See also Lenaerts et al (ibid) 759–62.

[50] Rules of Procedure of the Court of Justice, Art 123; Rules of Procedure of the General Court, Art 45.

[51] Rules of Procedure of the Court of Justice, Art 21(4); Rules of Procedure of the General Court, Art 24(6). The purpose of the notice on the C series of the Official Journal is to put EU institutions, Member States and legal and natural persons on notice of the proceedings, giving them the opportunity of intervening. Special rules apply with the notification to the Commission, the European Parliament and the Council (Art 125 of the Rules of Procedure of the Court of Justice and Art 24(7) of the Rules of Procedure of the General Court).

[52] Rules of Procedure of the Court of Justice, Art 124(1); Rules of Procedure of the General Court, Art 46(1). For the content of the defence, see the same; see also Lenaerts et al (n 49) 759–62.

[53] Rules of Procedure of the Court of Justice, Art 124(3); Rules of Procedure of the General Court, Art 46(3).

[54] Rules of Procedure of the Court of Justice, Art 126(1) and (2); Rules of Procedure of the General Court, Art 47(1) and (2).

[55] Rules of Procedure of the Court of Justice, Art 59(1); Rules of Procedure of the General Court, Art 52(1). Note that in proceedings before the General Court the court may decide, after hearing the Advocate General, that a second exchange of pleadings is unnecessary because the documents before it are sufficiently comprehensive to enable the parties to elaborate their pleas and arguments in the course of the oral procedure (Rules of Procedure of the General Court, Art 47(1)).

[56] Or the General Court decided that the application and the defence do not need supplementing.

[57] Rules of Procedure of the Court of Justice, Art 59(1); Rules of Procedure of the General Court, Art 52(1).

General Court may decide to give judgment 'by default'.[58] Before doing so, the Court of Justice or General Court, after hearing the Advocate General, considers whether the application initiating proceedings is admissible, whether the appropriate formalities have been complied with and whether the application appears to be well founded.[59] The court will then decide whether to open the oral hearing relating to the application or to grant the applicant's claim. In such cases, only the applicant will be heard.

(2) *Oral hearing:* The oral procedure consists of 'the hearing by the Court of agents, advisers and lawyers and of the submission of the Advocate General, as well as the hearing, if any, of witnesses and experts', as noted in Article 20(3) of the Statute of the Court of Justice.

The oral part should not be considered as a default moment of the procedure. First of all, there is no oral hearing if the court deems the case manifestly inadmissible or manifestly unfounded.[60] Furthermore, under Article 76 of the Rules of Procedure of the Court of Justice, the Court of Justice may decide without an oral hearing if both parties agree or if, on a proposal from the judge-rapporteur and after hearing the Advocate General, it considers, on reading the written pleadings or observations lodged during the written part of the procedure, that it has sufficient information to give a ruling. There is no equivalent of this provision in the Rules of Procedure of the General Court, so proceedings before the General Court must include a hearing.

At the hearing, the parties present their arguments orally, after which the president, judge and Advocate General may put questions to the agents, advisers or lawyers of the parties.[61] This gives the possibility of elucidating any aspects remaining unclear. The oral part is closed by the president after the Advocate General has been heard.[62] After the closure of the oral proceedings, the parties listed in Article 23 of the Statute of the Court of Justice will be informed of a date when the judgment of the court will be delivered.

(3) *Expedited procedure:* It is possible for the president of the court to agree to an expedited procedure for a hearing in appropriate cases.[63] In cases where the expedited procedure is used before the CJEU, the parties will not ordinarily be permitted to submit a written reply or rejoinder in the proceedings unless the president of the court, after hearing the judge-rapporteur and Advocate General, decides that this

[58] Statute of the Court of Justice, Art 41; Rules of Procedure of the Court of Justice, Art 152(1); Rules of Procedure of the General Court, Art 122(1). See, eg Case C-274/93 *Commission v Luxembourg* ECLI:EU:C:1996:160.

[59] Rules of Procedure of the Court of Justice, Art 152(3); Rules of Procedure of the General Court, Art 122(2).

[60] Rules of Procedure of the Court of Justice, Art 151; and Rules of Procedure of the General Cour, Art 111t.

[61] Rules of Procedure of the Court of Justice, Art 80; Rules of Procedure of the General Court, Art 58.

[62] Rules of Procedure of the Court of Justice, Art 81; for the General Court, where an AG has not been designated or has presented his conclusions in writing at the end of the hearing, see Arts 60 and 61(2) of the Rules of Procedure of the General Court.

[63] Rules of Procedure of the Court of Justice, Arts 133–35. Similar rules can be found in Arts 151–55 of the Rules of Procedure of the General Court.

is necessary.[64] In the expedited procedure, this has the effect of enhancing the importance of the oral part of the proceedings, as this is where the arguments of the parties will be supplemented and evidence will be provided.[65]

5.2.C DUAL-STAGE PROCEEDINGS IN A MONISTIC COURT SYSTEM: ENGLAND AND WALES

The process in England and Wales is different to that in the other jurisdictions under consideration in a number of respects, not least because one might argue that the system as a whole, even that for the lodging of a judicial review claim, is focused on resolving the dispute between the parties without the need for legal proceedings. It was noted in Chapter 2 that there is an expectation that all public authorities should have in place an intra-administrative objection procedure, and the courts will normally expect this to be followed prior to the lodging of a judicial review claim.[66] In addition to this, the vast majority of claimants are expected to follow the pre-action protocol before commencing judicial review proceedings.

Pre-action Protocol for Judicial Review[67] **5.12 (EW)**

The letter before claim

14. In good time before making a claim, the claimant should send a letter to the defendant. The purpose of this letter is to identify the issues in dispute and establish whether they can be narrowed or litigation can be avoided.

15. Claimants should normally use the suggested standard format for the letter outlined at Annex A.

…

16. The letter should contain the date and details of the decision, act or omission being challenged, a clear summary of the facts and the legal basis for the claim. It should also contain the details of any information that the claimant is seeking and an explanation of why this is considered relevant.

…

The letter of response

20. Defendants should normally respond within 14 days using the standard format at Annex B. Failure to do so will be taken into account by the court and sanctions may be imposed unless there are good reasons. Where the claimant is a litigant in person, the defendant should enclose a copy of this Protocol with its letter.

21. Where it is not possible to reply within the proposed time limit, the defendant should send an interim reply and propose a reasonable extension, giving a date by which the defendant expects to respond substantively. Where an extension is sought, reasons

[64] Rules of Procedure of the Court of Justice, Art 134(1). Similar rules can be found for the General Court in Arts 154–55 of the Rules of Procedure of the General Court.

[65] Rules of Procedure of the Court of Justice, Art 135(2).

[66] See Chapter 2, section 2.7 for more detail on this issue.

[67] Available at www.justice.gov.uk/courts/procedure-rules/civil/protocol/prot_jrv.

should be given and, where required, additional information requested. This will not affect the time limit for making a claim for judicial review, nor will it bind the claimant where he or she considers this to be unreasonable. However, where the court considers that a subsequent claim is made prematurely it may impose sanctions.

22. If the claim is being conceded in full, the reply should say so in clear and unambiguous terms.

23. If the claim is being conceded in part or not being conceded at all, the reply should say so in clear and unambiguous terms, and–

(a) where appropriate, contain a new decision, clearly identifying what aspects of the claim are being conceded and what are not, or, give a clear timescale within which the new decision will be issued;

(b) provide a fuller explanation for the decision, if considered appropriate to do so;

(c) address any points of dispute, or explain why they cannot be addressed;

(d) enclose any relevant documentation requested by the claimant, or explain why the documents are not being enclosed;

(e) where documents cannot be provided within the time scales required, then give a clear timescale for provision. The claimant should avoid making any formal application for the provision of documentation/information during this period unless there are good grounds to show that the timescale proposed is unreasonable;

(f) where appropriate, confirm whether or not they will oppose any application for an interim remedy; and

(g) if the claimant has stated an intention to ask for a protective costs order, the defendant's response to this should be explained.

Note

Parties seeking to bring a judicial review claim and defendant public authorities are not required by law to follow the pre-action protocol. However, failure by either the claimant or the defendant to follow the pre-action protocol may have consequences in terms of the award of costs, as the court may decide to make an order of costs with adverse consequence to the parties that do not comply.[68] The pre-action protocol itself makes it clear that engaging steps required by the pre-action protocol does not pause the time limit for bringing a claim for judicial review, so it is important for the parties to be aware of this fact.[69] The provisions of the protocol acknowledge that its use would not be appropriate in urgent cases, such as in those cases where the claim relates to impending removal of an individual from the UK in immigration cases or in cases relating to homelessness where state support for housing has been refused.[70]

Senior Courts Act 1981 **5.13 (EW)**

Section 31 (3) No application for judicial review shall be made unless the leave of the High Court has been obtained in accordance with rules of court; and the court shall

[68] See, eg *R (Aegis Group Plc) v Inland Revenue Commissioners* [2005] EWHC 1468 (Ch), [2006] STC 23.
[69] See para 1 of the Pre-Action Protocol.
[70] See para 6 of the Pre-Action Protocol.

not grant leave to make such an application unless it considers that the applicant has a sufficient interest in the matter to which the application relates.

(3C) When considering whether to grant leave to make an application for judicial review, the High Court–

(a) may of its own motion consider whether the outcome for the applicant would have been substantially different if the conduct complained of had not occurred, and

(b) must consider that question if the defendant asks it to do so.

(3D) If, on considering that question, it appears to the High Court to be highly likely that the outcome for the applicant would not have been substantially different, the court must refuse to grant leave.

(3E) The court may disregard the requirement in section (3D) if it considers that it is appropriate to do so for reasons of exceptional public interest.

(3F) If the court grants leave in reliance on section (3E), the court must certify that the condition in section (3E) is satisfied.

Civil Procedure Rules **5.14 (EW)**

Rule 54.4 The court's permission to proceed is required in a claim for judicial review whether started under this section or transferred to the Administrative Court.

…

Rule 54.6 (1) In addition to the matters set out in rule 8.2 (contents of the claim form) the claimant must also state–

(a) the name and address of any person he considers to be an interested party;

(b) that he is requesting permission to proceed with a claim for judicial review; and

(c) any remedy (including any interim remedy) he is claiming; and

(d) where appropriate, the grounds on which it is contended that the claim is an Aarhus Convention claim.

…

(2) The claim form must be accompanied by the documents required by Practice Direction 54A.

Service of claim form

Rule 54.7 The claim form must be served on–

(a) the defendant; and

(b) unless the court otherwise directs, any person the claimant considers to be an interested party,

within 7 days after the date of issue.

…

Rule 54.10 (1) Where permission to proceed is given the court may also give directions.

(2) Directions under paragraph (1) may include–

(a) a stay of proceedings to which the claim relates;

…

Rule 54.11 The court will serve–

(a) the order giving or refusing permission; and

(ai) any certificate (if not included in the order) that permission has been granted for reasons of exceptional public interest in accordance with section 31(3F) of the Senior Courts Act 1981; and

(b) any directions,
on–
(i) the claimant;
(ii) the defendant; and
(iii) any other person who filed an acknowledgment of service.

Rule 54.11A (1) This rule applies where the court wishes to hear submissions on–

(a) whether it is highly likely that the outcome for the claimant would not have been substantially different if the conduct complained of had not occurred; and if so

(b) whether there are reasons of exceptional public interest which make it nevertheless appropriate to give permission.

(2) The court may direct a hearing to determine whether to give permission.

(3) The claimant, defendant and any other person who has filed an acknowledgment of service must be given at least 2 days' notice of the hearing date.

(4) The court may give directions requiring the proceedings to be heard by a Divisional Court.

(5) The court must give its reasons for giving or refusing permission.

Rule 54.12 (1) This rule applies where the court, without a hearing–

(a) refuses permission to proceed; or
(b) gives permission to proceed–
(i) subject to conditions; or
(ii) on certain grounds only.

(2) The court will serve its reasons for making the decision when it serves the order giving or refusing permission in accordance with rule 54.11.

(3) Subject to paragraph (7), the claimant may not appeal but may request the decision to be reconsidered at a hearing.

(4) A request under paragraph (3) must be filed within 7 days after service of the reasons under paragraph (2).

(5) The claimant, defendant and any other person who has filed an acknowledgment of service will be given at least 2 days' notice of the hearing date.

(6) The court may give directions requiring the proceedings to be heard by a Divisional Court.

(7) Where the court refuses permission to proceed and records the fact that the application is totally without merit in accordance with rule 23.12, the claimant may not request that decision to be reconsidered at a hearing.

Note

An application for judicial review in England and Wales will not be heard unless the court has granted permission to proceed. Once the claimant has submitted the claim form[71] and the associated evidence and documents, a date for the hearing of the claim will be set.[72] The usual practice is that permission cases are submitted on paper,

[71] The claim form, known as Form N461, is available at http://formfinder.hmctsformfinder.justice.gov.uk/n461-eng.pdf.

[72] The requirements are to be found in Rule 54.6 CPR and Practice Direction 54A, paras 5.6–5.8, available at www.justice.gov.uk/courts/procedure-rules/civil/rules/part54/pd_part54a.

and hearings will only be ordered where the court deems it to be necessary in light of the complexities of the claim or uncertainties in the written documents, or where the claim on the papers is initially refused and the applicant seeks an oral hearing. If the claimant is not successful at the written stage of proceedings, it is possible for a re-submission of an application to take place. At this stage, the claimant will be given an oral hearing.[73] In the oral hearing, it is primarily for the claimant to make the case that permission should be granted, taking into account the reasons given by the judge for refusal of permission at the initial stage. The defendant may attend the proceedings and contest any grant of permission, although it has generally been held that the oral hearing on the issue of permission is not an appropriate time to rehearse all of the factual matters pertaining to the case, but should simply offer an overview of the main reasons why permission is being sought and, if the public authority is present and represented, its main reasons for resisting the permission application.[74] It should be noted that since 2013, Rule 54.12(7) of the Civil Procedure Rules (CPR) has contained a provision permitting the court hearing a written application to declare it 'totally without merit'. If this is done, it is not possible for the claimant to seek an oral re-hearing of the permission application. The courts have adopted a narrow interpretation of when a claim may be said to be 'totally without merit' and generally require that cases should only be certified 'totally without merit' if the judge is convinced that the claim is certain to fail.[75] If the application is refused at the oral hearing, it is possible for a claimant to seek the permission of the Court of Appeal to appeal against the refusal of permission.[76] Very few claimants, having failed at both the written and oral hearing stage in the High Court, seek to pursue this route.

House of Lords, 2 November 2000[77] **5.15 (EW)**

R v Secretary of State for Trade and Industry, ex parte Eastaway

JURISDICTION; APPEAL; PERMISSION STAGE

Eastaway

The House of Lords does not have jurisdiction to hear an appeal from the Court of Appeal concerning the permission stage of judicial review proceedings.

Facts: Eastaway was facing disqualification as a company director through proceedings brought against him by the Secretary of State. Eastaway claimed judicial review of the Secretary of State's decision to proceed against him and was denied permission to proceed both by the High Court and on appeal to the Court of Appeal. The Court of Appeal refused to grant Eastaway permission to appeal to the House of Lords and Eastaway sought to appeal the refusal.

[73] See Rule 54.12(3) CPR.

[74] *R (Mount Cook Land Ltd) v Westminster City Council* [2003] EWCA Civ 1346, [2017] PTSR 1166.

[75] See, eg *R (Grace) v Secretary of State for the Home Department* [2014] EWCA Civ 1091, [2014] 1 WLR 3432.

[76] See Part 52 CPR for the process.

[77] [2000] 1 WLR 2222 (HL).

Held: The House of Lords held not to have jurisdiction to hear Eastaway's appeal.

Judgment: Lord Bingham: The requirement of permission to apply for judicial review is imposed primarily to protect public bodies against weak and vexatious claims. The requirement of permission to appeal is imposed primarily to protect the courts against the burden of hearing and adjudicating on appeals with no realistic chance of success. The purpose of these filters is different, even though there is an incidental benefit to the courts in the first case and the successful litigant (or both litigants) in the second.

Despite the applicant's argument, I see no escape from this conclusion. Nor should the House, in my opinion, seek to escape from it. In its role as a supreme court the House must necessarily concentrate its attention on a relatively small number of cases recognised as raising legal questions of general public importance. It cannot seek to correct errors in the application of settled law, even where such are shown to exist. In this case it is not suggested that the decision of Buxton L.J. raises any legal question of general public importance. The House has not, because of its decision on jurisdiction, heard argument on the merits of the applicant's complaint, but these have now been considered in detail by two judges of the High Court and one Lord Justice of Appeal, and it would both stultify the requirement of permission to appeal to the Court of Appeal and subvert the true function of the House if it were now open to the applicant to invite the House to review the merits of his complaint for a fourth time. Whatever sympathy one may have for the applicant personally, the House must apply the law as it stands and adhere to its true constitutional role.

Note

The purpose of the permission stage is to act as a filter – claimants without standing will not be permitted to proceed and the court will also consider whether there is an arguable case should the claim be permitted to go forward to a full hearing. As the *Eastaway* case demonstrates, there is no appeal to what is now the Supreme Court if the Court of Appeal ultimately denies the request for permission to proceed.

Civil Procedure Rules **5.16 (EW)**

Part 8

Rule 8.1 (1) The Part 8 procedure is the procedure set out in this Part.

...

Rule 8.2 Where the claimant uses the Part 8 procedure the claim form must state–

(a) that this Part applies;

(b)

(i) the question which the claimant wants the court to decide; or

(ii) the remedy which the claimant is seeking and the legal basis for the claim to that remedy;

(c) if the claim is being made under an enactment, what that enactment is;

(d) if the claimant is claiming in a representative capacity, what that capacity is; and

(e) if the defendant is sued in a representative capacity, what that capacity is.

...

Rule 8.5 (1) The claimant must file any written evidence on which he intends to rely when he files his claim form.

(2) The claimant's evidence must be served on the defendant with the claim form.

(3) A defendant who wishes to rely on written evidence must file it when he files his acknowledgment of service.

(4) If he does so, he must also, at the same time, serve a copy of his evidence on the other parties.

(5) The claimant may, within 14 days of service of the defendant's evidence on him, file further written evidence in reply.

(6) If he does so, he must also, within the same time limit, serve a copy of his evidence on the other parties.

(7) The claimant may rely on the matters set out in his claim form as evidence under this rule if the claim form is verified by a statement of truth.

...

Rule 8.8 (1) Where the defendant contends that the Part 8 procedure should not be used because–

(a) there is a substantial dispute of fact; and

(b) the use of the Part 8 procedure is not required or permitted by a rule or practice direction,

he must state his reasons when he files his acknowledgment of service.

(2) When the court receives the acknowledgment of service and any written evidence it will give directions as to the future management of the case.

Part 54

Rule 54.18

The court may decide the claim for judicial review without a hearing where all the parties agree.

Practice Direction 54A – Judicial Review[78] **5.17 (EW)**

Skeleton arguments

15.1 The claimant must file and serve a skeleton argument not less than 21 working days before the date of the hearing of the judicial review (or the warned date).

15.2 The defendant and any other party wishing to make representations at the hearing of the judicial review must file and serve a skeleton argument not less than 14 working days before the date of the hearing of the judicial review (or the warned date).

15.3 Skeleton arguments must contain:

(1) a time estimate for the complete hearing, including delivery of judgment;

(2) a list of issues;

(3) a list of the legal points to be taken (together with any relevant authorities with page references to the passages relied on);

(4) a chronology of events (with page references to the bundle of documents (see paragraph 16.1);

[78] Available at www.justice.gov.uk/courts/procedure-rules/civil/rules/part54/pd_part54a.

(5) a list of essential documents for the advance reading of the court (with page references to the passages relied on) (if different from that filed with the claim form) and a time estimate for that reading; and

(6) a list of persons referred to.

Bundle of documents to be filed

16.1 The claimant must file a paginated and indexed bundle of all relevant documents required for the hearing of the judicial review when he files his skeleton argument.

16.2 The bundle must also include those documents required by the defendant and any other party who is to make representations at the hearing.

Note

Once permission to proceed has been granted, the court will give directions as to the next steps, and a date for the full hearing of the case will be set. The usual practice is for the parties to produce an agreed statement of facts (as illustrated by the fact that Rule 54.6 CPR refers directly to a claim procedure under Part 8 CPR, which deals with claims where there is no substantial dispute of facts). This is illustrated by the approach to skeleton arguments (the indication of the arguments to be put forward by the parties, and the case law and legislation relied upon to support the legal submissions) and the bundle of documents, which envisages that the parties will collaborate on its content. The full hearing will thus focus on the legal arguments of the parties, led by the advocates for the parties or the parties themselves (if the parties are not represented). It is not usual for the court to engage in any aspect of a contested procedure, such as the hearing of witnesses or experts, although this is possible should the case require it.[79] Once the parties have put forward their arguments, the court will deliver judgment. It is possible that judgment will be delivered orally at the end of the hearing, with written reasons to follow, or, in appropriate cases, the judge will reserve judgment and then a judgment will be delivered at a later date to be set by the court.

5.2.D COMPARATIVE REMARKS

There is a fundamental difference between the approach of the systems in France, the Netherlands and Germany when contrasted with that in England and Wales. The French, German and Dutch legal systems all allow claims to proceed to court without any initial scrutiny of their suitability, whereas the system in England and Wales requires each potential claimant to seek permission to proceed before a judicial review claim can proceed to full hearing. The EU system evidently draws upon the civilian legal tradition in its approach, as in direct actions there is no process of filtering, although there are strict requirements in terms of standing, as illustrated in Chapter 4.[80]

[79] See section 5.3.B below; see also the *Tweed* case, excerpt 5.32.

[80] See on this point Chapter 4, section 4.4.

Other than at the EU level, each system under analysis endeavours to reduce the number of disputes coming before the courts in judicial review through the use of intra-administrative objection procedures.[81] In addition to this, in England and Wales there is an additional expectation that claimants for judicial review will follow the pre-action protocol, delivering a further opportunity for the dispute to be resolved prior to the commencement of judicial review proceedings. This does not appear to be a feature of any other legal system under analysis.

As noted above, there is a clear distinction to be drawn between the two-stage procedure in England and Wales and the single-stage process in all other systems under analysis. However, although the process for bringing the claim is different, it may be that the practical differences that this brings about are not so great. In the French and EU legal systems, judges have the power to issue summary judgments to dispose of cases that are manifestly ill-founded or otherwise unsuitable to proceed further. In Germany and the Netherlands, it is also possible for cases that are manifestly well-founded to succeed at the stage of summary judgment. In England and Wales, these cases would be filtered out at the permission stage. So, in all systems there are processes that deliver a similar function, although in France, the EU and England and Wales it is only possible for a claimant to be unsuccessful in summary proceedings as the court will be taking steps to dispose of the case as it is ill-founded, whereas in Germany and the Netherlands there is also the potential to dispose of cases in such a manner that the claimant can succeed.

In the Netherlands, it is possible for judges to pause judicial review proceedings in order to offer the opportunity for the parties to resolve their dispute if this is deemed to be appropriate by the judge. This is not possible in the other systems, or at least, there are no specific legal provisions that provide for this opportunity. In England and Wales, it may be that after the hearing at the permission stage the parties resolve the dispute without proceeding to full hearing, but there is little reliable statistical evidence to reveal how frequently this occurs. It is possible for the parties to seek the judge's consent to stay proceedings in order to seek a resolution to their dispute out of court, but if this is done and a new decision is reached, it is not generally possible for a claimant to seek to restart the proceedings in order to challenge the new decision – this is generally possible only by commencing new proceedings.[82]

In each legal system under analysis, judges enjoy broad powers to manage the case, including powers to hear evidence, call witnesses and require the parties to provide information to the court. The major difference between the systems, as we will see as the chapter progresses, lies in the practice of the court in the way that these powers are used. In England and Wales, powers to call witnesses, require discovery of documents or hear additional evidence are very seldom used because the expectation is that the parties will have resolved any disputes of fact in advance of the hearing. The French, German and EU legal systems adopt a more inquisitorial approach, where such powers are more regularly used, although, as the discussion in section 5.3 below will illustrate, there are still

[81] See on this point Chapter 2, section 2.7.

[82] *R (on the application of Bhatti) v Bury MBC* [2013] EWHC 3093 (Admin), (2014) 17 CCL Rep 64.

substantial differences in approach between the evidence regimes adopted in the different jurisdictions under examination.

5.3 EVIDENCE REGIME

The evidence regime in each jurisdiction is important as this is the method through which claimants can support the claims that they bring. Legal systems that adopt an inquisitorial approach frequently allow for a detailed evidence regime in administrative law cases in order to fully test the arguments put forward in the case. In the systems where the approach is adversarial, or where judicial review proceedings focus mainly or exclusively on questions of law, evidence regimes may be more limited, allowing less opportunity for claimants to adduce evidence before the court. Some systems also limit the potential for substantial evidential disputes and extensive provision of evidence in order to expedite proceedings and to reduce the burden on administrative courts. This section of the chapter will examine a number of issues, with a focus on whether proceedings might have a significant oral element or are predominantly written, the means through which the court may receive evidence and the burden of proof incumbent on the parties.

Case 199/82, 9 November 1983[83] **5.18 (EU)**

Amministrazione delle Finanze dello Stato v SpA San Giorgio

EVIDENCE; BURDEN OF PROOF; PRINCIPLES OF EQUIVALENCE AND EFFECTIVENESS

San Giorgio

National rules on the provision of evidence in cases involving the vindication of rights accrued from EU law must not violate the principles of equivalence or effectiveness.

Facts: The claimant brought proceedings against the Italian Ministry of Finance seeking recovery of charges paid for the inspection of its produce. The charges had been declared unconstitutional by the Italian Constitutional Court due to their incompatibility with the requirements of EU law. The Ministry of State resisted the repayment of the charges because the claimant was unable to provide documentary proof that no part of the charges that it had been paid had been passed on to another party. The claimant argued that such a rigid and restrictive rule of evidence was contrary to EU law, and the President of the Tribunale di Trento made a preliminary reference to the CJEU requesting clarification on whether restrictive rules of evidence such as the one in this case were contrary to EU law.

Held: If a rule of evidence in national law is very restrictive, it may offend the principle of effectiveness contained in EU law.

Judgment: 12 In that connection it must be pointed out in the first place that entitlement to the repayment of charges levied by a Member State contrary to the rules of Community law is a consequence of, and an adjunct to, the rights conferred on individuals by the Community provisions prohibiting charges having an effect equivalent to customs duties or, as the case may be, the discriminatory application of internal taxes. Whilst it is true

[83] ECLI:EU:C:1983:318.

that repayment may be sought only within the framework of the conditions as to both substance and form, laid down by the various national laws applicable thereto, the fact nevertheless remains, as the court has consistently held, that those conditions may not be less favourable than those relating to similar claims regarding national charges and they may not be so framed as to render virtually impossible the exercise of rights conferred by Community law …

13 However, as the court has also recognized in previous Decisions, and in particular in the aforesaid judgment in *Just v Ministry for Fiscal Affairs*, Community law does not prevent a national legal system from disallowing the repayment of charges which have been unduly levied where to do so would entail unjust enrichment of the recipients. There is nothing in Community law therefore to prevent courts from taking account, under their national law, of the fact that the unduly levied charges have been incorporated in the price of the goods and thus passed on to the purchasers. Thus national legislative provisions which prevent the reimbursement of taxes, charges, and duties levied in breach of Community law cannot be regarded as contrary to Community law where it is established that the person required to pay such charges has actually passed them on to other persons.

14 On the other hand, any requirement of proof which has the effect of making it virtually impossible or excessively difficult to secure the repayment of charges levied contrary to Community law would be incompatible with Community law. That is so particularly in the case of presumptions or rules of evidence intended to place upon the taxpayer the burden of establishing that the charges unduly paid have not been passed on to other persons or of special limitations concerning the form of the evidence to be adduced, such as the exclusion of any kind of evidence other than documentary evidence. Once it is established that the levying of the charge is incompatible with Community law, the court must be free to decide whether or not the burden of the charge has been passed on, wholly or in part, to other persons.

…

16 The national court also asks the Court of Justice whether rules restricting the repayment of charges levied contrary to Community law are compatible with the principles of the EEC Treaty when they are not applied identically to every national tax, charge or duty. In that regard it refers to the judgments in which, after stating that the extent to which it is possible to contest charges unlawfully claimed or to recover charges unduly paid differs in the various Member States, and even within a single Member State, according to the type of tax or charge in question … the court emphasized that individuals who seek to enforce rights by virtue of provisions of Community law may not be treated less favourably than persons who pursue similar claims on the basis of domestic law.

17 It must be pointed out in that regard that the requirement of non-discrimination laid down by the court cannot be construed as justifying legislative measures intended to render any repayment of charges levied contrary to Community law virtually impossible, even if the same treatment is extended to taxpayers who have similar claims arising from an infringement of national tax law. The fact that rules of evidence which have been found to be incompatible with the rules of Community law are extended, by law, to a substantial number of national taxes, charges and duties or even to all of them is not therefore a reason for withholding the repayment of charges levied contrary to Community law.

18 The reply to the first question must therefore be that a Member State cannot make the repayment of national charges levied contrary to the requirements of Community law conditional upon the production of proof that those charges have not been passed on to

other persons if the repayment is subject to rules of evidence which render the exercise of that right virtually impossible, even where the repayment of other taxes, charges or duties levied in breach of national law is subject to the same restrictive conditions.

Note

The *San Giorgio* case demonstrates that, while Member States are free to decide upon their own rules of evidence autonomously, the principles of equivalence and effectiveness in EU law apply to national rules of evidence where these rules impact upon the ability of a claimant to vindicate rights that flow to them by virtue of EU law. In particular, on the basis of the principle of effectiveness, any requirement of proof which has the effect of making it virtually impossible or excessively difficult to secure enforcement of the rights conferred by EU law would be incompatible with this principle.

Charter of Fundamental Rights of the European Union **5.19 (EU)**

Article 47 Right to an effective remedy and to a fair trial

...

Everyone is entitled to a fair and public hearing within a reasonable time by an independent and impartial tribunal previously established by law. Everyone shall have the possibility of being advised, defended and represented.

Note

The Charter of Fundamental Rights of the European Union secures the right to a fair trial in relation to all rights and obligations flowing from EU law. In addition to the provisions of Article 47 of the Charter of Fundamental Rights, one can also consider the role of Article 6 ECHR in influencing the jurisprudence of the CJEU on the fairness of evidence regimes.

Case C-276/01, 10 April 2003[84] **5.20 (EU)**

Joachim Steffensen

EVIDENCE REGIME, PRINCIPLES OF EQUIVALENCE AND EFFECTIVENESS; ARTICLE 6(1) ECHR

Steffensen

National rules on evidence must comply with the principles of equivalence and effectiveness and must also be compliant with the requirements of Article 6(1) ECHR in order to meet the requirements of EU law.

Facts: Mr Steffensen worked for a German food manufacturer. Samples of the company's products were taken on behalf of the relevant German administrative authority from some retailers where its products were

[84] ECLI:EU:C:2003:228.

stocked and were analysed at a laboratory. These tests determined that the products did not meet the requirements of German food standards legislation. It was not possible for Mr Steffensen or his employers to get a second opinion from another laboratory on the tests as samples were not available. German law permitted the evidence gleaned from the samples to be admitted in court as evidence despite the fact that it was not possible for Mr Steffensen or his employers to challenge that evidence through the seeking of a second opinion. Mr Steffensen argued that the admission of evidence such as this was contrary to the principles of equivalence and effectiveness, and also infringed Article 6(1) ECHR.

Held: The national court must determine, in light of the procedural rules that operate in the case before it, whether the rules permit the principles of equivalence and effectiveness to be met and for Article 6(1) ECHR to be satisfied. The court must ensure that each of these requirements is met in order to ensure compliance with EU law.

Judgment: 54. Mr Steffensen claims that it follows from, in particular, the fundamental right to a fair hearing and the principle of equality of arms arising from that right that the results of analyses of foodstuff samples which, as in the case in the main proceedings, it was not possible to challenge by way of a second opinion cannot be used as evidence.

55. The German Government submits essentially that the question whether such evidence is to be excluded if it is obtained improperly is a procedural matter which is not governed by Community law and therefore falls within the scope of national law, subject, however, to observance of the Community principles of equivalence and effectiveness.

56. According to the German Government, in a case such as that at issue in the main proceedings German law does not impose a general prohibition on the admission of evidence obtained in an improper administrative procedure. The principles of German procedural law, in particular those relating to *ex officio* investigations and the free evaluation of evidence, make it possible to challenge the results of irregular analyses. In addition, those national principles are not contrary to the Community principles of equivalence and effectiveness.

...

58. The Commission submits that neither the Directive nor the fundamental rights guaranteed by Community law establish an absolute prohibition on the use of the results of analyses on which it has not been possible to obtain a second opinion.

59. That view is supported by the use of the word 'may' in the second subparagraph of Article 7(1), which confirms that a second opinion need not be possible in all cases but only in those cases in which it may prove useful to the defence of the rights of the person subject to inspection. Moreover, the Commission concurs with the Danish Government's argument that the fundamental right to a fair hearing is not applicable in the case in the main proceedings since it concerns an administrative act and not judicial proceedings.

...

64. It must therefore be examined whether national rules such as the provisions of German law on the taking of evidence referred to in paragraph 56 of this judgment are compatible with the abovementioned principles of equivalence and effectiveness.

65. The Court notes that there is nothing in the case documents submitted to it which casts doubt on the compatibility of those provisions of German law with the principle of equivalence. However, the national court must consider that point in the light of all the factual and legal evidence available to it in order to guarantee observance of that principle.

66. With respect to the principle of effectiveness, the Court observes that each case which raises the question whether a national procedural provision renders application of Community law impossible or excessively difficult must be analysed by reference to the role of that provision in the procedure, its progress and its special features, viewed

as a whole, before the various national instances and that, in the light of that analysis, the basic principles of the domestic judicial system, such as protection of the rights of the defence, the principle of legal certainty and the proper conduct of procedure, must, where appropriate, be taken into consideration (see Case C-312/93 *Peterbroeck* [1995] ECR I-4599, paragraph 14).

67. Thus, the German procedural rule that evidence, such as the results of analyses, which has been obtained in an irregular administrative procedure remains, as a general rule, admissible in subsequent appeal proceedings can, according to the German Government, be explained by certain basic principles of German law, in particular those relating to *ex officio* investigations and the free evaluation of evidence, which make it possible to challenge that evidence effectively.

68. In the main proceedings, the national court must consider whether, in the light of all the factual and legal evidence available to it, the provisions of German law governing the taking of evidence do in fact allow an infringement of the right to a second opinion to be taken into consideration so that the application of those provisions to the case in the main proceedings cannot be regarded as rendering enjoyment of the guarantees provided by that right to a second opinion impossible or excessively difficult.

72. In this case, account must be taken, more specifically, of the right to a fair hearing before a tribunal, as laid down in Article 6(1) of the ECHR and as interpreted by the European Court of Human Rights.

...

75. It should be noted, next, that, it follows from the case-law of the European Court of Human Rights that Article 6(1) of the ECHR does not lay down rules on evidence as such and, therefore, it cannot be excluded as a matter of principle and in the abstract that evidence obtained in breach of provisions of domestic law may be admitted. According to that case-law, it is for the national courts to assess the evidence they have obtained and the relevance of any evidence that a party wishes to have produced (see *Mantovanelli v France*, judgment of 18 March 1997, Reports of Judgments and Decisions 1997-II, § 33 and 34; and *Pélissier and Sassi v France*, judgment of 25 March 1999, Reports of Judgments and Decisions 1999-II, § 45).

76. However, according to the same case-law, the review carried out by the European Court of Human Rights under Article 6(1) of the ECHR of the fairness of a hearing – which requires essentially that the parties be given an adequate opportunity to participate in the proceedings before the court – relates to the proceedings considered as a whole, including the way in which evidence was taken.

77. Lastly, it should be observed that the European Court of Human Rights has held that, where the parties are entitled to submit to the court observations on a piece of evidence, they must be afforded a real opportunity to comment effectively on it in order for the proceedings to reach the standard of fairness required by Article 6(1) of the ECHR. That point must be examined, in particular, where the evidence pertains to a technical field of which the judges have no knowledge and is likely to have a preponderant influence on the assessment of the facts by the court (see *Mantovanelli*, cited above, § 36).

78. It is for the national court to assess whether, in the light of all the factual and legal evidence available to it, the admission as evidence of the results of the analyses at issue in the main proceedings entails a risk of an infringement of the adversarial principle and, thus, of the right to a fair hearing. In the context of that assessment, the national court will have to examine, more specifically, whether the evidence at issue in the main proceedings pertains to a technical field of which the judges have no knowledge and is likely to have a preponderant influence on its assessment of the facts and, should this be

the case, whether Mr Steffensen still has a real opportunity to comment effectively on that evidence.

79. If the national court decides that the admission as evidence of the results of the analyses at issue in the main proceedings is likely to give rise to an infringement of the adversarial principle and, thus, of the right to a fair hearing, it must exclude those results as evidence in order to avoid such an infringement.

Note

The *Steffensen* case and later decisions of the Court of Justice have emphasised the requirement that evidence regimes applicable where rights and obligations flowing from EU law are at stake should be complaint with Article 6(1) ECHR. This has been further considered by the Court of Justice in later cases, all of which have emphasised that the requirements of Article 6(1) are an important aspect of the requirements of EU law in respect of evidence.[85]

5.3.A REGIMES OPEN TO EVIDENCE AT THE ORAL HEARING AND ALSO IN WRITING

Some regimes frequently hear much of the evidence at the oral hearing. This might be expected to some extent in systems that adopt an inquisitorial approach, as such an approach allows the judge to challenge the evidence and seek additional information. In Germany, the Netherlands, the EU and France, much evidence will be provided to the court in advance of the hearing in writing, although each system also permits the hearing of evidence at the oral hearing. The balance to be struck between the written and oral parts of the proceedings depends, as will be seen, on the approach adopted in each of the systems under consideration.

5.3.A.1 GERMANY

Verwaltungsgerichtsordnung **5.21 (DE)**

§96 (1) The court shall take evidence at the oral hearing. It may in particular inspect evidence and question witnesses, expert witnesses and those concerned, and consult certificates.

…

§97 Those concerned shall be informed of all evidence-taking dates and can attend the taking of evidence. They may address pertinent questions to witnesses and to expert witnesses. If an objection is raised against a question, the court shall decide.

[85] See, eg Case C-300/11 *ZZ v Secretary of State for the Home Department* ECLI:EU:C:2013:363; Case C-437/13 *Unitrading Ltd v Staatssecretaris van Financiën* ECLI:EU:C:2014:2318.

§98 Unless this Act contains any derogations, §§358 to 444 and 450 to 494 of the Code of Civil Procedure shall apply mutatis mutandis to the taking of evidence.

...

§100 (1) Those concerned can inspect the court files and the files submitted to the court. Those concerned can ask at their own costs duplicates, excerpts, printouts and copies from the registry. ...

§108 (1) The court shall rule in accordance with its free conviction gained from the overall outcome of the proceedings. The judgment shall state the grounds which were decisive in forming the conviction of the court.

(2) The judgment may only be based on facts and results of evidence on which those concerned have been able to make a statement.

Notes

(1) As a general rule, all proceedings in the administrative courts are oral (*Grundsatz der Mündlichkeit*) unless provided otherwise.[86] An appeal on grounds of fact and law (*Berufung*) can take place without an oral hearing if there are only questions of law to be decided.[87] Any other exceptions to the requirement of oral proceedings must be made by law. For example, according to §47(5), the VwGO procedure to review by-laws and executive regulations may also be decided without an oral hearing by order.[88] A violation of the right to an oral hearing constitutes a procedural error within the meaning of §132(2), No 3 VwGO[89] and §138, No 3 VwGO, which allows the aggrieved party to appeal on points of law. Furthermore, the right to an oral hearing is also embedded in Article 6(1) ECHR.[90]

As a matter of principle, the parties or their legal representatives shall be present during the court proceedings. The court can even order the parties to attend in person, and may threaten them with an administrative fine in the event of non-attendance.[91] Nonetheless, as noted above, §102(2) VwGO also allows the court to decide on the case in the absence of the parties, if the parties were informed about this beforehand. However, it is beneficial to the parties to be present in person or legally represented as the court takes evidence during the oral hearing.[92]

(2) The proceedings are characterised by the principle of direct evidence (*Grundsatz der Unmittelbarkeit*) in the sense that all evidence is recorded during the oral proceedings in the court except when a judge is authorised by law to record it on

86 §101(1)–(3) VwGO.

87 BVerwG, NVwZ 2004, 108.

88 However, according to BVerwGE 110, 203 and BVerwG, NVwZ 2002, 87, a hearing must be held in case of an action according to §47 VwGO if Art 6(1) ECHR is at stake.

89 BVerwG, NJW 1995, 2308; BVerwG, NVwZ 2003, 1130.

90 Therefore, the Bundesverfassungsgericht interprets the provisions on the appeals decision in light of Art 6 ECHR: §125(2), second sentence and §130a VwGO, which allow for a decision without oral hearing by order, are compatible with Art 6(1) ECHR only if the parties have a right to one oral hearing with regard to the review of the facts, BVerwG, NVwZ 2004, 108, 109.

91 §95 VwGO.

92 §96 VwGO.

commission or some other court has been requested to record it.[93] Thus, during the oral hearing, the court performs the examination of eye witnesses, experts and parties, and the documents produced upon request.[94] Moreover, a judgment may only be rendered by the judges and honorary judges who took part in the proceedings on which the judgment is based (as only these judges will have heard the evidence adduced by the parties).[95] In addition, the judgment is to be based solely on facts and evidence on which parties have had an opportunity to be heard.[96] An exception to the principle of direct evidence is made by §96 VwGO, which allows the court to appoint one judge acting as a commissioned judge to take evidence prior to the court hearing or request another court to take specific evidence in suitable cases.[97] However, this is only legitimate where the indirect gathering of evidence is sufficient to enable the court to provide a well-reasoned judgment even though the court had no direct personal impression on that particular piece of evidence.[98]

According to §97 VwGO, the parties are informed of all the dates when evidence is taken and are entitled to be present during all evidence hearings. They may address expedient questions to normal witnesses and to expert witnesses. If an objection is raised against a question, the court decides.

(3) The court may order the administrative authority to provide any information and to submit certificates or files, or transmit electronic documents, relevant to the disposal of a dispute.[99] The competent supreme or supervisory authority may, however, decline to obey if, in its opinion, the disclosure of the content of a document or record, or any other information, will be detrimental to the interests of the federation or state, or if the law or the nature of the proceedings requires them to be kept confidential and secret.[100] The opinion of the authority in this regard is not conclusive. On request of a party, the court may examine whether the legal requirements for not transmitting any document, record or information are satisfied.[101] If the court is satisfied that substantial reasons exist for not submitting a document, record or information, it may uphold the claim of the administrative authority and ask it to produce the required document, record or information, as the case may be. If the authority still fails to provide the document, an adverse interference may be drawn against it.

(4) According to §86 VwGO, the court investigates the facts *ex officio*. Only where the court cannot clarify the facts and a non liquet occurs, the burden of proof becomes relevant in German administrative court procedure law. In respect of an action for annulment (*Anfechtungsklage*), the public authority has the burden of proof with

[93] See further W Berg, 'Grundsätze des verwaltungsgerichtlichen Verfahrens' in H-U Erichsen, W Hoppe and A von Mutius (eds), *System des verwaltungsgerichtlichen Rechtsschutzes, Festschrift für Ch-F Menger* (Cologne, Carl Heymanns, 1985) 537–56; Roth (n 31 above).
[94] §96(1) VwGO.
[95] §112 VwGO.
[96] §108(2) VwGO.
[97] §96(2) VwGO. See also BVerwG NJW 1998, 3369.
[98] See BVerwG, NJW 1994, 1975.
[99] §99 VwGO.
[100] §99(2) and (3) VwGO.
[101] §99(2) VwGO.

regard to all facts which support the decision of the authority in its issuance of a burdensome administrative act. In an action seeking the issuance of an administrative act (*Verpflichtungsklage*), the burden of proof rests with the public authority, which has to demonstrate why the citizen is not granted a certain permission if the refusal of the permission interferes with fundamental rights. However, there are exceptions.[102]

(5) Generally, illegally gathered evidence can also be considered by administrative courts. Only where the gathering or the utilisation of the evidence seriously infringes the general right of privacy of a person may the evidence be excluded.[103]

5.3.A.2 THE NETHERLANDS

Algemene Wet Bestuursrecht **5.22 (NL)**

Article 8:60 (1) The administrative judge may summon witnesses and appoint experts and interpreters.

(2) A witness who has been summoned or an expert or interpreter who has accepted his appointment and is summoned by the administrative judge shall be required to comply with the summons. …

(3) The invitation [to the hearing] shall, as far as possible, state the names and addresses of the witnesses and experts who have been summoned and the facts about which they will be heard or the instructions to be carried out.

(4) The parties may bring witnesses and experts or summon witnesses and experts by registered letter or bailiff's writ, provided they have sent the administrative court and the other parties notice thereof, stating names and addresses, at least ten days before the date of the hearing ….

Article 8:63 …

(2) The administrative judge may decide not to hear witnesses and/or experts brought or called by a party if he considers that this cannot reasonably be expected to contribute to the assessment of the case.

Notes

(1) The key approach of the evidence regime is the fact that the administrative judge is *dominus litis* and investigates the facts of the case actively. However, scholars have argued that the Dutch legal system has witnessed a change to a more adversarial process where the parties, rather than the judge, get the lead role and the role

[102] See WR Schenke, *Verwaltungsprozessrecht*, 15edn (Heidelberg, CF Müller, 2017) para 22 ff.

[103] For details, see M Dawin, in F Schoch, J-P Schneider and W Bier (eds) *Verwaltungsgerichtsordnung*, 32nd edn (Munich, CH Beck, 2016) §86 para 113 ff.

of the judge is more limited and lenient.[104] In diverse areas of administrative law, there are tailor-made evidence rules which apply only to the respective decision or area of law.[105] There are very few general (written) rules about the evidence regime. Most important is Article 8:60 AWB, containing both the right of the administrative judge to appoint experts and to summon experts or witnesses to be present at the hearing and the right of the parties to bring their own witnesses and experts to the hearing. At the hearing, the administrative judge will generally hear these witnesses and experts, although he may refrain from hearing party witnesses and experts if he considers that this cannot reasonably contribute to the assessment of the case (Article 8:63(2) AWB).

The administrative judge will generally also hear the parties or their representatives about evidential issues. These issues may include witness and expert statements and expert reports, but also all other documents and statements that have been brought forward by the other party or the court itself during the preliminary investigations or at the hearing. In the Netherlands, there is no rule under which all evidence should be taken orally. The judge may use all facts, statements of witnesses, expert opinions, written documents and oral contributions to the hearing as evidence. He may, in principle, weigh all those elements freely.

(2) If evidence is gathered illegally, this does not necessarily mean that it may not be taken into account. In this regard, the administrative judge is not required to be as strict as the criminal judge. Illegally gathered evidence is, however, excluded if an 'important' rule is 'substantially' violated.[106]

(3) According to Article 3:2 AWB, the administrative authority is obliged to examine the facts of a case brought before it in order to be able to take a sound decision. Hence, the burden of proof is not always, as in civil law cases, on the one who makes a claim, but is often on the administrative authority that was obliged to examine the facts of the case. However, this requirement is not absolute. If, as an example, the applicant for a certain decision is the only one able to deliver the relevant information necessary to decide on his application, he is obliged to deliver this information and the authority's duty to investigate is limited accordingly.[107] Furthermore, citizens have to cooperate in order to make the investigations by the authorities possible.[108] The burden of proof shifts if the party who had the burden of proof has proven facts to a reasonable level.

[104] YE Schuurmans, *Bewijslastverdeling in het bestuursrecht* (Deventer, Kluwer, 2005) para 3.2. M Schreuder-Vlasblom, *Rechtsbescherming en bestuurlijke voorprocedure* (Deventer, Kluwer, 2013) 649 ff; HD Van Wijk, W Konijnenbelt and R Van Male, *Hoofdstukken van bestuursrecht*, 16th edn (Deventer, Kluwer, 2014) 558.

[105] See, eg ABRvS 2 June 2004, ECLI:NL:RVS:2004:AP0342, JV 2004, 425; ABRvS 25 January 2012, ECLI:NL:RVS:2012:BV1835, JB 2012, 62; ABRvS 19 September 2012, ECLI:NL:RVS:2012:BX7704.

[106] ECLI:NL:HR:2004:AM2533.

[107] Art 4:2 AWB.

[108] ECLI:NL:CRVB:2002:AF1669.

Raad van State, 1 April 2009[109] **5.23 (NL)**

De besloten vennootschap met beperkte aansprakelijkheid Extrabox v Mayor and Aldermen of Zaanstad

NATURE OF THE BURDEN OF PROOF

Extrabox

An applicant must demonstrate facts to support the claim before the burden of proof is shifted onto the public authority.

Facts: In a letter dated 20 July 2007, the claimant had lodged an intra-administrative objection against a decision of 12 June 2007. He had asked the authority to grant him time to supplement the grounds for the objection until 31 August 2007. With an unregistered letter sent on 30 July 2007, the claimant was given the opportunity to do so within four weeks of the date on which the letter was sent. The claimant claimed not to have received the letter sent by the authority.

Held: The appeal was rejected. The judgment of the district court, declaring that the claim was not admissible, was upheld.

Judgment: 2.1. Extrabox maintains the following. In a letter dated 20 July 2007, it lodged an objection against the decision of 12 June 2007. It asked to be granted time to supplement the grounds for the objection until 31 August 2007.

With a non-registered letter sent on 30 July 2007, Extrabox was given the opportunity to do so within four weeks of the sending of that letter. However, Extrabox did not receive this letter. In the municipality of Zaanstad, problems are frequent in the processing and dispatch of mail. The postal delivery at the location of the business is also poor.

According to Extrabox, the court failed to recognise that failure to submit the grounds of the objection within the prescribed period is, under these circumstances, excusable.

2.1.1. As the Judicial Division has previously considered (judgment of 27 April 2004 in Case No. 200402504/1; www.raadvanstate.nl), it is up to the relevant administrative authority, in the event of non-registered dispatch of decisions or other legally relevant documents of importance, to be able to prove that the document is sent. If it has done this, it is up to the recipient, if appropriate, to deny the receipt of the latter in a plausible way. Only after that has happened, is it for the administrative authority to prove the reception of the document by the addressee.

2.1.2. By submitting a printed copy of the computerized records, in which the date of dispatch of 30 July 2007 and the subject of the letter are indicated, and a copy of the letter, in which the name and address of Extrabox are been stated correctly, the major and aldermen, taking into account that the aforementioned is proven to be the common practice, has demonstrated that the letter of 30 July 2007 was sent to Extrabox.

Extrabox was unable to demonstrate that in the corresponding period there have been any problems in the processing and delivery of mail in the municipality of Zaanstad.

It had asked the mayor and aldermen in its objection of 20 July 2007 to offer it an opportunity to supplement the grounds for the objection until 31 August 2007. It did not claim that it has checked with the board, when, as it claims, it did not receive a reply to

[109] ECLI:NL:RVS:2009:BH9231.

this request. At the time of the decision of 5 September 2007 the mayor and aldermen still had not received the supplements of the grounds of the objection. Extrabox has also not proved that the postal service at the site of its business is poor.

The receipt of the letter of 30 July 2007 is therefore not denied in a plausible manner. It must therefore be assumed that Extrabox has received the letter shortly after 30 July 2007.

Under these circumstances, the district court has correctly, albeit not entirely on correct grounds, held that the municipality rightly declared the objection of Extrabox against the decision of 12 June 2007 inadmissible.

Note

In this case, the question of the burden of proof is illustrated strongly – Extrabox was unable to demonstrate any evidence that the letter had not been sent, so was unable to reverse the burden of proof onto the public authority.

5.3.A.3 THE EUROPEAN UNION

Statute of the Court of Justice of the European Union **5.24 (EU)**

Article 24 The Court of Justice may require the parties to produce all documents and to supply all information which the Court considers desirable. Formal note shall be taken of any refusal.

The Court may also require the Member States and institutions, bodies, offices and agencies not being parties to the case to supply all information which the Court considers necessary for the proceedings.

Article 26 Witnesses may be heard under conditions laid down in the Rules of Procedure.

Article 27 With respect to defaulting witnesses the Court of Justice shall have the powers generally granted to courts and tribunals and may impose pecuniary penalties under conditions laid down in the Rules of Procedure.

Article 28 Witnesses and experts may be heard on oath taken in the form laid down in the Rules of Procedure or in the manner laid down by the law of the country of the witness or expert.

Article 29 The Court of Justice may order that a witness or expert be heard by the judicial authority of his place of permanent residence.

The order shall be sent for implementation to the competent judicial authority under conditions laid down in the Rules of Procedure. The documents drawn up in compliance with the letters rogatory shall be returned to the Court under the same conditions.

The Court shall defray the expenses, without prejudice to the right to charge them, where appropriate, to the parties.

Article 30 A Member State shall treat any violation of an oath by a witness or expert in the same manner as if the offence had been committed before one of its courts with jurisdiction in civil proceedings. At the instance of the Court of Justice, the Member State concerned shall prosecute the offender before its competent court.

Note

The European courts may play an active role in fact-finding provided that the parties have been able to define their position as regards the facts on which the court bases its judgment. However, the parties must prove their assertions, so evidence submitted by the parties must constitute at least prima facie evidence for the allegation.[110] Only if the evidence satisfies this condition will the court decide to investigate the allegations further by means of so-called 'measures of organisation of procedure' or 'measures of inquiry'.[111]

Rules of Procedure of the Court of Justice **5.25 (EU)**

Article 61 Measures of organisation prescribed by the Court

(1) In addition to the measures which may be prescribed in accordance with Article 24 of the Statute, the Court may invite the parties or the interested persons referred to in Article 23 of the Statute to answer certain questions in writing, within the time-limit laid down by the Court, or at the hearing. The written replies shall be communicated to the other parties or the interested persons referred to in Article 23 of the Statute.

(2) Where a hearing is organised, the Court shall, in so far as possible, invite the participants in that hearing to concentrate in their oral pleadings on one or more specified issues.

…

Article 63 Decision on measures of inquiry

(1) The Court shall decide in its general meeting whether a measure of inquiry is necessary.

(2) Where the case has already been assigned to a formation of the Court, the decision shall be taken by that formation.

Article 64 Determination of measures of inquiry

(1) The Court, after hearing the Advocate General, shall prescribe the measures of inquiry that it considers appropriate by means of an order setting out the facts to be proved.

(2) Without prejudice to Articles 24 and 25 of the Statute, the following measures of inquiry may be adopted:

(a) the personal appearance of the parties;
(b) a request for information and production of documents;
(c) oral testimony;
(d) the commissioning of an expert's report;
(e) an inspection of the place or thing in question.

(3) Evidence may be submitted in rebuttal and previous evidence may be amplified.

…

[110] So, for example, if a party is requesting the opposing party to produce a document, the requesting party must provide some minimum information concerning the utility of that document for the purposes of the proceedings. Case C-185/95 P *Baustahlgewebe v Commission* ECLI:EU:C:1998:608.

[111] Case T-53/96 *Syndicat des producteurs de viande bovine and others v Commission* ECLI:EU:T:1996:170.

Article 66 Oral testimony

(1) The Court may, either of its own motion or at the request of one of the parties, and after hearing the Advocate General, order that certain facts be proved by witnesses.

(2) A request by a party for the examination of a witness shall state precisely about what facts and for what reasons the witness should be examined.

(3) The Court shall rule by reasoned order on the request referred to in the preceding paragraph. If the request is granted, the order shall set out the facts to be established and state which witnesses are to be heard in respect of each of those facts.

(4) Witnesses shall be summoned by the Court, where appropriate after lodgment of the security provided for in Article 73(1) of these Rules.

...

Rules of Procedure of the General Court **5.26 (EU)**

Article 64 (1) The purpose of measures of organisation of procedure shall be to ensure that cases are prepared for hearing, procedures carried out and disputes resolved under the best possible conditions. They shall be prescribed by the General Court, after hearing the Advocate General.

(2) Measures of organisation of procedure shall, in particular, have as their purpose:

(a) to ensure efficient conduct of the written and oral procedure and to facilitate the taking of evidence;

(b) to determine the points on which the parties must present further argument or which call for measures of inquiry;

(c) to clarify the forms of order sought by the parties, their pleas in law and arguments and the points at issue between them;

(d) to facilitate the amicable settlement of proceedings.

(3) Measures of organisation of procedure may, in particular, consist of:

(a) putting questions to the parties;

(b) inviting the parties to make written or oral submissions on certain aspects of the proceedings;

(c) asking the parties or third parties for information or particulars;

(d) asking for documents or any papers relating to the case to be produced;

(e) summoning the parties' agents or the parties in person to meetings.

Article 65 Without prejudice to Articles 24 and 25 of the Statute, the following measures of inquiry may be adopted:

(a) the personal appearance of the parties;

(b) a request for information and production of documents;

(c) oral testimony;

(d) the commissioning of an expert's report;

(e) an inspection of the place or thing in question.

Notes

(1) Apart from those foreseen by Article 24 of the Statute of the Court of Justice, 'measures of organisation' entail in essence the possibility for the European courts to ask questions in writing or at the hearing: they have the aim of ensuring the smooth conduct of the written and oral proceedings, and to determine the points on which the

parties must present further arguments. 'Measures of inquiry' include the personal appearance of the parties; a request for information and production of documents; oral testimony; the commissioning of an expert's report; and an inspection of the place or thing in question. Measures of inquiry are intended to prove the veracity of the facts alleged by one of the parties in support of its pleas. The parties may be present at the measures of inquiry.[112]

(2) The classic apportionment of the burden of proof, whereby each party must prove the facts on which its claim is based, is applicable in EU law. However, the judge is permitted to mitigate the inequalities of the parties in terms of their ability to prove the necessary facts.[113] So, for example, a party may be obliged by the court to release information to which only it has access in order to enable the opponent to provide the necessary evidence.[114]

(3) EU law does not lay down specific rules on the use of evidence. All means of proof are admissible except for evidence obtained improperly[115] and internal documents. Those internal documents should not be disclosed unless the production of these documents has been authorised by the institution concerned or ordered by the court.[116] It is notable that although EU law precludes the ability of claimants to rely on improperly obtained evidence, no clear definition of this concept has been developed in EU law.

5.3.A.4 FRANCE

Code de justice administrative **5.27 (FR)**

Article R623-1 The court may, either at the request of the parties or *ex officio*, order an investigation into the facts which it deems useful to ascertain for the preparation of the case.

Article R623-2 The decision in which the investigation is ordered should indicate which facts should be covered and specified, depending on the case, whether it is to take place before a court formation or an investigation formation, or before one of its members who, if necessary, will visit the location. This is notified to the parties.

Article R623-3 The parties are invited to present their witnesses on the day and at the place set in the decision ordering the investigation.

They may summon witnesses to attend, at their expense, using the services of a judicial officer.

The court formation or investigation formation, or the judge who carries out the investigation may, *ex officio*, convene or hear any person whose testimony may be helpful to determine the truth.

[112] Rules of Procedure of the Court of Justice, Art 65(3); Rules of Procedure of the General Court Art, 67(2).

[113] Case 10/55 *Mirossevick v High Authority* ECLI:EU:C:1956:14.

[114] Case 45/64 *Commission v Italy* ECLI:EU:C:1969:49.

[115] Joined Cases 197-200, 243, 245 and 247/80 *Ludwigshafener Walzmühle and others v Council and Commission* ECLI:EU:C:1981:311, para 16.

[116] Case C-445/00 *Austria v Council* ECLI:EU:C:2003:445.

Article R623-4 When the investigation is ordered, counter evidence may be brought by witnesses without any new decision.

Anyone may be heard as a witness, except for persons who do not have the legal capacity to testify in legal proceedings.

Persons who cannot testify may, however, be heard under the same conditions, without making a sworn statement.

...

Notes

(1) Judicial review proceedings in France are predominantly written proceedings, with evidence being provided in writing. The courts have the power to order an investigation and hear witnesses, but tend to do so only in complex cases, particularly those involving complex economic disputes. Whenever an investigation is undertaken by the courts, copies of the records of the investigation (specifically, the record of any investigation undertaken or witness heard) are provided to the parties to the dispute.[117] There is no specific provision in the Code of Administrative Justice requiring that written evidence that is submitted to the court should be provided to all parties.

(2) The issue of the burden of proof remains significant in French administrative proceedings as the factual elements of the case are often important in determining the application of the relevant legal rules. The paramount duty lies with the parties to bring relevant evidence to the court to support their claims, and the approach of the court is to allow freedom to the parties in the evidence that they bring.

(3) In principle, all types of evidence, including testimony, photographs, letters and all kinds of documentary evidence, are accepted, whatever method has been used to acquire them, including evidence that has been unlawfully acquired. The judge in the proceedings then has the freedom to determine whether the evidence provided is conclusive or not.

Conseil d'État, 28 May 1954[118] **5.28 (FR)**

Barel and others v Director of National School of Administration

EVIDENCE REGIME; EQUALITY BETWEEN PARTIES

Barel

The burden of proof of the facts which ground the decision is on the public authority.

Facts: Mr Barel and other students were not permitted to participate in the competition organised to determine entry into the National School of Administration by the Secretary of State in charge of competition.

117 Code de justice administrative, Art R623-7.
118 N° 28238.

They challenged this decision before the Council of State, alleging that this refusal was grounded on the fact that they were communist and, therefore, that this refusal violated the principle of equality.

Held: The decision was quashed.

Judgment: Considering that the applicants, whom the Secretary of State to the presidency of the Council has, by the challenged decisions, denied the permission to participate in the competition opened in 1953 for the admission to the National School of Administration, maintain that they have been removed from the list of candidates, issued by decision by aforesaid Secretary of State, only because of political views that have been imputed to them; that they invoke, in support of their allegations, circumstances and specific facts that constitute serious presumptions; that, nevertheless, the Secretary of State, in his submissions on the appeal, when contesting the significance of the abovementioned circumstances and facts, only indicated, further, that is it for the Council of State to look among the items added to the files for those [items] that allow to identify the grounds of the adopted decisions and in that way abstained from disclosing the grounds of his decisions.

That in this state of the proceedings, the Litigation Section, tasked with the investigation of the applications, using the power that belongs to the Council of State to request the competent administration to provide all documents that are adequate to establish the facts before the court and to allow a control of the allegations of the applicants, requested, by deliberation of 19 March 1954, the Secretary of State to provide the files dealing with the application of each of the applicants; that, as far as Mr Barel and Bedjaoui are concerned, the Secretary of State has not complied with this request; that, concerning Mr Guyader, Fortuné and Lingois, the Litigation Section stated, in response to a letter of the Secretary of State of 13 May 1954 concerning those three candidates, that the files which the Council of State asked for, comprised all the items, reports and documents in the light of which the challenged decisions have been taken.

That this last request has not been fulfilled with the submissions made on 25 May 1954; that it results from all the circumstances of the case that the grounds alleged by the authors of the appeal must be regarded as ascertained; that, therefore, the applicants are justified in maintaining that the decisions brought before the Council of State are based on a ground tainted with an error of law and, consequently, in requesting their annulment through an action for annulment (*recours pour excès de pouvoir*).

Note

This case demonstrates that, where appropriate, the court must recognise the likelihood that a public authority is in a better position than a claimant to support its case with evidence and must adapt the evidence regime accordingly. The approach in French law is that it is frequently the case that the factual elements of the case are known only by the administration and thus the obligation incumbent on the claimant to prove the claims made is consequently reduced. When the claimant makes an allegation, it is for the administrative body to bring forward evidence to rebut the claims made by the claimant, such as providing details of the grounds for the decision that has been made. If the administrative authority fails to do this, the case will be concluded in favour of the claimant.

5.3.B REGIMES ADOPTING A RESTRICTIVE APPROACH TO EVIDENCE GATHERING: ENGLAND AND WALES

Pre-action Protocol for Judicial Review[119] **5.29 (EW)**

Requests for information and documents at the pre-action stage

13. Requests for information and documents made at the pre-action stage should be proportionate and should be limited to what is properly necessary for the claimant to understand why the challenged decision has been taken and/or to present the claim in a manner that will properly identify the issues. The defendant should comply with any request which meets these requirements unless there is good reason for it not to do so. Where the court considers that a public body should have provided relevant documents and/or information, particularly where this failure is a breach of a statutory or common law requirement, it may impose costs sanctions.

Civil Procedure Rules **5.30 (EW)**

Rule 18.1 (1) The court may at any time order a party to–

(a) clarify any matter which is in dispute in the proceedings; or

(b) give additional information in relation to any such matter,

whether or not the matter is contained or referred to in a statement of case.

(2) Paragraph (1) is subject to any rule of law to the contrary.

(3) Where the court makes an order under paragraph (1), the party against whom it is made must–

(a) file his response; and

(b) serve it on the other parties,

within the time specified by the court.

(Part 22 requires a response to be verified by a statement of truth)

...

Rule 22.1 (1) The following documents must be verified by a statement of truth–

(a) a statement of case;

(b) a response complying with an order under rule 18.1 to provide further information;

(c) a witness statement;

...

Rule 32.1(1) The court may control the evidence by giving directions as to–

(a) the issues on which it requires evidence;

(b) the nature of the evidence which it requires to decide those issues; and

(c) the way in which the evidence is to be placed before the court.

(2) The court may use its power under this rule to exclude evidence that would otherwise be admissible.

(3) The court may limit cross-examination

...

Rule 32.6 (1) Subject to paragraph (2), the general rule is that evidence at hearings other than the trial is to be by witness statement unless the court, a practice direction or any other enactment requires otherwise.

[119] Available at www.justice.gov.uk/courts/procedure-rules/civil/protocol/prot_jrv.

(2) At hearings other than the trial, a party may, rely on the matters set out in–

(a) his statement of case; or

(b) his application notice, if the statement of case or application notice is verified by a statement of truth.

Rule 32.7 (1) Where, at a hearing other than the trial, evidence is given in writing, any party may apply to the court for permission to cross-examine the person giving the evidence.

(2) If the court gives permission under paragraph (1) but the person in question does not attend as required by the order, his evidence may not be used unless the court gives permission.

Rule 32.15 (1) Evidence must be given by affidavit instead of or in addition to a witness statement if this is required by the court, a provision contained in any other rule, a practice direction or any other enactment.

(2) Nothing in these Rules prevents a witness giving evidence by affidavit at a hearing other than the trial if he chooses to do so in a case where paragraph (1) does not apply, but the party putting forward the affidavit may not recover the additional cost of making it from any other party unless the court orders otherwise.

Rule 54.16 …

(2) No written evidence may be relied on unless–

(a) it has been served in accordance with any–

(i) rule under this section; or

(ii) direction of the court; or

(b) the court gives permission.

Notes

(1) Under Part 18 CPR, the court enjoys broad powers to require parties to clarify elements of the claim that has been submitted or to require parties to provide additional information in relation to the claim to the court. This may be exercised by the court in judicial review cases, but the exercise of this power is subject to the general principle according to which the courts are reluctant to engage in substantial disputes in relation to evidence in judicial review claims.

(2) The general rule in all civil proceedings (administrative proceedings are treated as civil proceedings in the law of England and Wales) is that the predominant mode of providing evidence to the court is through written witness statements, accompanied by a statement of truth, as set out in Rules 22.1 and 32.6 CPR. It is also possible, and is often the case, for witnesses and others giving evidence to the court to do so by affidavit (sworn statement). Rule 32.1 offers the judge broad discretion over the evidence to be admitted and empowers the court to make orders relating to the evidence that might be required to reach a decision in the case.

(3) In general, the practice of the courts in judicial review is to determine cases based on the documents which are pertinent to the case and the sworn affidavits of the individuals who are relevant to the case (claimant, relevant public officials, possible witnesses, etc). Both parties are under a 'duty of candour', and must therefore

make a full and frank disclosure of the relevant facts to the court,[120] which includes a duty to update the court when any circumstances change.[121] As a result of the duty of candour, the court will not ordinarily order disclosure of evidence,[122] although it will do so where the documents concerned have not been exhibited by the state yet may be material to the justice of the case.[123]

(4) Under Rule 32.7 CPR, it is possible for either party to seek permission to cross-examine those who have submitted witness statements or affidavits. In judicial review claims, this will seldom be ordered, but must be permitted when the circumstances of the case require it in order to secure fairness for the parties.[124]

House of Lords, 13 December 2006[125] **5.31 (EW)**

Tweed v Parades Commission

JUDICIAL REVIEW CLAIMS; EVIDENCE; DISCLOSURE OF DOCUMENTS

Tweed

Disclosure of documents may be ordered where the justice of the case requires it.

Facts: The claimant brought judicial review proceedings against a decision of the Parades Commission in Northern Ireland, restricting the route of a march to be held by the Orange Order (a political group in Northern Ireland). As part of the claim, he requested disclosure of five documents, including a police report, an internal memorandum and two other reports held by the Parades Commission.

Held: The documents should be disclosed to the judge in the first instance, as in this case there was a dispute of fact and the documents could assist Tweed in supporting his case.

Judgment: Lord Bingham of Cornhill: … 2 The disclosure of documents in civil litigation has been recognised throughout the common law world as a valuable means of eliciting the truth and thus of enabling courts to base their decisions on a sure foundation of fact. But the process of disclosure can be costly, time-consuming, oppressive and unnecessary, and neither in Northern Ireland nor in England and Wales have the general rules governing disclosure been applied to applications for judicial review. Such applications, characteristically, raise an issue of law, the facts being common ground or relevant only to show how the issue arises. So disclosure of documents has usually been regarded as unnecessary, and that remains the position.

3 In the minority of judicial review applications in which the precise facts are significant, procedures exist in both jurisdictions, as my noble and learned friends explain, for disclosure of specific documents to be sought and ordered. Such applications are likely to

[120] See, eg *Cocks v Thanet DC* [1983] 2 AC 286 (HL) (in relation to the claimant's duty) and *R (Quark Fishing Ltd) v Secretary of State for Foreign and Commonwealth Affairs* [2002] EWCA Civ 1409.

[121] See, eg *R (Tshikangu) v Newham LBC* [2001] EWHC (Admin) 92, *The Times*, 27 April 2001.

[122] *Quark Fishing* (n 123 above).

[123] See, eg *R v Inland Revenue Commissioners, ex parte J Rothschild Holdings Plc* [1986] STC 410 (QB).

[124] See, eg *R (on the application of Wilkinson) v Broadmoor Hospital* [2001] EWCA Civ 1545, [2002] 1 WLR 419.

[125] *Tweed v Parades Commission* [2006] UKHL 53, [2007] 1 AC 650.

increase in frequency, since human rights decisions under the Convention tend to be very fact-specific and any judgment on the proportionality of a public authority's interference with a protected Convention right is likely to call for a careful and accurate evaluation of the facts. But even in these cases, orders for disclosure should not be automatic. The test will always be whether, in the given case, disclosure appears to be necessary in order to resolve the matter fairly and justly.

4 Where a public authority relies on a document as significant to its decision, it is ordinarily good practice to exhibit it as the primary evidence. Any summary, however conscientiously and skilfully made, may distort. But where the authority's deponent chooses to summarise the effect of a document it should not be necessary for the applicant, seeking sight of the document, to suggest some inaccuracy or incompleteness in the summary, usually an impossible task without sight of the document. It is enough that the document itself is the best evidence of what it says. There may, however, be reasons (arising, for example, from confidentiality, or the volume of the material in question) why the document should or need not be exhibited. The judge to whom application for disclosure is made must then rule on whether, and to what extent, disclosure should be made.

Notes

(1) Where documents are ordered to be disclosed in judicial review proceedings, it may be the case that the public authority seeks to have all or part of them withheld due to the information within them being confidential, or that it is in the public interest to have the documents withheld. In such circumstances, the court will often consider whether the documents should be subject to public interest immunity. It is notable that in cases concerning arguments about the proportionality of the action taken by a public authority, or where claims relate to the Human Rights Act 1998, disclosure of documents and other aspects of the law relating to factual dispute are more likely to come into play due to the sensitive nature of some of these proceedings.

(2) The issue of improperly obtained evidence has not been considered to any significant extent in judicial review proceedings in England and Wales, perhaps because of the duty of candour. It is clear that the courts will generally consider all forms of evidence, including hearsay evidence and evidence that may have been gathered illegally, when deciding judicial review proceedings.[126] It is clear, however, that evidence procured by torture should be excluded.[127]

(3) As English administrative law cases are heard as civil proceedings, the burden of proof is on the civil standard, ie it is for the parties to prove factual issues on the balance of probabilities. As a general principle, the onus to prove facts to support the claim lies with the claimant.[128] The courts have often held that where an administrative

[126] See, eg *R v Camden London Borough Council, ex parte Adair* (1997) 29 HLR 236, 248 (QB).

[127] *A v Secretary of State for the Home Department (No 2)* [2005] UKHL 71, [2006] 2 AC 221.

[128] See, eg *R v Birmingham City Council, ex parte O* [1983] 1 AC 578, 597 (HL) (Lord Brightman); *R (Ireneschild) v Lambeth London Borough Council* [2007] EWCA Civ 234, [2007] HLR 34, [45]; *Standard Commercial Property Securities Ltd v Glasgow City Council* [2006] UKHL 50, [2007] JPL 758, [61].

decision has been made, there is a presumption that it is lawful unless the claimant can demonstrate otherwise.[129] However, it is important to note that the courts have always adopted an approach of requiring the public authority to provide evidence supporting action (essentially reversing the burden of proof) in cases where fundamental rights or the liberty of the claimant is at stake.[130] There are also examples where the court has reversed the burden of proof in circumstances where the public authority has acted in an unusual or unexpected way, such as by failing to follow statutory guidance.[131]

5.3.C COMPARATIVE REMARKS

The evidence regimes adopted in the different jurisdictions vary somewhat, although there are some clear commonalities in the approach adopted in Germany and the Netherlands and under EU law. In Germany, the inquisitorial process is most evidently in place, with the principle of 'direct evidence' (*Grundsatz der Unmittelbarkeit*) leading to the judge being in a position to gather and determine what evidence is appropriate in the case. Nonetheless, in cases of a *non liquet*, the burden of proof becomes relevant. In principle, each party must present and prove the facts favourable to them, unless the law provides for a reversal of the burden of proof. In the Netherlands, the judge is also considered to be the master of the proceedings, though there is a greater onus on the claimant to support the case, with a requirement that the claimant can demonstrate suitable factual evidence to offer a basis for the claim being made in advance of the burden of proof being reversed onto the public authority. Under EU law and in France, the approach is generally to permit the parties to make out their case, although the judges have substantial powers to control the evidence-gathering process and to require the parties to provide additional evidence to support their case. A significant difference in approach is apparent in England and Wales, where the courts are reluctant to address significant evidential disputes in judicial review proceedings, with the courts hearing evidence only in cases where there is a clear need to do so. As the case of *Tweed* demonstrates, the requirements of Article 6 ECHR have required a more permissive approach to disputes of fact and evidence gathering where fairness requires it.

It is important to note that, in all systems, the written submission of the case and evidence is crucially important – even in Germany, where the judge is active in gathering evidence, the claimants must be able to demonstrate that they have an arguable case and

[129] See, eg *Stancliffe Stone Co Ltd v Peak District National Park Authority* [2005] EWCA Civ 747, [2006] Env LR 7, [47]–[48].

[130] This is a long-held principle. See, eg *Eshugbayi Eloko v Government of Nigeria* [1931] AC 662 (PC), where it was held that if the executive wished to interfere with the liberty or property of an individual, this could only be done if evidence could be provided to the court in support of the action. In the modern context, the same principle arises whenever the executive proposes to interfere in an ECHR right protected by the Human Rights Act 1998. See, eg *R (Suryananda) v Welsh Ministers* [2007] EWCA Civ 893, [69].

[131] *R v Islington London Borough Council, ex parte Rixon* [1997] ELR 66 (QB).

some appropriate evidence to support it, as without this the case may be dealt with under the summary procedure and disposed of as being manifestly unfounded. This is also the case in France, the Netherlands and the EU – claims that are not adequately supported by the written submissions face the likelihood of being disposed of via summary proceedings. In England and Wales, the written submissions of the parties at the permission stage are important because first, they will determine whether or not permission to proceed is granted, and secondly, if permission is granted, the grounds raised at the permission stage will frame the dispute at the substantive hearing.

If one steps back and examines the substance of the rules of evidence in each of the regimes considered above, it is apparent that all the legal systems under consideration provide the courts with similar and relatively extensive powers to require the provision of evidence from witnesses, to call witnesses for cross-examination and to require the production of documentary evidence. The key issue of variation is the approach of the courts to the use of these powers. The approach to the evidence regime is clearly linked with the general approach to claims: where the contours of the case are defined by the parties, disputes of fact are infrequently considered. However, where judges have greater powers to frame the dispute and adopt a more inquisitorial approach, a more open and comprehensive approach to evidence gathering is required, although it is important to emphasise that even within systems that adopt an inquisitorial approach the extent to which judges engage in evidence gathering and require such evidence to be taken at the hearing varies considerably. The judges are most heavily involved in Germany, due to the principle of 'direct evidence'. In the Netherlands and the EU, there is evidence that judges are willing to use the powers to order the production of evidence on a relatively frequent basis and to take an active approach in the management of the case. Despite the fact that the French system is inquisitorial in nature, judges are generally less willing to exercise the powers to gather evidence, preferring to leave the onus on the parties to support their own cases. In England and Wales, the court enjoys substantial powers to require the parties to provide evidence and the judge enjoys great discretion to direct the parties in relation to the evidence that should be provided. However, in practice, such powers are infrequently used.

The approach adopted to improperly obtained evidence varies between the systems. The EU courts generally exclude such evidence, whereas in Germany, the Netherlands and England and Wales, the courts are willing to consider evidence that is improperly obtained in most circumstances. The approach in France is much more open, permitting all forms of evidence, however obtained, to be considered by the court.

In France, Germany, the Netherlands and the EU, the burden of proof is generally applied in a manner that is sympathetic to claimants, reflecting the fact that public authorities are frequently in a stronger position to bring evidence than claimants because they hold the necessary information and the claimant is often not in a position to access this information. In each of these jurisdictions, the judge may require administrative authorities to discharge the burden of proof in order to support the action that has been taken or the decision that has been made. The position is less clear in some respects in England and Wales. The general rule is that applied in civil cases – that the burden of proof lies with the claimant to demonstrate that the action or decision of the public authority is unlawful. This might be argued to be less favourable to claimants than in the other jurisdictions under consideration. However, the courts have not adhered rigidly to this principle, and where a public authority appears to be taking action that is unusual, or where the action taken infringes the principle of liberty or other fundamental rights of the claimant (including the Convention rights protected by the Human Rights Act 1998), then the burden of proof is reversed and the requirement will be that the public authority must demonstrate facts that support its action. Furthermore, one might argue that the 'duty of candour' inherent in the law in England and Wales assists a claimant with the burden of proof because the expectation is that parties will reveal information to the court even if it is disadvantageous to their argument. In many respects, there is considerable similarity between the systems, as the courts retain substantial discretion to adjust the burden of proof in order to deliver fairness to the parties, and particularly to the claimant, who is often in a disadvantageous position.

This section of the chapter commenced with an examination of the approach of the Court of Justice of the European Union to issues of evidence gathering and has also addressed the approach of the European Court of Human Rights to the equality of arms principle. The excerpts above demonstrate that there has been a coming together of the approaches of the CJEU and the ECtHR on standards of fairness in the evidentiary process. However, as demonstrated by the discussion of *San Giorgio* and *Steffensen*, although both EU law and the case law under the European Convention on Human Rights require certain principles of effectiveness, equivalence and fairness to be adhered to, there is no overriding set of procedural requirements that are imposed – legal systems still enjoy significant levels of procedural autonomy. It can also be observed that the requirements of Article 6(1) ECHR have led to modifications of approach in some jurisdictions – the discussion of *Tweed* being such an example.

5.4 ROLE OF EXPERTS AND AMICI CURIAE

Experts and amici curiae can provide a useful way for parties to support their submissions with expert evidence and may also provide a useful mechanism through which the court can understand issues of particular technical complexity, which might arise frequently in administrative law cases in areas such as public procurement and disputes over medical treatment. A distinction can be drawn between experts who are brought to court as a result of their particular expertise and an amicus curiae (friend of the court), who may not necessarily be an expert on a technical issue but could advise the court on matters where he has practical experience or knowledge, or may be appointed by the court to assist where there is a one-sided approach to particular issues. Much like many of the other issues in this chapter, the extent to which the courts are open to hearing expert evidence often turns on the nature of the regime in which the case is heard – those jurisdictions where proceedings are predominantly written and focused predominantly on issues of law are generally less willing to permit the hearing of expert evidence than those which adopt an approach of permitting greater oral argument or which are more inquisitorial.

5.4.A EUROPEAN INFLUENCES

This section will start out by considering European influences on the approach to expert evidence, as it is possible to identify some commonalities which are perhaps driven by the case law of the European Court of Human Rights and legislation in this area. Once the European case law has been examined, the approach adopted in each national system (and the specific rules at the level of the European Union) will be considered in order to assess the extent that general principles of law at the European level have impacted upon the development of the national rules in this area.

5.4.A.1 THE EUROPEAN UNION

Council Regulation (EC) No 1/2003 of 16 December 2002
on the implementation of the rules on competition laid down
in Articles 81 and 82 of the Treaty[132] **5.32 (EU)**

Article 15 Cooperation with national courts

...

3. Competition authorities of the Member States, acting on their own initiative, may submit written observations to the national courts of their Member State on issues relating to the application of Article 81 or Article 82 of the Treaty. With the permission of the court in question, they may also submit oral observations to the national courts of their Member State. Where the coherent application of Article 81 or Article 82 of the Treaty so requires, the Commission, acting on its own initiative, may submit written observations to courts of the Member States. With the permission of the court in question, it may also make oral observations.

For the purpose of the preparation of their observations only, the competition authorities of the Member States and the Commission may request the relevant court of the Member State to transmit or ensure the transmission to them of any documents necessary for the assessment of the case.

4. This Article is without prejudice to wider powers to make observations before courts conferred on competition authorities of the Member States under the law of their Member State.

Note

Article 15(3) of Regulation 1/2003 requires that both national competition authorities and the European Commission are given the opportunity on their own initiative to submit observations relating to relevant cases involving the interpretation and application of what are now Articles 101 and 102 TFEU. In some Member States, such as the Netherlands, this has led to specific legislative provisions being put in place to facilitate amicus curiae interventions of competition authorities in appropriate cases.[133] Given that Regulation 1/2003 is directly applicable, there is no need for national

[132] [2003] OJ L1/1.
[133] See Art 8:45a AWB.

implementing measures to be put in place, and in England and Wales, for example, courts have followed the requirements of Article 15(3) without implementing measures being in place.[134] This provision opens up the potential for amici curiae to be heard in relevant cases even where the national system at hand does not otherwise allow for their hearing (as is the case in the Netherlands) wherever judicial review proceedings involve interpretation of Articles 101 and 102 TFEU.

5.4.A.2 THE EUROPEAN COURT OF HUMAN RIGHTS

European Court of Human Rights, 18 March 1997[135] **5.33 (COE)**

Mantovanelli v France

EXPERT EVIDENCE; EQUALITY OF ARMS; OPPORTUNITY TO CHALLENGE EXPERT REPORT

Mantovanelli

The equality of arms principle inherent in Article 6 ECHR requires that the parties are given the opportunity to challenge expert reports before they are finalised and taken into account by the court.

Facts: The claimants were parents of a young woman who had died after undergoing a number of surgeries. The parents sought damages from the hospital, alleging that the reason for the death of their daughter was medical negligence through the excessive administration of a particular anaesthetic which was known to cause liver damage in large or repeated doses. The parents asked the court, which agreed, to order an expert report to address disagreements over the facts between the parents and the hospital. The expert report was compiled, but in the course of this, the Mantovanellis' lawyer was not advised of the dates when interviews of relevant parties were undertaken by the expert, so did not have the opportunity to question the evidence of these parties and also did not receive copies of documents that the hospital disclosed to the expert in the process of the report being compiled. As such, the Mantovanellis did not have the opportunity to comment on the evidence gathered by the expert, or to ask the expert to undertake additional investigations in advance of the compilation of the expert report. The claimants alleged that this was a breach of Article 6 ECHR.

Held: In the circumstances, the failure to allow the claimants to comment on the evidence gathered by the expert before the finalisation of the report was considered a breach of Article 6 ECHR.

Judgment: 30. Mr and Mrs Mantovanelli maintained that the procedure followed in preparing the expert medical opinion ordered by the Nancy Administrative Court had not been in conformity with the adversarial principle and had given rise to a violation of their right to a fair hearing as secured by Article 6 para. 1 of the Convention (art. 6-1), which provides:

'In the determination of his civil rights and obligations ..., everyone is entitled to a fair ... hearing ... by [a] ... tribunal ...'

Contrary to the former Article R. 123 of the Administrative Courts and Administrative Courts of Appeal Code, neither they nor their counsel had been informed of the dates of the interviews conducted by the expert. The expert had also referred in his report to

[134] See, eg *National Grid Electricity Transmission Plc v ABB Ltd* [2012] EWHC 869 (Ch), [2012] UKCLR 220.

[135] ECLI:CE:ECHR:1997:0318JUD002149793.

documents which they had not seen and which it had been pointless to ask the hospital management to produce.

They had thus been deprived of the opportunity to examine the persons who gave evidence to the expert, to submit comments to him on the documents examined and on the witness evidence taken and to ask him to carry out additional investigations.

Admittedly, the expert report had later been communicated to the applicants, who could thus have challenged it in the administrative court. They had nevertheless been prevented from participating on an equal footing in the production of the report.

31. The Commission submitted that compliance with the principle of adversarial procedure meant that where a court ordered the production of an expert report, the parties should be able to challenge before the expert the evidence he had taken into account in carrying out his instructions. There were three reasons for this: an expert report of this kind, produced under a court's authority for its own enlightenment, was an integral part of the proceedings; as the court was unable to assess for itself all the technical issues considered, the expert's investigation tended to replace the taking of evidence by the court itself; and merely being able to challenge the expert report in court did not permit an effective application of the adversarial principle as the report had become final by then.

In the present case Mr and Mrs Mantovanelli had been unable to attend the expert's interviews with the witnesses (all members of the CHRN's medical staff) and the report referred to documents which they had not seen. The Nancy Administrative Court had refused their application for a second expert report and had reproduced the findings of the report in order to dismiss their claims. There had therefore been a breach of Article 6 para. 1 (art. 6-1).

32. The Government maintained that in French law it was for the administrative courts to assess the outcome of investigative measures they ordered. They had discretion to take into account an expert report produced in breach of the provisions of the former Article R. 123 of the Administrative Courts and Administrative Courts of Appeal Code.

In this case the expert report, despite its irregularity, had fulfilled its purpose of enlightening the court. The issue actually being raised by the applicants was the court's assessment of the evidence, which was not subject to review by the Convention institutions.

Furthermore, as to observance of the adversarial principle, only the proceedings in court were of importance. The expert report had been communicated to the applicants on 19 July 1985 and could therefore have been the subject of adversarial argument in the administrative court. In any event, some of the documents examined by the expert had been filed by the applicants themselves; as to the other documents, parties were allowed, under case-law, to request access to a medical file through the intermediary of a doctor designated by them for that purpose (Conseil d'État, Judicial Assembly, 22 January 1982, *Administration générale de l'assistance publique à Paris*, Actualité juridique, Droit administratif, June 1982, p. 395).

33. The Court notes that one of the elements of a fair hearing within the meaning of Article 6 para. 1 (art. 6-1) is the right to adversarial proceedings; each party must in principle have the opportunity not only to make known any evidence needed for his claims to succeed, but also to have knowledge of and comment on all evidence adduced or observations filed with a view to influencing the court's decision (see, *mutatis mutandis*, the *Lobo Machado v. Portugal* and *Vermeulen v. Belgium* judgments of 20 February 1996, Reports of Judgments and Decisions 1996-I pp. 206-07, para. 31, and p. 234, para. 33, respectively, and the *Nideröst-Huber v. Switzerland* judgment of 18 February 1997, Reports 1997-I, p. 108, para. 24).

In this connection, the Court makes it clear at the outset that, just like observance of the other procedural safeguards enshrined in Article 6 para. 1 (art. 6-1), compliance with the adversarial principle relates to proceedings in a 'tribunal'; no general, abstract principle may therefore be inferred from this provision (art. 6-1) that, where an expert has been appointed by a court, the parties must in all instances be able to attend the interviews held by him or to be shown the documents he has taken into account. What is essential is that the parties should be able to participate properly in the proceedings before the 'tribunal' (see, *mutatis mutandis*, the *Kerojärvi v. Finland* judgment of 19 July 1995, Series A no. 322, p. 16, para. 42 in fine).

34. Moreover, the Convention does not lay down rules on evidence as such. The Court therefore cannot exclude as a matter of principle and in the abstract that evidence obtained in breach of provisions of domestic law may be admitted. It is for the national courts to assess the evidence they have obtained and the relevance of any evidence that a party wishes to have produced. The Court has nevertheless to ascertain whether the proceedings considered as a whole, including the way in which the evidence was taken, were fair as required by Article 6 para. 1 (art. 6-1) (see, *mutatis mutandis*, the *Schenk v. Switzerland* judgment of 12 July 1988, Series A no. 140, p. 29, para. 46).

...

36. However, while Mr and Mrs Mantovanelli could have made submissions to the administrative court on the content and findings of the report after receiving it, the Court is not convinced that this afforded them a real opportunity to comment effectively on it. The question the expert was instructed to answer was identical with the one that the court had to determine, namely whether the circumstances in which halothane had been administered to the applicants' daughter disclosed negligence on the part of the CHRN. It pertained to a technical field that was not within the judges' knowledge. Thus although the administrative court was not in law bound by the expert's findings, his report was likely to have a preponderant influence on the assessment of the facts by that court.

Under such circumstances, and in the light also of the administrative courts' refusal of their application for a fresh expert report at first instance and on appeal (see paragraphs 19-22 above), Mr and Mrs Mantovanelli could only have expressed their views effectively before the expert report was lodged. No practical difficulty stood in the way of their being associated in the process of producing the report, as it consisted in interviewing witnesses and examining documents. Yet they were prevented from participating in the interviews, although the five people interviewed by the expert were employed by the CHRN and included the surgeon who had performed the last operation on Miss Mantovanelli, and the anaesthetist. The applicants were therefore not able to cross-examine these five people who could reasonably have been expected to give evidence along the same lines as the CHRN, the opposing side in the proceedings. As to the documents taken into consideration by the expert, the applicants only became aware of them once the report had been completed and transmitted.

Mr and Mrs Mantovanelli were thus not able to comment effectively on the main piece of evidence. The proceedings were therefore not fair as required by Article 6 para. 1 of the Convention (art. 6-1). There has accordingly been a breach of that provision (art. 6-1).

Note

The above case demonstrates that where a court-appointed expert undertakes investigations leading to a report which is likely to be significant in influencing the outcome of the case, all of the parties should have the opportunity to see the evidence that is given to the expert and to comment on it, and all parties should have the opportunity to seek further investigations from the expert. This is not such an essential requirement in systems where experts are brought by the parties, because the expert report is subject to the adversarial process. However, as will be demonstrated in the next excerpt, it may still be problematic from the perspective of Article 6 ECHR if one party has significantly greater financial resources than the other (as is frequently the case in administrative law cases, as the state is generally well-resourced and experienced in such litigation).

European Court of Human Rights, 8 January 2016[136] **5.34 (COE)**

Korošec v Slovenia

EXPERT EVIDENCE; EQUALITY OF ARMS; FINANCIAL SUPPORT OF CLAIMANT

Korošec

The equality of arms principle inherent in Article 6 ECHR requires that the court should appoint an expert at public expense to assist the claimant in appropriate cases.

Facts: The claimant was seriously disabled and made an application for financial support to assist him with his care needs under the provisions of Slovenian law. His initial assessment determined that he was eligible for support at 70% of the maximum permitted by law. As the claimant's condition worsened, his family doctor applied for an increase in the amount of the allowance. This claim was tested by a Commission appointed by the state and constituted of a number of medical experts appointed by the Commission and was rejected. The claimant then appealed and the case was considered by a second Commission, also constituted of state-appointed experts. They upheld the rejection of the application. The claimant then proceeded through the hierarchy of national courts in order to pursue an appeal and was unsuccessful, as the courts upheld the decision of the Commissions, in part due to the weight of expert evidence. The claimant then brought a claim to the European Court of Human Rights, arguing that it was contrary to Article 6 ECHR for the courts to refuse to appoint medical experts on his behalf to support his claims against the decisions to deny him increased financial support.

Held: In the circumstances of this case, it was considered contrary to Article 6 ECHR for the courts to refuse to appoint appropriate experts to support the claimant in taking forward his case.

Judgment: 49. The Court initially notes that the disability allowance claimed by the applicant was purely financial in nature; it was determined on the basis of specific criteria and not dependent on the discretion of a state authority. The Court considers that the domestic proceedings concerned the applicant's civil rights within the meaning of Article 6 (see Feldbrugge, cited above, § 40; *Deumeland v Germany*, 29 May 1986, § 74, Series A no. 100; *Francesco Lombardo v Italy*, 26 November 1992, § 17, Series A no. 249-B; and *Mihailov v Bulgaria*, no. 52367/99, § 34, 21 July 2005).

50. It also observes that under domestic legislation the social courts serve as judicial bodies which have full jurisdiction to review the decisions taken by the administrative authorities (see, *mutatis mutandis*, *Grande Stevens and Others v Italy*, nos. 18640/10, 18647/10, 18663/10, 18668/10 and 18698/10, § 139, 4 March 2014).

[136] ECLI:CE:ECHR:2015:1008JUD007721212.

51. The Court notes that in the present case the opinions of the Institute's disability commissions were neither ordered by the domestic courts nor were they explicitly referred to by the domestic courts as expert opinions. They were, however, obtained and treated as such in the pre-judicial proceedings before the Institute (later the opposing party in the applicant's judicial proceedings). Moreover, they were, for all practical purposes, regarded by the domestic courts as expert medical evidence. The present case therefore has similarities to those cases in which the Court examined the issue of neutrality of court-appointed experts (see *Bönisch v Austria*, 6 May 1985, § 33, Series A no. 92; *Sara Lind Eggertsdóttir*, cited above, § 47; and *Placì*, cited above, § 79; see also, *mutatis mutandis*, *Yvon*, cited above, § 37).

52. The Court reiterates that in *Sara Lind Eggertsdóttir* (cited above, §§ 47-55) it found a violation of Article 6 § 1 on account of non-compliance with the principle of equality of arms by taking into account three factors: (1) the nature of the task entrusted to the experts; (2) the experts' position within the hierarchy of the opposing party; and (3) their role in the proceedings, in particular the weight attached by the court to their opinions.

53. As to the first factor, the Court observes that the task of the disability commissions was to provide medical expertise to the administration of the Pensions and Invalidity Institute when deciding on claims for allowances based on national insurance schemes.

54. As to the second factor, the Court notes that the disability commissions were dependent on the Institute since their members were appointed by the board of the Institute following nomination by the Institute's director (see paragraph 28 above). Therefore the method of their appointment justifiably gave rise to the applicant's suspicion that they would not be able to act impartially (see, *mutatis mutandis*, *Mihailov*, cited above, § 37). While such suspicions may have a certain importance, they are not decisive; what is decisive is whether the doubts raised by appearances can be objectively validated (see *Brandstetter v Austria*, 28 August 1991, § 44, Series A no. 211).

55. In this connection, and with reference to the third factor (the experts' role in proceedings), the Court agrees with the applicant that it appears from both the first- and second-instance courts' decisions that the first-instance court based its judgment on the opinions of the disability commissions (see paragraphs 15 and 17 above). It notes that in the proceedings before the Institute the task of the commissions was to examine whether the applicant's condition had deteriorated to the extent that he would have been entitled to a higher allowance. They were not required to give general advice on a particular subject, but rather to make findings on specific facts and to assess the applicant's state of health. The aim was to assist the Institute in deciding whether the applicant was entitled to a higher allowance with regard to his exact state of health at that time (see, similarly, *Sara Lind Eggertsdóttir*, cited above, § 51; *Shulepova v Russia*, no. 34449/03, § 65, 11 December 2008; and *Placì*, cited above, § 77). The conclusions of the disability commissions were directly decisive in assessing the rights at issue (see, similarly, *Mihailov*, cited above, § 34).

56. The Court further notes that the applicant did not have the opportunity to challenge the findings of the commissions since his application to have the courts appoint an independent expert were dismissed on the grounds that the commissions had already made an adequate assessment of the documentation in the applicant's medical file (see paragraph 15 above). The appellate court confirmed this decision of the first-instance court, also stating that it was based on the opinions of the commission. This left the opinions of the commission as the decisive evidence relied on by the courts to determine the issue in a case which certainly required expert knowledge, arguably not at hand in

the court itself. Such reasoning by the domestic courts further highlights the dominant role of the Institute's disability commissions (see, similarly, *Placì*, cited above, § 78). In this light, the fact that the domestic court also heard testimony from the applicant and had regard to other material in the file before dismissing the claim, is not sufficient for the Court to decide that the proceedings complied with the Convention requirements.

57. The Court is therefore unable to conclude that the applicant's procedural position was on a par with that of his adversary, a State-run social protection body, as required by the principle of equality of arms.

There has accordingly been a violation of Article 6 of the Convention.

Note

The case above illustrates that when the European Court of Human Rights considers whether there has been a breach of the equality of arms principle, three predominant factors should be considered. The first is the nature of the task entrusted to the experts. If their role is to specifically advise the public body on the applicability of rules in individual cases and they are appointed for that purpose, then the argument that the experts are likely to focus on the position of the state may be strengthened. The second factor to be considered is the relationship of the expert to the state – if experts are independently appointed and protected from removal by law, it may be argued that the experts retain an adequate degree of independence to be neutral in the opinions that they offer. However, if an expert is appointed by a particular state body and can be removed by that same body, the likelihood is that the expert may be said to lack independence and will likely favour the position of the state. The final question that must be considered under the equality of arms principle is the approach of review bodies and courts to the expert's report. If the expert report is considered to be largely conclusive of the issues of fact, then it is likely to be held that where a claimant does not have the financial resources to appoint an expert to support his case, the court should do so at public expense.

5.4.B REGIMES PROVIDING FOR EXPERT TESTIMONY BUT NO AMICUS CURIAE

5.4.B.1 GERMANY

Zivilprozessordnung **5.35 (DE)**

§402 Applicability of the rules for witnesses

Unless otherwise provided for by the provisions below, the rules in place for the evidence provided by witnesses shall apply mutatis mutandis to the evidence provided by experts.

§403 Offer to provide evidence

Evidence shall be offered by designating the issues regarding which a report is to be prepared.

§404 Selection of the expert

(1) The court hearing the case shall select the experts to be involved and shall determine their number. It may limit itself to appointing a single expert. It may appoint other experts to take the stead of the expert first appointed.

(2) Before the appointment, the parties can be heard on the choice of the expert.

(3) Should experts have been publicly appointed for certain types of reports, other persons shall be selected only if particular circumstances so require.

(4) The court may ask the parties to propose persons who are suited to be examined as experts.

(5) Should the parties agree on certain persons to be appointed as experts, the court is to comply with what they have agreed; however, the court may limit the selection made by the parties to a certain number.

…

§406 Rejection of an expert

(1) An expert may be rejected for the same reasons that permit the rejection of a judge. However, the fact that the expert has been examined as a witness cannot be taken as ground for rejecting him.

(2) The petition for rejection is to be filed with the court or judge by whom the expert has been appointed, prior to the expert being examined; at the latest, however, within two weeks following the pronouncement or service of the order concerning the appointment. Any such rejection shall be admissible at a later date only if the petitioner demonstrates to the satisfaction of the court that he was prevented, through no fault of his own, from asserting and filing the reasons for rejecting the expert earlier. The petition may be recorded with the registry for the files of the court.

…

§407 Obligation to submit a report

(1) The person appointed as expert is to comply with this appointment if he is a publicly appointed expert responsible for the submission of reports of the type required, or if he publicly pursues, as an economic activity, the science, art or commercial activities, the knowledge of which is a pre-requisite for preparing the report, or if he has been publicly appointed or authorised for the exercise of such activities.

(2) Any person who has declared before the court that he is willing to submit such a report shall be under obligation to do so.

§407a Other obligations of the expert

(1) The expert shall review, without undue delay, whether the task allocated to him by the court in fact falls within his field and whether it can be completed without involving further experts. Should this not be the case, the expert is to notify the court of this fact without undue delay.

…

(3) The expert does not have authority to transfer the task allocated to him by the court to another person. To the extent the expert avails himself of the collaboration of another person, he shall provide that person's name and set out the scope of the work of that person, unless the work so done concerned ancillary services of minor significance.

(4) Should the expert be in doubt as to the content and scope of the task allocated to him by the court, he is to procure clarification from the court without undue delay. If it is foreseeable that costs will accrue that are clearly disproportionate to the value of the

subject matter being litigated or that significantly exceed the requested advance on the costs, he shall draw the attention of the court to this circumstance in due time.

(5) Should the court so demand, the expert shall submit or communicate, without delay, the files and any other documents he has used to prepare his report, as well as any results of his investigations. Should he fail to comply with this obligation, the court shall order the submission.

(6) The court shall advise the expert of his obligations.

§408 Right to refuse to prepare a report

(1) The same grounds that entitle a witness to refuse to testify shall entitle an expert to refuse to prepare a report. The court may also release an expert from the obligation to prepare a report for other reasons.

(2) When examining judges, civil servants, and other persons in the public service, the specific stipulations of civil service law shall apply. The special rules governing the actions of members of the federal government or of a state government shall apply for these persons.

(3) Anyone who has assisted with a judicial ruling may not be examined as an expert regarding questions that were the subject matter of the court's decision.

...

§411 Written report

(1) If it is ordered that the report be submitted in writing, the court shall set the expert a time period within which he is to transmit his signed report.

(2) Should an expert who is obliged to submit the report fail to meet the deadline imposed on him, a coercive fine shall be levied against him. A warning that a coercive fine may be levied must have been previously issued, with a period of grace being set in the warning. Should the deadline be missed in repeated instances, the coercive fine may be levied once again in the same manner. A single coercive fine may not exceed 3,000 Euro. §409 (2) shall apply mutatis mutandis.

(3) The court may order the expert to appear before it for the purpose of explaining the written report. The court can also order a written explanation or supplementation of the report.

(4) Within a reasonable period of time, the parties are to communicate to the court their objections to the report, any petitions with regard to the preparation of the report, and supplementary questions to the written report. The court may set a deadline for this; §296 (1) and (4) shall apply mutatis mutandis.

§411a Use of expert reports prepared in other proceedings

The preparation of a written report may be replaced with re-using an expert report that has been obtained by the court or the public prosecution office in other court proceedings.

...

§414 Expert witnesses

Insofar as knowledgeable persons are to be examined in order to obtain evidence regarding past facts and circumstances, or situations given in the past, the perception of which required special technical competence, the rules governing the taking of evidence by hearing witnesses shall be applicable.

Notes

(1) There is no superiority of one kind of evidence over the other in German law. The court decides the case before it according to its free conviction formed from the overall result of the proceedings, and not on the basis of evidence alone. With regard to experts, the provisions of the Code of Civil Procedure (Zivilprozessordnung) apply according to §98 VwGO. The evidence of experts is delivered by submitting a report. As German administrative court proceedings are guided by the inquisitorial principle, the court directs the expert in terms of his activities and may issue instructions concerning their nature and scope. Where the facts of a case are at issue, the court shall determine the facts on which the expert is to base his report.

According to §404 of the Code of Civil Procedure, the court also selects the experts. It may limit itself to appointing a single expert. Should experts have been publicly appointed for certain types of reports, other persons shall be selected only if particular circumstances so require. The court may also ask the parties to designate persons who are suited to be examined as experts. Should the parties to the dispute agree on certain persons being appointed as experts, the court is to comply with what they have agreed; however, the court may limit the selection made by the parties to a certain number.

(2) The concept of 'amicus curiae' is not common in German administrative law. There is the concept of 'expert witnesses' (*sachverständiger Zeuge*), but they are procedurally treated as normal witnesses and do not become parties of the proceedings. According to §93 VwGO, in conjunction with §414 of the Code of Civil Procedure, expert witnesses can be examined in order to obtain evidence regarding past facts and circumstances which required special technical competence in order to be understood.

5.4.B.2 THE NETHERLANDS

Algemene Wet Bestuursrecht **5.36 (NL)**

Article 8:47 (1) The administrative judge may appoint an expert to carry out an examination.

(2) The appointment will state the instructions to the expert and the time limit as referred to in section 4.

(3) The parties shall be informed of the intention to appoint an expert as referred to in section 1. The administrative judge may give the parties the opportunity to express their wishes concerning the investigation to the court in writing within a time limit set by the administrative judge.

(4) The administrative judge shall set the expert a time limit for submitting his written report of the examinations.

(5) The parties may express their views on the report in writing within four weeks of the date on which the report is sent to them. …

Article 8:60 (1) The administrative judge may summon witnesses and appoint experts and interpreters.

(2) A witness who has been summoned and an expert or interpreter who has accepted his appointment and has been summoned by the administrative judge shall be obliged

to comply with the summons. Articles 172 and 187 of the Code of Civil Procedure shall apply mutatis mutandis. The summons issued to the expert shall specify the assignment to be carried out, the time and place at which the assignment must be carried out and the consequences of a failure to appear.

...

(4) The parties may bring witnesses and experts or summon witnesses and experts by registered letter or bailiff's writ, provided they have sent the court and the other parties notice thereof, stating names and addresses, at least ten days before the day of the hearing. ...

Article 8:63 (1) ...

(2) The administrative judge may decide not to hear witnesses and experts brought or summoned by a party if it considers that this testimony cannot reasonably be expected to contribute to the assessment of the case.

(3) If a witness or expert called by a party has not appeared, the administrative judge may summon him. In that case the administrative judge shall stay the proceedings at court.

Notes

(1) Experts may get involved in an administrative dispute in two ways: namely, on initiative of the administrative judge or on initiative of a party. The administrative judge may appoint an expert during the preliminary investigation of a case (Article 8:47(1) AWB) and/or at the trial stage (Article 8:60(1) AWB). In both situations, the expenses of the expert and the examinations will be paid by the administrative court itself. The parties are entitled to submit in the proceedings expert reports drawn up on their request. In addition, they may bring an expert to the hearing, provided that they have informed the court and the other parties thereof at least ten days before the date of the hearing (Article 8:60(4) AWB). In that case, the expenses of the expert and the examination have to be paid by the party itself.

(2) A topic which has recently been discussed in the Netherlands is whether the administrative judges may be under an obligation to appoint an expert at the request of a party who has too limited financial means to hire an expert himself, in order to provide him with a reasonable opportunity to defend himself effectively against an administrative decision based on the opinion of a non-neutral expert working for the authority. If the latter opinion otherwise might be decisive for the court's judgment, this right may, under certain circumstances, be derived from the equality of arms requirement of Article 6 ECHR, as interpreted by the ECtHR in cases such as *Korošec* and *Letinčić*.[137] In Dutch case law, such right is recognised in medical cases, but only in a limited way.[138] The starting point of the case law is that the party involved should in principle submit medical documents which raise at least some doubts as regards the correctness of the opinion of the authority's expert. In practice, such documents

[137] See section 5.4.A.2 above. See also the decisions of the ECtHR in *Letinčić v Croatia* ECLI:CE:ECHR:2016:0503JUD000718311. In the same vein, see ECtHR, *Spycher v Switzerland* ECLI:CE:ECHR:2015:1117DEC002627512.

[138] ECLI:NL:CRVB:2017:2226; ECLI:NL:RVS:2017:1674.

are produced, for instance, by the family doctor or a medical specialist. Only if the submission of such documents cannot reasonably be expected from a party may the administrative judge be under an obligation to provide for compensation, for instance by appointing an independent medical advisor. Under what circumstances submission of documents 'cannot reasonably be expected' from a party is not yet clear, as the case law is very recent.

(3) In Dutch law, there is a specialist expert body, the Stichting Advisering Bestuursrechtspraak (Foundation of Independent Court Experts in Environmental and Planning Law; StAB). This is an independent foundation, funded by the government, with the sole task of advising, on request, the administrative courts (the district courts and the Judicial Division of the Council of State) on technical issues in environmental and/or planning law cases. The StAB has a broad expertise in all technical aspects in this area. It is for the courts to decide whether they are in need for an advisory opinion of the StaB in a specific case. The opinion is not binding for the court, although it is very influential in practice. The StAB's advisory opinion enables the judge to review the merits of such cases without being a technical expert in these areas himself, and is thus a unique instrument of judicial review of administrative decisions in these areas.

(4) Until fairly recently, the amicus curiae was an unknown phenomenon in Dutch administrative law. This changed in 2013, when Article 8:45a was included in the AWB. According to this provision, the European Commission, as guardian of the EU competition rules, and the Dutch competition authority (Autoriteit Consument en Markt, Consumer and Market Authority) are entitled to make written remarks in a case if they communicate the wish thereto, and may be allowed by the administrative judge to make oral remarks as well. Both possibilities are mandatorily prescribed by Regulation 1/2003 on the enforcement of the competition rules of Articles 81 and 82 of the Treaty (currently Article 101 and 102 TFEU).[139] Thus, this amicus curiae is in fact an EU transplant in the AWB. To date, neither the competition authority nor the Commission has made use of this possibility. If the provisions are used, the AWB guarantees that the parties can be present at the hearing where the authorities make their oral remarks. If the national or EU competition authorities, acting as amici curiae, submit their opinions or other materials to the court, the parties are entitled to respond to these documents or pleadings.

5.4.C SYSTEMS WHERE EXPERTS AND AMICI CURIAE ARE INFREQUENTLY USED

5.4.C.1 THE EUROPEAN UNION

Statute of the Court of Justice of the European Union **5.37 (EU)**

Article 25 The Court of Justice may at any time entrust any individual, body, authority, committee or other organisation it chooses with the task of giving an expert opinion.

[139] See section 5.4.A.1 above.

Rules of Procedure of the Court of Justice **5.38 (EU)**

Article 70 (1) The Court may order that an expert's report be obtained. The order appointing the expert shall define his task and set a time-limit within which he is to submit his report.

(2) After the expert has submitted his report and that report has been served on the parties, the Court may order that the expert be examined, the parties having been given notice to attend. At the request of one of the parties or of his own motion, the President may put questions to the expert.

Article 72 (1) If one of the parties objects to a witness or an expert on the ground that he is not a competent or proper person to act as a witness or expert or for any other reason, or if a witness or expert refuses to give evidence or to take the oath, the matter shall be resolved by the Court.

(2) An objection to a witness or an expert shall be raised within two weeks after service of the order summoning the witness or appointing the expert; the statement of objection must set out the grounds of objection and indicate the nature of any evidence offered.

Rules of Procedure of the General Court **5.39 (EU)**

Article 70 (1) The General Court may order that an expert's report be obtained. The order appointing the expert shall define his task and set a time-limit within which he is to make his report.

(2) The expert shall receive a copy of the order, together with all the documents necessary for carrying out his task. He shall be under the supervision of the Judge- Rapporteur, who may be present during his investigation and who shall be kept informed of his progress in carrying out his task.

The General Court may request the parties or one of them to lodge security for the costs of the expert's report.

(3) At the request of the expert, the General Court may order the examination of witnesses. Their examination shall be carried out in accordance with Article 68.

(4) The expert may give his opinion only on points which have been expressly referred to him.

(5) After the expert has made his report, the General Court may order that he be examined, the parties having been given notice to attend.

Subject to the control of the President, questions may be put to the expert by the representatives of the parties. …

Article 73 (1) If one of the parties objects to a witness or to an expert on the ground that he is not a competent or proper person to act as witness or expert or for any other reason, or if a witness or expert refuses to give evidence, to take the oath or to make a solemn affirmation equivalent thereto, the matter shall be resolved by the General Court.

(2) An objection to a witness or to an expert shall be raised within two weeks after service of the order summoning the witness or appointing the expert; the statement of objection must set out the grounds of objection and indicate the nature of any evidence offered.

Notes

(1) It is possible for experts to be called and expert reports to be used in the course of proceedings, although this is seldom done.

(2) Neither the Court of Justice nor the General Court has any provision for hearing an amicus curiae.

5.4.C.2 FRANCE

Code de justice administrative **5.40 (FR)**

Article R621-1 The court may, either *ex officio*, or at the request of the parties or of one of them, order, before the judgment, an expert examination to be carried out on the points specified in its decision. The expert can be entrusted with the task of mediation. He can also, with the consent of the parties, take the initiative of such mediation.

...

Article R621-6 The experts or persons with expert knowledge of the subject area mentioned in Article R621-2 may be objected to for the same reasons as the judges. If the expert or person with expert knowledge is a legal entity, the objection may relate to the legal entity itself or the natural person or persons who carry out the assignment in its name. Any party that intends to object to the expert or person with expert knowledge must do so before the operations begin or as soon as the reason for the objection is discovered. If the expert or person with expert knowledge considers that he may be objected to, he must immediately declare this fact to the president of the court or, at the Council of State, to the President of the Litigation Section.

Article R621-6-3 Within one week of this notification, the expert must make known in writing whether he acquiesces to the objection, or the reasons why he opposes it.

Article R621-6-4 If the expert acquiesces to the objection, he is replaced immediately.

Otherwise, the court, in a decision for which no reason is given, makes a ruling on the objection, after a hearing in open court of which the expert and the parties have been informed.

...

The expert may not challenge the decision by which he is rejected.

Article R621-7 The parties are informed by the expert or experts of the days and times on which the expert examinations will be carried out, at least four days in advance, by recorded delivery letter. ...

The parties' observations made during the course of the operations are recorded in the report.

Article R621-9 Two copies of the report are filed at the court registry. The expert sends copies to the interested parties. With their agreement, the copies may be sent in electronic form.

The court registry may ask the expert to file his report in digital form. The communication of the report to the parties is then provided by the court registry.

The parties are invited by the court registry to submit their observations within a period of one month; an extension of the period may be granted.

Article R621-10 The court may decide that the expert or experts will appear before the court formation or one of its members, after the parties have been duly convened, in order to provide all useful additional explanations and more particularly to express their opinions on the findings collected in accordance with Article R621-9.

Notes

(1) Generally, the courts in France adopt a restrictive approach to expert evidence. Experts are used only in cases involving complex technical factual aspects, such as medical liability or in environmental matters, in order to assess the extent of damage. In such cases, the expert is commissioned by the court, either at the request of one of the parties or *ex officio*. The process is conducted by a registered independent expert and is open to challenge by the parties. The expert is requested only to explain the facts and shall not give an opinion on the legal aspects of the case.

(2) Despite the restrictive approach to expert evidence in French law, the Code of Administrative Justice sets out a comprehensive framework governing the appointment of experts, the right of the parties to object to an appointment and also, evidently in response to the *Mantovanelli* judgment,[140] a framework for the parties to comment upon the evidence adduced by the expert.

Code de justice administrative **5.41 (FR)**

Article R625-2 When a technical question does not require complex investigation, the court formation may appoint a person to deliver an opinion on the points that it determines. … The consultant, who is not provided with the file of the proceedings, shall not act in compliance with the requirements of adversarial procedure.

The opinion is registered in writing. It is sent to the parties by the court. …

Article R625-3 The formation that is responsible for the preparation of the case may invite any person whose competence or skills are of a nature to make a useful contribution to the solution of the claim, to provide observations of a general nature on the points that it determines.

The opinion is registered in writing. It is sent to the parties.

Under the same conditions, every person may be invited to present oral comments before the formation responsible for the preparation of the case or the court formation when the parties have been duly summoned.

Notes

(1) The court formation with responsibility for the preparation of the case may invite any person to submit observations of a general nature on points that it determines, provided that the person concerned has particular competence or knowledge useful to the judge in order to decide the case. An amicus curiae can be differentiated from an expert because an amicus curiae is not required to be independent and its intervention is not subject to the adversarial procedure, even if the communication of an amicus curiae has to be delivered to the parties. An example of a technical opinion given by an amicus curiae is one that is requested in a public procurement case to allow the court to understand the technical specifications of a tender.

[140] See section 5.4.A above.

(2) An amicus curiae brief may be filed before French administrative courts only at the request of the court, and it can consist of observations and analyses on points of law, or provide information to assist the court in understanding technical or factual elements of the case, to the exclusion of any analysis or appraisal of the documents contained in the case file.[141] The opinion is written and communicated to the parties. It is also open to the court to invite the person to submit comments orally, either at the stage of investigation of the case or at the time when the court is formed to reach judgment.

Conseil d'État, 14 February 2014[142] **5.42 (FR)**

Mrs Rachel Lambert and others v University Hospital of Reims

EXPERT EVIDENCE AND AMICI CURIAE; URGENT CASES

Rachel Lambert

Courts may, even in interim relief procedures, request an expert report and/or the intervention of amici curiae.

Facts: Mr Vincent Lambert, born in 1976, was victim of a car accident in 2008, resulting in him being quadriplegic and in a state of complete dependence, and in need to be fed artificially. After several years and thorough examination (in a public hospital), the doctors concluded that Mr Lambert was in a state of minimal consciousness but, nonetheless, was suffering from his state and from the treatment that was being administered to him. In light of the fact that Mr Lambert had previously given his consent to stop the treatments and with the agreement of a part of the family, the doctors eventually decided to stop any further treatment, including feeding him, pursuant to the Public Health Code (Code de la santé publique), which enables doctors to stop giving treatment when such treatment amounts to an unreasonable intervention that may leave the patient in a great deal of pain or with a serious disability. Other members of the family of Mr Lambert challenged that decision through a fundamental rights interim remedy (*référé-liberté*), which enables the judge to order any measure necessary to stop an infringement of a fundamental right.[143] The case was eventually brought before the Conseil d'État.

Held: The judge has the power to seek expert reports and the intervention of amici curiae even in interim relief cases.

Judgment: Considering that, under [Article L521-2], when an application is lodged to this end, the interim relief judge, upon the request of the applicant and in case of a specific urgency, has the power to order any measures necessary to safeguard a fundamental freedom allegedly breached in a serious and manifestly unlawful manner by an administrative authority; that these legislative provisions confer on the interim relief judge, who in principle acts alone and decides, in accordance with Article L511-1 of the Code of Administrative Justice, by measures of an interim nature, the power to order, without delay and on the basis of criteria of obviousness the necessary measures to protect fundamental freedoms;

[141] Conseil d'État, 6 May 2015, *Mr A v Prefect of Ille-et-Vilaine*, N° 375036.
[142] N° 375081.
[143] See further Chapter 7, section 7.8.C.4 (iii).

Considering, however, that the interim relief judge must exercise his powers in a particular way when hearing an application under Article L521-2 of the Code of Administrative Justice concerning a decision taken by a doctor on the basis of the Public Health Code (Code de la santé publique) which would lead to the cessation of or a failure to initiate treatment on grounds that this treatment would amount to an unreasonable intervention and the implementation of the decision would cause irreversible damage to life; that in such circumstances the judge, sitting where applicable as a member of a bench of judges, must take the necessary protective measures to prevent the decision in question from being implemented, when such measures may not be covered by one of the situations provided for by law, while striking a balance between the fundamental freedoms at issue, namely the right to respect for life and the patient's right to consent to medical treatment and not undergo treatment that amounts to an unreasonable intervention; that, in such a case, the interim relief judge or the bench to which he has referred the case may, as appropriate, after temporarily suspending the implementation of the measure and before ruling on the lodged application, order a medical expert report and, under Article R625-3 of the Code of Administrative Justice, seek the opinion of any person whose expertise or knowledge is able to usefully enlighten the court.

Note

The case above demonstrates that it is possible for the court to seek expert opinions and interventions from amici curiae even in interim relief cases where this might be necessary to protect the fundamental rights of the individuals who are subject to an administrative decision.

5.4.C.3 ENGLAND AND WALES

In England and Wales, a distinction is drawn between expert evidence and the hearing of amicus curiae. Expert evidence is evidence that is brought to the court and paid for by one or both parties in order to clarify a matter of factual dispute, or where there are technical issues at stake and the court may find it helpful to have an expert explanation of them. This might be contrasted with the hearing of an amicus curiae, which is requested by the court rather than the parties and may be used to assist the court in any way that the court considers appropriate. An amicus curiae will generally assist the court on a voluntary basis, or may be paid from public funds.

Civil Procedure Rules **5.43 (EW)**

Rule 35.1 Expert evidence shall be restricted to that which is reasonably required to resolve the proceedings.

Rule 35.2 (1) A reference to an 'expert' in this Part is a reference to a person who has been instructed to give or prepare expert evidence for the purpose of proceedings.

(2) 'Single joint expert' means an expert instructed to prepare a report for the court on behalf of two or more of the parties (including the claimant) to the proceedings.

Rule 35.3 (1) It is the duty of experts to help the court on matters within their expertise.

(2) This duty overrides any obligation to the person from whom experts have received instructions or by whom they are paid.

Rule 35.4 (1) No party may call an expert or put in evidence an expert's report without the court's permission.

(2) When parties apply for permission they must provide an estimate of the costs of the proposed expert evidence and identify–

(a) the field in which expert evidence is required and the issues which the expert evidence will address; and

(b) where practicable, the name of the proposed expert.

(3) If permission is granted it shall be in relation only to the expert named or the field identified under paragraph (2). The order granting permission may specify the issues which the expert evidence should address.

...

Rule 35.5 (1) Expert evidence is to be given in a written report unless the court directs otherwise.

...

Rule 35.6 (1) A party may put written questions about an expert's report (which must be proportionate) to–

(a) an expert instructed by another party; or

(b) a single joint expert appointed under rule 35.7.

(2) Written questions under paragraph (1)–

(a) may be put once only;

(b) must be put within 28 days of service of the expert's report; and

(c) must be for the purpose only of clarification of the report,

unless in any case–

(i) the court gives permission; or

(ii) the other party agrees.

(3) An expert's answers to questions put in accordance with paragraph (1) shall be treated as part of the expert's report.

High Court (Queen's Bench Division), 10 December 2003[144] **5.44 (EW)**

Lynch v General Dental Council

APPOINTMENT OF EXPERTS IN JUDICIAL REVIEW CASES

Lynch

The court may hear expert witnesses in a judicial review case if it is necessary in order to clarify points of significant technical complexity.

Facts: Mr Lynch was a dental surgeon who had trained in Australia. He had worked in the UK for some time, and had considerable experience and expertise in orthodontic treatment. Mr Lynch thus applied to the General Dental Council (GDC) (the regulator for the dental profession in the UK) for inclusion on the specialist list of

[144] [2003] EWHC 2987 (Admin), [2004] 1 All ER 1159.

orthodontists. The GDC declined Mr Lynch's application, arguing that Mr Lynch had not provided sufficient evidence of his experience and expertise in the field of orthodontics to justify his inclusion on the list. Mr Lynch then brought a claim for judicial review, arguing that the GDC's refusal to include him on the list was irrational. As part of the claim, Mr Lynch sought to have expert testimony to explain to the court the nature of expertise in orthodontics.

Held: In a case such as the one at stake, where there are issues of great technical complexity, it may be necessary to hear an expert witness in order to be fair to the claimant.

Judgment: Collins J.: 22. I have no doubt that fresh evidence involving expert evidence should in general not be admitted … However, it is and has always been recognised that irrationality is an error of law which can lead to a decision being quashed. If the decision in question is made by an expert tribunal or indeed by anyone dealing in a field involving consideration of matters which would not obviously be fully understood by a layman without some assistance from an expert in that field, it may be necessary at the very least to have some explanation of any technical terms …

23. Mr. Havers submitted that, particularly in a case such as this, it was necessary that the Court should understand not only the meaning of the technical terms but also their significance. The nature of the treatments which the claimant had carried out could no doubt be explained, but the Court would be unable to judge whether the decision was irrational without appreciating their significance. Unless the claimant was able, for example, to show that they were the sorts of treatments which only a specialist would be expected to carry out, he could not establish his claim and this was manifestly unfair.

24. It is clear that the Court's function must not be usurped. But it seems to me that the Court must be enabled to carry out its function. To do this it must understand the material which is put before it. There is in my view a real distinction between a report from an expert which seeks to explain what is involved in a particular process (in this case, treatment) and how complicated that process is and one which goes on to opine that it was irrational for the body to have reached the conclusion it did. I recognise that in this jurisdiction the obtaining by a defendant of a report which disagrees with the views of the claimant's expert may neutralise those views since the Court cannot and will not decide the issue of fact. However, it seems to me that in a truly technical field, where the significance of a particular process is in issue expert evidence can be admitted to explain the process and its significance. Cases where this can be permitted will be very rare and what I have said should not be regarded as opening the door to the admissibility of experts' reports in all cases such as this which involve judicial review of an expert tribunal or body. Equally, the court must be careful to recognise and to apply the distinction to which I have referred, albeit in some instances it may be somewhat difficult to see where the line should be drawn.

25. This is, I appreciate, some extension … of the possibility of admitting fresh evidence. But its purpose is in reality to explain to the court matters which it needs to understand in order to reach a just conclusion. It is difficult to see why, where such need is established, that should not in principle be permitted. But a word of caution is appropriate. Where the tribunal or body is itself composed of experts or has been advised by an expert assessor (which can happen in appeals in cases such as the present), it will be virtually impossible to justify the submission of expert evidence which goes beyond explanation of technical terms since it will almost inevitably involve an attempt to challenge the factual conclusions and judgment of an expert. That is something which is inappropriate for a reviewing court.

Notes

(1) Part 35 CPR provides a framework for the admission of expert evidence. Such expert evidence may only be brought to the court by a party to the proceedings (or the parties to the proceedings) with the permission of the court. Although the evidence is adduced by the parties, the expert is under a duty to the court. As such, it should be impartial and aim to assist the court in the determination of the case, rather than to assist the claim of the instructing party. Other than in exceptional cases, expert reports and any questions on an expert report must be submitted in writing, although under Rule 35.5 CPR the court may instruct the expert to offer oral testimony and then, under the rules of evidence in Rule 32 CPR, may permit the expert to be cross-examined.[145] It should also be noted that although expert evidence must be adduced by an expert appointed by a party or parties to the proceedings and cannot be sought directly by the court on its own volition, this does not mean that the court cannot seek such evidence in the sense that, under the powers of the court in Rule 32.1 CPR, it is possible for the court to advise the parties that it is likely to be assisted by an expert report on a specific issue or issues and that they should thus seek to bring an expert witness to assist their case.

(2) As noted above in section 5.2.C, as the parties are generally expected to agree on a statement of facts prior to the full hearing in judicial review proceedings, it is not usual for the court to hear from expert witnesses. However, it has been held in some cases that an expert witness is needed to explain technical issues so that the court can reach a conclusion on the legality of the public authority's decision. In any case where expert witnesses are heard, their role is to assist the court in relation to issues of factual difficulty or complexity, rather than to opine that a decision of a public authority was lawful or unlawful. Their role should also be limited to explaining terms of particular complexity to the court, rather than seeking to interpret or reinterpret evidence. It is important to emphasise that in cases where expert witnesses are heard, they are under a duty to assist the court.

High Court (Queen's Bench Division), 19 April 2005[146] **5.45 (EW)**

R (Ministry of Defence) v Swindon and Wiltshire Coroner

APPOINTMENT OF AMICUS CURIAE

Swindon and Wiltshire Coroner

An amicus curiae may be appointed to assist the court or represent parties who may be unable to represent themselves, although the amicus curiae must be appointed by the Attorney General where he is to be paid from public funds.

Facts: The Swindon and Wiltshire Coroner (an official who investigates unexplained, suspicious or violent deaths) delivered a verdict of unlawful killing in relation to the death of an army serviceman in 1953 as a result

[145] See the discussion of the rules of evidence in section 5.3.B.1 above.

[146] *R (Ministry of Defence) v Swindon and Wiltshire Coroner* [2005] EWHC 889 (Admin), [2006] 1 WLR 134.

of a non-therapeutic experiment carried out by the Ministry of Defence involving sarin nerve gas. The Ministry of Defence brought a claim for judicial review, arguing that the Coroner's summing up of the evidence was not fair. As part of the proceedings, the Ministry of Defence sought disclosure of the tape recordings of the proceedings before the Coroner so that the court might hear the tone of voice and approach of the Coroner to the evidence. The Coroner argued that he should be entitled to a Protective Costs Order restricting his liability for costs[147] if he was unsuccessful in defending the claim. As part of the proceedings, the question arose as to whether the court ought to seek the appointment of an amicus curiae to represent the interests of the family of the deceased, given that they were not in a position to represent themselves at the judicial review hearing and the Coroner was not necessarily in a position to represent the interests of the families.

Held: The court held that the tape recordings should be disclosed and that the Coroner was not entitled to a Protective Costs Order. The court discussed the circumstances when an amicus curiae should be appointed and determined to seek advice from the Attorney General on what representation might be appropriate in this case.

Judgment: Collins J.: 38 I should however make this point. It is obvious that if the coroner does not appear and take an active role, there is someone who is going to have to do so. That someone will either be the family, supported by public funds, or an amicus, equally supported by public funds, and it may be that there is a more general concern that in an exceptional situation such as this, and I do not doubt that it is an exceptional situation, the matter is of more general concern than just for the County of Wiltshire and it may be considered to be more appropriate that, in some form or other, central funds should bear the burden. Whether it is the ministry or some other central funds perhaps does not at this stage matter.

39 But that argument, as it seems to me, is something that should be raised by the county council and put to whoever is responsible in central government, whichever department is the appropriate one. No doubt that can relatively easily be ascertained. If it is an amicus, as I understand it, the vote is that of the Treasury Solicitor. If it is to be legal aid, the vote is that of the Department of Constitutional Affairs. Otherwise of course, so far as the ministry is concerned, these proceedings are brought and will be paid for, so far as necessary, out of the ministry's vote. But all will be, in one form or another, out of central funds.

...

41 However, going back to what I said earlier about an amicus, since the coroner is not likely to argue the points which the family might want to raise, it may well be that the sensible course to adopt here is to ask for an amicus. I do not propose to make that decision finally now, because I think it would be sensible to enable a little time to be taken so that the parties can sort out, if possible, who is to be represented and on what sort of basis, having regard to my decision today. Equally, there will be a little time because, until Mr Havers has had the opportunity to consider the disk and to decide whether the allegations in relation to what I have called tone of voice are to be pursued, there is no point in reaching any final conclusion as to how this case is to proceed. But the decision whether an amicus is appropriate is one that the court is going to have to make shortly.

42 I should add of course that even if the court does decide that an amicus is desirable it does not mean that the court will get an amicus because the procedure is, if I correctly recall it, for the court to ask the Attorney General to appoint an amicus, and of course it is open to him to take the view that in all the circumstances that is not necessary.

43 What I suggest is done is that this is put to the Attorney General now, not on the basis of a formal request for an amicus, but so that my concerns are indicated to him and he may involve himself in deciding at an early stage, or persuading others who may

[147] See Chapter 7, sections 7.4 and 7.9.B.1 (iv).

decide at an early stage, what may be the appropriate approach to funding and to representation in what I regard as the somewhat exceptional circumstances of this case. As I said, I make it clear that I am not making a formal request for an amicus yet because there are other things to be decided and the position of the family may be clarified within a relatively short time, or at least clarified temporarily, as Mr Brown put it, in the sense that he could not guarantee that whatever decision was reached now would necessarily prevail for the whole time. There might be a need to reconsider. But obviously whatever decision is made on representation should be made on the basis of the fullest possible information.

Note

In England and Wales, it is possible for the court to seek the appointment of an amicus curiae to avoid a one-sided argument or to advise the court on a legal issue that is of particular importance. This power arises at common law, rather than from the Civil Procedure Rules. As noted in the *Swindon and Wiltshire Coroner* case, the court has no power to require that an amicus curiae be provided, as this is a matter for the Attorney General (the government's chief law officer). Such requests are infrequent, as the court must always be mindful of the cost to public funds.[148]

5.4.D COMPARATIVE REMARKS

Each of the systems studied permits the hearing of expert evidence to some degree, although this is always in line with the philosophy in respect of the hearing of evidence. In the Netherlands and Germany, the practice of calling experts is more common than in the EU courts, France or England and Wales. In all the systems that are studied, it is most common for expert witnesses to be called to assist the courts with issues of particular factual technicality. In England and Wales, the expectation is that experts will ordinarily assist the court only with factual matters and are not generally permitted to make observations on matters of law. This requirement does not appear to be imposed strictly in the other systems, although in the Netherlands there is a general expectation that experts will not address points of law, although this is not set down in law. In France, by contrast, it is possible for experts to advise on points of law.

One particular point of interest from a comparative perspective is the right of the parties to challenge or object to expert evidence in the court proceedings. It is clear that in Germany, France and before the European courts there is a specific legal right or process available to allow the parties to challenge the appointment and evidence of an expert witness. In the Netherlands, there is a practice of allowing the parties to do this, but there is no requirement in legislation. In England and Wales, there is the potential under Rule 35.6 CPR for the parties to pose written questions to a provider of expert evidence. Furthermore, there is potential for either of the parties to the proceedings to ask for the expert to be cross-examined on their evidence should there be any dispute

[148] *London Borough of Islington v Camp* [2004] LGR 58 (QB).

over it. There is evidence, particularly in France, that the framework for the appointment and challenging of expert evidence has been influenced by the decisions of the European Court of Human Rights.

The appointment of an amicus curiae or the power of the court to hear an amicus curiae is a subject of some variance between the systems. In Germany and France, there appears to be overlap between the roles of experts and amici curiae in the sense that both adopt similar functions and are appointed by the court. There is no concept of an amicus curiae at the European level, so it is not possible for the courts to hear such submissions. In England and Wales, the concepts of experts (which are brought by the parties) and an amicus curiae (whose appointment is sought by the court) are separate, although neither are heard regularly in judicial review proceedings and in the case of an amicus curiae, although the court has the power to seek such assistance, the decision over whether it is provided lies with the Attorney General.

5.5 POWER OF THE COURT TO DECIDE ISSUES *ULTRA PETITA*

The power of the court to grant a remedy not sought by the parties (ie *ultra petita*) is determined by the approach of the legal system concerned. In all jurisdictions, the dispute before the court is ultimately framed by the parties, and it is not possible for the court, acting under its own volition, to add to it. Rules requiring courts not to act *ultra petita* also prevent a so-called *reformatio in peius*, ie the situation that a claim places an individual in a less favourable position than he would have been had he not lodged the claim. The CJEU has held that the prohibition of a *reformatio in peius* applies in EU law on the basis of the traditions of Member States and the principles of effective judicial protection, and also that the rule ensures the protection of the rights of defence and legal certainty.[149]

5.5.A GERMANY

Verwaltungsgerichtsordnung **5.46 (DE)**

§88 The court may not go beyond what is requested in the action, but is not bound by the wording of the statement of claim.

Note

In Germany, the administrative court is bound by the claims made by the parties, but may interpret the wording of the statement of claim in order to clarify the claims made by the parties. Thus, *reformatio in peius* is prohibited in administrative court proceedings. The court may not decide to the detriment of the claimant if there is no corresponding counterclaim. The provision of §88 VwGO also serves to prevent courts from acting *ultra petita*.

[149] Case C-455/06 *Heemskerk & Schaap* ECLI:EU:C:1999.14.

5.5.B FRANCE

As a matter of practice in France, the courts do not act *ultra petita*, although this is not specifically provided for in legislation.[150] The administrative court is bound by the claims of the parties. The rationale for the prohibition of *ultra petita* is drawn from the desire to prevent the court from behaving like an administrator. Consequently, the court may ignore illegalities of an act if they are not expressly challenged by the parties or he may not annul an administrative decision which was not challenged by the applicant.[151] Furthermore, it cannot either annul an administrative decision in its entirety if only the partial annulment was requested[152] or order a compensation whose amount is higher than that requested by a party.[153] However, the administrative court may sometimes use powers of interpretation to reformulate the challenges brought by the parties if this enables the court to clarify the objectives of the claim.[154]

5.5.C THE NETHERLANDS

Algemene Wet Bestuursrecht **5.47 (NL)**

Article 8:69 (1) The administrative judge shall give judgment on the basis of the act introducing the claim, the documents lodged, the proceedings during the preliminary investigations and the investigations in court.

Explanatory memorandum to Article 8:69 AWB[155] **5.48 (NL)**

We [the ministers of Justice and Interior Affairs, responsible for AWB] are of the opinion that the scope of the dispute, to be decided by the court, is in principle determined by the scope of the act introducing the claim. Consistently with the primary function of administrative justice, namely to provide for legal protection, there is no reason for the court to rule beyond the claim [*ultra petita*]. Moreover, from the viewpoint of legal certainty of the parties involved, it would be unfortunate if it were possible for the court to exceed the limits of the dispute as presented to it by the parties.

The foregoing implies, in the first place, that the court should not rule on parts of the decision which are not contested. However, it should be noted in this respect that the court should not assess this matter solely on the basis of the grounds that have been formulated in the act introducing the claim. After all, from the absence of certain grounds it cannot be inferred that a claimant deliberately did not raise certain defects of the decision .... It is consistent with the active role of the court in the proceedings that the claimant is granted the opportunity to react thereto.

150 Conseil d'État, 8 August 1919, *Delacour*, N° 56377.
151 Conseil d'État, 27 February 1974, *Broch*, N° 87063.
152 Conseil d'État, 5 November 1975, *Société Pavita*, N° 95530.
153 Conseil d'État, 28 October 1977, *Martin*, N° 00791.
154 For a discussion of this issue, see B Seiller, M Guyomar, *Contentieux administratif*, 4th edn (Paris, Dalloz, 2017) 80.
155 PG Awb II, 463.

In the second place, bringing a claim for judicial review should not lead to the situation that a claimant would be placed in a less favourable position. In that respect, a *reformatio in peius* in the strict sense should not be possible. …

Notes

(1) According to Article 8:69(1) AWB, as interpreted in the Explanatory Memorandum, the scope of administrative disputes is, in principle, determined by the act introducing the claim – and the grounds raised therein against the decision contested – and by the discussions during the preliminary investigations and the hearing. This implies in the first place that the administrative judge may not rule *ultra petita*. Thus, judicial review does not check the contested decision entirely, not even where the administrative judge recognises that the decision has (major) legal flaws. The prohibition of *reformatio in peius* is guarded strictly by the courts.[156]

(2) It can be derived from the Explanatory Memorandum to Article 8:69(1) AWB that the grounds raised by the claimant are in principle decisive for the scope of the dispute to be decided by the court. In the grounds, the claimant indicates why he believes that the decision is unlawful. The grounds may be formulated in laymen's terms – in the Netherlands, there is no requirement that claimants must be represented by a lawyer. If the intentions of the claimant are not clear, the administrative court should discuss the scope of the grounds at the hearing. To this extent, the Dutch administrative judges are still active judges. However, if the claimant does not raise a certain ground at all, the court cannot address it. The 'scope of the dispute' is (partly) decisive for the judicial obligation to apply the law *ex officio*.[157]

5.5.D THE EUROPEAN UNION

Rules of Procedure of the Court of Justice **5.49 (EU)**

Article 120 An application of the kind referred to in Article 21 of the Statute shall state:

…

(d) the form of order sought by the applicant;

Rules of Procedure of the General Court **5.50 (EU)**

Article 119 (1) An application of the kind referred to in Article 21 of the Statute shall state:

…

(d) the form of order sought by the applicant;

[156] See ECLI:NL:RVS:1999:AD6700.

[157] See section 5.6.C below.

Note

In an application before the European courts, the party must state clearly the form of order sought, ie which decision it is claiming that the court should give. This indication must express exactly the *petitum* of the applicant so that the European courts do not decide *ultra petita*.[158]

5.5.E ENGLAND AND WALES

As noted above,[159] judicial review proceedings in England and Wales are adversarial and the dispute is framed by the parties. The judge will not seek to add to or otherwise change the dispute as framed by the parties, nor will he seek to decide issues that are not raised by the parties in the statement of claim.

There is no evidence that the English courts have considered the issue of *reformatio in peius* in the case law, although this is perhaps unsurprising, given the adherence to the grounds submitted by the claimant.

5.5.F COMPARATIVE REMARKS

In all of the systems studied, it is not usually possible for the court to act *ultra petita*. In Germany and the Netherlands, such action is specifically precluded by legislative provisions, whereas in France and England and Wales, the rule is drawn from the practice of the courts or the approach of the common law, respectively. In direct actions, the Court of Justice of the European Union adheres to a similar rule – it is not possible for the court to act *ultra petita*. The rationale for the adherence to a rule that courts will not act *ultra petita* is drawn primarily from a desire to ensure legal certainty – if the court is willing to act *ultra petita*, then this may create considerable uncertainty about the scope of a dispute and may lead to the determination of issues that had not been contemplated by the parties. Furthermore, it will be inherently difficult for the courts to create a legal framework through which they might act *ultra petita* that would be sufficient to ensure legal certainty. Furthermore, if courts are willing to act *ultra petita*, this will almost certainly impact upon the rights of defence enjoyed by the parties if the court determines such issues without allowing parties the opportunity to argue on these points. The refusal to act *ultra petita* also brings with it the notable advantage that it prevents the potential for a *reformatio in peius*.

The evident disadvantage of a refusal to act *ultra petita* is that there is considerable potential for unlawful acts to stand and parties to a claim to be denied a remedy. This is particularly likely in circumstances where a claimant is not represented by a lawyer and has thus omitted certain issues in the claim submitted to the court.

[158] See Case C-296/01 *Commission v France* ECLI:EU:C:2003:626, para 121; Joined Cases 46/59 and 47/59 *Meroni & Co, Erba – Meroni & Co, Milan v High Authority of the European Coal and Steel Community* ECLI:EU:C:1962:44.

[159] See section 5.2.C above.

5.6 POWER OF THE COURT TO CONSIDER ISSUES *EX OFFICIO*

The power of a court to act *ex officio* concerns the power to go beyond the ambit of the dispute framed by the parties and to draw on facts and legal and public policy arguments not raised by the parties. There may be important reasons of public policy that allow courts to act *ex officio*, but most systems tend to restrict the ability of the court to act *ex officio* or preclude the possibility entirely.

Joined Cases C-222/05 to C-225/05, 7 June 2007[160] **5.51 (EU)**

J van der Weerd and Others v Minister van Landbouw, Natuur en Voedselkwaliteit

EX OFFICIO; EU LAW; DUTY OF NATIONAL COURTS

van der Weerd

EU law does not require national courts to conduct an examination of their own motion of the compatibility of national administrative decisions with EU law.

Facts: The claimants brought proceedings in the Netherlands arguing that the Dutch authorities had acted contrary to national law in declaring their herds of cattle to be infected with foot and mouth disease and ordering their destruction. The national court rejected their arguments based on Dutch law, but sent preliminary question to the CJEU seeking clarification of whether the principles of equivalence and effectiveness in EU law require the court to raise issues of compatibility with EU law *ex officio*.

Held: It was held that there is no requirement that national courts should raise issues of compatibility with EU law *ex officio*.

Judgment: Question 1

20. By this question, the national court essentially asks whether Community law requires a national court, in actions such as the main proceedings, to conduct an examination of its own motion of the validity of an administrative measure by having regard to pleas in law which allege that Articles 11 and 13 of Directive 85/511 have been infringed.

...

Substance

28. It is clear from the case-law that, in the absence of Community rules in the field, it is for the domestic legal system of each Member State to designate the courts and tribunals having jurisdiction and to lay down the detailed procedural rules governing actions for safeguarding rights which individuals derive from Community law, provided, first, that such rules are not less favourable than those governing similar domestic actions (principle of equivalence) and, secondly, that they do not render virtually impossible or excessively difficult the exercise of rights conferred by Community law (principle of effectiveness) (Joined Cases C-430/93 and C-431/93 *Van Schijndel and van Veen* [1995] ECR I-4705, paragraph 17, and Case C-129/00 *Commission v Italy* [2003] ECR I-14637, paragraph 25).

[160] ECLI:EU:C:2007:318.

29. As regards the principle of equivalence, it is clear from the order for reference that the College van Beroep voor het bedrijfsleven is competent to raise of its own motion issues relating to the infringement of rules of public policy, which are construed in Dutch law as meaning issues concerning the powers of administrative bodies and those of the court itself, and provisions as to admissibility. Those rules lie at the very basis of the national procedures, since they define the conditions in which those procedures may be initiated and the authorities which have the power, within their area of responsibility, to determine the extent of the rights and obligations of individuals.

30. The provisions of Directive 85/511 which are at issue do not occupy a similar position within the Community legal order. They govern neither the conditions in which procedures relating to the control of foot-and-mouth disease may be initiated nor the authorities which have the power, within their area of responsibility, to determine the extent of the rights and obligations of individuals.

31. Those provisions cannot therefore be considered as being equivalent to the national rules of public policy referred to above. As a result, the application of the principle of equivalence does not mean, as regards the present cases, that the national court is obliged to conduct of its own motion an examination of the validity of the administrative measures in question by having regard to criteria based on Directive 85/511.

32. Moreover, were those provisions to form part of public health policy, they would have been put forward in the main proceedings essentially in order to take account of the private interests of individuals who had been the object of measures to control foot-and-mouth disease.

33. As regards the principle of effectiveness, it is clear from the Court's case-law that each case which raises the question whether a national procedural provision renders the exercise of rights conferred by the Community legal order on individuals impossible or excessively difficult must be analysed by reference to the role of that provision in the procedure, its progress and its special features, viewed as a whole, before the various national instances. In that context, it is necessary to take into consideration, where relevant, the principles which lie at the basis of the national legal system, such as the protection of the rights of the defence, the principle of legal certainty and the proper conduct of the proceedings (see, to that effect, Case C-312/93 *Peterbroeck* [1995] ECR I-4599, paragraph 14, and *Van Schijndel and van Veen*, paragraph 19).

34. In the cases which gave rise to the judgment in *Van Schijndel and van Veen*, the Court examined the compatibility with the principle of effectiveness of a principle of national law which provided that the power of the court to raise pleas of its own motion in domestic proceedings was limited by its obligation to keep to the subject-matter of the dispute and to base its decision on the facts put before it.

35. The Court held that that limitation on the power of the national court was justified by the principle that, in a civil suit, it is for the parties to take the initiative, and that, as a result, the court is able to act of its own motion only in exceptional cases involving the public interest. That principle safeguards the rights of the defence and ensures the proper conduct of proceedings by, in particular, protecting them from the delays inherent in examination of new pleas (see, to that effect, *Van Schijndel and van Veen*, paragraph 21).

36. On the basis of that reasoning, the Court held that the principle of effectiveness does not preclude a national provision which prevents national courts from raising of their own motion an issue as to whether the provisions of Community law have been infringed, where examination of that issue would oblige them to abandon the passive role assigned to them by going beyond the ambit of the dispute defined by the parties themselves and relying on facts and circumstances other than those on which the party

with an interest in application of those provisions has based his claim (see *Van Schijndel and van Veen*, paragraph 22).

37. In the present case, the *College van Beroep voor het bedrijfsleven* (High Administrative Court for Trade and Industry) indicates that the procedure followed before it does not differ, in that regard, from the procedure at issue in *Van Schijndel and van Veen*. In particular, to examine of the court's own motion issues not put forward by the appellants in the main proceedings would go beyond the ambit of the dispute as put before it. Those two procedures differ only in so far as, in the present case, the High Administrative Court for Trade and Industry is not ruling as a court of last instance, as in that judgment, but as a court of first and last instance.

38. That matter alone does not place the parties to the main proceedings in a special situation which is capable of calling into question the principles referred to above. Accordingly, it cannot lead to a different conclusion from that reached by the Court in *Van Schijndel and van Veen*. That point does not affect the fact that, in the context referred to in the preceding paragraph, the taking into consideration by the national court of its own motion of issues not put forward by the parties to the main proceedings is, as in that judgment, capable of infringing the rights of the defence and the proper conduct of proceedings and, in particular, of leading to the delays inherent in the examination of new pleas.

…

41. It follows that the principle of effectiveness does not, in circumstances such as those which arise in the main proceedings, impose a duty on national courts to raise a plea based on a Community provision of their own motion, irrespective of the importance of that provision to the Community legal order, where the parties are given a genuine opportunity to raise a plea based on Community law before a national court. Since the appellants in the main proceedings have had a genuine opportunity to raise pleas based on Directive 85/511, the principle of effectiveness does not require the national court to examine of its own motion a plea based on Articles 11 and 13 of that Directive.

42. In the light of the foregoing, the answer to Question 1 should be that Community law does not require the national court, in an action of the kind which forms the basis of the main proceedings, to raise of its own motion a plea alleging infringement of the provisions of Community legislation, since neither the principle of equivalence nor the principle of effectiveness require it to do so.

Notes

(1) The judgment of the Court of Justice in this case is helpful in illustrating the policy reasons for limiting or excluding the potential for courts to act *ex officio*. In particular, if the courts were under such an obligation, then this would add considerable complexity and delay in many cases. There might also be considerable problems in the sense that the rights of defence available to the parties could be compromised by the raising of issues *ex officio* in the sense that the legal representatives may not have an adequate opportunity to research and respond to them.

(2) The judgment is also important because it sets minimum harmonisation requirements to be respected by national courts with regard to their *ex officio* powers. According to the case law of the Court of Justice, national courts are not required to raise points *ex officio* if there is no power to do so in national law. However, where

there is discretion on the part of national courts to consider issues *ex officio* in domestic law, this implies an obligation to consider EU law *ex officio* if such a bar would impair the principle of effectiveness. In order to make that assessment, according to the Court, a national procedural provision must be analysed by reference to the role of that provision in the procedure, its progress and its special features, viewed as a whole, before the various national instances. In that context, it is necessary to take into consideration, where relevant, the principles which lie at the basis of the national legal system, such as the protection of the rights of the defence, the principle of legal certainty and the proper conduct of the proceedings.[161] Furthermore, according to the Court, certain EU law provisions which have the character of public order provisions should always be raised *ex officio*. In thc context of arbitration, for example, it has been held that Article 101 TFEU has the character of a public order provision and should, according to the principle of equivalence, always be applied *ex officio*.[162]

5.6.A FRANCE

Code de justice administrative **5.52 (FR)**

Article R611-7 When the president of the court formation or, at the Council of State, the chamber charged with the preparation of the case, considers that the decision may be based on an argument raised *ex officio*, he informs the parties of this before the sitting at which the case will be judged and determines a time limit within which they may submit their observations on the argument sent to them. The fact that the preparations may be closed shall not interfere with this process.

Notes

(1) On the whole, the court in France is required to abide by the pleas set out in the application to the court and the response of the defendant. However, it is possible for the court to act *ex officio* in certain circumstances, where these pleas concern issues relating to the public interest or public order. *Ex officio* pleas are predominantly raised in relation to three issues, knowing that there is no exhaustive list of what could be raised *ex officio*.

The first issue is that the court may raise a plea in relation to its own jurisdiction. Secondly, there might be a plea on the admissibility of the case, whether this relates to

[161] Case C-430/93 *Jeroen van Schijndel & Johannes Nicolaas Cornelis van Veen v Stichting Pensioenfonds voor Fysiotherapeuten* ECLI:EU:C:1995:441. For a detailed account of the obligations imposed on national courts to consider EU law *ex officio*, see R Ortlep and RJGM Widdershoven, 'Judicial Protection' in JH Jans, S Prechal and RJGM Widdershoven (eds), *Europeanisation of Public Law* 2nd edn (Groningen, Europa Law Publishing, 2015) 333–434.

[162] Case C-126/97 *Eco Swiss China Time Ltd v Benetton International NV* ECLI:EU:C:1999:269, as interpreted in Joined Cases C-295/04 to C-298/04 *Vincenzo Manfredi v Lloyd Adriatico Assicurazioni SpA* ECLI:EU:C:2006:461.

the legal capacity of the applicant, standing[163] or compliance with the time limits, etc. The third possible *ex officio* plea arises depending on the nature of the remedy that is sought and the legal grounds raised in the case which are related to the substance of the case. Pleas that can be raised *ex officio* by the court are pleas, for example, challenging the retroactivity of a regulatory decision,[164] the inexistence of an administrative decision[165] or the nullity of a contract based on the fact that it is seriously vitiated (because the consent of the parties is lacking).[166]

(2) The court may raise such pleas *ex officio* only if they emerge clearly from the files submitted by the parties. The pleas have to be communicated to the parties, and the parties have a right to respond to the pleas and contradict the claims made therein. In such cases, when the judge raises pleas *ex officio*, it is often introduced by the words 'without it being necessary to rule on the pleas submitted by the parties' (*sans qu'il soit besoin d'examiner les moyens de la requête*), meaning that the pleas presented by the parties would not be reviewed, a plea *ex officio* being regarded as taking priority.

5.6.B GERMANY

Grundgesetz **5.53 (DE)**

Article 19 (4) Should any person's rights be violated by a public authority, he shall have recourse to the courts.

Article 20 …

(3) The legislature shall be bound by the constitutional order, the executive and the judiciary by law and justice.

Verwaltungsgerichtsordnung **5.54 (DE)**

§86 (1) The court shall investigate the facts of the case *ex officio*; those concerned shall be consulted in doing so. It shall not be bound to the submissions and to the motions for the taking of evidence of those concerned.

Note

The 'inquisitorial principle' (*Untersuchungsgrundsatz*) has a constitutional basis in the right to effective legal protection in Article 19(4) of the Basic Law and the rule of law principle, enshrined in Article 20 of the Basic Law. The inquisitorial principle is to be interpreted as the duty of the court to establish the facts acting *ex officio*. The court is not limited to the allegations and evidence provided by the parties, but

163 Conseil d'État, 23 October 2015, *Janin*, N° 392550.
164 Conseil d'État, 25 March 1983, *Coz*, N° 8699.
165 Conseil d'État, 15 May 1981, *Maurice*, N° 33041.
166 Conseil d'État, 28 December 2009, *Commune de Béziers*, N° 304802.

should decide on a complete and correct basis of the facts. In the lower administrative courts, parties are under no obligation to engage a lawyer. As a result, they may suffer from lack of technical information and knowledge about the proper procedure as well as the law. Moreover, in some cases, a party may not be in a position to engage a lawyer. Therefore, the law imposes a certain duty to assist the parties to overcome the asymmetry of information and ability to express oneself. To take care of the factors mentioned, the courts are under an obligation to help the citizen to set the record straight.

5.6.C THE NETHERLANDS

Algemene Wet Bestuursrecht **5.55 (NL)**

Article 8:69 (1) The administrative judge shall decide on the basis of the act introducing the claim, the documents lodged, the proceedings during the preliminary investigations and the investigations in court.

(2) The administrative judge shall supplement the legal grounds of his own motion.

(3) The administrative judge may supplement the facts of his own motion.

Explanatory memorandum to Article 8:69 AWB[167] **5.56 (NL)**

The application of the provisions concerning competence and admissibility are of public order and are not freely definable by the parties. Thus, the judge will indeed not conform itself to, for example, the incorrect interpretation of the term 'decision' or an unlawfully excused exceedance of a fatal time limit. This also applies if the parties have agreed to not invoke the lack of competence or the inadmissibility.

Notes

(1) The *ex officio* activities of the Dutch administrative courts can be distinguished between the obligation to supplement *ex officio* the legal grounds of the dispute and the obligation to apply *ex officio* provision of public order.[168] The former is prescribed by Article 8:69(2) AWB, according to which the judge is obliged, within the scope of the dispute determined by the grounds raised by the claimant,[169] to supplement on its own motion the legal grounds. In other words, the judge should apply the appropriate legal rules to the grounds that have been raised by the claimant, and thus 'translate' the latter grounds into legal grounds. Since 1994, there has been a tendency to apply the obligation of Article 8:69(2) AWB quite restrictively. The adversarial character of the procedure and the duty to keep the procedure within the limits of the case set out by the parties is adhered to more rigidly than in the past.

[167] PG Awb II, 464.

[168] For more details on both *ex officio* activities, see Schreuder-Vlasblom (n 107 above) 550–648.

[169] Art 8:69(1) AWB; see section 5.5.I.C above.

Furthermore, according to Article 8:69(3) AWB, the judges may, within the scope of the dispute, supplement the facts on their own motion. In principle, the judge has an active role in exploring the facts of a case. However, there is a delicate balance between the (limited) responsibility of the judge to explore the facts of the case (the judge 'may' supplement the facts) and the responsibility of the parties to deliver the facts and as much evidence as possible to strengthen their pleas.

(2) The administrative judges are always obliged to examine and apply *ex officio* questions of public order, even beyond the scope of the dispute (as determined by the grounds raised by the parties). Issues that qualify as 'public order' are the competence of the court, the admissibility of the claim, the impartiality of the court[170] and the most fundamental rules of due process.[171] In addition, the court will quash a decision *ex officio* if it is obvious that the administration lacked the competence to take it (pursuant to the legality principle).

The obligation to apply questions of public order *ex officio* is an exception to the rule that the dispute is generally framed by the parties, and prevails above the prohibition of *reformatio in peius*.[172]

5.6.D THE EUROPEAN UNION

The European courts are bound by the subject matter of the case as stated in the application,[173] and the pleas in law must be identifiable from the text of the application. It must be possible to identify the factual and legal particulars on which the pleas are based.[174] The European courts are bound by the legal arguments set out by the applicant and cannot raise new legal grounds of their own motion. This limitation has been considered to be in compliance with the principle of effective judicial protection which has been held not to require 'that the General Court – which is indeed obliged to respond to the pleas in law raised and to carry out a review of both the law and the facts – should be obliged to undertake of its own motion a new and comprehensive investigation of the file'.[175]

Similarly to the French legal system, EU courts can intervene *ex officio* when certain public policy grounds are at stake. The conditions governing the admissibility of an action are a matter of public policy, so the EU courts may check of its own motion bars to the proceedings, which include bars relating to the time limit for bringing an action,[176]

[170] ABRvS 26 November 2003, ECLI:NL:RVS:2003:AN8790, JB 2004, 46.

[171] ABRvS 26 January 2011, ECLI:NL:RVS:2011:BP2536, AB 2011, 83. For another example, see ABRvS 3 May 2006, ECLI:NL:RVS:2006:AW7323.

[172] See section 5.5.C above.

[173] Case 232/78 *Commission v France* ECLI:EU:C:1979:215.

[174] eg Case 111/63 *Lemmerz-Werke GmBH v High Authority* ECLI:EU:C:1965:76; Case C-52/90 *Commission v Denmark* ECLI:EU:C:1992:151.

[175] Case C-295/12 P *Telefónica and Telefónica de España v Commission* ECLI:EU:C:2014:2062.

[176] Case 4/67 *Collignon v Commission* ECLI:EU:C:1967:51; Case 108/79 *Belfiore v Commission* ECLI:EU:C:1980:146, para 3.

whether the contested measure is of a challengeable nature,[177] the interest of the applicant in obtaining the annulment of the measure,[178] the standing to bring proceedings[179] and the *lis pendens* objection.[180]

Furthermore, in relation to the merits of particular actions, the case law has clarified that certain pleas amongst those contained in Article 263 TFEU should be raised *ex officio* by the European courts, namely lack of competence[181] and the infringement of an essential procedural requirement.[182]

5.6.E ENGLAND AND WALES

The precise scope of the court's ability to act *ex officio* in judicial review proceedings is not entirely clear. Where a party to a case has raised an issue in their grounds of claim or grounds of appeal but have then not submitted argument on that point, it has been held that the court will raise the issue of its own motion (ie *ex officio*) and seek the submissions of the parties on that issue.[183] Similarly, it has been accepted that where an issue of compatibility with EU law arises in judicial review proceedings but has not been raised by the parties, the court might raise it *ex officio*.[184] The precise scope of the requirement to raise points *ex officio* is uncertain, however. It appears that such an obligation does not extend to circumstances where the court identifies a possible breach of ECHR rights under the Human Rights Act 1998.[185]

5.6.F COMPARATIVE REMARKS

The power of the court to act *ex officio* on public policy grounds, or to consider substantive rules of law or procedure, varies between the systems that are studied. Germany offers the broadest scope for the courts to raise issues *ex officio*, with the entire process of evidence gathering being *ex officio* and in the hands of the judge, who also enjoys the

[177] Case T-308/02 *SGL Carbon v Commission* ECLI:EU:T:2004:119; Case T-29/03 *Comunidad Autonoma de Andalucia v Commission* ECLI:EU:T:2004:235.

[178] Case T-310/00 *MCI v Commission* ECLI:EU:T:2004:275.

[179] Case C-298/00 P *Italy v Commission* ECLI:EU:C:2004:240, para 35; Case T-239/94 *EISA v Commission* ECLI:EU:T:1997:158, para 27; Joined Cases T-107/01 and T-175/01 *Société de Mines de Salicior-Lormines v Commission* ECLI:EU:T:2004:213, paras 51–52.

[180] Joined Cases 45/70 and 49/70 *Bode v Commission* ECLI:EU:C:1971:56, para 11; Case 75/72 *Perinciolo v Council* ECLI:EU:C:1973:52, para 5.

[181] Joined Cases T-12/99 and T-63/99 *UK Coal v Commission* ECLI:EU:T:2001:188; Case T-147/00 *Laboratoires Servier v Commission* ECLI:EU:T:2003:17; Joined Cases T-134/03 and 135/03 *Common Market Fertilizer v Commission* ECLI:EU:T:2005:339.

[182] Case C-265/97 *P VBA v Florimex and others* ECLI:EU:C:2000:170, para 114; Case T-266/99 *Metropole Television v Commission* ECLI:EU:T:2000:88, para 43.

[183] See, eg *R (Tesfay) v Secretary of State for the Home Department* [2016] EWCA Civ 415, [2016] 1 WLR 4853, [46]–[47], where the Court of Appeal required the Secretary of State to submit argument on the point of jurisdiction in relation to costs, raised in the grounds of appeal but not considered in argument.

[184] See, eg *R v Hammersmith and Fulham LBC, ex parte Council for the Protection of Rural England (No 1)* [2000] Env LR 532, 539.

[185] See, eg *R (JL) v Secretary of State for Defence* [2013] EWCA Civ 449, [2013] PTSR 1014, [40].

power to raise new points of law even if these have not been raised by the parties. This is at least in part a reflection of the desire in the German system to address the inequality of resources that often exists between the citizen and the state. The courts in the Netherlands also enjoy broad powers to act *ex officio* in order to supplement the legal and factual grounds submitted by the claimant under Article 8:69 AWB, although the judge has discretion over whether to act *ex officio* in determining the facts. In addition to the discretionary character of the powers in Article 8:69 AWB, the Dutch courts are obliged in general to act *ex officio* to raise a number of 'public order' grounds, including the competence of the court to hear the claim, the admissibility of the claim or potential bias on the part of the court in reaching its decision.

In France and the EU, the courts have the power to act *ex officio* only on public policy grounds, such as lack of jurisdiction, arguments that the claim is inadmissible and lack of standing. The European courts may also raise *ex officio* certain of the grounds in Article 263 TFEU, such as lack of competence and infringement of an essential procedural requirement, if these are not raised by the parties. On the whole, one might say that the approach in France and the EU is more passive than that in the Netherlands and Germany, and is generally isolated to *ex officio* interventions on issues of public policy.

England and Wales offers the most uncertain picture – it is possible for courts to raise issues on their own motion (ie *ex officio*), and there is evidence that they will do this in judicial review proceedings. The power to do so arises from the inherent jurisdiction of the court rather than from any legislative source, which leads to uncertainty over when the power will be used. There is evidence that the courts may be willing to raise issues of compatibility with EU law *ex officio*, and it will also seek argument on points raised by the parties in the statement of claim or appeal but then not further explored. However, there are no clear authorities on the scope of the power to raise issues *ex officio* in judicial review proceedings.

The power to raise issues *ex officio* is an important one that may, at least in some cases, ensure that important legal issues or evidence are considered. This may sometimes be valuable in ensuring that imbalances in resources that exist between state and claimant do not serve to prevent effective redress. However, the legal systems under examination vary in their approach, from the expansive approaches adopted in Germany and the Netherlands to the more limited approaches adopted in France and the EU and the uncertain picture in England and Wales.

As a final point, it should be mentioned that the case law of the CJEU in this area has led to only minimal harmonisation, since the CJEU does not unconditionally require national courts to raise points of EU law *ex officio* which the parties have not brought forward, but instead encourages the courts to balance the possibility to raise grounds of EU law *ex officio* with the respect for the principle of defence.

5.7 EQUALITY OF THE PARTIES

The equality of the parties is a fundamental aspect of the rule of law. The challenge for both the EU legal system and the legal systems of the Member States is that, while they all adhere to the principle of formal equality of the parties (ie all parties have the right to be heard by the court and defendant government authorities do not enjoy a privileged position), the substantive equality of the parties is much more difficult to deliver and has a multiplicity of components. The defendant public authority is almost invariably in a better position than the claimant in the sense that it will be in possession of a greater degree of information and documentation relating to the case and will almost always be in a stronger position than the claimant to utilise its legal and financial resources in order to support its case. This section of the chapter will offer some consideration of the formal equality of the parties, although this will not be the central focus because all systems, whether through explicit constitutional guarantees or through implicit recognition of what is a fundamental element of the rule of law. The section will also examine the way in which the systems address issues of substantive (in)equality. Many of the procedural issues discussed in this chapter may have a significant bearing on the substantive equality of the parties. The ability of the court to assist the claimant through an inquisitorial process, the nature of the burden of proof, the ability of courts to appoint experts without imposing a financial burden on the claimant and so on may all be important elements that can determine the substantive equality of the parties. The availability of legal aid[186] is also likely to be an important element influencing the substantive equality of the parties.

A helpful starting point is an examination of the approach to the European Court of Human Rights in a case which considered the application of Article 6 ECHR where a claimant is facing complex legal proceedings.

European Court of Human Rights, 9 October 1979[187] **5.57 (COE)**

Airey v Ireland

RIGHT TO FAIR TRIAL; COMPLEXITY OF PROCEEDINGS; LEGAL AID

Airey

Where it is necessary for citizens to follow complex legal procedures in order to vindicate their rights, it may be a breach of Article 6 ECHR to fail to provide appropriate support for them, whether through civil legal aid or other methods.

Facts: The applicant was a married woman who earned relatively little. She wished to seek an order of judicial separation from her husband. In Ireland, this could only be obtained from the High Court, which would require the claimant to incur substantial legal costs. The claimant argued that the complex procedure and the lack of availability of civil legal aid in Ireland for cases such as hers were in breach of Article 6(1) ECHR.

Held: In the circumstances in this case, the court held that the conditions imposed by Irish law were in breach of Article 6(1) ECHR.

Judgment: 24. The Government contend that the application does enjoy access to the High Court since she is free to go before that court without the assistance of a lawyer.

The Court does not regard this possibility, of itself, as conclusive of the matter. The Convention is intended to guarantee not rights that are theoretical or illusory but

[186] See further on this point Chapter 4, section 4.10.
[187] ECLI:CE:ECHR:1981:0206JUD000628973.

rights that are practical and effective (see, *mutatis mutandis*, the judgment of 23 July 1968 in the 'Belgian Linguistic' case, Series A no. 6, p. 31, paras. 3 in fine and 4; the above-mentioned *Golder* judgment, p. 18, para. 35 in fine; the *Luedicke, Belkacem and Koç* judgment of 28 November 1978, Series A no. 29, pp. 17-18; para. 42; and the *Marckx* judgment of 13 June 1979, Series A no. 31, p. 15, para. 31). This is particularly so of the right of access to the courts in view of the prominent place held in a democratic society by the right to a fair trial (see, *mutatis mutandis*, the *Delcourt* judgment of 17 January 1970, Series A no. 11, p. 15, para. 25). It must therefore be ascertained whether Mrs. Airey's appearance before the High Court without the assistance of a lawyer would be effective, in the sense of whether she would be able to present her case properly and satisfactorily.

Contradictory views on this question were expressed by the Government and the Commission during the oral hearings. It seems certain to the Court that the applicant would be at a disadvantage if her husband were represented by a lawyer and she were not. Quite apart from this eventuality, it is not realistic, in the Court's opinion, to suppose that, in litigation of this nature, the applicant could effectively conduct her own case, despite the assistance which, as was stressed by the Government, the judge affords to parties acting in person.

In Ireland, a decree of judicial separation is not obtainable in a District Court, where the procedure is relatively simple, but only in the High Court. A specialist in Irish family law, Mr. Alan J. Shatter, regards the High Court as the least accessible court not only because 'fees payable for representation before it are very high' but also by reason of the fact that 'the procedure for instituting proceedings ... is complex particularly in the case of those proceedings which must be commenced by a petition', such as those for separation (*Family Law in the Republic of Ireland*, Dublin 1977, p. 21).

Furthermore, litigation of this kind, in addition to involving complicated points of law, necessitates proof of adultery, unnatural practices or, as in the present case, cruelty; to establish the facts, expert evidence may have to be tendered and witnesses may have to be found, called and examined. What is more, marital disputes often entail an emotional involvement that is scarcely compatible with the degree of objectivity required by advocacy in court.

For these reasons, the Court considers it most improbable that a person in Mrs. Airey's position (see paragraph 8 above) can effectively present his or her own case. This view is corroborated by the Government's replies to the questions put by the Court, replies which reveal that in each of the 255 judicial separation proceedings initiated in Ireland in the period from January 1972 to December 1978, without exception, the petitioner was represented by a lawyer (see paragraph 11 above).

The Court concludes from the foregoing that the possibility to appear in person before the High Court does not provide the applicant with an effective right of access and, hence, that it also does not constitute a domestic remedy whose use is demanded by Article 26 (art. 26) (see paragraph 19 (b) above).

...

26. The Government's principal argument rests on what they see as the consequence of the Commission's opinion, namely that, in all cases concerning the determination of a 'civil right', the State would have to provide free legal aid. In fact, the Convention's only express provision on free legal aid is Article 6 para. 3 (c) (art. 6-3-c) which relates to criminal proceedings and is itself subject to limitations; what is more, according to the Commission's established case law, Article 6 para. 1 (art. 6-1) does not guarantee any

right to free legal aid as such. The Government add that since Ireland, when ratifying the Convention, made a reservation to Article 6 para. 3 (c) (art. 6-3-c) with the intention of limiting its obligations in the realm of criminal legal aid, a fortiori it cannot be said to have implicitly agreed to provide unlimited civil legal aid. Finally, in their submission, the Convention should not be interpreted so as to achieve social and economic developments in a Contracting State; such developments can only be progressive.

The Court is aware that the further realisation of social and economic rights is largely dependent on the situation – notably financial – reigning in the State in question. On the other hand, the Convention must be interpreted in the light of present-day conditions (above-mentioned *Marckx* judgment, p. 19, para. 41) and it is designed to safeguard the individual in a real and practical way as regards those areas with which it deals (see paragraph 24 above). Whilst the Convention sets forth what are essentially civil and political rights, many of them have implications of a social or economic nature. ...

It would be erroneous to generalize the conclusion that the possibility to appear in person before the High Court does not provide Mrs. Airey with an effective right of access; that conclusion does not hold good for all cases concerning 'civil rights and obligations' or for everyone involved therein. In certain eventualities, the possibility of appearing before a court in person, even without a lawyer's assistance, will meet the requirements of Article 6 para. 1 (art. 6-1); there may be occasions when such a possibility secures adequate access even to the High Court. Indeed, much must depend on the particular circumstances.

In addition, whilst Article 6 para. 1 (art. 6-1) guarantees to litigants an effective right of access to the courts for the determination of their 'civil rights and obligations', it leaves to the State a free choice of the means to be used towards this end. The institution of a legal aid scheme – which Ireland now envisages in family law matters (see paragraph 11 above) – constitutes one of those means but there are others such as, for example, a simplification of procedure. In any event, it is not the Court's function to indicate, let alone dictate, which measures should be taken; all that the Convention requires is that an individual should enjoy his effective right of access to the courts in conditions not at variance with Article 6 para. 1 (art. 6-1) (see, *mutatis mutandis*, the National Union of Belgian Police judgment of 27 October 1975, Series A no. 19, p. 18, para. 39, and the above-mentioned *Marckx* judgment, p. 15, para. 31).

Note

As noted in the *Airey* case, substantive equality between the parties is required to some extent by Article 6(1) ECHR. It is important to note the argument of the European Court of Human Rights in paragraph 26 of the judgment, where it is noted that the availability of legal aid should not be seen as the sole or, indeed, the central indicator of substantive equality. The simplification of the procedural aspects of the claim and other characteristics of the judicial proceedings, including those considered earlier in this chapter, such as the level of assistance provided to the claimant by the nature of the process (so one might argue that inquisitorial processes tend to offer greater assistance to claimants than adversarial processes), the burden of proof and the ability of the judge to act *ex officio*, are all relevant when determining whether the requirements of substantive equality are met.

5.7.A FRANCE

Code de justice administrative **5.58 (FR)**

Article L5 The investigation of a case is adversarial. The requirements of adversarial procedure are adapted to those of urgency, of secrecy of national security and of the protection of the safety of persons.

Notes

(1) In France, the principle of equality of the parties is not explicitly recognised in legislation, but should be regarded as a general principle of law. Insofar as the principle is recognised in legislation, the focus is upon the adversarial nature of the proceedings. The principle of equality of the parties is then ensured by the powers of the judge to require the provision of information and documents to the parties, and to ensure that all information provided by each party is then provided to the other litigants.[188] A further example of the way in which the French system has sought to enhance the equality of the parties is from the reform to the public rapporteur, whose comments are now open to response by the parties and who may no longer sit with the judges on the case while they deliberate the decision.[189]

(2) The substantive equality of the parties is supported by some aspects of the procedural steps of the hearing in French law. The process in the French courts is inquisitorial, although the judge is generally more passive than in the German or Dutch systems. The court has extensive powers to manage the evidentiary process, and the burden of proof is adjusted to acknowledge the relative power of the parties.[190] The court may also have the power to call expert witnesses and seek the opinion of an amicus curiae to assist proceedings if necessary,[191] although this power is relatively seldom exercised. Each of these devices may assist the substantive equality of the parties. The French courts are, however, relatively passive in their use of the power to raise issues *ex officio*, as shown in section 5.6.A above.

5.7.B GERMANY

Grundgesetz **5.59 (DE)**

Article 3 (1) All persons shall be equal before the law.

(2) Men and women shall have equal rights. The state shall promote the actual implementation of equal rights for women and men and shall take steps to eliminate the disadvantages that now exist.

[188] The process is outlined above in sections 5.3.A.4 and 5.4.C.2.

[189] For an account of these changes, see J Bell, 'From Government Commissioner to Public Reporter: A Transformation in French Administrative Court Procedure' (2010) 16 *European Public Law* 533. See also the further discussion in Chapter 2, section 2.2.A.1.

[190] See section 5.3.A.4 above.

[191] As illustrated above in section 5.4.C.2.

(3) No person shall be favoured or disfavoured because of sex, descent, race, language, homeland and origin, faith, or religious or political opinions. No person shall be disfavoured because of disability.

Article 103 (1) Before the court, every person shall be entitled to a hearing in accordance with law.

...

Notes

(1) In the German legal system, administrative authorities are not privileged in administrative court proceedings. Articles 3 and 103 of the Basic Law prohibit unequal treatment of a party of the administrative judicial proceedings. To reach substantive equality of the parties, Article 101(1), sentence 2 of the Grundgesetz includes not only the right to the judge foreseen by law (*gesetzlicher Richter*), but also the right to an impartial judge (*unparteilicher Richter*).[192] Another aspect ensuring the equality of the parties is the provision of legal aid.[193] It is also notable, as outlined in sections 5.2.A.2 (ii) and 5.3.A.1 above, that the inquisitorial process adopted by the German courts is likely to be of considerable assistance to parties without substantial means to fund legal advice or assistance.

(2) In Germany, the procedure is the strongest example of an inquisitorial process. As shown in section 5.3.A.1 above, the judge generally leads the process of evidence gathering, and in most cases the burden of proof does not lie with either party. The court also enjoys extensive powers to call upon expert witnesses, which are used on a relatively frequent basis, as shown in section 5.4.B.1 above. In addition to this, the court has broad powers to raise issues *ex officio*, which are relatively frequently used, as shown in section 5.6.B above.

5.7.C THE NETHERLANDS

Although the parties in administrative disputes have the same procedural rights to be heard by the court and to defend their views in the proceedings (formal equality), there may be a structural or substantive inequality between the strong and well-equipped administrative authority, which, as a repeat player, is usually in a good position to participate in litigation, and the citizen, who is generally engaging in such proceedings for the first time and has less knowledge and resources than an administrative authority. In the primarily inquisitorial process before the AWB came into force in 1994, it was stressed that the court should compensate for this (substantive) inequality, in particular by applying *ex officio* all relevant law to the case at hand. This compensation was and is referred to as the principle of inequality compensation (*ongelijkheidscompensatie*).[194]

[192] BVerfG, NVwZ 1996, 885.

[193] §166 VwGO in conjunction with §114 and §569(3), No 2 of the Zivilprozessordnung. According to BVerfGE 78, 104, 120, the requirements to obtain legal aid must not be too restrictive and render participation in the administrative judicial process impossible.

[194] See the Explanatory Memorandum to the AWB, PG AWB II, 172.

Since 1994, the practice of administrative law proceedings has moved from being primarily inquisitorial to more adversarial, and this process is still ongoing. The principle of equality compensation no longer plays a very important role, although it has not disappeared completely. Elements of it are still visible, eg in the courts' practice to interpret the 'laymen's' grounds leniently in line with the intention of the claimant and the obligation to apply *ex officio* all appropriate legal rules to these grounds,[195] and in the court's practice to appoint (and finance) experts in medical and environmental cases to compensate for the expertise of the authorities.[196] Nevertheless, the function of administrative proceedings to compensate for structural inequality has been reduced. There is a tension between this development and the fact that applicants do not need to be represented by lawyers during the court proceedings. In practice, judges do take more care of the procedural interests of parties who do not have professional legal assistance, but they are less active than they were in the past.[197] The availability of legal aid and the principle of one-way cost shifting[198] are important financial instruments to compensate inequality.

5.7.D THE EUROPEAN UNION

Charter of Fundamental Rights of the European Union **5.60 (EU)**

Article 20 Equality before the law

Everyone is equal before the law.

Article 21 Non-discrimination

(1) Any discrimination based on any ground such as sex, race, colour, ethnic or social origin, genetic features, language, religion or belief, political or any other opinion, membership of a national minority, property, birth, disability, age or sexual orientation shall be prohibited.

(2) Within the scope of application of the Treaties and without prejudice to any of their specific provisions, any discrimination on grounds of nationality shall be prohibited.

Article 47 Right to an effective remedy and to a fair trial

Everyone whose rights and freedoms guaranteed by the law of the Union are violated has the right to an effective remedy before a tribunal in compliance with the conditions laid down in this Article.

Everyone is entitled to a fair and public hearing within a reasonable time by an independent and impartial tribunal previously established by law. Everyone shall have the possibility of being advised, defended and represented.

Legal aid shall be made available to those who lack sufficient resources in so far as such aid is necessary to ensure effective access to justice.

[195] See sections 5.6.C above.

[196] See section 5.4.B.2 above.

[197] For more details, see S Prechal and RJGM Widdershoven, 'The Dutch General Administrative Law Act: Europe-proof?' (2008) 14 *European Public Law* 81; A Mallan, *Lekenbescherming in het bestuursrprocesrecht* (*Layman's Protection in Administrative Procedural Law*) (Oisterwijck, Wolf Legal Publishers, 2014) (with summary in English).

[198] See Chapter 4, section 4.9.B.2.

Notes

(1) The Charter of Fundamental Rights of the European Union guarantees formal equality before the law and non-discrimination. These provisions might be regarded as being drawn from the legal position in each of the Member States. Similarly, the fundamental aspects of a fair trial are set out in Article 47 of the Charter, along with the right to an effective remedy. There is also some acknowledgement of the challenge of substantive equality, with a guarantee of legal aid to those who are particularly in need of it.[199]

(2) As noted above in section 5.3.A.3, the Court of Justice and the General Court have powers to invoke measures of inquiry where these are deemed necessary. This process is inquisitorial and may be used in order to ensure that appropriate evidence is put before the court, which may aid the substantive equality between the parties. Similarly, the burden of proof is adjusted in order to acknowledge that the position of the parties may be unequal. In addition to this, it is demonstrated in section 5.4.C.1 that, although they are infrequently used, the court may draw upon expert witnesses in order to assist the case. Each of these procedural devices may be used to assist claimants who might otherwise find difficulty in supporting a case. The EU courts generally take a passive approach to raising issues *ex officio*, as noted in section 5.6.D above, so this is unlikely to allow the court to assist claimants where they have omitted to raise important legal issues.

5.7.E ENGLAND AND WALES

AV Dicey, Lectures Introductory to the Law of the Constitution[200] **5.61 (EW)**

We mean in the second place, when we speak of the 'rule of law' as a characteristic of our country, not only that with us no man is above the law, but (what is a different thing) that here every man, whatever be his rank or condition, is subject to the ordinary law of the realm and amenable to the jurisdiction of the ordinary tribunals. In England the idea of legal equality, or of the universal subjection of all classes, to one law administered by the ordinary Courts, has been pushed to its utmost limit. With us every official, from the Prime Minister down to a constable or a collector of taxes, is under the same responsibility for every act done without legal justification as any other citizen.

Notes

(1) In the unwritten constitution of the UK, there is no explicit constitutional guarantee of formal equality before the law, although it has been accepted that such formal equality is a fundamental aspect of the rule of law for many years and is expressed clearly in the excerpt from *Dicey* set out above.

[199] See Chapter 4, section 4.10 for further information on this issue.
[200] AV Dicey, *Lectures Introductory to the Law of the Constitution* (London, MacMillan & Co, 1885) 177–78.

(2) In England and Wales, the process of judicial review litigation is adversarial, and it is for the parties, whether represented by a lawyer or not, to advance their case before the court. The evidence regime, as demonstrated above in section 5.3.B, allows the court to manage the evidentiary process to a significant extent, seeking clarification from the parties on particular points and advising the parties on what evidence may best assist the court. However, unlike in the inquisitorial systems, the power of the court to actually engage in the evidence-gathering process is relatively limited – it is for the parties to adduce the evidence. One might argue that the existence of the duty of candour in judicial review cases, where both parties are required to produce all evidence, whether favourable to their case or not, seeks to address the imbalance of power between the state and the individual. As shown above in section 5.4.C.3, the court may seek the assistance of an amicus curiae, but this is seldom done, and where there is recourse to public funds in order to pay the amicus curiae, the consent of the Attorney General is required. Expert witnesses can only be brought forward by the parties at their expense, so this has the potential to strengthen the imbalance between the parties where a claimant is unable to finance the delivery of such expert evidence. It may, however, be difficult to determine the impact of the approach to evidence. The court does have the ability to raise points of law *ex officio*, but this power is used relatively infrequently and there is no overarching framework of rules governing its use, as shown in section 5.6.E. Legal aid is available in some but not in all judicial review cases, so not every claimant has legal representation.[201] The court is likely (though not required) to assist litigants in person in relation to procedural matters insofar as it is able, but there is no doubt that those who are unable to obtain legal representation will be at a disadvantage when compared with the public authority.

5.7.F COMPARATIVE REMARKS

In systems where the approach to the proceedings is adversarial rather than inquisitorial, little assistance is offered to the claimant in the steps of the proceedings. In each system under examination, aspects of the procedure are designed to facilitate a degree of substantive equality between the parties. In a strongly inquisitorial system such as Germany, it is likely that substantive equality is facilitated by the role of the judge in leading the proceedings. A similar argument might be made in the case of France and the European Union, although in these systems the impact of the inquisitorial approach is much less pronounced. All of the systems under analysis acknowledge in some way that the public authority is likely to have the upper hand in terms of access to information germane to the proceedings, so may adjust the burden of proof or require a duty of candour, where the public authority is required to disclose information to the court even where this information may be prejudicial to its case.

Trends in relation to the substantive equality of the parties are difficult to discern. One might argue that the German, French and EU legal systems contain many of the

[201] See further Chapter 4, section 4.10.

aspects that one might expect to increase the substantive equality of the parties. In contrast, one might argue that, since 1994, the Dutch system has retreated from some elements of procedure that are more likely to deliver substantive equality. In England and Wales, one might argue that substantive equality is at its weakest. The availability of civil legal aid to bring judicial review proceedings has been reduced, the procedure is strongly adversarial and is framed by the parties, and the court will not generally act *ex officio* in order to assist claimants. Furthermore, the burden of proof, while to some extent flexible, generally remains with the claimant. Some of the systems under analysis acknowledge that the assistance of a lawyer may greatly assist a claimant in the formulation of a strong case and endeavour to support those who do not have the means to do so through legal aid schemes, offering public support for those who cannot afford to obtain legal representation.[202] However, in times of austerity in the public sector, some jurisdictions have heavily reduced such support or limited the circumstances in which it can be claimed.[203] It would be too simplistic, though, to focus solely on the availability of legal aid as a true indicator of the substantive equality of the parties.

5.8 THE USE OF INFORMATION TECHNOLOGY AND EFFICIENCY MEASURES IN PROCEEDINGS

Courts have become increasingly interested in the use of technology to assist in expediting judicial review proceedings and to simplify the process of collating court files and evidence. All of the systems under investigation have adopted technological solutions to aspects of the proceedings, or have allowed for electronic filing of documents.

5.8.A FRANCE

Code de justice administrative **5.62 (FR)**

Article R414-1 When submitted by an attorney, an attorney to the Council of State and to the Court of Appeal, a person governed by public law other than a municipality of less than 3,500 inhabitants or a private-law entity entrusted with the permanent performance of a public service, the application shall, in order to be admissible, be sent to the court electronically by means of a dedicated software, which may be accessed via the internet. The same obligation applies to other statements of the applicant.

When submitted by a municipality with less than 3,500 inhabitants, the application may be sent by means of this software.

Legal persons tasked, on the basis of Article R553-14 of the Code of Entry and Residence of Foreigners and of Asylum Law (Code de l'entrée et du séjour des étrangers et du droit d'asile), with informing foreigners placed in an administrative detention centre and with helping them to exercise their rights can send the applications submitted by those foreigners to the court electronically and by means of this software.

202 ibid.
203 See Chapter 4, section 4.10.

Article R414-1-1 The technical characteristics of the software specified in Article R414-1 shall guarantee the reliability of the identification of the parties or their representative, the integrity of the documents sent and the security and confidentiality of the exchanges between the parties and the court. They shall also allow to establish with certainty the date and time that a document has been made available and of its first consultation by its recipient. An administrative decision (*arrêté*) of the Ministry of Justice, defines those characteristics, the technical requirements that shall be respected by the users of the software and the conditions of registration in the software by the persons specified in Article R414-1.

Article R414-2 The identification of the author of the application, according to the conditions provided by the administrative decision specified in Article R414-1, is to be considered a signature for the application of the provisions of the present code. However, when the application does not contain an electronic signature in the sense of Article 1367, second section, of the Civil Code, the applicant or his representative can, if necessary, be obliged to provide a copy of his application with his hand-written signature. …

Note

Parties who are registered to use a special dedicated system and website, known as *telerecours*,[204] may file a request in electronic form in accordance with the relevant legal provisions. Only lawyers and public bodies are entitled to register at present. If both parties are registered, the entire proceedings are conducted in electronic form and all exchanges are made through the web platform, which has been designed to guarantee the confidentiality, safety and authenticity of the proceedings. Although it is not generalised yet, the internal work of a growing number of administrative courts (preparation of judgments, deliberations and hearings) is conducted in completely dematerialised fashion, with electronic case files and collaborative work on documents.[205]

5.8.B GERMANY

Verwaltungsgerichtsordnung **5.63 (DE)**

§55a (1) Preparatory pleadings and their annexes, applications to be submitted in writing and declarations by the parties concerned, as well as information, to be submitted in writing, expert assessments, translations and declarations of third parties may, in accordance with sections 2 to 6, be filed with the court as electronic documents.

(2) The electronic document must be suitable for processing by the court. The Federal Government shall determine the technical framework conditions suitable for transmission and processing by executive regulation with the consent of the Federal Council.

(3) The electronic document must be accompanied by a qualified electronic signature of the person responsible or signed by the person responsible and must be submitted via a secure means of transmission.

[204] www.telerecours.fr.

[205] See Code de justice administrative, Art R611-8-2.

(4) Secure means of transmission are

1. the Mailbox and mailing service of a De-Mail account, if the sender is securely registered in the sense of § 4 (1) Sentence 2 of the De-Mail Act when sending the message and he confirms the security of the application pursuant to § 5(5) of the De-Mail Act,

2. the transmission between the special electronic lawyer's mailbox according to §31a of the Federal Bar Code (Bundesrechtsanwaltsordnung) or a corresponding electronic mailbox established on a legal basis and the electronic mailing office of the Court,

3. the transmission between the mailbox of an authority or a legal person of public law, established after an identification procedure has been implemented, and the electronic mail office of the Court; the details are provided in the executive regulation referred to in the second sentence of section 2,

4. other federally standardized means of transmission, as determined by a federal government's executive regulation with the consent of the Federal Council, which guarantee the authenticity and integrity of the data as well as the accessibility.

(5) An electronic document has been received as soon as it is stored on the device of the court designated for reception. The sender shall receive an automated confirmation of the date of receipt. The provisions of this Act on additional copies for the other parties are not applicable.

(6) If an electronic document is not suitable for processing by the court, the sender must be immediately notified of the fact, with reference to the invalidity of the receipt and the applicable technical framework conditions. The document shall be deemed to have been received at the time of the earlier filing, provided that the sender submits it immediately in a form suitable for the court to be processed and demonstrates that it complies with the content of the first submitted document.

(7) In so far as a handwritten signature by the judge or the registrar of the office is required, this requirement is complied with by a record as an electronic document, if the persons responsible add their names at the end of the document and the document is provided with a qualified electronic signature.

§55b (1) The process files can be managed electronically. The federal government and the governments of the states (*Länder*) determine by executive regulation, each for their area, the date from which the process files may be managed electronically. In the executive regulation, the organisational and technical framework conditions for the formation, management and safekeeping of electronic files must be laid down. The governments of the states may delegate the authorization to the highest state authorities responsible for administrative jurisdiction. The use of electronic files may be restricted to individual courts or procedures; where this possibility is exercised, the executive regulation may determine that, by means of an administrative direction which has to be publicly announced, the procedures in which the proceedings are to be carried out electronically shall be defined. The executive regulation of the federal government does not require the approval of the Federal Council.

(2) If the files are conducted in paper form, a paper copy of all electronic documents has to added to the files. A paper copy is not necessary if it cannot be made with regards to attachments to preparatory pleadings or only can be made with disproportionate effort. In such a case, the data are to be stored permanently. The location of this storage must be documented.

(3) If the electronic document is submitted via a secure means, this has to be placed on record.

(4) If the electronic document is provided with a qualified electronic signature and it is not submitted via a secure means, the copy of the document must contain a note detailing:

1. the result of the integrity check of the document,
2. who, according to the signature check, is the holder of the signature,
3. the time, according to the signature check, the signature was affixed.

(5) In cases of section 2, a submitted electronic document may be deleted after six months.

(6) If the files are conducted electronically, documents submitted in paper form and other writs shall be transferred to an electronic document in accordance with the state of the art. The conformity with the documents and other writs as far as their content and image is concerned must be ensured. Documents and other writs submitted in paper form may be destroyed six months after they have been transferred, unless they are subject to return to the provider.

Notes

(1) The use of IT in Germany has been strengthened by a reform in 2005. According to §55a VwGO, the participants of administrative court proceedings may convey electronic documents. In order to secure the electronic communication, specific electronic signatures have to be used and must be submitted via a secure means of transmission.[206]

(2) Furthermore, §55b VwGO allows procedural files to be kept in electronic form. The federal government and the state governments shall determine in each case under their remit by executive regulation the time from when the procedural files are kept in electronic form. By 2026, all procedural files and records shall be kept electronically. If a document that has been submitted in paper form has been converted into an electronic document, it must contain a note as to when and by whom the conversion was carried out. If an electronic document has been converted into paper form, the printout must contain a note as to the result yielded by the integrity check of the document, the individual who is identified by the signature check as the owner of the signature and the time the signature check shows for affixing the signature.

5.8.C THE NETHERLANDS

Algemene Wet Bestuursrecht **5.64 (NL)**

Article 8:36a (1) A claim for judicial review should be lodged electronically.

(2) Parties and other persons involved should submit all other documents electronically electronic route, unless the administrative judge determines differently ....

...

(5) If the obligations deriving from [section 1 and 2] ... are not complied with, the administrative judge will provide the party or other persons involved the opportunity

[206] Regulation No 910/2014 of the European Parliament and of the Council of 23 July 2014 on electronic identification and trust services for electronic transactions in the internal market and repealing Directive 1999/93/EC [2014] OJ L257/73.

to repair this flaw within a time-limit set by the judge. If the party or the other persons involved do not make use of this opportunity, the claim may be declared inadmissible, or the administrative judge may refuse to consider the document.

Article 8:36b 1. The obligation to conduct the proceedings electronically does not apply to natural persons …, unless they are represented by a third person offering professional legal assistance.

Notes

(1) Since 1 January 2017, the Act on simplification and digitisation of procedural law (Wet vereenvoudiging en digitalisering van het procesrecht) has amended the Algemene Wet Bestuursrecht.[207] According to its provisions, Dutch judicial proceedings will be digitised step by step in the years to come. At the moment, asylum law cases are in practice already conducted only by electronic means. The implementation of the new rules in other areas of administrative law is foreseen in the near future.

(2) Under the new rules, in principle, in a claim for judicial review before the administrative court documents must be submitted by using electronic means, via a single digital portal, Mijn Rechtspraak (My Judiciary). All other communication between the parties and the court will take place through this digital portal as well. An exception is made only for natural persons who are not represented by a legal professional. They are still allowed to a claim for judicial review and submit documents in paper form. However, legal persons and natural persons represented by a legal professional must use the digital portal. If they fail to do so, the judge may declare their appeal inadmissible or refuse to consider the documents that are submitted by other means.

5.8.D THE EUROPEAN UNION

Decision of the General Court of 14 September 2011
on the lodging and service of procedural documents
by means of e-Curia[208] **5.65 (EU)**

Article 1 The information technology application known as 'e-Curia', common to the three constituent courts of the Court of Justice of the European Union, allows the lodging and service of procedural documents by electronic means under the conditions laid down by this Decision.

…

Article 3 A procedural document lodged by means of e-Curia shall be deemed to be the original of that document for the purposes of the first subparagraph of Article 43(1) of the Rules of Procedure where the representative's user identification and password have

[207] Stbl 2016, 288.
[208] [2011] OJ C289/9.

been used to effect that lodgment. Such identification shall constitute the signature of the document concerned.

Article 4 A document lodged by means of e-Curia must be accompanied by the Annexes referred to therein and a schedule listing such Annexes.

It shall not be necessary to lodge certified copies of a document lodged by means of e-Curia or of any Annexes thereto.

Article 5 A procedural document shall be deemed to have been lodged for the purposes of Article 43(3) of the Rules of Procedure at the time of the representative's validation of lodgment of that document.

The relevant time shall be the time in the Grand Duchy of Luxembourg.

Article 6 Procedural documents, including judgments and orders, shall be served on the parties' representatives by means of e-Curia where they have expressly accepted this method of service or, in the context of a case, where they have consented to this method of service by lodging a procedural document by means of e-Curia.

Procedural documents shall also be served by means of e-Curia on Member States, other States which are parties to the Agreement on the European Economic Area and institutions, bodies, offices or agencies of the Union that have accepted this method of service.

Article 7 The intended recipients of the documents served referred to in Article 6 shall be notified by e-mail of any document served on them by means of e-Curia.

A procedural document shall be served at the time when the intended recipient (representative or his assistant) requests access to that document. In the absence of any request for access, the document shall be deemed to have been served on the expiry of the seventh day following the day on which the notification e-mail was sent.

Where a party is represented by more than one agent or lawyer, the time to be taken into account in the reckoning of time-limits shall be the time when the first request for access was made.

The relevant time shall be the time in the Grand Duchy of Luxembourg.

Note

For proceedings before both the Court of Justice and the General Court, it is possible for claimants to use the e-Curia system, which allows applicants to upload documents through a special portal. The advantage of this system is that it is possible to send a single original of a document, without the need to sign the document[209] or to send certified copies. The system also allows for the electronic exchange of documents. The system has been in operation since 2011, when both courts adopted decisions in relation to its use.[210]

[209] Pursuant to Art 43(7) of the Rules of Procedure of the General Court.

[210] See Decision of the Court of Justice of 13 September 2011 on the lodging and service of procedural documents by means of e-Curia [2011] OJ C289/7; Decision of the General Court of 14 September 2011 on the lodging and service of procedural documents by means of e-Curia [2011] OJ C289/9.

5.8.E ENGLAND AND WALES

Civil Procedure Rules **5.66 (EW)**

Rule 5.5 (1) A practice direction may make provision for documents to be filed or sent to the court by–

(a) facsimile; or

(b) other electronic means.

(2) Any such practice direction may–

(a) provide that only particular categories of documents may be filed or sent to the court by such means;

(b) provide that particular provisions only apply in specific courts; and

(c) specify the requirements that must be fulfilled for any document filed or sent to the court by such means.

Practice Direction 5B – Communication and Filing of Documents by Email[211] **5.67 (EW)**

2.1 Subject to paragraphs 2.2 and 2.3, a party may e-mail the court and may attach or include one or more specified documents to or in that e-mail.

2.2 In the High Court–

(a) a party must not e-mail an application or other document to the court where a fee is payable for that document to be filed with the court; and

(b) the length of any attachments and total size of an e-mail must not exceed the maximum which the appropriate court office has indicated it can accept.

Note

Parties are permitted to file documents by email to the High Court (Queen's Bench Division) in accordance with the provisions of Practice Direction 5B, annexed to the CPR. The technical standards for the transmission of documents are also found in the Practice Direction.[212] Although some divisions of the High Court, such as the Chancery Division, have adopted wider use of information technology in the conduct and recording of court proceedings, this has not yet extended in any systematic manner to the Administrative Court. It is proposed that there will be far greater use of digital systems throughout the court system, including in the civil courts and tribunals.[213] This is likely to include a process for the commencement of proceedings and filing of the documents in administrative law cases, together with the potential for online hearings in place of physical hearings in appropriate cases. In its response to the feedback

[211] Practice Direction 5B – Communication and Filing of Documents by Email. Available at www.justice.gov.uk/courts/procedure-rules/civil/rules/part05/pd_part05b.

[212] ibid, Rule 3.

[213] Ministry of Justice *Transforming our Justice System: Summary of Reforms and Consultation* (Cm 9321, 2016).

received through the consultation process, the government is clear that the electronic processes will not be obligatory.[214]

5.8.F COMPARATIVE REMARKS

Each of the systems that have been analysed demonstrate some move towards a greater use of information technology to drive the efficiency of the proceedings. The German system is by far the most advanced in this regard, having had a comprehensive system of rules in place since 2005. France is also relatively advanced, having specific legal provisions in place to require the use of an electronic portal for the submission of claims, although this is open only to lawyers and public bodies at the moment. The European Union courts also have the potential for comprehensive use of IT.

The Netherlands is developing the use of information technology in administrative court proceedings. The requirement for lawyers and public bodies to use an electronic portal for the submission of claims is laid down in statutory law. Ultimately, it is clear that the objective in the Dutch system is to create a comprehensive framework for the electronic submission and management of administrative proceedings. This system is already compulsory for legal professionals and legal persons, but individuals who do not have legal representation are not obliged to use the system.

In England and Wales, the CPR permit the filing of documents by email and there have been efforts to introduce a more comprehensive IT system for the submission and management of proceedings in some other courts, but this has not so far extended to the Administrative Court. There do not appear to be any specific plans to extend the use of information technology in the Administrative Court at the present time.

The adoption of a comprehensive system for electronic filing and management of administrative proceedings may bring with it many advantages for the courts, for public authorities and for lawyers dealing with the court. However, from the perspective of the equality of the parties and access to justice, the adoption of a requirement that electronic means be used to submit and then participate in administrative proceedings could serve as a significant barrier to those without IT skills and access to suitable IT equipment. At present, this does not appear to be a barrier in any of the legal systems studied because none of the systems studied *requires* the use of such electronic systems for all (natural) persons. However, as the use of such systems is extended, the issue of access for the citizen is an issue of some concern.

5.9 LANGUAGE ISSUES, TRANSLATION AND INTERPRETERS

Language issues and translation may be important issues during legal proceedings. Evidently, it is crucial that those who participate in legal proceedings are able to understand

[214] Ministry of Justice, *Transforming our Justice System: Assisted Digital Strategy, Automatic Online Conviction and Statutory Standard Penalty, and Panel Composition In Tribunals – Government Response* (London, 2017).

and follow the proceedings. Articles 5(2) and 6(3)(e) ECHR specifically require defendants in criminal proceedings to be informed of the charges against them in a language that they understand and then to have the services of an interpreter free of charge in order that they might participate in the proceedings against them. No such obligation is inherent in civil matters, although many administrative law decisions in areas such as taxation may lead to criminal consequences in some circumstances, so claimants may be required to receive the support of an interpreter in such cases.[215] If claimants or witnesses are to give evidence or address the court, it is also important for the court to be able to understand the information that they are providing. It is clear that such language issues might affect the fairness of the proceedings, so each system has taken steps to ensure that translation is available in appropriate cases.

5.9.A THE NETHERLANDS

The official language is Dutch or, within the Province of Friesland, Frysan (Article 2:5 ff AWB). The use of another language may be accepted if its use is more effective and the interests of third persons are not disproportionately harmed (Article 2:5(2) AWB). Administrative appeal bodies of universities, for example, often allow pleas in English and the submission of documents in English without translation. If a notice of objection or a claim for judicial review is written in a language other than Dutch and a translation is necessary for the objection or the claim to be properly dealt with, the applicant shall arrange for the translation (Article 6:5(3) AWB). The same applies to any other documents for which the judge deems a translation to be necessary in order to ensure due process. The judge can appoint an interpreter (Article 8:49 and Article 8:60(1) AWB). If he does so, the costs for the interpreter are for the government to bear (Article 8:39(1) AWB).

5.9.B GERMANY

Similar to the Dutch rules, §184 of the Court Constitution Act (Gerichtsverfassungsgesetz) declares that the court language in Germany is German. Thus, if persons are participating in the hearing who do not speak the German language, an interpreter is called in (§185(1) of the Gerichtsverfassungsgesetz). The costs of the interpreter form part of the process costs. However, an interpreter may be dispensed with if all the persons involved (judges, lawyers, participants of the court procedure) have command of the foreign language (§185(2) of the Gerichtsverfassungsgesetz). No additional record shall be made in the foreign language; however, testimony and declarations given in the foreign language should also be included in the record or appended thereto in the foreign language if and to the extent that the judge deems this necessary in view of the importance of the case. Where appropriate, a translation to be certified by the interpreter should be annexed to the record.

[215] An example of such a case in the context of tax proceedings is *Cuscani v United Kingdom* ECLI:CE:ECHR:2002:0924JUD003277196.

5.9.C ENGLAND AND WALES

There are no clear requirements as to interpretation or translation in judicial review claims, but the general rule is that in civil proceedings (judicial review is considered to be a civil matter in England and Wales), the claimant must meet the cost of any interpretation or translation that is required.[216] If the judge in proceedings believes that it is necessary for the claimant or a witness to have an interpreter in order to participate in proceedings and that the party concerned cannot afford to pay an interpreter, the judge may order that an interpreter be provided by the court.[217]

It is arguable that the Equality Act 2010 may require that anyone with a disability leaving them in need of assistance with translation or interpretation of court proceedings must be provided with this at the expense of the court.

A final issue to note is that section 22 of the Welsh Language Act 1993 allows any person who wishes to do so to address the court in Welsh. This right applies only to court hearings based in Wales, so claimants who wish to exercise this right must seek to get the case transferred to the Administrative Court Office in Cardiff. The court will likely arrange for simultaneous translation of English to Welsh and vice versa, although some judges are able to speak Welsh.[218]

5.9.D FRANCE

Code de justice administrative **5.68 (FR)**

Article R776-23 In cases where a foreigner who does not speak French adequately and in case he requests it, the President shall appoint an interpreter who is obliged to swear to provide assistance to justice according to his honour and conscience. This request may be made as soon as the application commencing proceedings has been filed. At the time of the registration of the application, the registry shall, if necessary, inform the interested person that it is possible to file such a request. The costs of the interpretation shall be paid according to the conditions provided for in Article R122 of the Criminal Procedure Code.

Note

In France, the language of the proceedings is French. Any request formulated in another language will be dismissed as inadmissible. Parties who submit evidence in foreign languages must bear the costs of translation. However, in immigration cases, the cost is to be borne by the court rather than the parties if interpretation or translation is necessary.

[216] A requirement that parties pay the cost of translation is imposed for the filing of affidavits in a foreign language by Practice Direction 32, para 10.2, and for witness statements in the same Practice Direction, para 23.2. The general expectation that claimants or witnesses in need of a translator to participate in proceedings should be financed by the claimant or party seeking to call the witness is found in HM Courts and Tribunals Service, *The Administrative Court Judicial Review Guide 2016* (London, 2016) s 9.3.

[217] HM Courts and Tribunals Service (ibid) s 9.3.

[218] ibid, s 10.3.

5.9.E THE EUROPEAN UNION

In an approach that differs from these national provisions, the EU courts apply a very unique and very costly regime. The linguistic regime applicable before the European courts is governed in detail by the Rules of Procedure of the Court of Justice and of the General Court. Currently, the languages of procedure before the European courts are all official languages of the EU.[219] The choice of language is performed by the applicant, unless (1) the defendant is a Member State (in which case the language of the case is the – or one of the – official language(s) of the Member State); (2) the parties jointly request a change of language; or (3) one of the parties unilaterally requests a change of language. In the latter two cases, the change of language is decided by the president of the competent court.[220] In appeals proceedings, the language is in principle the same as the first instance proceedings, while in preliminary ruling proceedings, the language is in principle the language of the referring court or tribunal.[221] Where a party seeks to submit documents that are not in the language of the case, the general requirement is that the party submitting the documents should bear the costs of translation.[222] In cases where experts or witnesses cannot use the language of the case, then the cost of translation is borne by the court, even if the language of the expert or witness is not an official language of the EU.[223]

Judgments of the European courts are handed down in the language of the procedure. Translation is not always available in all official languages.

5.9.F COMPARATIVE REMARKS

Each system addresses the issue of language and translation to some extent. In each of the Member States under consideration, the general expectation is that the language of the proceedings will be that of the state concerned, although in the Netherlands and Germany there is some flexibility if all parties to the case can communicate in an alternative language, and in England and Wales and the Netherlands there is some endeavour to permit minority languages to be used. In the European Union, the *acquis* necessitates that all languages used in Member States are languages of the court, with the choice of language generally lying with the applicant. Where parties seek to submit documents in a language other than that of the case, they are generally expected to provide translations at their own expense. Where a witness or expert gives oral testimony and does not speak the language of the case, the costs of translation are borne by the court.

[219] Rules of Procedure of the Court of Justice, Art 94(1); Rules of Procedure of the General Court, Art 35(1).

[220] Rules of Procedure of the Court of Justice, Art 94(1); Rules of Procedure of the General Court, Art 35(2).

[221] Rules of Procedure of the Court of Justice, Art 36(3).

[222] Rules of Procedure of the Court of Justice, Art 38(2); Rules of Procedure of the General Court, Art 35(3). See also the order of the Court of First Instance of 25 July 2012 in Case T-11/95 *BP Chemicals Ltd v Commission* ECLI:EU:T:1996:91.

[223] Rules of Procedure of the Court of Justice, Art 38(7); Rules of Procedure of the General Court, Art 45(4).

In the Netherlands, France and England and Wales, the starting point in terms of the costs of translation or interpretation is that they should be borne by the claimant or party who is in need of the service. However, in the Netherlands and England and Wales, the judge retains some discretion to order the provision of translation or interpretation funded by the court if this is deemed to be necessary in order to ensure the fairness of the proceedings, and in Germany, if translation is required, it forms a part of the process costs of the proceedings and is borne by the court.

5.10 COMPARATIVE OVERVIEW

The comparative material in this chapter illustrates that, although there are some significant differences in the approach adopted by the legal systems that are studied to the organisation of the courts that deal with administrative law cases and also in the approach taken to certain of the issues, there are also many similarities and commonalities. This is perhaps unsurprising, as both EU law and the European Convention on Human Rights and Fundamental Freedoms have had an impact on each national legal system, and the EU system is inspired by principles drawn from national law.[224] As a result, this has led to a degree of procedural harmonisation over time.

In addition to this driver of harmonisation, it is evident that the policy reasons for adopting many of the procedural rules in existence are the result of common needs in all legal systems, such as the needs to manage the duration of proceedings, to manage the cost of litigation and to maximise the efficiency of the use of court time. Therefore, each legal system has rules that deliver upon these underlying policy objectives.

If we consider the legal systems under examination, there are two core areas of division. The first is that some systems adopt an inquisitorial approach, as in Germany, France and the EU, whereas England and Wales adopts an adversarial approach to litigation in administrative law cases. The approach in the Netherlands has become more adversarial in nature, but still demonstrates significant inquisitorial elements. The German system might be characterised as the strongest example of the manifestation of an inquisitorial system, with the French and EU legal systems retaining an inquisitorial approach, but perhaps placing greater onus upon the parties to put forward their case. In the adversarial systems, England and Wales is an example of a system that has always been based upon the adversarial approach, whereas the Netherlands moved from the inquisitorial to the adversarial in the 1990s, so there are still some examples of situations (such as the approach to the burden of proof, or the role of the judge in leading and managing the progress of the proceedings) which demonstrate facets similar to those adopted in inquisitorial systems.

[224] For a general account of the impact of European legal systems on one another and of the EU and ECHR systems on national orders and vice versa, see P Birkinshaw, *European Public Law*, 2nd edn (Deventer, Kluwer, 2014). For an account of the way in which national procedural law might have been impacted, see M Eliantonio, *Europeanisation of Administrative Justice? The Influence of the ECJ's Case Law in Italy, Germany and England* (Groningen, Europa Law Publishing, 2009); D-U Galetta, *Procedural Autonomy of EU Member States: Paradise Lost?* (Berlin, Springer, 2010).

The fundamental differences between the adversarial and inquisitorial approaches are best illustrated by the approach to the evidence regime, where the judge has a dominant role in inquisitorial systems, whereas in adversarial systems the provision of evidence is left in the hands of the parties. That said, the distinction between the inquisitorial and adversarial approaches is not as considerable as one might expect.

All of the systems under examination do not generally allow the court to consider issues *ultra petita*. The approach to permitting the court to raise issues *ex officio* is rather more variable, with the German and Dutch legal systems proving to be the most open to the raising of points *ex officio*. The EU and French legal systems take a more limited approach to the *ex officio* raising of points of law, generally limiting this to issues of public order. The courts in England and Wales enjoy a substantial discretion to raise points *ex officio*, but do so relatively infrequently and without a clear framework governing when the power to do so should be used.

All of the systems under examination allow for the admission of expert evidence in appropriate cases, although it is clear that the systems which adopt an inquisitorial approach are perhaps more open to the use of this, perhaps because such experts are called by the courts. In adversarial systems, it is for the parties to seek permission to use expert testimony, and in these cases it may be that claimants are deterred by the potential expense of doing so.

The other major distinction to be drawn between the legal systems under examination is that in England and Wales and the European Union (bearing in mind the *sui generis* nature of the CJEU) there is a single, unified court structure, whereas in Germany, France and the Netherlands there is a separate system of administrative courts.

From the perspective of procedure, this does not appear to lead to significant differences – the contrast between the inquisitorial and adversarial approaches is far more significant in this regard. Insofar as there are differences, these are most apparent when one contrasts the approach to the bringing of administrative law proceedings in England and Wales with those in the other systems under consideration. The bringing of an administrative law claim in England and Wales is a two-stage procedure, including a permission stage, designed to test the standing of the claimant and to consider whether the claimant has an arguable case, whereas in all of the other systems under examination proceedings have a single stage. However, the difference here is perhaps more in form than function, because in France, Germany, the Netherlands and the EU it is possible for the courts to dispose of cases that are ill-founded or otherwise unsuitable to proceed to full hearing through summary proceedings, whereas in England and Wales such cases would be filtered out at the permission stage. Whichever way this is done, the system is designed to achieve the same policy objectives, ie the removal of cases that are ill-founded or otherwise unable to proceed from the system at an early stage in order to minimise the usage of the court's resources on such cases. An important point to note is that, in Germany and the Netherlands, the courts may also deal with cases that are manifestly well founded through summary proceedings and find in favour of the claimant, whereas this is not true in any of the other legal systems. This could be very valuable for claimants in such cases. Another element of the Dutch system which is not replicated in any of the other systems under examination is that the judge can pause the proceedings specifically to allow, or even request, the authority to repair certain flaws of the decision within a period of time determined by the court (the so-called administrative loop). This often allows the final resolution of a case without the need to annul the decision and refer the case back to the authority in order for it to take a new decision.

A final trend that has been shown in this chapter is the rise of electronic processes for the origination of proceedings and the submission of documents and evidence to the court. Each system under consideration has adopted electronic working to some extent. At the present time, England and Wales and the EU legal system are perhaps the least developed in this regard, while France and Germany appear to be furthest along in the process of adopting digital means. The Netherlands has seen some adoption of IT, but much of this is not yet being fully used in the courts. Similarly, England and Wales saw a proposal by the Ministry of Justice in 2016 which is likely to lead to a radical expansion of the use of IT in the determination of a range of cases, including administrative law cases and cases before tribunals. This is likely to include not only the commencement of proceedings and the submission of documents, but also the conducting of some hearings online. These changes could be valuable in increasing the efficiency of the courts and reducing costs, but there may also be some significant negative consequences – adequate account must be taken of the needs of those who do not or cannot make effective use of digital means. Furthermore, the conduct of hearings online, while potentially advantageous in reducing costs, could also have the consequence of changing the nature of court proceedings by reducing the effectiveness of oral testimony (as it may not be so easy to see non-verbal responses and cues from witnesses) and will require substantial investment in technology by the court systems.

FURTHER READING

Eliantonio, M, *Europeanisation of Administrative Justice? The Influence of the ECJ's Case Law in Italy, Germany and England* (Groningen, Europa Law Publishing, 2009).

Galetta, D-U, *Procedural Autonomy of EU Member States: Paradise Lost?* (Berlin, Springer, 2010).

Grashof, F, *National Procedural Autonomy Revisited* (Groningen, Europa Law Publishing, 2016).

Ortlep, R and Widdershoven, RJGM, 'Judicial Protection' in JH Jans, S Prechal and RJGM Widdershoven (eds), *Europeanisation of Public Law*, 2nd edn (Groningen, Europa Law Publishing, 2015) 333–434.

CHAPTER 6
GROUNDS OF REVIEW AND STANDARD OF REVIEW

Hermann Pünder and Anika Klafki

6.1 INTRODUCTION

In order to determine the effectiveness of judicial review of administrative action, the grounds of review as well as the standard of review must be examined. Both elements are intertwined. Systems with far-reaching grounds of judicial review but a low standard of review might provide just as effective judicial protection as systems with very limited grounds of judicial review but a high intensity of judicial scrutiny.[1]

[1] M Kayser, in A von Bogdandy, S Cassese and PM Huber (eds), *Handbuch Ius Publicum Europaeum, Band V: Verwaltungsrecht in Europa* (Heidelberg, CF Müller, 2014) §91, para 101 ff.

At the centre of administrative judicial review throughout Europe stands the question of the legality or illegality of administrative action. Even though the judicial review of administrative action evolved domestically long before the European integration process and is still above all a matter of national sovereignty, Europeanisation has had harmonising effects on the different systems.[2] In 1950, Article 6 of the European Convention on Human Rights (ECHR) established a right to judicial review of actions determining 'civil rights and obligations' or 'criminal charges' and the right to a fair trial. Arbitrary decisions are thereby prohibited. Even though Article 6 ECHR is not directly applicable to all administrative decisions, the broad understanding of the terms 'civil rights and obligations' and 'criminal charges' by the European Court of Human Rights (ECtHR) has led to the inclusion of various fields of law, which are considered as administrative lawsuits under the national legal order.[3] Therefore, Article 6 ECHR also broadened the scope of review of administrative action and serves as an important source of inspiration for the judicial rights and guarantees in EU and national law.[4] The Court of Justice subsequently set the level of scrutiny with which the national courts must comply when dealing with cases that relate to EU law.[5] However, pursuant to the case law of the Court of Justice, EU law does not require that national courts must be empowered to substitute the assessment by the public authority with their own assessment of the facts of the case.[6] Thus, the Court of Justice accepts different levels of scrutiny on the Member State level, as long as the Member States 'provide remedies sufficient to ensure effective legal protection in the fields covered by Union law', according to Article 19(1) of the Treaty on European Union (TEU). The basic EU norms concerning effective judicial review are thus based on the idea of a common European understanding of the basic functions that judicial review should fulfil to ensure an effective protection of individual rights.

In this chapter, different aspects of the grounds and the scope of review will be analysed. First, the question of whether judicial review of administrative action is structured around specific grounds of judicial review will be examined. Then the scope of review of discretionary administrative decisions will be analysed. This affects fundamental understandings of the national legal systems concerning the separation of powers between the executive, the judiciary and the legislature. Third, the role of human rights and principles in court decisions will be considered. Judicial protection in Europe encompasses

[2] *cf* CD Classen, *Die Europäisierung der Verwaltungsgerichtsbarkeit* (Tübingen, Mohr Siebeck, 1996) 182 ff.

[3] See, eg ECtHR *Van Kück v Germany* ECLI:CE:ECHR:2003:0612JUD003596897, concerning the medical necessity for hormone replacement therapy and gender reassignment surgery which is considered as a social law and, thus, a public law dispute in Germany law.

[4] See J Schwarze, 'Judicial Review of European Administrative Procedure' (2004–2005) 68 *Law and Contemporary Problems* 85, 103; E Schmidt-Aßmann, *Kohärenz und Konsistenz des Verwaltungsrechtsschutzes* (Tübingen, Mohr Siebeck, 2015) 34 ff. For the high significance of Art 6 ECHR for the Dutch judicial review of administrative action, see section 6.4.B.1 below.

[5] See, eg Case 294/83 *Les Verts v Parliament* ECLI:EU:C:1986:166, para 23 (neither the Member States nor the European institutions can avoid judicial review; also, parliamentary decisions are reviewable).

[6] Case C-120/97 *Upjohn v Licensing Authority established by the Medicines Act 1968* ECLI:EU:C:1999:14, paras 29, 32 ff, 35; Case C-55/06 *Acor v Germany* ECLI:EU:C:2008:244, para 163 ff. See also J Schwarze, *Administrative Law under European Influence* (Baden-Baden, Nomos, 1996) 789, 808 ff.

the right of citizens not only to review administrative action because of its substantive illegality, but also to challenge administrative action because of formal flaws, such as incompetence, procedural errors or defects of form (eg lack of written form).[7] Nonetheless, the judicial review of breaches of formalities can be limited, as will be explained in section 6.6. This is due to the fact that, with regard to the annulment of administrative decisions on formal grounds, all legal systems have to balance the protection of procedural guarantees and the need for effective and speedy judicial protection.[8] Finally, issues such as the recognition of the direct effect of EU law and the principle of consistent interpretation with EU law in the national legal systems will be studied. The chapter ends with a comparative overview of the grounds of review and the scope of review of administrative action.

6.2 GROUNDS OF REVIEW

Concerning the grounds of review, it is remarkable that some legal systems, such as France, England and Wales, and the EU, are centered around a fixed set of grounds of judicial review, whereas other legal systems, such as Germany and the Netherlands, allow a more general judicial review of administrative action, without explicitly mentioning a strict set of grounds.

6.2.A SYSTEMS ORGANISED AROUND GROUNDS OF JUDICIAL REVIEW

The grounds of judicial review are not to be understood in a dogmatic way; rather, they serve procedural purposes. The grounds of judicial review should be understood as different pleas in law supporting the claim. They do not necessarily have a limiting effect on the scope of review. Especially in France, the *violation de la loi* ground serves as a catch-all clause, with the effect that a broad judicial review is guaranteed.

6.2.A.1 FRANCE

C Broyelle, Contentieux administratif[9] **6.1 (FR)**

The roles of the parties and the judge respectively

Intervention of the judge – If the parties must provide the judge with the grounds, meaning they must expose the reasons for which it would be suitable to accept their claims, they are not obliged to express these grounds in legal terms. Also, often, the

[7] Kayser (n 1 above) §91, para 101 ff.

[8] For a comparative perspective, see H Pünder, 'German Administrative Procedure in a Comparative Perspective – Observations on the Path to a Transnational *Ius Commune Proceduralis* in Administrative Law' (2013) 11 *International Journal of Constitutional Law* 940; Ch Backes, M Eliantonio and S Jansen, *Quality and Speed in Administrative Decision-Making: Tension or Balance?* (Antwerp, Intersentia, 2016).

[9] C Broyelle, *Contentieux administratif*, 4th edn (Paris, Librairie générale de droit et de jurisprudence, 2017) 137–38.

'grounds' provided by the parties are presented as a set of factual evidence. For example: 'I have been subjected to a disciplinary sanction, without ever having been informed beforehand of the very existence of such objections raised against me'; or: 'While I was crossing the road, I tripped in a pot hole and I got injured'. The parties are authorised to present raw data which require, to become legal grounds, the intervention of the judge.

With regard to the story told by the applicants, the judge identifies the legal rule raised by the applicant and then proceeds to the translation of the facts into legal terms. For example, the applicant asks for the annulment of a disciplinary sanction on the grounds that he has not been previously informed of the objections raised against him; these conclusions are then related to a ground of *illégalité externe*, derived from the violation of the rights of the defence. ...

This translation exercise is carried out during the preparation stage and rarely perceived in the judgment, unless the ruling used formulas such as the applicant 'must be regarded as having invoked (such) grounds'.

Conseil d'État, 4 April 1914[10] **6.2 (FR)**

Gomel v Prefect of Paris

LEGAL ASSESSMENT OF FACTS

Gomel

The administrative courts may review the legal assessment of the facts on which the decision is based.

Facts: The prefect of Paris had refused a building permit in Paris because he argued that the planned building would affect the architectural value of the square in which the building would be located.

Held: The decision was annulled.

Judgment: Considering that, in the terms of Article 3 of the Decree of 26 March 1852, 'all house builders, before they start the works, must request the alignment and levelling on a public road in front of their land and comply with it'; that Article 4 of the same decree, modified by Article 118 of the law of 14 July 1911, states: 'Similarly, they should send a plan of the planned cuts of the constructions to the administration, and comply with the prescriptions that will be made in the interest of public security, of safety and of the conservation of existing views of architectural value and of the squares, except in case of appeal to the Council of State'; considering that this last article, completed by the law of 13 July 1911, is intended to confer to the prefect the right to refuse, by way of individual decision, a building permit in case the submitted project infringes upon an existing view of architectural value; considering that the only restrictions made to the powers of the prefect, the exercise of which the law has not subordinated to a prior classification as an existing view of architectural value, are those which result from the necessity to reconcile the conservation of said perspectives with the respect owed to the property right. But considering that it is for the Council of State to verify whether the location of the planned

[10] N° 55125.

construction is included in an existing view of architectural value and, in the affirmative, whether this construction, as it is proposed, would be of a nature to infringe upon it; considering that Place Beauvau would not be regarded as a whole as forming a view of architectural value; considering also that, by refusing to grant the applicant the building permit by the challenged decision, the prefect of the Seine has incorrectly applied of Article 118 of the aforementioned law of 13 July 1911.

Notes

(1) Judicial review in France is structured around certain grounds of judicial review.[11] The first two grounds concern so-called 'external illegality' (*illégalité externe*). From this perspective, a decision may be unlawful due to lack of competence (*incompetence*) if the decision was not taken by the person, or the body, who was empowered to issue it. The second ground of review linked to *illégalité externe* is procedural or formal irregularity (*vice de forme ou de procédure*), which means that the decision has a flaw in its form or that the correct procedure for its adoption was not followed.[12]

(2) The other grounds concern the so-called 'internal illegality' (*illégalité interne*) of the decision. Within 'internal illegality', a first ground is the so-called 'violation of the law' (*violation de la loi*). Within this ground, the court may assess the compliance of the challenged decision with higher norms, such as legislation, constitutional norms or EU law. In order to assess where a 'violation of the law' has occurred, the court may assess the correctness of the facts on which the decision was grounded (*contrôle de l'exactitude matérielle des faits*). If the facts are incorrect, the judge will consider that the factual ground of the decision is missing. This is the case, for example, when a decision is adopted to sanction a civil servant for the destruction of public goods but the goods are not actually destroyed. Furthermore, in order to assess a 'violation of the law', the court may also review the 'legal assessment of the facts' (*qualification juridique des faits*). There is a wrong legal assessment of the facts when, for example, the public authorities adopt a decision to sanction a fault committed by a civil servant while the behaviour of the civil servant is not considered unlawful under the applicable laws. A second ground of review concerning the 'internal illegality' of an administrative decision is 'misuse of power' (*détournement de pouvoir*). This ground of review applies when a decision is not taken in the public interest or, while being in the public interest, it is not taken for the specific interest for which, according to the law, it should have been taken.

[11] For a good overview, see E Steiner, *French Law: A Comparative Approach* (Oxford, Oxford University Press, 2010) 269 f; G Bermann and E Picard, 'Administrative Law' in G Bermann and E Picard (eds), *Introduction to French Law* (Alphen aan de Rijn, Kluwer Law International, 2008) 57, 94 ff; JB Auby, L Cluzel-Métayer and Lamprini Xenou, 'Administrative Law in France' in R Seerden (ed), *Administrative Law of the European Union, its Member States and the United States*, 4th edn (Antwerp, Intersentia, 2018) 38 ff.

[12] For more information on the treatment of procedural errors, see section 6.6.B.1 below.

(3) These grounds of review developed historically and are by no means mutually exclusive. In principle, it is for the plaintiff to state the grounds under which the court will review the decision. However, the court always has the possibility to raise *ex officio* the grounds which are 'of public order' (*moyens d'ordre public*), the main one being lack of competence.[13]

6.2.A.2 ENGLAND AND WALES

House of Lords, 22 December 1984[14] **6.3 (EW)**

Council of Civil Service Unions v Minister for the Civil Service

GROUNDS OF REVIEW IN ENGLISH LAW

GCHQ

The common law recognises three grounds of judicial review: 'illegality', 'irrationality' and 'procedural impropriety'.

Facts: The Prime Minister (acting in her role as Minister for the Civil Service) decided to ban all trade union activity at GCHQ (the government's communication headquarters, which plays a major role in gathering and interpreting information for the security services, police and intelligence services) due to national security concerns. The trade unions objected to the proposed ban and brought a claim for judicial review of the decision. The issue in the case was whether or not the decision to ban trade union activity was unlawful.

Held: The House of Lords held that the ban was lawful.

Judgment: Lord Diplock: Judicial review has, I think, developed to a stage today when without reiterating any analysis of the steps by which the development has come about, one can conveniently classify under three heads the grounds upon which administrative action is subject to control by judicial review. The first ground I would call 'illegality', the second 'irrationality', and the third 'procedural impropriety'. That is not to say that further development on a case by case basis may not in the course of time add further grounds. I have in mind particularly the possible adoption in the future of the principle of 'proportionality' which is recognised in the administrative law of several of our fellow members of the European Economic Community; but to dispose of the instant case the three already well-established heads that I have mentioned will suffice.

By 'illegality' as a ground for judicial review I mean that the decision-maker must understand correctly the law that regulates his decision-making power and must give effect to it. Whether he has or not is par excellence a justiciable question to be decided, in the event of dispute, by those persons, the judges, by whom the judicial power of the state is exercisable.

[13] LN Brown and J Bell, *French Administrative Law* (Oxford, Clarendon Press, 1998) 239; J Massot, 'The Powers and Duties of the French Administrative Judge' in S Rose-Ackerman and PL Lindseth (eds), *Comparative Administrative Law* (Cheltenham, Edward Elgar, 2010) 415, 421; Auby et al (n 11 above) 6, 28 ff. See further also Chapter 5, section 5.5.

[14] [1985] AC 374.

By 'irrationality' I mean what can by now be succinctly referred to as 'Wednesbury unreasonableness' (*Associated Provincial Picture Houses Ltd. v. Wednesbury Corporation* [1948] 1 KB 223). It applies to a decision which is so outrageous in its defiance of logic or of accepted moral standards that no sensible person who had applied his mind to the question to be decided could have arrived at it. Whether a decision falls within this category is a question that judges by their training and experience should be well equipped to answer, or else there would be something badly wrong with our judicial system. To justify the court's exercise of this role, resort I think is today no longer needed to Viscount Radcliffe's ingenious explanation in *Edwards v. Bairstow* [1956] AC 14 of irrationality as a ground for a court's reversal of a decision by ascribing it to an inferred though unidentifiable mistake of law by the decision-maker. 'Irrationality' by now can stand upon its own feet as an accepted ground on which a decision may be attacked by judicial review.

I have described the third head as 'procedural impropriety' rather than failure to observe basic rules of natural justice or failure to act with procedural fairness towards the person who will be affected by the decision. This is because susceptibility to judicial review under this head covers also failure by an administrative tribunal to observe procedural rules that are expressly laid down in the legislative instrument by which its jurisdiction is conferred, even where such failure does not involve any denial of natural justice. But the instant case is not concerned with the proceedings of an administrative tribunal at all.

Note

In common law, traditionally three grounds of review are accepted: illegality, irrationality and procedural impropriety.[15] Illegality arises when the executive oversteps its decision-making competence, which is particularly difficult to decide where Parliament confers discretion to the administration or where the wording of the law is ambiguous or very open.[16] The concept of irrationality is closely connected to the *Wednesbury* unreasonableness, which will be explained in depth when the judicial review of discretion is examined.[17] However, the Human Rights Act led to an extension of judicial review in the UK due to the ECHR rights taking effect in English law.[18] The last ground of review, procedural impropriety, concerns administrative procedure and procedural fairness.[19] The focus of judicial review in England and Wales used to place greater focus on procedural errors and illegality, with only limited control of the substance of administrative decisions. However, with Europeanisation, the courts have become increasingly willing to scrutinise the substance of administrative decisions.[20]

[15] For a comprehensive overview, see K Thompson, 'Administrative Law in the United Kingdom' in Seerden (n 11 above) 197, 246 ff.

[16] See A Tomkins, 'The Struggle to Delimit Executive Power in Britain' in P Craig and A Tomkins (eds), *The Executive and Public Law* (Oxford, Oxford University Press, 2006) 16, 42 ff.

[17] See sections 6.3.B.3 and 6.5.A.5 below.

[18] See Tomkins (n 16 above) 16, 42.

[19] ibid, 16, 44. For details, see section 6.6.A.1 below.

[20] See section 6.3.B.3 below.

6.2.A.3 THE EUROPEAN UNION

Treaty on the Functioning of the European Union **6.4 (EU)**

Article 263 The Court of Justice of the European Union shall review the legality of legislative acts, of acts of the Council, of the Commission and of the European Central Bank, other than recommendations and opinions, and of acts of the European Parliament and of the European Council intended to produce legal effects vis-à-vis third parties. It shall also review the legality of acts of bodies, offices or agencies of the Union intended to produce legal effects vis-à-vis third parties.

It shall for this purpose have jurisdiction in actions brought by a Member State, the European Parliament, the Council or the Commission on grounds of lack of competence, infringement of an essential procedural requirement, infringement of the Treaties or of any rule of law relating to their application, or misuse of powers. ...

Article 265 Should the European Parliament, the European Council, the Council, the Commission or the European Central Bank, in infringement of the Treaties, fail to act, the Member States and the other institutions of the Union may bring an action before the Court of Justice of the European Union to have the infringement established. This Article shall apply, under the same conditions, to bodies, offices and agencies of the Union which fail to act. ...

Notes

(1) In the European system, a fixed set of grounds for judicial review exists. In Article 263 of the Treaty on the Functioning of the European Union (TFEU), which stipulates the requirements for an action for annulment, specific reasons are listed. The claim can only be based 'on grounds of lack of competence, infringement of an essential procedural requirement, infringement of the Treaties or of any rule of law relating to their application, or misuse of powers'. Thus, complaints based on procedural grounds as well as claims based on the infringement of substantive law are covered. The ground of lack of competence means that the body that adopted the act did not have the power to do so. The ground of 'infringement of an essential procedural requirement' concerns, for example, the duty to state reasons, consultation requirements and the right to be heard.[21] The third ground of review, the infringement of the Treaty or another rule of law, encompasses a wide variety of possible claims. Examples include where an EU institution has breached the principle of non-discrimination; breaches of proportionality[22] and breaches of legitimate expectations.[23] Finally, the ground of 'misuse of power' concerns situations in which the EU institutions have used their power for improper purposes. For example, an unsuccessful applicant for a job at the European Commission successfully challenged the Commission's job

[21] See section 6.6.B.2 below. See also eg Case T-450/93 *Lisrestal and others v Commission* ECLI:EU:T:1994:290.

[22] See section 6.5.A.2 below.

[23] See section 6.5.B.5 below.

competition on the ground that the Commission had held the job competition solely for the purpose of promoting an existing Commission employee to a higher grade. This was found to be a misuse of the Commission's power to hold a recruitment exercise.[24]

(2) An action for failure to act, according to Article 265, may be brought when the failure to act is allegedly 'in infringement of the Treaties'. This should be taken to mean, in accordance with the case law of the Court of Justice, the violation of any rule of EU law which is binding on the defendant institution and contains a duty to act.[25]

(3) The grounds for review were originally taken from the French legal system,[26] but the grounds themselves, as well as the procedural consequences, differ considerably today from the original French model.

6.2.B SYSTEMS WITHOUT SPECIFIC GROUNDS OF REVIEW

6.2.B.1 GERMANY

Grundgesetz **6.5 (DE)**

Article 19 (4) Should any person's rights be violated by a public authority, he shall have recourse to the courts. …

Notes

(1) The German constitution guarantees the right to effective judicial protection. The German Constitutional Court has a far-reaching understanding of this fundamental right.[27] Thus, the grounds for judicial review are not restricted to certain categories, and the level of scrutiny, as will be further analysed with regard to the control of discretionary choices, is particularly high.[28]

(2) However, legal doctrine does differentiate between formal illegality and substantive illegality. Formal illegality includes lack of competence, procedural flaws and defects of form, such as insufficient reasoning or the violation of a written formal requirement.[29] Substantive illegality covers all sorts of flaws relating to the merits of the decision, such as the requirement of a legal basis for burdensome administrative action, violation of the applicable law, lack of clarity, errors in exercising

[24] Case 105/75 *Giuffrida v Council* ECLI:EU:C:1976:128.

[25] Cases 10 and 18/68 *Società 'Eridania' Zuccherifici Nazionali and others v Commission* ECLI:EU:C:1969:66.

[26] M Kotzur, in R Geiger, DE Khan and M Kotzur (eds), *European Union Treaties: A Commentary* (Munich, CH Beck, 2015) Art 263, para 34.

[27] See eg BVerfGE 103, 142, 156 f.

[28] See E Schmidt-Aßmann and C Möllers, 'The Scope and Accountability of Executive Power in Germany' in Craig and Tomkins (n 16 above) 268, 285; see also F Erath, 'Scope of Judicial Review in German Administrative Law' (1997) 8 *Stellenbosch Law Review* 192, 196 ff.

[29] See H Pünder, 'German Administrative Law' in FJ Heidinger and A Hubalek (eds), *Anglo-Amerikanische Rechtssprache, Anglo-American Legal Language* Vol 3 (Vienna/Berlin, LexisNexis/BDÜ, 2016) 79, 86 ff. For more details, see Pünder (n 8 above).

discretion (*Ermessensfehler*),[30] proportionality and the legal or factual impossibility of execution. In principle, the administrative courts scrutinise the entire administrative action unless the law, by exception, grants the administration special freedoms, such as discretion or a margin of interpretation.[31] Thus, in Germany, the last authoritative interpretation of administrative law generally rests with the administrative courts.[32] Furthermore, in contrast to the rather objective judicial review system in France,[33] the focus of judicial review of administrative action in Germany lies on the protection of individual rights. Thus, flaws which do not infringe subjective rights of the claimant will in principle not lead to the annulment of an administrative decision.[34]

6.2.B.2 THE NETHERLANDS

Algemene Wet Bestuursrecht **6.6 (NL)**

Article 8:77 (2) If the district court finds the claim for judicial review (*beroep*) well-founded, the judgment shall state which written or unwritten rule of law or which general principle of law is found to have been violated.

Notes

(1) The only provision in the Algemene Wet Bestuursrecht (General Administrative Law Act, AWB) which provides for information about the grounds for review is Article 8:77(2) AWB. This provision presumes that the administrative courts review administrative decisions on the grounds of written and unwritten rules of law and of general principles of law. According to the *travaux preparatoires* on the provision, together these categories cover the law as a whole.[35] They do not intend to set any restrictions as regards the grounds for judicial review.

(2) 'Written rules of law' include not only EU law, international law, Acts of Parliament and lower or delegated legislation, but also those principles of good administration that have been codified in the AWB, such as the principle of due care (Article 3:2 AWB), the principle of *detournement de pouvoir* (Article 3:3 AWB) and the principle requiring reasons to be stated (Articles 3:46 and 3:47 AWB).[36] 'Unwritten rules of law' are the principles of good administration that have not yet been codified, such

[30] See section 6.3.A below.
[31] ibid. See also Schmidt-Aßmann and Möllers (n 28 above) 268, 286.
[32] For an overview, see W Kahl, in von Bogdandy et al (n 1 above) §74, para 127 ff.
[33] See Chapter 1, section 1.5.
[34] For details on the distinction between objective and subjective judicial review systems, see Chapter 1, section 1.5; with regard to standing, see Chapter 4, section 4.4.
[35] PG AWB II, 501.
[36] For more information on the role of principles in judicial review, see section 6.5 below.

as the principles of legitimate expectations and legal certainty. 'General principles of law' consist of unwritten principles of law which also apply to areas other than administrative law (private law, criminal law). Examples mentioned in the *travaux preparatoires* are the principles of *ne bis in idem* and proportionality (both also applicable in the area of criminal law) and the principle of unjust enrichment (also applicable in the area of private law).

(3) Similarly to Germany, Dutch doctrine differentiates between formal illegality and substantive illegality. The former includes lack of competence, flaws in the decision-making process and defects regarding the reasoning of the decision. Material illegality covers all sorts of flaws relating to the merits of the decision.

(4) Finally, it should be noted that the Netherlands have recently introduced a so-called 'relativity requirement' (*relativiteitsvereiste*), according to which the administrative courts cannot annul a decision on the grounds that it is inconsistent with a written or unwritten rule of law or a general principle, if this rule or principle clearly does not intend to protect the interests of the party relying on it (Article 8:69a AWB).[37] This requirement resembles the German 'protection of rights doctrine',[38] but is applied in a less strict way.

6.3 REVIEW OF DISCRETION

If the law defines exactly what the administration must do if certain facts are demonstrated, the authority is fully bound and does not have any discretion. The judge has to fully review such administrative acts. However, all legal systems often grant discretionary powers to the administrative branch in order to achieve individual justice in the course of executing the law.[39] The idea of separation of powers demands that courts do not interfere with the powers of the legislature – which assigns the tasks to the administration – or the powers of the executive. Nonetheless, the rule of law requires the courts to assess whether public authorities have violated the law. Thus, all legal systems that have been examined allow judicial review of discretionary administrative decisions in principle, but limit the level of scrutiny.[40] However, the limits applying to judicial review of discretionary administrative decisions differ considerably with regard to the underlying legal doctrine and the scope of application.

Furthermore, the terminology for the freedom of manoeuvre of the administration differs between the analysed legal systems. Whereas some legal systems subsume all kinds of decision-making independence of the administration under the term 'discretion', in Germany and in the Netherlands a distinction is made between factual assessments and choices of the administration concerning the legal consequences.

[37] See further Chapter 4, section 4.4.G.

[38] *Schutznormtheorie*; see Chapter 4, section 4.4.B.

[39] J Schwarze, *European Administrative Law: Revised First Edition* (London, Sweet & Maxwell, 2006) 209, 210.

[40] See S Ranchordás and B de Waard, 'Concluding Remarks' in S Ranchordás and B de Waard (eds), *The Judge and the Proportionate Use of Discretion. A Comparative Study* (London, Routledge, 2016) 191, 193 f.

6.3.A SYSTEMS DISTINGUISHING BETWEEN MARGIN OF INTERPRETATION AND DISCRETION

6.3.A.1 GERMANY

Verwaltungsgerichtsordnung **6.7 (DE)**

§114 Insofar as the administrative authority is empowered to exercise discretion, the court shall also examine whether the administrative act or the refusal or omission of the administrative act is unlawful because the statutory limits of discretion have been overstepped or discretion has been used in a manner not corresponding to the purpose of the empowerment …

Verwaltungsverfahrensgesetz **6.8 (DE)**

§40 Where an authority is empowered to act at its discretion, it shall do so in accordance with the purpose of such empowerment and shall respect the legal limits of such discretionary powers.

Bundesverwaltungsgericht, 25 April 2007[41] **6.9 (DE)**

MARGIN OF INTERPRETATION

The indefinite legal term 'suitable' in the Act on the Legal Status of Soldiers provides for a margin of interpretation for the competent authority. Thus, the judicial review of the administration's evaluation of whether a candidate is suitable is limited to specific errors of assessment (Beurteilungsfehler).

Facts: The federal Minister of Defence had appointed a soldier with the rank of a colonel doctor to a vacant position, for which the claimant had also applied. The claimant, a doctor with the rank of a general, opposed this decision.

Held: The Minister of Defence was ordered to decide again in compliance with the ruling of the court.

Judgment: 44. Since 'suitability' (*Eignung*), 'qualification' (*Befähigung*) and 'performance' (*Leistung*) are indefinite legal terms with an evaluative content, the competent hierarchical authority has a right to a margin of interpretation when deciding about the suitability (*Eignung*) of a soldier for a certain purpose in the sense of §3(1) of the Act of the Legal Status of Soldiers. This margin of interpretation will need to be exercised with regard to the service which the soldier needs to perform … . Consequently, judicial review of the suitability is limited to the control of whether the hierarchical authority has, when making the decision, misjudged the indefinite legal term or the margin of justice resulting thereof. This is the case when the public authority started from a wrong premise, disregarded generally accepted standards, took irrelevant matters into consideration or infringed procedural rules. …

51. Regardless of the question – presently left open by the Senate – whether a procedural error occurred, the decision made by the Minister and contested by the claimant is

[41] BVerwGE 128, 329–42.

erroneous because generally valid value scales concerning the suitability of the candidate were misjudged. Generally accepted standards [for the assessment of the suitability of the candidate] have not been respected adequately. The decision is therefore to be set aside and the Minister is to be obliged to take a new decision on the filling of the position … considering the legal position of the court.

Notes

(1) With regard to freedom in administrative decision-making, German law differentiates between the administrative 'margin of interpretation' (*Beurteilungsspielraum*) of 'indefinite legal terms' (*unbestimmte Rechtsbegriffe*) and 'discretion' (*Ermessen*) to choose between different actions.[42] Margin of interpretation relates to factual assessments, while discretion relates to the legal consequences of a certain administrative action.

(2) Generally, indefinite legal terms such as 'suitable', 'appropriate' or 'reliable', which require interpretation, are fully reviewable by the administrative courts due to the constitutional guarantee to judicial review contained in Article 19(4) of the Grundgesetz.[43] However, exceptionally, a 'margin of interpretation' is acknowledged, which entitles the administration to an autonomous factual assessment and thus limits the scope of judicial review.[44] German administrative law recognises only a very few areas where a 'margin of interpretation' is granted to the administration. This is the case, for example, with examinations in schools or universities, selection decisions (as was the case in the excerpt above) or appraising decisions of pluralist bodies of experts (for example, in the field of nuclear law). Here, it would be inappropriate for the courts to substitute the administration's factual findings with their own. The courts therefore limit their review to certain 'specific errors of assessment' (*Beurteilungsfehler*): the judiciary only examines whether procedural rules were observed, the facts on which the administrative decision is based were correct, no irrelevant factors were taken into account and whether 'generally accepted evaluation standards' (*allgemein anerkannte Beurteilungsmaßstäbe*) were observed.

(3) With regard to the legal consequences, administrative discretion is generally only acknowledged where the law explicitly offers a choice of action to the administration (norms containing, for example, 'may' or 'can'). §40 of the Verwaltungsverfahrensgesetz (Administrative Procedure Act, VwVfG) reiterates the rule-of-law principle in respect of discretionary decisions, and makes clear that the administration

[42] For a brief summary of the German concept of administrative freedoms, see H Pünder and A Klafki, 'Administrative Law in Germany' in Seerden (n 11 above) 49, 88 ff. See also N Marsch and V Tünsmeyer, 'Proportionality: German Administrative Law' in Ranchordás and de Waard (n 40 above) 13, 18 ff. However, the distinction between margin of interpretation on the one hand and discretion on the other hand is contested in doctrinal writing; see M Jestaedt, in D Ehlers and H Pünder (eds), *Allgemeines Verwaltungsrecht*, 15th edn (Berlin, De Gruyter, 2016) §11.

[43] See BVerfGE 129, 1.

[44] The leading case for this is BVerwGE 39, 197. For details see Schwarze (n 39 above) 273, 274.

must exercise its discretion in accordance with the purpose of the legal empowerment and shall respect the legal limits of its discretionary powers. In order to ensure that the court will not simply substitute the discretionary decision of the administration by its own, §114 of the Verwaltungsgerichtsordnung (Administrative Court Procedure Act, VwGO) limits judicial review to 'discretionary errors' (*Ermessensfehler*). Accordingly, administrative courts may not freely decide whether another decision would have been more appropriate or reasonable. The court may only annul the decision if it establishes that the decision is based on a discretionary error.

(4) There are three types of discretionary errors. First, if the authority fails to realise that it had discretionary freedoms in decision-making, this constitutes a 'failure to use discretion' (*Ermessensnichtgebrauch*). For example, if an administrative body issues a request for reimbursement of a subsidy and states that it is obliged to do so in the reasoning of the administrative act, even though this is a discretionary decision according to the applicable law, the addressee may claim that the administration failed to exercise its discretion properly. Secondly, in situations in which the administration failed to investigate all relevant aspects of the case or has considered irrelevant aspects, an 'unreasonable way of exercising discretion' (*Ermessensdefizit*) is established. In building law, it would, for example, constitute an unreasonable way of exercising discretion if the administration did not consider the interests of neighbours at all when granting a building permit for a nightclub. Thirdly, if the administration exceeds its discretion by acting in a disproportionate manner, this error constitutes 'excess of discretion' (*Ermessensüberschreitung*).[45] 'Excess of discretion' (*Ermessensüberschreitung*) in particular leads to a very high level of scrutiny of administrative courts, which in practice is carried out through the proportionality principle. Due to Germany's historic background, the rule of law principle (*Rechtsstaatsprinzip*) has led to a very strict application of the proportionality test in judicial review.[46] Wherever fundamental rights are affected, the administrative courts closely scrutinise the weighing process, as well as the merits of administrative decisions.[47] De facto, nearly all administrative decisions are therefore tested with regard to proportionality by the courts in Germany.

6.3.A.2 THE NETHERLANDS

Algemene Wet Bestuursrecht **6.10 (NL)**

Article 3:4 (1) An administrative authority shall consider the interests directly affected by a decision, subject to any limitations following from a legal rule or the nature of the power to be exercised.

(2) The adverse consequences of a decision for one or more interested parties may not be disproportionate to the purposes to be served by the decision.

[45] For a brief overview, see H Pünder and A Klafki, 'Administrative Law in Germany' in Seerden (n 11 above) 49, 90; Marsch and Tünsmeyer (n 42 above) 13, 21 f.

[46] Schwarze (n 39 above) 270 ff.

[47] For more details, see section 6.5.A below.

Raad van State, 9 May 1996[48] **6.11 (NL)**

Mayor and Aldermen of Venlo v Kwantum Nederland and Maxis Praxis

REVIEW OF DISCRETIONARY ADMINISTRATIVE DECISIONS

Maxis Praxis

Judicial review of discretionary administrative decisions is limited to whether there is such an imbalance of the weighing of the interests involved that it must be concluded that the administrative authority could not reasonably have come to the contested decision.

Facts: The mayor and aldermen of Venlo had granted Kwantum Nederland an exemption from the provisions of a development plan in order to allow the construction of a large shop. Maxis Praxis (a competitor) contested the decision before the district court. The district court annulled it on the grounds that the exemption violated Article 3:4(2) AWB as the adverse consequences of the decision for Maxis Praxis were disproportionate compared with the advantages for Kwantum. The board of mayor and aldermen and Kwantum appealed against this judgment before the Judicial Division of the Council of State.

Held: The judgment of the district court was annulled on the ground that the district court did not show enough restraint when assessing the decision.

Judgment: Article 3:4(2) AWB requires that the consequences of a decision are not disproportionate for one or more interested parties in relation to the objectives the decision aims to serve. With this provision, which addresses the administration, the legislator has not intended to intensify the judicial scrutiny of decisions compared to the case law developed under the regime of Article 8 of the (former) Law on Administrative Jurisdiction against Administrative Decisions (Wet Administratieve rechtspraak overheids beschikkingen). From the *travaux preparatoires* it appears that the wording of Article 3:4(2) AWB, which includes a double negation ('not disproportionate'), is intended to force the judge to show restraint when assessing the weighing of interests carried out by the administration.

The district court should have restricted itself to the question of whether there is such an imbalance of the weighing of the interests involved that it must be concluded that the board could not reasonably have come to the decision granting the exemption. The judgment is annulled.

Raad van State, 24 April 2007[49] **6.12 (NL)**

Mayor and Aldermen of Dordrecht v PMN Holding BV, PMN Exploitatie BV and 'Parkeer Management Nederland CV'

REVIEW OF DISCRETIONARY ADMINISTRATIVE DECISIONS

PMN

The courts have to show restraint in assessing discretionary administrative decisions, but may scrutinise whether there is such an imbalance in the consideration of the interests involved that the administrative body could not reasonably have come to that decision.

[48] ECLI:NL:RVS:1996:ZF2153.

[49] ECLI:NL:RVS:2007:BA4135.

Facts: The mayor and aldermen of Dordrecht had decided to enlarge the area in the city centre where cars are allowed only for exceptional reasons (an area of limited car use). The claimants, which were companies that operated car parks within the city of Dordrecht, objected against this decision and argued that their interests had not been weighed properly. In the end, the case was brought before the Judicial Division of the Council of State.

Held: The decision was annulled.

Judgment: 2.4.1 The Judicial Division presupposes that the board of mayor and aldermen has a broad margin of discretion when making a traffic order. It is for the board, when taking such a decision, to take all interests involved into account and weigh these interests against each other. The judge will have to show restraint in assessing such a decision and should assess whether the decision was not contrary to statutory provisions and whether there is such an imbalance in the consideration of the interests involved that the administrative body could not reasonably have come to that decision. …

Raad van State, 3 September 2008[50] **6.13 (NL)**

Council of Dutch of Caribbean Background v the Data Protection Authority, the Minister of Integration and the mayors of 21 municipalities

MARGIN OF INTERPRETATION

Reference Index Antilleans

Where a margin of interpretation is granted to a public authority, the courts may review the choices of the authorities, but may not substitute the authority's assessment with their own assessment.

Facts: By a decision of 11 December 2006, the Data Protection Authority (DPA) had granted exemptions under several conditions to the Minister of Integration and the mayors of 21 municipalities for processing personal data regarding ethnicity in the Reference Index Antilleans. This decision was contested by the Council of Dutch of Caribbean Background before the district court. The district court annulled the decision, stating that it was under an obligation to fully review the question of whether the processing of personal data was necessary on the ground of a compelling general interest, as the DPA enjoyed no margin of interpretation in this respect. The DPA, the Minister and the mayors filed an appeal against the judgment before the Judicial Division of the Council of State.

Held: The judgment of the district court was annulled.

Judgment: 2.9.1 The district court has held that, from the wording of Article 23 (1) sub (e) of the Law on the Protection of Personal Data, it does not appear that the DPA enjoys a margin of interpretation in the interpretation of the notion 'necessary on the ground of a compelling general interest'. Taking the national and international legal provisions on the prohibition of discrimination into account, the district court is of the opinion that the DPA's interpretation must be fully reviewed.

2.9.2 [According to the Judicial Division] [N]ecessity and the question of whether there are compelling grounds for a decision are inherently concepts of the applicable legal provisions, the interpretation of which requires a certain margin of interpretation. In its decision-making, the DPA should develop this margin further. This implies that, notwithstanding the fact that, in light of the strict regime for the processing of sensitive personal

[50] ECLI:NL:RVS:2008:BE9698.

data laid down in Articles 16 to 24 of the *Wet bescherming persoonsgegevens* (Law on the Protection of Personal Data) and the ban on discrimination, an intensive judicial review is in place, the district court has unlawfully substituted the assessment of the DPA with its own assessment. The appeal is well-founded. The judgment is annulled.

Notes

(1) On the surface, the Dutch approach appears to be similar to the German system, as it also distinguishes between discretion (*beleidsruimte*) and margin of interpretation (*beoordelingsruimte*) with regard to administrative freedom in decision-making.[51] As in German law, discretion refers to the freedom of choosing legal consequences, whereas the margin of interpretation concerns factual assessments.

(2) The Dutch system does, however, differ from the German system in some respects.[52] In particular, in the Netherlands, many norms convey a certain, often wide, margin of discretion to the administration, including in areas in which German law would not provide for administrative discretion or would reduce it to zero because fundamental rights are affected. For example, the Dutch authorities have discretion when deciding on an environmental permit, whereas the German authorities are considered not to have any discretion in the decision concerning the same environmental permit in Germany (*immissionsschutzrechtliche Genehmigung*).

(3) As is clear from the excerpts from *Maxis Praxis* and *PMN*, the need for judicial restraint in reviewing discretionary decisions is emphasised more vigorously than in Germany, as Dutch courts are limited to scrutinising only whether there is such an imbalance in the consideration of the interests involved that the administrative body could not reasonably have come to the challenged decision. This test leads to a looser application of the proportionality principle in the Netherlands than in Germany.[53]

(4) The courts fully review the interpretation of legal terms by the administration. However, when the authorities are given a margin of interpretation, for example with regards to certain vague terms (beoordelingsruimte), the courts may review the interpretation by the administration only to a certain extent. This means concretely that the courts will only intervene on the way in which the administration used its margin of interpretation if the ensuing decision is unreasonable or infringes other principles of good administration. This leads, in general, to a more limited review of factual assessment than in Germany. Exceptionally, however, when fundamental rights are at stake, as in the case of Reference Index Antilleans, Dutch courts review the interpretation of vague legal terms more intensively.

(5) Finally, it should be noted that the level of judicial scrutiny in both situations (discretion and margin of interpretation) has increased over time due to the development of various principles of good administration, which are henceforth applied in

[51] For details, see B de Waard, 'Proportionality: Dutch Administrative Law' in Ranchordás and de Waard (n 40 above) 109, 127 ff.

[52] See further AP Klap, 'Rechterlijke toetsing aan vage normen in Nederland en Duitsland' in AP Klap, FT Groenewegen and JR van Angeren (eds), *Toetsing aan vage normen door de bestuursrechter in het Nederlandse, Duitse, Engelse en Franse recht* (Oisterwijk, Wolf Legal Publishers, 2014) 1–78.

[53] See section 6.5.A.4 below.

the judicial review of administrative decisions.[54] In particular, the principle to state sufficient reasons for a decision has proven to be useful in this respect. In practice, the exercise of discretion or of a margin of interpretation by the administration is judicially assessed quite intensively with regard to the compliance with this and other principles.[55] Obviously, the relevance of general principles of good administration is greater if the authority has discretion or a margin of interpretation. In case of legal norms which tell the authority precisely what it has to do, there is less room for the application of general principles.

6.3.B SYSTEMS WITH AN ALL-ENCOMPASSING UNDERSTANDING OF 'DISCRETION'

6.3.B.1 FRANCE

Conseil d'État, 16 December 1988[56] **6.14 (FR)**

Bleton and others v Prime Minister and Minister for National Education, Youth and Sport

MANIFEST ERROR OF ASSESSMENT

Bleton

The power of the court to control an administrative decision that appoints an individual to a public office is limited to the review of a manifest error of assessment.

Facts: Mr Gérard I was appointed by a decree of 13 February 1986 to the position of general inspector of libraries. The decree was challenged before the Council of State by several applicants, who considered that Mr Gérard I did not have the professional skills to hold such position.

Held: The decree was annulled.

Judgment: Considering that the assessment by the appointing authority of the candidates' abilities must be carried out by taking account of the powers conferred on the members of the body concerned and the conditions under which they perform their duties;

Considering that the members of the General Inspectorate of Libraries, governed by the decree of 31 December 1969 on the Statute for Scientific Personnel of Libraries, are responsible for the technical and scientific control as well as the operation of university libraries, central lending libraries and many municipal libraries; that they must carry out within the powers delegated by the Minister the annual rating of the curators and all senior library staff; that the body of the General Inspectorate of Libraries has only four members; that, therefore, each of them is necessarily charged to fulfil alone important

[54] For a detailed historical analysis of the limitation of judicial review of discretionary action, see T Barkhuysen and M L van Emmerik, 'Deference to the Administration in Judicial Review: The Case of the Netherlands' in LPW van Vliet (ed), *Netherlands Reports to the Twentieth International Congress of Comparative Law Fukuoka 2018* (Oisterwijk, Wolf Legal Publishers, 2018) 23 ff.

[55] See R Widdershoven and M Remac, 'General Principles of Law in Administrative Law under European Influence' (2012) 20 *European Review of Private Law* 381.

[56] N° 77713.

functions of a technical and scientific nature; that, in addition, apart from the statutory missions of any general inspectorate, the members of the General Inspectorate of Libraries exercise responsibilities such as the chairmanship of juries for the recruitment of library supervisory staff or the participation in different managing boards or higher education and research institutions (charter school, national library school, national library);

Considering that Mr I., after starting his career in the merchant navy, was responsible for associations addressing social inclusion, and was appointed in 1983 as delegate assistant to the inter-ministerial delegation to the professional and social inclusion of young people in difficulty; that it does not appear from the documents in the file that he possessed any experience in the field of libraries and scientific and technical information; that, consequently, taking the above-mentioned characteristics of the General Inspectorate of Libraries into account, the authors of the contested decree, in considering that Mr I. had the requested capacities to be named as a member of this body, have, whatever may be the merits of the person concerned, made a manifest error of assessment; that the applicants are therefore right in claiming that the contested decree is tainted with a misuse of discretionary powers …

Conseil d'État, 28 May 1971[57] **6.15 (FR)**

Minister for Infrastructure and Housing v Federation of defence of the persons concerned by the project currently called 'Ville Nouvelle Est'

COST—BENEFIT ANALYSIS

Ville Nouvelle-Est

When assessing whether a manifest error of assessment has occurred, the courts may carry out a 'costs–benefits' analysis.

Facts: In 1966, the government decided to build a university district in the eastern part of the city of Lille. The scheme required the confiscation and destruction of the properties of about a hundred citizens. Its 'public utility' was challenged in court and the Council of State was called upon to decide the appropriate standard of review.

Held: The request of the Federation of defence of the persons concerned by the project currently called 'Ville Nouvelle Est' was dismissed.

Judgment: On the utility of the operation: Considering that an operation can only legally be declared to be of public utility if the restrictions on private property rights, its financial cost and that the long term disadvantages to the social order that it involves are not excessive in regard to the benefit that it delivers; considering that it results from elements of the case file that the planning of the area, which is the object of the declaration of public utility, has been designed in such a way that the university buildings, planned there, shall not be separated from the sectors dedicated to housing; that the administration demonstrated that it had, in order to guarantee such planning, incorporated in this area a certain number of parcels of land, including buildings which should be demolished; considering that under these conditions, and in view of the importance of the entire project, the circumstance that its execution implies the disappearance of a hundred houses, is not of a nature to deny to the operation its character of public utility.

[57] N° 78825.

Notes

(1) In France, the intensity of judicial review of administrative decisions depends on the margin of discretion afforded to the administrative authority. In this regard, two situations have to be distinguished: first, situations in which the public authority has no choice with regard to the decision to be adopted once the facts are determined in compliance with the law. This situation is a case of *compétences liées*; and secondly, there are situations in which the authority has discretion and has the freedom to weigh the legal consequences of facts (*pouvoir d'appréciation*).[58] In the case of *compétences liées*, the court performs a control of normal intensity, meaning that all errors of fact and of law in the decisions are fully reviewable. In case of discretion,[59] a limited review (*contrôle minimum*) is performed, meaning that the content of an administrative decision can only be contested on the ground of a 'manifest error of assessment' (*erreur manifeste d'appréciation*).[60] As can be seen in the *Bleton* case, the court limited its review to the question of whether a manifest error of assessment occurred when the public authority had assessed whether the individual had the required skills to be appointed to a public office. The court concluded that the public authority had committed a 'manifest error of assessment' by adopting the decision of appointment, as the candidate had no experience in the field the position was concerned with. It is worth noting that cases of review limited to a 'manifest error of assessment' are increasingly rare. Initially, during the twentieth century, the development of the 'manifest error of assessment' test was seen as an improvement of judicial review of administrative discretionary powers, since it constituted the first step towards controlling decisions which used to be outside the scope of judicial review altogether. Progressively, judicial review has evolved towards a control of normal intensity and, when sanctions are at stake or decisions limiting fundamental freedoms are under consideration by the courts, the most intense form of control (which will be dealt with in note (3) below). For example, in the *Lebon* case in 1978,[61] a French court reviewed for the first time a disciplinary sanction applied to a civil servant, considering that the public authority, adopting a decision imposing compulsory retirement, had not committed any 'manifest error of assessment'. In 2007, the court applied a control of normal intensity to a similar decision.[62] Nowadays, the 'manifest error of assessment' test is still used to review technical and complex decisions, or decisions imposed on civil servants acting in very specific fields, such as the military forces.[63]

(2) When reviewing cases of 'manifest error of assessment', French courts have developed the technique of the so-called 'cost–benefit analysis' (*contrôle bilan coûts-avantages*). In such cases, the court reviews the balance made by the administrative

[58] See Bermann and Picard (n 11 above) 57, 96.
[59] For an overview of the judicial review of discretion in France, see Schwarze (n 39 above) 261 ff.
[60] See section 6.3.B.1 above, excerpt 6.14.
[61] Conseil d'Etat, 9 June 1978, *Lebon*, N° 05911.
[62] Conseil d'Etat, 22 June 2007, *MA*, N° 272650.
[63] Conseil d'Etat, 12 January 2011, *Matelly*, N° 338461.

authority between the costs and the benefits of a decision, as can be seen in the *Ville Nouvelle-Est* case. In this judgment, the court weighed the costs against the benefits of a project in order to determine its utility. The court found that the disadvantages of the project, such as the demolition of a number of buildings, were compensated by the important advantages of the project. The court therefore recognised the public utility of the project and hence held it to be lawful. This cost–benefit analysis test is applied when the courts have to review complex technical or economic assessments made by the administration (as is often the case in environmental and urban planning matters) and various – often conflicting – interests have to be balanced against each other. However, the cost–benefit analysis still constitutes a limited form of review, since the courts annul decisions only if they consider that a manifest error in weighing the costs and the benefits has been committed by the public authority. The French courts do not substitute their analysis with the one of the public authority. The cases of annulment following a cost–benefit analysis are, thus, very rare.

(3) In some cases, the most intense scale of review (*contrôle maximum*) is applied. This form of review involves a full proportionality assessment.[64] It is exercised where civil liberties or fundamental rights are at stake, such as in police law.[65] Another relevant field is the right to strike.[66]

6.3.B.2 THE EUROPEAN UNION

Case C-331/88, 13 November 1990[67] **6.16 (EU)**

The Queen v Ministry of Agriculture, Fisheries and Food, ex parte FEDESA and Others

REVIEW OF DISCRETIONARY CHOICES

FEDESA

In matters where the EU legislature enjoys broad discretionary powers, such as the common agricultural policy, the Court of Justice of the European Union (CJEU) may only scrutinise whether the decision is manifestly inappropriate having regard to the objective which the competent institution is seeking to pursue.

Facts: The Queen's Bench Division of the High Court had sent questions for a preliminary ruling to the Court of Justice. The questions, relating to the validity of Directive 88/146/EEC, arose in proceedings brought by FEDESA and Others against the Minister for Agriculture, Fisheries and Food and the Secretary of State for Health. The questions brought before the Court of Justice by the national court dealt with the principles of legal certainty, proportionality and equality.

Held: The Court ruled that the questions raised did not affect the validity of Directive 88/146/EEC.

[64] See section 6.5.A.3 below. See further Y Sanchez, 'Proportionality: French Administrative Law' in Ranchordás and de Waard (n 40 above) 41, 61 f.

[65] Sanchez (ibid) 41, 50 ff.

[66] ibid 41, 52.

[67] ECLI:EU:C:1990:391.

Judgment: 13. The Court has consistently held that the principle of proportionality is one of the general principles of Community law. By virtue of that principle, the lawfulness of the prohibition of an economic activity is subject to the condition that the prohibitory measures are appropriate and necessary in order to achieve the objectives legitimately pursued by the legislation in question; when there is a choice between several appropriate measures recourse must be had to the least onerous, and the disadvantages caused must not be disproportionate to the aims pursued.

14. However, with regard to judicial review of compliance with those conditions it must be stated that in matters concerning the common agricultural policy, the Community legislature has a discretionary power which corresponds to the political responsibilities given to it by Articles 40 and 43 of the Treaty. Consequently, the legality of a measure adopted in that sphere can be affected only if the measure is manifestly inappropriate having regard to the objective which the competent institution is seeking to pursue (see in particular the judgment in Case 265/87 Schräder [1989] ECR 2237, paragraphs 21 and 22).

Case C-12/03, 15 February 2005[68] **6.17 (EU)**

Commission v Tetra Laval BV

REVIEW OF COMPLEX ECONOMIC AND SCIENTIFIC CHOICES

Tetra Laval

Even when the EU institutions enjoy a margin of discretion with regard to economic matters, the CJEU is entitled to review not only whether the evidence relied on is factually accurate, reliable and consistent, but also whether that evidence contains all the information which must be taken into account in order to assess a complex situation and whether it is capable of substantiating the conclusions drawn from it.

Facts: The Commission had issued a decision through which it had declared the acquisition of Sidel SA by Tetra Laval BV incompatible with the common market. The claimants brought a claim before the Court of First Instance, which held that the Commission had committed manifest errors of assessment in its findings with regard to the leveraging and strengthening of Tetra's dominant position in the carton sector and therefore annulled the contested decision. The ruling in first instance was appealed by the Commission, which claimed that the Court of First Instance had not confined itself to a review of legality, but had also placed itself in the Commission's position.

Held: The appeal was dismissed.

Judgment: 39. Whilst the Court recognises that the Commission has a margin of discretion with regard to economic matters, that does not mean that the Community Courts must refrain from reviewing the Commission's interpretation of information of an economic nature. Not only must the Community Courts, inter alia, establish whether the evidence relied on is factually accurate, reliable and consistent but also whether that evidence contains all the information which must be taken into account in order to assess a complex situation and whether it is capable of substantiating the conclusions drawn from it. Such a review is all the more necessary in the case of a prospective analysis required when examining a planned merger with conglomerate effect.

[68] ECLI:EU:C:2005:87. See also the first instance case T-5/02 *Tetra Laval BV v Commission* ECLI:EU:T:2002:264.

Notes

(1) The CJEU understands the administrative interpretation of undefined legal terms and the choice of the legal consequences as two dimensions of administrative discretion, which encompass the entirety of administrative freedom in decision-making. Thus, the German approach is not followed and the French model is not adopted. In fact, the European judicature has developed an autonomous understanding of discretion.

(2) The intensity of judicial review of discretionary decisions depends on the subject matter and has developed over time.[69] Where individual rights are affected, the European courts generally apply quite a strict version of the proportionality principle.[70] However, the CJEU has traditionally been reluctant to fully assess decisions where complex economic and scientific choices are at stake, as one can see in the *FEDESA* case.[71] In such cases, the test used by the European courts is that of 'manifest error of assessment'. However, as can be seen in the *Tetra Laval* case, the Court of Justice has applied, over time, a stricter version of the 'manifest error of assessment' test and currently looks at 'whether the evidence relied on is factually accurate, reliable and consistent but also whether that evidence contains all the information which must be taken into account in order to assess a complex situation and whether it is capable of substantiating the conclusions drawn from it'.[72]

6.3.B.3 ENGLAND AND WALES

Court of Appeal (Civil Division), 10 November 1947[73] **6.18 (EW)**

Associated Provincial Picture Houses v Wednesbury Corporation

Wednesbury

WEDNESBURY UNREASONABLENESS

The courts can only interfere with a decision made by a public authority in the exercise of discretion within its sphere of competence when the decision is so unreasonable that no reasonable authority could ever have come to it.

Facts: A local authority was empowered by section 1 of the Sunday Entertainments Act 1932 to license cinema performances 'subject to such conditions as the authority thinks fit to impose'. Taking into account the well-being and physical and moral health of children likely to visit the cinema, the authority imposed a condition that no child under 15 should be admitted to such performances, whether accompanied by an adult or not. P brought an action for a declaration that the condition was ultra vires.

[69] For more details, see P Craig, 'The Locus and Accountability of the Executive in the European Union' in Craig and Tomkins (n 16 above) 315, 338; C Haguenau-Moizard and Y Sanchez, 'Proportionality: European Law' in Ranchordás and de Waard (n 40 above) 142, 156 ff; J Mendes, 'Administrative Discretion in the EU: Comparative Perspectives' in S Rose-Ackerman, PL Lindseth and B Emerson, *Comparative Administrative Law*, 2nd edn (Cheltenham, Edward Elgar Publishing, 2017), 632 ff.

[70] See, eg the in-depth proportionality test in Case 44/79 *Hauer v Land Rheinland-Pfalz* ECLI:EU:C:1979:290. See further section 6.5.A.2 below.

[71] See also Craig (n 69 above) 315, 340 f.

[72] See, eg Joined Cases 142 and 156/84 *British-American Tobacco Company L and RJ Reynolds Industries v Commission* ECLI:EU:C:1987:490; Case T-13/99 *Pfizer Animal Health v Council* ECLI:EU:T:2002:209.

[73] [1948] 1 KB 223.

Held: The action was dismissed.

Judgment: Lord Greene M.R.: It is clear that the local authority is entrusted by Parliament with the decision on a matter which the knowledge and experience of that authority can best be trusted to deal with. The subject-matter with which the condition deals is one relevant for its consideration. They have considered it and come to a decision upon it. It is true to say that, if a decision on a competent matter is so unreasonable that no reasonable authority could ever have come to it, then the courts can interfere. That, I think, is quite right; but to prove a case of that kind would require something overwhelming, and, in this case, the facts do not come anywhere near anything of that kind. I think Mr. Gallop in the end agreed that his proposition that the decision of the local authority can be upset if it is proved to be unreasonable, really meant that it must be proved to be unreasonable in the sense that the court considers it to be a decision that no reasonable body could have come to. It is not what the court considers unreasonable, a different thing altogether. If it is what the court considers unreasonable, the court may very well have different views to that of a local authority on matters of high public policy of this kind. Some courts might think that no children ought to be admitted on Sundays at all, some courts might think the reverse, and all over the country I have no doubt on a thing of that sort honest and sincere people hold different views. The effect of the legislation is not to set up the court as an arbiter of the correctness of one view over another. It is the local authority that are set in that position and, provided they act, as they have acted, within the four corners of their jurisdiction, this court, in my opinion, cannot interfere. …

… The court is entitled to investigate the action of the local authority with a view to seeing whether they have taken into account matters which they ought not to take into account, or, conversely, have refused to take into account or neglected to take into account matters which they ought to take into account. Once that question is answered in favour of the local authority, it may be still possible to say that, although the local authority have kept within the four corners of the matters which they ought to consider, they have nevertheless come to a conclusion so unreasonable that no reasonable authority could ever have come to it. In such a case, again, I think the court can interfere. The power of the court to interfere in each case is not as an appellate authority to override a decision of the local authority, but as a judicial authority which is concerned, and concerned only, to see whether the local authority have contravened the law by acting in excess of the powers which Parliament has confided in them.

Supreme Court, 24 June 2015[74] **6.19 (EW)**

Lumsdon v Legal Service Board

PROPORTIONALITY REVIEW; EU LAW

Lumsdon

In cases where rights flowing from EU law are at stake, the proportionality test applies when the courts review the discretionary choices of the administration.

Facts: In response to serious concerns over professional standards in criminal advocacy, the legal profession's approved regulatory body (the Legal Services Board) devised a scheme of accreditation. It classified criminal

[74] [2015] UKSC 41, [2016] AC 697.

cases at four levels: full accreditation for carrying out work at the upper levels required an assessment as 'competent' by a trial judge. There was no right of appeal against such an assessment. In making its decision to approve, the Legal Services Board had regard to the 'Better Regulation Principles' in section 3(3) of the Legal Services Act 2007, which stated that regulatory activities should be 'transparent, accountable, proportionate, consistent and targeted only at cases in which action is needed'. Some barristers sought judicial review of the Legal Services Board's decision on a variety of grounds, all of which were rejected by the courts. Permission to appeal to the Supreme Court was given on the question of whether the decision was contrary to Regulation 14 of The Provision of Services Regulations 2009. Since those provisions were derived from Directive 2006/123 on services in the internal market, and had to be interpreted so as to give effect to that Directive, the argument was in substance a submission that the scheme fell within the ambit of the Directive and failed to comply with Articles 9(1)(b) and 9(1)(c) of the Directive. The barristers argued that the scheme failed to meet the conditions set out in Regulations 14(2)(b) and (c), namely that the 'need for an authorisation scheme is justified by an overriding reason relating to the public interest' and that 'the objective pursued cannot be attained by means of a less restrictive measure'.

Held: The scheme of accreditation brought about by the Legal Services Board was considered lawful and not disproportionate to the aim pursued.

Judgment: Lord Reed: 31. Where the proportionality principle is applied by a national court, it must, as a principle of EU law, be applied in a manner which is consistent with the jurisprudence of the court: as is sometimes said, the national judge is also a European judge.

32. The jurisprudence in relation to the principle of proportionality is, however, not without complexity. As will be explained, the principle has been expressed and applied by the court in different ways and in different contexts. In order for national judges to know how the principle should be applied in the cases before them, it is necessary for them to understand the nature and rationale of these differences, and to identify the body of case law which is truly relevant. …

34. Apart from the questions which need to be addressed, the other critical aspect of the principle of proportionality is the intensity with which it is applied. … It is, however, important to avoid an excessively schematic approach, since the jurisprudence indicates that the principle of proportionality is flexible in its application. The court's case law applying the principle in one context cannot necessarily be treated as a reliable guide to how the principle will be applied in another context: it is necessary to examine how in practice the court has applied the principle, in the particular context in question.

35. Subject to that caveat, however, it may be helpful to describe the court's general approach in relation to three types of case: the review of EU measures, the review of national measures relying upon derogations from general EU rights, and the review of national measures implementing EU law.

36. As a generalisation, proportionality as a ground of review of EU measures is concerned with the balancing of private interests adversely affected by such measures against the public interests which the measures are intended to promote. Proportionality functions in that context as a check on the exercise of public power of a kind traditionally found in public law. The court's application of the principle in that context is influenced by the nature and limits of its legitimate function under the separation of powers established by the Treaties. In the nature of things, cases in which measures adopted by the EU legislator or administration in the public interest are held by the EU judicature to be disproportionate interferences with private interests are likely to be relatively infrequent.

37. Proportionality as a ground of review of national measures, on the other hand, has been applied most frequently to measures interfering with the fundamental freedoms

guaranteed by the EU Treaties. Although private interests may be engaged, the court is concerned first and foremost with the question whether a member state can justify an interference with a freedom guaranteed in the interests of promoting the integration of the internal market, and the related social values, which lie at the heart of the EU project. In circumstances of that kind, the principle of proportionality generally functions as a means of preventing disguised discrimination and unnecessary barriers to market integration. In that context, the court, seeing itself as the guardian of the Treaties and of the uniform application of EU law, generally applies the principle more strictly. Where, however, a national measure does not threaten the integration of the internal market, for example because the subject-matter lies within an area of national rather than EU competence, a less strict approach is generally adopted. That also tends to be the case in contexts where an unregulated economic activity would be harmful to consumers, particularly where national regulatory measures are influenced by national traditions and culture. …

38. Where member states adopt measures implementing EU legislation, they are generally contributing towards the integration of the internal market, rather than seeking to limit it in their national interests. In general, therefore, proportionality functions in that context as a conventional public law principle. On the other hand, where member states rely on reservations or derogations in EU legislation in order to introduce measures restricting fundamental freedoms, proportionality is generally applied more strictly, subject to the qualifications which we have mentioned.

Notes

(1) English law has not developed an elaborate approach to concepts of administrative discretion and the legality of administrative decision-making within the sphere of competence granted by such discretion, although the control of discretion continues to develop through the case law and is becoming increasingly context sensitive.[75] Traditionally, the courts in England and Wales have abstained from reviewing administrative decisions in substance. Only where a claimant could establish that an administrative decision was 'so unreasonable that no reasonable authority could ever have come to it' could the decision be found to be unlawful, according to the *Wednesbury* test.[76] Thus, the scope of scrutiny was very low and only a few administrative decisions were annulled on grounds of unreasonableness.[77]

(2) The increasing Europeanisation of English administrative law by EU law, as well as by the ECHR, which is incorporated through the Human Rights Act 1998, has introduced stricter standards for reviewing the substance of administrative decisions.[78] Where EU law or human rights are concerned, the standard of review

[75] *cf* C Hilson, 'The Europeanization of English Administrative Law: Judicial Review and Convergence' (2003) 9 *European Public Law* 125, Schwarze (n 39 above) 697.

[76] *Associated Provincial Picture Houses v Wednesbury Corporation* [1948] 1 KB 223, 234.

[77] See, eg *Mixnam's Properties Ltd v Chertsey Urban DC* [1965] AC 735; *Wheeler v Leicester City Council* [1985] 2 All ER 1106. For a comprehensive overview of judicial review of discretionary decisions in English law, see ACL Davies and JR Williams, 'Proportionality: English Law' in Ranchordás and de Waard (n 40 above) 73, 74 ff.

[78] For a brief overview, see Hilson (n 75 above) 131 ff.

is particularly increased, and in a number of cases the proportionality test has been applied.[79] However, the relationship between *Wednesbury* reasonableness and the proportionality test has not yet been resolved.[80] While some argue that they represent competing tests,[81] the Supreme Court in the *Lumsdon* case treats them as coexisting concepts rooted in the same principle. According to that judgment, the intensity of judicial review depends on the context of the administrative decision rather than the applied test.

6.3.C COMPARATIVE REMARKS

Whereas in most legal systems discretion refers to all areas in which the administration has the freedom to decide autonomously, in Germany and the Netherlands a doctrinal distinction is made with regard to factual assessments (for which the administration may enjoy a margin of interpretation) and the selection of different legal consequences (which is linked to the concept of discretion).[82] The CJEU has developed an autonomous understanding of discretion which is independent from that of the national legal systems. With regard to the scope of judicial review, German courts are particularly rigorous,[83] whereas English courts traditionally abstain from reviewing discretionary decisions.[84] Even though English law scrutinises breaches of EU law and fundamental rights under the Human Rights Act more rigorously, the overall level of scrutiny in the review of discretionary choices seems to be lower than in the other systems. The Netherlands and France lie somewhere in between, with the level of scrutiny in the Netherlands tending to be stricter than that in France. In the EU, similarly to France, the intensity of judicial review of discretionary decisions depends on the subject matter. Despite the different approaches, recent judgments in all of the legal systems examined reveal a tendency towards a more rigorous review of discretionary choices.

6.4 ROLE OF HUMAN RIGHTS

The infringement of human rights is an important cause for judicial review of administrative action and may alter the level of scrutiny in many legal systems. Whereas in most European countries there is already a strong constitutional protection of fundamental

[79] See further section 6.5.A.5 below.
[80] See Davies and Williams (n 77 above) 73, 79 ff.
[81] Hilson (n 75 above) 136.
[82] For a comparative legal analysis, see Schwarze (n 39 above) 261 ff.
[83] G Nolte, 'General Principles of German and European Administrative Law: A Comparison in Historical Perspective' (1994) 57 *The Modern Law Review* 191, 197; Y Arai-Takahashi, 'Discretion in German Administrative Law: Doctrinal Discourse Revisited' (2000) 6 *European Public Law* 69; Kayser (n 1 above) §91, para 106.
[84] For the 'Europeanisation' of administrative law in the UK, see Hilson (n 75 above) ff.

rights which compels the courts to review alleged breaches strictly, in the Netherlands and England the role of human rights is traditionally different. However, the Europeanisation process brought by the ECHR and EU law has increased the importance of human rights protection in the judicial review of administrative action in both the Dutch and English systems. The human rights regime on the European level also affects the protection of fundamental rights in the national legal systems. It creates a multi-level system of human rights protection in which different interpretations of the scope of the various rights can cause conflicts and may require adjustments of domestic legal doctrine.[85]

6.4.A SYSTEMS WITH A STRONG CONSTITUTIONAL PROTECTION OF HUMAN RIGHTS

6.4.A.1 GERMANY

The fundamental rights which are provided in the Grundgesetz (Basic Law) serve as a framework for administrative judicial review in Germany. Due to the dreadful experiences under the dictatorship of the National Socialists, the guarantees of fundamental rights were deliberately placed at the beginning of the Grundgesetz (Articles 1–19) and bind all state power (Article 1(3)).[86] Article 19(4) of the Grundgesetz explicitly guarantees recourse to the courts.[87] Administrative bodies are thus bound by national fundamental rights.

Furthermore, the administration must also respect the EU fundamental rights when acting in the sphere of EU law.[88] Also, the significance of the ECHR and its interpretation by the ECtHR is increasing in German administrative law. Even though international law ranks lower than national constitutional law in Germany according to Articles 25 and 59(2) of the Grundgesetz, there is a general principle of legal interpretation in conformity with international law (*Grundsatz der völkerrechtskonformen Auslegung*).

In Germany, the administrative courts play an important role in the protection of fundamental rights and constitutional principles. As fundamental rights bind all state power according to Article 1(3) of the Grundgesetz, the courts must ensure that the public authorities observe the 'supremacy of the law' (Article 20(3) of the Grundgesetz). Any burdensome measure adopted by the public administration constitutes an interference with fundamental rights in Germany law. The freedom to act (Article 2(1) of the Grundgesetz) serves as a catch-all clause in this respect.[89] Hence, the administrative

[85] *cf* B Kingsbury, N Krisch and RB Stewart, 'The Emergence of Global Administrative Law' (2005) 68 *Law and Contemporary Problems* 15, 30 f.

[86] For details, see Pünder, 'German Constitutional Law' (n 29 above) 27.

[87] See excerpt 6.5 under section 6.2.B.1 above.

[88] See P Craig and G de Burca, *EU Law: Text, Cases and Materials*, 4th edn (Oxford, Oxford University Press, 2008) 378 ff. However, actions of EU bodies cannot be challenged in front of the German Constitutional Court on the basis that they infringe national fundamental rights. Only in the case of ultra vires actions by the EU would the German Constitutional Court scrutinise acts of the EU on the basis of German fundamental rights. See BVerfGE 89, 155, 174 ff (*Maastricht*); BVerfGE 102, 147, 164 (*Bananenmarkt*).

[89] W Cremer, 'The Basic Right to "Free Development of the Personality" – Mere Protection of Personality Development versus General Right of Freedom of Action' in H Pünder and C Waldhoff (eds), *Debates in German Public Law* (Oxford, Hart Publishing, 2013) 57 ff.

courts must always examine whether interference with citizens' rights has been authorised by a statute as well as the proportionality of the administrative decision. The constitutional foundations of administrative law are thus particularly important in Germany.[90] Administrative law has even been called 'specified constitutional law' (*Verwaltungsrecht als konkretisiertes Verfassungsrecht*) by German scholars.[91]

6.4.A.2 FRANCE

Fundamental rights and public liberties play an essential role in French administrative law and in the case law of French administrative courts. They are guaranteed by constitutional provisions, as well as by legal texts which are also considered to have constitutional value, such as the Déclaration des droits de l'homme et du citoyen (Declaration of the Rights of Man and of the Citizen), the Preamble of the 1946 Constitution de la République française (French Constitution) and the Charte de l'environnement (Environmental Charter). Furthermore, the Council of State has developed several general principles of law that help to protect human rights.[92] Additionally, the ECHR and the Charter on Fundamental Rights of the European Union are directly applicable within their scope and can be invoked by litigants in administrative courts while challenging an administrative decision. They prevail over Acts of Parliament.

The immediate applicability of the ECHR and the EU Charter of fundamental Rights derives from the monist character of the French legal system and from general provisions related to international Treaties. Unlike in Germany, all international law can be immediately applied in courts; there is no need for a law to transpose the international norm into domestic law (Article 55 of the French Constitution).[93]

6.4.A.3 THE EUROPEAN UNION

Treaty on the European Union **6.20 (EU)**

Article 6 (1) The Union recognises the rights, freedoms and principles set out in the Charter of Fundamental Rights of the European Union of 7 December 2000, as adapted at Strasbourg, on 12 December 2007, which shall have the same legal value as the Treaties.

The provisions of the Charter shall not extend in any way the competences of the Union as defined in the Treaties. The rights, freedoms and principles in the Charter shall be interpreted in accordance with the general provisions in Title VII of the Charter governing its interpretation and application and with due regard to the explanations referred to in the Charter, that set out the sources of those provisions.

[90] D Ehlers, 'Verwaltung und Verwaltungsrecht im demokratischen und sozialen Rechtsstaat' in Ehlers and Pünder (n 42 above) 7, 239 ff. For a comprehensive overview of the constitutional foundations of administrative law in English, see MP Singh, *German Administrative Law in Common Law Perspective* (Berlin, Springer 2001) 10 ff. See also Pünder and Klafki (n 11 above) 49, 55 ff.

[91] F Werner, 'Verwaltungsrecht als konkretisiertes Verfassungsrecht' (1959) 74 *Deutsches Verwaltungsblatt* 527.

[92] See section 6.5 below.

[93] For details, see Bermann and Picard (n 11 above) 57, 74 f.

(2) The Union shall accede to the European Convention for the Protection of Human Rights and Fundamental Freedoms. Such accession shall not affect the Union's competences as defined in the Treaties.

(3) Fundamental rights, as guaranteed by the European Convention for the Protection of Human Rights and Fundamental Freedoms and as they result from the constitutional traditions common to the Member States, shall constitute general principles of the Union's law.

Note

The current constitutional framework of the EU provides a strong commitment to the protection of human rights. However, these developments are quite recent and, for many years, human rights as a standard of review in EU law were solely recognised and upheld by the case law of the CJEU.[94] With regard to international sources of human rights, the CJEU declared in the *Nold* case that international human rights play an important role in the interpretation of human rights protection in the EU.[95] Special significance is being given to the ECHR and the case law of the ECtHR.[96]

6.4.B SYSTEMS WITH TRADITIONALLY LESS FOCUS ON HUMAN RIGHTS

6.4.B.1 THE NETHERLANDS

In the Dutch legal system, fundamental rights guaranteed by the Dutch constitution do not play a substantial role in judicial review. The function that (national) human rights have in other legal systems (such as in Germany) is taken over mainly by the general principles of proper administration,[97] and partly by the human rights codified in European law and international treaties (which, under certain conditions, are directly applicable in the monistic Dutch legal system). Dutch judicial review has been shaped most intensively by Article 6 ECHR and its interpretation by the ECtHR. Article 6 ECHR has specifically influenced the constitutional structure of judicial review in the Netherlands.[98]

[94] While at the very beginning the Court of Justice had resisted the attempts by claimants to recognise human rights protected by domestic legal systems (Case 1/58 *Stork v High Authority* ECLI:EU:C:1959:4; Case C-40/64 *Sgarlata and others v Commission* ECLI:EU:C:1965:36), in the *Stauder* case, there was a change in attitude: in this case, the ECJ recognised human rights as general principles of (then) EC law and as a standard of review of EU measures. See Case 26/69 *Stauder v City of Ulm* ECLI:EU:C:1969:57; as a follow up of this case, see Case 11/70 *Internationale Handelsgesellschaft v Einfuhr- und Vorratsstelle für Getreide und Futtermittel* ECLI:EU:C:1970:114.

[95] Case 4/73 *Nold v Commission* ECLI:EU:C:1974:51.

[96] Case 36/75 *Rutili v Ministry for the Interior* ECLI:EU:C:1975:137.

[97] For a brief explanation of the most relevant Dutch administrative principles, see R Seerden and D Wenders, 'Administrative Law in the Netherlands' in Seerden (n 11 above) 135–41.

[98] Especially ECtHR, *Benthem v the Netherlands* ECLI:CE:ECHR:1985:1023JUD000884880. See Chapter 1, section 1.2.B.2. There are still discussions whether the Council of State, which hosts a division

Furthermore, the right of review within due time has shaped the compensation scheme for overly long court proceedings.[99]

6.4.B.2 ENGLAND AND WALES

House of Lords, 23 May 2001[100] **6.21 (EW)**

R v Secretary of State for the Home Department, ex parte Daly

PROPORTIONALITY TEST IN HUMAN RIGHTS CASES

Daly

In human rights cases under the Human Rights Act 1998, the proportionality test is to be applied by the courts, which partly overlaps with the traditional grounds of review in the common law.

Facts: The Home Secretary had introduced a policy in 1995 governing the searching of prisoners' cells. The policy required prisoners to leave their cell whilst it was being searched and to leave all items, including privileged legal correspondence, in the cell. The rules permitted staff to examine privileged legal correspondence in the absence of the prisoner in order to ensure that it did not conceal anything else, but not to read it. If privileged legal correspondence was to be read, the prisoner had to be informed and the correspondence had to be read in the presence of the prisoner. D brought a claim for judicial review arguing that the policy was unlawful as it contravened the common law right to privilege of legal correspondence and also because it infringed Article 8 ECHR.

Held: The claim was successful and the policy was quashed.

Judgment: Lord Steyn: … The Master of the Rolls concluded, at p 857, para 40: 'When anxiously scrutinising an executive decision that interferes with human rights, the court will ask the question, applying an objective test, whether the decision-maker could reasonably have concluded that the interference was necessary to achieve one or more of the legitimate aims recognised by the Convention. When considering the test of necessity in the relevant context, the court must take into account the European jurisprudence in accordance with section 2 of the 1998 Act.' …

26. The explanation of the Master of the Rolls in the first sentence of the cited passage requires clarification. It is couched in language reminiscent of the traditional Wednesbury ground of review …, and in particular the adaptation of that test in terms of heightened scrutiny in cases involving fundamental rights as formulated in *R v Ministry of Defence, Ex p Smith* [1996] QB 517, 554E–G per Sir Thomas Bingham MR. There is a material difference between the Wednesbury and Smith grounds of review and the approach of proportionality applicable in respect of review where convention rights are at stake.

27. The contours of the principle of proportionality are familiar. In *de Freitas v Permanent Secretary of Ministry of Agriculture, Fisheries, Lands and Housing* [1999] 1 AC 69 the

advising the legislator and a judicial review division, should be split up into two separate bodies or not. See ECHR 6 May 2003, AB 2003, 211, available at www.kabinetsformatie2012.nl/actueel/documenten/regeerakkoord.html, 28.

[99] See Chapter 11, section 11.8.

[100] [2001] UKHL 26, [2001] AC 532.

Privy Council adopted a three stage test. Lord Clyde observed, at p 80, that in determining whether a limitation (by an act, rule or decision) is arbitrary or excessive the court should ask itself: 'whether: (i) the legislative objective is sufficiently important to justify limiting a fundamental right; (ii) the measures designed to meet the legislative objective are rationally connected to it; and (iii) the means used to impair the right or freedom are no more than is necessary to accomplish the objective.'

Clearly, these criteria are more precise and more sophisticated than the traditional grounds of review. What is the difference for the disposal of concrete cases? ... The starting point is that there is an overlap between the traditional grounds of review and the approach of proportionality. Most cases would be decided in the same way whichever approach is adopted. But the intensity of review is somewhat greater under the proportionality approach. ... I would mention three concrete differences without suggesting that my statement is exhaustive. First, the doctrine of proportionality may require the reviewing court to assess the balance which the decision maker has struck, not merely whether it is within the range of rational or reasonable decisions. Secondly, the proportionality test may go further than the traditional grounds of review inasmuch as it may require attention to be directed to the relative weight accorded to interests and considerations. Thirdly, even the heightened scrutiny test developed in *R v Ministry of Defence, Ex p Smith* [1996] QB 517, 554 is not necessarily appropriate to the protection of human rights. It will be recalled that in Smith the Court of Appeal reluctantly felt compelled to reject a limitation on homosexuals in the army. ... The European Court of Human Rights came to the opposite conclusion .... The court concluded, at p 543, para 138: 'the threshold at which the High Court and the Court of Appeal could find the Ministry of Defence policy irrational was placed so high that it effectively excluded any consideration by the domestic courts of the question of whether the interference with the applicants' rights answered a pressing social need or was proportionate to the national security and public order aims pursued, principles which lie at the heart of the court's analysis of complaints under article 8 of the Convention.'

In other words, the intensity of the review, in similar cases, is guaranteed by the twin requirements that the limitation of the right was necessary in a democratic society, in the sense of meeting a pressing social need, and the question whether the interference was really proportionate to the legitimate aim being pursued.

28. The differences in approach between the traditional grounds of review and the proportionality approach may therefore sometimes yield different results. It is therefore important that cases involving convention rights must be analysed in the correct way. This does not mean that there has been a shift to merits review. ... And Laws LJ rightly emphasised in Mahmood, at p 847, para 18, 'that the intensity of review in a public law case will depend on the subject matter in hand'. That is so even in cases involving Convention rights. In law context is everything.

Notes

(1) The judicial protection of human rights in England and Wales has undergone a unique development. As there is no written constitution, there were no statutorily granted fundamental rights until the introduction of the Human Rights Act (HRA) 1998, which incorporates the ECHR into English law. The Human Rights Act creates a duty of consistent interpretation – ie domestic law should, wherever possible, be interpreted so that it is in conformity with the requirements of the articles of

the ECHR.[101] If the courts are not able to interpret legislation in conformity, then they must issue a declaration of incompatibility under section 4 of the Human Rights Act. The declaration of incompatibility is not a legally binding instrument but is, in essence, a request to Parliament to intervene and render legislation in compliance with the ECHR.[102] Public authorities and bodies that exercise public functions (including the courts) are precluded from acting in contravention of ECHR rights, other than where the body is required to act in a non-compliant way by provisions of domestic legislation.[103]

(2) Human rights had also developed in the common law constitution before the introduction of the Human Rights Act. A significant instance of invocation of such common law rights came in the *Ahmed v HM Treasury* decision.[104] From the 1980s, courts had built on traditions of statutory construction so that only clear and precise words could defeat what today are referred to as human rights, although examples pre-date that period.[105] Its clearest enunciation came in *Simms*.[106] What has happened since is an unfolding of specific rights under the common law: sustenance, right to life, access to justice,[107] protection of property and, most recently, transparency, following on from the earlier case law on freedom of speech and open justice.[108] Furthermore, there is a common law basis in English case law for the right to fair procedures and open justice independent of the ECHR.[109]

(3) English courts are somewhat reluctant to replace the assessment made by public authorities with their own judgment. Thus, historically, courts scrutinised the exercise of discretion of administrative authorities with comparatively low intensity by applying the above-mentioned *Wednesbury* test.[110] However, under the pressure of the European case law and of the ECtHR, the national courts increasingly apply the proportionality test in human rights cases and thereby increase the level of scrutiny. Nonetheless, the courts continually emphasise that the English reasonableness test is by no means abolished but that both tests supplement each other and are equally applicable in English law, depending on the context of the concrete case.[111]

[101] On the whole, the courts have perhaps not been as expansive in their use of this provision as they have in the case of the duty of consistent interpretation under EU law. See, eg *Re S (Minors)* [2002] UKHL 10, [2002] 2 AC 291; *Bellinger v Bellinger* [2003] UKHL 21, [2003] 2 WLR 1174; *Ghaidan v Mendoza* [2004] 3 WLR 113.

[102] See, eg *A v Secretary of State for the Home Department* [2004] UKHL 56, [2005] 2 WLR 87.

[103] *R (on the application of AB) v Secretary of State for the Home Department* [2013] EWHC 3453 (Admin), [2014] 2 CMLR 22, [14].

[104] [2010] UKSC 2, [2010] 2 AC 534.

[105] *Anisminic v FCC* [1969] 2 AC 147.

[106] *R v Secretary of State for the Home Department ex p Simms* [2000] 2 AC 115 (HL).

[107] Case 222/84 *Johnston v CC RUC* ECLI:EU:C:1986:206.

[108] *AG v Guardian Newspapers* [1990] 1 AC 109 (HL); *R (Guardian News Ltd) v City of Westminster Magistrates' Court* [2012] EWCA Civ 420, 2013 QB 618.

[109] See *Osborn v The Parole Board* [2013] UKSC 61, [2014] AC 1115 on the common law of access to fairness and oral procedure in parole hearings for prisoners. See the same judge in *A v BBC* [2014] UKSC 25, [2015] AC 588 – but *cf R (T) v Secretary of State for the Home Department* [2014] UKSC 35, [2015] AC 49, where the ECHR was found to be the basis of privacy protection under the Data Protection Act.

[110] See section 6.3.B.3, excerpt 6.18 above.

[111] See further below, section 6.5.A.5.

6.5 ROLE OF PRINCIPLES

In all of the legal systems analysed in this book, general principles have been at the centre of the development of administrative law. In all jurisdictions, the administrative law regime has been shaped by the case law of the courts applying certain general principles, before the administrative law was codified by the legislature.[112] At the national level as well as in the EU, functionally comparable general principles of administrative law have evolved.[113] Many of these principles of administrative law are rooted in the rule of law principle.[114] Some principles of administrative law can meanwhile be found in statutory law; others remain unwritten principles shaped by case law. In France and the Netherlands, as well as in England and Wales, principles still play a particularly important role in the judicial review of administrative action, even though they have different functions in the different legal systems.

In France, after the Second World War, there was a lack of statutory provisions in the field of administrative law, as there had not been many legislative sources dealing with the position of individuals in relation to the administration. The general principles of law were thus developed by the courts in order to specifically review the administrative action. Even though the situation in France has changed, the role of principles is still comparatively strong.[115] The numerous principles can be categorised into three groups. First, many principles are directly derived from fundamental and civil rights, such as the principle of equality, the freedom of commerce and industry, individual freedom and the freedom of movement. Secondly, many principles are linked to the guarantees conferred to citizens in their relationship with administrative authorities, such as the right to be heard, the principle of impartiality of administrative authorities and the principle of uninterrupted public service. Many principles, lastly, are related to very specific fields of administrative action, such as the principle prohibiting dismissing pregnant women in the civil service, the principle of adversarial procedures and the principle of unity of the family in asylum law.

In England and Wales, principles play an important role due to the common law system. General administrative law to date has mainly been rooted in case law, ie court precedents. The ultra vires and natural justice principles have steadily been restricted and extended by the courts in various cases through history.[116] Furthermore, the doctrine of parliamentary sovereignty has had a strong impact on the development of judicial review in England, and has often led to a lower level of scrutiny in England than in the other analysed systems.[117] No systematic theory of the underpinnings of administrative law has evolved in England yet, but the understanding of the principles guiding administrative law is in constant development.[118]

[112] *cf* Schwarze (n 39 above) cx ff.
[113] See in depth Schwarze (n 39 above).
[114] KP Sommermann, in von Bogdandy et al (n 1 above) §86 para 28.
[115] See also Bermann and Picard (n 11 above) 57, 76 ff.
[116] *cf* P Craig, *Administrative Law*, 7th edn (London, Sweet & Maxwell, 2012) para 1-003 ff.
[117] See sections 6.3.B.3 and 6.4.B.2 above.
[118] *cf* Schwarze (n 39 above) 145.

Principles also play a very important role in the judicial review of administrative action in the Netherlands. This is historically rooted in the weak statutory role of fundamental rights in administrative law. In the Netherlands, national human rights are still relatively undeveloped.[119] Hence, general principles partly take over their function. Some general principles have been codified, mainly in the Algemene Wet Bestuursrecht (General Administrative Law Act); others still only exist in case law. The most important principles are the principle of fairness (Article 2:4 AWB), the principle of due care (Article 3:2 AWB), the specificity principle, which is comparable to the legality principle (Articles 3:3 and 3:4(1) AWB), the prohibition of arbitrariness and the principle of proportionality (Article 3:4(2) AWB), the principle of *égalité devant les charges publiques* (Article 4:126 AWB),[120] the principle of sound reasoning (Article 3:46 AWB), the principle of legitimate expectations and legal certainty, and the principle of equality.[121] The latter three principles are not codified.

So, too, in Germany do general principles play a significant role in judicial review. However, many of the governing principles have been incorporated in the Grundgesetz (Basic Law) or in statutory law.[122] For example, the legality principle is set out in Articles 1(3) and 2(3) of the Grundgesetz. Furthermore, administrative principles governing the administrative procedure, such as the right to be heard, have been codified in the Verwaltungsverfahrensgesetz (Administrative Procedure Act) (§28 VwVfG). Thus, in most cases, the law is simply applied by the administrative courts without explicitly referring to certain general administrative principles. Notably, however, the principle of proportionality, an important principle in German administrative law, is not codified.

On the supranational level of the European Union, no precise classification of the general administrative law principles exists yet. The general principles of administrative law serve an important function in the case law of the CJEU as an aid for interpretation and filling gaps.[123] The CJEU derives the principles from the common traditions of the Member States and thereby fosters the development of common EU administrative law principles. General principles of administrative law which are recognised or codified at EU level include the principle of legality, the principle of proportionality, the principle of non-discrimination, the principle of legal certainty and legitimate expectations, and the principle of good administration.[124]

Even though similar principles can be found in all of the legal systems analysed here, they may be quite differently categorised and defined in each legal system.[125] As no comprehensive analysis of all the principles of administrative law can take place at this

[119] See section 6.3.B.3 above.
[120] Note that this provision is not yet in force.
[121] For a brief explanation of the most relevant Dutch administrative principles, see Seerden and Wenders (n 97 above).
[122] J Schwarze, *European Administrative Law: Revised First Edition* (London, Sweet & Maxwell, 2006) 120.
[123] ibid 65.
[124] See further H Hofmann, G Rowe and A Türk, *Administrative Law and Policy of the European Union* (Oxford, Oxford University Press, 2001) ch 7.
[125] Schwarze (n 122 above) 1445 ff.

point, the role of general principles in judicial review shall be exemplified by the proportionality principle, the principles of legal certainty and legitimate expectations, and the principle of equality.[126]

6.5.A PROPORTIONALITY

The proportionality principle, which was developed in the Prussian administrative law in the late nineteenth century, serves to control the administrative discretion.[127] It can be described as a core principle of German public law. This section will examine whether and to what extent the proportionality principle found its way into EU law and is applied in the other legal systems compared here.[128] An important question to address will be whether Europeanisation has led to an implementation of this principle in legal systems where this was unknown or less well known in first instance.

6.5.A.1 GERMANY

Bundesverfassungsgericht, 20 April 2016[129] **6.22 (DE)**

PROPORTIONALITY PRINCIPLE

Federal Criminal Police Office Act

According to the principle of proportionality, administrative action must always pursue a legitimate aim, and must be suitable, necessary and, in the strict sense, proportionate to achieve this aim.

Facts: The case originates from a number of constitutional complaints which were directed against the provisions of the Bundeskriminalamtgesetz (Federal Criminal Police Office Act). The federal legislature assigned the Federal Criminal Police Office tasks extending beyond its previous law enforcement duties, reaching into the domain of the protection against threats from international terrorism. An additional subject matter of the constitutional complaints was the previously existing provision in the Federal Criminal Police Office Act on the transfer of data to third countries, the scope of which had been extended by the newly attributed powers.

Held: Several provisions of the Federal Criminal Police Office Act were declared void because they were held to be disproportionate.

Judgment: 93. The constitutionality of the powers depends on the limits arising from each of these fundamental rights and the proportionality requirements which must be determined for each of the powers. According to the principle of proportionality, the

[126] KP Sommermann, in von Bogdandy et al (n 1 above) §86, paras 32, 33; Schwarze (n 122 above) 625 ff, 867 ff.

[127] M Cohen-Eliya and I Porat, 'American Balancing and German Proportionality: The Historical Origins' (2010) 8 *International Journal of Constitutional Law* 263, 271. See also Schwarze (n 122 above) 678 f; S Ranchordás and B de Waard, 'Proportionality Crossing Borders' in Ranchordás and de Waard (n 40 above) 1.

[128] See also J Mathews, 'Proportionality Review in Administrative Law' in Rose-Ackerman et al (n 69 above) 405 ff.

[129] BVerfGE 141, 220, ECLI:DE:BVerfG:2016:rs20160420.1bvr096609. For an English translation, see www.bundesverfassungsgericht.de/SharedDocs/Entscheidungen/EN/2016/04/rs20160420_1bvr096609en.html.

granting of these powers must always pursue a legitimate aim and must be suitable, necessary and, in the strict sense, proportionate to achieving this aim ....

96. The powers pursue a legitimate aim. They provide the Federal Criminal Police Office with means of gathering information which it can use in fulfilling its new task of protecting against threats from international terrorism. ... The provision of effective means of gathering information for protecting against terrorism constitutes a legitimate aim and is of great significance for a democratic and free basic order ....

97. The granting of the surveillance and investigative powers in question is suitable for achieving this aim. They provide the Federal Criminal Police Office with the means for gathering information that can play a role in countering the threat of international terrorism. The different powers are, at least in principle, necessary for this. Each power allows specific measures that cannot always be replaced by others. Less intrusive measures that provide equally effective and broad possibilities for gathering information for protecting against international terrorism are not apparent. Evidently, this does not affect the fact that in each individual case, the exercise of these powers, too, must be in accordance with the concepts of suitability and necessity.

98. Limitations result mainly from the requirements of proportionality in the strict sense. Accordingly, the surveillance and investigative powers must be appropriately designed with a view to the weight of the interference. It is the legislature's task to balance the seriousness of the interferences with fundamental rights of the potentially affected persons that are at issue here, on the one hand, with the duty of the state to protect the fundamental rights of its citizens, on the other.

105. With regard to the detailed design of the individual powers, what matters substantially for their appropriateness as well as the required specificity is that they should be tailored to the weight of each codified interference. The more seriously the surveillance measures interfere with privacy and thwart legitimate expectations of confidentiality, the stricter the requirements must be. The surveillance of private homes and the access to information technology systems constitute particularly serious interferences with privacy.

Note

The proportionality principle (*Verhältinsmäßigkeitsgrundsatz*) is firmly rooted in the German administrative case law, as well as in the literature.[130] According to German doctrine, the proportionality assessment encompasses three stages: first, the measure must be suitable to achieve or facilitate a legitimate interest of the state (*Geeignetheit*); secondly, the suitable measure must also be necessary in the sense that there is no less restrictive means available to achieve the legitimate interest (*Erforderlichkeit*); and finally, the measure must be proportionate in the strict sense (*Angemessenheit*). The measure serving the legitimate interest and the benefits it delivers must not be excessive in relation to the burden imposed on the affected citizen. Thus, the competing interests must be balanced. Every administrative decision that interferes with the fundamental rights of citizens is assessed on the basis of the proportionality principle in Germany. The proportionality principle can thus be described as a core principle of German public law.[131]

[130] For a comprehensive overview of the German concept, see Schwarze (n 122 above) 685 ff; Marsch and Tünsmeyer (n 42 above) 13 ff.

[131] *cf* E Grabitz, 'Der Grundsatz der Verhältnismäßigkeit in der Rechtsprechung des Bundesverfassungsgerichts' (1973) 98 *Archiv des öffentlichen Rechts* 568.

6.5.A.2 THE EUROPEAN UNION

Treaty on the European Union **6.23 (EU)**

Article 5 (1) The limits of Union competences are governed by the principle of conferral. The use of Union competences is governed by the principles of subsidiarity and proportionality. …

(4) Under the principle of proportionality, the content and form of Union action shall not exceed what is necessary to achieve the objectives of the Treaties.

The institutions of the Union shall apply the principle of proportionality as laid down in the Protocol on the application of the principles of subsidiarity and proportionality.

Notes

(1) In the EU, as in Germany, the proportionality principle is recognised as the overriding principle for the purposes of setting limits to the legal measures of the Union that impose burdens on EU citizens.[132] As in Germany, proportionality as applied by the CJEU generally involves a three-stage test, aimed at checking: (i) if the measure was suitable, ie appropriate to achieve the desired result; (ii) if the measure was necessary, ie if less restrictive means could have achieved the same result; and (iii) if the measure was excessive, ie if the means employed went beyond the aim sought. It is not completely straightforward whether this third limb is applied by the EU courts.[133] Even though the German concept of proportionality was the main source of inspiration for the CJEU at the outset, the court has developed its own proportionality doctrine with different levels of intensity of review.[134]

(2) The level of scrutiny varies with regard to the decision-maker (national authorities or EU institutions) and to the subject matter.[135] While the proportionality review has, thus far, been rather limited with regard to measures of general application,[136] the scrutiny is somewhat more intense with implementing measures.[137] With regard to acts of individual application, however, the CJEU is quite reluctant to apply a strict proportionality review in cases in which complex economic choices and wide discretionary powers are at stake.[138] Yet, in the area of sanctions and charges, and cases involving fundamental rights, the proportionality test is rather vigorously applied.[139]

[132] See *Internationale Handelsgesellschaft* (n 94 above). See also Haguenau-Moizard and Sanchez (n 69 above) 142, 151 ff.

[133] P Craig, EU Administrative Law, 2nd edn (Oxford University Press, 2012) 592.

[134] Haguenau-Moizard and Sanchez (n 69 above) 142, 152.

[135] Haguenau-Moizard and Sanchez (n 69 above) 142, 157.

[136] See Case C-310/04 *Spain v Council* ECLI:EU:C:2006:521, para 98, where the threshold was that of 'manifestly inappropriate'.

[137] See Case T-72/98 *Astilleros Zamacona v Commission* ECLI:EU:T:2000:79, para 89; Case T-55/99 *CETM v Commission* ECLI:EU:T:2000:223, para 163; Case T-59/99 *Ventouris v Commission* ECLI:EU:T:2003:334, para 219.

[138] See section 6.3.B.2 above. Case T-9/98 *Mitteldeutsche Erdöl-Raffinerie v Commission* ECLI:EU:T:2001:271, para 114; Case T-333/99 *X v ECB* ECLI:EU:T:2001:251, para 224; Case T-180/00 *Astipesca v Commission* ECLI:EU:T:2002:249, para 79.

[139] See, eg Case 181/84 *R. v IBAP ex parte ED&F Man (Sugar)* ECLI:EU:C:1985:359.

6.5.A.3 FRANCE

Conseil d'État, 19 May 1933[140] **6.24 (FR)**

Benjamin v City of Nevers

PROPORTIONALITY PRINCIPLE

Benjamin

When reviewing an administrative decision limiting the exercise of a fundamental freedom, the courts use the proportionality test.

Facts: The claimant challenged the legality of two administrative decisions of the mayor of Nevers prohibiting two demonstrations that the claimant had organised.

Held: The administrative decisions were annulled.

Judgment: On the legality of the contested decisions: considering that, if the mayor, by virtue of Article 97 of the law of 5 April 1884, has to take measures to preserve the public order, he must reconcile the exercise of his powers with the respect of freedom of assembly guaranteed by the laws of 30 June 1881 and 20 March 1907; considering that, in order to prohibit the conferences of Mr René Benjamin, which were part of the programme of literature galas organised by the Tourist Office of Nevers, which both displayed the features of public conferences, the mayor relied on the fact that the venue of Mr Benjamin in Nevers was of a nature to jeopardise the public order; considering that it results from the case file that the possibility of disorder, alleged by the mayor of Nevers, did not display a degree of gravity such that the mayor of Never could not have, without prohibiting the conference, maintained the order by enacting the measures of police which he was empowered to take; considering that, therefore, without reviewing the ground of abuse of power (*détournement de pouvoir*), the applicants are right in claiming that the contested decisions are unlawful; ....

Conseil d'État, 9 January 2014[141] **6.25 (FR)**

Minister of Internal Affairs v Société Les Productions de la Plume et M Dieudonné M'Bala M'Bala

BREACH OF FREEDOM OF EXPRESSION; PROPORTIONALITY PRINCIPLE

Dieudonné M'Bala

When reviewing an administrative decision limiting the exercise of a fundamental freedom, the courts use the proportionality test.

Facts: Mr Dieudonné was a comedian who, during public shows, made anti-Semitic remarks. In order to preserve the public order, the prefect had banned the performance of a show in the city of Saint-Herblain.

Held: The administrative decision was upheld.

[140] N° 17413 17520.
[141] N° 374508.

Judgment: Considering that the exercise of freedom of expression is a condition of democracy and one of the guarantees of respect of other rights and freedoms; considering that it is the task of the authorities in charge of administrative police to take the necessary measures to enforce the freedom of assembly; considering that the interference with the exercise of those fundamental freedoms must be necessary, suitable and proportionate to achieve the requirements of public order; …

5. Considering that, when prohibiting the performance of the show 'Le Mur' at Saint-Herblain, previously performed in the theatre of La Main d'Or in Paris, the prefect of Loire-Atlantique has indicated that this show, as it is designed, contains statements of anti-Semitic character which incite to racial hatred and, in breach of the dignity of the human person, glorify discrimination, persecution and exterminations committed during the Second World War; considering that the challenged decision of the prefect reminds that M.B … D … has received nine criminal convictions, of which seven are definitive, for statements of the same nature; considering that this finally indicates that the reactions to the show of 9 January reveal, in a climate of high tension, that there are serious risks of disturbances to the public order which would be very difficult for the police forces to control;

6. Considering that the reality and the gravity of the risks of disturbances to the public order mentioned by the challenged judgment are established by elements contained in the case file as well as resulting from the discussions held during the public hearing; considering that, in regard to the planned show as it has been announced and programmed, the allegation according to which the statements which are criminally reprehensible and of a nature to affect national cohesion as seen in the sessions held in Paris would not be mentioned in Nantes, is not sufficient to exclude the serious risk that the show would again jeopardise the respect of the values and principles, notably the dignity of the human person protected by the Declaration of the Man and of the Citizen and the republican tradition; considering that, furthermore, it is the task of the administrative authority to take measures of such nature to avoid that criminal offences are committed; considering that, by basing itself on the risks that the planned show represents for the public order and the breach of the principles of which the state authorities have to ensure the respect, the prefect of Loire-Atlantique has not acted illegally in a serious and manifest manner in the exercise of its powers of administrative police ….

Notes

(1) In France, there is no legal rule that enshrines proportionality as a general principle of administrative law. In general, French administrative law is predominantly judge-made, and the concept of *proportionnalité* was implicitly introduced through case law as a means of control of the administrative discretion in specific situations. Thus, to date, proportionality is not understood as an overriding principle of public law, but is only applied in certain fields of law which are specifically related to human rights (eg the law relating to police powers). There is no clear system determining when the Council of State applies the proportionality principle,[142] but it does so within the ground of review of *violation de la loi*.[143]

[142] Sanchez (n 64 above) 41 ff.

[143] See section 6.2.A.1 above.

(2) The recognition of the proportionality principle is often traced back to the *Benjamin* case, even though the Council of State does not explicitly refer to *proportionalité* in the judgment. Nonetheless, in this case, the Council of State engaged in balancing the competing interests. In particular, it assessed the necessity of the decision taken and its adequacy, namely if there were no decision which would have been less restrictive for the individual's freedom whilst achieving the same goal. The court balanced the public interest in the public order against the freedom of assembly of the applicant and finally quashed the contested administrative decisions as the applicant's interests prevailed. This rather 'liberal' reasoning was rather novel at the time and is therefore seen as the offspring of proportionality in French law.[144] Since then, where civil liberties and fundamental rights are concerned, especially in the field of the law relating to police powers, the administrative courts apply a proportionality assessment, using so-called 'intense scrutiny' (*contrôle maximum*), meaning that the judge imposes strong limits on the margin of discretion of public authorities,[145] as the excerpt of *Dieudonné M'Bala* case demonstrates. This case considered a situation where Dieudonné performed a show where he made anti-Semitic remarks. Such remarks constituted a criminal offence, and since there were huge demonstrations each time the show was performed, the court considered the decision banning the show to be lawful, even though this measure constituted a significant limitation on freedom of expression. In this case, a proportionality test was applied.

(3) However, the proportionality principle plays a smaller role in the French case law than in Germany.[146] Whereas, in Germany, the proportionality principle is understood as a core principle of judicial review in public law, French administrative courts apply the proportionality test less regularly. Furthermore, the application of the proportionality test is less distinct.[147] Instead of the German three-stage method, the Council of State generally applies two steps: first, it checks the suitability of the measure to reach a legitimate interest of the state; and secondly, it engages in an extensive balancing of the interests at stake, thereby also assessing whether the aim could not have been reached by a less restrictive measure.[148]

6.5.A.4 THE NETHERLANDS

Algemene Wet Bestuursrecht **6.26 (NL)**

Article 3:4 (1) The administrative authority weighs the interests directly affected by the decision in as far as no limitation follows from a legal rule or from the nature of the power to be exercised.

[144] Sanchez (n 64 above) 41, 45.
[145] See section 6.3.B.1 above.
[146] *cf* Schwarze (n 122 above) 680 ff.
[147] See also Sanchez (n 64 above) 41, 44.
[148] J Ziller, 'Verwaltungsgerichtsbarkeit: Frankreich' in A von Bogdangy, P Cruz Villalón and PM Huber (eds), *Ius Publicum Europaeum, Band VIII. Grundlagen und Grundzüge staatlichen Verfassungsrechts*, 2nd edn (Heidelberg, CF Müller, forthcoming).

(2) The disadvantageous consequences of a decision for one or more parties concerned may not be disproportionate to the purposes to be served by the administrative decision.

Notes

(1) According to the case law, Article 3:4(2) AWB, which expressly stipulates the proportionality principle, covers both the prohibition to act in an arbitrary manner and the proportionality principle. Thus, the proportionality principle is acknowledged in Dutch law. However, the courts do not usually apply the three-stage test employed by Germany, but concentrate on the question of whether all relevant public and private interests involved have been balanced, whether there is a sound motivation for the outcome of this balancing process and whether the adverse effects for one of the parties are not entirely disproportionate (proportionality *stricto sensu*).[149] Although it is also acknowledged that the administration may not take measures which interfere with the interests of parties more than is necessary,[150] this necessity test is not always applied, at least not explicitly.[151]

(2) With regard to the intensity of judicial review, the courts can only interfere in the exercise of discretion by the administration if the weighing of interests has led to an evidently unreasonable outcome.[152] The level of scrutiny is thus lower than in Germany with regard to discretionary decisions.

6.5.A.5 ENGLAND AND WALES

Supreme Court, 19 June 2013[153] **6.27 (EW)**

Bank Mellat v HM Treasury

PROPORTIONALITY REVIEW; BREACH OF A CONVENTION RIGHT

Bank Mellat

The concept of proportionality must be used in cases where there is an alleged breach of an ECHR right. The proportionality test may also be used in appropriate cases outside the scope of the ECHR.

Facts: The Treasury restricted the access of the claimant bank and its subsidiaries to UK financial markets using powers under schedule 7, part 3, para 13 of the Counter-Terrorism Act 2008. Bank Mellat argued that this was unlawful as it was contrary to common law standards on irrelevant considerations and error of fact,

[149] For a brief overview, see Schwarze (n 122 above) 700 f. For a more detailed analysis of the concept of proportionality in Dutch law, see de Waard (n 51 above) 109 ff.

[150] ABRvS 26 February 2003, ECLI:NL:RVS:2003:AF5025.

[151] ECLI:NL:RBBRE:2008:BC2577.

[152] See section 6.3.A.2 above; ECLI:NL:RVS:1996:ZF2153 (leading case); see also case note at AB 1997, 93.

[153] [2013] UKSC 39.

and also that the Treasury's decision to take action without offering the protections of natural justice was contrary to Article 6 ECHR. The bank also contended that the decision to prevent it from dealing in the UK was contrary to its rights under Article 1, Protocol 1 ECHR.

Held: By a majority, the Supreme Court held that the Treasury's action was a disproportionate interference with the rights of Bank Mellat.

Judgment: Lord Reed (Dissenting judgment):

The concept of proportionality

68. The idea that proportionality is an aspect of justice can be traced back via Aquinas to the Nicomachean Ethics and beyond. … The idea that the state should limit natural rights only to the minimum extent necessary developed in Germany into a public law standard known as *Verhältnismäßigkeit*, or proportionality. From its origins in German administrative law, where it forms the basis of a rigorously structured analysis of the validity of legislative and administrative acts, the concept of proportionality came to be adopted in the case law of the European Court of Justice and the European Court of Human Rights. From the latter, it migrated to Canada, where it has received a particularly careful and influential analysis, and from Canada it spread to a number of other common law jurisdictions.

69. Proportionality has become one of the general principles of EU law, and appears in article 5(4) of the Treaty on European Union ('TEU'). … The intensity with which the test is applied – that is to say, the degree of weight or respect given to the assessment of the primary decision-maker – depends upon the context.

70. As I have mentioned, proportionality is also a concept applied by the European Court of Human Rights. … The intensity of review varies considerably according to the right in issue and the context in which the question arises. Unsurprisingly, given that it is an international court, its approach to proportionality does not correspond precisely to the various approaches adopted in contracting states.

71. An assessment of proportionality inevitably involves a value judgment at the stage at which a balance has to be struck between the importance of the objective pursued and the value of the right intruded upon. The principle does not, however, entitle the courts simply to substitute their own assessment for that of the decision-maker. … One important factor in relation to the Convention is that the Strasbourg court recognises that it may be less well placed than a national court to decide whether an appropriate balance has been struck in the particular national context. For that reason, in the Convention case law the principle of proportionality is indissolubly linked to the concept of the margin of appreciation. That concept does not apply in the same way at the national level, where the degree of restraint practised by courts in applying the principle of proportionality, and the extent to which they will respect the judgment of the primary decision maker, will depend upon the context, and will in part reflect national traditions and institutional culture. For these reasons, the approach adopted to proportionality at the national level cannot simply mirror that of the Strasbourg court.

72. The approach to proportionality adopted in our domestic case law under the Human Rights Act has not generally mirrored that of the Strasbourg court. In accordance with the analytical approach to legal reasoning characteristic of the common law, a more clearly structured approach has generally been adopted, derived from case law under Commonwealth constitutions and Bills of Rights, including in particular the Canadian Charter of Fundamental Rights and Freedoms of 1982. …

74. The judgment of Dickson CJ in Oakes provides the clearest and most influential judicial analysis of proportionality within the common law tradition of legal reasoning.

… The approach adopted in Oakes can be summarised by saying that it is necessary to determine (1) whether the objective of the measure is sufficiently important to justify the limitation of a protected right, (2) whether the measure is rationally connected to the objective, (3) whether a less intrusive measure could have been used without unacceptably compromising the achievement of the objective, and (4) whether, balancing the severity of the measure's effects on the rights of the persons to whom it applies against the importance of the objective, to the extent that the measure will contribute to its achievement, the former outweighs the latter. … In essence, the question at step four is whether the impact of the rights infringement is disproportionate to the likely benefit of the impugned measure.

Applying the proportionality test

83. There is no doubt that the objective of the order – to reduce access by entities involved in Iran's nuclear weapons programme to the UK financial sector, and thereby inhibit the development of nuclear weapons by Iran and the consequent risk to the national interests of this country – is sufficiently important to justify an interference with Bank Mellat's enjoyment of its possessions. The question under paragraph 9(6) of Schedule 7, and under the Human Rights Act, is whether the remaining three criteria of proportionality are satisfied. Lord Sumption identifies the central issue as being whether the singling out of Bank Mellat has been justified, and considers that issue in the context of the second and, more briefly, the third and fourth criteria: whether the measure is rationally connected to its objective, whether a less intrusive measure would have been equally effective, and whether the measure is proportionate having regard to its effects upon Bank Mellat's rights. …

Proportionate effect

126. If, as I would hold, (1) the Government's objective was sufficiently important to justify limiting the rights of Bank Mellat, (2) the requirements imposed by the direction were rationally connected to that objective and (3) no less intrusive measure would have been equally effective in achieving the objective, the question remains whether (4) having regard to the severity of its effect on Bank Mellat's rights, the direction was justified by the importance of the objective. Lord Sumption concludes that it was not, given that, in his view, the direction would make little if any contribution to the achievement of its objective. For the reasons I have explained, I do not agree with that assessment. On the basis that the direction would make a worthwhile contribution to the achievement of the Government's objective, I agree with Mitting J that its impact upon the rights of Bank Mellat is proportionate. …

Note

(1) The proportionality principle as such has no roots in English law. Measures which are unsuitable to reach the objective, and hence would be reviewed under the heading of proportionality in the other legal systems, have traditionally been assessed under the *Wednesbury* test to determine whether they are ultra vires.[154] Furthermore, the English constitutional system in principle grants Parliament unlimited powers. Thus, the judges refrained from any balancing with regard to legislative and policy decisions. As seen above (section 6.3.B.3), the traditional *Wednesbury* reasonableness

[154] See Craig (n 116 above) para 1-003 ff.

test strictly limits judicial review to the irrationality of discretionary administrative decisions.

(2) However, with the coming into force of the Human Rights Act and judicial review concerning EU law issues, the proportionality principle has been introduced into the English legal system. In the *Bank Mellat* case, Lord Reed describes the different steps of the proportionality test, which are similar to the German test, as follows: 'it is necessary to determine (1) whether the objective of the measure is sufficiently important to justify the limitation of a protected right, (2) whether the measure is rationally connected to the objective, (3) whether a less intrusive measure could have been used without unacceptably compromising the achievement of the objective, and (4) whether, balancing the severity of the measure's effects on the rights of the persons to whom it applies against the importance of the objective, to the extent that the measure will contribute to its achievement, the former outweighs the latter.' Nonetheless, he emphasises that the intensity of review 'will depend upon the context and will in part reflect national traditions and institutional culture'.

(3) At the same time, different scales of the traditional reasonableness test with varying intensities of review developed in the common law.[155] As seen above, the relationship between the proportionality principle and the traditional reasonableness test is still unclear and needs further development.[156] To date, both tests have been applied by the courts in England and Wales with varying intensity of review, depending on the subject matter of the case. As the excerpts above illustrate, the courts always use the proportionality test when considering cases under the Human Rights Act 1998 or where they involve matters of EU law.

6.5.A.6 COMPARATIVE REMARKS

The proportionality principle was first created in German public law in the late nineteenth century. Here, the full three-stage test was developed, and it is still applied with regard to every administrative decision that interferes with the fundamental rights of the citizens. It therefore serves as a core instrument with which to control administrative discretion.

The proportionality principle is also an important means for the protection of individual rights against the administrative action in EU law. The German concept has served as the main source of inspiration for the CJEU when developing this principle in its case law. However, the court has an own proportionality doctrine, with different levels of intensity of review. The third limb of the three-stage test is not always applied.

In the Netherlands, the principle of proportionality is codified in Article 3:4(2) AWB. However, the courts do not usually apply the three-stage test. In particular, the necessity of an administrative measure is not explicitly examined. The Dutch courts concentrate on the question of whether all relevant public and private interests involved have been balanced, whether there is a sound motivation for the outcome of this balancing process

[155] For details, see Davies and Williams (n 77 above) 71, 85 ff.

[156] See sections 6.3.B.3 and 6.4.B.2 above.

and on the proportionality *stricto sensu*. It is doubtful whether the proportionality principle was introduced into the Dutch legal system due to European influences. Rather, the development of the concept in Dutch law was a genuine Dutch process.

In France and England and Wales, the situation is different. In both legal systems, the proportionality principle is not recognised as a general legal principle. In France, the principle is mainly applied in certain fields of law which are particularly related to human rights (eg the law related to police powers). Even in cases in which the principle is applied, the test is less elaborated than, for example, in Germany. Usually, only the first two steps of the test are applied. In England and Wales, the proportionality test was not known as a general principle. Due to constitutional constraints, the traditional *Wednesbury* reasonableness test strictly limited judicial review to the irrationality of discretionary administrative decisions. However, in this legal system we can observe the clearest influence of European law on the national legal order. Within the application of the Human Rights Act and judicial review concerning EU law issues, the proportionality principle has been introduced into the English legal system in order to comply with EU law and to meet the requirements of the Human Rights Act 1998. When applied, the test is very similar to the German three-stage test. The intensity of the review depends upon the context. Furthermore, the relationship between the proportionality test and the *Wednesbury* unreasonableness test is not yet resolved, although there is evidence to suggest that the *Wednesbury* test is developing into something closer to the proportionality test, with the intensity of review varying depending on the subject matter of the case.[157]

6.5.B LEGAL CERTAINTY, LEGITIMATE EXPECTATIONS AND WITHDRAWAL OF ADMINISTRATIVE ACTS

The principle of legal certainty is recognised in all of the legal systems analysed and may be described as a general legal principle throughout the EU.[158] However, the scope and extent of this principle seems to differ from system to system. These differences will be highlighted in this section. The principles of legitimate expectations and legal certainty play a role in respect of the withdrawal of administrative decisions, with the public interest in the withdrawal of the act having to be balanced against the principle of legal certainty, but also with regard to changes in legislation. Furthermore, whether the protection of legal certainty and legitimate expectations can lead to the compensation of the citizens will also be discussed.

6.5.B.1 GERMANY

Verwaltungsverfahrensgesetz **6.28 (DE)**

§48 (1) An unlawful administrative act may, even after it has become final and non-appealable, be withdrawn wholly or in part either retroactively or with effects for the

[157] See, eg the decision of the Supreme Court in *Kennedy v Information Commissioner* [2014] UKSC 20, [2015] AC 455 and the judgment of Lord Mance at [51]–[54].
[158] Schwarze (n 122 above) 868 ff.

future. An administrative act which gives rise to a right or an advantage relevant in legal proceedings or confirms such a right or advantage (beneficial administrative act) may only be withdrawn subject to the restrictions of sections 2 to 4.

(2) An unlawful administrative act which provides for a one-time or continuous payment of money or a divisible benefit in kind, or is a condition for it, may not be withdrawn in so far as the beneficiary has relied upon the administrative act and his reliance deserves protection when weighed against the public interest in a withdrawal. …

(3) If an unlawful administrative act which does not fall under section 2 is withdrawn, the authority shall, upon application, compensate the person concerned for the disadvantage he suffered as a consequence of his reliance on the administrative act to the extent that his reliance deserves protection when weighed against the public interest the public interest. …

§49 (1) A lawful, non-beneficial administrative act may, even after it has become final and non-appealable, be revoked wholly or in part with effects for the future, except if an administrative act of the same content would have to be issued or if revocation is not allowed for other reasons.

(2) A lawful, beneficial administrative act may, even when it has become final and non-appealable, be revoked in whole or in part with effects for the future only when:

1. revocation is permitted by law or the right of revocation is provided for in the administrative act itself;

2. the administrative act is combined with an obligation which the beneficiary has not complied with fully or not within the time limit set;

3. the authority would be entitled, as a result of a subsequent change in circumstances, not to issue the administrative act and if failure to revoke it would be contrary to the public interest;

4. the authority would be entitled, as a result of an amendment to a legal provision, not to issue the administrative act where the beneficiary has not availed himself of the benefit or has not received any benefits derived from the administrative act and when failure to revoke would be contrary to the public interest, or

5. in order to prevent or remove serious harm to the common good. …

(6) When a beneficial administrative act is revoked in the cases covered by section 2, no. 3 to 5, the authority shall, upon application, compensate the person concerned for the disadvantage which he incurred as a consequence of his reliance on the continued existence of the act to the extent that his reliance deserves protection. …

Bundesverwaltungsgericht, 23 April 1998[159] **6.29 (DE)**

LEGITIMATE EXPECTATIONS; REVOCATION OF ILLEGAL SUBSIDIES

Alcan

In cases concerning EU subsidies, the protection of legitimate expectations under §48 VwVfG can be limited because of the increased public interest in withdrawal due to the influence of EU law.

Facts: The claimant, an international company, had received subsidies which were incompatible with EU law. The administrative authority therefore withdrew the approval of the grant and asked the claimant to repay the

[159] BVerwGE 106, 328 ff.

subsidies it had received. The claimant appealed against the repayment decision on the basis of §48 VwVfG, which provided for the protection of its legitimate expectations. The Federal Administrative Court therefore referred to the Court of Justice a question for preliminary ruling. In particular, it asked whether the protection of legitimate expectations can protect a company from repaying subsidies which are illegal under EU law. The Court of Justice answered the question in the negative. The claimant argued that the decision of the CJEU was ultra vires.

Held: The claim was dismissed.

Judgment: As the 11th Senate of the Federal Administrative Court has accurately held in its judgment of 17 February 1993 ..., the reliance of a recipient of subsidies – deviating from the 'rule' of §48(2) sentence 2 VwVfG – can be unworthy of protection, independently of the conditions set in §48(2) sentence 3 VwVfG, because of the increased public interest in withdrawal due to the influence of Community law; such is the situation in the case at hand: the protection of legitimate expectations of the beneficiary in principle diminishes when the state aid was granted without the mandatory monitoring procedure prescribed in Article 93 EC, ie without the control of the Commission. This is because a secure basis for the trust of the substantive lawfulness of the state aid only exists when the monitoring procedure as a precondition of the correctness of the state aid was respected. It is possible for a careful commercial company to assure itself of whether this precondition is fulfilled. If the prescribed monitoring procedure – as in this case – has not been carried out then the trust of the state aid recipient is only worthy of protection when special circumstances lead to this conclusion ....

Note

(1) According to the German understanding, the principles of legal certainty and of the protection of legitimate expectations are vested in Articles 20(3) and 28(1) of the Grundgesetz (GG), which enshrine the rule of law principle (*Rechtsstaatsprinzip*).[160]

(2) In respect of executive regulations,[161] the Federal Constitutional Court draws a distinction between 'real' retroactivity (*echte Rückwirkung*) – concerning measures which change circumstances that have been concluded in the past – and 'apparent' retroactivity (*unechte Rückwirkung*) – referring to measures which apply to past actions the consequences of which extend to the present.[162] Whereas real retroactivity is generally unlawful and only permissible in exceptional circumstances,[163] apparent retroactivity is generally permissible and only illegal in exceptional circumstances.[164] In both cases, the public interest, which can lead to changes in the rules, is weighed against the interest of the individuals to have their legitimate expectations protected.

(3) With regard to the withdrawal and revocation of administrative acts, the principle of legitimate expectations is implemented in the applicable laws (see §§48 and 49 VwVfG). The law differs between the revocation of lawful administrative decisions

[160] BVerfGE 8, 155, 172; E 30, 367, 386; E 30, 392, 401 ff.
[161] *Rechtsverordnungen*, see Chapter 3, section 3.3.B.2.a.
[162] For a summary, see Schwarze (n 122 above) 899.
[163] BVerfGE 13, 261, 272 ff.
[164] BVerfGE 36, 73, 82; E 63, 312, 329.

(*Rücknahme*) and the withdrawal of unlawful administrative acts (*Widerruf*), limits the revocation and withdrawal of beneficial administrative acts, and grants compensation under certain circumstances.[165]

(4) When illegal EU subsidies are granted, the administrative discretion to withdraw the beneficial administrative act is limited to only one lawful decision to withdraw the act. According to the *Alcan* judgment of the Federal Administrative Court, which follows the CJEU case law, in these cases, the legitimate expectations of the addressee always weigh less than the public interest to ensure the effectiveness of the EU law.[166]

6.5.B.2 FRANCE

Conseil d'État, 24 March 2006[167] **6.30 (FR)**

Société KPMG v Prime Minister

PRINCIPLE OF LEGAL CERTAINTY

KPMG

According to the principle of legal certainty, administrative authorities are obliged to adopt transitory measures in order to protect contractual relationships.

Facts: After the Enron scandal (the bankruptcy of this US company revealed that the audit company Arthur Anderson had helped to make false statements to the financial market), the French parliament intervened to strengthen the independence of auditors, by separating audit from advice, according to the law of 1 August 2003 on financial security relating to the ethics and the independence of statutory auditors. Based on this law, a Code of Ethics was adopted. The Decree of 16 November 2005 approved the Code, which was considered to be immediately applicable, including to existing contractual obligations.

Held: The decree was annulled.

Judgment: Considering that the provisions of the law of 1 August 2003 on financial security related to the ethics and to the independence of statutory auditors, implemented by the Code of Ethics, are, due to requirements of public order on which they are grounded, designed to apply to members of the profession thus regulated and organised without their effect being postponed at the expiry of the mandate to which the interested parties are contractually bound; considering that, however, in the absence of any transitional provision in the challenged decree, the requirements and prohibitions which result from the code would involve disturbances in the contractual relations legally instituted before its enforcement, which, because of their excessive nature in the light of the objective

[165] See also Pünder and Klafki (n 11 above) 49, 77 f.
[166] Case C-24/95 *Land Rheinland Pfalz v Alcan* ECLI:EU:C:1997:163; M Ruffert, in Ehlers and Pünder (n 42 above) §24, para 17.
[167] N° 288460.

pursued, are contrary to the principle of legal certainty; considering that, accordingly, it is appropriate to set aside the challenged decree insofar as it does not include transitional measures related to the existing mandates of statutory auditors at the date of its entry into force ....

Code des relations entre le public et l'administration **6.31 (FR)**

Article L241-1 Subject to the requirements arising from European Union law and the special legislative provisions and regulations, the rules applicable to the abrogation and the withdrawal of a unilateral administrative act taken by the administration are set by the provisions under the present title.

Article L241-2 By derogation to the provisions of the present title, a unilateral administrative act obtained through fraud can be abrogated or withdrawn at any time.

Article L242-1 The administration cannot abrogate or withdraw a decision creating rights on its own initiative or on the demand of a third party except if this decision is unlawful and if the abrogation or withdrawal intervenes within the time period of four months after the adoption of the decision.

Article L243-1 A regulatory act or a non-regulatory act which does not create rights can, for any reason and without conditions as to time limits, be modified or abrogated, subject to, if applicable, the enactment of transitory measures under the conditions provided for under Article L221-6.

Article L243-2 The administration is bound to expressly abrogate an unlawful regulatory act or an act devoid of purpose, whether this situation exists since its enactment or whether it results from subsequent legal or factual circumstances, except where it has ceased to be illegal.

The administration is bound to expressly abrogate a non-regulatory act which does not create rights and which has become unlawful or devoid of purpose in light of legal or factual circumstances which have arisen after its enactment, except if it has ceased to be illegal.

Article L243-3 The administration can withdraw a regulatory act or a non-regulatory act not creating any rights only if it is illegal and if the withdrawal is adopted within the time period of four months following its enactment.

Notes

(1) There is no principle of legitimate expectations recognised in French law, as this principle is considered to contravene the objective conception of administrative law, which serves the promotion of the general interest.[168] In French law, as a matter of principle, individual expectations cannot limit the freedom of the administration in its pursuit of the public interest.

[168] For details, see Chapter 1, section 1.5.3.

(2) However, because the principle of legal certainty is a general principle of EU law, French courts apply the principle of legal certainty in cases where EU law is enforced.[169] Recently, French administrative courts have even recognised the principle of legal certainty as a more general principle of administrative law. Thus, the principle is meanwhile also applied to purely domestic administrative law disputes, as shown in the *KPMG* case. The recognition of the principle of legal certainty has been an important step in integrating EU law into the national administrative law system. Nevertheless, the principle of legal certainty is always balanced with the legality principle.[170]

(3) The principle of legal certainty applies to the revocation of single-case decisions, measures of general scope and legislation with varying intensity.[171] With regard to the retroactivity of legislative acts, just as in Germany, a distinction is drawn between retroactive effects on cases which have already ceased in the past (retroactivity in the narrow sense) and circumstances where the law has implications in cases which originate in the past but are not yet concluded.[172] Whilst retroactivity in the narrow sense is strictly forbidden, the legality of retroactivity in the second case depends on the extent to which this encroaches on an individual right.[173] As seen in the *KPMG* case, transitory measures may be required to lessen the intrusion on individual rights to render retroactive legislative acts legal.

(4) Administrative decisions can be withdrawn by the administration in two ways: through withdrawal (*retrait*) and through abrogration (*abrogation*), as outlined in the Code des relations entre le public et l'administration (Code of Relations between the Administration and the Members of the Public). These instruments are to be distinguished according to their effects in time, and they also differ as to their applicability to lawful and unlawful administrative acts.[174] Through withdrawal (*retrait*), the effects both for the future and for the past are cancelled (*ex tunc*); abrogation only cancels the administrative decision for the future (*ex nunc*). An administrative decision which confers rights on an individual may in principle only be revoked *ex tunc* if it is unlawful and would also be annulled by a court for one of the reasons mentioned above (lack of competence – *incompétence*, formal irregularity – *vice de forme*, misuse of power – *détournement de pouvoir*, or illegality – *violation de la loi*).[175] In case of lawful regulatory acts,[176] withdrawal and abrogation are always possible, without any time limit (Article L243-1). On the contrary, in case of lawful non-regulatory acts creating rights, the withdrawal is in principle impossible (Article L242-1).

[169] Conseil d'État, 9 May 2001, *Entreprise personnelle de transports Freymuth*, N° 210944.
[170] For the importance of the legality principle in French law, see Bermann and Picard (n 11 above) 57, 69 ff.
[171] *cf* Schwarze (n 122 above) 874 ff.
[172] ibid 885.
[173] ibid 886.
[174] ibid 875.
[175] See section 6.2.A.1 above.
[176] For details on 'regulatory acts', see Chapter 3, section 3.3.

6.5.B.3 THE NETHERLANDS

Centrale Raad van Beroep, 31 October 1935[177] **6.32 (NL)**

X v Provincial Executive of Utrecht

PRINCIPLE OF LEGAL CERTAINTY

Utrecht

The principle of legal certainty has to be recognised as an unwritten general principle of law.

Facts: On 19 March 1935, the provincial executive of Utrecht laid down a decision which implied a reduction in the salary of its civil servants, including the claimant, with retroactive effect to 1 April 1934. The decision was contested by the claimant, in final instance, before the Central Appellate Court.

Held: As far as the decision has retroactive effect to 1 April 1934, it was considered contrary to legal certainty, a general principle of law.

Judgment: Considering that the civil servant's legal certainty, also in respect of salary that is lawfully obtained, is such a precious right, that it cannot be affected by a decision, which interferes with the period for which he, according to the then applicable valid rules, has obtained salary, and which would alter these rules with retroactive effect in an unfavourable way.

Considering that the general principle of law, which forbids lawfully acquired rights from being affected, should be respected even if it has not been laid down in written law. Therefore, the decision of the provincial executive of Utrecht of 19 March 1935 lacks legal force as far as it determines that the reduction of the claimant's salary has retroactive effect to 1 April 1934.

Hoge Raad, 12 April 1978[178] **6.33 (NL)**

X v Tax Authority

PRINCIPLE OF LEGITIMATE EXPECTATIONS; *CONTRA LEGEM* APPLICATION

Tax Authority

In certain cases, the principle of legitimate expectations may require that the law is not applied.

Facts: The tax authorities had imposed several taxes on, amongst others, the claimant. These decisions were consistent with the applicable legislation, but deviated from several tax resolutions (a form of policy rules) of the Minister of Finance which 'obliged' the authorities to deviate from the legislation in favour of certain groups of taxpayers (to which the claimant belonged). The decision was, in final instance, brought before the Supreme Court.

Held: The decision was annulled.

[177] ECLI:NL:CRVB:1935:AM3312.
[178] ECLI:NL:HR:1978:AX3264.

Judgment: Considering that, under certain circumstances, a strict application of the law (an Act of Parliament), from which a tax debt directly flows, is to such an extent contrary to one or more general principles of good administration, that such application is not allowed;

Considering that the question under which circumstances the latter applies in general should be answered from case to case by weighing the principle that the law should be applied against one or more applicable principles of good administration; considering that it is a principle of good administration that the administration should honour expectations which it has raised on the part of an interested party in respect of a course of action to be followed by the administration and on which the party may reasonably rely; considering that this principle in the weighing process of the principles mentioned above is of overriding importance if the taxpayer may derive such expectations from statements of the Ministers which are responsible for the tax authorities, or if such statements are included in a ministerial tax resolution … which has become public …; considering that therefore, if the taxpayer relies on the expectations which he has derived from these statements, the tax decision should be determined in conformity with them, even if the law does not provide for any discretion for the tax authorities.

Notes

(1) In 1935, the principle of legal certainty was the first unwritten general principle of law to be recognised by an administrative court, the Central Appellate Court in the *Utrecht* case. The principle of legitimate expectations has been developed by the administrative courts since the Second World War. It is recognised as a separate principle of good administration, although it partly overlaps with legal certainty.[179] In general terms, it requires the administrative authority to act as far as possible in conformity with the justified expectations that it has raised by making assurances and promises of a specific and precise nature, by laying down policy rules, as the *Tax Authority* case shows, and by concluding so-called competence contracts, ie contracts in which an administrative authority agrees with a private partner to exercise its public law competences in a certain way.[180] Legal certainty and legitimate expectations are accepted as principles of proper administration, but also extend to the legislature.

(2) As is clear from the *Utrecht* case, the principle of legal certainty forbids retroactive application of new rules which would affect lawfully acquired rights of individuals in an unfavourable way. The courts also acknowledge legitimate expectations if a claimant relies on them and the relevant conditions are met. The principle has been further developed since 1935, and nowadays it may even limit sudden revocation of certain benefits, for example a subsidy decision, for the future without

[179] For details, see JBJM ten Berge and RJGM Widdershoven, 'The Principle of Legitimate Expectations in Dutch Constitutional and Administrative Law' in EH Hondius (ed), *Netherlands Report to the Fifteenth International Congress of Comparative Law, Bristol 1998* (Antwerp, Intersentia, 1998) 421–52.

[180] For more details on policy rules and competence contracts, see Chapter 3, sections 3.3.B.2.b. and 3.5.B, respectively.

an adaption period.[181] However, revocation of decisions, even with retroactive effect, is not impossible in all cases. If, for example, the addressee of the decision has informed the authority wrongfully about circumstances which were decisive for the decision, the decision can be revoked retroactively.[182] Moreover, the principle of legal certainty requires decisions containing obligations for individuals to be clear and precise.[183]

(3) In the Netherlands, the principle of legitimate expectations features very strongly in two-party disputes. Such disputes exist in, for example, in the areas of taxes, subsidies and social security benefits. In these areas – as is shown in the *Tax Authority* case – the principle may even take precedence over the written law, and require a decision *contra legem*. However, in three-party disputes in, for example, environmental law, planning law or economic law, the interests of the individual relying on the expectations have to be balanced against the interests of third parties and the public interest. As a rule, the latter interests prevail.

(4) In Dutch case law, if claimants are to rely on legitimate expectations in two-party disputes, the requirements are less strict than those prescribed by the CJEU in the area of European subsidies, as the CJEU does not recognise the application of the principle *contra legem* and applies a higher standard of good faith for the recipient to be able to rely on the principle.[184] This led to a conflict between EU law, which requires the withdrawal of a wrongfully paid European subsidy, and Dutch law, under which the legitimate expectations of the recipient would take precedence.[185] Ultimately, this conflict was resolved by the Judicial Division of the Council of State interpreting the Dutch principle – as codified in the area of subsidies in the AWB[186] – in such a way as to reach a result that is consistent with EU law.[187] As a result, the Dutch principle is in fact set aside.

(5) There is no general statutory provision in the AWB on withdrawal (*intrekking*) and revocation (*herroepen*) of administrative decisions. If the applicable acts are silent, the principles of legal certainty and legitimate expectations provide the applicable legal regime.

(6) The principle of legitimate expectations is not only addressed to the administration, but also has to be taken into account by the legislator. There are even some, albeit quite rare, cases in which the courts have declared that legislation cannot be applied because it is in conflict with legitimate expectations. That may, for example, be the case if the legislator, without urgent need, drastically changes the conditions

[181] This is explicitly codified in Art 4:51 AWB.

[182] ECLI:NL:RVS:2013:BZ9071. A case in which revocation was nevertheless not allowed because of legal certainty can be found in ECLI:NL:CBB:1998:ZG0269.

[183] ECLI:NL:RVS:2001:AL3065; ECLI:NL:CBB:2011:BP9342.

[184] For details, see JH Jans, S Prechal and RJGM Widdershoven (eds), *Europeanisation of Public Law*, 2nd edn (Groningen, Europa Law Publishing, 2015) 207–35.

[185] Joined Cases C-383/06 to C-385/06 *Vereniging Nationaal Overlegorgaan Sociale Werkvoorziening and others v Minister van Sociale Zaken en Werkgelegenheid and Sociaal Economische Samenwerking West-Brabant* ECLI:EU:C:2008:165.

[186] See Arts 4:46, 4:47 and 4:57 AWB.

[187] ECLI:NL:RVS:2008:BG8284.

for obtaining a subsidy or removes the subsidy without any transitional period.[188] However, the legislator has a very large margin of discretion. Furthermore, one has to take into account that, according to Article 120 of the Dutch Constitution, judges may not review whether (formal) legislation is in accordance with the constitution. This also concerns general principles which may be derived from the Constitution. The question of whether legislation is in accordance with general principles of law is therefore discussed before the courts only with regard to compliance with international law.[189]

6.5.B.4 ENGLAND AND WALES

Court of Appeal (Civil Division), 9 July 2008[190] **6.34 (EW)**

R (on the Application of Niazi) v Secretary of State for the Home Department

PRINCIPLE OF LEGITIMATE EXPECTATIONS

Niazi

The power of public authorities to change policy is constrained by the legal duty to be fair, otherwise the sudden change of a policy is deemed to be an abuse of power.

Facts: N was a prisoner who alleged that there had been a miscarriage of justice in his case and had begun a claim for compensation, which had not yet been submitted, under a discretionary scheme introduced by the Secretary of State. Before N made his application, the Secretary of State withdrew the scheme. N argued that there should have been consultation before the scheme was withdrawn and that there should have been clear advance notice of the withdrawal date, so that prospective claimants could make their applications prior to withdrawal. N's solicitors were paid fees at a generous private client rate to support N in bringing his application, but on the date that the scheme was withdrawn the fees paid were reduced to a less generous rate. N's solicitors argued that they had a legitimate expectation that the private client rate would be paid in relation to all the clients where they were retained to support an application to the scheme, but where no application had yet been submitted.

Held: The appeal was dismissed.

Judgment: Laws LJ: 43. Authority shows that where a substantive expectation is to run the promise or practice which is its genesis is not merely a reflection of the ordinary fact (as I have put it) that a policy with no terminal date or terminating event will continue in effect until rational grounds for its cessation arise. Rather it must constitute a specific undertaking, directed at a particular individual or group, by which the relevant policy's continuance is assured. Lord Templeman in Preston referred … to 'conduct … equivalent to a breach of contract or breach of representations'.

188 See, eg ECLI:NL:RBSGR:2012:BU9921; ECLI:NL:RBSGR:2012:BX0977.

189 Both judgments mentioned in the previous footnote provide examples for the scrutiny of the courts on whether Dutch legislation complies with international law.

190 *R (on the Application of Niazi) v Secretary of State for the Home Department* [2008] EWCA Civ 755, *The Times*, 21 July 2008.

46. These cases illustrate the pressing and focussed nature of the kind of assurance required if a substantive legitimate expectation is to be upheld and enforced. ... Though in theory there may be no limit to the number of beneficiaries of a promise for the purpose of such an expectation, in reality it is likely to be small, if the court is to make the expectation good. There are two reasons for this, and they march together. First, it is difficult to imagine a case in which government will be held legally bound by a representation or undertaking made generally or to a diverse class. ...

The second reason is that the broader the class claiming the expectation's benefit, the more likely it is that a supervening public interest will be held to justify the change of position complained of. ...

50. A very broad summary of the place of legitimate expectations in public law might be expressed as follows. The power of public authorities to change policy is constrained by the legal duty to be fair (and other constraints which the law imposes). A change of policy which would otherwise be legally unexceptionable may be held unfair by reason of prior action, or inaction, by the authority. If it has distinctly promised to consult those affected or potentially affected, then ordinarily it must consult (the paradigm case of procedural expectation). If it has distinctly promised to preserve existing policy for a specific person or group who would be substantially affected by the change, then ordinarily it must keep its promise (substantive expectation). If, without any promise, it has established a policy distinctly and substantially affecting a specific person or group who in the circumstances was in reason entitled to rely on its continuance and did so, then ordinarily it must consult before effecting any change (the secondary case of procedural expectation). To do otherwise, in any of these instances, would be to act so unfairly as to perpetrate an abuse of power.

Notes

(1) Even though legal certainty has been inherent in the common law as a part of the rule of law principle,[191] the doctrine of legitimate expectations has had a fairly uncertain history. For many years, the law has accepted the concept of a legitimate expectation to the procedure,[192] whereas substantive legitimate expectation is a much more recent development.[193]

(2) Even though the judges accepted the doctrine of substantive legitimate expectations in the *Niazi* case, they still rejected the claims. Controversy has been caused in English law by the question of the extent to which the claimant must have acted to his detriment in order to make the expectation legitimate. The majority of cases all suggest that some form of detrimental reliance is necessary.[194] Furthermore, unlike in the

[191] See, eg *R (Anufrijeva) v Secretary of State for the Home Department* [2003] UKHL 36, [2004] 1 AC 604 (claimant must have proper notice of an administrative decision before it may produce legal effects); *R (L) v Secretary of State for the Home Department* [2003] EWCA Civ 25, [2003] 1 WLR 1230 (Secretary of State could not rely on a provision in legislation prior to its proper publication).

[192] For early examples, see, eg *Cinnamond v British Airports Authority* [1980] 1 WLR 582 (CA); *R v Liverpool Corporation, ex parte Taxi Fleet* [1972] 2 QB 299 (CA).

[193] For an early example of the substantive legitimate expectation principle, see *R v Ministry of Agriculture, Fisheries and Food, ex parte Hamble* [1995] 1 CMLR 533 (QB).

[194] See, eg ibid [47]–[49]; *R (On the Application of Abdi and Nadarajah) v SoS for the Home Department* [2005] EWCA Civ 1363, *The Times*, 14 December 2005, where Laws LJ gives a relatively detailed account of the need or otherwise for detrimental reliance at [55]–[58].

Dutch system, legitimate expectations cannot be created by an ultra vires promise.[195] Finally, even where a legitimate interest can be established, public authorities can depart from it if they act because of an 'overriding public interest'.[196]

(3) In English law, it is possible for public authorities to revoke lawful administrative decisions, provided that this is done in a manner that the courts would consider to be fair and in accordance with the principle of legitimate expectations. In the *Unilever* case,[197] the Court of Appeal held that it was lawful for the tax authorities to stop a practice of waiving time limits in relation to claims for tax relief. However, it was held that this was lawful only because the tax authority proposed to revoke the practice prospectively, having given appropriate notice of its intention to do so. Similarly, in cases such as *Hamble*[198] and *Niazi*, the revocation of policies that favoured the claimants was held to be unlawful because the state could demonstrate a public interest in the withdrawal and, in the case of *Niazi*, appropriate transitional measures were adopted to limit the negative impact on those who were presently gaining the benefit of the policy. The issue of whether or not a public authority can revoke an unlawful decision or policy is not an issue that has been considered widely in England and Wales because the courts are not willing to enforce ultra vires legitimate expectations.

6.5.B.5 THE EUROPEAN UNION

Case 112/77, 3 May 1978[199] **6.35 (EU)**

August Töpfer & Co GmbH v Commission

PRINCIPLE OF LEGITIMATE EXPECTATIONS; GENERAL PRINCIPLES OF EU LAW

Töpfer

The principle of legitimate expectations is part of the EU legal order.

Facts: The claimant requested the Court of Justice to annul a Commission regulation regarding sugar exported under certain tendering arrangements and, alternatively, to declare that the Commission was liable for the damage which the claimant alleged it had suffered as a result of that regulation. The dispute related to the application of the EU rules governing the consequences of the alterations in the value of the unit of account used for the common agricultural policy as far as export licences involving the advance fixing of amounts to be paid or refunded were concerned. The claimant had a large number of export licences, which gave it the right to a certain amount of compensation if it proceeded to export. However, because of an amendment to the relevant rules, the amount of compensation decreased. The claimant claimed that the amendment was a breach of the principle of legitimate expectations.

195 See *R (Theophilus) v London Borough of Lewisham* [2002] EWHC 1371 (Admin), [2002] 3 All ER 851.
196 See, eg *Hamble* (n 193 above); see also the judgment in *R v North and East Devon Health Authority, ex parte Coughlan* [2000] 2 WLR 622 (CA), especially [76].
197 *Niazi* (n 190 above).
198 *Hamble* (n 193 above).
199 ECLI:EU:C:1978:94.

Held: The court dismissed the claim, despite the existence of the principle of legitimate expectations, because the claimant could not rely on the amount of the first compensation, since the base of calculation went beyond the objective of the regulations it was based on.

Judgment: 19. The submission that there has been a breach of this principle (of legitimate expectations) is admissible in the context of proceedings instituted under Article 173, since the principle in question forms part of the Community legal order with the result that any failure to comply with it is an 'infringement of this Treaty or of any rule of law relating to its application' within the meaning of the article quoted.

Notes

(1) The principles of legal certainty and of legitimate expectations have been accepted by the case law of the CJEU, as can be seen in the *Töpfer* case.[200] The principle of legal certainty has been described as a 'basic principle' of the legal order of the EU.[201]

(2) In the EU legal system, the revocation of lawful acts is in principle prohibited.[202] With regard instead to unlawful acts, their revocation with retroactive effect is possible provided that the revocation occurs within a reasonable time frame and the legitimate expectations of the individuals are adequately balanced with the public interest in the maintenance of legality of EU law.[203]

(3) As in the national legal systems, a distinction is made in EU law between actual and apparent retroactivity. Actual retroactivity concerns situations in which a rule governs events which have already been concluded. These situations are in principle prohibited under EU law,[204] unless 'the purpose to be attained so requires and the legitimate expectations of the persons concerned are properly respected'.[205] In other words, actual retroactivity will be allowed when this is necessary to achieve a public interest and when this public interest overrides the private interest in the maintenance of the situation. Furthermore, actual retroactivity will be allowed when it is capable of placing the person concerned in a more favourable position.[206] Apparent retroactivity, on the other hand, concerns situations in which a rule governs events which originated in the past but have not yet definitively been concluded. These situations were considered worthy of protection by the CJEU,[207] although legitimate expectations will

[200] See also Case 111/63 *Lemmerz-Werke v High Authority of the ECSC* ECLI:EU:C:1965:76, where the concept of protection of legitimate expectations was first discussed.

[201] See AG Roemer in Case 59/70 *Netherlands v Commission* ECLI:EU:C:1971:63. See also Schwarze (n 122 above) 871.

[202] See Joined Cases 7/56 and 3/57 to 7/57 *Algera and others v Common Assembly* ECLI:EU:C:1957:7.

[203] See, eg Case T-251/00 *Lagardère and Canal+ v Commission* ECLI:EU:T:2002:278.

[204] Case 98/78 *Racke v Hauptzollamt Mainz* ECLI:EU:C:1979:14, para 20.

[205] Case C-110/97 *Netherlands v Council* ECLI:EU:C:2001:620, para 151.

[206] Case T-7/99 *Medici Grimm v Council* ECLI:EU:T:2000:175, para 91.

[207] Case 74/74 *Comptoir national technique agricole v Commission* ECLI:EU:C:1976:84.

not be readily honoured if the change in legal circumstances was foreseeable.[208] In an area such as that of the common market, which is in need of frequent adjustments to meet its goals, European courts have considered that traders cannot entertain legitimate expectations in their legal situation to remain stable when the authorities have acted within the limits of their discretion.[209] Furthermore, no legitimate expectations can arise if there is the lack of a clear and explicit assurance on the part of the authority.[210] Finally, it should be noted that, as in cases of actual retroactivity, the CJEU will balance the legitimate interest of the claimant with the need to protect the public interest.[211]

6.5.B.6 COMPARATIVE REMARKS

Although the principles of legal certainty and of legitimate expectations have been applied by the Court of Justice for many decades and the EU courts have qualified the principle of legal certainty as a 'basic principle' of the legal order of the EU,[212] these principles are not fully recognised or applied in all the other legal systems discussed in this book.

Whilst both principles have been qualified as general legal principles for many years, and have been partly codified in Germany and the Netherlands, the situation is (at least partly) different in France and in England and Wales. In France, the principle of legitimate expectations is not recognised as a general principle. For a long time, this was also true for legal certainty. However, the European integration process enhanced the role of this principle, which is now also accepted in French case law in purely French cases.

Whilst legal certainty has been inherent in the common law as part of the rule of law principle,[213] the principle of legitimate expectations was not widely accepted until recently. The courts began by accepting the concept of procedural legitimate expectation, whereas the development of the principle of substantive legitimate expectation has only been seriously developed by the courts over the past 20 years.

In detail, the conditions for accepting a claim based on legitimate expectations differ between the legal systems, but always comprise a balance of the legitimate interest of the claimant with the need to protect the public interest. Dutch and German law seem the only legal systems which accept, under certain conditions, a *contra legem* application

[208] Case 78/77 *Lührs v Commission* ECLI:EU:C:1978:20, para 6; Case C-350/88 *Delacre and others v Commission* ECLI:EU:C:1990:71.

[209] Joined Cases T-64/01 and T-65/01 *Afrikanische Frucht-Compagnie v Council* ECLI:EU:T:2004:37, para 83; Case 230/78 *Eridania v Minister of Agriculture and Forestry* ECLI:EU:C:1979:216, para 21.

[210] Case T-347/03 *Branco v Commission* ECLI:EU:T:2005:265.

[211] Case 84/78 *Tomadini v Amministrazione delle Finanze dello Stato* ECLI:EU:C:1979:129, para 20.

[212] See AG Roemer in *Netherlands v Commission* (n 201 above). See also Schwarze (n 122 above) 871.

[213] See, eg *Anufrijeva* (n 191 above) (claimant must have proper notice of an administrative decision before it may produce legal effects); see also *L* (n 191 above) (Secretary of State could not rely on a provision in legislation prior to its proper publication).

of the principle of legitimate expectations. Even expectations which were created *contra legem* (ultra vires, as English lawyers would say) may, under certain conditions, create legitimate expectations. This is not possible in the EU, France or England and Wales. If EU law is applied by national authorities, then, due to the principle of effectiveness of EU law, a *contra legem* application is also forbidden in Germany and in the Netherlands, even in cases where, if they were purely national, this would have been accepted. In such cases, the Dutch courts interpret Dutch law in such a way as to reach a result that is consistent with EU law. This is a clear example of the Europeanisation of Dutch law.

As far as changes in legislation are concerned, one has to distinguish between actual and apparent retroactivity. Actual retroactivity concerns situations in which a rule retroactively governs events which have already been concluded. These situations are prohibited in principle in all legal systems and are only allowed in some under very limited conditions. In cases of apparent retroactivity, in which a rule governs events which originated in the past but have not yet definitively been concluded, the room for changes in the legal regime is much broader.

6.5.C EQUALITY

The equality principle is one of the oldest democratic principles and is firmly rooted in all of the legal systems analysed in this book.[214] As the principle is dependent on what is regarded as equal, the principle is dependent on societal views and is thus a rather dynamic principle. A question which has to be addressed with regard to the different legal systems concerns the level of judicial scrutiny.

6.5.C.1 FRANCE

Conseil d'État, 9 March 1951[215] **6.36 (FR)**

Society of Concerts of the Conservatory v President of the Council of Ministers

EQUALITY PRINCIPLE

Société des concerts du conservatoire

The administrative authority has to comply with the equality principle when regulating access to public services.

Facts: A sanction was inflicted on two members of the Society of Concerts of the Conservatory. Consequently, the broadcasting public authority decided to suspend any radio broadcasts of the concerts given by the Society.

[214] Schwarze (n 122 above) 545 ff.
[215] N° 92004.

The Society was thereby temporarily banned from public service broadcasting, whereas other philharmonic societies were broadcasted by the public service.

Held: The administrative decision was annulled and damages were granted.

Judgment: Considering that, by imposing on the applicant company a measure of exclusion for reason of related incidents without any reason stemming from the general interest justifying this decision, the administration of the French radio broadcast has made use of its powers for a different purpose than the one for which they are conferred and has disregarded the principle of equality which governs the functioning of public services and according to which the applicant company, treated previously as the other large philharmonic companies, could be called, where appropriate, to contribute to the emissions of radio broadcasting; considering that this fault (*faute*) establishes the liability of the state; considering that, in view of the loss established by the elements brought forward by the applicant company, a fair assessment of the circumstances of the case will be made by convicting the State to pay the Society of Concerts of the Conservatory 50,000 francs with interest at the statutory rates from 24 February 1947, which is the date of the receipt of the application for monetary damages by the President of the Council of Ministers.

Note

The equality principle is a general principle of law in France and, as part of the Déclaration des droits de l'homme et du citoyen (Declaration of Rights of Man and of the Citizen), it is also accepted as a part of the modern French constitution by inclusion in the preamble.[216] It applies to administrative acts as well as to the legislature. In substance, the courts scrutinise whether like cases are treated equally and unequal situations are treated unequally, and whether this can be justified by general interests. The case law of the Council of State has shaped the equality principle in different areas of law, such as the equality of the genders and equality before public charges (*égalité devant les charges publiques*).

6.5.C.2 GERMANY

Grundgesetz **6.37 (DE)**

Article 3 (1) All persons shall be equal before the law.

(2) Men and women shall have equal rights. The state shall promote the actual implementation of equal rights for women and men and take steps to eliminate the disadvantages that now exist.

(3) No person shall be favoured or disfavoured because of sex, descent, race, language, homeland and origin, faith, or religious or political opinions. No person shall be disfavoured because of disability.

[216] Schwarze (n 122 above) 556–57.

Bundesverfassungsgericht, 21 June 2011[217] **6.38 (DE)**

EQUALITY PRINCIPLE

Mediziner-BAföG

Depending on the object of regulation and the distinguishing features, the general principle of equality leads to different levels of judicial scrutiny, varying from the loose test of arbitrariness to the strict proportionality test. The less the individual can influence the distinguishing characteristics or the more they approximate to the characteristics enumerated in Article 3(3) GG, the more intense the judicial review is.

Facts: Educational support according to the Bundesausbildungsförderungsgesetz (Federal Training Aid Act, BAföG), which is dependent on individual need, is granted to university students in the form of an interest-free loan. According to §18b BAföG, the loan could be partly waived upon the successful completion of studies. According to §18b(3) BAföG, 5,000 DM of the loan would be remitted if the student successfully completed his degree within a time period of at least four months before expiry of the maximum support term (large partial remission); if the time period amounted to only two months, 2,000 DM would be remitted (small partial remission). However, after the German reunification, it was temporarily objectively impossible for medical students in the new federal states (of the former East Germany) to achieve a large partial remission, as the minimum duration of the medical studies were almost as long as the time period for the maximum support term. In other study programmes, there was no minimum duration of study or the maximum support term was fixed in such a way that the completion of the programme within four months before the end of the maximum support term remained possible.

Held: The first Senate of the German Constitutional Court decided that §18b(3) BAföG was incompatible with the general principle of equality (Article 3(1) of the Grundgesetz), as far as it was objectively impossible for students to receive the large partial remission.

Judgment: 63. Pursuant to Article 3(1) GG, the general principle of equality requires the legislator to treat equally what is essentially equal and to treat unequally what is essentially unequal … This is true for unequal burdens as well as for unequal privileges … Inequitable exclusion from a privilege which is granted to one group of people, but which is withheld from others, is also forbidden …

64. The general principle of equality leads to, depending on the object of regulation and the distinguishing features, different limits for the legislator. Those limits can reach from the loosened test of arbitrariness to the strict requirements of proportionality … Differentiations always require a justification through substantive reasons, which are appropriate with regard to the goal of the differentiation and with regard to the extent of the different treatment. Article 3(1) Grundgesetz does not only state that the differentiation must relate to justified criteria, but also requires an inner connection between the factual differences and the distinguishing regulation, which proves to be a factually justifiable point of differentiation with sufficient weight. The principle of equality is violated if a group addressed by the norm or affected by the norm is treated differently in comparison to another group, although there are no differences of such nature or weight between both groups that could justify the different treatment …

65. There exists a standard of review oriented at the principle of proportionality. The limits of review cannot be defined abstractly, but can only be determined according to

[217] BVerfGE 129, 49.

the respective factual and regulatory sectors concerned. A stricter test must be applied when the differentiation relates to personal characteristics. The constitutional restraints intensify the more, the less the individual can influence those personal characteristics … or the more they approximate to the characteristics enumerated in Article 3(3) Grundgesetz (sex, descent, race, language, homeland and origin, faith, religious or political opinions, disability) …

Note

The principle of equality is firmly rooted in Article 3 of the Grundgesetz. With regard to judicial scrutiny in the application of the equality principle, there is some unsteadiness in the case law of the Constitutional Court with regard to the applicable test.[218] The case law of the Constitutional Court is of particular importance in this respect as it also influences and shapes the application of constitutional principles by the administrative courts.[219] At the outset, the Constitutional Court quashed arbitrary administrative decisions by applying a test which is similar to the reasonableness test in English law.[220] The Court later introduced a 'new formula' (*Neue Formel*) to test the conformity of administrative acts or legislation which affect fundamental freedoms of the addressee. This new formula increased the level of scrutiny and allows the courts to engage in a balancing process.[221] In the *Mediziner-BAföG* decision, the Constitutional Court emphasised that the judicial test for reviewing decisions in light of the equality principle is closely linked to the proportionality test. However, the level of scrutiny is dependent on the context of the case. In situations where the unequal treatment is based on criteria of human conduct and behaviour, judicial scrutiny may be less strict than where the criteria cannot be influenced by such conduct. Furthermore, the review is more intense where the criteria for the unequal treatment of two groups approximates to the characteristics enumerated in Article 3(3) of the Grundgesetz (sex, descent, race, language, homeland and origin, faith, religious or political opinions, disability).

[218] For a summary of the development of case law with regard to Art 3(1) GG, see U Kischel, in V Epping and C Hillgruber (eds), *Beck'scher Onlinekommentar Grundgesetz*, 27th edn (Munich, CH Beck, 2016) Art 3, para 28 ff.

[219] In Germany, the administrative courts play a vivid role in the protection of fundamental rights: see section 6.4.A.1 above.

[220] BVerfGE 1, 14, 52: 'The principle of equality is infringed if a sound reason for legal differentiation or equal treatment, resulting from the nature of things or which is otherwise objectively plausible, cannot be found, in short, if the provision must be described as arbitrary.'

[221] See, eg BVerfGE 55, 72, 88 f.

6.5.C.3 THE NETHERLANDS

Raad van State, 18 February 1997[222] **6.39 (NL)**

WHF Beurskens v Provincial Executive of Noord-Brabant

PRINCIPLE OF *ÉGALITÉ DEVANT LES CHARGES PUBLIQUES*

Beurskens

The principle of égalité devant les charges publiques *(equality before public charges) may constitute a basis for public liability and the award of damages.*

Facts: On 31 March 1993, the claimant (Beurskens) submitted an application to the provincial executive of the province of Noord-Brabant for compensation as defined in Article 24 of the Verordening grondwaterbeschermingsgebieden Provincie Noord-Brabant (Regulation on the groundwater protection areas in the province of Noord-Brabant), supplemented by a request for compensation based on the general principles of good administration. The provincial executive rejected the supplementary request because it considered that a right to compensation could not be based on any general principle of good administration. Beurskens challenged the decision before the Judicial Division of the Council of State.

Held: The Council of State declared itself incompetent to hear the case and forwarded the claim to the district court of 's Hertogenbosch.

Judgment: The Judicial Division further considers that the decision of the defendants on the supplementary application for compensation for damage allegedly suffered as a result of the designation of the area as a groundwater protection area, although it is not based on a specific legal basis, is to be regarded as a decision as defined in Article 1:3 AWB.

The competence to take a decision on an application for damages, insofar as the application is concerned with damage caused by the lawful application of a public law competence, is based on the legal principle of *'égalité devant les charges publiques'* (equality before public charges), which also underlies Article 3:4(2) AWB. On the basis of this principle, administrative authorities are obliged to compensate disproportionate damages – ie damages which go beyond the normal societal risk and constitute a burden for a limited group of citizens – caused in the legal relation between the authority and this group when exercising the public law competence.

Raad van State, 2 November 2016[223] **6.40 (NL)**

X v Mayor of Vlaardingen

PRINCIPLE OF EQUALITY; COMPETITIVE DISTRIBUTION OF LIMITED PERMITS

Vlaardingen

The principle of equality implies that administrative authorities, when distributing limited permits, should offer (potential) interested parties the opportunity to compete in respect of the available permits.

Facts: According to the Verordening Speelautomaten Vlaardingen (Regulation on games of chance of the Municipality of Vlaardingen), the number of permits for the exploitation of gambling halls was limited to one.

[222] ECLI:NL:RVS:1997:ZF2587.
[223] ECLI:NL:RVS:2016:2927.

The municipality thereby wanted to limit the number of gambling locations to prevent gambling addiction. By a decision of 19 December 2012, the mayor of Vlaardingen granted a permit to Hommerson. By a decision of 28 December 2012, the mayor refused the application for such a permit to the claimant as the only permit had already been granted to Hommerson. The claimant contested both decisions before the district court, but his claim was rejected. He appealed against this decision to the Judicial Division of the Council of State.

Held: The appeal was upheld and the judgment of the district court as well as the decision of the Mayor were annulled.

Judgment: 8. The Judicial Division shares the opinion of the Advocate General that in Dutch law a legal norm exists which implies that administrative authorities, when distributing limited permits, should offer (potential) interested parties the opportunity to compete in respect of the available permit(s). This legal norm is based on the principle of equality which in this context aims at offering equal opportunities.

It flows from this legal norm that limited permits in principle cannot be granted indefinitely, but only temporarily. Granting the permit indefinitely would disproportionately favour the permit holder, as it would be virtually impossible for a new operator to join the market.

The Judicial Division shares the opinion of the Advocate General that the administrative authorities, in order to grant equal opportunities, should ensure an adequate level of transparency as regards the availability of the limited permits, the procedure for distribution, the application time limit and the criteria applicable. In this respect, the authority should publicly provide, in a way that would enable potential parties to inform themselves, clear information about these aspects in a timely manner and before the start of the application process.

Note

(1) Although Article 1 of the Dutch constitution codifies the equality principle, this norm does not play a significant role in judicial practice. When relying on the equality principle, claimants refer to equality as a general principle of administrative law rather than to Article 1 of the Dutch constitution. However, relying on the equality principle is not often successful,[224] mainly because the administration can justify unequal treatment in most cases as the circumstances in different cases are in general not completely equal.[225] Moreover, if the authority made an error when applying the law and someone benefited from that error, another person cannot rely on the equality principle to gain the same benefits.

(2) Nevertheless, two applications of the principle deserve attention. First, a peculiarity of Dutch law, taken over from French law, is the application of the principle of *égalité devant les charges publiques*, which is called by its French name and is applied frequently.[226] As appears from the case of *Beurskens*, it first offers an (unwritten) legal basis for decisions about financial compensation for lawful administrative action.

[224] ECLI:NL:RVS:2011:BP2786; ECLI:NL:RVS:2005:AU2637.
[225] ECLI:NL:RVS:2011:BP2786.
[226] See ECLI:NL:CRVB:1994:ZB0806; ECLI:NL:RVS:1997:ZF2587.

Furthermore, the principle provides for a right or entitlement to compensation of disproportionate damages, ie damages which go beyond the normal societal risk and constitute a disproportionate burden for a specific and limited group of citizens.[227]

(3) Secondly, as the Judicial Division of the Council of State clarified in the *Vlaardingen* case, the principle of equality implies that administrative authorities, when distributing limited permits, should offer (potential) parties the opportunity to compete in respect of the available permit(s), as there may be more candidates than permits. This application of the equality principle also implies that limited permits in principle cannot be granted indefinitely, but only temporarily. Moreover, to grant equal opportunities to all possible candidates, the authority is under an obligation to ensure an adequate level of transparency. The judgment of the Council of State is inspired by the case law of the CJEU in cases such as *Betfair* and *Trijber & Harmsen*.[228] In these cases, the CJEU based the Member States' obligation to ensure effective competition when distributing limited services permits on the freedom of establishment and services (Articles 49 and 56 TFEU) in conjunction with the EU principle of equality, or on the Services Directive 2006/123/EC, which codifies the above-mentioned case law.[229] However, in the judgment of the Council of State, the obligation to ensure competition is extended to purely internal situations in which EU law is not applicable and to all limited permits, ie also to permits which are not concerned with services. This extensive understanding is based on the Dutch principle of equality.

6.5.C.4 ENGLAND AND WALES

Supreme Court, 19 October 2016[230] **6.41 (EW)**

R (Johnson) v Secretary of State for the Home Department

ARTICLE 14 ECHR; EQUALITY PRINCIPLE

Johnson

Administrative decisions taken contrary to the equality principle contained in Article 14 ECHR are unlawful and legislative provisions contrary to the same principle can be subject to a declaration of incompatibility.

Facts: The claimant in this case was the son of a Jamaican mother and English father who were unmarried. Under the provisions of the relevant nationality legislation at the time, the claimant was thus not entitled to

[227] For more details, see Chapter 11, section 11.4.A.

[228] Case C-203/08 *Sporting exchange v Minister of Justice* ECLI:EU:C:2010:307; Joined Cases C-340/14 and 341/14 *Trijber & Harmsen v Mayor of Amsterdam* ECLI:EU:C:2015:641.

[229] Directive 2006/123/EC of the European Parliament and of the Council of 12 December 2006 on services in the internal market [2006] OJ L376/36.

[230] [2016] UKSC 56, [2017] AC 365.

British citizenship, though he would have been had his mother, rather than his father, been a British national or if his parents had been married, whether before or after he was born. In 2008, the claimant was convicted of manslaughter and in 2011 the Secretary of State informed the claimant that upon completion of his imprisonment for the offence he would be deported to Jamaica under the provisions of section 32(5) of the Borders Act 2007. The claimant commenced judicial review proceedings and the Secretary of State then certified that the claimant's claim was clearly unfounded and thus that he had no right of appeal within the UK against the decision. The core of the claimant's claim was that the decision to deport him and the failure to grant him citizenship because his parents were unmarried constituted discrimination for the purposes of Article 14 ECHR when read alongside Article 8 ECHR.

Held: The Supreme Court held that the provisions of nationality law denying citizenship to individuals in the claimant's position were contrary to Articles 8 and 14 of the ECHR and issued a declaration of incompatibility accordingly. The court also held that the Secretary of State's certification of the claimant's claim as being clearly unfounded was unlawful and quashed that decision.

Judgment: Lady Hale: 23. The issue, therefore, is whether an appeal against the decision that section 32(5) of the 2007 Act applies to the appellant, on the basis that to deport the appellant now would be a breach of the UK's obligations under the Human Rights Convention, is clearly unfounded. That depends upon (1) whether it is sufficiently within the ambit of article 8 of the Convention to bring into play the prohibition of discrimination in the enjoyment of the Convention rights in article 14; (2) whether the discrimination had a 'one off effect' at birth or whether it has continuing consequences which may amount to a present violation of the Convention rights; and (3) whether such discriminatory effect can be justified. The discrimination complained of in this case is that he is liable to deportation whereas he would not be if (a) his mother and father had been married to one another at the time of his birth; (b) his mother and father had been married to one another at any time after his birth; (c) his mother had been British and his father Jamaican; or (d) an application had been made to register him as a citizen before he was 18.

Article 8

24. Although article 15.1 of the Universal Declaration of Human Rights says that 'Everyone has the right to a nationality', the European Convention says nothing about the right to a nationality. ...

25. In *Genovese v Malta* (2014) 58 EHRR 25, the complaint was that the denial of Maltese citizenship to the son of a British mother and a Maltese father who were not married to one another was in breach of article 14 read with article 8. ... Malta was not obliged to recognise the right to citizenship by descent, but as it did so, it had to ensure that the right was secured without discrimination. The discrimination could not be justified by the argument that 'motherhood is certain, whereas fatherhood is not': in that case, paternity had been established scientifically and in legal proceedings. ...

27. It is clear, therefore, that the denial of citizenship, having such an important effect upon a person's social identity, is sufficiently within the ambit of article 8 to trigger the application of the prohibition of discrimination in article 14. ...

Article 14

...

30. As has been said many times, 'For the purpose of article 14, a difference in treatment is discriminatory if it has no objective and reasonable justification, that is, if it does not pursue a legitimate aim or if there is not a reasonable relationship of proportionality between the means employed and the aim sought to be realised' (see, for example, *Inze v Austria* (1988) 10 EHRR 394, para 41; *Genovese v Malta*, para 43). It is also clear that birth

outside wedlock falls within the class of 'suspect' grounds, where 'very weighty reasons' are required to justify discrimination. ...

34. But in this case what needs to be justified is the current liability of the appellant, and others whose parents were not married to one another when they were born or at any time thereafter, to be deported when they would not be so liable had their parents been married to one another at any time after their birth. That is a present distinction which is based solely on the accident of birth outside wedlock, for which the appellant is not responsible, and no justification has been suggested for it. It is impossible to say that his claim that Exception 1 applies, based on article 14 read with article 8, is 'clearly unfounded'.

Conclusion

35. It follows that I would allow this appeal and quash the Secretary of State's certificate. The consequence, as I understand it, is that his appeal against the Secretary of State's decision of 23 November 2012 must be allowed to proceed and, for the reasons given earlier, is certain to succeed.

Notes

(1) In England and Wales, the principle of formal equality – the idea that all individuals, whether citizens or non-citizens, can have access to the courts in judicial review, where they meet the requirements in the procedural bars – is a fundamental principle.

(2) However, substantive equality is rather addressed in relation to the ultra vires doctrine, ie when administrative authorities exceed the limits of the powers which were conferred upon them by statute.[231] Moreover, there are a number of cases which deal with a more substantive concept of equality, predominantly drawn from EU law. There are cases where judicial review has been successfully predicated on non-discrimination provisions as between men and women in the EU Treaties,[232] and there are also many cases predicated on the free movement provisions of the Treaty.[233] The Equality Act 2010 implements EU non-discrimination law in the UK and the duties therein extend to the public sector. There seems to be little doubt that any measure which offends the principle of equality (whether in the free movement sense or in the sense of discrimination on personal or group characteristics) would be considered unlawful by the English courts in a judicial review claim. In addition to these developments, the increasing importance of claims for judicial review citing a breach of Article 14 of the ECHR bringing a further dimension to claims relating to the equality principle can also be observed.

[231] Schwarzc (n 122 above) 559.

[232] See eg *R v Secretary of State for Employment, ex parte Seymour Smith* [1999] 2 AC 554 (HL).

[233] See eg Case C-5/94 *R v Ministry of Agriculture, Fisheries and Food, ex parte Hedley Lomas (Ireland) Ltd* ECLI:EU:C:1996:205; *R (International Transport Roth GmbH) v Secretary of State for the Home Department* [2002] EWCA Civ 158, [2003] QB 728.

6.5.C.5 THE EUROPEAN UNION

Joined Cases 117/76 and 16/77, 19 October 1977[234] **6.42 (EU)**

Albert Ruckdeschel & Co and Others v Hauptzollamt Hamburg St Annen

EQUALITY PRINCIPLE; GENERAL PRINCIPLES OF EU LAW

St Annen

The general principle of equality is one of the fundamental principles of EU law.

Facts: On 8 November 1976 and 18 January 1977, the Finanzgericht Hamburg referred to the Court of Justice two questions concerning the validity of provisions of regulations relating to production refunds.

Held: The Court of Justice ruled that the provisions of the challenged regulations were incompatible with the principle of equality insofar as they provided for different treatments in respect of production refunds.

Judgment: The second subparagraph of article 40(3) of the Treaty provides that the common organization of agricultural markets 'shall exclude any discrimination between producers or consumers within the community'. Whilst this wording undoubtedly prohibits any discrimination between producers of the same product it does not refer in such clear terms to the relationship between different industrial or trade sectors in the sphere of processed agricultural products. This does not alter the fact that the prohibition of discrimination laid down in the aforesaid provision is merely a specific enunciation of the general principle of equality which is one of the fundamental principles of community law. This principle requires that similar situations shall not be treated differently unless differentiation is objectively justified.

Note

The equality principle is firmly rooted in many Treaty provisions (eg Articles 2, 4 and 9 TEU, Articles 10, 18, 36, 37, 65 and 157 TFEU), as well as in acts of secondary legislation. Beyond that, the CJEU has accepted the equality principle as one of the 'fundamental principles' of EU law and thus also applies it in areas where no explicit equality provision can be found.[235]

6.5.C.6 COMPARATIVE REMARKS

The equality principle is recognised in all legal systems. In most of them, it has constitutional status. In France and the Netherlands, the principle of *égalité devant les charges publiques* serves as an (unwritten) legal basis for decisions about financial compensation

[234] ECLI:EU:C:1977:160.

[235] For a brief analysis of the CJEU case law on the equality principle, see Schwarze (n 122 above) 625 ff.

for lawful administrative action. With regard to the level of scrutiny of the equality principle by the courts, England and Wales differs considerably from the other analysed legal systems. Whereas in Germany, France and the EU, the intensity of review is rather high, the level of scrutiny is traditionally much lower in the England and Wales. However, much like in other areas, the Europeanisation process has led to an increase in the intensity of review.

6.5.D COMPARATIVE REMARKS

The role of principles in administrative law is particularly interesting with regard to the separation of powers between the courts and the legislative branch. By forming general principles of law without statutory embedding, the courts converge into the field of law-making.[236] Therefore, general principles traditionally play a weaker role in judicial review in England and Wales, where parliamentary sovereignty finds the highest recognition. In Germany, most general principles can be deduced from the constitution or statutory law, and are only shaped through case law. In the Netherlands, many principles can be found in the Algemene Wet Bestuursrecht (General Administrative Law Act). However, the courts also developed general principles independently. Many general administrative principles have an important function in the protection of human rights, as, unlike in Germany, the constitutional guarantees are rarely applied in administrative law cases. In the French and European legal systems, case law plays a more important role in the creation of principles of administrative law. The CJEU furthermore has been strongly influenced by the law of the Member States in the creation of the general principles.

With regard to the principles of proportionality, legal certainty, legitimate expectations and equality that have been analysed, it can be seen that, on the surface, all the legal systems studied here now provide for these principles in judicial review of administrative action (at least where EU law is at stake). The greatest differences between the analysed legal systems occur with regard to legal certainty and legitimate expectations, which have traditionally not been fully recognised by French law. EU law has had strong harmonising effects on the recognition of general principles of administrative law in the various national legal systems. The scope and the application of the different principles in court, however, differ considerably. Furthermore, the intensity of review with regard to the different principles is far from uniform.

6.6 JUDICIAL REVIEW AND THE BREACH OF FORMALITIES

All legal systems within the European law area provide procedural guarantees in administrative decision-making in order to ensure legitimacy, a fair process and

[236] R Drago, 'The General Principles of the Law in the jurisprudence of the French Conseil d'Etat' (1962) 11 *American University Law Review* 126, 132.

rationality.[237] Well-known procedural safeguards include the right to an oral hearing, the obligation of the administration to give reasons for its decisions, the rules on competence of public authorities, anti-bias provisions, the consultation of other public bodies and non-judicial redress mechanisms. Although there are vast differences concerning the rigidity of the legal consequences of procedural errors in administrative law, there is no legal system in which every procedural deficiency leads to the invalidity of administrative action, nor is there a legal regime where the breaches of procedural provisions are always ignored.[238] The following comparative analysis will first discuss the extent to which it is possible to heal procedural errors by rectification. Secondly, it will address the issue of the circumstances under which procedural errors will not lead to annulment.

6.6.A SYSTEMS WITH A STRONG PROTECTION OF PROCEDURE AND FORMALITIES

6.6.A.1 ENGLAND AND WALES

Court of Appeal (Civil Division), 9 November 1990[239] **6.43 (EW)**

Anderson v Army Board of the Defence Council, ex parte Anderson

RIGHT TO BE HEARD

Anderson

There must be a proper hearing of a complaint in the sense that the public authority must consider all the relevant evidence and contentions before reaching its conclusions.

Facts: A was a black soldier who faced physical and verbal abuse from his fellow soldiers due to his race. A went absent without leave as a result of it and complained about the abuse that he had received. The complaint was first investigated by A's commanding officer, who rejected the complaint. A then escalated the matter to the Army Board of the Defence Council, which had the power to determine complaints provided that any two of its members acted in tandem. The members examined the case on the papers and rejected A's complaint. A claimed judicial review of the decision, arguing that the Board should have met in person; that it should have allowed A access to all documentation and allowed him to make representations in relation to the evidence; and also that there should have been an oral hearing in his case.

[237] For a comparative perspective on the various functions of administrative procedure, see J Barnes, 'Towards a Third Generation of Administrative Procedure' in Rose-Ackerman and Lindseth (n 13 above) 336, 340; H Pünder, 'Administrative Procedure – Mere Facilitator of Material Law versus Cooperative Realization of Common Welfare' in Pünder and Waldhoff (n 89 above) 240 ff; Pünder (n 8 above).

[238] R Grote, 'Procedural Deficiencies in Administrative Law: A Comparative Analysis' (2002) 18 *South African Journal on Human Rights* 475 ff.

[239] [1992] QB 169 (CA).

Held: The decision was annulled.

Judgment: Taylor LJ: What procedural requirements are necessary to achieve fairness when the Army Board considers a complaint of this kind? ... The Army Board as the forum of last resort, dealing with an individual's fundamental statutory rights, must by its procedures achieve a high standard of fairness. I would list the principles as follows.

(1) There must be a proper hearing of the complaint in the sense that the board must consider, as a single adjudicating body, all the relevant evidence and contentions before reaching its conclusions. This means, in my view, that the members of the board must meet. ...

(2) The hearing does not necessarily have to be an oral hearing in all cases. There is ample authority that decision-making bodies other than courts and bodies whose procedures are laid down by statute, are masters of their own procedure. Provided that they achieve the degree of fairness appropriate to their task it is for them to decide how they will proceed and there is no rule that fairness always requires an oral hearing .... Whether an oral hearing is necessary will depend upon the subject matter and circumstances of the particular case and upon the nature of the decision to be made. It will also depend upon whether there are substantial issues of fact which cannot be satisfactorily resolved on the available written evidence. This does not mean that whenever there is a conflict of evidence in the statements taken, an oral hearing must be held to resolve it. Sometimes such a conflict can be resolved merely by the inherent unlikelihood of one version or the other. ... Even when such a hearing is necessary, it may only require one or two witnesses to be called and cross-examined.

... The Quartermaster General said: 'Elements of the complaint can be dismissed on technical grounds. There is no provision for disclosure of documentation or for an oral hearing in a complaint of this nature.' Those observations suggest that the board fettered its discretion and failed to consider the request for an oral hearing in the present case on its own merits.

(3) The opportunity to have the evidence tested by cross-examination is again within the Army Board's discretion. ...

(4) Whether oral or not, there must be what amounts to a hearing of any complaint under the Act of 1976. This means that the Army Board must have such a complaint investigated, consider all the material gathered in the investigation, give the complainant an opportunity to respond to it and consider his response.

But what is the board obliged to disclose to the complainant to obtain his response? Is it sufficient to indicate the gist of any material adverse to his case or should he be shown all the material seen by the board? ... Because of the nature of the Army's Board's function pursuant to the Race Relations Act 1976, already analysed above, I consider that a soldier complainant under that Act should be shown all the material seen by the board, apart from any documents for which public interest immunity can properly be claimed.

... In my judgment the errors of law and procedure in their handling of this complaint when viewed in the aggregate are such as requires the court to quash their decision. Accordingly, I would grant an order of certiorari. I conceive it to be unnecessary in those circumstances to grant an order of mandamus, since I am confident that the complaint will be reheard by a freshly constituted Army Board.

Supreme Court, 29 October 2014[240] **6.44 (EW)**

Moseley v Haringey London Borough Council

RIGHT TO CONSULTATION

Moseley

The duty to consult can follow from statutory law, but may also result from the general common law duty to act fairly.

Facts: M was a single mother who had been in receipt of full council tax benefit until 1 April 2013, when H's council tax reduction scheme came into effect. In its 2010 spending review, the central government had announced that, as part of its programme for the reduction of the national deficit, it would from April 2013 transfer to each local authority the responsibility for making and operating a scheme for providing relief from council tax; it was said that in 2013–2014 the reimbursement by the central government to each local authority in respect of whatever it provided by way of relief from council tax would be fixed at about 90 per cent of the amount which the government would have paid in the previous year. H's consultation document, which was sent to 36,000 households, contained no reference to options for meeting that shortfall other than by a reduction in relief from council tax (the other options being increasing council tax, reducing the funding of H's services and applying its deployable reserves of capital).

Held: The council's failure to consult over the alternatives to its favoured proposal rendered the consultation process ineffective and thus unlawful.

Judgment: Lord Wilson: A public authority's duty to consult those interested before taking a decision can arise in a variety of ways. Most commonly, as here, the duty is generated by statute. Not infrequently, however, it is generated by the duty cast by the common law upon a public authority to act fairly. The search for the demands of fairness in this context is often illumined by the doctrine of legitimate expectation; .... But irrespective of how the duty to consult has been generated, that same common law duty of procedural fairness will inform the manner in which the consultation should be conducted.

... First, the requirement 'is liable to result in better decisions, by ensuring that the decision-maker receives all relevant information and that it is properly tested' (para 67). Second, it avoids 'the sense of injustice which the person who is the subject of the decision will otherwise feel' (para 68). Such are two valuable practical consequences of fair consultation. But underlying it is also a third purpose, reflective of the democratic principle at the heart of our society. This third purpose is particularly relevant in a case like the present, in which the question was not 'Yes or no, should we close this particular care home, this particular school etc?' It was 'Required, as we are, to make a taxation-related scheme for application to all the inhabitants of our Borough, should we make one in the terms which we here propose?' ...

Two further general points emerge from the authorities. First, the degree of specificity with which, in fairness, the public authority should conduct its consultation exercise may be influenced by the identity of those whom it is consulting. ... 'the demands of fairness

240 [2014] UKSC 56, [2014] 1 WLR 3947.

are likely to be somewhat higher when an authority contemplates depriving someone of an existing benefit or advantage than when the claimant is a bare applicant for a future benefit'.

Sometimes, particularly when statute does not limit the subject of the requisite consultation to the preferred option, fairness will require that interested persons be consulted not only upon the preferred option but also upon arguable yet discarded alternative options. …

But, even when the subject of the requisite consultation is limited to the preferred option, fairness may nevertheless require passing reference to be made to arguable yet discarded alternative options. …

Notes

(1) The handling of procedural guarantees in England and Wales differs considerably from the continental approach. In principle, any violation of procedural requirements renders the decision ultra vires and void. However, there are fewer procedural requirements acknowledged than, for example, in France and Germany, and their scope may vary in different contexts. Furthermore, a correction of procedural errors in the course of court proceedings is possible and is at the discretion of the court.[241] Accordingly, the focus of judicial review lies on the issue of whether a procedural error occurred at all, rather than which legal consequences such an error creates.

(2) Concerning the possibility to bypass procedural errors, Section 31(2A) of the Senior Courts Act 1981 requires the court to refuse a remedy in a case where it considers that it is highly likely that the decision taken by the public authority would not have been substantially different had the error not been made. This legislative requirement exists in addition to the broader discretion enjoyed by the courts over the granting of a remedy, whereby in some circumstances an administrative decision is not quashed if the procedural flaw had no consequence for the merits of the decision.[242]

(3) Sources of formal requirements are parliamentary statutes as well as the established case law concerning the principles of 'natural justice'. The principle of natural justice comprises two elemental rules of fair procedure, namely that no one may be judge in his own case (*nemo judex in causa sua*) and the right to be heard (*audi alteram partem*).[243] Apart from that, there is no general act of administrative procedure with a set of formal requirements in English law, but statutory procedural requirements can only be found in special fields of administrative law.[244] Thus, there is no general obligation to give reasons for administrative action unless it is required specifically by

[241] *cf Calvin v Carr* [1980] AC 574 (HL).

[242] *cf Malloch v Aberdeen Corp (No 1)* [1971] 1 WLR 1578 (HL); *Glynn v Keele University* [1971] 1 WLR 487 (QB); more recently, *Walton v Scottish Ministers* [2012] UKSC 44, [2013] 1 CMLR 28; see further Chapter 7, section 7.2.B.3.

[243] E Pircher-Eschig and P Eschig, 'Introduction to Administrative Law in England and Wales' in Heidinger and Hubalek (n 29 above) 71, 75 ff.

[244] For a brief overview of the administrative procedural law, see Pünder (n 8 above) 955 ff.

statute, although the common law has imposed a duty to give reasons in many cases where this may be necessary to ensure fairness[245] or to facilitate judicial review of administrative action.[246]

6.6.A.2 THE NETHERLANDS

Algemene Wet Bestuursrecht **6.45 (NL)**

Article 6:22 A body deciding on an intra-administrative objection or a claim for judicial review (*beroep*) may uphold the challenged decision despite the fact that a written or unwritten rule of law or a general principle has been violated, if it is plausible that the parties concerned do not thereby incur any disadvantages.

Raad van State, 11 February 2015[247] **6.46 (NL)**

Claimants v Municipal Council of Maastricht

CONSEQUENCES OF PROCEDURAL ERRORS

Maastricht

If the procedural requirement to investigate and weigh all relevant interests was violated, but the procedural error has not affected the parties concerned, the error may be bypassed and the administrative decision is upheld.

Facts: On 18 February 2014, the municipal council of the municipality of Maastricht established the spatial plan 'Tramline Flanders – Maastricht'. Several claimants contested the plan before the Judicial Division of the Council of State on multiple grounds. One of the grounds was the low-frequency noise which would allegedly be caused by the planned tramline. From the facts of the case, it was clear that the municipal council of Maastricht had not conducted any research in respect of this noise. While the case was pending before the Council of State, such research was conducted and resulted in a report concerning vibration.

Held: The Council of State upheld the spatial plan.

Judgment: 10.6. The Judicial Division considers that, when establishing the spatial plan, no research was conducted in respect of the possible occurrence of low-frequency noise as a result of the tramline. Insofar the plan has not been prepared with due care. Hence, the Council has violated Article 3:2 AWB …

10.8. In respect of the possible nuisance caused by low-frequency noise, the updated vibration report provides for a prognosis. Moreover, the report describes the measures to be taken to prevent these problems. Therefore, the council may have reasonably

245 See eg *Doody v Home Secretary* [1994] 1 AC 531.

246 See eg *R (On the Application of Farrakhan) v Secretary of State for the Home Department* [2002] EWCA Civ 606, [2002] QB 1391. For a detailed overview of the development of the duty to give reasons in English law, see M Elliott 'Has the Common Law Duty to Give Reasons Come of Age Yet?' (2011) *Public Law* 56.

247 ECLI:NL:RVS:2015:353.

come to the decision that noise nuisance caused by low-frequency noise will be reduced sufficiently. …

As research to low-frequency noise has been conducted and the claimants … have had the opportunity to react on it, the Judicial Division decides to bypass the error established in point 10.6, by applying Article 6:22 AWB. The Judicial Division considers that it is plausible that other parties concerned are not affected by the foregoing [bypass of the defect], as the spatial plan is not altered by it.

Notes

(1) The Dutch approach to judicial review of breaches of formalities used to be quite similar to the English model. Thus, until the first few years of the new millennium, breaches of procedural norms generally resulted in quashing the decision and referring the case back to the administrative authority to take a new decision after repairing the error. The violation of the need to investigate and weigh all relevant interests (Article 3:4 AWB) and the need to properly motivate decisions (Article 3:46 AWB) were often used by administrative courts as the basis to quash a decision and refer the case back to the administration.

(2) However, in the last ten years, the public concern to solve judicial disputes in a timely manner has led to a shift towards the continental approach. In 2012, Article 8:41a was added to the AWB (General Administrative Law Act), which obliges the judge to strive to decide disputes in a manner which is as definitive as possible. The shift is particularly visible in Article 6:22 AWB, as amended in 2012, which empowers the administrative courts to uphold a decision, despite an infringement of a legal rule or principle, if it is plausible that the infringement has not prejudiced the interests of any interested party. Therefore, procedural, but also material, errors, including errors in respect of the competence of the authority, may be bypassed by the courts if it is plausible that nobody's interests are harmed. Before 2012, this possibility was limited to procedural errors.

(3) In practice, Article 6:22 AWB is mainly used to bypass procedural errors, including quite serious ones, as is illustrated in the *Maastricht* case. In respect of material errors, the courts tend to use another remedy provided for by Article 8:72(3) AWB, namely the possibility to determine that the legal consequences of an annulled decision remain effective.[248] In that case, the court will annul the decision because of the material error, but uphold its legal consequences if it can be assumed that the error did not harm anybody's interests. The main reason to choose this remedy instead of Article 6:22 AWB is that, under the AWB, the annulment of a decision implies a statutory right to compensation of the court fee paid and of the costs of legal assistance. This right does not exist if the claim for judicial review is rejected after bypassing an error on the ground of Article 6:22 AWB.

(4) Correction of procedural errors is also possible in the Netherlands and it takes place mostly through the so-called 'administrative loop', as examined in depth in Chapter 7, section 7.2.B.5.

[248] This remedy is discussed at length in Chapter 7, section 7.2.B.5.

6.6.B SYSTEMS (TRADITIONALLY) DISTINGUISHING BETWEEN ESSENTIAL AND NON-ESSENTIAL PROCEDURAL REQUIREMENTS

6.6.B.1 FRANCE

Conseil d'État, 5 May 1944[249] **6.47 (FR)**

Dame veuve Trompier Gravier v Prefect of the Seine

RIGHT TO BE HEARD

Trompier Gravier

As a general principle of law, the rights of defence have to be respected in the administrative decision-making process.

Facts: The addressee was sanctioned by the administration without having been heard.

Held: The Council of State annulled the administrative sanction.

Judgment: Considering that it is established that the challenged decision, by which the prefect of the Seine withdrew lady widow Trompier-Gravier's authorisation to sell newspapers in a kiosk located on the boulevard Saint-Denis in Paris, was grounded on a fault (*faute*) which the claimant was responsible for; considering that, taking the nature of the withdrawal of the authorisation in the aforementioned circumstances into account and the severity of this sanction, such a measure could not legally be adopted without lady widow Trompier-Gravier having been given the opportunity to discuss the objections brought against her; considering that the applicant, who was not previously asked to present her defences, can validly argue that the challenged decision was made under irregular conditions by the prefect of the Seine and, therefore, is tainted by an abuse of power (*excès de pouvoir*).

Conseil d'État, 24 July 1981[250] **6.48 (FR)**

Belasri v Minister of the Interior

VIOLATION OF THE DUTY TO GIVE REASONS

Belasri

Where a statute requires that the reasons of a decision must be provided, it is unlawful to provide an exceptionally general statement of reasons.

Facts: An administrative decision of deportation was adopted towards Mr Belasri, based on general public order grounds.

Held: The Council of State annulled the decision.

Judgment: Considering that, according to the wording of Article 1 of the law of 11 July 1979, the 'decisions which restrict the exercise of public liberties, or, generally, constitute a measure of police' shall be motivated, and that Article 3 of the same law states that

[249] N° 69751.
[250] N° 31488.

'the reasons required by the present law must be written and must contain the statement of the considerations in law and in fact which constitute the basis of the decision'; considering that the challenged decision of the Minister of the Interior of 26 August 1980 which orders Mr Y … to leave the French territory, refers as a reason to the fact that 'Mr Y …. committed acts infringing the security of the people and (that) the presence of this foreigner on the French territory is of nature to jeopardize the public order'; considering that by failing to specify the elements of the action which are the basis of the contested police measure, the Minister of the Interior has not complied with the requirements of the law of 11 July 1979. …

Conseil d'État, 23 December 2011[251] **6.49 (FR)**

Danthony v Prime Minister

CONSEQUENCES OF PROCEDURAL ERRORS

Danthony

Where a procedural error occurred, the decision taken is only considered illegal if the evidence proves that the procedural error was likely to have an influence on the decision taken or that it deprived the interested parties of a safeguard.

Facts: The challenged administrative decision was procedurally erroneous because a public body had not been consulted, even though its consultation was compulsory by law.

Held: The Council of State annulled the administrative decision because the infringement of procedural requirements was deemed to have consequences on the content of the decision. However, due to the significant consequences of the annulment of the decision, the court postponed the annulment for six months.

Judgment: Considering that these provisions provide, with regard to irregularities which are committed during the consultation of a body, a rule which takes inspiration from the principle according to which, although administrative measures must be taken according to the forms and in compliance with the procedures laid down by the laws and the regulations, an error affecting the course of a prior administrative procedure, followed on a mandatory or optional basis, may affect the lawfulness of the decision taken only if it results from the elements of the case file that it was likely, in this case, to have an influence on the decision taken or that it deprived the interested parties of a safeguard; …

Conseil d'État, 27 February 2015[252] **6.50 (FR)**

Minister of the Interior – Communauté Urbaine de Lyon v Association Carton Rouge

CONSEQUENCES OF PROCEDURAL ERRORS

Communauté Urbaine de Lyon

Infringement of formal requirements does not lead to the annulment of a decision if the infringement did not have influence on the outcome.

Facts: In order to develop the area surrounding a stadium, the prefect of Lyon had adopted three administrative decisions (*arrêté*) declaring the 'public utility' of the projects. Due to the importance of the projects,

[251] N° 335033.
[252] N° 382502.

the decisions had to fulfil certain procedural requirements, such as an environmental impact assessment. A group of citizens challenged the administrative decisions, and the Court of Appeal of Lyon annulled the decisions. The Minister of the Interior and the Urban Community of Lyon appealed against this ruling.

Held: The appeal was upheld and the case was remitted to the Court of Appeal of Lyon.

Judgment: Considering that, if the administrative authority is empowered to open the public inquiry and ensure its publicity, under the conditions set up by the provisions of the Code de l'environnement (Environmental Code) previously cited, the disregard of those provisions is nevertheless of a nature to vitiate the legal process and therefore to lead to the unlawfulness of the decision adopted at the end of the public inquiry, only if it has not allowed adequate information of all persons interested in the process or if it has been of such nature to have an influence on the results of the inquiry and, therefore, on the decision of the administrative authority.

Notes

(1) In France, administrative decisions are subject to annulment by the administrative courts on grounds of formal illegality. Unlike in Germany and the Netherlands,[253] there are no written provisions concerning procedural errors in French administrative law. However, with regard to the potential annulment of administrative decisions on grounds of procedural errors, two important limits apply, which have been developed by the case law of the Council of State.

(2) First, there is no annulment of administrative acts on procedural grounds where there is no discretion on the part of the competent authority and only one decision on the merits is possible (*théorie des moyens inopérants en cas de compétence liée*). In that case, an annulment would only delay the administrative work and serve no further purpose because the public authority would have to issue the exact same decision after the quashing of the initial decision.[254] However, unlike in German law, in most cases, some discretion is deemed to exist.[255]

(3) Secondly, there used to be a distinction between essential formalities (*formalités substantielles*) and non-essential formalities (*formalités accessoires*). The breach of essential formalities always led to annulment unless, as mentioned above, no other administrative decision was deemed possible. The obligation of the administration to give reasons for its decisions (*motivation*),[256] the competence of the public servant taking the administrative decision and the right to be heard before a burdensome administrative decision is taken were, inter alia, considered to be such essential procedural guarantees. When non-essential formalities were violated, the administrative decision was only quashed for formal illegality if it could be shown that the procedural error had had an influence on the merits of the decision. However, the distinction between essential and non-essential formalities has been questioned by

[253] See below, section 6.6.C.
[254] See Grote (n 238 above), 490.
[255] ibid.
[256] See Code des relations entre le public et l'administration (Code of Relations between Administration and Members of the Public), Arts L211-2, L211-5.

the more recent case law. Since the *Danthony* case, an infringement of a procedural rule only leads to the annulment of the decision if this infringement has consequences on the content of the decision or has deprived individuals of procedural safeguards. The *Communauté Urbaine de Lyon* case has confirmed that the administrative courts no longer refer to the categories of essential or non-essential formalities. The decisive criteria are rather whether an infringement of the procedural rule denies the claimant an essential procedural protection or if a failure to follow procedural requirements has an influence on the content of the decision. In the *Communauté Urbaine de Lyon* case, despite its importance for decision-making, the omission of an environmental impact assessment did not lead to the annulment of the decision, since the court considered that the omission had no influence on the content of the decision or on the extent of the procedural guarantees afforded to the individuals.

(4) As regards rectification of procedural errors, this is only possible in very limited circumstances, as discussed in Chapter 7, section 7.2.B.4.

6.6.B.2 THE EUROPEAN UNION

Case 138/79, 29 October 1980[257] **6.51 (EU)**

SA Roquette Frères v Council

REQUIREMENT TO CONSULT THE EUROPEAN PARLIAMENT

Roquette Frères

The consultation of the European Parliament, as required by the Treaties, is an essential procedural requirement the non-observance of which leads to annulment.

Facts: The claimant brought a claim to ask the Court of Justice to declare Council Regulation 1293/79 void insofar as the regulation amended Council Regulation 1111/77 and fixed the production quota for isoglucose, thereby affecting the claimant. The claimant argued that the Council adopted Council Regulation 1293/79 without having received the opinion of the European Parliament as required by Article 43(2) of the EEC Treaty (currently Article 49 TFEU), which would constitute an infringement of an essential procedural requirement within the meaning of Article 173 of the EEC Treaty (currenly Article 263 TFEU).

Held: The Court of Justice declared Council Regulation 1293/79 void.

Judgment: The consultation provided for in the third subparagraph of Article 43(2), as in other provisions of the Treaty, is the means which allows the Parliament to play an actual part in the legislative process of the Community. Such power represents an essential factor in the institutional balance intended by the Treaty. Although limited, it reflects at Community level the fundamental democratic principle that people should take part in the exercise of power through the intermediary of a representative assembly. Due consultation of the parliament in the cases provided for by the Treaty therefore constitutes an essential formality regardless of the means by which the measure concerned is void.

[257] ECLI:EU:C:1980:249.

Notes

(1) The approach of the EU to dealing with breaches of formalities is inspired by the French model. As used to be the case in France, a distinction is made between 'essential' procedural requirements and 'non-essential' formalities. According to Article 263(2) TFEU, only the infringement of an essential procedural requirement can justify the annulment of acts of European authorities. Pursuant to the CJEU's case law, essential procedural requirements are procedural rules aimed at ensuring that measures are formulated with due care.[258] The most important essential procedural requirements are the requirement to hear the addressee of an onerous decision,[259] the requirement to consult certain EU institutions[260] and the duty to reason administrative decisions.[261]

(2) Formal errors of a minor nature can be remedied if the necessary procedural steps are carried out effectively before the beginning of the court proceedings.[262]

6.6.C SYSTEMS EMPHASISING THE SERVING FUNCTION OF PROCEDURE: GERMANY

Verwaltungsverfahrensgesetz **6.52 (DE)**

§44 (1) An administrative act shall be invalid where it is tainted by particularly serious errors and this is apparent when all relevant circumstances are duly considered.

(2) Regardless of the conditions laid down in section 1, an administrative act shall be invalid if:

1. it is issued in written or electronic form but fails to identify the issuing authority;
2. by law it can be issued only by means of the delivery of a document, and this method is not followed;
3. it has been issued by an authority acting beyond its powers as defined in §3(1) and without authorisation thereto; …

§45 (1) An infringement of the provisions governing procedure or form which does not render the administrative act invalid under §44 shall be ignored if:

1. the application necessary for the issuing of the administrative act is subsequently filed;
2. the necessary statement of grounds is subsequently provided;
3. the necessary hearing of a participant is subsequently held;
4. the decision of a committee whose collaboration is required in the issuing of the administrative act is subsequently taken;

[258] See Art 296(2) TFEU; Case 6/54 *Netherlands v High Authority* ECLI:EU:C:1955:5.

[259] Case 17/74 *Transocean Marine Paint Association v Commission* ECLI:EU:C:1974:106; Case 85/76 *Hoffmann la Roche v Commission* ECLI:EU:C:1979:36, para 9.

[260] Case 138/79 *Roquette Freres v Council* ECLI:EU:C:1980:249, para 33; Case C-21/94 *European Parliament v Council* ECLI:EU:C:1995:220, para 17.

[261] Case 18/57 *Nold v High Authority of the ECSC* ECLI:EU:C:1959:6, paras 51–52; Case C-269/90 *Technische Universität München v Main customs office Munich* ECLI:EU:C:1991:438, paras 26–27.

[262] See, eg Joined Cases C-329/93, C-62/95 and 63/95 *Germany and others v Commission* ECLI:EU:C:1996:394, paras 22, 48; Case T-30/91 *Solvay v Commission* ECLI:EU:T:1995:115, para 98.

5. the necessary collaboration of another authority is subsequently obtained.

(2) Actions referred to in section 1 may be made good until the final instance ruling on facts. …

§46 Application for annulment of an administrative act which is not invalid under §44 cannot be made solely on the ground that the act came into being through the infringement of provisions governing procedure, form or local competence, where it is evident that the infringement has not influenced the decision on the substance.

Notes

(1) Major procedural rights are covered by the Verwaltungsverfahrensgesetz (Administrative Procedure Act). It contains, inter alia, the right of an addressee of a burdensome administrative decision to be heard (§28(1) VwVfG), the duty to give reasons (§39(1) VwVfG), anti-bias provisions (§§20, 21 VwVfG) and the duty of the administration to investigate the case *ex officio* (§24 VwVfG).[263]

(2) Even though the German Constitutional Court has strengthened the value of procedural rules by acknowledging the constitutional requirement to protect fundamental rights through administrative procedure (*Grundrechtsschutz durch Verfahren*),[264] according to traditional German legal doctrine, procedural norms have a mere 'auxiliary function' (*dienende Funktion*) for the content of administrative decisions.[265] Thus, as a general rule, administrative decisions which were adopted through an erroneous administrative procedure are valid unless the procedural error exceptionally constitutes a grave error according to §44(1) or (2) VwVfG, which renders the administrative act void.

(3) Nonetheless, an administrative act which is unlawful in terms of procedural law (*formell rechtswidrig*) is voidable by the administrative courts.[266] However, §45 VwVfG provides that certain procedural errors, such as the right to a hearing, can be rectified until the final instance ruling on facts (*letzte Tatsacheninstanz*). Even if a procedural error cannot or has not been rectified by subsequent action according to §45 VwVfG, administrative courts may not annul an administrative decision because of procedural error 'where it is evident that the infringement has not influenced the decision on the matter' (§46 VwVfG). This is true for mandatory decisions, where the public authority has no discretion in its choice of action anyway, as well as in situations where, due to the circumstances of the case, only one decision appears to be

[263] For an overview, see Pünder and Klafki (n 11 above) 49, 73 ff.

[264] BVerfGE 53, 30, 65; H Pünder, in Ehlers and Pünder (n 42 above) §13, para 12.

[265] From a comparative perspective, see H Pünder, 'Administrative Procedure – Mere Facilitator of Material Law versus Cooperative Realization of Common Welfare' in Pünder and Waldhoff (n 89 above) 240, 243 ff; Pünder (n 8 above) 942 ff.

[266] For a comparative analysis of voidness and voidability of administrative acts, see GB Hola, 'Voidness and Voidability of Unilateral Administrative Acts in the Western Tradition' in Rose-Ackerman et al (n 69 above) 420 ff. For an overview of judicial review of administrative procedure in Germany, see Pünder and Klafki (n 11 above) 49–106.

lawful ('discretion reduced to zero' – *Ermessensreduzierung auf Null*).[267] However, the Federal Administrative Court has accepted that some 'absolute procedural errors' which protect the general interest (such as the consultation of environment protection agencies in certain cases) are never irrelevant according to §46 VwVfG.[268] While German law is, as has been seen above, very strict in the substantive control of administrative decisions, procedural errors on the other side are handled less rigorously by the courts.

6.6.D COMPARATIVE REMARKS

At first glance, the approaches to judicial review of procedural requirements seem to differ considerably in the legal systems examined.

Despite the differences that are apparent in the legal detail, all legal systems strike a balance between the protection of procedural guarantees and the need for effective and speedy legal remedies.[269] Remarkably, the German, French, and lately also the Dutch and English systems apply a flexible approach regarding the consequences of breaches of formalities in judicial review in respect of their effect on the content of the decision.[270]

In general, the different treatment of formal deficiencies is an effect of a deeper distinction of the concepts of administrative judicial review. Whilst the German law emphasises the control of the substance of administrative decisions in order to protect individual rights, the other legal systems take greater account of the objective function of judicial review of administrative action.[271] It is important to note that the German understanding of procedural requirements as merely serving the merits of the administrative decision has been found by the Court of Justice to be in conflict with EU law.[272] Important adjustments have been made to German law, particularly in the field of environmental law. For example, according to §4(1) Umweltrechtsbehelfsgesetz (Environmental Remedies Act), the infringement of procedural rules concerning an environmental impact assessment always leads to annulment of the respective administrative decision even if the infringement had no effect on the merits of the decision. Thereby, the general rule of §46 VwVfG is set aside with regard to the environmental impact assessment in order to comply with EU law.[273] Despite these ad hoc changes of law, formal errors still generally play a subordinate role in the judicial review of administrative action in Germany.[274] On the other hand, one can identify a trend, which is particularly visible in France and England, towards the de-potentiation of procedural errors, and the limitation

[267] See Grote (n 238 above), 488.
[268] ibid 475, 489; Pünder (above n 264) §14, para 87.
[269] *cf* Pünder (n 8 above) 960.
[270] *cf* Grote (n 238 above), 499.
[271] ibid 475, 499 ff.
[272] See Case C-72/12 *Altrip v Land Rheinland Pfalz* ECLI:EU:C:2013:712.
[273] See H Pünder, 'Verwaltungsverfahren' in Ehlers and Pünder (n 42 above) §15, para 58.
[274] See also U Kischel, *Rechtsvergleichung* (Munich, CH Beck 2015), §6, para 291.

of the cases in which the latter errors will lead to the annulment of a decision. In this sense, there seems to be a phenomenon of convergence, whereby, in the German legal system, procedural errors have risen in importance, and elsewhere they have become less important.

6.7 DIRECT EFFECT OF EU LAW IN DIFFERENT SITUATIONS

Treaty on the Functioning of the European Union **6.53 (EU)**

Article 288 (1) To exercise the Union's competences, the institutions shall adopt regulations, directives, decisions, recommendations and opinions.

(2) A regulation shall have general application. It shall be binding in its entirety and directly applicable in all Member States.

(3) A directive shall be binding, as to the result to be achieved, upon each Member State to which it is addressed, but shall leave to the national authorities the choice of form and methods.

(4) A decision shall be binding in its entirety. A decision which specifies those to whom it is addressed shall be binding only on them.

(5) Recommendations and opinions shall have no binding force.

Note

(1) Article 288 TFEU lists the forms of the legal acts of the EU. According to this provision, only regulations and decisions are directly applicable in the Member States, whereas directives are only binding 'as to the results to be achieved', and thus need implementation into the national legal order to create binding legal effects. The CJEU has accepted that both regulations[275] and decisions[276] can have direct effect if their provisions are sufficiently precise and unconditional.

(2) Nonetheless, the CJEU has ruled that, under certain circumstances, directives may also have direct effect, enabling EU citizens to bring claims to the national courts based on the violation of EU directives that have not yet been implemented or have been implemented wrongly. Even though the direct effect of directives evolved 45 years ago in the case law of the Court of Justice, it is still coloured by differing national legal doctrine at the Member State level.[277] Thus, some considerable differences have evolved in the application of the direct effect doctrine. Two issues have emerged: the first issue concerns the question of when and under what circumstances direct effect of directives arises. Secondly, there is some uncertainty as to whether directives can also have horizontal direct effect and thus influence legal relations between citizens.

[275] Case C-93/71 *Orsolina Leonesio v Ministry of Agriculture and Forestry of the Italian Republic* ECLI:EU:C:1972:39.

[276] Case C-9/70 *Franz Grad v Finanzamt Traunstein* ECLI:EU:C:1970:78.

[277] For a brief apt analysis, see S Prechal, 'Does Direct Effect Still Matter?' (2000) 37 *Common Market Law Review* 1047, 1053 ff.

6.7.A THE EUROPEAN UNION

Case 41/74, 4 December 1974[278] **6.54 (EU)**

Van Duyn v Home Office

VERTICAL DIRECT EFFECT; DIRECTIVES

van Duyn

If a Member State fails to implement a directive correctly, the citizens to whom rights are granted by the directive may invoke these rights against the Member State.

Facts: The claimant, a Dutch national, was denied an entry permit to work at the Church of Scientology on the basis of UK law. She argued that the UK acted in violation of EU law, in particular of Article 3(1) of Directive 64/221/EC. The UK court referred to the Court of Justice the question whether the Directive was directly applicable so as to confer on individuals rights enforceable by them in the courts of a Member State.

Held: The Court of Justice ruled that the Directive confers individual rights to the claimant.

Judgment: 12. If, however, by virtue of the provisions of Article 189 regulations are directly applicable and, consequently, may by their very nature have direct effects, it does not follow from this that other categories of acts mentioned in that Article can never have similar effects. It would be incompatible with the binding effect attributed to a directive by Article 189 to exclude, in principle, the possibility that the obligation which it imposes may be invoked by those concerned. In particular, where the Community authorities have, by directive, imposed on Member States the obligation to pursue a particular course of conduct, the useful effect of such an act would be weakened if individuals were prevented from relying on it before their national courts and if the latter were prevented from taking it into consideration as an element of Community law. Article 177, which empowers national courts to refer to the Court questions concerning the validity and interpretation of all acts of the Community institutions, without distinction, implies furthermore that these acts may be invoked by individuals in the national courts. It is necessary to examine, in every case, whether the nature, general scheme and wording of the provision in question are capable of having direct effects on the relations between Member States and individuals.

13. By providing that measures taken on grounds of public policy shall be based exclusively on the personal conduct of the individual concerned, Article 3 (1) of Directive No 64/221 is intended to limit the discretionary power which national laws generally confer on the authorities responsible for the entry and expulsion of foreign nationals. First, the provision lays down an obligation which is not subject to any exception or condition and which, by its very nature, does not require the intervention of any act on the part either of the institutions of the Community or of Member States. Secondly, because Member States are thereby obliged, in implementing a clause which derogates from one of the fundamental principles of the Treaty in favour of individuals, not to take account of factors extraneous to personal conduct, legal certainty for the persons concerned requires that they should be able to rely on this obligation even though it has been laid down in a legislative act which has no automatic direct effect in its entirety.

[278] ECLI:EU:C:1974:133.

14. If the meaning and exact scope of the provision raise questions of interpretation, these questions can be resolved by the courts …

15. Accordingly, in reply to the second question, Article 3 (1) of Council Directive No 64/221 of 25 February 1964 confers on individuals rights which are enforceable by them in the courts of a Member State and which the national courts must protect.

Case C-152/84, 26 February 1986[279] **6.55 (EU)**

Marshall v Southampton and South-West Hampshire Area Health Authority

DIRECT EFFECT; DIRECTIVES; STATE ACTING AS AN EMPLOYEE; DISTINCTION BETWEEN VERTICAL AND HORIZONTAL DIRECT EFFECT

Marshall

Provisions from unimplemented or incorrectly implemented directives also give rise to direct effect against the state if the state acts as an employer under civil law norms.

Facts: The claimant alleged that her dismissal because of her age violated the Equal Treatment Directive (Directive 76/207/EEC). She was an employee of an Area Health Authority (AHA), a body established by the UK government under the National Health Service Act. The AHA's policy was that women should compulsorily retire at 60, but men at 65. Given that the claimant suffered financial loss, namely the difference between her earnings as an employee and her pension, she initiated proceedings before the national courts. The English Court of Appeal referred two questions for preliminary ruling to the Court of Justice. First, whether the defendant's dismissal on the grounds that she was a woman who had passed the normal retiring age was an act of discrimination prohibited by the Directive. Secondly, if the answer to the first would be affirmative, whether or not the Equal Treatment Directive could be relied upon by the claimant in the circumstances at stake.

Held: The Court of Justice answered both questions in the affirmative, ie the dismissal constituted discrimination under the Directive and the court had to apply the Directive's provisions that have direct effect.

Judgment: 41. In support of that view, the appellant points out that directives are capable of conferring rights on individuals which may be relied upon directly before the courts of the Member States; national courts are obliged by virtue of the binding nature of a directive, in conjunction with Article 5 of the EEC Treaty, to give effect to the provisions of directives where possible, in particular when construing or applying relevant provisions of national law (judgment of 10 April 1984 in Case 14/83 von Colson and *Kamann v Land Nordrhein-Westfalen* [1984] ECR 1891). Where there is any inconsistency between national law and Community law which cannot be removed by means of such a construction, the appellant submits that a national court is obliged to declare that the provision of national law which is inconsistent with the directive is inapplicable. …

46. It is necessary to recall that, according to a long line of decisions of the Court (in particular its judgment of 19 January 1982 in Case 8/81 *Becker v Finanzamt Münster-Innenstadt* [1982] ECR 53), wherever the provisions of a directive appear, as far as their subject-matter is concerned, to be unconditional and sufficiently precise, those provisions may be relied upon by an individual against the State where that State fails to implement the directive in national law by the end of the period prescribed or where it fails to implement the directive correctly. …

[279] ECLI:EU:C:1986:84.

48. With regard to the argument that a directive may not be relied upon against an individual, it must be emphasized that according to Article 189 of the EEC Treaty [Article 288 TFEU] the binding nature of a directive, which constitutes the basis for the possibility of relying on the directive before a national court, exists only in relation to 'each Member State to which it is addressed'. It follows that a directive may not of itself impose obligations on an individual and that a provision of a directive may not be relied upon as such against such a person. It must therefore be examined whether, in this case, the respondent must be regarded as having acted as an individual.

49. In that respect it must be pointed out that where a person involved in legal proceedings is able to rely on a directive as against the State he may do so regardless of the capacity in which the latter is acting, whether employer or public authority. In either case it is necessary to prevent the State from taking advantage of its own failure to comply with Community law. ...

51. The argument submitted by the United Kingdom that the possibility of relying on provisions of the directive against the respondent qua organ of the State would give rise to an arbitrary and unfair distinction between the rights of State employees and those of private employees does not justify any other conclusion. Such a distinction may easily be avoided if the Member State concerned has correctly implemented the directive in national law.

Case C-201/02, 7 January 2004[280] **6.56 (EU)**

R v Secretary of State for Transport, Local Government and the Regions, ex parte Wells

DIRECT EFFECT; DIRECTIVES; NEGATIVE EFFECTS ON THIRD PARTIES

Delena Wells

The negative repercussions on the rights of third parties do not justify preventing an individual from invoking the provisions of a directive against the Member State concerned.

Facts: Mrs Wells, the claimant, had requested the English Secretary of State to take appropriate action, namely revocation or modification of a planning permission of a quarry, in order to remedy the lack of an environmental impact assessment in the consent procedure. Since she received no reply to her request, she brought proceedings before the High Court of Justice. The question which arose in the national proceedings was whether the claimant could rely on the provisions of Directive 85/337, as this would bring about negative consequences for the quarry owners.

Held: The negative repercussions on the rights of third parties do not justify preventing an individual from invoking the provisions of a directive against the Member State concerned.

Judgment: 55 According to the United Kingdom Government, acceptance that an individual is entitled to invoke Article 2(1) of Directive 85/337, read in conjunction with Articles 1(2) and 4(2) thereof, would amount to inverse direct effect directly obliging the Member State concerned, at the request of an individual, such as Mrs Wells, to deprive another individual or individuals, such as the owners of Conygar Quarry, of their rights.

[280] ECLI:EU:C:2004:12.

56 As to that submission, the principle of legal certainty prevents directives from creating obligations for individuals. For them, the provisions of a directive can only create rights (see Case 152/84 *Marshall* [1986] ECR 723, paragraph 48). Consequently, an individual may not rely on a directive against a Member State where it is a matter of a State obligation directly linked to the performance of another obligation falling, pursuant to that directive, on a third party ….

57 On the other hand, mere adverse repercussions on the rights of third parties, even if the repercussions are certain, do not justify preventing an individual from invoking the provisions of a directive against the Member State concerned ….

58 In the main proceedings, the obligation on the Member State concerned to ensure that the competent authorities carry out an assessment of the environmental effects of the working of the quarry is not directly linked to the performance of any obligation which would fall, pursuant to Directive 85/337, on the quarry owners. The fact that mining operations must be halted to await the results of the assessment is admittedly the consequence of the belated performance of that State's obligations. Such a consequence cannot, however, as the United Kingdom claims, be described as inverse direct effect of the provisions of that directive in relation to the quarry owners.

Notes

(1) According to the case law of the CJEU, unimplemented or incorrectly implemented directives have vertical direct effect if their provisions are sufficiently precise and unconditional, and the transposition period has elapsed.[281] As a rule, the direct effect can only be invoked *against* the Member State ('vertical direct effect'). That means that a Member State cannot invoke provisions of a directive directly against an individual without implementing them into national law ('no reverse vertical direct effect').

(2) Furthermore, there is, in principle, no 'horizontal direct effect' of directives between private parties.[282] However, in the *Marshall* case, the Court of Justice made it clear that a Member State cannot escape from vertical direct effect by acting under private law.[283] Hence, provisions from unimplemented or incorrectly implemented directives also unfold direct effect against a Member State if it acts as an employer under civil law norms. The Court of Justice defines a public body as 'a body, whatever its legal form, which has been made responsible, pursuant to a measure adopted by the state, for providing a public service under the control of the state and has for that purpose special powers beyond those which result from the normal rules applicable in relations between individuals'.[284]

(3) The CJEU also accepted in the *Delena Wells* case that an individual could rely on the direct effect of a directive against the state when such reliance would result in a disadvantage to a third party.

[281] Case 41/74 *van Duyn v Home Office* ECLI:EU:C:1974:133; C-346/97 *Braathens Sverige v Riksskatteverket* ECLI:EU:C:1999:291. For the criterion of precision and clarity, see *Braathens Sverige*, para 27 ff.

[282] Case 152/84 *Marshall v Southampton* ECLI:EU:C:1986:84, para 48.

[283] ibid para 49.

[284] Case C-188/89 *A Forster v British Gas plc* ECLI:EU:C:1990:313, para 20.

(4) Finally, it should be noted that, according to the case law of the CJEU, even before the expiry of the implementation period of a directive, the Member States must not introduce measures which could seriously compromise the results of the directive.[285]

6.7.B GERMANY

Grundgesetz **6.57 (DE)**

Article 23 (1) With a view to establishing a united Europe, the Federal Republic of Germany shall participate in the development of the European Union that is committed to democratic, social and federal principles, to the rule of law and to the principle of subsidiarity, and that guarantees a level of protection of basic rights essentially comparable to that afforded by this Basic Law. …

W Schroeder, Article 288 TFEU[286] **6.58 (DE)**

106 According to the case law, directives cannot have direct effect, but only individual provisions of a directive. Direct effect requires that: (1) the deadline for transposition of the Directive has expired without the Member State having fully and correctly implemented it; and (2) the specific provision of the directive is formulated without further conditions and is sufficiently clear. (3) It is controversial whether a further requirement is that the directive in question should grant individuals subjective public rights or, in any event, protect their legal interests. (4) Finally, directives which contain legal obligations for private persons cannot be directly applied.

Bundesverwaltungsgericht, 19 May 1998[287] **6.59 (DE)**

DIRECT EFFECT OF A DIRECTIVE PRIOR TO THE END OF THE TRANSPOSITION PERIOD

Ostsee-Autobahn

Even if the implementation period of a directive has not elapsed, Member States are under a 'pre-emptive' obligation of conduct to avoid contradictions with the objectives of a directive.

Facts: The State Office for Road Construction in Schleswig-Holstein adopted a zoning decision concerning a federal highway. The plan foresaw that the highway should cross a small river, the Wakenitz. The claimants, two nature conservation associations, alleged inter alia that the Habitats Directive (Directive 92/43/EEC), which had not been implemented by the time of the planning decision, had not been respected by the State Office.

Held: The action was dismissed. Even though there might have been a procedural flaw resulting in a breach of the Habitats Directive, this would not have resulted in the annulment of the zoning decision, as the alleged infringement would not have influenced the decision on the matter.

285 Case C-129/96 *Inter-Environnement Wallonie v Region Wallonne* ECLI:EU:C:1997:628.
286 W Schroeder, in R Streinz (ed), *EUV/AEUV*, 2nd edn (Munich, CH Beck, 2012) Art 288, para 106.
287 BVerwGE 107, 1.

Judgment: 77. ... In favour of the claimant, it is to be assumed that even, before the expiry of the implementation period, a Member State is obliged not to act contrary to the goals of the Directive and not to create a *fait accompli* which will later no longer allow it to comply with the Directive and the Treaty obligations contained in Article 5(2) in conjunction with Article 189(3) EC. This duty follows from the requirement of compliance with the Treaty. In that sense, the Member State may also be under the 'early' Treaty obligation, which can be understood as a duty to prevent contradictions with the goals of the Directive or as a duty to 'stand still' as a pre-effect of Community law. The pre-effect is aimed at preventing the destruction or damage of areas worthy of protection before they are put under protection under national law. However, no absolute development freeze exists. Despite a Member State's conduct which is contrary to the Treaty, a Member State cannot be burdened with consequences, which would go above any restriction which is envisaged by the Directive itself in case of correct implementation.

78. Such a duty of Community law to 'stand still' should especially apply where a Member State – as in the case at hand – contrary to its Treaty obligations did not implement a directive into national law on time. ...

82. This means: Even before 5 June 1998, planning procedures had to investigate whether road planning affected areas which could (potentially) be considered as conservation areas and – in case of the affirmative – whether the protection regime contained in Articles 6 (2)–(4) of the Directive was observed. ...

Notes

(1) According to Article 23 of the Grundgesetz, Germany participates in the development of the EU.[288] With regard to the direct effect of directives, German legal doctrine is closely aligned to the case law of the CJEU. However, there is some academic debate about whether EU directives have to confer specific 'individual rights' to have direct effect.[289] This dispute is rooted in the German principle of judicial protection of individual rights (*Individualrechtsschutz*), which is discussed in depth in Chapter 4 (section 4.4.B.1).

(2) In accordance with the CJEU's case law,[290] German courts abstain from giving directives horizontal direct effect between individuals (*unmittelbare Horizontalwirkung*).

(3) There is some academic dispute about whether the vertical direct effect of directives applies if other individuals are affected negatively as a consequence (*horizontale Drittwirkung*). This problem arises in situations where an administrative decision has different effects on different parties. For example, in public procurement law, the acceptance of a tender works in favour of the selected bidder, but is at the same time burdensome for the competing bidders. In these cases, the acceptance of the

[288] See Pünder, 'German Constitutional Law' (n 29 above) 36.

[289] See M Ruffert, 'Rights and Remedies in European Community Law: A Comparative View' (1997) 34 *Common Market Law Review* 307, 320; B Wegener, 'Subjective Public Rights – Historical Roots versus European and Democratic Challenges' in Pünder and Waldhoff (n 89 above) 219 ff.

[290] Case C-91/92 *Faccini Dori v Recreb* ECLI:EU:C:1994:292.

direct effect of directives technically only applies to the administration and can thus be qualified as 'vertical', but de facto also affects individuals (as a sort of 'horizontal side effect'). Nonetheless, the German administrative courts, following the view of the CJEU, accept the vertical direct effect of directives, even if they have burdensome side effects on individuals.[291]

(3) Lastly, in the *Ostsee-Autobahn* decision, the Federal Administrative Court acknowledged that even if the implementation period of a directive has not lapsed, the Member States are under a 'pre-emptive' obligation of conduct, which can be understood as a duty to avoid contradictions with the objectives of the directive or as an obligation to 'stand still' as a Community law precaution. In this respect, German literature uses the term *Vorwirkung* (pre-effect) of directives.[292]

6.7.C THE NETHERLANDS

Raad van State, 7 July 1997[293] **6.60 (NL)**

Metten v Minister of Finance

SUPREMACY OF EU PROVISIONS WHICH ARE NOT DIRECTLY APPLICABLE

Metten

Even EU provisions which are not directly applicable to the Member States, such as those concerning the obligation of the Commission to maintain confidentiality, may prevail over national law.

Facts: Metten, a Dutch member of the European Parliament, requested the Dutch Minister of Finance, on the basis of the Wet openbaarheid van bestuur (Act on openness of the administration), to disclose certain documents of the meetings of the Ecofin Council. The Minister denied the request. The case was ultimately brought before the Judicial Division of the Council of State.

Held: The Council of State dismissed the appeal.

Judgment: The Court of Justice has established in several judgments that the legal order of the EC is incorporated in the legal systems of the Member States, and that Community law takes precedence over national law. …

Community law consists not only of the Treaties establishing the European Community, but also of decisions of the institutions. Pursuant to Article 5 of the Merger Treaty, the rules which the Council has adopted are such a decision and they therefore are part of Community law. These rules have therefore, at least insofar as they bind the Member States, supremacy over national rules. …

[291] See M Schröder, in R Streinz (ed), *EUV/AEUV*, 2nd edn (Munich, CH Beck 2012) Art 288 TFEU, para 118.
[292] VI Gronen, *Die 'Vorwirkung' von EG-Richtlinien* (Baden-Baden, Nomos, 2006).
[293] ECLI:NL:RVS:1995:AN5284.

The supremacy of Community law constitutes one of the essential features of the Community legal order. According to the *Costa/ENEL* judgment, EC law can, as stemming from an independent source, by virtue of its unique nature, not be put aside by any rule of national law 'without losing its character as Community law and without the legal basis of the Community itself being affected'. ... The Judicial Division concludes ... that the principle of supremacy of Community law also applies to non-directly applicable provisions.

More specifically, the Judicial Division considers, with regard to the rules at stake, that they constitute, at least in regard to the obligation of confidentiality laid down in Article 18 of the Rules of Procedure of the Council of the European Union, a binding decision, despite the fact that they are not shaped in one of the kind of measures explicitly mentioned in Article 189, first to fourth paragraphs, EC Treaty. It cannot be intended, in the light of the objective of uniform effect of Community law in all Member States, that, depending on the law of the Member State of the person submitting a request for disclosure, access to the documentation of the Council is granted or not. This would also undermine the effectiveness of the provision, which in principle follows from the aforementioned judgment *W. Wilhelm and Others/Bundeskartellamt* and also underlies the supremacy of Community law. ...

Lastly, with regard to the plea of the appellant that the Rules of Procedure of the Council of the European Union would only concern the internal functioning of the institution and therefore would not have direct effect, the Judicial Division is exempted from the obligation to provide a judgment as it has already stated above that also non-directly effective provisions of Community law have precedence over national law and that the obligation to maintain confidentiality binds the members of the Council and therefore the state as well.

In view of the above, the Judicial Division is of the opinion that the defendant correctly rejected the request of the appellant for access to the minutes of the Ecofin Council meeting on the basis of the Wet openbaarheid van bestuur (WOB) (Law on the openness of the administration) because of the Community obligation to maintain confidentiality. The Judicial Division therefore sees no reason to refer the question to the Court of Justice for a preliminary ruling.

Raad van State, 5 December 2007[294] **6.61 (NL)**

'De Ingensche Waarden BV', Vught, and others v Provincial Executive of Gelderland

DIRECT EFFECT; NEGATIVE EFFECTS ON THIRD PARTIES

Ingensche Waarden

In general, administrative authorities must not apply EU law provisions to the detriment of citizens. However, if a third party relies on the directly applicable provisions of EU law, the administrative authority has to apply the provision, even if it causes negative side effects for another citizen.

Facts: By a decision of 12 September 2006, the defendant was granted a permit for certain alterations as regulated in the Wet milieubeheer (Environmental Management Act) to use a former gravel pit at the 'Ingensche

[294] ECLI:NL:RVS:2007:BB9488.

Waarden' to store dredging residues (class 0–4). The permit was granted indefinitely (ie without time restrictions). The claimants brought a claim against the permit. One of the claimants argued that the permit infringed Article 11 of the Groundwater Directive (Directive 80/68/EEC), which, according to him, was not properly implemented into Dutch law.

Held: The Council of State annulled the decision.

Judgment: Claimant sub 4 argues that the decision of the defendant infringes Directive 80/68/EEC (hereafter: Groundwater Directive) and that this Directive is not correctly transposed into national law. Regarding this point, the claimant argues that ... the defendant has infringed Article 11 of the Directive by granting the permit for an indefinite period of time. Regarding the temporary nature of the licence, the defendant states that the Environmental Management Act does not allow for the requested activity, by derogation from the request, to grant a permit for a limited period of time. It therefore granted the licence indefinitely. Neither Article 8.17, second paragraph, of the Environmental Management Act, nor any other provision of national law in such respect, provides for the possibility to grant a temporary licence. ...

Given the above, Article 11 of the Groundwater Directive is not implemented properly into national law. In the light of the Environmental Management Act regime regarding the granting of licences of indefinite time and the ensuing the exceptions on this made in Article 8.17 of this law, the Judicial Division considers that it is not possible for national law, on this point, in the light of the wording and purpose of Article 11 of the Groundwater Directive, to be interpreted in conformity with the Directive.

Given the unconditional and sufficiently precise wording of Article 11 of the Groundwater Directive, an individual can directly rely on this provision.

Raad van State, 7 November 2007[295] **6.62 (NL)**

Claimant v Committee for the Safety of Medicines

DIRECT EFFECT OF A DIRECTIVE PRIOR TO THE END OF THE TRANSPOSITION PERIOD

Safety of Medicines

Even before the end of the transposition period of a directive, the public authorities of the Member States must, as far as possible, refrain from any interpretation of national law which could, after the expiry of the implementation period, seriously compromise the objective pursued by that directive.

Facts: By decisions of 20 June 2003, the Committee for the Assessment of Medicines rejected the request of the claimant for the registration of 18 products at the register for homeopathic pharmaceutical products. The claimant filed intra-administrative objections against the decisions, but these were rejected with a decision of 31 March 2005. The claimant contested the latter decision before the district court and raised a ground based on Directive 2004/27/EC on Medical Products for Human Use, a directive the transposition period of which had not yet expired. The district court rejected the claim. The claimant appealed against the judgment before the Judicial Division of the Council of State.

Held: The Judicial Division confirmed the judgment of the district court.

[295] ECLI:NL:RVS:2007:BB7305.

Judgment: 2.6.1 At the time of the decision of 31 March 2005, the period for implementation of Directive 2004/27/EC, amending Directive 2001/83/EC, had not yet expired.

It has to be examined whether Community law obliged the Committee to interpret Article 4 of the Besluit homeopathische farmaceutische producten 1991 (Executive Regulation on homeopathic and pharmaceutical products 1991) as far as possible in the light of the wording and purpose of Article 15 of Directive 2001/83/EC, as amended by Directive 2004/27/EC. …

In its judgment of 14 June 2007 in Case C-422/05 (*Commission/Belgium*), point 62, the Court of Justice has recalled that, although the Member States are not obliged to implement a directive before the end of the prescribed period, they must, during that period, refrain from taking any measure that seriously compromises the result prescribed by the directive. In the judgment of 4 July 2006 in Case C-212/04 (*Adeneler and Others*), point 123, the Court has held that, from the date of entry into force of a directive, the judicial authorities of the Member States must, as far as possible, refrain from any interpretation of national law which could, after expiry of the implementation period, seriously compromise the objective pursued by that Directive. …

In the preamble of Directive 2004/27/EC it is held that … new measures are necessary to take away the remaining impediments to free movement. At the same time, according to the preamble, a high level of protection of public health should be achieved.

Insofar as Directive 2004/27/EC entails an amendment to Article 15 of Directive 2001/83/EC, the objectives pursued by Directive 2004/27/EC are not seriously compromised by continuing to apply Directive 2001/83/EC, as this provision was formulated before the entry into force of Directive 2004/27/EC, until the end of the implementation period of Article 15 Directive 2001/83/EC. In this regard, it is taken into consideration that products which are registered using the simplified procedure should have such a degree of dilution, that their harmlessness is guaranteed and that regarding these products no evidence of any therapeutic effect is required. The protection of human health is therefore not endangered.

Therefore, the district court has lawfully held that the Committee could require from the claimant that his application for the simplified procedure be accompanied by a dossier in which the homeopathic nature of the products was supported by a thorough bibliography.

Notes

(1) The Dutch judiciary is very EU law-friendly, and thus applies the principle of direct effect in a comparatively broad manner. This is shown in particular in the case of *Metten*, in which the Judicial Division of the Council of State observes that, on the basis of the case law of the CJEU, the principle of supremacy even applies to provisions of EU law that do not have direct effect.

(2) The excerpt of *Ingensche Waarden* provides an example of a case in which an administrative court applied a directly effective provision of a directive. The excerpt illustrates two other issues. In the first instance, it illustrates that the Judicial Division of the Council of State, before arriving at the possible direct effect of the provision, first considers that the implementation error cannot be remedied by a consistent interpretation of national law, as this would constitute an interpretation *contra legem*

national law.[296] Secondly, the judgment illustrates a limitation of the instrument of direct effect, namely that, as a matter of principle, it cannot be applied to the detriment of an individual (prohibition of reverse direct vertical effect). However – as was decided by the CJEU in the case of *Wells*,[297] to which the Judicial Division refers – this limitation does not apply to so-called 'negative side effects' in a triangular situation, ie a situation in which one individual relies on a directly effective directive provision in his relationship with an administrative authority and this has detrimental effects in respect of another individual.[298] In this situation, the negative side effects on the latter individual are considered to be 'collateral damage' resulting from the right of the first individual to rely on the directly effective provision in his relationship with the authority.

(3) Finally, the *Safety of Medicines* case provides an example of the obligation of the authorities of a Member State, including the courts, based on Article 4(3) TEU in conjunction with Article 288 TFEU, to refrain from adopting any measure which may seriously compromise the result prescribed by a directive in the period between the entering into force of the directive and the end of the transposition period.[299] Thus, similarly to the German courts, the Dutch courts also accept a 'pre-effect' of directives. In this case, the application of the obligation did not lead to the annulment of the decision contested, as the Judicial Division of the Council of State was of the opinion that the objectives pursued by the new directive of which the transposition period had not expired yet were not seriously compromised by a continuous application of the old version of the directive.

6.7.D FRANCE

Conseil d'État, 22 December 1978[300] **6.63 (FR)**

Cohn Bendit v Minister of the Interior

DIRECT EFFECT; SINGLE-CASE DECISIONS; DIRECTIVES

Cohn Bendit

An individual cannot invoke a directive to challenge an individual decision, since it does not create individual rights directly.

Facts: Because of his involvement in the protests of May 1968, Daniel Cohn Bendit was subject to a decision of expulsion from France adopted by the Minister of the Interior. Being a German citizen, and therefore falling within the scope of EU law, he challenged the decision on the ground that it infringed Directive 64/221 on the co-ordination of special measures concerning the movement and residence of foreign nationals which are justified on grounds of public policy, public security or public health.

Held: The appeal was dismissed.

[296] For details on the priority of consistent interpretation over direct effect, see section 6.8.B below.
[297] See excerpt 6.56.
[298] For more details, see Jans et al (n 184 above) 111–17.
[299] For more details, see Jans et al (n 184 above) 102–06.
[300] N° 11604.

Judgment: Considering that, under Article 56 of the Treaty establishing the European Economic Community of 25 March 1957, no provision of which authorizes an institution of the European Communities to adopt any regulations directly applicable in the Member States in the field of public policy, the coordination of laws and regulations 'providing for a special regime for foreign nationals and justified on grounds of public policy, public security or public health' is the subject matter of Council directives on a proposal from the Commission and after consulting the Assembly; considering that it is clear from Article 189 of the Treaty of 25 March 1957 that, if those Directives bind the Member States 'as to the result to be achieved' and if, in order to achieve the result which they prescribe, national authorities are obliged to adapt the laws and regulations of the Member States to the Directives addressed to them, those authorities remain solely competent to decide on the form to be given to the implementation of the directives and to decide for themselves, under the supervision of the national courts, the means to bring them into force in their domestic laws; considering therefore that, irrespective of the details which they contain for the Member States, the directives cannot be relied on by the nationals of those States in support of an action brought against an individual decision (*décision individuelle*); considering that, by consequence, Mr X could not successfully argue, in order to ask the Administrative Court of First Instance of Paris to annul the decision of the Minister of the Interior dated 2 February 1976, that this decision violated the directive adopted on 25 February 1964 by the Council of the European Communities with a view to coordinating, under the conditions laid down in Article 56 of the Treaty of Rome, special measures concerning the movement and residence of foreign nationals justified on grounds of 'public order, public security and public health'; considering that, in the absence of any challenge to the legality of the regulatory decisions (*decisions réglementaires*) taken by the French Government to comply with the directives adopted by the Council of the European Communities, the solution to be given to Mr X's application can in any case not be subject to the interpretation of the Directive of 25 February 1964; considering that, therefore, without the need to consider the grounds of appeal, the Minister of the Interior is right in maintaining that it was not correct for the Administrative Court of First Instance of Paris, through the judgment under appeal dated 21 December 1977, to refer to the Court of Justice of the European Communities some questions relating to the interpretation of that Directive and to stay the proceedings until the decision of the Court. …

Conseil d'État, 30 October 2009[301] **6.64 (FR)**

Perreux v Minister of Justice

DIRECT EFFECT; DIRECTIVES

Perreux

Provisions of a directive having direct effect can lead to the annulment of single-case decisions.

Facts: Ms Perreux was a magistrate and challenged the appointment of Ms Durand for a specific post in the administration. She argued that her application was rejected because of her belonging to a union. She claimed that Article 10 of Directive 2000/78/CE should shift the burden of proof of discrimination in this type of case.

[301] N° 298348.

Held: The Council of State dismissed the claim.

Judgment: Considering that the transposition of Community directives into national law, which is an obligation resulting from the Treaty Establishing the European Community, has, furthermore, in accordance with Article 88-1 of the Constitution, the nature of a constitutional obligation; considering that, for those two reasons, it is incumbent upon the national judge, as the ordinary judge who applies Community law, to guarantee the effectiveness of the rights that every person holds as a result of this obligation against the public authorities; that every litigant can, as a consequence, ask for the annulment of the regulatory provisions which would be contrary to the objective defined by the directives and, in order to challenge an administrative decision, assert that, after the expiry of the implementation period, the national authorities may neither let regulatory provisions continue to exist, nor continue to apply those national rules, written or unwritten, which would not be compatible with the objective set up by the directives; considering that, furthermore, every litigant may rely, in support of an action against a non-regulatory administrative act, on the precise and unconditional provisions of a directive, when the state has not taken, within the timeframe given by this directive, the necessary measures of transposition.

Notes

(1) According to Article 55 of the French Constitution, international law that is duly ratified or approved prevails over national legislation. Nevertheless, at the outset, French courts have been quite reluctant to accept the direct effect of directives in accordance with the case law of the CJEU. For decades, the Council of State has refused to review single-case decisions (*décisions individuelles*) that were argued to contravene an EU Directive, since, according to the Council of State, a directive does not confer rights to individuals, but only sets obligations for the Member States, which have a margin of discretion when implementing them. Consequently, an individual could only invoke a directive when challenging a decision of general scope (*décision règlementaire*), because the latter does not aim to protect individual rights, but seeks to promote the general interest.[302] The applicants in the *Cohn Bendit* case adapted their clams in light of this restrictive interpretation, using the plea of illegality against a decision of general scope in order to challenge indirectly an individual decision which was considered in violation of an EU directive.[303] Parting from this view, in the *Perreux* case, the Council of State accepted for the first time that an individual can challenge a single-case decision directly on the basis of rights conferred to him by an EU directive.

(2) In France, there is no specific debate related to the adverse consequences of direct effect on third parties. This may be explained by the objective conception of judicial review.[304] Indeed, since the aim of judicial review is to ensure legality,

[302] On these concepts in the French legal system, see Chapter 3, sections 3.2.A.3. and 3.3.
[303] On the plea of illegality in the French legal system, see Chapter 7, section 7.7.B.
[304] For details, see Chapter 1, section 1.5.

the potential consequences of the direct effect of provisions of an EU directive on third parties, even when creating burdens and obligations, is not taken into consideration.

Conseil d'État, 10 January 2001[305] **6.65 (FR)**

France Nature Environnement v Minister of Environment

DIRECT EFFECT OF A DIRECTIVE PRIOR TO THE END OF THE TRANSPOSITION PERIOD

France Nature Environnement

Even if the implementation period has not expired, national authorities cannot enact measures of such a nature as to seriously jeopardise the achievement of the goal prescribed by a directive.

Facts: The Minister of Environment had adopted, on 26 September 1999, an administrative decision (*arrêté*) related to the conditions and thresholds applicable to the assessment of the waste produced by nuclear plants. An association dealing with environmental protection challenged the decision, on the ground that it was in breach of Directive 96/29/Euratom of 13 May 1996 laying down basic safety standards for the protection of the health of workers and the general public against the dangers arising from ionising radiation.

Held: The claim was dismissed.

Judgment: Considering that, in accordance with Article 192, indent two, of the Treaty establishing the European Atomic Energy Community, Member States 'shall abstain from any measure which could jeopardize the attainment of the objectives of this Treaty'; considering that, by virtue of Article 161 of the same treaty, the directives of the Council of the European Union bind the Member States 'as to the result to be achieved, while leaving to the national instances the competence regarding the form and the means'; considering that if, to achieve this result within the timeframe imposed by the directive, the national authorities have sole jurisdiction to decide upon the form of the enforcement of those directives and to determine themselves, under the control of the national courts, the proper means to render them effective under national law, they cannot legally take, as specified by the Court of Justice of the European Communities in the ruling of 18 December 1997 in the case C-129/96, during the time-limit imposed by the directive, measures of such a nature to seriously jeopardise the achievement of the goal prescribed by the directive.

Note

Although a directive can have direct effect only after the transposition period has expired, the administrative courts consider that it can produce some effects even before the implementation period. In the *France Nature Environnement* case, the court

305 N° 217237.

implicitly grounded its reasoning on the duty of loyal cooperation in order to prevent public authorities from acting in a way contrary to the goals of the directive, thereby preserving the interest of its future implementation.

6.7.E ENGLAND AND WALES

Court of Appeal (Civil Division), 8 March 2000[306] **6.66 (EW)**

R v Durham County Council, ex parte Huddleston

Huddleston

REVERSE VERTICAL DIRECT EFFECT

The principle of vertical direct effect is applicable even if third parties are affected adversely thereby.

Facts: A company, Sherburn, applied to register a dormant permission to undertake quarrying pursuant to section 22 of the Planning and Compensation Act 1991. The effect of registration would be to allow Sherburn to undertake mining and quarrying in the area subject to the permission. Under the provisions of the legislation, there was no requirement for Sherburn to produce an environmental impact assessment. The legislative scheme was contrary to the provisions of the Environmental Impact Assessment Directive (Directive 85/337/EEC). Huddleston claimed judicial review of the Council's registration of the permission, arguing that although the Council was bound to register the permission due to the provisions of the legislation, he could challenge the provisions of the legislation and the registration because they were a breach of provisions of a directive that have direct effect. Counsel for Sherburn argued that to allow Huddleston to succeed in a claim for judicial review such as the one he was pursuing would be to give the Directive horizontal direct effect and create obligations between Huddleston and Sherburn, contrary to the case law of the CJEU.

Held: The Court of Appeal found in favour of Huddleston, holding that in circumstances such as these permitting Huddleston to proceed in judicial review did not create obligations between Huddleston and Sherburn.

Judgment: Sedley LJ: 8. The first step in the process is no longer contentious. Once it is established, as the decision of the House of Lords in Ex parte Brown has now established, that a section 22 determination is a development consent for the purposes of the Directive, it follows that the United Kingdom must require an environmental impact assessment as a precondition of making the determination. This the legislation not only manifestly fails to do ...; it positively encourages a developer to withhold a statement in the knowledge that the resulting deadlock will shortly be resolved by operation of law in the developer's favour. Recognising this, government is now at an advanced stage of consultation on the best means of bringing national law into conformity with the Directive. In the interim it has strongly advised voluntary compliance.

9. The second question is whether, notwithstanding the present situation, remedial action at law has to take the form of new primary legislation or, failing that, of proceedings brought by the Commission against the United Kingdom. The answer is to be found

[306] [2000] 1 WLR 1484 (CA).

in the broad proposition that there are means by which a Directive can be given effect in domestic law otherwise than by implementing legislation, but that these stop short both of rewriting the statute book and of giving direct effect to the Directive as between individuals. For the Secretary of State and the developer it has been urged that any attempt at convergent construction would fall into the first of these vices, and that the deeming provision cannot be disapplied without falling into the second.

10. For reasons which in the end were common ground and so do not need to be rehearsed, I accept that to construe the statutory provisions so as to converge with the Directive by 'writing in' further words would set off a chain reaction likely to disrupt the whole planning regime for mineral extraction. This makes it unnecessary to decide the potentially important question of whether the doctrinal objection to horizontal direct effect is logically relevant at all to the process of convergent construction. Instead one moves directly to the question of whether the possibility of giving the Directive direct effect by disapplying the deeming provision is precluded by the consequence that to do so will impermissibly alter the legal relations between two persons, Mr. Huddleston and Sherburn, neither of whom is part of the state. In other words, is this the forbidden territory of horizontal direct effect? …

14. … If further illumination is needed it can be found in the classic exposition of principle set out in the opinion of Advocate General Sir Gordon Slynn in Marshall's case [1986] Q.B. 401, 411–414. The present case on this analysis is not one in which treating an environmental impact statement as a uniform prerequisite of a determination touches any legal relationship between Sherburn and Mr. Huddleston. They have no legal relationship akin, for example, to that of employer and employee or even neighbour and neighbour. They confront one another in these proceedings only because each has a distinct interest recognised by law in Durham's function as a mineral planning authority, the one as a developer with an extant mining permission, the other as a member of the public concerned that the environment should be suitably protected when mining starts. In Lord Hoffmann's words, the case on both sides 'concerns the rights and duties of the citizen as against the state'; it 'brings into question the legal relations between the individual and the state.' …

15. If, however, to give effect to rights and duties against the state is also to impose obligations upon an individual, Lord Hoffmann's test would appear at lowest to cut both ways and at highest, as Mr. Findlay has submitted it does, to support Sherburn's case. In my view it does neither. This is not only because it is plain that the categories described by Lord Hoffmann are intended to be mutually exclusive; it is because there is a fundamental difference between imposing legal obligations on an individual which limit his freedom of action vis-a-vis other individuals and placing conditions upon that individual's entitlement to secure a benefit from the state. The latter, which is what Sherburn are facing, seems to me to come in the category of permitted transposition from Community to domestic law as surely as the former does not.

16. For the most part the Community cases which counsel have cited illustrate this distinction. Most recently, in *World Wildlife Fund v. Autonome Provinz Bozen* (Case C-435/97) The Times, 12 October 1999, the Court of Justice of the European Communities held that an individual could call the state to account for the non-implementation of the requirements of the present Directive for environmental impact assessments, in a case in which a developer was directly and adversely affected by the intervention. The analogy with the present case is close, both in fact and, more important, in principle. I find Mr. Elvin's submission that the present point was not addressed in it a surprising one for the Secretary of State to make, since both the United Kingdom and the adversely affected developer were

parties to the proceedings. The outcome simply could not have been reached by the court if it had been perceived as involving horizontal direct effect. The more convincing explanation is the obvious one: everyone involved recognised that if the case was otherwise well founded no question of horizontal direct effect arose.

Notes

(1) Many of the CJEU cases on direct effect have arisen in England. Once the position has been clarified by the CJEU, English courts have willingly followed the mandated approach. It is thus accepted that directives may have vertical direct effect.[307]

(2) Similarly to the Dutch and German approach, the Court of Appeal ruled in *Huddleston* that in cases where one private party challenges an administrative act that favours another citizen (eg building permission) on the basis of a directive, direct effect applies. In the *Huddleston* case, the court argued that there was no horizontal relationship between the parties as no private law relationship existed between them and hence this was a case of vertical direct effect.[308]

(3) There has not been a significant consideration of the issue of pre-effect of directives in the case law of the courts in England and Wales. However, where the issue has arisen, it is accepted that there is an obligation incumbent on administrative authorities not to take steps that are inconsistent with directives that have not yet reached their implementation deadline.[309]

6.7.F COMPARATIVE REMARKS

According to the case law of the CJEU, unimplemented or incorrectly implemented directives have vertical direct effect against public authorities if their provisions are sufficiently precise and unconditional, and the transposition period has elapsed. On the contrary, public authorities cannot invoke provisions of a directive directly against an individual without implementing them into national law ('no reverse vertical direct effect'). Furthermore, directives do not create horizontal direct effects between individuals.

All of the legal systems considered in this book accept and apply the above requirements of EU law in their national system. However, in Germany there is some discussion whether EU directives, in order to create direct effect, have to confer specific 'individual rights'. This debate cannot be found in the other legal systems, at least not any longer. The acceptance of the direct effect doctrine has taken the longest time in France. For decades, the Council of State has refused to apply directives directly. Only in 2009, in the *Perreux* case, did the Council of State accept for the first time that an individual could challenge a single-case decision directly on the basis of rights conferred to him by an EU directive.

[307] See, eg *van Duyn v Home Office* (n 281 above); *Marshall v Southampton and South West Hampshire AHA (No 2)* [1994] 1 AC 530.

[308] *R v Durham CC, ex parte Huddleston* [2000] 1 WLR 1484 (CA).

[309] See eg *R (on the application of T-Mobile (UK) Ltd) v Competition Commission* [2003] EWHC 1566 (Admin), [2003] Eu LR 769, [67]–[71].

If individuals rely on the vertical direct effect of directives, this can negatively affect other individuals as a consequence. Such indirect negative consequences for individuals that arise as a result of vertical direct effect are accepted in all legal systems under different labels. Similarly, all legal systems apply, under different names, an obligation to refrain from any measure which may seriously compromise the result prescribed by the directive in the period between the entering into force of a directive and the end of the transposition period if the directive has not yet been properly transposed.

6.8 CONSISTENT INTERPRETATION WITH EU LAW

The direct effect of EU law has to be distinguished from the principle of consistent interpretation. In the former case, an EU rule is applied as an autonomous source of law. In the latter case, EU law is used to interpret a rule of the national legal order. Consistent interpretation thus has an 'indirect' effect on the national legal order.[310] Thereby, the principle of consistent interpretation may evoke legal issues about the relationship between parliament and judiciary in the Member States. The principle of consistent interpretation of national law with EU law has been established by the case law of the CJEU.[311] Furthermore, according to the case law of the CJEU, secondary EU law also has to be interpreted in conformity with primary EU law.[312]

6.8.A THE EUROPEAN UNION

6.8.A.1 CONSISTENT INTERPRETATION OF SECONDARY EU LAW

Case C-449/04, 9 March 2006[313] **6.67 (EU)**

Hans Werhof v Freeway Treffic Systems GmbH & Co KG

CONSISTENT INTERPRETATION OF SECONDARY EU LAW WITH PRIMARY EU LAW

Werhof

Secondary EU legislation is to be interpreted in accordance with the general principles of EU law.

Facts: Mr Werhof, the claimant, claimed that he should have got the benefit of a wage increase under a 2002 collective agreement. His employer was no longer a member of an employers' association due to the splitting of the former company, for which Mr Werhof worked. The newly founded company had got Mr Werhof to sign an agreement waiving all of the individual employment rights that he could claim under the prior collective agreement in return for a one-off wage payment under a new collective agreement. Mr Werhof claimed that he

[310] See G Betlem and A Nollkaemper, 'Giving Effect to Public International Law and European Community Law?' (2003) 14 *European Journal of International Law* 569, 572.

[311] See Case 14/83 *Von Colson and Kamann v NRW* ECLI:EU:C:1984:153, para 26; Case 79/83 *Harz v deutsche Tradax* ECLI:EU:C:1984:155.

[312] Case C-449/04 *Werhof v Freeway Traffic Systems* ECLI:EU:C:2006:168, para 32.

[313] ECLI:EU:C:2006:168.

was entitled to the wage increases as updated in the collective agreement. He argued that the rights from the collective agreement had been transferred from his old employer (transferor) to his new employer (transferee) under German law and under the EU Business Transfers Directive (Directive 77/187/EEC). The court referred to the Court of Justice the question of whether, under the aforementioned Directive, the transferee is bound by the collective wage agreement.

Held: In order to determine the scope of the rights under a directive, the latter must be interpreted accordance with the general principles of EU law.

Judgment: 31. In addition, although in accordance with the objective of the Directive the interests of the employees concerned by the transfer must be protected, those of the transferee, who must be in a position to make the adjustments and changes necessary to carry on his operations, cannot be disregarded.

32. In this connection, in accordance with the Court's settled case-law, when interpreting the provisions of a directive, account must be taken of the principle of the coherence of the Community legal order which requires secondary Community legislation to be interpreted in accordance with the general principles of Community law (see, to that effect, Case C-1/02 *Borgmann* [2004] ECR I-3219, paragraph 30).

Note

The principle of consistent interpretation with primary EU law – consisting of the European Treaties (TEU, TFEU) and the protocols attached – and with the general principles of EU law developed by the Court of Justice applies to all secondary EU law.[314] The EU basic freedoms, as well as the fundamental rights contained in the Charter of Fundamental Rights of the European Union, are of particular relevance in this context.[315]

6.8.A.2 PRINCIPLES FOR CONSISTENT INTERPRETATION OF MEMBER STATES' LAW

Case C-14/83, 10 April 1984[316]
Sabine von Colson and Elisabeth Kamann v Land Nordrhein-Westfalen **6.68 (EU)**

CONSISTENT INTERPRETATION OF NATIONAL LAW WITH EU LAW

von Colson

National courts are required to interpret their national law in the light of the wording and the purpose of a directive.

Facts: On 6 December 1982, the Labour Court of Hamm referred several questions on the interpretation of Directive 76/107/EEC on Equal Treatment for Men and Women as Regards Access to Employment to the

[314] Joined Cases C-402/07 and C-432/07 *Sturgeon v Condor Flugdienst* ECLI:EU:C:2009:716, para 48.

[315] For more details, see S Leible and R Domröse, in K Riesenhuber (ed), *Europäische Methodenlehre*, 3rd edn (Berlin, De Gruyter, 2015) §8, para 7 ff.

[316] ECLI:EU:C:1984:153.

Court of Justice. Two social workers, Sabine von Colson and Elisabeth Kamann, had applied for a position in a prison for which two male candidates were appointed. The women brought an action against the German state Nordrhein-Westfalen, arguing that they had been refused the post solely on the basis of their sex. They claimed that the defendant state had to be ordered to offer them a contract of employment or, in the alternative, to pay them damages amounting to six months' salary. These claims could not be accommodated under German law. The German court referred to the Court of Justice the question of whether the Directive conferred upon the claimants the rights that they were claiming.

Held: The Court of Justice ruled the Directive did not impose a sanction by way of an obligation on the employer who is responsible for discrimination to conclude a contract of employment with the candidate discriminated against. Furthermore, the court held that Member States were free to choose between the different solutions suitable for achieving the Directive's objective, but the national court had to ensure that legislation implementing the Directive is applied and interpreted in conformity with the requirements of Community law. The Directive did not contain any unconditional and sufficiently precise obligation as to impose on the employer the sanction to conclude a contract of employment with the candidate discriminated against. However, Member States were under an obligation to impose effective sanctions. It was for the national court to interpret and apply the legislation adopted for the implementation of the Directive in conformity with the requirements of Community law, insofar as it was given discretion to do so under national law.

Judgment: However, the Member States' obligation arising from a directive to achieve the result envisaged by the directive and their duty under Article 5 of the Treaty to take all appropriate measures, whether general or particular, to ensure the fulfilment of that obligation, is binding on all the authorities of Member States including, for matters within their jurisdiction, the courts. It follows that, in applying the national law and in particular the provisions of a national law specifically introduced in order to implement directive no 76/207, national courts are required to interpret their national law in the light of the wording and the purpose of the directive in order to achieve the result referred to in the third paragraph of article 189.

Notes

(1) The principle of consistent interpretation of national law with EU law applies in all cases where the implementation of EU rules is to some extent incomplete or insufficient. According to the Court of Justice, 'it is for the national court, within the limits of its discretion under national law, when interpreting and applying domestic law, to give to it, where possible, an interpretation which accords with the requirements of the applicable community law and to the extent that this is not possible, to hold such domestic law inapplicable'.[317] Thus, the European law does not require an interpretation *contra legem*. Where the domestic law cannot be interpreted consistently, the national legal rule is set aside because of the primacy of EU law.[318] The Court of Justice demands that national law is interpreted in such a way that the result envisaged by

[317] Case C-157/86 *Murphy v An Bord Telecom* ECLI:EU:C:1988:62, para 11.

[318] Case C-200/91 *Colorell Pension Trustees v Russel and others* ECLI:EU:C:1994:348, para 29; Case C-165/91 *van Munster v Rijksdienst voor Pensioenen* ECLI:EU:C:1994:359, para 34; Joined Cases C-270/97 and C 271/97 *Deutsche Post v Sievers and Schrage* ECLI:EU:C:2000:76, para 62; Case C-262/97 *Rijksdienst voor Pensioenen v Engelbrecht*, para 39 ff; Case C-8/02 *Leichtle* ECLI:EU:C:2004:161, para 58.

EU law is achieved in law and fact.[319] The principle of consistent interpretation with EU primary law is based on Article 4(3) TEU.

(2) With regard to directives, the requirement of consistent interpretation follows from Article 288(3) TFEU.[320] It requires the national courts to interpret domestic legal provisions, 'so far as possible, in the light of the wording and purpose of the directive concerned in order to achieve the result sought by the directive'.[321] It is irrelevant whether the national law provisions were adopted before or after the directive.[322] However, the obligation to interpret national law consistently with directives only applies within the ambit of the directive and only after the transposition period has lapsed.[323]

6.8.B THE NETHERLANDS

Raad van State, 27 April 2000[324] **6.69 (NL)**

Claimant v Minister of Agriculture, Nature Management and Fisheries

PRIORITY OF CONSISTENT INTERPRETATION OVER DIRECT EFFECT

Hamster

Before considering the question of whether a provision of a directive has direct effect, the court should first examine whether the applicable national law can be interpreted in conformity with the directive.

Facts: By decision of 6 August 1998, the Minister of Agriculture, Nature Management and Fisheries granted an exemption from the prohibitions contained in Article 24 of the Natuurbeschermingswet (Nature Protection Act) to the municipality of Heerlen, allowing the municipality to catch, trying to catch and transport a protected type of hamster (*Cricetus cricetus*) and disrupt and damage its nest or den. The exemption applied to the areas of the zoning plans called 'Beitel-Zuid' and 'Transboundary Company Area GOB Aachen-Heerlen'. The claimant filed an intra-administrative objection against this decision. After the rejection of the objection, the claimant contested the decision before the Judicial Division of the Council of State.

Held: The decision was annulled.

Judgment: 2.6.1. ... According to the settled case law of the Court of Justice of the European Communities, when determining the effect of a directive, one has to distinguish between a correct and an incorrect implementation of the directive and that question of direct effect of the directive provisions can only arise in the event of incorrect implementation.

[319] Case C-300/95 *Commission v UK* ECLI:EU:C:1997:255, para 22 ff; see also Betlem and Nollkaemper (n 311 above) 576.

[320] Joined Cases C-397/01 to C-403/01 *Pfeiffer and others v Deutsches Rotes Kreuz* ECLI:EU:C:2004:584, para 113 ff; C-306/12 *Spedition Welter* ECLI:EU:C:2013:650.

[321] *Pfeiffer and others* (ibid) para 113.

[322] Case C-106/89 *Marleasing SA v La Comercial Internacional de Alimentación SA* [1990] ECR I-4135.

[323] Case C-212/04 *Adeneler* [2006] ECR I-6057, para 115; Joined Cases C-378/07 to C-380/07 *Angelidaki* [2009] ECR I-3071, para 201.

[324] ECLI:NL:RVS:2000:AA6571, AB 2000/303.

2.6.2. It is settled case law of the Court (case 14/83 *Von Colson and Kamann*, 10 April 1984, ECR 1984, p. 1891; case 106/89, *Marleasing*, 13 November 1990, ECR 1990, p. I-4135) that national courts, when applying national law, should as far as possible interpret this law in the light of the wording and purpose of the directive, in order to achieve the result sought. Therefore, the Judicial Division should, before it considers the question of whether a provision of a directive has direct effect, first examine whether the applicable national law is in conformity with the directive and, if that is not the case, whether it can be interpreted in conformity with the directive.

2.6.3. Article 12 paragraph 1 of the Habitats Directive provides …: Member States shall take the necessary measures to establish a system of strict protection for the animal species listed in Annex IV, point a) in their natural range, prohibiting: …

b. deliberate disturbance of these species, particularly during the period of breeding, rearing, hibernation and migration; …

d. deterioration or destruction of breeding sites or resting places; …

2.6.5. The defendant, when granting the exemption from the prohibition of Article 24, section 3, of the Nature Protection Act, did not attribute any meaning to the word 'necessity', as defined in Article 24, section 3, of the Nature Protection Act. Thus, the defendant applied Article 24, section 3 in accordance with the Directive. The Judicial Division will therefore disregard the question of whether Article 12 section 1 under b and d of the Directive is correctly implemented in Article 24, section 3, of the Nature Protection Act.

Raad van State, 22 February 2001[325] **6.70 (NL)**

Netherlands Association for the Protection of Birds v Minister of Agriculture, Nature Management and Fisheries

CONSISTENT INTERPRETATION

Ventjagersplaat

National law has to be interpreted in conformity with EU directives.

Facts: By a decision of 24 November 2000, the Minister of Agriculture had granted a fishing company the permission to professionally catch eel within some areas in the Haringvliet area which were protected by the Natuurbeschermingswet (Nature Protection Act). The claimant brought an action before the Judicial Division of the Council of State against the permit, insofar it allowed fishing with bow nets in the Ventjagersplaat area north of Hellegatsdam in July and August, when the area is closed to the public to prevent disturbances to the waterfowl. The claimant argued that the whole area, including the Ventjagersplaat, functioned as a breeding and resting place for the waterfowl, and that the fishing activities would substantially interfere with this function. Moreover, the claimant argued that the authority unlawfully failed to undertake an impact assessment, prescribed by Article 6 of the Habitats Directive 92/43/EEC.

Held: The decision was declared in breach of Article 12 of the Nature Protection Act, interpreted in conformity with Article 6, second paragraph, of the Habitats Directive. The decision was annulled.

Judgment: 2.1 Pursuant to Article 12, first paragraph, of the Nature Protection Act, it is prohibited to perform actions or condone harmful activities to the natural integrity or the scientific importance of a protected natural monument or to disfigure a protected natural

[325] ECLI:NL:RVS:2002:AE9209.

monument without a permit or contrary to the permit conditions. Pursuant to the second paragraph, acts that interfere with the essential characteristics of a protected natural monument in any event qualify as being harmful to the natural integrity or the scientific significance of a protected natural monument. …

2.3.3 As the Judicial Division has stated in its judgment of 31 March 2000 (E01.97.0178, AB 2000, 302), the Nature Protection Act does not provide for any rules that are expressly intended to implement the obligation contained in Article 6, second paragraph, of the Habitats Directive, to ensure that the quality of the natural habitats and the habitats of species will not deteriorate and that no disturbances will occur to the extent that these factors could have a significant effect. Moreover, it has not been shown that any other general binding regulations, which are intended to implement the obligations stemming from Article 6, second paragraph, of the Habitats Directive, apply to the Haringvliet.

However, the Judicial Division is of the opinion that Article 12 of the Nature Protection Act can be interpreted in conformity with the Directive. Therefore, the legal regime that follows from the assignment as protected natural monument and as interpreted in conformity with the Directive applies. This means that the prohibition contained in the article not to conduct, unless licensed, an action that is detrimental to the ecological values of the area designated, also covers actions that lead to a deterioration in the quality of a habitat or can lead to a disruption of the species as referred to in Article 6, second paragraph, of the Habitats Directive …

2.9. … Moreover, the Judicial Division considers that the defendant, when interpreting Article 12 of the Nature Protection Act in conformity with the Directive …, should not have attached importance to the economic interests of the fishing company (the permit holder) and to the fact that the case concerned existing activities.

Note

EU law provides for two 'instruments' to remedy the incorrect implementation of an EU directive: direct effect and consistent interpretation. As regards the relationship between both instruments (if they are both applicable), the Dutch courts – as appears from the *Hamster* case – first try to interpret national law in conformity with EU law before moving to direct application of directly effective EU law provisions if consistent interpretation is not possible. This priority sequence is in line with the judgment of the CJEU in the case of *Dominguez*.[326] In practice, in the Netherlands, most implementation flaws are remedied by consistent interpretation, even if national law provides for a very 'thin' legal base.[327] However, this instrument cannot be used if the interpretation would constitute an interpretation *contra legem* of national law.[328] In that case, the instrument of direct effect is applied (if, of course, the provision of EU law qualifies for direct effect).[329]

[326] Case C-282/10 *Dominguez v Centre informatique du Centre Ouest Atlantique and Préfet de la région Centre* ECLI:EU:C:2012:33.

[327] See S Haket, 'Coherence in the Application of the Duty of Consistent Interpretation of EU Law' (2015) 8 *Review of European Administrative Law* 215.

[328] See section 6.8.A.2 above.

[329] For an example, see excerpt 6.61.

6.8.C GERMANY

Bundesgerichtshof, 26 November 2008[330] **6.71 (DE)**

CONSISTENT INTERPRETATION

Quelle

German legal doctrine differs between legal interpretation (Auslegung) and judicial law-making (Rechtsfortbildung). With regard to the duty of consistent interpretation, both methods must be fully used.

Facts: The claimant was a consumer association. The defendant operated a mail-order business. In summer 2002, the buyer B bought a so-called 'Stove Set' for her own private usage. The goods were delivered in August 2002. In January 2004, the claimant noticed that the enamel layer on the inner side of the 'Stove Set' oven had detached. As it was not possible to repair the oven, the defendant exchanged it in January 2004. The device originally delivered was given back to the defendant by the buyer. For its usage, the defendant claimed compensation in line with §439(4) of the German Civil Code, which the buyer paid to the defendant. According to this rule, the seller can, in case of a replacement, demand compensation for the usage of the initially delivered good. The claimant demanded the repayment of the compensation and the omission of demanding compensation for the usage of defective goods from consumers. The district court granted the payment request but dismissed the rest of the claim. Both parties appealed to the appellate court. The appellate court rejected the appeal of the defendant (against the order to pay compensation) and, in regard to the aforementioned request for omission, also the appeal of the claimant. With his appeal on grounds of law, the defendant aimed at dismissing the claim for payment. The claimant continued to pursue the injunctive relief with his appeal. The Federal Court of Justice suspended the proceedings and referred a preliminary question to the Court of Justice on whether Directive 1999/44/EG on the Sale of Consumer Goods prohibited national rules providing the seller with the right to demand compensation for usage of a defective good.

Held: The appeal of the defendant was considered unfounded; the appeal of the claimant was considered well founded.

Judgment: 21. The principle of consistent interpretation with EU law, strongly influenced by the Court of Justice of the European Communities, demands from the national courts more than just an interpretation in the stricter sense. In its usage of the term 'interpretation', the Court of Justice did not distinguish between the terms 'interpretation' (in the stricter sense) (*Auslegung*) and 'judicial law-making' (*Rechtsfortbildung*), which is common in the German legal system, different from other European legal systems. Also, the restriction as phrased by the Court of Justice of the European Communities, according to which the interpretation in accordance with the Directive cannot serve as the basis of a *contra legem* interpretation of national law, does not refer to the distinction between the two terms. The term *contra legem* interpretation is to be understood in a rather functional way; it refers to cases in which consistent interpretation with EU law would be inadmissible according to the national methods of legal interpretation. The principle of consistent interpretation therefore also demands that national law, whenever this is necessary and possible, be developed in conformity with the Directive … In the case at hand, a teleological reduction of §439(4) BGB is required in order to ensure that its content is in conformity with the Directive and that it does not contradict Article 3 of the Directive. …

[330] BGHZ 179, 27.

22. Judicial law-making through teleological interpretation requires a hidden regulatory gap in the sense of an incompleteness of the law. This requirement is fulfilled. …

24. It follows that the intention of the legislator was on the one hand to grant the seller a right to compensation, in case of a replacement delivery. However, on the other hand … the legislator also aimed to create a rule which is in conformity with the Directive. However, the Court of Justice of the European Communities has now determined, with binding effect, that granting this compensation to the seller is unlawful. …

31. The courts may not alter unambiguous decisions of the legislator on the basis of their own policy ideas. However, through the abovementioned judicial law-making (by teleological reduction of the norm), the recognisable will of the legislator is not set aside. Rather, the legal reasoning shows that a legal gap exists and explains in what way this gap it to be filled. The concrete intention of the legislator to create a regulation which is in conformity with the Directive can – as mentioned above – be found in the legislative materials …

Note

German courts closely follow the legal principle of consistent interpretation as it has been developed by the CJEU. However, in German legal doctrine, a distinction is drawn between 'legal interpretation' (*Auslegung*) and 'judicial law-making' (*Rechtsfortbildung*). The *canones* of legal interpretation are limited to textual interpretation, systematic interpretation, historic interpretation and purposive interpretation. Where the meaning of the legal provision cannot be reconciled with EU law by these means of legal interpretation, the courts also have to apply the principle of judicial law-making (*Rechtsfortbildung*), according to the Federal Court of Justice. By way of analogy, the scope of a legal rule may be broadened or it may be narrowed by 'teleological reduction' (*teleologische Reduktion*).[331] In the *Quelle* judgment, the Federal Court of Justice (*Bundesgerichtshof*) accepted that legal interpretation as well as judicial law-making is to be applied to ensure consistent interpretation of national legal norms with EU law.

6.8.D ENGLAND AND WALES

House of Lords, 16 March 1989[332] **6.72 (EW)**

Litster v Forth Dry Dock & Engineering Company

CONSISTENT INTERPRETATION

Forth Dry Dock

Courts are supposed to apply a purposive construction to legislation and, where necessary, to supply words by implication in order to give effect to the UK's Treaty obligations under EU law.

Facts: The Forth Dry Dock & Engineering Company became insolvent. L and others were employees of the company at the time of its insolvency and were advised that they would no longer be paid or receive monies

[331] For more details, see WH Roth and C Jope, in Riesenhuber (n 316 above) §13, para 39 ff.
[332] [1990] 1 AC 546 (HL).

owed to them by the company (such as unpaid wages or holiday pay) because no funds were available to make such payments. L and the other claimants were informed at 3.30 pm on 6 February 1984 that the company no longer had resources to pay them and their employment would be terminated. At 4.30 pm on the same day, the company was sold by the receivers to a new company, known as Forth Estuary. L and the other employees were not re-employed by Forth Estuary and so L and others claimed unfair dismissal against the Forth Dry Dock & Engineering Company, arguing that Forth Estuary should be liable for any compensation due because it had acted contrary to the transfer of undertakings provisions in Directive 77/187/EEC on the Safeguarding of Employees' Rights in the Event of Transfers of Undertakings. The case thus turned on the interpretation of Regulation 5(3) of the regulations implementing the directive into UK law, which provided 'Any reference in paragraph (1) or (2) above to a person employed in an undertaking or part of one transferred by a relevant transfer is a reference to a person so employed immediately before the transfer, including, where the transfer is effected by a series of two or more transactions, a person so employed immediately before any of those transactions'.

Held: The House of Lords held in favour of L and the other workers, holding that the duty of consistent interpretation required a purposive reading of the regulation.

Judgment: Lord Oliver of Aylmerton: ... Regulation 8(1) does not follow literally the wording of article 4(1). It provides only that if the reason for the dismissal of the employee is the transfer of the business, he has to be treated 'for the purposes of Part V of the 1978 Act' as unfairly dismissed so as to confer on him the remedies provided by sections 69 to 79 of the Act (including, where it is considered appropriate, an order for reinstatement or re-engagement). If this provision fell to be construed by reference to the ordinary rules of construction applicable to a purely domestic statute and without reference to Treaty obligations, it would, I think, be quite impermissible to regard it as having the same prohibitory effect as that attributed by the European Court to article 4 of the Directive. But it has always to be borne in mind that the purpose of the Directive and of the Regulations was and is to 'safeguard' the rights of employees on a transfer and that there is a mandatory obligation to provide remedies which are effective and not merely symbolic to which the Regulations were intended to give effect. The remedies provided by the Act of 1978 in the case of an insolvent transferor are largely illusory unless they can be exerted against the transferee as the Directive contemplates and I do not find it conceivable that, in framing Regulations intending to give effect to the Directive, the Secretary of State could have envisaged that its purpose should be capable of being avoided by the transparent device to which resort was had in the instant case. *Pickstone v. Freemans Plc.* [1989] A.C. 66, has established that the greater flexibility available to the court in applying a purposive construction to legislation designed to give effect to the United Kingdom's Treaty obligations to the Community enables the court, where necessary, to supply by implication words appropriate to comply with those obligations: ... Having regard to the manifest purpose of the Regulations, I do not, for my part, feel inhibited from making such an implication in the instant case. The provision in regulation 8(1) that a dismissal by reason of a transfer is to be treated as an unfair dismissal, is merely a different way of saying that the transfer is not to 'constitute a ground for dismissal' as contemplated by article 4 of the Directive and there is no good reason for denying to it the same effect as that attributed to that article. In effect this involves reading regulation 5(3) as if there were inserted after the words 'immediately before the transfer' the words 'or would have been so employed if he had not been unfairly dismissed in the circumstances described in regulation 8(1).' For my part, I would make such an implication which is entirely consistent with the general scheme of the Regulations and which is necessary if they are effectively to fulfil the purpose for which they were made of giving effect to the provisions of the Directive. ...

In the instant case it is quite clear that the reason for the dismissal of the appellants was the transfer of the business which had just been agreed and was going to take place almost at once. The effect of regulation 5, construed as I have suggested that it should be, is that their employment continued with Forth Estuary. I would therefore allow the appeal. …

Note

English courts have demonstrated considerable flexibility in departing from the interpretation of statutory wording in order to foster compliance with EU law. Nonetheless, the limit of the interpretative obligation is drawn where such interpretation would amount to statutory amendment.[333] Thus, the separation of powers principle and the principle of the supremacy of Parliament prohibit impermissible creative interpretation of the national law.[334] In general, English courts base their interpretation of the law on the assumption that Parliament has no interest in contravening European or international law provisions unless a parliamentary provision unmistakably and purposefully aims to violate European or international law.[335]

6.8.E FRANCE

Conseil d'État, 1st March 2013[336] **6.73 (FR)**

Société Natiocrédimurs v Commune d'Issoire

CONSISTENT INTERPRETATION

Commune d'Issoire

The court is under a duty of consistent interpretation of national legislative provisions which implement an EU directive.

Facts: The mayor of Issoire adopted a decision requiring the company Natiocrédimurs to clean up the pollution on fields that they own, grounded on provisions of the Environmental Code stating the responsibility of depollution. The company challenged the decision before the Administrative Court of First Instance, which annulled it. The Administrative Court of Appeal annulled the ruling of the lower court. Subsequently, the company challenged the ruling before the Council of State.

Held: The Council of State annulled the ruling of the Administrative Court of Appeal due to the misinterpretation of the national provisions.

333 *Webb v Emo Air Cargo (UK) Ltd* [1993] 1 WLR 49, 59 (HL).
334 See Betlem and Nollkaemper (n 311 above) 587 ff.
335 *cf* P Craig, in M Andenas and F Jacobs (eds), *European Community Law in the English Courts* (Oxford, Oxford University Press, 1998) 46 ff; M Schillig, in Riesenhuber (n 316 above) §25, para 32 ff.
336 N° 354188.

Judgment: 3. Considering that the person responsible for the waste within the meaning of Article L541-3 of the Environmental Code, as interpreted in light of the aforementioned provisions of the Directive of 5 April 2006, refers only the producers or other holders of waste; that if, in the absence of any producer or any other known holder of waste, the owner of the land on which the waste is located may be regarded as its holder within the meaning of Article L541-2 of the Environmental Code, in particular in case of his negligence in the abandonment of such waste on his land, and therefore may be subject to the obligation to dispose of such waste, the responsibility of the landowner for the waste is only subsidiary to that incurred by the producer or other holders of such waste and may be investigated if it appears that any other holder of such waste is unknown or has disappeared; ...

Note

French administrative courts used to be reluctant to interpret national law in conformity with EU law. However, since 2000, the French courts have adopted a more flexible approach towards consistent interpretation. Consistent interpretation of national provisions (especially statutory provisions) is viewed as a duty fulfilled by national administrative courts in the course of their function as EU law courts. Insofar as it is possible, national (statutory) provisions falling within the scope of EU law will be consistently interpreted with the latter.

6.9 COMPARATIVE OVERVIEW

The grounds for review and the standard of review are far from uniform in the analysed legal systems. Judicial review of administrative action is largely a nation-state affair. Although the Europeanisation process has brought some harmonisation, the national legal systems still preserve their domestic legal traditions, changing the grounds and standard of review on a case-by-case basis and doing so gradually. Despite the differences in the judicial review of administrative action, however, the systems often produce similar outcomes. For example, in the Netherlands, the protection of human rights, derived from the national constitution, plays a relatively weak role in the judicial review process. However, this alleged deficit is compensated for by the strong role of general principles in the Dutch judicial review of administrative action. Similarly, with regard to the judicial review of procedure and formalities, three different approaches could be identified, some emphasising the role of formal legality more than others. Nonetheless, the results of the judicial review might be quite similar. In England and Wales, where, in principle, every breach of procedural and formal requirements leads to the annulment of an administrative decision,[337] fewer procedural requirements are acknowledged and

[337] However, it should be noted that English remedies have a discretionary nature. See further on this point in Chapter 7, section 7.2.B.3.

their scope is more limited than in systems that have a procedure that allows for correcting deficiencies or ignoring minor formal defects that have no effect on the merits of the administrative decision.[338] The overall level of scrutiny, however, differs considerably in the various legal systems. Germany represents a very strict system of judicial review with regard to the content of the administrative action, whereas in England and Wales the executive is often granted much more freedom. These differences are the result of the socio-historic contexts of the countries, which lead to different understandings of democracy.[339] These differences affect the distribution of power between the legislative, the executive and the judiciary, and thus influence the intensity of judicial review of the exercise of public power.[340]

FURTHER READING

Bell, J, 'France: French Administrative Law and the Supremacy of European Laws' (2005) 11 *European Public Law* 487.

Craig, P and Tomkins, A (eds), *The Executive and Public Law: Power and Accountability in Comparative Perspective* (Oxford, Oxford University Press, 2006).

Grote, R, 'Procedural Deficiencies in Administrative Law: A Comparative Analysis' (2002) 18 *South African Journal on Human Rights* 457.

Haket, S, 'Coherence in the Application of the Duty of Consistent Interpretation of EU Law' (2015) 2 *Review of European Administrative Law* 215.

Kayser, M, 'Rechtsschutz und Kontrolle' in A von Bogdandy, S Cassese and PM Huber (eds), *Handbuch Ius Publicum Europaeum*, vol 5 (Heidelberg, CF Müller, 2014) §91.

Pünder, H, 'German Administrative Procedure in a Comparative Perspective – Observations on the Path to a Transnational *Ius Commune Proceduralis* in Administrative Law' (2013) 11 *International Journal of Constitutional Law* 940.

Pünder, H, 'Administrative Procedure – Mere Facilitator of Material Law versus Cooperative Realization of Common Welfare' in H Pünder and C Waldhoff (eds), *Debates in German Public Law* (Oxford, Hart Publishing, 2013) 240–60.

Ranchordás, S and de Waard, B (eds), *The Judge and the Proportionate Use of Discretion. A Comparative Study* (London, Routledge, 2016).

Schwarze, J, 'Judicial Review of European Administrative Procedure' (2004–2005) 68 *Law and Contemporary Problems* 85.

Seerden, R (ed), *Comparative Administrative Law. Administrative Law of the European Union, Its Member States and the United States* (4th ed, Cambridge, intersentia, 2018).

Temple Lang, J, 'Developments, Issues and New Remedies – The Duties of National Authorities and Courts under Article 10 of the EC Treaty' (2003) 27 *Fordham International Law Journal* 1904.

Widdershoven, RJGM and Remac, M, 'General Principles of Law in Administrative Law under European Influence' (2012) 20 *European Review of Private Law* 381.

[338] For an in-depth analysis, see Pünder (n 8 above) 958 ff.

[339] *cf* Schwarze (n 122 above) 86. For the importance of context in the translation of international to national law, see AK Mangold, 'The Persistence of National Peculiarities: Translating Representative' (2014) 21 *Indiana Journal of Global Legal Studies* 223, 225. For the socio-historic development of the strong judicial review in Germany, see Nolte (n 83 above) 198 ff.

[340] *cf* Grote (n 238 above), 499 f.

CHAPTER 7
REMEDIES AND CONSEQUENCES OF COURT DECISIONS

Emilie Chevalier

7.1 INTRODUCTION

This chapter deals with the remedies provided for in the legal systems addressed by this book when the administrative action is challenged. When administrative action is challenged, an applicant will typically seek the annulment of an administrative decision. However, an applicant may also ask the court to restrain the public authority from acting unlawfully, to order the public authority to perform its duties, to declare the rights and duties of the parties, to order the public authority to pay compensation for the loss suffered by the applicant or to adopt interim measures while the main proceedings are pending.

Each of the legal systems studied in this book provide different types of remedies for these possible claims. First of all, all of the legal systems provide for an action to seek the annulment of an administrative act. Secondly, as annulment may not always be the most appropriate solution, remedies are provided to restrain the public authority from acting unlawfully or to order the public authority to perform its duties. Thirdly, more specific remedies exist in order to obtain a declaration of the court's view of a certain legal position. Furthermore, in all the legal systems studied there are remedies which allow for the compensation of losses when liability of public authorities is found. However, the relation of such remedies with the action for annulment differs, depending on the legal system under analysis. In some legal systems, two separate actions are needed; in others, annulment and restitution of damages can be combined into one action. Moreover, the available remedies and their potential use are closely linked to the authority of rulings, determined by the scope of the res judicata principle. The acknowledgement of res judicata is considered to be a fundamental principle in the legal systems studied, and it limits the potential to reopen a case which has become final. Finally, two other categories of remedies of a slightly different nature are analysed in this chapter: legal systems may provide for the possibility to challenge acts through an indirect challenge procedure; and individuals may also seek interim relief. Interim measures are of a temporary nature and aim to preserve and protect the interests of the parties pending the final hearing, and the effectiveness of the final ruling.

In administrative matters, the organisation of remedies is linked not only to the upholding of the rule of law, but also to the protection of individual rights, especially fundamental constitutional rights. The right to effective judicial protection is in itself a fundamental right, guaranteed at the national, European and international levels.

Charter of Fundamental Rights of the European Union **7.1 (EU)**

Article 47 – Right to an effective remedy and to a fair trial

Everyone whose rights and freedoms guaranteed by the law of the Union are violated has the right to an effective remedy before a tribunal in compliance with the conditions laid down in this Article.

Everyone is entitled to a fair and public hearing within a reasonable time by an independent and impartial tribunal previously established by law. Everyone shall have the possibility of being advised, defended and represented.

Legal aid shall be made available to those who lack sufficient resources in so far as such aid is necessary to ensure effective access to justice.

Convention for the Protection of Human Rights and Fundamental Freedoms **7.2 (COE)**

Article 13 – Right to an effective remedy

Everyone whose rights and freedoms as set forth in this Convention are violated shall have an effective remedy before a national authority notwithstanding that the violation has been committed by persons acting in an official capacity.

UNECE Convention on Access to Information,
Public Participation in Decision-making and Access to Justice
in Environmental Matters (Aarhus Convention) **7.3 (UN)**

Article 9 – Access to justice

...

(4) In addition and without prejudice to paragraph 1 above, the procedures referred to in paragraphs 1, 2 and 3 above shall provide adequate and effective remedies, including injunctive relief as appropriate, and be fair, equitable, timely and not prohibitively expensive. Decisions under this article shall be given or recorded in writing. Decisions of courts, and whenever possible of other bodies, shall be publicly accessible.

Note

The right to effective judicial protection has become increasingly important in the European and international legal systems. At the European level, this right has a general scope and covers all rights conferred by EU law. In contrast, the Aarhus Convention is specific, since its scope is limited to remedies available in environmental matters. Nevertheless, the Aarhus Convention has played an important role within the EU Member States, and to a certain extent within the EU itself. It has become clear that in some of the legal systems under study there have been some deficiencies in guaranteeing adequate and effective remedies in environmental matters.[1]

7.2 ANNULMENT

Judicial review aims first and foremost to ensure that the administrative action is legal. To promote respect for the rule of law, the action for annulment aims to review the legality of an administrative decision. If the challenged decision is found to be illegal, it will be annulled. The annulment (or quashing) of an act leads to its retroactive (*ex tunc*) annulment. The annulment of a decision therefore implies, in principle, the removal of all of its legal consequences.

However, in some legal systems and in some situations, a court can mitigate the retroactive effects of an annulment ruling. The administrative decision in this case is not removed from the legal system *ab initio.* Either the decision may be annulled with *ex nunc* effects or the effects of the annulment ruling may be postponed. These possibilities have the aim of adapting the consequences of an annulment ruling to the specific case in order to preserve legal certainty.[2]

Furthermore, a trend is developing in the studied legal systems which permits the court to avoid the annulment of a decision, even though the decision is considered illegal by the court. In this respect, the court may be given powers to ignore or repair a certain type of illegality, or even substitute its own decision with the decision of the

[1] On the consequences of the Aarhus Convention on standing, see Chapter 4, section 4.4.E.
[2] Section 7.2.A below.

administrative authority, without referring the case back to the authority, which would have to prepare and take a new decision.[3]

7.2.A MITIGATION OF RETROACTIVITY (OF *EX TUNC* EFFECTS)

In all of the legal systems under analysis, when a decision is annulled, the consequence, in principle, is its retroactive disappearance from the legal order. However, in all of the legal systems except for Germany, the courts have the discretion to mitigate this consequence in order to reconcile the demands of the rule of law with those of legal certainty.

7.2.A.1 GERMANY

German law distinguishes between several different kinds of court actions[4] for the judicial review of administrative action. These different types of actions correlate with different types of remedies. This distinction is very important, as the prerequisites for admissibility as well as the effects of the remedies are different. The question of which type of action is admissible depends on the claim and the remedies sought (§88 of the Verwaltungsgerichtsordnung (VwGO)) and, crucially, on whether or not an 'administrative act' (*Verwaltungsakt*) is involved.[5] Consequently, it is crucial for the applicant to determine exactly what outcome is sought in order to choose the relevant action. To provide effective judicial protection, different actions can, in general, easily be (and in practice are) combined in one claim.

Verwaltungsgerichtsordnung **7.4 (DE)**

§42 (1) By legal action, the annulment (*Aufhebung*) of an administrative act (action for annulment (*Anfechtungsklage*)) as well as the order to issue a refused or omitted administrative act (action seeking the issuance of an administrative act (*Verpflichtungsklage*)) may be requested.

§ 113 (1) Insofar as the administrative act is unlawful and the claimants' rights have been violated, the court shall annul the administrative act and any decision on an objection ....

Notes

(1) If the claimant asks for the annulment of a burdensome administrative act, such as a demolition order, he will lodge an 'action for annulment' (*Anfechtungsklage*), such as provided for by the first alternative of §42(1) VwGO.

[3] Section 7.2.B below.

[4] See H Pünder and A Klafki, 'Administrative Law in Germany' in R Seerden (ed), *Administrative Law of the European Union, its Member States and the United States*, 4th edn (Antwerp, Intersentia, 2018) 49–106.

[5] On the notion of *Verwaltungsakt*, see Chapter 3, section 3.2.A.1.

(2) The consequence of an annulment in the German legal system is its complete or partial retroactive disappearance.[6] There is no possibility for the court to mitigate the consequences of an annulment ruling.

(3) If the claimant instead asks for the annulment of an administrative act containing a refusal, he will lodge an 'action seeking the issuance of an administrative act' (*Verpflichtungsklage*), such as provided for by the second alternative of §42(1) VwGO. The consequences of a successful *Verpflichtungsklage* will be examined under section 7.3.B.2 below.

7.2.A.2 ENGLAND AND WALES

In England and Wales, the main remedies that can be sought through the judicial review process come through what are known as the 'prerogative orders', which are public law remedies. The judicial review process can also be used to seek private law remedies against the actions of public authorities. The private law remedies that can be sought are the injunction and declaration. For many years, prerogative remedies and private law remedies used against public authorities had to be sought through separate actions. One of the consequences of the judicial reform is to provide for a single procedure, named the 'application for judicial review', when remedies are being sought against the actions of public authorities.[7] Consequently, when the administrative action is challenged through an application for judicial review, the claimant can ask the court to provide one or more of those remedies, depending on the purpose of the claim.

Senior Courts Act 1981 **7.5 (EW)**

Section 31 Application for judicial review

(1) An application to the High Court for one or more of the following forms of relief, namely –

(a) a mandatory, prohibiting or quashing order;

(b) a declaration or injunction under subsection (2); or

(c) an injunction under section 30 restraining a person not entitled to do so from acting in an office to which that section applies,

shall be made in accordance with rules of court by a procedure to be known as an application for judicial review.

(2) A declaration may be made or an injunction granted under this subsection in any case where an application for judicial review, seeking that relief, has been made and the High Court considers that, having regard to –

(a) the nature of the matters in respect of which relief may be granted by mandatory, prohibiting or quashing orders;

[6] For details, see D Ehlers, 'Anfechtungsklage' in D Ehlers and F Schoch (eds), *Rechtsschutz im Öffentlichen Recht* (Berlin, De Gruyter, 2009) 603–40.

[7] See further Chapter 1, section 1.2.A.4.

(b) the nature of the persons and bodies against whom relief may be granted by such orders; and

(c) all the circumstances of the case,

it would be just and convenient for the declaration to be made or the injunction to be granted, as the case may be.

Civil Procedure Rules **7.6 (EW)**

Rule 54.2

The judicial review procedure must be used in a claim for judicial review where the claimant is seeking–

(a) a mandatory order;

(b) a prohibiting order;

(c) a quashing order; or

(d) an injunction under section 30 of the Supreme Court Act 1981 (restraining a person from acting in any office in which he is not entitled to act).

Rule 54.3

(1) The judicial review procedure may be used in a claim for judicial review where the claimant is seeking–

(a) a declaration; or

(b) an injunction.

Note

In England and Wales, a claimant who seeks the annulment of a decision[8] will request a quashing order. A quashing order is one of the 'prerogative orders'.

P Craig, Administrative Law[9] **7.7 (EW)**

… the foundational proposition that invalid acts are retrospectively void has on occasion been obscured by judicial use of the term voidable to describe the consequences of invalid action, rather than void. The rationale for doing so has varied, but the general answer is that some courts have sought to escape from the conclusions that will follow if they find that the contested decision was made outside jurisdiction and hence retrospectively invalid. They have used the term voidable in order to express the conclusion that the contested order should only be ineffective from the date when it was found to be invalid by the court, and not from the date when it was first made.

Note

If the court rules that an administrative decision is illegal, the decision is declared void *ab initio*, which means it is retroactively annulled, in whole or in part. The retroactive character is seen as an essential element of the rule of law in the legal system of England and Wales. However, the concept of 'voidness' in the English legal

[8] On the concept of a decision in the English legal system, see Chapter 3, section 3.2.B.1.

[9] P Craig, *Administrative Law*, 8th edn (London, Sweet & Maxwell, 2016) 733.

system is not always clear, and has been used in some cases in a relative manner, and adapted to the concrete circumstances of the case. The court, using its remedial discretion, has the possibility to limit the application of this fundamental principle, sometimes ordering that the judicial decision operates only prospectively. The decision is then declared void, but, where circumstances require, such as practical ones of administrative convenience, in order to avoid excessive disruption in the administrative system, the effects of the annulment are confined to the future. The current approach of English law, which in theory holds all ultra vires acts void, while seeking to ameliorate the effects of such findings in cases where the impact of holding an act to be void has significant consequences for the administrative system, has been criticised, with some authors suggesting that the approach to void decisions should be modified.[10]

Supreme Court, 4 February 2010[11] **7.8 (EW)**

Ahmed and Others v HM Treasury

QUASHING ORDER; RETROACTIVITY

Ahmed

The court may limit the consequences of the annulment of an act on the ground of a significant public interest.

Facts: The Supreme Court was asked to suspend the effects of its judgment in *A v HM Treasury*,[12] which found secondary legislation created to facilitate the freezing of the assets of the claimants and other claimants pursuant to UN Security Council resolutions to be ultra vires. The government asked for the effects of the judgment of the court (which rendered the secondary legislation void) to be suspended for a period of eight weeks to allow Parliament to pass primary legislation to rectify the deficiencies that were found with the secondary legislation that was subject to the challenge.

Held: The Supreme Court refused to suspend the effects of its judgment.

Judgment: Lord Phillips of Worth Matravers PSC: 1 When judgment was given on 27 January 2010 an issue arose in respect of the order that the court proposed to make. The court has held that the TO and article 3(1)(b) of the AQO were ultra vires. This means that the restrictions imposed on individuals pursuant to these Orders have been imposed without authority and are of no effect in law. Because this has not been appreciated there has been compliance with these restrictions, not least by third parties, including banks holding funds of those purportedly affected by the Orders. Thus the Orders have, in practice, achieved the effect that the Treasury intended when making them.

2 The Treasury is anxious that this state of affairs should persist until the invalid restrictions can be replaced by restrictions that have the force of law. To this end Mr Swift has

[10] See, eg T Adams, 'The Standard Theory of Administrative Unlawfulness' (2017) 76 *Cambridge Law Journal* 289.

[11] [2010] UKSC 5, [2010] 2 AC 534.

[12] ibid.

submitted that the court should suspend the operation of the orders that it proposes to make declaring the TO and article 3(1)(b) of the AQO ultra vires and quashing them, in the case of the former for a period of eight weeks to 25 March 2010 and in the case of the latter for a period of six weeks to 11 March 2010.

3 This submission is a variation and extension of a limited suspension to the operation of its orders that Lord Hope of Craighead DPSC had proposed that the court should make in para 84 of his judgment. I had concurred in this proposal, but having considered the matter further I have concluded that it would not be appropriate to suspend any part of the court's order.

4 Mr Swift submitted that this court has power to suspend the effect of any order that it makes. Counsel for the appellants conceded that this was correct and that concession was rightly made. The problem with a suspension in this case is, however, that the court's order, whenever it is made, will not alter the position in law. It will declare what that position is. It is true that it will also quash the TO and part of the AQO, but these are provisions that are ultra vires and of no effect in law. The object of quashing them is to make it quite plain that this is the case.

5 The effect of suspending the operation of the order of the court would be, or might be, to give the opposite impression. It would suggest that, during the period of suspension of the quashing orders, the provisions to be quashed would remain in force. Mr Swift acknowledged that it might give this impression. Indeed, he made it plain that this was the object of seeking the suspension.

6 Mr Swift's submissions are described in the dissenting judgment of Lord Hope DPSC. He did not suggest that the court could or should give temporary validity to the unlawful provisions. He did not suggest that the court could or should purport prospectively to overrule them. He did not suggest that suspension was necessary in order to permit action by the executive which might otherwise appear to be flouting the decision of the court, as it was in *Koo Sze Yiu v Chief Executive of the Hong Kong Special Administrative Region* (2006) 9 HKCFAR 441. He did not suggest that the suspension would have any effect in law.

7 Mr Swift urged the court to suspend the operation of its judgment because of the effect that the suspension would have on the conduct of third parties. He submitted that the banks, in particular, would be unlikely to release frozen funds while the court's orders remained suspended. I comment that if suspension were to have this effect this would only be because the third parties wrongly believed that it affected their legal rights and obligations.

8 The ends sought by Mr Swift might well be thought desirable, but I do not consider that they justify the means that he proposes. This court should not lend itself to a procedure that is designed to obfuscate the effect of its judgment. Accordingly, I would not suspend the operation of any part of the court's order ....

Note

In this case, the majority of the Justices of the Supreme Court sitting in this case agreed with the judgment of Lord Phillips. Lord Hope DPSC dissented, arguing that in a case such as this, where there is a significant public interest in national security, the court should be willing to suspend the impact of the quashing order.

7.2.A.3 THE EUROPEAN UNION

Treaty on the Functioning of the European Union **7.9 (EU)**

Article 263 (1) The Court of Justice of the European Union shall review the legality of legislative acts, of acts of the Council, of the Commission and of the European Central Bank, other than recommendations and opinions, and of acts of the European Parliament and of the European Council intended to produce legal effects vis-à-vis third parties. It shall also review the legality of acts of bodies, offices or agencies of the Union intended to produce legal effects vis-à-vis third parties.

Article 264 (1) If the action is well founded, the Court of Justice of the European Union shall declare the act concerned to be void.

Notes

(1) In the EU legal system, an action for annulment can be brought against different forms of administrative action, including measures of denial.[13] The consequence of a successful action for annulment is the total or partial[14] annulment of the contested measure. While the Treaty provision contains the phrase 'declare the act void', the outcome of an annulment action is to be considered of a 'constitutive' and not mere declaratory nature.

(2) The annulment of an act causes it to be annulled from the date on which it came into force (therefore a ruling upholding the applicant's claim has *ex tunc* effects) so that the parties to the proceedings are restored to the situation which they were in before the act entered into force.[15]

Treaty on the Functioning of the European Union **7.10 (EU)**

Article 264 (2) However, the Court shall, if it considers this necessary, state which of the effects of the act which it has declared void shall be considered as definitive.

Note

The European courts may decide to preserve the effects of the annulled act[16] or even declare that it is to remain in force until the competent institution has taken all the necessary measures to give effect to the judgment annulling the act.[17]

[13] On this point, see Chapter 3, sections 3.2.B.2 and 3.3.B.1 (iii).

[14] Partial annulment is only possible where the elements to be annulled are severable from the remainder of the act. See Case 17/74 *Transocean Marine Paint v Commission* ECLI:EU:C:1974:106, para 21.

[15] Case 22/70 *Commission v Council* ECLI: ECLI:EU:C:1971:32, para 59-60; Joined Cases 97/86, 99/86, 193/86 and 215/86 *Asteris and other v Commission* ECLI:EU:C:1988:199, para 30.

[16] Case 45/86 *Commission v Council* ECLI:EU:C:1987:163, para 23; Case C-22/96 *European Parliament v Council* ECLI:EU:C:1998:258, para 42.

[17] Joined Cases C-164/97 and C-165/97 *European Parliament v Council* ECLI:EU:C:1999:99, paras 22–24; Case C-211/01 *Commission v Council* ECLI:EU:C:2003:452, paras 54–57.

Case C-402/05 P, 3 September 2008[18] **7.11 (EU)**

Kadi and others v Commission

ACTION FOR ANNULMENT; MITIGATION OF THE EFFECTS OF ANNULMENT

Kadi

The court can decide, after having annulled a measure, that it remains effective, if public interest requires so.

Facts: The appellants sought the annulment of Council Regulation (EC) 467/2001, which provided the legal basis for the freezing of their assets. The Regulation mandated the freezing of assets owned or controlled by persons associated with Osama bin Laden.

Held: The judgment of the Court of First Instance was set aside. The Regulation was annulled on the ground of the violation of the appellants' right to be heard. However, the Regulation was permitted to remain effective for a maximum of three months after the date of delivery of the judgment to allow the Council to adopt substitute measures to ensure that the assets remained frozen.

Judgment: 372 It follows from all the foregoing that the contested regulation, so far as it concerns the appellants, must be annulled.

373 However, the annulment to that extent of the contested regulation with immediate effect would be capable of seriously and irreversibly prejudicing the effectiveness of the restrictive measures imposed by the regulation and which the Community is required to implement, because in the interval preceding its replacement by a new regulation Mr Kadi and Al Barakaat might take steps seeking to prevent measures freezing funds from being applied to them again.

374 Furthermore, in so far as it follows from this judgement that the contested regulation must be annulled so far as concerns the appellants, by reason of breach of principles applicable in the procedure followed when the restrictive measures introduced by that regulation were adopted, it cannot be excluded that, on the merits of the case, the imposition of those measures on the appellants may for all that prove to be justified.

375 Having regard to those considerations, the effects of the contested regulation, in so far as it includes the names of the appellants in the list forming Annex I thereto, must, by virtue of Article 231 EC, be maintained for a brief period to be fixed in such a way as to allow the Council to remedy the infringements found, but which also takes due account of the considerable impact of the restrictive measures concerned on the appellants' rights and freedoms.

376 In those circumstances, Article 231 EC will be correctly applied in maintaining the effects of the contested regulation, so far as concerns the appellants, for a period that may not exceed three months running from the date of delivery of this judgement.

Note

A decision of the European courts stating that the effects of an annulled measure are to remain in force is exceptional, and may only be granted where there are compelling reasons relating to the principle of legal certainty.

[18] ECLI:EU:C:2008:461.

7.2.A.4 FRANCE

In the French system, the remedies available before administrative courts are classified according to two main categories of actions: the action for annulment (*recours pour excès de pouvoir*) and the 'full jurisdiction remedy' (*recours de plein contentieux* or *recours de pleine juridiction*). Such a division is made according to the types of powers granted to the court. In the case of the action for annulment, the power of the court used to be limited to ruling on the legality of the decision and, if necessary, annulling it. Hence, an individual would use the action for annulment if he sought only the annulment of a decision, whether it be a burdensome decision or a decision containing a refusal. The aim of the full jurisdiction remedy is not to ensure legality as such, but is primarily to safeguard the legal rights of the individual. The powers of the court in the full jurisdiction remedy are diverse, including not only the annulment of the decision, but also the correction and substitution of the challenged decision, and, if relevant, the award of a sum of money. The full jurisdiction remedy may be used to challenge an administrative law contract[19] and to bring a claim for liability of public authorities.[20]

However, the distinction between the two forms of action is no longer strict, since, in the action for annulment, the court's powers are no longer limited to solely the annulment of a decision.[21]

Code de justice administrative **7.12 (FR)**

Article L311-4 The Council of State is competent, at first and last instance, to grant a 'full jurisdiction remedy' (*recours de pleine juridiction*) in the cases that are attributed to it by virtue of:

1. Paragraph IV of Article L612-16 of the Monetary and Financial Code (Code monétaire et financier) against decisions to impose sanctions taken by the Prudential Supervisory and Resolution Authority (Autorité de contrôle prudentiel et de résolution);
2. Article L342-14 and L342-15 of the Construction and Housing Code (Code de la construction et de l'habitation) against decisions to impose sanctions taken by the Ministers in charge of housing and local entities;
3. Articles L5-3 and L36-11 of the Post and Electronic Communications Code (Code des postes et des communications électroniques) against decisions to impose sanctions taken by the Post and Electronic Communications authority (Autorité de régulation des communications électroniques et des postes);
4. Article L824-14 of the Commercial Code (Code du commerce);
5. Article 42-8 of Law N° 86-1067 of 30 September 1986, against the decisions of the Higher Council for the Audiovisual Sector (Conseil supérieur de l'audiovisuel) referred to in Articles 42-1, 42-3 and 42-4 of said law;
6. Article 71 of Law N° 96-597 of 2 July 1996 against decisions to impose sanctions taken by the Financial Markets authority (Autorité des marchés financiers) against approved providers of investment services;
7. Article L623-3 of the Monetary and Financial Code;

[19] On this concept, see Chapter 3, section 3.5.C.
[20] On liability of public authorities in France, see Chapter 11.
[21] See further section 7.3.A.3 below.

8. Articles L232-24 and L241-8 of the Sport Code (Code du sport);

9. Article 40 of Law N° 2000-108 of 10 February 2000 against decisions to impose sanctions taken by the Energy authority (Commission de régulation de l'énergie);

10. Article 17 of Law N° 2009-1503 of 8 December 2009 relating to the organisation and regulation of rail transport and containing various provisions relating to transportation, against decisions to impose sanctions taken by the Rail and Road Activities authority (Autorité de régulation des activités ferroviaires et routières).

Notes

(1) The classification of a remedy as belonging to one of the two categories of action is not expressly indicated as such in the Code de justice administrative. Consequently, whether a claim is brought as an action for annulment or a full jurisdiction remedy is not a decision for the claimant, but results from the court's examination of what the claimant is seeking.[22] Article L311-4 of the Code de justice administrative is an exception in this respect, as it specifically mentions which cases are to be brought as full jurisdiction remedy. In these cases, an individual can ask not only for the annulment of a challenged decision, but also for its substitution by a decision of the Conseil d'État or compensation for the damages suffered.

(2) The classification of an action into one of the two categories not only is relevant in determining the powers of the judge, but also has procedural consequences. Most notably, the assistance of an attorney is needed in cases where the full jurisdiction remedy is sought, whereas this is not required in actions for annulment.[23] Furthermore, if the remedy of annulment is sought under the full jurisdiction remedy, the applicable time limit is two months, as for the action for annulment, whereas for other remedies – such as compensation following an illegality – there is no time limit applicable.[24]

Conseil d'État, 11 May 2004[25] **7.13 (FR)**

Association AC! and others v Minister for Social Affairs, Labour and Solidarity

ACTION FOR ANNULMENT; MITIGATION OF EFFECTS OF ANNULMENT DECISION

Association AC!

If the general interest requires it, the court may limit the effects of an annulment ruling.

Facts: The claimants were pursuing the annulment of decrees (*arrêtés*) adopted on 5 February 2003, by which the Minister of Social Affairs, Labour and Solidarity had approved agreements related to the conditions for the granting of assistance to unemployed people.

[22] See in general on remedies in the French legal system, F Melleray, *Essai sur la structure du contentieux administratif* (Paris, Librairie générale de droit et de jurisprudence, 2001); S Doumbe-Billé, 'Recours pour excès de pouvoir et recours de plein contentieux' (1993) *Actualité Juridique de Droit Administratif* 3.

[23] See Chapter 4, section 4.3.C.

[24] See Chapter 4, section 4.7.D.2.

[25] N° 255886.

Held: The ministerial acts were annulled, but annulment of some provisions was postponed to a later date. The annulment of the other provisions had no retroactive effect.

Judgment: On the consequences of the illegality of the challenged decrees:

As regards the court's duty:

Whereas the annulment of an administrative measure implies in principle that this measure is deemed never to have existed; nevertheless, if it appears that the retroactive effect of this annulment is such that there are obviously excessive consequences due to the effects that this measure has brought about and the situations which could have arisen when it was in force and the general interest that may be linked to the temporary maintenance of its effects, it is the responsibility of the administrative court – after having received the parties' observations on this point and examined *ex officio* all the grounds of public order and all grounds raised by the parties which could affect the legality of the measure in question – to take into consideration, firstly, the consequences of the retroactive status of the annulment on the various public or private interests concerned, and, secondly, the disadvantages which, with regard to the principle of legality and the litigants' right to an effective remedy, a time limit imposed on the effects of the annulment would cause; whereas it is the court's duty to assess, by weighing these elements, if they can justify that, exceptionally, a departure should be made from the principle of retroactive effect of the disputed annulments and, if so, to make provision in its ruling that, subject to legal proceedings undertaken on the date thereof against the measures issued on the basis of the measure in question, all or part of the effects of this measure prior to its annulment shall be regarded as final or even, where required, that the annulment should only take effect on a later date that it determines;

As regards the application of these principles to the disputed decrees:

As regards the decrees relating to the agreement of 1 January 2004:

Whereas, however, it follows from the provisions of the above mentioned Labour Code (Code du travail) that the law obliges the most representative organisations of employers and workers and the minister responsible for labour and, failing this, the Prime Minister, to take the measures necessary to guarantee the continuity of the unemployment insurance system; whereas accordingly, it necessarily falls to the public authorities, in the event of the annulment of the decree by which the minister responsible for labour approved agreements entered into for the application of the provisions of Article L351-8, to take promptly the measures that these provisions require; whereas, having regard to the interest attached to the continuity of the payment of unemployment benefits and the collection of contributions, to which a retroactive annulment of the provisions of the challenged decrees …, would be clearly excessively harmful, it is appropriate, in order to allow the minister of labour or, failing that, the Prime Minister, to take the necessary steps to ensure this continuity, to rule that the decision is annulled, subject to the rights of persons who have initiated legal proceedings on the date of the ruling, only as of 1 July 2004; …

Notes

(1) When, in an action for annulment, an administrative decision[26] is found to be unlawful, it will be retroactively annulled. In some cases, when the annulment of the whole decision would be disproportionate, the court might opt, upon the request of

[26] For the concept of *décision* in the French legal system, see Chapter 3, section 3.1.A.2.

the applicant or *ex officio*, for the partial annulment of the unlawful provisions if only a part of the decision is unlawful and this part is severable.[27]

(2) In rare cases, exceptions to the principle of retroactive annulment are made if these serve the general interest. From the *Association AC!* case, it follows that the administrative court has been granted the power to mitigate the consequences of an annulment ruling in two different ways: it can decide that an act is not annulled *ex tunc*, but only *ex nunc*; and it can decide that the retroactive effects will not commence *ex tunc*, but from a later date. Such a prerogative is only used when a compelling ground of general interest is at stake, mainly when the principle of legal certainty requires that the administrative decisions based on the challenged act not be called into question. In such circumstances, financial considerations are often decisive. This prerogative is also used to allow the legislator sufficient time to adopt adequate measures, in order to prevent a legal vacuum which would affect the general interest.

7.2.A.5 THE NETHERLANDS

Algemene Wet Bestuursrecht **7.14 (NL)**

Article 8:72 (1) If the administrative judge declares the claim for judicial review (*beroep*) well-founded, he annuls the contested decision as defined in Article 1:3 AWB (*besluit*) in whole or in part.

(2) The annulment of an administrative decision or of a part of an administrative decision entails the annulment of the legal consequences of that administrative decision or of the annulled part thereof.

...

Notes

(1) In the Dutch legal system, only certain types of administrative decisions (*besluit*), namely single-case decisions (*beschikkingen*) (including the refusal to issue a single-case decision) and 'concretising decisions of general scope' (*concretisierende besluiten van algemene strekking*), may be challenged in a claim for judicial review.[28] If the claim for judicial review is well founded, the Dutch administrative court is, in principle, obliged to annul, in whole or in part, the contested decision.

(2) The annulment is effective *ex tunc*. Hence, the legal effects of the decision disappear, as if the decision had never been taken. In exceptional circumstances, however, if legal certainty requires, the court is allowed to decide whether the effect of the annulment ruling is to be postponed.[29] However, courts hardly ever apply this possibility.

[27] Conseil d'État, 1 June 1970, *Association Défense et promotion des langues de France*, N° 06410.

[28] For these concepts in the Dutch administrative legal system, see Chapter 3, sections 3.1.A.1, 3.2.A.2, 3.3.A.1 (iii).

[29] See, eg ECLI:NL:CBB:2011:BQ9602.

(3) The annulment may concern the decision as a whole or only a part of it, for instance, a condition attached to the decision. The annulment of a decision entails the annulment only of the legal consequences of that decision, not of the factual consequences. So, for example, the annulment of a building permit renders the development of a building on the ground of that permit *ex tunc* unlawful. However, to have such a building demolished – and bring the factual situation in line with the legal situation – the administrative authority must take a separate enforcement measure.

Algemene Wet Bestuursrecht **7.15 (NL)**

Article 8:41a The administrative judge is obliged to decide the dispute in a manner which is as definitive as possible.

Article 8:72 … (3) the administrative judge may determine that:
a. the legal consequences of the annulled administrative decision or the annulled part thereof remain effective in whole or in part; or …

Note

If a decision is annulled, the Dutch administrative judge is under a legal obligation to decide the dispute in a manner which is as definitive as possible (Article 8:41a AWB), and to avoid, if possible, a so-called 'bald' annulment, ie an annulment only (and a referral of the case back to the administrative authority in order for the latter to issue a new decision). In this light, according to Article 8:72(3)(a) AWB, the judge has the competence to uphold the legal consequences of the annulled decision.

Raad van State, 21 October 2009[30] **7.16 (NL)**

Mayor and Aldermen of Lansingerland v X

ANNULMENT DECISION; CONSEQUENCES OF ANNULMENT

Fence Lansigerland

If the administrative authority has discretion after an annulment ruling, certain conditions have to be met to uphold the legal consequences of a decision.

Facts: By decision of 24 July 2007, the board of mayor and aldermen of Lansingerland had refused to grant a building permit to install a fence on the premises of the applicant. The district court annulled this decision because, originally, it had not well been reasoned. However, during the court proceedings, the authority added a new, sufficient reasoning. In reaction to this, the district court annulled the decision, but upheld its legal consequences.

[30] ECLI:NL:RVS:2009:BK0806.

Held: In the circumstances of the case, the district court could lawfully uphold the legal effects of the annulled decision.

Judgment: 2.3.1 As the Judicial Division has previously decided, the ability of the court to uphold the legal effects of a decision which has been annulled does not require that only one decision is possible. In the present case, where a decision has been invalidated due to lack of sound reasoning, in view of the discretion available to the administrative body, the legal effects of the decision may, from the point of view of procedural economy, be upheld, provided that the administrative body keeps to its decision and provides the necessary statement of reasons and the other parties have sufficient opportunity to respond. Thereby, it is decisive whether the content of the invalidated decision, once the new reasoning is provided, could pass the test of judicial review.

According to the contested judgment of the district court, the board of mayor and aldermen made clear, by writing a letter from 25 November 2008 and through a hearing, the considerations on the basis of which the legal effects of the annulled decisions could be upheld. The Judicial Division agrees with this assessment. The appeal is rejected.

Notes

(1) As is shown by the case of *Fence Lansingerland*, the power to uphold the effects of an annulled decision may, for example, be used if a decision is annulled on the ground of lack of sound reasoning but the authority, while the case is pending before the court, provides stronger reasoning in support of that decision.

(2) In the past, the court used to be able to uphold the legal effects of a decision only in situations where the administrative authority did not enjoy any remaining discretion. The *Fence Lansingerland* case shows that this requirement is no longer applied. The current standard that the courts apply in order to determine when they can use such power is whether the decision whose legal consequences are upheld 'can pass the test of judicial review', meaning that it is lawful. In order to apply this instrument, it is necessary to give the parties to the dispute the opportunity to make representations prior to their use.

7.2.B BYPASSING FLAWS, REPARATION AND SUBSTITUTION

Section 7.2.A. has shown that, in the studied legal systems, there is a tendency to grant powers to the court that permit the mitigation of the consequences of an annulment ruling in specific circumstances. This section deals with a more far-reaching power, namely the possibility for the judge to avoid the annulment of a decision even though it is found to be illegal. The consequence is that, after the ruling, the original decision has to be considered to be legal and is fully enforceable, both *ex tunc* and *ex nunc*.

For example, the court may have the power to bypass the flaws of a decision. In some legal systems, the court proceedings may also be the place, to various extents, to engage in the redrafting of the illegal decision, or may sometimes be the forum where the court itself adopts a new decision. These possibilities all serve the aim of preventing the case from being referred back to the administrative authority, which would have to start the decision-making process again.

7.2.B.1 GERMANY

In the German legal system, the courts have instruments to avoid the annulment of a decision, through repairing or bypassing the flaws in an administrative act, when there is no need to quash the challenged decision in order to protect the rights of the claimant.[31]

Verwaltungsverfahrensgesetz **7.17 (DE)**

§45 (1) An infringement of the provisions governing procedure or form which does not render the administrative act invalid under §44 shall be ignored if:

1. the application necessary for the issuing of the administrative act is subsequently filed;
2. the necessary statement of grounds is subsequently provided;
3. the necessary hearing of a participant is subsequently held;
4. the decision of a committee whose collaboration is required in the issuing of the administrative act is subsequently taken;
5. the necessary collaboration of another authority is subsequently obtained.

(2) Actions referred to in section 1 may be made good until the final instance ruling on facts.

(3) Where an administrative act lacks the necessary statement of grounds or has been issued without the necessary prior hearing of a participant, so that the administrative act could not have been contested in good time, failure to observe the period for legal remedy shall not be regarded as the fault of the applicant. The event resulting in restoration of the *status quo ante* under §32(2) shall be deemed to occur when the omission of the procedural action is made good.

§46 Application for annulment of an administrative act which is not invalid under §44 cannot be made solely on the ground that the act came into being through the infringement of regulations governing procedure, form or local competence, where it is evident that the infringement has not influenced the decision on the substance.

Note

(1) §45 of the Verwaltungsverfahrensgesetz (VwVfG) provides that certain procedural errors – for example, the failure to fulfil the right to a hearing – can be rectified up until the final instance ruling on facts (*letzte Tatsacheninstanz*).

(2) Even if a procedural error cannot or has not been rectified by subsequent action according to §45 VwVfG, the administrative courts may not annul an administrative decision because of a procedural error 'where it is evident that the infringement has not influenced the decision on the matter' (§46 VwVfG).

[31] For more detail, see Chapter 6, section 6.6.C.

Verwaltungsgerichtsordnung **7.18 (DE)**

§114 ... The administrative authority may also supplement its discretionary considerations as to the administrative act in the proceedings before the administrative courts.

Notes

(1) In order to avoid annulment, the administrative authority can provide elements to complement the considerations of its decision during the court proceedings, developing, for example, the factual grounds on which it based its decision, in order to address the insufficient motivation of its original decision.

(2) The administrative court cannot substitute its own decision for that of the authority. If §114 VwGO could not successfully be applied, the judge finds the decision unlawful and §45 VwVfG does not apply, the court will pronounce the annulment of the decision, and the matter will be referred back to the competent administrative authority.

7.2.B.2 THE EUROPEAN UNION

Treaty on the Functioning of the European Union **7.19 (EU)**

Article 263 (2) It shall for this purpose have jurisdiction in actions brought by a Member State, the European Parliament, the Council or the Commission on grounds of lack of competence, infringement of an essential procedural requirement, infringement of the Treaties or of any rule of law relating to their application, or misuse of powers.

Notes

(1) In the European Union, according to Article 263(2) of the Treaty on the Functioning of the European Union (TFEU), only the infringement of an essential procedural requirement can justify the annulment of acts of European institutions. This means that the violation of non-essential procedural requirements will not lead to the annulment of a decision.

(2) Furthermore, formal errors can be repaired if the necessary procedural steps are carried out effectively before the beginning of the court proceedings or during the court proceedings. However, this is possible only if it concerns minor formal errors.[32]

(3) The European courts have no power of substitution of their own decision in place of the illegal decision.

[32] See, eg Joined Cases C-329/93, C-62/95 and C-63/95 *Germany and others v Commission* ECLI:EU:C:1996:394, paras 22, 48; Case T-30/91 *Solvay v Commission* ECLI:EU:T:1995:115, para 98.

7.2.B.3 ENGLAND AND WALES

Senior Courts Act 1981 **7.20 (EW)**

Section 31

(2A) The High Court –

(a) must refuse to grant relief on an application for judicial review, and

(b) may not make an award under subsection (4) on such an application,

if it appears to the court to be highly likely that the outcome for the applicant would not have been substantially different if the conduct complained of had not occurred.

(2B) The court may disregard the requirements in subsection (2A)(a) and (b) if it considers that it is appropriate to do so for reasons of exceptional public interest.

(2C) If the court grants relief or makes an award in reliance on subsection (2B), the court must certify that the condition in subsection (2B) is satisfied.

...

(5) If, on an application for judicial review, the High Court quashes the decision to which the application relates, it may in addition–

...

(b) substitute its own decision for the decision in question.

(5A) But the power conferred by subsection (5)(b) is exercisable only if–

(a) the decision in question was made by a court or tribunal,

(b) the decision is quashed on the ground that there has been an error of law, and

(c) without the error, there would have been only one decision which the court or tribunal could have reached.

(5B) Unless the High Court otherwise directs, a decision substituted by it under subsection (5)(b) has effect as if it were a decision of the relevant court or tribunal.

Civil Procedure Rules **7.21 (EW)**

Rule 54.19

(1) This rule applies where the court makes a quashing order in respect of the decision to which the claim relates.

(2) The court may–

... (b) in so far as any enactment permits, substitute its own decision for the decision to which the claim relates.

Notes

(1) In addition to the possibility provided for in section 31(5)(a) of the Senior Courts Act[33] permitting the court to remit the quashed decision to the decision-maker, the court has also the power, in accordance with Section 31(5)(b), to take the decision itself when there is no purpose to be served by remitting the matter to the

[33] For more detail on this point, see section 7.3.A below.

decision-maker where the decision-maker was a court or tribunal.[34] However, this possibility is seldom used.

(2) The Crime and Courts Act 2015 introduced section 31(2A) into the Senior Courts Act 1981. This provision requires that the courts must not grant a remedy where the decision or action of a public authority would not have been substantially different if the conduct complained of had not occurred. This introduced for the first time a specific legislative requirement for bypassing flaws. The courts still retain considerable discretion in the application of section 31(2A), as the 'substantially different' test is subject to interpretation by the courts, and in a number of cases the court has found that failures to comply with procedural requirements may have made a substantial difference and thus has still granted a remedy.[35] However, the Court of Appeal has made it clear that section 31(2A) has broad scope and requires the court to refuse to grant a remedy where either procedural or substantive errors committed by a decision-maker have made no difference to the decision made by a public authority.[36] As of yet, there is no case law that has engaged in any detail with the requirements of sections 31(2B) and 31(2C) involving the court's discretion to ignore the requirement of section 31(2A) in cases of exceptional public interest.

(3) In addition to this statutory power, the grant of a remedy is at the discretion of the court in public law cases, so the court may decide not to grant a remedy if there is a good reason not to do so. As such, some flaws may be bypassed or corrected either because of the requirements of section 31(2A) or because the court decides, in its discretion, to refuse to grant a remedy. Such a remedy might be denied where this would lead to a substantial disadvantage to the public administration and the error would make no difference to the decision,[37] such as creating uncertainty for a large number of rent payers;[38] where the remedy would have no effect, such as where the challenge was to regulations that had subsequently been amended prior to the hearing;[39] or where the grant of a remedy would have a severe effect on third parties.[40] The courts have been clear that the discretion over the grant of a remedy has not been entirely replaced by section 31(2A) of the Senior Courts Act 1981, although the interface between the requirements of section 31(2A) and the courts' discretion to refuse to grant a remedy has not yet been fully explored in the case law.

[34] In England and Wales, a distinction is drawn between 'superior courts of record', which are not subject to control through judicial review (the High Court, Court of Appeal and Supreme Court are examples), and 'inferior courts', such as the magistrates' courts (to deal with less serious criminal offences) and the county court (which deals, amongst other things, with civil cases of lower value). Inferior courts are subject to the judicial review jurisdiction of the High Court.

[35] See, eg *R (Lensbury) v Richmond-upon-Thames District Council* [2016] EWCA Civ 814, [2017] JPL 96, [41]–[44] (Sales LJ).

[36] *R (on the application of Goring-on-Thames Parish Council) v South Oxfordshire District Council* [2018] EWCA Civ 860, [47]–[53].

[37] See, eg *Walton v Scottish Ministers* [2012] UKSC 44, [2013] PTSR 51.

[38] See, eg *R v Paddington Valuation Officer and Another, ex parte Peachey Property Corporation Ltd* [1966] 1 QB 380 (CA).

[39] *R v Secretary of State for Social Services, ex p Association of Metropolitan Authorities* [1986] 1 WLR 1 (QB).

[40] *R v Panel on Take-overs and Mergers, ex p Datafin plc* [1987] QB 815 (DC).

7.2.B.4 FRANCE

Conseil d'État, 3 December 2003[41] **7.22 (FR)**

Prefect of Seine-Maritime v El Bahi

SUBSTITUTION OF LEGAL GROUNDS

El Bahi

Once it has ruled that a decision is illegal because it was based on an illegal ground, the administrative court has the power to substitute the illegal ground with the correct legal ground in order to avoid annulling the decision.

Facts: On 23 October 2001, the prefect of Seine-Maritime adopted an expulsion decision against Mr El Bahi, a Morrocan national. The decision was based on the fact that he had entered the French territory illegally. However, Mr El Bahi had entered in possession of a valid visa delivered by the Italian authorities. Mr El Bahi challenged the decision.

Held: The decision of expulsion was not annulled, even though it was based on the wrong legal basis. The Conseil d'État decided to substitute the legal ground of the decision with the correct one (that the applicant remained unlawfully on French territory three months after his entry without any valid authorisation).

Judgment: Considering that it follows from the documents of the file that, contrary to the grounds of the challenged administrative decision (*arrêté*), Mr Y was the holder of a valid residence permit issued by the Italian authorities on the day of his entry to France in August 2000; that thus, he is proven to have entered France lawfully; that, consequently, the decision to deport the claimant could not have been taken on the basis of the aforementioned provisions of Article 22-I-1° of the Ordinance of 2 November 1945;

Considering, nevertheless, that, where he ascertains that a contested decision before him could have been taken lawfully on the basis of another legal provision than the one that is subject of challenge, the judge competent to rule on the annulment action may substitute this basis for the one that served as the legal basis of the challenged decision, provided that the concerned individual was given the guarantees provided by the rule on the basis of which the decision should have been taken; that such a substitution falls within the scope of the jurisdiction of the judge and he may carry the substitution out on his own initiative, with regard to the documents of the file, but provided that, in this case, he has given the opportunity to the parties to bring forward comments on this point; ...

Notes

(1) Through case law, the administrative courts have developed the potential to 'rescue' an unlawful decision from annulment in order not to require a new decision-making process. First, the judge can avoid the annulment of a decision which

[41] N° 240267.

was adopted in infringement of procedural or formal requirements. The judge, in his ruling, can bypass procedural or formal flaws if these infringements did not have consequences to the content of the decision or deprived individuals of procedural safeguards.[42]

(2) Apart from bypassing certain flaws in the decision, the French courts also have certain limited 'healing' powers, as shown by *El Bahi*. In this case, the decision was illegal since it was based on the wrong legal or factual grounds. However, the public authority would have adopted the same decision once it had been grounded on the correct legal or factual basis. In order to avoid what is considered a 'useless' annulment, the court can change the legal or factual ground,[43] by referring to the lawful ones, while dismissing the claim.

(3) According to the *El Bahi* case, the requirements to substitute the legal grounds are the following: the provision which will be substituted must have an 'equivalent scope' to the legal basis wrongfully used; the administrative authority must hold the same margin of discretion; and the applicant must have benefited from the guarantees (formal and procedural) he would have had if the correct legal basis had been applied. The parties must also have the opportunity to comment on the substitution before the court carries it out.

(4) The French court cannot substitute its own decision for the illegal decision. Indeed, the possibility to substitute the legal or factual grounds of a decision, as established in *El Bahi*, is conditioned by the fact that the substitution has no consequences on the substance of the final decision.

7.2.B.5 THE NETHERLANDS

Algemene Wet Bestuursrecht **7.23 (NL)**

Article 8:41a The administrative judge is obliged to decide the dispute in a manner which is as definitive as possible.

Article 6:22 A body deciding on an intra-administrative objection or a claim for judicial review (*beroep*) may uphold the challenged decision despite the fact that a written or unwritten rule of law or a general principle has been violated, if it is plausible that the parties concerned do not thereby incur any disadvantages.

Article 8:72 … (3) the administrative judge may determine that:

a. the legal consequences of the annulled administrative decision or the annulled part thereof remain effective in whole or in part; or

b. his ruling takes the place of the annulled administrative decision or of the annulled part thereof.

[42] See further Chapter 6, section 6.6.B.1.

[43] Conseil d'État, 6 February 2004, *Hallal*, N° 240560.

Raad van State, 21 March 2012[44] **7.24 (NL)**

X v Mayor and Aldermen of Helmond

UNLAWFUL DECISION; SUBSTITUTION

Sand Depot Helmond

Having ruled that a decision is unlawful, the court has the power to replace a decision of the administration by its own decision.

Facts: By a decision of 22 February 2011, mayor and aldermen granted a permit to develop a storage area for sand (including a road leading to the area) for a period of five years as an exemption from the local development plan. In its judgment of 4 May 2011, the interim relief judge (*voorzieningenrechter*) decided that the claim against this permit was well-founded, because the exemption from the local development plan, which was a prerequisite for granting the permit to develop the sand depot, did not contain any conditions. The judge quashed the decision and replaced it by adding to the decision of 22 February 2011 the conditions that the activities should be undertaken only outside the breeding season of birds and also that disturbance of bats by using lights in the evening and at night had to be avoided. The court declared that the judgment replaced the original decision of the authority. The decision of the district court was appealed before the Council of State.

Held: The judgment of the district court was quashed.

Judgment: 2.4. The interim relief judge found no reason to rule that the board of mayor and aldermen had not been able to reasonably provide an exemption from the development plan. The interim relief judge further considered that the authority infringed the duty to state reasons, because, in spite of what had been announced in the policy document prepared by the authority, no reasons have been provided in the decision to grant the exemption. The interim relief judge, applying Article 8:72(4) AWB [now Article 8:72(3)(b) AWB], replaced the decision of the authority with his own decision, by connecting the missing conditions to the exemption.

...

2.9. The claimant sub 2, the board of mayor and aldermen and the claimant sub 1 argue that the interim relief judge incorrectly applied Article 8:72(4) AWB by attaching the condition to the decision of 22 February that the activities should be undertaken outside the breeding season of birds. According to the board and the claimant sub 2, this requirement is too far-reaching and according to the claimant sub 1 the term breeding season is not sufficiently specific to allow enforcement of the decision. The claimant sub 1 also argues that the provision which has been added to the decision by the interim relief judge, according to whom all disturbance of the bats resulting from light had to be prevented, is too vague.

2.9.1. When using the competence permitting the replacement of a decision of an authority by his own decision, the judge must be convinced that the result of the dispute, in case the board of mayor and aldermen would again decide on the application, is in accordance with the law. In the case before the court, however, the board argued that the provision attached to the exemption by the court that the work must be carried out

[44] ECLI:NL:RVS:2012:BV9463.

outside the breeding season is too general and that there is no reason to provide further protection than that arising from the Flora and Fauna Act (Flora- en Faunawet).

Assuming that the claimant sub 2 will apply aforementioned code of conduct when he performs his activities, this code of conduct already prescribes precautionary measures that aim to prevent destruction of nests in the working area and that the claimant sub 2, based on this code of conduct, must already take the breeding season of birds into account, there is no reason to add an extra condition to the exemption, according to which the activities may only take place outside the breeding season of birds. In view of this, the judge incorrectly replaced the authorities' decision by his own decision by adding to the decision the condition that the activities must be performed outside the breeding season of birds. The claims are successful. The challenged decision must be quashed insofar as it is contrary to Article 8:72(4) AWB.

Notes

(1) According to the AWB, the administrative courts are obliged to 'decide the dispute in a manner which is as definitive as possible'. This implies that, having declared a decision unlawful, the ruling should not lead to a legal vacuum that needs to be filled by a subsequent decision but, rather, should solve the dispute directly.[45]

(2) A first instrument to deciding the dispute definitively as far as possible is to treat flaws as being insignificant where this is possible. According to Article 6:22 AWB, all legal flaws, whether they concern procedural or substantial requirements, can be ignored if it may be assumed that this error has not affected the interested parties.[46]

(3) To come to a definitive judgment in the case, Article 8:72(3) provides for two more instruments. First, Article 8:72(3)(a) grants the court the power to uphold the legal consequences of the annulled decision, as discussed above.[47] Secondly, the court may take a decision that substitutes the annulled decision (Article 8:72(3)(b)). As with the situation in which the court upholds the legal consequences of an annulled decision, and in case the court wants to substitute the annulled decision with its own, the standard to be applied in order to use this power is whether the new decision 'can pass the test of judicial review'. In this case, it is also necessary to give the parties to the dispute the opportunity to make representations prior to the substitution of the annulled decision.

Algemene Wet Bestuursrecht **7.25 (NL)**

Article 8:51a (1) The administrative judge may grant the administrative authority the opportunity to repair or have repaired a flaw in the contested decision. …

(2) The administrative judge shall determine the time limit within which the administrative authority may repair the flaw. He may extend this time limit.

[45] R Seerden and D Wenders, 'Administrative Law in the Netherlands' in R Seerden (ed), *Comparative Administrative Law*, 4th edn (Antwerp, Intersentia, 2017) 162 ff.

[46] This provision was dealt with in more detail and with an excerpt from case law in Chapter 6, section 6.6.A.2.

[47] See section 7.2.A above.

Article 8:51b … (2) If the authority uses the opportunity to repair the flaw, it shall inform the judge as soon as possible in writing about the way in which the flaw has been repaired.

(3) Parties may, within four weeks after the information referred to in section 2 has been sent to them, submit their views in writing about the way in which the flaw has been repaired. The judge may extend this time limit.

Article 8:51c The administrative judge shall inform the parties about the way in which the proceedings will continue within four weeks.

… c. it has received the view of the parties.

Article 8:80a (1) The administrative judge pronounces the application of Article 8:51a AWB by means of an interlocutory judgment (*tussenuitspraak*).

(2) The interlocutory judgment states as far as possible the way in which the defect may be repaired.

…

Raad van State, 8 December 2010[48] **7.26 (NL)**

X v Mayor and Aldermen of Leeuwarden

ADMINISTRATIVE LOOP

Administrative Loop Leeuwarden

If a decision is illegal, the judge can pause the proceedings and provide the administrative authority with the opportunity to repair a flaw.

Facts: On 16 September 2010, the mayor and aldermen of Leeuwarden ordered the claimant to scrap his ship and remove waste from the quay.

Held: By way of interlocutory judgment, the mayor and aldermen were ordered to provide the claimant with the opportunity to respond to the report of the inspection carried out on 17 May 2010. Their order to remove the ship was suspended until the final decision of the court.

Judgment: 2.7.1. By letter of 17 August 2010, the board of mayor and aldermen announced to the appellant its intention to amend the decision of 5 January 2010. In addition, the appellant was given the opportunity to put forward his views on this subject. However, as has been demonstrated at the hearing, the inspection report of 17 May 2010, which forms the basis for the aforementioned amendment, was not made available in advance of the decision of 16 September 2010. Due to the fact that information necessary to permit the claimant to make representations against the proposed decisions was not made available to the claimant, the decision is not adequately and carefully prepared.

2.7.2. The conclusion is that the decision of 16 September 2010 violates Article 3:2(1) AWB.

2.8. The court, recognising the importance of a swift end to the dispute in accordance with Article 49(6) Council of State Act (Wet op de Raad van State), orders the rectification of the aforementioned defect contained in the decision of 16 September 2010.

[48] ECLI:NL:RVS:2010:BO6641.

The board of mayor and aldermen shall provide the claimant with the opportunity to offer a response to the facts as set out in the report of the inspection carried out on 17 May 2010 within four weeks, for example by means of an expert report. The board of mayor and aldermen must respond within another four weeks by assessing the arguments of the claimant and must send the transcript of this review to the court. If necessary, the board of mayor and aldermen must take a new decision within this period.

Notes

(1) To facilitate definitive dispute resolution by the administrative courts, the AWB provides for the so-called 'administrative loop' procedure. This instrument is applied where the defects in the decision-making process or in the decision itself are such that it is impossible for the court to apply the finalisation instruments of Articles 6:22 and 8:72(3) AWB. In such a case, the court may render an interlocutory judgment (Article 8:80a AWB), in which it offers the administration the opportunity to repair the defects in the decision within a certain time limit. According to Article 8:51d AWB, a final instance court can even order the administrative authority to (try to) repair the decision. A decision may be repaired by altering the decision (hence taking a new one)[49] or, if possible, without altering the decision, eg by organising a public hearing, by repairing an insufficient mandate to decide and/or by improving the reasoning of the decision.[50] In the *Administrative Loop Leeuwarden* case, the Judicial Division of the Council of State prescribed the way in which the authority should act to guarantee the right of defence to the applicant, which were violated when the contested decision was taken.

(2) After the administration has acted to repair the decision (eg by holding the missing hearing), the court procedure continues. The parties may make representations on the results of the repair. Often, there is no second hearing. The court then takes its definitive (second) decision. If the administration successfully repaired the decision, the final judgment may be that the first decision is quashed and the claim against the second decision is rejected (if there is a second decision),[51] or that the decision is quashed but the legal consequences of the decision are upheld.[52] Other dicta are possible, too. The advantage of this procedure is that the delay which would result if the decision were quashed and the whole decision-making process would have to be carried out again can be circumvented.

(3) The authority must inform the administrative court of the way in which it has repaired or tried to repair the defects as soon as possible, and in any case within the time limit set by the court. If the other parties do not agree with the way in which the decision is repaired, the judicial review procedure continues. Hence, the 'administrative loop' procedure is distinct from the possibility offered in some other

[49] Eg ECLI:NL:RVS:2012:BW8876.

[50] Eg ECLI:NL:RVS:2010:BL7777.

[51] C Backes and others, *Evaluatie Bestuurlijke Lus en internationale rechtsvergelijking* (The Hague, Ministerie van Justitie WODC, 2014) para 4.7.2.

[52] ECLI:NL:RVS:2011:BP2798.

legal systems (and also in Dutch law) to provide guidance addressed to administrative authorities,[53] since the redrafting of the decision is taken during the judicial proceedings, under the supervision of the court.

(4) Apart from the 'administrative loop' procedure, which is court-driven, the administration may also, of its own accord, repair a flaw in a decision while judicial proceedings are pending, as follows from Article 6:19 AWB.

7.2.C COMPARATIVE REMARKS

All the legal systems studied provide for an action for annulment to challenge acts adopted by the public authorities. Annulment can be regarded as a core remedy in administrative matters in order to ensure the legality of administrative action. In this regard, the principle of retroactive effects of an annulment ruling is acknowledged in all legal systems, as a guarantee to the rule of law.

In England and Wales, the Netherlands, France and the EU, when an action for annulment is successful, the court can mitigate the retroactive effects of the annulment ruling, by limiting or postponing the consequences of an annulment ruling if the interests of the claimant or the general interest require it. However, it is important to note that, in all legal systems providing for this possibility, the use of such powers remains exceptional. The outlier in this context is Germany, where the remedy of annulment is strictly limited to the retroactive removal of the challenged decision.

Annulment is, however, never the only power of the court in administrative matters.

The courts may, firstly, *bypass* flaws if the illegalities have not influenced the decision on the matter and/or the interests of the parties have not been affected. In Germany, this possibility only concerns infringements of most procedural requirements; in the Netherlands, infringements of all kind of legal requirements can be ignored if it is plausible that the infringement has not affected any interested parties. The same is true in France, but only in cases of infringement of procedural or formal requirements. In the EU, procedural flaws are only relevant if they are essential, which means that they may have influenced the content of the decision at stake. In the opposite case, they will not lead to the annulment of the contested decision. The law in England and Wales has only recently created an official process for bypassing flaws in decisions. However, even prior to the introduction of the legislative provision, the fact that remedies are discretionary allowed the courts considerable scope to bypass errors either where the errors are deemed not to be significant or where granting a remedy could have negative effects for the public administration or for third parties. An examination of the approach of the courts under the new legislative provision on the bypassing of flaws and the law on the discretion over the grant of a remedy suggests that the approach under both provisions is similar.

The courts also have, to different extents, the power to *repair* flaws in the decision during the judicial proceedings. The aim of these instruments is to accelerate the resolution of the dispute between the parties. In Germany, certain kinds of procedural flaws can be

[53] On this point, see section 7.3 below.

repaired during the court proceedings. In the Netherlands, the possibility for the authorities to repair a flaw in a decision concerns all flaws. Moreover, the 'administrative loop' provides a procedural, court-driven, instrument to heal potentially all illegalities during the court proceedings. In France, the court may repair certain flaws concerning legal or factual grounds of the decision by substituting a new legal or factual basis, as long as the process does not change the content of the challenged decision. In the EU, the repairing of flaws during the proceedings is very limited and concerns only minor flaws, while in England and Wales, the reparation is subject to the discretion of the court.

Another instrument to prevent a case from being referred back to the administrative authority if this is not necessary is the court's power of *substitution* of the authority's decision by a decision of the court itself. This instrument is known in England and Wales (although rarely used), and particularly so in the Netherlands. Whilst a prerequisite for such a substitution in England and Wales is that, after the annulment, there is no discretion left to the administration on how to respond to the judgment, in the Netherlands, substitution is, under certain conditions, even possible if the authority still has some discretion remaining. However, the conditions for substitution in such cases ensure that the judge does not take over the task of the administration. In France, the power of substitution only exists in the 'full jurisdiction remedy' (*recours de pleine juridiction*) and not in the action for annulment.[54]

All in all, the Dutch legal system seems to offer the most far-reaching instruments aimed at preventing the need to refer the case back to the administration if the decision at stake is found to be unlawful. The general requirement contained in Article 8.41a AWB that the judge is obliged to decide the dispute in a manner which is as definitive as possible is responsible for this 'mindset'.

7.3 ORDERS AND GUIDANCE TO THE PUBLIC AUTHORITIES

When challenging the administrative action, the circumstances of the case may be such that the applicant may not seek the annulment of a decision, but instead may seek an order obliging public authorities to behave in a certain way or towards a certain end. In the different legal systems studied, these claims are dealt with either through autonomous and specific actions or through an action for annulment.

In all the studied legal systems, the court can order, to different extents, the public authority to act or to abstain from acting. When doing so, and depending on the conditions of the case, it can indicate to the authority how it should act.

It is not self-evident to what extent such powers are granted to the judge, because, if the scope of these powers is too wide, they could be regarded as infringing the principle of separation of powers. Such powers may exceed the limits of the scope of the judicial function, which is the determination of a dispute. Developing a solution for a case and adopting decisions to this end may be seen as being outside of the competence of the court and lying instead with the executive. However, the need to increase the efficiency

[54] See section 7.2.A.4 above.

of the decision-making process has affected the classical boundaries of the separation of powers. In this respect, one can observe a more interventionist role of the administrative courts with the aims of ensuring that the public authorities perform their task in compliance with the requirements of legality and that the rights of individuals are effectively protected.

7.3.A ORDERS AND GUIDANCE TO THE PUBLIC AUTHORITIES AS A CONSEQUENCE OF ANNULMENT

In all the studied legal systems apart from Germany, it is possible for the courts, as a consequence of an annulment ruling, to issue more or less detailed and more or less binding instructions to the authority as to how to act.

7.3.A.1 THE EUROPEAN UNION

Treaty on the Functioning of the European Union **7.27 (EU)**

Article 266 The institution whose act has been declared void or whose failure to act has been declared contrary to the Treaties shall be required to take the necessary measures to comply with the judgement of the Court of Justice of the European Union.

This obligation shall not affect any obligation which may result from the application of the second paragraph of Article 340.

Joined Cases 97, 99, 193 and 215/86, 26 April 1988[55] **7.28 (EU)**

Asteris AE and others and Hellenic Republic v Commission

ACTION FOR ANNULMENT; CONSEQUENCES FOR EU INSTITUTIONS

Asteris AE

The European courts have the power to give guidance to the European institutions on how to comply with a ruling.

Facts: In 1985, the Court of Justice declared Commission Regulation No 1615/83, fixing coefficients to be applied to production aid for tomato concentrates for the 1983/84 marketing year, to be void to the extent to which it resulted in unequal treatment of Greek producers, and obliged the Commission to fix new coefficients. As a result, the Commission adopted Regulation No 381/86, fixing additional aid only for the marketing years 1983/84. The applicants – 15 companies and the Greek state – claimed that the judgment also required action in respect of the previous and subsequent marketing years, and called upon the Commission to act. The Commission refused to act, declaring that it has fulfilled its obligations under the judgment by adopting the regulation concerning the marketing years 1983/84.

Held: The Commission's refusal to act was declared void.

[55] ECLI:EU:C:1988:199.

Judgment: In order to adjudicate upon the application for annulment of the Commission's refusal to act, in pursuance of the procedure initiated against it for failure to act, it is necessary first to determine what measures an institution is obliged to take under article 176 in order to comply with a judgement of the court of justice annulling a measure adopted by it.

In order to comply with the judgement and to implement it fully, the institution is required to have regard not only to the operative part of the judgement but also to the grounds which led to the judgement and constitute its essential basis, in so far as they are necessary to determine the exact meaning of what is stated in the operative part. It is those grounds which, on the one hand, identify the precise provision held to be illegal and, on the other, indicate the specific reasons which underlie the finding of illegality contained in the operative part and which the institution concerned must take into account when replacing the annulled measure.

However, although a finding of illegality in the grounds of a judgement annulling a measure primarily requires the institution which adopted the measure to eliminate that illegality in the measure intended to replace the annulled measure, it may also, in so far as it relates to a provision with specific scope in a given area, give rise to other consequences for that institution.

In cases such as this one, where the effect of the annulled regulation is limited to a clearly defined period (namely the 1983/84 marketing year), the institution which adopted the measure is first of all under an obligation to ensure that new legislation adopted following the judgement annulling the previous measure and governing the marketing years subsequent to that judgement contains no provisions having the same effect as the provisions held to be illegal.

However, by virtue of the retroactive effect of judgements by which measures are annulled, the finding of illegality takes effect from the date on which the annulled measure entered into force. It follows that in the present case the institution concerned is also under an obligation to eliminate from the regulations already adopted when the annulling judgement was delivered and governing marketing years after 1983/84 any provisions with the same effect as the provision held to be illegal.

Notes

(1) As a consequence of an annulment action, the EU authorities have a duty to comply with the annulment ruling. However, the European courts have always insisted that they have no power to indicate which measures should be taken by the defendant institutions to comply with the courts' rulings.[56] However, even though they cannot order the defendant institution whose act has been declared void to take a particular course of action, the European courts have, in certain instances, provided guidance as to how to implement their judgments.[57]

[56] Case 53/85 *AKZO Chemie v Commission* ECLI:EU:C:1986:256, para 23; Case T-75/95 *Gunzler Aluminium v Commission* ECLI:EU:T:1996:74, para 18.

[57] Joined Cases T-94/01, T-152/01 and T-286/01 *Hirsch and others v ECB* ECLI:EU:T:2003:3.

(2) The institution must be given a reasonable time in order to comply with a judgment.[58] What constitutes a reasonable time depends on the nature of the measures needed in order to carry out the requirements of the judgment. In the event that there are special difficulties in giving effect to the judgment annulling the contested act, the institution may comply with its obligation by adopting any measure which offers fair compensation for the disadvantage suffered by the applicant.[59]

7.3.A.2 ENGLAND AND WALES

Senior Courts Act 1981 **7.29 (EW)**

Section 31 …

(5) If, on an application for judicial review, the High Court quashes the decision to which the application relates, it may in addition–

(a) remit the matter to the court, tribunal or authority which made the decision, with a direction to reconsider the matter and reach a decision in accordance with the findings of the High Court, …

Civil Procedure Rules **7.30 (EW)**

Rule 54.19 (1) This rule applies where the court makes a quashing order in respect of the decision to which the claim relates.

(2) The court may–

(a)

(i) remit the matter to the decision-maker; and

(ii) direct it to reconsider the matter and reach a decision in accordance with the judgment of the court; …

Note

Since the enactment of the Senior Courts Act 1981, the court can, in addition to quashing a decision, also remit the case to the original decision-maker, asking the authority to reconsider the case and adopt a new decision in the light of the judgment. This power is available only where a quashing order has been granted against the initial decision.

[58] Case 266/82 *Turner v Commission* ECLI:EU:C:1984:3, para 5; T-120/89 *Stahlwerke Peine-Salzgitter v Commission* ECLI:EU:T:1991:32, para 66.

[59] Case T-73/95 *Estabelecimentos Isidoro M Oliveira SA v Commission* ECLI:EU:T:1997:39, para 41.

7.3.A.3 FRANCE

7.3.A.3 (i) Guidance to Authority Contained in Annulment Ruling

Conseil d'État, 25 June 2001[60] **7.31 (FR)**

Société Toulouse Football Club v National Football League

ANNULMENT; CONSEQUENCES FOR PUBLIC AUTHORITIES

Société Toulouse Football Club

The court has the power to give guidance to the competent authority on how to comply with an annulment ruling.

Facts: The applicant, Toulouse Football Club, claimed before the National Football League that two players from the Club of Saint-Etienne used false passports in order to be eligible to play as European citizens. They asked the National Football League to sanction the Club of Saint-Etienne by reversing the result of the match between the teams in Toulouse's favour, which was one of the sanctions available to the League in a case such as this. The National Football League validated the results of the match. The Toulouse Football Club lodged an appeal against the decision before the Federal Commission of Appeal of the National Football League, which dismissed the claim. The applicant challenged the decision before the Conseil d'État.

Held: The decision of the National Football League was annulled.

Judgment: And regarding the match of 2 December 2000:

... that, thus, by refusing to impose the sanction deciding that the match shall be considered as lost by the Club of Saint-Etienne and by deciding to confirm the results of the match, although it has appeared that two players of this club had used passports that were issued under fraudulent conditions, the Federal Commission of Appeal of the French Football League has disregarded the provisions of Article 187 of the general rules; that the illegality of the decision of this commission taints, in this regard, the legality of the attacked decision, which is of an indivisible character;

Considering that it results from the foregoing that the company, 'Toulouse Football Club', which has a sporting object, seeks the annulment of the decision of the commission of the organisation of competitions of the National Football League of 22 May 2001 recognising the final ranking of the professional championship of France of the first League for the season 2000–2001; considering that the claim is well-founded;

Considering that the present decision has necessarily as a consequence that, called upon to rule anew on the recognition of the final ranking of the said championship, the Commission for the Organisation of Competitions of the National Football League applies to the match of 2 December 2000 the sanction envisaged by Article 187 of the general rules, by taking away three points from the club of Saint-Etienne and allocating them to the Toulouse Football Club; that it is also incumbent upon it, if this is the case, to impose the same sanction to any other match of which the results have not yet been finally recognised due to an admissible and still pending objection, and in respect of which one of the violations mentioned under Article 187 have been ascertained;

[60] N° 234363.

Notes

(1) An annulment ruling does not usually indicate precisely which measures are to be adopted to enforce it, leaving the administration free to decide how to use its margin of discretion. However, the court may provide for guidance addressed to the public authorities when reconsidering the case of the claimant.

(2) In some cases, such as the *Société Toulouse Football Club* case, the administrative courts may also state clearly what the administrative authority should do to comply with the ruling. In this case, the administrative court is particularly prescriptive, since it indicates which sanction the authority concerned would have to adopt towards not only the football club concerned by the case, but also to any other club which may have committed the same offence.

7.3.A.3 (ii) Injunction

When an action for annulment (*recours pour excès de pouvoir*) is lodged against a decision, the court may, at the same time as pronouncing the annulment of the challenged decision, issue an injunction. This power is therefore to be distinguished to the power discussed under section 7.3.A.3 (i), which concerns the possibility for courts to give guidance to authorities in the annulment ruling.

Code de justice administrative **7.32 (FR)**

Article L911-1 Where its ruling requires a legal person governed by public law or an entity governed by private law charged with the performance of a public service to adopt a specific measure of execution, the court, having heard submissions to this effect, shall order the legal entity to adopt the measure in the same ruling, accompanied, where appropriate, of a time limit for its execution.

Article L911-2 Where its ruling necessarily requires a legal person governed by public law or an entity governed by private law charged with the performance of a public service to take a decision again, after undertaking a further investigation of the case, the court, having heard submissions to this effect, shall order, in the same ruling, that the new decision must be taken within a specified time limit.

Article L911-3 Having heard submissions to this effect, the court may, in the same ruling, in addition to the injunctions imposed in accordance with Articles L911-1 and L911-2, impose a periodic penalty, under the conditions laid down in this book, for which it determines the date on which it takes effect.

Notes

(1) In France, there has traditionally been a reluctance to provide the courts with powers to grant injunctive relief, as this was seen as an encroachment upon the powers of the administration. According to the old position of case law, the administrative

courts could not depart from the fundamental principle according to which 'it is not for the administrative court to address injunctions to the administration'.[61] However, the absence of explicit powers of injunction was criticised by the doctrine.[62]

(2) The adoption of the law of 8 February 1995[63] provided the administrative courts with powers to grant injunctive relief grounded on three new provisions of the Code de justice administrative, namely Articles L911-1 to L911-3. Two conditions are to be met for an applicant to be able to seek an injunction. First, the injunction must be requested by a party. Secondly, the case must fall within the scope of application of Articles L911-1 and L911-2. These provisions require that either the administrative authority has to adopt a specific decision in order to implement the ruling (Article L911-1) or the authority has to take a new decision, after having reconsidered the case (Article L911-2).

(3) Moreover, the court can order a periodic penalty, pursuant to Article L911-3, until the judgment is complied with, the amount of which must be paid before a deadline defined by the order. The determination of the amount of penalty is at the discretion of the administrative court. Part of the penalty must be paid to the applicant and part transferred to the state budget.

Conseil d'État, 4 July 1997[64] **7.33 (FR)**

Bourezak v Minister of Foreign Affairs

INJUNCTION; NO ADMINISTRATIVE DISCRETION

Bourezak

The administrative court has, if requested, the power to indicate what kind of measure the administrative authority must adopt.

Facts: By a decision of 22 December 1993, the Minister of Foreign Affairs refused to grant a visa to Mr Bourezak to enter the French territory. Mr Bourezak challenged the decision, alleging that it infringed Article 8 of the European Convention on Human Rights (ECHR) and his right to privacy.

Held: The refusal was annulled, and the Council of State ordered the administrative authority to grant the visa.

Judgment: On the findings that the issuance of a visa to Mr X shall be prescribed, and that a periodic penalty shall be imposed:

[61] This formula is frequently used by the administrative judge himself, see Conseil d'État, 22 November 1968, *Miss Y*, N° 67843.

[62] J Rivero, 'Le Huron au Palais-Royal ou réflexions naïves sur le recours pour excès de pouvoir' (1962) *Dalloz* 37; F Moderne, 'Etrangère au pouvoir du juge, l'injonction, pourquoi le serait elle ?' (1990) *Revue Française de Droit Administratif* 798.

[63] Law N° 95-125 of 8 February 1995 on the organisation of courts and civil, criminal and administrative proceedings (Loi relative à l'organisation des juridictions et à la procédure civile, pénale et administrative). See also J-M Sauvé, 'L'injonction – la loi du 8 février 1995 après vingt ans de pratique', available at www.conseil-etat.fr/Actualites/Discours-Interventions/L-injonction-la-loi-du-8-fevrier-1995-apres-vingt-ans-de-pratique.

[64] N° 156298.

Considering that, according to Article 6-1 inserted into the law of 16 July 1980 by the law of 8 February 1995: 'Where it settles a dispute on the merits through a ruling that necessarily requires a specific enforcement measure, the Council of State, before which submissions in that sense were brought, prescribes this measure and may attach to its ruling a penalty starting on a date which it determines'; that, with regard to the grounds of the present ruling, its execution implies in principle the issuance of a visa to Mr X ...; that, however, it is for the Council of State, when a request to this end is submitted, on the basis of the aforementioned provisions, to prescribe a specific measure to be adopted, to rule on these submissions, taking the legal and factual situation at the time of its decision into consideration; that, having been invited by letter of the president of the second sub-section of the Litigation section of the Council of State to inform the court on whether the situation of Mr X ... since the intervention of the disputed decision had been modified, in fact or in law, in such a way that his request would have become moot, or that circumstances subsequent to the date of the said decision allowed going forward to substantiate, in law, a new decision to reject, the parties responded that no change had occured in the situation of Mr X ...; that, consequently, there is reason for the Council of State to require the competent authority to issue Mr X ..., within a time period of a month, a visa for entry into France; that under the circumstances at stake, there is no reason to attach to this injunction a penalty payment; ...

Note

When the administrative court receives a request from a party to grant an injunction against a public authority following the annulment of a decision, it may decide if such a measure is appropriate and, if so, it can order the public authority to adopt a specific measure, where the authority has no remaining discretionary power with regard to the circumstances of the case, as in the *Bourezak* case.

Conseil d'État, 7 February 2003[65] **7.34 (FR)**

Société civile d'exploitation agricole Le haras d'Achères II v City of Achères-la-Forêt

INJUNCTION; DISCRETION OF THE AUTHORITY

Haras d'Achères II

When using its powers to grant injunctive relief, the court must take the extent of the discretion of the public authority into account.

Facts: By decision of 18 November 1996, the mayor of Achères-la-Forêt refused to grant a building permit to the Haras d'Achères II (Stud Farm of Achères II). The stud farm challenged the refusal and requested that the Council of State order the administrative authority to issue the building permit.

Held: The refusal to grant the building permit was annulled. The mayor of Achères-la-Forêt was ordered to reconsider the case within a time period of two months.

[65] N° 220215.

Judgment: On the findings for the purposes of an injunction: Considering that the annulment of the administrative decision (*arrêté*) adopted by the mayor of Achères-la-Forêt on 18 November 1996 refusing to grant the Haras d'Achères II the building permit that it had requested, necessarily requires that the mayor of Achères-la-Forêt must reconsider the request of the company; that, even if the company's request for the building permit is rejected, it is appropriate, however, for the Council of State to order the mayor of Achères-la-Forêt to reconsider this request within a time period of two months from the notification of the present ruling, in accordance, especially, with the provisions of Article L600-2 of the Code de l'Urbanisme (Planning Code); that there is no reason for the Council of State to impose a penalty; …

Note

Whenever an administrative authority is given a margin of discretion, an injunction can only require the reconsideration of the case, and cannot determine the content of the decision to be taken by the authority. In the case above, the Council of State did not order the public authority to grant a building permit, but only to reconsider the request of the applicant within a time period of two months.

Conseil d'État, 29 June 2001[66] **7.35 (FR)**

Vassilikiotis v Minister of Culture and Minister of Home Affairs

INJUNCTION POWERS; EU LAW

Vassilikiotis

When the challenged act implements EU law, the administrative court has the power to grant injunctive relief.

Facts: Mr Vassilikiotis, the applicant, challenged an interministerial decision (*arrêté*) of 15 April 1999 relating to the conditions of issuance and withdrawal of a licence determining the qualifications of the persons who may work as guides in museums.

Held: The decision was partially annulled to the extent that its provisions were held not to be in compliance with EU law. Furthermore, the Council of State required the competent public authorities to act in a specific way, while waiting for the adoption of a new decision which would be in compliance with EU law.

Judgment: Considering that the decision (*arrêté*) of 15 April 1999, adopted to enforce the aforementioned provisions, established the list of French certificates and diplomas that entitle to the issuance of the professional card referred to under Article 86 of the Decree of 15 June 1994; that Mr Y … asserts that this decision disregards the provisions of the Treaty Establishing the European Community regarding the freedom to provide services as it does not provide for, and neither does any other regulatory text, the conditions under

[66] N° 213229.

which the certified guides with certificates and diplomas issued by the other Member States of the European Union may exercise their profession on the French territory as service providers; …

Considering that, as noted above, the challenged decision of 15 April 1999 is restricted to providing the conditions governing the issuance of the different licenses to persons who hold one of the French certificates or diplomas listed in the decision; that it creates in that way, between the persons that hold a French certificate or diploma and the others, a difference in treatment that is incompatible with Articles 49 and 50 of the Treaty Establishing the European Community; that, thus, the claim of Mr Y is well-founded …;

Considering, however, that such a partial annulment of the challenged decision cannot have the effect to maintain in the French legal system a situation of discrimination contrary to the requirements of Community law; that, consequently, there is a need to specify the scope of the annulment decision by referring to the grounds that constitute its necessary basis;

Considering, on the one hand, that the present decision has necessarily as a consequence that the competent authorities are obliged to take, within a reasonable time limit, the measures provided for by the Decree of 15 June 1994, modified for the granting of professional cards to Community nationals who do not possess a French certificate of diploma; that they have, in particular, to arrange for a system of equivalence or to determine the conditions that allow, in conformity with the requirements of the rules of Community law regarding the freedom to provide services, to check that the certificates or diplomas issued in other Member States are equivalent to those required by French national law.

Considering, on the other hand, that, while waiting for the enactment of this additional regulation, the annulment resulting from the present ruling has necessarily the effect of prohibiting the authorities from preventing the exercise by a Community national of the profession of guide at historical museums and monuments on the ground that he does not hold the certificates and diplomas that are required by the Decree of 15 June 1994 and the decision of 15 April 1999; that it is the responsibility of the competent authorities, until the decision of 15 April 1999 has been amended in accordance with the conditions explained above, to issue the Community nationals who request so a professional card by deciding, on a case by case basis, under the control of the courts, whether the certificates and diplomas submitted can be considered as providing, from the perspective of the general interests the safeguard of which is the objective of Article 13 of the law of 13 July 1992, equivalent standards to the ones that result from the holding of a French certificate or diploma;

Note

When EU law is at stake, regardless of the request of the applicant, the administrative court can order the administration to adopt all the necessary measures to comply with EU law and to provide for transitional measures. The court's powers to grant an injunction are not grounded on Articles L911-1 and L911-2 of the Code of Administrative Justice in such cases. Hence, the court does not need to check whether the conditions provided in these provisions are met, as the injunctive powers of the court are instead grounded on the duty to ensure an effective judicial protection of rights stemming from EU law. In the *Vassilikiotis* case, since the measures implementing EU law were not deemed adequate to comply with the EU requirements on mutual recognition, the challenged decision was annulled, as it was considered to be in violation of EU law. The Council of State also made use of its injunctive powers in order to require the competent authority to assess any individual application to obtain recognition of certain professional qualifications, while waiting for the enactment of new implementing measures.

7.3.A.4 THE NETHERLANDS

Algemene Wet Bestuursrecht **7.36 (NL)**

Article 8:72 …

(4) The administrative judge may, if application of the third section is not possible, instruct the administrative authority to issue a new administrative decision or to perform another act, in accordance with his instructions. In doing so, he may:

a. determine that legal rules are wholly or partly disapplied in the preparation of the new administrative decision or other act;

b. set a time limit for the administrative authority to issue the new administrative decision or perform the other act.

(5) The administrative judge may, if necessary, adopt a provisional measure. He determines the time at which the provisional measure expires.

(6) The administrative judge may determine that, if or as long as the administrative authority does not comply with the judgment, the administrative authority is liable to the payment of a penalty to be fixed in the judgment to a party designated by him. Articles 611a (4), 611, parts b. to d. and 611, part g. of the Code of Civil Procedure apply mutatis mutandis.

Notes

(1) If it is not possible to uphold the consequences of the annulled decision or to replace the decision by a new one (Article 8:72(3) AWB), the Dutch administrative courts may order the public authority to adopt a new decision in accordance with the further instructions given in the ruling (Article 8:72(4) AWB). The provision explicitly mentions some procedural instructions which may be inserted in the ruling (section 4, subsections a and b of Article 8:72 AWB). Other procedural instructions, such as the parties which should be heard (again) before deciding, are also possible. Moreover, the court can give instructions concerning the substance of the decision. This, however, is only possible as far as such instructions follow from binding legal provisions which do not leave any discretion for how the authority should act. Self-evidently, the court has to respect the discretion of the administrative authorities.

(2) The public authority must adopt a new decision within the time limit set by the judge. If the public authority does not comply with the instruction, it can be held liable and could be subject to the payment of a penalty.

7.3.B ORDERS TO THE PUBLIC AUTHORITIES WHICH ARE AUTONOMOUS FROM ANNULMENT

In England and Wales, as well as in Germany, orders to public authorities to behave in a certain manner are to be requested through a specific remedy, which is autonomous from the annulment action. The European Union also provides for a specific remedy to order the EU authorities to act, but, unlike in Germany and England and Wales, it cannot be used when there has been an explicit decision of refusal.

7.3.B.1 ENGLAND AND WALES

Civil Procedure Rules **7.37 (EW)**

Rule 54.2 The judicial review procedure must be used in a claim for judicial review where the claimant is seeking–

(a) a mandatory order;
(b) a prohibiting order;
(c) a quashing order; or
(d) an injunction under section 30 of the Supreme Court Act 1981 (restraining a person from acting in any office in which he is not entitled to act)

Note

In England and Wales, a citizen adversely affected by a decision of a public authority may seek a variety of remedies available in judicial review through the judicial review procedure. In addition to the power to quash a decision,[67] the court may also grant remedies in order to restrain the public authority from acting in an unlawful way or require the authority to perform its duties in a lawful manner, which imply different powers granted to the judge.

Court of Appeal (Civil Division), 27 July 1923[68] **7.38 (EW)**

R v Electricity Commissioners ex parte London Joint Electricity Committee Co

PROHIBITING ORDER; SCOPE

Electricity Commissioners

A prohibiting order can be granted to prevent unlawful action contemplated by a public authority.

Facts: The Electricity Commissioners, as empowered by their constitutive act, constituted an electricity district and formulated a scheme providing for the incorporation of a joint electricity authority which purported to be

[67] See section 7.2.A.2 above.
[68] [1924] 1 KB 171.

representative of the authorised undertakers, both local authorities and electricity companies, in the district so constituted. The scheme provided that, at its first meeting, the joint authority should appoint two committees. Certain companies affected by the scheme applied for writs of prohibition and certiorari on the ground that the scheme was ultra vires insofar as it compelled the joint authority to appoint the two committees and delegate to them powers and duties of the joint authority.

Held: An order was granted prohibiting the Electricity Commissioners from implementing the proposed regulatory scheme, which was found to be unlawful.

Judgment: Atkin LJ: The question now arises whether the persons interested are entitled to the remedy which they now claim in order to put a stop to the unauthorized proceedings of the Commissioners. The matter comes before us upon rules for writs of prohibition and certiorari which have been discharged by the Divisional Court. Both writs are of great antiquity, forming part of the process by which the King's Courts restrained courts of inferior jurisdiction from exceeding their powers. Prohibition restrains the tribunal from proceeding further in excess of jurisdiction; certiorari requires the record or the order of the court to be sent up to the King's Bench Division, to have its legality inquired into, and, if necessary, to have the order quashed. It is to be noted that both writs deal with questions of excessive jurisdiction, and doubtless in their origin dealt almost exclusively with the jurisdiction of what is described in ordinary parlance as a Court of Justice. But the operation of the writs has extended to control the proceedings of bodies which do not claim to be, and would not be recognized as, Courts of Justice. Wherever any body of persons having legal authority to determine questions affecting the rights of subjects, and having the duty to act judicially, act in excess of their legal authority they are subject to the controlling jurisdiction of the King's Bench Division exercised in these writs … I can see no difference in principle between certiorari and prohibition, except that the latter may be invoked at an earlier stage. If the proceedings establish that the body complained of is exceeding its jurisdiction by entertaining matters which would result in its final decision being subject to being brought up and quashed on certiorari, I think that prohibition will lie to restrain it from so exceeding its jurisdiction. Reference was made to the case of *In re Clifford and O'Sullivan 72*, where an attempt was made to prohibit the proceedings of so-called military courts of the Army in Ireland acting under proclamations which had placed certain Irish districts in a time of armed disturbance under martial law. Prohibition, it was held in the House of Lords, would not lie because the so-called courts were not claiming any legal authority other than the right to put down force by force, and because the so-called courts were *functæ officio*. I am satisfied that the observations of the Lord Chancellor in that case were directed to the first point, and that he had no intention of overruling, or indeed questioning, the long line of authority which has extended the writs in question to bodies other than those who possess legal authority to try cases, and pass judgments in the strictest sense.

Notes

(1) A prohibiting order is aimed at preventing a public authority from acting beyond the scope of its powers. This remedy has a wide scope, since it can be claimed against any public authority.[69]

[69] HWR Wade and CF Forsyth, *Administrative Law*, 11th edn (Oxford, Oxford University Press, 2014) 513.

(2) The case of *R v Electricity Commissioners ex parte London Joint Electricity Committee Co* accurately illustrates the evolution of the nature of the prerogative remedies that could be granted by the court in its judicial review jurisdiction. In practice, the quashing order and the prohibiting order are closely related. They can either be used alone, or, often, in conjunction. Indeed, what the case law shows is that quashing and prohibiting orders frequently go hand in hand, particularly in circumstances where a quashing order is sought to quash a decision and a prohibiting order is sought to restrain its execution.

House of Lords, 14 February 1968[70] **7.39 (EW)**

Padfield v Minister of Agriculture, Fisheries and Food

MANDATORY ORDER

Padfield

The court can grant a mandatory order when a public authority refuses to use its powers in a lawful manner.

Facts: This case arose at the time when the production and sale of milk was subject to considerable state involvement. For the purposes of the operation of the scheme, England and Wales had been divided into seven regions. Producers of milk were required to sell their milk to the Milk Marketing Board, which determined a set price for the milk in each of the regions. The price differed in each region, particularly as it was acknowledged that there were significant differences in the cost of transportation. Should farmers in any region be unhappy about the price paid for milk, they could make representations to the Secretary of State, who had the discretion to refer the issue of milk pricing to an independent committee, which could recommend changes in prices. Padfield and others argued that the sums paid to them in respect of transportation were not adequate. The Secretary of State refused to refer the issue of milk prices to the Committee, stating that the referral would be contrary to the public interest as it would cause instability in milk prices throughout all the regions. Padfield and others then brought a claim for judicial review, arguing that the Secretary of State's decision was unlawful.

Held: A mandatory order was granted, requiring the Secretary of State to excise his discretionary power in accordance with the law.

Judgment: Lord Reid: The question at issue in this appeal is the nature and extent of the Minister's duty under section 19 (3) (b) of the Act of 1958 in deciding whether to refer to the committee of investigation a complaint as to the operation of any scheme made by persons adversely affected by the scheme. The respondent contends that his only duty is to consider a complaint fairly and that he is given an unfettered discretion with regard to every complaint either to refer it or not to refer it to the committee as he may think fit. The appellants contend that it is his duty to refer every genuine and substantial complaint, or alternatively that his discretion is not unfettered and that in this case he failed to exercise his discretion according to law because his refusal was caused or influenced by his having misdirected himself in law or by his having taken into account extraneous or irrelevant considerations.

[70] [1968] AC 997.

In my view, the appellants' first contention goes too far. There are a number of reasons which would justify the Minister in refusing to refer a complaint. For example, he might consider it more suitable for arbitration, or he might consider that in an earlier case the committee of investigation had already rejected a substantially similar complaint, or he might think the complaint to be frivolous or vexatious. So he must have at least some measure of discretion. But is it unfettered?

It is implicit in the argument for the Minister that there are only two possible interpretations of this provision either he must refer every complaint or he has an unfettered discretion to refuse to refer in any case. I do not think that is right. Parliament must have conferred the discretion with the intention that it should be used to promote the policy and objects of the Act, the policy and objects of the Act must be determined by construing the Act as a whole and construction is always a matter of law for the court. In a matter of this kind it is not possible to draw a hard and fast line, but if the Minister, by reason of his having misconstrued the Act or for any other reason, so uses his discretion as to thwart or run counter to the policy and objects of the Act, then our law would be very defective if persons aggrieved were not entitled to the protection of the court. So it is necessary first to construe the Act.

When these provisions were first enacted in 1931 it was unusual for Parliament to compel people to sell their commodities in a way to which they objected and it was easily foreseeable that any such scheme would cause loss to some producers. Moreover, if the operation of the scheme was put in the hands of the majority of the producers, it was obvious that they might use their power to the detriment of consumers, distributors or a minority of the producers. So it is not surprising that Parliament enacted safeguards.

The approval of Parliament shows that this scheme was thought to be in the public interest, and in so far as it necessarily involved detriment to some persons, it must have been thought to be in the public interest that they should suffer it. But in sections 19 and 20 Parliament drew a line. They provide machinery for investigating and determining whether the scheme is operating or the board is acting in a manner contrary to the public interest.

The effect of these sections is that if, but only if, the Minister and the committee of investigation concur in the view that something is being done contrary to the public interest the Minister can step in. Section 20 enables the Minister to take the initiative. Section 19 deals with complaints by individuals who are aggrieved. I need not deal with the provisions which apply to consumers. We are concerned with other persons who may be distributors or producers. If the Minister directs that a complaint by any of them shall be referred to the committee of investigation, that committee will make a report which must be published. If they report that any provision of this scheme or any act or omission of the board is contrary to the interests of the complainers and is not in the public interest, then the Minister is empowered to take action, but not otherwise. He may disagree with the view of the committee as to public interest, and, if he thinks that there are other public interests which outweigh the public interest that justice should be done to the complainers, he would be not only entitled but bound to refuse to take action. Whether he takes action or not, he may be criticised and held accountable in Parliament but the court cannot interfere.

...

As the Minister's discretion has never been properly exercised according to law, I would allow this appeal. It appears to me that the case should now be remitted to the Queen's Bench Division with a direction to require the Minister to consider the complaint of the appellants according to law. The order for costs in the Divisional Court should stand.

The appellants should have their costs in the Court of Appeal but, as extra expense was caused in this House by an adjournment of the hearing at their motion, they should only have two-thirds of their costs in this House.

Note

A mandatory order is an order issued to a public authority to require it to act in accordance with its duties. It addresses a wrongful failure to act, where the public authority refuses to consider the case, has misinterpreted the law or has grounded its decision on extraneous or irrelevant considerations. The mandatory order has been used in a variety of situations, including to compel a minister to refer a matter to a statutory committee, as in the *Padfield* case, to require an authority empowered to set rents but which had declined to do so to act in accordance with its legal duty[71] and to require Inland Revenue officials to act after they had delayed action for a lengthy period.[72]

Court of Appeal (Civil Division), 23 August 1967[73] **7.40 (EW)**

Bradbury v Enfield London Borough Council

INJUNCTION

Bradbury

The court will grant an injunction in order to uphold the rule of law and ensure that an authority abides by statutory requirements.

Facts: The defendant council proposed to change the organisation of and funding arrangements for schools in its local area. When such changes were to be made, section 13 of the Education Act 1944 required councils to give notice to local residents that such changes were to occur. In this case, the council did not give such notice, and the claimant sought an injunction to prevent the council from making any changes to the organisation or funding of schools until the requirements of the statute had been satisfied.

Held: An injunction was granted in order to ensure that the council abided by the statutory requirements as to process.

Judgment: Lord Denning MR: I come now to the last point. Ought an injunction to be granted against the council? It has been suggested by the chief education officer that, if an injunction is granted, chaos will supervene. All the arrangements have been made for the next term, the teachers appointed to the new comprehensive schools, the pupils allotted their places, and so forth. It would be next to impossible, he says, to reverse all these arrangements without complete chaos and damage to teachers, pupils and the public.

I must say this: If a local authority does not fulfil the requirements of the law, this court will see that it does fulfil them. It will not listen readily to suggestions of 'chaos.'

71 *R v Camden London Borough Rent Officer, ex parte Ebiri* [1981] WLR 881.
72 *Wang v Commissioner of the Inland Revenue* [1994] 1 WLR 1286.
73 [1967] 1 WLR 1311.

The Department of Education and the local education authority are subject to the rule of law and must comply with it, just like everyone else. Even if chaos should result, still the law must be obeyed. But I do not think that chaos will result. The evidence convinces me that the 'chaos' is much over-stated. If an injunction is granted now, there will be much less chaos than if it were sought to reverse the situation in a year or so. After all, the injunction will only go as to the eight schools, and not as to the remaining twenty or so schools in the borough.

And in regard to these eight schools, it will only affect the new intake coming in at the bottom forms. I see no reason why the position should not be restored, so that the eight schools retain their previous character until the statutory requirements are fulfilled. I can well see that there may be a considerable upset for a number of people, but I think it far more important to uphold the rule of law. Parliament has laid down these requirements so as to ensure that the electors can make their objections and have them properly considered. We must see that their rights are upheld.

I have only to add this: It is still open to the education authority to fulfil the statutory requirements, that is, to give the public notices so that objections can be submitted to and considered by the Minister. I will not venture to predict what the results will be, but that is the least that must be done in order that the law should be observed.

Notes

(1) Injunctions, although in principle a private law remedy, may also be claimed in judicial review proceedings, although they are not often sought as a final remedy.[74] In private law, the injunction may be used in a variety of circumstances, including where the grant will prevent the commission or continuance of any tort or breach of contract. In public law, it is also used against unlawful action by public bodies, and may even be granted where this action would not constitute a tort or breach of contract. Although prerogative remedies and private law remedies are presented distinctly and are autonomous, they are sometimes used in conjunction. For example, in the case of *Wheeler*, the House of Lords issued a quashing order to quash a council's decision to prevent a rugby club from training on its land, but acknowledged that a further remedy, an injunction, could be necessary to prevent the council from acting to remove the club and left it open to the claimant to return to the High Court to seek an injunction if this were needed.[75] The case of *Wheeler* serves to illustrate the main distinction between the use of the mandatory or prohibitory order and the use of the mandatory and prohibitory injunction as a final remedy. Mandatory and prohibitory orders will be granted as a final remedy where such is needed to require or prevent the use of public law powers. By contrast, in a case such as *Wheeler*, the House of Lords granted a quashing order to quash the public decision taken by the authority, but remained open to the grant of a prohibitory injunction as a final remedy if required in order to prevent the public authority from using its private law powers (in this case, private

[74] It is also important to note that all injunctions are subject to the 'balance of convenience' test outlined in excerpt 7.89 below, which is an additional hurdle for claimants that does not exist in a claim for a prohibitory or mandatory order.

[75] *Wheeler v Leicester City Council* [1985] AC 1054.

law powers in respect of ownership and management of facilities) to eject the club. Injunctions have sometimes been used as final remedies to prevent public authorities from acting in an unlawful way where the unlawful action of the public authority is procedural, rather than substantive, such as in *Bradbury*. The reason for using the injunction rather than the prohibiting order in a case like this is unclear, but may stem from the differing procedural requirements for the grant of these remedies prior to the unification of the process for claiming remedies by the Senior Courts Act 1981.

(2) There are two types of injunctions: a *prohibitory* injunction is an order made by the court to prevent a public body from acting in an unlawful way. It is also possible for the court to grant a *mandatory* injunction, requiring a public authority to take a particular action. Such an injunction is sought only infrequently, because the court has the prerogative remedy of the mandatory order at its disposal to achieve the same purpose.[76] The main distinction is that mandatory injunctions are usually used only in interim proceedings, whereas mandatory orders are used as a remedy when the court reaches its final judgment. Similarly, in the case where a prohibitory injunction is granted, this is often granted in interim proceedings, but may not be necessary after a final hearing if the claimant is successful, because if, in the final hearing, the court decides that a decision of a public authority is unlawful, then the decision will likely be quashed and thus the authority will have no lawful basis upon which to take the action that was previously restrained by the injunction.

7.3.B.2 GERMANY

In Germany, different actions are available to order the public authority to act or to restrain it from acting. Which action is to be sought depends on whether factual action (*Realakt*) or an administrative act (*Verwaltungsakt*) is the object of the claim.[77]

Verwaltungsgerichtsordnung **7.41 (DE)**

§42 (1) By legal action, the annulment (*Aufhebung*) of an administrative act (action for annulment (*Anfechtungsklage*)) as well as the order to issue a refused or omitted administrative act (action seeking the issuance of an administrative act (*Verpflichtungsklage*)) may be requested.

§113 (1) Insofar as the administrative act is unlawful and the claimants' rights have been violated, the court shall annul the administrative act and any ruling on an objection ....

(5) Insofar as the rejection or omission of the administrative act is unlawful and the claimants' rights are thereby violated, the court shall require the administrative authority to give effect to the requested act, if the case is one where the administrative authority has no remaining discretion. Otherwise, it shall require the administrative authority to make a decision on the application, taking the decision of the court into consideration.

[76] For a case considering the circumstances in which a mandatory injunction will be granted in the context of public law, see *Meade v Haringey London Borough Council* [1979] 1 WLR 637.

[77] These terms are discussed in Chapter 3, sections 3.1.A.3 and section 3.4.A.

Notes

(1) If the claimant wishes to obtain a beneficial administrative act, such as a building permit, which has been refused or if the claimant has applied for the issuance of a beneficial administrative action and the administration has not made a decision in respect of this application,[78] an 'action seeking the issuance of an administrative act' (*Verpflichtungsklage*) (second alternative of §42(1) and §113(5) VwGO) must be filed.[79] If the issuance of the administrative act constitutes a discretionary decision, the claimant can generally only demand a 'decision free from discretionary errors' through his action for issuing an administrative act (*ermessensfehlerfreie Entscheidung*, second sentence of §113(5) VwGO). If the authority retains discretion, the court may only require the authority to reconsider the case, taking the decision of the court into consideration. Only if the 'discretion is reduced to zero' (*Ermessensreduzierung auf Null*) in a specific case (first sentence of §113(5) VwGO) can the claimant demand a judgment to compel the administration to issue the administrative act that has been requested.

(2) If a claimant wishes to bring a claim against factual action of public authorities or if he demands a certain factual action of the administration, he may bring a 'general action for performance' (*allgemeine Leistungsklage*).[80] By this action, a claimant can seek performance of an administrative action which does not qualify as an 'administrative act'. For example, by means of a general action for performance, the claimant may require that a public construction site surrounding the claimant's shop be better secured so that his customers do not injure themselves. In an approach similar to that in relation to the 'action seeking the issuance of an administrative act' (*Verpflichtungsklage*), only if the administrative discretion is reduced to zero will the court compel the administration to take a specific factual action.

7.3.B.3 THE EUROPEAN UNION

In the case of action for annulment in the European Union, the courts have no power to compel the competent authorities to act. It is only through the action for failure to act that an individual can complain that an authority has failed to perform its duties.

Treaty on the Functioning of the European Union **7.42 (EU)**

Article 265 Should the European Parliament, the European Council, the Council, the Commission or the European Central Bank, in infringement of the Treaties, fail to act, the Member States and the other institutions of the Union may bring an action before the Court of Justice of the European Union to have the infringement established.

[78] On administrative silence in the German legal system, see Chapter 3, section 3.6.A.

[79] D Ehlers, 'Verpflichtungsklage' in Ehlers and Schoch (n 6 above) 641–58.

[80] For details, see D Ehlers, 'Allgemeine verwaltungsgerichtliche Leistungsklage' in Ehlers and Schoch (n 6 above) 659–71.

This Article shall apply, under the same conditions, to bodies, offices and agencies of the Union which fail to act.

The action shall be admissible only if the institution, body, office or agency concerned has first been called upon to act. If, within two months of being so called upon, the institution, body, office or agency concerned has not defined its position, the action may be brought within a further period of two months.

Any natural or legal person may, under the conditions laid down in the preceding paragraphs, complain to the Court that an institution, body, office or agency of the Union has failed to address to that person any act other than a recommendation or an opinion.

Note

(1) The subject matter of an action for failure to act is an enquiry as to whether the failure to issue a decision was unlawful.[81] According to the case law, a failure to take a decision is unlawful only if the institution was under a duty to act. Such duties can be derived from a provision of primary or secondary EU law.[82] For example, the General Court ruled that the fact that the Commission did not manage to adopt delegated acts, according to Article 290 TFEU, within the time limit mandated by the relevant secondary law was a failure to act.[83]

(2) In order for the action to be admissible, certain preliminary steps need to be taken. First of all, an action for failure to act will be admissible only if the institution concerned has first been called upon to act. The case law requires that the applicant's request must be specific, in that it is must be clear what decision the institution should have taken.[84] There is no time limit within which the request must be made. The court has held, however, that the applicant may not delay the exercise of his rights indefinitely.[85] If, within two months of this request, the institution concerned has not defined its position, an action may be brought under Article 265 TFEU. If it acts to comply with the request, the institution will have defined its position. The courts have clarified that the same can be considered when an institution adopts a decision different from that which the applicant requested.[86] Secondly, if an action for failure to act is brought by a natural or legal person, it will only be admissible if it concerns the institution's failure to adopt a binding act.[87] If, in contrast, the action for failure to act is brought by an institution or a Member State, this limitation does not apply.[88]

[81] On administrative silence in the EU legal system, see Chapter 3, section 3.6.E.

[82] Case C-141/02 P *Commission v T-Mobile Austria* ECLI:EU:C:2005:98; Case T-277/94 *AITEC v Commission* ECLI:EU:T:1996:66.

[83] Case T-521/14 *Kingdom of Sweden v Commission* ECLI:EU:T:2015:976.

[84] Case 25/85 *Nuovo Campsider v Commission* ECLI:EU:C:1986:195, para 8.

[85] Case 59/70 *Netherlands v Commission* ECLI:EU:C:1971:77, para 19.

[86] Joined Cases 166/86 and 220/86 *Irish Cement Ltd v Commission* ECLI:EU:C:1988:549, para 17.

[87] Art 265 TFEU mentions 'any act other than a recommendation or an opinion'.

[88] For example, an action may be brought against the Commission if it fails to submit a proposal for a legislative measure to the Council relating to a matter on which the EU is under an obligation to legislate. See, eg Case 13/83 *European Parliament v Council* ECLI:EU:C:1985:220

(3) If the Court of Justice finds that an EU institution or organ has failed to act, that institution is required to take the necessary steps to comply with the judgment. The EU courts cannot issue directions on what act to take.[89] In circumstances in which the institution has an obligation to take a specific action, however, the institution has very little discretion left on how to comply with the Court's ruling.[90]

7.3.C COMPARATIVE REMARKS

In all the studied legal systems, the administrative courts have the power not only to annul an administrative act, but also to influence the content of the subsequent decision or action of the public authorities, through the possibility to provide guidance or orders to the public authorities.

This possibility for courts to influence the content of the subsequent decision or action of the public authorities can be linked to or may be autonomous from an annulment action. In legal systems where annulment is the main remedy and which do not provide for a separate action seeking the issuance of an administrative act or a separate claim concerning an omission to act, namely France and the Netherlands, this possibility is linked to an annulment ruling. However, one main difference between France and the Netherlands is that, in France, a differentiation can be observed between 'soft' guidance, given by courts as a consequence of annulment ruling, and 'hard' injunction powers, which have to meet specific legislative requirements. This demarcation is not known in the Dutch legal system. The courts also make use of the possibility to provide for guidance in the EU system, but, in the action for annulment, such measures are never binding.

At the other end of the spectrum from France and the Netherlands are the EU, Germany and England and Wales, where orders to the authorities must be sought separately and are not dependent on the annulment of a decision.

However, there are two differences between these legal systems. First of all, in England and Wales and the EU, orders to the authorities are independent from the annulment action, but it is nevertheless possible for courts to issue guidance to the authorities in an annulment ruling. This possibility does not exist in Germany. This might be justified by the strict separation of 'actions', which is at the core of the German system of administrative justice, whereby each action has one and only one specific purpose: annulment in the action for annulment, and injunction in the action seeking the issuance of an administrative act.

Secondly, whereas, in England and Wales and Germany, the relevant remedies to give orders to public authorities can be exercised both in cases of refusal and in cases of omission, this is not the case in the EU, as the action for failure to act is limited to omissions.

[89] T-395/04 *Air One v Commission* ECLI:EU:T:2006:123, para 24.
[90] K Lenaerts et al, *EU Procedural Law*, 2nd edn (Oxford, Oxford University Press, 2014) 440.

A common trend that is shared by all the studied legal systems apart from the EU is that the content of the order of the court depends on the discretion granted to the public authority when acting or adopting a decision. The greater the discretion is, the softer the courts' intervention is. When ordering the adoption of an act, the court can only interfere with the content of an act where the public authority has no discretion. In contrast, in cases where an authority enjoys any remaining discretion, the court can only order public authorities to take a new decision, taking the court's ruling into account. This correlation between intensity of injunctive powers and discretion of the court does not seem to find a correspondence in the EU, as the EU courts will not readily mandate a specific action even in those situations in which no remaining discretion exists.

7.4 DECLARATORY JUDGMENTS

With a declaratory action, the judge can be asked to declare an act lawful or unlawful, to offer a view on a controversial legal issue or to declare the status of legal relationship of the parties. The peculiarity of declaratory judgments is that the declaration has no legal effect and it is not accompanied by any sanction or means of enforcement. The purpose of asking for a declaratory judgment is to clarify a legal situation or relationship, which sometimes opens the way for the use of other remedies.

7.4.A LEGAL SYSTEMS ALLOWING DECLARATORY JUDGMENTS

7.4.A.1 ENGLAND AND WALES

Senior Courts Act 1981 **7.43 (EW)**

Section 31 …

(2) A declaration may be made or an injunction granted under this subsection in any case where an application for judicial review, seeking that relief, has been made and the High Court considers that, having regard to –

(a) the nature of the matters in respect of which relief may be granted by [mandatory, prohibiting or quashing orders];

(b) the nature of the persons and bodies against whom relief may be granted by such orders; and

(c) all the circumstances of the case,

it would be just and convenient for the declaration to be made or the injunction to be granted, as the case may be.

Civil Procedure Rules **7.44 (EW)**

Rule 54.3 (1) The judicial review procedure may be used in a claim for judicial review where the claimant is seeking–

(a) a declaration; or

(b) an injunction.

Note

According to Article 54.3 of the Civil Procedure Rules (CPR) and Section 31(2) of the Senior Courts Act, an applicant can seek a declaration as a remedy. Whilst this remedy plays a role in private law and is a tool that is sometimes used to settle disputes between private parties, it is also applicable to disputes between individuals and public authorities. Historically, the courts have been reluctant to introduce a declaratory judgment in public law matters and against public authorities. Nowadays, such a declaration is used as a remedy where this is deemed by the court to be 'just and convenient',[91] and when a prerogative remedy would not be granted. The declaration is valuable in clarifying the legal relationship between an applicant and a public authority. A declaratory judgment merely states the court's view of an existing legal situation. It does not require anyone to do anything. A declaration may be granted to settle a doubtful question of law, for example where a company wishes to know whether a planning permission is required for certain operations.[92] A declaration might be sought along with an injunction to restrain a public authority from taking a particular step or mandating that a certain action should be taken.

P Craig, Administrative Law[93] **7.45 (EW)**

However, as time progressed the courts became more aware of its potential, especially when contrasted with the limitations surrounding the prerogative orders. Judicial statements countenanced the broad reach of the declaration and its freedom from constraint.

The declaration can operate both as an original and a supervisory remedy. In the former instance a court will declare what rights the parties have, for example, under a contract or over a land. In the latter case, the remedy will control decisions made by other bodies, such as declaring the attachment of planning conditions to be invalid. This duality strengthens the declaration. It allows a court to declare invalid action by a public body in pursuance of the supervisory role, and then, if appropriate, to pronounce on the parties' rights, in pursuance of the original role.

Note

In the excerpt, Craig stresses the ambivalence of the declaration remedy. In principle, a declaration is not a remedy used to solve a dispute or rule on a case, because of its declaratory nature. However, with regard to its conditions of enforcement, the declaration remedy has been considered a useful tool for applicants who do not have access to a prerogative remedy, perhaps because no decision that could be subject to challenge has yet been taken. Indeed, the declaration is more accessible, as it is a

[91] See *Dyson v Attorney-General* (1911) 1 KB 410 (CA).

[92] *Pyx Granite Co Ltd v Ministry of Housing and Local Government* [1960] AC 260 (HL).

[93] Craig (n 9 above) 805.

way for the individual to get a statement of his rights that may be binding on public authorities. Declarations are often sought to clarify whether particular regulations are lawful or have correctly implemented an EU directive,[94] or where the claimant wishes to seek a declaration as to the scope of procedural protection (such as the right to a hearing or the right to be given reasons for a decision) applicable in his case.[95]

High Court (Queen's Bench Division), 24 June 1999[96] **7.46 (EW)**

Mayor and Burgesses of the London Borough of Islington v Sheila Camp

DECLARATION

Sheila Camp

A declaration may be sought in the absence of any dispute.

Facts: C was employed by the London Housing Unit (a joint committee of the London Borough of Islington and other local authorities in London) and was elected as a councillor in Islington. Under section 80 of the Local Government Act 1972, employees of local authorities are disqualified from being elected members of an authority to which their employment also relates. In C's case, the application of section 80 was uncertain and the chief executive of Islington London Borough Council determined that it would be necessary to seek a declaration from the court to determine whether section 80 precluded C from holding elected office in Islington.

Held: The declaration in this case was refused, as in this case the council had applied for the declaration even though it would have had no power to seek C's removal as a councillor.

Judgment: Richards J: It is common ground before me that the court has jurisdiction to entertain the present application. The power of the court to entertain an application for a merely declaratory judgment is carried through into the CPR by Schedule 1, RSC Order 15 rule 16:

'No claim or other proceeding shall be open to objection on the ground that a merely declaratory judgment or order is sought thereby, and the court may make binding declarations of right whether or not any consequential relief is or could be claimed.'

There is, however, a very real question as to whether it is appropriate for the court to entertain these proceedings. Islington contends that it is appropriate. The defendant shares that view, subject however to the preliminary issue of whether Islington is entitled to act under section 86 of the 1972 Act even if the defendant is disqualified. Mr Jones, as amicus, contends that the proceedings are inappropriate, principally because (i) the claimant does not put forward a positive case on the issues in respect of which a declaration is sought and (ii) there are deficiencies and uncertainties in the factual evidence which call for further evidence and cross-examination, but the procedure adopted precludes that possibility. He accepts, however, that in the circumstances the court should determine

[94] See, eg *R (Infant and Dietetics Foods Association Ltd) v Secretary of State for Health* [2008] EWHC 575 (Admin), [2009] Eu LR 1.
[95] *R v Secretary of State for the Home Department, ex parte Doody* [1994] 1 AC 531 (HL).
[96] [2004] BLGR 58 (QB).

the issue under section 86 and certain other legal issues on which there is a real dispute between the parties.

...

Miss Baxendale has referred me to a number of cases which, it is said, point towards the appropriateness of the court entertaining proceedings of this kind. In *Attorney General v. Fiona Jones* (*The Times*, 3 May 1999) the Divisional Court granted a declaration on the application of the Attorney General by way of originating summons (equivalent to the new procedure under CPR Part 8) that the defendant was entitled under the Representation of the People Act 1983 to sit in Parliament following the quashing of her conviction of an election offence. The court seems to have accepted without argument or question the appropriateness of such a procedure. Counsel for the Attorney General argued in favour of the declaration granted but also advanced a number of other arguments in a quasi-amicus role.

In *Ruislip-Northwood UDC v. Lee* (1931) 145 LT 208 the plaintiff council sought a declaration from the court that the defendants had erected 'temporary buildings' within the meaning of the relevant statute. The statute gave the council the power to pull down temporary buildings erected without permission. The council sought a declaration in advance, in order to know whether it had the power to pull down the buildings, rather than run the risk of pulling them down and being told after the event that it had done so unlawfully. The court held that there was a real dispute between the parties on the point raised and that the court had the jurisdiction to grant, and should grant, the declaration sought.

Other examples of the grant of declarations in unusual circumstances in the public law field are *Ealing LBC v. Race Relations Board* [1972] AC 342 and *Gillick v. West Norfolk and Wisbech Health Authority* [1986] AC 112. The discussion of these and other cases in de Smith, Woolf & Jowell, *Judicial Review of Administrative Action*, 5th ed., para 18-018, refers to the value of the courts giving 'advisory opinions' in the form of declarations in appropriate cases, even where the issue is theoretical in the sense that, for example, there is no dispute in existence. The authors state that 'the courts can be relied upon to ensure that the cases where relief is granted are confined to those where there is a real public interest in the relief being available.' They suggest that –

'In the end what should be determinative is whether the declaration will serve some useful purpose. If it will, then subject to the pragmatic considerations such as the burden on the court of resolving additional litigation, the more useful will be the declaration the more ready should be the court to grant the declaration, albeit that the issues are properly regarded as theoretical'.

Perhaps unsurprisingly, similar views are expressed in Zamir & Woolf, *The Declaratory Judgment*, 2nd ed., paras 4.043–4.052 and 4.086.

Account should also be taken of the observations of Sir John Laws, both judicially in *R v. Home Secretary, ex parte Mehari* [1994] QB 474 at 491 ('I have no doubt that there are circumstances in which the public law court ought to exercise the jurisdiction, which it certainly possesses, to give advisory opinions; but this is not one of them') and extrajudicially in his article on Judicial Remedies and the Constitution (1994) 57 MLR 213, which examines the issue of advisory opinions in some detail.

The authorities, textbooks and articles on the availability of declaratory relief in the public law field provide important guidance notwithstanding that the present case was transferred by the Divisional Court into the general Queen's Bench list. The case is still redolent of public law. The matters that the court is asked to decide are all matters that the court would be called upon to decide in proceedings in the Crown Office list if Islington were to declare the defendant's office vacant pursuant to section 86 of the 1972 Act and that decision were then subject to challenge by way of judicial review.

...

Such considerations are important matters to weigh in the balance but are not a fatal objection to the present proceedings. The general comments to which I have referred concerning the grant of declaratory relief in the public law field show that the existence of a dispute is not a necessary feature: a declaration may be appropriate even where the issues are properly regarded as theoretical.

Notes

(1) The courts have developed the concept of an 'advisory declaration' where there is not yet a dispute between the parties. These declarations are granted only rarely and in exceptional circumstances. However, they can be regarded as a useful tool to limit the retroactive annulment of decisions.[97] These declarations should not be designed to look retroactively at previous conduct, but should seek to guide future conduct of public authorities.[98] Their purpose is to reinforce legal certainty, giving the possibility to individuals to know their legal rights and obligations. In addition, the public authority against which a declaration is sought is bound by the ruling of the court. The question asked through declaration should not be hypothetical.

(2) The jurisdiction to grant declaration is wide, even if the judge may as a matter of discretion impose limits in its use, noticeably on matters of high policy and those that are controversial. In *R (Campaign for Nuclear Disarmament) v Prime Minister*,[99] the court refused to make a declaration that the invasion in Iraq in 2003 was unlawful in international law because it was contrary to public interest.

7.4.A.2 FRANCE

In the French system, the scope of declaratory judgments through a direct action is very limited. They are more frequent in case of indirect action in the case where an ordinary court must first solve the question of the legality of an administrative decision before ruling on the case. However, ordinary courts have no competence, in principle, to decide such an issue. Consequently, they must suspend the proceedings and refer a question on interpretation or on the validity of an administrative decision to the administrative court.[100] In such cases, the judgment adopted by the administrative court has a declaratory nature.

[97] See above section 7.2.A.2.
[98] *R v Minister of Agriculture, Fisheries and Food, ex parte Live Sheep Traders Ltd* [1995] COD 297.
[99] See *R (Campaign for Nuclear Disarmament) v Prime Minister* [2002] EWHC 2759 (Admin).
[100] See Art 49 of the Code of Civil Procedure (Code de procédure civile).

Conseil d'État, 26 May 1971[101] **7.47 (FR)**

Minister for Infrastructure and Housing v Société le Val d'Oise

DECLARATION REMEDY; INTERPRETATION

Société le Val d'Oise

Through a declaratory remedy, the applicant may seek the interpretation of an act if there is a current and existing dispute.

Facts: The mayor of Parmain Val-d'Oise adopted three decisions (*arrêtés*), on 20 September, 7 October and 8 December 1961, issuing a building permit to the Societé le Val d'Oise. However, the prefect disagreed with the scope of the permit, preventing the delivery of a certificate, which was required to pursue the development of a housing project that the society wished to pursue. Consequently, the society sought a declaratory remedy on the interpretation of the permits. The Administrative Court of First Instance confirmed that the decisions granted a building permit. The ruling was challenged.

Held: The Council of State confirmed the interpretation delivered by the Administrative Court of First Instance, interpreting the decisions as requiring the competent authority to grant the building permit taking the subsequent modifications of the plan of allotment into account.

Judgment: On the admissibility of the claim for interpretation of the municipal decisions (*arrêtés municipaux*) of 20 September, 7 October and 8 December 1961 lodged by the Société le Val d'Oise before the Administrative Court of First Instance of Versailles: Considering that, while the above mentioned decisions adopted by the mayor of Parmain clearly granted a building permit to the Société le Val d'Oise, the scope of the decisions could be interpreted in different ways and the question of whether those decisions (*arrêtés*) should be regarded as granting an authorization for a housing estate is such that the dispute on this issue between the claimant and the administration had led to prevent the prefect from delivering the certificate based on Article 9 of the Decree n° 58-1466 of 31 December 1958 and, consequently, to prevent the sale or the rent of the assets already authorised by a building permit; that, in these circumstances, there was an existing and open dispute when the Société le Val d'Oise introduced before the Administrative Court of First Instance of Versailles a claim for the interpretation of the above mentioned decisions (*arrêtés*);

On the substance of the case: Considering that the decisions adopted on 20 September, 7 October and 8 December 1961 by the mayor of Parmain granting the building permit refer explicitly to plans which modify the initial plan of the housing estate; that, consequently, it shall be considered that the authority which delivered those permits after the positive opinion of the department of the Minister for Infrastructure and Housing, must have implicitly but necessarily authorized those modifications; that the decisions which are the object of the dispute must be hence interpreted in that they also grant an authorization for the housing estate as provided for by Article 2 of the Decree N° 58-1466 of 31 December 1958; ...

Notes

(1) A declaratory remedy is rarely granted through direct action, where an individual lodges such a claim before the administrative court. It is mainly used in contractual

[101] N° 77323.

matters as part of the full jurisdiction remedy (*recours de pleine jurisdiction*) and relates to the interpretation of contractual obligations.

(2) Through a declaratory remedy, a party can also seek the court's view on the interpretation of a decision, as demonstrated by the *Société le Val d'Oise* case. In order for the claim to be admissible, there needs to be an existing and open dispute. The interpretation must be necessary, meaning that there must be real doubts on the content or meaning of the decision. For example, in the *Société le Val d'Oise* case, the judge had to interpret a decision granting a building permit, in order to determine the precise scope of that building permit. The declaratory remedy is also used to clarify the legal assessment of the facts, in order to establish, for example, the applicable rules in a specific situation[102] or the scope of a regulatory decision (*décision réglementaire*).[103] A declaratory ruling is binding on the public authorities.

(3) In housing matters, a specific declaratory remedy is provided for by the Law of 5 March 2007. It aims at recognising the existence of a housing right granted to an individual.[104]

(4) Another declaratory remedy is the remedy declaring the voidness of a decision. It concerns decisions which are vitiated by a severe illegality, such as decisions adopted by an authority which is not competent to adopt such a decision.[105] This remedy is admissible without any time limit, and the act is declared to never have existed.[106]

(5) A declaration remedy may also be related to the interpretation of a court ruling which aims at clarifying an obscure or ambiguous issue in the ruling.[107]

7.4.A.3 THE EUROPEAN UNION

Statute of the Court of Justice of the European Union **7.48 (EU)**

Article 43 If the meaning or scope of a judgment is in doubt, the Court of Justice shall construe it on application by any party or any institution of the Union establishing an interest therein.

Note

In the EU system, declaratory judgments are limited to a single action. This type of proceedings, called 'judgment of interpretation', is meant neither to amend the

[102] Conseil d'État, 7 February 2007, *M et Mme Sable*, N° 280373.
[103] Conseil d'État, 30 July 2003, *Marcelin et syndicat CDMT-ANPE*, N° 246771. On the concept of *décision réglementaire* in the French legal system, see Chapter 3, section 3.3.C.
[104] Arts R778-1 to R778-9 Code de justice administrative.
[105] Conseil d'État, 1 October 1990, *Bourreil*, N° 77030.
[106] Conseil d'État, 8 November 1974, *Epoux Figueras*, N° 83517.
[107] Conseil d'État, 23 November 2005, *Société Eiffage TP*, N° 271329.

substance of an existing judgment nor for third parties to be able to influence a ruling. It aims only at clarifying the meaning of the judgment, by clarifying its scope or the obligations resulting from it, in order to aid its enforcement.[108]

7.4.A.4 GERMANY

In the German legal system, there are two forms of declaratory actions.

Verwaltungsgerichtsordnung **7.49 (DE)**

§43 (1) By legal action, the declaration of the existence or non-existence of a legal relationship or of the voidness *ab initio* (*Nichtigkeit*) of an administrative act may be requested if the claimant has a legitimate interest in a speedy declaration (action for declaration) (*Feststellungsklage*).

(2) The declaration may not be requested as far as the claimant is able or could have been able to pursue his rights through an action for modification of a right or legal relationship (*Gestaltungsklage*) or by an action for performance (*Leistungsklage*). This does not apply where a declaration of the invalidity of a void act is requested.

Note

In Germany, the action for declaration (*Feststellungsklage*) is directed to situations where the court is asked to declare the existence or non-existence of a legal relationship or the voidness *ab initio* of an administrative act (*Verwaltungsakt*) in cases of severe illegality. It does not lead to the imposition of obligations. Rather, it declares the binding nature of a legal situation. Its expressly declared subsidiary function vis-à-vis the other types of court actions reflects the principle of procedural economy.

Verwaltungsgerichtsordnung **7.50 (DE)**

§47 (1) The Higher Administrative Court shall adjudicate on application within the boundaries of its jurisdiction on the validity of

1. by laws issued under the provisions of the Federal Building Code (Baugesetzbuch) and executive regulations issued on the basis of §246(2) of the Federal Building Code,

2. other legal provisions ranking below state legislation, to the extent that this is provided in state law.

…

(5) The Higher Administrative Court shall adjudicate by handing down a judgment or, if it does not consider oral proceedings to be necessary, it shall hand down an order. Should the Higher Administrative Court come to the conclusion that the legal provision is invalid, it shall declare it to be null and void; in this case, the ruling shall be binding *erga omnes*, and the respondent shall be required to publish the ruling in exactly the same

[108] Joined Cases 41/73, 43/73 and 44/73 *Société anonyme Générale sucrière and others v Commission* ECLI:EU:C:1977:41.

manner as the legal provision would be required to be made public. §183 shall apply mutatis mutandis in respect of the effect of the decision.

(6) On application, the court may issue a temporary injunction where this is urgently required in order to avert serious disadvantages or for other compelling reasons.

Note

By way of the procedure to review by-laws and executive regulations (*Normenkontrollverfahren*), the validity of abstract and general measures, ie executive regulations (*Rechtsverordnungen*) and by-laws (*Satzungen*), can be challenged.[109] If the claimant is successful, the court will declare the respective regulation or by-law invalid. A judgment on this action has *erga omnes* effects (§47(1) VwGO), whereas all other actions only lead to judgments with *inter partes* effects. The competent courts for this procedure are the Higher Administrative Courts (Oberverwaltungsgerichte). This type of action is particularly important in the context of development plans (*Bebauungspläne*). Besides development plans, §47(1), sub 1, review of by-laws and executive regulations is only possible if the German states have introduced this possibility into their legal orders. Some states have done so fully, some have done so to only a very limited extent and others have not done so at all.[110]

7.4.B LEGAL SYSTEMS WITHOUT DECLARATORY JUDGMENTS: THE NETHERLANDS

A declaratory action does not exist in the Netherlands as the only action is the claim for judicial review (*beroep*), which leads to annulment. For public law measures which cannot be challenged before administrative courts,[111] a declaration of illegality of these measures, without their annulment, may be issued by the civil courts in the course of a liability action.

7.4.C COMPARATIVE REMARKS

With the exception of the Netherlands, a declaratory remedy exists in all the legal systems studied. The conception of a declaratory action is similar in a number of respects.

First, in all legal systems providing for such a remedy, a declaration may concern the interpretation of an act (as is the case in France) or the declaration of the existence of a legal relationship (as is the case in Germany and England and Wales). Secondly, both in France and in Germany, the declaratory remedy may be used in cases of severe illegality of an administrative decision, where the measure at stake is so seriously flawed that

[109] For an explanation of the concepts of executive regulations and by-laws in the German legal system, see Chapter 3, sections 3.1.A and 3.7.A.

[110] See also Chapter 3, section 3.3.B.2 (i).

[111] See further Chapter 3. See also Seerden and Wenders (n 45 above) 166 ff.

it may be regarded as never having taken effect. Thirdly, particularly in England and Wales and in France, the point is explicitly made that the request for an interpretative declaration must be related to a concrete dispute, although this is interpreted in a flexible manner. Fourthly, the declaratory remedy has a somewhat ambiguous status. It is distinct from an action for annulment in the sense that it does not have any constitutive effects. However, the interpretation given is still binding on public authorities in the sense that, in its decision, the court can determine the scope of an act and the extent of a right, and the public authorities must comply with this interpretation. The authority of the ruling is even more important when a declaratory remedy can be requested in conjunction with other remedies, as is the case in England and Wales. Finally, it should be noted that the scope of declaratory remedies is quite narrow in the European Union, since the remedy only relates to the interpretation of a judgment.

7.5 LIABILITY DICTA

The notion of liability dicta refers to the situation in which courts having annulled a decision declare public authorities liable. In such a case, the public authority is held liable on the ground of the unlawful act which was quashed by the court. This case ought to be distinguished from a liability action, brought separately, the exclusive purpose of which is to seek damages from a public authority not necessarily in connection to the unlawfulness of an administrative act. The liability actions which exist in all the studied legal systems as autonomous actions are analysed in Chapter 11.

Liability dicta connected to annulment actions do not exist in all the legal systems subject to analysis in this book.

7.5.A LEGAL SYSTEMS WITHOUT THE POSSIBILITY OF LIABILITY DICTA THROUGH THE ACTION FOR ANNULMENT

7.5.A.1 GERMANY

In Germany, administrative courts are, in principle, not competent to deal with liability issues, damages or compensation.[112] Such legal disputes are dealt with by the civil courts. Damages and compensation claims before the civil courts are sought by way of an 'action for performance' (*Leistungsklage*), according to the rules of the Code of Civil Procedure (*Zivilprozessordnung*).

The annulment of an administrative act can only be ordered by an administrative court.[113] Thus, an action to annul an administrative act cannot be combined with an action for damages or compensation, because two different courts are competent.

[112] See Chapter 11, section 11.2.B.1. Only public liability cases resulting from public law contracts, civil service law and withdrawal of unlawful administrative acts remain within the jurisdiction of the administrative courts according to §40(2) VwGO.

[113] See section 7.2.A.1 above.

7.5.A.2 THE NETHERLANDS

Algemene Wet Bestuursrecht **7.51 (NL)**

Article 8:88 (1) The administrative judge is competent, upon the request of a party concerned, to order an administrative authority to compensate damage which the party concerned has suffered or will suffer as a result of:

(a) an unlawful decision;

(b) another unlawful act for the preparation of an unlawful decision;

(c) failure to issue a decision in due time;

(d) another unlawful act of an administrative authority wherein a person within the meaning of Article 8:2(1)(a), his survivors, or his legal successors are parties concerned.

(2) Section (1) does not apply where the decision is exempt from judicial review before the administrative judge.

Note

In the Netherlands, the administrative courts cannot rule on a liability claim in the same procedure in which the administrative decision (causing damage) has been annulled. Thus, there is no liability dictum. If the claimant seeks compensation for damage caused by the annulled decision, he must bring a separate procedure, either before the administrative courts (Article 8:88 AWB), which are exclusively competent in liability matters in the area of taxation and social security, or before the (general) civil courts.[114]

7.5.B LIABILITY DICTA COMBINED WITH ACTION FOR ANNULMENT

7.5.B.1 THE EUROPEAN UNION

Case T-713/14, 13 December 2016[115] **7.52 (EU)**

International and European Public Services Organisation in the Federal Republic of Germany (IPSO) v European Central Bank

ACTION FOR ANNULMENT; LIABILITY

International and European Public Services Organisation (IPSO)

A claim for liability can be joined to an action for annulment.

Facts: The International and European Public Services Organisation in the Federal Republic of Germany (IPSO) is a professional trade union which, in accordance with its statutes, represented the interests of persons employed in or working for international and European organisations established in Germany. The organisation lodged an action for annulment against a decision of the European Central Bank (ECB) Executive Board of 20 May 2014 limiting the maximum period during which the ECB may use the services

[114] See Chapter 11, section 11.2.B.2.

[115] ECLI:EU:T:2016:727.

of the same temporary agency worker for administrative and secretarial tasks to two years. At the same time, the organisation lodged an application to claim compensation for a non-material harm based on the illegality of the decision.

Held: The challenged decision was annulled on the ground that the applicant had not been duly consulted during the decision-making process. However, the claim for compensation was rejected since the non-material harm of the applicant was fully compensated by the annulment of the decision and by the obligation imposed on the ECB to initiate a social dialogue on the contested subject.

Judgment: ... 147. Consequently, unless it is to undermine the effectiveness of the obligation to consult, the administration must comply with that obligation whenever consultation of workers' representatives is such as to have an influence on the substance of the measure to be adopted (see, to that effect and by analogy, judgement of 20 November 2003, *Cerafogli and Poloni v ECB*, T-63/02, EU:T:2003:308, paragraph 23).

148. It follows that, in adopting the contested act without first having involved the applicant, even though the subject matter of the act came under the discussions in the working group, and without awaiting the working group's report, the ECB did not respect the applicant's rights to be informed and consulted, which form part of its rights and powers as the trade union representing the persons concerned, in breach of Article 27 of the Charter of Fundamental Rights, defined by Directive 2002/14 and implemented by the framework agreement as extended to cover agency staff by the creation of the working group.

149. That finding is not invalidated by the ECB's argument that the contested act was adopted, for the purpose of sound administration, in anticipation of a future amendment of the AÜG, with which the ECB would, in any event, be required to comply.

150. As noted in paragraphs 29 to 32 above, it cannot be considered that the contested act was adopted simply in anticipation of a future amendment of the AÜG.

151. The first plea in law must therefore be upheld, without there being any need to consider the applicant's complaints alleging a breach of Directive 2008/104 or to rule on the admissibility of those complaints, which is challenged by the ECB. Consequently, the contested act must be annulled without any need to consider the second plea in law.

The claim for damages

152. The applicant claims that it suffered non-material harm that can be separated from the illegality on which the annulment of the contested act is based and cannot be compensated for in full by that annulment, and it seeks payment of EUR 15000 by way of compensation. It argues that it was denied its position as a social partner because the contested act was adopted in disregard of the social dialogue. It points out that it made requests for the contested act to be withdrawn or suspended until the working group had completed its work.

...

154. First of all, it should be noted that, pursuant to the second paragraph of Article 340 TFEU, the European Union must, in accordance with the general principles common to the laws of the Member States, make good any damage caused by its institutions or by its servants in the performance of their duties. However, pursuant to the third paragraph of Article 340 TFEU, in derogation from the second paragraph, the ECB is, in accordance with the general principles common to the laws of the Member States, to make good any damage caused by it or its servants in the performance of their duties.

155. According to settled case-law, applicable mutatis mutandis to the non-contractual liability of the ECB provided for in the third paragraph of Article 340 TFEU,

the European Union's non-contractual liability under the second paragraph of Article 340 TFEU for the unlawful conduct of its bodies depends on fulfilment of a set of conditions, namely: the unlawfulness of the conduct alleged against the institutions, the fact of damage and the existence of a causal link between that conduct and the damage complained of (see judgements of 27 November 2007, *Pitsiorlas v Council and ECB*, T-3/00 and T-337/04, EU:T:2007:357, paragraph 290 and the case-law cited; of 23 May 2014, *European Dynamics Luxembourg v ECB*, T-553/11, not published, EU:T:2014:275, paragraph 342 and the case-law cited; and of 7 October 2015, *Accorinti and Others v ECB*, T-79/13, EU:T:2015:756, paragraph 65 and the case-law cited).

156. In the present case, it is evident from paragraph 148 above that the contested act is unlawful in that it was adopted in breach of the applicant's rights to be informed and consulted, thus infringing Article 27 of the Charter of Fundamental Rights, defined by Directive 2002/14 and implemented by the framework agreement as extended to cover agency staff by the creation of the working group.

157. Without there being any need to rule on whether that unlawful conduct by the ECB constitutes a sufficiently serious breach for the purposes of the case-law (judgement of 4 July 2000, *Bergaderm and Goupil v Commission*, C-352/98 P, EU:C:2000:361, paragraph 42), or whether the other conditions for the ECB to incur non-contractual liability, set out in paragraph 155 above, are met in the present instance, it should be noted that, even if that were the case, the annulment of the contested act constitutes, contrary to the applicant's claims, adequate and sufficient compensation for the non-material harm which allegedly resulted from the disregarding of the social dialogue and of its position as a social partner.

158. In so far as the non-material harm alleged by the applicant results from the illegality of the contested act, it is settled case-law that such harm is, in principle, sufficiently compensated for by the court's finding of illegality, unless the applicant can show that it suffered non-material harm that can be separated from the illegality on which the annulment is based and cannot be compensated for in full by that annulment ....

159. The applicant does not provide any evidence in support of its allegation that the non-material harm it suffered can be separated, in the present case, from the illegality of the contested act.

160. By contrast, the annulment of the contested act has the effect of requiring the ECB, pursuant to Article 266 TFEU, to take the necessary measures to comply with the present judgement and to initiate or continue social dialogue with the applicant on the issue that was the subject matter of the contested act, which will have the effect of compensating in full for the non-material harm alleged by the applicant and resulting from the disregarding of the social dialogue and of its position as a social partner.

161. Consequently, the claim for damages must be dismissed.

Note

In the EU legal system, a party can claim for compensation on the ground of liability of the EU institutions, while at the same time bringing an action for annulment. In such cases, the court, after having reviewed the legality of the challenged decision, assesses the possibility of imposing liability on EU authorities according to the general requirements of liability. If the court rules that there is no illegality, the action for compensation is be rejected.[116] Moreover, not all forms of illegality are sufficient to ground a claim in liability. Where the challenged decision is adopted in a field where EU institution has a wide discretion, the illegality must result from a sufficiently serious breach, meaning that the public authority manifestly and gravely disregarded the limits on its discretion.[117] Furthermore, as the *IPSO* case demonstrates, the liability of the EU institutions is conditional upon the proof of a harm suffered by the applicant.[118] In this case, the General Court considered that the annulment of the challenged decision had fully repaired its non-material harm. Finally, the applicant has also to show that there is a causal link between the illegality of the decision and the harm suffered. For example, the illegal refusal to grant access to documents by the European Commission was not considered to be the cause of the deterioration in the mental health of the applicant.[119]

7.5.B.2 ENGLAND AND WALES

Senior Courts Act **7.53 (EW)**

Section 31 …

(4) On an application for judicial review the High Court may award to the applicant damages, restitution or the recovery of a sum due if –

(a) the application includes a claim for such an award arising from any matter to which the application relates; and

(b) the court is satisfied that such an award would have been made if the claim had been made in an action begun by the applicant at the time of making the application.

Civil Procedure Rules **7.54 (EW)**

Rule 54.3 …

(2) A claim for judicial review may include a claim for damages, restitution or the recovery of a sum due but may not seek such a remedy alone.

Note

Section 31(4) of the Supreme Court Act sets out the circumstances in which the court may award damages, restitution or the recovery of a sum due on a claim for judicial review.

[116] Case T-31/07 *Du Pont de Nemours (France) SAS and Others v Commission* ECLI:EU:T:2013:167; Case T-476/07 *Evropaïki Dynamiki – Proigmena Systimata Tilepikoinonion Pliroforikis kai Tilematikis AE v European Agency for the Management of Operational Cooperation at the External Borders of the Member States of the European Union (Frontex)* ECLI:EU:T:2012:366.

[117] See Chapter 11, section 11.3.A.3.

[118] See also Case T-133/12 *Mehdi Ben Tijani Ben Haj Hamda Ben Haj Hassen Ben Ali v Council of the European Union* ECLI:EU:T:2014:176.

[119] Case T-221/08 *Guido Strack v Commission* ECLI:EU:T:2016:242.

Court of Appeal (Civil Division), 27 January 2005[120] **7.55 (EW)**

ID and Others v Home Office

REMEDIES; DAMAGES

ID

It is not possible to claim damages as a remedy in judicial review proceedings unless the claimant is also seeking a public law remedy and can also demonstrate that the unlawful act of the public authority infringes private law rights.

Facts: The claimants, who were members of a Czech family of Roma ethnic origin, were detained by immigration officers on their entry to the UK and were held in a detention centre while their asylum claims (which ultimately failed) were processed. The claimants made claims for declarations that their detention was unlawful and contrary to the Human Rights Act 1998, and also sought damages for the tort of wrongful imprisonment and infringement of their human rights.

Held: The Court of Appeal held that immigration officers did not enjoy immunity from such claims, but that in this case the claimants had been unsuccessful in showing that they had a cause of action to enable such recovery.

Judgment: Brooke LJ: [57] The second is that there is on the face of it nothing in the slightest bit peculiar about an individual bringing a private law claim for damages against an executive official who has unlawfully infringed his private rights. For this proposition it is unnecessary to go much further than AV Dicey, *Introduction to the Study of the Law of the Constitution*, 8th Edition (being the last edition for which the original author was responsible) at p 114:

'In England the idea of legal equality, or of the universal subjection of all classes to one law administered by the ordinary Courts, has been pushed to its utmost limit. With us every official, from the Prime Minister down to a constable or a collector of taxes, is under the same responsibility for every act done without legal justification as any other citizen. The Reports abound with cases in which officials have been brought before the Courts, and made, in their personal capacity, liable to punishment, or to the payment of damages, for acts done in their official character but in excess of their jurisdiction.'

See, also, Wade and Forsyth, *Administrative Law*, 9th Edition (2004) at p 751:

'Public authorities, including ministers of the Crown, enjoy no dispensation from the ordinary law of tort and contract, except in so far as statute gives it to them. Unless acting within their powers, they are liable like any other person for trespass, nuisance, negligence and so forth. This is an important aspect of the rule of law.'

[58] It should be noted in this context that although CPR Pt 54 now permits the Administrative Court to award damages in addition to other relief on an application for judicial review, it has no jurisdiction to entertain a claim for damages alone (see CPR 54.3(2)).

[59] The difficult questions we have to determine are whether the law grants any form of immunity to an immigration officer in respect of what would normally be regarded as an unlawful act causing a loss of liberty, and whether a complainant's remedy is limited to a declaration that the act was unlawful and/or a quashing order, or whether it sounds in damages as well, or as an alternative remedy.

[120] [2005] EWCA Civ 38.

Note

Claims for damages or compensatory remedies are granted in private law. Consequently, as a principle, damages alone cannot be sought through the judicial review procedure, but should ordinarily be brought through private law procedures (ie in debt, restitution or the law of tort, etc). However, under Article 54.3 CPR and section 31(4) of the Senior Courts Act 1981, a claimant for judicial review may seek damages or restitution together with quashing, mandatory, declaratory or prohibiting orders.[121] Such claims are not frequently made and damages are not frequently awarded as part of a judicial review claim, so liability dicta arise only infrequently.

7.5.B.3 FRANCE

R Rouquette, Petit Traité du procès administratif[122] **7.56 (FR)**

§1 The choice between challenging the legality of a decision or action, claiming for liability and the combination of both actions

This discussion refers to the classical case where two kinds of litigation are possible: the first one to request the annulment of an administrative decision, a second one to claim for the liability of the authority which adopted the decision. … Several strategies are available …. The action for annulment (*recours pour excès de pouvoir*) is usually simpler than the full jurisdiction remedy (*recours de pleine juridiction*), mainly because it is often the case that an administrative decision exists and can thus be challenged, so it is not necessary to go before the administrative authority to ask for a decision (*décision préalable*).[123] The most common case is when there is an illegal decision having caused damage. If an action for annulment is lodged, only illegality has to be demonstrated. If a claim for liability is introduced, one needs to demonstrate, in addition, the existence of damage, a causal link between the illegal decision and the damage and the amount of the damages. Considering the fact that litigation for damages is more expensive (costs of expert witnesses if necessary, lawyers' fees), a good strategy may be to defer the liability claim to the moment in which the chances of success of the action for annulment are relatively low or if it seems possible to get an informal resolution of the dispute related to damages ….

Note

In principle, if a decision is considered unlawful in an action for annulment (*recours pour exces de pouvoir*), this may lead to liability of the administration. A liability claim can be brought forward either in an autonomous liability action or within the action for annulment. In principle, an application has only one objective

[121] *Page Motor Ltd v Epsom and Ewell BC* (1982) 80 LGR 337 (CA).
[122] R Rouquette, *Petit Traité du Procès administratif*, 7th edn (Paris, Dalloz, 2016) 277–78.
[123] On this notion, see Chapter 4, section 4.7.C.4.

for one specific remedy. Hence, the annulment action and the action for liability are autonomous actions. However, in order to assist the claimant, and also for reasons of sound and efficient administration of justice, claimants are authorised to present in a single application both a claim concerning the legality of the challenged act and one related to liability of the public authority.[124] The administrative court can then rule on the two issues in a single judgment. In order to be admissible, both claims must be sufficiently connected (namely the challenged act must be the basis for liability). This system constitutes an example of the action for annulment and the 'full jurisdiction remedy' (*recours de pleine jurisdiction*) coming together. In such cases, the relevant procedural requirements are those applicable to full jurisdiction remedy. Nevertheless, the two claims are assessed separately by the administrative court, especially with regard to their admissibility. Furthermore, as the excerpt above demonstrates, it is mainly a matter of strategy to decide whether it is more appropriate to claim for liability while bringing an action for annulment or to bring two separate actions. One of the main considerations in this context is that of costs: since an action for liability is considerably more expensive than an action for annulment, it will generally be in the claimant's interest to bring an action for annulment in the first instance and then launch an action in respect of liability if the action for annulment is successful. Only in cases where a claimant is confident that the action taken by the public authority is unlawful will it be advisable to proceed directly with an action for damages.

7.5.C COMPARATIVE REMARKS

The possibility of liability dicta is directly linked to the division of competences between ordinary and administrative courts. Consequently, the legal solutions chosen by the legal systems. When judicial review is dealt with by ordinary courts, such as in England and Wales, liability dicta can be sought in judicial review proceedings (although with certain limitations). In contrast, in countries such as Germany and the Netherlands, the administrative courts are rarely competent to determine liability actions against public authorities. Consequently, liability claims within an action for annulment are not possible. Finally, in the French and EU systems, the same court is competent to hear actions for annulment and liability actions against public authorities. Therefore, actions combining both claims are admissible, although specificities of both claims from a procedural and substantive point of view apply. In particular, the classical requirements for liability need to be met. The possibility offered to the claimant to combine both claims in one procedure serves a sound administration of justice goal, promoting both the effectiveness of the judiciary and the effective protection of rights, since it contributes to the acceleration of proceedings are very different.

[124] Conseil d'État, 31 March 1911, *Blanc, Argaing et Bezie*, Rec Lebon, paras 407, 409, 410.

7.6 THE REVISION OF FINAL JUDGMENTS AND THE PRINCIPLE OF RES JUDICATA

The res judicata principle is a fundamental principle in all the legal systems studied in this book. According to this principle, judicial decisions become final after all possibilities for judicial review have been exhausted or after the expiry of the time limits for starting such actions. At that point, a final judicial decision cannot, in principle, be called into question, even when it is certain that the decision is inconsistent with the law. The res judicata principle is closely connected to the principle of legal certainty. It ensures the stability of legal relations, which is essential because the parties will shape their legal positions in conformity with a final judicial decision. It also contributes to the sound administration of justice, because it prevents parties litigating the same issue repeatedly.

Although all studied legal systems recognise the binding authority of res judicata as a matter of principle, they also provide for some exceptions to the principle. Under some limited circumstances, it might be possible to have a final judgment reconsidered, revised or rectified.

7.6.A INFLUENCE OF EUROPEAN UNION LAW ON THE PRINCIPLE OF RES JUDICATA

Case C-213/13, 10 July 2014[125] **7.57 (EU)**

Impresa Pizzarotti & C. SpA v Comune di Bari ea

RES JUDICATA; EFFECTIVENESS OF EU LAW

Impresa Pizzarotti

The principles of equivalence and effectiveness of EU law require a national judge to reopen a case which has become definitive only if national law permits such a possibility.

Facts: The company Impresa Pizzarotti applied for a public 'market investigation' notice published by the municipality of Bari, with the objective of building, as soon as possible, a new single headquarters which would be suitable and appropriate to host all the courts of Bari. The proposal of Pizzarotti was accepted, although there was a continuing reduction in the availability of financial resources for the project. Nevertheless, the municipality notified the company that it wished to proceed with the works. The municipality gave no further indication to the company, which brought a claim in order require the authority to take action. A ruling of the Italian Council of State confirmed that the municipality was required to resolve the issue. However, by subsequent rulings, it appeared that the ruling of the Council of State was not in compliance with EU law. By judgment N° 4267/2007, the Council of State ruled that the municipality had to reach a decision to explore the possibility of proceeding with the works. The municipality introduced a claim to challenge this ruling.

[125] ECLI:EU:C:2014:2067.

Held: The principles of equivalence and effectiveness require a national judge to reopen a case which has become definitive only if such a possibility exists under national law.

Judgment: By its second question, the referring court asks, in essence, whether it may decide that a ruling which it has made which has led to a situation which is incompatible with the EU legislation on public works contracts is ineffective.

In that regard, it should be borne in mind that, in the absence of EU legislation in this area, the rules implementing the principle of res judicata are a matter for the national legal order, in accordance with the principle of the procedural autonomy of the Member States, but must be consistent with the principles of equivalence and effectiveness (see, to that effect, the judgement in *Fallimento Olimpiclub*, C2/08, EU:C:2009:506, paragraph 24 and the case-law cited).

In its request for a preliminary ruling, the referring court indicates that, according to its case-law, it may, under certain conditions, supplement the original operative part of one of its judgements by implementation decisions, that possibility giving rise to what it terms 'progressively formed res judicata'.

If – and it is for the referring court to ascertain whether this is the case – the conditions for applying that procedure are met in respect of the decision in Judgement No 4267/2007, a decision which is mentioned in paragraph 15 of this judgement and which – according to the order for reference – alone has the force of res judicata in the present case, it is for that court, having regard to the principle of equivalence, to make use of that procedure, favouring, from among 'the numerous different possibilities of implementation' which it states may be used in respect of that decision, the solution which, in accordance with the principle of effectiveness, ensures compliance with the EU legislation on public works contracts.

As has been stated by the Comune di Bari, that solution could consist of an order, supplementing that decision, to terminate the market investigation procedure without accepting any of the proposals, which would then permit the launch of a new procedure, in compliance with the EU legislation on public works contracts.

On the other hand, if the referring court is led to the view that the correct application of that legislation conflicts, having regard to the applicable domestic rules of procedure, with its Judgement No 4267/2007 or with its decisions of 15 April and 3 December 2010 implementing that judgement, attention should be drawn to the importance, both in the legal order of the European Union and in national legal systems, of the principle of res judicata. In order to ensure both stability of the law and legal relations and the sound administration of justice, it is important that judicial decisions which have become definitive after all rights of appeal have been exhausted or after expiry of the time-limits provided for in that connection can no longer be called into question ....

Therefore, EU law does not require a national court to disapply domestic rules of procedure conferring finality on a judgement, even if to do so would make it possible to remedy a domestic situation which is incompatible with EU law ....

Accordingly, EU law does not require a judicial body automatically to go back on a judgement having the authority of *res judicata* in order to take into account the interpretation of a relevant provision of EU law adopted by the Court after delivery of that judgement.

...

That said, if the applicable domestic rules of procedure provide the possibility, under certain conditions, for a national court to go back on a decision having the authority of *res judicata* in order to render the situation compatible with national law, that possibility must prevail if those conditions are met, in accordance with the principles of equivalence and effectiveness, so that the situation at issue in the main proceedings is brought back into line with the EU legislation on public works contracts.

...

In the light of the foregoing, the answer to the second question is that, to the extent that it is authorised to do so by the applicable domestic rules of procedure, a national court – such as the referring court – which has given a ruling at last instance, without a reference having first been made to the Court of Justice under Article 267 TFEU, that has led to a situation which is incompatible with the EU legislation on public works contracts must either supplement or go back on that definitive ruling so as to take into account any interpretation of that legislation provided by the Court subsequently.

Notes

(1) The Court of Justice attaches great value to the principle of res judicata, both in the legal order of the European Union and in the national legal systems of Member States.[126] The principle ensures the stability of the law, and the legal relations and sound administration of justice. Therefore, as a matter of principle, EU law does not unconditionally require a national court to revoke or revise a final judicial decision, having the authority of res judicata, even when this decision is contrary to EU law. The Court decided in *Kapferer*[127] that EU law does not require a national court to disapply national rules of procedure conferring finality on a decision, even if reopening a case would be necessary to remedy an infringement of EU law.[128] Thus, as a matter of principle, the principle of res judicata prevails above the effectiveness principle.

(2) Despite its importance in the EU legal order, the Court of Justice allows a few exceptions to the principle. According to the *Impresa Pizzarotti* case, such exceptions may result from the EU principles of equivalence and effectiveness,[129] two principles that must always apply in national cases in which the enforcement of EU law is at stake. The case itself provides for an example of the application of the principle of equivalence. Italian law provided for an opportunity to limit the res judicata of an incorrect judicial decision under certain circumstances in purely domestic cases. Therefore, the national court is – on the ground of the principle of equivalence – obliged to use this possibility under the same circumstances if the judicial decision is contrary to EU law. Besides that, the Court of Justice requires that a national court reopens a case when it does not comply with EU law requirements only in exceptional

[126] On this topic, see JH Jans, S Prechal and RJGM Widdershoven (eds), *Europeanisation of Public Law*, 2nd edn (Groningen, Europa Law Publishing, 2015) 396–99.

[127] Case C-234/04 *Rosmarie Kapferer v Schlank & Schick GmbH* ECLI:EU:C:2006:178.

[128] See Jans et al (n 126 above) 396–99.

[129] For a limitation of the res judicata principle on the basis of the principle of effectiveness, see Case C-2/08 *Amministrazione dell'Economia e delle Finanze and Agenzia delle entrate v Fallimento Olimpiclub Srl* ECLI:EU:C:2009:506.

circumstances. Such circumstances were at stake in the *Lucchini* case,[130] concerning the application of EU law on state aid. The Court of Justice ruled that the principle of primacy of European law requires that a national court must refuse to apply any provision likely to conflict with it, including a provision that seeks to lay down the principle of res judicata. Such a situation was at stake in *Lucchini*, as the res judicata nature of a national judicial decision prevented the recovery of state aid which the Commission established in a final decision was incompatible with the internal market.

7.6.B ENGLAND AND WALES

Judicial decisions are generally considered to be final due to the principle of res judicata. The general principle adopted by the courts is that a judgment can be reopened at any point prior to the sealing of the final order (as to remedy or outcome) in the case by the court.

High Court (Queen's Bench Division), 25 July 2016[131] **7.58 (EW)**

R (Veolia ES Landfill Limited, Veolia ES Cleanaway (UK) Limited) v The Commissioners for HM Revenue and Customs

RES JUDICATA; REOPENING OF JUDICIAL DECISIONS; CLERICAL ERRORS

Veolia ES

The court is free to reopen a draft judgment and address errors or omissions contained within it but, after the court seals the final order, this is no longer possible.

Facts: In a tax dispute between the claimant and the tax authorities, the judge in the case circulated a draft judgment to the parties for their comment (as is the usual practice). Counsel for the claimant argued that the judgment was incorrect as it stated that one of the parties had not made a claim in respect of a certain issue when, in fact, it had. There was then some dispute between the parties as to the extent of the power of the court to reopen a draft judgment and reconsider issues raised in the case.

Held: At any point prior to the sealing of the final order in the case, the court can reopen the proceedings to address any errors or omissions. Once the final order has been sealed, the principle of res judicata is applied.

Judgment: Nugee J.: 220 I circulated a draft judgment in the above form to counsel for the parties inviting them to submit any typographical corrections and other obvious errors in writing in the usual way. I received a response from Mr Grodzinski asking me to reconsider the substance of the draft judgment, specifically the statement in paragraph 214 above that Veolia had not made any claim in respect of its internals (see also paragraphs 82 and 215), which he said was factually incorrect. I replied that I would

[130] Case C-119/05 *Ministero dell'Industria, del Commercio e dell'Artigianato v Lucchini SpA* ECLI:EU:C:2007:434.

[131] [2016] EWHC 1880 (Admin), [2017] Env LR 15.

be prepared to re-consider the draft judgment, and subsequently through my clerk indicated that I was vacating the hand-down and invited submissions. That led to further submissions from first Mr Grodzinski and then Mrs Hall, and a request from Mr Grodzinski to file reply submissions and/or hold a further oral hearing.

221 That raises a number of issues, which I will try and disentangle.

222 First, this point only affects Veolia and has no impact on Viridor's case. I will therefore dismiss Viridor's application for the reasons given above.

223 Second, I have no difficulty in principle with the Court being invited to reconsider a part of the draft judgment. The purpose of circulating a draft judgment is primarily to enable counsel to draw to the attention of the Court minor corrections or amendments before the judgment is formally handed down; to prepare, and if possible agree, drafts of orders giving effect to the judgment; and to prepare submissions on consequential matters such as costs and permission to appeal: see Civil Procedure (the White Book) 2016 §40.2.5. But the draft is a draft and not a final judgment, and for precisely that reason the Court retains the ability to reconsider and revise the judgment, whether invited to do so by the parties, or on the judge's own initiative if, on re-reading the draft, he or she thinks it appropriate to do so: *R (Mohamed) v Secretary of State for Foreign and Commonwealth Affairs (No 2)* [2010] EWCA Civ 158 ('*Mohamed*') at [3]. The jurisdiction to alter a draft judgment is therefore not in doubt: *Robinson v Bird* [2003] EWCA Civ 1820 at [91].

224 The Court indeed retains a jurisdiction to re-open its judgment even after it has been handed down, provided that it has not been perfected by the order being sealed. This was confirmed by the Court of Appeal in *re Barrell Enterprises* [1973] 1 WLR 19, and the leading case is now *re L (Children) (Preliminary Finding: Power to Reverse)* [2013] UKSC 8, in which the Supreme Court disapproved statements to the effect that the jurisdiction is limited to exceptional circumstances, and held that it should be exercised in accordance with the overriding objective. Whatever the limits on this jurisdiction, the ability of a judge to alter a draft judgment that has not been handed down cannot be any narrower, and is probably in theory at least entirely unfettered.

225 Third, it follows that if a draft judgment contains a demonstrable error of fact, it is open to a judge to correct it. Not only is this so, but I would have thought he or she should normally do so. Otherwise the judgment will be handed down despite containing a factual error. If the error makes no difference to the result, there is no reason not to correct it; if however it does make a difference to the result, to decline to correct it would mean the judgment was flawed, and no doubt lead to an appeal where one might otherwise have been unnecessary.

226 Fourth, the circulation of a draft judgment is not however intended to provide an opportunity for the unsuccessful party to re-open or re-argue the case, or to repeat submissions made at the hearing, or to deploy fresh ones: *Mohamed* at [4]. A fortiori, the circulation of a draft judgment is not intended to provide an opportunity for the unsuccessful party to change his case, or adduce new evidence. It is not in the interests of efficient case management for a litigant, having seen from a draft judgment in detail why he has lost (or is about to lose), to be permitted to try and make good any gaps that the judge has found in his case by new evidence or argument. The trial is the opportunity for a litigant to put forward his case and the evidence he relies on; trial is not, and should not be allowed to become, an iterative process. That is not to say that there may not be circumstances where fresh evidence can be admitted after trial (and even after judgment has been handed down), but such applications are rare and not to be encouraged: see *Charlesworth v Relay Roads* [2000] 1 WLR 230.

227 Fifth, although the Court can in an appropriate case be invited to look again at a draft judgment, the Court is not obliged to hold a hearing. If having looked at what it is invited to do and why, the Court sees no reason to alter the draft, it must be open to the Court to decline the invitation without more. One of the facets of the overriding objective is that a case should be allotted, so far as is practicable, an appropriate share of the Court's resources, while taking into account the need to allot resources to other cases. In practical terms that means that it must be open to a judge to draw a line under the debate and finalise the judgment. In the present case I have extensive written submissions from Mr Grodzinski. I do not think it necessary in order to address the point he makes either to have further submissions or a further hearing.

Notes

(1) The practice of the courts in England and Wales is to release a draft judgment to the parties (as in the excerpt above) for their comment, including their comment on any clerical errors in the judgment.

(2) The above decision illustrates the general rule, drawn from a decision of the Court of Appeal,[132] that a judgment of the court can be reopened at any point prior to it being perfected by the court sealing the order of the court. Once the judgment is sealed, it is not generally possible for the court to reopen the proceedings on any grounds. The grounds for reopening the decision are generally restricted to errors of fact, although there is no binding rule to require this.

House of Lords, 25 April 1991[133] **7.59 (EW)**

Arnold v National Westminster Bank Plc

RES JUDICATA; ESTOPPEL

Arnold

There are two types of estoppel which support the res judicata principle in English law – cause of action estoppel and issue estoppel.

Facts: A lease agreement between the claimant and the defendants provided for rent reviews on a five-yearly basis. A dispute arose between the parties as to the interpretation of the rent review provisions in the contract, and this was litigated and a determination on the appropriate interpretation of the provisions was decided by the High Court. Subsequently, the appellate authority (not involving the parties) determined that the judge's decision on the interpretation was not correct. The claimant then brought further proceedings regarding the construction of the lease and the correct interpretation of the rent review provisions, and the defendant argued that the latter point could not be raised again in proceedings as the res judicata principle prevented this.

Held: The principle of res judicata (in this case, one of issue estoppel) did not prevent the claimant from raising the issue that was subject of the instant case. Where it could be shown that a first instance decision had been

[132] *Re Barrell Enterprises* [1973] 1 WLR 19 (CA).
[133] [1991] 2 AC 93 (HL).

overruled in later cases, the party who suffered from that mistake was not barred from reopening the issue in later proceedings.

Judgment: Lord Keith of Kinkel: It is appropriate to commence by noticing the distinction between cause of action estoppel and issue estoppel. Cause of action estoppel arises where the cause of action in the later proceedings is identical to that in the earlier proceedings, the latter having been between the same parties or their privies and having involved the same subject matter. In such a case the bar is absolute in relation to all points decided unless fraud or collusion is alleged, such as to justify setting aside the earlier judgment. The discovery of new factual matter which could not have been found out by reasonable diligence for use in the earlier proceedings does not, according to the law of England, permit the latter to be re-opened. ... Cause of action estoppel extends also to points which might have been but were not raised and decided in the earlier proceedings for the purpose of establishing or negativing the existence of a cause of action. In *Henderson v. Henderson* (1843) 3 Hare 100, 114–115, Sir James Wigram V.-C. expressed the matter thus:

'In trying this question, I believe I state the rule of the court correctly, when I say, that where a given matter becomes the subject of litigation in, and of adjudication by, a court of competent jurisdiction, the court requires the parties to that litigation to bring forward their whole case, and will not (except under special circumstances) permit the same parties to open the same subject of litigation in respect of matter which might have been brought forward as part of the subject in contest, but which was not brought forward, only because they have, from negligence, inadvertence, or even accident, omitted part of their case. The plea of res judicata applies, except in special cases, not only to points upon which the court was actually required by the parties to form an opinion and pronounce a judgment, but to every point which properly belonged to the subject of litigation, and which the parties, exercising reasonable diligence, might have brought forward at the time.'

...

Issue estoppel may arise where a particular issue forming a necessary ingredient in a cause of action has been litigated and decided and in subsequent proceedings between the same parties involving a different cause of action to which the same issue is relevant one of the parties seeks to re-open that issue. This form of estoppel seems first to have appeared in *Duchess of Kingston's Case* (1776) 20 St.Tr. 355. A later instance is *Reg. v. Inhabitants of the Township of Hartington Middle Quarter* (1855) 4 E. & B. 780. The name 'issue estoppel' was first attributed to it by Higgins J. in the High Court of Australia in *Hoysted v. Federal Commissioner of Taxation* (1921) 29 C.L.R. 537, 561. It was adopted by Diplock L.J. in *Thoday v. Thoday* [1964] P. 181. Having described cause of action estoppel as one form of estoppel per rem judicatam, he said, at p. 198:

'The second species, which I will call 'issue estoppel,' is an extension of the same rule of public policy. There are many causes of action which can only be established by proving that two or more different conditions are fulfilled. Such causes of action involve as many separate issues between the parties as there are conditions to be fulfilled by the plaintiff in order to establish his cause of action; and there may be cases where the fulfilment of an identical condition is a requirement common to two or more different causes of action. If in litigation upon one such cause of action any of such separate issues as to whether a particular condition has been fulfilled is determined by a court of competent jurisdiction, either upon evidence or upon admission by a party to the litigation, neither party can, in subsequent litigation between one another upon any cause of action which depends upon the fulfilment of the identical condition, assert that the condition was fulfilled if the court has in the first litigation determined that it was not, or deny that it was fulfilled if the court in the first litigation determined that it was.'

Issue estoppel, too, has been extended to cover not only the case where a particular point has been raised and specifically determined in the earlier proceedings, but also that where in the subsequent proceedings it is sought to raise a point which might have been but was not raised in the earlier.

...

In the present case I consider that abuse of process would be favoured rather than prevented by refusing the plaintiffs permission to reopen the disputed issue. Upon the whole matter I find myself in respectful agreement with the passage in the judgment of Sir Nicolas Browne-Wilkinson V.-C. where he said [1989] Ch. 63, 70–71:

'In my judgment a change in the law subsequent to the first decision is capable of bringing the case within the exception to issue estoppel. If, as I think, the yardstick of whether issue estoppel should be held to apply is the justice to the parties, injustice can flow as much from a subsequent change in the law as from the subsequent discovery of new facts. In both cases the injustice lies in a successful party to the first action being held to have rights which in fact he does not possess. I can therefore see no reason for holding that a subsequent change in the law can never be sufficient to bring the case within the exception. Whether or not such a change does or does not bring the case within the exception must depend on the exact circumstances of each case.'

I am satisfied, in agreement with both courts below, that the instant case presents special circumstances such as to require the plaintiffs to be permitted to reopen the question of construction decided against them by Walton J., that being a decision which I regard as plainly wrong.

Notes

(1) As the case above defines it, 'cause of action estoppel' arises 'where the cause of action in the later proceedings is identical to that in the earlier proceedings, the latter having been between the same parties or their privies and having involved the same subject matter'. In such a case, the bar is absolute, and it is never possible to have the case reopened, even if a new fact arises. Furthermore, res judicata then applies to all the action, even on the points which had not been raised before the judge.

(2) Concerning the second case, the 'issue estoppel' arises where 'a particular issue forming a necessary ingredient in a cause of action has been litigated and decided and in subsequent proceedings between the same parties involving a different cause of action to which the same issue is relevant one of the parties seeks to reopen that issue'. Then an issue can be heard again by the judge if there is a new fact which could not, by reasonable diligence, have been determined previously by the party who now wishes to rely on it; there is a change in the law relating to the original decision; or fraud or collusion is alleged.

(3) The excerpt above is from private law proceedings in relation to a lease. It is possible for both cause of action estoppel and issue estoppel to be raised in judicial review proceedings, but it is difficult to find examples of cause of action estoppel

being raised in public law proceedings, although it is possible that they could be raised in private law actions against a public authority (for example, actions in tort or for breach of contract). In principle, although issue estoppel is primarily a creature of private law, it could apply to public law proceedings; however, the courts have generally adopted a flexible approach to the issue.

Court of Appeal (Civil Division), 31 January 1984[134] **7.60 (EW)**

R v Secretary of State for the Environment, ex parte Hackney London Borough Council

RES JUDICATA; ISSUE ESTOPPEL; JUDICIAL REVIEW

Hackney London Borough Council

Although it is possible for issue estoppel to arise in public law proceedings, it will seldom do so.

Facts: The Secretary of State had powers in legislation to determine and vary the amount of central government support payable to local authorities. The claimant local authority had previously been successful in a judicial review claim arguing that the Secretary of State had acted unlawfully in reducing the payment due to it as he had failed to consider the representations made by the authority. At a later date, the Secretary of State sought to reintroduce the funding reduction and the authority claimed judicial review of that decision. In the second judicial review hearing, the issue of whether some of the grounds of the claim could not be heard due to issue estoppel arose.

Held: Issue estoppel did not apply.

Judgment: Dunn LJ: The final ground of appeal was that the Secretary of State was estopped from denying that as at the date of the present application for judicial review Camden was entitled to receive the full amounts of rate support grant on the dates set out in the letters of 9 January 1980 and 6 January 1981. The passages in the judgment in Ex parte Brent London Borough Council [1982] Q.B. 593 relied on as raising an issue estoppel are set out in the judgment of the Divisional Court under appeal [1983] 1 W.L.R. 524, and the argument in support at pp. 535–536. The Divisional Court rejected the argument for the reasons given at p. 537, which I adopt.

In my judgment no issue estoppel arose in the present case. Although not necessary for my decision I also incline to the view that the Divisional Court was right to hold that the doctrine of issue estoppel cannot be relied on in applications for judicial review, although the court has an inherent jurisdiction as a matter of discretion in the interests of finality not to allow a particular issue which has already been litigated to be re-opened. This depends upon the special nature of judicial review under R.S.C., Ord. 53 which makes it different both from ordinary civil litigation inter partes and from criminal proceedings. Like the Divisional Court, I adopt the passage from Professor Wade's *Administrative Law*, 5th ed. (1982), p. 246, set out in the judgment of the Divisional Court at p. 539.

Lord Donaldson MR: … I share the doubts … as to the applicability of issue estoppel in judicial review proceedings.

[134] [1984] 1 WLR 592 (CA).

Note

The courts have generally been consistent in the approach that issue estoppel arises in judicial review claims.[135] For example, the House of Lords decided that issue estoppel may also arise in relation to planning decisions where the issues in a claim for judicial review have already been considered on appeal.[136] However, the overall judicial approach is that the res judicata principle should be treated flexibly in public law cases and the courts should be open to reconsideration of issues raised previously where appropriate.

7.6.C THE NETHERLANDS

Algemene Wet Bestuursrecht **7.61 (NL)**

Article 8:119 (1) The administrative judge may, on request of a party, reconsider an irrevocable judgment [having the force of *res judicata*] on the ground of facts and circumstances which:

a. took place before the judgment,

b. were unknown and could not reasonably have been known to the requesting party before the judgment, and

c. if the administrative court would have known earlier, could have had led to a different judgment.

Notes

(1) On the basis of Article 8:119 AWB, a court that has given a final judgment is allowed to revise it in exceptional circumstances, specifically on the basis of facts and circumstances that took place before the judgment was delivered, which were unknown and could not reasonably have been known by the requesting party, and which, if the court had known earlier, could have led to a different judgment.

These cumulative conditions for revising a judgment having force of res judicata are interpreted restrictively. The phrase 'facts and circumstances' only includes factual *nova*. Therefore, new case law favourable to the claimant, including case law of the Court of Justice and the European Court of Human Rights (ECtHR), does not qualify as such (as it is not factual). Moreover, such case law does not meet the condition according to which a ground for reopening must have been in place before the judgment was delivered, as the new case law 'took place' after the judgment which has in the meantime become final was delivered. Therefore, new case law does not constitute a reason for revision of the judgment.[137] In Dutch case law, it is correctly assumed

[135] See also *R (Barber) v Secretary of State for Work and Pensions* [2002] EWHC 1915 (Admin), [2002] 2 FLR 1181, [45]; *R (on the application of Munjaz) v Mersey Care NHS Trust, R (on the application of S) v Airedale NHS Trust* [2003] EWCA Civ 1036, [2004] QB 395, [79].

[136] *Thrasyvoulou v Secretary of State for the Environment* [1990] 2 AC 273 (HL).

[137] Hoge Raad, 24 June 2011, ECLI:NL:HR:2011:BM9272.

on the basis of the case law of the Court of Justice, for instance the case of *Impresa Pizzarotti*,[138] that EU law does not require a court to disapply Article 8:119 AWB.[139]

(2) Although written law does not provide for an explicit legal basis to do so, the administrative courts are allowed to rectify manifest 'administrative' errors in a judgment.[140] An example of such an error is, for instance, an incorrect date. Before a judgment can be rectified, the parties are given the opportunity to express their views on the rectification.

(3) In addition, the courts may, in very exceptional circumstances, declare a judgment expired (*vervallen verklaren*). This power is used in cases where a party's fundamental procedural rights have manifestly been violated, for instance if the invitation for the hearing was sent to the wrong address or if the court incorrectly assumed that a party had not paid the obligatory court fee.[141] The power to do this is not expressly provided in written law.

7.6.D THE EUROPEAN UNION

Statute of the Court of Justice of the European Union **7.62 (EU)**

Article 44 An application for revision of a judgment may be made to the Court of Justice only on discovery of a fact which is of such a nature as to be a decisive factor, and which, when the judgment was given, was unknown to the Court and to the party claiming the revision.

The revision shall be opened by a judgment of the Court expressly recording the existence of a new fact, recognising that it is of such a character as to lay the case open to revision and declaring the application admissible on this ground.

No application for revision may be made after the lapse of 10 years from the date of the judgment.

Note

In the European Union, only when several cumulative conditions are met can a final judgment of the Court of Justice or the General Court be revised. In the first place, revision can only be based on the discovery of a fact which was, when the judgment was given, unknown to the court and the party claiming the revision. The fact concerned must have existed before the judgment was delivered, and it is for the applicant to prove that he discovered it after the delivery of the judgment. Secondly, which is a result of the first condition, subsequent case law of the Court of Justice or the General Court is not a reason for revision, as it does not qualify as a new fact.[142]

[138] See section 7.6.A above.
[139] See Centrale Raad van Beroep, 17 November 2006, ECLI:NL:CRVB:2006:AZ2586; Centrale Raad van Beroep, 31 December 2007, ECLI:NL:CRVB:2007:BC2676.
[140] Centrale Raad van Beroep, 7 April 2011, ECLI:NL:CRVB:2011:BQ2229.
[141] Centrale Raad van Beroep, 19 July 2002, ECLI:NL:CRVB:2002:AE6842.
[142] Case C-403/85 REV *Ferrandi v Commission* ECLI:EU:C:1991:119.

Thirdly, the fact concerned should be 'of such a nature as to be decisive'. To meet this condition, it is necessary that the fact, if the court had known it, would have led to a different judgment.[143]

Rules of Procedure of the Court of Justice **7.63 (EU)**

Article 154 Rectification

(1) Without prejudice to the provisions relating to the interpretation of judgments and orders, clerical mistakes, errors in calculation and obvious inaccuracies may be rectified by the Court, of its own motion or at the request of a party made within two weeks after delivery of the judgment or service of the order.

(2) Where the request for rectification concerns the operative part or one of the grounds constituting the necessary support for the operative part, the parties, whom the Registrar shall duly inform, may submit written observations within a time-limit prescribed by the President.

(3) The Court shall take its decision after hearing the Advocate General.

(4) The original of the rectification order shall be annexed to the original of the rectified decision. A note of this order shall be made in the margin of the original of the rectified decision.

Note

Clerical mistakes, errors in calculation and obvious inaccuracies in a judgment or order of the Court of Justice may be rectified by an order setting out the rectified text. A similar provision applies with regard to the General Court.[144]

7.6.E FRANCE

Code civil **7.64 (FR)**

Article 1355 The authority of res judicata applies only to the *ratio decidendi* of the judgment. It applies when the claim is seeking the same remedy; when the claim is based on the same cause of action; and when the claim concerns the same parties and is brought by these parties and against these parties acting in the same capacities.

Note

In the French system, the res judicata principle is applicable before administrative courts, drawing inspiration from civil law and more specifically from Article 1355 of the Civil Code (Code civil). The principle aims to preclude any further litigation

[143] Case C-185/90 P-REV *Gill v Commission* ECLI:EU:C:1991:380

[144] Rules of Procedure of the General Court, Art 84.

(except an appeal) between the same parties on the same issue and the same grounds. There is a distinction between the relative and absolute scope of the res judicata principle. In the first case, the case cannot be reopened between the same parties, but other individuals can challenge the decision on different grounds. In case of absolute authority of the ruling, even other individuals cannot challenge the administrative decision anymore. This is particularly the case when an administrative act is declared void.[145]

Conseil d'État, 17 December 2007[146] **7.65 (FR)**

City of Angles v Marion A

RES JUDICATA; SCOPE

Commune des Angles

Res judicata applies not only to the operative part of the ruling, but also to its grounds.

Facts: The City of Angles was held liable for the injuries caused to Marion A, resulting from an accident that was caused by the lack of maintenance of a ski slope. The City challenged the first instance ruling since the ruling was grounded on an error of law and on an error in the legal assessment of the facts. However, the time limit for an appeal on points of law (*recours en cassation*) had expired.

Held: The request of the City of Angles to annul the first instance ruling was rejected.

Judgment: Considering that, in first place, neither any legislative or regulatory provision nor any general rule of procedure extends the time limit for appeal on points of law against an interlocutory (*avant dire droit*) judgment of an Administrative Court of First Instance, ruling in first and last instance until the expiry of the time limit of the appeal against the judgment ruling on the merits of the dispute; that as the City of Angles has not lodged an appeal on points of law against the interlocutory judgment of 11 March 2004, the latter has become final; that this final character prevents the City of Angles from calling into question, in its appeal against the judgment of 2 June 2004, the *res iudicata* which is applicable to both the operative part of the judgment and the grounds which are its necessary basis; that, consequently, the grounds raised, concerning the fact that the Court of First Instance had, by the judgment of 11 March 2004, on the one hand, committed an error in law by ruling on the rejection of the request of Ms A and by retaining *ex officio* the regime of responsibility for damages of public works and had, on the other hand, incorrectly qualified the facts with regard to their type by ruling that the ski slope at stake had the character of public work, are not admissible. …

Note

The excerpt illustrates the importance the Conseil d'État attaches to the principle of res judicata of a judgment that has become final because it was not contested within

[145] See section 7.2.A.4 above.
[146] N° 271482.

the prescribed time limit. As a result, a judgment cannot be called into question even though it might have been based on incorrect legal or factual grounds. Moreover, the res judicata principle applies to both the operative part of the judgment and the grounds on which it is based.

Code de justice administrative **7.66 (FR)**

Article R834-1

Appeals seeking to have a decision revised on the grounds of error of fact or law may only be lodged against a decision of the Council of State rendered in *inter partes* proceedings in the following circumstances:

1. If it was rendered on the basis of forged documents;

2. If a party was found liable because he failed to produce a decisive document that had not been disclosed by the opposing party;

3. If the decision was made without taking account of the provisions of this code relating to the composition of the court formation, the holding of hearings and the form and delivery of the decision.

Article R834-2

Appeals as defined in this chapter must be lodged within the same time limit and are admitted in the same way as objections to decisions rendered *in absentia*.

In the cases referred to in points 1. and 2. of the foregoing article, the time limit only runs as from the day on which the party became aware of the reason for the revision on which the appeal is based.

Notes

(1) The grounds for revision of a final judgment of the Conseil d'État on the grounds of error of fact or law are defined in a very limited way by Article R834-1 of the Code de justice administrative. Three grounds may be raised. The first two relate to fraudulent behaviour by the parties, relating to the withholding of relevant materials or the submission of forged materials. The third ground is concerned with the violation by the Conseil d'État of important procedural rules, such as the rules on the composition of the court formation and the requirement of a public hearing.[147] In respect of the latter, a possible reason for revising a judgment is a violation of the court's obligation to inform the parties of the date of the hearing.[148]

(2) An action for revision must be lodged within two months either from the moment 'when the party became aware of the reason for the revision on which the appeal is based' (Article R834-2), meaning two months from the notification of the ruling, or from the day on which the party discovered the forged or fraudulent character of the submitted materials. If the appeal is declared admissible and considered as well-founded, the court annuls the challenged ruling and has to rule again on the case.

[147] Conseil d'État, 10 May 1995, *Paris*, N° 142984.

[148] Conseil d'État, 7 April 2011, *Amnesty International sect. française*, N° 343595.

Code de justice administrative **7.67 (FR)**

Article R833-1

When a decision of an Administrative Court of Appeal or the Council of State is affected by a clerical error that might have had an influence on the judgment of the case, the party concerned may lodge an appeal seeking to have the decision rectified, before the court that delivered the decision.

Appeals of this type must be lodged following the same formalities as the initial application. Appeals of this type must be lodged within a period of two months, which runs from the day on which the decision whose rectification is sought was notified or served.

The provisions of books VI and VII apply.

Article R833-2 The provisions of Article R811-5 apply to appeals seeking to have a clerical error corrected.

Note

Article R833-1 of the Code de justice administrative provides for a remedy for the parties to have so-called administrative errors rectified (*recours en rectification d'erreur matérielle*). These are errors which have been made by the court unintentionally (for instance, a clearly incorrect date or the incorrect spelling of a name). If the error might have had an influence on the ruling of the case, the party concerned may apply to have it rectified.

7.6.F GERMANY

Verwaltungsgerichtsordnung **7.68 (DE)**

§121 Final judgments shall be binding insofar as a ruling has been handed down on the subject-matter of the dispute

1. upon those concerned and their legal successors, and
2. in cases falling under §65(3), upon those persons who did not make a request for subpoena or did not do so in good time.

Bundesverwaltungsgericht, 8 December 1992[149] **7.69 (DE)**

The principle of res judicata prohibits the issuance of a new administrative act with the same content against the addressee in the future.

Facts: In 1977, the city B prohibited the claimant from organising a used car market for non-commercial providers on Sundays and public holidays. The action for annulment brought by the claimant against that decision was successful on appeal. The Higher Administrative Court annulled the administrative act by a final judgment of 13 October 1983 because it held that the car market did not contradict the law concerning the protection of Sundays and public holidays. However, in its judgment of 3 May 1988, the Federal Administrative Court ruled in another case that car markets on Sundays and public holidays generally contradict the

[149] BVerwGE 91, 256.

constitutional purpose of the protection of Sundays and holidays – regardless of whether a specific disturbance has been established. Recalling that decision, the city B prohibited the organisation of the claimant's car market on Sundays and public holidays by issuing a new administrative act. The claimant brought an action for annulment against that administrative act based on the res judicata effect of the former judgment by the Higher Administrative Court.

Held: The newly issued administrative act prohibiting the claimant's car market was annulled.

Judgment: 1. In the event of a successful annulment action the resulting final judgment does not only affect the administrative act which was challenged at the time according to §121 VwGO. The defeated administrative authority is precluded from adopting a new administrative act under unchanged factual and legal circumstances against the claimant on the same grounds.

2. The res iudicata effect occurs even if the final judgment was substantially flawed. It is therefore irrelevant if a subsequent decision of a higher court confirms that the earlier final judgment was incorrect.

Note

In Germany, the principle of res judicata is an important principle. From the excerpt, it is clear that this principle prevails even if the final judgment is substantively flawed. Moreover, in the event of a successful annulment action, the res judicata of the final judgment not only affects the administrative act that was challenged, but also impinges on subsequent administrative acts. Therefore, the defeated administrative authority in the first case is precluded from adopting a new administrative act under unchanged factual and legal circumstances against the claimant on the same grounds even where the judgment of the court is later found to be incorrect by a higher court.

Verwaltungsgerichtsordnung **7.70 (DE)**

§153 (1) Proceedings which are final may be resumed in accordance with the provisions of Book Four of the Code of Civil Procedure.

(2) The power to lodge an action for declaration of voidness (*Nichtigkeitsklage*) and an action for retrial of the case (*Restitutionsklage*) shall also be held by the representative of the public interest, in the proceedings before the Federal Administrative Court at first and final instance also by the Representative of the Interests of the Federation at the Federal Administrative Court (Vertreter des Bundesinteresses beim Bundesverwaltungsgericht).[150]

Zivilprozessordnung **7.71 (DE)**

§579 – Action for declaration of voidness

(1) An action for declaration of voidness (*Nichtigkeitsklage*) may be brought:

1. Where the composition of the court hearing the case was not compliant with the relevant provisions;

[150] The permanent representatives of the public interest and the Representative of the Interests of the Federation may engage as a party in any administrative law proceedings pending before the courts. Only 6 out of 16 states have made use of the possibility to appoint a representative of the public interest.

2. Where a judge was involved in the decision who, by law, was prohibited from holding judicial office, unless this impediment had been asserted by a motion to recuse a judge or by filing appellate remedies and the motion or appeal were refused;

3. Where a judge was involved in the decision although he had been recused for fear of bias and the motion to so recuse him had been declared justified;

4. Where a party to the proceedings had not been represented in accordance with the stipulations of the law, unless that party had expressly or tacitly approved the litigation.

(2) No complaint may be filed in the cases set out under numbers 1 and 3 if it was possible to enforce such annulment by appellate remedies.

§580 – Action for retrial of the case

An action for retrial of the case (*Restitutionsklage*) may be brought:

1. Where the opponent, by swearing an oath regarding his testimony, on which the judgment had been based, has intentionally or negligently committed perjury;

2. Where a record or document on which the judgment was based had been prepared based on misrepresentations of fact or had been falsified;

3. Where, in a testimony or report on which the judgment was based, the witness or experts violated their obligation to tell the truth, such violation being liable to prosecution;

4. Where the judgment was obtained by the representative of the party or its opponent or the opponent's representative by a criminal offence committed in connection with the legal dispute;

5. Where a judge contributed to the judgment who, in connection with the legal dispute, violated his official duties vis-à-vis the party, such violation being liable of prosecution;

6. Where a judgment by a court of general jurisdiction, by a former special court, or by an administrative court, on which the judgment has been based, is reversed by another judgment that has entered into force;

7. Where the party

a) finds, or is put in the position to avail itself of a judgment that was handed down in the same matter and that has become final and binding earlier, or where it

b) finds, or is put in the position to avail itself of, another record or document that would have resulted in a decision more favourable to that party's interests;

8. Where the European Court of Human Rights has established that the European Convention for the Protection of Human Rights and Fundamental Freedoms or its protocols have been violated, and where the judgment is based on this violation.

Notes

(1) According to §153 VwGO in conjunction with §§579 and 580 of the Zivilprozessordnung (Code of Civil Procedure), proceedings concluded with a final judgment having the force of res judicata may be reopened by either an 'action for declaration of voidness' (*Nichtigkeitsklage*) or an 'action for retrial of the case' (*Restitutionsklage*).

(2) The grounds for declaring a final judgment void (action for declaration of voidness) are listed in §579 of the Zivilprozessordnung. They include the situation in which the composition of the court is not compliant with the relevant provisions and the situation where a judge is involved in the decision who, by law, is prohibited from holding judicial office.

(3) The grounds for an action for retrial are listed in §580 of the Zivilprozessordnung. They include several situations in which the fact-finding in the case was affected by the criminal behaviour of an actor involved (perjury by the opponent, falsification of records and documents, violation of the obligation to tell the truth by witnesses or experts). In addition, an action for retrial may be brought where a party avails itself of a record or document that would have resulted in a judicial decision more favourable to that party's interest.

(4) Mere clerical errors may be corrected by the court at any time according to §118 VwGO.

7.6.G COMPARATIVE REMARKS

From the foregoing, it is clear that, as has been stated by the Court of Justice in a consistent line of case law, the principle of res judicata is a fundamental principle, both in the legal order of the European Union and in the national legal systems. The importance of the principle of res judicata has been confirmed in all the legal systems studied in this book. The principle contributes to legal certainty in general, and the stability of the law and legal relations and the sound administration of justice in particular. Therefore, as a matter of principle, final judgments are not to be called into question.

However, the res judicata principle is not absolute. All the legal systems provide for one or more remedies aimed at having final judgments reopened or rectified under specific conditions.

The first set of conditions concerns situations in which a new fact has come to light which could not have been known when the ruling was issued and which is decisive for the outcome of the case. This circumstance provides an exception of the principle of res judicata in the Netherlands, England and Wales and the European Union, and – under the specific conditions listed in §580 of the Zivilprozessordnung – also in Germany. A second set of possibilities to bypass the principle of res judicata concerns situations in which there is forgery of documents, fraud or another form of criminal behaviour. This is the case in Germany, France and England and Wales. Thirdly, exceptions to the principle of res judicata are made in Germany and France when procedural issues, such as with court formation, are at stake.

A further similarity between all legal systems is that incorrect application of law, including EU law, is not as such a reason for the revision of a final judgment. The only action which is possible for individuals if a judgment is manifestly in breach of EU law is an action in liability, grounded on the fault of the judiciary.[151] Finally, new case law, decided after the original hearing of the case, favourable to the applicant, including case law of the Court of Justice and the ECtHR, does not provide grounds to reopen a case under judicial review. In Germany, however, §153 VwGO, in conjunction with §580 of the Zivilprozessordnung, explicitly states that 'where the European Court of Human

[151] See Chapter 11, section 11.6.

Rights has established that the European Convention for the Protection of Human Rights and Fundamental Freedoms or its protocols have been violated, and where the judgment is based on this violation', an action for the retrial of the case may be brought against the judgment.

7.7 INDIRECT REVIEW

It is possible to challenge an administrative decision in judicial review not only through a direct action, but also indirectly, through a so-called indirect review. The indirect control of illegality is generally exercised through a plea of illegality, which is an action that allows the claimant to challenge the act which constitutes the legal basis for the decision that is the subject of the direct challenge. This is the case, for example, when a claimant challenges through a direct action for annulment a single-case decision which denies him an authorisation to open a shop. One possible ground raised in order to obtain the annulment of this decision is to claim that the measure on which the decision in respect of the permit is grounded (for example, the measure which sets out the conditions to be fulfilled for the authorisation to be granted) is unlawful.

The existence of this possibility is justified by the need to protect the rule of law. This is because judicial review of administrative action is conditioned first upon the introduction of an application, and secondly by the conditions of admissibility of the action. These relate not only to the need to demonstrate standing, but also to the very possibility to challenge a specific form of administrative action in a direct action before the administrative courts.[152] Indirect review may be seen as a way to address these limitations, since it is a way for individuals to challenge an act concerning an individual which would not have standing in a direct action, or an act which, according to the applicable procedural rules, cannot be challenged in a direct action. Indirect review is most often used to challenge measures of general scope (and specifically general and abstract measures) concerning which an applicant would typically not fulfil the standing requirements (as is the case, for example, in the European Union), or which are excluded from direct actions before the administrative court altogether (as is the case, for example, in the Netherlands).

While indirect actions and direct actions are similar in the sense that they both aim to review the legality of administrative action, indirect actions have specific characteristics concerning the type of acts which may be challenged, the time limits applicable and the consequences of a ruling of unlawfulness. Furthermore, the consequences of a finding of illegality through an indirect action are most of the time more limited than those applicable in a direct action for annulment, as the authority of the ruling is generally limited to the parties.

[152] For more detail, see Chapter 3 on the forms of administrative action and Chapter 4, section 4.4 on standing.

7.7.A ENGLAND AND WALES

House of Lords, 2 April 1998[153] **7.72 (EW)**

Boddington v British Transport Police

COLLATERAL CHALLENGE; ADMISSIBILITY

Boddington

It is possible for an applicant to challenge a by-law through collateral challenge, thus avoiding the need to bring a direct claim through the judicial review procedure.

Facts: B was convicted of the offence of smoking a cigarette in a railway carriage where smoking was prohibited, contrary to Byelaw 20 of the British Railways Board's Byelaws 1965, which, in turn, were created under statutory authority in section 67(1) of the Transport Act 1962. B challenged the validity of the by-law, arguing that the by-law itself was ultra vires. The divisional court identified the question to what extent subordinate legislation can be challenged by defendants subject to criminal charges laid under that subordinate legislation.

Held: B could challenge the by-law through a collateral challenge. The by-law was not considered to be invalid.

Judgment: Lord Irvine of Lairg L.C.: Mr. Boddington's primary defence, therefore, raises the question of the extent to which a defendant to a criminal charge may defend himself by pointing to the unlawfulness of subordinate legislation, or an administrative act made under that legislation, the breach of which is alleged to constitute his offence. The Divisional Court held that Mr. Boddington was not entitled to put forward his public law defence in the criminal proceedings against him.

These arguments are regularly raised in the courts in cases in the public law field, concerned with applications for judicial review. The issue is whether the same arguments may be deployed in a criminal court as a defence to a criminal charge.

Challenge to the lawfulness of subordinate legislation or administrative decisions and acts may take many forms, compendiously grouped by Lord Diplock in *Council of Civil Service Unions v. Minister for the Civil Service* [1985] A.C. 374 under the headings of illegality, procedural impropriety and irrationality. Categorisation of types of challenge assists in an orderly exposition of the principles underlying our developing public law. But these are not watertight compartments because the various grounds for judicial review run together. The exercise of a power for an improper purpose may involve taking irrelevant considerations into account, or ignoring relevant considerations; and either may lead to an irrational result. The failure to grant a person affected by a decision a hearing, in breach of principles of procedural fairness, may result in a failure to take into account relevant considerations.

The question of the extent to which public law defences may be deployed in criminal proceedings requires consideration of fundamental principle concerning the promotion of the rule of law and fairness to defendants to criminal charges in having a reasonable opportunity to defend themselves. However, sometimes the public interest in orderly administration means that the scope for challenging unlawful conduct by public bodies may have to be circumscribed.

[153] [1999] 2 AC 143 (HL).

Where there is a tension between these competing interests and principles, the balance between them is ordinarily to be struck by Parliament. Thus whether a public law defence may be mounted to a criminal charge requires scrutiny of the particular statutory context in which the criminal offence is defined and of any other relevant statutory provisions. That approach is supported by authority of this House.

...

However, in every case it will be necessary to examine the particular statutory context to determine whether a court hearing a criminal or civil case has jurisdiction to rule on a defence based upon arguments of invalidity of subordinate legislation or an administrative act under it. There are situations in which Parliament may legislate to preclude such challenges being made, in the interest, for example, of promoting certainty about the legitimacy of administrative acts on which the public may have to rely.

The recent decision of this House in *Reg. v. Wicks* [1998] A.C. 92 is an example of a particular context in which an administrative act triggering consequences for the purposes of the criminal law was held not to be capable of challenge in criminal proceedings, but only by other proceedings. The case concerned an enforcement notice issued by a local planning authority and served on the defendant under the then current version of section 87 of the Town and Country Planning Act 1971. The notice alleged a breach of planning control by the erection of a building and required its removal above a certain height. One month was allowed for compliance. The appellant appealed against the notice to the Secretary of State, under section 174 of the Town and Country Planning Act 1990, but the appeal was dismissed. The appellant still failed to comply with the notice and the local authority issued a summons alleging a breach of section 179(1) of the Act of 1990. In the criminal proceedings which ensued, the appellant sought to defend himself on the ground that the enforcement notice had been issued ultra vires, maintaining that the local planning authority had acted in bad faith and had been motivated by irrelevant considerations. The judge ruled that these contentions should have been made in proceedings for judicial review and that they could not be gone into in the criminal proceedings. The appellant then pleaded guilty and was convicted. This House upheld his conviction. Lord Hoffmann, in the leading speech, emphasised that the ability of a defendant to criminal proceedings to challenge the validity of an act done under statutory authority depended on the construction of the statute in question. This House held that the Town and Country Planning Act 1990 contained an elaborate code including provision for appeals against notices, and that on the proper construction of section 179(1) of the Act all that was required to be proved in the criminal proceedings was that the notice issued by the local planning authority was formally valid.

...

Lord Nicholls of Birkenhead noted in *Reg. v. Wicks*, at pp. 106–107, that there may be cases where proceedings in the Divisional Court are more suitable and convenient for challenging a byelaw or administrative decision made under it than by way of defence in criminal proceedings in the magistrates' court or the Crown Court. None the less Lord Nicholls held that 'the proper starting point' must be a presumption that 'an accused should be able to challenge, on any ground, the lawfulness of an order the breach of which constitutes his alleged criminal offence:' see p. 106. No doubt the factors listed by Lord Nicholls may, where the statutory context permits, be taken into account when construing any particular statute to determine Parliament's intention, but they will not usually be sufficient in themselves to support a construction of a statute which would preclude the right of a defendant to raise the legality of a byelaw or administrative action taken under it as a defence in other proceedings. This is because of the strength of the presumption against a construction which would prevent an individual being able to vindicate his rights in court proceedings in which he is involved.

Lord Slynn of Hadley: There is, above all, another matter which strikes at the root of the decision in *Bugg's* case. That decision contemplates that, despite the invalidity of a byelaw and the fact that consistently with *Reg. v. Wicks* such invalidity may in a given case afford a defence to a charge, a magistrate court may not rule on the defence. Instead the magistrates may convict a defendant under the byelaw and punish him. That is an unacceptable consequence in a democracy based on the rule of law. It is true that *Bugg's* case allows the defendant to challenge the byelaw in judicial review proceedings. The defendant may, however, be out of time before he becomes aware of the existence of the byelaw. He may lack the resources to defend his interests in two courts. He may not be able to obtain legal aid for an application for leave to apply for judicial review. Leave to apply for judicial review may be refused. At a substantive hearing his scope for demanding examination of witnesses in the Divisional Court may be restricted. He may be denied a remedy on a discretionary basis. The possibility of judicial review will, therefore, in no way compensate him for the loss of *the right* to defend himself by a defensive challenge to the byelaw in cases where the invalidity of the byelaw might afford him with a defence to the charge. My Lords, with the utmost deference to eminent judges sitting in the Divisional Court I have to say the consequences of *Bugg's* case are too austere and indeed too authoritarian to be compatible with the traditions of the common law

Notes

(1) Indirect control of legality is exercised in the English legal system through a claim called 'collateral challenge'. The possibility to bring a claim for collateral challenge is deemed to be an important part of the rule of law. Although there is some historical case law suggesting that the right to bring collateral challenge is restricted, *Boddington* sought to emphasise the protection of the citizen's ability to bring a collateral challenge, even if the House of Lords dismissed the action on its merits.

(2) The indirect control of legality is used to challenge general and abstract measures, both by-laws and statutory instruments,[154] where a public authority is proposing to rely on these to impose criminal liability or civil liability[155] on the claimant. As the excerpt above illustrates, any ground of challenge available in a direct action is available to a claimant bringing a collateral challenge.

(3) Collateral challenge is used in those cases in which it would in principle be possible for the claimant to bring judicial review proceedings via the direct route of challenge, but such a challenge will often be prevented by the reasons outlined by Lord Slynn in the excerpt above. If the indirectly challenged decision is invalid, it will be quashed.

[154] On these concepts, see Chapter 3, section 3.3.B.1 (i).

[155] A local authority's tenant, sued for increased rent, may contend in his defence that the increase was ultra vires and void. See *Wandsworth LBC v Winder* [1985] AC 461 (HL).

(4) There are, however, some limits with regard to access to indirect challenge. This may be the case where such proceedings are expressly excluded by statute[156] or when a specific statutory remedy exists. For example, indirect challenge is excluded on the ground that legislation in the planning sphere provides for a specific regime, designed to make enforcement notices in this area effective without excessive delay.[157]

7.7.B FRANCE

Code de justice administrative **7.73 (FR)**

Article R312-3 The Administrative Court of First Instance that has territorial competence to hear a main application is also competent to hear any additional or interlocutory application, or any counter claim that falls within the jurisdiction of the Administrative Court of First Instance. It is also competent to hear any pleas or objections that fall within the competence of an administrative court.

Notes

(1) An indirect action can be lodged before any court which has jurisdiction to hear an action for annulment (*recours pour excès de pouvoir*). It is also possible, but less frequently done, to introduce a plea of illegality while lodging an action for liability. The indirect action aims to challenge indirectly a regulatory decision (*décision reglementaire*) (namely *décrets, ordonnances* and *arrêtés*) or an individual decision (*décision individuelle*) while also challenging directly a regulatory or individual decision which is based upon the former.[158] While the indirect action is available at any time for a regulatory act,[159] an indirect action against a non-regulatory act is only admissible if the act is not final, meaning that it may be still the object of a direct challenge.[160]

(2) When regulatory acts are at stake, the use of indirect actions by a claimant is a way to bypass the time limit requirement for a direct action – for example, in case a regulatory act was adopted at a time in which the claimant did not know of or was not concerned by its illegality, or the regulatory act became illegal due to a factual or legal change. The rationale for indirect review is different for non-regulatory acts, as in these cases indirect review is mainly available to compensate for a lack of standing in a direct action, ie the applicant would not have been able to show sufficient interest to challenge the decision which is the subject matter of the indirect action.[161]

156 *Manchester City Council v Cochrane* [1999] 1 WLR 809 (CA).

157 *R v Wicks* [1998] AC 92 (HL) (W applied for planning permission which was not granted and then built the building and sought collateral challenge of the demolition order. The House of Lords held that W was precluded from collateral challenge partly due to the need to ensure the integrity of the planning process and partly as W had failed to claim judicial review of the refusal of permission).

158 On these concepts, see Chapter 3.

159 Conseil d'État, 29 May 1908, *Poulin*, N° 25488.

160 For time limits before the French administrative courts, see Chapter 4, section 4.7.

161 For standing before the French administrative court, see Chapter 4, section 4.4.

(3) Concerning the grounds to be raised in an indirect action, an applicant may challenge an act either because it is contrary to national law – the action is in this case called a classical and *stricto sensu* indirect review (*exception d'illégalité*) – or because it is contrary to EU law, to the ECHR or to other international law – the action is then called a 'plea of incompatibility' (*exception d'inconventionalité*). It is worth noting that, as an exception, civil courts also have jurisdiction to rule on an indirect challenge of a regulatory decision when the question of the legality of the regulatory decision has to be solved in order to rule on a claim brought before a civil court where it is claimed that the act is in breach of EU law.[162]

(4) In 2018, the Council of State ruled that in indirect actions, grounds related to procedural or formal requirements can no longer be raised.[163]

Conseil d'État, Opinion, 30 December 2013[164] **7.74 (FR)**

Oksoun v Prefect of Seine-Maritime

INDIRECT REVIEW; ADMISSIBILITY

Oksoun

An indirect action against a regulatory decision is admissible only if the act challenged through a direct action has sufficient ties with it.

Facts: Mrs Oksoun challenged before the Administrative Court of First Instance of Rouen the decision of the prefect of Rouen of 2 July 2012, which refused to grant the applicant a temporary residence permit allowing her to remain in France. Before deciding on the merits of the case, the judge decided to stay proceedings and referred to the Council of State a question related to a possible indirect challenge of the provisions of a regulatory decision.

Held: The regulatory decision could not be indirectly challenged since it was not the basis for the individual decision.

Judgment: 6. The illegality of an administrative act, whether it is regulatory or not, can only be invoked by indirect action in support of submissions against a later administrative decision, if this latter decision has been taken in order to enforce the first act or if the first act constitutes the legal basis of the act challenged directly. When a regulatory act is at stake, such indirect action may be brought at any time, even after the expiry of the time limit for a direct action against this act. When a non-regulatory act is at stake, the indirect action is, by contrast, only available if this act has not become final on the day on which the action is brought, except for the case where the act and the later decision constitute elements of the same proceedings. In such circumstances, the unlawfulness of the act can be raised regardless of the final character of this act.

[162] Tribunal des Conflits, 17 October 2011, *SCEA du Chéneau v INAPORC*, N° 3828-3829. On this point, see E Chevalier, 'La spécificité du contrôle des actes administratifs par rapport au droit de l'Union par le juge judiciaire français' (2011) 2 *Cahiers de droit européen* 522.
[163] Conseil d'État, 18 May 2018, *Fédération des finances et affaires économiques de la CFDT*, N° 414583.
[164] N° 367615.

The decisions by which the prefect refuses, at the end of the proceedings, residence to the foreigner whose request for asylum has been rejected by the OFPRA (French Office for the Protection of Refugees and Stateless Persons) and obliges that person to leave the French territory, are not taken in application of the decision by which the prefect rules, at the beginning of the procedure, on the temporary residence permit. The decision taken on the residence permit does not constitute the legal basis for the refusal of the residence permit and the obligation to leave the French territory.

Consequently, the illegality of the refusal to grant a temporary residence permit to an asylum seeker, especially for the failure to present the information document provided for in the last paragraph of Article R742-1, cannot be raised in an action against the decisions by which the prefect, after the notification of the OFPRA of the request for asylum, … refuses the residence permit and obliges the foreigner to leave the French territory.

Notes

(1) One of the conditions for the admissibility of an indirect action is that the directly challenged act enforces or at least has sufficient ties with the act that is the object of the indirect action. Instances of indirect action concern, for example, the challenge against a general and abstract measure on which an individual decision is based or against an individual decision on which the individual decision that is the subject of the direct challenge is based. This is the case, for example, when an individual decision to refuse the grant of state aid is challenged, because the regulatory decision setting the conditions for the award of such aid is deemed illegal.[165] It has also been considered that a decree requiring that the marriage of civil servants of the Ministry of Foreign Affairs needs the prior authorisation of the minister can be indirectly challenged when bringing a direct action against the refusal to authorise a wedding.[166] However, as the excerpt above demonstrates, an indirect challenge against a decision of a prefect determining the right to stay temporarily on the territory was not considered admissible as the act challenged indirectly was not considered sufficiently linked to the decision of refusal of stay and the decision of deportation which were being directly challenged.

(2) In order to ensure legal certainty in the field of planning law, a more restrictive approach is applied. Indeed, individual planning authorisations, such as building permits, are not regarded as implementation measures of general planning measures. Consequently, while challenging a refusal to grant a building permit, an applicant cannot raise the illegality of the local urban plan, because of insufficient ties between the general decision and the individual decision.[167] It is still possible to bring an indirect action against the plan, while challenging directly a decision which implements it, on the ground of formal flaws, but only within a six-month time limit, hence this type of act cannot be subject to indirect action for an indefinite period.[168]

[165] Conseil d'État, 9 December 2005, *Grangeon*, N° 273327.
[166] Conseil d'État, 18 January 1980, *Bargain*, N° 14397.
[167] Conseil d'État, 12 December 1986, *Société Gépro*, N° 54701.
[168] Code de l'urbanisme, Art L600-1.

Conseil d'État, 27 May 2002[169] **7.75 (FR)**

SA Transolver Service v Prime Minister

INDIRECT REVIEW; BINDING FORCE

SA Transolver

A ruling in an indirect action is binding on the public authorities.

Facts: The company Transolver challenged Ordinance N° 2000-912 of 18 September 2000 based upon the legislative part of the Commerce Code (Code du commerce), since it codified certain provisions which the Council of State had annulled in a previous ruling.

Held: The appeal was dismissed.

Judgment: ...

Considering that, under Article L627-1 of the Commerce Code, the challenged ordinance has codified the provisions of Article 173 of the Decree of 27 December 1985 in the following wording: 'No objection or execution proceedings of any nature whatsoever on amounts paid to the Public Investment Authority [a body charged with supporting public investment in order to aid national economic development] (Caisse des depots et consignations) is admissible'; that, by its ruling of 19 January 2000, the Council of State, has declared unlawful, without annulling them, these provisions of the Decree of 27 December 1985, on the ground that they belonged to the field of competence of the legislator; that this decision could not have the effect of removing from the legal order Article 173 from the Decree of 27 December 1985; that the government, by codifying these provisions in the legislative part of the Code of Commerce, far from disregarding the principle of res judicata, has undertaken modifications that had become necessary by the abovementioned decision of the Council of State, in order to ensure the respect of the hierarchy of norms, as it was empowered by the law of 16 December 1999; that, consequently, the government could, without disregarding its powers or misusing its of power, insert Article 173 of the Decree of 27 December 1985 into the legislative part of the Code of Commerce annexed to the challenged ordinance;

Note

Where a general and abstract measure is considered to be unlawful in an indirect action, the unlawfulness is declared, but the act is not annulled. However, such a statement has the consequence of depriving the regulatory decision of any legal effects, not only in the case brought before the court, but also in general.[170] Indeed, administrative authorities are bound by such a ruling, and should take all necessary measures to enforce it. Consequently, the competent authorities have to set the challenged act aside or possibly, depending on the ground of illegality, they must abrogate[171] the regulatory

[169] N° 227338.

[170] B Seiller, 'Les effets de la déclaration d'illégalité sur l'ordonnancement juridique' (2014) *Revue Française de Droit Administratif* 721.

[171] See Chapter 6, section 6.5.B.2.

decision or amend it. Indeed, as the above excerpt shows, the public authority has to take measures 'that had become necessary by the abovementioned decision of the Council of State'.

7.7.C THE EUROPEAN UNION

Treaty on the Functioning of the European Union **7.76 (EU)**

Article 277 Notwithstanding the expiry of the period laid down in Article 263, sixth paragraph, any party may, in proceedings in which an act of general application adopted by an institution, body, office or agency of the Union is at issue, plead the grounds specified in Article 263, second paragraph, in order to invoke before the Court of Justice of the European Union the inapplicability of that act.

Case 92/78, 6 March 1979[172] **7.77 (EU)**

SpA Simmenthal v Commission

PLEA OF ILLEGALITY; ADMISSIBILITY

Simmenthal

The plea of illegality is complementary to the direct action for annulment.

Facts: The applicant challenged, under Article 184 of the EEC Treaty (currently Article 277 TFEU), a Commission decision fixing minimum selling prices for frozen beef. The decision was based on regulations and on a notice of invitation to tender. The wording of Article 184 of the EEC Treaty, however, provided only for the challenging of 'regulations'. The Court of Justice held the challenge admissible regarding the Commission decision and regulations, but questioned whether Article 184 of the EEC Treaty also applies to notices of tender since they are not in the strict sense measures laid down by regulation.

Held: The application was considered admissible in relation not only to the regulations, but also to the notice of invitation to tender, although the latter was not in the strict sense a measure laid down by regulation.

Judgment: 39 … Article 184 of the EEC treaty gives expression to a general principle conferring upon any party to proceedings the right to challenge, for the purpose of obtaining the annulment of a decision of direct and individual concern to that part, the validity of previous acts of the institutions which form the legal basis of the decision which is being attacked, if that party was not entitled under article 173 of the treaty [currently Article 277 TFEU] to bring a direct action challenging those acts by which it was thus affected without having been in a position to ask that they be declared void.

40 The field of application of the said article must therefore include acts of the institutions which, although they are not in the form of a regulation, nevertheless produce similar effects and on those grounds may not be challenged under article 173 by natural or legal persons other than Community institutions and Member States.

[172] ECLI:EU:C:1979:53.

41 This wide interpretation of article 184 derives from the need to provide those persons who are precluded by the second paragraph of article 173 from instituting proceedings directly in respect of general acts with the benefit of a judicial review of them at the time when they are affected by implementing decisions which are of direct and individual concern to them.

Notes

(1) An indirect action (which, at the European Union level, is often referred to as 'plea of illegality') can in principle be raised in any direct action brought before the European courts, but it is mostly used in the context of actions for annulment.[173] In an indirect action, according to Article 277 TFEU, the applicant can raise any argument which can be raised in the context of an action for annulment.[174]

(2) Such an action can be used to challenge measures of general application. The essential function of the indirect action is to allow for the control of EU measures which a natural or legal person would have no standing to challenge in a direct action under Article 263 TFEU because of the restrictive standing conditions for direct actions[175] in cases where such a person seeks the annulment of a single-case decision adopted on the basis of those measures. The plea of illegality can be lodged at any time.

(3) Article 277 TFEU requires the measure of general application in respect of which the indirect action is raised to be 'at issue'. This means that there should be a real connection between the measure subject to direct challenge and that whose invalidity is raised in the indirect action. This criterion has been interpreted as meaning that the general measure against which the plea of illegality is raised must be the legal basis of the measure that has been directly challenged.[176] In some other cases, however, the judge has accepted that the necessary connection does not need to be framed in terms of legal basis.[177]

(4) According to the case law, whereas the plea of illegality may be used as a way to circumvent the limits of the conditions of standing for action for annulment,[178] it cannot be used to challenge the legality of a measure where the applicant could have applied for an action for annulment of that measure.[179] This is because the applicant would otherwise be allowed to challenge a decision after the time limit for the action

[173] Case 33/80 *Albini v Council and Commission* ECLI:EU:C:1981:186, para 17; Case C-239/99 *Nachi Europe v Hauptzollamt Krefeld* ECLI:EU:C:2001:101, para 33.

[174] Lenaerts et al (n 90 above) para 9.18.

[175] On this point, see Chapter 4, section 4.4.B.5.

[176] Case 21/64 *Macchiorlati Dalmas e figli v High Authority* ECLI:EU:C:1965:30, paras 187–88; Joined Cases T-222/99, T-327/99 and T-329/99 *Martinez and others v European Parliament* ECLI:EU:T:2001:242, para 136.

[177] Thus an exception of illegality may be raised against the Commission's guidelines on the method of setting fines in an annulment action brought against a decision imposing fines, although the guidelines do not constitute the legal basis of the fines. See Joined Cases C-189/02 P, C-202/02 P, C-205 to 208/02 P, C-213/02 P *Dansk Rorindustri v Commission* ECLI:EU:C:2005:408, paras 212 and 213.

[178] See Chapter 4, section 4.4.B.5.

[179] Case 156/77 *Commission v Belgium* ECI:EU:C:1978:180, paras 20–21.

for annulment has expired, which would have a significant adverse impact on legal certainty.

(5) If an indirect action is successful, the act of general application is declared inapplicable for the purposes of the proceedings in which the objection was raised and, therefore, only in relation to the parties to the proceedings and not to third parties.[180] Doctrine suggests that the institution which adopted the act that is declared inapplicable is, however, under a duty to withdraw or adjust the act in order to eliminate the illegality found.[181]

7.7.D GERMANY

In Germany, the possibility to bring an indirect action, which, in the German legal system, is referred to as 'incidental control' (*Inzidentkontrolle*), applies with regard to general and abstract measures (namely executive regulations (*Rechtsverordnungen*) and by-laws (*Satzungen*)), as they do not qualify as an administrative act (*Verwaltungsakt*) and cannot be challenged in a direct action for annulment (*Anfechtungsklage*). If, for example, an administrative act was issued on the basis of an executive regulation (*Rechtsverordnung*), the claimant may argue that the administrative act is illegal due to the illegality of the executive regulation. The court will then examine the legality of the executive regulation in order to decide whether the administrative act must be annulled. If the court finds that the executive regulation on which the administrative act is based is illegal, it will set the regulation aside, as it is illegal.

The decision taken by the court in an *Inzidentkontrolle* only applies *inter partes*. If the claimant wants a general and abstract measure to be annulled with an *erga omnes* effect, he needs to file an action to review by-laws and executive regulations (*Normenkontrollverfahren*) directly against the measure itself, if such an action is possible. This special procedure, set out in §47 VwGO, is, however, only applicable under limited circumstances.[182]

7.7.E THE NETHERLANDS

In the Netherlands, the indirect action against a measure on which the challenged measure depends is called 'incidental review' (*exceptieve toetsing*). In the Netherlands, the jurisdiction of the administrative courts is limited, as all of the so-called decisions of general scope (*besluiten van algemene strekking*), except for the 'concretising decisions of general scope' (*concretiserende besluiten van algemene strekking*), cannot be

[180] Joined Cases 15–33, 52–53, 57–109, 116, 117, 123, 132 and 135–137/73 *Kortner and others v Council and others* ECLI:EU:C:1974:16, para 36; Case C-434/98 P *Council v Busacca and others* ECLI:EU:C:2000:546, para 26.

[181] Lenaerts et al (n 90 above) 455.

[182] See Chapter 3, section 3.3.B.2 (i).

challenged directly through a claim for judicial review (*beroep*).[183] As a consequence, these acts cannot become final, since they are not subject to the review of the courts within a time limit. Therefore, they are frequently subject to incidental review.

Raad van State, 20 July 2016[184] **7.78 (NL)**

X v Mayor and Aldermen of Landert

INCIDENTAL REVIEW

Peelweg 20 Landert

Facts: The defendant took a decision to bundle together several procedures relating to the issuance of permits regarding a dairy farm. As a consequence of this bundling, the procedural rules for the decisions which were bundled were changed in order to speed up decision-making. On the basis of this decision to bundle the different permitting procedures, the defendant granted a building permit for the farm. The claimants brought a claim for judicial review against the building permit, arguing that the decision to bundle the proceedings on which the building permit was based was unlawful.

Held: The claim was rejected.

Judgment: 5.2. In view of Article 8:5(1) AWB, read in conjunction with Article 1 of Appendix 2 to the AWB, no claim for judicial review can be filed against a decision taken on the basis of Article 3.30(1) of the Spatial Planning Act (Wet ruimtelijke ordening – Wro). This does not mean, however, that this decision to bundle the various permitting procedures cannot be reviewed. Article 8:5(1) AWB, read in conjunction with Article 1 of Appendix 2 AWB, does not preclude the possibility of incidental review (*exceptieve toetsing*). Incidental review of the decision to apply the rules on the bundling of procedures will result in the decision being set aside if it is in conflict with a statutory provision or if it is in conflict with a general principle of law ....

5.3. The Judicial Division considers that the plan and the environmental permit both aim at the realization of a part of the municipal spatial policy as referred to in Article 3.30 Wro. This article does not stipulate that the rules on bundling the permitting procedures may not be applied to individual projects.

In light of the foregoing, there is no ground for the opinion that the bundling decision infringes a statutory provision or a general principle of law. This decision is therefore not set aside.

Notes

(1) Although there is no explicit legal norm requiring a connection between the directly challenged decision and the indirectly challenged measure which forms the legal basis for the challenged decision, the courts will only scrutinise decisions of general scope if the act which was directly challenged is based on this general

[183] On these concepts see Chapter 3, section 3.3.B.2 (ii).
[184] ECLI:NL:RVS:2016:2015.

decision and its legality depends on the legality of the general decision. Otherwise, the claimant has no legitimate interest to ask the court to scrutinise the legality of the general measure.

(2) If such an indirect action is well founded, this may result either in the declaration that the act challenged indirectly is considered not to be binding or in the act being set aside.[185] The general measure is considered not to be binding by the administrative courts if the unlawfulness of the act is so fundamental that any application of it would be unlawful. This declaration applies *erga omnes*. The general measure is instead set aside if lawful application of the act may still be possible. In such a case, the declaration applies *inter partes* only. The result in both situations is that the directly contested single-case decision is annulled on the ground that the legal basis for it has 'vanished' (either in general or in the specific case).

(3) On 14 July 2017, the Judicial Division of the Council of State requested Advocate General Widdershoven to reflect on several issues regarding the scope and limits of incidental appeal. The opinion of the Advocate General was published on 22 December 2017.[186] The Advocate General suggested that scrutiny in incidental review should, at least in many cases, be more intensive than in the past. Moreover, he made a number of recommendations concerning the application of the relativity requirement.[187]

7.7.F COMPARATIVE REMARKS

All the legal systems studied in this book provide for the possibility for applicants to challenge the administrative action indirectly. In all legal systems, indirect review is seen as a possibility to challenge measures of general scope, for which a direct challenge would not otherwise be available or would be available only under limited circumstances.

However, the rationale justifying indirect challenges in the studied legal systems is different. There is indeed a distinction between legal systems which apply an objective conception of actions for annulment and legal systems where actions for annulment rather have a subjective function.[188] The former refers to systems of the EU, France and England and Wales, in which the enforcement of legality in the general interest is a core value of the rule of law. Although, in these legal systems, direct challenges against measures of general scope are, in principle, possible, it may nevertheless be important for claimants to challenge general acts indirectly. In the EU, direct actions against measures of general scope will often be rejected as a matter of standing, because of the very restrictive standing conditions applicable to direct actions under Article 264(3) TFEU. In France, a direct action against a measure of general scope

[185] See RJB Schutgens, *Onrechtmatige wetgeving* (Deventer, Kluwer, 2009) 9–10.
[186] ECLI:NL:RVS:2017:3557.
[187] See on this concept, Chapter 4, section 4.4.G.
[188] See Chapter 1, section 1.5.

could be rejected for lack of standing, but this is not often the case, due to the wide conception of standing.[189] Most often, indirect review is a way to circumvent the time limit requirement for direct actions. This is also the case in England and Wales.

Germany and the Netherlands, on the other hand, only allow direct challenges against single-case decisions and decisions which are general and concrete. In these two systems, the possibility of indirect review supplements the impossibility to directly challenge general and abstract measures.

7.8 INTERIM RELIEF

Procedures for interim relief aim to promote the effectiveness of judicial protection and to ensure that the court's judgment in the main procedure is still able to deliver a remedy which is useful for the applicant.

Court proceedings necessarily take a certain amount of time. If it were impossible to prevent the execution of the contested decision while a case is pending before the court, this could lead to irreversible situations which could not be remedied by the final ruling. For instance, if an administrative decision prohibiting a show on a specific day is annulled by an administrative court, the decision of the court would have no consequence, since the ruling will be issued after the date of the show. Or, if a rubbish tip is authorised by an administrative decision which is ultimately annulled by an administrative court, the retroactive effect of the annulment would not remedy the effects already produced and the damage, sometimes irreversible, caused to the environment.

To prevent such situations, all legal systems provide for different forms of interim relief, allowing the courts to grant interim measures taking the urgency of the specific situation and the interests involved into account. The most common interim measure is the suspension of the contested act, pending the main proceedings. In addition, all legal systems provide for the possibility to order other 'positive' interim measures.

Although the differences between the legal systems should not be exaggerated, one striking difference can be observed. On the one side is Germany, in which an action for annulment has, in principle, suspensory effect, although there are several exceptions to that rule. On the other end of the scale are the European Union, the Netherlands, England and Wales and France. In these legal systems, an action in court has no suspensory effect, but all these systems provide for possibilities for interim relief.

7.8.A INFLUENCE OF EUROPEAN UNION LAW ON INTERIM RELIEF

The influence of EU law on the national rules of interim relief plays a role both in cases where interim relief is sought against a national measure, on the ground that this measure is allegedly inconsistent with EU law (so-called cases of interpretation), and in cases where interim relief is sought against a national decision, based on an EU act whose validity is disputed (so-called cases of validity).

[189] See Chapter 4, section 4.4.B.3.

Case C-213/89, 19 June 1990[190] **7.79 (EU)**

The Queen v Secretary of State for Transport, ex parte Factortame Ltd and others

INTERIM RELIEF; EFFECTIVENESS OF EU LAW

Factortame

A national judge must have the power to grant interim relief in order to ensure the effectiveness of EU law.

Facts: The applicants in the main proceedings had been denied a fishing licence under national law, but claimed to have a right to obtain such a licence under EU law. The applicants challenged the compatibility of the national law with EU law and sought interim relief. However, the national court had no competence under national law to grant interim relief and referred the question of whether national law had to be set aside if it precludes the possibility of interim relief.

Held: National courts must set aside a rule of national law that precludes the possibility of interim relief in a case concerning EU law.

Judgment: 19 In accordance with the case-law of the Court, it is for the national courts, in application of the principle of cooperation laid down in Article 5 of the EEC Treaty [now Article 4 (3) TEU], to ensure the legal protection which persons derive from the direct effect of provisions of Community law ….

20 The Court has also held that any provision of a national legal system and any legislative, administrative or judicial practice which might impair the effectiveness of Community law by withholding from the national court having jurisdiction to apply such law the power to do everything necessary at the moment of its application to set aside national legislative provisions which might prevent, even temporarily, Community rules from having full force and effect are incompatible with those requirements, which are the very essence of Community law ….

21 It must be added that the full effectiveness of Community law would be just as much impaired if a rule of national law could prevent a court seised of a dispute governed by Community law from granting interim relief in order to ensure the full effectiveness of the judgement to be given on the existence of the rights claimed under Community law. It follows that a court which in those circumstances would grant interim relief, if it were not for a rule of national law, is obliged to set aside that rule.

22 That interpretation is reinforced by the system established by Article 177 of the EEC Treaty whose effectiveness would be impaired if a national court, having stayed proceedings pending the reply by the Court of Justice to the question referred to it for a preliminary ruling, were not able to grant interim relief until it delivered its judgement following the reply given by the Court of Justice.

23 Consequently, the reply to the question raised should be that Community law must be interpreted as meaning that a national court which, in a case before it concerning Community law, considers that the sole obstacle which precludes it from granting interim relief is a rule of national law must set aside that rule.

[190] ECLI:EU:C:1990:257.

Notes

(1) The case *Factortame* is a so-called case of interpretation: English law on fishing licences was allegedly inconsistent with EU law. In this ruling, the Court of Justice recognised, on the basis of the principle of sincere cooperation (Article 4(3) TEU) and the principle of effectiveness inherent in EU law, the right to interim relief. The right to interim relief arises when an applicant challenges a measure of national law, adopted in violation of EU law, and the court is unable to give an instant ruling on the matter.[191] The need to provide for such a remedy is nowadays derived from the EU principle of effective judicial protection,[192] which implies the possibility of provisional and immediate judicial protection. Therefore, where a right conferred by EU law is at issue, the competent national court must have the possibility to grant interim relief, pending the final outcome of the main proceedings concerning that right, even where such power is not available to the courts under national law. If necessary, the national court has to set aside any incompatible national legislation.[193]

(2) On the basis of *Factortame*, Member States are therefore obliged to provide interim relief in their legal systems notwithstanding national procedural rules which would preclude the courts from doing so. However, on the ground of the principle of procedural autonomy, the Member States are allowed to apply their national rules concerning the criteria to be applied to obtain interim relief and other procedural matters as regards the remedy, provided that the principles of equivalence and effectiveness are met.

Joined Cases C-143/88 and C-92/89, 21 February 1991[194] **7.80 (EU)**

Zuckerfabrik Süderdithmarschen AG v Hauptzollamt Itzehoe and

Zuckerfabrik Soest GmbH v Hauptzollamt Paderborn

INTERIM RELIEF; VALIDITY OF EU LAW

Zuckerfabrik Süderdithmarschen

Under strict conditions, national courts are empowered to grant interim relief in cases concerning the validity of EU law.

Facts: The case referred for a preliminary ruling originated in cases brought by sugar factories that had been ordered through a national decision, based on Regulation No 1914/87, to pay sums in respect of a special levy for the 1986/87 sugar marketing years. The sugar factories argued that the regulation was invalid. One of them sought suspension of enforcement of the national decision. The competent court then referred to the Court

[191] See M Eliantonio, *Europeanisation of Administrative Justice?* (Groningen, Europa Law Publishing, 2009) 226 ff; Jans et al (n 126 above) 421–33.

[192] See Case C-432/05 *Unibet (London) Ltd and Unibet (International) Ltd v Justitiekanslern*, ECLI:EU:C:2007:163.

[193] For the consequences of the *Factortame* ruling in England and Wales, see section 7.8.C below.

[194] ECLI:EU:C:1991:65.

of Justice the question whether Article 189 EEC Treaty (currently Article 278 TFEU) precludes the power of a national court to suspend the enforcement of a national measure based on a regulation by way of interim measure.

Held: Article 278 TFEU does not preclude the power of national courts to suspend the enforcement of a national decision implementing a Community regulation. However, the suspension is subject to strict conditions.

Judgment: 14 The Finanzgericht Hamburg first seeks, in substance, to ascertain whether the second paragraph of Article 189 of the EEC Treaty [currently Article 278 TFEU] must be interpreted as meaning that it denies to national courts the power to suspend enforcement of a national administrative measure adopted on the basis of a Community regulation. ...

16 It should first be emphasized that the provisions of the second paragraph of Article 189 of the Treaty cannot constitute an obstacle to the legal protection which Community law confers on individuals. In cases where national authorities are responsible for the administrative implementation of Community regulations, the legal protection guaranteed by Community law includes the right of individuals to challenge, as a preliminary issue, the legality of such regulations before national courts and to induce those courts to refer questions to the Court of Justice for a preliminary ruling.

17 That right would be compromised if, pending the delivery of a judgement of the Court, which alone has jurisdiction to declare that a Community regulation is invalid (see judgement in Case 314/85 *Foto-Frost v Hauptzollamt Lübeck-Ost* [1987] ECR 4199, at paragraph 20), individuals were not in a position, where certain conditions are satisfied, to obtain a decision granting suspension of enforcement which would make it possible for the effects of the disputed regulation to be rendered for the time being inoperative as regards them.

18 As the Court pointed out in its judgement in *Foto-Frost*, cited above, (at paragraph 16), requests for preliminary rulings which seek to ascertain the validity of a measure, like actions for annulment, constitute means for reviewing the legality of acts of the Community institutions. In the context of actions for annulment, Article 185 of the EEC Treaty enables applicants to request suspension of the enforcement of the contested act and empowers the Court to order such suspension. The coherence of the system of interim legal protection therefore requires that national courts should also be able to order suspension of enforcement of a national administrative measure based on a Community regulation, the legality of which is contested.

19 Furthermore, in its judgement in Case C-213/89 (*The Queen v Secretary of State for Transport, ex parte Factortame Ltd and Others* [1990] ECR I-2433), delivered in a case concerning the compatibility of national legislation with Community law, the Court, referring to the effectiveness of Article 177, took the view that the national court which had referred to it questions of interpretation for a preliminary ruling in order to enable it to decide that issue of compatibility, had to be able to grant interim relief and to suspend the application of the disputed national legislation until such time as it could deliver its judgement on the basis of the interpretation given in accordance with Article 177.

20 The interim legal protection which Community law ensures for individuals before national courts must remain the same, irrespective of whether they contest the compatibility of national legal provisions with Community law or the validity of secondary Community law, in view of the fact that the dispute in both cases is based on Community law itself.

21 It follows from the foregoing considerations that the reply to the first part of the first question must be that Article 189 of the Treaty has to be interpreted as meaning that

it does not preclude the power of national courts to suspend enforcement of a national administrative measure adopted on the basis of a Community regulation.

22 The Finanzgericht Hamburg then goes on to ask under what conditions national courts may order the suspension of enforcement of a national administrative measure based on a Community regulation, in view of the doubts which they may have as to the validity of that regulation.

23 It must first of all be noted that interim measures suspending enforcement of a contested measure may be adopted only if the factual and legal circumstances relied on by the applicants are such as to persuade the national court that serious doubts exist as to the validity of the Community regulation on which the contested administrative measure is based. Only the possibility of a finding of invalidity, a matter which is reserved to the Court, can justify the granting of suspensory measures.

24 It should next be pointed out that suspension of enforcement must retain the character of an interim measure. The national court to which the application for interim relief is made may therefore grant a suspension only until such time as the Court has delivered its ruling on the question of validity. Consequently, it is for the national court, should the question not yet have been referred to the Court of Justice, to refer that question itself, setting out the reasons for which it believes that the regulation must be held to be invalid.

25 As regards the other conditions concerning the suspension of enforcement of administrative measures, it must be observed that the rules of procedure of the courts are determined by national law and that those conditions differ according to the national law governing them, which may jeopardize the uniform application of Community law.

26 Such uniform application is a fundamental requirement of the Community legal order. It therefore follows that the suspension of enforcement of administrative measures based on a Community regulation, whilst it is governed by national procedural law, in particular as regards the making and examination of the application, must in all the Member States be subject, at the very least, to conditions which are uniform so far as the granting of such relief is concerned.

27 Since the power of national courts to grant such a suspension corresponds to the jurisdiction reserved to the Court of Justice by Article 185 in the context of actions brought under Article 173, those courts may grant such relief only on the conditions which must be satisfied for the Court of Justice to allow an application to it for interim measures.

28 In this regard, the Court has consistently held that measures suspending the operation of a contested act may be granted only in the event of urgency, in other words, if it is necessary for them to be adopted and to take effect before the decision on the substance of a case, in order to avoid serious and irreparable damage to the party seeking them.

29 With regard to the question of urgency, it should be pointed out that damage invoked by the applicant must be liable to materialize before the Court of Justice has been able to rule on the validity of the contested Community measure. With regard to the nature of the damage, purely financial damage cannot, as the Court has held on numerous occasions, be regarded in principle as irreparable. However, it is for the national court hearing the application for interim relief to examine the circumstances particular to the case before it. It must in this connection consider whether immediate enforcement of the measure which is the subject of the application for interim relief would be likely to result in irreversible damage to the applicant which could not be made good if the Community act were to be declared invalid.

30 It should also be added that a national court called upon to apply, within the limits of its jurisdiction, the provisions of Community law is under an obligation to ensure that

full effect is given to Community law and, consequently, where there is doubt as to the validity of Community regulations, to take account of the interest of the Community, namely that such regulations should not be set aside without proper guarantees.

31 In order to comply with that obligation, a national court seized of an application for suspension must first examine whether the Community measure in question would be deprived of all effectiveness if not immediately implemented.

32 If suspension of enforcement is liable to involve a financial risk for the Community, the national court must also be in a position to require the applicant to provide adequate guarantees, such as the deposit of money or other security.

Notes

(1) The *Zuckerfabrik Süderdithmarschen* case concerns a question of validity of EU law. Interim relief was sought before the national court against a national decision implementing an EU regulation, on the ground that this regulation was allegedly invalid. In such cases, therefore, the request for interim relief is indirectly directed against the EU act in question. From the *Zuckerfabrik Süderdithmarschen* case, it appears that, despite the potential threats to the uniform application of EU law, in this situation national courts are permitted to grant interim relief. In this respect, the Court of Justice considers that 'interim legal protection which Community law ensures for individuals before national courts must remain the same, irrespective of whether they contest the compatibility of national legal provisions with Community law or the validity of secondary Community law, in view of the fact that the dispute in both cases is based on Community law itself' (paragraph 20 of the ruling).

(2) In validity cases, providing interim relief may run counter to the uniform application of EU law. After all, if interim relief is granted, the EU act in question is temporarily not applied in the Member State concerned. Therefore, the Court of Justice has set out strict and uniform conditions for assessing requests for interim relief in validity cases. According to these conditions, the national court may only grant the request for interim relief under the following circumstances:

(a) The national court has serious doubts as to the validity of the EU act.
(b) The relief granted should only have the character of an interim measure until the European Court of Justice has ruled on the question of validity; if the question is not yet brought to the European Court of Justice, a preliminary question of validity has to be asked.
(c) There should be urgency and a threat of serious and irreparable damage to the applicant seeking relief. Financial damage is only considered irreversible if there is a real threat of insolvency.
(d) The national court takes due account of the EU's interests.
(e) The national court must respect the judgments of the Court of Justice and the General Court on the lawfulness of EU acts when granting interim relief.

In order to enable the Court of Justice to determine the validity of the EU act concerned, the national court should refer a question of validity to the Court of Justice pursuant to Article 267 TFEU. After all, only the Court of Justice has the power to declare EU acts invalid.[195]

(3) The case of *Zuckerfabrik Süderdithmarschen* concerned the suspension of the application of an EU regulation. In the subsequent case of *Atlanta*, the Court of Justice decided that national courts are also empowered to take positive interim measures in cases of validity of EU law.[196]

7.8.B LEGAL SYSTEMS WITH AUTOMATIC SUSPENSORY EFFECT OF ACTIONS FOR ANNULMENT: GERMANY

7.8.B.1 INTRODUCTION

In Germany, lodging an intra-administrative objection against an administrative decision or filing an action for annulment (*Anfechtungsklage*) has, in principle, a suspensory effect. However, there are important exceptions to the principle of automatic suspension. Moreover, in certain circumstances, the administrative authority may order the immediate execution of an administrative act.

7.8.B.2 AUTOMATIC SUSPENSIVE EFFECT

Verwaltungsgerichtsordnung **7.81 (DE)**

§80 (1) An objection and an action for annulment shall have suspensory effect ....

(2) The suspensory effect shall not apply

1. if public charges and costs are at stake,

2. to non-postponable orders and measures by police enforcement officers,

3. in other cases prescribed by a Federal statute or for state law, by state statute, in particular with regard to objections and actions by third parties against administrative acts relating to investments or job creation,

4. in cases in which immediate execution is separately ordered in the public interest or in the overriding interest of a party concerned by the authority which has issued the administrative act or must decide on the objection.

The states may also determine that remedies do not have a suspensory effect insofar as they are directed against measures taken in administrative execution by the states in accordance with Federal law.

(3) In cases falling under section 2 No. 4, the special interest in immediate execution of the administrative act must be reasoned in writing. No special reasoning shall be required if the authority, in case of imminent danger, in particular with impending disadvantages to life, health or property, takes, in the public interest and by way of precaution, an emergency measure designated as such.

[195] Case 314/85 *Foto-Frost v Hauptzollamt Lübeck-Ost* ECLI:EU:C:1987:452.

[196] Case C-465/93 *Atlanta Fruchthandelsgesellschaft mbH and Others (I) v Bundesamt für Ernährung und Forstwirtschaft* ECLI:EU:C:1995:369.

Notes

(1) In order to protect citizens against the immediate effects of administrative decisions, §80(1) VwGO states that filing an intra-administrative objection or an action for annulment has an automatic suspensory effect on the decision challenged.[197] Hence, the decision does not need to be complied with and cannot be implemented, executed or enforced by the authority by means of coercion until the legal dispute has been decided. The suspension of an administrative act ends after the act has become final and non-appealable (*bestandskräftig*). This happens if either the citizen fails to file an action for annulment in due time after his intra-administrative objection has been rejected or the time limit for appeal against a judgment of the Administrative Court of First Instance has elapsed.[198]

(2) However, §80(2) VwGO provides for some important exceptions to this rule.[199] Pursuant to §80(2) VwGO, the suspensory effect of an objection or an action in court does not apply to administrative decisions imposing the payment of public charges and costs,[200] to urgent police measures, such as traffic measures or the decision to dissolve an unlawful assembly,[201] or to any other acts provided for by a federal statute or a statute of a *Land*.[202] The latter exception particularly aims at preventing the suspensory effect of objections and other actions instigated by third parties against administrative acts relating to investments or job creation.

(3) In addition, the authority may order the 'immediate execution' (*sofortige Vollziehung*) of an administrative act if this is necessary 'in the public interest or in the interest of the parties involved' (§80(2), no 4 VwGO). The authority must explicitly order the direct execution of the act (*Anordnung des Sofortvollzugs*) (§80(2), no. 4 VwGO), giving written reasons, although no such reasoning is necessary in case of emergency.[203]

JH Jans, S Prechal, RJGM Widdershoven (eds) Europeanisation of Public Law[204] **7.82 (DE)**

It will be clear that this form of interim judicial protection [automatic suspensory effect, unless the competent authority had ordered immediate execution of the decision concerned] could conflict with the effective application of Union acts in the national legal

[197] Pünder and Klafki (n 4 above). For further details, see F Schoch, 'Aufschiebende Wirkung und verwaltungsgerichtliches Aussetzungsverfahren' in Ehlers and Schoch (n 6 above) 785–850.

[198] For time limits in the German legal system, see Chapter 4, section 4.7.

[199] These exceptions are not, however, absolute and have been further restricted by law. Unless a federal law provides to the contrary, the administrative authority before which an objection against an administrative act is pending may suspend the execution of any administrative act covered.

[200] The rationale of this exception is the predictability for budget planning.

[201] This also applies to traffic signs and parking meters, BVerwG NJW 1978, 656; BVerwG NVwZ 1988, 623.

[202] eg German Residence Act (Aufenthaltsgesetz), §58/58a; Asylum Procedure Act (Asylverfahrensgesetz), §75; Building Code (Baugesetzbuch), §212a; Federal Civil Service Framework Act (Beamtenrechtsrahmengesetz), §126(3), no 3.

[203] §80(3) VwGO.

[204] Jans et al (n 126 above) 428–29.

order. In 1990, a year before the Court's judgement in *Zuckerfabrik*, this conflict resulted in Germany being held to have failed to fulfil its Treaty obligations in proceedings under Article 258 TFEU, because the competent authority had not ordered immediate enforcement of a decision implementing a Union regulation and the appeal against this decision had therefore automatic suspensive effect. The Court rejected the argument that there were serious objections under German law to the adoption of a decision ordering the immediate enforcement of the measures, on the ground that a Member State may not plead provisions, practices or circumstances existing in its internal legal system in order to justify a failure to comply with its obligations under Union law. The judgement in *Zuckerfabrik* (and later in *Atlanta*) may be seen as a reaction to the situation arising after the judgement in this case. In *Zuckerfabrik*, the Court on the one hand accommodated the German point of view, in that it gave the national court the power to suspend (temporarily) the operation of a Union act in cases concerning questions of validity, while on the other hand it attached strict, uniform European conditions to the exercise of this power.

Because of these strict European conditions there was still a conflict with German law regarding interim judicial protection even after *Zuckerfabrik*. In early 1995, in other words after *Zuckerfabrik* but before *Atlanta*, the *Bundesverfassungsgericht* (Federal Constitutional Court) quashed a decision of the *Verwaltungsgerichsthof Kassel* (Administrative Court of Appeal), in which the latter had rejected an application for an interim measure concerning national implementation of a European regulation, applying the *Zuckerfabrik* criteria. According to the constitutional court, the lower court should not have applied the *Zuckerfabrik* criteria, but those of Article 19(4) of the *Grundgesetz*. However, since *Atlanta* the German courts seem to have accepted the case law of the Court concerning interim relief in cases involving questions of validity. A factor that will undoubtedly have played a role is that the rules on interim judicial protection in Germany were changed in 1997. Since then, the rule that an appeal against an administrative decision has suspensive effect, has been limited considerably. In many cases – for instance concerning all decisions which contain a financial obligation – the suspensory effect of the appeal has been abolished. In these cases, the person concerned must now seek interim relief.

Note

Prior to 1997, German law did not provide for general exceptions to the rule of automatic suspensory effect and the authorities had only limited potential to order the immediate enforcement of decisions contested. These rules also applied to decisions imposing a levy, prescribed by EU law. In 1990, this led to a collision with EU law, as the Court of Justice, in the case of *Table Wine*,[205] was of the opinion that Germany had failed to fulfil its obligations under EU law, because the German authorities had not ordered the immediate enforcement of the imposition of a levy prescribed by an EU regulation, and the action against the levy therefore had an automatic suspensory effect.

Since that time, the German and EU approaches with regard to interim judicial protection have developed towards greater harmonisation with each other. On the one

[205] Case 217/88 *Commission v Germany (Table wine)* ECLI:EU:C:1990:290.

hand, the Court of Justice has, in the cases of *Zuckerfabrik Süderdithmarschen* and *Atlanta*,[206] empowered the national courts to provide for interim relief in cases in which the validity of an EU act is questioned. On the other hand, German law now provides for several exceptions to the rule of automatic suspensory effect of judicial review in both national and EU cases. The exception in respect of administrative acts requiring the payment of public charges and costs (§80(2) VwGO), is of particular importance for EU law, because many EU regulations are concerned with the imposition of public charges. As a result of both developments, the tension between EU law and German law has to large extent disappeared, although one cannot say that there is a causal link between the two developments. The reasons for the introduction in Germany of several exceptions to the rule of automatic suspensory effect were primarily internal.

7.8.B.3 SUSPENSION

Verwaltungsgerichtsordnung **7.83 (DE)**

§80 … (5) On request, the court seized of the main case may completely or partly order the suspensory effect in cases falling under section 2 Nos. 1–3, and may restore it completely or partly in cases falling under section 2 No 4. The request shall already be admissible prior to the filing of an action for annulment. If the administrative act has already been executed at the time of the decision, the court may order the rescission of the execution. The rescission of the suspensive effect may be made dependent on the provision of a security or on other requirements. It may also be time-limited.

Notes

(1) With regard to the administrative acts which fall under §80(2) nos. 1–3 VwGO and are, thus, directly enforceable, as well as for acts whose execution was separately ordered by the authority pursuant to §80(2) no. 4, §80(5) VwGO entitles an adversely affected citizen to file a request for a suspension of the administrative act (*einstweiliger Rechtsschutz*). Furthermore, where the execution of the administrative act has already begun, an application to the court on the basis of §80(5) VwGO to stop the execution of an administrative act and restore the status quo ante is also admissible. The admissibility of such a request for suspension is dependent on *locus standi*.[207] Therefore, the applicant must claim that his individual rights are infringed by the administrative act subject to challenge. In the procedure for suspension, the court does not take oral evidence and does not further examine the facts, but bases its decision on the facts derived from the documents submitted to the court as part of the claim.

[206] See section 7.8.A above.
[207] For details on standing in Germany, see Chapter 4, section 4.4.B.1.

(2) With regard to the merits of an application under §80(5) VwGO, the court has to examine whether the citizen's interest in the suspension of the execution of the administrative act outweighs the public interest in its immediate execution.[208] An important factor in this balancing process is whether the claim against the administrative act in the main proceedings (*Hauptsacheverfahren*) may be successful.[209] If the court finds that the administrative act appears to be unlawful and infringes the individual rights of the citizen, the application under §80(5) VwGO will be successful, and the court will order the suspension of the administrative act. However, if the administrative act seems to be lawful and there is a special public interest in the direct execution of the administrative act which outweighs the interest of the applicant, the application under §80(5) VwGO will be dismissed. If, on the basis of the facts in the file, no prognosis can be made on who will succeed in the main proceedings, the court only balances the interest of the parties.[210]

(3) Where a suspension of the execution of the administrative act is ordered, its duration is limited by §80b VwGO. According to this provision, the suspension shall come to an end when an action for annulment can no longer be brought or three months after the expiry of the time limit for seeking a legal remedy against the dismissal of the action by the Administrative Court of First Instance, whichever is first. Contrary to the situation in civil procedural law,[211] the Federal Administrative Court does not recognise the right to claim damages in cases of interim relief.[212] Against the refusal to adopt a decision according to §80(5) VwGO, a complaint may be lodged on the basis of §146 VwGO.

7.8.B.4 INTERIM INJUNCTION

Verwaltungsgerichtsordnung **7.84 (DE)**

§123 (1) On request, the court may, even prior to the lodging of an action, issue an interim order in relation to the subject matter of the dispute if the danger exists that the enforcement of a right of the plaintiff could be prevented or significantly impeded by an alteration of the existing situation. Interim orders shall also be admissible to determine an interim condition in relation to a contentious legal relationship if such regulation, particularly in the case of ongoing legal relationships, seems to be necessary in order to avert major disadvantages or imminent violence or for other reasons.

(2) The court seized of the main case is competent to for the issue interim orders. This shall be the court of first instance and, if the main case is pending in the proceedings for an appeal on points of fact and law, the court of appeal on points of fact and law. §80(8) shall apply mutatis mutandis.

[208] See, eg BVerfG, NVwZ 2005, 927.
[209] BVerfGE 69, 305, 315, 363.
[210] BVerwG, NVwZ-RR, 1991, 365.
[211] BGHZ 78, 128 on §945 ZPO.
[212] BverwG, NVwZ 1991, 270.

(3) §§920, 921, 923, 926, 928 to 932, 938, 939, 941 and 945 the Code of Civil Procedure shall apply mutatis mutandis to the issuance of interim orders.

(4) The court shall decide by means of an order.

(5) The provisions contained in sections 1 to 3 shall not apply to cases falling under §§80 and 80a.

Notes

(1) Interim protection on the basis of §123 VwGO applies where §§80 and 80a VwGO do not apply. This includes two situations, namely the situation where no administrative act is contested but the applicant desires an administrative action to be taken, and the situation where the case does not concern a burdensome administrative act but rather an administrative act conferring a benefit. In both situations, the court may grant an 'interim injunction' (*einstweilige Verfügung*) in respect of the matter in dispute, even before an action in the main proceeding has been lodged, if the danger exists that a change of the existing situation would seriously impede the enforcement of a right by the applicant.[213] In addition, a situation may be regulated on a provisional basis if 'such regulation, particularly in the case of ongoing legal relationships, seems to be necessary in order to avert major disadvantages or imminent violence, or for other reasons' (§123 VwGO). A distinction is made between an application to secure the status quo (*Sicherungsanordnung*) and an application to order the administration to do something (*Regelungsanordnung*). The former is intended to secure a temporary state of affairs in respect of a disputed legal relationship, whereas the latter might go beyond the status quo.

(2) In proceedings for an interim injunction, the court must, similar to the proceedings on suspension under §80(5) VwGO, balance the interests at stake. In the proceedings, no oral hearing takes place and no evidence apart from prima facie evidence (*Glaubhaftmachung*) is taken. The decision is made in the form of an order (*Beschluss*). In order for the request for an interim injunction to be granted, the applicant must duly show that he has a right to the administrative action desired (*Anordnungsanspruch*) and that the protection of the status quo or a positive administrative action is necessary because his right would otherwise be irreversibly infringed (*Anordnungsgrund*). The former requires a summary assessment of the prospects of success in the main action. The latter implies that there should be a state of urgency (*Dringlichkeit*). If, for example, the claimant acts against the illegal operation of a chemical factory and he wants the administrative authority to take enforcement measures against this operation, he should (try to) demonstrate that the factory operates unlawfully (*Anordnungsanspruch*) and that operating the chemical factory during the period until the decision on his request to take enforcement measures in the main proceedings will harm his interests, for example his health, and that therefore immediate action is urgent (*Dringlichkeit*).

[213] For details, see Schoch (n 194 above) 851–87.

Verwaltungsgerichtsordnung **7.85 (DE)**

§47 (1) The Higher Administrative Court shall adjudicate on application within the boundaries of its jurisdiction on the validity of

1. by-laws issued under the provisions of the Federal Building Code (Baugesetzbuch) and executive regulations issued on the basis of §246(2) of the Federal Building Code,
2. other legal provisions ranking below state legislation, to the extent that this is provided in state law.

...

(6) On application, the court may issue a temporary injunction where this is urgently required in order to avert serious disadvantages or for other compelling reasons.

Note

A specific form of interim relief can be found in the framework of §47 VwGO concerning the procedure to review by-laws and executive regulations (*Normenkontrollverfahren*).[214] According to this provision, courts can order a temporary injunction in respect of a by-law or executive regulation that is claimed to be unlawful.

7.8.C LEGAL SYSTEMS WITH INTERIM RELIEF ON REQUEST

7.7. C.1 ENGLAND AND WALES

7.8.C.1 (i) Introduction

Prior to the decision in the *Factortame* case, under a long-standing common law rule, the courts in England and Wales were not allowed to grant interim relief against the Crown or its officers.[215] As a result of *Factortame*, the courts had to set aside this rule in cases where national law was allegedly inconsistent with EU law. Therefore, according to the English academic literature, the case 'ranks as one of the most important decisions affecting UK government'.[216] In 1993, the House of Lords decided to extend the *Factortame* rule to purely domestic cases (where no EU right is at stake). In the case of *M v Home Office*, the House of Lords held that a court may grant interim relief against the Crown in a case governed exclusively by national law.[217] According to the House of Lords, it was unacceptable that the judicial protection of persons in a national context should be worse than where the case had a European dimension.

As a result of the foregoing, an important limitation on the remedy of interim relief in England and Wales no longer exists. Nevertheless, the possibilities for individuals to

[214] See Chapter 3, section 3.3.B.2 (i).

[215] See Eliantonio (n 188 above) 261 ff.

[216] J Jowell and P Birkinshaw, 'English Report' in J Schwarze (ed), *Administrative Law under European Influence: On the Convergence of the Administrative Law of the EU Member States* (London, Sweet & Maxwell/Nomos, 1996) 273–332, 302.

[217] *M v Home Office* [1994] 1 AC 377 (HL). See also *Woolwich Building Association v IRC (No 2)* [1993] AC 70 (HL).

apply for interim relief in public law cases are still somewhat more limited than in the other legal systems. In cases concerning a claim for judicial review, the courts in England and Wales may offer two interim remedies, namely declarations and injunctions, but requesting the latter is generally limited by the requirement of cross-undertakings in damages. Where injunctions are sought, they may be prohibitory (ie to prevent a public authority from taking a certain action) or mandatory (ie to require a public authority to take a particular action). In the vast majority of interim relief cases, claimants are likely to seek a prohibitory interim injunction, preventing a certain action prior to the full hearing.

7.8.C.1 (ii) Interim Injunctions and Declarations

Senior Courts Act 1981 **7.86 (EW)**

Section 37 (1) The High Court may by order (whether interlocutory or final) grant an injunction ... in all cases in which it appears to the court to be just and convenient to do so.

(2) Any such order may be made either unconditionally or on such terms and conditions as the court thinks just.

Civil Procedure Rules **7.87 (EW)**

Rule 25.1 Orders for interim remedies

(1) The court may grant the following interim remedies–

(a) an interim injunction;

(b) an interim declaration;

...

(4) The court may grant an interim remedy whether or not there has been a claim for a final remedy of that kind.

Notes

(1) In judicial review proceedings, the court may grant (a) an interim injunction and/or (b) an interim declaration. These interim remedies may be granted whether a claim for a final remedy has been lodged in the main proceedings or not. An order for interim remedies may be made at any time, including at the stage before proceedings are started and after a judgment has been delivered. Where an interim remedy is sought before a claim has been made, the court will only consider granting such a remedy where the matter is urgent, or it is otherwise desirable to do so in the interests of justice, and where a defendant may not apply for any of the orders listed in Rule 25.1(1) before he has filed either an acknowledgment of service or a defence (Rule 25.2 CPR).

(2) In the past, there was a question as to whether interim declarations were available against the Crown or its officers,[218] and whether it would be possible for the

[218] The notion of an interim declaration has been rejected in *International General Electric Co of New York v Customs and Excise Commissioners* (1962) Ch 784 (CA).

court to award an interim declaration. Indeed, 'declarations exist to tell people what their rights are and this cannot be achieved until the final judgment'.[219] The introduction of Rule 25.1(1)(b) CPR solved these issues. It explicitly provides the power for the courts to issue an interim declaration in judicial review proceedings. The most likely use of the interim declaration remains that of spelling out the basis upon which a particular law should be understood and applied by the public bodies, pending the final hearing of a claim for judicial review.[220]

Privy Council, 13 August 2003[221] **7.88 (EW)**

Belize Alliance of Conservation Non-Governmental Organisations v Department of the Environment (Interim Injunction)

INTERIM RELIEF; REQUIREMENT OF CROSS-UNDERTAKING

Belize

To be granted interim relief, an applicant must fulfil the requirement of the cross-undertaking in damages.

Facts: B applied for an interim injunction to halt construction works on a dam project in Belize pending the hearing of his substantive claim by the Privy Council. The issues for the Privy Council were whether it had jurisdiction to grant an interlocutory injunction halting work on the project, what principles should be applied if it did have jurisdiction, whether B had an arguable case and what the relative risks of injustice to both parties were.

Held: Interim relief was not available to the claimant in this case because it could not demonstrate that it had the necessary financial means to provide an appropriate cross-undertaking in damages.

Judgment: Lord Walker of Gestingthorpe: The circumstance in which an injunction could be granted in a public law case.

Counsel were agreed (in the most general terms) that when the court is asked to grant an interim injunction in a public law case, it should approach the matter on the lines indicated by the House of Lords in *American Cyanamid Company v Ethicon Limited* [1975] AC 396, but with modifications appropriate to the public law element of the case. The public law element is one of the possible 'special factors' referred to by Lord Diplock in that case (at page 409). Another special factor might be if the grant or refusal of interim relief were likely to be, in practical terms, decisive of the whole case; but neither side suggested that the present case is in that category.

The Court's approach to the grant of injunctive relief in public law cases was discussed (in particularly striking circumstances) by Lord Goff of Chieveley in *Queen v Secretary of State for Transport, ex parte Factortame Limited (No 2)* [1991] AC 603, 671-4. The whole passage calls for careful study. Lord Goff stated at page 672 that where the Crown is seeking to enforce the law, it may not be thought right to impose upon the Crown the

[219] Craig (n 9 above) 888.
[220] C Lewis, *Judicial Remedies in Public Law*, 3rd edn (London, Sweet & Maxwell, 2004) 228.
[221] [2003] UKPC 63.

usual undertaking in damages as a condition of the grant of injunctive relief. Lord Goff concluded (at page 674):

'I myself am of the opinion that in these cases, as in others, the discretion conferred upon the court cannot be fettered by a rule; I respectfully doubt whether there is any rule that, in cases such as these, a party challenging the validity of a law must – to resist an application for an interim injunction against him, or to obtain an interim injunction restraining the enforcement of the law – show a strong prima facie case that the law is invalid. It is impossible to foresee what cases may yet come before the courts; I cannot dismiss from my mind the possibility (no doubt remote) that such a party may suffer such serious and irreparable harm in the event of the law being enforced against him that it may be just or convenient to restrain its enforcement by an interim injunction even though so heavy a burden has not been discharged by him. In the end, the matter is one for the discretion of the court, taking into account all the circumstances of the case. Even so, the court should not restrain a public authority by interim injunction from enforcing an apparently authentic law unless it is satisfied, having regard to all the circumstances, that the challenge to the validity of the law is, prima facie, so firmly based as to justify so exceptional a course being taken.'

In some public law cases (such as *Queen v Servite Houses and Wandsworth LBC, ex parte Goldsmith* (2000) 3 CCLR 354) the issue is a straightforward dispute between a public or quasi-public body (in that case, a charity providing care services on behalf of a local authority) and citizens to whom the services are being provided. In such a case an injunction may be granted to the citizen, without any undertaking in damages, if justice requires that course. Swinton Thomas LJ took into consideration the public importance of the case, involving the closure of a residential care home; the very serious consequences for the elderly and infirm residents who would be moved from accommodation in which they were settled; their prospect of success at the full hearing; and the relatively short period for which the injunction would be in force pending the hearing of the appeal.

In *Queen v Inspectorate of Pollution, ex parte Greenpeace Limited* [1994] 1 WLR 570, on the other hand, a campaigning organisation was challenging an official decision which, if stayed, would have adverse financial implications for a commercial company (British Nuclear Fuels PLC) which was not a party to the proceedings. Brooke J had refused a stay and the Court of Appeal upheld this decision. Glidewell LJ said at page 574:

'At the hearing before Brooke J no offer was made by Greenpeace to give an undertaking as to damages suffered by BNFL should they suffer any; the sort of undertaking that would normally be required if an interlocutory injunction were to be granted. I bear in mind that the judge said that he was influenced by the evidence about Greenpeace's likely inability to pay for that financial loss, but he had earlier remarked that he had not been offered an undertaking. If we were dealing with this matter purely on the material which was before the judge, I would find no difficulty at all. This was essentially a matter for the discretion of the judge.'

Scott LJ said at page 577:

'But if the purpose of the interlocutory stay is, as here, to prevent executive action by a third party in pursuance of rights which have been granted by the decision under attack, then, in my judgment, to require a cross-undertaking in damages to be given is, as a matter of discretion, an entirely permissible condition for the grant of interlocutory relief and in general, I would think, unless some special feature be present, a condition that should be expected to be imposed.'

A similar approach has been taken by the Land and Environment Court of New South Wales in *Jarasius v Forestry Commission of New South Wales* (19 December 1989). Some observations of Lord Jauncey of Tullichettle in *Queen v Secretary of State for the Environment, ex parte The Royal Society for the Protection of Birds* [1997] Env LR 431, 440 are also consistent with the view that an undertaking in damages should normally be required, even in a public law case with environmental implications, if the commercial interests of a third party are engaged.

Both sides rightly submitted that (because the range of public law cases is so wide) the court has a wide discretion to take the course which seems most likely to produce a just result (or to put the matter less ambitiously, to minimise the risk of an unjust result). In the context Mr Clayton referred to the well-known decision of the Court of Appeal in *Allen v Jambo Holdings* [1980] 1 WLR 1252, which has had the result that in England a very large class of litigants (that is, legally assisted persons) are as a matter of course excepted from the need to give a cross-undertaking in damages. However their Lordships (without casting any doubt on the practice initiated by that case) do not think that it can be taken too far. The court is never exempted from the duty to do its best, on interlocutory applications with far-reaching financial implications, to minimise the risk of injustice. In *Allen v Jambo Holdings* Lord Denning MR said (at page 1257),

'I do not see why a poor plaintiff should be denied a Mareva injunction just because he is poor, whereas a rich plaintiff would get it'.

On the facts of that case, that was an appropriate comment. But there may be cases where the risk of serious and uncompensated detriment to the defendant cannot be ignored. The rich plaintiff may find, if ultimately unsuccessful, that he has to pay out a very large sum as the price of having obtained an injunction which (with hindsight) ought not to have been granted to him. Counsel were right to agree (in line with all the authorities referred to above) that the court has a wide discretion.

Note

An important limitation to the availability of interim injunctions is the obligation imposed on the claimant to pay a cross-undertaking in damages to compensate the defendant authority and/or possible third parties, when claiming for an interim injunction. A cross-undertaking in damages is an agreement by a claimant requesting an injunction to pay compensation to the party subject to the injunction in case where the court in the main proceedings decides that the injunction should not have been given and the party subject to the injunction suffers a quantifiable financial loss as a result of complying with that injunction. If the claimant is unsuccessful at the final hearing, the party restrained is compensated for any loss suffered in the interim. However, such a mechanism, which has as its aim the protection of the defendant or (more usually) third parties, obviously makes it more difficult to use interim relief procedures and to benefit from judicial protection, in particular when challenging decisions on large industrial or infrastructure projects. Indeed, the amount of the cross-undertaking corresponds to the potential loss of profit, which might be very large for such projects. The applicant might not be able to provide for such a sum of money, especially when the claimant is an individual or an environmental non-governmental organisation. The argument in favour of such a requirement is that the cross-undertaking is presented as a mechanism allowing the claimant for injunction to better anticipate the potential consequences of the outcome of the case. In its judgment against the UK of 13 February 2014,[222] the Court of Justice of the European Union had doubts whether the possibility to require the claimant to pay for cross-undertakings is in accordance with the requirement that judicial review proceedings (in the area covered by the EU directives transposing Article 9(2) of the Aarhus Convention) should not be prohibitively expensive.[223]

House of Lords, 19 June 1990[224] **7.89 (EW)**

R v Secretary of State for Transport, ex parte Factortame Ltd (No 2)

INJUNCTIONS; BALANCE OF CONVENIENCE

Factortame

In assessing the balance of convenience in public law cases, the court must consider not only whether damages would be an adequate remedy if the interim injunction was not granted and the claimant was ultimately successful, but also broader issues of public interest, including the public interest in allowing public authorities to uphold the law using the powers granted to them by law.

Facts: The Merchant Shipping Act 1988 and associated secondary legislation restricted the ability of owners of fishing vessels that were not owned and operated by UK nationals from being registered so that they could lawfully fish in British waters. A number of vessels were denied registration under the new regime on the basis that, although they were registered in the UK and the vessels were operated by companies registered in the UK, the vessels were either controlled from Spain or by Spanish nationals, or Spanish nationals held a significant proportion of the beneficial ownership of the shares in the operating companies. The claimants argued that the statutory regime was an infringement of their rights to non-discrimination and free movement under EU law and thus sought an interim injunction to prevent the Secretary of State from applying the new regime until a preliminary ruling had been issued by the Court of Justice.

Held: The interim injunction was granted.

Judgment: Lord Goff: The jurisdiction of courts to grant interim injunctions is to be found in section 37 of the Supreme Court Act 1981, under which the court has power to grant an injunction in all cases in which it appears to it to be just or convenient so to do, and has power to do so on such terms and conditions as it thinks fit. Guidelines for the exercise of the court's jurisdiction to grant interim injunctions were laid down by your Lordships' House in *American Cyanamid Co. v. Ethicon Ltd.* [1975] A.C. 396, in the speech of Lord Diplock in that case, with which the remainder of their Lordships concurred. I use the word 'guidelines' advisedly, because I do not read Lord Diplock's speech as intended to fetter the broad discretion conferred on the courts by section 37 of the Supreme Court Act 1981; on the contrary, a prime purpose of the guidelines established in the *Cyanamid* case was to remove a fetter which appeared to have been imposed in certain previous cases, viz., that a party seeking an interlocutory injunction had to establish a prima facie case for substantive relief. It is now clear that it is enough if he can show that there is

[222] Case C-530/11 *Commission v United Kingdom* ECLI:EUC:2014:67.
[223] See further Chapter 4, section 4.9.C.
[224] [1991] 1 AC 603.

a serious case to be tried. If he can establish that, then he has, so to speak, crossed the threshold; and the court can then address itself to the question whether it is just or convenient to grant an injunction.

Nothing which I say is intended to qualify the guidelines laid down in Lord Diplock's speech. But, before I turn to the question of public interest, which lies at the heart of the rival submissions in the present case, I must advert to the fact that Lord Diplock approached the matter in two stages. First, he considered the relevance of the availability of an adequate remedy in damages, either to the plaintiff seeking the injunction or to the defendant in the event that an injunction is granted against him. As far as the plaintiff is concerned, the availability to him of such a remedy will normally preclude the grant to him of an interim injunction. If that is not so, then the court should consider whether, if an injunction is granted against the defendant, there will be an adequate remedy in damages available to him under the plaintiff's undertaking in damages; if so, there will be no reason on this ground to refuse to grant the plaintiff an interim injunction.

At this stage of the court's consideration of the case (which I will for convenience call the first stage) many applications for interim injunctions can well be decided. But if there is doubt as to the adequacy of either or both of the respective remedies in damages, then the court proceeds to what is usually called the balance of convenience, and for that purpose will consider all the circumstances of the case. I will call this the second stage. Again, I stress that I do not wish to place any gloss upon what Lord Diplock said about this stage. I wish only to record his statement, at p. 408, that

'It would be unwise to attempt even to list all the various matters which may need to be taken into consideration in deciding where the balance lies, let alone to suggest the relevant weight to be attached to them. These will vary from case to case.'

And his further statement, at p. 409 (after referring to particular factors), that 'there may be many other special factors to be taken into consideration in the particular circumstances of individual cases.'

I turn to consider the impact upon these guidelines of the public interest, with particular reference to cases in which a public authority is seeking to enforce the law against some person, and either the authority seeks an interim injunction to restrain that person from acting contrary to the law, and that person claims that no such injunction should be granted on the ground that the relevant law is, for some reason, invalid; or that other person seeks an interim injunction to restrain the action of the authority, on the same ground.

I take the first stage. This may be affected in a number of ways. For example, where the Crown is seeking to enforce the law, it may not be thought right to impose upon the Crown the usual undertaking in damages as a condition of the grant of an injunction: see *F. Hoffmann-La Roche & Co. A.G. v. Secretary of State for Trade and Industry* [1975] A.C. 295. Again, in this country there is no general right to indemnity by reason of damage suffered through invalid administrative action; in particular, on the law as it now stands, there would be no remedy in damages available to the applicants in the present case for loss suffered by them by reason of the enforcement of the Act of 1988 against them, if the relevant part of the Act should prove to be incompatible with European law: see *Bourgoin S.A. v. Ministry of Agriculture, Fisheries and Food* [1986] Q.B. 716. Conversely, an authority acting in the public interest cannot normally be protected by a remedy in damages because it will itself have suffered none. It follows that, as a general rule, in cases of this kind involving the public interest, the problem cannot be solved at the first stage, and it will be necessary for the court to proceed to the second stage, concerned with the balance of convenience.

Turning then to the balance of convenience, it is necessary in cases in which a party is a public authority performing duties to the public that 'one must look at the balance of convenience more widely, and take into account the interests of the public in general to whom these duties are owed:' see *Smith v. Inner London Education Authority* [1978] 1 All E.R. 411, 422, per Browne L.J., and see also *Sierbien v. Westminster City Council* (1987) 86 L.G.R. 431. Like Browne L.J., I incline to the opinion that this can be treated as one of the special factors referred to by Lord Diplock in the passage from his speech which I have quoted. In this context, particular stress should be placed upon the importance of upholding the law of the land, in the public interest, bearing in mind the need for stability in our society, and the duty placed upon certain authorities to enforce the law in the public interest. This is of itself an important factor to be weighed in the balance when assessing the balance of convenience. So if a public authority seeks to enforce what is on its face the law of the land, and the person against whom such action is taken challenges the validity of that law, matters of considerable weight have to be put into the balance to outweigh the desirability of enforcing, in the public interest, what is on its face the law, and so to justify the refusal of an interim injunction in favour of the authority, or to render it just or convenient to restrain the authority for the time being from enforcing the law. This was expressed in a number of different ways by members of the Appellate Committee in the *Hoffmann-La Roche case* [1975] A.C. 295. Lord Reid said, at p. 341, that

'it is for the person against whom the interim injunction is sought to show special reason why justice requires that the injunction should not be granted or should only be granted on terms.'

Note

For an interim injunction to be granted, the court must examine whether there is a serious issue to be tried and whether there is imminent danger of irreparable injury. In this respect, the interim injunction will be granted if a remedy in damages would not be adequate. The strength of the case and the balance of convenience are crucial factors. The court's discretion is very broad,[225] although the court will be guided by the principles set out in the excerpt above, particularly the urgency of the need to obtain an interim measure, the risk of irreparable damage if the measure is not granted and the public interest (both in maintaining the status quo and permitting the state to proceed with the proposed course of action).

7.8.C.1 (iii) STAY OF PROCEEDINGS

Civil Procedure Rules **7.90 (EW)**

Rule 54.10 Permission given

(1) Where permission to proceed is given the court may also give directions.

(2) Directions under paragraph (1) may include–

(a) a stay of proceedings to which the claim relates;

(b) directions requiring the proceedings to be heard by a Divisional Court.

[225] *Smith v Inner London Education Authority* [1978] 1 All ER 411 (CA); *R (Miranda) v Home Secretary* [2013] EWHC 2609, [2014] ACD 26.

Court of Appeal (Civil Division), 28 June 2002[226] **7.91 (EW)**

R (H) v Ashworth Special Hospital Authority

STAY OF PROCEEDINGS

Ashworth

The court has jurisdiction to grant a stay of proceedings even where the proceedings might be said to be concluded.

Facts: H was a patient in the hospital with a history of violent conduct who was detained under the provisions of the Mental Health Act 1983. A mental health review tribunal ordered H's release from detention against the advice of a majority of the doctors and gave inadequate reasons for its decision. In the meantime, H did not leave the hospital as no suitable alternative accommodation was available and remained as a voluntary patient. The hospital sought a stay of the tribunal's decision pending the hearing of its judicial review claim against the decision of the tribunal. The hospital was ultimately successful in its claim and the tribunal's decision to release H was quashed, with H's application to seek judicial review of the decision of the doctors to continue his detention being denied. H appealed this decision and one of the issues that arose in the appeal (though it was no longer relevant in the instant case) was whether or not the court had the power to stay the decision of the tribunal.

Held: The court had the power to stay the decision of the tribunal.

Judgment: Dyson LJ: 42 The purpose of a stay in a judicial review is clear. It is to suspend the 'proceedings' that are under challenge pending the determination of the challenge. It preserves the status quo. This will aid the judicial review process and make it more effective. It will ensure, so far as possible, that, if a party is ultimately successful in his challenge, he will not be denied the full benefit of his success. In Avon, Glidewell LJ said that the phrase 'stay of proceedings' must be given a wide interpretation so as apply to administrative decisions. In my view it should also be given a wide interpretation so as to enhance the effectiveness of the judicial review jurisdiction. A narrow interpretation, such as that which appealed to the Privy Council in Vehicle and Supplies, would appear to deny jurisdiction even in case A. That would indeed be regrettable and, if correct, would *139 expose a serious shortcoming in the armoury of powers available to the court when granting permission to apply for judicial review. As I have said, this extreme position is not contended for by Mr Pleming. Thus it is common ground that 'proceedings' includes not only the process leading up to the making of the decision but the decision itself. The Administrative Court routinely grants a stay to prevent the implementation of a decision that has been made but not yet carried into effect, or fully carried into effect. A good example is where a planning authority grants planning permission and an objector seeks permission to apply for judicial review. It is not, I believe, controversial that, if the court grants permission, it may order a stay of the carrying into effect of the planning permission.

43 In some, and perhaps many, contexts the result desired by the court can be achieved by the grant of an injunction. This was, in effect, the point that was made by Lord Oliver in the passage that I have cited. But that would not be an appropriate remedy in a case concerning the detention of a patient pursuant to the Act. The judge recognised that, if there were no jurisdiction to grant a stay, there was a serious lacuna in the law, unless it

[226] [2002] EWCA Civ 923, [2003] 1 WLR 127.

could be overcome by a fresh admission to hospital. He said that there was power in the court under section 37 of the Supreme Court Act 1981 to grant an injunction prohibiting a patient from leaving hospital, and requiring him to agree to treatment. But, he added, he could not think of circumstances in which it would be proper to use this power. As he pointed out:

'The court should not deprive a person of liberty by injunction, or compel him to submit to treatment, except in the most exceptional cases. Moreover, an injunction cannot authorise a doctor to treat a patient: it can only require the patient to agree to treatment. If, notwithstanding the injunction, the patient does not agree to the treatment in question, the only remedy is committal for contempt. Difficulties would also arise in specifying the treatment in question.'

44 For these and other reasons, the judge held that the solution to the problem did not lie in the jurisdiction to grant an injunction. It was common ground before us that the judge was right, and I agree. Where the patient has actually left the hospital, the arguments in favour of an injunction have even less attraction. It is unthinkable that the court would grant an injunction to order the patient to return to hospital and submit to the regime of the Act.

45 I return, therefore, to the question whether the court has jurisdiction to grant a stay in cases B and C. As I have said, the essential effect of a stay of proceedings is to suspend them. What this means in practice will depend on the context and the stage that has been reached in the proceedings. If the inferior court or administrative body has not yet made a final decision, then the effect of the stay will be to prevent the taking of the steps that are required for the decision to be made. If a final decision has been made, but it has not been implemented, then the effect of the stay will be to prevent its implementation. In each of these situations, so long as the stay remains in force, no further steps can be taken in the proceedings, and any decision taken will cease to have effect: it is suspended for the time being.

46 I now turn to the third situation, which occurs where the decision has not only been made, but it has been carried out in full. At first sight, it seems nonsensical to speak of making an order that such a decision should be suspended. How can one say of a decision that has been fully implemented that it should cease to have effect? Once the decision has been implemented, it is a past event, and it is impossible to suspend a piece of history. At first sight, this argument seems irresistible, but I think it is wrong. It overlooks the fact that a successful judicial review challenge does in a very real sense rewrite history. Take a decision by a tribunal to discharge a patient. The order has effect for the purposes of being implemented, i e, releasing him into the community. But it also has effect in a more general sense: it declares that at the time it was made the tribunal was not satisfied that the criteria for the patient's continued detention were fulfilled. If the order is ultimately quashed it will be treated as never having had any legal effect at all: see *R (Wirral Health Authority) v Finnegan* [2001] EWCA Civ 1901. If that occurs it will be treated as if it had never been made, and the patient will once again become subject to the Mental Health Act regime to which he was subject before the order was made. It is, therefore, difficult to see why the court should not in principle have jurisdiction to say that the order shall temporarily cease to have effect, with the same result for the time being as will be the permanent outcome if it is ultimately held to be unlawful and is quashed. I would hold that the court has jurisdiction to stay the decision of a tribunal which is subject to a judicial review challenge, even where the decision has been fully implemented as in cases B and C.

Note

Under Rule 54.10(2)(a) CPR, if the relief sought is a quashing or prohibitory order, the court has the power, when the permission to proceed in the claim is granted, to order 'a stay of the proceedings to which the claim relates'. Such a stay takes effect until the determination of the substance of the case and is binding on the public authority subject to the stay. The 'stay of proceedings' differs from the two interim remedies discussed above, since it is not the interim version of a final remedy (so, in the case of an interim declaration or injunction, the final remedy sought will be a declaration or injunction, whereas in cases where a stay is sought the ultimate remedy sought will be one of the prerogative remedies); instead, it brings a pause to any administrative decision-making process or the execution of an administrative decision until the full hearing can take place. As such, the stay of proceedings is most often used where the final remedy sought will be a quashing, mandatory or prohibiting order, as none of these remedies are available in interim form. The scope of the 'stay of proceedings' is wide, since it can be granted against any public authority.[227] In most cases, the stay of proceedings delivers no practical benefit for the claimant over an injunction, as the court will still consider whether an effective cross-undertaking in damages can be offered and the balance of convenience when determining whether to grant a stay.[228]

7.8.C.2 THE EUROPEAN UNION

Treaty on the Functioning of the European Union **7.92 (EU)**

Article 278 Actions brought before the Court of Justice of the European Union shall not have suspensory effect. The Court may, however, if it considers that circumstances so require, order that application of the contested act be suspended.

Article 279 The Court of Justice of the European Union may in any cases before it prescribe any necessary interim measures.

Note

In the EU system, an action brought before the EU courts does not have suspensory effect on the challenged act. However, the Treaty provides for the possibility for the judge to suspend the act that is subject of challenge. In some cases, the mere suspension of the operation of a measure is not sufficient. Hence, Article 279 TFEU provides for the possibility to issue 'any necessary interim measures'. The range of measures

227 *R v Her Majesty's Inspectorate of Pollution & Another, ex p. Greenpeace Ltd* [1994] 1 WLR 570 (CA).
228 ibid.

in such cases is not predetermined, but the court that issues them may not exercise a power which is vested in another institution which would jeopardise the institutional balance.[229]

Rules of Procedure of the Court of Justice **7.93 (EU)**

Article 160 Application for suspension or for interim measures

(1) An application to suspend the operation of any measure adopted by an institution, made pursuant to Article 278 TFEU or Article 157 TEAEC, shall be admissible only if the applicant has challenged that measure in an action before the Court.

(2) An application for the adoption of one of the other interim measures referred to in Article 279 TFEU shall be admissible only if it is made by a party to a case before the Court and relates to that case.

(3) An application of a kind referred to in the preceding paragraphs shall state the subject-matter of the proceedings, the circumstances giving rise to urgency and the pleas of fact and law establishing a prima facie case for the interim measure applied for.

(4) The application shall be made by a separate document and in accordance with the provisions of Articles 120 to 122 of these Rules.

(5) The application shall be served on the opposite party, and the President shall prescribe a short time-limit within which that party may submit written or oral observations.

(6) The President may order a preparatory inquiry.

(7) The President may grant the application even before the observations of the opposite party have been submitted. This decision may be varied or cancelled even without any application being made by any party.

Notes

(1) Interim measures are ancillary to the main proceedings. Indeed, the Rules of Procedure of the two institutions make clear that an application to suspend the operation of a measure is only admissible if the applicant is challenging the measure in the main proceedings and that an application for any other interim measure must be made by a party within the scope of a pending case and must be related to that case.[230] The judge in the interim proceedings may not, in principle, examine the admissibility of the main action. However, as a consequence of the ancillary nature of the interim measure, the judge must assess if there are prima facie indications that the main action is inadmissible if the defendant contends that the main action is manifestly inadmissible. If this is the case, no interim measures will be granted.[231]

229 Case 109/75 R *National Carbonising v Commission* ECLI:EU:C:1975:133, para 8.

230 Similar requirements to Art 160 can be found in Art 156 of the Rules of Procedure of the General Court.

231 Case 123/80 R *B v European Parliament* ECLI:EU:C:1980:149; Joined Cases C-239/96 R and C-240/96 R *United Kingdom v Commission* ECLI:EU:C:1996:347 para 37.

(2) The application for an interim measure is assessed in a 'summary procedure' (Article 39 of the Statute of the European Court of Justice).[232] The decision is taken by the president of the competent court in the form of an order.[233] An appeal against a decision concerning interim measures of the General Court lies with Court of Justice, while there is no appeal against interim measures issued by the Court of Justice (Article 162(1) of the Rules of Procedure of the Court of Justice).

(3) Only 'enforceable' acts can be suspended. Therefore, the authorities' refusal to act cannot, in principle, be suspended.[234] This restriction prevents the interim relief judge from encroaching upon the executive power, as the suspension of a refusal to act would be equivalent to performing the act which is within the competence of the administrative authority.

Case C-149/95 P(R), 19 July 1995[235] **7.94 (EU)**

Commission v Atlantic Container Line AB and others

INTERIM RELIEF; CONDITIONS

Atlantic container line AB

In order to grant interim relief, several conditions must be fulfilled.

Facts: The defendants were party to the TAA (Trans-Atlantic Agreement), which fixed rates applicable to maritime transport. By Commission Decision 94/980/EC, the Commission found that agreement to be in violation of Community law and required the agreement to come to an end. The defendants sought suspension of that decision. Suspension was granted in part by order of the president of the court of first instance. The Commission appealed against that order.

Held: The appeal was dismissed.

Judgment: 22 It is thus open to the judge hearing an application to order the suspension of the operation of an act, or other interim measures, only if it is established that such an order is justified, prima facie, in fact and in law and that it is urgent in so far as, in order to avoid serious and irreparable damage to the applicant's interests, it must be made and produce its effects before a decision is reached in the main action. Such an order must further be provisional inasmuch as it must not prejudge the points of law or fact in issue or neutralize in advance the effects of the decision subsequently to be given in the main action.

232 See further Chapter 5, section 5.2.B.1. For the content of the application, see Art 160(3) of the Rules of Procedure of the Court of Justice and Art 156(2) of the Rules of Procedure of the General Court.

233 See Art 162(1) of the Rules of Procedure of the Court of Justice and Art 158(1) of the Rules of Procedure of the General Court.

234 See Case C-89/97 P *Moccia Irme v Commission* ECLI:EU:C:1997:226, para 45; Case T-369/03 R *Arizona Chemical and others v Commission* ECLI:EU:T:2004:9, para 62. For an exception to this rule, see Case 76/88 R *La Terza v Council* ECLI:EU:C:1988:169.

235 ECLI:EU:C:1995:257.

Notes

(1) Interim measures must be of a temporary nature, in the sense that (i) they only apply for a limited period of time and (ii) they 'must not prejudge the points of law or fact in issue or neutralise in advance the effects of the decision given in the main action'.[236] Concerning point (i), it should be noted that the period of time for which the measures are to apply may be expressly mentioned in the order awarding the interim measures. If, however, no time limit is mentioned, then the interim measure will by default expire when the judgment in the main proceedings is given. Point (ii) relates to the fact that the judge hearing applications for interim measures may not order measures which would create an irreversible situation,[237] or which would make the main application devoid of any purpose.[238]

(2) In order for an interim measure to be granted, three conditions must be fulfilled:

- — the application must establish a prima facie case, ie it must be established that the main action has a reasonable chance of success;
- — the application must be urgent; and
- — the applicant's interest in the imposition of interim measures must outweigh the other interests at stake in the proceedings.

As far as the prima facie case is concerned, the threshold seems to be that 'the arguments put forward by the applicant cannot be dismissed at that stage in the procedure without a more detailed examination'.[239] In other words, as doctrine has suggested, since the judge is not allowed to prejudge the decision in the main action, the prima facie requirement is turning from a *fumus boni iuris* requirement into a *fumus non mali iuris* one, where the threshold is that the judge has to be convinced that application is prima facie reasonable.[240]

The second requirement, urgency, implies that there must be a threat of 'serious and irreparable damage'.[241] Financial damage is generally not considered to be irreparable,[242] save for in exceptional circumstances, eg when an undertaking's very existence is threatened.[243] Furthermore, the damage must be serious, so that irreparable, but negligible, damage will not be sufficient for interim measures to be awarded.[244] The threat of serious and irreparable damage must be real, which means that it must be foreseeable with a sufficient degree of probability. Potential damage, therefore, does not suffice.[245]

[236] Case C-149/95 P(R) *Commission v Atlantic Container Line* ECLI:EU:C:1995:257, para 22; Case C-393/96 P(R) *Antonissen v Commission and Council* ECLI:EU:C:1997:42, para 27.

[237] Case 44/75 R *Konecke v Commission* ECLI:EU:C:1975:72, para 4.

[238] Case 91/76 R *De Lacroix v Court of Justice* ECLI:EU:C:1976:138, para 2.

[239] Case C-149/95 P(R) *Commission v Atlantic Container Line and Others* ECLI:EU:C:1995:257, para 26; Case T-83/00 R I *Hanseler v Commission* ECLI:EU:T:2000:249, para 32.

[240] Lenaerts et al (n 90 above) 597–98.

[241] Case C-39/03 P(R) *Commission v Artedogan and others* ECLI:EU:C:2003:418, para 41.

[242] Case T-369/03 R *Arizona Chemical and others v Commission* ECLI:EU:T:2004:9, para 75.

[243] Case C-152/88 R *Sofrinport v Commission* ECLI:EU:C:1990:259, paras 31 and 32.

[244] Case 20/81 R *Arbed v Commission* ECLI:EU:C:1981:61, para 14; Case 294/86 R *Technointorg v Commission* ECLI:EU:C:1986:497, para 28.

[245] Case T-83/00 R *Hanseler v Commission* ECLI:EU:T:2000:249, para 41.

Finally, the third condition involves a balancing exercise between the interest of the applicant in the interim measure and the public interest and the interests of third parties directly affected by the interim measure.[246] This means that even when a prima facie case has been shown and there is a threat of serious and irreparable damage, the court may refuse interim measures if the applicant's interest does not outweigh the possible effects of the measure on the interest of the defendant, of third parties or of the public interest.

7.8.C.3 THE NETHERLANDS

Algemene Wet Bestuursrecht **7.95 (NL)**

Article 6:16 Bringing an intra-administrative objection procedure or lodging a claim for judicial review (*beroep*) shall not halt the operation of the decision against which it is brought unless provided otherwise by or pursuant to a statutory provision.

Notes

As a rule, bringing an intra-administrative objection procedure before the administrative authority or lodging a claim for judicial review before the administrative court does not halt the operation of the contested decision. Thus, in principle, the administrative authority is empowered to apply or enforce the decision while the objection or judicial review proceedings are pending.

However, there are exceptions to this rule. Sometimes legislation provides for administrative decisions to be automatically suspended, for instance within the time limit for filing objections or lodging a claim for judicial review. An example can be found in Article 6.1(2) of the Environmental Licensing General Provisions Act (Wet algemene bepalingen omgevingsrecht), which prescribes that certain permits only come into force after the time limit for filing an objection or lodging a claim for judicial review has passed. If, within this period, an objection or claim for judicial review is lodged and a request for interim relief is requested, the permit only comes into force after the court has determined the request.

Algemene Wet Bestuursrecht **7.96 (NL)**

Article 8:81 (1) If a claim for judicial review has been lodged with the administrative judge against a decision, or if an objection … has been filed prior to a possible claim for judicial review before the administrative court, the judge in interlocutory proceedings (*voorzieningenrechter*) at the administrative court which has or may come to have jurisdiction over the main action may, on request, grant a provisional remedy where speed is of the essence in view of the interests involved.

[246] Case T-339/00 R *Bactria v Commission* ECLI:EU:T:2001:163, para 111.

(2) If a claim for judicial review has been lodged with the administrative judge, any party to the main action may file an application for interim relief.

...

Rechtbank Midden Nederland, 22 May 2017[247] **7.97 (NL)**

X v Mayor of the Municipality of Stichtse Vecht

INTERIM RELIEF; BALANCE OF INTERESTS

House trailer Stichtse Vecht

In interlocutory proceedings, the judge has to balance the applicant's interest in favour of an interim remedy against the opposing interests of the defendant authority.

Facts: By a decision of 10 April 2017, the mayor of the municipality of Stichtse Vecht decided to close down the applicant's home (a house trailer), including a barn belonging to it, for a period of three months, because of the discovery of a cannabis plantation in the barn. The applicant filed an objection against the decision. In addition, she filed an application for interim relief with the judge in interlocutory proceedings (*voorzieningenrechter*) of the district court Mid-Netherlands.

Held: The judge suspended the decision contested, as far as it related to the applicant's house trailer, for a period of six weeks starting from the day of the announcement of the decision on the objection.

Judgment: The assessment of the judge in interlocutory proceedings has an interlocutory character and does not bind the district court in (potential) main proceedings on the merits. When examining the request for an interim measure, the judge finds it of particular importance to assess whether the objection against the closure of the home has a reasonable chance of success. In this respect the judge in interlocutory proceedings balances the applicant's interest in favour of an interim remedy against the opposite interests of the defendant.

...

On the ground of Article 13b, first paragraph, of the Law on Opiates (Opiumwet), the mayor is competent to take enforcement actions in case in of a home where ... a substance as meant in annex I and II of the Law, is sold, delivered or present to be sold or delivered.

According to the applicant, the defendant has, in breach of the law, also decided to close down the house trailer. The cannabis plantation was discovered in the barn, which the applicant did not know was her property. From the decision it is unclear why it is necessary to shut down the house trailer as well. ... The defendant has stated that the barn and the trailer are situated on the same parcel of land and that both are connected in such a way that he is empowered to shut down the trailer as well.

The judge in interlocutory proceedings does not share the defendant's view. In the first place, the defendant has not provided reasons from which it appears that the applicant is responsible for exploiting the cannabis plantation. .... In addition, if it were established that the applicant is indeed the (co)-operator of the cannabis plantation, this mere fact would, in the circumstances of the case, be insufficient to close down the trailer as well as the barn. ... The cannabis plantation is discovered in an adjacent barn, around which five house-trailers are situated. ... From the trailer of applicant there is hardly any view

[247] ECLI:NL:RBMNE:2017:2559.

of the joint barn. Therefore, it is insufficient that the part of the joint barn where the cannabis plants have been discovered, contractually belongs to applicant's house trailer. It is important to establish in a reasonable way that the home [ie the trailer] played a role in the production and trade of the drugs. The defendant has failed to do so.

In addition, the applicant states that the defendant has insufficiently taken her interests into account. Closing down her home would mean that she and her three minor children would be homeless. The applicant does not have sufficient financial means to find an alternative accommodation at short notice and she cannot be taken care of by family or friends. In this regard, the defendant has taken the view that the applicant could stay with her mother, who is living in a house trailer on the neighbouring parcel of land … If that is, nevertheless, not an option, the applicant may turn to the social local welfare team, which may assist her when finding alternative accommodation. …

According to the judge in interlocutory proceedings the defendant has not demonstrated an appropriate weighing of interests, in so far as the impact of the decision on the applicant and her three children of seven, four and two years old in particular, is disproportionate when compared to the purposes pursued by the policy involved. …

Notes

(1) If a party in the main action wishes to prevent the operation of a decision while his objection or claim for judicial review against this decision is pending, he may request the judge in the interlocutory proceedings (*voorzieningenrechter*, also known as the 'interim relief judge') to grant interim relief. The competent interim relief judge is the judge of the administrative court that has jurisdiction (in the case of a claim for judicial review) or may come to have jurisdiction (in the case of an objection). From the foregoing, it appears that a request for interim relief is only possible if a main procedure on the merits, either on an objection or on judicial review, is already pending. Thus, for such a request to be admissible, the applicant must also challenge the decision in the main proceeding by filing an objection or lodging a claim for judicial review. This requirement is called the 'connectivity requirement' (*connexiteitseis*).

(2) The law does not indicate what kind of provisional remedy may be requested or granted. In practice, the most common provisional remedy is the suspension of the contested decision. However, positive interim measures are also possible – for instance, a party may be temporarily treated as if a permit that was refused is granted. If necessary, the judge may add conditions to this 'fictitious' permit. However, the provisional remedy may not lead to the result that the case is definitively decided at the interim relief stage or that measures are taken which are irreversible.

(3) A provisional remedy is temporary by definition. Unless the provisional relief judge has indicated otherwise, it ceases to have effect as soon as a decision has been taken in the main action, either on the objection by the administrative authority or in judicial review by the administrative court. In practice, the interim relief judge generally determines that the interim remedy ends six weeks after the decision in the main action has been taken, in order to extend the effects of the interim measure to the period available to applicants to lodge a claim for judicial review (if the interim relief was requested pending an objection procedure), or to lodge an appeal (if the interim

relief was granted pending judicial proceedings).[248] It is not possible to appeal the grant or refusal of an interim measure.

(4) According to Article 8:81 AWB, a provisional remedy is only granted'where speed is of the essence, in view of the interests involved'. This criterion implies two conditions. First, there must be an urgent need for the provisional measure. Thus, the need for a measure to be granted urgently is of the essence. Such a need exists if the immediate enforcement of the decision contested has irreversible consequences. Secondly, the judge must weigh the interests involved, ie the interest of the applicant in favour of a provisional remedy against the opposing interests of the administrative authority to enforce its decision immediately and possible interests of third parties. In this respect, the judge generally makes a provisional examination of the merits of the case ('provisional assessment on lawfulness'). If it is certain or very likely that the applicant will succeed in the main proceedings, his interest in a provisional order weighs more heavily. If it seems to be very likely that he will be unsuccessful, his interest is of lesser importance. If it is unclear or uncertain what the outcome of the main proceedings will be, the judge will apply a balancing of interests. The case in the excerpt provides an illustration of this assessment scheme, insofar as the judge takes the reasonable chance of success of the applicant in the main proceedings (in the case an objection) into account. From the assessment, it is clear that the judge has serious doubts as regards the lawfulness of, and in particular the reasons for, the contested decision to close down the applicant's home. In addition, the judge is of the opinion that the authority did not conduct a balanced weighing of interests involved, in particular the interest of the applicant and her minor children to retain access to their home, against the authorities interest to enforce its policy immediately. The 'urgent need' requirement is not tested explicitly, as it is obvious that this requirement is met.

(5) Financial interests are in principle no reason for granting interim relief. Financial interests are important only if would be 'unreasonably burdensome' (*onevenredig bezwarend*) for the applicant to wait for the judgment in the main proceedings.[249] Such a situation may, for instance, occur when a refusal of the request would endanger the survival of a company.

(6) In addition, it should be noted that in cases about compensation for damages the interim relief measure may, in exceptional circumstances, concern an advance partial payment of the compensation claimed. Such an advance payment is, however, only granted if it is almost certain that compensation will be granted in the main proceedings and if the interests of the claimant require this measure to be taken immediately.[250]

Algemene Wet Bestuursrecht **7.98 (NL)**

Article 8:86 (1) If the application is filed where a claim for judicial review has already been lodged with the administrative judge and the judge in interlocutory proceedings

[248] For time limits before Dutch administrative courts, see Chapter 4, section 4.7.
[249] ECLI:NL:RVS:1996:ZF3367, AB 1997/415; ECLI:NL:CBB:2005:AS5300.
[250] ECLI:NL:CBB:1998:ZG0116.

takes the view that further inquiry after the hearing ... cannot reasonably be expected to contribute to the assessment of the case, he may immediately rule on the merits. ...

Note

If the judge, ruling on the application for interim relief, after a hearing has taken place, considers that further inquiry cannot reasonably be expected to contribute to the assessment of the case in the main proceedings, he can immediately rule on the merits of the main action. This possibility is referred to as 'shortcutting' (*kortsluiten*). In some areas of law, for instance asylum law, this is done quite regularly. Shortcutting is only possible if interim relief is requested while the main case is already pending before the administrative court, and not where it is sought during an objection procedure.

7.8.C.4 FRANCE

7.8.C.4 (i) Introduction

In France, bringing an action for annulment has no suspensory effect on the contested decision. There are, however, several remedies that may be granted as interim relief.[251] They have been partly introduced by the law of 30 June 2000 concerning interim relief before the administrative courts (Loi relative au référé devant les juridictions administratives)[252] came into force. Prior to the coming into force of this law, the scope of interim relief available from the administrative courts was more limited and the existing procedures were inadequate, particularly where urgent intervention was required to prevent a violation of fundamental rights. Therefore, in these cases, claimants used to favour actions before the civil courts, which enjoyed the power to suspend administrative decisions.

Since 2000, several interim relief remedies have become available before the administrative courts. In respect of most of these remedies, urgency is an essential condition. The group of 'urgent' interim remedies includes three types of interim relief, the suspension (*référé-suspension*), the 'fundamental rights interim remedy' (*référé-liberté*) and the 'useful measure interim remedy' (*référé-mesure utile*). In addition to these 'urgent' interim remedies, the French interim relief judge is competent to take several other interim decisions of a mainly procedural nature. The different interim remedies and competences will be discussed in more depth below, after first introducing the competent judge.

Code de justice administrative **7.99 (FR)**

Article L511-1 The interim relief judge grants interim orders. He does not deal with the merits of the case and takes a decision as soon as possible.

[251] For an overview, see J Bell, 'Rapports: France: Interim Relief in French Administrative Court Procedure' (2001) 7 *European Public Law* 329.

[252] Loi n° 2000-597 du 30 juin 2000 relative au référé devant les juridictions administratives (JORF n° 151 du 1 juillet 2000, 9948).

Article L511-2 The Presidents of Administrative Courts of First Instance and Administrative Courts of Appeal act as interim relief judges.

Other judges who have at least two years' experience and have reached at least the grade of senior judge may also be appointed by the former to perform this role. If an appointee is absent or unable to act, these latter conditions may be waived.

With respect to disputes that fall within the competence of the Council of State, the President of the Litigation section acts as interim relief judge, as may the State Councillors that he appoints for that purpose.

Note

Interim relief measures are adopted by the president of the competent court, acting as 'interim relief judge' (*juge des référés*). The president does not rule on the merits of the case, but must decide whether specific orders need to be adopted in the relevant case. This decision is then adopted by means of an *ordonnance*. An *ordonnance* has no authority of res judicata. The judge who decides the main proceedings is not bound by the review exercised at the interim relief stage. However, the *ordonnance* is binding on the administrative authorities.

7.8.C.4 (ii) SUSPENSION

Code de justice administrative **7.100 (FR)**

Article L521-1 When an action for annulment or revision is lodged against an administrative decision, including a decision of rejection, the interim relief judge to whom the case has been referred may order the decision, or some of its effects, to be suspended or executed, when the urgent nature of the case justifies such a course of action and when a submission that is sufficient to create serious doubts regarding the legality of the decision, at the current stage of the proceedings, has been presented in evidence.

When the decision is suspended, the judge rules on the application to have the decision set aside or revised as soon as possible. The suspension will come to an end at the latest when the judge rules on the application to have the decision set aside or revised.

Notes

(1) Under Article L521-1 of the Code de justice administrative (Code of administrative justice), the applicant may ask for the suspension (*référé-suspension*) of an administrative decision in an action for annulment or, in the 'full jurisdiction remedy', an action for revision of the decision. The measure of suspension will be adopted by the administrative court if there is an urgent need to do so, and if there exists, in view of the evidence submitted by the applicant, a prima facie doubt of the legality of the challenged act.

(2) The decision of an administrative court of first instance is only subject to appeal on points of law (*cassation*)[253] before the Council of State.

[253] See further Chapter 8.

Conseil d'État, 19 January 2001[254] — 7.101 (FR)

Confédération nationale des radios libres
v Minister for Employment and Solidarity

INTERIM RELIEF; CONDITION OF URGENCY

Confédération nationale des radios libres

The assessment of the condition of urgency implies a balancing act of the interests at stake.

Facts: On 11 October 2000, the Minister for Employment and Solidarity adopted a decision (*arrêté*) which extended the operation of a collective agreement in the field of radio and broadcasting activities. The National Confederation of Independent Radio Stations lodged a claim for interim relief before the Council of State in order to ask for the suspension of the enforcement of the decision.

Held: The request was rejected as the condition of urgency was not met.

Judgment: Considering that it follows from these provisions ..., that the requirement of urgency, to which the ordering of a measure of suspension is subject, shall be regarded as fulfilled, when the contested administrative decision threatens in a sufficiently serious and immediate manner the public interest, the situation of the applicant or the interests it aims to defend; that this is so, even though this decision would have an object or repercussions which are purely financial and, in the event of annulment, its effects could be cleared by pecuniary reparation; that it is the task of the interim relief judge, ruling on a request for the suspension of such a decision, to assess in a concrete way, taking the submissions of the applicant into account, whether the effects of the decision on the situation of the applicant or, if applicable, of the persons concerned, are of a urgent nature justifying that the execution of the decision be suspended, without waiting for the judgment on the merits.

Note

The condition of urgency, which must be proven by the applicant, is met when the challenged decision has immediate and severe consequences on the public interest, on the individual's situation or on third parties' interests. This is the case, for example, when the refusal to grant a residence permit prevents the applicant from being with his children,[255] or where a regulatory decision has severe financial consequences on the income of a professional group.[256] Purely financial consequences may, in principle, justify the condition of urgency, provided that they are significant enough.[257] However, these disadvantages as such are not sufficient for ordering the suspension of a measure, but have to be balanced against other interests, particularly the general interest.

[254] N° 228815.
[255] Conseil d'État, 26 January 2011, *MA et Mme B*, N° 345352.
[256] Conseil d'État, 28 December 2010, *Fédération française des syndicats professionnels de pilote maritime*, N° 344754.
[257] Conseil d'État, 19 November 2010, *Benzoni*, N° 344286.

7.8.C.4 (iii) Fundamental Rights Interim Remedy

Code de justice administrative **7.102 (FR)**

Article L521-2 When dealing with an application of this type that is justified by the urgent nature of the case, the interim relief judge may order all measures required to safeguard a fundamental freedom that has been seriously infringed in a manner that is clearly unlawful by a legal person governed by public law or an organisation governed by private law with responsibility for the management of a public service in the exercise of its powers. The interim relief judge must issue a ruling within 48 hours.

Note

(1) The peculiarity of the 'fundamental rights interim remedy' (*référé-liberté*) is that the applicant can apply for it without having brought an action for annulment against the act which may affect his situation. It aims to protect the individual in cases of severe and manifest breaches of fundamental rights by the administration.

(2) Another specificity of this procedure is that the judge is required to decide on the question of interim relief within a very short time limit of 48 hours. The 'fundamental rights interim remedy' is very often requested to suspend administrative police measures, such as the prohibition of an event or demonstration. The *référé-liberté* is the only interim relief measure against which an appeal on points of fact and law (cassation) is possible. This appeal should be brought before the Conseil d'État within 2 weeks of the date of notification of interim measure at stake. The interim relief judge (*juge des référés*) of the Conseil d'État has to take a decision within 48 hours in such cases of appeal.[258]

(3) Since a fundamental freedom is at stake, the interim relief judge may adopt 'any necessary measure to protect' the freedom concerned, in order to stop the violation with immediate effect. In addition to suspension of the decision, these measures may include injunctions, such as an order to provide for housing for an individual within 24 hours or the order to return a passport.

Conseil d'État, 14 February 2014[259] **7.103 (FR)**

Mrs Rachel Lambert and others v University Hospital of Reims

FUNDAMENTAL RIGHTS INTERIM REMEDY; SCOPE

Lambert

The scope of the 'fundamental rights interim remedy' is not limited to constitutionalised rights.

Facts: Mr Vincent Lambert, born in 1976, was victim of a car accident in 2008, resulting in him being quadriplegic and in a state of complete dependence, and in need to be fed artificially. After several years and thorough

[258] Code de justice administrative, Art L523-1.
[259] N° 375081.

examination (in a public hospital), the doctors concluded that Mr Lambert was in a state of minimal consciousness but, nonetheless, was suffering from his state and from the treatment that was being administered to him. In light of the fact that Mr Lambert had previously given his consent to stop the treatments and with the agreement of a part of the family, the doctors eventually decided to stop any further treatment, including feeding him, pursuant to the Public Health Code (Code de la santé publique), which enables doctors to stop giving treatment when such treatment amounts to an unreasonable intervention that may leave the patient in a great deal of pain or with a serious disability. Other members of the family of Mr Lambert challenged that decision through a fundamental rights interim remedy (*référé-liberté*), which enables the judge to order any measure necessary to stop an infringement of a fundamental right. The case was eventually brought before the Conseil d'État.

Held: The Council of State decided to ask for an opinion of a medical expert.

Judgment: Considering that, under [Article L521-2], when an application is lodged to this end, the interim relief judge, upon the request of the applicant and in case of a specific urgency, has the power to order any measures necessary to safeguard a fundamental freedom allegedly breached in a serious and manifestly unlawful manner by an administrative authority; that these legislative provisions confer on the interim relief judge, who by principle acts alone and decides, in accordance with Article L511-1 of the Code of Administrative Justice, by measures of an interim nature, the power to order, without delay and on the basis of criteria of obviousness, the necessary measures to protect fundamental freedoms;

Considering, however, that the interim relief judge must exercise his powers in a particular way when hearing an application under Article L521-2 of the Code of Administrative Justice concerning a decision taken by a doctor on the basis of the Public Health Code (Code de la santé publique) which would lead to the cessation of or a failure to initiate treatment on grounds that this treatment would amount to an unreasonable intervention and the implementation of the decision would cause irreversible damage to life; that in such circumstances the judge, sitting where applicable as a member of a bench of judges, must take the necessary protective measures to prevent the decision in question from being implemented, when such measures may not be covered by one of the situations provided for by law, while striking a balance between the fundamental freedoms at issue, namely the right to respect for life and the patient's right to consent to medical treatment and not undergo treatment that amounts to an unreasonable intervention; that, in such a case, the interim relief judge or the bench to which he has referred the case may, as appropriate, after temporarily suspending the implementation of the measure and before ruling on the lodged application, order a medical expert report and, under Article R625-3 of the Code of Administrative Justice, seek the opinion of any person whose expertise or knowledge are able to usefully enlighten the court.

Note

(1) For a 'fundamental rights interim remedy' (*référé-liberté*) to be granted, four conditions must be fulfilled. First of all, the case should concern a breach of a fundamental right. The administrative judge is competent to define the material scope of Article L521-2 of the Code of Administrative Justice and to determine what qualifies as a fundamental right under Article L521-2.[260] While the courts generally consider

[260] L Favoreu, 'La notion de liberté fondamentale devant le juge administratif des référés', (2001) *Recueil Dalloz – Chronique* 1739.

this requirement to be fulfilled only if a fundamental right guaranteed by the French Constitution is at stake, in the *Lambert* case the Council of State ruled that a breach of the patient's right 'to consent to medical treatment' may meet the first condition for granting a 'fundamental right interim remedy' (*référé-liberté*), although this right is not expressly recognised as a constitutional freedom.

(2) The *Lambert* case also shows that in a sensitive case, involving the life of a human being, the interim relief judge has the power to order specific measures, such as requesting the opinion of a medical expert.[261]

Conseil d'État, 14 March 2011[262] **7.104 (FR)**

Commune de Galluis v Mr and Mrs A

INTERIM RELIEF; PRIMA FACIE ILLEGALITY

Commune de Galluis

A prima facie illegality may result from the manifest disproportionality of the measure.

Facts: On 4 February 2011, the mayor of Galluis ordered the placement of containers on the pavement of the city hall street, which was a public road. These containers prevented the circulation by car on this part of the street. The street was the only route of access to the home of Mr and Mrs A. Hence, they were deprived of the right to access their property by car. They brought an action for annulment (*recours pour excès de pouvoir*) before the Administrative Court of First Instance, seeking an order addressed to the mayor to remove the containers. The judge issued the interim order. The mayor, in the name of the city, appealed against this interim measure before the Council of State.

Held: The request of the city was rejected and the interim order was upheld.

Judgment: Considering that the free access of the residents to the public road is accessory to the right to property, which has the character of a fundamental liberty in the sense of Article L521-2 of the Code of Administrative Justice; that the deprivation of all access to the public road is liable to constitute a serious and manifestly illegal infringement of this liberty, capable of justifying the ruling, by the interim relief judge ruling on a claim regarding Article L521-2, on any measure necessary to protect this liberty;

Considering that it results from the investigation that the mayor of Galluis had, on 4 February 2011, placed containers in the street of the city hall, which had the character of a public road; that these containers were an obstacle, due to their weight, their volume, their placement and the width of the road, to the circulation of any motor vehicle on the part of the road on which they had been placed; that the street of the city hall gives access to the house of Mr and Mrs A, to which it constitutes, taking into account the configuration of the premises, the only access;

Considering, on the one hand, that the placement of these containers had the effect of preventing any motor vehicle from reaching the door of the house of Mr and Mrs A, thereby depriving them of the access from which they had benefited until then; that this

[261] See Chapter 5, section 5.4.C.2.
[262] N° 347345.

arrangement is not justified by the necessity of conservation of the public domain or the maintenance of the road; that if the municipality of Galluis invokes the provisions of the administrative decision (*arrêté*) of 3 October 2009 by which the mayor regulated the traffic and parking in this part of the street of the city hall in order to establish a pedestrian area there, it follows from the same stipulations of this administrative decision (*arrêté*) that it reserves for Mr and Mrs A the possibility to use the road to access their house; that, besides, if such an administrative decision (*arrêté*) can lawfully prohibit the parking and motor traffic on this road, such a measure cannot lawfully prohibit, in a general manner and under all circumstances, the access of vehicles to the house of the residents; that, thus, by installing, under the conditions present on the road, the containers in question on that public road, the mayor of Galluis has seriously and manifestly infringed the right to property;

Considering, on the other hand, that the deprivation, under the given circumstances, of all access of vehicles to their house constitutes, for Mr and Mrs A, a situation of urgency justifying that the interim relief judge makes use of the powers he holds under Article L521-2 of the Code of Administrative Justice; ...

Notes

(1) The second condition for granting a 'fundamental rights interim remedy' (*référé-liberté*) refers to prima facie illegality. The illegality of the decision concerned has to be evident, which is justified by the fact that, in an interim relief procedure, the court shall not rule on the merits of the case.[263] In the excerpt above, a general and absolute ban of all traffic in a public road, preventing people from accessing their home, was held to constitute a clear and disproportionate breach of their property right.

(2) The third condition is that the breach should be severe. The applicant must not only establish that a fundamental freedom is affected, but also that the violation is particularly serious. The judge then has to assess the concrete effects of the measure and the behaviour of the administration in the particular situation of the individual, and balance the individual interest with other interests. Exceptionally, some administrative decisions are presumed, de facto and de jure, to constitute a severe violation of a fundamental freedom, such as a decision on deportation from the French territory,[264] or a decision prohibiting migrants access to French territory and preventing them from claiming asylum protection.[265]

(3) Finally, the fourth condition relates to the urgency of the case. Although this condition also applies to the suspension remedy (*référé-suspension*), discussed above, the condition is assessed more restrictively in 'fundamental rights interim remedy' (*référé-liberté*) cases. The judge requires 'particular circumstances' in such cases.[266]

[263] J Schmitz, 'Le juge du référé-liberté à la croisée des contentieux de l'urgence et du fond' [2014] *Revue Française de Droit Administratif* 502.

[264] Conseil d'État, 30 October 2001, *Tliba*, N° 238211.

[265] Conseil d'État, 19 November 2010, *Ministère de l'Intérieur*, N° 344286.

[266] Conseil d'État, 6 June 2006, *Koubi*, N° 293935.

For example, it may be urgent to suspend the refusal of a hospital to admit an individual in detention since his medical condition is incompatible with his imprisonment, but not so urgent that the judge would have to rule within 48 hours.[267]

7.8.C.4 (iv) USEFUL MEASURE INTERIM REMEDY

Code de justice administrative **7.105 (FR)**

Article L521-3 When a case is urgent, the interim relief judge may order all useful measures without interfering with the execution of any administrative decision, on the basis of an application that will be admissible even if no administrative decision has already been taken.

Notes

(1) Article L521-3 provides for the 'useful measure interim remedy' (*référé-mesures utiles*), which empowers the judge to adopt 'all useful measures' with regard to the individual's situation. A procedural specificity is that this remedy can be sought even if the applicant has not lodged an action for annulment against the administrative decision which might have a negative effect on the applicant's situation.

(2) One of the requirements for granting a 'useful measure interim remedy' by the judge is that of urgency, which is fulfilled if the individual would be exposed to severe damage or a specific threat. In addition, the required measure should be useful, meaning that it should be a useful remedy for the needs of the individual, and that no other legal remedy would achieve such a result. There is no requirement of prima facie illegality, since the claim for such measures does not aim to prevent the enforcement of the challenged decision.

(3) The administrative judge can order a number of different measures, but cannot order the suspension of the act. Furthermore, the measure should not impair the enforcement of an administrative decision. For example, the applicant cannot ask the administrative judge to order the administrative authority to grant it access to a suitable room to celebrate a religious festivity after the administrative authority has implicitly rejected the applicant's request.[268] The administrative court can instead issue an injunction directed against individuals to, for example, leave public property, including highways, or an injunction to submit documents or to perform specific public works,[269] sometimes under threat of a penalty. The measures ordered must remain provisional.

7.8.C.4 (v) OTHER INTERIM MEASURES

Code de justice administrative **7.106 (FR)**

Article R531-1 If nothing more than a statement of findings of fact is requested, the interim relief judge may, on the basis of an application that may be submitted without

[267] Conseil d'État, 9 March 2007, *Guiot*, N° 302182.
[268] Conseil d'État, 29 December 2006, *Association culturelle musulmane de St-Nazaire*, N° 297992.
[269] Conseil d'État, 18 July 2006, *Elissondo Labat*, N° 283474.

the intervention of a lawyer, appoint an expert to promptly prepare a report on the facts that might give rise to a dispute before the court, even if no administrative decision has yet been taken. The potential respondents are informed of this immediately. ...

Article R532-1 The interim relief judge may, on the basis of an ordinary application and even if no administrative decision has yet been made, order any expert examination or preparatory measure that would prove useful.

He may, more particularly, appoint an expert to prepare, when public works are carried out, all reports relating to the state of buildings that are likely to be affected by the works and to the causes and extent of any damage that occurs during his assignment.

Applications made in accordance with this chapter do not require the intervention of a lawyer if they are linked to disputes that do not require the intervention of such a person.

Article R541-1 Even if no application has been made on the merits, the interim relief judge may grant an advance payment to a creditor that has referred his case to the authority, when the existence of the obligation is not seriously in doubt ....

Note

There are three other interim measures, which are distinct from the ones discussed previously because they are not conditional upon the requirement of urgency.

— Under Article R531-1 of the Code de justice administrative, an applicant can ask the court to appoint an expert to prepare a report on a specific situation, which may be useful in a future dispute (for instance on the state of a road).
— Under Article R532-1 of the Code de justice administrative, an individual may ask the judge to order any expert examination or preparatory measure that would prove useful (for example to assess damage).
— Finally, under Article R541-1 of the Code de justice administrative, an applicant can claim for the advance payment of an amount of money, which, according to the applicant, is due to him from the administrative authority. The administrative judge will only grant such a remedy if it is evident that the administrative authority has a debt towards the individual.

7.8.D COMPARATIVE REMARKS

Proceedings for interim relief are present in all the studied legal systems. The most striking difference is between Germany, which applies a system of automatic suspensory effect to decisions challenged in objection procedures and actions for annulment, although there are several exceptions to this rule, and the other legal systems, in which actions in court and objection procedures have no suspensory effect.

However, despite these differences, one can observe a clear convergence between the legal systems, partly under the influence of EU law. The *Factortame* case of the Court of Justice forced England and Wales to set aside the rule of common law, according to which the courts could not grant an injunction against the Crown. On the other hand, since 1997, Germany has introduced a number of exceptions to the rule of automatic suspensory effect, leading to the situation that in Germany individuals have to request for interim relief on a more frequent basis.

The importance of having rules concerning interim relief, preventing administrative decisions from having irreversible effects while an action is pending in the main proceedings, is recognised in every legal order. These rules ensure the effectiveness of judicial protection and prevent a situation where the court's judgment in the main proceedings may be useless for the applicant.

Interim measures are temporary by definition. The most common interim measure, available in every legal order, is the suspension of the contested administrative act. In addition, all legal systems provide for the potential to order interim injunctions or positive interim measures. In the EU, a request for interim relief is only possible if the applicant has filed a claim for judicial review. Other legal systems, such as those of Germany and England and Wales, offer the opportunity to file such a request independently of the main proceedings. This is also the case for the French fundamental rights interim remedy (*référé-liberté*), which may be requested without the commencement of a direct action for annulment against the decision concerned.

In all the legal systems studied, the requirements for granting a request for interim relief are quite similar. A common condition is the requirement of urgency, which is only met if the enforcement of the decision challenged would have severe or irreparable consequences for the applicant. The second common condition is that the decision contested should be prima facie unlawful. This condition stresses the fact that the review of the interim relief judge is different from the one exercised in the main proceedings. The interim relief judge does not rule on the merits of the case and the interim measure should not have the effect that the case is already definitively decided. Finally, an interim measure always requires the weighing of the interest of the applicant on one side and general interest and the interests of possible third parties on the other.

A special feature of the Dutch rules on interim relief is the so-called 'shortcutting' (*kortsluiten*) according to Article 8:86 AWB. If a hearing has taken place and the judge then considers that further inquiry cannot reasonably be expected to contribute to the assessment of the case in the main proceedings, he can immediately give a judgment in the main proceedings. Shortcutting is a very efficient instrument.

FURTHER READING

Eliantonio, M, *Europeanisation of Administrative Justice? The Influence of the ECJ's Case Law in Italy, Germany and England* (Groningen, Europa Law Publishing, 2009).

Galetta, D-U, *Procedural Autonomy of EU Member States: Paradise Lost?* (Berlin, Springer, 2010).

Grashof, F, *National Procedural Autonomy Revisited* (Groningen, Europa Law Publishing, 2016).

Ortlep, R and Widdershoven, RJGM, 'Judicial Protection' in JH Jans, S Prechal and RJGM Widdershoven (eds), *Europeanisation of Public Law*, 2nd edn (Groningen, Europa Law Publishing, 2015) 333–434.

CHAPTER 8
APPELLATE PROCEEDINGS

Rob Widdershoven

8.1 INTRODUCTION

This chapter will examine the appellate proceedings against the judgments of lower courts in administrative matters. The aspects of these proceedings which are regulated in a similar way as in first instance proceedings are not included, as they are discussed in other chapters.

In this chapter, appellate proceedings are mainly examined against the background of their possible functions. These functions are:[1]

— *The second chance function:* if this function is prevalent, the parties are permitted to repair mistakes committed in lower instance and bring forward new legal grounds and factual evidence which could have been, but were not, brought in lower instance.
— *Control or discipline function:* if this function is prevalent, the appellate proceedings is, as a matter of principle, directed to the judgment of the lower court (and not to the decision contested in lower instance) and the parties should in principle raise defects in this judgment. Moreover, the possibility for the parties to bring forward new grounds or evidence might be limited, as these grounds were not assessed by the lower court of first instance.

[1] For these functions, compare RJGM Widdershoven et al, *Hoger Beroep. Algemeen bestuursrecht 2001* (The Hague, Boom Juridisch, 2001) 20–27 (with a summary in English); M Schreuder-Vlasblom, *Rechtsbescherming en bestuurlijke voorprocedure*, 6th edn (Deventer, Kluwer, 2017) 1178–1232.

— *Guarantee legal unity and a uniform interpretation of the law:* if this function is prevalent, appellate proceedings are in principle limited to grounds of law only, and, in principle, it is not possible to raise new legal grounds. Furthermore, to facilitate this function, the access to appellate proceedings might be limited by a permission to appeal system or by other means.

These functions do not exclude each other per se. In fact, most appellate proceedings are, to a certain extent, a compromise between them. Nevertheless, several peculiarities of appellate proceedings, which are different in some jurisdictions, may depend on and can be explained by the importance that is attached to the prevalent function(s).

This is apparent in section 8.2, which not only provides an overview of the structure of appellate proceedings in the different jurisdictions, but also discusses, partly in the light of their main function(s), the scope of and standards for review in the different appellate proceedings. Access to appellate proceedings is discussed in section 8.3, and in particular the possible limitation of such access by means of a permission to appeal procedure. Section 8.4 examines some procedural aspects of appellate proceedings, with a focus on the possibility for the parties to raise new legal grounds and to introduce new factual evidence in these proceedings. In section 8.5, the remedies in appeal are examined. The comparative overview in section 8.6 returns to the functions of appellate proceedings in more general terms.

8.2 STRUCTURE, SCOPE AND EXCEPTIONS

All jurisdictions examined provide for the potential to commence appellate proceedings against judgments delivered by the lower courts to one or more higher court(s) in the hierarchy. How many layers of appellate courts exist varies between jurisdictions, with some with a single layer of appeal (the EU, the Netherlands) and others with two layers of appeal (Germany, England and Wales, France). This distinction structures this section. The scope of and standard for review in the different appellate proceedings, and thus the grounds to be raised by the parties, range from a full review of the lower judgment both in law and fact, to a review in law in general and a review on particular legal rules. Finally, in all the jurisdictions studied, with the exception of the EU, there are deviations from the general rule that administrative action can be contested in at least two instances, either because the possibility to commence appellate proceedings against a lower court's judgment is excluded or because some actions may be contested before a higher court in first and final instance only.

8.2.A SINGLE LAYER OF APPELLATE PROCEEDINGS: THE EUROPEAN UNION AND THE NETHERLANDS

8.2.A.1 THE EUROPEAN UNION

Treaty on the Functioning of the European Union **8.1 (EU)**

Article 256 (1) The General Court shall have jurisdiction to hear and determine at first instance actions or proceedings referred to in Articles 263, 265, 268, 270 and 272 ....

Decisions given by the General Court under this paragraph may be subject to a right of appeal to the Court of Justice on points of law only, under the conditions and within the limits laid down by the Statute.

Statute of the Court of Justice of the European Union **8.2 (EU)**

Article 58 An appeal to the Court of Justice shall be limited to points of law. It shall lie on the grounds of lack of competence of the General Court, a breach of procedure before it which adversely affects the interests of the appellant as well as the infringement of Union by the General Court. ....

Case C-53/92 P, 2 March 1994[2] **8.3 (EU)**

Hilti AG v Commission

APPEAL; ASSESSMENT OF EVIDENCE

Hilti

A distortion of evidence by the General Court constitutes a point of law reviewable on appeal by the Court of Justice.

Facts: Hilti manufactured a range of products used for fastening materials in place: nail guns, cartridge strips, cartridges and nails. Hilti brought an action for annulment against a Commission decision which held that Hilti had committed an abuse of its dominant position, in the meaning of (now) Article 102 of the Treaty on the Functioning of the European Union (TFEU). In particular, Hilti claimed that the Commission had wrongly defined the market, which is a necessary element in the assessment of dominance. The Court of First Instance dismissed the claim. On appeal, Hilti claimed, amongst others, that the CFI had wrongly appraised a survey, an opinion and econometric analyses which provided evidence for the determination of the relevant market.

Held: The Court dismissed the argument and the appeal.

Judgment: 42. It should be pointed out that the appraisal by the Court of First Instance of the evidence put before it does not constitute (save where the clear sense of that evidence has been distorted) a point of law which is subject, as such, to review by the Court of Justice.

43. Since Hilti challenges the appraisal by the Court of First Instance of certain evidence submitted to it but does not establish, or even, indeed, claim that the Court of First Instance distorted the clear sense of that evidence, its sixth plea is inadmissible and, for that reason, must be rejected.

Notes

(1) Every judgment delivered by the General Court (the former Court of First Instance) is subject to a right of appeal to the Court of Justice. In practice, most appellate proceedings are concerned with decisions of the General Court in actions

[2] ECLI:EU:C:1994:77.

for annulment under Article 263 TFEU, actions for failure to act under Article 265 TFEU and disputes relating to compensation for damages under Article 268 TFEU.

(2) Appellate proceedings before the Court of Justice are limited to questions of law. This limitation clearly serves the legal unity function. The Court of Justice has no jurisdiction to conduct findings of the fact, to order measures of inquiry or to assign experts.[3] The parties arc not entitled to contest the factual findings of the General Court, or to offer to adduce evidence of facts which were not found by the General Court.[4] However, as is ruled in, inter alia, the case of *Hilti*, distinguishing points of law from points of fact is not always that clear. From the case, it seems that in circumstances where the General Court distorted the clear sense of some evidence and, as a result, made a manifestly incorrect finding of facts, this may raise a point of law which is reviewable in appeal by the Court of Justice.

(3) According to Article 58 of the Statute of the Court of Justice, an appeal must be based on (a) pleas alleging a lack of competence of the General Court, (b) a breach of procedure by the General Court which adversely affects the interests of the claimant or (c) an infringement of EU law by the General Court. Possible breaches of procedure are infringements of the right to a fair hearing within a reasonable time,[5] of the right to submit a document necessary for the outcome of the case[6] or of the right to have the oral hearing reopened.[7] The general clause 'infringement of EU law' covers every infringement of EU law, whether primary or secondary law, or a general principle of EU law. From the grounds of appeal, it is apparent that appellate proceedings before the Court of Justice are directed to the first instance judgment, and also serve the control function.

8.2.A.2 THE NETHERLANDS

Algemene Wet Bestuursrecht **8.4 (NL)**

Article 8:104 (1) A party concerned and the administrative authority are entitled to lodge an appeal against:

a. a judgment of the district court within the meaning of Article 8:66(1) or Article 8:67(2),

b. a judgment of the interim relief judge of the district court within the meaning of Article 8:86(1),

c. a judgment of the district court on a request within the meaning of Article 8:88(1).

(2) No appeal can be lodged against:

a. a judgment of the district court adopted following application of Article 8:54(1).

…

c. a judgment of the district court within the meaning of Article 8:55(7).

[3] See further on these instruments, Chapter 5, section 5.3.A.3.
[4] Case C-320/92 P *Finsider v Commission* ECLI:EU:C:1994:414.
[5] Case C-185/95 P *Baustahlgewebe v Commission* ECLI:EU:C:1998:608, para 26.
[6] Case C-119/97 P *Ufex v Commission* ECLI:EU:C:1999:116, para 110.
[7] Case C-199/92 P *Huels v Commission* ECLI:EU:C:1999:358, para 94.

d. a judgment of the interim relief judge within the meaning of Article 8:84(1).

...

Article 8:105 An appeal can be lodged before the Judicial Division of the Council of State unless, pursuant to Chapter 4 of the Specification of Jurisdiction of Administrative Courts or another legal provision, another appellate court is competent.

Notes

(1) As a rule, a party concerned and the administrative authority are entitled to appeal final judgments of the first instance district courts before an appellate court.[8] According to Article 8:104(1) AWB, this right of appeal exists against a judgment based on Article 8:66 AWB (the regular judgment in first instance), a definite judgment of an interim relief judge based on Article 8:86 AWB (the so-called 'shortcutting' procedure[9]) and a judgment on a request for financial compensation based on Article 8:95 AWB.

(2) The most important appellate court is the Judicial Division of the Council of State (Afdeling bestuursrechtspraak van de Raad van State). It is competent by default, unless another appellate court is declared competent in the Specification of Jurisdiction of Administrative Courts (Bevoegdheidsregeling bestuursrechtspraak), an annex to the Algemene Wet Bestuursrecht (General Adminstrative Law Act). The other appellate courts are:

— the Central Appellate Court (Centrale Raad van Beroep), which is competent in social security and civil service matters.
— the High Administrative Court for Trade and Industry (College van Beroep voor het Bedrijfsleven), which is competent in matters of economic law, such as competition and telecommunications.
— the ordinary courts of appeal (*gerechtshoven*) and, in cassation, the Supreme Court (Hoge Raad), which are competent in tax matters. The appeal to the Supreme Court is on ground of law only (*cassatie*).

With the exception of appeal to the Supreme Court (in tax matters), the scope of appeal of the appellate courts is not limited; they may review both points of law and points of fact. The intensity of the judicial scrutiny of the appellate grounds is the same as in first instance. The Judicial Division of the Council of State, the Central Appellate Court and the High Administrative Court for Trade and Industry are within their competences courts in final instance, and should therefore guarantee legal unity as well.[10]

[8] See further R Seerden and D Wenders, 'Administrative Law in the Netherlands' in R Seerden (ed), *Comparative Administrative Law*, 4th edn (Antwerp, Intersentia, 2017) 173 ff.

[9] For details, see Chapter 7, section 7.8.C.3.

[10] How this function is reconciled with the second chance and control functions is discussed in more detail in section 8.4 below.

(3) There is no hierarchical relationship between the different appellate courts. Legal unity between them is enhanced by two instruments. The first is by means of consultations in the Committee Legal Unity (Commissie Rechtseenheid). This committee has been set by the appellate courts, and representatives of all appellate courts have been appointed to it. It has no legal basis. If the representatives in the committee agree on a certain line of case law, this line is generally applied by the appellate courts in their case law on a voluntary basis, sometimes through explicit reference to the case law of one or more other appellate courts. This instrument is applied to achieve legal unity in rather technical, procedural matters. The second instrument is the possibility for every appellate court to refer a case, in the interest of 'legal unity and legal development', to a so-called Grand Chamber (Grote Kamer, see Article 8:10a of the Algemene Wet Bestuursrecht (AWB)). A Grand Chamber consists of five judges, some of which have their main function in another appellate court. To make this possible, several judges of every appellate court are assigned as an honorary judge to the other appellate court (personal union). In cases referred to a Grand Chamber, generally an opinion is delivered by an Advocate General.[11]

Algemene Wet Bestuursrecht **8.5 (NL)**

Article 8:104 (2) No appeal can be lodged against:

a. a judgment of the district court adopted following application of Article 8:54(1).

...

c. a judgment of the district court within the meaning of Article 8:55(7).

d. a judgment of the interim relief judge within the meaning of Article 8:84(1).

...

Notes

(1) Some judgments of the district courts have been explicitly excluded from appeal in Article 104(2) AWB. Most important are judgments in a procedure for interim relief (Article 8:104(2)(c)) and judgments in summary proceedings, where no oral hearing has been held because the appeal was manifestly inadmissible, unfounded or well founded (Article 8:104(2)(a) AWB).[12] Against the latter judgments, a rehearing (*verzet*) before the district court itself is possible. Judgments in the rehearing procedure cannot be further appealed before a higher court (Article 8:104(2)(b) AWB).

(2) In some cases in particular, the Judicial Division of the Council of State and the High Administrative Court for Trade and Industry act as a court in first and last instance. The decisions concerned are mentioned in Annex b, Chapter 2 of the Specification of Jurisdiction of Administrative Courts (Bevoegdheidsregeling bestuursrechtspraak), attached to the Algemene Wet Bestuursrecht (General Administrative Law Act). According to the Annex, the Judicial Division of the Council of State is,

[11] For more details about the Grand Chamber and the Advocate-General, see Chapter 2, section 2.2.A.3.
[12] See for more details about this summary procedure, Chapter 5, section 5.2.A.1.(iii).

for example, competent in first and last instance in appeal procedures against several decisions in the area of environmental and planning law and decisions on the basis of the Election Act (Kieswet). The High Administrative Court for Trade and Industry is competent in first and last instance in appeal procedures against, for example, specific decisions on the basis of the Electricity Act (Electriciteitswet), the Gas Act (Gaswet), the Telecommunications Act (Telecommunicatiewet) and the Financial Supervision Act (Wet Financieel Toezicht).

8.2.B TWO LAYERS OF APPELLATE PROCEEDINGS: GERMANY, FRANCE AND ENGLAND AND WALES

8.2.B.1 GERMANY

Verwaltungsgerichtsordnung **8.6 (DE)**

§124 (1) The parties involved shall be entitled to an appeal on points of fact and law (*Berufung*) against final judgments, including the partial judgments in accordance with §110, and against interim judgments in accordance with §109 and 111, if such appeal is admitted by the Administrative Court of First Instance or the Higher Administrative Court.

§128 The Higher Administrative Court shall review the dispute within the application for appeal on points of fact and law (*Berufung*) to the same degree as the Administrative court of First Instance. It shall also consider newly submitted facts and evidence.

§132 (1) Those concerned shall have recourse to an appeal on points of law (*Revision*) to the Federal Administrative Court against the judgments of the Higher Administrative Court (§49 no 1), and against orders (*Beschlüsse*) in accordance with §47(5), first sentence, if the Higher Administrative Court, or the Federal Administrative Court in response to a complaint against non-admission, has admitted it.

§137 (1) The appeal on points of law may only be based on the challenged judgment being based on a violation

1. of federal law, or
2. of a provision of the Administrative Procedure Act (Verwaltungsverfahrensgesetz) of a state (*Land*), the wording of which is corresponds with the Administrative Procedure Act (Verwaltungsverfahrensgesetz) of the Federation.

Notes

(1) In German general administrative law, appellate proceedings consist of two layers: first, an appeal on points of fact and law (*Berufung*) to a Higher Administrative Court (Oberverwaltungsgericht), then an appeal on points of law only (*Revision*) to the Federal Administrative Court (Bundesverwaltungsgericht). In both instances, access to appeal is limited by means of a leave for appeal system.[13] The appellate

[13] See section 8.3 below.

form *Berufung* is concerned with both facts and law. A *Berufung* is well founded if the judgment of the first instance court violates the law and thereby violates the rights of the appellant. The points of law to be raised and assessed are not limited in any way. The intensity of the judicial scrutiny is the same as in first instance. As will be detailed below in section 8.4, the primary function of *Berufung* is the second chance function, although the control function also plays a minor role. Appeal on points of law (*Revision*) can only be based on the ground that the contested judgment is based on a violation of a federal law or of a provision of the administrative procedure act of a state, which is in conformity with the Verwaltungsverfahrensgesetz (Administrative Procedure Act) of the Federation (§137 of the Verwaltungsgerichtsordnung (VwGO)). The main function of *Revision* is clearly to guarantee legal unity at the federal level.

(2) Sometimes the Higher Administrative Court acts as a first instance court, for example against some decisions based on the Baugesetzbuch (Federal Building Code), decisions based on regulatory laws (such as the Energiewirtschaftsgesetz (Energy Act)) and bans on organisations which are imposed by the highest state authority. Appeal against such judgments of the Higher Administrative Courts on points of law (*Revision*) is possible to the Federal Administrative Court. Furthermore, the Federal Administrative Court is a court of first and last instance (on points of fact and law), for example, in non-constitutional disputes between the federal states or between the federation and those states, and in actions against the federal government in matters of the Federal Intelligence Service and diplomatic and consular affairs (§50 VwGO).

(3) In Germany, there are two specialised judicial branches which may be labelled 'administrative', in the areas of social security and taxes.[14] In the former branch, the appeal is two-layered, with the possibility of appeal on points of fact and law (*Berufung*) before the Higher Social Courts (Landessozialgerichte) and the possibility of appeal on points of law (*Revision*) before the Federal Social Court (Bundessozialgericht). In tax matters, the appellate proceedings are single-layered, namely appeal on the ground of law only (*Revision*) before the Federal Fiscal Court (Bundesfinanzhof). At federal level, two other courts exist: the Federal Court of Justice (Bundesgerichthof), competent in civil and criminal matters, and the Federal Labour Court (Bundesarbeitsgericht). To enhance legal unity between all federal courts, the German system provides for the so-called Joint Senate of the Highest Courts of the Federation (Gemeinsamer Senat der Obersten Bundesgerichte, Article 95 of the Grundgesetz).[15] If a federal court wants to deviate from a judgment of another federal court or of the Joint Senate itself, it should in principle refer the matter to the Joint Senate. The Joint Senate consists of the presidents of the five federal courts, together with the president and a member of the chambers involved in the difference of opinion.

[14] See Chapter 2, section 2.6.C.
[15] For details, see Chapter 2, section 2.5.B.1c.

8.2.B.2 FRANCE

Code de justice administrative **8.7 (FR)**

Article L211-2 The Administrative Courts of Appeal hear cases adjudicated in first instance by the Administrative Courts of First Instance, subject to the powers awarded to the Council of State (Conseil d'État) in its capacity as an appeal court and those stipulated in Articles L552-1 and L552-2.

Article L821-1 The rulings issued by the Administrative Courts of Appeal and, in general, all the decisions issued in last resort by the administrative courts can be brought before the Council of State (Conseil d'État) by way of cassation proceedings.

Article L111-1 The Council of State is the highest administrative court. It rules, without further possibility of appeal, on appeals on points of law (*cassation*) lodged against judgments rendered at the last instance by the various administrative courts and on cases of which it is seized as a court of first instance or as an appeal court.

Conseil d'État, 7 February 1947[16] **8.8 (FR)**

D'Aillières v Jury d'honneur

RIGHT TO APPEAL ON POINTS OF LAW

D'Aillières

Even where the law excludes judicial review, there is always a right to appeal on a point of law before the Council of State.

Facts: Mr X, a former member of parliament, was declared ineligible by an ordinance (*ordonnance*) of 21 April 1944, whose purpose was to declare ineligible any person who had an elective function during the Occupation period and who was regarded as being involved with the German occupant or the Vichy regime. He requested, before the *jury d'honneur*, the body competent for appeals against such decisions, to be declared eligible. The jury refused to declare Mr X eligible. The claimant subsequently challenged the decision of the *jury d'honneur* before the Council of State, although the relevant legislation provided that the decisions of this body could not be reviewed.

Held: The jury's decision was annulled.

Judgment: Considering that it results from the set of legislative provisions related to the *jury d'honneur* and notably those which concern both its composition and its powers and the judicial review of which it can be seized, that this body has the character of a court which, by nature of the cases on which it rules, belongs to the administrative order and falls in this regard within the scope of the review of the Council of State (*Conseil d'État*) in its litigation jurisdiction;

Considering that, according to the 3rd indent of Article 18*bis*, added to the ordinance of 21 April 1944 by the ordinance of 6 April 1945, which was in force when the request was introduced and of which the later modification by the ordinance of 13 September 1945 has had neither the goal, nor the effect, to change on this point the meaning,

[16] N° 79128.

'no further appeal shall be admitted' against the decision of the *jury d'honneur*; but considering that the expression which has been used by the legislator cannot be interpreted, in the absence of a contrary intention, clearly specified by the authors of this provision, as excluding cassation proceedings before the Council of State.

Notes

(1) As a rule, appeal on points of fact and law (*appel*) is possible to one of the eight Administrative Courts of Appeal (court administrative d'appel)[17] from the Administrative Courts of First Instance (tribunaux administratifs). Judgments of an Administrative Court of Appeal can be challenged before the Council of State (Conseil d'État) on matters of law only (*cassation*). In some areas of law, such as social welfare and refugee law, there are specialised administrative courts of first instance.[18] Judgments of these specialised courts can be challenged before the Council of State on matters of law only (*cassation*). The Council of State is the highest administrative court in France, and oversees all of the other administrative courts. Its main function is to guarantee legal unity.

(2) The review in appeal on points of fact and law (*appel*) is concerned with both points of fact and points of law. The points of law to be raised and assessed are not limited in any way. The intensity of the judicial scrutiny is the same as in first instance. The main function of appeal on points of fact and law (*appel*) is the second chance function, although the control function also plays a role.[19] Appeal to an Administrative Court of Appeal is not a right, but exists only if the law provides for one. Therefore, it is possible for the legislature to bypass the appellate procedure to the courts of appeal and to determine that judgments of a first instance court cannot be contested before an Administrative Court of Appeal, but only before the Council of State (on points of law).[20] This is the case, for example, in respect of decisions concerning local elections and driving licences. In some disputes, the Council of State is the first and last instance court, for example, against decrees of the Prime Minister and the President of the Republic, and against some important actions of regulatory bodies, for example, in the fields of energy and telecommunications.[21]

(3) Appeal on points of law is a matter of right. This statement is clearly supported by the case of *D'Aillières*. In this case, although the law excluded review ('the decision shall not be subjected to review'), the Council of State held that the expression used by parliament could not be interpreted, in the absence of a clearly articulated intention by the writers of the provision, so as to exclude review on a point of law to the Council of State.

[17] In French law, the word *appel* (appeal) had a precise meaning: it means a new trail where the questions of law and fact raised at first instance may be discussed again. Contrary to this, *cassation* means, in principle, that only points of law are reviewed.

[18] See further, Chapter 2, section 2.6.D.

[19] See section 8.4 below.

[20] See Art R811-1 of the Code de justice administrative (Code of Administrative Justice).

[21] For a list of cases heard in first and last instance by the Council of State, see Art R311-1 of the Code de justice administrative (Code of Administrative Justice).

8.2.B.3 ENGLAND AND WALES

Senior Courts Act 1981 **8.9 (EW)**

Section 16 (1) Subject as otherwise provided by this or any other Act ... the Court of Appeal shall have jurisdiction to hear and determine appeals from any judgment or order of the High Court.

Civil Procedure Rules **8.10 (EW)**

Rule 52.11 (3) The appeal court will allow an appeal where the decision of the lower court was

(a) wrong; or

(b) unjust because of a serious procedural or other irregularity in the proceedings in the lower court.

Constitutional Reform Act 2005 **8.11 (EW)**

Section 40 (1) The Supreme Court is a superior court of record.

(2) An appeal lies to the Court from any order or judgment of the Court of Appeal in England and Wales in civil proceedings.

Notes

(1) From the first instance High Court (Queen's Bench Division), appeal is generally possible to the Civil Division of the Court of Appeal. Judgments of the Court of Appeal can be challenged before the Supreme Court (formerly the House of Lords). The appeal to both the Court of Appeal and the Supreme Court is limited by a permission to appeal system.[22] When a decision can be contested before the First-Tier Tribunal,[23] the judgments of the tribunal can, after obtaining permission from the First-Tier Tribunal or the Upper Tribunal, be challenged before the Upper Tribunal. The appeal to the Upper Tribunal is generally limited to points of law and is not concerned with points of fact. Judgments of the Upper Tribunal can, if permitted by the Upper Tribunal or the Court of Appeal, be contested before the Court of Appeal (and further to the Supreme Court).

(2) The statutory standard in appellate proceedings before both appellate courts is the same, namely whether the decision of the lower court was either 'wrong' or 'unjust because of a serious procedural or other irregularity in the proceedings in the lower court' (Rule 52.11(3) of the Civil Procedure Rules (CPR)). The broad scope of the 'wrong' standard offers the possibility for the appellate courts to fully review both points of law and points of fact, and to overturn the factual findings of the lower court. However, in practice, the appellate courts generally leave findings of fact made by lower courts in place, because the Court of Appeal and Supreme Court do not usually

[22] See section 8.3 below.

[23] For more information about the English tribunal system, see Chapter 2, section 2.5.B.1 (iii).

hear witnesses and do not generally permit the introduction of new evidence. This rule is not absolute, but is generally adhered to.[24] Therefore, appellate proceedings are usually concerned with points of law only. The appellate courts enjoy a very broad jurisdiction to address appeals over points of law. From the foregoing, it seems that the appeal before both appellate courts serves all three functions of appeal (second chance, control, legal unity), but that the second chance function is limited in respect of the facts.[25]

Court of Appeal (Civil Division), 30 January 2004[26] **8.12 (EW)**

R (Aru) v Chief Constable of Merseyside

COURT OF APPEAL; JURISDICTION

Aru

The court of appeal is not competent to hear cases relating to a 'criminal cause or matter'.

Facts: Aru was given an official caution by the police, rather than facing prosecution for offences under section 5 of the Public Order Act 1986. Aru challenged the issue of the official caution by means of judicial review and the High Court rejected the claim, preferring the evidence offered by the police against that of Aru. Aru sought to appeal to the Court of Appeal.

Held: The subject matter of this case was held to relate to a 'criminal cause or matter' and was thus excluded from the appellate jurisdiction of the Court of Appeal by section 18(1) of the Senior Courts Act 1981.

Judgment: Maurice Kay LJ: 10. How then do these authorities assist in the taxonomy of the present case? First, it is important to keep in mind that the words used in section 18 of the 1981 Act are 'criminal cause or matters' and not, say, 'criminal proceedings'. The words 'or matter' denote a wider ambit. Secondly, although the administering of the caution put an end to the risk of prosecution and conviction in the Magistrates Court, I find it impossible to escape the conclusion that it was simply another way of disposing of a 'criminal matter'. On the face of it, and as found by Elias J [High Court judge in first instance], Mr. Aru was accepting his criminality and agreeing to be cautioned as an alternative to possible prosecution and conviction. Thirdly, it is necessary to have regard to the inherent and consequences of a caution, As Schieman LJ said in *R v Commissioner of Police of the Metropolis ex parte Thompson* [1997] 1 WLR 1519 (at page 1520):

'It is a method of disposal of criminal cases outside court which is more severe in possible consequences than a warning but usually less severe in its outcome than a successful prosecution.

A formal caution is not something to be regarded lightly. Records are kept of the administering of cautions. The Home Secretary has power to direct over what period of time records should be retained …

We understand … that in practice a record of caution will be kept for a minimum of three years. Such a caution, while carrying no immediate disagreeable consequences for

[24] *Powell v Streatham Manor Nursing Home* [1935] AC 243 (HL); *Higgins v J & CM Smith (Whiteinch) Ltd* [1990] SC (HL) 63; *Piglowska v Piglowski* [1999] 3 All ER 632 (HL). See also CPR, Rule 52.11(2).

[25] For further explanation, see section 8.4 below.

[26] [2004] EWCA Civ 199, [2004] 1 WLR 1697.

the recipient, has potential adverse consequences for him should he be accused of offending on a future occasion. He is more likely to be prosecuted for that offence and he will not be able to claim a good character before the trial court. If convicted, the existence of a prior formal caution may affect his sentence. ...'

This is to be contrasted with proceedings such as those relating to an application for an anti-social behaviour order which are civil because no criminal offence need to be established, no conviction or condemnation as guilty of an offence is implied, no penalty ensues (unless and until there is a subsequent breach) and the order does not go on the person's criminal record. For these reasons such order were classified by the House of Lords in *Clingham v Royal Borough of Kensington and Chelsea* [2002] UKHL 39 as not relating to a criminal cause or matter. They are civil, their purpose is preventive and they are akin to injunctions.

11. All this leads me to the conclusion that a caution falls on the other side of the line, and that the judgment and order of Elias J were undoubtedly made in a criminal case or matter.

Note

There exists one important exception to the structure of appeal set out above. Where a claim for judicial review is concerned with a 'criminal cause or matter', there is no possibility to appeal to the Court of Appeal, as it has no jurisdiction to hear such appeals by virtue of section 18(1) of the Senior Courts Act 1981. This exception may also apply to administrative action,[27] as is illustrated in the case of *R (Aru) v Chief Constable of Merseyside*. As a result, appeals against a first instance judgment concerning administrative action qualifying as 'criminal cause or matter' are to be made directly to the Supreme Court. There is a filter process in place for such appeals – in order for an appeal to be possible, the first instance High Court (Queen's Bench Division) must certify that 'a point of law of general public importance is involved in the decision'.[28] Either the High Court (Queen's Bench Division) or the Supreme Court may grant permission to appeal in such a case.

8.2.C COMPARATIVE REMARKS

There are some similarities between the appellate structure in the jurisdictions considered, but far more differences. One similarity is that in every jurisdiction there is some form of appeal against first instance judgments. As an exception to this rule, the highest administrative court(s) in Germany, France and the Netherlands may sometimes act as a first and last instance court. Moreover, in the Netherlands, some judgments of the first instance courts are not appealable to a higher court.

[27] The precise definition of what is a 'criminal cause or matter' where judicial review proceedings are concerned is not straightforward. It is not possible to list all of the possible circumstances in which judicial review claims might relate to a 'criminal cause or matter'. The Court of Appeal held in *R (South West Yorkshire Mental Health NHS Trust) v Bradford Crown Court* [2003] EWCA Civ 1857, [2004] 1 WLR 1664 that the general character of the proceedings must be considered to determine whether they have a criminal or a civil nature.

[28] Administration of Justice Act 1960, s 1(2).

The appellate structure is single layered in the EU and the Netherlands, and has two layers in England and Wales, Germany and France. Within the former group, in the EU, the scope of appeal is limited to points of law, which indicates that guaranteeing legal unity is the main function. In the Netherlands, there exist several appellate courts of final instance, reviewing first instance judgments on both points of fact and law. They combine all three possible functions of appellate proceedings.

Within the group of two-layered appellate proceedings, France and Germany make a comparable distinction between *appel/Berufung* on points of fact and law by the first appellate court (court administrative d'appel, Oberverwaltungsgericht) and *cassation/Revision* on points of law by the subsequent appellate court (Conseil d'État, Bundesverwaltungsgericht). The primary function of *appel/Berufung* is the second chance function, although the control function may play a role as well. The main function of *cassation/Revision* is to guarantee legal unity. In England and Wales, both the Court of Appeal and the Supreme Court are, in principle, competent to engage in a full review of points of fact and law, but, in practice, they generally leave findings of fact made by lower courts in place. So, the appeal before both appellate courts seems to serve all three functions of appeal, but the second chance function is limited in respect of the facts. In all jurisdictions within the group of two-layered appellate proceedings, the first layer appellate court can or should sometimes be bypassed.

Finally, it should be noted that in the EU, France, and England and Wales, there is only one highest court in final instance, while in the Dutch and German systems there are several. To ensure legal unity between these highest courts, Germany employs formal means (Joint Senate, Gemeinsamer Senat), and the Netherlands employs a mix of informal (Committee Legal Unity, Commissie Rechtseenheid) and formal means (Grand Chamber, Grote Kamer).

8.3 ACCESS TO APPELLATE PROCEEDINGS

In respect of access, the most important distinction between appellate proceedings in the different jurisdictions is that in two of them access in these proceedings is limited by a permission to appeal system (England and Wales, Germany), while in the other jurisdictions this mechanism does not exist (France, the EU, the Netherlands). This section will explore this important issue further. Moreover, the section will pay attention to the parties in appellate proceedings, and to some other particularities related to access in some jurisdictions.

8.3.A PERMISSION TO APPEAL SYSTEM: ENGLAND AND WALES AND GERMANY

8.3.A.1 ENGLAND AND WALES

Civil Procedure Rules **8.13 (EW)**

Rule 52.3 (1) A claimant or respondent requires permission to appeal–
(a) where the appeal is from a decision of a judge in the … High Court …

(2) An application for permission to appeal may be made–
(a) To the lower court at the hearing at which the decision to be appealed was made; or
(b) To the appeal court in an appeal notice.
(3) Where the lower court refuses an application for permission to appeal–
(a) a further application for permission may be made to the appeal court; and
...

Rule 52.6 (1) Except where rule 52.7 applies, permission to appeal may be given only where–
(a) the court considers that the appeal would have a real prospect of success; or
(b) there is some other compelling reason for the appeal to be heard.

Rule 52.8 (1) Where a permission to apply for judicial review has been refused at a hearing of the High Court, an application for permission to appeal may be made to the Court of Appeal.
...
(5) On an application under paragraph (1) and (2), the Court of Appeal may, instead of giving permission to appeal, give permission to apply for judicial review.
(6) Where the Court of Appeal gives permission to apply for judicial review in accordance with paragraph (5), the case will proceed in the High Court unless the Court of Appeal orders otherwise.

Court of Appeal (Civil Division), 12 July 2002[29] **8.14 (EW)**

R (Werner) v Inland Revenue Commissioners

APPEAL; PERMISSION; THRESHOLD FOR PERMISSION

Werner

Whether permission to appeal is granted depends on whether the appeal would have a 'real prospect of success'

Facts: Werner was in prison and was contacted by the Inland Revenue (the UK tax authority) to provide information about his financial affairs. Werner initially said that he would cooperate with the Inland Revenue and provide information while he was in prison, but ultimately refused to provide the information until he was released from prison on licence. In response to Werner's refusal to cooperate, the Inland Revenue served W with a notice under section 20(1) of the Taxes Management Act 1970, requiring disclosure of the information sought. Werner claimed judicial review of the decision to issue the notice but permission to proceed was refused by the High Court. Werner tried to appeal to the Court of Appeal against the refusal of permission to bring a judicial review claim.

Held: The Court of Appeal denied Werner permission to appeal, finding that his claim did not have any realistic prospect of success.

Judgment: Brooke LJ: 31. Under this scheme the Court of Appeal will apply the now familiar test of determining whether an appeal against a judge's refusal of permission would have a real prospect of success, in the sense that the prospect of success is not merely 'fanciful' (*Swain v Hillman* [2001] 1 All ER 91). In applying this test it will inevitably

[29] [2002] EWCA Civ 979, [2002] STC 1213.

examine the merits of the original application, and if it considers that the application is fit for consideration at a substantive judicial review hearing it will of course decide that the prospects of a successful appeal are not fanciful. It will probably go on to grant permission to apply for judicial review itself under CPR 52[8](3).

32. If it considers that there is a real prospect of the appellant being able to show at a contested appeal hearing that the application is fit for consideration at a substantive judicial review hearing but it wishes to hear the respondent on the matter, it will probably adjourn the application to be heard on notice, with the appeal to follow if permission is granted. This will represent a speedier and more convenient way of dealing with the matter than merely granting permission to appeal there and then, and then holding things up until a substantive appeal hearing can be heard on the question whether the appeal should be allowed and permission to apply for judicial review granted.

Notes

(1) Appeal is not available as a right. In order for an appeal to be brought, permission must be granted, either by the lower court making the decision to be appealed (High Court (Queen's Bench Division) or Court of Appeal) or, in appeal against the lower courts' refusal to grant permission, by the appellate courts (Court of Appeal or Supreme Court). In respect of appeal from the High Court (Queen's Bench Division) to the Court of Appeal, this system is regulated by Rule 52 CPR. In respect of appeal from the Court of Appeal to the Supreme Court, section 40(2) and (6) of the Constitutional Reform Act 2005 provides the legislative basis for a similar permission system.

(2) Permission to appeal can be granted either where 'the court considers that the appeal would have a real prospect of success' or where 'there is some other compelling reason why the appeal should be heard' (Rule 52.6(1) CPR). In cases where the former ground is the reason for permission to be granted, 'the word "real" means that the prospect of success must be realistic rather than fanciful' (*cf* Brooke LJ in the case *R (Werner) v Commissioners of Customs and Excise*). In the case of the latter ground, all turns to the importance of the issue at hand.[30]

(3) As already stated, if permission to proceed is refused, it is possible for an unsuccessful claimant to appeal the refusal.[31] This process is governed by Rule 52.8 CPR, which provides that wherever permission to bring judicial review proceedings has been refused by the High Court (Queen's Bench Division), the claimant may apply to the Court of Appeal to seek permission to appeal that decision (Rule 52.8(1) CPR). Unless this application is refused, the Court of Appeal may either grant permission to appeal, which will involve a substantive hearing of the permission to proceed stage in the Court of Appeal, or may simply grant permission to apply for judicial review (Rule 52.8(5) CPR). In the latter situation, the usual process is that the substantive

[30] See, eg *R (Ben-Abdelaziz) v Haringey LBC* [2001] EWCA Civ 803, [2001] 1 WLR 1485, where an appeal which was unlikely to succeed was permitted to proceed on the basis that it dealt with an important point of interpretation of the Human Rights Act 1998.

[31] Note that the defendant cannot appeal against the granting of permission: *R v Chief Constable of West Yorkshire Police, ex parte Wilkinson* [2002] EWHC 2353 (Admin), [2002] Po LR 328.

hearing will take place in the High Court (Queen's Bench Division), although Rule 52.8(6) CPR allows the Court of Appeal discretion to hear the substantive judicial review case itself without a hearing in the High Court (Queen's Bench Division). This is not usual, but may be done where the point of law at issue is one of considerable public importance,[32] or where the Court feels that the issue is unlikely to be disposed of by a hearing at first instance.[33]

(4) Permission to appeal can be requested by the parties in the procedure before the lower court. Although it is formally not required that the parties should be aggrieved by the first instance judgment, in practice, one or both parties are aggrieved or they would not request permission to appeal. In some cases, a third party may be permitted to appeal against judgments of a lower court. This is most usual where the Secretary of State concerned by a particular decision may seek to appeal.[34] This is, however, exceptional rather than usual.

8.3.A.2 GERMANY

8.3.A.2 (i) Parties in Appellate Proceedings

Both appellate possibilities, on points of fact and law (*Berufung*) and on points of law (*Revision*), are only admissible after a judicial grant of leave. Only participants in the preceding process may file an appeal. These may include intervening parties according to §65 VwGO or representatives of the public interest. In second and third instance proceedings, §67 VwGO requires a duty to legal representation. Appeals may only be filed by claimants who are aggrieved by the first instance judgment. Third parties who participated in the first (and second) instance proceedings are only considered aggrieved where the challenged judgment directly affects their individual rights.

8.3.A.2 (ii) Permission for Appeal on Points of Fact and Law (*Berufung*)

Verwaltungsgerichtsordnung **8.15 (DE)**

§124 (2) The appeal on points of fact and law shall only be admitted

1. if serious doubts exist as to the correctness of the judgment,
2. if the case has special factual or legal difficulties,
3. if the case is of fundamental significance,
4. if the judgment deviates from a ruling of the Higher Administrative Court, of the Federal Administrative Court, of the Joint Senate of the Highest Courts of the Federation, or of the Federal Constitutional Court, and is based on this deviation, or

[32] See, eg *R v Secretary of State for the Home Department, ex parte Sanusi* [1999] Imm AR 334 (CA).

[33] See, eg *R (Smith) v Parole Board* [2003] EWCA Civ 1014, [2003] 1 WLR 2548, later appealed to and decided by the House of Lords.

[34] See, eg *Wilson v First County Trust Ltd (No 2)* [2003] UKHL 40, [2004] 1 AC 816, where the Secretary of State was permitted to appeal a decision of the Court of Appeal issuing a declaration of incompatibility under s 4 of the Human Rights Act 1998; *R (Middleton) v West Somerset Coroner* [2004] UKHL 10, [2004] 2 AC 182, where the Secretary of State was permitted to appeal findings of the Court of Appeal in a case concerning coroners and the interpretation of Art 2 ECHR.

5. if a procedural shortcoming subject to the judgment of the Higher Administrative Court on points of fact and law is alleged which may have influenced the merits of the decision.

Bundesverwaltungsgericht, 14 June 2002[35] **8.16 (DE)**

JUDICIAL GRANT OF LEAVE FOR AN APPEAL ON POINTS OF FACT AND LAW (*BERUFUNG*) ON THE BASIS OF NEWLY SUBMITTED FACTS

The purpose of the appeal on points of fact and law is to ensure the correctness of the decision. Therefore, permission to appeal because of newly submitted facts is to be granted even if the claimant culpably missed introducing these facts in the first instance.

Facts: The legal successor of the claimant filed an appeal on points of fact and law (*Berufung*). He submitted new facts which were of high relevance to the legal dispute and which were already known but had not been submitted by the claimant during the first instance proceedings. The legal successor asked for a grant of permission to appeal on the basis of serious doubts as to the correctness of the judgment. The Higher Administrative Court requested a ruling from the Federal Administrative Court whether permission could be granted pursuant to §124(2) no 1 VwGO on the basis of newly submitted, decisive facts which had already existed at the time of the decision of the first instance and were not taken into account, because they were not submitted and were not to be determined *ex officio* as there was no indication of their existence.

Held: Permission was granted on the basis of §124(2) no 1 VwGO.

Judgment: (3) The Senate answers the question posed to it … to the effect that, in the decision regarding the grounds for admission of §124(2) no 1 VwGO, the court has to take facts into account which were submitted by the claimant for the first time within the period of application and which are relevant in regards to the substantive law, which were already present at the time of the decision of the Administrative Court, but which the Administrative Court did not take into account because the claimant failed to submit these facts and the court did not have to determine them *ex officio* as there was no indication of their existence.

The purpose of the admission procedure also requires such facts to be taken into account. §124(2) no 1 VwGO opens access to the Higher Administrative Court with regard to the projected outcome of the appeal sought. … [Legal remedies] should ensure the correctness in the individual case; the relevant question is therefore whether the case has been correctly decided. §124(2) no 1 VwGO therefore intends to open access to a substantive review of the contested judgment in an appeal procedure in cases where the correctness of the contested judgment requires further examination and the success of the intended appeal therefore seems possible. … It is therefore of no relevance whether the Administrative Court of First Instance has correctly decided on the matter in view of the apparent facts. In the light of that purpose, all the factual factors set out by the claimant which are relevant to the success of the appeal sought must be taken into account in the admission procedure. This also includes circumstances which the Administrative Court of First Instance could not take into account because the claimant had not submitted them. The appeal on points of fact and law (*Berufung*) still has the function of a second fact-finding procedure. For this purpose, the appeal includes a review of the contested judgment in fact. The appeal court must also take new facts and evidence into account … .

35 NVwZ-RR (2002) 894.

Notes

(1) In appellate proceedings on points of fact and law (*Berufung*), leave for appeal is normally granted by the Administrative Courts of First Instance in their judgments (§124a(1) to (3) VwGO). If the Administrative Court of First Instance has granted leave, the Higher Administrative Court is bound by this decision (§124a(1) VwGO). The claimant should lodge the appeal within one month of service of the reasoned judgment. The reasoning for the appeal can be filed within two months after service of the complete first instance judgment. If the Administrative Court of First Instance refuses leave in the first instance judgment, the claimant can apply for leave to the Higher Administrative Court within one month after service of the complete judgment. The Higher Administrative Court decides whether or not leave is granted. The criteria for granting leave for appeal are listed in §124(2) VwGO.

(2) The case of the Bundesverwaltungsgericht of 14 June 2002 contains a judgment in which the Federal Administrative Court clarifies how the first criterion for granting leave for appeal (serious doubts as to the correctness of the judgment) has to be applied in case the administrative court did not take into account certain essential facts because the claimant failed to submit them. According to the Federal Administrative Court, §124(2) no 1 VwGO aims at opening access to a substantive review of the contested judgment in an appeal procedure in cases where the correctness of the contested judgment requires further examination and the success of the intended appeal therefore seems possible. Therefore, the courts must take into account in the admission procedure all factual factors set out by the claimant which are relevant to the success of the appeal sought, including circumstances which the Administrative Court of First Instance could not take into account because the claimant had not submitted them. In the judgment, the Federal Administrative Court stresses the function of appeal on points of fact and law (*Berufung*) as 'a second fact-finding body'.[36]

8.3.A.2 (iii) Permission to Appeal on Points of Law (*Revision*)

Verwaltungsgerichtsordnung **8.17 (DE)**

§ 132 (2) The appeal on points of law shall only be admitted if

1. the legal case is of fundamental significance,

2. the judgment deviates from a ruling of the Federal Administrative Court, of the Joint Senate of the Highest Courts of the Federation or of the Federal Constitutional Court and is based on this deviation, or

3. a procedural flaw is alleged which may have influenced the merits of the decision.

Notes

(1) In appellate proceedings on points of law (*Revision*), leave for appeal is granted by the Higher Administrative Court, or by the Federal Administrative Court deciding

[36] For this aspect of the judgment, see section 8.4 below.

on a complaint against non-admission by the Higher Administrative Court (§132(1) VwGO). The criteria for granting permission are listed in §132(2) VwGO, and are difficult to meet.

(2) Where the Higher Administrative Court grants leave the Federal Administrative Court is bound by this decision even if it is wrongful (§132(3) VwGO). The appeal on points of law must be lodged in writing with the court whose decision is challenged within one month of service of the complete judgment (§139 VwGO). The reasoning, to which strict formal requirements apply, must be filed within two months of service of the reasoned judgment.

8.3.B NO PERMISSION TO APPEAL SYSTEM: FRANCE, THE EUROPEAN UNION AND THE NETHERLANDS

8.3.B.1 FRANCE

As stated in section 8.2.C.3 above, France employs a two-layered system of appeal: appeal on points of fact and law (*appel*) before the Administrative Courts of Appeal and appeal on points of law (*cassation*) before the Council of State.

8.3.B.1 (i) Appeal on Points of Fact and Law (*Appel*)

Code de justice administrative **8.18 (FR)**

Article R811-1 All parties present in proceedings before the Administrative Court of First Instance or who have been summoned in a correct manner can bring an appeal against any judicial decision taken in those proceedings even if they did not submit any defence.

Conseil d'État, 3 February 1999[37] **8.19 (FR)**

Hôpital of Cosne-Cours-sur-Loire v Spouses X

INTEREST TO APPEAL

Hôpital de Cosne-Cours-sur-Loire

If a judgment is favourable to a claimant, an appeal against its grounds is inadmissible, even if the grounds were incorrect.

Facts: The mayor had adopted a decision granting a planning permission to a hospital. This decision was challenged by Mr and Ms X. In the first instance proceedings, the Administrative Court of First Instance rejected the claim. However, the hospital challenged the ruling since, in the view of the hospital, the judgment was based on the wrong grounds as the ruling did not mention that the building permit was still valid.

[37] N° 126687.

Held: The appeal of the hospital was rejected.

Judgment: Considering, firstly, that by virtue of the challenged judgment, the Administrative Court of First Instance has rejected the pleadings of the spouses Y ... and the spouses X ... directed against the decision of 9 September 1988, granting a building permit to the Hospital of Cosne-Cours-sur-Loire for the reason that this permit had expired; considering that, if during the appeal proceedings against this judgment, the hospital asks the Council of State to hold that the building permit of which it has been the holder was still valid, those conclusions which are not directed against the ruling but against its grounds are not admissible.

Note

Appeal on points of fact and law (*appel*) can, in principle, be lodged by every party present or summoned at first instance. However, to have standing in appeal, a party should be aggrieved by the first instance judgment, in the sense that the judgment modifies its legal position. A party cannot challenge a first instance judgment that satisfied its original claim, even if the party does not agree with the reasoning of the ruling. The first instance judgment may be challenged either in part or totally. The claimant may ask for the quashing of the judgment and its reformation.

8.3.B.1 (ii) Appeal on Points of Law (*Cassation*): Admission System

Code de justice administrative **8.20 (FR)**

Article R822-1 Appeals on points of law to the Council of State sitting as a court of cassation must follow the preliminary admission procedure. Admission will be refused by court decision if the appeal on points of law is inadmissible or if there is no serious ground of appeal.

Article R822-2 If it appears that the application to appeal might be refused, the president of the chamber forwards the file to the public rapporteur for its registration; the appellant or his lawyer is notified of the day of the sitting.

Otherwise, the president of the chamber decides if it will proceed on the application to appeal under the ordinary conditions; the appellant or his lawyer is notified of this decision.

Notes

(1) Appeal on points of law (*cassation*) before the Council of State can only be lodged by the parties with regard to the final judgment.[38] In addition, to have standing, the parties must be aggrieved by the judgment in some way. A party whose claims have been satisfied by the judgment cannot appeal it.

[38] Conseil d'État, 30 July 1949, *Faucon*, Rec 409; Conseil d'État, 20 December 2000, *Commune de Ville d'Avray*, N° 209329.

(2) There is a special procedure which the Council of State follows to grant permission to appeal on points of law (*cassation*).[39] Such permission is refused if the appeal is inadmissible or lacks serious grounds. In this case, the appeal is rejected by the adoption of a ruling by a single judge. How this procedure is applied in practice is not very clear, because the Council of State is not obliged to give reasons for a refusal. However, the conclusions of the public rapporteur (*rapporteur public*)[40] may provide useful information to the claimant.[41]

8.3.B.2 THE EUROPEAN UNION

Statute of the Court of Justice of the European Union **8.21 (EU)**

Article 56 An appeal may be brought before the Court of Justice within two months of the notification of the decision appealed against, against final decisions of the General Court and decisions of that Court disposing of the substantive issues in part only or disposing of a procedural issue concerning a plea of lack of competence or admissibility.

Such an appeal may be brought by any party which has been unsuccessful, in whole or in part, in its submissions. However, interveners others than the Member States and the institutions of the Union may bring such an appeal only where the decisions of the General Court directly affects them.

With the exception of cases relating to disputes between the Union and its servants, an appeal may also be brought by Member States and institutions of the Union which did not intervene in the proceedings before the General Court. Such Member States and institutions shall be in the same position as Member States or institutions which intervened at first instance.

Case C-19/93 P, 19 October 1995[42] **8.22 (EU)**

Rendo NV, Centraal Overijsselse Nutsbedrijven NV and Regionaal Energiebedrijf Salland NV v Commission

PROCEDURAL INTEREST IN APPEAL

Rendo

For a claimant to have interest in bringing proceedings, the appeal must be likely, if successful, to procure an advantage to the party bringing it.

Facts: The claimants were local electricity distribution companies in the Netherlands. In May 1988, they made an application to the Commission against, among others, the company supplying them with energy and the

[39] For this procedure see J Massot, 'The Powers and Duties of the French Administrative Judge' in S Rose-Ackerman and PL Lindseth (eds), *Comparative Administrative Law* (Cheltenham, Edward Elgar Publishing, 2010) ch 24.

[40] See Chapter 2, section 2.2.A.1.

[41] J Massot, 'La Cassation' (1995) *L'Actualité juridique de droit administratif* 200.

[42] C-19/93 *Rendo NV v Commission* ECLI:EU:C:1996:158.

Samenwerkende Elektricteitsproduktiebedrijven NV (SEP), which was a company set up in 1949 by the Dutch electricity generating companies to serve as a vehicle for cooperation. The claimants alleged that various infringements of Articles 85 and 86 of the EEC Treaty (now Articles 101 and 102 TFEU) had been committed by SEP through the signing of an agreement restricting imports and exports of electricity to SEP alone and requiring the parties to the agreement to stipulate in supply contracts concluded with the undertakings distributing electric power that those undertakings will not import or export electricity. The Commission found that the agreement was indeed an agreement between undertakings within the meaning of Article 85(1) and that the prohibition of imports and exports of electricity by undertakings other than SEP restricted competition. Nevertheless, the claimants challenged the Commission's decision on the ground that the Commission's decision did not address the lawfulness of the Electricity Law which entered into force after the agreement had been concluded. The claim was dismissed by the Court of First Instance. The claimants appealed to the Court of Justice. Before the Court, the Commission questioned the claimants' interest in maintaining the appeal. In this respect, it stated that, after the appeal was lodged, it had initiated proceedings against the Kingdom of the Netherlands under Article 169 EEC (now 258 TFEU) concerning the Dutch Electricity Law.

Held: The Court of Justice dismissed the argument because the infringement procedure which the Commission referred to was not concluded at the time the appeal was being decided by the Court of Justice.

Judgment: 13. The Court may of its own motion raise the objection that a party has no interest in bringing or maintaining an appeal on the ground that an event subsequent to the judgment of the Court of First Instance removes the prejudicial effect thereof as regards the appellant, and declare the appeal inadmissible or devoid of purpose for that reason. For an claimant to have interest in bringing proceedings the appeal must be likely, if successful, to procure an advantage to the party bringing it.

Notes

(1) An appeal against a judgment of the General Court may be brought by any party which has been unsuccessful, in whole or in part, in its submissions (Article 56 of the Statute of the Court of Justice of the European Union). For a claimant to have interest in bringing appellate proceedings, the appeal must be likely, if successful, to procure an advantage to the party bringing it. The interest in bringing or maintaining an appeal may 'expire' if an event subsequent to the judgment in first instance removes the prejudicial effects thereof.

(2) Certain preclusion clauses apply in appeal proceedings. First, interveners in first instance proceedings, other than the Member States and the institutions of the EU, may bring such an appeal only where the appealed decision directly affects them. Doctrine suggests that the interest which an intervener must show is the same interest that has to be shown in order to obtain leave to intervene in the first instance proceedings. However, because of the fact-finding activity already carried out at first instance, the Court of Justice has a more concrete basis than the General Court when appraising the interest of the intervener. It is, therefore, possible that an intervener at first instance will be refused permission to appeal.[43]

[43] K Lenaerts et al, *EU Procedural Law*, 2nd edn (Oxford, Oxford University Press, 2014) 643.

8.3.B.3 THE NETHERLANDS

Algemene Wet Bestuursrecht **8.23 (NL)**

Article 8:104 (1) A party concerned and the administrative authority are entitled to lodge an appeal against:

a. a judgment of the district court within the meaning of Article 8:66(1) or Article 8:67(2),

b. a judgment of the interim relief judge of the district court within the meaning of Article 8:86(1),

c. a judgment of the district court on a request within the meaning of Article 8:88(1).

Article 8:110 (1) If a judgment has been appealed, any one who could have lodged an appeal, may also lodge an incidental appeal. ...

Raad van State, 6 August 2003[44] **8.24 (NL)**

X v Mayor and Aldermen of Brummen

SCOPE OF THE DISPUTE IN APPEAL

Brummen

If a judgment in first instance rejecting certain grounds explicitly and unconditionally is not appealed, the part of the ruling concerning those grounds gains the authority of res judicata.

Facts: The mayor and aldermen of the municipality of Brummen had imposed a periodic penalty payment on X, alleging that X used a piece of land contrary to the agrarian function allocated to the land in the zoning plan. After an unsuccessful intra-administrative objection procedure, X challenged the decision before the district court. The district court declared this claim partly well founded on the ground that some use of the land concerned was in its opinion not inconsistent with the agrarian function, and annulled the decision. In respect of other forms of land use, the grounds raised by X were explicitly and unconditionally rejected. The district court referred the case back to the mayor and aldermen in order to issue a new decision on the objection. In its new decision, the authority maintained the periodic penalty payment insofar as the district court had rejected the grounds raised by X. X challenged this decision again before the district court, claiming that these grounds had been unlawfully rejected by the district court in the first case. In the second case, the district court refused to assess these grounds as it had already assessed them in the first case. X appealed against this judgment before the Judicial Division of the Council of State.

Held: The appeal was dismissed.

Judgment: The appellant's appeal against the scope of the dispute, as determined by the district court, is unfounded.

Unlike in the past (*inter alia* the judgment of 23 March 1995, ECLI:NL:RVS:1995:ZF1905), the Judicial Division is now of the opinion that not lodging an appeal against an earlier judgment of the district court has as consequence that, if in appeal against the new decision on objection grounds have been put forward, which have been rejected by the district court explicitly and unconditionally in this earlier judgment, the district court shall assume that its earlier decision concerning these grounds is legally sound.

[44] ECLI:NL:RVS:2003:AI0801.

This opinion is founded on the consideration that a second assessment of grounds which have been rejected by the district court explicitly and unconditionally is inconsistent with the authority of the non-contested judgment. From the principle of legal certainty, it follows that the administrative authority involved and other interested persons may presume that, as far as these ground are concerned, the decision is lawful.

Notes

(1) Interested (natural or legal) persons and the administrative authority involved are entitled to lodge an appeal against the following judgments of the district court: a judgment within the meaning of Article 8:66 AWB (the regular judgment in first instance), a final judgment of an interim relief judge within the meaning of Article 8:86 AWB (the so-called 'shortcutting' proceedings) and the judgment on a request for financial compensation within the meaning of Article 8:95 AWB (Article 8:104(1) AWB). For an appeal to be admissible, the parties concerned or administrative authority should have *procesbelang* (a procedural interest). This requirement is not met where, as a consequence of legal or factual developments, there is no real dispute between the parties at the moment of the hearing or where the judgment in first instance was favourable for them in all respects.

(2) As a result of the *Brummen* case, parties concerned have a procedural interest in appellate proceedings – and are even forced to appeal in order to maximise their opportunities – in cases where the first instance court has found some grounds to be well founded (and has annulled the contested decision on these grounds and referred the case to the administration), but has rejected other grounds 'explicitly and unconditionally'. The same applies mutatis mutandis to the administrative authority.[45] If a judgment of the first instance court, which (also) rejects certain grounds explicitly and unconditionally is not appealed, these decisions will gain the authority of res judicata and cannot be contested in possible follow-up procedures (judicial review and higher appeal) against the new decision on objections of the administrative authority.

(3) Furthermore – and consistently with the *Brummen* line of reasoning – the scope of appellate proceedings is limited to the grounds which have been brought forward by the appellant(s). If other parties in first instance have not lodged an appeal against the first instance judgment, these parties cannot raise grounds themselves, but can only defend themselves against the grounds brought forward by the appellant(s). To remedy this 'inequality', in 2013 the legislature introduced the possibility of incidental appeal (Article 8:110 AWB). Such appeal can, once an appeal is lodged by a party, be brought forward by other parties which could have lodged an appeal (but did not do so initially). An incidental appeal has to be lodged within six weeks of the appellate court sending the grounds of the (regular) appeal to the party concerned. No court fee is required. The main reason for the introduction of the possibility of incidental appeal was that the government wanted to limit the numbers of appellate proceedings to some extent. Before the introduction of the system of incidental appeal, a party which appealed against a decision of the district court did not run

[45] ECLI:NL:RVS:2006:AX2074.

any risk, as the scope of the dispute was limited to the grounds put forward by him. By lodging an appeal on the last day of the period available to lodge an appeal, the party could even, to some extent, prevent the other party from also appealing. This is no longer possible as the other party always has the right to lodge an incidental appeal. Hence, each party that appeals has to take into account the risk of an incidental appeal by thc othcr party.

8.3.C COMPARATIVE REMARKS

In respect of access to appellate proceedings, the main distinction is that in two jurisdictions access is limited by a permission or leave to appeal system (England and Wales, Germany), while in the others (France, the EU, the Netherlands) such mechanism does not exist. Insofar as a permission to appeal system is applied, the threshold for granting permission seems to be lowest in the German *Berufung* (appeal on ground of fact and law) and arguably in the appeal to the Court of Appeal in England and Wales. In final instance, the criteria in the German *Revision* procedure (appeal on points of law) in particular are rather strict. Furthermore, it should be noted that the French Council of State is allowed to refuse admission for *cassation* (appeal on points of law) if the appeal is inadmissible or lacks serious grounds without stating reasons.

In all jurisdictions, the right of appeal is generally limited to the parties in first instance (and in some jurisdictions the interveners) who are aggrieved by the first instance judgment in some way. This excludes parties in first instance whose legal position has not been modified (France) or affected (Germany) by the judgment, for whom this judgment was favourable in all respects (the Netherlands) or for whom the appellate judgment cannot bring any advantage (the EU).

A particularity of the Dutch appellate system is the *Brummen* rule, which implies that, if a first instance court has found some of the grounds raised by a party to be well founded (and has annulled the contested decision to that extent), but has rejected other grounds explicitly and unconditionally, the party involved is forced to appeal against the latter decision, as otherwise this decision will gain the authority of res judicata and cannot be contested in possible follow-up procedures. To partially mitigate the consequences of the *Brummen* rule, in 2013 the Dutch legislator offered parties who were entitled to lodge an appeal, but initially did not do so, the possibility to bring an incidental appeal.

8.4 PROCEDURAL ASPECTS

In section 8.1 of this chapter, three possible functions of appellate proceedings were introduced: the second chance function, the control function and the legal unity function. In section 8.2, it was concluded that the latter function is the main function of the German *Revision*, the French *cassation* and the EU appellate proceedings. The relevance of the other functions in the other appellate proceedings in the jurisdictions involved will be discussed in this section, together with the question of how, if necessary, they can be reconciled with the legal unity function.

With a view to answering these questions, the main topic of this section is whether it is possible in appellate proceedings to raise new legal grounds and to introduce new evidence which could have been, but was not, brought in first instance. Furthermore, and also related to the functions mentioned, the question of whether the grounds of appeal should, as a matter of principle, be directed to the lower instance judgment, or that they can be a repetition of the grounds put forward in lower instance, will be examined. Furthermore, attention will be paid to the issue of the possible suspensory effect of the appellate proceedings.

8.4.A FRANCE

8.4.A.1 APPEAL ON POINTS OF FACT AND LAW (*APPEL*)

Code de justice administrative **8.25 (FR)**

Article L211-2 The Administrative Courts of Appeal hear cases adjudicated in first instance by the Administrative Courts of First Instance, subject to the powers awarded to the Council of State (Conseil d'État) in its capacity as an appeal court and those stipulated in Articles L552-1 and L552-2.

Conseil d'État, 10 July 1995[46] **8.26 (FR)**

City of La Tremblade v X

NEW GROUND FOR APPEAL; PROCEDURAL ILLEGALITY

Commune de La Tremblade

A new ground related to procedural illegality cannot be raised on appeal if only substantive grounds were raised during the first instance proceedings.

Facts: A decision of the city council of La Tremblade withdrew the decision which had allowed Mr X to perform the function of a police officer in the municipality. The Administrative Court of First Instance annulled it. The city council appealed the ruling to the Council of State.

Held: The ruling of the Administrative Court of First Instance was annulled.

Judgment: As far as the decision to withdraw the approval is concerned:

Considering, first and foremost, that the grounds submitted by Mr X … to the Administrative Court of First Instance of Poitiers concerned the internal legality of the challenged decision; that the plea that the concerned person would not have had the possibility to present his observations before the adoption of the decision is related to its external legality and cannot, therefore, be raised for the first time during the appeal proceedings.

[46] N° 148139.

Conseil d'État, 27 June 2005[47] **8.27 (FR)**

Laurent X v Minister of the Interior

GROUNDS OF APPEAL

Laurent X

For an appeal to be admissible, the claimant must raise specific grounds for his action, and not only copy the grounds presented at first instance.

Facts: By decision of 1 October 1999, the Minister of the Interior had removed Mr Mahdi from his function. The latter challenged the decision, first before the Administrative Court of First Instance and then before the Administrative Court of Appeal, both of which rejected his claim.

Held: The ruling of the Administrative Court of Appeal was annulled.

Judgment: Considering that, according to Article R87 of the Code of the Administrative Court of First Instance and the Administrative Courts of Appeal, applicable on the date of the registration of the appeal initiated by Mr X against the judgment of the Administrative Court of First Instance of Nice of 27 November 2000: 'The application ... shall include the presentation of the facts and the grounds. ... The initiator of an application not including any presentation of the grounds can regularise this application by filing observations presenting one or more grounds only until the expiry of the time limit for appeal';

Considering that, according to the case file submitted to the court hearing the substance of the case (*juge du fond*), Mr X has presented within the time limit for appeal before the Administrative Court of Appeal of Marseille an appeal which was not only the literal reproduction of his pleading of first instance but instead he presented, in a precise manner, the criticism addressed to the decision of which he had demanded the annulment before the Administrative Court of First Instance; considering that such statement of grounds complies with the conditions of aforementioned Article R87 of the Code of the Administrative Court of First Instance and the Administrative Courts of Appeal; considering that, therefore, by rejecting this application for appeal as inadmissible, the Administrative Court of Appeal has committed an error of law; considering that its ruling of 21 January 2003 shall be annulled.

Notes

(1) The appeal on points of fact and law (*appel*) combines elements of the second chance function and of the control function. In *appel*, it is possible to raise new legal grounds, but only if they are related to the same 'category' of grounds that were raised before the first instance court. In the action for annulment (*recours pour excès de pouvoir*), two main categories of grounds may be raised, namely grounds concerning the external illegality of the decision, in particular, lack of competence or procedural flaws (*illegalité externe*), and grounds concerning the internal or substantive illegality (*illegalité interne*).[48] If, for example, in first instance only grounds have been raised concerning the category of internal illegality of the contested decision,

[47] N° 259446.

[48] For more details, see Chapter 6, section 6.2.A.1.

it is possible to raise in appeal a new point concerning this category of grounds. However, as the case of *Commune de la Tremblade* shows, grounds concerning the external illegality will be declared inadmissible. Within the ground raised in first instance, a party in appeal is allowed to bring forward new evidence.

(2) Because of the control function of *appel* (appeal on points of fact and law), the claimant should, as a matter of principle, identify flaws in the first instance judgment and cannot solely rely on the arguments brought at first instance. Formally, the request shall contain the grounds for appeal. Thus, as the *Laurent X* case shows, the grounds of review should not be a copy of the grounds raised at first instance, otherwise the appeal may be declared inadmissible. However, case law is progressively changing, and grounds brought in appellate proceedings can increasingly be very similar, from a substantial point of view – and sometimes even identical – to those that have been raised in first instance.

(3) An appeal on points of fact and law (*appel*) does not suspend the first instance judgment (Article R811-14 of the Code de justice administrative). However, the Administrative Court of Appeal can order the suspension of the first instance judgment 'if the grounds raised by the applicant appear, in the current state of the proceedings, to be serious and sufficient to justify not only the annulment or the reformation of the challenged judgment, but also the rejection of the conclusions reached by this judgment to ground the annulment' (Article R811-15 of the Code de justice administrative).

8.4.A.2 APPEAL ON POINTS OF LAW (*CASSATION*)

Code de justice administrative **8.28 (FR)**

Article L821-1 The rulings issued by the Administrative Courts of Appeal and, in general, all the decisions issued in last resort by the administrative courts can be brought before the Council of State (Conseil d'État) by way of cassation proceedings.

Article L111-1 The Council of State is the highest administrative court. It rules, without further possibility of appeal, on appeals on points of law (*cassation*) lodged against judgments rendered at the last instance by the various administrative courts and on cases of which it is seized as a court of first instance or as an appeal court.

Conseil d'État, 2 February 1945[49] **8.29 (FR)**

Moineau v Ordre national des médecins

CASSATION; REVIEW OF THE ESTABLISHMENT OF THE FACTS (*CONTRÔLE DE LA MATÉRIALITÉ DES FAITS*)

Moineau

When acting in cassation proceedings, the Conseil d'État may review the way in which facts were established by the earlier instance courts.

[49] N° 76127.

Facts: Mr Moineau challenged the refusal of the National Medical Council (Ordre national de médecins) to register him as a doctor. The Administrative Court of First Instance and the Higher Administrative Court both rejected his claim.

Held: The action was rejected.

Judgment: Considering that it does not result of the case file on the basis of which the Chambre de Discipline de l'Ordre National des Médecins (Disciplinary Chamber of the National Medical Council) has decided that its decision was grounded on incorrect facts;

considering also that the assessment of the chamber on the value of certain methods used by Mr X … falls outside the scope of review of the judge of cassation;

considering finally that, taking this sovereign assessment into account, the alleged acts of the claimant were of a nature to motivate the refusal to register him with the National Medical Council.

Conseil d'État, 27 June 2005[50] **8.30 (FR)**

Conseil départemental de l'Ordre des chirugiens-dentistes des Bouches-du-Rhône v Ordre des chirurgiens-dentistes

CASSATION; REVIEW ON LEGAL ASSESSMENT OF THE FACTS (*QUALIFICATION JURIDIQUE DES FAITS*)

Conseil départemental de l'Ordre des chirugiens-dentistes des Bouches-du-Rhône

The review of the legal assessment of the facts is part of the jurisdiction of the court in case of appeal on points of law.

Facts: Following a claim introduced by a patient, Mr X was sanctioned by the National Dental Surgeons Council (Conseil national de l'ordre des chirurgiens-dentistes). He challenged this decision first before the disciplinary commission, which annulled the sanction since, according to the Commission, he had not breached any of his professional duties. The National Dental Surgeons Council challenged, in cassation, the ruling of the disciplinary commission.

Held: The claim of the National Dental Surgeons Council was rejected.

Judgment: Considering that if Mr X … has, as ruled by the court hearing the substance of the case (*juge du fond*), violated the aforementioned provisions of Article 27, thereby omitting to request the prior consent of his patient for the removal of three teeth, this mistake, under the circumstances of the case such as they result of the file submitted to the court hearing the substance of the case, did not have the character of misconduct, notably due to the fact that the total removal of teeth could have seemed necessary from a medical point of view to Mr X … because of the dental history of the patient, which could suggest that the three remaining teeth would, within a very short time, break down as the others; considering thus, noting that the committed fault was excused according to Article 11 of the law of 6 August 2002, that decision of the disciplinary commission of the National Dental Surgeons Council, which has not distorted the facts of the case and which has been sufficiently motivated, is not flawed either by an error of law, or by an error of legal assessment.

[50] N° 257623.

Notes

(1) The primary function of the appeal on points of law (*cassation*) before the Council of State is the legal unity function. In *cassation*, in principle, only legal grounds of *cassation* can be raised. These grounds are different from the grounds raised in first instance and in *appel*. The grounds developed at the *cassation* stage all aim at challenging the ruling against which the action is introduced. First, points can be related to the regularity of the ruling (competence, motivation, formal and procedural requirements applied to the ruling). Secondly, points may be related to the merits of the ruling, questioning the legal reasoning of the judge. At the *cassation* stage, it is not possible bring forward new factual evidence.

(2) Although *cassation* proceedings before the Council of State are concerned with points of law, some questions of fact may play a role. First, they can be raised insofar as the fact-finding in *appel* is incorrect. In this respect, the *cassation* judges can only intervene if there has been an error with regard to the way in which the facts were established by the earlier instance courts (*inexactitude matérielle des faits*) or an error in the way in which the facts were taken into account by the earlier instance courts (*dénaturation des faits*). Secondly, the *cassation* judges may in some cases review the legal assessment of the facts (*qualification juridique des faits*): did the appeal court deduce the correct legal consequences of the facts it found proven?[51] In this respect, the Council of State distinguishes the legal assessment of the facts (which it considers to be its task) from the establishment of the facts themselves (which it considers to be the task of the court hearing the substance of the case, the *juge du fond*). Obviously, this distinction is subject to criticism.[52]

(3) The appeal on grounds of law (*cassation*) does not suspend the contested judgment. However, suspension of the judgment can be ordered by the Council of State if two conditions are met: first, 'if this decision might have consequences that would be difficult to remedy'; and, secondly, 'if the arguments relied upon appear, in the current state of the proceedings, to be serious and sufficient to justify not only the setting aside of the judgment rendered at the last instance, but also the setting aside of the solution adopted by the court dealing with the merits' (Article R821-5 of the Code de justice administrative).

8.4.B GERMANY

Similar to France, Germany has a two-layered system of appeal: *Berufung* on points of fact and law before the Higher Administrative Court, and *Revision* on points of law before the Federal Administrative Court. Both appellate remedies have a suspensory effect with regards to the prior judgment (§124a(5) and 133(5) VwGO). Thus, they hinder the

[51] For another example in respect of the qualification of 'inhuman or degrading treatment', see Conseil d'État, 6 April 2001, *Djerrar*, N° 212106.

[52] F Raynaud and P Fombeur, 'Chronique générale de jurisprudence administrative française' (1998) *L'Actualité juridique: Droit administratif* 792.

entry into force of the prior judgment and lead to the continuation of the legal dispute. Lodging and admitting an appellate remedy does however not automatically continue the suspensive effect of lodging of a claim in first instance (§80 VwGO).[53]

8.4.B.1 APPEAL ON POINTS OF FACT AND LAW (*BERUFUNG*)

Verwaltungsgerichtsordnung **8.31 (DE)**

§124 (1) The parties involved shall be entitled to an appeal on points of fact and law (*Berufung*) against final judgements, including the partial judgments in accordance with §110, and against interim judgments in accordance with §§109 and 111, if such appeal is admitted by the Administrative Court of First Instance or the Higher Administrative Court.

§128 The Higher Administrative Court shall review the dispute within the application for appeal on points of fact and law (*Berufung*) to the same degree as the Administrative Court of First Instance. It shall also consider newly submitted facts and evidence.

§128a (2) Declarations and items of evidence which the Administrative Court of First Instance has rightly rejected shall also remain ruled out in the proceedings for an appeal on points of fact and law.

Notes

(1) The main function of the appeal of points of fact and law (*Berufung*) is the second chance function. This appears in §128 VwGO, which clearly states that the Higher Administrative Court shall review the dispute to the same degree as the Administrative Court of First Instance, and is stressed by the Federal Administrative Court in its judgment of 14 June 2002 (discussed in section 8.3.A.2 (i)). In *Berufung*, therefore, the Higher Administrative Court examines the dispute within the scope of the appeal in law and fact to the same extent as the first instance court, without being bound to the grounds for appeal. As the German system of judicial review of administrative acts follows the inquisitorial principle,[54] the court may also consider new legal aspects of the case which have been ignored by the first instance.[55] The Higher Administrative Court shall also consider newly submitted facts and items of evidence. Only evidence that was precluded in the first instance is in principle inadmissible in the second instance (§128a VwGO).

(2) The control function is also of some relevance in *Berufung*, insofar as the claimant should reason why there is a ground for appeal (§124 VwGO) and thereby direct the appeal against the first instance decision. Still, the substantive reasons for the appeal can be rooted in the initial arguments against the administrative decision.

[53] See in more detail, §80b(1) and (2) VwGO.

[54] §86 VwGO. See further Chapter 5, section 5.3.A.1.

[55] See W Roth, in Posser and Wolff (eds), *Beck'scher Online-Kommentar VwGO*, 39th edn (Munich, CH Beck, 2016) §128, para 1.

8.4.B.2 APPEAL ON POINTS OF LAW (*REVISION*)

Verwaltungsgerichtsordnung **8.32 (DE)**

§132 (1) Those concerned shall have recourse to an appeal on points of law (*Revision*) to the Federal Administrative Court against the judgments of the Higher Administrative Court (§49 no 1), and against orders (*Beschlüsse*) in accordance with §47(5), first sentence, if the Higher Administrative Court, or the Federal Administrative Court in response to a complaint against non-admission, has admitted it.

§137 (1) The appeal on points of law may only be based on the challenged judgment being based on a violation

1. of federal law, or
2. of a provision of the Administrative Procedure Act (Verwaltungsverfahrensgesetz) of a state, the wording of which corresponds with the Administrative Procedure Act of the Federation. …

§138 A judgment shall always be regarded as being based on the violation of federal law if

1. the deciding court was not composed according to the regulations,
2. a judge was involved in the ruling who had been excluded from the exercise of judicial office by force of law or had been successfully rejected for concerns regarding partiality,
3. a party concerned had been refused a legal hearing,
4. a party concerned in the proceedings was not represented in accordance with the provisions of the law, unless he explicitly or tacitly consented to the continuation of the proceedings,
5. the judgment was handed down on the basis of an oral hearing in which the provisions on the public nature of the proceedings were violated, or
6. the ruling is not reasoned.

Notes

(1) The primary function of the appeal on points of law (*Revision*) is to guarantee legal unity in the application of federal law.[56] Thus, this appeal may only concern violations of federal law or of a provision of the Administrative Procedure Act of a state (Landesverwaltungsverfahrensgesetz) which corresponds with the Administrative Procedure Act of the Federation (§137 VwGO). In §138 VwGO, some points for an appeal of law are listed which are always considered to violate federal law.

(2) In *Revision*, the Federal Administrative Court is, in principle, bound to the factual findings handed down in the impugned judgment. However, there are some exceptions to the latter principle. First, new facts may be taken into account if they are only relevant due to a change of the law which took place during the appeal procedure on points of law (*Revisionsverfahren*). In this case, the legal dispute is remitted to

[56] HJ Blanke in H Sodan and J Ziekow (eds), *Verwaltungsgerichtsordnung*, 4th edn (Baden-Baden, Nomos, 2014) §124, para 14.

the previous instance. Secondly, in exceptional circumstances, new undisputed facts, which need no submission of evidence, can be considered by the Federal Administrative Court for reasons of efficiency, namely to prevent remitting the case to the lower court. Thirdly, obvious facts, which need no submission of evidence, may be taken into account.[57] Furthermore, if the appellant rightly claims that procedural norm in respect of the fact finding have been infringed, the court is no longer bound by the facts. In this case, the Federal Administrative Court will remit the case back to the prior instance for fact finding.

8.4.C ENGLAND AND WALES

Similar to Germany and France, England and Wales has a two-layered system of appeal: first to the Court of Appeal and then to the Supreme Court. In contrast to the former jurisdictions, appeal to both appellate courts may be concerned with both points of law and (although in practice it seldom is[58]) points of fact.

House of Lords, 24 February 2005[59] **8.33 (EW)**

R (Williamson) v Secretary of State for Education and Employment

NEW GROUNDS IN APPEAL

Williamson

Where a point of law is important to the resolution of an appeal, the court is likely to permit it to be raised even if it was not in the original grounds of appeal.

Facts: The case concerned a challenge to the prohibition of the use of corporal punishment in private schools. The parents claimed, inter alia, that the prohibition of corporal punishment was an infringement of the right to freedom of religious belief in Article 9 of the European Convention on Human Rights (ECHR). The Administrative Court and the Court of Appeal were of the opinion that the prohibition did not engage the Article 9 rights of the parents and, as such, dismissed the claim. The Council for the Secretary of State sought to introduce a novel point of appeal, namely that even if Article 9 was engaged in the case, the prohibition could be justified under Article 9(2) ECHR. The appeal ultimately turned upon the issue of justification, which was only raised during the hearing before the House of Lords (now the Supreme Court).

Held: The House of Lords permitted the consideration of the new ground of appeal and found that the prohibition was justified under Article 9(2) ECHR.

Judgment: Lord Nicholls: 42. The final step is to consider whether this interference is justified. In the case of article 9 the issue is whether the Secretary of State can show that section 548 satisfies the requirements of article 9(2). Here there is a procedural complication. The issue was raised at first instance. Elias J dismissed the Secretary of State's

[57] For details, see W Neumann in Sodan and Ziekow (ibid) §137, para 146 ff.
[58] See section 8.2.C.3 above.
[59] [2005] UKHL 15, [2005] 2 AC 246.

submission with a degree of briskness: 2002 2 ELR 214, 229, para 59. He said this is not one of those exceptional cases where the potential harm resulting from the manifestation of a belief is so plan that it is obvious on what ground the state has banned it. …

43. In the Court of Appeal the Secretary of State did not raise this issue again. This was a considered and deliberate decision. Rix LJ expressed his 'unhappiness' that, in consequence, the submissions before the Court of Appeal did not include argument that a government ought to be entitled to legislate against all corporal punishment in schools, on an ultimate balance of the competing rights and interests involved ….

44. Before your Lordships' House the Secretary of State in his written case sought to resurrect this point. Mr Dingemans QC objected to this. He submitted that if the Secretary of State were given leave to raise the justification issue again, the hearing should be adjourned to enable the claimants to bring forward evidence on this issue.

45. Without expressing any view on this procedural point the appellate committee invited both parties' council to present any oral arguments they wished, additional to their written arguments, on this justification issue. Council did so.

46. I am in no doubt that, despite having abandoned the justification defence in the Court of Appeal, the Secretary of State should be at liberty to raise this point again. Clearly it would be unfortunate if this important issue were to be left unresolved … .

Court of Appeal (Civil Division), 2 February 2004[60] **8.34 (EW)**

E v Secretary of State for the Home Department

FRESH FACTUAL EVIDENCE IN APPEAL

E

In exceptional circumstances it is possible for the Court of Appeal to permit fresh factual evidence during the hearing of an appeal.

Facts: After his claim for asylum had been rejected by the Secretary of State, E went on to appeal before an adjudicator and then subsequently to the Immigration Appeal Tribunal (IAT). Both the adjudicator and the tribunal confirmed the Secretary of State's decision. In the time between the hearing before the IAT and the announcement of the decision on the appeal, new evidence came to light. The IAT declined to hear this fresh evidence and, in this case, the relevant statutory scheme limited appeals to the Court of Appeal to matters of law only, and was restricted to matters raised before the IAT at the hearing. However, there was an additional power for the IAT to order a rehearing of the case if there was a good reason to do so. In this case, the IAT refused to admit this fresh evidence, reasoning that it could only consider evidence that was before it in the initial appeal and which had been before the adjudicator.

Held: The Court of Appeal permitted the admission of fresh factual evidence.

Judgment: Carnwath LJ: 22. Account must be taken of the general rules governing appeals to the Court of Appeal. For the purpose of appeal the Court of Appeal generally has 'all authority and jurisdiction' of the tribunal appealed against: Supreme Court Act 1981, section 15(3). Rule 52.11(1) provides that the appeal will be limited to a 'review of the decision of the lower court, unless the court considers that ''in the circumstances of an individual appeal it would be in the interest of justice to hold a rehearing'. Rule 52.11(2)

[60] [2004] EWCA Civ 49, [2004] QB 1044.

provides that, unless otherwise is ordered, the court will not receive (a) oral evidence; or (b) evidence which was not before the lower court.

23. Although that rule gives the court discretion to admit new evidence, it is not unlimited. (i) The discretion is subject to any statutory limitations of the appeal: see CPR r 52.1(4). Thus, where the appeal is limited to questions of law, the power to admit new evidence cannot be used to turn it into an appeal on issues of pure fact (cf. *Green v Minister of Housing and Local Government* [1967] 2 QB 606, 615, under the old rules). New evidence will normally be admitted only in accordance with 'Ladd v Marshall principles' (see Ladd v Marshall [1954] 1 WLR 1489), applied with some additional flexibility under the CPR, see Hertfordshire Investments Ltd v Bubb [2000] 1 WLR 2318, 2325 and CFR r. 52.11(2). The Ladd v Marshall principles are, in summary: first, that the fresh evidence could not have been obtained with reasonable diligence for use at the trial; secondly, that if given, it probably would have had an important influence on the result; and, thirdly, that it is apparently credible although not incontrovertible. As a general rule, the fact that the failure to adduce the evidence was that of the party's legal advisers provides no excuse: see R v Secretary of State for the Home Department, Ex p Al-Mehdawi [1990] 1 AC 876. We will need to consider below to what extent those principles are further relaxed in asylum cases. …

82. We would respectfully accept the statement of Sir John Donaldson MR quoted in the previous paragraph as accurately reflecting the law applicable in a case of this kind (whether it takes the form of a direct appeal from the IAT to the Court of Appeal, or comes by way of judicial review of the IAT's refusal of leave to appeal). However, we would not regard it as showing that Ladd v Marshall principles have 'no place' in public law. Rather it shows that they remain the starting point, but there is discretion to depart from them in exceptional circumstance.

83. One can perhaps draw three lessons from that decision: (i) not all (or even most) Court of Appeal decisions in this area should be seen as laying down propositions of law; the decisions in this area are unusually fact-sensitive; (ii) it provides another good example of the need for a residual ground of review for unfairness arising from a simple mistake of fact; (iii) it illustrates the intrinsic difficulty in many asylum cases of obtaining reliable evidence of the facts giving rise to the fear of persecution, and the need for some flexibility in the application of Ladd v Marshall principles.

Notes

(1) The question of whether the appellate courts are able to hear points of law *de novo* that have not been raised before the lower court is frequently addressed in the Supreme Court and remains controversial. In cases involving the Human Rights Act 1998, the Supreme Court (formerly the House of Lords) is willing to accept new points of law during the course of the appeal, even – as is illustrated in the case of *Williamson* – where the party involved deliberately did not raise the issue before the Court of Appeal. In addition, the case of *Maye* demonstrates that, in recent times, the Supreme Court has been willing to introduce novel points of law during appeal proceedings even where matters of human rights or EU law are not engaged.[61] However, the

[61] *Re Maye* [2008] UKHL 9, [2008] 1 WLR 315.

appellate courts are not under a general obligation to allow new points of law as a matter of right; it will depend on the circumstances of the case.

(2) In respect of the introduction of new evidence in appeal cases, the default position is that new evidence will not be permitted, but the court retains discretion to permit new evidence where necessary. In the case of *Ladd v Marshall*,[62] the Court of Appeal held that for new evidence to be admitted on appeal, three conditions must usually be fulfilled: first, that the fresh evidence could not have been obtained with reasonable diligence for use at the trial before the lower court; secondly, that if given, it probably would have had an important influence on the result; and, thirdly, that it is apparently credible although not incontrovertible. From the case of *E v Secretary of State for the Home Department*, it is clear that these conditions apply in public law cases as well, although there may be some need for departure from a strict application if the interests of justice require this, in particular in asylum cases. The *Simms* case offers a good example of both the Court of Appeal[63] and the House of Lords[64] permitting the introduction of additional evidence at the appeal stage, although this should be seen as the exception rather than the rule.

(3) From the foregoing, it is apparent both that appellate proceedings may offer parties a second chance, but also that this function is limited. New points of law may be permitted by the appellate courts and, particularly in human rights cases, they increasingly are. However, the courts are not under a general obligation to allow new points of law as a matter of right. New evidence is only admitted under rather strict conditions, although these conditions may be applied in a more flexible way in public law cases. Arguably, these limitations are an indication that the other functions of appellate proceedings, the control and legal unity functions, are of relevance in the English appellate system as well. Furthermore, in order for permission to appeal to be granted, it is imperative to direct appellate grounds to the judgment contested. As already stated in section 8.2 above, an appeal will only be allowed if the decision of the lower court was wrong or unjust because of a serious procedural or other irregularity in the proceedings (Rule 52.11(3) CPR). This illustrates the relevance of the control function as well.

(4) Unless the appeal court or the lower court orders otherwise, an appeal does not operate as a stay of any order or decision of the lower court (Article 52.16 CPR). In deciding on a request for granting a stay pending the hearing in appeal, the appellate court conducts a balancing exercise which relates not to the merits of the appeal itself, but to the different effects that, on the one hand, granting a stay would have and, on the other hand, not granting a stay would have. In this balancing exercise, the public interest obviously has to be taken into account. Whether it will prevail depends on its importance in the particular case and the importance of the opposite interests of the party requesting the stay.[65]

[62] *Ladd v Marshall* [1954] 1 WLR 1489 (CA).

[63] *R v Secretary of State for the Home Department, ex parte Simms* [1999] QB 349 (CA).

[64] *R v Secretary of State for the Home Department, ex parte Simms* [2000] 2 AC 115 (HL).

[65] For a case in which the Court of Appeal approved the stay because the latter interest prevailed, see *R (Muck It Ltd) v The Transport Tribunal* [2005] EWCA Civ 668.

8.4.D THE NETHERLANDS

As stated in section 8.2.B.2 above, there are several appellate courts judging cases in final instance in the Netherlands, namely the Judicial Division of the Council State (Afdeling bestuursrechtspraak Raad van State) (competent by default), the Central Appellate Court (Centrale Raad van Beroep) (competent for social security and civil servants), the High Administrative Court for Trade and Industry (College van Beroep voor het Bedrijfsleven) (competent for economic cases) and the Courts of Appeal/ Supreme Court (Hoge Raad) (competent for tax cases). Their vision of the primary function of appellate proceedings differs.[66]

Raad van State, 29 April 2009[67] **8.35 (NL)**

X v Mayor and Aldermen of Ede

NEW GROUNDS IN APPEAL

Ede

In principle, it is not possible to raise new legal grounds in appeal.

Facts: On 5 February 2007, the claimant requested that the mayor and aldermen of Ede require the holder of a building permit to bring a building in line with what the building permit allowed. By a decision of 9 February, the authority refused the request. In its judgment of 15 April 2008, the district court of Arnhem dismissed the claim for judicial review against the refusal. In appeal before the Judicial Division of the Council of State, the claimant raised a new legal ground which was not raised at first instance.

Held: The new ground was not admitted.

Judgment: The grounds of the (claimant) against the construction of the building facility have not been raised before the district court. Since the appeal is directed against the first instance judgment, and there is no reason why this ground for appeal could not have been put forward before the district court – and this, in the view of the function of appeal, should have been done – this ground of appeal is not admitted.

Centrale Raad van Beroep, 14 October 1999[68] **8.36 (NL)**

A v Regional Police Manager of Groningen

NEW GROUNDS IN APPEAL

Groningen

In principle, it is possible to raise new legal grounds in appeal.

[66] On this topic, see M Schreuder-Vlasblom, *Rechtsbescherming en bestuurlijke voorprocedure*, 6th edn (Alphen aan den Rijn, Wolters Kluwer, 2017) 1178–1232; RJGM Widdershoven, 'Het bestuursrechtelijk appel revisited' in GH Addink et al (eds), *Grensverleggend Bestuursrecht* (Alphen aan den Rijn, Wolters Kluwer, 2008) 475–96.

[67] ECLI:NL:RVS:2009:BI2678.

[68] ECLI:NL:CRVB:1999:AA4696.

Facts: A claimant appealed against a judgment of the district court in which his claim for judicial review had been rejected. In appeal before the Central Appellate Court, he brought forward a large number of new grounds, which had not been raised in first instance.

Held: The new grounds were admitted.

Judgment: The Court considers in the first place that, in the current case, it does not share the complaint of the defendant against raising new grounds in appeal. By reference to its judgment of 16 October 1998, published in AB 1999/48, the Court is of the opinion that, if a party concerned has made known his grounds to the Court in time and the defendant has been able to give a reasoned reaction to these grounds, no rule of written or unwritten law prevents their assessment by the court.

It cannot be said that the claimant has exceeded the scope of the dispute and it has not appeared that he intentionally did not raise (possible) defects of the contested decision at an earlier stage.

Notes

(1) According to the Judicial Division of the Council of State (Afdeling bestuursrechtspraak Raad van State), the main function of appeal is the control function. This vision is clearly expressed in the *Ede* case, in which this appellate court ruled that it was not possible to raise in the appellate stage new legal grounds which could – and thus should – have been raised in first instance. This opinion is linked to the fact that the appeal is directed against the judgment of the district court (in line with the control function). It obviously also serves the legal unity function. In the past, the Judicial Division of the Council of State applied this strict line to new evidence as well, but its approach is currently more lenient. If the evidence is brought in appeal in time (ten days before the hearing, pursuant to Article 8:58 AWB), and the defendant is able to react to it, the evidence is generally allowed.[69] In such a case, the appeal also serves the second chance function.

(2) The other appellate courts favour instead the second chance function.[70] In line with the judgment of the Central Appellate Court (Centrale Raad van Beroep) in the *Groningen* case, they allow new grounds to be raised in appeal, as long as the defendant is able to give a reasoned reaction to them (in line with the requirements of due process) and the claimant did not intentionally refrain from raising possible defects of the contested decision at an earlier stage. The latter reason for not allowing a new ground has never occurred in case law. Furthermore, it is perfectly possible in appellate proceedings before the other appellate courts – within the limits of due process – to bring forward new evidence at the appellate stage.[71] Even evidence which was lawfully excluded in first instance for due process reasons can be brought in at the appellate stage, as long as this is done in time and the defendant is able to react to it.[72]

[69] ECLI:NL:RVS:2003:AI0807; ECLI:NL:RVS:2006:AX9487.

[70] See High Administrative Court for Trade and Industry, 1 April 2004, ECLI:NL:CBB:2004:AO8207; as regards the courts of appeal in tax matters, see, eg Court of Appeal 's-Hertogenbosch, 21 July 2006, ECLI:NL:GHDB:2006:AY8155; Court of Appeal Amsterdam, 13 June 2006, ECLI:NL:GHA:2006:AX9346.

[71] ECLI:NL:CRVB:2013:CA2803; ECLI:NL:HR:2010:BO6786.

[72] ECLI:NL:GHARN:2006:AY8155.

(3) In the view of the control function, the object of appeal is the judgment in first instance, and only indirectly the decision contested in first instance (Article 8:104(1) AWB). Therefore, the grounds of appeal should, as a matter of principle, be directed to this judgment. A mere copy-and-paste of the first instance grounds by the claimant is no reason for declaring the appeal inadmissible, but might lead to a summary judgment rejecting the appeal under reference to the judgment in first instance.[73] Also in this respect, the practice of the Council of State is stricter than the practice of the other appellate courts.

(4) As a rule, lodging an appeal does not suspend the first instance judgment automatically (Article 6:16 AWB). However, it is possible for all parties to apply for an interim relief measure in accordance with Article 8:81 AWB. In addition, in social security (the area of the Central Appellate Court) and tax matters (the area of the Court of Appeal), this rule is set aside, and lodging an appeal suspends the first instance judgment, first during the appellate period and, if an appeal is lodged, up until the moment that a judgment is given by the appellate court (Article 8:106(1) AWB). The reason for this exception is that in these financial matters it might be difficult (or even impossible) in practice to redress the financial consequences of the first instance judgment.

8.4.E THE EUROPEAN UNION

Joined Cases C-24/01 P and C-25/01 P, 7 November 2002[74] **8.37 (EU)**

Glencore Grain Ltd and Compagnie Continentale (France) SA v Commission

NEW GROUNDS IN APPEAL

Glencore

On appeal to the Court of Justice, parties are not entitled to seek an order relating to a plea not raised before the General Court.

Facts: In a complex case about medium-term loans to the Soviet Union and its constituent Republics, the Commission had refused to approve a certain amendment to the contracts as initially concluded between the claimants and their suppliers. Both claimants brought a claim against this decision, which was rejected by the Court of First Instance. On appeal to the Court of Justice, they argued, inter alia, that the Court of First Instance had failed to take account of the Commission's administrative practice and the obligations arising from it, and of the rights of the defence.

Held: The pleas not raised before the Court of First Instance were dismissed.

Judgment: 62. As regards the complaint that the Court of First Instance failed to check whether the Commission had followed its usual administrative practice and had had

[73] ABRvS 4 May 2005, ECLI:NL:RVS:2005:AT5105, point 2.2.
[74] ECLI:EU:C:2002:642.

regard for the rights of the defence, suffice it to observe that that complaint was not raised at first instance. To allow a party to put forward for the first time before the Court of Justice a plea in law which it has not raised before the Court of First Instance would be to allow it to bring before the Court, whose jurisdiction in appeals is limited, a dispute of wider ambit than that which came before the Court of First Instance. In an appeal the Court's jurisdiction is confined to review of the findings of law on the pleas argued before the Court of First Instance.

Case C-48/96 P, 14 May 1998[75] **8.38 (EU)**

Windpark Groothusen GmbH & Co Betriebs KG v Commission

REPETITION OF PLEAS OF FIRST INSTANCE IN APPEAL; INADMISSIBILITY

Windpark Groothusen

An appeal which merely repeats the pleas in law previously submitted to the CFI is inadmissible.

Facts: On 27 November 1992, the claimant submitted to the Commission an application for aid of ECU 1,933,495 for the construction of a wind turbine park. By a letter of 13 January 1994, addressed to the claimant, the Commission stated that the claimant's project could not be granted financial support in 1993, owing to the lack of appropriate budgetary credits. Windpark brought an action before the Court of First Instance, claiming that the Court should annul the Commission's decision of 13 January 1994. The Court of First instance dismissed the action. On appeal before the Court of Justice, Windpark argued, inter alia, that the Commission failed to adopt a proper position in respect of its application. According to Windpark, its project satisfied the requirements for such financial support and the requisite funds were in fact available.

Held: The Court of Justice dismissed this argument and the appeal.

Judgment: 56. It is sufficient to note in this regard that this plea is inadmissible insofar as it is based on Article 175 of the Treaty. The action before the Court of First Instance was not based on that provision. Insofar as it questions the propriety of the decision of 13 January 1994, the action is confined to repeating the pleas in law which this Court has already rejected. However, pursuant to Article 51, first paragraph, of the EC Statute of the Court of Justice and Article 112(1)(c) of its Rules of Procedure, an appeal must indicate precisely the contested elements of the judgment which the appellant seeks to have set aside, and also the legal arguments specifically advanced in support of the appeal. That requirement is not satisfied by an appeal which confines itself to repeating or reproducing word for word the pleas in law and arguments previously submitted to the Court of First Instance, including those based on facts expressly rejected by that court.

Notes

(1) In addition to the legal unity function, the second important function of the appellate proceedings before the Court of Justice is the control function. In view of the latter, the Court cannot change the subject matter of the proceedings from the

[75] ECLI:EU:C:1998:223.

proceedings before the General Court (formerly Court of First Instance).[76] Or, in other words, the ambit or scope of the dispute in appeal cannot be wider than in first instance. As a consequence, a claimant is not entitled to seek a new form of order, ie an order relating to a plea not raised before the General Court. However, he remains free to further develop his legal pleas by way of new (legal) arguments as long as this does not amount to putting forward new legal pleas.[77] With a view to the legal unity function, appellate proceedings before the Court of Justice are limited to questions of law (Article 58 of the Statute of the Court of Justice and Article 256(1) TFEU). Obviously, it is not possible to bring forward new evidence that could have been brought in first instance.

(2) Related to the control function, the appeal must indicate precisely the contested elements of the judgment which the appellant seeks to have set aside, and also the legal arguments specifically advanced in support of the appeal. An appeal which merely repeats the pleas in law previously submitted to the General Court does not satisfy that requirement and it will be dismissed.

(3) According to Article 278 TFEU, an appeal brought before the Court of Justice does not have a suspensory effect. The Court may, however, if it considers that circumstances so require, order that application of the contested act be suspended (Article 178 TFEU), or prescribe any other necessary interim measures (Article 179 TFEU).

8.4.F COMPARATIVE REMARKS

With a view to the dominant function of appeal, the various appellate proceedings in the jurisdictions involved can be ranked in a spectrum, which goes from primarily serving the second chance function to primarily serving the control and/or legal unity function.

At one end of the spectrum are the German and French appeals on points of fact and law (*Berufung*, *appel*), and the Dutch appeal before appellate other courts than the Judicial Division of Council of State (Afdeling bestuursrechspraak Raad van State). In all these appellate proceedings, the second chance function clearly prevails. The possibility to raise in appeal new legal grounds and bring forward new evidence is restricted only in a limited way, namely on the ground of due process considerations, and, in the French *appel*, to the category of grounds (external or internal illegality) raised in first instance as well. In these proceedings, the control function plays a modest role, insofar as the grounds raised in appeal should, in principle, be directed against the first instance judgment (and not against the decision contested in first instance), and a mere copy-and-paste of the first instance grounds may lead to the dismissal or inadmissibility of the appeal.

[76] Rules of Procedure of the Court of Justice, Art 170(1).

[77] Case C-76/93 P *Scaramuzza v Commission* ECLI:EU:C:1993:881, para 8.

In practice, however, the grounds raised in appeal can be very similar to those raised in first instance.

At the other end of the spectrum are the appellate proceedings before the European Court of Justice, and the German and French appeal on points of law (*Revision, cassation*). The review in these proceedings is limited to questions of law, although factual matters may exceptionally play a role, and their primary functions are the control function and the legal unity function. In all three proceedings, new pleas of law and new factual evidence are not allowed. Moreover, the grounds raised in appeal proceedings must be directed to the judgment contested.

Somewhere in between are the appellate proceedings in England and Wales before the Court of Appeal and the Supreme Court, and those before the Dutch Judicial Division of Council of State. In the latter, the control function prevails: appeal should be directed to the first instance judgment and, in principle, it is not possible to raise new legal grounds in the appellate stage. These limitations also serve the legal unity function. However, and insofar as the second chance function is also visible, new evidence is nowadays generally allowed by the Council of State. As regards the appellate proceedings in England and Wales, it has been observed that they may offer parties a second chance, but also that the possibility to raise new points of law and to admit new factual evidence is restricted in various ways. These limitations serve the control function and the legal unity function. With a view to the latter functions, appellate grounds should generally be directed to the judgment contested as well (and not to the decision contested in first instance).

In most jurisdictions (France, England and Wales, the Netherlands and the EU), lodging an appeal before an appellate court does not, in principle, suspend the judgment contested. However, in all jurisdictions, the appellate courts – and in England and Wales, the lower courts too – may, under certain circumstances and on request, order the suspension of the judgment or another interim measure. In some jurisdictions, lodging an appeal has instead a suspensory effect (Germany and the Netherlands in tax and social security cases).

8.5 REMEDIES

This section examines the remedies existing in appellate proceedings in the different jurisdictions. An appeal against a lower court's judgment can be either well founded or ill-founded. In the latter case, the appeal is rejected. If the appeal is well founded, the question can be raised of whether this should always lead to the annulment of the judgment contested, or whether it is possible for the appellate court to uphold the judgment if it is supported by other legal grounds. This question will be discussed hereafter. Furthermore, attention is paid to the issue of whether, if the contested judgment is annulled, the appellate court can decide on the merits of the case or should refer the case back to a lower court.

8.5.A THE EUROPEAN UNION

Statute of the Court of Justice of the European Union **8.39 (EU)**

Article 61 If the appeal is well founded, the Court of Justice shall quash the decision of the General Court. It may itself give final judgment in the matter, where the state of the proceedings so permits, or refer the case back to the General Court for judgment.

Where a case is referred back to the General Court, that Court shall be bound by the decision of the Court of Justice on points of law.

Case C-36/92 P, 19 May 1994[78] **8.40 (EU)**

Samenwerkende Elektriciteits-Produktiebedrijven (SEP) NV v Commission

APPEAL; INCORRECT GROUNDS; CORRECTION OPERATIVE PART

SEP

If the grounds of a judgment of the General Court disclose a breach of EU law but the operative part appears well founded for other reasons of law, the appeal must be dismissed.

Facts: The Commission had opened an investigation against the claimant for the alleged violation of EU competition law. In this framework, the Commission had adopted a decision requiring the claimant to sent it certain documents relating to the investigation. The claimant refused to produce these documents and the matter was eventually brought to the attention of the Court of First Instance. The court dismissed the claim. The judgment was appealed before the Court of Justice.

Held: The Court of Justice upheld the arguments of the claimant, but dismissed the appeal.

Judgment: 32. By interpreting Article 20 as it did, the Court of First Instance therefore infringed Community law.

33. It does not necessarily follow that the appeal must be upheld. … (i)f the grounds of a judgment of the Court of First Instance disclose a breach of Community law but the operative part appears well founded for other reasons of law, the appeal must be dismissed.

34. In the appeal, the appellant wrongly assumes that Article 10 of Regulation No 17, which states that 'the Commission shall forthwith transmit to the competent authorities of the Member States … copies of the most important documents lodged with the Commission …', obliges the Commission automatically to transmit the Statoil contract to the Dutch authorities.

35. Firstly, the wording of Article 10 itself gives the Commission power to determine which are the most important documents, with a view to transmitting them to the authorities of the Member States.

36. Secondly, Article 10(1) must be interpreted in the light of the general principle of the right of undertakings to protect their business secrets, a principle which is expressed in Article 214 of the Treaty and various provisions of Regulation No 17, such as Articles 19(3), 20(2) and 21(2) … .

37. In cases such as the present one where an undertaking has expressly raised before the Commission the confidential nature of a document against the competent national

[78] ECLI:EU:T:1991:71.

authorities, on the ground that it contains business secrets, and where that argument is not irrelevant, the general principle of the protection of business secrets, referred to above, may limit the Commission's obligation under Article 10(1) to transmit the document to the competent national authorities. …

41. It follows that the obligation to produce the Statoil contract, imposed on SEP by the contested decision, does not necessarily mean that the contract can be transmitted to the Dutch authorities.

42. Accordingly, notwithstanding legally defective reasoning, the under appeal rightly rejected the plea alleging breach of the principle of proportionality.

Notes

(1) Pursuant to Article 61 of the Statute of the Court of Justice, if the Court of Justice finds the appeal to be well founded, it will quash the decision of the General Court. As stated in the *SEP* case, such quashing will only occur if the judgment of the General Court is vitiated by an error of law which had an impact on the operative part of the ruling. This implies that if the reasoning of the General Court is vitiated but its operative part is nevertheless lawful on another ground, the appeal will be dismissed and the Court of Justice will set out the 'correct' grounds in the ruling.

(2) If the appeal is well founded and the judgment of the General Court is quashed, the Court of Justice will either refer the case back to the General Court or decide to judge the matter itself (Article 61 of the Statute of the Court of Justice). The latter option will be used if taking the decision does not require any additional fact-finding. In this case, the Court of Justice avails itself of all remedies available to the General Court.[79] Referrals back to the General Court instead are, for example, likely to happen if the General Court erroneously declared an application inadmissible,[80] or declared a certain legal plea (erroneously) well founded and therefore did not examine other legal pleas.[81] If the case is referred back to the General Court, the latter is bound by the decision of the Court of Justice on points of law.

8.5.B THE NETHERLANDS

Algemene Wet Bestuursrecht **8.41 (NL)**

Article 8:113 (1) The appellate court confirms the judgment of the district court, either confirming or improving the grounds, or, after annulling all or part of the judgment, does what the district court ought to do.

Article 8:115 (1) The appellate court refers the case back to the district court that decided the case in first instance if:

(a) the district court has ruled itself incompetent or has declared the appeal inadmissible, and the appellate court has annulled this judgment, declaring that the district court is competent, or the appeal is admissible, or

[79] On remedies, see Chapter 7.

[80] Case C-404/96 P *Glencore v Commission* ECLI:EU:C:1998:196, para 57.

[81] Case C-316/97 P *Parliament v Gaspari* ECLI:EU:C:1998:558, para 37.

(b) the appellate court is of the opinion that the case should be heard again before the district court for other reasons.

Notes

(1) According to Articles 8:113(1) and 8:115(1) AWB, the appellate court has three remedial options. First, it may confirm the judgment of the lower court, either by upholding it or by improving the grounds. Thus, it is possible that the judgment of the lower court is upheld even though it was based on insufficient grounds. Secondly, it can quash the judgment of the lower court in whole or in part, and do what the lower court ought to do. In this case, the appellate court avails itself of all the remedies available to the lower courts.[82] Thirdly, it can quash the judgment of the lower court and refer the case back to the court that dealt with the case in first instance. This obligation exists in two situations: (a) when the first instance court did not rule on the merits of the case, because it incorrectly decided that it was not competent or that the appeal was inadmissible, and (b) when the appellate court for other reasons is of the opinion that a retrial at first instance is necessary. In practice, the latter reason for referral is hardly applied as it is contrary to the principle of procedural economy.

(2) When the judgment of the appellate court results in the administrative authority taking a new decision, the appellate court may rule that a new appeal has to be brought directly before the appellate court (and not before the first instance district court). This possibility is called the 'judicial loop' (*rechterlijke lus*).

8.5.C FRANCE

Conseil d'État, 22 March 1993[83] **8.42 (FR)**

Hôpital de Brest v Ms Fraboul

APPEAL; DISCRETION OF THE COURT

Fraboul

An Administrative Court of Appeal has discretion to decide whether, after the annulment of a first instance judgment, to refer the case back to a lower court or to rule on the merits of the case.

Facts: After her husband's death, Ms Fraboul sought damages from Brest hospital. The Administrative Court of Appeal, after annulling the Administrative Court of First Instance's judgment, awarded her damages. The hospital challenged the ruling before the Council of State (Conseil d'État) in cassation.

Held: The claim of the hospital was rejected.

Judgment: Considering that, in order to annul the interim judgment of the Administrative Court of First Instance of Rennes of 6 February 1988 ordering medical expertise for the

[82] On remedies, see Chapter 7.
[83] N° 129052.

purpose of assessing the existence and the consequences of the delay in the intervention of the medical resident and of the anesthetist on the chances of survival of Mr X … on the ground that ordering this expertise was unreasonable, the Administrative Court of Appeal of Nantes, to support its findings, referred to the case file and notably to the expert report requested by the criminal court; considering that, by relying on factual elements presented to it, the court has carried out a sovereign assessment which shall not be reconsidered by the judge of cassation;

considering that, since it annulled the judgment of the Administrative Court of First Instance for the aforementioned reason, the Administrative Court of Appeal of Nantes has not committed an error of law by ruling on the merits of the matter; considering that, by deciding that it was justified to rule on the merits of the case, it has carried out an assessment which falls outside of the review of the judge of cassation.

Note

In *appel* proceedings (appeal on points of fact and law), the Administrative Court of Appeal can either, if necessary after improving the grounds of the first instance judgment, confirm or quash it. In the latter situation, it has discretion to either decide on the case itself (as in the *Fraboul* case) or refer it back to the lower court. In practice, it almost always chooses the first option (for various reasons, such as speed of justice or to inform future judgments). In this case, it avails itself of the same remedies as the lower courts.[84] The second option, referring the case back to the lower court, is used if the lower court did not rule on the merits of the case because of presumed lack of competence or of presumed inadmissibility of the action for annulment, and sometimes because of lack of information or in order to 'punish' the first instance court. In this case, a new appeal will be open against the 'second' first instance ruling.

Code de justice administrative **8.43 (FR)**

Article L821-2 When it annuls a decision of an administrative court ruling at the last instance, the Council of State (Conseil d'État) may either refer the case to the same court, ruling in a different formation, unless it is impossible due to the nature of the court, or refer the case to another court of the same type, or determine the merits of the case if this is justified in the interests of the good administration of justice.

When the case is subject of a second appeal to the Council of State sitting as a court of cassation, the Council will rule on the case definitively.

Note

In *cassation* proceedings (appeals on points of law), the Council of State either quashes or confirms the contested judgment. If the judgment is quashed, the Council of State can return the case to the court that took the contested judgment, refer it to

[84] On remedies, see Chapter 7.

a different court of appeal or decide on the merits of the case itself 'in the interest of the good administration of justice'. The latter is hardly ever done. However, if the case is subject to a second *cassation* appeal, the Council of State should make a final ruling.

8.5.D GERMANY

Verwaltungsgerichtsordnung **8.44 (DE)**

§129 The judgment of the Administrative Court of First Instance may only be altered insofar as an alteration has been applied for.

§130 (1) The Higher Administrative Court shall take the necessary evidence and shall rule on the merits itself.

(2) The Higher Administrative Court may only refer the case to the Administrative Court of First Instance, insofar as a further hearing on the case is necessary, by annulling the judgment and the proceedings

1. insofar as the proceedings before the Administrative Court of First Instance suffer from a major shortcoming and because of this shortcoming a comprehensive or laborious taking of evidence is necessary, or

2. if the Administrative Court of First Instance has not yet ruled on the merits itself and a party concerned applies for referral to the Administrative Court of First Instance.

(3) The Administrative Court of First Instance shall be bound by the legal assessment of the ruling on the appeal on points of fact and law.

§144 (1) If the appeal on points of law is inadmissible, the Federal Administrative Court shall dismiss it by order.

(2) If the appeal on points of law is ill-founded, the Federal Administrative Court shall reject the appeal on points of law.

(3) If the appeal on points of law is well-founded, the Federal Administrative Court may

1. rule on the case itself,

2. quash the challenged judgment and refer the case for court hearing and a ruling in other respects. …

(4) If the reasoning for the decision reveals a violation of the law, but the ruling itself proves to be correct for other reasons, the appeal on points of law shall be dismissed.

(5) …

(6) The court to which the case has been remitted for hearing and ruling shall base its ruling on the legal assessment of the court which ruled on points of law (*Revisionsgericht*).

Notes

(1) In proceedings for *Berufung* (appeal on points of fact and law), the Higher Administrative Court may alter the judgment of the administrative court only to the extent that an alteration of the initial judgment has been applied for (§129 VwGO). So if, for example, a party has claimed only for a partial annulment, *casu quo* partial alteration, of the judgment, the appellate court cannot annul or alter the entire judgment.

As *Berufung* is a continuation of the first instance proceedings, the Higher Administrative Court generally shall rule on the merits itself (§130(1) VwGO). In doing so, it avails itself of all the remedies available in first instance.[85] The appeal will be dismissed if the appellants' claim is unfounded even though flaws occurred in first instance. The Higher Administrative Court may only remit the case to the Administrative Court of First Instance if a further hearing on the case is necessary. That may be so where the proceedings before the Administrative Court of First Instance suffer from a major shortcoming and a comprehensive or laborious taking of evidence is necessary because of this shortcoming, or if the Administrative Court of First Instance has not yet ruled on the merits itself – for example, because it held the claim to be inadmissible – and one of the parties concerned applies for remittal (see §130(2) VwGO). In case of remittal, the administrative court shall be bound by the legal assessment of the ruling of the higher instance (§130(3) VwGO).

(2) With regard to decisions of the Federal Administrative Court (Bundesverwaltungsgericht) in a procedure for *Revision* (appeal on points of law), §144 VwGO stipulates that if the appeal on points of law is inadmissible, it will be dismissed by means of an order. If the appeal on points of law is ill-founded, the Federal Administrative Court will reject it. The appeal will also be dismissed if the reasoning for the contested judgment reveals a violation of the law, but the ruling proves to be correct for other reasons. If the appeal on points of law is well founded, the Federal Administrative Court may either rule on the case itself or quash the impugned judgment and remit the case to the Higher Administrative Court for settlement and a ruling in other respects. The former is done if the facts of the case are clear.

8.5.E ENGLAND AND WALES

Civil Procedure Rules **8.45 (EW)**

Rule 52.20 (1) In relation to an appeal the appeal court has all powers of the lower court.

(2) The appeal court has the power to–

(a) affirm, set aside or vary any order or judgment made or given by the lower court;

(b) refer any claim or issue for determination by the lower court;

(c) order retrial or hearing;

(d) make orders for payment of interest;

(e) make a cost order.

Note

Both appellate courts, the Court of Appeal and the Supreme Court, have the power to affirm, set aside or vary any order or judgment made or given by the lower court. If the lower judgment was flawed in some way, but the claimants' claim is ultimately

[85] On remedies, see Chapter 7.

unfounded, the judgment is affirmed. If the judgment is set aside or varied, the appellate courts avail themselves of all remedies available to the lower court.[86] They may, however, opt to refer a claim or issue for a new determination by the lower court, or order a retrial or hearing. Appellate courts are most likely to refer a matter back to a lower court if, after determination of a point of law, there needs to be a further consideration of the facts in order to reach a decision. In many administrative law cases, where factual disputes are not often at issue in appeals, it is usual for the appellate court to make a new order where the appeal is successful, rather than refer the issue back to the lower court.

8.5.F COMPARATIVE REMARKS

The remedies available in appellate procedures in the different jurisdictions are, although different at a technical level, quite similar in substance. First, in all jurisdictions, a contested judgment is not quashed if its operative part (the ruling), although based on unlawful grounds, is correct. In this respect, the appellate courts are competent to improve or supplement the grounds on which the contested judgment was based. Secondly, with an exception of the appeal on points of law in France (*cassation*) and Germany (*Revision*), the general rule in all appellate proceedings is that, if the first instance judgment is quashed or set aside, the appellate courts decide on the merits of the case. In doing so, they avail themselves of the same remedies as the lower courts. A general exception to this rule exists where the lower court did not rule on the merits of the case, for example, because it erroneously declared the action to be inadmissible. If the case is referred to a lower court, this court is bound by the legal assessment of the appellate court.

8.6 COMPARATIVE OVERVIEW

Appellate proceedings in the jurisdictions under analysis are regulated in different ways. Most similar are the appellate proceedings in Germany and France. Both countries provide for a two-layered system, in which a distinction is made between *Berufung/appel* on points of fact and law before the first appellate court (court administrative d'appel, Oberverwaltungsgericht) and *Revision/cassation* on points of law before the subsequent appellate court (Conseil d'Etat, Bundesverwaltungsgericht). The primary function of *Berufung/appel* is to offer a second chance to the parties. With a view to this function, in both appellate proceedings, it is possible to raise new legal grounds, although in the French *appel* this possibility may be limited by the category of grounds (concerning the internal or external illegality of the decision) brought forward in first instance, and to bring forward new factual evidence. The control function is also of some relevance for

[86] On remedies, see Chapter 7.

both appellate proceedings, as the appellate grounds should as a matter of principle be directed to the first instance judgment and should not be a copy of the grounds raised in first instance against the decision contested. However, in practice, they can be very close. In both appellate proceedings, only aggrieved parties have access. A difference between the two jurisdictions is that access to the German *Berufung* is limited by a permission to appeal system, a mechanism that does not exist in the French *appel*. In practice, this German permission system in *Berufung* is applied in a fairly relaxed manner.

The main function of *Revision/cassation* is to guarantee legal unity. The appeal is limited to legal grounds (in Germany, concerning federal law), and new legal grounds cannot be raised. The same obviously applies to (new) factual evidence. In Germany, the access to *Revision* is limited by a permission to appeal system. In France, such a mechanism does not exist. However, if the appeal in *cassation* is inadmissible or lacks serious grounds, the Council of State can reject it without giving any reason. Another difference between the two countries is that, in France, the Council of State is the only highest court overseeing all administrative courts, whereas there are several (administrative) highest federal courts in Germany. Legal unity between these courts is ensured by the Joint Senate of the Highest Courts of the Federation (Gemeinsamer Senat der obersten Gerichtshöfe des Bundes).

Similar to Germany and France, the appellate system in England and Wales is two-layered. In contrast to both countries, the English appellate courts, the Court of Appeal and the Supreme Court, are, in principle, competent to fully review points of law and fact. In practice, however, they tend to leave findings of the facts made by lower courts in place. Raising new legal grounds in appeal is possible, but is not allowed as a right. As regards new factual evidence, the default position is that it will not be permitted, although the Court of Appeal may allow it under fairly strict conditions. The access to both appellate proceedings is restricted by a permission to appeal procedure. Both English appellate proceedings combine, in a comparable way, elements of second chance, control and enhancing legal unity.

The Netherlands employs a single-layered system of appeal, in which several appellate courts decide in final instance on both points of law and fact. Appeal is not limited by a permission for appeal system. According to the – by default competent – Judicial Division of the Council of State, the main function of appeal is the control function. Therefore, the grounds should, as a matter of principle, be directed to the first instance judgment, and raising new legal grounds in appeal which could have been brought in first instance is forbidden. However, the Judicial Division permits new factual evidence concerning grounds that were already raised in first instance. The other appellate courts (Central Appellate Court, High Administrative Court for Trade and Industry and Courts of Appeal in tax cases) favour the second chance function, and allow new legal grounds and new factual evidence to be raised in appeal. With a view to the control function, parties should direct their grounds against the first instance judgment, but these grounds can be very similar to those raised in first instance. All appellate courts should guarantee legal unity within their specific competence. Legal unity between the different highest courts is enhanced by formal and informal means.

The single-layered appellate proceedings before the Court of Justice in the EU system is limited to grounds of law. In appeal, the claimant may develop the legal pleas, raised before the General Court, by way of new legal arguments, but he or she is not allowed to raise new legal pleas. Nor can the claimant bring forward new factual evidence. The main functions are the legal unity function and the control function.

FURTHER READING

Benetti, J, 'La définition de l'office du juge d'appel par le Conseil d'Etat, le juge administratif face au principe du réalisme' (2008) 40 *Actualité Juridique Droit Adminisratif* 2206.

Boucher, J and Crepey, E, 'Le Conseil d'Etat juge de cassation et la qualification juridique des faits' in MD Labetoulle (ed), *Mélanges en l'honneur de Daniel Labetoulle* (Paris, Dalloz, 2007).

Deguergue, M, 'Le double degré de juridiction' (2006) 24 *Actualité Juridique Droit Administratif* 1308.

Drewry, G, Blom-Cooper, L and Blake, C, *The Court of Appeal* (Oxford, Hart Publishing, 2007).

Massot, J et al, *Le Conseil d'Etat: Juge de cassation* (Boulogne Billancourt, Berger-Levrault, 2001).

Pouyaud, D, 'La recevabilité des moyens en cassation' [2004] *Revue française de droit administratif* 156.

Paterson, A, *Final Judgment: The Last Law Lords and the Supreme Court* (Oxford, Hart Publishing, 2013).

Widdershoven, RJGM, 'Het bestuursrechtelijk appel revisited' in GH Addink et al (eds), *Grensverleggend Bestuursrecht* (Alphen aan den Rijn, Wolters Kluwer, 2008).

Widdershoven, RJGM et al, *Hoger Beroep. Algemeen bestuursrecht 2001* (The Hague, Boom Juridisch, 2001).

CHAPTER 9
STRUCTURE AND STYLE OF JUDGMENTS

Chris Backes

9.1 INTRODUCTION

To understand the case law of the different legal systems dealt with in this book, it is necessary to examine how judgments are structured and drafted. For this purpose, in this chapter, examples of judgments of administrative law cases are provided and compared. The elements of judgments, their style and their structure are not accidental. They mirror the legal culture and traditions of the particular systems, and are also influenced by elements of procedural law. Therefore, this chapter also deals with the question of whether and to what extent a system of precedent is applied in the legal systems under examination, whether dissenting opinions are possible and whether judgments reflect the use of international and foreign law, even in cases where international or foreign rules are not directly binding on the case pending before the court. Hence, the chapter is not only about the outside appearance of judgments, but also about some substantive elements of procedural law that have not been dealt in Chapter 5.

9.2 NECESSITY OF A CERTAIN STRUCTURE OR STYLE

The structure and style of judgments in a certain legal system may be determined by historical factors or by fundamental principles of procedure, but may also mirror the course of the (oral) proceedings. Structure and style differ substantially in the legal systems examined. This chapter starts, therefore, with examples of (shortened) judgments from all legal systems dealt with in this book.[1]

9.2.A GERMANY

Verwaltungsgerichtsordnung **9.1 (DE)**

§117 (1) The judgment shall be handed down 'in the name of the people'. It shall be drawn up in writing and signed by the judges who were involved in the ruling. If a judge is prevented from adding his signature, this shall be noted under the judgment, along with the reason why he is prevented from attending, by the presiding judge or, if he is unable to attend, by the most senior associate judge. The honorary judges shall not be required to sign.

(2) The judgment shall contain

1. the designation of those concerned, of their legal representatives and of the authorized representatives by names, occupations, places of residence and by their status in the proceedings,
2. the designation of the court and the names of the members who have contributed towards the ruling,
3. the ruling,
4. the facts,
5. the reasoning for the ruling, and
6. the notification of the right to appeal.

(3) The statement of facts shall contain the essential content of the state of the facts and of the dispute in concise form, emphasising the relief sought. In respect of the details, reference should be made to written statements, minutes and other documents insofar as the state of the facts and of the dispute is sufficiently clear from these documents.

(4) …

(5) The court may refrain from a further exposition of the reasoning for the ruling insofar as it concurs with the reasoning of the administrative act or of the decision on the objection and this is established in its ruling.

(6) The clerk of the registry shall note on the judgment the date of service, and in cases falling under §116(1), first sentence, the date of the pronouncement, and shall sign this note. If the files are kept in electronic form, the clerk of the registry shall record the note in a separate document. The document shall be inseparably bound together with the judgment.

Notes

(1) §117 of the Verwaltungsgerichtsordnung (VwGO) lays down in quite some detail what judgments should contain and how they should be structured. In practice, this structure is applied.

(2) The formulation of the ruling depends upon the kind of action brought before the court and whether the claim is upheld or dismissed. In the case of an action for

[1] As the purpose of these excerpts is to demonstrate the structure and style of judgments and not to illustrate a certain point, the format of the excerpts may be slightly different from those contained in the other chapters.

annulment of an administrative act (*Anfechtungsklage*), the court must, for instance, rule that the original administrative act is annulled if the action is successful. If an action seeking the issuance of an administrative act (*Verpflichtungsklage*) is upheld and there is no discretion left to the administrative authority, the operative part of the judgment must state that the defendant administrative authority must issue the requested administrative act. If the administration retains discretion, the court will only rule that the defendant administrative authority must take a decision in accordance with the ruling of the court.[2] If an action for damages is brought, the court will mention the sum which the defendant is under an obligation to pay. Furthermore, the operative part of the judgment must always state who bears the costs of the proceedings.

Verwaltungsgericht Berlin, 17 December 2008[3] **9.2 (DE)**

Facts: See the first part of the judgment.

Held: See the part of the judgment called 'Decision'.

Judgment:
VG 72 A 245.08

Proclaimed on 17 December 2008
Eckert
Secretary of Justice
As authenticating officer of the court registry

(Sign of the Administrative Court Berlin)
ADMINISTRATIVE COURT BERLIN

JUDGMENT
In the name of the people

In the administrative dispute
of …

Claimant,

Counsel: …

a g a i n s t

Broadcast Berlin-Brandenburg,
public agency – legal department -;
represented by the director,
Masurenallee 8-14, 14057 Berlin,

Respondent,

[2] See Chapter 7, section 7.3.B.2.
[3] VG 27 A 245.08.

the administrative court Berlin, 27th chamber, has, after the oral hearing of 17 December 2008 by the presiding judge at the administrative court Neumann as single judge, ruled:

The notification of the broadcast Berlin-Brandenburg of 1 July 2008 as modified in the decision on the objection of 25 July 2008 is repealed.

The respondent is obliged to pay to the claimant €121,03 plus 5% interest charges above the base rate, starting from day the action has been pending at the court.

The costs of the proceedings are to be paid by the respondent.

In respect of the costs, the judgment is provisionally enforceable.

Facts

The parties involved disputed whether web-enabled personal computers (PCs) which have been used exclusively for professional use qualified as a 'new kind of radio receiver' and were therefore subject to broadcasting charges (a television or radio licence, required if one is to use a device to receive television or radio programmes), or whether the duty to pay broadcasting charges for these devices was satisfied when a different chargeable person who lives in the same property, has paid the broadcasting charges for a conventional radio receiver.

...

The claimant brought his claim on 29 August 2008. He argued that PCs, as multifunctional devices, which are not intended for use in the reception of radio broadcasting, were not subject to broadcasting charges. ...

The claimant sought to annul the notification of charges of the respondent of 1 June 2008 as modified in the decision on the objection and to order the respondent to pay to him €142,70 plus 5% interest charges above the base rate starting from day the action was pending at the court.

The respondent sought the claim to be dismissed.

He argued that web-enabled PCs should be subject to charges since 1 January 2007, as they can receive public broadcasting services through the internet.

Reasoning

In accordance with the decision of the chamber to transfer the case to a single judge, it was possible to decide the claim by the reporting judge, acting as a single judge (§6(1) VwGO).

The claim is admissible as a combined action for annulment and action seeking the issuance of an administrative act, as the notification of charges of 1 June 2008 and the decision on the objection of 25 July 2008 are unlawful and infringe upon the claimant's rights (§113(1) VwGO). The claim for restitution of the broadcasting charges paid is only partially founded, namely only insofar as the broadcasting charges paid by the claimant were not ultimately fixed by the notification of 4 July 2008.

...

9.3. The ancillary decisions are based on §§154(1) VwGO and 167(2) VwGO, as the fact that the claim was partially unsuccessful is of no importance for the decision as to costs, as the value in dispute remains within the same category.

Right to appeal

The respondent has a right to appeal against this ruling if the appeal is admitted by the Higher Administrative Court (Oberverwaltungsgericht).

The application for admission of the appeal has to be made within one month of the notification of the judgment. The application needs to identify the judgment it seeks to challenge.

Within two months of the notification of the judgment, the statement of grounds of appeal must be laid out in writing. The reasoning is, as far as it has not already been presented with the application, to be submitted to the Higher Administrative Court (Oberverwaltungsgericht) Berlin, Kirchstraße 7, 10557 Berlin.

Before the Higher Administrative Court (Oberverwaltungsgericht), the parties involved must be represented by attorneys of record. This also holds for the application for the admission of the appeal. Lawyers and professors of law at a university in the sense of the Framework Act for Higher Education (Hochschulrahmengesetz) as attorneys of record are allowed. Further, the persons identified in §67(2) sentence 2 no 3-7 VwGO can act. Public authorities and juridical persons of public law, including the associations set up to fulfil the tasks of the public authorities, can be represented by employees qualified as judges; the employment relationship can also extend to a different public authority, juridical person of public law or one of the associations as defined above. Judges cannot act before the court and lay judges cannot act before the chamber of which they are a member.

Neumann

Drawn up
Court employee
As authenticating officer of the court registry

9.2.B NETHERLANDS

Algemene Wet Bestuursrecht **9.3 (NL)**

Article 8:77 (1) The written judgment shall state:

a. the names of the parties and their representatives or agents,
b. the grounds for the decision,
c. the decision,
d. the name or names of the judge or judges hearing the case,
e. the date on which the decision was delivered,
f. by whom, within which period and before which court, which kind of legal recourse may be sought.

(2) If the district court finds the claim for judicial review to be well-founded, the judgment shall state what written or unwritten rule of law or which general principle of law is found to have been violated.

(3) The judgment shall be signed by the presiding judge and the registrar. If the presiding judge or registrar is unable to sign, this shall be stated in the judgment.

Note

Article 8:77 of the Algemene Wet Bestuursrecht (AWB) sums up all the elements which must be contained in a judgment.

Rechtbank Noord-Holland, 19 April 2013[4] **9.4 (NL)**

Stichting bevordering kwaliteit leefomgeving Schipholregio

Facts: The claimant, who lived close to Schiphol Airport, asked the respondent, the Schiphol Region Quality of Life Foundation (Stichting bevordering kwaliteit leefomgeving Schipholregio), for financial compensation because of the detrimental effects of the intensified use of Schiphol airport, which had been permitted by law.

Held: The district court held that it lacked the competence to hear the case.

Judgment:

DISTRICT COURT OF NOTHERN HOLLAND
Venue Alkmaar
Administrative Law
Case number HAA 12/4740
Judgment of the chamber of three judges of 19 April 2013 in the dispute between
[name of claimant], [residence of claimant], claimant
and
Schiphol Region Quality of Life Foundation (*Stichting bevordering kwaliteit leefomgeving Schipholregio*), respondent
(representative mr. F.A. Mulder)

Process sequence

By decision of 12 September 2012 (the disputed decision), the respondent rejected the objections raised in the intra-administrative objection procedure.

The claimant has applied for judicial review of the disputed decision.

The respondent has put forward a statement of defense.

The oral hearing took place on 12 March 2013.

The claimant was present. The respondent was represented by his representative as well as R.V. Gort, the program manager, and M.J. Meulen, the secretary of the intra-administrative objection procedure committee (*bezwaarschriftencommissie*), both employees of the Stichting bevordering kwaliteit leefomgeving Schipholregio (hereafter: the Stichting).

Considerations

1. Before considering the substance of the claim for judicial review, the district court has to assess whether the Stichting can be considered an administrative authority as defined in Article 1:1 AWB, and thus if the disputed decision is subject to judicial review by the administrative courts.

2. In Article 1:1(1) AWB an administrative authority is defined as:

(a) an organ of a legal entity which has been established under public law, or

(b) another person or body which is invested with any public authority.

In Article 1:3(1) AWB a decision (*besluit*) is defined as: a written decision by an administrative authority containing a legal act under public law.

2. From the Stichting's articles of association it follows that the Stichting was established by the province Noord-Holland and N.V. Luchthaven Schiphol (Schiphol airport)

[4] ECLI:NL:RBNHO:2013:BZ8741.

with the aim of improving the quality of life, in the broadest sense, within the Schiphol region. The Stichting tries to achieve its goals *inter alia* by granting benefits, whether or not paid in kind, in individual cases where very severe circumstances are demonstrated by the applicant. These grants have to meet the criteria put forward in the Stichting's regulations, which have to be approved by the board of directors. In the claim for judicial review at hand, the denial of a benefit paid in kind to the claimant is in dispute.

3. The Stichting is not a legal person established by public law in the sense of Article 1:1(1) AWB, but a legal person established under private law. As a result of this fact, the question at hand is whether the Stichting constitutes a person or body to whom public powers are attributed as defined under Section b of this provision.

4. The Stichting argues that it is to be regarded as an administrative authority.

5. According to settled jurisprudence of the Judicial Division of the Council of State (judgment of 30 November 1995, LJN ZF1850, and 15 July 2009, LJN BJ2607) in order to establish whether a person or a body has to be considered an administrative authority within the definition of Article 1:1(1) under b AWB, it is relevant to consider whether the Stichting, when deciding on benefits, is executing public powers in the sense meant in this article. In the case of a legal person established under private law to which no public powers are given to fulfill a public task, this must be considered not to be the case, unless extraordinary circumstances lead to a different judgment. The following conditions are in the jurisprudence of the Division deemed to be extraordinary: the execution of a public task by a legal person established under private law, the transfer of financial means to the legal person by the government and the setting of criteria for the spending of these financial means by the government.

6. The court finds no execution of any public power. This finding is based on the following considerations. It is not in dispute that no public task was given to the Stichting to which public powers are attributed. Therefore, the conclusion must be that the Stichting's decisions in granting benefits in severe cases are not made in execution of any public powers. Furthermore, there are no other conditions that lead to a different judgment.

The conclusion is that in the case of the Stichting there are no special circumstances concerning its tasks and the granting of financial means in severe cases, so the decisions made by the Stichting are not made in the execution of public powers.

7. These considerations lead to the conclusion that the court lacks competence to hear the case because the Stichting cannot be deemed to be an administrative authority as defined in Article 1:1 AWB. Therefore, the letter of 12 September 2012 cannot be regarded as a decision under the statutory definition of Article 1:3(1) AWB.

8. There is no cause for an order to compensate for legal costs.

9. In the instance where the respondent regarded the claimant to have standing in the intra-administrative objection procedure and has explicitly mentioned in the disputed decision that the decision was open to judicial review, the court finds that the respondent has to pay back the court fees to the claimant.

Decision

The court:

— holds that it lacks the competence to hear the case;

— orders the respondent to compensate the claimant for the amount of €156 paid in court fees.

This judgment was issued by Mr WJAM van Brussel, president, and Mr IM Ludwig and Mr SM van Velsen, members of the court, in presence of Mr YR Boonstra-van Herwijnen, clerk.

Remedies

This judgment is open to appeal before the Judicial Division of the Council of State. The appeal can be brought within six weeks after the notification of the judgment. When the appeal is submitted, a provisional remedy to stay or alter the current decision can be requested from the interim relief judge of the appellate court.

Notes

(1) Written judgments in general contain five elements, as can be seen from the example above. Some elements follow from the AWB and other elements are based on practice.

(a) A heading in which the specific court, the date of the judgment and the parties are indicated. For a judgment in an appeal, the court decision against which the appeal is brought is also stated.

(b) The first (introductory) part of the judgment starts with a summary of the proceedings and sets out the relevant decision(s) of the administrative authority (and possibly the court in first instance). It also states the date of the court hearing and who has attended (if there was a court hearing, see Article 8:54 AWB).[5]

(c) The second (substantive) part of the judgment is the most important. It deals with the content of the administrative decision (or in appeal, the court decision of first instance) and the grounds of appeal. It also outlines the relevant legal provisions applicable to the substance of the case and above all it states the considerations of the court applicable to the grounds of the claim; for instance, that the administrative decision will be annulled and a new decision has to be taken.

(d) The third part deals with the dictum or dicta that are a consequence of the second part. This part is concluded by the indication of the names of the judge(s) and the clerk, as well as the date of the notification of the judgment.

(e) The judgments (of the lower courts) close with a notice of the possibility of appeal, or if an appeal is not possible, this will be stated. In cases where it is possible to appeal, the time period for bringing an appeal and the relevant court are indicated.

(2) The style of writing is an issue that from time to time has led to some debate (how long should a judgment be, can it easily be read and understood by non-lawyers, etc). In practice, at least within the same court, there is an effort to write texts in a uniform and consistent manner. Since February 2016, the Judicial Division of the Council of State (Afdeling Bestuursrechtspraak Raad van State) has developed a 'readability project'. It has changed the structure and style of its judgments in order to enhance readability, especially for persons who are not used to reading judgments and do not have a legal background. One of the measures taken is that legal provisions are no longer quoted in the text itself, but in an appendix. Another measure is that the judgment starts with a summary of the case and of what the parties sought from the court in non-legal terms.[6]

[5] For more detail, see Chapter 5, section 5.2.A.1 (iii).

[6] G van der Bruggen, 'Een kleine stap voor de rechter, een reuzensprong voor de rechtspraak' (2016) *JBplus* 109.

9.2.C FRANCE

Code de justice administrative **9.5 (FR)**

Article R741-2 The decision must state that the hearing was held in open court, unless the provisions of Article L731-1 were applied. In this latter case, the decision states that the hearing was held or continued in camera.

It includes the names of the parties, an analysis of the submissions and statements of the case and references to the statutory or regulatory provisions that the decision applies.

It mentions that the judge rapporteur and the public rapporteur and, where appropriate, the parties, their agents or defence counsels and any person heard on the basis of a decision by the president by virtue of Article R731-3(2), were heard.

When, in accordance with Article R732-1-1, the public rapporteur has not been required to deliver conclusions, this is mentioned.

If a memorandum was submitted to the court during the deliberations, the decision also records this fact.

The decision states the date of the hearing and the date on which the decision was rendered.

Note

The compulsory requirements of the judgments are prescribed by Article R741-2 of the Code of Administrative Justice. The structure and other recurring elements of judgments, however, are based on practice.

Conseil d'État, 28 December 2009[7] **9.6 (FR)**

Commune de Béziers v Commune de Villeneuve-lès-Béziers

Commune de Béziers

Facts: Two local authorities concluded a contract to proceed with the development of a new industrial area. The mayor of one authority decided to terminate the contract due to the breach of procedural requirements. The other authority claimed for damages.

Held: The contract was upheld because of the minor character of the breach.

Judgment:
Conseil d'État
N° 304802
ECLI:FR:CEASS:2009:304802.20091228
Published in digest Lebon

Assembly

M. Xavier Domino, rapporteur SCP NICOLAY, DE LANOUVELLE, HANNOTIN; ODENT, representatives

Reading of Monday, 28 December 2009

[7] N° 304802.

FRENCH REPUBLIC
IN THE NAME OF THE FRENCH PEOPLE

Considering the summary of the claim and the supplementary submission, registered on 16 April and 13 June 2007 at the litigation secretariat of the Litigation Section of the Conseil d'État, presented on behalf of the MUNICIPALITY OF BEZIERS, represented by its Mayor; the MUNICIPALITY OF BEZIERS requests the Conseil d'État:

1) to set aside the judgment of 12 February 2007 of the Administrative Court of Appeal of Marseille, insofar as, having annulled the judgment of the Administrative Court of First Instance of Montpellier of 25 March 2005, it dismissed its request that the municipality of Villeneuve-lès-Béziers be ordered to pay it compensation of €591,103.78, for the amounts that this municipality should have paid it pursuant to the clauses of an agreement signed on 10 October 1986 as well as €45,374.70 in damages;

2) settling the case on the merits, to grant the appeal;

3) to order the municipality of Villeneuve-lès-Béziers to pay the sum of €5,000 pursuant to Article L7611 of the Code of Administrative Justice;

Considering the other materials of the case;

Considering the General code on local authorities (Code général des collectivités territoriales);

Considering the Code of Administrative Justice;

Having heard in open court:

— the report by Mr Xavier Domino, Auditor,

— the observations of SCP[8] Nicolaÿ, de Lanouvelle, Hannotin, counsel for the MUNICIPALITY OF BEZIERS and Me[9] Odent, counsel for the municipality of Villeneuve-lès-Béziers,

— the submissions by Mr Emmanuel Glaser, public rapporteur;

SCP Nicolaÿ, de Lanouvelle, Hannotin, counsel for the MUNICIPALITY OF BEZIERS

and Me Odent, counsel for the municipality of Villeneuve-lès-Béziers, having again addressed the court.

Considering that it appears from the evidence of the case submitted to the court hearing the substance of the case that, as part of a multipurpose inter-municipal association they had created to this end, the municipalities of BEZIERS and Villeneuve-lès-Béziers concluded a project extending an industrial estate located entirely on the territory of the municipality of Villeneuve-lès-Béziers; that, by an agreement signed by their two mayors on 10 October 1986, these local authorities agreed that the municipality of Villeneuve-lès-Béziers would pay to the MUNICIPALITY OF BEZIERS a part of the money that it would collect in respect of business tax, in order to reflect the decrease in revenue resulting from the relocation of businesses that until that time were located on the territory of the MUNICIPALITY OF BEZIERS to the industrial estate thus created; that, by letter of 22 March 1996, the Mayor of Villeneuve-lès-Béziers informed the mayor of BEZIERS of his intention to terminate this agreement with effect from 1 September 1996; considering that, by a judgment of 25 March 2005, the Administrative Court of First Instance of Montpellier, before which the case was brought by the MUNICIPALITY OF BEZIERS, dismissed the latter's application seeking that the municipality of Villeneuve-lès-Béziers be ordered to pay it compensation of €591,103.78 in respect of the amounts not paid since the termination

[8] SCP signifies '*société civile professionnelle*'.
[9] Me is the acronym for '*maître*'.

of the contract, as well as a sum of €45,374.70 in damages; that, by an order of 13 June 2007, against which the MUNICIPALITY OF BEZIERS appealed on points of law, the Administrative Court of Appeal of Marseille ruled, after having annulled the judgment of the Administrative Court of First Instance of Montpellier because a violation of the law, that the contract of 10 October 1986 should be declared 'void' and dismissed the application by the MUNICIPALITY OF BEZIERS;

Without need to consider the other grounds of the appeal;

Considering that, firstly, the parties to an administrative contract may lodge a claim for a full jurisdiction remedy (*recours de plein jurisdiction*) challenging the validity of the contract which binds them;

Considering that it is the court's responsibility, where it finds the existence of irregularities, to assess their importance and consequences, after having checked that the irregularities of which the parties avail themselves are among those which, given the requirement of fairness of contractual relations, they may invoke before it;

...

Considering that, secondly, when the parties put before the court a dispute relating to the performance of the contract which binds them, it is in principle the court's responsibility, given the requirement of fairness of contractual relations, to require the contract to be applied;

...

Considering that, therefore, by ruling that the contract concluded on 10 October 1986 between the municipalities of Villeneuve-lès-Béziers and Béziers must be declared 'void' on the sole ground that the deliberations of 29 September 1986 and 3 October 1986 authorising the mayors of these municipalities to sign it were only communicated to the sub-prefecture on 16 October 1986 and that such a circumstance was an obstacle to the stipulations of the contract being invoked in the context of the dispute before it, the Administrative Court of Appeal of Marseille committed an error of law;

Considering that, accordingly, the MUNICIPALITY OF BEZIERS is justified in requesting the annulment of the judgment that it contests;

Considering that the provisions of Article L761-1 of the Code of Administrative Justice preclude the MUNICIPALITY OF BEZIERS which is not, in this case, the losing party from making payment to Villeneuve-lès-Béziers of the amount sought in respect of the expenses incurred by it and not included in the costs;

Considering that it is appropriate, on the basis of the same provisions, to order Villeneuve-lès-Béziers to pay a sum of €3,000 to the MUNICIPALITY OF BEZIERS;

DISPOSITION:

Article 1: The judgment of the Administrative Court of Appeal of Marseille of 12 February 2007 is set aside insofar as it dismisses the application of the MUNICIPALITY OF BEZIERS.

Article 2: The case is referred back to the Administrative Court of Appeal of Marseille to this extent.

Article 3: The municipality of Villeneuve-lès-Béziers shall pay to the MUNICIPALITY OF BEZIERS the sum of €3,000 pursuant to Article L761-1 of the Code of Administrative Justice.

Article 4: The submissions presented by the municipality of Villeneuve-lès-Béziers on the basis of Article L761-1 of the Code of Administrative Justice are dismissed.

Article 5: This decision shall be notified to the MUNICIPALITY OF BEZIERS and to the municipality of Villeneuve-lès-Béziers. A copy shall be sent for information to the Ministry of Budget, Public Accounts, Civil Service and State Reform.

Notes

(1) All French administrative courts follow the same structure and style of judgments. The judgment is divided into three parts:

(a) At the beginning of the judgment it is expressed that the judgment is rendered in the name of the French people, and the name of the applicant, the date of the judgment, and the names of the judge rapporteur, the public rapporteur and the judge chairing the panel are stated. This part contains the list (one by one) of the different submissions of the parties, their claims and the pleas, as well as the legal texts explicitly or implicitly used in the reasoning (for example: 'Considering the Constitution; Considering the European Convention on Human Rights; Considering statute number …')

(b) The second part contains the reasoning of the judgment. This reasoning is drafted in indirect style, each paragraph beginning by 'considering that …'. The order of the paragraphs must reveal the syllogism used by the court to deduce the solution from the general rule and from the facts.

(c) The final part is the 'decision' itself, written in articles. The signatures of the justices and the clerk follow.

(2) A substantial reform occurred in 2015 regarding the structure and style of the judgments of administrative courts. Some judging panels in the Council of State, the Administrative Courts of First Instance and the Administrative Courts of Appeal are experimenting with different means of conveying their judgments. The project will eventually lead to strengthening the phrasing of the reasoning and the courts will write judgments in a direct style, without using 'considering that'.

9.2.D THE EUROPEAN UNION

Rules of Procedure of the Court of Justice **9.7 (EU)**

Article 87 Content of a judgment

A judgment shall contain:

(a) a statement that it is the judgment of the Court,

(b) an indication as to the formation of the Court,

(c) the date of delivery,

(d) the names of the President and of the Judges who took part in the deliberations, with an indication as to the name of the Judge Rapporteur,

(e) the name of the Advocate General,

(f) the name of the Registrar,

(g) a description of the parties or of the interested persons referred to in Article 23 of the Statute who participated in the proceedings,

(h) the names of their representatives,

(i) in the case of direct actions and appeals, a statement of the forms of order sought by the parties,

(j) where applicable, the date of the hearing,

(k) a statement that the Advocate General has been heard and, where applicable, the date of his Opinion,

(l) a summary of the facts,
(m) the grounds for the decision,
(n) the operative part of the judgment, including, where appropriate, the decision as to costs.

Note

Article 87 of the Rules of Procedure of the Court of Justice and Article 81 of the Rules of Procedure of the General Court provide for certain requirements for the content of a judgment. Importantly, the judgments should contain a summary of the facts, the grounds for the decision and the operative part of the judgment, including, where appropriate, the decision as to costs.

Joined Cases 46/87 and 227/88, 21 September 1989[10] **9.8 (EU)**

Hoechst AG v Commission

Hoechst AG

Facts: See Sections 1–3 of the judgment.

Held: The claim was dismissed.

Judgment:

HOECHST v COMMISSION
JUDGMENT OF THE COURT
21 September 1989*

In Joined Cases 46/87 and 227/88

Hoechst AG, a company incorporated under German law whose registered office is in Frankfurt am Main, represented by Hans Hellmann, Rechtsanwalt, Cologne, with an address for service in Luxembourg at the Chambers of Marc Loesch, 8, rue Zithe,

applicant,

v

Commission of the European Communities, represented by its Legal Adviser, Norbert Koch, acting as Agent, with an address for service in Luxembourg at the office of Georgios Kremlis, a member of its Legal Department, Wagner Centre,

defendant,

APPLICATION

...

THE COURT

...

Judgment

1. By applications lodged at the Court Registry on 16 February 1987 and 5 August 1988 respectively, Hoechst AG brought two actions under the second paragraph of Article 173 of the EEC Treaty for declarations that three Commission decisions ... were void. ...

[10] ECLI:EU:C:1989:337.

2. Having grounds for suspecting the existence, as between certain producers and suppliers of PVC and polyethylene in the Community, of agreements or concerted practices concerning the fixing of prices and delivery quotas for those products, the Commission decided to carry out an investigation into several undertakings, including the applicant in respect of which it adopted the abovementioned contested decision of 15 January 1987 (hereinafter referred to as 'the decision ordering the investigation').

3. On 20, 22 and 23 January 1987, the Commission sought to carry out the investigation in question, but the applicant refused to submit to the investigation on the ground that it constituted an unlawful search. The applicant expressed the same point of view in its reply to a telex in which the Commission called upon it to undertake to submit to the investigation and set a periodic penalty payment, in the event of non-compliance, of ECU 1,000 for each day of delay. The Commission then adopted the abovementioned contested decision of 3 February 1987, in which it imposed the periodic penalty payment mentioned above on the applicant (hereinafter referred to as 'the decision imposing the periodic penalty payment').

...

(a) The Commission's powers of investigation

10. The applicant considers that the contested decision is unlawful inasmuch as it permitted the Commission's officials to take steps which the applicant describes as a search, which are not provided for under Article 14 of Regulation No 17 and which infringe on fundamental rights recognized by Community law. It adds that if that provision is to be interpreted as empowering the Commission to carry out searches, it is unlawful on the ground that it is incompatible with fundamental rights, for the protection of which it is necessary that searches should be carried out only on the basis of a judicial warrant issued in advance.

11. The Commission contends that its powers under Article 14 of Regulation No 17 extend to the adoption of measures which, under the law of some Member States, would be regarded as searches. It nonetheless considers that the requirements of judicial protection deriving from fundamental rights, which it does not contest in principle, are fulfilled insofar as the addressees of decisions ordering investigations have an opportunity, on the one hand, to contest those decisions before the Court and, on the other, to apply for suspension of their operation by way of interim order, which permits the Court to check rapidly that the investigations ordered are not arbitrary in nature. Such review is equivalent to a judicial warrant issued in advance.

12. It should be noted, before the nature and scope of the Commission's powers of investigation under Article 14 of Regulation No 17 are examined, that that article cannot be interpreted in such a way as to give rise to results which are incompatible with the general principles of Community law and in particular with fundamental rights.

13. The Court has consistently held that fundamental rights are an integral part of the general principles of law the observance of which the Court ensures, in accordance with constitutional traditions common to the Member States, and the international treaties on which the Member States have collaborated or of which they are signatories (see, in particular, the judgment of 14 May 1974 in Case 4/73 *Nold v Commission* (1974) ECR 491). The European Convention for the Protection of Human Rights and Fundamental Freedoms of 4 November 1950 (hereinafter referred to as 'the European Convention on Human Rights') is of particular significance in that regard (see, in particular, the judgment

of 15 May 1986 in Case 222/84 *Johnston v Chief Constable of the Royal Ulster Constabulary* (1986) ECR 1651).

...

36. In the light of the foregoing, it must be held that the measures which the contested decision ordering the investigation permitted the Commission's officials to take did not exceed their powers under Article 14 of Regulation No 17. Article 1 of that decision merely requires the applicant 'to permit officials authorized by the Commission to enter its premises during normal office hours, to produce for inspection and to permit copies to be made of business documents related to the subject-matter of the enquiry which are requested by the said officials and to provide immediately any explanations which those officials may seek'.

37. During the proceedings before the Court, the Commission did indeed argue that its officials are entitled, when making investigations, to carry out searches without the assistance of the national authorities and without respecting the procedural guarantees provided for under national law. However, that misinterpretation of Article 14 of Regulation No 17 cannot render unlawful decisions adopted on the basis of that provision.

38. The submission alleging that the Commission exceeded its powers of investigation must therefore be rejected.

(b) The statement of reasons

(c) The procedure under which the decision was adopted

...

66. It follows from the foregoing that the applications must be dismissed.

Costs

67. Under Article 69(2) of the Rules of Procedure, the unsuccessful party is to be ordered to pay the costs if they have been asked for in the successful party's pleading. Since the applicant has failed in its submissions, it must be ordered to pay the costs.

On those grounds,

THE COURT

hereby:

(1) Dismisses the applications;

(2) Orders the applicant to pay the costs.

...

Note

As can be seen from the excerpt above, rulings of the European Courts always start with an indication of the parties, the type of request and the judges composing the court giving the ruling. Thereafter the facts are summarised, and the claim and the grounds of the ruling are provided. Often this part is sub-divided into sub-parts when there is more than one contention made by the application. The ruling is concluded with the decision on costs and the operative part.

9.2.E ENGLAND AND WALES

High Court (Queen's Bench Division), 4 October 2016[11] **9.9 (EW)**

Forest of Dean District Council v Secretary of State for Communities and Local Government and Gladman Developments Limited

Gladman

Facts: The Forest of Dean District Council applied for judicial review of the decision of an inspector appointed by the Secretary of State to allow Gladman's appeal against the Council's decision to refuse planning permission for a development of up to 95 developments. The Council's argument was that the inspector had erred in his definition of the concept of a 'valued landscape' as referred to in the relevant National Planning Policy Framework. The question was whether the inspector's definition of a 'valued landscape' in his decision was erroneous.

Held: See judgment, section 43.

Judgment:

Neutral Citation Number: [2016] EWHC 2429 (Admin)
Case No: CO/978/2016

IN THE HIGH COURT OF JUSTICE
QUEEN'S BENCH DIVISION
PLANNING COURT

Bristol Civil Justice Centre
2 Redcliff Street
Bristol
04/10/16

Before:
MR JUSTICE HICKINBOTTOM

Between:
FOREST OF DEAN DISTRICT COUNCIL
Claimant
- and -
(1) SECRETARY OF STATE FOR COMMUNITIES AND LOCAL GOVERNMENT
(2) GLADMAN DEVELOPMENTS LIMITED
Defendants

Peter Wadsley and Philip Robson (instructed by Forest of Dean District Council Legal Services) for the Claimant
Gwion Lewis (instructed by the Government Legal Department) for the First Defendant
Peter Goatley (instructed by Irwin Mitchell LLP) for the Second Defendant
Hearing date: 4 October 2016

---

[11] [2016] EWHC 2429 (Admin).

Mr Justice Hickinbottom:

Introduction

1. This is an application under section 288 of the Town and Country Planning Act 1990 ('the 1990 Act'), in which the Claimant local planning authority ('the Council') seeks to quash a decision dated 14 January 2016 of an inspector appointed by the First Defendant Secretary of State, namely George Baird BA (Hons) MA MRTPI ('the Inspector'), to allow an appeal under section 78 of the 1990 Act against its decision dated 10 December 2014 and to grant planning permission for up to 95 dwellings and associated development at land north of Gloucester Road, Tutshill, Chepstow, Gloucestershire ('the Site') on the application of the Second Defendant ('the Developer'). The Site is immediately adjacent to the village of Tutshill, being separated from other dwellings by Gloucester Road and Elm Road.

...

4. The sole extant ground is straightforward, discrete and narrow. Briefly, the Council through Mr Wadsley contends that the Inspector erred in the manner in which he dealt with landscape. Paragraph 109 of the National Planning Policy Framework ('the NPPF') states that: 'The planning system should contribute to and enhance the natural and local environment by ... protecting and enhancing valued landscapes ...'. That requires a planning decision-maker to determine whether the relevant landscape is 'valued'; and then, if it is, to recognise that enhanced planning status by taking into account the policy that such landscapes should be protected and enhanced. The Inspector erred (it is said) by equating 'valued landscape' with a landscape that is designated to have a particular landscape quality. The landscape here is not the subject of any designation; but the Inspector erred in finding that, consequently, it was necessarily also not 'valued'. He ought to have assessed whether the landscape was a 'valued landscape' for the purposes of paragraph 109 of the NPPF; and, had he done so, it cannot be assumed that he would definitely have concluded that it was not; and it cannot be assumed that his decision to grant the application for planning permission would have been the same. The Inspector's error was therefore material, and his decision ought to be quashed.

...

The Relevant Law and Policy

7. The relevant law and policy is uncontroversial.

8. Section 70(2) of the 1990 Act provides that, in dealing with an application for planning permission, a decision-maker must have regard to the provisions of 'the development plan', as well as 'any other material consideration'. 'The development plan' sets out the local planning policy for an area, and is defined by section 38 of the Planning and Compulsory Purchase Act 2004 ('the 2004 Act') to include adopted local plans.

9. Section 38(6) of the 2004 Act provides:

'If regard is to be had to the development plan for the purpose of any determination to be made under the planning Acts the determination must be made in accordance with the plan unless material considerations indicate otherwise.'

Section 38(6) thus raises a presumption that planning decisions will be taken in accordance with the development plan, but that presumption is rebuttable by other material considerations.

10. The relevant adopted local plan for the Site was the Council's Core Strategy adopted in February 2012 ('the Core Strategy') together with saved policies from the Council's Local Plan 2005. There was also an emerging Allocations Plan.

11. Policy CSP1 of the Core Strategy provides that the design and construction of new development must take into account important characteristics of the environment and conserve, preserve or otherwise respect them in a manner that maintains or enhances their contribution to the environment, including their wider context. Mr Wadsley emphasised the disjunctive nature of 'maintained or enhanced', compared with paragraph 109 of the NPPF in which the terms are used conjunctively ('protected and enhanced'), such that the status conferred by paragraph 109 is the greater. In achieving that, Policy CSP1 sets out a number of matters that must be considered, including: 'The effect of the proposal on the landscape including [Areas of Outstanding Natural Beauty] and any mitigation/enhancement that is necessary or desirable'. Paragraph 6.5 of the notes to the Core Strategy states:

'Overall the variety of landscapes is an outstanding feature of the Forest of Dean District and it is vital that development proposals take account of this, as well as any nature conservation or archaeological and/or historical interests. The impact on the landscape will primarily be evaluated using the Council's Landscape Supplementary Planning Document and the Landscape Assessment. It will be a key consideration in the evaluation of any development proposal.'

...

<u>The Issue</u>

20. The Inspector had to consider a number of key issues, including the adverse impact of the proposed development on the character and appearance of the area. One element of that, raised by the Council for the first time in the appeal, was whether the Site was located in an area of 'valued landscape' for the purposes of paragraph 109 of the NPPF.

21. It was not suggested by any party that a 'valued' landscape was restricted to an area which had been the subject of some form of landscape designation; but, in its submissions to the Inspector, the Council contended that the Site, although not designated, fell within a 'valued landscape' as defined in Stroud (see, e.g., paragraph 10 of the Council's Opening Statement and paragraphs 6–7 of its Closing Submissions). The Council's case on this issue was supported by expert evidence from Peter Radmall MA BPhil CMLI. His evidence was that the GLVIA makes clear that 'highly valued landscapes are normally designated', but 'the absence of designation does not necessarily indicate an absence of value' (paragraph 6.3 of his July 2015 Report). He appended a copy of the Stroud judgment, to which he referred in his report; and he made an assessment of landscape value on the basis of the GLVIA criteria, before concluding that, in his opinion, 'the Site and its surroundings demonstrate sufficient physical attributes to suggest that they fall within a locally valued landscape' so that it was 'worthy of a commensurate degree of protection and enhancement under NPPF paragraph 109' (paragraphs 6.10 and 6.11).

...

<u>The Inspector's Decision</u>

24. The Inspector identified 'the effect [of the proposal] on the character and appearance of the area' as a major issue with which he had to grapple (paragraph 10 of his Decision). He dealt with it in paragraphs 11–19.

...

<u>The Ground of Challenge</u>

28. As I have already indicated, there is a single ground of challenge; and it is simply put.

29. In paragraph 16 of the Decision, the Inspector proceeded on the basis that a 'valued landscape' must be a landscape that is 'considered to be of value because of particular

attributes that have been designated through the adoption of a local planning document' (paragraph 16). Mr Wadsley submits that, in the context of landscape, the Inspector erred in interpreting paragraph 109 of the NPPF, in effectively eliding, or otherwise failing to distinguish between, designation and value. As a result of that failure, he made no proper assessment of whether the landscape was valued; as the landscape was not designated, he simply proceeded on the basis that it was also not valued. Mr Wadsley makes no complaint about the planning balancing exercise performed by the Inspector on the basis that landscape did not have the enhanced status given by paragraph 109; but, he submits, if it was properly a 'valued landscape', then, in the planning balance exercise, it ought to have been granted the enhanced status given by paragraph 109 of the NPPF. Therefore, his failure to consider whether it was 'valued landscape' could have resulted in a different determination of the planning application.

...

Conclusion

43. For those reasons, this application is refused.

Note

The outline of the judgment provided above is a fairly typical example of the structure that is generally used in administrative law cases. Prior to the judgment of the court itself, the name of the court, its location, the name(s) of the judge(s), the names of the parties and the names of their legal representatives are set out. Information about the case number, the neutral citation[12] and the date(s) of the hearing are also included. In the judgment, there is usually an introduction, consideration of the relevant law, the factual situation, consideration of the way in which the law applies to the facts and then a conclusion. However, this structure is not in any way mandated and each judgment may differ in the way in which these issues are presented. Other decisions may not have a structure such as that above and might be presented as a transcript of the proceedings. In the appellate courts (or the Divisional Court), there may be a judgment from each judge sitting in the case, or there might be a composite judgment of the court or the majority or minority. It is important to emphasise that the approach to the reporting of judicial decisions in England and Wales is quite different from that adopted in the other legal systems under consideration.

9.2.F COMPARATIVE REMARKS

Not only are the elements of a judgment quite similar in the EU, France, Germany and the Netherlands, but so, too, are the structure and style of the judgments. In most of these

[12] The 'neutral citation' of a case is one that does not refer to a specific law report, but gives details of the case by reference to the year, the court that decided the case and the case number. The system was introduced in 2001 by a practice direction issued by the Lord Chief Justice. For further details, see *Practice Direction (Judgments: Form and Citation)* [2001] 1 WLR 194.

legal systems, statutory law prescribes these elements and, by doing so, also determines the structure of the judgments to a certain extent. Contrary to this, there are no statutory requirements for the elements and structure of judgments in England and Wales and the structure and elements of judgments can differ widely, particularly when first instance and appellate courts are considered. However, it is important that the judgment contains sufficient reasons to allow the parties to understand the motivation for the decision and the common law contains principles which support this requirement.[13] Within these formal limits and requirements, the structure and style of judgments are mainly determined by traditions. They are therefore very diverse throughout the legal systems examined. Courts choose different styles to explain their reasoning. In France, the deduction of the findings from the legal provision as the starting point seems to be the most important structuring element. Reference to and quoting from earlier case law can be found in all legal systems. However, as the role of precedent differs in the legal systems under examination,[14] the intensity of this element also differs.

In the Netherlands and France, reforms have aimed to make judgments more easily understandable, especially for parties without legal representation. In France and the Netherlands, in 2015 and 2016 respectively, reforms with the aim of enhancing the readability of judgments for readers who do not have a legal education and are not used to reading judgments were commenced. The goal of these reforms is to draft the verdicts in more common language and to prevent the use of structures and jargon that is only understandable to insiders. In France, this has led, or is likely to lead, to the use of more direct language and shorter sentences without lengthy enumerations (in the form of 'considering that …').

Whether references to scholarly writings are made or to what extent the arguments of the parties are referred to seem mainly to depend on traditions. German judgments are much more extensive and comprehensive than Dutch and French ones. Judgments of the French Council of State are particularly brief.

In contrast to the other legal systems, judgments in England and Wales often look more like a transcript of the proceedings than an announcement of the verdict plus a motivation of that verdict. Judgments in England and Wales may be the longest of all.

9.3 REASONING

9.3.A GERMANY

Verwaltungsgerichtsordnung **9.10 (DE)**

§117 (1) …

(2) The judgment shall contain

1. the designation of those concerned, of their legal representatives and of the authorized representatives by names, occupations, places of residence and by their status in the proceedings,

[13] See *Flannery v Halifax Estate Agents*, excerpt 9.16 below.

[14] See section 9.3 below.

2. the designation of the court and the names of the members who have contributed towards the ruling,
3. the ruling,
4. the facts,
5. the reasoning for the ruling, and
6. the notification of the right to appeal.

(3) …

(4) …

(5) The court may refrain from a further exposition of the reasoning for the ruling insofar as it concurs with the reasoning of the administrative act or of the decision on the objection and this is established in its ruling.

(6) The clerk of the registry shall note on the judgment the date of service, and in cases falling under §116(1), first sentence, the date of the pronouncement, and shall sign this note. If the files are kept in electronic form, the clerk of the registry shall record the note in a separate document. The document shall be inseparably bound together with the judgment.

Note

No structure is prescribed by law in respect of the reasoning of the ruling. Even though the textbooks contain a number of model structures for the reasoning regarding admissibility and the substantive decision, there is no legal requirement to apply a certain order or a particular model. Generally, legal terminology, categorisation and systematisation are very important in German law and scholarly legal writings. As German law is codified in great detail, the judgments generally make many references to the relevant statutory provisions. Formal correctness is one of the characterising elements of German court decisions, which includes making extensive mention of scholarly works and their stances on a given issue and the weighing of minority and majority arguments based on scholarly writings anticipating future or hypothetical legal problems.

9.3.B THE EUROPEAN UNION

Statute of the Court of Justice of the European Union **9.11 (EU)**

Article 36 Judgments shall state the reasons on which they are based. They shall contain the names of the Judges who took part in the deliberations.

Note

According to the rather short provision of Article 36 of the Statute of the Court of Justice of the European Union, judgments of the European courts shall state the reasons on which they are based. This leaves considerable potential for different levels of detail and approaches to the written presentation of the reasoning. The General Court's rulings tend to be much more detailed and clearer than the European Court of Justice's rulings, probably because the General Court is empowered to rule on questions of fact as well as questions of law.[15] Because there are no dissenting opinions,[16] rulings of the European Court of Justice may be ambiguous in matters which are important or controversial. Moreover, while the Advocate General's opinion[17] discusses all the points relevant to the case, the European Court of Justice only decides on those points which are directly relevant to the decision.

Case C-376/98, 15 October 2000[18] **9.12 (EU)**

Germany v Parliament and Council

Germany v Parliament and Council

Facts: Germany, supported by three other Member States and the European Commission, applied for the annulment of Directive 98/43/EC of the European Parliament and of the Council of 6 July 1998 on the approximation of the laws, regulations and administrative provisions of the Member States relating to the advertising and sponsorship of tobacco products.

Held: The directive was annulled.

Judgment: 97. In the case, for example, of periodicals, magazines and newspapers which contain advertising for tobacco products, it is true, as the applicant has demonstrated, that no obstacle exists at present to their importation into Member States which prohibit such advertising. However, in view of the trend in national legislation towards ever greater restrictions on advertising of tobacco products, reflecting the belief that such advertising gives rise to an appreciable increase in tobacco consumption, it is probable that obstacles to the free movement of press products will arise in the future.

98. In principle, therefore, a Directive prohibiting the advertising of tobacco products in periodicals, magazines and newspapers could be adopted on the basis of Article 100a of the Treaty with a view to ensuring the free movement of press products, on the lines of Directive 89/552, Article 13 of which prohibits television advertising of tobacco products in order to promote the free broadcasting of television programmes.

99. However, for numerous types of advertising of tobacco products, the prohibition under Article 3(1) of the Directive cannot be justified by the need to eliminate obstacles to the free movement of advertising media or the freedom to provide services in the field of advertising. That applies, in particular, to the prohibition of advertising on posters, parasols, ashtrays and other articles used in hotels, restaurants and cafés, and the prohibition of advertising spots in cinemas, prohibitions which in no way help to facilitate trade in the products concerned. 100. Admittedly, a measure adopted on the basis of Articles 100a, 57(2) and 66 of the Treaty may incorporate provisions which do not contribute to the elimination of obstacles to exercise of the fundamental freedoms provided that they are necessary to ensure that certain prohibitions imposed in pursuit of that purpose are not circumvented. It is, however, quite clear that the prohibitions mentioned in the previous paragraph do not fall into that category.

[15] For more details see Chapter 5, section 5.3.B.2.
[16] See section 9.5.B below.
[17] See further Chapter 2, section 2.2.B.2.
[18] ECLI:EU:C:2000:544.

Note

As can be seen from this very short extract from a judgment, which is 37 pages in total, the Court sometimes gives very detailed reasoning, which carries an almost 'instructional' message.

9.3.C FRANCE

Code de justice administrative **9.13 (FR)**

Article L9 Judgments have to give reasons.

Note

Any judgment of the French administrative courts must present the legal and factual aspects of the case and the reasoning that leads to the solution. Despite this requirement, judgments rendered by French administrative courts are traditionally rather brief, presenting only the most important aspects of the reasoning. This is especially so compared with, for example, judgments of international courts or of other national courts. Seven to ten pages for a judgment on a normal case of the Council of State is considered to be quite long. Judgments are longer in appeal and in first instance.

9.3.D THE NETHERLANDS

Grondwet **9.14 (NL)**

Article 121 Except where deviations are laid down in a statute, court hearings are open to the public and the judgments include the grounds on which they are based. The judgments are delivered in open court.

Vreemdelingenwet **9.15 (NL)**

Article 91 (2) If the Judicial Division of the Council of State decides that the grounds for review put forward by the applicant cannot lead to an annulment of the decision, it may limit the reasoning of its decision to this finding.

Note

It should be noted that, in some areas of Dutch law, the duty for the court to give reasons is explicitly restricted. This is in accordance with Article 121 of the Constitution (Grondwet), which allows deviation by statute. For instance, this is the case in asylum and migration law (Article 91(2) of the Aliens Act).

9.3.E ENGLAND AND WALES

Court of Appeal (Civil Division), 18 February 1999[19] **9.16 (EW)**

Flannery v Halifax Estate Agencies Ltd.

Flannery

Facts: Flannery brought a claim against the defendant in the County Court, arguing that the defendants had failed to undertake a satisfactory survey of the property that they had purchased, as the survey report (for which Flannery had paid) suggested that there were no concerns about structural movement in relation to the property that Flannery ultimately purchased. When Flannery came to sell the property, it was discovered that some structural movement had taken place and Flannery's buyer withdrew. At the hearing, the judge dismissed Flannery's claim, stating that he preferred the evidence of Halifax Estate Agencies' expert as opposed to that of Flannery, but did not explain the reasons for so doing.

Held: The appeal from the initial decision of the county court was allowed and a fresh trial was ordered.

Judgment: Lord Judge: (1) The duty [to give reasons for a judgment] is a function of due process, and therefore of justice. Its rationale has two principal aspects. The first is that fairness surely requires that the parties – especially the losing party – should be left in no doubt why they have won or lost. This is especially so since without reasons the losing party will not know (as was said in Ex p. Dave) whether the court has misdirected itself, and thus whether he may have an available appeal on the substance of the case. The second is that a requirement to give reasons concentrates the mind; if it is fulfilled, the resulting decision is much more likely to be soundly based on the evidence than if it is not.

(2) The first of these aspects implies that want of reasons may be a good self-standing ground of appeal. Where because no reasons are given it is impossible to tell whether the judge has gone wrong on the law or the facts, the losing party would be altogether deprived of his chance of an appeal unless the court entertains an appeal based on the lack of reasons itself.

(3) The extent of the duty, or rather the reach of what is required to fulfil it, depends on the subject-matter. Where there is a straightforward factual dispute whose resolution depends simply on which witness is telling the truth about events which he claims to recall, it is likely to be enough for the judge (having, no doubt, summarised the evidence) to indicate simply that he believes X rather than Y; indeed, there may be nothing else to say. But where the dispute involves something in the nature of an intellectual exchange, with reasons and analysis advanced on either side, the judge must enter into the issues canvassed before him and explain why he prefers one case over the other. This is likely to apply particularly in litigation whereas here there is disputed expert evidence; but it is not necessarily limited to such cases.

(4) This is not to suggest that there is one rule for cases concerning the witnesses' truthfulness or recall of events, and another for cases where the issue depends on reasoning or analysis (with experts or otherwise). The rule is the same: the judge must explain why he has reached his decision. The question is always, what is required of the judge to do so; and that will differ from case to case. Transparency should be the watchword.

[19] [2000] 1 WLR 377.

Notes

(1) Transcripts of the court proceedings are required in the High Court.[20] In some circumstances, judges will give their detailed reasons for a decision orally, but in most judicial review cases they do so in writing. The reported judgments of the court are sometimes made by court reporters, who take note of proceedings and then produce a public report. In addition to these reports, all judgments will be published in the form of approved transcripts of the judgment of the court, or published as written reasons of judges. In the appellate courts, it is common for the court, or sometimes each individual judge, to produce a written judgment, which is then published. In the Supreme Court, the oral giving of reasons (which are truncated versions of the written reasoning) and the hearings themselves can be watched online.[21]

(2) There is no specific statutory requirement for courts to give reasons for decisions, although a failure to give adequate reasons for a decision in a judgment is grounds for an appeal. The Court of Appeal has considered this issue in a number of cases, as the above excerpt shows,[22] and has permitted a number of appeals where judicial reasoning has not been adequate.

9.3.F COMPARATIVE REMARKS

The reasoning of the court has to be laid down in the judgments in all legal systems. This may be seen as a general principle, which is guaranteed by Article 6 of the European Convention on Human Rights (ECHR), at least insofar as administrative proceedings fall within the scope of this article.[23] In all the legal systems under consideration except for England and Wales, the duty to give reasons is codified in statutory law. In the Netherlands, this is a requirement contained in the constitution.

In England and Wales, the notion or requirement that judgments should give reasons is not contained in statutory law, but is a tradition contained in the common law. There is a fundamental difference between England and Wales and the other legal systems. The tradition in common law countries such as England and Wales is that the judgment is either a summary or a literal transcript of the court proceedings. The reader then has to find the reasoning leading to the outcome of the case from the transcript of the proceedings. However, the judgments are often structured in such a fashion as to make the

[20] There is a requirement in Practice Direction 39A, rule 6.1 of the Civil Procedure Rules (www.justice.gov.uk/courts/procedure-rules/civil/rules/part39/pd_part39a#IDAPEXKC) that High Court proceedings are recorded unless the judge directs otherwise. Under rule 6.3, transcripts of the recording can be requested by any party to the proceedings.

[21] See www.supremecourt.uk/news/catch-up-on-court-action-supreme-court-launches-video-on-demand-service.html.

[22] See also *English v Emery Reimbold & Strick* [2002] EWCA Civ 605, [2002] 1 WLR 2409; *Re v (A Child) (Inadequate Reasons for Findings of Fact)* [2015] EWCA Civ 274, [2015] 2 FLR 1472.

[23] ECtHR, *Van de Hurk v The Netherlands* ECLI:CE:ECHR:1994:0419JUD0016003490; ECtHR, *Hansen v Norway* ECLI:CE:ECHR:2014:1002JUD001531909; W Peukert, 'Die Garantie des "fair trial" in der Strassburger Rechtsprechung' (1980) *Europäische Grundrechte-Zeitschrift* 247, 267; BWN de Waard, *Leerstukken van bestuursprocesrecht* (Deventer, Kluwer, 2015) 43 ff and 56 ff.

reasoning apparent. Sometimes, the reasoning of the judgment is given orally. In the other legal systems, the court, after having reported the main arguments of the parties, explains its findings and reasoning to 'justify' its judgment.

There are great differences both within and between the legal systems regarding the depth of (the required) reasoning, and general estimates of the length and comprehensibility of the reasoning are difficult to give. For example, the reasoning in a Dutch judgment where the resolution of the case is simple may be only two or three sentences long, whereas in some cases the judgments of Dutch administrative courts can exceed 100 pages. However, by way of cautious classification, one may say that, in similar cases, French judgments, especially judgments of the Council of State, are significantly shorter than German judgments, and that the EU courts and the courts in the Netherlands seem to be somewhere in the middle. German courts seem to be the only ones to regularly refer to scholarly work.

9.4 USE OF PRECEDENT

Judges, when finding the law, rely on earlier decisions in similar cases and do not deviate from them without a justification for doing so. The use of earlier case law as a source of law ensures stability, legal certainty and legitimacy of court decisions.[24]

A distinction must be drawn between a 'strict use of precedent', whereby an appeal court would quash a lower court's decision when a precedent is not correctly adhered to, and a 'loose use of precedent', entailing the use by courts of prior courts' rulings on similar matters. In general terms, common law legal systems contrast with civil law systems, the former regarding a 'strict use of precedent' as the norm and the latter adhering to a 'loose use of precedent'.

The case law of the European Court of Justice has further imposed restrictions of the binding nature of precedents when EU law is at stake.

Case 166-73, 16 January 1974[25] **9.17 (EU)**

Rheinmühlen-Düsseldorf v Einfuhr- und Vorratsstelle für Getreide und Futtermittel

EU LAW; BINDING NATURE OF PRECEDENTS

Rheinmühlen

National courts cannot be precluded from sending a preliminary reference to the European Court of Justice despite a procedural rule whereby a court is bound on points of law by the judgments of the court superior to it.

Facts: In an action pending before the Federal Fiscal Court (Bundesfinanzhof) between Rheinmühlen-Düsseldorf and Einfuhr- und Vorratsstelle für Getreide und Futtermittel, the Federal Fiscal Court asked the European

[24] See, eg J Esser, *Vorverständnis und Methodenwahl der Rechtsfindung* (Frankfurt am Main, Fischer, 1972) 74 ff.

[25] ECLI:EU:C:1974:3.

Court of Justice for a preliminary ruling under Article 177 of the EEC Treaty (now Article 267 TFEU) on the interpretation of the second paragraph of that article.

Held: The existence of a rule of domestic law whereby a court is bound on points of law by the rulings of a court superior to it cannot of itself take away the power provided for by Article 177 of the EEC Treaty to refer cases to the European Court of Justice.

Judgment: ... On the other hand the inferior court must be free, if it considers that the ruling on law made by the superior court could lead it to give a judgment contrary to Community law, to refer to the Court questions which concern it.

If inferior courts were bound without being able to refer matters to the Court, the jurisdiction of the latter to give preliminary rulings and the application of Community law at all levels of the judicial systems of the Member States would be compromised.

Note

When an inferior court is confronted with a judgment of a superior court which it, as a consequence of a national rule of precedent, should apply to a case pending before it and this ruling seems to wrongly apply EU law, this court has to deal with two conflicting requirements. On the one hand, it should follow the ruling of the superior court. On the other hand, it should not adopt a ruling which, potentially or perhaps certainly, infringes EU law. This conflict can be solved by referring preliminary questions on the interpretation of the respective provisions of EU law to the European Court of Justice under Article 267 of the Treaty on the Functioning of the European Union. National rules of precedent may not forbid the reference of preliminary questions on the correct interpretation of EU law to the European Court of Justice even if superior courts applied the relevant EU law provisions without referring such questions. This limitation of the rule of precedent in all national legal systems is necessary to ensure the primacy of EU law.[26]

9.4.A STRICT USE OF PRECEDENT: ENGLAND AND WALES

Befitting the common law nature of England and Wales, all courts are bound by a strict doctrine of precedent. If the *ratio decidendi* of a case at hand corresponds with a previous judgment, the courts are bound by precedent. There is a possibility of disagreement about whether a previous case is sufficiently similar to the present case and therefore whether the principle of *stare decisis* applies, but it is clear that precedents form a key part of the common law legal system. Decisions of the Court of Appeal and the Supreme Court, as higher courts, have particular value within the system of precedent.

Exceptions to this system of binding precedents exist. There are, for example, legal rules (to be found in case law) permitting the Court of Appeal to depart from a previous

[26] See also Case C-173/09 *Georgi Ivanov Elchinov v Natsionalna zdravnoosiguritelna kasa* ECLI:EU:C:2010:581; see further M Eliantonio and CW Backes, 'Taking Constitutionalization One Step Too Far? The Need for Revision of the *Rheinmühlen* Case Law in the Light of the AG Opinion and the ECJ's Ruling in *Elchinov*' (2012) 23 *European Review of Public Law* 839.

decision,[27] though only in certain limited circumstances. Furthermore, the House of Lords (now Supreme Court) issued a Practice Statement in 1966[28] indicating when it might depart from previous judgments, but has done so on relatively few occasions.[29] A similar Practice Statement has not been issued by the Supreme Court, but logic dictates that the Supreme Court too has the ability to depart from a decision, either from a decision of the House of Lords or one of its own decisions, if it deems it fit to do so.

Supreme Court, 9 December 2009[30] **9.18 (EW)**

R v Horncastle

RULE OF PRECEDENT; DECISIONS OF THE ECTHR MAY REQUIRE TO DEVIATE FROM DOMESTIC (CASE) LAW

Horncastle

There may be some circumstances where domestic courts are required to deviate from domestic precedent and follow the jurisprudence of the European Court of Human Rights (ECtHR).

Facts: H was convicted of the offence of committing grievous bodily harm with intent on the basis of written evidence submitted against him where the witnesses were not present in court to be cross-examined (known as 'hearsay evidence'). The victim in the case gave evidence implicating the defendant, but subsequently died (of causes unrelated to the alleged offence) prior to trial. H argued that the provisions of the Criminal Justice Act 2003, which allowed the admission of hearsay evidence in circumstances such as those that arose in his case, were contrary to Article 6 of the ECHR and thus appealed the decision of the trial judge to allow the evidence to be admitted. The Court of Appeal dismissed H's appeal and the case came before the Supreme Court.

Held: The appeals were dismissed and the Supreme Court declined to follow the decision of the Chamber of the ECtHR in Al-Khawaja.

Judgment: Lord Phillips of Worth Matravers PSC: 9. Article 43(1) of the Convention provides that within a period of three months from the date of judgment of the Chamber any party may, in an exceptional case, request that the case be referred to the Grand Chamber. Article 43(2) provides that a panel of five judges of the Grand Chamber shall accept the request if the case raises a serious question affecting the interpretation or application of the Convention or its Protocols, or a serious issue of general importance.

[27] See *Young v Bristol Aeroplane* [1944] KB 718 (CA).

[28] Practice Statement (Judicial Precedent) [1966] 1 WLR 1234.

[29] Prior to 1980, Paterson found that the House of Lords had departed from its own previous decision on eight occasions. See A Paterson, *The Law Lords* (London, Palgrave Macmillan, 1982). An issue here is that, as Paterson acknowledges, it was sometimes difficult to discern whether the House of Lords was using the Practice Statement to depart from a previous decision or whether it was distinguishing the previous decision. Since 1980, the House has used the Practice Statement to depart from one of its previous decisions on at least nine other occasions. The cases are *Khawaja v Secretary of State for the Home Department and Another* [1984] AC 74 (HL); *R v Shivpuri* [1987] AC 1 (HL); *R v Howe* [1987] AC 417; *Patel v Immigration Appeal Tribunal* [1988] AC 910 (HL); *Murphy v Brentwood District Council* [1991] 1 AC 398 (HL); *Pepper (Inspector of Taxes) v Hart* [1993] AC 593 (HL); *R v G* [2003] UKHL 50, [2004] 1 AC 1034; *Horton v Sadler and Another* [2006] UKHL 27, [2007] 1 AC 307; *A v Hoare* [2008] UKHL 6, [2008] 2 WLR 311.

[30] *R v Horncastle* [2009] UKSC 14, [2010] 2 AC 373.

On 16 April 2009, the United Kingdom requested that the decision of the Chamber in Al-Khawaja be referred to the Grand Chamber. On 5 June 2009, the panel of the Grand Chamber adjourned consideration of that request pending our judgment in the present case.

10. Mr Tim Owen QC, for Mr Horncastle and Mr Blackmore, submitted that we should treat the judgment of the Chamber in Al-Khawaja as determinative of the success of these appeals. He submitted that this was the appropriate response to the requirement of section 2(1) of the Human Rights Act 1998 that requires a court to 'take into account' any judgment of the European Court of Human Rights in determining any question to which such judgment is relevant. He submitted that the decision of the House of Lords in *Secretary of State for the Home Department v AF (No 3)* [2010] 2 AC 269 exemplified the correct approach to a decision of the European court. In that case the committee held itself bound to apply a clear statement of principle by the Grand Chamber in respect of the precise issue that was before the committee. Mr Owen submitted that we should adopt precisely the same approach to the decision of the Chamber in Al-Khawaja.

11. I do not accept that submission. The requirement to 'take into account' the Strasbourg jurisprudence will normally result in the domestic court applying principles that are clearly established by the Strasbourg court. There will, however, be rare occasions where the domestic court has concerns as to whether a decision of the Strasbourg court sufficiently appreciates or accommodates particular aspects of our domestic process. In such circumstances, it is open to the domestic court to decline to follow the Strasbourg decision, giving reasons for adopting this course. This is likely to give the Strasbourg court the opportunity to reconsider the particular aspect of the decision that is in issue, so that there takes place what may prove to be a valuable dialogue between the domestic court and the Strasbourg court. This is such a case.

…

Lord Brown of Eaton-under-Heywood JSC: 117. I recognise, however, the distinct possibility that the Strasbourg court in Al-Khawaja really did intend to lay down an absolute principle along the lines here contended for and it may be, indeed, that the outcome of that very case itself tends to support such a view. In this event the question then arises: what should this court do? Should we accept and apply this absolute principle with the inevitable result that these appeals must be allowed or should we instead decline to follow the Strasbourg decision in Al-Khawaja and in effect join with the United Kingdom Government in inviting the Grand Chamber to overrule it (the Grand Chamber panel having adjourned the UK's request for such a reference until the pronouncement of our decision on these appeals)?

118. I have not the least doubt that the latter course is to be preferred. This case seems to me a very far cry from *Secretary of State for the Home Department v AF (No 3)* [2010] 2 AC 269 where the House of Lords was faced with a definitive judgment of the Grand Chamber in *A v United Kingdom* (2009) 49 EHRR 625 on the very point at issue and where each member of the Committee felt no alternative but to apply it. Lord Rodger put it most succinctly, at para 98: 'Argentoratum locutum, iudicium finitum – Strasbourg has spoken, the case is closed.'

119. Moreover, not merely was the Strasbourg ruling in a clear and authoritative but, whatever view individual members of the committee may have taken about it (and it is evident that, whilst many agreed with it, others did not), it expressed an entirely coherent view.

120. The contrasts with the present situation are striking. In the first place, we are faced here not with a Grand Chamber decision but rather with the possible need for one.

Moreover, not merely is the court's ruling in Al-Khawaja not as authoritative as a Grand Chamber decision, but it is altogether less clear than was the decision in A. Indeed, as I have already suggested, it is far from certain that Al-Khawaja stands for any absolute principle of the sort here contended for. I would reject the appellant's argument that not merely is the court's judgment in Al-Khawaja clear but, unlike the position in A, it is supported by a whole stream of consistent earlier Strasbourg case law and consequently more, rather than less, authoritative than the ruling in A. For the reasons fully elaborated by the Court of Appeal and now by Lord Phillips PSC, I cannot accept that the earlier cases support, still less compel, an absolute principle such as Al-Khawaja is now said to stand for.

Note

The case of *AF v Secretary of State for the Home Department (No 3)* considered circumstances where the claimants had successfully brought a case against the UK for a breach of Article 6 ECHR in relation to the fairness of their trials.[31] The Supreme Court felt bound to follow the decision of the ECtHR despite the fact that it departed from domestic jurisprudence, as noted in paragraph 118 of Lord Brown's judgment set out above. However, in cases where there is no Grand Chamber decision that is directly analogous to the case before the UK court, the obligation to 'take account' of the jurisprudence of the Strasbourg court does not necessarily bind the court to follow the Strasbourg jurisprudence, as illustrated by the *Horncastle* case.

9.4.B LOOSE USE OF PRECEDENT

9.4.B.1 FRANCE

In France, precedents are in principle not legally binding, but the administrative courts regularly adhere to precedents. This results not only from the judge-made nature which has predominantly defined French administrative law for many years, but also from the necessity to ensure the consistency of the case law of all courts in order to maintain legal certainty.

The existing doctrine of precedent stems from the way in which administrative judges work. The preparatory phase of a case revolves to a great extent around the search for precedents that might be relevant to a case at hand, on matters both of facts and of law. In practice, administrative judges will always adhere to general principles and interpretations of statutes delivered by the Council of State that apply to a specific case regarding matters of law.

[31] *AF v Secretary of State for the Home Department (No 3)* [2007] UKHL 46, [2008] 1 AC 440.

Conseil d'État, 9 January 2014[32] **9.19 (FR)**

Minister of Internal Affairs v Société Les Productions de la Plume et M Dieudonné M'Bala M'Bala

USE OF PRECEDENT; EXPLICIT REFERENCE TO PREVIOUS CASE LAW

Dieudonné

The Council of State expressly refers to previous case law.

Facts: Mr Dieudonné was a comedian who, during public shows, made anti-Semitic remarks. In order to preserve the public order, the prefect had banned the performance of a show in the city of Saint-Herblainhe police authorities and the mayor had banned an anti-Semitic show.

Held: The administrative decision was upheld.

Judgment: In light of the decisions of the Council of State, ruling in the disputes of Benjamin of 19 May 1933, Commune de Morsang-sur-Orge of 27 October 1995 and Mme Hoffman-Glemane of 16 February 2009;

...

5. Considering that, when prohibiting the performance of the show 'Le Mur' at Saint-Herblain, previously performed in the theatre of La Main d'Or in Paris, the prefect of Loire-Atlantique has indicated that this show, as it is designed, contains statements of anti-Semitic character which incite to racial hatred and, in breach of the dignity of the human person, glorify discrimination, persecution and exterminations committed during the Second World War; considering that the challenged decision of the prefect reminds that M.B ... D ... has received nine criminal convictions, of which seven are final, for statements of the same nature; considering that the reactions to the show of 9 January reveal, in a climate of high tension, that there are serious risks of disturbances to the public order which would be very difficult for the police forces to control;

6. Considering that the reality and the gravity of the risks of disturbances to the public order mentioned by the challenged judgment are established by elements contained in the case file as well as resulting from the discussions held during the public hearing; considering that, in regard to the planned show as it has been announced and programmed, the allegation according to which the statements which are criminally reprehensible and of a nature to affect national cohesion as seen in the sessions held in Paris would not be mentioned in Nantes, is not sufficient to exclude the serious risk that the show would again jeopardise the respect of the values and principles, notably the dignity of the human person protected by the Declaration the Rights of Man and of the Citizen and the republican tradition; considering that, furthermore, it is the task of the administrative authority to take measures of such nature to avoid that criminal offences are committed; considering that, by basing itself on the risks that the planned show represents to the public order and the breach of the principles of which the state authorities have to ensure the respect, the prefect of Loire-Atlantique has not acted illegally in a serious and manifest manner in the exercise of its powers of administrative police.

[32] N° 374508.

Note

In this ruling the Council of State quoted three of its previous decisions:

— *Benjamin* of 19 May 1933,[33]
— *Commune de Morsang-sur-Orge* of 27 October 1995,
— *Mme Hoffman-Glemane* of 16 February 2009.

The *Benjamin* case is the landmark case establishing the stringent proportionality test when a public authority decides to ban a show for reasons of public order, thereby limiting the right of freedom of expression. The *Commune de Morsang-sur-Orge* case further established that moral questions form a part of the public order. The *Hoffman-Glemane* case concerned the liability of the French State for the deportation of Jews when the public administration facilitated their deportation.

9.4.B.2 GERMANY

D Ehlers, §2 Rechtsquellen und Rechtsnormen der Verwaltung[34] **9.20 (DE)**

Judge-made law. When exercising their mandate to provide judicial protection, judges have the duty, in a dispute, to construe, substantiate and apply the law with ultimately binding force. Their decisions often reach beyond the individual case because they determine the future jurisprudence and guide the practice. This also applies when [the decisions] have no force of law or general binding force …, but apply only *inter partes*. A consequence is that the deviation of the administration from the jurisprudence of the highest instance, without new and substantial reasons, gives rise, in case of damage, to public liability. If a formation of a court wishes to deviate from the jurisprudence of a chamber that is at least of equal rank it can be obliged to submit [the case] to a Federal court or to refer it to the Joint Senate of the Highest Courts of the Federation. This shows at the same time that, in appeal stages and in the multi-layered system, the courts, especially the highest courts, regularly interact in a network.

Note

No strict system of precedent exists in Germany. Judgments of the Federal Constitutional Court form the only exception to this civil law tradition. Case law of the Federal Constitutional Court is legally binding upon all federal and state courts.[35]

[33] For more detail, see Chapter 6, section 6.5.A.3.
[34] D Ehlers, in D Ehlers and H Pünder (eds), *Allgemeines Verwaltungsrecht*, 15th edn (Berlin, de Gruyter, 2016) §2, para 65.
[35] Federal Constitutional Court Act (Bundesverfassungsgerichtsgesetz), §31(1).

9.4.B.3 THE NETHERLANDS

Raad van State, 17 September 2014[36] **9.21 (NL)**

X v WEW Trust

USE OF PRECEDENT; EXPLICIT DEPARTURE FROM PRIOR CASE LAW

Stichting WEW

The Judicial Division of the Council of State expressly deviates from its own case law, which has been steady for many years, and takes the consequences of this change into account.

Facts: In its letter of 24 October 2012, the WEW Trust, a body entrusted with providing deposits in the form of mortgage guarantees, informed the claimant of its refusal to return the amounts of money which had been paid to the creditor on the basis of his declaration of losses. In its letter of 18 June 2013, the WEW Trust rejected the objection of the claimant. In its judgment of 18 December 2013, the district court rejected the claimant's action brought against this decision. The claimant appealed against this judgment.

Held: The judgment of the district court was upheld.

Judgment: 1. In the light of today's judgments of the Grand Chamber in the cases 201304908/1/A2 and 201307828/1/A2, the Judicial Division *ex officio* wonders whether the WEW Trust can still be qualified as an administrative authority. …

1.6 The Trust cannot be qualified as being an administrative authority in the sense of Article 1:1 AWB. The decisions of the Trust concerning granting the mortgage guarantees … are, as a consequence, no decisions as defined in Article 1:3 AWB. Therefore, lodging an objection or lodging a claim for judicial review against these decisions is not possible.

1.7 The Judicial Division admits that this judgment contravenes its own case law which has been steady for many years and on which practice has developed. In order to enable all the parties which dealt with the WEW Trust to adapt to the change which this case entails, in order to enable the WEW Trust to adapt to this change, and to prevent undesirable consequences for on-going proceedings, the Judicial Division of the Council of State decides that all decisions on granting a national mortgage guarantees and all decisions on waiving of debts following payments to creditors on the basis of declarations of losses which have been taken prior to 1 March 2015, are deemed to be decisions as defined in Article 1:3 AWB.

The chamber of three judges has transferred the case to the Grand Chamber. The president of the Judicial Division has asked the Advocate General Mr R.J.G.M. Widdershoven to draft a conclusion as mentioned in Article 8.12a AWB.

Notes

(1) In the Netherlands, no rules exist on the strict use of precedent. In practice, administrative judges rely on and repeat previous judgments, but they are not obliged to do so. Moreover, lower courts are not bound by the case law of higher courts and

[36] ECLI:NL:RVS:2014:4568.

may as a result deviate from rulings of a higher court whenever they deem fit. At the same time, higher courts may alter their opinions whenever they hold this to be appropriate and are therefore not restricted by their own case law, as can be seen in the judgment above.

(2) At the Judicial Division of the Council of State (Afdeling bestuursrechtspraak Raad van State), a few cases concerning the notion of what an 'administrative authority' is (Article 1:1 AWB) had been pending. The Judicial Division transferred two of the cases to the Grand Chamber and asked Advocate General Widdershoven to deliver an opinion on this question. The other cases were stayed. As the excerpt shows, the court followed the opinion of the Advocate General – which, however, meant a substantial change in its steady case law. As many parties had relied on this case law, the Judicial Division ensured that the new line of the case law would be applied only after a certain transitional period.

9.4.B.4 THE EUROPEAN UNION

The CJEU does not consider itself bound by a strict doctrine of precedent. It does, though, build upon and develop previous case law. This is shown by the references it makes to previous judgments when substantiating its reasoning. The CJEU does not generally state that it is departing from previous case law or that a previous case is overruled.[37] However, exceptions to this general principle do exist.[38]

Case C-10/89, 17 October 1990[39] **9.22 (EU)**

SA CNL-SUCAL NV v HAG GF AG

USE OF PRECEDENT; DEPARTURE FROM PRIOR CASE LAW

CNL-SUCAL/HAG

The Court of Justice refers to a previous ruling and expressly departs from it.

Facts: In the action pending before the Bundesgerichtshof (Federal Court of Justice) between SA CNL-SUCAL NV and HAG GF AG, the Bundesgerichtshof sought a preliminary ruling under Article 177 of the EEC Treaty (currently Article 267 TFEU) on the interpretation of various provisions of the EEC Treaty.

Held: Articles 30 and 36 of the EEC Treaty do not preclude national legislation from allowing an undertaking which is the proprietor of a trademark in a Member State to oppose the importation from another Member State of similar goods lawfully bearing in the latter state an identical trademark or one which is liable to be confused with the protected trademark. This is the case even if the trademark under which the goods in dispute are imported originally belonged to a subsidiary of the undertaking which opposes the importation and was acquired by a third undertaking following the expropriation of that subsidiary.

[37] For more on this point, see A Arnull, 'Owing Up to Fallibility: Precedent and the European Court of Justice' (1993) 30 *Common Market Law Review* 247.

[38] See also Joined Cases C-267/91 and C-268/91 *Keck and Mithouard* ECLI:EU:C:1993:905, para 16.

[39] ECLI:EU:C:1990:359.

Judgment: Bearing in mind the points outlined in the order for reference and in the discussions before the Court concerning the relevance of the Court's judgment in Case 192/73 *Van Zuylen v HAG* [1974] ECR 731 to the reply to the question asked by the national court, it should be stated at the outset that the Court believes it necessary to reconsider the interpretation given in that judgment in the light of the case-law which has developed with regard to the relationship between industrial and commercial property and the general rules of the Treaty, particularly in the sphere of the free movement of goods.

Note

In the hierarchical relationship between the General Court as court of first instance and the Court of Justice as the supreme body of the European Court of Justice, the former is not formally bound by the rulings of the latter. Since the Court of Justice provides for a system of 'cassation' in relation to judgments of the General Court, the judgments of the Court of Justice still bind the General Court in a factual sense.

9.5 DISSENTING OPINIONS

A dissenting opinion expresses that one or more judges disagree with the majority opinion of the court which gives a judgment. If a legal system allows dissenting opinions, they are usually published together with the judgment. Dissenting opinions contribute to the quality and intensity of the discussion of the legal questions which have been dealt with in a judgment. They reflect the fact that a judgment aims to decide the case at hand, but not at finally determining the discussion on a certain doctrinal question. Dissenting opinions can be used to spur a change in the law, and a later case may result in a majority opinion adopting an approach previously advocated in dissent. Furthermore, the difference in opinion between the dissenting faction and the majority opinion can illuminate the precise scope of the majority opinion. It can therefore contribute to better reasoning in the majority judgment and to the better understanding of the judgment.

However, dissenting opinions also have disadvantages. Dissenting opinions may decrease the authority of a judgment and its potential to offer a final determination of a certain legal question. They may limit the contribution of judgments to legal certainty. They may even do harm to the understanding of the judgment as laymen may not (precisely) understand the legal dispute between the majority and the minority of the judges. Furthermore, dissenting opinions can limit the guidance that judgments provide for legal practice and therefore can jeopardise legal certainty.[40]

[40] See further R Raffaeli, *Dissenting Opinions in the Supreme Courts of the Member States* (European Parliament, Directorate General for Internal Policies, 2012), available at www.europarl.europa.eu/document/activities/cont/201304/20130423ATT64963/20130423ATT64963EN.pdf.

9.5.A LEGAL SYSTEMS WHICH USE DISSENTING OPINIONS: ENGLAND AND WALES

Supreme Court, 29 June 2011[41] **9.23 (EW)**

R (G) v Governors of X School

DISSENTING OPINION

Governors of X School

Facts: G was a teaching assistant at the (undisclosed) school. The parents of a 15-year-old pupil at the school alleged that they had discovered evidence that there was a sexual relationship between G and the pupil. The school suspended G, conducted an investigation and then held a disciplinary hearing at which G was refused legal representation. The school found G guilty of having an inappropriate relationship with the pupil and thus dismissed him. The High Court held that the school had breached Article 6 ECHR and ordered a new disciplinary investigation to be held by a differently constituted disciplinary panel. The Court of Appeal dismissed the School's appeal. The Supreme Court allowed the school's appeal from the Court of Appeal, with a dissent by Lord Kerr.

Held: The Supreme Court allowed the school's appeal from the Court of Appeal.

Judgment: Lord Kerr (dissenting): 105. As Lord Dyson has said (at para 76) 'ISA is expected to form its own assessment of the facts on the basis of all the available evidence' and (at para 79) 'ISA is required to make its own findings of fact and bring its own independent judgment to bear as to their seriousness and significance before deciding whether it is appropriate to place the person on the barred list'. The question that these statements raise is whether, because ISA must reach its own view as to whether the facts, as they have found them to be, are sufficient to support the conclusion that an individual should be placed on the barred list, insulates that process from substantial influence by the earlier disciplinary hearing. Supplying an answer to that question does not involve the application of principle. It is an exercise in deduction as to what is likely to happen when the case officers of ISA consider all the available information, including the report on the disciplinary proceedings. On that account alone, I have grave misgivings about the propriety of this court finding that the Court of Appeal was wrong to conclude that it was inevitable that the views of the disciplinary panel and the report of the evidence given to it were likely to have a substantial influence on the decision of ISA.

106. It appears to be implicit in the view of the majority that it would be improper for ISA to allow itself to be heavily influenced by the findings that emerged from the disciplinary proceedings. Regretfully, I cannot subscribe to that view.

...

114. Lord Brown has said that a less than satisfactory feature of the Court of Appeal's decision is that while requiring school disciplinary panels to allow legal representation, it does not require them to be independent and impartial. But this is to assume that all the requirements of article 6 must be supplied at the disciplinary proceedings stage of the process. That is not so.

[41] [2011] UKSC 30, [2012] 1 AC 167.

Note

In any court where there is more than one judge sitting (so mainly in the Court of Appeal and the Supreme Court – the appellate courts),[42] it is possible to have a dissenting opinion or opinions, which will be available to the public. It is also possible for majority decisions to be reached on different grounds by the judges in the majority. It is fairly common to have dissenting opinions in England and Wales, which are often helpful for demonstrating judicial debate on certain issues of particular difficulty or complexity.[43] Dissents are also sometimes used to advocate a change in the law's approach to a particular issue.[44]

9.5.B LEGAL SYSTEMS WHICH DO NOT USE DISSENTING OPINIONS: THE EUROPEAN UNION, GERMANY, FRANCE AND THE NETHERLANDS

B Wägenbaur, Court of Justice of the European Union[45] **9.24 (EU)**

IV. Room for dissenting opinions?

1. Overview

Dissenting opinions are not recorded in the reports of deliberations or decisions, let alone are they published. This is in contrast to common practice at e.g. the German Federal constitutional court, the United States Supreme Court and in a number of inter-, or supranational Courts, such as the European Court of Human Rights.

2. Pro and contra

This point has served as a source of criticism of the ECJ. Arguments in favour of the publication of dissenting opinion cite the concept of transparency and democracy, and also, to a lesser extent, the judge's individual rights to freedom of conscience and independence. On the other hand, leaving aside the fact that the publication of dissenting opinions does not exist in every national legal system of the EU and is thus not a *common* tradition of the Member States, it might be detrimental to the ECJ's mission to ensure the unity of Union law. Dissenting opinions would inevitably become a means in order to criticize or question such or such judgment. This would have little added value as compared to the political damage it would be bound to create. What would be left of the authority of the ECJ's judgements, if every major judgement e.g. in institutional matters, such as applications of the Commission against the Council or the Parliament and vice versa, were to result in dissenting opinions being published and then extensively commented by

42 See Chapter 2, section 2.2.B.1 (i).

43 See *YL v Birmingham City Council* [2007] UKHL 27, [2008] 1 AC 95, where Lord Bingham and Lady Hale both dissented against the finding of the majority that the care home was not exercising a 'public function' for the purposes of s 6 of the Human Rights Act 1998; *R (G) v Governors of X School* [2011] UKSC 30, [2012] 1 AC 167, where Lord Kerr gave a strong dissent from the view of the majority on the issue of whether Art 6 was engaged in school disciplinary proceedings.

44 As in Lord Bingham's dissent in *JD v East Berkshire HA* [2005] UKHL 23, [2005] 2 AC 373, where Lord Bingham advocated a change in approach to the tort liability of public authorities away from grounding liability on the question of whether a duty of care exists to the seriousness of the breach. Lord Nicholls gives the major speech for the majority, in which he analyses some of Lord Bingham's arguments.

45 B Wägenbaur, *Court of Justice of the European Union* (Munich, CH Beck, 2013) 235.

politicians, the media, etc.? Next, dissenting opinions in referrals for preliminary questions would be simply unthinkable, since the national Court or tribunal expects to be given answer to its questions, rather than something which might look like a cacophony. Finally, if dissenting opinions were to be published, 'the secret of the deliberations' would be no longer fully protected.

J-P Ancel, Les opinions dissidentes **9.25 (FR)**

Cycle de conférences annuelles sur les méthodes de jugement[46]

The dissenting opinion is almost a taboo of our procedure, a sort of ghost. Dealing with it, thus, is a matter of provocation, if not subversion, as it is true that this practice is profoundly foreign to our legal and, especially, our judicial culture.

Those who criticise this instrument see in it, primarily, an intolerable infringement of the secrecy of deliberations, and, incidentally, an infringement of the authority of the decisions of the court, through the weakening of its conception and its application.

It is true that the publication of the opinion of one or several deliberating judges shatters this secrecy that the judge commits himself, by oath, to keep 'religiously'. This argument is therefore decisive in the current state of our law. This argument remains true for the publication of the dissenting opinion with the signature of the dissenting judge or judges.

In addition, the publication of the dissenting opinion weakens the decision, thereby showing … but thereby showing what, in fact? What weakness, in reality? This weakness is perceived in a wrong way. Would this weakness affecting the judgment be due to the fact that it was not unanimous? But then, would that mean that only the decisions taken unanimously would hold authority? Or, worse, that it should be pretended that each decision of a court has been taken with the consent of all participants in the deliberations? But who could subscribe to such a fiction?

Let us acknowledge that, on the logical and rational level, the argument is somewhat surprising. Who would dream of criticising – in order to underline its 'weakness' – a decision of the Strasbourg Court, on the ground that it has been taken with only a majority vote?

The other criticism that is directed to the practice of the dissenting opinion is the necessary guarantee of the independence of the judge, that his anonymity protects him from coercion, from threats, even from reprisals.

There are, thus, several ideas in the rejection of the dissenting opinion: the respect of an absolute secrecy of the creative work of the judge, for the protection of his independence by means of anonymity, and the guarantee of the authority of his decision, which is considered monolithic, in a way imperial, and, as such, forcing respect. …

I consider myself authorised – but authorised by myself only – to issue a dissenting opinion regarding dissenting opinions.

I think, in fact, that it would be beneficial to allow a publication of a minority opinion under certain specified conditions:

— the *first requirement* is a publication in anonymous form, by insertion of a short and summarised notice, drafted by the judges who have issued this opinion, under the

[46] Available at www.courdecassation.fr/IMG/File/opinions_dissidentes_jp_ancel.pdf.

control of the president and of the chamber of the dean,[47] in order to avoid the risks inherent to such an exercise: sterile controversy, ideological involvement, deviation for self-satisfaction, or appeals to the media.

This prerequisite addresses, it seems to me, the objection concerning a violation of the secrecy of deliberations. Secrecy is respected since the identity of the dissenting judges is not revealed.

— the *second requirement* is that publication of dissents should be limited to cases that present not only an important and controversial legal question but equally a societal question. These are cases that put into question the balance that is to be struck between conflicting interests, which the judge is tasked to arbitrate in the pursuit of the 'common good'. …

To sum up, the proposed system – anonymous publication of the minority opinion in cases that generate an intense legal debate and that entail an essential question on a societal matter – allows the improvement of the comprehensibility of the discussion before the Court of Cassation, and would lead to more transparency in our methods of adjudication.

Would this not simply enhance *democracy*? It seems to me that this question deserves to be asked. I add that, when considering our international environment, especially the practices of our European neighbours, it seems to me that we cannot keep absolute secrecy, full opacity of the legal content of deliberations for much longer, and that, one day, an evolution will be inevitable.

But I am aware that this is, for the moment, a minority opinion.

Note

As the excerpts above demonstrate, there has been a debate on allowing dissenting opinions in the CJEU and in France. With the exception of England and Wales, the national legal systems dealt with in this book do not permit dissenting opinions in administrative courts. In Germany, dissenting opinions are used by the Federal Constitutional Court (Bundesverfassungsgericht).[48] Constitutional jurisprudence, however, does not concern judicial review of administrative action, and constitutional courts are not within the scope of this book.

9.5.C COMPARATIVE REMARKS

Only England and Wales make use of dissenting opinions. Whilst most constitutional courts in the EU use this instrument,[49] it is much less common in administrative courts.

[47] The dean is the most experienced judge within the chamber dealing with the case.

[48] The possibility of a dissenting opinion has not always been in existence. The reasons for the introduction of dissenting opinions can be found in the explanatory notes of the draft act, BTDrs VI, 388, sub 10.

[49] R Raffaeli, *Dissenting Opinions in the Supreme Courts of the Member States* (European Parliament, Directorate General for Internal Policies 2012), available at www.europarl.europa.eu/document/activities/cont/201304/20130423ATT64963/20130423ATT64963EN.pdf 7.

9.6 USE OF INTERNATIONAL AND FOREIGN LAW

The focus of this section is whether international law or foreign law, which is not directly decisive for the case at hand, is used as a source of inspiration for the judges and whether the judgments demonstrate the use of such law. Therefore, the focus of this section is not the question of whether the courts apply international legal norms, such as the ECHR, where this is legally required, but the cases where non-binding instruments of international or foreign law may be used to influence the outcome of domestic cases.

9.6.A USE OF INTERNATIONAL LAW

9.6.A.1 LEGAL SYSTEMS WHERE INTERNATIONAL LAW DOES NOT PLAY A SIGNIFICANT ROLE AS A SOURCE OF INSPIRATION: GERMANY AND THE NETHERLANDS

In Germany and the Netherlands, international law which is not directly applicable and decisive for cases does not seem to be used very often as a source of inspiration for the courts. Judges may occasionally make use of international law when they consider the case behind closed doors. However, administrative law judgments generally do not refer to such considerations.

9.6.A.2 LEGAL SYSTEMS WHERE INTERNATIONAL LAW IS REFERRED TO AS A SOURCE OF INSPIRATION: FRANCE, ENGLAND AND WALES AND THE EUROPEAN UNION

9.6.A.2 (i) France

The ECHR and the case law of the ECtHR are frequently used and referred to by the French administrative courts when deciding a case, regardless of whether the case falls directly under the scope of the treaty and the case law or not. The ECHR is not the only instrument of international law which is used by French courts. However, the use of international law which is not directly binding upon the case to be decided is always implicit.

9.6.A.2 (ii) England and Wales

Court of Appeal (Civil Division), 15 May 2012[50] **9.26 (EW)**

Burnip v Birmingham City Council

REFERENCE TO INTERNATIONAL LAW

Burnip

Facts: B suffered from severe disabilities and needed a live-in carer to support him. B's housing benefit was assessed by the council on the basis of him being a single person in need of accommodation with one bedroom

[50] [2007] EWCA Civ 624, [2008] HLR 8.

when, in fact, he needed two. B claimed judicial review of this decision. The basis of B's claim was that to assess him as a single person needing only one bedroom was unlawful discrimination on grounds of his disability, contrary to Article 14 ECHR. The attention of the court was also drawn to the United Nations Convention on the Rights of Persons with Disabilities, to which the UK is a state party.

Held: The appeal was allowed and a declaration that the regulations were unlawful was granted.

Judgment: 19. It follows that, in my judgment, the appellants fall within Article 14, subject to justification. I feel able to reach this conclusion even without resort to the United Nations Convention on the Rights of Persons with Disabilities (CRPD), which is relied upon by Mr Richard Drabble QC and further expounded upon by Ms Helen Mountfield QC on behalf of the Equality and Human Rights Commission. Mr Eicke seeks to marginalise the CRPD for present purposes by relying on *Reg (NM) v London Borough of Islington* [2012] EWHC 414 (Admin), in which Sales J, obiter, was inclined to disregard the CRPD as an aid to ascertaining the scope of Article 14 (see paragraphs 99–108). However, in *AH v West London MHT* [2011] UKUT 74 (AAC), the Upper Tribunal, presided over by Carnwath LJ, had taken a more expansive view (at paragraphs 15 and 16):

'The CRPD prohibits discrimination against people with disabilities and promotes the employment of fundamental rights for people with disabilities on an equal basis with others …

The CRPD provides the framework for Member States to address the rights of persons with disabilities. It is a legally binding international treaty that comprehensively clarifies the human rights of persons with disabilities as well as corresponding obligations on state parties. By ratifying a Convention, a state undertakes that wherever possible its laws will conform to the norms and values that the Convention enshrines.'

20. The CRPD was adopted by the General Assembly on 13 December 2006. It was ratified by the United Kingdom on 7 August 2009 and by the European Union on 23 December 2010. Article 4 obliges State Parties to:

'take all appropriate measures, including legislation, to modify or abolish existing laws, regulations, customs or practices that constitute discrimination against persons with disabilities.'

Article 5(3) provides that:

'in order to promote equality and eliminate discrimination, State Parties shall take all appropriate steps to ensure that reasonable accommodation is provided.'

Article 19 provides:

'State Parties … recognise the equal right of all persons with disabilities to live in the community, with choices equal to others, and shall take effective and appropriate measures to facilitate full engagement by persons with disabilities of this right and their full inclusion and participation in the community by ensuring that

(a) Persons with disabilities have the opportunity to choose their place of residence and where and with whom they live on an equal basis with others and are not obliged to live in a particular living arrangement;

(b) Persons with disabilities have access to a range of in-home, residential and other community support services, including personal assistance necessary to support living and inclusion in the community and to prevent isolation or segregation from the community;

(c) Community services and facilities are available on an equal basis to persons with disabilities and are responsive to their needs.'

These provisions resonate in the present case, even though they do not refer specifically to the provision of a state subsidy such as HB.

21. In the recent past, the Strasbourg Court has shown an increased willingness to deploy other international instruments as aids to the construction of the ECHR. In *Demir and Baykara v Turkey* (2009) 48 EHRR 54, the Grand Chamber said (at paragraph 85) that:

'in defining the meaning of terms and notions in the text of the [ECHR], [it] can and must take into account elements of international law other than the [ECHR], the interpretation of such elements by competent organs and the practice of European States reflecting their common values.'

22. The response of the Secretary of State is to seek to limit this approach by drawing fine distinctions as between different international instruments and in relation to their maturity or chronology. It seems to me, however, that such rearguard action is inappropriate. If the correct legal analysis of the meaning of Article 14 discrimination in the circumstances of these appeals had been elusive or uncertain (and I have held that it is not), I would have resorted to the CRDP and it would have resolved the uncertainty in favour of the appellants. It seems to me that it has the potential to illuminate our approach to both discrimination and justification.

Note

Although the UK is a dualist legal system, the courts make regular reference to the UK's international obligations, and the UK's international obligations may be considered as an interpretive aid in a case even if these international obligations have not been brought into domestic law. However, courts will not ordinarily create directly enforceable obligations from international treaties at common law where these have not been brought about through legislation.[51]

9.6.A.2 (iii) The European Union

Case 4/73, 14 May 1974[52] **9.27 (EU)**

Nold, Kohlen- und Baustoffgroßhandlung v Commission

REFERENCE TO THE ECHR

Nold

Facts: Nold, a German wholesale coal and construction materials business, requested that the Court of Justice annul the Commission's decision authorising the new terms of business of Ruhrkohle AG. The applicant was of the opinion that this decision indirectly and illegally withdrew the status of being a direct wholesaler of Ruhrkohle AG. Nold argued that the decision violated its property rights and its right to the free pursuit of business activity.

Held: The action was dismissed.

[51] *JH Rayner (Mincing Lane) Ltd v Department of Trade and Industry* [1990] 2 AC 418 (HL). See, however, Lord Kerr's dissent in *R (JS) v Secretary of State for Work and Pensions* [2015] UKSC 16, [2015] 1 WLR 1449 for an alternative point of view.

[52] ECLI:EU:C:1974:51.

Judgment: As for the question of fundamental rights, the protection of property ownership constitutes without any doubt one of the guarantees recognised by Community law which, in this connection, is based on the constitutional traditions of Member States and on acts of public international law, such as the Convention for the Protection of Human Rights and Fundamental Freedoms.

Notes

(1) While, in its early days, the European Court of Justice had resisted the attempts by applicants to recognise human rights protected by domestic legal systems,[53] there was a change of attitude in the *Stauder* case. In this case, the European Court of Justice recognised human rights as general principles of (then) European Community law and as a standard of review of European Community measures.[54] Although the European Community was not (and the EU is not) a party to the ECHR and neither Article 6 of the Treaty on European Union nor the Charter of Fundamental Rights were in force, in the *Nold* case, the European Court of Justice identified the sources of human rights to be protected in international human rights treaties and the common constitutional traditions,[55] with special significance being given to the ECHR.[56]

(2) In competition policy, the Commission has wide powers of investigation and sanctioning, and affected parties have repeatedly brought human rights claims to control the Commission's exercise of its powers, although the EU was not directly bound to the treaties ensuring such human rights.[57]

9.6.B USE OF FOREIGN LAW

The question dealt with in section 9.4.A above is also relevant with regard to the law of other legal systems which is not directly decisive for the case at hand, but may be used as a source of comparative inspiration. As the judges consider and reach their decisions behind closed doors, we cannot know whether they refer to foreign law in their deliberations. What can be compared is whether such comparative considerations appear in the judgments themselves.

[53] Case 1/58 *Stork v High Authority* ECLI:EU:C:1959:4; Case 40/64 *Sgarlata and others v Commission* ECLI:EU:C:1965:36.

[54] Case 26/69 *Stauder v City of Ulm* ECLI:EU:C:1970:67. As a follow-up of this case, see Case 11/70 *Internationale Handelsgesellschaflt* ECLI:EU:C:1970:114.

[55] Case 4/73 *Nold v Commission* ECLI:EU:C:1975:114.

[56] Case 36/75 *Rutili v Ministry for the Interior* ECLI:EU:C:1975:137. See further, eg S Douglas-Scott, 'The European Union and Human Rights after the Treaty of Lisbon' (2011) 11 *Human Rights Law Review* 645.

[57] Case 347/87 *Orkem v Commission* ECLI:EU:C:1989:387; Case T-99/04 *Treuhand AG v Commission* ECLI:EU:T:2008:256; Case T-69/04 *Schunk v Commission* ECLI:EU:T:2008:415; Case 322/81 *Michelin v Commission* ECLI:EU:C:1983:313.

9.6.B.1 THE NETHERLANDS

The law of other states and judgments of foreign national courts are quoted or used very rarely. This is the case even if a rule of European law, eg a provision of a European directive, is decisive for the case and that rule is interpreted differently by courts of other Member States.[58]

9.6.B.2 GERMANY

Similar to the position in relation to Dutch case law, there are hardly any occasions where the German administrative courts cite foreign national law or case law. Furthermore, the German Federal Constitutional Court (Bundesverfassungsgericht) essentially relies on its own authorities, with little inclination to look for inspiration from abroad.[59]

9.6.B.3 FRANCE

Comparative law is seen by leading administrative French judges as an important aspect of the judicial process. A comparative learning process has thus been developed by the Council of State. Since 2008, the Council of State has institutionalised and professionalised comparative legal research, notably through the creation of the Comparative Law Unit (Cellule de droit comparé). This is a team of foreign lawyers working under the supervision of the Research and Legal Dissemination Centre (Centre de recherches et de diffusion juridiques, CRDJ).

The Cellule contributes to the research activity of the CRDJ in order to provide support for the Judicial and Advisory Chambers of the Council of State. While the Cellule may have been somewhat improvised at its inception – it only had two part-time lawyers – it has since been provided with significant resources (including extensive databases), thanks to the growing importance of comparative law at the Council of State.

The importance of comparative law is obvious from both a qualitative and a quantitative standpoint. Whilst there were indeed examples of comparative law being drawn upon in an ad hoc way prior to the Cellule, the institutional creation of a centre of expertise for comparative law means that resort to such information has now become commonplace in important cases. It should thus be stressed that most cases decided by the Conseil d'Etat in enlarged panels are subject to comparative legal research. Those comparative reports, however, are part of the proceedings and are therefore covered by the principle of confidentiality of judicial investigations. The conclusions of the public rapporteur very regularly refer to foreign law and include comparative considerations.

[58] CW Backes, 'Een plicht tot rechtsvergelijkende motivering? Over de vraag hoe bestuursrechters omgaan met de interpretatie van EU-recht door hun buitenlandse collega's' in AT Marseille et al (eds), *Behoorlijk bestuursprocesrecht: Opstellen aangeboden aan prof mr BWN de Waard over grondslagen, beginselen en vernieuwingen van het bestuursprocesrecht* (The Hague, Boom Juridische Uitgevers) 313–30, para 2.2.

[59] For a detailed empirical analysis, see S Graf von Kielmansegg, 'Foreign Precedents in Constitutional Litigation' in M Schmidt-Kessel (ed), *German National Reports on the 19th International Congress of Comparative Law* (Tübingen, Mohr Siebeck, 2014) 643–78.

Despite this vivid importance of comparative law in the decision-making process, the Council of State never quotes foreign rulings and judgments in its judgments: the function of comparative law and of foreign rulings helps to assert or challenge the legitimacy of the Council of State's case law, but is not considered as binding.

9.6.B.4 ENGLAND AND WALES

House of Lords, 18 May 2000[60] **9.28 (EW)**

Three Rivers District Council v Bank of England

REFERENCE TO FOREIGN LAW

Three Rivers District Council

Facts: T and other depositors who had lost money following the collapse of the Bank of Credit and Commerce International appealed against a decision upholding an order striking out their action against the Bank of England, alleging misfeasance in public office. The Bank argued that the claim should be struck out due to the inadequacy of the pleadings and as an abuse of process.

Held: The appeal was allowed. However, the question of whether the evidence supported misfeasance in public office was a matter for the trial judge to determine.

Judgment: Lord Hope: The judgments of the High Court of Australia in *Northern Territory of Australia v. Mengel* (1995) 69 A.L.J.R. 527 and the judgment of the Court of Appeal of New Zealand in *Garrett v. Attorney-General* [1997] 2 N.Z.L.R. 332 are the second factor which leads me to reject the wider ambit of the second limb of the tort contended for by the plaintiffs. In those two cases, there was a full discussion of the issue now before this House (save that in *Mengel* the distinction between foresight by the public officer and objective foreseeability was not directly considered) and in both cases it was held that it was insufficient for the plaintiff to show a knowing breach of duty by a public officer coupled with resultant injury.

In *Mengel* stock inspectors employed by the defendant, without statutory or other authority, wrongly quarantined the plaintiffs' cattle whereby the plaintiffs suffered loss. Before the High Court of Australia, the plaintiffs contended that they were entitled to succeed on a claim for misfeasance in public office, and they argued that the mental element of that tort is made out if the public officer either knows or ought to know that he is acting without authority and the unlawful exercise of the power results in damage.

Note

It is common to see the courts consider decisions from other common law jurisdictions, such as Canada and Australia. In the *Three Rivers District Council* case judgment quoted here, what follows is a lengthy and intense discussion of the judgments of the High Court of Australia and the Court of Appeal of New Zealand.

[60] [2000] WLR 1220 (HL).

9.6.B.5 THE EUROPEAN UNION

Joined Cases 7/56 and 3 to 7/57, 12 July 1957[61] **9.29 (EU)**

Algera and Others v Common Assembly

COMPARATIVE METHOD; REFERENCE TO THE LEGAL SYSTEMS OF THE MEMBER STATES

Algera

Facts: In 1955, the Common Assembly of the European Coal and Steel Community reshaped its secretariat. This led to some decisions resulting in a change of the legal position and salary of the claimants. The claimants asked for annulment of these decisions and for the award of damages.

Held: Some of the decisions were annulled, one decision was upheld.

Judgment: The possibility of withdrawing such measures is a problem of administrative law, which is familiar in the case-law and learned writing of all the countries of the Community, but for the solution of which the Treaty does not contain any rules. Unless the Court is to deny justice, it is therefore obliged to solve the problem by reference to the rules acknowledged by the legislation, the learned writing and the case-law of the member countries.

It emerges from a comparative study of this problem of law that in the six Member States an administrative measure conferring individual rights on the person concerned cannot in principle be withdrawn, if it is a lawful measure; in that case, since the individual right is vested, the need to safeguard confidence in the stability of the situation thus created prevails over the interests of an administration desirous of reversing its decision. This is true in particular of the appointment of an official.

If, on the other hand, the administrative measure is illegal, revocation is possible under the law of all the Member States. The absence of an objective legal basis for the measure affects the individual right of the person concerned and justifies the revocation of the said measure. It should be stressed that whereas this principle is generally acknowledged, only the conditions for its application vary.

French law requires that the withdrawal of the illegal measure should be pronounced before the expiry of the time-limit for instituting legal proceedings and, if proceedings have been instituted, before judgment is delivered; with certain small differences, Belgian, Luxembourg and Dutch law seem to follow similar rules.

German law, on the other hand, does not set any time-limit for the exercise of the right of evocation, except where such a time-limit is laid down by a special provision. Thus Article 13 of the Bundesbeamtengesetz (Federal law governing Civil Servants) allows the withdrawal of an appointment only within a period of six months. However, it is generally acknowledged that unduly late withdrawal, occurring considerably later than the date on which withdrawal could have been pronounced, is contrary to the principle of good faith (*Treu und Glauben*). In this connection, case-law and learned writing found themselves also upon the concepts of waiver (*Verzicht*) and of forfeiture (*Verwirkung*) of the right of revocation.

Italian law is particularly clear on the question. Any administrative measure which is vitiated by lack of competence, infringement of the law or abuse of powers (*eccesso di*

[61] ECLI:EU:C:1957:7.

potere) may be annulled *ex tunc* by the administrative authority which issued it, irrespective of the individual rights to which it might have given rise. Such withdrawal may be declared at any time (*in qualsiasi momento*); thus, there is no time-limit prescribed for withdrawal. However, according to learned writing and case-law, unduly late withdrawal can constitute abuse of powers; measures which have been in force for a long time (*fatti avvenuti da lunga data*) should be kept in force, even if they were contrary to the law, unless overriding reasons require their withdrawal in the public interest.

Thus, the revocability of an administrative measure vitiated by illegality is allowed in all Member States.

In agreement with the Advocate-General's opinion, the Court accepts the principle of the revocability of illegal measures at least within a reasonable period of time, such as that within which the decisions in question in the present dispute occurred.

Note

The European courts regularly refer to the law of the Member States. According to scholarly writings, this may be seen as a method of law finding, which was and still is used to develop general principles of European law.[62] The most classical example for this is the *Algera* case, which is contained in the excerpt above. However, the European courts do not use this comparative method systematically, but only on a case-by-case basis.

9.6.B.6 COMPARATIVE REMARKS

The law of foreign legal systems, including judgments of foreign courts, are very rarely referred to in judgments of courts dealing with administrative law issues in most of the legal systems under study. This is true even for areas of law where there is a predominant influence of EU law and national courts all have to apply the same legal provisions as their colleagues in other Member States, such as asylum law and some parts of environmental law. 'The empirical findings reveal a surprising lack of transnational use of national jurisprudence'[63] also in these cases. However, the situation is different in France, especially at the French Council of State, where comparison of the law of other jurisdictions is an important method through which the courts find and develop the law. This was mainly fostered by creating the Cellule de droit comparé, a comparative law unit. However, the use of foreign law and its influence on the considerations in French cases are not explicitly outlined in the judgments. In England and Wales, the importance of the Commonwealth and the history of the development of independent Commonwealth legal systems have a bearing on the approach. Whilst comparisons with (case) law of other EU

[62] See, eg CH Hofman, GC Rowe and AH Türk, *Administrative Law and Policy of the European Union* (Oxford, Oxford University Press, 2011) 144 ff.

[63] H Lambert, 'Transnational Judicial Dialogue, Harmonisation and the Common European Asylum System' (2009) 58 *International and Comparative Law Quarterly* 519, 522. See also E Mak, 'Globalisation of the National Judiciary and the Dutch Constitution' (2013) 9 *Utrecht Law Review* 36, 45 ff; Backes (n 58 above) para 2.2.

Member States are rare, use of case law of other Commonwealth members, particularly, but not exclusively, Australia, Canada and New Zealand, are much more common.

The position and practice of the EU courts with regard to 'foreign' law is different from the position of the courts of the Member States. The EU courts regularly, but not systematically, use the comparative method and rely on legal traditions common to all (or some) Member States when interpreting or developing the law to fill gaps in the EU legal order.

FURTHER READING

Antoine, A and Fairgrieve, D, 'Écrire les décisions de justice … une comparaison franco-britannique' (2014) 3 *Revue du droit public* 759.

Arnull, A, 'Owning Up to Fallibility: Precedent and the Court of Justice' (1993) 30(2) *Common Market Law Review* 247.

Backes, CW, 'Een plicht tot rechtsvergelijkende motivering? Over de vraag hoe bestuursrechters omgaan met de interpretatie van EU-recht door hun buitenlandse collega's' in AT Marseille, ACM Meuwese, FCMA Michiels and JCA de Poorter (eds), *Behoorlijk bestuursprocesrecht. Opstellen aangeboden aan prof. mr. B.W.N. de Waard over grondslagen, beginselen en vernieuwingen van het bestuursprocesrecht* (The Hague, Boom Juridische Uitgevers, 2015) 313–30.

Blom-Cooper, L, 'Style of Judgments' in L Blom-Cooper, B Dickson and G Drewry (eds), *The Judicial House of Lords 1876–2009* (Oxford, Oxford University Press, 2009) 159–63.

Graf von Kielmansegg, S, 'Foreign Precedents in Constitutional Litigation' in M Schmidt-Kessel (ed), *German National Reports on the 19th International Congress of Comparative Law* (Tübingen, Mohr-Siebeck, 2014) 643–78.

Groppi, T and Ponthoreau, M-C, *The Use of Foreign Precedents by Constitutional Judges* (Oxford, Hart Publishing, 2013).

Jacob, M, *Precedents and Case-based Reasoning in the European Court of Justice* (Cambridge, Cambridge University Press, 2014).

Komarek, J, 'Judicial Lawmaking and Precedent in Supreme Courts: The European Court of Justice Compared to the US Supreme Court and the French Cour de cassation' (2008–09) 11 *Cambridge Yearbook of European Legal Studies* 399.

Mak, E, 'Comparative Law before the Supreme Courts of the UK and the Netherlands: An Empirical and Comparative Analysis' in M Andenas and D Fairgrieve (eds), *Courts and Comparative Law* (Oxford, Oxford University Press, 2015) 407–33.

Mak, E, 'Foreign Precedents in Constitutional Litigation' in L van Vliet (ed), *Netherlands Reports to the Nineteenth International Congress of Comparative Law: Vienna 2014* (Antwerp, Intersentia, 2015) 277–94.

Mak, E, *Judicial Decision-making in a Globalised World: A Comparative Analysis of the Changing Practices of Western Highest Courts* (Oxford, Hart Publishing, 2013).

Malhière, F, *La brièveté des décisions de justice (Conseil constitutionnel, Conseil d'État, Cour de cassation): contribution à l'étude des représentations de la justice* (Paris, Dalloz, 2013).

Paterson, A, *Final Judgment: The Last Law Lords and the Supreme Court* (Oxford, Hart Publishing, 2013).

de S-O-l'E Lasser, M, *Judicial Deliberations: A Comparative Analysis of Transparency and Legitimacy* (Oxford, Oxford University Press, 2004).

CHAPTER 10
NON-JUDICIAL REDRESS MECHANISMS

Mike Varney

10.1 INTRODUCTION

It is important to analyse systems of non-judicial redress for a number of reasons. Such mechanisms may be important because non-judicial redress may be able to offer citizens a remedy where judicial review could not because such systems often address issue not necessarily covered by the principle of legality, such as where the service offered by a public body has been poor, or where processes have led to frustration, delay or inconvenience.[1] In addition to providing a remedy for individuals where none would otherwise be available, these processes might also offer an effective learning opportunity for public bodies, allowing them to modify future conduct in order to improve decision-making and avoid further grievances and possible legal disputes between public bodies and the subjects of their decisions.[2] It is also possible that these non-judicial means of redress can provide an important avenue for reducing the overall caseload of the judicial system, with the potential to reduce the overall cost of resolving administrative disputes and also possibly increasing access to administrative dispute resolution mechanisms in systems where the cost of seeking judicial review is high.

In the systems where ombudsmen exist, these bodies generally play a dual role. As noted above, one of these roles is to provide a mechanism for the investigation and possible provision of redress for individual grievances. This objective was the reason for the creation of the ombudsmen in England and Wales, for instance.[3] In addition to this main

[1] For an overview of the ways in which non-judicial remedies might bring value to a system of administrative justice see, eg T Mullen, 'A Holistic Approach to Administrative Justice?' in M Adler (ed), *Administrative Justice in Context* (Oxford, Hart Publishing, 2010) 383–420; P Birkinshaw, 'Grievances, Remedies and the State Revisited and Reappraised' in the same volume, 353–87.

[2] See, eg C Harlow and R Rawlings, *Law and Administration*, 3rd edn (Cambridge, Cambridge University Press, 2009) ch 10.

[3] See, eg Sir J Whyatt, *The Citizen and the Administration* (London, Justice, 1961), available at https://2bquk8cdew6192tsu41lay8t-wpengine.netdna-ssl.com/wp-content/uploads/2014/04/The-Citizen-and-the-Administration-1961.pdf.

function, many ombudsmen also provide for an effective means of system surveillance, where the information gleaned from investigations can be fed back to the legislature in order to inform legislators and provide opportunities for law reform.

These factors all create a need for the consideration of non-judicial mechanisms for redress. The Council of Europe has also made a recommendation that systems of administrative justice should have a mechanism for non-judicial redress of grievance.

Council of Europe Recommendation Rec(2001)9 of the Committee of Ministers to Member States on Alternatives to Litigation between Administrative Authorities and Private Parties **10.1 (COE)**

... 13. Recommends that the governments of member states promote the use of alternative means for resolving disputes between administrative authorities and private parties by following, in their legislation and their practice, the principles of good practice contained in the appendix to this recommendation.

Appendix to Recommendation Rec(2001)9

I. General provisions

1. Subject of the recommendation

i. This recommendation deals with alternative means for resolving disputes between administrative authorities and private parties.

ii. This recommendation deals with the following alternative means: internal reviews, conciliation, mediation, negotiated settlement and arbitration.

iii. Although the recommendation deals with resolving disputes between administrative authorities and private parties, some alternative means may also serve to prevent disputes before they arise; this is particularly the case in respect of conciliation, mediation and negotiated settlement.

2. Scope of alternative means

i. Alternative means to litigation should be either generally permitted or permitted in certain types of cases deemed appropriate, in particular those concerning individual administrative acts, contracts, civil liability, and generally speaking, claims relating to a sum of money.

ii. The appropriateness of alternative means will vary according to the dispute in question.

3. Regulating alternative means

i. The regulation of alternative means should provide either for their institutionalisation or their use on a case-by-case basis, according to the decision of the parties involved.

ii. The regulation of alternative means should:

a. ensure that parties receive appropriate information about the possible use of alternative means;

...

c. guarantee fair proceedings allowing in particular for the respect of the rights of the parties and the principle of equality;

d. guarantee, as far as possible, transparency in the use of alternative means and a certain level of discretion;

e. ensure the execution of the solutions reached using alternative means.

iii. The regulation should promote the conclusion of alternative procedures within a reasonable time by setting time-limits or otherwise.

iv. The regulation may provide that the use of some alternative means to litigation will in certain cases result in the suspension of the execution of an act, either automatically or following a decision by the competent authority.

II. Relationship with courts

i. Some alternative means, such as internal reviews, conciliation, mediation and the search for a negotiated settlement, may be used prior to legal proceedings. The use of these means could be made compulsory as a prerequisite to the commencement of legal proceedings.

...

iv. In all cases, the use of alternative means should allow for appropriate judicial review which constitutes the ultimate guarantee for protecting both users' rights and the rights of the administration.

v. Judicial review will depend upon the alternative means chosen. Depending on the case, the types and extent of this review will cover the procedure, in particular the respect for the principles stated under section I.3.ii.a, b, c, and d, and/or the merits.

vi. In principle and subject to the law, the use of alternative means should result in the suspension or interruption of the time-limits for legal proceedings.

III. Special features of each alternative means

1. Internal reviews

i. In principle, internal reviews should be possible in relation to any act. They may concern the expediency and/or legality of an administrative act.

ii. Internal reviews may, in some cases, be compulsory, as a prerequisite to legal proceedings.

iii. Internal reviews should be examined and decided upon by the competent authorities.

2. Conciliation and mediation

i. Conciliation and mediation can be initiated by the parties concerned, by a judge or be made compulsory by law.

ii. Conciliators and mediators should arrange meetings with each party individually or simultaneously in order to reach a solution.

iii. Conciliators and mediators can invite an administrative authority to repeal, withdraw or modify an act on grounds of expediency or legality.

3. Negotiated Settlement

i. Unless otherwise provided by law, administrative authorities shall not use a negotiated settlement to disregard their obligations.

ii. In accordance with the law, public officials participating in a procedure aimed at reaching a negotiated settlement shall be provided with sufficient powers to be able to compromise.

Note

This recommendation is exceptionally broad and provides for a wide range of possibilities for non-judicial redress of grievance. It also appears to impose requirements in excess of those mandated by most of the national systems that are the subject of this study. However, the recommendation emphasises the importance of such systems of alternative redress of grievances and also underlines a further important point – often, the purpose of internal grievance redress is not necessarily to remove or exclude judicial protection, but to provide an additional opportunity for disputes to be settled without the need for judicial review. The recommendation also notes that internal review is not necessarily concerned solely with issues of legality, but might also consider issues of expediency.

10.2 NON-JUDICIAL REDRESS MECHANISMS OTHER THAN OMBUDSMEN

All legal systems under examination have alternative methods of grievance redress. This section will consider the potential for complaints to be addressed to administrative authorities and whether the right exists in law or through administrative practice.

10.2.A SYSTEMS PROVIDING FOR REDRESS MECHANISMS IN LAW

Some systems have a legal right to complain to or address administrative authorities and create a corresponding legal right to a response. A failure to respond to such a complaint creates the opportunity for the complainant to bring a complaint before the courts, which may then mandate a response from the competent authority. Furthermore, some systems have in place additional systems mandated in legislation, which may be sector specific or system-wide, to deliver redress outside of the judicial system.

10.2.A.1 FRANCE

Ordonnance n° 58-1100 du 17 novembre 1958 relative au fonctionnement des assemblées parlementaires **10.2 (FR)**

Article 4 It is prohibited to bring petitions to the two parliamentary chambers.

The rules of procedure of the two chambers shall set the conditions according to which written petitions can be submitted.

All violations of the above provisions, all provocations through public speeches, or through writings which are printed, exposed or distributed in a public gathering with the aim of discussing, preparing or submitting a petition, a declaration or a statement to one of the parliamentary chambers shall be punished with six months imprisonment and a fine of 7500 Euro, whether the provocation produced any effect or not.

Règlement de l'assemblée nationale **10.3 (FR)**

Article 147 (1) Petitions shall be addressed to the President of the Assembly. They may also be presented by any member of National Assembly, who shall mention and sign the submission.

(2) No petition brought or transmitted by a public gathering shall be received or tabled by the President.

(3) Every petition shall specify the petitioner's place of residence and shall bear his signature.

Article 148 (1) Petitions shall be entered on a general list in the order in which they are received. All petitioners shall be notified of the serial numbers of their petitions.

(2) The President of the National Assembly shall refer petitions to the committee competent to consider them by virtue of Article 36. The committee shall appoint a rapporteur.

(3) After hearing the recommendations of the rapporteur the committee shall decide, on a case by case basis, to take no further action on the petition, or to refer it to another standing committee of the Assembly or to a minister, or to submit it to the Assembly. Each petitioner shall be notified of the committee's decision concerning his petition.

(4) Where a petition is referred to another standing committee of the Assembly, that committee may decide to take no further action on it, or to refer it to a minister, or to submit it to the Assembly. Each petitioner shall be notified of the committee's decision concerning his petition.

(5) The minister's reply shall be communicated to the petitioner. If the minister has not replied within three months to a petition referred to him by a committee, the committee may decide to submit the petition to the Assembly.

(6) Where a committee decides, under paragraph 3, 4 or 5, to submit a petition to the Assembly it tables a report reproducing the full text of the petition; the report shall be printed and distributed.

Article 149 (1) A bulletin summarising petitions and the relevant decisions shall be distributed periodically to the members of the National Assembly.

(2) Within eight days of the distribution of a bulletin publishing a committee's decision to take no further action on a petition or to refer it to a minister or another committee, any member of Parliament may request the President to submit the petition to the Assembly; any such request shall be transmitted to the Conference of Presidents, which shall decide.

(3) After this time has elapsed, or if the Conference of Presidents refuses the request, the committee's decision shall stand confirmed and shall be published in the Official Journal.

(4) If the Conference of Presidents grants the request, the report on the petition which has been published in the Official Journal shall be tabled, printed and distributed; the report shall reproduce the full text of the petition.

Note

There is a right to petition the National Assembly in France contained in the Ordonnance of 17 November 1958 (Ordonnance n° 58-1100 du 17 novembre 1958 relative au fonctionnement des assemblées parlementaires) and Articles 147–151 of the Rules of Procedure of the National Assembly (Règlement de l'assemblée nationale). This right is relatively seldom used by citizens, as citizens generally prefer to make use of the Defender of Rights (Defenseur des Droits).[4] The result of this is that

[4] See section 10.3.A.1 (ii) below.

the right of petition, while in existence, is used only infrequently as a mechanism of administrative dispute resolution.

Code des relations entre le public et l'administration **10.4 (FR)**

Article L340-1 The Commission for access to administrative documents (Commission d'accès aux documents administratifs) is an independent administrative authority.

It is responsible for ensuring respect for the freedom of access to administrative documents and public archives and for the application of Title II of this Book under the conditions laid down in this Book and in Title I of Book II of the Heritage Code (Code du patrimoine).

Article L342-1 The Commission for access to administrative documents issues notices when it is seized by a person who is opposed to a refusal to communicate or a refusal to publish an administrative document under Title I, a refusal to consult or to communicate public archival documents, with the exception of the documents mentioned in Article L211-4 of the Heritage Code and of acts and documents produced or received by parliamentary assemblies, or an adverse decision on the re-usage of public information.

Referral to the Commission for an opinion is a mandatory prerequisite for the exercise of a court action.

Article R343-1 The person concerned shall have two months from the date of notification of the refusal or the expiry of the period provided for in Article R311-13 to refer the matter to the Commission for access to administrative documents.

The Commission shall be seized by letter, fax or electronic means. The referral shall specify its purpose and, where appropriate, the provisions on which it is based. It shall indicate, when the applicant is a natural person, his full name and address and, in the case of a legal person, his form, name, registered office and the full name of the person representing it. It shall be accompanied by a copy, as the case may be, of the refusal decision or the unanswered request. The Commission shall register the application if it contains all of these elements after having, where appropriate, invited the applicant to complete it. It then acknowledges receipt without delay.

The Commission shall forward requests for opinions to the administration concerned.

Article R343-2 The administration concerned shall, within the time limit prescribed by the chairman of the Committee, communicate to the latter all relevant documents and information and provide it with the necessary assistance.

The members of the Committee, as well as the rapporteurs appointed by the president, may carry out any on-site investigation necessary for the accomplishment of their mission.

The chairman may call to participate in the work of the Committee, in an advisory capacity, a representative of the administration concerned by the deliberation.

Article R343-3 The Commission shall notify the person concerned and the administration concerned of its opinion within one month of the registration of the application to the Secretariat. That administration shall inform the Commission, within one month of receipt of such notice, of the action it intends to take on the application.

Article R343-4 The silence kept during the period provided for in Article R343-5 by the administration in question amounts to a decision of refusal.

Article R343-5 The period after which the implied decision of refusal referred to in Article R343-4 comes into effect shall be two months from the date of the registration of the applicant's application by the Commission.

Note

In addition to the right of petition noted above, the French system has developed independent administrative authorities which are competent to regulate one specific field, often in relation to technical subject matters. In the excerpt above, the example of the Commission d'accès aux documents administratifs (Commission for access to administrative documents) is offered. This Commission is competent to deal with complaints lodged by individuals who were refused access to administrative documents by an administrative decision. Referral to the Commission is compulsory before any challenge of the administrative refusal before the administrative courts and has the objective of diverting complaints in this specialised field away from the courts insofar as is possible.

10.2.A.2 GERMANY

Grundgesetz **10.5 (DE)**

Article 17 Every person shall have the right individually or jointly with others to address written requests or complaints to competent authorities and to the legislature.

Note

The right of petition allows for complaints to be addressed to any state institution. The right to have a petition examined and answered is enforceable before the courts.[5] This does not, however, create a right to a remedy, and the administrative authority may reject the complaint in its response.

10.2.A.3 THE NETHERLANDS

Grondwet **10.6 (NL)**

Article 5 Everyone shall have the right to submit a petition in writing to the competent authorities.

Notes

(1) In the Netherlands, the right of petition may be qualified as the mother of all political rights and freedoms. It goes back to the end of the Middle Ages, when citizens had no right to participate in political decision-making at all. They were,

[5] BVerwG, DÖV 1976, 315; BVerfG, NJW 1992, 3033 (no right to motivation).

however, entitled to submit petitions to the authorities, and frequently did so. Indeed, the Dutch War of Independence (1568–1648) started after a petition of noblemen had been rejected by the Spanish authorities.

(2) Over the years, the right of petition has been developed into a right to complain against the authorities' actions. Constitutionally, the right does not imply an accompanying right to receive an answer. Such right is, however, statutorily guaranteed in the complaint regulations regarding the different branches of government. In the next excerpt, internal complaint mechanisms against administrative authorities will be presented. In addition to these mechanisms, special mention should be made of the Committee of Petitions (Commissie voor de verzoekschriften) of the Second Chamber of the Parliament. The Committee receives hundreds of petitions yearly. Most of them are transferred to the national ombudsman. However, in some cases, the Committee may start an investigation, leading to a report which is discussed with the government.

Algemene Wet Bestuursrecht **10.7 (NL)**

Article 9:1 (1) Any person has the right to lodge a complaint with an administrative authority about its conduct towards him or another person in a particular matter.

(2) The conduct of a person working under the authority of an administrative authority is considered conduct of the administrative authority.

Article 9:2 An administrative authority shall ensure that oral and written complaints about its conduct and conduct of administrative authorities operating under its responsibility are handled properly.

Article 9:3 A decision on the handling of a complaint about the conduct of an administrative authority is not open to judicial review.

Article 9:4 (1) If a written complaint relates to conduct towards the complainant and satisfies the requirements of section 2, Articles 9:5 to 9:12 apply.

(2) The notice of complaint must be signed and shall in any event contain:

(a) the name and address of the person lodging the complaint;

(b) the date;

(c) a description of the conduct against which the complaint is directed.

. . .

Article 9:7 (1) Complaints shall be handled by a person who was not involved in the conduct to which the complaint relates.

(2) Section 1 does not apply if the complaint relates to conduct of the administrative authority itself or its chairman or one of its members.

Article 9:8 (1) An administrative authority is not required to deal with complaints relating to conduct:

. . .

(b) which occurred more than one year before the complaint was lodged;

(c) against which the complainant could have lodged an objection (*bezwaar*);

(d) against which the complainant can still lodge a claim for judicial review, unless the conduct consists of failure to take a decision in due time, or could have lodged a claim for judicial review;

(e) which is or has been the subject of a ruling in proceedings instituted before a court other than an administrative court, or

(f) …

(2) An administrative authority is not required to deal with a complaint if the complainant's interest is manifestly not sufficiently substantial or the conduct manifestly not sufficiently serious.

…

Article 9:9 The person whose conduct is the subject of the complaint shall be sent a copy of the notice of complaint and of any documents enclosed with it.

Article 9:10 (1) The administrative authority shall give the complainant and the person to whose conduct the complaint relates the opportunity to be heard.

(2) The administrative authority may decide not to hear the complainant if:

(a) the complaint is manifestly unfounded,

(b) the complainant has stated that he does not wish to exercise the right to be heard or

(c) the complainant does not indicate, within a reasonable period, determined by the administrative authority, that he wants to be heard.

(3) A record shall be drawn up of the hearing.

Article 9:11 (1) The administrative authority shall deal with the complaint within six weeks or – if division 9.1.3 applies – within ten weeks after receiving the notice of complaint.

(2) The administrative authority may postpone dealing with the complaint by four weeks at most. The postponement shall be communicated in writing to the complainant and the person to whose conduct the complaint relates.

Article 9:12 (1) The administrative authority shall notify the complainant, in writing and stating reasons, of the findings of the investigation into the complaint, of its opinion on the complaint and the consequences, if any, it will attach to it.

(2) When sending this notification, the administrative authority shall state with which ombudsman and within what time limit the complainant may subsequently file a request for investigation of the complaint.

Article 9:12a The administrative authority shall keep a register of the written complaints lodged with it. The complaints registered shall be published annually.

…

Article 9:14 (1) A person or committee may be made responsible by law or by decision of the administrative authority with handling and advising on complaints.

(2) The administrative authority may give the person or committee only general instructions.

Article 9:15 …

(2) If the complainant and the person to whose conduct the complaint relates are heard, the hearing shall be conducted by the person or committee referred to in Article 9:14. If a committee has been established, it may entrust the conduct of the hearing to the chairman or a committee member.

(3) The person or committee shall decide whether or not to apply Article 9:10(2).

(4) The person or committee shall send a report of the findings, together with the opinion and recommendations, if any, to the administrative authority. The report shall include the record of the hearing.

Article 9:16 If the conclusions of the administrative authority differ from the opinion, the reason for this difference shall be stated in the conclusions and the opinion shall be enclosed with the notification referred to in Article 9:12.

Notes

(1) *General:* Article 9:1 of the Algemene Wet Bestuursrecht (AWB) provides for a right for any person to raise complaints with an administrative authority about the authority's conduct or conduct of a person working under the authority's responsibility towards the person concerned or another person. In principle, this internal complaint procedure must be followed before the person can file a complaint with an (external) ombudsman. Therefore, the assessment standards in internal complaint procedures are the same as those applied by an ombudsman. Both the complaint procedure before an ombudsman and the assessment standards will be discussed in depth in sections 10.3.A.2 (iv) and 10.3.A.3 (i) part iii below. Generally, complaints are concerned with factual (in)action of the authorities or their civil servants, and sometimes with private law actions, but not with decisions as defined in Article 1:3 AWB (*besluiten*).[6] Against the latter, an interested party should, within the strict limit of six weeks, file an intra-administrative objection (*bezwaar*) to the administrative authority as a prerequisite for instigating an action for judicial review (*beroep*) before the district court.[7] Then again, the rules for handling internal complaints are fairly similar to those applicable to the procedures for objections, although they are less strict.

(2) *Access:* according to Article 9:4 AWB, a complaint should, in principle, be in writing, and should contain the name and address of the complainant, the date and a description of the conduct against which the complaint is directed. Filing a complaint is free of charge. An administrative authority is not required to deal with a complaint relating to conduct which occurred more than one year ago (Article 9:8(1)(b) AWB), or where the complainant's interest is manifestly not of sufficient weight or the conduct is manifestly not sufficiently serious (Article 9:8(2) AWB). In addition, the authority is not obliged to handle a complaint if the conduct concerned qualifies as a decision as defined in Article 1:3 AWB (*besluit*) and could have been contested in the intra-administrative objection procedure (Article 9:8(1)(c) AWB), and, thereafter, by means of a claim for judicial review (*beroep*) before an administrative court (Article 9:8(1)(d) AWB). In practice, a 'complaint' (*klacht*) of a citizen is sometimes concerned with both an administrative decision and with improper conduct of a civil servant in the course of taking it. In that case, the authority may decide to handle it in a combined procedure for objections and complaints (at least if the 'complaint'

[6] For the meaning of *besluit* in the Dutch legal system, see Chapter 3, section 3.1.A.1.

[7] For the procedure of intra-administrative objection in the Netherlands, see Chapter 2, section 2.5.B.1 (ii).

was raised within the six-week time limit for filing objections), and decide on both. In this respect, it is convenient that the procedural rules for handling objections and complaints are fairly similar. As regards private law actions, the complaint procedure may function as a more accessible, costless small claims alternative for the civil courts. If the citizens choose to bring the action before the civil courts, the authorities are no longer required to deal with a complaint regarding the same private law action (Article 9:8(1)(e) AWB).

(3) *Procedure:* the procedure for handling complaints is straightforward. After a complaint has been filed, the person whose conduct is the subject of it is sent a copy of the complaint and of any documents enclosed with it. Subsequently, the administrative authority generally will offer both parties the opportunity to be heard, and will decide about the complaint, in principle, within six weeks of receiving the notice of complaint (Article 9:11(1) AWB). Finally, the authority will notify the complainant, in writing and stating reasons, of the findings of the investigation into the complaint, its opinion on the complaint and the consequences it will attach to it (Article 9:12(1) AWB). The notification should state with which ombudsman the complainant may subsequently file a request for investigation of the complaint (Article 9:12(2) AWB). A decision on the handling of a complaint is not open to judicial review before a court (Article 9:3 AWB). Complaints are, in principle, handled by a person who was not involved in the conduct to which the complaint relates (Article 9:7(1) AWB). In order to enhance the impartiality of the complaints process, the authority may attribute the complaint handling and the giving of advice on the complaint to a person or committee (Article 9:14(1) AWB). In that case, the committee (or person) will hear the parties involved (Article 9:15(2) AWB). The time limit for deciding on the complaint is ten weeks after receipt of the complaint. At the end of the process, the committee gives an opinion on how to deal with the complaint. This opinion is not binding on the authority. However, if the authority wants to deviate from it, the reason for this should be stated in the conclusions (Article 9:16 AWB).

10.2.A.4 THE EUROPEAN UNION

Treaty on the Functioning of the European Union **10.8 (EU)**

Article 227 Any citizen of the Union, and any natural or legal person residing or having its registered office in a Member State, shall have the right to address, individually or in association with other citizens or persons, a petition to the European Parliament on a matter which comes within the Union's fields of activity and which affects him, her or it directly.

Note

The only horizontal non-judicial remedy available in the EU legal system is the petition to the Petitions Committee of the European Parliament, which is competent to receive complaints on any matter within the Union's fields of competence and which affects the petitioner directly. The outcome of the procedure does not have the force of law and is a recommendation.

10.2.B SYSTEMS PROVIDING FOR REDRESS MECHANISMS AS ADMINISTRATIVE PRACTICE

While some systems do not provide for a means of complaint in the Constitution or in statute, there is an expectation that administrative bodies will have a mechanism for the handling of complaints. Although the system does not necessarily create a right to complain to the courts if the complainant does not receive a response (as in the systems outlined in section 10.2.A), the complaints system still provides an important mechanism for the resolution of grievances, and is adopted and adhered to by public authorities as a matter of administrative good practice.

10.2.B.1 ENGLAND AND WALES

Parliamentary and Health Service Ombudsman, Principles of Good Complaints Handling[8] **10.9 (EW)**

Summary

1. Getting it right

Acting in accordance with the law and relevant guidance, and with regard for the rights of those concerned.

Ensuring that those at the top of the public body provide leadership to support good complaint management and develop an organisational culture that values complaints.

Having clear governance arrangements, which set out roles and responsibilities, and ensure lessons are learnt from complaints.

Including complaint management as an integral part of service design.

Ensuring that staff are equipped and empowered to act decisively to resolve complaints.

Focusing on the outcomes for the complainant and the public body.

Signposting to the next stage of the complaints procedure, in the right way and at the right time.

Having clear and simple procedures.

Ensuring that complainants can easily access the service dealing with complaints, and informing them about advice and advocacy services where appropriate.

Dealing with complainants promptly and sensitively, bearing in mind their individual circumstances.

Listening to complainants to understand the complaint and the outcome they are seeking.

Responding flexibly, including co-ordinating responses with any other bodies involved in the same complaint, where appropriate.

2. Being customer focused

Publishing clear, accurate and complete information about how to complain, and how and when to take complaints further.

Publishing service standards for handling complaints.

Providing honest, evidence-based explanations and giving reasons for decisions.

Keeping full and accurate records.

[8] Parliamentary and Health Service Ombudsman, *Principles of Good Complaints Handling* (London, 2009).

3. Being open and accountable

Treating the complainant impartially, and without unlawful discrimination or prejudice.

Ensuring that complaints are investigated thoroughly and fairly to establish the facts of the case.

Ensuring that decisions are proportionate, appropriate and fair.

Ensuring that complaints are reviewed by someone not involved in the events leading to the complaint.

Acting fairly towards staff complained about as well as towards complainants.

4. Acting fairly and proportionately

Acknowledging mistakes and apologising where appropriate.

Providing prompt, appropriate and proportionate remedies.

Considering all the relevant factors of the case when offering remedies.

Taking account of any injustice or hardship that results from pursuing the complaint as well as from the original dispute.

5. Putting things right

Using all feedback and the lessons learnt from complaints to improve service design and delivery.

Having systems in place to record, analyse and report on the learning from complaints.

Regularly reviewing the lessons to be learnt from complaints.

Where appropriate, telling the complainant about the lessons learnt and changes made to services, guidance or policy.

6. Seeking continuous improvement

Good complaint handling is not limited to providing an individual remedy to the complainant: public bodies should ensure that all feedback and lessons learnt from complaints contribute to service improvement.

Learning from complaints is a powerful way of helping to improve public service, enhancing the reputation of a public body and increasing trust among the people who use its service. Public bodies should have systems to record, analyse and report on the learning from complaints. Public bodies should feed that learning back into the system to improve their performance.

It is good practice for public bodies to report publicly on their complaint handling performance. This should include reporting on the number of complaints received and the outcome of those complaints. Where complaints have led to a change in services, policies or procedures, public bodies could report those changes.

...

Notes

(1) There is no legal requirement for public bodies to have a complaints handling scheme and there is no legal right for service users to be able to complain to public bodies. However, administrative practice on complaints handling has existed for a long time in England and Wales.[9] In 1991, the Conservative government launched the Citizen's Charter, which, amongst other things, had the objective of making public

[9] For early study on this issue, see P Birkinshaw and N Lewis, *When Citizens Complain: Reforming Justice and Administration* (Oxford, Oxford University Press, 1993).

bodies more responsive to the needs of the citizen and more responsive to complaints. The current practice is that all public bodies should have a complaints procedure to deal with complaints made by members of the public. The excerpt above illustrates the principles that the Parliamentary Commissioner for Administration expects such complaints systems to support. The principles envisage complaints not only as a method for providing redress to those who are aggrieved, but also as a means of improving the future delivery of public services.

(2) Given that there is no legal requirement to have a complaints system, there is therefore no mandated process for dealing with complaints. It was noted in a parliamentary report that the result of this lack of consistent process was that the handling of complaints remains inconsistent between government bodies and departments.[10] Most departments adopt a written procedure for the handling of complaints and expect that this will be followed by individual complainants. There is no requirement in law for departments to acknowledge complaints that have been made, there are no specific deadlines for response and there are no uniform processes for the investigation or resolution of complaints. However, most public bodies are likely to seek to follow best practice as recommended by the Parliamentary Commissioner for Administration or, in the case of local authorities, the Local Government and Social Care Ombudsman.

(3) The submission of a complaint about the decision or action of a public body is likely to constitute a refreshment of the three-month time limit for the claim of judicial review,[11] as the ultimate response to the claim is likely to be treated as a fresh decision by the courts, which is thus subject to judicial review. In general, the courts are unlikely to entertain a judicial review claim unless a claimant can demonstrate that internal complaints mechanisms have been exhausted.[12]

10.2.C COMPARATIVE REMARKS

Each of the systems under examination has some method for handling complaints against public bodies made by individuals. In France, Germany, the Netherlands and the EU, these methods are enshrined in law. In Germany, there is a legal right to receive a response enshrined in the German Constitution. France and the Netherlands also guarantee a right to response, but this is contained in a statute, rather than in the Constitution.[13] In Germany, the right is to petition any institution of the state, and a response must be provided. In France and the EU, the right to petition is limited to complaints to Parliament, with a petition to the General Assembly in France and to the Petitions Committee of the European Parliament in the EU. This process is not often used by citizens, perhaps because the process is relatively lengthy and the ultimate remedy only has the force of recommendation. It may also be that the existence of ombudsmen in both France and

[10] Public Administration Select Committee, *More Complaints Please!* (2013–2014, HC 229) paras 19–20 and 23–25.

[11] See the discussion of time limits in Chapter 4, section 4.7.B.5.

[12] See, eg *R v Secretary of State for the Home Department, ex parte Swati* [1986] 1 WLR 477.

[13] Art 9:12 AWB.

the EU reduces the attractiveness of the petition to complainants as it may be possible for the ombudsman to provide a more effective remedy. In all of the legal systems where there is a legal right to have a complaint considered, the complaints process tends to be separate from judicial review, rather than being mandatory before judicial review can take place.

In England and Wales, there is no legal right to make a complaint or to receive a response, but administrative practice, in part driven by government action and ideology and in part driven by the ombudsman, has made complaints handling an important part of public administration, with the potential to deliver appropriate redress to complainants and also to lead to possible improvements in service delivery. In both the French system and that of England and Wales, it is interesting to note that there is a stronger interface between complaints and judicial review. In France, the making of a complaint can be mandatory if provided by statute (as in the process in relation to access to administrative documents set out in section 10.2.A.2 above), but is generally facultative. In English law, there is a general expectation that claimants for judicial review will have pursued the complaints process in advance of bringing a judicial review claim.

The complaints systems characterise certain differences that exist within the systems under examination. In the Netherlands and Germany,[14] complaints processes are predominantly seen as a way to address complaints that arise outside of the realm of judicial protection, rather than as a means of reducing the caseload of administrative courts. Much the same might be said of France and the EU, where the right to bring a petition before the European Parliament is not a significant means of redress for those who are aggrieved by the actions of the authorities at the EU level when contrasted with the ability to submit a complaint to the European ombudsman or seek judicial redress. This position might be contrasted with that in England and Wales. The latter system seeks to reduce the incidence of judicial review claims through the use of complaints systems. In France, these are mandated only in specific sectors where the legislature has sought to impose such a requirement, whereas in England and Wales, the expectation is generally that if there are internal complaints mechanisms, then these should have been exhausted in advance of any claim for judicial review.[15]

10.3 OMBUDSMEN

10.3.A SYSTEMS WITH A LEGALLY MANDATED OMBUDSMAN

The majority of systems subject to analysis in this book have a legally mandated ombudsman of some kind, operating at the national level in the Member States or at the EU level. The powers, nature of the appointment and jurisdiction of the ombudsman in each system vary, although, because that the concept of the ombudsmen shares a common

[14] For a piece that argues this in relation to Germany, see U Stelkens, 'Administrative Appeals in Germany' in DC Dragos and B Neamtu (eds), *Alternative Dispute Resolution in European Administrative Law* (Berlin, Springer, 2014) 3–57, 34.

[15] See further Chapter 2, section 2.7.A.2.

historical origin in the Scandinavian countries, there are likely to be some commonalities. Some ombudsmen have been established for a considerable period of time and thus have a large body of investigations behind them, whereas others are relative newcomers, or have generally been less well used by aggrieved citizens and thus may have had less impact in their respective systems.

10.3.A.1 THE APPOINTMENT AND JURISDICTION OF THE OMBUDSMAN

Each system has its own approach to the appointment and jurisdiction of the ombudsman. Most ombudsmen tend to be tied to parliaments, so the appointment of the ombudsman and the accountability of the ombudsman are predominantly in the hands of the parliament. However, it is possible that some ombudsmen have stronger links to the executive, although this could lead to questions of independence and impartiality from those who may be subject to investigation.

10.3.A.1 (i) The European Union

Treaty on the Functioning of the European Union **10.10 (EU)**

Article 228 (1) A European Ombudsman, elected by the European Parliament, shall be empowered to receive complaints from any citizen of the Union or any natural or legal person residing or having its registered office in a Member State concerning instances of maladministration in the activities of the Union institutions, bodies, offices or agencies, with the exception of the Court of Justice of the European Union acting in its judicial role. He or she shall examine such complaints and report on them.

In accordance with his duties, the Ombudsman shall conduct inquiries for which he finds grounds, either on his own initiative or on the basis of complaints submitted to him direct or through a Member of the European Parliament, except where the alleged facts are or have been the subject of legal proceedings. Where the Ombudsman establishes an instance of maladministration, he shall refer the matter to the institution, body, office or agency concerned, which shall have a period of three months in which to inform him of its views. The Ombudsman shall then forward a report to the European Parliament and the institution, body, office or agency concerned. The person lodging the complaint shall be informed of the outcome of such inquiries.

The Ombudsman shall submit an annual report to the European Parliament on the outcome of his inquiries.

(2) The Ombudsman shall be elected after each election of the European Parliament for the duration of its term of office. The Ombudsman shall be eligible for reappointment.

The Ombudsman may be dismissed by the Court of Justice at the request of the European Parliament if he no longer fulfils the conditions required for the performance of his duties or if he is guilty of serious misconduct.

(3) The Ombudsman shall be completely independent in the performance of his duties. In the performance of those duties he shall neither seek nor take instructions from any Government, institution, body, office or entity. The Ombudsman may not, during his term of office, engage in any other occupation, whether gainful or not.

(4) The European Parliament acting by means of regulations on its own initiative in accordance with a special legislative procedure shall, after seeking an opinion from the Commission and with the consent of the Council, lay down the regulations and general conditions governing the performance of the Ombudsman's duties.

Notes

(1) The European Ombudsman was created by the Maastricht Treaty, and the first ombudsman was elected by the European Parliament in 1995. The Treaty provides for a broad jurisdiction for the Ombudsman, with the only notable exception being that the Ombudsman is not entitled to investigate the Court of Justice or General Court when they are acting in their judicial capacities. The second possible limitation on the jurisdiction of the European Ombudsman is that it is not possible to investigate any matter which is or has been the subject of legal proceedings. The scope of who might make a complaint is very broad, as the Ombudsman may investigate complaints from citizens of the European Union and from those who are resident in a Member State or have a registered office there. As such, even those who do not have citizenship of the European Union may make a complaint to the European Ombudsman if they have a connection with a Member State.

(2) The process of appointment of the Ombudsman is through election by the European Parliament for the duration of its term of office (Article 228(2) of the Treaty on the Functioning of the European Union (TFEU)), with the potential for extension. It is clear that the Ombudsman is to be independent of all institutions and is not an institution for the purposes of Article 265 TFEU.

(3) The European Parliament is granted considerable power to regulate the activities of the Ombudsman by Article 228(4) TFEU. Parliament has adopted Decisions in order to further regulate the activities of the Ombudsman and the investigatory powers of the office.

Decision 94/262/ECSC, EC, Euratom of the European Parliament of 9 March 1994 on the regulations and general conditions governing the performance of the Ombudsman's duties[16] **10.11 (EU)**

Article 2 (1) Within the framework of the aforementioned Treaties and the conditions laid down therein, the Ombudsman shall help to uncover maladministration in the activities of the Community institutions and bodies, with the exception of the Court of Justice and the Court of First Instance acting in their judicial role, and make recommendations with a view to putting an end to it. No action by any other authority or person may be the subject of a complaint to the Ombudsman.

(2) Any citizen of the Union or any natural or legal person residing or having his registered office in a Member State of the Union may, directly or through a Member of the European Parliament, refer a complaint to the Ombudsman in respect of an instance of maladministration in the activities of Community institutions or bodies, with the exception of the Court of Justice and the Court of First Instance acting in their judicial role. The Ombudsman shall inform the institution or body concerned as soon as a complaint is referred to him.

[16] [1994] OJ L113/15, and amended by its decisions of 14 March 2002 [2002] OJ L92/13 and 18 June 2008 [2008] OJ L189/25.

(3) The complaint must allow the person lodging the complaint and the object of the complaint to be identified; the person lodging the complaint may request that his complaint remain confidential.

(4) A complaint shall be made within two years of the date on which the facts on which it is based came to the attention of the person lodging the complaint and must be preceded by the appropriate administrative approaches to the institutions and bodies concerned.

(5) The Ombudsman may advise the person lodging the complaint to address it to another authority.

(6) Complaints submitted to the Ombudsman shall not affect time-limits for appeals in administrative or judicial proceedings.

(7) When the Ombudsman, because of legal proceedings in progress or concluded concerning the facts which have been put forward, has to declare a complaint inadmissible or terminate consideration of it, the outcome of any enquiries he has carried out up to that point shall be filed definitively.

(8) No complaint may be made to the Ombudsman that concerns work relationships between the Community institutions and bodies and their officials and other servants unless all the possibilities for the submission of internal administrative requests and complaints, in particular the procedures referred to in Article 90(1) and (2) of the Staff Regulations, have been exhausted by the person concerned and the time limits for replies by the authority thus petitioned have expired.

(9) The Ombudsman shall as soon as possible inform the person lodging the complaint of the action he has taken on it.

Article 6 (1) The Ombudsman shall be appointed by the European Parliament after each election to the European Parliament for the duration of its mandate. He shall be eligible for reappointment.

(2) The Ombudsman shall be chosen from among persons who are Union citizens, have full civil and political rights, offer every guarantee of independence, and meet the conditions required for the exercise of the highest judicial office in their country or have the acknowledged competence and experience to undertake the duties of Ombudsman.

Article 7 (1) The Ombudsman shall cease to exercise his duties either at the end of his term of office or on his resignation or dismissal.

(2) Save in the event of his dismissal, the Ombudsman shall remain in office until his successor has been appointed.

(3) In the event of early cessation of duties, a successor shall be appointed within three months of the office's falling vacant for the remainder of the parliamentary term.

Article 8 An Ombudsman who no longer fulfils the conditions required for the performance of his duties or is guilty of serious misconduct may be dismissed by the Court of Justice of the European Communities at the request of the European Parliament.

Article 9 (1) The Ombudsman shall perform his duties with complete independence, in the general interest of the Communities and of the citizens of the Union. In the performance of his duties he shall neither seek nor accept instructions from any government or other body. He shall refrain from any act incompatible with the nature of his duties.

(2) When taking up his duties, the Ombudsman shall give a solemn undertaking before the Court of Justice of the European Communities that he will perform his duties with complete independence and impartiality and that during and after his term of office he

will respect the obligations arising therefrom, in particular his duty to behave with integrity and discretion as regards the acceptance, after he has ceased to hold office, of certain appointments or benefits.

Article 10 (1) During his term of office, the Ombudsman may not engage in any political or administrative duties, or any other occupation, whether gainful or not.

(2) The Ombudsman shall have the same rank in terms of remuneration, allowances and pension as a judge at the Court of Justice of the European Communities.

(3) Articles 12 to 15 and Article 18 of the Protocol on the Privileges and Immunities of the European Communities shall apply to the Ombudsman and to the officials and servants of his secretariat.

Article 11 (1) The Ombudsman shall be assisted by a secretariat, the principal officer of which he shall appoint.

(2) The officials and servants of the Ombudsman's secretariat shall be subject to the rules and regulations applicable to officials and other servants of the European Communities. Their number shall be adopted each year as part of the budgetary procedure.

(3) Officials of the European Communities and of the Member States appointed to the Ombudsman's secretariat shall be seconded in the interests of the service and guaranteed automatic reinstatement in their institution of origin.

(4) In matters concerning his staff, the Ombudsman shall have the same status as the institutions within the meaning of Article 1 of the Staff Regulations of Officials of the European Communities.

Notes

(1) The European Parliament has acted, in its Decision, to impose some important limitations on complaints to the Ombudsman. In particular, it clarifies that all complaints must be brought within two years of the complainant becoming aware of the alleged maladministration. Although this might be criticised as limiting access, such limitations are important in providing certainty for the EU institutions and also in managing the caseload of the Ombudsman. It also clarifies that the Ombudsman can request that a complainant addresses the complaint to another authority, although the extent to which this power is used or the manner of its use are not further clarified. A final point of interest is that the Ombudsman is able to insist that all staff complaints should have first exhausted all internal grievance mechanisms before making a complaint, but this is not the case in relation to other complaints. This may be explained, at least in part, because a uniform complaints procedure in respect of the actions of the EU institutions does not exist, so aggrieved citizens may not have the same mechanisms of redress enjoyed by staff complainants.

(2) The requirement for complete independence on the part of the Ombudsman is made particularly apparent in the Decision of the Parliament. The requirement of independence is reiterated in Article 9, with each office holder being required to give an undertaking before the Court of Justice of the European Union (CJEU) that he will observe the behavioural standards that are expected. Furthermore, there is

elaboration of the requirement that the Ombudsman must not engage in any administrative or political duties, or any occupation, whether gainful or not. The inclusion of reference to political or administrative duties is an elaboration upon the provisions found in Article 228(3) TFEU.

10.3.A.1 (ii) France

Constitution de la République française **10.12 (FR)**

Article 71-1 The Defender of Rights (Défenseur de droits) shall ensure the due respect of rights and freedoms by state administrations, local authorities, public legal entities, as well as by all bodies carrying out a public service mission or by those that the organic law decides fall within his remit.

Referrals to the Defender of Rights may be made, in the manner determined by an organic law, by every person who considers his rights to have been infringed by the operation of a public service or of a body mentioned in the first section. He may act without referral.

The organic law shall set the mechanisms for action and powers of the Defender of Rights. It shall determine the manner in which he may be assisted by third parties in the exercise of certain of his powers.

The Defender of Rights shall be appointed by the President of the Republic for a six-year, non-renewable term, after the application of the procedure provided for in the last section of Article 13. This position is incompatible with membership of the Government or membership of Parliament. Other incompatibilities shall be determined by the organic law.

The Defender of Rights is accountable for his actions to the President of the Republic and to Parliament.

Notes

(1) The position of Defender of Rights was created in the Constitution by reforms brought about by President Sarkozy in 2008, and its broader powers and procedure were set out in a law of 2011.[17] The Defender of Rights integrates four bodies that previously had separate status – the Mediator of the Republic (Médiateur de la République), the Children's Ombudsman, the Equal Opportunities and Anti-Discrimination Commission, and the body responsible for regulating the conduct of the police and security services.[18] The reform is notable because it changes the status of all of these bodies from being independent administrative agencies to having constitutional status, although the practical impact of this is open to question.[19]

[17] Loi organique n° 2011-333 du 29 mars 2011 relative au Défenseur des droits (Organic Law concerning the Defender of Rights).

[18] For more details on the historical development of the Defender of Rights, see R Bousta and A Sagar, 'Alternative Dispute Resolution in French Administrative Proceedings' in Dragos and Neamtu (n 14 above) 57–85, 78.

[19] ibid.

(2) The Defender of Rights is appointed by the President, rather than by the Parliament, for a single non-renewable term. Article 71-1 of the French Constitution notes that the Defender of Rights is accountable to both the President and the Parliament, and the holder of the position may not be a member of the government or of the Parliament.[20] The link to the executive may be argued to be relatively strong in France – the line of accountability to the President and the President's power of appointment secure this to a significant extent.

(3) The jurisdiction of the Defender of Rights is broad. In Article 71-1(1), the Constitution allows the Defender of Rights to ensure that rights and freedoms are respected by a broad range of public bodies. The Defender of Rights is also not limited by the need for a referral – Article 71(2) makes it clear that it is possible for 'own-initiative' investigations to be undertaken.

10.3.A.1 (iii) England and Wales

The Parliamentary Commissioner Act 1967[21] **10.13 (EW)**

1 Appointment and tenure of office

(1) For the purpose of conducting investigations in accordance with the following provisions of this Act there shall be appointed a Commissioner, to be known as the Parliamentary Commissioner for Administration.

(2) Her Majesty may by Letters Patent from time to time appoint a person to be the Commissioner.

(2A) A person appointed to be the Commissioner shall hold office until the end of the period for which he is appointed.

(2B) That period must be not more than seven years.

(2C) Subsection (2A) is subject to subsections (3) and (3A).

(3) A person appointed to be the Commissioner may be–

(a) relieved of office by Her Majesty at his own request, or

(b) removed from office by Her Majesty, on the ground of misbehaviour, in consequence of Addresses from both Houses of Parliament.

(3A) Her Majesty may declare the office of Commissioner to have been vacated if satisfied that the person appointed to be the Commissioner is incapable for medical reasons–

(a) of performing duties of his office; and

(b) of requesting to be relieved of it.

(3B) A person appointed to be the Commissioner is not eligible for re-appointment.

4 Departments etc subject to investigation

(1) Subject to the provisions of this section and to the notes contained in Schedule 2 to this Act, this Act applies to the government departments, corporations and unincorporated bodies listed in that Schedule; and references in this Act to an authority to which this Act applies are references to any such corporation or body.

(2) Her Majesty may by Order in Council amend Schedule 2 to this Act by the alteration of any entry or note, the removal of any entry or note or the insertion of any additional entry or note.

[20] This point is given further definition by Art 3 of the Organic Law concerning the Defender of Rights.
[21] Chapter 13.

(3) An Order in Council may only insert an entry if–

(a) it relates–

(i) to a government department; or

(ii) to a corporation or body whose functions are exercised on behalf of the Crown; or

(b) it relates to a corporation or body–

(i) which is established by virtue of Her Majesty's prerogative or by an Act of Parliament or on Order in Council or order made under an Act of Parliament or which is established in any other way by a Minister of the Crown in his capacity as a Minister or by a government department;

(ii) at least half of whose revenues derive directly from money provided by Parliament, a levy authorised by an enactment, a fee or charge of any other description so authorised or more than one of those sources; and

(iii) which is wholly or partly constituted by appointment made by Her Majesty or a Minister of the Crown or government department.

...

(8) In this Act–

(a) any reference to a government department to which this Act applies includes a reference to any of the Ministers or officers of such a department; and

(b) any reference to an authority to which this Act applies includes a reference to any members or officers of such an authority.

5 Matters subject to investigation

(1) Subject to the provisions of this section, the Commissioner may investigate any action taken by or on behalf of a government department or other authority to which this Act applies, being action taken in the exercise of administrative functions of that department or authority, in any case where–

(a) a written complaint is duly made to a member of the House of Commons by a member of the public who claims to have sustained injustice in consequence of maladministration in connection with the action so taken; and

(b) the complaint is referred to the Commissioner, with the consent of the person who made it, by a member of that House with a request to conduct an investigation thereon.

...

(2) Except as hereinafter provided, the Commissioner shall not conduct an investigation under this Act in respect of any of the following matters, that is to say–

(a) any action in respect of which the person aggrieved has or had a right of appeal, reference or review to or before a tribunal constituted by or under any enactment or by virtue of Her Majesty's prerogative;

(b) any action in respect of which the person aggrieved has or had a remedy by way of proceedings in any court of law:

Provided that the Commissioner may conduct an investigation notwithstanding that the person aggrieved has or had such a right or remedy if satisfied that in the particular circumstances it is not reasonable to expect him to resort or have resorted to it.

...

(3) Without prejudice to subsection (2) of this section, the Commissioner shall not conduct an [investigation under subsection (1) of this section] in respect of any such action or matter as is described in Schedule 3 to this Act.

(4) Her Majesty may by Order in Council amend the said Schedule 3 so as to exclude from the provisions of that Schedule such actions or matters as may be described in

the Order; and any statutory instrument made by virtue of this subsection shall be subject to annulment in pursuance of a resolution of either House of Parliament.

(4A) Without prejudice to subsection (2) of this section, the Commissioner shall not conduct an investigation pursuant to a complaint under subsection (1A) of this section in respect of–

(a) action taken by or with the authority of the Secretary of State for the purposes of protecting the security of the State, including action so taken with respect to passports, or

(b) any action or matter described in any of paragraphs 1 to 4 and 6A to 11 of Schedule 3 to this Act.

(4B) Her Majesty may by Order in Council amend subsection (4A) of this section so as to exclude from paragraph (a) or (b) of that subsection such actions or matters as may be described in the Order.

(4C) Any statutory instrument made by virtue of subsection (4B) of this section shall be subject to annulment in pursuance of a resolution of either House of Parliament.

(5) In determining whether to initiate, continue or discontinue an investigation under this Act, the Commissioner shall, subject to the foregoing provisions of this section, act in accordance with his own discretion; and any question whether a complaint is duly made under this Act shall be determined by the Commissioner.

...

6 Provisions relating to complaints

(1) A complaint under this Act may be made by any individual, or by any body of persons whether incorporated or not, not being–

(a) a local authority or other authority or body constituted for purposes of the public service or of local government or for the purposes of carrying on under national ownership any industry or undertaking or part of an industry or undertaking;

[(b) any other authority or body within subsection (1A) below.

(1A) An authority or body is within this subsection if–

(a) its members are appointed by–

(i) Her Majesty;

(ii) any Minister of the Crown;

(iii) any government department;

(iv) the Scottish Ministers;

(v) the First Minister; or

(vi) the Lord Advocate, or

(b) its revenues consist wholly or mainly of–

(i) money provided by Parliament; or

(ii) sums payable out of the Scottish Consolidated Fund (directly or indirectly)].

(2) Where the person by whom a complaint might have been made under the foregoing provisions of this Act has died or is for any reason unable to act for himself, the complaint may be made by his personal representative or by a member of his family or other individual suitable to represent him; but except as aforesaid a complaint shall not be entertained under this Act unless made by the person aggrieved himself.

(3) A complaint shall not be entertained under this Act unless it is made to a member of the House of Commons not later than twelve months from the day on which the person aggrieved first had notice of the matters alleged in the complaint; but the Commissioner may conduct an investigation pursuant to a complaint not made within that period if he considers that there are special circumstances which make it proper to do so.

(4) ... a complaint shall not be entertained under this Act unless the person aggrieved is resident in the United Kingdom (or, if he is dead, was so resident at the time of his death) or the complaint relates to action taken in relation to him while he was present in the United Kingdom or on an installation in a designated area within the meaning of the Continental Shelf Act 1964 or on a ship registered in the United Kingdom or an aircraft so registered, or in relation to rights or obligations which accrued or arose in the United Kingdom or on such an installation, ship or aircraft.

...

SCHEDULE 2 Departments etc. subject to investigation

Administration of Radioactive Substances Advisory Committee.

Advisory Committee on Animal Feeding Stuffs.

Advisory Committee on Clinical Excellence Awards.

Advisory Committee on Consumer Engagement.

...

SCHEDULE 3 Matters not subject to investigation

...

1 Action taken in matters certified by a Secretary of State or other Minister of the Crown to affect relations or dealings between the Government of the United Kingdom and any other Government or any international organisation of States or Governments.

2 (1) Action taken, in any country or territory outside the United Kingdom, by or on behalf of any officer representing or acting under the authority of Her Majesty in respect of the United Kingdom, or any other officer of the Government of the United Kingdom other than,

(a) action which is taken by an officer (not being an honorary consular officer) in the exercise of a consular function on behalf of the Government of the United Kingdom;

...

3 Action taken in connection with the administration of the government of any country or territory outside the United Kingdom which forms part of Her Majesty's dominions or in which Her Majesty has jurisdiction.

[4 Action taken by the Secretary of State under the Extradition Act 2003.]

5 Action taken by or with the authority of the Secretary of State for the purposes of investigating crime or of protecting the security of the State, including action so taken with respect to passports.

[6 The commencement or conduct of civil or criminal proceedings before any court of law in the United Kingdom, of service law proceedings (as defined by section 324(5) of the Armed Forces Act 2006) (anywhere)], or of proceedings before any international court or tribunal.

[6A Action taken by any person appointed by the Lord Chancellor as a member of the administrative staff of any court or tribunal, so far as that action is taken at the direction, or on the authority (whether express or implied), of any person acting in a judicial capacity or in his capacity as a member of the tribunal.]

[6B (1) Action taken by any member of the administrative staff of a relevant tribunal, so far as that action is taken at the direction, or on the authority (whether express or implied), of any person acting in his capacity as a member of the tribunal.

(2) In this paragraph, 'relevant tribunal' has the meaning given by section 5(8) of this Act.]

...

7 Any exercise of the prerogative of mercy or of the power of a Secretary of State to make a reference in respect of any person to the High Court of Justiciary or the Court Martial Appeal Court.

...

9 Action taken in matters relating to contractual or other commercial transactions, whether within the United Kingdom or elsewhere, being transactions of a government department or authority to which this Act applies or of any such authority or body as is mentioned in paragraph (a) or (b) of subsection (1) of section 6 of this Act and not being transactions for or relating to–

(a) the acquisition of land compulsorily or in circumstances in which it could be acquired compulsorily;

(b) the disposal as surplus of land acquired compulsorily or in such circumstances as aforesaid.

10 (1) Action taken in respect of appointments or removals, pay, discipline, superannuation or other personnel matters, in relation to–

(a) service in any of the armed forces of the Crown, including reserve and auxiliary and cadet forces;

(b) service in any office or employment under the Crown or under any authority [to which this Act applies]; or

(c) service in any office or employment, or under any contract for services, in respect of which power to take action, or to determine or approve the action to be taken, in such matters is vested in Her Majesty, any Minister of the Crown or any such authority as aforesaid.

...

11 The grant of honours, awards or privileges within the gift of the Crown, including the grant of Royal Charters.

...

Notes

(1) The Parliamentary Commissioner for Administration (PCA) is the ombudsman who deals with complaints relating to maladministration by the central government and bodies connected to central government. There is a separate ombudsman (the Local Commissioner for Administration, or Local Government and Social Care Ombudsman) to deal with complaints of maladministration in relation to local government.[22] The Local Government and Social Care Ombudsman will not be considered in detail here, although many of the provisions of the Local Government Act 1974 are similar in nature to those applicable to the Parliamentary Commissioner. In addition to the Parliamentary Commissioner's jurisdiction to hear complaints of maladministration in respect of central government, the Parliamentary Commissioner

[22] The Local Commissioners for Administration were created by the Local Government Act 1974, which still sets out the legislative framework for the operation of the Local Government and Social Care Ombudsman, although this framework has been amended on many occasions since the creation of the office.

also serves as the Health Service Commissioner, dealing with complaints about the National Health Service.[23]

(2) As the excerpt illustrates, the Parliamentary Commissioner's jurisdiction is limited in a number of important ways. The main issues to note are that the Commissioner can only consider complaints of maladministration if the body concerned is listed in schedule 2 of the Act. An example of a listing in Schedule 2 is provided in the excerpt. Many hundreds of bodies are listed in Schedule 2, including government departments and other bodies created by or linked to the activities of central government. It is important to note that since devolution of power to Scotland, Wales and Northern Ireland, the Act does not include departments or bodies of the devolved administrations, as these are subject to separate ombudsmen for Scotland, Wales and Northern Ireland. A second significant limitation on the jurisdiction of the ombudsman is that he may only consider complaints of administration that have been referred by a Member of Parliament (MP) – aggrieved citizens do not have direct access. The reason for this is that when the office was created it was felt that the link between MPs and constituents would be strengthened if complaints of maladministration had to be filtered by the MPs because this would make the MPs aware of maladministration that might be suffered by their constituents and may also allow the MP to assist constituents in resolving complaints without the need for referral to the PCA, thus reducing demand on the PCA's time and resources. A further limitation on the ability to hear complaints is that the PCA should ordinarily refuse to hear complaints made more than 12 months after the complainant became aware of the issue complained of, although, once again, in section 6(3) of the Act, the Commissioner has the discretion to investigate complaints made out of time.

(3) In addition to the requirement that bodies should be listed in schedule 2 of the Act and that the complaint must be referred by an MP, there are other important limitations on the jurisdiction of the PCA. Schedule 3 lists a number of issues which cannot be investigated by the PCA, including issues in relation to foreign affairs, extradition, matters in relation to legal proceedings, complaints of maladministration in relation to employment and service in the civil service, and matters in relation to contractual and commercial transactions. Section 5 of the Act also provides that the PCA cannot deal with complaints where the claimant has or had available an alternative route of appeal or has or could have had recourse to legal proceedings in relation to the matter complained of. However, this exclusion is not absolute, and the PCA retains discretion to investigate such complaints where the PCA decides that it would not have been reasonable for the complainant to have had recourse to these alternative mechanisms. In practice, this discretion is frequently exercised in favour of complainants.

(4) The entire regime for public services ombudsmen in England and Wales is likely to be reformed in the near future. The government published a consultation

[23] This is done under the provisions of the Health Service Commissioners Act 1993.

paper on reform of public services ombudsmen in 2015[24] and a draft bill has since been published by the government.[25] This is presently subject to a parliamentary inquiry, considering the proposals. The main thrust of the proposals is that the separate offices of the Parliamentary Commissioner, the Local Government Ombudsman and the Health Services Commissioner (bearing in mind that the Parliamentary Commissioner and the Health Services Commissioner are already in practice a single office, despite being created by separate pieces of legislation) will be abolished and a single office of the Public Service Ombudsman will be created to deal with all complaints about maladministration in the public sector. Another significant element of the proposal is that the requirement for complaints about central government to be referred by an MP will be removed.

10.3.A.1 (iv) The Netherlands

Grondwet **10.14 (NL)**

Article 78a (1) The National Ombudsman (Nationale Ombudsman) shall investigate, on request or of his own accord, actions taken by administrative authorities of the State and other administrative authorities designated by or pursuant to Act of Parliament.

(2) The National Ombudsman and a alternate ombudsman shall be appointed by the Second Chamber of the Parliament for a period to be determined by Act of Parliament. They may resign or retire on attaining an age to be determined by Act of Parliament. They may be suspended or dismissed by the Second Chamber of the Parliament in instances specified by Act of Parliament. Their legal status shall in other respects be regulated by Act of Parliament.

(3) The powers and functioning of the National Ombudsman shall be regulated by Act of Parliament.

…

Wet Nationale Ombudsman **10.15 (NL)**

Article 1a (1) This act applies to the conduct of the following administrative authorities:

a. Our Ministers;

b. Administrative authorities of provinces, municipalities, public bodies, water boards and joint arrangements, unless these authorities have established their own arrangement for the handling of complaints [under their respective laws].

c. Administrative authorities to which, by or pursuant to a statutory provision, a task in respect of the police has been attributed, as far as the exercise of this task is concerned.

…

e. Other administrative authorities, also including administrative authorities of public bodies, as far as not excluded by a general applicable regulation.

[24] Cabinet Office, *A Public Services Ombudsman* (London, HM Government, 2015).

[25] Cabinet Office, *Draft Public Service Ombudsman Bill* (London, HM Government, 2016).

(2) The conduct of a civil servant, performed in the exercise of his functions, is considered to be conduct of the administrative authority under whose responsibility the civil servant works.

Article 2 (1) There is a National Ombudsman.

(2) The Ombudsman is appointed by the Second Chamber of the Parliament …

(3) The appointment applies for a period of six years.

Article 9 (1) The Second Chamber of the Parliament assigns at the request of the Ombudsman one or more persons as alternate ombudsman and designates the alternative ombudsmen who will have the function of Children's Ombudsman or Ombudsman for Veterans.

2. The assignment of an alternate ombudsman applies for the term of office of the Ombudsman on request of whom he is assigned, plus an additional year.

Notes

(1) The National Ombudsman was established in 1981 by the National Ombudsman Act (Wet Nationale Ombudsman, WNO). Two years later, the National Ombudsman was included in Article 78a of the Constitution. The National Ombudsman is appointed by the Second Chamber of the Parliament for a period of six years. This period may be renewed. He enjoys special protection against interim dismissal or suspension, comparable to the judiciary. At the request of the National Ombudsman, the Second Chamber of the Parliament may assign alternate ombudsmen. The WNO provides for two specialised national ombudsmen, the Children's Ombudsman, appointed since 2011, and the Ombudsman for Veterans, appointed since 2014. Both have the status of alternate ombudsman and are part of the National Ombudsman's office. In contrast to other alternate ombudsmen, they have an independent legal status and are not subordinated to the National Ombudsman.

(2) The jurisdiction of the National Ombudsman is regulated in the WNO and in the AWB. The WNO determines which authorities citizens may file a complaint against before the ombudsman. The AWB regulates matters of access. According to Article 1a(1)(a) and (e) WNO, the National Ombudsman enjoys exclusive jurisdiction in respect of conduct of central administrative authorities and of the employees working under their responsibility.[26] Central administrative authorities include ministers, independent authorities, eg the Authority for Consumer and Markets, and other civil services, eg the tax authorities and the Organisation for Social Security (Article 1a(1)(e) WNO).[27] In addition, the National Ombudsman is exclusively

[26] The limitation to 'administrative authorities' implies that the National Ombudsman is not competent to investigate complaints against Parliament and the courts. As regards the courts, the Act on the Judicial Organization provides for a special complaint procedure before the Supreme Court. The Judicial Division of the Council of State investigates complaint against councillors of state.

[27] The statutory possibility of Art 1a(1)(e) WNO, to exclude the National Ombudsman's competence by general applicable regulation is only used exceptionally. The most important examples are the statutory tasks of the Authority of Financial Markets and of the Dutch Central Bank.

competent in respect of authorities to which a police task has been attributed (Article 1a(1)(c) WNO). As regards conduct of decentralised authorities and their employees, the National Ombudsman is competent by default (Article 1a(1)(b) WNO). This category includes authorities of provinces, municipalities, water boards, public bodies such as the Bar Association, and joint arrangements between municipalities. These authorities may opt for an (external) ombudsman or a committee of ombudsmen of their own. In that case, these institutions take the place of the National Ombudsman and enjoy the same investigatory and other powers as the National Ombudsman. If a decentralised authority chooses not to set up an external complaint arrangement of its own, the National Ombudsman is competent to deal with complaints against it. In practice, the vast majority of decentralised authorities have opted for the latter option. Only a few large municipalities, such as Amsterdam and Rotterdam, have a municipal ombudsman.

Algemene Wet Bestuursrecht **10.16 (NL)**

Article 9:17 'Ombudsman' means:

a. the National Ombudsman, or

b. an Ombudsman or Committee of Ombudsmen (*ombudscommissie*) established pursuant to the Municipalities Act (Gemeentewet), the Provinces Act (Provinciewet), the Water Management Boards Act (Waterschapswet) or the Joint Arrangements Act (Wet gemeenschappelijke regelingen).

Article 9:18 (1) Any person has the right to request an Ombudsman, in writing, to investigate the manner in which an administrative authority has acted towards him or another person in a particular matter.

(2) If a request is filed with an Ombudsman who does not have jurisdiction, it shall as soon as possible be forwarded to the Ombudsman having jurisdiction, and this shall be communicated to the complainant at the same time.

(3) Unless Article 9:22, 9:23 or 9:24 applies, the Ombudsman is required to act on a request as referred to in section 1.

Article 9:20 (1) Before filing a request with an Ombudsman, the complainant must first lodge a complaint about the conduct with the administrative authority concerned, unless he cannot reasonably be expected to do so.

...

Article 9:22 An Ombudsman has no competence to start or continue an investigation if the request relates to:

a. a matter falling under general government policy, including law enforcement policy, or under the general policy of the administrative authority concerned;

b. a general binding regulation;

c. conduct which is open to judicial review, unless the conduct consists of failure to take a decision in due time, or conduct against which a claim for judicial review ... is pending;

d. conduct on which an administrative judge has passed judgment;

e. conduct which is the subject of a procedure pending before a court other than an administrative court, or in respect of which appeal lies against a judgment given in such a procedure;

...

Article 9:23 The Ombudsman is not required to start or continue an investigation if:

a. the request does not satisfy the requirements referred to in Articles 9:28(1) and 9:28(2);

b. the request is manifestly unfounded;

c. the complainant's interest in an investigation by the ombudsman or the gravity of the conduct is manifestly insufficient;

d. the complainant is a person other than the person towards whom the conduct occurred;

e. the request relates to conduct against which an objection (*bezwaar*) may be lodged, unless it consists of failure to take a timely decision, or is conduct against which an objection procedure is pending;

f. the request relates to conduct against which the complainant could have lodged an objection or claim for judicial review ...;

g. the request relates to a conduct on which a court other than an administrative court has given judgment;

h. the requirement of Article 9:20(1) is not satisfied;

...

Article 9:24 (1) In addition, the Ombudsman is not required to start or continue an investigation if the request is filed more than one year:

a. after the administrative authority has given notice of the findings of its investigation, or

...

Article 9:27 (2) If a court has given a judgment with respect to the conduct to which the Ombudsman's investigation relates, the Ombudsman shall be bound by the legal grounds on which the judgment is based.

...

Article 9:28 (1) A request to investigate a complaint must be signed and shall in any event contain:

a. the name and address of the complainant;

b. the date;

c. a description of the conduct to which the request relates, particulars of the person whose conduct is the subject of the complaint and particulars of the person affected by the conduct, if this is not the complainant;

d. the grounds for the request;

e. the manner in which the complaint was lodged with the administrative authority, and if possible the findings of the administrative authority's investigation into the complaint, its opinion on the complaint and the consequences, if any, which the administrative authority has attached to it.

...

(3) If the requirements of this article are not satisfied, the Ombudsman shall give the complainant the opportunity to remedy the omission within a time limit set by him.

Notes

(1) *General:* the way the National Ombudsman or a decentralised ombudsman or committee (hereafter Ombudsman) has to deal with a complaint against an authority within their respective competence is regulated in the AWB. According to Article 9:18(1) AWB, any person has the right to request an Ombudsman, in writing, to investigate the manner in which an administrative authority has acted towards him or another person in a particular matter. Unless the access to the Ombudsman is restricted, he is required to act on the complaint (Article 9:18(3) AWB). The AWB distinguishes between two kinds of restrictions, namely situations in which the Ombudsman lacks competence to start or continue an investigation and situations in which the Ombudsman is not required to handle a complaint.[28] In the latter case, the Ombudsman enjoys discretion to deal with the complaint, and may do so in exceptional situations. The procedure before an Ombudsman is free of charge.

(2) *Lack of competence:* the situations in which the Ombudsman lacks competence to start or continue an investigation of a request are mentioned in Article 9:22 AWB. They include: matters of general government policy and of the general policy of the administrative authority concerned; conduct which is open for judicial review before the administrative courts or against which a claim of judicial review is pending; conduct on which an administrative court has passed judgment; and conduct which is the subject of a procedure pending before a civil court. From these exclusions, it is clear that an Ombudsman is not supposed to interfere with general policies, with possible and actual procedures before an administrative court or with actual procedures before a civil courts.

(3) *No obligation to investigate:* in a number of situations, mentioned in Articles 9:23 and 9:24 AWB, the Ombudsman is not required to start or continue an investigation, but may do so in exceptional situations. They include several situations related to the complaint or complainant. For example, the Ombudsman is not required to investigate a complaint if the request does not satisfy the formal requirements of Article 9:28 AWB (the complaint should contain the name and address of the complainant, the date, a description of the conduct to which the request relates, the grounds for the request and the outcome of the internal complaint procedure) or is manifestly unfounded, in cases where the complainant's interest is manifestly insufficient and if the request is filed more than one year after the conclusion of the internal complaint procedure. In addition, the Ombudsman is not obliged to start an investigation if the request relates to conduct against which an objection may be, could have been or has been lodged, or against which a civil court has given judgment.[29] Finally, such obligation does not exist if the complainant did not first lodge a complaint with the administrative authority (Article 9:20 AWB).[30]

[28] For more details, see M Remac, *Coordinating Ombudsmen and the Judiciary* (Antwerp, Intersentia, 2014) 28–32.

[29] If, in the latter case, the Ombudsman nevertheless decides to investigate the case, he is bound to the legal grounds on which the civil courts judgment is based (Art 9:27(2) AWB).

[30] See section 10.2.A.2 above.

(4) *In sum:* similar to the internal complaint procedure, 'external' complaint procedures before an Ombudsman are not intended as a means for contesting decisions as defined in Article 1:3 AWB (*besluiten*). These should, in principle, be contested in an objection procedure, and afterwards before an administrative court. As regards private law actions of administrative authorities, the Ombudsman may function as an accessible small claims 'court', as an alternative to the civil courts. However, if a citizen starts a procedure before the civil courts against private law actions, the Ombudsmen will generally not interfere with this issue anymore. As a result, the main object of Ombudsman procedures are factual actions of administrative authorities.[31]

10.3.A.1 (v) Comparative Remarks

Given that all systems of Ombudsmen draw their inspiration from the original Scandinavian models, it is perhaps unsurprising to see that all systems share a great deal in terms of the approach to jurisdiction and also that there is general commonality in the method of appointment. The major distinction that one might draw is between the French system and the systems in England and Wales, the European Union and the Netherlands. In the French system, the executive (in the form of the President) appoints the Ombudsman and then holds the Ombudsman accountable. In England and Wales, the Crown (ie the executive) appoints the Ombudsman, but then the Ombudsman's accountability is to Parliament. In the Netherlands and in the EU, Parliament appoints and provides the major accountability mechanisms for the Ombudsman and it is Parliament that plays a major role in supporting the work of the Ombudsman. In all systems there is a specific provision for the independence of the Ombudsman and it is not entirely apparent what impact a link to the executive might have on the work of an Ombudsman. The Ombudsman in England and Wales has proven to be strongly independent, but although the appointment flows from the executive, the accountability is to Parliament. The French system is perhaps rather different in the sense that the Defender of Rights is appointed by and predominantly accountable to the President first of all and then the Parliament,[32] although the importance of independence is emphasised by the Constitution.

In all four systems, those who serve as Ombudsmen are precluded from adopting other positions in government that might be incompatible with the independence of the position. This is clearly an endeavour to ensure that the respective Ombudsmen are able to complete their work without conflict of interest and also perhaps to ensure that the office holder maintains a focus on the work of the Ombudsman.

In each system under examination, the predominant role of the Ombudsman is to investigate complaints made by aggrieved individuals in relation to the delivery of public services and the action or inaction of public bodies. In France, the Netherlands and the European Union, the Ombudsmen may also launch 'own-initiative' investigations without the need for a complaint, but this is not possible in England and Wales.

[31] For the concept of factual action in the Netherlands, see Chapter 3, section 3.4.B.1.
[32] Bousta and Sagar (n 18 above) 78.

It might be argued that England and Wales has the greatest number of limitations on the jurisdiction of the Ombudsman because, in addition to the requirement that there is a complaint, there is the requirement that the complaint is referred by an MP, and schedule 3 of the 1967 Act also imposes a number of significant limitations on the issues that can be investigated, excluding matters such as extradition, commercial dealings of the government, national security, the investigation of crime and a number of other issues, as illustrated above. These limitations do not exist to the same extent in the other systems under consideration. An important common thread is that none of the systems under examination permit a complaint to the Ombudsman where court proceedings are available or pending in respect of the same issue. In general, in each of the systems, judicial review and investigations by the Ombudsman are seen to be alternatives, rather than adjuncts.

10.3.A.2 INVESTIGATORY POWERS OF THE OMBUDSMAN

It is evident that in order to carry out investigations, Ombudsmen need to have investigatory powers. This section will consider the scope of the powers enjoyed by the Ombudsman in each of the systems under investigation, and will examine, in particular, the scope of the powers to demand documents and information, to call and examine witnesses, and to gather evidence as the Ombudsman deems appropriate.

10.3.A.2 (i) The European Union

Decision 94/262/ECSC, EC, Euratom of the European Parliament of 9 March 1994 on the regulations and general conditions governing the performance of the Ombudsman's duties **10.17 (EU)**

Article 3 (1) The Ombudsman shall, on his own initiative or following a complaint, conduct all the enquiries which he considers justified to clarify any suspected maladministration in the activities of Community institutions and bodies. He shall inform the institution or body concerned of such action, which may submit any useful comment to him.

(2) The Community institutions and bodies shall be obliged to supply the Ombudsman with any information he has requested from them and give him access to the files concerned. Access to classified information or documents, in particular to sensitive documents within the meaning of Article 9 of Regulation (EC) No 1049/2001, shall be subject to compliance with the rules on security of the Community institution or body concerned.

The institutions or bodies supplying classified information or documents as mentioned in the previous subparagraph shall inform the Ombudsman of such classification.

For the implementation of the rules provided for in the first subparagraph, the Ombudsman shall have agreed in advance with the institution or body concerned the conditions for treatment of classified information or documents and other information covered by the obligation of professional secrecy.

The institutions or bodies concerned shall give access to documents originating in a Member State and classed as secret by law or regulation only where that Member State has given its prior agreement.

They shall give access to other documents originating in a Member State after having informed the Member State concerned.

In both cases, in accordance with Article 4, the Ombudsman may not divulge the content of such documents.

Officials and other servants of Community institutions and bodies must testify at the request of the Ombudsman; they shall continue to be bound by the relevant rules of the Staff Regulations, notably their duty of professional secrecy.

(3) The Member States' authorities shall be obliged to provide the Ombudsman, whenever he may so request, via the Permanent Representations of the Member States to the European Communities, with any information that may help to clarify instances of maladministration by Community institutions or bodies unless such information is covered by laws or regulations on secrecy or by provisions preventing its being communicated. Nonetheless, in the latter case, the Member State concerned may allow the Ombudsman to have this information provided that he undertakes not to divulge it.

(4) If the assistance which he requests is not forthcoming, the Ombudsman shall inform the European Parliament, which shall make appropriate representations.

...

Article 4 (1) The Ombudsman and his staff, to whom Article 287 of the Treaty establishing the European Community and Article 194 of the Treaty establishing the European Atomic Energy Community shall apply, shall be required not to divulge information or documents which they obtain in the course of their inquiries. They shall, in particular, be required not to divulge any classified information or any document supplied to the Ombudsman, in particular sensitive documents within the meaning of Article 9 of Regulation (EC) No 1049/2001, or documents falling within the scope of Community legislation regarding the protection of personal data, as well as any information which could harm the person lodging the complaint or any other person involved, without prejudice to paragraph 2.

(2) If, in the course of inquiries, he learns of facts which he considers might relate to criminal law, the Ombudsman shall immediately notify the competent national authorities via the Permanent Representations of the Member States to the European Communities and, in so far as the case falls within its powers, the competent Community institution, body or service in charge of combating fraud; if appropriate, the Ombudsman shall also notify the Community institution or body with authority over the official or servant concerned, which may apply the second paragraph of Article 18 of the Protocol on the Privileges and Immunities of the European Communities. The Ombudsman may also inform the Community institution or body concerned of the facts calling into question the conduct of a member of their staff from a disciplinary point of view.

Article 4a The Ombudsman and his staff shall deal with requests for public access to documents, other than those referred to in Article 4(1), in accordance with the conditions and limits provided for in Regulation (EC) No 1049/2001.

Article 5 (1) In so far as it may help to make his enquiries more efficient and better safeguard the rights and interests of persons who make complaints to him, the Ombudsman may cooperate with authorities of the same type in certain Member States provided he complies with the national law applicable. The Ombudsman may not by this means demand to see documents to which he would not have access under Article 3.

(2) Within the scope of his functions as laid down in Article 195 of the Treaty establishing the European Community and Article 107d of the Treaty establishing the European Atomic Energy Community and avoiding any duplication with the activities of the other

institutions or bodies, the Ombudsman may, under the same conditions, cooperate with institutions and bodies of Member States in charge of the promotion and protection of fundamental rights.

Decision of the European Ombudsman adopting Implementing Provisions[33] **10.18 (EU)**

Article 2: Receipt of complaints

2.1. The Ombudsman shall accept complaints submitted in writing, either electronically or on paper. The Ombudsman shall take appropriate measures to assist persons with disabilities to exercise their right to submit a complaint to the Ombudsman.

2.2. A complainant shall identify any information in the complaint that the complainant considers confidential. The identification of any such information as confidential by a complainant shall not prevent the Ombudsman, for the purposes of carrying out an inquiry, from communicating the information to the institution concerned.

2.3. The Ombudsman shall treat a petition transferred to the Ombudsman by the European Parliament with the consent of the petitioner as a complaint.

2.4. In appropriate cases, and with the consent of the complainant, the Ombudsman may transfer a complaint to another competent authority.

Article 3: Initial processing of complaints

3.1. The Ombudsman shall determine whether a complaint is within the mandate and, if so, whether it is admissible pursuant to Article 2 of the Statute. The Secretariat may request the complainant to provide further information or documents to enable the Ombudsman to make that determination.

3.2. If a complaint is outside the mandate of the Ombudsman, or is inadmissible, the Ombudsman shall close the file on the complaint.

3.3. The Ombudsman shall decide whether there are grounds to inquire into an admissible complaint. If the Ombudsman considers that there are no grounds to conduct an inquiry, the Ombudsman shall close the file on the complaint.

Article 4: Information gathering actions during inquiries

4.1. When the Ombudsman finds grounds to open an inquiry, the Ombudsman shall identify the allegations made by the complainant that fall within the scope of the inquiry.

4.2. The Ombudsman may ask the institution concerned to provide a reply in relation to those allegations. The Ombudsman may also ask the institution concerned to set out in its reply its views on specific aspects of the allegations and on specific issues arising from or related to the complaint.

4.3. The Ombudsman may ask an institution to send information or documents to the Ombudsman. The Ombudsman may, after consulting with the institution concerned, also arrange to inspect relevant documents.

4.4. The institution's replies on the matters referred to in paragraphs 4.2 and 4.3 shall be made within the timeframe specified by the Ombudsman, which shall normally not exceed three months. The precise timeframe for providing a reply shall be reasonable,

[33] Available at www.ombudsman.europa.eu/en/resources/provisions.faces.

taking into account the complexity and urgency of the inquiry. If the Ombudsman considers that the inquiry is of public interest, the timeframe for responding shall be as short as is reasonably possible. If the institution concerned is not in a position to provide a reply to the Ombudsman within the set timeframe, it shall make a reasoned request for an extension.

4.5. The Ombudsman may ask the institution concerned to organise a meeting with the Ombudsman in order to clarify issues falling within the scope of the inquiry.

4.6. The Ombudsman may require officials or other servants of an institution to testify in accordance with the rules laid down in the Statute. The Ombudsman may decide that the person testifying shall do so in confidence.

4.7. The Ombudsman may, for the purposes of carrying out an inquiry, request a Member State, through its Permanent Representation, to provide information or documents relating to the alleged maladministration by an institution, in accordance with the rules set out in the Statute.

4.8. When an institution or a Member State provides information or documents to the Ombudsman pursuant to paragraph 4.2, 4.3, 4.5 or 4.7, they shall clearly identify any information they consider to be confidential. The Ombudsman will not disclose any such confidential information, either to the complainant or to the public, without the prior agreement of the institution or the Member State concerned.

4.9. If an institution or a Member State does not provide the Ombudsman with the assistance described in paragraph 4.2, 4.3, 4.5 or 4.7, the Ombudsman shall remind the institution or Member State concerned why that assistance is necessary. If, after discussion with the institution or Member State concerned, the matter cannot be resolved to the satisfaction of the Ombudsman, the Ombudsman shall inform the European Parliament and request it to take whatever action it considers appropriate.

4.10. The Ombudsman may, for the purposes of carrying out an inquiry, ask the complainant or any third party to provide the Ombudsman with information or documents, or to clarify information or documents already provided to the Ombudsman. The Ombudsman may also request a meeting with the complainant in order to clarify issues falling within the scope of the inquiry.

4.11. The Ombudsman may commission any studies or expert reports that he or she considers relevant to the inquiry.

Article 9: Points of procedure

9.1. If the Ombudsman considers it appropriate to do so, the Ombudsman may take steps to ensure that a complaint is dealt with as a matter of priority, taking into account strategic objectives.

9.2. The Ombudsman shall, to the extent necessary, keep the complainant informed about the progress of an inquiry. If the Ombudsman considers it necessary to clarify with the complainant any aspect of an institution's reply to the Ombudsman, the Ombudsman may decide to provide the complainant with the reply of the institution concerned. If the Ombudsman decides to do so, the Ombudsman may also provide the complainant with a copy of the Ombudsman's letter to the institution requesting a reply.

9.3. The Ombudsman may make public non-confidential information about the progress of an inquiry. In particular, in inquiries of public interest, the Ombudsman may publish the letters the Ombudsman sends to the institutions or Member States, and the replies thereto.

9.4. The Ombudsman shall retain possession of documents obtained from an institution or a Member State during an inquiry, and declared to be confidential by that institution or Member State, only for so long as the inquiry is ongoing and the period of time for dealing with any request for review has not expired. The Ombudsman may request an institution or Member State to retain such documents for a period of at least five years following a notification to them that the Ombudsman no longer retains the documents.

9.5. The complainant shall be entitled to see the Ombudsman's file on the complaint when making a request for review pursuant to Article 10 of this Decision, with the exception of documents declared confidential by an institution, a Member State or the Ombudsman, and of any other confidential information in the file.

9.6. The Ombudsman shall adopt rules on public access to documents based on Regulation (EC) No 1049/2001.

9.7. The Ombudsman may, for the protection of the legitimate interests of the complainant or of a third party, classify information in a complaint or in other documents as confidential on the Ombudsman's own initiative.

9.8. The Ombudsman shall deal with abusive communications and with complaints that amount to an abuse of process in accordance with guidelines adopted by the Ombudsman for this purpose.

9.9. The Ombudsman may decide to discontinue an inquiry at the request of the complainant. This shall not prevent the Ombudsman from opening an own-initiative inquiry into the subject matter of the complaint.

9.10. The Ombudsman may close an inquiry where the complainant has failed to provide any requested information or any requested comments.

Article 10: Requests for review

10.1. A complainant shall have the right to request a review of a decision taken pursuant to Articles 3.2 and 3.3 of this Decision, and of any finding in a decision closing an inquiry with the exception of a finding of maladministration.

10.2. The detailed rules on how the Ombudsman deals with requests for review shall be set out in a decision of the Ombudsman.

Article 11: Delegation of complaint handling

The Ombudsman may delegate to the Secretariat parts of the complaint-handling process. The Secretariat shall inform the complainant of the right to request the Ombudsman to review any decision taken by the Secretariat.

Article 12: Cooperation with ombudsmen and similar bodies in Member States

The Ombudsman may cooperate with ombudsmen and similar bodies in the Member States, including through the European Network of Ombudsmen.

Article 13: Languages

13.1. Any person may write to the Ombudsman in any Treaty language, on any matter falling within the Ombudsman's competence. The Ombudsman shall draft the response in that Treaty language.

13.2. A complaint may be submitted to the Ombudsman in any Treaty language. The Ombudsman shall communicate with a complainant in that language.

13.3. In exceptional circumstances, the Ombudsman may request the institutions to provide copies of relevant documents in the language of the complaint. In making such a request, the Ombudsman shall act proportionately to the needs of the complainant and reasonably with regard to the resources of the institutions.

Notes

(1) The first step to be taken in the complaints handling process of the European Ombudsman is to inform the institution or body that an investigation is to be undertaken and to allow a response from that institution or body. This may be a valuable means of resolving some issues without the need for further investigation.

(2) The Parliament offers the Ombudsman broad powers to seek documents both from EU institutions and from the Member States. In the case of the institutions of the Union, if the Ombudsman seeks access to classified documents, then any such documents must be handled in accordance with the rules of security adopted by the institution concerned and shall only be used and disclosed in a manner agreed with the institution in advance. In the case of documents originating from the Member States that are sought from the EU institutions, such access can only be granted to non-classified documents if the Member State concerned is informed and, in the case of documents that are classified or otherwise secret, only with the consent of the Member State concerned. In the case of documents originating in a Member State that are supplied by the Union institutions, the Ombudsman is not permitted to disclose the content of these documents.

(3) If the Ombudsman wishes to seek documents that originate in Member States and are not in the possession of the EU institutions, then he may do so via the permanent representation of the Member State concerned. The Member State concerned is then obliged to provide such information unless it is classified or secret according to the domestic law of the Member State, in which case the Member State has the discretion to withhold or release the information. In cases where the information sought is not disclosed, the Ombudsman is given the power to refer the matter to the European Parliament so that this can be pursued with the Member State concerned.

(4) The Ombudsman also has powers to require any member of staff of the EU institutions to testify in investigations, although this power is seldom used.

10.3.A.2 (ii) France

Loi organique n° 2011-333 du 29 mars 2011 relative au Défenseur des droits **10.19 (FR)**

Article 18 The Defender of Rights can request an explanation from any natural or legal person subject to investigation before him. For this purpose, he can hear any person whose contribution would be useful for him.

The natural or legal persons subject to investigation shall facilitate the performance of his mandate.

Bodies subject to investigation are obliged to authorise their civil servants and agents to comply with his requests. Civil servants and agents are obliged to comply with the requests for explanation that he addresses to them and to comply with its summons. The summons shall mention the object of the hearing.

When the Defender of Rights has to deal with a case, the persons whose explanations are requested may seek assistance from a counsel of their choice. A report of their statements is drawn up and provided to them.

If the Defender of Rights requests so, the ministers must order the inspection bodies to carry out, within the scope of their competence, all examinations or investigations. They must then inform the Defender of Rights of the actions taken upon these requests.

Article 19 The Defender of Rights may request the vice president of the Council of State or the first president of the Court of Auditors to order to proceed with any investigations.

Article 20 Natural or legal persons subject to investigation are required to disclose to the Defender of Rights, upon his reasoned request, all information and documents that are useful for the performance of his mandate.

On the facts that have been brought to his attention, the Defender of Rights may obtain any information that he deems necessary regardless of the fact that such information is deemed to be secret or confidential, except in matters of secrecy concerning national defence, state security or foreign policy. The secrecy of examination and investigation cannot be claimed against him.

The information covered by medical confidentiality or by professional secrecy applicable to the relations between a lawyer and his client may only be disclosed to him in case of the express request of the concerned person. However, the information covered by medical confidentiality can be passed on to him without the consent of the person concerned where it concerns physical, sexual or psychological deprivations, abuses or violence committed against a minor or a person who is not capable of protecting himself due to his age or physical or psychological incapacity.

The persons bound by professional secrecy may not face proceedings under Article 226-13 of the Criminal Code for information of a secret character which they have disclosed to the Defender of Rights, provided that this information falls within the field of competence of the latter, as provided under Article 4 of the present organic law.

Article 21 When his requests, formulated in accordance with Article 18, apart from the final section, or with Article 20, are not followed by action, the Defender of Rights may request the concerned persons to reply within a time limit that he sets.

When the request is not followed by action, he may bring before the interim relief judge a reasoned request to order any measure he deems useful.

Article 22 (1) The Defender of Rights may carry out

1. on-site investigations at administrative or private premises of persons under investigation;

2. on side investigations at places, premises, publicly accessible means of transport and professional premises exclusively dedicated to this use.

Throughout his on-site investigations, the Defender of Rights may hear any person likely to provide information.

(2) The competent authority may object to on-site investigations at administrative premises of a public entity, under one of the competences provided by numbers 1 to 3 and 5 of Article 4, due to imperative and serious reasons related to national defence or public security.

The competent authority must then provide reasons to the Defender of Rights with the explanation of its objection.

The Defender of Rights may bring before the interim relief judge a reasoned request for the authorisation of the on-site investigations. The checks then take place under the authority and the control of the judge who authorised them. He may access the administrative premises during the operation. He may decide for the termination or interruption of the on-site investigations at any time.

(3) A person responsible for private premises is informed beforehand of his right to object to the visit or the on-site investigation. When he exercises this right, the visit or on-the-spot investigation may only take place after the authorisation of the judge responsible for matters relating to liberty and detention in the regional court in whose judicial district the premises to be visited are located, who decides according to the requirements prescribed by decree of the Council of State. However, if the urgency or severity of the facts that underlie the inspection or the risk of destruction, or the concealment of documents justify it, the visit may take place without the person in charge of the premises having been informed thereof, upon the prior authorisation of the court responsible for matters relating to liberty and detention. In this case, the person responsible for the premises cannot object to the visit.

The visit takes place under the authority and surveillance of the judge responsible for matters relating to liberty and detention who authorised it, in the presence of the occupant of the premises or his representative who may seek assistance of a counsel of his choice or, otherwise, in the presence of two witnesses who are not placed under the authority of the persons that are charged with the enforcement of the inspection.

The ordinance that authorised the visit is directly enforceable, without the need to wait for notification to be made to the subject. It mentions that at any moment a request for interruption or termination of the visit can be brought before the judge who authorised this visit. It specifies the time limit and the type of recourse available. The ordinance can be subject, according to the rules provided by Code of Civil Procedure, to an appeal on points of fact and law before the first president of the Court of Appeal. The latter is also competent to rule on appeals against the execution of the visiting operations.

Article 23 When a case is addressed to the Defender of Rights, or if the Defender of Rights acts *ex officio*, concerning facts that give rise to a preliminary investigation, or an investigation of flagrant breach, or for which a judicial investigation is open or for which judicial proceedings are on-going, he must obtain the prior consent of the seized jurisdictions or of the public prosecutor, depending on the case, for the application of Article 18, except for the last section, or of Articles 20 and 22. When it comes within the competence laid down in number 3 of Article 4, he must also obtain the prior consent:

— of the seized jurisdictions or of the public prosecutor, for the application of Article 26 and of the first section of Article 28, when the facts give rise to a preliminary investigation or an investigation for flagrancy or for which a judicial investigation is open or for which judicial proceedings are on-going;

— of the public prosecutor, for the application of the second section of Article 28, when the facts give rise to a preliminary investigation or an investigation for flagrancy.

Article 24 The Defender of Rights assesses whether the facts that are subject to a complaint or that are reported to him call for an intervention by him.

He provides the grounds for which he decides not to pursue a request.

Article 31 When a complaint is lodged before the Defender of Rights, that has not been raised before a judicial authority, and that raises a question affecting the interpretation or the scope of a legislative or regulatory provision, he may consult the Council of State. The Defender of Rights may publish this opinion. The latter is delivered under the conditions prescribed by a decree of the Council of State.

Notes

(1) The Defender of Rights is given broad powers to request information from individuals in the course of an investigation. Article 20 of the Organic Law concerning the Defender of Rights gives the Defender the power to seek information without significant limitation. In general, the rules on secrecy and confidentiality of information do not apply, although Article 20(2) excludes information on national security, national defence and international relations. Furthermore, the provisions of Article 20(3) limit the ability of the Defender to seek information that may be subject to lawyer–client privilege or constitutes confidential medical information. Such information may be disclosed only with the consent of the subject of the information.

(2) Article 22 of the Organic Law gives the Defender broad powers to visit and enter the premises of those under investigation and also to take evidence from those present at any premises that are visited. However, prior to any such visit, the Defender must warn the occupier and inform him of his right to object to such a visit. If an objection is made, the Defender may only enter premises if a judge grants an order permitting such entry.

(3) The Defender of Rights is given a number of important investigatory powers in the Organic Law concerning the Defender of Rights. Article 18 creates the power to call any individual or body corporate to give evidence in relation to a complaint and, if necessary, to compel such attendance. Where a person is called to give evidence, the process is adversarial, and the person may be assisted by a lawyer of their choosing.

(4) If, in the course of an investigation, the Defender of Rights requires judicial interpretation of a piece of legislation, this may be sought from the Conseil d'Etat and the interpretation can be made public. This demonstrates a stronger link with the judiciary than that which is enjoyed by other Ombudsmen.

(5) The Defender of Rights is under no obligation to launch an investigation when seized of a complaint, although Article 24 of the Organic Law concerning the Defender of Rights requires that if the decision is taken not to investigate, the reasons for not doing so must be communicated to the complainant.

10.3.A.2 (iii) England and Wales

The Parliamentary Commissioner Act 1967[34] **10.20 (EW)**

7 Procedure in respect of investigations

(1) Where the Commissioner proposes to conduct an investigation pursuant to a complaint under section 5(1) of this Act, he shall afford to the principal officer of the department or authority concerned, and to any person who is alleged in the complaint to have taken or authorised the action complained of, an opportunity to comment on any allegations contained in the complaint.

[34] Chapter 13.

(1A) Where the Commissioner proposes to conduct an investigation pursuant to a complaint under section 5(1A) of this Act, he shall give the person to whom the complaint relates an opportunity to comment on any allegations contained in the complaint.

(2) Every [investigation under this Act] shall be conducted in private, but except as aforesaid the procedure for conducting an investigation shall be such as the Commissioner considers appropriate in the circumstances of the case; and without prejudice to the generality of the foregoing provision the Commissioner may obtain information from such persons and in such manner, and make such inquiries, as he thinks fit, and may determine whether any person may be represented, by counsel or solicitor or otherwise, in the investigation.

(3) The Commissioner may, if he thinks fit, pay to the person by whom the complaint was made and to any other person who attends or furnishes information for the purposes of an investigation under this Act–

(a) sums in respect of expenses properly incurred by them;

(b) allowances by way of compensation for the loss of their time,

in accordance with such scales and subject to such conditions as may be determined by the Treasury.

(4) The conduct of an investigation under this Act shall not affect any action taken by the department or authority concerned [or the person to whom the complaint relates], or any power or duty of [that department, authority or person] to take further action with respect to any matters subject to the investigation; but where the person aggrieved has been removed from the United Kingdom under any Order in force under the Aliens Restriction Acts 1914 and 1919 or under the Commonwealth Immigrants Act 1962, he shall, if the Commissioner so directs, be permitted to re-enter and remain in the United Kingdom, subject to such conditions as the Secretary of State may direct, for the purposes of the investigation.

8 Evidence

(1) For the purposes of an investigation under section 5(1) of this Act the Commissioner may require any Minister, officer or member of the department or authority concerned or any other person who in his opinion is able to furnish information or produce documents relevant to the investigation to furnish any such information or produce any such document.

(1A) For the purposes of an investigation pursuant to a complaint under section 5(1A) of this Act the Commissioner may require any person who in his opinion is able to furnish information or produce documents relevant to the investigation to furnish any such information or produce any such document.

(2) For the purposes of any investigation under this Act the Commissioner shall have the same powers as the Court in respect of the attendance and examination of witnesses (including the administration of oaths or affirmations and the examination of witnesses abroad) and in respect of the production of documents.

(3) No obligation to maintain secrecy or other restriction upon the disclosure of information obtained by or furnished to persons in Her Majesty's service, whether imposed by any enactment or by any rule of law, shall apply to the disclosure of information for the purposes of an investigation under this Act; and the Crown shall not be entitled in relation to any such investigation to any such privilege in respect of the production of documents or the giving of evidence as is allowed by law in legal proceedings.

(4) No person shall be required or authorised by virtue of this Act to furnish any information or answer any question relating to proceedings of the Cabinet or of any committee of the Cabinet or to produce so much of any document as relates to such proceedings; and for the purposes of this subsection a certificate issued by the Secretary of the Cabinet with the approval of the Prime Minister and certifying that any information, question, document or part of a document so relates shall be conclusive.

(5) Subject to subsection (3) of this section, no person shall be compelled for the purposes of an investigation under this Act to give any evidence or produce any document which he could not be compelled to give or produce in civil proceedings before the Court.

Notes

(1) The process of investigation requires that the government department concerned and any individual who is subject of a complaint of maladministration must have the opportunity to make representations about the complaint. The Commissioner is granted extensive discretion over how the investigation will be conducted by section 7 of the Parliamentary Commissioner Act 1967. In order to try and deliver a degree of equality of arms between the parties, the Commissioner has the power to cover expenses incurred by complainants and others who give evidence, and also to compensate them for the loss of their time if it is appropriate to do so.

(2) The Parliamentary Commissioner enjoys very broad powers of investigation, including the power to demand documents from ministers, government departments and public bodies, and also from any other person who may hold documents or information relevant to an investigation. The Parliamentary Commissioner's powers to require the production of documents and information and to examine witnesses is the same as that of a High Court judge according to section 8(2) of the Act. In general, the Parliamentary Commissioner cannot be refused access to documents or information simply because the information is classified or otherwise deemed to be secret – the information must generally be disclosed to the Commissioner, although section 11 of the Act then places restrictions on what information might be made public in reports. The only exception to this principle is to be found in section 8(4), where the Parliamentary Commissioner is not empowered to require production of documents relating to proceedings of the Cabinet. Any failure to comply with a valid request for access to documents, or a failure to attend in person to testify if subpoenaed to do so, will be a contempt of court and can be subject to criminal sanction through the process outlined in section 9 of the Act.

(3) The Parliamentary Commissioner enjoys the same powers as a High Court judge to demand the attendance of witnesses and may examine them accordingly. If a witness fails to attend if called by the Commissioner, then that witness could be subject to criminal sanction under section 9 of the Parliamentary Commissioner Act 1967.

10.3.A.2 (iv) The Netherlands

Algemene Wet Bestuursrecht **10.21 (NL)**

Article 9:30 (1) The Ombudsman shall give the administrative authority, the person to whose conduct the request relates and the complainant the opportunity to explain their positions.

(2) The Ombudsman shall decide whether their explanations will be given in writing or orally and whether or not in each other's presence.

Article 9:31 (1) The administrative authority, the persons working under its responsibility – even after termination of their activities –, the witnesses and the complainant shall provide the Ombudsman with the necessary information and shall appear before him upon being invited to do so. Collegial bodies are subject to the same requirements, save that the collegial body shall determine which of its members is to fulfil the requirements, unless the Ombudsman designates one or more specific members. The Ombudsman may order persons who have been called up to appear in person.

...

(3) At the Ombudsman's written request and within a time limit to be determined by him, the documents in the possession of the administrative authority, of the person to whose conduct the request relates and of other persons shall, for the purposes of the investigation, be submitted to the Ombudsman.

Article 9:32 (1) The Ombudsman may instruct experts to perform work for the purposes of the investigation. He may also summon experts and interpreters in the interest of the investigation.

(2) Experts or interpreters summoned by the Ombudsman shall appear before him, and shall perform their services impartially and to the best of their ability. Articles 9:31(2) to 9:31(6) apply mutatis mutandis to experts who are also public employees.

(3) The Ombudsman may direct that witnesses and interpreters shall first take the oath or affirmation before they are heard or permitted to perform their duties. In that case witnesses shall swear or affirm that they will tell the whole truth and nothing but the truth and interpreters that they will conscientiously perform their duties as an interpreter.

...

Article 9:34 (1) The Ombudsman may carry out an on-site investigation. For this purpose he shall, in so far as reasonably necessary for the performance of his duties, have access to any place with the exception of a dwelling if he does not have the occupant's consent.

(2) Administrative authorities shall cooperate as required in the interest of the investigation referred to in section 1.

(3) A record shall be drawn up of the investigation.

Article 9:35 (1) Before closing the investigation the Ombudsman shall communicate his findings in writing to:

a. the administrative authority concerned;

b. the person to whose conduct the request relates;

c. the complainant.

(2) The Ombudsman shall give them the opportunity to comment on the findings within a time limit to be determined by him.

Article 9:36 (1) After closing an investigation the Ombudsman shall prepare a report, in which he lays down his findings and his opinion. ...

M Remac, Coordinating ombudsmen and the judiciary[35] **10.22 (NL)**

An investigation can be conducted as an *intermediation* (*tussenkomst*) or as a *thorough investigation* (*uitgebreid onderzoek*). An *intermediation* can best be described as a speedy and very informal investigation. It can be exercised through *intervention* (*interventie*) or *mediation* (*bemiddeling*). These tools are aimed at restoring the trust of an individual in the administration in concrete situations. An example of an *intermediation* is a case where a complainant is in financial need because his allowance or his benefit has not been paid in time or if he has to wait for an administrative decision for a long time. During the intermediation the National Ombudsman contacts the administrative authority concerned usually by telephone or email and proposes a solution. An intermediation provides the body concerned with the possibility to react speedily and often enables an expeditious solution to a problem or a dispute. If the National Ombudsman is satisfied with the (proposed) solution of an administrative authority he informs the complainant about the solution and winds down the investigations. Intermediation does not lead to written and published reports. However, if the National Ombudsman is not satisfied with the solution, he will proceed with a *thorough investigation*. An intermediation is a popular way of dealing with a complaint. Most cases that are received by the National Ombudsman are dealt with by this particular method.

Notes

(1) The investigation powers of the Ombudsman are regulated in the AWB. The Ombudsman may make use of them if a complaint leads to a 'thorough investigation' (*uitgebreid onderzoek*), and in investigations on its own initiative.[36] The latter are discussed below, in section 10.3.A.5 (iv). In practice, most complaints are not dealt with through a thorough investigation, but in a so-called 'intermediation' (*tussenkomst*). An intermediation may be exercised through mediation or through intervention. It does not lead to a formal report. In practice, most cases are dealt with through interventions. For example, in 2015,[37] the National Ombudsman resolved 3506 complaints through intervention and 24 through mediation, and in only 176 cases did the National Ombudsman conduct thorough investigations, leading to a formal report.

(2) The 'thorough investigation' undertaken by the Ombudsman is clearly of an inquisitorial nature. The Ombudsman is actively investigating and enjoys far-reaching competences to collect all facts that he thinks are necessary to assess and decide the case. Administrative authorities, their employees, witnesses and the complainant are under an obligation to provide the Ombudsman with the information necessary for the

[35] Remac (n 28 above) 31–32.

[36] See P Langbroek et al, 'The Dutch System of Dispute Resolution in Administrative Law' in Dragos and Neamtu (n 14 above) 113–53, 134–35, for statistics regarding the output of the National Ombudsman.

[37] For these figures, see www.nationaleombudsman.nl.

investigation, and must appear in person before him when summoned (Article 9:31(1) AWB). The Ombudsman may ask for any document in the possession of the administrative authority and, in principle, the authority is obliged to submit them to the Ombudsman (Article 9:31(3) AWB). In addition, the Ombudsman may instruct experts to perform work in the interest of the investigation (Article 9:32 AWB), and is entitled to conduct on-site investigations (Article 9:34 AWB). In respect of the rights of defence of the parties involved, the Ombudsman is obliged to give the administrative authority, the person to whose conduct the request relates and the complainant the opportunity to explain their positions, either in writing or orally (Article 9:30 AWB). Moreover, before closing the investigation, the Ombudsman should communicate his findings to them in writing and give them the opportunity to comment on those findings within a time limit set by him (Article 9:35 AWB). After closing the investigation, the Ombudsman shall prepare a report, in which he lays down his findings and his opinion (Article 9:36 AWB).

10.3.A.2 (v) Comparative Remarks

In each system analysed above, the Ombudsmen enjoy similar powers of investigation. In all four systems, the Ombudsmen can seek documents and information from public authorities and may require this to be provided to them. In England and Wales, this power is strengthened by the potential for criminal sanction. Similarly, in each system, the Ombudsman enjoys the power to call witnesses and may examine them accordingly. The practice in this regard varies, but appears to be most seldom used in the European Union, whereas it is more commonly used in the Member State systems.

It is interesting to note that the law in England and Wales and the law in France both explicitly lift obligations of secrecy that would ordinarily apply to certain categories of information when it is sought by the Ombudsman, whether in the form of documents or through the questioning of witnesses. The position of the European Ombudsman is contrary to this, with the relevant legal provisions stating explicitly that the rules on secrecy still apply to any information sought by the Ombudsman. In Dutch law, this issue does not appear to be addressed.

In French and Dutch law, the Ombudsman enjoys the power to conduct site visits and enter premises, whereas this power is not offered to the Parliamentary Commissioner for Administration in England and Wales or to the European Ombudsman.

10.3.A.3 CONCEPTS OF FAULT OR MALADMINISTRATION

In most systems, Ombudsmen consider complaints in light of principles of maladministration. The maladministration concept is a fluid one in most systems and certainly extends beyond the principles of legality applicable in judicial review cases. Maladministration tends to focus upon and include issues that are not considered by the principle of legality in the courts. It is also important to note that the maladministration concept is one that has developed over the years and remains fluid. In most systems, Ombudsmen are free to add to the definition on a regular basis because maladministration is not usually the subject of detailed legal definition. In the French system, rather than relying on a maladministration concept, there is a focus on a substantive breach of the rights of the complainant, which will be explored further below.

10.3.A.3 (i) Systems with a Concept of Maladministration

i) The European Union

European Ombudsman, Problems with the EU? Who Can Help You?[38] **10.23 (EU)**

The Ombudsman may find maladministration if an institution fails to respect fundamental rights, legal rules or principles, or the principles of good administration. This covers administrative irregularities, unfairness, discrimination, abuse of power, failure to reply, refusal of information, and unnecessary delay, for example.

Note

There is no clear definition of the concept of maladministration offered in the EU Treaties or any of the implementing provisions in relation to the Ombudsman. The concept is a flexible one, and could encapsulate many kinds of action and inaction by the institution that is the subject of the complaint. Instead of providing a definitive list of what might constitute maladministration, the European Ombudsman has, instead, created a set of principles of good administration, and a failure by an institution to act in a manner consistent with these is likely to result in a finding of maladministration.

European Ombudsman, The European Code of Good Administrative Behaviour[39] **10.24 (EU)**

Article 4 Lawfulness

The official shall act according to law and apply the rules and procedures laid down in EU legislation. The official shall in particular take care to ensure that decisions which affect the rights or interests of individuals have a basis in law and that their content complies with the law.

Article 5 Absence of discrimination

1. In dealing with requests from the public and in taking decisions, the official shall ensure that the principle of equality of treatment is respected. Members of the public who are in the same situation shall be treated in a similar manner.

2. If any difference in treatment is made, the official shall ensure that it is justified by the objective relevant features of the particular case.

3. The official shall in particular avoid any unjustified discrimination between members of the public based on nationality, sex, race, colour, ethnic or social origin, genetic

[38] European Ombudsman, *Problems with the EU? Who Can Help You?* (Strasbourg, European Union, 2015), 5.

[39] European Ombudsman, *The European Code of Good Administrative Behaviour* (Strasbourg, European Union, 2015).

features, language, religion or belief, political or any other opinion, membership of a national minority, property, birth, disability, age, or sexual orientation.

Article 6 Proportionality

1. When taking decisions, the official shall ensure that the measures taken are proportional to the aim pursued. The official shall in particular avoid restricting the rights of the citizens or imposing charges on them, when those restrictions or charges are not in a reasonable relation with the purpose of the action pursued.

2. When taking decisions, the official shall respect the fair balance between the interests of private persons and the general public interest.

Article 7 Absence of abuse of power

Powers shall be exercised solely for the purposes for which they have been conferred by the relevant provisions. The official shall in particular avoid using those powers for purposes which have no basis in the law or which are not motivated by any public interest.

Article 8 Impartiality and independence

1. The official shall be impartial and independent. The official shall abstain from any arbitrary action adversely affecting members of the public, as well as from any preferential treatment on any grounds whatsoever.

2. The conduct of the official shall never be guided by personal, family, or national interest or by political pressure. The official shall not take part in a decision in which he or she, or any close member of his or her family, has a financial interest.

Article 9 Objectivity

When taking decisions, the official shall take into consideration the relevant factors and give each of them its proper weight in the decision, whilst excluding any irrelevant element from consideration.

Article 10 Legitimate expectations, consistency, and advice

1. The official shall be consistent in his or her own administrative behaviour as well as with the administrative action of the institution. The official shall follow the institution's normal administrative practices, unless there are legitimate grounds for departing from those practices in an individual case. Where such grounds exist, they shall be recorded in writing.

2. The official shall respect the legitimate and reasonable expectations that members of the public have in light of how the institution has acted in the past.

3. The official shall, where necessary, advise the public on how a matter which comes within his or her remit is to be pursued and how to proceed in dealing with the matter.

Article 11 Fairness

The official shall act impartially, fairly, and reasonably.

Article 12 Courtesy

1. The official shall be service-minded, correct, courteous, and accessible in relations with the public. When answering correspondence, telephone calls, and e-mails, the official shall try to be as helpful as possible and shall reply as completely and accurately as possible to questions which are asked.

2. If the official is not responsible for the matter concerned, he or she shall direct the citizen to the appropriate official.

3. If an error occurs which negatively affects the rights or interests of a member of the public, the official shall apologise for it and endeavour to correct the negative effects

resulting from his or her error in the most expedient way and inform the member of the public of any rights of appeal in accordance with Article 19 of the Code.

...

Article 14 Acknowledgement of receipt and indication of the competent official

1. Every letter or complaint to the institution shall receive an acknowledgement of receipt within a period of two weeks, except if a substantive reply can be sent within that period.

2. The reply or acknowledgement of receipt shall indicate the name and the telephone number of the official who is dealing with the matter, as well as the service to which he or she belongs.

3. No acknowledgement of receipt and no reply need be sent in cases where letters or complaints are abusive because of their excessive number or because of their repetitive or pointless character.

Article 15 Obligation to transfer to the competent service of the institution

1. If a letter or a complaint to the institution is addressed or transmitted to a Directorate General, Directorate, or Unit which has no competence to deal with it, its services shall ensure that the file is transferred without delay to the competent service of the institution.

2. The service which originally received the letter or complaint shall inform the author of this transfer and shall indicate the name and the telephone number of the official to whom the file has been passed.

3. The official shall alert the member of the public or organisation to any errors or omissions in documents and provide an opportunity to rectify them.

Article 16 Right to be heard and to make statements

1. In cases where the rights or interests of individuals are involved, the official shall ensure that, at every stage in the decision-making procedure, the rights of defence are respected.

2. Every member of the public shall have the right, in cases where a decision affecting his or her rights or interests has to be taken, to submit written comments and, when needed, to present oral observations before the decision is taken.

Article 17 Reasonable time-limit for taking decisions

1. The official shall ensure that a decision on every request or complaint to the institution is taken within a reasonable time-limit, without delay, and in any case no later than two months from the date of receipt. The same rule shall apply for answering letters from members of the public and for answers to administrative notes which the official has sent to his or her superiors requesting instructions regarding the decisions to be taken.

2. If a request or a complaint to the institution cannot, because of the complexity of the matters which it raises, be decided upon within the above mentioned time-limit, the official shall inform the author as soon as possible. In such a case, a definitive decision should be communicated to the author in the shortest possible time.

Article 18 Duty to state the grounds of decisions

1. Every decision of the institution which may adversely affect the rights or interests of a private person shall state the grounds on which it is based by indicating clearly the relevant facts and the legal basis of the decision.

2. The official shall avoid making decisions which are based on brief or vague grounds, or which do not contain an individual reasoning. passed.

3. If it is not possible, because of the large number of persons concerned by similar decisions, to communicate in detail the grounds of the decision and where standard replies are therefore sent, the official shall subsequently provide the citizen who expressly requests it with an individual reasoning.

Article 19 Indication of appeal possibilities

1. A decision of the institution which may adversely affect the rights or interests of a private person shall contain an indication of the appeal possibilities available for challenging the decision. It shall in particular indicate the nature of the remedies, the bodies before which they can be exercised, and the time-limits for exercising them.

2. Decisions shall in particular refer to the possibility of judicial proceedings and complaints to the Ombudsman under the conditions specified in, respectively, Articles 263 and 228 of the Treaty on the Functioning of the European Union.

Article 20 Notification of the decision

1. The official shall ensure that persons whose rights or interests are affected by a decision are informed of that decision in writing, as soon as it is taken.

2. The official shall abstain from communicating the decision to other sources until the person or persons concerned have been informed.

...

Article 22 Requests for information

1. The official shall, when he or she has responsibility for the matter concerned, provide members of the public with the information that they request. When appropriate, the official shall give advice on how to initiate an administrative procedure within his or her field of competence. The official shall take care that the information communicated is clear and understandable.

2. If an oral request for information is too complicated or too extensive to be dealt with, the official shall advise the person concerned to formulate his or her demand in writing.

...

Article 23 Requests for public access to documents

1. The official shall deal with requests for access to documents in accordance with the rules adopted by the institution and in accordance with the general principles and limits laid down in Regulation (EC) 1049/2001.

2. If the official cannot comply with an oral request for access to documents, the citizen shall be advised to formulate it in writing.

Article 24 Keeping of adequate records

The institution's departments shall keep adequate records of their incoming and outgoing mail, of the documents they receive, and of the measures they take.

Notes

(1) The above principles of good administration are stated by the Ombudsman to be an elaboration of the right to good administration to be found in Article 41 of the Charter of Fundamental Rights of the European Union. They should be considered alongside the Ombudsman's publication of ethical standards for civil servants in the

European Union.[40] Any behaviour by civil servants or institutions that can be said to contravene these principles is likely to be found to be maladministration.

(2) The European Code of Good Administrative Behaviour can be argued to have two functions: it may act as a guide, both to the institutions and members of the public, as to what maladministration might be; and it may also play an important function in relation to the channelling of administrative behaviour – institutions can use the Code in order to develop and improve administrative practice, which can avoid future complaints of maladministration.

ii) England and Wales

Hansard, Parliamentary Commissioner Bill[41] **10.25 (EW)**

What about the definition of maladministration? In the first place I can define it to some extent negatively. It does not extend to policy, which remains a matter for Parliament. Nor do we include under maladministration that whole group of discretionary decisions which Sir John Whyatt treated separately in the first part of his Report. Discretionary decision, properly exercised, which the complainant dislikes but cannot fault the manner in which it was taken, is excluded by this Clause.

A positive definition of maladministration is far more difficult to achieve. We might have made an attempt in this Clause to define, by catalogue, all of the qualities which make up maladministration, which might count for maladministration by a civil servant. It would be a wonderful exercise – bias, neglect, inattention, delay, incompetence, inaptitude, perversity, turpitude, arbitrariness and so on. It would be a long and interesting list.

We have not tried to define injustice by using such terms as 'loss or damage'. These may have legal overtones which could be held to exclude one thing which I am particularly anxious shall remain – the sense of outrage aroused by unfair or incompetent administration, even where the complainant has suffered no actual loss. We intend that the outraged citizen who persuades his Member to raise a problem shall have the right to an investigation, even where he has suffered no loss or damage in the legal sense of those terms, but is simply a good citizen who has nothing to lose and wishes to clear up a sense of outrage and indignation at what he believes to be a maladministration.

Notes

(1) The above excerpt is taken from the parliamentary debate held when the Parliamentary Commissioner Bill was debated by the House of Commons. It is clear that the government's deliberate intention was that the maladministration concept should not be defined in the statute, but should be open and flexible in order that the concept might develop over time. The initial examples offered in the second paragraph of the term have become known as the 'Crossman catalogue' and have often been considered to be a starting point for the definition of the maladministration concept.

[40] European Ombudsman, *Public Service Principles for the EU Civil Service* (Strasbourg, European Union, 2012).

[41] HC Deb 18 October 1966, vol 734, col 51 (Mr Richard Crossman).

(2) The speech above also serves to reinforce the point that Parliament did not intend to define the concept of maladministration so that it could be refined and developed over time.

Sir William Reid, Annual Report 1993–1994[42] **10.26 (EW)**

The terms given in 1966 by Mr Richard Crossman were bias, neglect, inattention, delay, incompetence, inaptitude, perversity, turpitude, arbitrariness and so on. To that, I have added rudeness (though that is a matter of degree); an unwillingness to treat an individual as a person with rights; a refusal to answer reasonable questions; neglecting to inform an individual on request of his or her rights or entitlement; knowingly giving advice which is misleading or inadequate; ignoring valid advice or overruling considerations which would produce an uncomfortable result for the person overruling; offering no redress or manifestly disproportionate redress; showing bias whether because of colour, sex, or any other grounds; an omission to notify those who thereby lost a right of appeal; a refusal to inform adequately of the right of appeal; faulty procedures; the failure to monitor compliance with adequate procedures; cavalier disregard of guidance which was intended to be followed in the interest of the equitable treatment of those who use a service; partiality; and failure to mitigate the effects of rigid adherence to the letter of the law where that produces manifestly inequitable treatment.

Note

Sir William Reid, who was the Parliamentary Commissioner for Administration from 1990 to 1996, developed the 'Crossman catalogue' further and added to the types of action that might be said to constitute maladministration. This report has been influential in the development of the maladministration concept and demonstrates how the PCA has developed the concept over time in light of the information gained.

Parliamentary and Health Service Ombudsman, Principles of Good Administration[43] **10.27 (EW)**

Summary

Good administration by public bodies means:

1. Getting it right

Acting in accordance with the law and with regard for the rights of those concerned.
Acting in accordance with the public body's policy and guidance (published or internal).
Taking proper account of established good practice.
Providing effective services, using appropriately trained and competent staff.
Taking reasonable decisions, based on all relevant considerations.

[42] Public Administration Select Committee Annual Report of the Parliamentary Commissioner for Administration 1993–1994 (1993–1994, HC 290) para 7.
[43] Parliamentary and Health Service Ombudsman, *Principles of Good Administration* (London, 2009).

2. Being customer focused

Ensuring people can access services easily.

Informing customers what they can expect and what the public body expects of them.

Keeping to its commitments, including any published service standards

Dealing with people helpfully, promptly and sensitively, bearing in mind their individual circumstances

Responding to customers' needs flexibly, including, where appropriate, co-ordinating a response with other service providers

3. Being open and accountable

Being open and clear about policies and procedures and ensuring that information, and any advice provided, is clear, accurate and complete.

Stating its criteria for decision making and giving reasons for decisions

Handling information properly and appropriately.

Keeping proper and appropriate records

Taking responsibility for its actions

4. Acting fairly and proportionately

Treating people impartially, with respect and courtesy.

Treating people without unlawful discrimination or prejudice, and ensuring no conflict of interests.

Dealing with people and issues objectively and consistently.

Ensuring that decisions and actions are proportionate, appropriate and fair.

5. Putting things right

Acknowledging mistakes and apologising where appropriate.

Putting mistakes right quickly and effectively.

Providing clear and timely information on how and when to appeal or complain.

Operating an effective complaints procedure, which includes offering a fair and appropriate remedy when a complaint is upheld.

6. Seeking continuous improvement

Reviewing policies and procedures regularly to ensure they are effective.

Asking for feedback and using it to improve services and performance.

Ensuring that the public body learns lessons from complaints and uses these to improve services and performance.

These Principles are not a checklist to be applied mechanically. Public bodies should use their judgment in applying the Principles to produce reasonable, fair and proportionate results in the circumstances. The Ombudsman will adopt a similar approach in deciding whether maladministration or service failure has occurred.

Note

The Parliamentary Commissioner for Administration (PCA) now publishes a set of principles of good administration as an adjunct to the other sources which might be said to assist in the definition of the concept (not only those excerpts outlined above, but also the annual reports of the PCA and the reports produced in relation to investigations undertaken). As with other legal systems, it might be presumed that if the action of the authority under investigation is not compliant with the principles of good administration, then it is likely to be found to be maladministration.

iii) The Netherlands

National Ombudsman, Guidance on proper administration[44] **10.28 (NL)**

The essence of proper conduct of administrative authorities may be summarized in four core values: A. Open and clear B. Respectful C. Concerned and solution-focused D. Fair and trustworthy.

A. Open and clear

1. Transparent

Actions of public authorities are open and transparent so that it is clear for citizens why government is taking a particular action.

2. Provide adequate information

Public authorities ensure that citizens receive the information they need and that the information is correct, complete and clear. Public authorities provide information proactively, not just when citizens ask for it.

3. Listen to citizens

Public authorities listen to citizens actively, so that citizens feel that they have been heard and seen.

4. Adequate reasons

Public authorities explain their actions and decision in a clear manner. They indicate the statutory base for their actions and decisions, the facts taken into consideration, and the way individual citizens' interests have been taken into account. Citizens should be able to understand the reasons.

B. Respectful

5. Public authorities respect the fundamental rights of citizens. Some of these fundamental rights guarantee protection against government action. For example: the right to physical integrity, the right to privacy, the right of inviolability of the home, the right to personal freedom and the prohibition of non-discrimination. By contrast, other fundamental rights guarantee that public authorities will actively take certain action. For example: the right to education and the right to health.

6. Promotion of active public participation

Public authorities maximize public involvement in their actions.

7. Courtesy

Public authorities are respectful, courteous and helpful towards citizens.

8. Fair play

Public authorities give citizens the opportunity to utilize their procedural opportunities and ensure fair play in this respect.

9. Proportionality

In pursuing its aims, a public authority avoids measures that unnecessarily interfere in the life of the citizen and that are disproportionate to the aims concerned.

[44] Nationale Ombudsman, Behoorlijkheidswijzer, available at www.nationaleombudsman.nl/system/files/infomateriaal/Behoorlijkheidswijzer%20NL%20oktober%202016.pdf.

10. Special care

When individuals are in government custody and therefore reliant on public authorities for their physical care, the authorities should provide for that care.

C. Concerned and solution focused

11. Individualised approach

Public authorities are willing to depart from general policies or rules in order to prevent unintended or undesirable consequences.

12. Cooperation

Public authorities cooperate spontaneously with other (governmental) institutions in the interest of the citizen and do not send citizens from pillar to post.

13. Leniency

When mistakes have been made, public authorities show leniency and flexibility in remedying them. They do not deny reasonable claims and do not burden citizens with unnecessary and complicated procedures and demands for proof.

14. Promptness

Administrative authorities act as prompt and effective as possible.

15. De-escalation

In its contacts with individual citizens, public authorities seek to prevent or limit escalation. Communications skills and a solution focused attitude are essential in this respect.

D. Fair and trustworthy

16. Integrity

Public authorities act with integrity and use their powers only for the purpose for which they were conferred.

17. Trustworthiness

Public authorities act within the framework of the law. They are honest and fair-minded. They do what they say and comply with judgments of the courts.

18. Impartiality

Public authorities act impartial and are unprejudiced in their actions.

19. Reasonableness

Before taking any decision, public authorities weigh the different interests involved. The outcome of this process is not unreasonable.

20. Careful preparation

Public authorities collect all the information necessary to take a well-considered decision.

21. Effective organisation

Public authorities ensure that their organisation and administrative systems promote the standard of their services to the public. They work meticulously and avoid mistakes. Possible errors are corrected as quickly as possible.

22. Professionalism

Public authorities ensure that their employees work in accordance with relevant professional standards. Citizens are entitled to expect from them particular expertise.

Notes

(1) According to Article 9:27(1) AWB, the Dutch normative standard for mal- or good administration is (im)propriety (*(on)behoorlijkheid*). As, during the adoption of the Wet Nationale Ombudsman, there was no consensus about the precise meaning of this standard, the legislator decided to leave this matter at the discretion of the National Ombudsman. Over the years, the different office holders have developed this concept further.[45] They were 'forced' to do so because, if they find conduct to be improper, they are under a statutory obligation to state in the report which requirement of properness is violated (Article 9:36(2) AWB). Initially, the Ombudsman's standards for properness resembled the standards for judicial review by the courts, although the Ombudsman applied them less strictly. Since the new millennium, the Ombudsman has chosen to develop its own standards of properness that are less legalistic in their nature and better connect to the expectations that citizens may have of good administration.[46] The result can be found in the Guidance on Proper Administration.

(2) The Guidance still contains standards that are also applied by the courts. Examples are the principle of transparency, the duty to state adequate reasons, fundamental rights, the principles of fair play, proportionality, reasonableness and impartiality, and the duty of careful preparation. In addition, it contains several citizen rights that do not have a legal nature, such as the authority's duty to listen to citizens and to promote active participation, and the rights to courtesy, leniency and de-escalation. Finally, the Guidance includes some organisational standards, in particular the authority's duty to have an effective and professional organisation. Where the Ombudsman's standards overlap with the standards applied by the courts, their application is in general less strict than the courts' application. This does not pose a problem, because the Ombudsman's opinion is not legally binding and does not lead to annulment (see section 10.3.A.4 (iv) below). Because of this distinction and because the Ombudsman also applies standards which are not known as legal principles and standards, properness and lawfulness are distinctive normative standards. In this respect, the National Ombudsman has developed the so-called 'quadrant of propriety and lawfulness'.[47] This quadrant includes four situations, namely the situation that an action is both lawful and proper, the situation that it is unlawful and improper, the situation that it is lawful but improper and the situation that it is unlawful but proper. Obviously, the last situation is quite exceptional.[48]

(3) In addition to the Guidance on Proper Administration, the National Ombudsman has developed guidance documents applicable to specific administrative action or to specific forms of conduct.[49] Most of them are directed towards administrative

[45] Langbroek et al (n 36 above) 132–33.

[46] The National Ombudsman had developed this Guidance in cooperation with the municipal ombudsmen.

[47] Annual report of the National Ombudsman 2005, 20. *cf* Langbroek et al (n 36 above) 133.

[48] For a rare example, see National Ombudsman, 18 July 2006, Report 2006/247, mentioned in Remac (n 28 above) 95–96.

[49] Remac (n 28 above) 35–36.

authorities and contain standards for specific forms of administrative action. Examples are the Guidance on Proper Correspondence (Correspondentiewijzer), the Guidance on Proper Telephone Contact (Telefoonwijzer), the Guidance on Proper Compensation (Schadevergoedingswijzer) and the Guidance for Enforcement (Handhavingswijzer). Some of them are addressed to individuals, such as the 'Stop discrimination card' (Stop discriminatie kaart) or the 'Stop bullying homosexuals card' (Stop homopesten kaart). Both contain norms of proper societal behaviour as well. Finally, some guidance documents are addressed to both the administration and to individuals. Examples of this category are the Guidance on Participation (Participatiewijzer) and the Guidance for Public Demonstrations (Demonstratiewijzer).

10.3.A.3 (ii) Systems without a Concept of Maladministration: France

Loi organique n° 2011-333 du 29 mars 2011 relative au Défenseur des droits **10.29 (FR)**

Article 4 The Defender of Rights is in charge:

1. of defending the rights and freedoms in the context of relations with the authorities of the state, local authorities, public institutions and bodies vested with a public service mandate;
2. of defending and promoting the child best interests and rights, enshrined by law or by an international obligation that is ratified in due form or approved by France;
3. of combatting discrimination, direct or indirect, that is prohibited by law or by an international obligation that is ratified in due form or approved by France, as well as to promote equality;
4. of safeguarding the respect for ethics by persons who exercise security activities on the territory of the Republic;
5. of forwarding to the competent authorities each person who reports an alert under the conditions prescribed by law, to safeguard the rights and liberties of this person.

Note

The concept of maladministration is not used in the French system. Whereas this notion was implicitly taken into consideration in the mandate of the former Mediator of the Republic (Médiateur de la République), the conception attached to the Defenseur des droits, created in 2008, is right-based. This right-based approach might consider issues that are broader than simply the conduct of public administration and the relationship between individuals and public authorities in the sense that many issues that come before the Defenseur des droits may relate to fundamental rights and freedoms rather than maladministration, as in the other systems under investigation. It may be, however, that as a result of this, the work of the Defenseur des droits is significantly less focused on failures of public administration that are not necessarily addressed by the principle of legality.

10.3.A.3 (iii) Comparative Remarks

The maladministration concept is very similar in the European Union, England and Wales and the Netherlands. Some aspects of the maladministration concept overlap with principles of legality (each system, for instance, mentions proportionality and non-discrimination as being a part of the maladministration concept) and each system also covers a range of issues, such as courtesy, offering appropriate advice and, in various ways, offering good service to those who seek to interact with public authorities through, for example, ensuring courtesy, efficient and effective use of information, and so on.

Maladministration is a concept that has been Europeanised to a considerable extent. It is evident that there has been cross-fertilisation between the systems, and, although one might argue that the England and Wales system is perhaps more focused on the citizen as consumer than either the Dutch or the EU system, at the same time, all of the systems adopt a very similar approach to the expectations imposed on public authorities.

The only exception to the above observations lies in the French system, where the approach is somewhat different and considers not whether there has been maladministration, but whether a relevant right of the individual has been infringed.

10.3.A.4 REMEDIES FROM THE OMBUDSMAN

The question of remedies from Ombudsmen is invariably challenging because, in general, Ombudsmen cannot mandate a remedy, but may only make recommendations for redress. This section will examine the approach of the Ombudsmen to giving a remedy and will also seek to consider the effectiveness of the remedy, including the level of compliance with recommendations and any potential support from the judicial process should a recommendation not be followed.

10.3.A.4 (i) The European Union

Treaty on the Functioning of the European Union **10.30 (EU)**

Article 228 (1) A European Ombudsman, elected by the European Parliament, shall be empowered to receive complaints from any citizen of the Union or any natural or legal person residing or having its registered office in a Member State concerning instances of maladministration in the activities of the Union institutions, bodies, offices or agencies, with the exception of the Court of Justice of the European Union acting in its judicial role. He or she shall examine such complaints and report on them.

In accordance with his duties, the Ombudsman shall conduct inquiries for which he finds grounds, either on his own initiative or on the basis of complaints submitted to him direct or through a Member of the European Parliament, except where the alleged facts are or have been the subject of legal proceedings. Where the Ombudsman establishes an instance of maladministration, he shall refer the matter to the institution, body, office or agency concerned, which shall have a period of three months in which to inform him of its views. The Ombudsman shall then forward a report to the European Parliament and the institution, body, office or agency concerned. The person lodging the complaint shall be informed of the outcome of such inquiries.

…

Decision 94/262/ECSC, EC, Euratom of the European Parliament on the regulations and general conditions governing the performance of the Ombudsman's duties **10.31 (EU)**

Article 3 ... (5) As far as possible, the Ombudsman shall seek a solution with the institution or body concerned to eliminate the instance of maladministration and satisfy the complaint.

(6) If the Ombudsman finds there has been maladministration, he shall inform the institution or body concerned, where appropriate making draft recommendations. The institution or body so informed shall send the Ombudsman a detailed opinion within three months.

(7) The Ombudsman shall then send a report to the European Parliament and to the institution or body concerned. He may make recommendations in his report. The person lodging the complaint shall be informed by the Ombudsman of the outcome of the inquiries, of the opinion expressed by the institution or body concerned and of any recommendations made by the Ombudsman.

(8) At the end of each annual session the Ombudsman shall submit to the European Parliament a report on the outcome of his inquiries.

Decision of the European Ombudsman adopting Implementing Provisions **10.32 (EU)**

Article 5: Proposals for solutions

5.1. If the Ombudsman considers that a complaint can be resolved, the Ombudsman shall seek a solution with the institution concerned.

5.2. The institution concerned shall reply to the Ombudsman's proposal for a solution within a specified timeframe, which shall normally not exceed three months. The precise timeframe for providing a reply shall be reasonable, taking into account the complexity and urgency of the inquiry. If the Ombudsman considers that the inquiry is of public interest, the timeframe for responding shall be as short as is reasonably possible. If the institution concerned is not in a position to provide a reply to the Ombudsman within the set timeframe, it shall make a reasoned request for an extension.

5.3. The Ombudsman shall provide the complainant with a copy of the proposal for a solution and the institution's reply to that proposal after obtaining the reply of the institution concerned. The complainant may submit comments to the Ombudsman within one month.

Article 6: Findings and recommendations

6.1. The Ombudsman may make suggestions for improvement regarding issues related to the inquiry in the course of an inquiry.

6.2. Where the Ombudsman finds no maladministration, that a solution has been found or that no further inquiries are justified, the inquiry shall be closed with a decision setting out findings. The Ombudsman shall send the decision to the complainant and to the institution concerned.

6.3. Where the Ombudsman finds maladministration, the Ombudsman shall make any appropriate recommendation(s) to the institution concerned in accordance with Article 3(6) of the Statute and ask the institution concerned to provide an opinion on the recommendation(s) within three months. The opinion shall state whether and, if so, how the institution has implemented or intends to implement the recommendation(s).

The Ombudsman shall forward the opinion to the complainant, who may submit comments on it within one month.

6.4. Where the Ombudsman becomes aware that the matter under investigation by the Ombudsman has become the subject of legal proceedings, the Ombudsman shall close the inquiry and inform the complainant and the institution.

Article 7: Closure of inquiries finding maladministration and reports to Parliament

7.1. The Ombudsman, after analysing the opinion of the institution concerned and any comments submitted by the complainant in accordance with Article 6.3 of this Decision, may close the inquiry setting out definitive findings.

7.2. The Ombudsman shall report to the European Parliament on his or her inquiries on a regular basis, including by way of an annual report.

7.3. The Ombudsman may submit a Special Report to the European Parliament on any inquiry in which the Ombudsman finds maladministration and which the Ombudsman considers to be of significant public interest.

Notes

(1) The above excerpts elaborate on the approach adopted in Article 228 TFEU. The European Ombudsman does not enjoy the power to mandate a legally enforceable remedy. The Ombudsman operates on the basis that, in the initial phase, endeavours will be made to find a solution between the parties, in accordance with Article 5 of the Decision adopting the Implementing Provisions. Both parties are given the opportunity to comment upon a proposed solution and if it is mutually acceptable, then the inquiry can be closed and a report of findings sent to both the institution and the complainant in accordance with Article 6.2 of the Decision adopting the Implementing Provisions.

(2) The Ombudsman may close any inquiry where no maladministration is found or which does not merit further investigation by issuing a report of findings to the institution and to the complainant.

(3) In cases where maladministration is found, the Ombudsman may make recommendations to the institution concerned and ask it to provide an opinion on the report and recommendations within three months. The institution must respond to the findings and indicate whether it intends to adopt some or all of the recommendations that have been made. The complainant then has the opportunity, within one month of receiving the opinion of the institution from the Ombudsman, to make comments upon it. Once this process is completed, after consideration of the opinion and comments received, the Ombudsman will close the inquiry and set out definitive findings. If the report finds maladministration and a matter of significant public interest, the report may be communicated to the European Parliament as a Special Report, which will then be considered by the Parliament. It is important to note that the number of Special Reports that have been submitted to the Parliament is very low – in most years, no such reports are submitted, and in years where Special Reports have been submitted, there is usually only one submission, occasionally two or three.

(4) The Ombudsman produces an annual report to the European Parliament each year, setting out the nature of the work undertaken and summarising the main heads

of complaint that have been investigated over the year. These reports[50] are interesting as they illustrate that the Ombudsman commences inquiries in around 15% of cases and finds maladministration in around 10% of the inquiries that are concluded. The compliance rate with the recommendations of the Ombudsman varies somewhat, with around 80% of recommendations being followed in most years.

Decision of the European Ombudsman closing the inquiry into complaint 178/2014/AN against the European Investment Bank[51] **10.33 (EU)**

Facts: Impresa Pizzarotti & C SpA submitted a tender for a bridge building project in Bosnia & Herzegovina. The project was financed by the European Investment Bank (EIB). The EIB excluded Impresa Pizzarotti & C SpA from the tender despite the fact that its bid was the lowest on the basis that the EIB had determined that the company did not meet all of the requirements of the tender. Impresa Pizzarotti & C SpA complained about this decision through the EIB's complaints process, arguing that the EIB had made an error in the interpretation of the tender and that it did meet the requirements, and their complaint was upheld. The EIB still refused to permit the tender to be considered, and the project was subsequently awarded to and commenced by another bidder. The Ombudsman was asked to investigate whether the interpretation of the tender document was correct and lawful, and whether misinterpretation would constitute maladministration.

Held: The EIB committed an act of maladministration and interpreted the tender document incorrectly.

Arguments presented to the Ombudsman

6. The EIB endorsed, in substance, the BiH promoter's view that the construction methodology proposed by the complainant in its bid was different from the one required by the tender documentation, which did not allow for any deviations.

7. The EIB also considered that the construction methodology proposed by the complainant would have implied significant additional time, not only to carry out a re-design, but also to obtain a new set of administrative permits from BiH authorities. The BiH promoter's decision to exclude the complainant's bid, on the basis that it did not meet the requirements of the tender documentation, was supported by three external experts commissioned by the promoter. Moreover, the EIB commissioned a fourth international expert to review the case who agreed with the latter's view. In addition, the EIB's own technical services also concluded that the complainant's bid did not meet the tender requirements.

8. One of the external experts also observed that the tender documentation was clear and unambiguous. In particular, the EIB considered that the required construction methodology was expressed in sufficiently clear and precise manner so as to enable a reasonably experienced civil engineer to understand what exactly was required. This is obvious, according to the EIB, from the absence, during the clarification procedure, of any question from the tenderers in relation to the construction methodology, and from the fact that all the other tenderers submitted bids based on the correct construction methodology.

9. In light of the Complaints Mechanism's recommendation to re-examine the non-objection, the EIB services re-examined the case and reaffirmed the initial non-objection. The EIB thus maintained its decision.

[50] The Reports can be found at www.ombudsman.europa.eu/en/press/publications.faces.

[51] Available at www.ombudsman.europa.eu/en/cases/decision.faces/en/58171/html.bookmark.

10. The complainant, on its side, believed that the tender documentation did not require a particular construction methodology, and therefore its proposed methodology could not be considered as deviating from the tender specifications. This view was also endorsed by the Complaints Mechanism. The complainant said repeatedly that its exclusion from the tender not only caused it significant economic damage, but also led the EIB to finance a bid which was 11% more expensive, entailing extra-spending of about 18 million euros.

The Ombudsman's assessment

11. The parties' diverging positions in this case include technical arguments related to civil engineering questions. It is neither appropriate nor necessary for the Ombudsman to take a position in relation to these matters, because the core issue turns on the legal meaning of the tender documents, in particular the provisions concerning the degree of technical freedom left to the bidders in preparing their offers.

12. The legal issue that lies at the heart of the dispute is whether the tender specifications clearly and unambiguously required a particular construction methodology, as the EIB claimed, or whether they left room for other methodologies, as the complainant and the Complaints Mechanism believed.

14. Having inspected the EIB's complete file in relation to the tender, the Ombudsman shares the view of the complainant and of the Complaints Mechanism that the tender documentation does not state clearly and unambiguously which construction methodology should be used. There is nothing in that regard in the written part. Moreover, as the EIB acknowledged in its opinion, the Drawings provided to the tenderers referred to 'main design', with no mention whatsoever that such main design was final. On the contrary, section 1.1.2 of the Bill of Quantities contains an item meant to cover the estimated cost for modification of the main design, which shows that the latter was not viewed as immutable in the tender documentation.

20. It follows that the EIB's decision to maintain its non-objection to the exclusion of the complainant's tender was based on a legally incorrect reading of the tender documents. This was an instance of maladministration.

21. The maladministration is particularly serious because, as the OECD has recognised, getting procurement procedures right is a key instrument in fighting corruption in the public sector. According to the OECD, procurement is the government activity most vulnerable to waste, fraud and corruption due to the size of the financial flows involved. Integrity in public procurement is essential in maintaining citizens' trust in government[2].

22. Furthermore, it is in the interests of the EIB's good reputation as a major provider of EU funding and as a respectable EU institution in the eyes of third country authorities, promoters and contractors that participants in tenders financed from EIB loans in third countries should have access to a fully operational internal redress mechanism within the EIB. This is particularly important where the EIB is involved in countries which have underdeveloped or ineffective systems for the administration of justice.

23. In this context, the Ombudsman notes the following statement contained in the European Commission's 2013 Progress Report on Bosnia and Herzegovina (COM(2013) 700 final): No substantial improvements can be reported as regards the legal system in Bosnia and Herzegovina, which remains complex and challenging. The standard of legislation is relatively high in some areas; nevertheless the practical implementation of laws is often poor due to the weak enforcement capacity of key institutions. The judicial system often does not function efficiently and does not cover commercial activities adequately.

Enforcement of commercial contracts remains a lengthy process, which involves 37 procedures and takes an average of 595 days, unchanged from the previous year. Overall, a weak rule of law, corruption, and unreliable contract enforcement continue to hamper the business environment.

24. Against this background, the approach taken by the EIB in this case is wholly unacceptable. It risks putting into question not only the EIB's own reputation but also the Union's commitment to strengthening the rule of law in Bosnia and Herzegovina. This reputational damage could have been avoided if the EIB had followed the advice of its own internal Complaints Mechanism.

25. Article 3(5) of the European Ombudsman's Statute provides that, when an instance of maladministration is identified, the Ombudsman shall as far as possible seek a solution with the institution concerned to eliminate the maladministration. In the present case, the serious nature of the maladministration and its potential systemic implications are such that it would be inappropriate to seek such a solution. In any event, in this case no solution is possible now, given that the construction project was awarded to another bidder and the construction began several months ago. The complainant in this case has not sought to be compensated for the costs of preparing a tender application which, because of an illegality, was excluded from the tender process. Accordingly, the Ombudsman will not recommend financial compensation for those costs. Consequently, the Ombudsman will close the inquiry with a critical remark and will also send a copy of this decision to the Presidents of the European Parliament, the Council of the European Union and the European Commission, for information.

26. The Ombudsman trusts that the Bank will follow up the critical remark by learning appropriate lessons from this case for the future. She will also consider opening an own-initiative inquiry into the systemic issues raised by the case.

Conclusion

On the basis of the inquiry into this complaint, the Ombudsman closes it with the following critical remark:

The EIB's decision to maintain its non-objection to the exclusion of the complainant's tender was based on a legally incorrect reading of the tender documents. This was an instance of maladministration.

The EIB's activities affect the reputation of the European Union and should be consistent with the Union's values and principles. The EIB's maladministration in this case risks putting into question not only the EIB's own reputation but also the Union's commitment to strengthening the rule of law in Bosnia and Herzegovina. This reputational damage could have been avoided if the EIB had followed the advice of its own internal Complaints Mechanism.

Note

The above excerpt demonstrates a typical report of the European Ombudsman into an allegation of maladministration brought by an individual complainant. It adopts a typical structure and approach in addressing the facts and arguments presented to the Ombudsman, the assessment of the facts and arguments, and then a conclusion and recommendations or remarks. As noted above, the Ombudsman's reports do not carry the force of law, although there is generally a high level of compliance with the findings of the Ombudsman. In this report, the Ombudsman offers a 'critical remark', in the expectation that this will be considered by administrative authorities at the EU level and their practice will be modified for the future. This report also illustrates the challenges that are posed for the Ombudsman in terms of offering effective redress in some cases, as in the above case the tender had been awarded to another bidder and work had commenced on the project, so there was no prospect of recommending that the process be rerun in a proper manner.

Decision of the European Ombudsman closing her own-initiative inquiry OI/10/2015/NF concerning EPSO's procedure for dealing with requests for review made by candidates in open competitions[52] **10.34 (EU)**

Facts: The European Ombudsman received a number of complaints from applicants for positions in the EU civil service, arguing that the European Personnel Selection Office (EPSO) had created excessive delays in dealing with review requests made by unsuccessful applicants in selection competitions for positions in the European civil service.

Held: EPSO had generally taken too long to respond to requests for review, although there was some evidence of improvement. Recommendations were made to guide further improvement.

The Ombudsman's assessment

8. This inquiry raises issues faced by every public administration on a daily basis: how, with limited resources, can a public administration provide a timely, tailored, well-reasoned and ultimately correct response to individual citizens. The Ombudsman appreciates that EPSO has made genuine efforts to prepare for peaks in its request for review workload, to tackle the delays it has faced and to improve, generally, the information it provides to candidates to reassure them that their requests are being handled in accordance with the principles of good administration.

9. The Ombudsman is pleased to learn that the situation has improved significantly since the Ombudsman's inquiry was opened. EPSO has now succeeded in eliminating its backlog of pending requests for review. This development should allow EPSO the necessary time to reflect on the suggestions set out below, so that the request for review procedure serves its purpose as an effective internal review mechanism, through which candidates receive a duly considered, well-reasoned, but also timely response.

...

The time aspect and procedural issues

13. While EPSO has made a considerable effort to manage the workload resulting from the sharp increase in requests for review received since 2014, the time taken to deal with such requests has continued to fluctuate. While, on average, it took EPSO 3.75 months to handle requests for review in 2013, EPSO needed 5.75 months to deal with requests for review in 2014. This fell to 3.5 months on average for requests for review received in the first half of 2015. For the full year 2015, the average time to deal with requests for review increased again to 4.75 months. In 2016, EPSO has succeeded in eliminating its backlog of pending requests for review and has reduced the average handling time.

[52] Available at www.ombudsman.europa.eu/en/cases/summary.faces/en/75540/html.bookmark.

14. The situation has certainly improved significantly compared to the situation which led the Ombudsman to open the inquiry. However, these figures, coupled with complaints that the Ombudsman has continued to receive, lead the Ombudsman to conclude that, despite EPSO's commendable efforts of late, there were, for a period of time, excessively long delays.

15. The improvement in the time being taken to deal with requests for review is very welcome. To some extent, however, this improvement is a reflection of a temporary drop in the level of EPSO activity more generally. The fewer competitions EPSO runs in a given period, the fewer requests for review it is going to receive.

16. It is thus important to reflect further on the functioning of the request for review procedure in order to ensure that, in the event of another peak in workload, similar delays do not reoccur in the future. The Ombudsman thus encourages EPSO to do its utmost to continue to seek systemic improvements in the request for review procedure and how it is applied to ensure that all candidates who make a request for review receive a timely answer, in accordance with Article 17 of the European Code of Good Administrative Behaviour on reasonable time-limits for taking decisions.

17. Of particular relevance is the fact that, following the decision of the selection board on a request for review, it often takes EPSO a number of months to draw up a reply communicating the selection board's decision to the candidate. As EPSO has explained, the selection board usually decides within two weeks whether a candidate's request for review has been successful or not. The candidate, however, is not informed of this decision until EPSO writes to him or to her. While EPSO reacts immediately whenever the outcome of the review is positive, the reply may not be sent out for up to five months where the outcome of the request for review is negative. It is difficult to justify, on objective grounds, the discrepancy between the relatively limited time it takes the selection board to decide on a candidate's exclusion or readmission with the time taken by EPSO to communicate the reasoned decisions to candidates.

18. It appears that this delay occurs because EPSO must, when preparing replies to candidates, link the reasoning set out by the selection boards for their decisions with the facts present in candidates' files and the arguments raised by candidates in their review requests. EPSO also takes care to set out, in its letters conveying a negative review decision, the detailed reasons for that negative decision. EPSO and the selection boards share responsibility for the smooth functioning of the request for review procedure. Within their respective remit, both should thus make efforts to facilitate the processing of review requests by ensuring that the selection boards' decisions can easily be translated into reasoned replies to candidates.

19. As regards the selection boards' remit, the Ombudsman is of the view that this delay could be minimised if selection boards took greater responsibility to provide EPSO with more detailed reasons for their decisions. In particular, the selection boards should make sure to link the reasoning underpinning their decisions to the facts present in a candidate's file and to the arguments put forward in a candidate's review request (which the selection board should have in front of it when it carries out the review).

...

21. Given that EPSO sometimes publishes the reserve lists of successful candidates before providing replies to all requests for review, the Ombudsman welcomes EPSO's statement that, by prioritising requests for review which have obtained a positive selection board decision, it is always able to readmit these successful candidates to the next stage of the competition.

22. In addition to the suggestions mentioned above, the Ombudsman has some further suggestions to help EPSO address delays in the procedure. First, EPSO should consider placing even more emphasis on estimating the number of requests for review it expects to receive and allocating staff resources accordingly to ensure it is adequately prepared for possible peaks in workload. An under-resourced request for review team seems to have been a factor contributing to the delays.

23. Second, EPSO should seek to identify technological solutions. EPSO's recent decision to overhaul its IT system, which had been identified as a source of complication in processing requests for review, is welcome. The Ombudsman invites EPSO, in its follow-up to this inquiry, to inform her of progress in this area.

24. In the event of an unforeseeable peak in review requests and the consequent delays, EPSO should consider quickly informing candidates who have submitted a request for review of possible delays. Communicating this information to candidates as soon as possible could help reduce the number of time-consuming individual requests for information EPSO receives about the procedure, and could free up resources for the actual handling of requests for review.

25. EPSO could at the same time indicate that it will give priority to replying to those requests for review which the selection board has deemed to be justified. This information could also be included in the information EPSO provides online regarding the request for review procedure (for example, in its general rules governing open competitions or on the FAQ page on its website).

Conclusion

The Ombudsman commends EPSO's efforts thus far on this issue and closes the inquiry with the following conclusion:

There are no grounds for further inquiries at present.

EPSO will be informed of this decision.

Suggestions for improvement

With a view to further improving the handling of requests for review, the Ombudsman suggests that EPSO:

1) Provide better support to selection boards so that they can give more detailed, and fact-based, reasons for their decisions on requests for review by

— revising the template ('fiche jury') used by selection boards to record their decisions;

— revising the guidance EPSO gives to selection boards on the practicalities involved in documenting decisions;

— providing additional training to selection board members on complaint handling and the practicalities of dealing with requests for review;

— giving greater responsibility to EPSO's permanent selection board members in coordinating how selection board decisions are recorded.

2) Further examine technological solutions to streamline the request for review procedure.

3) Take steps to estimate the number of requests for review it expects to receive and allocate staff resources accordingly.

4) Quickly inform candidates who have submitted a request for review of expected delays whenever there is an unforeseeable peak in requests. To help EPSO reconcile delays with its commitment to readmit candidates to the competition in the event of a positive reply, such a message to candidates could explain that EPSO will give priority to replying

to those candidates whose request for review has been successful. This information could also be included in the information EPSO provides online regarding the request for review procedure.

5) Include more information online on the request for review procedure, including information on the most commonly used unsuccessful arguments for requesting a review.

6) Report, on a regular basis, to its Management Board on the matter of requests for review and on any problems in their processing. The Management Board represents the EU institutions on behalf of which EPSO runs the selection competitions and should thus be made aware of any existing or potential problems in this area.

Notes

The excerpt above concerns a report published by the Ombudsman in response to an 'own-initiative' investigation which makes recommendations on a more systematic level in order to address issues of ongoing maladministration. This demonstrates that at the EU level, the Ombudsman may adopt an own-initiative investigation and may issue a report with broad systemic recommendations. The above excerpt also serves to demonstrate the importance of complaints even within this context, as it was the Ombudsman's realisation that the practice of the EPSO was generating a large number of complaints that ultimately triggered the own-initiative investigation.

10.3.A.4 (ii) France

Loi organique n° 2011-333 du 29 mars 2011 relative au Défenseur des droits **10.35 FR**

Article 25 The Defender of Rights may adopt any recommendation that he deems of a nature to guarantee the respect of the rights and freedoms of the aggrieved person and to address the grievances raised before him or to prevent their repetition.

He may recommend a settlement of the situation which was brought before him according to equity.

The authorities or persons concerned must inform the Defender of Rights, within the time limit he sets, of the action that was taken with regard to his recommendations.

In case of absence of information within this time limit, or if the Defender of Rights determines, with regard to the information received, that a recommendation has not been acted upon, the Defender of Rights may order the subject of the investigation to take the necessary measures within a time limit he sets.

When his order has not been acted upon, the Defender of Rights must draft a special report which is sent to the subject of the investigation. The Defender of Rights publishes this report and, if applicable, the reply of the subject of the investigation, in accordance with the conditions he determines.

Article 26 The Defender of Rights may amicably resolve the disputes that are brought to his attention through a process of mediation.

The observations made and the statements collected during the mediation may neither be produced nor invoked at a later stage before civil or administrative courts without the consent of the persons concerned, except if the disclosure of the agreement is necessary for its enforcement or if grounds of public order require so.

Article 29 The Defender of Rights may bring before the authority that is vested with the power to initiate disciplinary action the facts which he is aware of, and which seem to him of a nature to justify a sanction.

This authority must inform the Defender of Rights of the follow-up of its action and if it has not initiated any disciplinary proceedings, of the grounds of its decision.

In the case of absence of information within the time limit he sets, or if the Defender of Rights determines, with regard to the information received, that his request has not been followed by the necessary measures, the Defender of Rights may draft a special report which is sent to the authority specified under the first section. He may publish this report and, if applicable, the reply of this authority, in accordance with the conditions he determines.

The preceding section does not apply to the person that might be subject to the motion of the High Council of the Judiciary provided for in the penultimate section of Article 65 of the Constitution.

Article 36 (1) The Defender of Rights may, after having informed the subject of the investigation of it, decide to publish his opinions, recommendations or decisions with, if applicable, the reply of the subject of the investigation, in accordance with the conditions he determines.

(2) He submits, every year, to the President of the Republic, to the President of the National Assembly, and to the President of the Senate:

1. a report that gives account on his general activity and that comprises a thematic annex concerning each of his fields of competence listed in Article 4. This report is submitted before the 1st of June …

The reports referred to under number 1 … are published and may be subject of a communication by the Defender of Rights before any of the two chambers.

(3) The Defender of Rights may also submit any other report to the President of the Republic, to the President of the National Assembly, and to the President of the Senate. These reports are published.

Notes

(1) The Defender of Rights does not have the power to grant a legally enforceable remedy, but is empowered by Article 25 of the Organic Law to make recommendations in order to resolve the complaint received, protect the rights of a complainant and, on a broader systemic basis, prevent the issues that are the subject of the complaint from arising again. The recommendations should seek to ensure that the complainant's issues are resolved in an equitable manner (Article 25(2)). The recommendation must be accompanied by an appropriate time limit for implementation. If the recommendation is not followed, or if the Defender does not receive any indication that it will be followed within the time limit, the Defender may then make a formal request of the body concerned, requiring them to follow the recommendation Article 25(4). If this formal request is not followed, the Defender is empowered to make a special report, delivered to the body that is the subject of the complaint. The report is made public, along with any response received from the respondent to the complaint. Article 25(6). There is no scope for escalation of the report beyond making it

available to the public. In addition to the powers in Article 25, Article 29 of the Organic Law grants the Defender the power to recommend the institution of disciplinary proceedings where it is felt that these are justified. If the competent authority does not institute proceedings, or does not act within the time limit specified by the Defender, a special report can be made on a similar basis to that outlined by Article 25.

(2) Under Article 26 of the Organic Law, the Defender of Rights has the specific power to resolve disputes by mediating between the parties. This mediation and its results are not disclosed without the consent of the parties unless there are reasons of public policy or the disclosure is needed in order to secure the enforcement of the results of the mediation.

(3) Article 36 of the Organic Law permits the Defender of Rights to publish findings of investigations and recommendations, along with any responses received, as it sees fit. There is then a requirement for the Defender to make an annual report to the President and the presidents of both houses of the Parliament each year. These reports must cover all of its areas of activity and must be made public. Finally, the Defender of Rights may make other reports to the President and the presidents of each of the houses of Parliament on any other issue. These reports must also be made public. However, there is no formal mechanism for doing this if recommendations are not followed.

Décision du Défenseur des droits n° 2017-018, 21 Février 2017[53] **10.36 (FR)**

Facts: The claimant (a Chilean National) was refused a 10-year residence card because she was unable to provide proof of payment of residence tax. The claimant argued that such a requirement was not present in law, so should not be imposed in a case such as this.

Held: The requirement was considered unlawful and the authorities were requested to stop the practice of requiring such proof of payment.

Summary of Findings

The Defender of Rights has received a complaint concerning the refusal to issue a 10-year residence card to a Chilean national on the grounds that, as she was hosted for free by her employer, she was not able to provide a proof of payment of the residence tax in her name. Since such a condition is not provided for by law or by any regulatory text and the proof of residence provided for in the regulation in force can be provided by other means, this refusal is illegal and constitutes a violation of a right of a user of a public service. On these grounds, the Defender of Rights recommends to the competent prefectoral authority: – to re-examine the situation of the complainant with regard to the issuing of a resident card in conformity with the applicable regulations; – to end the

[53] Available at https://juridique.defenseurdesdroits.fr/#type=DEC&id=21215.

challenged practice by reminding the competent public agents, via an internal memo, of the applicable law and of the only documents that can be required in the context of an investigation concerning a request for a resident card, in accordance with Articles R314-1 and R314-1-1 of the Code de l'entrée et du séjour des ètrangers (Code of entry and stay of foreigners and of asylum law), with the circular of the Minister of the Interior of 3 January 2004 (NOR:INTK1400231C) and with the Guide de l'agent d'accueil des ressortissants étrangers en préfecture (Guide to civil servants dealing with foreign nationals in a prefecture) and specifying, also via an internal memo, that the proof of the payment of the residence tax mentioning the name of the applicant shall not be the only admissible document to show that the concerned party fulfils the requirement linked to the existence of an appropriate dwelling.

Note

This decision demonstrates that the Defender of Rights will intervene in cases where there is a substantive breach of the rights of a claimant, including the right to have an administrative procedure followed. This demonstrates some similarities with the approach in other jurisdictions, although there is a far greater focus on the need for an infringement of a right in the French system.

10.3.A.4 (iii) England and Wales

The Parliamentary Commissioner Act 1967[54] **10.37 (EW)**

10 Reports by Commissioner

(1) In any case where the Commissioner conducts an investigation under this Act or decides not to conduct such an investigation, he shall send to the member of the House of Commons by whom the request for investigation was made (or if he is no longer a member of that House, to such member of that House as the Commissioner thinks appropriate) a report of the results of the investigation or, as the case may be, a statement of his reasons for not conducting an investigation.

(2) In any case where the Commissioner conducts an investigation under section 5(1) of this Act, he shall also send a report of the results of the investigation to the principal officer of the department or authority concerned and to any other person who is alleged in the relevant complaint to have taken or authorised the action complained of.

...

(3) If, after conducting an investigation under section 5(1) of this Act, it appears to the Commissioner that injustice has been caused to the person aggrieved in consequence of maladministration and that the injustice has not been, or will not be, remedied, he may, if he thinks fit, lay before each House of Parliament a special report upon the case.

...

(4) The Commissioner shall annually lay before each House of Parliament a general report on the performance of his functions under this Act and may from time to time lay

[54] Chapter 13.

before each House of Parliament such other reports with respect to those functions as he thinks fit.

(5) For the purposes of the law of defamation, any such publication as is hereinafter mentioned shall be absolutely privileged, that is to say–

(a) the publication of any matter by the Commissioner in making a report to either House of Parliament for the purposes of this Act;

(b) the publication of any matter by a member of the House of Commons in communicating with the Commissioner or his officers for those purposes or by the Commissioner or his officers in communicating with such a member for those purposes;

(c) the publication by such a member to the person by whom a complaint was made under this Act of a report or statement sent to the member in respect of the complaint in pursuance of subsection (1) of this section;

(d) the publication by the Commissioner to such a person as is mentioned in subsection …

Notes

(1) The Parliamentary Commissioner cannot issue recommendations that are legally binding. Where an investigation is undertaken, the Commissioner produces a report including recommendations addressed to the public authority concerned and the public authority must then decide whether to comply with the recommendations that are made. A copy of the report must be provided to the Member of Parliament who referred the complaint and also to the principal officer of the department or body which is subject of the complaint, along with any other party who is subject of the complaint. If the public authority refuses to follow the recommendations of the Parliamentary Commissions, a special report may be issued to the Public Administration Select Committee in Parliament by virtue of section 10(3) of the Parliamentary Commissioner Act 1967 (1967 Act), which has the function of exerting political pressure on the authority concerned to comply with the report. Rates of compliance with recommendations of the Commissioner are remarkably high, with only seven special reports made since 1967.[55] In one case where the government declined to follow the recommendations of the Parliamentary Commissioner and aggrieved complainants have claimed judicial review of the decision not to comply with the recommendations, the Court of Appeal held that the recommendations could not be enforced through judicial review, but that there was an obligation incumbent on the relevant government department to give reasons for its decision not to follow the recommendations. The decision not to follow the recommendations could then be subject to substantive judicial review on grounds of rationality, although the claimants were not successful in their claim.[56]

(2) The system of issuing the report is interesting because the complainant is not entitled as a matter of law to receive a copy of the report that has been made – it is

[55] L Maer and M Everett, 'The Parliamentary Ombudsman: Role and Proposals for Reform' (House of Commons Library Research Briefing Paper CBP7496, 2016).

[56] *R (Bradley) v Secretary of State for Work and Pensions* [2008] EWCA Civ 36, [2009] QB 114 (CA).

instead to be provided to the Member of Parliament who made the referral. As a matter of practice, reports are usually made available to complainants, but this may not be the case if the report contains sensitive information. It is also important to note that the Parliamentary Commissioner does not enjoy a general power to disclose all reports to the public, although summaries of reports are sometimes published and made available online.[57]

(3) In cases where a number of complaints are made in relation to a particular body or there are issues of particular public interest, a more detailed report might be published, as arose recently in the cases of the Driver and Vehicle Licensing Agency and its management of those who have medical conditions that might impact on their ability to drive,[58] or the cases of home owners who faced compulsory acquisition of their homes by the state-owned company that is charged with building the High Speed 2 rail line.[59] Such reports are published under the power contained in section 10(4) of the 1967 Act and are much more substantial and detailed than the case summaries published online. In addition to these reports, the Parliamentary Commissioner is required to lay an annual report before Parliament each year, outlining the activities undertaken each year. These reports also contain useful summaries of the major investigations completed in that year.

Parliamentary Commissioner for Administration
Case Summary 938, May 2015[60] **10.38 (EW)**

Facts: Due to an error by the UK Visas and Immigration service, an elderly woman who was entitled to return to the UK as she had been granted indefinite leave to remain was prevented from returning to the UK and was left stranded in Eastern Europe. This necessitated family members travelling out to Eastern Europe in order to care for the lady, leading them to engage in significant expenditure so that they could do so. The family complained that they had been the victims of maladministration. The issue was whether the actions of the UK Visa and Immigration service constituted maladministration.

Held: There had been maladministration and an apology, and compensation had to be granted accordingly.

What happened

Mrs P was an East European citizen who had indefinite leave to enter the UK. When she and her late husband visited Eastern Europe in 2009, he became ill and could not travel back to the UK. After Mr P's death in 2013, Mrs P applied to return to the UK to live with her daughter and son-in-law but her application was refused on the basis that she did not meet paragraph 18 of the Immigration Rules because she had been away from the UK for more than two years. The entry clearance officer also said she did not meet paragraph 19 because she had only lived in the UK for fifteen months. Mrs P was severely sight impaired with a number of other diagnosed health problems. Her daughter

[57] These can be found at www.ombudsman.org.uk/about-us/how-our-casework-makes-difference/case-summaries.

[58] Parliamentary and Health Service Ombudsman, *Driven to Despair* (2016, HC 660).

[59] Parliamentary and Health Service Ombudsman, *Report on an Investigation into complaints about High Speed Two Limited* (2015, HC 620).

[60] Available at www.ombudsman.org.uk/about-us/how-our-casework-makes-difference/case-summaries/938.

and son-in-law were not able to remain with her in Eastern Europe and were extremely anxious about her health and welfare. Mrs P's grandson had to go to Eastern Europe to care for her. UKVI reviewed its decision six weeks later and revoked the refusal, granting her a returning resident visa.

What we found

UKVI [UK Visas and Immigration service] did not properly and fully consider Mrs P's application at first. It should have taken into account Mrs P's strong ties with the UK and the fact that her stay in Eastern Europe was prolonged through no fault of her own. We found that, on the balance of probabilities, had UKVI acted properly, it would have granted Mrs P a visa. We found that Mrs P's daughter and son-in-law experienced a lot of stress and anxiety because of UKVI's failings and they incurred financial losses. This included loss of income for Mrs P's daughter, travel and other expenses involved in extra journeys to Eastern Europe to care for Mrs P. We also found that they had to employ a solicitor to prepare for an appeal (the decision was revoked before the appeal was heard), which also involved additional expense.

Putting it right

UKVI accepted our findings, apologised and paid Mrs P's daughter, son-in-law and grandson £3,429 in respect of their additional expenses. It also made a consolatory payment of £500 to Mrs P, her daughter and son-in-law in recognition of the distress and anxiety caused.

Note

The excerpt above demonstrates the approach that is adopted by the Parliamentary Commissioner in investigations of complaints against government bodies. It is notable that each of the summaries and reports where maladministration is found contain a clear section on 'putting it right' in accordance with the *Principles of Good Administration* discussed in section 10.3.A.3 (i) part ii above. This will include financial compensation where there is evidence of loss and the requirement of an apology is usually imposed.

10.3.A.4 (iv) The Netherlands

Algemene Wet Bestuursrecht **10.39 (NL)**

Article 9:27 …

(3) The Ombudsman may make recommendations to the administrative authority based on his investigation.

Article 9:36 (1) After closing an investigation, the Ombudsman shall prepare a report, in which he lays down his findings and his opinion.

…

(4) If the Ombudsman makes a recommendation as referred to in Article 9:27(3) to the administrative authority, the latter shall inform the Ombudsman within a reasonable time what action will be taken on the recommendation. If the administrative authority considers not following the recommendation, it shall communicate this to the Ombudsman, stating reasons.

Report of the National Ombudsman, 21 December 2015[61] **10.40 (NL)**

Facts: On 1 September 2013, the Municipality of Leiden abolished the possibility for citizens to pay at a service desk in cash. From that date, it was only possible to pay electronically. In 2013, 12 complaints were filed against this decision and a further five were made in 2014. Therefore, the National Ombudsman started an investigation in respect of the question whether some citizens would encounter problems if municipalities would accept electronic payments only.

Held: The decision to accept electronic payments only was considered inconsistent with the requirement of an individualised approach and is therefore improper.

Report

The Ombudsman assesses whether the municipal choice of allowing electronic payment only is consistent with the requirements of proper administration. In this case, the Ombudsman applies the requirement of an individualised approach. It is a requirement of proper administration according to which the authorities are willing to depart from general policies or rules in order to prevent unintended or undesirable consequences. This *inter alia* implies that the authorities, after switching over to electronic payments, still should offer the opportunity to pay by other means, besides paying electronically, to those who cannot or do not want to pay electronically.

... The Municipality where a citizen resides is the only institution where citizens may apply for certain documents, such as an extract from the population register, an identity card or a driving licence. These documents are indispensable in societal relations.

... Some citizens are not able to pay (independently) by electronic means. In respect of those citizens, the choice for electronic payments only has rendered excessively difficult the access to the public authority and obtainment of documents. The accessibility of the municipality has been restricted too far. ... Therefore the National Ombudsman is of the opinion that the choice to accept electronic payments only is improper.

Recommendation

The National Ombudsman recommends informing citizens clearly of what steps they should take should they want to pay in cash.

Report of the National Ombudsman, 7 January 2015[62] **10.41 (NL)**

Facts: The complainants filed a complaint against the negative advice of the Commission of Experts on Public Notaries in respect of the business plan filed by Mrs B, in order to operate a notary's office in the municipality X.

Held: The complaint regarding the action investigated was considered to be well founded on the ground of a violation of the requirement of transparency.

Report

In sum, the National Ombudsman is of the opinion that the Commission, by communicating in the advisory stage the requirements for the business plan in an insufficiently clear way, has acted in violation of the requirement of transparency.

Conclusion

The complaint regarding the action of the Commission of Experts on Public Notaries is well-founded on the ground of a violation of the requirement of transparency.

[61] No 2015/172, AB 2016/99.
[62] No 2015/004, AB 2015/150.

Recommendation

The National Ombudsman suggests to the Commission of Experts to consider compensating, for reasons of leniency, the amount of money that was paid by complainant for obtaining the advice.

Notes

(1) After closing an investigation, the Ombudsman prepares a report, in which he lays down his findings and his opinion. The opinion is either that the action investigated was improper or that it was not improper. In the former case, the Ombudsman is obliged to state which requirement of properness has been violated. In addition, the Ombudsman may make a recommendation to the administrative authority based on his investigation (Article 9:27(3) AWB).

(2) Recommendations are either individual or structural. Individual recommendations contain advice to the authority on how to remedy the violation of a standard of proper administration in a specific case. In practice, individual recommendations may suggest that the authority should reconsider a decision taken, to compensate damages sustained,[63] to have an open discussion about the issue with complainants, to apologise for certain conduct, etc. In structural recommendations, the Ombudsman advises the authority to adapt working processes in order to prevent future violations of certain standards. An example is the recommendation to the municipal authorities to inform citizens on how they can pay in cash for certain municipal services.[64] Other structural recommendations may be concerned with the formulation of an official document or application process, active communication with citizens, the question of when and how to use telephone contact, etc. Structural recommendations may form the basis for a guidance document.[65]

(3) The Ombudsman's opinion and possible recommendations are not binding upon the authorities. An authority is obliged to inform the Ombudsman within a reasonable time in respect of the action it will take on a recommendation. Moreover, if the authority considers that it will not follow a recommendation, it shall communicate this to the Ombudsman (Article 9:36(4) AWB). However, in the latter case, neither citizens nor the Ombudsman have at their disposal any legal means to enforce the recommendation. Nevertheless, in practice, compliance with the Ombudsman's recommendations is high, on average 92%.[66] This compliance rate can be explained by the authority of the National Ombudsman and, arguably, by the reasonableness of its opinions. In addition, the special relationship between the National Ombudsman and the Parliament may be of importance. As stated in section 10.3.A.1 (iv) above, the National Ombudsman is appointed by the Second Chamber of the Parliament. Every year, he submits to both chambers of the Parliament an annual report, which includes a detailed analysis of his work during the past year and highlights several particular

[63] See excerpt 10.41.
[64] See excerpt 10.40.
[65] See excerpt 10.28 above.
[66] Remac (n 28 above) 33, based on the annual reports of the National Ombudsman, 2008–2012.

issues concerning the relation between the authorities and the citizens. Moreover, he may also send a report of a specific case to the Second Chamber. The annual report or specific report might be reason for the Parliament to force the government to follow the Ombudsman's opinion or recommendation. The annual report and all reports in particular cases are available to the press and the public at large, as they are published on the internet. Therefore, public pressure may enhance compliance with the Ombudsman's reports as well.

10.3.A.4 (v) Comparative Remarks

As with many other parts of the analysis of Ombudsmen, the systems show considerable similarity in their approach. In the EU, England and Wales and the Netherlands, there is a very strong link between the Ombudsman and the relevant parliament. While it is not possible for any of these Ombudsmen to require compliance with their recommendations, this link to parliament and general respect for the decisions of the Ombudsmen within the relevant administrative systems mean that the rates of compliance with recommendations are very high. In the European and Dutch systems, it is possible to have 'own-initiative' investigations, where the recommendations are systemic and designed to address deficiencies in the administrative process, rather than to deal with individual complaints. A similar power is available to the Defender of Rights in France, but, as the institution is relatively new, it is difficult to assess the impact of this power at present. In England and Wales, the Parliamentary Commissioner lacks the power to conduct an 'own-initiative' investigation, although the disadvantage that this might bring in terms of remedies that can address systemic failings is questionable, as the Parliamentary Commissioner can issue a special report under section 10(4) of the 1967 Act and has often used this power to make systemic recommendations where a significant number of complaints have been received about a particular body or area of activity.[67]

The French system offers the potential for the Defender of Rights to make recommendations, to mediate a solution between the parties and also to seek disciplinary action against public officials deemed to be at fault. However, the effectiveness of these remedies may be open to question as none of them can be legally mandated and, although Article 36 of the Organic Law provides some link both with the President and the Parliament, along with publicity, the work of the Defender of Rights does not appear to enjoy the same level impact within the administrative system as the work of the other Ombudsmen, although this could be because the institution is relatively new in its current form when compared with the Ombudsmen in the other systems.

10.3.A.5 THE 'SYSTEM SURVEILLANCE' ROLE OF THE OMBUDSMAN

It has been argued throughout this chapter that Ombudsmen may have a dual role. The predominant part of the role is to deal with complaints from members of the public and

[67] As in the case of *Driven to Despair* (n 62 above).

to make recommendations in cases that are investigated in order to offer redress of grievance. The second role could be described as a 'system surveillance' role, whereby the Ombudsman might examine particular bodies or areas of administrative activity in order to improve administrative practice or consider issues of significant underperformance. This section will examine the scope for such 'system surveillance' in each of the systems under consideration.

10.3.A.5 (i) The European Union

Decision of the European Ombudsman adopting Implementing Provisions **10.42 (EU)**

Article 8 Own-initiative inquiries

8.1. The Ombudsman shall conduct own-initiative inquiries for which the Ombudsman finds grounds.

8.2. The procedures applicable to inquiries opened following a complaint shall apply, to the extent that they are relevant, to own-initiative inquiries.

Note

It is clear from Article 228(1) TFEU that the Ombudsman enjoys a power of own-initiative investigation. This is a very valuable tool that allows the Ombudsman to undertake a systematic investigation of administration in areas where there may be concern. It is important to emphasise that relatively few own-initiative investigations are launched each year, with 10–20 being a typical number.[68] Within this category of own-initiative inquiries, the Ombudsman draws a distinction between own-initiative inquiries launched because a complaint has been received from an individual who is not a citizen of the Union (so-called technical own-initiative inquiries) and strategic own-initiative inquiries, where the Ombudsman launches an investigation due to concerns about administration in relation to a particular issue, or in relation to a particular institution. Strategic inquiries are launched less frequently, perhaps numbering no more than five in an average year.[69]

10.3.A.5 (ii) France

Loi organique n° 2011-333 du 29 mars 2011 relative au Défenseur des droits **10.43 (FR)**

Article 36 (1) The Defender of Rights may, after having informed the subjects of the investigation of it, decide to publish his opinions, recommendations or decisions with, if applicable, the reply of the implicated person, in accordance with the conditions he determines.

[68] This figure is determined through an examination of the annual reports of the European Ombudsman over the past ten years.

[69] ibid.

(2) He submits, every year, to the President of the Republic, to the President of the National Assembly, and to the President of the Senate:

1. a report that accounts on his general activity and that comprises a thematic annex regarding each of his fields of competence listed in Article 4 ...;

2. a report dedicated to the rights of the child on the occasion of the international day of the rights of the child.

The reports referred to under number 1 ... are published and may be the subject of a message of the Defender of Rights before any of the two chambers.

10.3. – The Defender of Rights may also submit any other report to the President of the Republic, to the President of the National Assembly, and to the President of the Senate. These reports are published.

Note

The excerpt above demonstrates that the Defender of Rights has the power to act without referral of a complaint. However, there is relatively little evidence that the Defender has so far acted to engage in a significant level of system oversight. There are two reports that could be considered to address broader systemic issues rather than individual complaints, but these are presently somewhat exceptional.[70]

10.3.A.5 (iii) England and Wales

The Parliamentary Commissioner's 'system surveillance' role is limited, as there is no power to undertake an 'own initiative' investigation. It is possible that the Parliamentary Commissioner can lay a report before Parliament on a matter not directly related to a complaint received under the powers in section 10(4) of the 1967 Act but this would not include the power to undertake investigation in the absence of a complaint. In the proposed reform of the Ombudsman, the government does not support the granting of a power of 'own-initiative' investigation.[71] As noted above, the impact of this lack of 'own-initiative' investigation is likely to be limited, given the large number of complaints that the Parliamentary Commissioner receives each year, as these will give data on the bodies and areas of activity with the great number of complaints and thus permit investigation of these, with the potential to issue a section 10(4) report if systemic issues are discovered.

[70] See, eg *Enquête sur l'accès aux droits: Volume 2 – Relations des usagères et usagers avec les services publics: le risque du non-recours* (Paris, Defenseur des Droits, 2017), available at www.defenseurdesdroits.fr/sites/default/files/atoms/files/enquete-relations-usagers-servpublics-v6-29.03.17_0.pdf; *Rapport d'observation: démantèlement des campements et prise en charge des exilés* (Paris, Defenseur des Droits, 2016), available at https://defenseurdesdroits.fr/sites/default/files/atoms/files/rapp-demantelement-v6.pdf.

[71] *Draft Public Service Ombudsman Bill* (n 25 above), where no power of own-initiative investigation has been included.

10.3.A.5 (iv) The Netherlands

Algemene Wet Bestuursrecht **10.44 (NL)**

Article 9:26 Unless Article 9:22 applies, the Ombudsman may of his own initiative start an investigation into the manner in which an administrative authority conducted itself in a particular matter.

Notes

(1) The 'system surveillance' role of the Ombudsman in the Netherlands is of huge importance. In this respect, the Ombudsman is allowed to start an investigation of his own initiative. The investigation powers in such investigations are the same as those in investigations on complaint. Investigations of his own initiative may be conducted when the Ombudsman has received signals from citizens, journalists, social workers, whistleblowers, lawyers, etc on a possible instance of structural maladministration in the central government or in a local authority. Own-initiative investigations are not very frequent, but they are influential. In practice, the National Ombudsman conducts such investigations ten times per year on average.[72]

(2) The 'system surveillance' role is also visible in the National Ombudsman's practice of combining several complaints regarding a certain issue in one investigation, which then leads to an opinion regarding both the individual complaints and the structural problems underlying them. Moreover, in recent years, the National Ombudsman has sometimes opened a complaint line in the course of an investigation of his own initiative, urging citizens to bring to his attention instances of maladministration concerning a certain issue. This is an effective means of gathering relevant facts regarding areas where there may be a systemic problem.

10.3.A.5 (v) Comparative Remarks

In the Netherlands and the European Union, we can see the way in which a 'system surveillance' role has been designed into the operation of the system, as the Ombudsmen have the power of 'own-initiative' investigation. The reality is that these powers are used relatively infrequently when compared with the number of investigations into complaints that are undertaken, but these powers may serve an important purpose in allowing investigations into areas where there could be systemic problems that need to be addressed. The French Defender of Rights enjoys a similar power to undertake own-initiative investigations, but this appears to have been seldom used so far.

The situation in England and Wales differs because there is no power for the PCA to undertake an investigation in the absence of a complaint. However, the importance of

[72] Langbroek et al (n 36 above) 134.

this issue should not be overstated because through the use of the power to issue special reports in section 10(4) of the 1967 Act, the Parliamentary Commissioner is still able to issue special reports into particular issues. The absence of an ability to engage in an own-initiative investigation may not be significant in these circumstances because a great deal of the data that any Ombudsman will use to determine whether there are systemic problems suitable for investigation will be drawn from the complaints that are received.

10.3.A.6 JUDICIAL REVIEW OF THE OMBUDSMAN

The final issue that will be considered in this section of the chapter will be the extent to which Ombudsmen are subject to judicial control. If it is possible for both complainants and public bodies to pursue frequent judicial review claims against the Ombudsman or to bring an action in damages against the Ombudsman, then this might have a significant impact on the effectiveness of the work that the ombudsman is to undertake. However, it might be argued that it is important for Ombudsmen to be accountable and that, although the recommendations do not have legal effect, they can have significant practical impact and should thus be subject to judicial control in certain circumstances.

10.3.A.6 (i) The European Union

Case T-103/99, 22 May 2000[73] **10.45 (EU)**

Associazione delle Cantine Sociali Venete v European Ombudsman and European Parliament

FAILURE TO ACT; JUDICIAL REVIEW OF OMBUDSMAN

Associazione delle Cantine Sociali Venete

The European Ombudsman is not subject to judicial review for failure to act.

Facts: The claimant organisation requested access to certain documents held by the Commission and the request was refused. The claimant organisation then complained to the European Ombudsman, arguing that the Commission's refusal constituted maladministration. The Ombudsman undertook an inquiry, sent the Commission's opinion to the claimant and sought the claimant's response. The claimant then wrote to the Ombudsman seeking the Ombudsman's definitive opinion on the issue, which was not provided within the requisite two-month period. The claimant sought judicial review of the Ombudsman's alleged failure to act. The issue in this case was whether the Ombudsman could be subject to judicial review for failure to act in a case such as this.

Held: The court held that the Ombudsman could not be subject to judicial review for failure to act.

Judgment: 43. According to the third paragraph of Article 175 of the Treaty, [a]ny natural or legal person may, under the conditions laid down in the preceding paragraphs,

[73] ECLI:EU:T:2000:135.

complain to the [Court of First Instance] that an institution of the Community has failed to address to that person any act other than a recommendation or an opinion.

44. According to Article 4 of the Treaty, the realisation of the tasks entrusted to the Community are to be carried out by the European Parliament, the Council, the Commission, the Court of Justice and the Court of Auditors. Each of these institutions is to act within the limits of the powers conferred on it by the EC Treaty. In addition, the Treaty provides for a European Central Bank (Article 4a of the EC Treaty (now Article 8 EC)) and also for a European Investment Bank (Article 4b of the Treaty (now Article 9 EC)), which are also to act within the limits of the powers and responsibilities conferred on them by the Treaty and the statutes annexed to it.

45. Lastly, under Article 11(4) of Decision 94/262, in matters concerning his staff, the Ombudsman shall have the same status as the institutions within the meaning of Article 1 of the Staff Regulations of Officials of the European Communities.

46. It follows from these provisions that the Ombudsman is not a Community institution within the meaning of Article 175 of the Treaty, so that the application, to the extent that it refers to a failure to act on the Ombudsman's part, must be declared inadmissible.

Notes

(1) Although the above case concerned failure to act on the part of the Ombudsman, the provisions of Article 263 TFEU concerning judicial review of acts of the institutions are worded in a similar fashion, so judicial review of acts of the Ombudsman is also likely to be precluded. This argument appears to be strengthened as Article 263(1) refers to the CJEU's ability to 'review the legality of acts of bodies, offices or agencies of the Union intended to produce legal effects vis-à-vis third parties'. As the Ombudsman's findings do not have legal effect, such review would appear to be precluded.

(2) It has been held that the Ombudsman could face liability in an action for damages under EU law. However, in order for such a claim to be successful, it would be necessary to demonstrate that the Ombudsman has made a manifest error in the performance of his duties.[74] Such actions are seldom likely to be successful, given the broad discretion offered to the Ombudsman in terms of methods of investigation and recommendation of remedies.

10.3.A.6 (ii) France

In France, it is not possible for the Defenseur des Droits to be subject to judicial review or actions for damages.

[74] Case C-234/02 P *Lamberts v Ombudsman* ECLI:EU:C:2004:174.

10.3.A.6 (iii) England and Wales

High Court (Queen's Bench Division), 19 October 1993[75] **10.46 (EW)**

R v Parliamentary Commissioner for Administration, ex parte Dyer

JUDICIAL REVIEW OF OMBUDSMAN

Dyer

The Parliamentary Commissioner for Administration is subject to judicial review, although the courts will generally be reluctant to intervene.

Facts: Miss Dyer made a complaint to the Parliamentary Commissioner for Administration regarding the handling of her claims for invalidity benefit and a number of other state benefits. The Parliamentary Commissioner found maladministration and recommended that Miss Dyer be paid £500 compensation and receive an apology. Miss Dyer claimed judicial review of the Parliamentary Commissioner's conduct of the investigation, refusal to show Miss Dyer the draft report and refusal to reopen the investigation and hear further complaints was unlawful. The main issue in this case was whether and in what circumstances the Parliamentary Commissioner could be subject to judicial review.

Held: The Parliamentary Commissioner was considered subject to judicial review, although the circumstances in which a decision of the Parliamentary Commissioner might be found to be unlawful are limited.

Judgment: Simon Brown LJ: … Although, as stated, her challenge in form is directed to the Commissioner's refusal to re-open his investigation, that is but one of her complaints; in substance she challenges the manner in which the Commissioner carried out the original investigation. Put shortly, the main criticisms which she directs at the Commissioner are these: First, that he investigated some only of her original complaints, omitting several which she regarded as of importance (and in one instance investigating an earlier problem about which she was no longer complaining). Second, that although he gave the department an opportunity to comment upon the report in draft he gave her no such opportunity. Third, that he refused to re-open the investigation when, after reading the final report, she pointed out his failure to consider a number of her complaints, and, indeed, wrongly regarded himself as precluded from re-opening it.

This is the first substantive application for judicial review of the Commissioner to come before the courts, an application for leave in an earlier case having been refused. The first question raised for decision upon it concerns the proper ambit of this court's supervisory jurisdiction over the Commissioner. Mr. Stephen Richards on his behalf submits to us that, certainly so far as the Commissioner's discretionary powers are concerned, this court has no review jurisdiction whatever over their exercise. In the alternative he submits that the court should intervene only in the most exceptional cases of abuse of discretion, essentially on the same limited basis held by the House of Lords in *Reg. v. Secretary of State for the Environment, Ex parte Nottinghamshire County Council* [1986] A.C. 240 and *Reg. v. Secretary of State for the Environment, Ex parte Hammersmith and Fulham London Borough Council* [1991] 1 A.C. 521, to be appropriate in the particular area of decision-making there in question.

…

Shortly after the Act of 1967 came into force, we are told, a House of Commons Select Committee on the Parliamentary Commissioner for Administration was appointed

[75] [1994] 1 WLR 621 (QB).

specifically with regard to the Commissioner, to examine his reports and consider any matters in connection with them.

As to his wider proposition, that this court has literally no right to review the Commissioner's exercise of his discretion under the Act of 1967 (not even, to give the classic illustration, if he refused to investigate complaints by red-headed complainants), Mr. Richards submits that the legislation is enacted in such terms as to indicate an intention that the Commissioner should be answerable to Parliament alone for the way he performs his functions. The Commissioner is, he suggests, an officer of the House of Commons, and, the argument runs, the Parliamentary control provided for by the statute displaces any supervisory control by the courts. Mr. Richards relies in particular on these considerations: first, the stipulation under section 5 that a complaint must be referred to the Commissioner by a member of Parliament before ever his powers of investigation are engaged; second, the requirement under section 10(1) to report back to the member of Parliament (and, in certain circumstances, to each House of Parliament: see section 10(3)); third, the requirement under section 10(4) annually to lay a general report before Parliament; fourth, the provision under section 1(3) of the Act for the Commissioner's removal from office only in the event of addresses from both Houses of Parliament. Mr. Richards points also to the Commissioner being always answerable to the Select Committee.

Despite these considerations, I for my part, would unhesitatingly reject this argument. Many in government are answerable to Parliament and yet answerable also to the supervisory jurisdiction of this court. I see nothing about the Commissioner's role or the statutory framework within which he operates so singular as to take him wholly outside the purview of judicial review.

All that said, however, and despite my rejection of both Mr. Richards' submissions on the question of jurisdiction, it does not follow that this court will readily be persuaded to interfere with the exercise of the Commissioner's discretion. Quite the contrary. The intended width of these discretions is made strikingly clear by the legislature: under section 5(5), when determining whether to initiate, continue or discontinue an investigation, the Commissioner shall 'act in accordance with his own discretion;' under section 7(2), 'the procedure for conducting an investigation shall be such as the Commissioner considers appropriate in the circumstances of the case.' Bearing in mind too that the exercise of these particular discretions inevitably involves a high degree of subjective judgment, it follows that it will always be difficult to mount an effective challenge on what may be called the conventional ground of Wednesbury unreasonableness (*Associated Provincial Picture Houses Ltd. v. Wednesbury Corporation* [1948] 1 K.B. 223).

Recognising this, indeed, one may pause to wonder whether in reality the end result is much different from that arrived at by the House of Lords in the two cases referred to, where the decisions in question were held 'not open to challenge on the grounds of irrationality short of the extremes of bad faith, improper motive or manifest absurdity.' True, in the present case 'manifest absurdity' does not have to be shown; but inevitably it will be almost as difficult to demonstrate that the Commissioner has exercised one or other of his discretions unreasonably in the public law sense.

Notes

(1) This case confirms the principle that, as a creature of statute and exercising discretionary power granted by statute, the Parliamentary Commissioner is subject to

judicial review. Relatively few judicial review claims have been brought and very few have been successful. In the first claim for judicial review against the Parliamentary Commissioner, the claimant sought a mandatory order[76] to oblige the Parliamentary Commissioner to investigate a complaint where he had declined to do so. The Court of Appeal held that a mandatory order would not be granted as the Parliamentary Commissioner enjoys a broad discretion in section 5(1) of the Parliamentary Commissioner Act 1967 to decide which cases to investigate.[77] There have been three successful claims for judicial review against the Parliamentary Commissioner arising in the *Balchin* investigation, which was an investigation into 'planning blight' and compensation where the value of property was impacted by the grant of planning permission for a new road. In the first case, it was held that the Parliamentary Commissioner had not considered all of the relevant factors in his report;[78] in the two subsequent cases, it was held that the report did not disclose adequate reasons for the Parliamentary Commissioner's findings on particular issues.[79] Ultimately, the approach is that the Parliamentary Commissioner is subject to judicial review, but in most cases, and particularly where the Parliamentary Commissioner is exercising a discretionary power, such as the power to recommend remedies, to open or reopen an investigation or to investigate only some of a number of complaints put forward by the complainant claims for judicial review are unlikely to be successful.

(2) It is possible that the findings of the Parliamentary Commissioner and the information contained in the Parliamentary Commissioner's reports can be relied upon as evidence in judicial review proceedings.[80] However, the fact that the Parliamentary Commissioner has found maladministration in relation to a particular issue does not necessarily mean that a judicial review claim in respect of the same point will be successful, given the different standards being applied by the courts and the Ombudsman.

10.3.A.6 (iv) The Netherlands

As explained in section 10.3.A.4 (iv), the report of the Ombudsman is not binding and does not have legal consequences. Therefore, it does not qualify as a decision as defined in Article 1:3 AWB[81] that can be contested before the administrative court.[82] In theory, a citizen may start a lawsuit before a civil court, claiming that the Ombudsman report or the investigation qualifies as tort in the meaning of Article 6:162 of the Civil Code. As yet, however, no such claim has ever been filed in practice.[83]

[76] On this type of remedy, see Chapter 7, section 7.3.B.1.
[77] *Re Fletcher's Application* [1970] 2 All ER 527.
[78] *R v Parliamentary Commissioner for Administration, ex parte Balchin (No 1)* [1998] 1 PLR 1 (QB).
[79] *R v Parliamentary Commissioner for Administration, ex parte Balchin (No 2)* (2000) 2 LGLR 87 (QB); *R v Parliamentary Commissioner for Administration, ex parte Balchin (No 3)* [2002] EWHC 1876 (Admin).
[80] See, eg *R (Elias) v Secretary of State for Defence* [2006] EWCA Civ 1293, [2006] 1 WLR 3213.
[81] On this concept, see Chapter 3, section 3.1.A.1.
[82] ECLI:NL:RVS:1987:AD4181.
[83] Remac (n 28 above) 52.

In addition, it should be noted that, as a matter of principle, the courts are not bound by the Ombudsman's assessment of an authority's conduct. This flows from the fact that the Ombudsman's standard of assessment – 'improperness' – is not the same as finding the action to be unlawful.[84] Therefore, the courts are not bound by the conclusion of the Ombudsman that a certain conduct was 'improper'.[85] On the other hand, the fact-finding in an Ombudsman's report might have some evidential force in court proceedings.

10.3.A.6 (v) Comparative Remarks

This section has considered the amenability of Ombudsmen to judicial review. In the European Union, France and the Netherlands. it is not possible for the Ombudsman to be subject to judicial review, given the characterisation of the Ombudsman in France and the EU and of its decisions in the Netherlands. In England and Wales, it is possible for the Ombudsman to be subject to judicial review, but the impact of this is limited as there have been very few claims and the general approach of the courts has been to offer the Parliamentary Commissioner for Administration a broad margin of appreciation in the exercise of discretionary powers. In the European Union, there is also the potential for the Ombudsman to be liable in an action for damages, and this may well also be the case in some of the other systems under examination, although this issue is not something that has been explored in the jurisprudence. However, it appears unlikely that such liability would flow on a frequent basis, given the wide discretion enjoyed by Ombudsmen in their investigatory powers and recommendations as to remedy.

10.3.B SYSTEMS WITH NO GENERAL OMBUDSMAN: GERMANY

In Germany, there is no general Ombudsman at the federal level. The prevailing opinion is that, due to the functioning administrative judicial review system and the constitutional right to petition (Article 17 of the Grundgesetz), no general Ombudsman is needed in Germany.[86] Nonetheless, two states, namely Rhineland-Palatinate and Schleswig-Holstein, have introduced Ombudsmen (Bürgerbeauftragte). Their task is to strengthen the position of the citizens in their interaction with the authorities. They also have the right to petition the public authorities and the legislature.[87]

There are, however, numerous Ombudsmen for specific administrative fields. For example, there is an Ombudsman for data protection (Datenschutzbeauftragter) and an

[84] See section 10.3.A.3 (i) part iii above.

[85] ECLI:NL:RBSGR:1994:AW2685, 36; ECLI:NL:CRVB:2006:AX3238.

[86] H Pünder, 'Wahlrecht und Parlamentsrecht als Gelingensbedingungen repräsentativer Demokratie' (2013) 72 *Veröffentlichung der Vereinigung der Deutschen Staatsrechtslehrer* 191, 247–48; HP Bull and V Mehde, *Allgemeines Verwaltungsrecht mit Verwaltungslehre*, 9th edn (Heidelberg, Hüthig Jehle Rehm, 2015) para 412; W Kahl, 'Grundzüge des Verwaltungsrechts in gemeineuropäischer Perspektive: Deutschland' in A Bogdandy, S Cassese and PM Huber (eds), *Handbuch Ius Publicum Europaeum* (Heidelberg, CF Müller, 2014) §74, para 139.

[87] See §§1 and 2 of the Landesgesetz über den Bürgerbeauftragten des Landes Rheinland-Pfalz und den Beauftragten für die Landespolizei; §§1 and 2 of the Gesetz über die Bürgerbeauftragte oder den Bürgerbeauftragten für soziale Angelegenheiten des Landes Schleswig-Holstein.

Ombudsperson for gender equality (Gleichstellungsbeauftragter). They are supposed to control administrative behaviour in their particular field of action. Furthermore, there are internal representatives, who have specific control tasks, such as the 'budget officer' (Beauftragter für den Haushalt) in the Federal Ministries.[88] However, Ombudsmen play a minor role as a redress mechanism in German law.

10.4 COMPARATIVE OVERVIEW

In each system under examination, there is an endeavour to provide forms of non-judicial grievance redress. The extent to which non-judicial mechanisms are embraced turns upon the nature and history of the administrative system and the approach to judicial redress of grievance. In Germany, there is a strong culture of judicial protection from the administrative courts, and access to this mechanism for those with a grievance is readily available. As such, alternative methods of redress have less prominence in the German system, although the right of petition contained in Article 17 of the Constitution should not be ignored as a means of redress.[89] It is also notable that, due to the judicial protection available in Germany, there has been less impetus to develop a strong system of protection from Ombudsmen, though these have been developed in some states (*Länder*) and in some sectors. A similar pattern exists in France, where judicial protection has generally been strong and readily available, so complaints mechanisms and an Ombudsman, while undoubtedly enjoying greater prominence than in Germany, have not developed to the same extent that they have in the Netherlands or England and Wales. Although the original Ombudsman (the Mediateur de la République) was created in France in 1973, this institution did not develop the same prominence and influence in the French administrative system as the Parliamentary Commissioner for Administration has garnered in England and Wales. The creation of the Defender of Rights does not appear to have created a significant change in this position, at least so far. It is interesting, however, to see that complaints processes have become more significant, and, indeed, have become mandatory in some areas (largely where there is the potential for a large number of disputes), demonstrating a desire to reduce the number of cases and the judicial workload in the administrative courts.

The system in England and Wales might be argued to have developed from a rather different starting point. Although judicial review has always been available to correct errors of law made by administrative authorities, judicial review is less accessible than in France, Germany or the Netherlands because of the high costs of bringing a claim.[90] Further, the desire of the courts to ensure that all other avenues of redress have been pursued before hearing a judicial review claim means that there are significantly fewer judicial review claims in England and Wales than in the other systems under examination. In addition to the courts, there are also tribunals,[91] although these are available only

[88] Bundeshaushaltsordnung, §9.
[89] See Stelkens (n 14 above).
[90] On the costs of proceedings in the English legal system, see Chapter 4, section 4.9.
[91] On the English Tribunals, see Chapter 2, section 2.2.B.1 (ii).

on a sectoral basis where Parliament has provided a tribunal with jurisdiction, so this is not a universal means of grievance redress. This, combined with a government ideology developed during the years of the Conservative government of Margaret Thatcher from 1979 to 1991 and then further developed by later governments has led to a culture of customer service in the provision of public services. This has necessitated the corresponding development of a complaints culture that supports this approach to the delivery of public services.[92] The result of this has been a stronger culture of dealing with grievances through the use of complaints mechanisms and a judicial approach that generally demands that such processes have been exhausted before a judicial review claim will be heard. Despite the importance of complaints processes in England and Wales, there is still little uniformity in the handling of complaints, and it is acknowledged that the quality of complaints handling throughout government is somewhat variable. The Ombudsman in England and Wales has also developed a stronger presence than in some other systems because the concept of 'maladministration' covers many issues that do not overlap with the principle of legality. Particularly given that the principle of legality and the tools available to the courts in their judicial review jurisdiction have developed most strongly over the past 30 years, it is understandable that the Parliamentary Commissioner for Administration has developed an important role in dealing with individual complaints and has also influenced the system of complaints handling through the issuing of reports dealing with individual complaints, special reports under section 10(4) of the Parliamentary Commissioner Act 1967 and annual reports. These have all made a significant impact on administrative practice.

The Dutch system has much in common with the German and French systems in the sense that judicial review is accessible and there are administrative courts that are inexpensive. However, there has been a greater endeavour to create an Ombudsman that can deal with grievances that are not necessarily actionable in the administrative courts and there is also a legal right to petition public authorities. Over time, the Ombudsman has enjoyed an increase in powers and has developed an increasingly important system surveillance role.

The system in the European Union is a peculiar hybrid. There is a strong Ombudsman to deal with complaints about the Union institutions, along with a right to petition the European Parliament, both of which have clearly been drawn from traditions in the Member States. It is interesting to see that, outside of the process for petitions to the European Parliament, the European institutions have not done a great deal to develop a framework for complaints about their own actions, so the impact and effectiveness of the ombudsman is crucial in this regard. It might be argued that, given that it is the Member States who are responsible for the implementation of the vast majority of EU law, it is not so important for effective complaints handling at the European level. At the same time, it might be argued that the growth of European agencies and other bodies that might

[92] For an outline of the developments in this respect, see P Birkinshaw, 'Grievances, Remedies and the State Revisited and Reappraised' in M Adler (ed), *Administrative Justice in Context* (Oxford, Hart Publishing, 2015) 353–87; C Harlow and R Rawlings, *Law and Administration*, 3rd edn (Cambridge, Cambridge University Press, 2009) ch 2.

have an impact directly on the lives of citizens may increase the need for a more uniform approach to complaints handling in the future.

FURTHER READING

Adler, M (ed), *Administrative Justice in Context* (Oxford, Hart Publishing, 2010).
Buck, T, Kirkham, R and Thompson, B, *The Ombudsman Enterprise and Administrative Justice* (Abingdon, Routledge, 2010).
Dragos, D and Neamtu, B (eds), *Alternative Dispute Resolution in European Administrative Law* (Berlin, Springer, 2014).
Remac, M, *Coordinating Ombudsmen and the Judiciary* (Antwerp, Intersentia, 2014).
Seneviratne, M, *Ombudsmen: Public Services and Administrative Justice* (London, Butterworths, 2002).

CHAPTER 11
LIABILITY OF THE ADMINISTRATION

Hermann Pünder and Anika Klafki

11.1 INTRODUCTION

Non-contractual public liability is based on the rule of law principle.[1] The focus of this chapter is on the liability of public authorities rather than on the liability of the acting public servants. The chapter will first analyse which courts deal with liability issues in the different legal orders. Then it will examine the conditions under which the state is liable for unlawful action and whether the legal systems under study provide for a system of liability for lawful action of the state. Another important issue is the scope of liability

[1] See O Dörr, Staatshaftung in Europa: Nationales und Unionsrecht (Berlin, De Gruyter, 2014) 1, 3.

claims. While most systems grant full damages, in some systems only 'just compensation', which does not cover the full amount of losses, is awarded to the damaged party. Special attention will be given to the liability of the judiciary, which is highly restricted in most legal systems. Finally, the liability for breaches of EU law and breaches of the reasonable time requirement of Article 6 of the European Convention on Human Rights (ECHR) will be discussed.

Public liability developed independently in all of the systems analysed in the course of democratisation throughout Europe during the nineteenth and twentieth centuries.[2] Common principles for public liability in Europe were first formulated in 1984 in recommendations from the Council of Europe. According to these recommendations, public liability should comprise legal remedies for damages caused by wrongful action of public authorities as well as reparation for lawful acts based on equity considerations. Despite the quite detailed recommendations of the Council of Europe, the legal landscape concerning public liability today is far from uniform. In fact, a variety of legal doctrines concerning public liability have flourished across Europe. However, the case law of the Court of Justice of the European Union (CJEU) has set the stage for a more harmonised legal development of public liability law in the European Union.

Council of Europe, Recommendation No R (84) 15
of the Committee of Ministers to Member States
Relating to Public Liability[3] **11.1 (COE)**

The Committee of Ministers, under the terms of Article 15.b of the Statute of the Council of Europe, ...

Recommends the governments of member states:

a. to be guided in their law and practice by the principles annexed to this recommendation;

b. to examine the advisability of setting up in their internal order, where necessary, appropriate machinery for preventing obligations of public authorities in the field of public liability from being unsatisfied through lack of funds.

Appendix to Recommendation No. R (84) 15

Scope and definitions

1. This recommendation applies to public liability, that is to say the obligation of public authorities to make good the damage caused by their acts, either by compensation or by any other appropriate means (hereinafter referred to as 'reparation').

2. The term 'public authority' means:

a. any entity of public law of any kind or at any level (including state; region; province; municipality; independent public entity); and

b. any private person, when exercising prerogatives of official authority.

[2] See G della Cananea, 'Verwaltungsrechtliche Paradigmen' in A von Bogdandy, S Cassese and P Huber (eds), *Handbuch Ius Publicum Europaum*, vol 3 (Heidelberg, CF Müller, 2010) § 52, paras 46–48.

[3] When this recommendation was adopted, and in application of Art 10.2.c of the Rules of Procedure for the meetings of the Ministers' Deputies, the representative of Sweden reserved the right of his government to comply with it or not and the representatives of Denmark and Norway reserved the right of their governments to comply or not with Principle II thereof.

3. The term 'act' means any action or omission which is of such a nature as to affect directly the rights, liberties or interests of persons.

4. The acts covered by this recommendation are the following:

a. normative acts in the exercise of regulatory authority;

b. administrative acts which are not regulatory;

c. physical acts.

5. Amongst the acts covered by paragraph 4 are included those acts carried out in the administration of justice which are not performed in the exercise of a judicial function.

6. The term 'victim' means the injured person or any other person entitled to claim reparation.

Principles

I Reparation should be ensured for damage caused by an act due to a failure of a public authority to conduct itself in a way which can reasonably be expected from it in law in relation to the injured person. Such a failure is presumed in case of transgression of an established legal rule.

II (1) Even if the conditions stated in Principle I are not met, reparation should be ensured if it would be manifestly unjust to allow the injured person alone to bear the damage, having regard to the following circumstances: the act is in the general interest, only one person or a limited number of persons have suffered the damage and the act was exceptional or the damage was an exceptional result of the act.

(2) The application of this principle may be limited to certain categories of acts only.

III If the victim has, by his own fault or by his failure to use legal remedies, contributed to the damage, the reparation of the damage may be reduced accordingly or disallowed.

The same should apply if a person, for whom the victim is responsible under national law, has contributed to the damage.

IV The right to bring an action against a public authority should not be subject to the obligation to act first against its agent.

If there is an administrative' conciliation system prior to judicial proceedings, recourse to such system should not jeopardize access to judicial proceedings.

V Reparation under Principle I should be made in full, it being understood that the determination of the heads of damage, of the nature and of the form of reparation falls within the competence of national law.

Reparation under Principle II may be made only in part, on the basis of equitable principles. …

Final provisions

This recommendation should not be interpreted as:

a. limiting the possibility for a member state to apply the principles above to categories of acts other than those covered by the recommendation or to adopt provisions granting a wider measure of protection to victims;

b. affecting any special system of liability laid down by international treaties;

c. affecting special national systems of liability in the fields of postal and telecommunications services and of transportation as well as special systems of liability which are internal to the armed forces, provided that adequate reparation is granted to victims having regard to all the circumstances;

d. affecting special national systems of liability which apply equally to public authorities and private persons.

11.2 WHICH COURTS DEAL WITH LIABILITY ISSUES?

11.2.A ONEFOLD COURT SYSTEMS: ENGLAND AND WALES AND THE EUROPEAN UNION

The jurisdiction for public liability issues is fairly unproblematic in legal systems which do not have separate administrative court systems, such as England and Wales and the EU. In England and Wales, the common law courts[4] are competent, and at the EU level public liability issues are dealt with by the CJEU.

Treaty on the Functioning of the European Union **11.2 (EU)**

Article 256 (1) The General Court shall have jurisdiction to hear and determine at first instance actions or proceedings referred to in Articles 263, 265, 268, 270 and 272, with the exception of those assigned to a specialised court set up under Article 257 and those reserved in the Statute for the Court of Justice. The Statute may provide for the General Court to have jurisdiction for other classes of action or proceeding.

Article 268 The Court of Justice of the European Union shall have jurisdiction in disputes relating to compensation for damage provided for in the second and third paragraphs of Article 340.

Senior Courts Act 1981 **11.3 (EW)**

Section 31 Application for judicial review

(4) On an application for judicial review the High Court may award to the applicant damages, restitution or the recovery of a sum due if–

(a) the application includes a claim for such an award arising from any matter to which the application relates; and

(b) the court is satisfied that such an award would have been made if the claim had been made in an action begun by the applicant at the time of making the application.

Notes

(1) Articles 256 and 268 of the Treaty on the Functioning of the European Union (TFEU) establish the jurisdiction of the CJEU in liability claims concerning the EU institutions.

[4] On the court system in England and Wales, see Chapter 2, section 2.1.C.

(2) Section 31 of the English Senior Courts Act 1981 provides that courts can only give a monetary award in a judicial review claim if such a claim would have succeeded under a relevant cause of action in private law that commenced at the same time as the judicial review claim.

11.2.B DUAL COURT SYSTEMS

Difficulties concerning the competent court arise in legal systems which distinguish between administrative and civil courts or – as in the Netherlands – between administrative and civil court divisions within an ordinary court.[5] The allocation to one of the branches is delicate: on the one hand, civil courts are more experienced with regard to actions for damages; on the other hand, it is the core competency of administrative courts to establish whether public authorities acted unlawfully and should hence be held liable. Whereas Germany and the Netherlands address the jurisdiction by statutory regulation and refer most of the public liability cases to the civil branch, in France the administrative courts developed a separate set of rules on public liability for which they are predominantly competent.[6]

11.2.B.1 JURISDICTION DIVIDED BETWEEN CIVIL AND ADMINISTRATIVE COURTS IN GERMANY

Grundgesetz **11.4 (DE)**

Article 34 If any person, in the exercise of a public office entrusted to him, violates his official duty to a third party, liability shall rest principally with the state or public body that employs him. ... Recourse to ordinary courts shall not be precluded for claims for compensation or indemnity.

Verwaltungsgerichtsordnung **11.5 (DE)**

§40 (1) Recourse to the administrative courts shall be available in all public law disputes of a non-constitutional nature insofar as the disputes are not explicitly allocated to another court by a federal statute. ...

(2) Recourse shall be available to the ordinary courts for property claims from sacrifice for the public good and from bailment by public authorities, as well as for compensation claims arising from the violation of public law obligations which are not based on a public law contract; ...

[5] For an overview of the different court systems, see Chapter 2, section 2.1.

[6] For the historic development in France, see KM Scherr, 'Public Liability for Administrative Acts under French Law' (2008) 14 *European Public Law* 213, 221.

Notes

(1) Public liability issues in Germany are mainly dealt with by the civil courts, which are part of the so-called 'ordinary' court branch (*ordentliche Gerichtsbarkeit*).[7] This is explicitly set out in Article 34(2) of the Grundgesetz and, more generally, in §40(2) of the Verwaltungsgerichtsordnung (VwGO). However, public liability cases resulting from public-law contracts,[8] civil service law[9] and withdrawal of unlawful administrative acts[10] remain within the jurisdiction of the administrative courts according to §40(2) VwGO.

(2) The assignment of the majority of the public liability cases to the civil courts in Germany has historically developed from a deeply rooted mistrust in the administrative courts, which, at the beginning of the nineteenth century, were internal judicial bodies instead of independent courts. The profound mistrust in these administrative courts can be illustrated by §182 of the Paulskirchenverfassung 1849 (Constitution of St Paul's Church of 1849), which was proclaimed by the Frankfurt Parliament after the Revolution of 1848, but never came into force. It provided that the administrative jurisdiction would cease and all violations of rights would be decided by the ordinary courts, which were independent from the state executive.[11]

11.2.B.2 JURISDICTION DIVIDED BETWEEN CIVIL AND ADMINISTRATIVE COURT DIVISIONS IN THE NETHERLANDS

Algemene Wet Bestuursrecht **11.6 (NL)**

Article 8:88 (1) The administrative judge is competent, upon request by a party concerned, to order an administrative authority to compensate damage which the party concerned has suffered or will suffer as a result of:

(a) an unlawful decision;
(b) another unlawful act for the preparation of an unlawful decision;
(c) failure to issue a decision in due time;
(d) another unlawful act of an administrative authority wherein a person within the meaning of Article 8:2(1)(a), his survivors, or his legal successors are parties concerned.

(2) Section 1 does not apply where the decision is exempt from judicial review (beroep) to the administrative judge.

[7] See also Arts 14(3)(3) and 34(2) GG.

[8] Verwaltungsverfahrensgesetz (VwVfG), §54 ff. For an overview of contracts concluded by the administration, see Chapter 3, section 3.5.

[9] See the Bundesbeamtengesetz (Federal Civil Service Act) and Gesetz zur Regelung des Statusrechts der Beamtinnen und Beamten in den Ländern (Civil Status Servants Act) for details.

[10] §48 VwVfG.

[11] For more details on the history of judicial review of administrative action in Germany, see Chapter 1, section 1.1. See also H Pünder and A Klafki, 'Administrative Law in Germany' in R Seerden (ed), *Administrative Law of the European Union, its Member States and the United States* (Cambridge, Intersentia, 2018) 49–106.

Article 8:89 (1) If damage has been caused by a decision on which the Central Appellate Court or the Supreme Court is competent to rule in only instance or highest instance, the administrative judge is exclusively competent.

(2) In all other cases, the administrative judge is competent if the compensation requested does not exceed €25,000, including interest owed until the day of the request, notwithstanding the right of the applicant to ask for compensation on the basis of other statutory provisions.

(3) In the cases referred to in the second section, the administrative judge is not competent if the applicant has lodged his request after he file a suit for compensation of his damage with the civil court.

(4) As long as the request of the party concerned is pending before the administrative judge the civil court must declare a request for compensation inadmissible.

Notes

(1) According to Article 8:88 of the Algemene Wet Bestuursrecht (AWB), the administrative judge is competent with regard to compensation claims for damage caused by an unlawful decision, its preparation or a failure to take a decision in due time if such a decision could be challenged before the administrative judge. However, Article 8:88 AWB has to be read in conjunction with Article 8:89 AWB, which provides that compensation claims are exclusively allocated to the administrative judge only in some specific areas of law (Article 8:89(1) AWB). In all other cases, the jurisdiction depends on the amount in dispute: for claims of up to €25,000, the claimant may choose between the civil division and the administrative division of the district court. If the claim exceeds €25,000, the competence is always with the civil division of the district court. If a form of public action other than those stipulated in Article 8:88(1) AWB causes the loss (eg factual action,[12] unlawful legislation), the civil divisions of the district courts are always competent. As a result of these comparatively complicated rules, the majority of the public liability cases are adjudicated by the civil judges.

(2) With regard to compensation for lawful action,[13] the rules on the allocation of jurisdiction are diverse and complicated. For the most part, the aggrieved party can choose to bring a claim either to the administrative division or to the civil division of the district court. Which division of the district court is competent depends on the legal basis of the claim. Currently, compensation claims for lawful public action may be based on one of the following:

— any explicit basis in a (formal) legal provision, a general binding regulation or policy rule.[14] The administrative judge is competent for such claims;
— the general administrative law principle of *égalité devant les charges publiques*. The administrative judge is competent for such claims;

[12] For judicial review of factual action in the Netherlands, see Chapter 3, section 3.4.B.1.
[13] See section 11.4.A.2 below.
[14] For more on these concepts, see Chapter 3, section 3.3.

— tort liability for public action which is as such lawful, but turns out to be unlawful because those disproportionately affected by the (as such lawful) action did not receive any compensatory payment. The civil judge is competent for such claims.

As a result, this means that if there is an explicit formal legal basis for a compensation claim, the administrative judge is competent. If not, the claimant may choose between a public law claim, based on the *égalité* principle, and a civil law claim, based on tort law. It is expected that, sometime in the future, with the advent of Article 4:126 AWB, a new, general public law basis for liability claims for lawful administrative action will be created.[15] In that case, nearly all liability claims for lawful administrative action would fall within the jurisdiction of the administrative division of the district court. It is not yet foreseeable when Article 4:126 AWB will enter into force.

11.2.B.3 JURISDICTION OF ADMINISTRATIVE COURTS IN FRANCE

Tribunal des Conflits, 8 February 1873[16] **11.7 (FR)**

Blanco v Prefect of Gironde

DISTINCTION BETWEEN CIVIL AND PUBLIC LIABILITY

Blanco

The administrative courts are competent to decide on matters of public liability.

Facts: The claimant asked for damages to compensate the injury caused to his daughter by a state-owned company.

Held: The case was remitted to the competent administrative court.

Judgment: Considering that Mr Blanco brought a suit against the prefect of the department of Gironde, representing the state, claiming that the state was liable under Articles 1382, 1383 and 1384 of the Civil Code for the damage suffered by his daughter as a result of the conduct of workers employed by the state owned tobacco company; considering that the principles contained in the Civil Code which regulate the relations between individuals are inapplicable to the possible liability of the state for damage caused to individuals by persons employed in the performance of a public service; considering that the responsibility of the state, being neither general nor absolute, is subject to special rules which vary depending on the needs of the public service and the need to reconcile the rights of the state with the rights of private persons; considering that accordingly, under the laws cited above, the jurisdiction to rule on these matters is vested exclusively in the administrative courts.

[15] See further section 11.4.A.2 below.
[16] N° 00012.

Notes

(1) The *Blanco* case was a landmark decision in France, which established that public liability is to be handled differently from private liability cases.[17] From *Blanco* onwards, the Council of State and the other administrative courts have evolved a separate set of non-codified rules on public liability.[18] Other than in the other legal systems, where the public liability regime is at least partly based on tort law, France established an entirely autonomous public liability system that is based on fault with regard to unlawful action and on the risk and equality principle with regard to lawful public action. As long as the liability issue derives from the exercise of a prerogative of public powers or from the performance of a public service (as opposed to industrial and commercial public services), generally the administrative courts deal with liability issues.[19]

(2) In France, public liability claims are brought with a so-called 'full jurisdiction remedy' (*recours de pleine juridiction*).[20]

Conseil d'État, 26 July 1918[21] **11.8 (FR)**

Epoux Lemonnier v Municipality of Roquecourbe

TWO-FOLD BASIS OF LIABILITY: CIVIL AND PUBLIC LIABILITY

Epoux Lemonnier

Even where the public servant is personally liable under civil law, damages based on public liability can be claimed in the administrative courts.

Facts: On one side of the river in the city of Roquecourbe, there was a fair at which games with firearms were offered. On the other side of the river, some pedestrians were injured by the shots. Although the mayor had been warned about the risks, he failed to adequately protect the pedestrians on the other side of the river. Thus, the claimants were injured because of the failure of the mayor to act.

Held: The city was held liable. However, the Council of State ruled that the claimants could only be compensated once. Thus, the damages resulting from the personal liability of the mayor were imposed upon the city.

Judgment: Considering that the circumstances of the accident seem to be the fault of an administrative officer in charge of a public service, and this fault is a personal one which could lead to the personal liability of the officer before the ordinary courts, requiring the administrative officer to pay damages, and, even if this award of damages would effectively be granted by the ordinary court, this could not have the consequence of depriving the victim of the accident of the right to introduce an action directly against the public

[17] For more details, see Scherr (n 6 above) 220 ff.

[18] See also G Bermann and E Picard, 'Administrative Law' in G Bermann and E Picard (eds), *Introduction to French Law* (Alphen aan de Rijn, Kluwer Law International, 2008) 57, 79 ff.

[19] There are a few exceptions, eg vehicle accidents, indirect taxation, confiscation. See Scherr (n 6 above) 222. On public service and the concept of prerogative of public powers, see Chapter 2, section 2.5.A.4.

[20] For more details, see Chapter 7, section 7.2.A.4.

[21] N° 49595 55240.

body which was in charge of the public service and thereby to receive compensation for the loss suffered.

Considering that it is solely for the administrative court, if a fault arising in the conduct of a public duty which may lead to the liability of the public body is established, to take any necessary measures, when assessing the recoverable amount and the form of damages to be awarded, to ensure that its decision would not grant the victim higher compensation than the total value of the damage suffered, because of the damages it could or can obtain before other courts for the same accident.

Note

Despite the *Blanco* decision, in the *Epoux Lemonnier* case, the Council of State clarified that a public-service-related fault, causing public liability, can simultaneously also qualify as a personal fault in very serious cases, which can give rise to private law remedies. In such a case, the claimant can either seek damages against the civil servant before the civil courts, arguing that the requirements of the *Code Civil* (Civil Code) are met, or file a claim against the public authority before an administrative court on the basis of the rules governing public liability. However, the personal liability of a civil servant is very rare.

11.3 LIABILITY FOR UNLAWFUL ACTION

All legal systems provide a remedy for unlawful acts of the administration which have caused an individual to suffer loss. Common requirements of public liability for unlawful acts are that, first, the harmful behaviour must be attributed to a public office and, secondly, there must be a causal link between the damage and the unlawful act.[22] In all the analysed legal systems, further limiting requirements apply to public liability. Some legal systems require that the law that is violated serves to protect individual rights (Germany, England and Wales, the Netherlands), some require that the violation was sufficiently serious (Germany, the EU) and some require fault of the public authority (France, partly Germany). A distinction can be drawn between systems which provide for a special public liability regime, such as France, Germany and the EU, and systems that integrate public liability into the civil tort law regime without further specifications, such as England and Wales and the Netherlands.

11.3.A LEGAL SYSTEMS WITH A SPECIAL PUBLIC LIABILITY LAW REGIME: FRANCE, GERMANY, THE EUROPEAN UNION

In this section, the analysis focuses on the requirements for public liability in legal systems with a special regime for the determination of public liability.

[22] See for an in-depth analysis of the causation requirement in the EU, K Bitterich, 'Elements of an Autonomous Concept of Causation in European Community Law Concerning Liability' (2007) 106 *Zeitschrift für Vergleichende Rechtswissenschaft* 12.

11.3.A.1 FAULT CRITERION IN FRANCE

Conseil d'État, 3 February 1911[23] **11.9 (FR)**

Anguet v Minister of Trade, Industry, Posts and Telegraphs

PUBLIC LIABILITY FOR MISDEMEANOUR OF CIVIL SERVANTS

Anguet

Fault in the fulfilment of public duties leads to public liability irrespective of whether the acting officer is liable on a civil law basis.

Facts: The claimant was brutally ejected from a post office, which was closing earlier than usual.

Held: The state was held liable.

Judgment: Considering that, according to the case file, the public entrance to the post office located at 1 rue des Filles-du-Calvaire had been closed on 11 January 1908 before the normal closing hours and before Mr Anguet, who was inside, could have finished his monetary transactions; considering that only following the instructions of one employee and because there were no other exits, Mr Anguet left the post office through the part of the building dedicated to public servants; considering that, in these circumstances, the accident of which the claimant has been a victim, resulting from the brutal ejection from this part of the post office, shall be attributed, regardless of the extent of the personal liability of the agents who initiated the expulsion, to an error in the delivery of a public service; considering that, therefore, Mr Anguet is entitled to request compensation from the state for the loss suffered as a result of this accident; considering that in the circumstances of the case, a fair assessment of the loss suffered leads to the judgment that the state must pay 20,000 francs in damages to Mr Anguet, this amounting to full compensation, covering both the principal sum and the interest.

Conseil d'État, 30 November 1923[24] **11.10 (FR)**

Couitéas v Minister of Foreign Affairs

PUBLIC LIABILITY FOR OMISSION OF THE EXECUTION OF A JUDGMENT

Couitéas

An omission of the enforcement of a judicial decision can constitute a fault that leads to public liability.

Facts: The claimant had successfully asked for the eviction of certain tribes in Tunisia, but the decision was not executed by the government of the colony. This caused him an injury for which he sought compensation.

Held: The state was held liable.

Judgment: But considering that the litigant, disposing of an enforceable judicial decision, has the right to rely on the support of the public power to ensure the enforcement of the

[23] N° 34922.
[24] N° 38284 48688.

title thus delivered to him; considering that if the government has the duty to assess the conditions of this enforcement and the right to decline to use armed force insofar as it considers that there is a security threat, the loss suffered by such a refusal, if it exceeds a certain period of time, cannot be qualified as a normal burden imposed to the person involved, and it is within the powers of a judge to decide to what extent it should be borne by the public as a whole.

Considering that the total and unlimited deprivation of enjoyment resulting from the measures taken vis-à-vis the applicant, imposed on the latter, in the general interest, a loss for which he is entitled to demand monetary compensation; hence the Foreign Minister was wrong to deny him any right to compensation; that it is appropriate to remit the matter to the said Minister to proceed, in the absence of amicable settlement, and taking all the legal and factual circumstances into account, to determine the quantum of damages which should be granted to the applicant.

Notes

(1) The French public liability system is based on fault (*faute simple*), which is understood broadly.[25] When damage results from an administrative decision, any violation of the law is considered in and by itself as a fault.[26] For example, where the administration illegally violates a property right (*emprise irrégulière*)[27] or illegally destroys property (*démolition*),[28] no further evidence of fault is needed. However, that principle has a noteworthy limit: illegality will not lead to liability where it appears that a decision which is only illegal because of procedural flaws is justified in fact and in substance, since this illegality would not lead to the annulment of the decision.[29] Apart from illegality, there are various other types of fault. These range from negligence and omission to excessive slowness and broken promises.

(2) In particularly difficult administrative fields, for example police activities and in the fiscal domain, gross fault (*faute lourde*) is required. However, cases in which the courts require *faute lourde* are becoming increasingly rare. The general principle is that *faute simple* is sufficient to claim damages.

(3) The proof of the fault is sometimes facilitated by a presumption mechanism in certain fields, for example in cases where damages are caused by simple medical acts in hospital leading to severe injuries,[30] or where the damage is inflicted by public works.[31]

[25] For details, see Berman and Picard (n 18 above) 81 ff.

[26] Conseil d'État, 26 January 1973, *Ville de Paris contre Driancourt*, N° 84768.

[27] Tribunal des Conflits, 9 December 2013, *Epoux Panizzon*, N° 3931.

[28] Tribunal des Conflits, 15 December 2008, *M. A*, N° C3673.

[29] For more details on the consequences of procedural errors in judicial review, see Chapter 6, section 6.6.B.1.

[30] Conseil d'État, 9 December 1988, *Cohen*, N° 65087.

[31] Conseil d'État, 14 March 1980, *Communauté Urbaine de Bordeaux*, N° 13780.

11.3.A.2 FAULT AND SCOPE OF THE NORM CRITERION OR SACRIFICIAL/ EXPROPRIATORY ENCROACHMENT IN GERMANY

Grundgesetz **11.11 (DE)**

Article 14 (3) Expropriation shall only be permissible for the public good. It may only be ordered by or pursuant to a law that determines the nature and extent of compensation. Such compensation shall be determined by establishing an equitable balance between the public interest and the interests of those affected.

Article 34 If any person, in the exercise of a public office entrusted to him, violates his official duty to a third party, liability shall rest principally with the state or public body that employs him. In the event of intentional wrongdoing or gross negligence, the right of recourse against the individual officer shall be preserved.

Einleitung zum Preußischen Allgemeinen Landrecht[32] **11.12 (DE)**

§74 The furthering of the common good takes precedence over individual rights and privileges of the members of the state if a genuine conflict (collision) exists between these two positions.

§75 The state is, however, bound to compensate anybody who is forced to sacrifice his particular rights and privileges for the common good.

Bürgerliches Gesetzbuch **11.13 (DE)**

§839 (1) If an official intentionally or negligently breaches the official duty incumbent upon him in relation to a third party, he must compensate the third party for damages resulting thereof. If the official is responsible only due to negligence, he may only be held liable if the injured person is not able to obtain compensation in another way.

§249 (1) A person who is liable in damages must restore the position that would exist if the circumstance obliging him to pay damages had not occurred.

(2) Where damages are payable for injury to a person or damage to real property or chattels, the claimant may demand the required monetary amount in lieu of restoration.

Bundesgerichtshof, 28 June 1984[33] **11.14 (DE)**

LIABILITY FOR UNLAWFUL ACTION ON THE BASIS OF EXPROPRIATORY ENCROACHMENT

Unlawful action which causes damages resulting from expropriatory encroachment impacting upon the claimant's property has to be compensated if the loss suffered constitutes a typical consequence of the illegal public action and would not have occurred without the public wrong.

Facts: The claimant operated a farm in the local community G. The municipality had passed a building plan which allowed residential development in the immediate neighbourhood. After the plan had been passed, the

[32] The General Land Law for the Prussian States was issued in 1794. It goes back to the Prussian King Friedrich the Great. §§ 74 and 75 of the introduction of the law are still quoted today, when it comes to substantiate the sacrificial encroachment compensation as customary law.

[33] (1984) NJW 2516.

claimant had requested permission to build a pigsty, which was rejected by the municipality due to the neighbouring residential buildings. The building plan was later annulled by the Higher Administrative Court, as the municipality had not balanced the interests of the concerned parties adequately. The claimant sought compensation, arguing that the erection of the residential buildings in his neighbourhood on the basis of the unlawful building plan had prevented him from building a pigsty on his land at reasonable cost.

Held: The case was remitted to the lower instance. The Federal Court of Justice held that the claimant should be compensated if the prerequisites for an action on the basis of expropriatory encroachment were met.

Judgment: The Senate handing down the judgment reiterates, as it has decided recently, that for unlawful sovereign interferences with property, compensation must be provided in accordance with the principles developed by the jurisprudence concerning expropriation-like encroachment.

The issuing of the unlawful development plan and its execution constitute a direct interference with the legal position of the claimants which is protected by Article 14(1) GG, as it is a precondition for expropriation-like encroachment, according to the Senate's consistent jurisprudence. …

There would not only be a causal link between the issuing of the illegal development plan and the (supposedly) incorrect notice given …, but the notice of rejection would also constitute a result which is based on the nature of the faulty development planning on the part of the defendant and which is a typical consequence thereof. The decision of the District Administrator's Office concerning the preliminary application of the claimant became significantly more onerous and complicated because of the fact that, due to the wrongful planning of the respondent, the housing development had come closer to the source of pollution caused by the firm owned by the claimants. Therefore, the fact that the administration has wrongly assessed the protection of the rights of existing property owners does form part of the typical consequences of the wrongful planning of the respondent. The regional court will have to consider that the claimants have to accept without compensation those disadvantages, which they also would have incurred (without any compensation) in the case of lawful construction planning. It cannot be excluded that the claimants, in the case of lawful construction planning, could have been burdened with obligations to take the interests of approved residential buildings into account, that have been allowed within a certain safety distance … In this case, the legal position of the claimants would be restricted accordingly …

Notes

(1) German public liability law is rooted in two different systems with differing compensatory consequences. On the one hand, there is tortious liability for unlawful acts committed by a public authority (§839 of the Bürgerliches Gesetzbuch (Civil Code, BGB) in conjunction with Article 34 of the Grundgesetz (GG)). The requirements for this system of liability are that, first, any person who is performing an official public function must have breached an official duty (*Amtspflichtverletzung*). Secondly, the public duty must protect third parties, and the claimant must fall within the scope of the protected group. Thirdly, there must be a causal link between the breach of the official duty and the damages suffered. Lastly, the tort law provision contained in §839 BGB requires fault on the part of the actor. Thus, public liability,

according to §839 BGB in conjunction with Article 34 GG, is limited by both the 'fault' criterion and the 'scope of the norm' criterion.

(2) On the other hand, even if the requirements of §839 BGB are not met, compensation can be obtained for unlawful 'sacrificial encroachment' (*Aufopferung*, §§74 and 75 of the Einleitung zum Preußischen Allgemeinen Landrecht (EinlALR)) or 'expropriatory encroachment' (*Enteignung*, Article 14(3) of the Grundgesetz) if the suffered loss results 'immediately' (*unmittelbar*) from the unlawful action and constitutes a typical consequence of the public action in question. Unlawful action which causes material damages can be compensated under an encroachment claim if the following prerequisites are met: (a) a property right or the physical integrity or the freedom of a person must be violated; (b) the violation resulted from an unlawful action of public authorities; (c) the violation was a typical consequence of the unlawful action of the public authority; and (d) the public authority acted in the general interest of the public. The Federal Court of Justice (Bundesgerichtshof), in its judgment of 28 June 1984, clarified that only those disadvantages that resulted directly from the unlawful administrative action will be compensated. Losses which would also have occurred where lawful action was taken by the administration are excluded from compensation, unless the prerequisites of liability for lawful action are met.[34]

11.3.A.3 SUFFICIENTLY SERIOUS BREACH CRITERION IN THE EUROPEAN UNION

Charter of Fundamental Rights of the European Union **11.15 (EU)**

Article 41 (3) Every person has the right to have the Union make good any damage caused by its institutions or by its servants in the performance of their duties, in accordance with the general principles common to the laws of the Member States.

Treaty on the Functioning of the European Union **11.16 (EU)**

Article 340 … In the case of non-contractual liability, the Union shall, in accordance with the general principles common to the laws of the Member States, make good any damage caused by its institutions or by its servants in the performance of their duties.

Note

In Article 41(3) of the Charter of Fundamental Rights of the European Union, liability of the EU for losses caused by its organs is generally guaranteed. On the basis of Article 340 TFEU and the public liability law traditions of the Member States, the CJEU has created an autonomous European system of liability for unlawful acts attributable to a Union institution or body.

[34] See section 11.4.A.3 below.

Case C-352/98 P, 4 July 2000[35] **11.17 (EU)**

Laboratoires Pharmaceutiques Bergaderm SA and others v Commission

SUFFICIENTLY SERIOUS BREACH CRITERION

Bergaderm

EU law confers a right to reparation where three conditions are met: the rule of law infringed must be intended to confer rights on individuals; the breach must be sufficiently serious; and there must be a direct causal link between the breach of the obligation resting on the EU and the damage sustained by the injured parties. The breach is sufficiently serious if the public authority manifestly and gravely disregarded the limits on its discretion.

Facts: Laboratoires Pharmaceutiques Bergaderm SA brought a claim for compensation for the damage that they purportedly suffered as a result of the preparation and adoption of Commission Directive 95/34/EC of 10 July 1995 adapting to technical progress, Annexes II, III, VI and VII to Council Directive 76/768/EEC, on the approximation of the laws of the Member States relating to cosmetic products. The Court of First Instance had dismissed the claim, considering that the Commission has not acted unlawfully. The company brought an appeal before the Court of Justice.

Held: The appeal was dismissed.

Judgment: 39. The second paragraph of Article 215 of the Treaty provides that, in the case of non-contractual liability, the Community is, in accordance with the general principles common to the laws of the Member States, to make good any damage caused by its institutions or by its servants in the performance of their duties.

40. The system of rules which the Court has worked out with regard to that provision takes into account, inter alia, the complexity of the situations to be regulated, difficulties in the application or interpretation of the texts and, more particularly, the margin of discretion available to the author of the act in question …

41. The Court has stated that the conditions under which the state may incur liability for damage caused to individuals by a breach of Community law cannot, in the absence of particular justification, differ from those governing the liability of the Community in like circumstances. The protection of the rights which individuals derive from Community law cannot vary depending on whether a national authority or a Community authority is responsible for the damage (*Brasserie du Pêcheur and Factortame*, paragraph 42).

42. As regards Member State liability for damage caused to individuals, the Court has held that Community law confers a right to reparation where three conditions are met: the rule of law infringed must be intended to confer rights on individuals; the breach must be sufficiently serious; and there must be a direct causal link between the breach of the obligation resting on the state and the damage sustained by the injured parties (*Brasserie du Pêcheur and Factortame*, paragraph 51).

43. As to the second condition, as regards both Community liability under Article 215 of the Treaty and Member State liability for breaches of Community law, the decisive test for finding that a breach of Community law is sufficiently serious is whether the Member State or the Community institution concerned manifestly and gravely disregarded the limits on its discretion …

[35] ECLI:EU:C:2000:361.

Joined Cases 83/76, 94/76, 4/77, 15/77 and 40/77, 25 May 1978[36] **11.18 (EU)**

Bayerische HNL Vermehrungsbetriebe GmbH & Co KG and others v Council and Commission

EU LIABILITY IN CASE OF DISCRETIONARY MEASURES

HNL

In legislative fields of wide discretion, such as the agricultural market, the EU does not incur liability unless the institution concerned has manifestly and gravely disregarded the limits imposed on the exercise of its powers.

Facts: The claimants sought damages in respect of the loss allegedly suffered by them as a result of the effects of Council Regulation (EEC) No 563/76 of 15 March 1976 on the compulsory purchase of skimmed-milk powder held by intervention agencies for use in feeding stuffs.

Held: The application was dismissed as unfounded.

Judgment: The finding that a legislative measure such as the regulation in question is null and void is however insufficient by itself for the Community to incur non-contractual liability for damage caused to individuals under the second paragraph of Article 215 of the EEC Treaty [Article 340 TFEU]. The Court of Justice has consistently stated that the Community does not incur liability on account of a legislative measure, which involves choices of economic policy unless a sufficiently serious breach of a superior rule of law for the protection of the individual has occurred.

In the present case there is no doubt that the prohibition on discrimination laid down in the second subparagraph of the third paragraph of Article 40 of the Treaty and infringed by Regulation No 563/76 is in fact designed for the protection of the individual .... To determine what conditions must be present in addition to such breach for the Community to incur liability in accordance with the criterion laid down in the case law of the Court of Justice it is necessary to take into consideration the principles in the legal systems of the Member States governing the liability of public authorities for damage caused to individuals by legislative measures. Although these principles vary considerably from one Member State to another, it is, however, possible to state that the public authorities can only exceptionally and in special circumstances incur liability for legislative measures, which are the result of choices of economic policy. This restrictive view is explained by the consideration that the legislative authority, even where the validity of its measures is subject to judicial review, cannot always be hindered in making its decisions by the prospect of applications for damages whenever it has occasion to adopt legislative measures in the public interest, which may adversely affect the interests of individuals.

It follows from these considerations that individuals may be required, in the sectors coming within the economic policy of the Community, to accept within reasonable limits certain harmful effects on their economic interests as a result of a legislative measure without being able to obtain compensation from public funds even if that measure has been declared null and void. In a legislative field such as the one in question, in which one of the chief features is the exercise of a wide discretion essential for the implementation of the Common Agricultural Policy, the Community does not therefore incur liability unless the institution concerned has manifestly and gravely disregarded the limits on the exercise of its powers.

[36] ECLI:EU:C:1978:113.

This is not so in the case of a measure of economic policy such as that in the present case, in view of its special features. In this connection it is necessary to observe first that this measure affected very wide categories of traders, in other words all buyers of compound feeding-stuffs containing protein, so that its effects on individual undertakings were considerably lessened .... The effects of the regulation on the profit-earning capacity of the undertakings did not ultimately exceed the bounds of the economic risks inherent in the activities of the agricultural sectors concerned.

In these circumstances the fact that the regulation is null and void is insufficient for the Community to incur liability under the second paragraph of Article 215 of the Treaty.

Joined Cases T-198/95, T-171/96, T-230/97, T-174/98 and T-225/99, 12 July 2011[37] **11.19 (EU)**

Comafrica SpA and Dole Fresh Fruit Europe Ltd & Co v Commission

EU LIABILITY IN CASE OF NON-DISCRETIONARY MEASURES

Comafrica

Where the institution in question has only limited or no discretion, the mere infringement of EU law may be sufficient to establish the existence of a sufficiently serious breach.

Facts: The claimants contested a number of regulations adopted by the Commission fixing the single reduction coefficient for the determination of the quantity of bananas to be allocated to each operator in categories A and B within the tariff quota for the years 1995–1999.

Held: The Court of First Instance dismissed the claims for annulment as inadmissible and dismissed the claims for damages as unfounded.

Judgment: As regards the liability of the Community for damage caused to individuals, the conduct alleged against the Commission must involve sufficiently serious breach of a rule of law intended to confer rights on individuals. The decisive test for finding that a breach of Community law is sufficiently serious is whether the Community institution concerned has manifestly and gravely disregarded the limits on its discretion. Where the institution in question has only a considerably reduced or even no discretion, the mere infringement of Community law may be sufficient to establish the existence of a sufficiently serious breach (see judgment of the Court in Case C-352/98 P *Bergaderm and Goupil v Commission* [2000] ECR I-5291, paragraphs 41 to 44). In particular, a finding of an error which, in analogous circumstances, an administrative authority exercising ordinary care and diligence would not have committed, will support the conclusion that the conduct of the Community institution was unlawful in such a way as to render the Community liable under Article 215 of the Treaty.

Note

As a first limitation to EU liability, the European courts require that the violated rule of law intend to confer rights on individuals. Secondly, *discretionary acts* only

[37] ECLI:EU:T:2001:184.

lead to liability of the EU if they entail a sufficiently serious breach of EU law. In contrast, liability for *non-discretionary* actions also arises where there is only a mere finding of illegality. This limits liability of EU institutions considerably. Wherever complex decision-making is involved, the 'sufficiently serious breach' criterion creates a high threshold for public liability claims. Thirdly, in order to establish liability, a causal link between the breach committed by the EU institutions and the damage suffered by the individual must be established.

11.3.B APPLICABILITY OF GENERAL TORT LAW: ENGLAND AND WALES AND THE NETHERLANDS

11.3.B.1 ENGLAND AND WALES

House of Lords, 29 June 1995[38] **11.20 (EW)**

X (Minors) v Bedfordshire County Council

LIABILITY OF PUBLIC AUTHORITIES

X (Minors)

Public authorities can only be liable where the claimant can demonstrate that the authority has committed a tort.

Facts: The claimants were all children who brought claims for breach of statutory duty and negligence, as they claimed that they had suffered personal injury as a result of Bedfordshire County Council's failure to exercise its statutory powers to take them into care and protect them from abuse by their parents.

Held: The claims were dismissed.

Judgment: Lord Browne-Wilkinson: ... Private law claims for damages can be classified into four different categories, viz: (A) actions for breach of statutory duty simpliciter (ie irrespective of carelessness); (B) actions based solely on the careless performance of a statutory duty in the absence of any other common law right of action; (C) actions based on a common law duty of care arising either from the imposition of the statutory duty or from the performance of it; (D) misfeasance in public office, ie the failure to exercise, or the exercise of, statutory powers either with the intention to injure the plaintiff or in the knowledge that the conduct is unlawful. ...

(A) Breach of statutory duty simpliciter

This category comprises those cases where the statement of claim alleges simply (a) the statutory duty, (b) a breach of that duty, causing (c) damage to the plaintiff. ... The basic proposition is that in the ordinary case a breach of statutory duty does not, by itself, give rise to any private law cause of action. However, a private law cause of action will arise if it can be shown, as a matter of construction of the statute, that the statutory duty was imposed for the protection of a limited class of the public and that Parliament intended

[38] [1995] 2 AC 633 (HL).

to confer on members of that class a private right of action for breach of the duty. ... The cases where a private right of action for breach of statutory duty has been held to arise are all cases in which the statutory duty has been very limited and specific as opposed to general administrative functions imposed on public bodies and involving the exercise of administrative discretions.

(B) The careless performance of a statutory duty – no common law duty of care

... In my judgment the correct view is that in order to found a cause of action flowing from the careless exercise of statutory powers or duties, the plaintiff has to show that the circumstances are such as to raise a duty of care at common law. The mere assertion of the careless exercise of a statutory power or duty is not sufficient.

(C) The common law duty of care

In this category, the claim alleges either that a statutory duty gives rise to a common law duty of care owed to the plaintiff by the defendant to do or refrain from doing a particular act or (more often) that in the course of carrying out a statutory duty the defendant has brought about such a relationship between himself and the plaintiff as to give rise to a duty of care at common law. A further variant is a claim by the plaintiff that, whether or not the authority is itself under a duty of care to the plaintiff, its servant in the course of performing the statutory function was under a common law duty of care for breach of which the authority is vicariously liable.

1. Co-existence of statutory duty and common law duty of care

It is clear that a common law duty of care may arise in the performance of statutory functions. But a broad distinction has to be drawn between: (a) cases in which it is alleged that the authority owes a duty of care in the manner in which it exercises a statutory discretion; (b) cases in which a duty of care is alleged to arise from the manner in which the statutory duty has been implemented in practice.

2. Discretion: Justiciability and the policy/operational test

(a) Discretion

Most statutes which impose a statutory duty on local authorities confer on the authority a discretion as to the extent to which, and the methods by which, such statutory duty is to be performed. It is clear both in principle and from the decided cases that the local authority cannot be liable in damages for doing that which Parliament has authorised. Therefore, if the decisions complained of fall within the ambit of such statutory discretion, they cannot be actionable in common law. However, if the decision complained of is so unreasonable that it falls outside the ambit of the discretion conferred upon the local authority, there is no a priori reason for excluding all common law liability.

(b) Justiciability and the policy/operational dichotomy

... Where Parliament has conferred a statutory discretion on a public authority, it is for that authority, not for the courts, to exercise the discretion: nothing which the authority does within the ambit of the discretion can be actionable at common law. If the decision complained of falls outside the statutory discretion, it can (but not necessarily will) give rise to common law liability. However, if the factors relevant to the exercise of the discretion include matters of policy, the court cannot adjudicate on such policy matters and therefore cannot reach the conclusion that the decision was outside the ambit of the statutory discretion. Therefore a common law duty of care in relation to the taking of decisions involving policy matters cannot exist.

3. If justiciable, the ordinary principles of negligence apply

If the plaintiff's complaint alleges carelessness, not in the taking of a discretionary decision to do some act, but in the practical manner in which that act has been performed (eg the running of a school), the question whether or not there is a common law duty of care falls to be decided by applying the usual principles. … Was the damage to the plaintiff reasonably foreseeable? Was the relationship between the plaintiff and the defendant sufficiently proximate? Is it just and reasonable to impose a duty of care? …

In accordance with the principles I have discussed, I propose to approach each of these cases as follows. I will consider first (if such claim is advanced) whether the statutory provisions by themselves give rise to a private law claim in damages (Category (A)). I will turn then to consider whether in each case there is a common law duty of care owed to the plaintiff. I will consider the following matters in turn, to the extent that they are relied upon.

(1) Direct duty of care owed by the local authority

(a) Is the negligence relied upon negligence in the exercise of a statutory discretion involving policy considerations: if so, the claim will pro tanto fail as being non-justiciable; (b) were the acts alleged to give rise to the cause of action within the ambit of the discretion conferred on the local authority; if not, (c) is it appropriate to impose on the local authority a common law duty of care?

(2) Vicarious liability of the local authority

(a) Is the duty of care alleged to be owed by the servant of the local authority consistent with the proper performance of his duties to the local authority; if so, (b) is it appropriate to impose on the servant the duty of care alleged?

House of Lords, 18 May 2000[39] **11.21 (EW)**

Three Rivers District Council v Bank of England

MISFEASANCE IN PUBLIC OFFICE

Three Rivers DC

In order to claim damages on the basis of misfeasance in public office, the damage must be caused by a public officer who exercised public power and thereby injured the claimant intentionally or with reckless indifference.

Facts: T and other depositors who had lost money following the collapse of the Bank of Credit and Commerce International appealed against a decision upholding an order striking out their action against the Bank of England alleging misfeasance in public office. The Bank of England argued that the claim should be struck out due to the inadequacy of the pleadings and as an abuse of process.

Held: The appeal was allowed. However, the question of whether the evidence supported misfeasance in public office was a matter for the trial judge to determine.

Judgment: Lord Steyn: It is now possible to consider the ingredients of the tort. …

(1) The defendant must be a public officer

It is the office in a relatively wide sense on which everything depends. Thus a local authority exercising private-law functions as a landlord is potentially capable of being sued. … In the present case it is common ground that the Bank satisfies this requirement.

(2) The second requirement is the exercise of power as a public officer

… The conduct of the named senior officials of the Banking Supervision Department of the Bank was in the exercise of public functions. …

[39] [2000] 2 WLR 1220 (HL).

(3) The third requirement concerns the state of mind of the defendant

The case law reveals two different forms of liability for misfeasance in public office. First there is the case of targeted malice by a public officer, ie conduct specifically intended to injure a person or persons. This type of case involves bad faith in the sense of the exercise of public power for an improper or ulterior motive. The second form is where a public officer acts knowing that he has no power to do the act complained of and that the act will probably injure the plaintiff. It involves bad faith inasmuch as the public officer does not have an honest belief that his act is lawful. ... The present case is not one of targeted malice. If the action in tort is maintainable it must be in the second form of the tort. ...

The basis for the action lies in the defendant taking a decision in the knowledge that it is an excess of the powers granted to him and that it is likely to cause damage to an individual or individuals. ... The alternative form of liability requires an element of bad faith. This leads to what was a disputed issue. Counsel for the Bank pointed out that there was no precedent in England before the present case which held recklessness to be a sufficient state of mind to ground the tort. Counsel argued that recklessness was insufficient. The Australian High Court and the Court of Appeal of New Zealand have ruled that recklessness is sufficient. ...

The Court of Appeal accepted the correctness of this statement of principle ... The policy underlying it is sound: reckless indifference to consequences is as blameworthy as deliberately seeking such consequences. It can therefore now be regarded as settled law that an act performed in reckless indifference as to the outcome is sufficient to ground the tort in its second form.

Notes

(1) In other legal systems, clear prerequisites for public liability have evolved which satisfy the need to limit public liability to a reasonable level on the one hand, but also grant citizens an effective legal remedy on the other. By contrast, in England and Wales, public liability has been integrated in the general tort law regime by the judiciary. This causes trouble, since the relationship between equal individuals is different from that between the state and its subordinated citizens. As a result, the judiciary has developed various tests and factors to set limits to public liability within the general tort law system. However, the case law is not always consistent and fails to provide a clear set of prerequisites that is generally applicable to public liability issues. The English approach to public liability is thus more complex and less comprehensible, and creates more legal uncertainty in many respects.

(2) As public liability is covered by general tort law in England and Wales, public liability usually requires that a public authority infringes a duty of care owed towards the citizen and thereby causes damage or that it is vicariously liable for its officials. Generally, there is no duty of care towards the public unless a provision imposes such a duty. Established causes for public liability in England and Wales are negligence, breach of statutory duty – if the duty was imposed for the protection of a limited class of the public, and Parliament intended to confer on members of that class a private right of action for breaches of the duty – and misfeasance in public office.

(3) Misfeasance in public office traditionally requires a condemnable state of mind. However, in the *Three Rivers DC* case, the court found that 'recklessness' sufficed

and thereby broadened the scope of the tort. Nonetheless, misfeasance in public office remains difficult to prove because of these subjective requirements and the narrow test of damage and remoteness.[40] In summary, public liability in England and Wales provides for very strict restrictions in comparison with other legal systems.

11.3.B.2 THE NETHERLANDS

Burgerlijk Wetboek **11.22 (NL)**

Article 6:162 (1) He who commits a wrongful act against another, which can be attributed to him, is obliged to compensate the damage suffered by that other as a consequence thereof.

(2) A wrongful act is considered to be a violation of a right and an act or omission contrary to a legal obligation or what according to unwritten law has to be regarded as acceptable social conduct, insofar as there was no justification for this behaviour.

Notes

(1) The common tort law requirements apply to public liability claims. According to Dutch law, any tort law liability claim is founded if five requirements are fulfilled: first, there has to be an unlawful action of a public body; secondly, damage must be suffered; thirdly, there must be a causal link between the action and the damage sustained; fourthly, an unlawful action must be attributed to the public body; and finally, the law which is infringed must intend to protect the interests which were harmed (the so-called 'scope of the norm' requirement, which follows from Article 6:163 of the Civil Code).[41] Any form of subjective fault or *culpa* is not required. Furthermore, as a matter of principle, unlawful actions are always attributed to the public body which committed the unlawfulness.

(2) Potentially, any kind of action of a public body (or non-action when there is a duty to act) can give rise to public liability.[42] In practice, however, there is a noteworthy limitation: if a single-case decision is at issue, the claimant must first seek primary legal protection against the decision within due time through the intra-administrative objection procedure[43] or, if that is not successful, ask for annulment of the decision before the administrative court. If he does not do so in time, the decision will become final and hence is deemed to be legal. Thus, the individual cannot claim damages for the incurred losses. There are only a few exemptions to this rule, for example, if the authority informed the claimant wrongly about the possibility to object to the decision.

[40] S Hannett, 'Misfeasance in Public Office: The Principles' (2005) 10 *Judicial Review* 227, 231.

[41] See excerpt 11.23 below.

[42] LJA Damen et al, *Bestuursrecht*, 5th edn (The Hague, Boom Juridisch, 2016) para 11.3.1. For the liability for unlawful statutory legislation which infringes international law or Union law, see section 11.7.B below.

[43] On the intra-administrative objection procedure in the Netherlands, see Chapter 2, section 2.7.B.1 (ii).

Burgerlijk Wetboek **11.23 (NL)**

Article 6:163 There is no obligation to pay damages where the violated norm does not intend to offer protection against the damage as suffered by the wronged person.

Hoge Raad, 7 May 2004[44] **11.24 (NL)**

Van Hasselt v Defendants and the State

PUBLIC LIABILITY; RELATIVITY REQUIREMENT

Duwbak Linda

Damages can only be awarded where the violated norm intends to offer protection against the damage suffered by the claimant.

Facts: A lighter (named Linda) sunk in the river Meuse, due to the heavy rusting of its base plates. A year before, the lighter had been checked by a state expert. The expert had issued a certificate, explaining that the lighter was safe and in good condition. The certificate was valid for seven years. The claimant tried to hold the state liable for damages caused by the fact that the certificate was not issued in accordance with the applicable safety and inspection rules.

Held: The claim was dismissed as unfounded.

Judgment: 3.4.3 ... Against this backdrop, the verdict must be that the required due diligence during the inspections conducted to issue a certification, which stems from the State's general obligation to ensure safe maritime traffic, does not aim to protect in principle an unlimited group of third parties against monetary damages, which often occur in an unpredictable fashion, caused by a defect or the unsafe condition of a ship that did not come to light due to error or oversight during the inspections made by the State or under the responsibility of the State. Therefore, third parties cannot derive claims for damages against the State, or private third parties charged with the inspections, from the circumstance that the inspection was conducted negligently.

Note

In the Dutch system, an unlawful action that causes damage only results in public liability if the violated law intends to protect the interests that were harmed (so-called 'relativity requirement'). This 'scope of the norm' requirement is fulfilled if a subjective right of the claimant is infringed or if the purpose of the legal rule is to protect specific individual interests. Apart from the 'scope of the norm' requirement, there is no other limitation of public liability for unlawful actions of public administrative bodies.

11.4 LIABILITY FOR LAWFUL ACTION

In addition to public liability for unlawful action, France, the Netherlands and Germany also recognise public liability for lawful actions if the suffered damages were unusual

[44] ECLI:NL:HR:2004:AO6012.

and particularly severe. In France, specific risks of lawful administrative action can cause public liability. In the Netherlands and partly also in France, compensation for lawful action is based on the equality principle. Conversely, in Germany, liability for lawful action rests upon the fundamental right to property or physical integrity.

In the EU and in England and Wales, there is no express claim for damages resulting from lawful public action. However, in England and Wales, the administration sometimes grants *ex gratia* payments if citizens suffer unusual, severe damages from lawful administrative action.

11.4.A SYSTEMS ACKNOWLEDGING LIABILITY FOR LAWFUL ACTION: FRANCE, THE NETHERLANDS, GERMANY

11.4.A.1 COMPENSATION ON THE BASIS OF THE EQUALITY AND THE RISK PRINCIPLE IN FRANCE

Conseil d'État, 28 March 1919[45] **11.25 (FR)**

Regnault-Desrozier v Minister of War

LIABILITY FOR FAULTLESS ACTION BECAUSE OF DANGEROUS PUBLIC ACTIVITY

Regnault-Desroziers

Even if no fault of the administration can be proven, public liability may result from particularly risky behaviour of the administration.

Facts: The military had stored grenades in a warehouse, which exploded, thereby causing significant damage to surrounding persons and property.

Held: The state was held liable.

Judgment: Considering that it follows from the investigation that, since the year 1915, the military authority had accumulated a vast amount of grenades in the pillboxes of the Fort de la Double-Couronne, located close to a residential area of an important agglomeration; that, furthermore, it continuously handled these dangerous devices, in order to supply the armed forces in the battlefield quickly; considering that those operations, carried out with poor organisation due to the influence of military necessity, involved risks which exceeded the limits of those risks which normally result from living in the vicinity, and that those risks were of a nature, in case of an accident arising independently of any act of war, to incur, independently of any fault, state liability; considering that it is not challenged that the explosion of Fort de la Double-Couronne, which occurred on 4 March 1916, was the consequence of the operations described above; that, therefore, the applicant's claim that the state must repair the damage caused by this accident is well-founded.

Notes

(1) Even though the French public liability system is built on the concept of fault, it is well established that lawful action of the state can also cause liability where specific

[45] N° 62273.

risks are created by public authorities.[46] Liability based on the notion of risk can arise, first, when the administrative action is essentially dangerous; secondly, where private parties assist to fulfil public tasks without being public employees; thirdly, for damage to third parties caused by public works; and finally, with regard to damages caused by demonstrations.

(2) Furthermore, damages are granted exceptionally where the equality principle (*principe d'égalité*) would otherwise be infringed.[47] Liability for special and abnormal damages based on the equality principle are granted, for example, where damages are caused by continuous public works.

11.4.A.2 COMPENSATION ON THE BASIS OF THE EQUALITY PRINCIPLE IN THE NETHERLANDS

Raad van State, 6 May 1997[48] **11.26 (NL)**

Van Vlodrop Holding BV v Minister of Housing, Spatial Planning and the Environment

LIABILITY FOR LAWFUL ACTION BASED ON THE EQUALITY PRINCIPLE

Van Vlodrop

On the basis of the equality principle, special damages which fall outside the scope of the general risk of the public and create a special burden to the citizen must be compensated.

Facts: The Minister of Housing, Spatial Planning and the Environment changed his policy with regard to certain kinds of waste. The claimant asserted that he had suffered losses as a consequence of this 'sudden' change of policy and asked for compensation. No explicit provision for compensation for lawful public action applied in this case. The previous instances therefore rejected the claim for damages.

Held: The previous ruling was quashed and the case was referred to the lower court.

Judgment: … the power to take a decision on a request to compensate damage, that was caused by lawful action on the basis of a public law power, is based on the … general principle of *égalité devant les charges publiques*. On the basis of this principle, administrative authorities are obliged to compensate disproportionate damage, which falls out of the scope of the risk of the general public, and which creates a special burden for a certain group of citizens and which occurred in a legal relationship caused by an administrative action based on public law power.

Algemene Wet Bestuursrecht **11.27 (NL)**

Article 4:126 (1) If a public authority, making lawful use of its public powers or tasks, causes any damage which exceeds what usually may be socially expected to be acceptable,

[46] For details, see Berman and Picard (n 18 above) 83 ff.
[47] For more details, see Scherr (n 6 above) 228 ff; see also Berman and Picard (n 18 above) 84 ff.
[48] ECLI:NL:RVS:1997:AA6762.

and which affects the claimant, compared with others, disproportionately, the authority must decide to grant compensation on request of the one who suffered the damage.[49]

Notes

(1) In the Netherlands, liability for lawful action has a long and colourful history.[50] Although there have been certain public law acts which have contained explicit compensation provisions for damages for lawful administrative action for almost 100 years, there is still no general compensatory provision in force. Nevertheless, civil courts have been willing to hold the government liable for abnormal damages resulting from lawful action, even if there was no special compensatory provision.[51] In these cases, the Supreme Court acknowledged that the action of the state as such was legal, but held that the action became illegal because the public authority did not compensate the affected person for the excessive damage. Hence, technically, the Supreme Court established a tort liability (Article 1401 of the Burgerlijk Wetboek (BW); currently Article 6:162 BW) for special damages resulting from lawful administrative action.

(2) The administrative courts developed a compensation mechanism for abnormal damages suffered from legal administrative action without a legal basis. First, the administrative judges, similar to the civil branch, based the liability for lawful action on the failure of the administration to balance all relevant interests when taking a decision (Article 3:4(2) AWB). Thus, the public authority could be held liable for lawful action because of a failure to balance the financial interests of the damaged rights and interests in the correct way, and by not granting just compensation.[52] Later, the administrative courts based the compensation for lawful action on the equality principle inspired by the French system (*égalité devant les charges publiques*). The equality principle was regarded as a general principle of Dutch administrative law and as a sufficient legal basis for liability claims because of lawful public action (*zelfstandig schadebesluit*), although usually, general principles of administrative law do not provide a sufficient legal basis for administrative decisions. However, since the *Van Vlodrop* case, decisions about compensation payments for lawful public action can be based on the *égalité* principle.

(3) For decades, there has been intense discussion aimed at creating a sufficient legal basis for public liability for lawful action. Eventually, in January 2013, Article 4:126 AWB was introduced, which could serve as a very broad, general legal basis for claims to compensate disproportionate effects of lawful administrative

[49] This provision is not yet in force.

[50] For details, see the English summary of MKG Tjepkema, *Nadeelcompensatie op basis van het égalitébeginsel: een onderzoek naar nationaal, Frans en Europees recht* (Deventer, Kluwer, 2010) 959–80.

[51] This important case law, of which the prime examples are *Haagse Duinwaterleiding* (1944) NJ 226 and *Voorste Stroom* (1943) NJ 312, proved that the Supreme Court was willing to recognise an extra-legal right to damage compensation in certain circumstances.

[52] (1982) AB 299 (*Paul Krugerbrug*).

action (although it does not cover damages caused by legislation). According to this provision, three conditions must be met. First, the damage must have been caused in the exercise of a public law competence or task (*bevoegdheid of taak*). Secondly, there must be an abnormal burden for the claimant. Thirdly, the suffered damage must be special, which means that a single person or limited group must be more severely affected than others.[53] However, Article 4:126 AWB leaves many important questions open. It is unclear, for example, how it relates to the explicit compensation clauses in specific acts. Furthermore, some scholars and politicians fear that the very broad scope of Article 4:126 AWB will cause a (very expensive) flood of compensation claims.[54] Therefore, Article 4:126 AWB has not yet entered into force. It may take several more years before it does enter into force, and the provision may perhaps be altered or supplemented before it does. Until then, damages for lawful action have to be based on one of the following: if there is an explicit legal basis for a compensation claim, this has to be chosen. If not, the person who suffered the damage may choose between a public law claim, based on the *égalité* principle, and a civil law claim, based on tort law.

11.4.A.3 COMPENSATION FOR SACRIFICIAL AND EXPROPRIATORY ENCROACHMENT IN GERMANY

Bundesgerichtshof, 19 February 1953[55] **11.28 (DE)**

SACRIFICIAL ENCROACHMENT

Damages not resulting from expropriatory interferences with property, but rather resulting from the damage to physical welfare suffered in the course of legal state actions, may also lead to public liability.

Facts: The claimant asserted damage resulting from vaccination. The district court had granted compensation for the damage resulting from vaccination. The court of appeal had denied compensation because compensation was intended only for interferences with property.

Held: The appeal judgment was reversed.

Judgment: An *Aufopferungsanspruch* (claim to compensation for sacrificial encroachment) can, according to the legal principle contained in § 75 EinlALR, also be granted in cases of legal intervention and intrusion in physical welfare (adverse effects of vaccination). The contradicting judgment of the court of appeal … is reversed.

[53] E Engelhard et al, 'Let's Think Twice before We Revise! Égalité as the Foundation of Liability for Lawful Public Sector Acts' (2014) 10 *Utrecht Law Review* 55, 58 ff.

[54] For details on the critique regarding Art 4:126 AWB, see Engelhard et al (ibid) 60 ff.

[55] (1953) NJW 1217.

Bundesgerichtshof, 14 March 2013[56] **11.29 (DE)**

EXPROPRIATORY ENCROACHMENT

The precondition of a 'special sacrifice' in expropriatory encroachment claims is subject to a broad interpretation.

Facts: The claimant was a co-owner of an apartment. The apartment was damaged during a police search. The search warrant had been granted because of a suspicion that the tenant of the flat illegally traded large quantities of narcotic drugs. The claimant was aware of the tenant's past participation in drug-related crimes.

Held: The judgment of the higher civil court, which established that there was no right to compensation, was reversed and the case was referred back to the lower court.

Judgment: The property rights of the claimant have been infringed for the purposes of criminal prosecution and, thus, in the public interest. The claimant – and his father as co-owner – have been exposed to state intervention which forced them, as opposed to other owners, to make a self-sacrifice (*Aufopferung*) in the public interest. However, according to the jurisprudence of the Senate, it is not possible to speak of a special sacrifice (*Sonderopfer*) having been demanded in the public interest, and thereby of inequitable state behaviour requiring compensation, if the negatively affected party has voluntarily put itself into a dangerous situation. ... In this case, though, it cannot be said, that the claimant put himself in a dangerous position solely with regard to the fact that the owner, by renting out an apartment, exposes himself to a, although rather remote, danger that his tenant engages in criminal offences and that therefore as a result of judicial measures, damage to the apartment may occur.

... [A] claim for compensation does not fail, contrary to the view of the defendant, because of the fact that the actual damage amounts to merely €802. Under the law of expropriation, only a considerable tangible impairment of a legal property asset can amount to liability for compensation of the victim; minor impairments do not qualify .... However, in case of the intended damages or destruction of property through criminal law enforcement, such a tangible impairment of the concerned property lies already in the destruction of property (*Substanzverletzung*) which – except for petty offences – suffices for the acceptance of an unacceptable special sacrifice. In order to answer the question of whether the aggrieved party has been demanded in the public interest and by sovereign force to make a special sacrifice in an inequitable manner, it is generally irrelevant whether the aggrieved party has claims against third parties from the occurrence of the damage. A special sacrifice that must be compensated does usually not amount to an acceptable disadvantage by means of referring the aggrieved party to claims towards a third party and by thereby burdening him with the risk of enforceability of these claims.

Note

In Germany, lawful actions which cause an unusual loss, ie a 'special sacrifice', may cause public liability where the suffered loss is deemed to constitute an 'immediate' consequence of the legal state action. In case of the 'expropriatory encroachment' claim (*enteignender Eingriff*), immediacy requires that the suffered special sacrifice

[56] (2013) NJW 1736.

is an unforeseeable and unavoidable consequence of the lawful act, harming the property of the victim.[57] The claim for compensation resulting from 'sacrificial encroachment' (*Aufopferungsanspruch*) encompasses all cases where intangible assets, such as physical integrity, are affected by the lawful action of a public authority and cause the loss.[58] In all these cases, the claimant must have suffered an unusual loss. According to the judgment of the Federal Court of Justice (*Bundesgerichtshof*) of 14 March 2013, a 'special sacrifice' requires 'tangible' damage. Thus, minor damages resulting from lawful action will not be regarded as a special sacrifice but as a socially acceptable detriment which is not compensable. However, the destruction of property or intentional damage – except for petty detriment – is always regarded as a compensable special sacrifice.

11.4.B SYSTEMS WITHOUT A LIABILITY REGIME FOR LAWFUL ACTION

11.4.B.1 THE EUROPEAN UNION

Joined Cases C-120/06 P and C-121/06 P, 9 September 2008[59] **11.30 (EU)**

FIAMM and others v Council and Commission

COMPENSATION FOR LAWFUL ACTION

FIAMM

There is generally no compensation for lawful action of EU institutions.

Facts: The claimants had brought a claim for compensation for the damage allegedly suffered by them on account of the increased customs duty which the Dispute Settlement Body (the DSB) of the World Trade Organization (WTO) authorised the United States of America to levy on imports of their products, following a finding by the DSB that the Community regime governing the import of bananas was incompatible with the agreements and understandings annexed to the Agreement established by the WTO. The Court of First Instance had dismissed their claim. The claimants appealed against the judgment.

Held: The appeal was dismissed.

Judgment: 164. It should be pointed out first of all that, in accordance with the settled case law ..., the second paragraph of Article 288 EC means that the non-contractual liability of the Community and the exercise of the right to compensation for damage suffered depend on the satisfaction of a number of conditions relating to the unlawfulness of the conduct of which the institutions are accused, the fact of damage and the existence of a causal link between that conduct and the damage complained of.

[57] For details, see B Grzeszick, in D Ehlers and H Pünder (eds), *Allgemeines Verwaltungsrecht*, 15th edn (Berlin, De Gruyter, 2016) §45, para 86 ff.
[58] ibid para 100 ff.
[59] ECLI:EU:C:2008:476.

165. The Court has also repeatedly pointed out that the liability cannot be regarded as having been incurred without satisfaction of all the conditions to which the duty to make good any damage, as defined in the second paragraph of Article 288 EC, is thus subject (*Oleifici Mediterranei v EEC*, paragraph 17). …

167. The Court's case law enshrining, in accordance with the second paragraph of Article 288 EC, both the existence of the regime governing the non-contractual liability of the Community for the unlawful conduct of its institutions and the conditions for the regime's application is thus firmly established. By contrast, that is not so in the case of a regime governing non-contractual Community liability in the absence of such unlawful conduct.

169. As the Court of Justice noted in particular in *Dorsch Consult v Council and Commission*, paragraph 18, … the Court has on the contrary hitherto limited itself, as set out in settled case law, to specifying some of the conditions under which such liability could be incurred in the event of the principle of Community liability for a lawful act being recognised in Community law (see also, in similar terms, Case 59/83 *Biovilac v EEC* [1984] ECR 4057, paragraph 28). It was solely on that basis that the Court noted in *Dorsch Consult v Council and Commission*, paragraph 19, that if the principle of such liability came to be recognised, at the very least three conditions, comprising the fact of damage, the existence of a causal link between it and the act concerned and the unusual and special nature of the damage, would all have to be satisfied in order for liability to be incurred. …

175. Finally, it is clear that, while comparative examination of the Member States' legal systems enabled the Court to make at a very early stage the finding recalled in paragraph 170 of the present judgment concerning convergence of those legal systems in the establishment of a principle of liability in the case of unlawful action or an unlawful omission of the authority, including of a legislative nature, that is in no way the position as regards the possible existence of a principle of liability in the case of a lawful act or omission of the public authorities, in particular where it is of a legislative nature.

176. In the light of all the foregoing considerations, it must be concluded that, as Community law currently stands, no liability regime exists under which the Community can incur liability for conduct falling within the sphere of its legislative competence in a situation where any failure of such conduct to comply with the WTO agreements cannot be relied upon before the Community courts.

Note

The EU does not acknowledge liability for lawful actions of EU institutions. Although, in the *Dorsch Consult* case,[60] the Court of Justice seemed not to exclude this possibility completely, in *FIAMM*, it denied the existence in EU law of a specific remedy for non-fault liability. The central consideration of the Court of Justice was that such a principle has been recognised in only a limited number of Member States.

[60] Case C-327/98 P *Dorsch Consult Ingenieursgesellschaft mbH v Council and Commission* ECLI:EU:C:2000:321.

11.4.B.2 ENGLAND AND WALES

Parliamentary and Health Service Ombudsman **11.31 (EW)**

Principles for Remedy London: PHSO[61]

Where maladministration or poor service has led to injustice or hardship, public bodies should try to offer a remedy that returns the complainant to the position they would have been in otherwise. If that is not possible, the remedy should compensate them appropriately. Remedies should also be offered, where appropriate, to others who have suffered injustice or hardship as a result of the same maladministration or poor service.

There are no automatic or routine remedies for injustice or hardship resulting from maladministration or poor service. Remedies may be financial or non-financial.

An appropriate range of remedies will include:

An apology, explanation, and acknowledgement of responsibility; remedial action, which may include reviewing or changing a decision on the service given to an individual complainant; revising published material; revising procedures to prevent the same thing happening again; training or supervising staff; or any combination of these; financial compensation for direct or indirect financial loss, loss of opportunity, inconvenience, distress, or any combination of these.

Public bodies should:

Calculate payments for financial loss by looking at how much the complainant has demonstrably lost or what extra costs they have incurred; apply an appropriate interest rate to payments for financial loss, aimed at restoring complainants to the position they would have been in if the maladministration or poor service had not occurred; consider what interest rate to pay and explain the reasons for the chosen rate.

Factors to consider when deciding the level of financial compensation for inconvenience or distress should include:

The impact on the individual – for example whether the events contributed to ill health, or led to prolonged or aggravated injustice or hardship; the length of time taken to resolve a dispute or complaint; the trouble the individual was put to in pursuing the dispute or complaint. Remedies may need to take account of injustice or hardship that results from pursuing the complaint as well the original dispute. Financial compensation may be appropriate for:

Costs that the complainant incurred in pursuing the complaint; any inconvenience, distress or both that resulted from poor complaint handling by the public body.

Remedial action may include improvements to the public body's complaints policy or procedures.

Notes

(1) Generally, in England and Wales, public authorities are not liable for losses suffered in consequence of lawful administrative action. There can, of course, be liability for expropriation of property.[62] However, the requirements are difficult to meet.

[61] See www.ombudsman.org.uk/sites/default/files/page/Principles%20for%20Remedy.pdf.

[62] *Burmah Oil Company Ltd v Lord Advocate* [1965] AC 75 (HL); *Attorney-General v De Keyser's Royal Hotel Limited* [1920] AC 508 (HL).

Otherwise, public authorities in England and Wales may grant *ex gratia* payments, ie non-compulsory payments, to the victim if they suffer special losses in consequence of lawful administrative action.

(2) *Ex gratia* payments have been accepted, for example, for those who have been injured by vaccinations,[63] or, until 2004, for those who have been wrongly convicted.[64] Yet, no monetary compensation is awarded in cases where the claimant's legitimate expectations have been infringed. Administrative self-regulation replaces legal regulation in this respect.[65]

(3) In addition to the *ex gratia* payments outlined above, it is possible for the Parliamentary Commissioner for Administration or Local Commissioner for Administration to make a recommendation that compensation be paid to a victim of maladministration.[66] The Parliamentary Commissioner for Administration has also produced some 'Principles for Remedy', offering guidance to public authorities on the appropriate approach to adopt when offering redress for maladministration.

11.5 DAMAGES OR MERE 'JUST COMPENSATION'

With regard to the scope of liability claims, damages, punitive damages and compensation must be distinguished. Which compensatory relief is granted may depend on the nature of the liability claim. In cases of tortious liability, as well as in liability cases based on fault, full damages are granted. 'Equitable remedies', such as the German 'just compensation' (*Entschädigung*) for expropriatory or sacrificial encroachment claims, in contrast, only deliver compensation which does not cover the entire losses suffered. Where damages are granted, the claimant is put in the position he would have been in if the breach had not occurred. In comparison, 'just compensation' only comprises a reasonable indemnisation, which is aligned with the loss suffered but does not generally put the plaintiff in the hypothetical financial position he would have been in without the harmful event.[67] Thus, lost profit is mostly not included in compensation. Furthermore, punitive damages, also called 'exemplary damages', exist in the common law system of England and Wales. Punitive damages may exceed the actual suffered loss in order to punish the tortfeasor. They are only granted in exceptional cases, for example in cases of misfeasance in public office or malicious cases of defamation.

[63] Such compensation is made available via the Vaccine Damage Payment Scheme. Information on the scheme can be found at www.gov.uk/vaccine-damage-payment/overview.

[64] Compensation for wrongful conviction is now only possible where the claimant can establish a successful claim under s 133 (as amended) of the Criminal Justice Act 1988. For a recent interpretation of the requirements of s 133, see *R (Adams) v Secretary of State for Justice* [2011] UKSC 18, [2012] 1 AC 48.

[65] J Bell and A Bradley, *Governmental Liability: A Comparative Study* (London, United Kingdom National Committee of Comparative Law, 1991) 17, 43.

[66] For more information on the ombudsmen in the UK, see Chapter 10, section 10.3.A.

[67] In Germany, where both compensatory mechanisms can be found, the distinction between damages and compensation is very important. See C Ernst, in *Münchener Kommentar zum Bürgerlichen Gesetzbuch: BGB*, 6th edn (Munich, CH Beck, 2013) §903, para 109.

11.5.A LEGAL SYSTEMS GRANTING FULL COMPENSATION OF DAMAGES

11.5.A.1 THE EUROPEAN UNION

Joined Cases C-104/89 and C-37/90, 19 May 1992[68] **11.32 (EU)**

JM Mulder and others and Otto Heinemann v Council and Commission

DAMAGES FOR NON-CONTRACTUAL LIABILITY

Mulder

With regard to the scope of the compensatory relief, the amount of compensation payable by the EU should correspond to the damage which it caused.

Facts: In order to restore a fair balance on the milk market, in 1977, the European Commission had introduced a premium system for the non-marketing of milk through Council Regulation 1078/77. The claimants therefore refrained from trading milk products for several years. During that time, in 1984, new Council Regulations (856/84 and 857/84) were introduced, which set a reference quantity for milk producers based on the quantity of milk they had delivered in 1981. An additional levy was introduced for any milk that was traded in addition to the reference quantity, in order to discourage producers from oversupplying the market. As the claimants did not trade any milk in 1981 in consequence of the premium system, they suffered losses because they were not granted a reference quantity and thus could not market milk without the additional levy. In consequence of the subsequent case law, Council Regulation 764/89 introduced a new provision in 1989 which provided a special calculation base for reference quantities for milk producers who had not traded milk products in 1981 because of the premium system.

Held: The Council and Commission were held liable and were ordered to make good the damages suffered by the claimants from 1984 to 1989.

Judgment: As regards the extent of the damage which the Community should make good, in the absence of particular circumstances warranting a different assessment, account should be taken of the loss of earnings consisting in the difference between, on the one hand, the income which the applicants would have obtained in the normal course of events from the milk deliveries which they would have made if, during the period between 1 April 1984 (the date of entry into force of Regulation No 857/84) and 29 March 1989 (the date of entry into force of Regulation No 764/89), they had obtained the reference quantities to which they were entitled and, on the other hand, the income which they actually obtained from milk deliveries made during that period in the absence of any reference quantity, plus any income which they obtained, or could have obtained, during that period from any replacement activities. ... It follows that the amount of compensation payable by the Community should correspond to the damage which it caused.

Note

Article 340 TFEU, which governs non-contractual liability, does not contain any substantive provision but merely refers to the 'general principles common to the laws

[68] ECLI:EU:C:1992:217.

of the Member States' as a source of inspiration for the conditions under which the Union may be held liable. While the CJEU drew inspiration from national law, over time, it has created an autonomous European system of liability. With regard to the assessment of the damage in cases of unlawful action, the *Mulder* case suggests that the general objective is to place the victim in the same situation in which he would have been if the wrong had not been committed. To this end, the damage must first be certain, although the courts have sometimes accepted claims for imminent damages if they are foreseeable with sufficient certainty.[69] Secondly, the damage must be specific, in the sense that it must affect the applicant's interest in a special and individual way.[70] Thirdly, the damage must be proven by the applicant.[71] Finally, the damage must be quantifiable. This includes the losses actually sustained and lost profits if they were foreseeable with sufficient certainty.[72]

11.5.A.2 FRANCE

C Paillard, Le préjudice indemnisable en droit administratif[73] **11.33 (FR)**

Even if compensable loss is clearly a category in evolution, it is nevertheless possible to present a typology. This is indeed indispensable to present the variety of types of compensable loss. The typology is widely grounded on the distinction between damage and loss. When the damage is considered as a breach, damages shall be classified according to the object of the breach, whereas the classification of losses must be established according to their nature. This approach leads to the adoption of a tripartite classification of damage (damage to a good, damage to a situation or an activity, physical damage) and a binary classification of the loss resulting from this damage (namely, pecuniary and non-pecuniary loss) ....

The application of this classification leads to the consideration of three cases. First, pecuniary and non-pecuniary loss can result from damage to a movable or immovable good. It is not excluded that such a damage could be the source of non-pecuniary loss (for example, in cases of changes in the conditions of existence, or disturbances of enjoyment) even if the damage mainly results in a pecuniary loss (in the form of material loss, including repair works, caused by the infringement to property and/or non-material loss, meaning the financial loss such as the loss of rents due to the destruction of an immovable property).

Moreover, a pecuniary and/or non-pecuniary loss may result from a breach of the situation or activity of a person (other than an infringement to his bodily integrity). This infringement covers various scenarios: a breach impacting on a commercial activity,

[69] Joined Cases 5/66, 7/66 and 13–24/66 *Kampffmeyer v Commission* ECLI:EU:C:1967:31, para 741.

[70] Joined Cases 83/76, 94/76, 4/77, 15/77 and 40/77 *Bayerische HNL Verhmehrungsbetriebe v Council and Commission* ECLI:EU:C:1978:113.

[71] Case 26/68 *Fux v Commission* ECLI:EU:C:1969:26, para 156.

[72] *Kampffmeyer* (n 70 above) paras 266–67.

[73] C Paillard, 'Le préjudice indemnisable en droit administratif' (2011) 1 *Droit administratif* 7.

a breach of an artist's moral rights to his work, a breach impacting someone's honour and reputation, a breach of a fundamental freedom, etc.

Finally, pecuniary and/or non-pecuniary losses may result from a physical injury, meaning a violation of physical integrity of the human person: injuries, paralysis, diseases, infections, death. Physical injury is the category which leads to the greatest diversification of the types of compensable loss: for a long time, the administrative judge has compensated the *pretium doloris*, aesthetical loss, the disturbance in living conditions, the loss of amenity, moral loss, moral suffering, this list is not exhaustive.

Note

In the past, in France, only pecuniary compensation was granted to the claimant in public liability cases.[74] However, since the *Le Tisserand* case,[75] lost profits as well as pain and suffering are generally compensable.[76] This is equally true for liability for lawful and for unlawful actions. Traditionally, the compensation in administrative courts was lower than in civil courts. Today, the two court branches increasingly adjust compensatory relief in order to achieve parity.

11.5.B SYSTEMS WITH MORE COMPLEX COMPENSATORY MECHANISMS

11.5.B.1 GERMANY

Bürgerliches Gesetzbuch **11.34 (DE)**

§249 (1) A person who is liable in damages must restore the position that would exist if the circumstance obliging him to pay damages had not occurred.

(2) Where damages are payable for injury to a person or damage to real property or chattels, the claimant may demand the required monetary amount in lieu of restoration.

§252 The awarded damages also comprise lost profits. Only those lost profits are compensable, which in the normal course of events or in the special circumstances, particularly due to the measures and precautions taken, could probably be expected.

§253 (2) If damages are to be paid for an injury to body, health, freedom or sexual self-determination, reasonable compensation in pecuniary form may also be demanded for any damage that is not pecuniary loss.

[74] See MA Latournerie, 'The Law of France' in J Bell and A Bradley (eds), *Governmental Liability: A Comparative Study* (London, United Kingdom National Committee of Comparative Law, 1991) 220.

[75] Conseil d'État, 24 November 1961, *Le tisserand*, N° 48841.

[76] N Marsch, 'Frankreich' in O Dörr (ed), *Staatshaftung in Europa: Nationales und Unionsrecht* (Berlin, De Gruyter, 2014) 195, 218.

Notes

(1) As seen above, German public liability law is rooted in two different systems, with differing compensatory consequences.[77] On the one hand, there is a tortious liability for unlawful acts committed by a public authority (§839 BGB in conjunction with Article 34 of the Grundgesetz[78]). In this case, the claimant is entitled to the full award of damages, including lost profit and damages for pain and suffering to the victim, according to §249 ff BGB.

(2) On the other hand, public liability – especially for lawful public action – can be derived from the idea of sacrificial encroachment (*Aufopferung*, §§74 and 75 EinlALR)[79] and expropriation (*Enteignung*, Article 14(3) of the Grundgesetz).[80] In these cases, the civil law provisions do not apply and the victim can only claim just compensation for suffering, which generally excludes compensation for lost profits and pain and suffering.

11.5.B.2 THE NETHERLANDS

In the Netherlands, the scope of compensation differs in cases of liability for unlawful action and cases of liability for lawful action. If all requirements of public liability for unlawful action are fulfilled, in general all damages which occur as a consequence of the unlawful action of the administrative authority will be compensated (ie full compensation will be awarded). In very exceptional cases, the judge may reduce the amount of compensation if full compensation would 'obviously be unacceptable' (Article 6:109 BW). Hence, lost profits and compensation for pain and suffering are included in principle. However, one should take into account that compensation for lost profits is only possible if the legal requirement which was infringed had as one of its purposes to protect the financial interests of the plaintiff, especially his interest to earn profits (Article 6:163 BW, *Relativiteitsvereiste*, relativity requirement).[81] Often, a public law requirement will not have the function of protecting the interests of private parties to make profits. The courts are also quite reluctant to acknowledge compensation for pain and suffering.

As seen above,[82] compensation for damage caused by lawful action can only be compensated if the damage goes beyond what is socially acceptable and if the claimant is disproportionally affected compared with others. Therefore, compensation of damage caused by lawful public action will almost never result in full compensation. Normally, a certain amount of the damages suffered because of a lawful public action will be regarded as a socially acceptable detriment which is not compensable.

[77] See section 11.3.A.2 above.
[78] See section 11.3.A.2 above.
[79] See section 11.3.A.2, excerpt 11.12 above.
[80] See sections 11.3.A.2. and excerpt 11.11 above.
[81] See section 11.3.B.2 above.
[82] See section 11.4.A.2 above.

11.5.B.3 ENGLAND AND WALES

House of Lords, 13 February 1880[83] **11.35 (EW)**

Livingstone v Rawyards Coal Company

MEASURE OF DAMAGES IN TORT

Livingstone

The damages awarded should put the party who has been injured, or who has suffered, in the same position as he would have been in had he not suffered the loss for which compensation is sought.

Facts: As a result of a mistaken belief that they had the legal right to do so, R mined and sold the coal from L's land. L sued R, seeking compensation for the loss.

Held: The claimant was awarded damages.

Judgment: Lord Blackburn: ... I do not think there is any difference of opinion as to its being a general rule that, where any injury is to be compensated by damages, in settling the sum of money to be given for reparation of damages you should as nearly as possible get at that sum of money which will put the party who has been injured, or who has suffered, in the same position as he would have been in if he had not sustained the wrong for which he is now getting his compensation or reparation. That must be qualified by a great many things which may arise – such, for instance, as by the consideration whether the damage has been maliciously done, or whether it has been done with full knowledge that the person doing it was doing wrong.

Note

As public liability in England and Wales is based on civil tort law, full damages are usually awarded to the victims. In the case of damages for breach of a Convention Right under the Human Rights Act 1998, the measure of compensation will be in line with the principle of just satisfaction developed in the jurisprudence of the European Court of Human Rights (ECtHR).[84] Thus, claims for pecuniary losses, including those for lost profit, might be made in appropriate cases.[85] Similarly, in appropriate cases, there can be claims for pain and suffering (the most common being for unlawful detention under Article 5 ECHR), but this is less common in the jurisprudence of the ECtHR. It is possible in some circumstances for a claimant to claim 'exemplary damages', which are essentially punitive in nature, although this only tends to arise in cases of deliberate wrongdoing under the tort of misfeasance in

[83] [1875] 5 App Cas 25 (HL).

[84] It is generally felt that the measure will therefore be lower, in accordance with the 'just satisfaction' principle adopted by the European Court of Human Rights. See the detailed treatments in *Anufrijeva* [2003] EWCA Civ 1406, [2004] QB 1124; *Greenfield* [2005] UKHL 14, [2005] 1 WLR 673.

[85] *Jain v Trent Strategic Health Authority* [2009] UKHL 4, [2009] 1 AC 853.

public office.[86] These are potentially available only in cases of unconstitutional or oppressive action by a public authority, or where the wrongdoing is calculated to make a profit.[87]

11.6 LIABILITY IN RESPECT OF JUDICIARY

The legal landscape of public liability for judicial action is very diverse. All legal systems have to balance the competing principles of individual justice on the one hand and res judicata and the independence of the judiciary on the other hand. In England and Wales, there is traditionally no domestic legal remedy for judicial wrongdoing, whereas in the other legal orders strict limitations apply with regard to public liability for judicial acts. The Court of Justice established Member States' public liability for judicial breaches of EU law in the *Köbler* judgment.[88]

11.6.A EUROPEAN REQUIREMENTS

Case C-224/01, 30 September 2003[89] **11.36 (EU)**

Gerhard Köbler v Austria

MEMBER STATE JUDICIAL LIABILITY FOR BREACHES OF EU LAW

Köbler

Member States are also liable for unlawful adjudication of last instance courts if the conditions for state liability are met.

Facts: Mr Köbler had been employed as an ordinary university professor in Austria. In 1996, he applied for the special length-of-service increment for university professors. His request was denied, because the duration of his service in universities of other Member States was not taken into consideration. Upon refusal of his application, Mr Köbler brought proceedings before the Austrian courts, arguing that such a requirement constituted indirect discrimination contrary to EU law. The administrative court of last instance made a reference on that point to the Court of Justice of the European Communities. Following a judgment of the Court of Justice in a similar case, the Austrian court withdrew its request for a preliminary ruling and dismissed Mr Köbler's action on the grounds that the special length-of-service increment was a loyalty bonus which justified a derogation from the provisions on freedom of movement for workers. This ruling was confirmed by the final instance appellate court in Austria. Mr Köbler subsequently brought an action for damages against the Republic of Austria before the Civil Court, on the grounds that the judgment of the highest administrative court was contrary to EU law. The referring court submitted certain questions to the Court of Justice, amongst which was the question of whether Austria was liable for the wrongful adjudication of the administrative court of last instance.

[86] *Kuddus v Chief Constable of Leicestershire Constabulary* [2001] UKHL 29, [2002] 2 AC 122.
[87] ibid.
[88] For a critical review, see the comparative study of KM Scherr, 'Comparative Aspects of the Application of the Principle of State Liability for Judicial Breaches' (2012) 12 *ERA Forum* 565, 572 ff.
[89] ECLI:EU:C:2003:513.

Held: Member States are liable for unlawful adjudication of final instance courts if the conditions for state liability are met. However, in this case, the breach of Community law was not considered to be sufficiently manifest to cause liability.

Judgment: 30. First, as the Court has repeatedly held, the principle of liability on the part of a Member State for damage caused to individuals as a result of breaches of Community law for which the State is responsible is inherent in the system of the Treaty …

33. In the light of the essential role played by the judiciary in the protection of the rights derived by individuals from Community rules, the full effectiveness of those rules would be called in question and the protection of those rights would be weakened if individuals were precluded from being able, under certain conditions, to obtain reparation when their rights are affected by an infringement of Community law attributable to a decision of a court of a Member State adjudicating at last instance. …

36. Consequently, it follows from the requirements inherent in the protection of the rights of individuals relying on Community law that they must have the possibility of obtaining redress in the national courts for the damage caused by the infringement of those rights owing to a decision of a court adjudicating at last instance …

37. In that regard the importance of the principle of *res judicata* cannot be disputed … In order to ensure both stability of the law and legal relations and the sound administration of justice, it is important that judicial decisions which have become definitive after all rights of appeal have been exhausted or after expiry of the time-limits provided for in that connection can no longer be called in question. …

39. However, it should be borne in mind that recognition of the principle of State liability for a decision of a court adjudicating at last instance does not in itself have the consequence of calling in question that decision as *res judicata*. … The applicant in an action to establish the liability of the State will, if successful, secure an order against it for reparation of the damage incurred but not necessarily a declaration invalidating the status of *res judicata* of the judicial decision which was responsible for the damage. In any event, the principle of State liability inherent in the Community legal order requires such reparation, but not revision of the judicial decision which was responsible for the damage. …

50. It follows from the foregoing that the principle according to which the Member States are liable to afford reparation of damage caused to individuals as a result of infringements of Community law for which they are responsible is also applicable where the alleged infringement stems from a decision of a court adjudicating at last instance. It is for the legal system of each Member State to designate the court competent to adjudicate on disputes relating to such reparation.

51. As to the conditions to be satisfied for a Member State to be required to make reparation for loss and damage caused to individuals as a result of breaches of Community law for which the State is responsible, the Court has held that these are threefold: the rule of law infringed must be intended to confer rights on individuals; the breach must be sufficiently serious; and there must be a direct causal link between the breach of the obligation incumbent on the State and the loss or damage sustained by the injured parties …

52. State liability for loss or damage caused by a decision of a national court adjudicating at last instance which infringes a rule of Community law is governed by the same conditions.

53. With regard more particularly to the second of those conditions and its application with a view to establishing possible State liability owing to a decision of a national

court adjudicating at last instance, regard must be had to the specific nature of the judicial function and to the legitimate requirements of legal certainty, as the Member States which submitted observations in this case have also contended. State liability for an infringement of Community law by a decision of a national court adjudicating at last instance can be incurred only in the exceptional case where the court has manifestly infringed the applicable law.

54. In order to determine whether that condition is satisfied, the national court hearing a claim for reparation must take account of all the factors which characterise the situation put before it.

55. Those factors include, in particular, the degree of clarity and precision of the rule infringed, whether the infringement was intentional, whether the error of law was excusable or inexcusable, the position taken, where applicable, by a Community institution and non-compliance by the court in question with its obligation to make a reference for a preliminary ruling under the third paragraph of Article 234 EC.

56. In any event, an infringement of Community law will be sufficiently serious where the decision concerned was made in manifest breach of the case-law of the Court in the matter …

126. The reply to the fourth and fifth questions must therefore be that an infringement of Community law, such as that stemming in the circumstances of the main proceedings from the judgment of the Verwaltungsgerichtshof of 24 June 1998, does not have the requisite manifest character for liability under Community law to be incurred by a Member State for a decision of one of its courts adjudicating at last instance.

Note

As shown in section 11.3.A.3 above, the CJEU established three requirements for EU liability based on the requirements specifically set for Member States' liability for breaches of European law, namely: that the rule of law infringed must be intended to confer rights on individuals; that the breach must be sufficiently serious; and there must be a direct causal link between the breach of the obligation incumbent on the state and the loss or damage sustained by the injured parties. In the *Köbler* judgment, the CJEU also applied these criteria to judicial wrongdoing of final instance rulings in the Member States. At the same time, the Court increased the threshold for the 'sufficiently serious breach' criterion in cases of judicial violations of EU law at last instance.[90] Member States can only be held liable for last instance judgments in the exceptional case that the court *manifestly* infringes the applicable law.

11.6.B NO JUDICIAL LIABILITY IN ENGLAND AND WALES

Crown Proceedings Act 1947 **11.37 (EW)**

Section 2 (5) No proceedings shall lie against the Crown by virtue of this section in respect of anything done or omitted to be done by any person while discharging or purporting to discharge any responsibilities of a judicial nature vested in him, or any responsibilities which he has in connection with the execution of judicial process.

[90] See Scherr (n 88 above) 570.

Court of Appeal (Civil Division), 12 May 2010[91] **11.38 (EW)**

Cooper v HM Attorney General

LIABILITY OF JUDICIARY FOR BREACHES OF EU LAW

Cooper

'Köbler *liability' is in principle available in the law of England and Wales, but it will be necessary to demonstrate a 'manifest infringement' of the applicable law.*

Facts: C brought a claim in tort for damages concerning two decisions of the Court of Appeal interpreting the requirements of the Environmental Impact Assessment Directive 85/337/EEC, which were subsequently found to be incorrect by the Court of Justice. C had been involved in both of these two cases and claimed in tort for the costs orders that had been made against him as an unsuccessful claimant.

Held: No state liability was established.

Judgment: Plender J: 64. In *Köbler* the Court of Justice explained that there were three conditions for member state liability for the acts of national supreme courts …

65. As to the second condition, the Court of Justice held:

'53. … State liability for an infringement of Community law by a decision of a national court adjudicating at last instance can be incurred only in the exceptional case where the court has manifestly infringed the applicable law.

54. In order to determine whether that condition is satisfied, the national court hearing a claim for reparation must take account of all the factors which characterise the situation put before it.

55. Those factors include, in particular, the degree of clarity and precision of the rule infringed, whether the infringement was intentional, whether the error of law was excusable or inexcusable, the position taken, where applicable, by a Community institution, and non-compliance by the court in question with its obligation to make a reference for a preliminary ruling under the third paragraph of article 234 EC.

56. In any event, an infringement of Community law will be sufficiently serious where the decision concerned was made in manifest breach of the case law of the Court of Justice in the matter: …

69. … It is clear that for a breach to be manifest it must be evident that there is a breach. It may be evident that it is a breach because the Court of Justice has already decided the point or it may follow from the case law of the Court of Justice that a particular set of circumstances constitutes a breach. However, in our judgment, when in paragraph 56 of its judgment the Court of Justice refers to a breach of Community law being sufficiently serious if it is in 'manifest breach' of its own case law, the Court did not intend to exclude from consideration the other factors 'which characterise the situation' …

70. It is helpful to consider what is not a manifest breach. In our judgment, a breach is not manifest if the answer to the question before the court is not evident in the sense just given. It will also not be manifest if it represents the answer to which the court has come through undertaking a normal judicial function. Interpretation of Community legislation is part of the normal judicial function and liability would no longer be exceptional

[91] [2010] EWCA Civ 464, [2011] QB 976.

if it could arise whenever the interpretation was shown to be wrong – if only because the Court of Justice often adopts an innovative interpretation or one motivated by policy insights that would not necessarily be available to the national court. There is in our judgment no member state liability simply because the national court arrives at the wrong answer: this is because 'regard is [required to be] had to the specific nature of the judicial function'.

71. This point is shown by the facts of *Köbler* itself. ... It must follow that the failure to make a reference because the court did not appreciate that the issue before it raised a question of Community law does not automatically result in *Köbler* liability unless it is obvious from Community law that there is a Community issue and an absence of mitigating circumstances. ...

74. If the decision of the national court was not in manifest breach of the case law, it may have been in manifest breach of some legislative requirement of Community law ...

76. That leads to the question: what errors of Community law are relevant? Although the first preliminary issue asks in this case what errors were made as a matter of Community law, in our judgment *Köbler* liability is only concerned with errors that were material for the purposes of that cause of action. The fact that other errors of Community law were made along the way is not relevant and gives rise to no claim. Thus, for example, the court's failure to deal with an argument on direct effect would not be material unless there was some relevant right conferred by the EIA Directive that had not been transposed into domestic law which was appropriately enforced through direct effect. It is therefore sufficient to ask whether there was some relevant right conferred by the EIA Directive to which effect should have been given by either of the impugned decisions and which would have led to a result in favour of CPRE.

77. Difficult questions might arise if a point was argued on one basis, which was bound to fail, but which would have succeeded if made on another basis. *Köbler* liability does not attach in our judgment in those circumstances unless it can be said that the court should itself have taken the point that would have succeeded. In *Kraaijeveld*, the Court of Justice held that where a court had power to take a point of national law, it should be under a duty to do so also in relation to 'binding rules' of Community law: ...

78. We proceed on the basis that a 'binding rule' is one which a party either does not, or cannot, waive.

79. A national judge applying Community law is not expected to do more, by way of taking a point of his own motion, than a judge would normally be entitled or bound to do in his jurisdiction. ... An analogy can be drawn with statutory interpretation. Even when undertaking a conforming interpretation a national judge is only required by Community law to interpret national legislation in conformity with Community legislation if that can be achieved under domestic principles of statutory interpretation: ... In England and Wales, in public law, the court may, if it is aware of the point, within certain limits take a point of law that has not previously been put forward by any party but which it considers has an important bearing on the case. Mr McCracken relies on this principle to assist his case where the argument put forward on behalf of CPRE did not make some submission which (if the court had not acted in breach of Community law) might have won the day.

82. ... We note that, although the Court of Justice in *Köbler* lists non-compliance with the obligation to make a reference as a factor which may result in the breach being characterised as sufficiently serious (see *Köbler*, paragraph 55), it is not described as a manifest breach in itself. This lends support to the argument that a breach of Community law may not be relevant unless it results in a breach of substantive Community law. ...

83. Alternatively, it may be that the breach of the obligation to refer should always be treated as insufficiently serious unless the answer to the question that ought to have been referred would have been that the order, which the national court made constituted a breach of a substantive rule of Community law.

Notes

(1) In England and Wales, judicial acts enjoy special immunity. The immunity of the Crown for judicial actions is explicitly stated in the Crown Proceedings Act. Thus, generally, there is no public liability for judicial wrongdoing in England and Wales.

(2) Nonetheless, in light of *Köbler*, the English courts accept that it may be possible for the judiciary to be liable for an erroneous decision which is contrary to EU law. However, the requirement of a 'manifest breach' establishes a high threshold. In the *Cooper* case, the Court of Appeal gave some indications as to which factors have to be taken into account regarding the question of whether a manifest infringement of EU law has occurred.

11.6.C JUDICIAL LIABILITY WITH STRICT LIMITATIONS IN FRANCE, GERMANY AND THE NETHERLANDS

Code de l'organisation judiciaire **11.39 (FR)**

Article L141-1 The state shall compensate the damage caused by wrongful actions of the judiciary. Unless provided otherwise, this liability only applies in cases of gross negligence (*faute lourde*) or denial of justice.

Bürgerliches Gesetzbuch **11.40 (DE)**

§839 (2) If a public official breaches his official duties when issuing a ruling in legal proceedings, he is only responsible for any damage arising from this if the breach of duty constitutes a criminal offence. This provision is not applicable to an illegal refusal to exercise or delay in the exercise of a public function.

Strafgesetzbuch **11.41 (DE)**

§332 (2) A judge or an arbitrator who allows himself to be promised or accepts a benefit for himself or for a third person in return for the fact that he performed or will in the future perform a judicial act and thereby violated or will violate his judicial duties shall be liable to imprisonment from one to ten years.

§339 A judge, another public official or an arbitrator who in conducting or deciding a legal matter perverts the course of justice for the benefit or to the detriment of a party shall be liable to imprisonment from one to five years.

Hoge Raad, 3 December 1971[92] **11.42 (NL)**

X te Bussum v the State

JUDICIAL LIABILITY

Bussum

The state is only liable for judicial wrongdoings if general principles of law have been infringed which are so fundamental that one cannot any longer speak of a fair and impartial trial, and there is and has been no further possibility of appeal.

Facts: On 29 July 1955, the Utrecht district court decided on a suspension of an employment agreement between the claimant and company Y. The Court based its judgment on the written statements of some witnesses, who were not heard in court.

Held: The claimant was not compensated for the judicial wrongdoing.

Judgment: … also with regard to the diligence of judicial procedures, it is only possible to complain by making use of any kind of appeal provided by statute, since a discussion on the diligence of the preparation of the judgment and its influence on the outcome of the case would question the validity of the judgment itself …

Only if, when preparing the judgment, general principles of law have been infringed which are so fundamental that one cannot any longer speak of a fair and impartial trial, and there is and has been no further possibility of appeal, may the state be liable for the infringement of the rights deriving from Article 6 of the European Convention on Human Rights and the damage occurring from such an infringement. However, apart from the question of whether Dutch law provides any basis which allows a judge to rule on such a question, the appeal does not contain any complaints about such an infringement.

Notes

(1) In French, German and Dutch domestic public liability law, there is a high threshold for legal remedies with regard to judicial errors committed at the final instance. In France, gross negligence (*faute lourde*) or a denial of justice is required. Similarly, in Dutch law, it is required that 'general principles of law have been infringed which are so fundamental that one cannot any longer speak of a fair and impartial trial, and there is and has been no further possibility of appeal'.[93] In Germany, according to §839(2) BGB, liability for judicial action requires that the breach of the judicial duty constitutes a criminal offence. The German state is, thus, only liable for an unlawful action of a judge if he or she perverts the course of justice for the benefit or to the detriment of one party (*Rechtsbeugung*, §339 of the Strafgesetzbuch (StGB)) or when the judge has accepted bribes (*Bestechlichkeit*, §332(2) StGB).

(2) Where EU law is at stake, these strict limitations conflict with the *Köbler* case law. In its *Traghetti del Mediterraneo* decision, the CJEU held that a similarly

[92] ECLI:NL:HR:1971:AB6788.
[93] ibid.

restrictive Italian provision was incompatible with the law of the Union.[94] Thus, many scholars in Germany argue that §839(2) BGB should not be applicable within the scope of EU law.[95]

(3) In the Netherlands, similar voices have been heard since the *Köbler* case. According to academics, the Dutch courts should apply the *Köbler* criteria in EU cases, in addition to the restrictive criteria set out in the leading case *X te Bussum*.[96] Recently, the lower courts have indeed followed this line in the first Dutch case, *State v KLM pilots*,[97] in which the state was held liable for an alleged manifest infringement of EU law by the Supreme Court in an earlier judgment.[98] The claim has, however, been rejected by both lower courts in substance because, according to them, the Supreme Court did not breach EU law at all (let alone manifestly). The case is currently pending before the Supreme Court. It is expected that the Supreme Court will uphold the contested judgment.

(4) In the French system, the liability of the state on the ground of a breach of EU law by a judicial decision did not lead to any change in the liability regime established by Article L141-1 of the Code de l'organisation judiciaire. The *Gestas* case is an example of a case of state liability for judicial error due to a violation of EU law where the national liability regime (and the gross negligence – *faute lourde* – requirement) was applied.[99]

11.7 PUBLIC LIABILITY FOR BREACHES OF EU LAW

Having analysed the public liability regimes of the different legal systems above, this section examines public liability for breaches of EU law. According to the settled case law of the CJEU, Member States are liable to private parties for damage resulting from the breach of EU law by public authorities.[100] The Member States have implemented EU liability for breaches of EU law in different ways.[101] In the Netherlands,

[94] Case C-173/03 *Traghetti del Mediterraneo v Italy* ECLI:EU:C:2006:391, para 38.

[95] For the German discussion, see F Kremer, 'Staatshaftung für Verstöße gegen Gemeinschaftsrecht durch letztinstanzliche Gerichte' (2004) *Neue Juridische Wochenschrift* 480, 482; W Frenz and V Götzkes, 'Staatshaftung für Gerichtsentscheidungen bei auslegungsbedürftigem Recht' (2009) *Europarecht* 622, 641 and references therein.

[96] See R Ortlep and RJGM Widdershoven, 'Schendingen van EG-recht door rechters' (2004) 2 *O&A* 34; for the current discussion, see, eg T Barkhuysen and ML van Emmerik, 'Onrechtmatige rechtspraak na 100 jaar Noordwijkerhout/Guldemond' in RJN Schlössels et al (eds), *De burgerlijke rechter in het publiekrecht* (Deventer, Kluwer, 2015) 179–99.

[97] Rechtbank Den Haag, 3 June 2015, ECLI:NL:RBDHA:2015:6222, affirmed in appeal by Hof Den Haag, 25 October 2016, ECLI:NL:GHDHA:2016:2981.

[98] In the judgment (2012) NJ 547.

[99] Conseil d'État, 18 June 2008, *Gestas*, N° 295831.

[100] Joined Cases C-6/90 and C-9/90 *Francovich and Bonifaci and others v Italy* ECLI:EU:C:1991:428; Joined Cases C-178/94, C-179/94, C-188/94, C-189/94 and C-190/94 *Dillenkofer and others v Germany* ECLI:EU:C:1996:375; Joined Cases C-46/93 and C-48/93 *Brasserie du Pêcheur v Germany* ECLI:EU:C:1996:79.

[101] For a more detailed comparative study, see BJ Hartmann, 'Alignment of National Government Liability Law in Europe after Francovich' (2012) 12 *ERA Forum* 613.

public liability law is broad enough to include the violation of European law in the general public liability system.[102] In contrast, England and Wales and Germany have established independent claims for breaches of EU law alongside domestic public liability claims.[103] In France, administrative acts which violate EU law fall under the general doctrinal set of public law rules and are treated equally to violations of national law. However, special rules have been created in case law for legislative violations of EU law, because the thresholds applicable to domestic public liability claims for legislative acts are too high. Thus, even though the EU law harmonised public liability within its limited scope, England and Wales, Germany and France refrained from generally adapting their domestic public liability regimes to the EU standards.

11.7.A EUROPEAN REQUIREMENTS

11.7.A.1 LIABILITY OF THE MEMBER STATES FOR BREACHES OF EU LAW

Joined Cases C-6/90 and C-9/90, 19 November 1991[104] **11.43 (EU)**

Francovich and others v Italy

MEMBER STATE LIABILITY FOR FAILURE TO IMPLEMENT AN EU DIRECTIVE

Francovich

A Member State is required to compensate losses caused to individuals by failure to implement directives within the implementation period.

Facts: Under the Insolvency Protection Directive 80/987, EU Member States were expected to implement rules in their national law to give a minimum level of insurance to employees whose wages would be unpaid if their employers became insolvent. Mr Francovich was entitled to 6 million lira, and Mr Bonifaci and 33 of his colleagues were together entitled to 253 million lira after their company had become insolvent, according to the Directive. The Directive had to be implemented by 1983, but five years later they had been paid nothing, as the company liquidators had informed them that no money remained. They brought a claim against the Italian state, arguing that it had to pay damages to compensate for their losses instead, on account of a failure to implement the Directive. The national courts referred several questions to the Court of Justice in order to clarify whether the Italian state could be held liable for the suffered losses.

Held: A Member State is required to make good losses caused to individuals by failure to implement directives within the implementation period.

Judgment: 33. The full effectiveness of Community rules would be impaired and the protection of the rights which they grant would be weakened if individuals were unable to obtain redress when their rights are infringed by a breach of Community law for which a Member State can be held responsible.

[102] EU law breaches are thus treated in the same way as national law violations.

[103] In both countries, there is an academic controversy about whether it would be preferable to include the principles of the EU liability in the general rules governing public liability instead of handling it as a separate action. For the discussion in Germany, see F Schoch, 'Staatshaftung wegen Verstoßes gegen Europäisches Gemeinschaftsrecht' (2002) *Jura* 837, 840 ff; for the discussion in England and Wales, see M Amos, 'Extending the Liability of the State in Damages' (2001) 21 *Legal Studies* 1, 9 ff.

[104] ECLI:EU:C:1991:428.

34. The possibility of obtaining redress from the Member State is particularly indispensable where, as in this case, the full effectiveness of Community rules is subject to prior action on the part of the State and where, consequently, in the absence of such action, individuals cannot enforce before the national courts the rights conferred upon them by Community law.

35. It follows that the principle whereby a State must be liable for loss and damage caused to individuals as a result of breaches of Community law for which the State can be held responsible is inherent in the system of the Treaty. …

39. Where, as in this case, a Member State fails to fulfil its obligation under the third paragraph of Article 189 of the Treaty to take all the measures necessary to achieve the result prescribed by a directive, the full effectiveness of that rule of Community law requires that there should be a right to reparation provided that three conditions are fulfilled.

40. The first of those conditions is that the result prescribed by the directive should entail the grant of rights to individuals. The second condition is that it should be possible to identify the content of those rights on the basis of the provisions of the directive. Finally, the third condition is the existence of a causal link between the breach of the state's obligation and the loss and damage suffered by the injured parties.

41. Those conditions are sufficient to give rise to a right on the part of individuals to obtain reparation, a right founded directly on Community law.

42. Subject to that reservation, it is on the basis of the rules of national law on liability that the state must make reparation for the consequences of the loss and damage caused. In the absence of Community legislation, it is for the internal legal order of each Member State to designate the competent courts and lay down the detailed procedural rules for legal proceedings intended fully to safeguard the rights which individuals derive from Community law …

43. Further, the substantive and procedural conditions for reparation of loss and damage laid down by the national law of the Member States must not be less favourable than those relating to similar domestic claims and must not be so framed as to make it virtually impossible or excessively difficult to obtain reparation …

Joined Cases C-46/93 and C-48/93, 5 March 1996[105] **11.44 (EU)**

Brasserie du Pêcheur SA v Bundesrepublik Deutschland and The Queen v Secretary of State for Transport, ex parte: Factortame Ltd and others

MEMBER STATE LIABILITY FOR BREACHES OF EU LAW BY THE LEGISLATURE

Brasserie du Pêcheur

Where a Member State acts in a field where it has a wide discretion, the conditions under which it may incur liability must, in principle, be the same as those under which the Community institutions incur liability in a comparable situation.

Facts: Each of the two national courts in *Brasserie du Pêcheur* and *Factortame* asked whether the Member States were obliged to compensate damage caused to individuals by a Member State's legislation that breached Community law.

[105] ECLI:EU:C:1996:79.

Held: Where a breach of Community law by a Member State is attributable to the national legislature acting in a field in which it has a wide discretion to make legislative choices, individuals suffering loss or injury thereby are entitled to reparation.

Judgment: 18. The German, Irish and Netherlands Governments contend that Member States are required to make good loss or damage caused to individuals only where the provisions breached are not directly effective … In so far as national law affords individuals a right of action enabling them to assert their rights under directly effective provisions of Community law, it is unnecessary, where such provisions are breached, also to grant them a right to reparation founded directly on Community law.

19. That argument cannot be accepted.

20. The Court has consistently held that the right of individuals to rely on the directly effective provisions of the Treaty before national courts is only a minimum guarantee and is not sufficient in itself to ensure the full and complete implementation of the Treaty. … As appears from paragraph 33 of the judgment in *Francovich and Others*, the full effectiveness of Community law would be impaired if individuals were unable to obtain redress when their rights were infringed by a breach of Community law. …

36. Consequently, … the principle that Member States are obliged to make good damage caused to individuals by breaches of Community law attributable to the State is applicable where the national legislature was responsible for the breach in question. …

47. … [W]here a Member State acts in a field where it has a wide discretion … the conditions under which it may incur liability must, in principle, be the same as those under which the Community institutions incur liability in a comparable situation. …

51. In such circumstances, Community law confers a right to reparation where three conditions are met: the rule of law infringed must be intended to confer rights on individuals; the breach must be sufficiently serious; and there must be a direct causal link between the breach of the obligation resting on the State and the damage sustained by the injured parties. …

55. As to the second condition, … the decisive test for finding that a breach of Community law is sufficiently serious is whether the Member State or the Community institution concerned manifestly and gravely disregarded the limits on its discretion.

56. The factors which the competent court may take into consideration include the clarity and precision of the rule breached, the measure of discretion left by that rule to the national or Community authorities, whether the infringement and the damage caused was intentional or involuntary, whether any error of law was excusable or inexcusable, the fact that the position taken by a Community institution may have contributed towards the omission, and the adoption or retention of national measures or practices contrary to Community law.

74. Accordingly, … where a breach of Community law by a Member State is attributable to the national legislature acting in a field in which it has a wide discretion to make legislative choices, individuals suffering loss or injury thereby are entitled to reparation where the rule of Community law breached is intended to confer rights upon them, the breach is sufficiently serious and there is a direct causal link between the breach and the damage sustained by the individuals. Subject to that reservation, the State must make good the consequences of the loss or damage caused by the breach of Community law attributable to it, in accordance with its national law on liability. However, the conditions laid down by the applicable national laws must not be less favourable than those relating to similar domestic claims or framed in such a way as in practice to make it impossible or excessively difficult to obtain reparation. …

80. … [P]ursuant to the national legislation which it applies, reparation of loss or damage cannot be made conditional upon fault (intentional or negligent) on the part of the organ of the State responsible for the breach, going beyond that of a sufficiently serious breach of Community law. …

90. … [R]eparation by Member States of loss or damage which they have caused to individuals as a result of breaches of Community law must be commensurate with the loss or damage sustained. In the absence of relevant Community provisions, it is for the domestic legal system of each Member State to set the criteria for determining the extent of reparation. However, those criteria must not be less favourable than those applying to similar claims or actions based on domestic law and must not be such as in practice to make it impossible or excessively difficult to obtain reparation. National legislation which generally limits the damage for which reparation may be granted to damage done to certain, specifically protected individual interests not including loss of profit by individuals is not compatible with Community law. Moreover, it must be possible to award specific damages, such as the exemplary damages provided for by English law, pursuant to claims or actions founded on Community law, if such damages may be awarded pursuant to similar claims or actions founded on domestic law. Extent of the period covered by reparation (question 4(b) in Case C-46/93) …

93. … [T]he breach of Community law must have been sufficiently serious. The fact that there is a prior judgment of the Court finding an infringement will certainly be determinative, but it is not essential in order for that condition to be satisfied …

96. Accordingly, … the obligation for Member States to make good loss or damage caused to individuals by breaches of Community law attributable to the State cannot be limited to damage sustained after the delivery of a judgment of the Court finding the infringement in question.

Notes

(1) According to the *Francovich* case, in order to establish a Member State's liability for breaches of EU law, three conditions must be met. First, a public authority must have infringed an EU law provision that confers rights to individuals. Secondly, in cases where the rights are based on directives, it should be possible to identify the content of those rights on the basis of the provisions of the directive. Thirdly, there must be a causal link between the violation and the damage suffered.

(2) In the *Brasserie du Pêcheur* case, the Court of Justice made clear that Member States' liability for breaches of EU law may also occur in fields where the Member States' legislature has wide discretion. The Court of Justice held that the infringement of EU law must be 'sufficiently serious'. In addition, the Court developed some factors that should be considered by the national courts in order to establish whether the breach of the Member State is sufficiently serious. These factors include: the clarity and precision of the rule breached; the measure of discretion left by that rule to the national or EU authorities; whether the infringement and the damage caused was intentional; whether any error of law was excusable; the fact that the position taken by an EU institution may have contributed to the omission; and the adoption or retention of national measures or practices contrary to EU law. Furthermore, the Court clarified that state liability for breaches of EU law cannot be made conditional upon fault.

With regard to the extent of the compensation, the Court ruled that, in the absence of EU law provisions, it is generally for the domestic legal system of the Member State to determine the scope of the compensatory relief, as long as it is no less favourable than the compensation for similar claims based on domestic law. However, it is not compatible with the EU law to generally exclude compensation for loss of profits. Furthermore, the damages have to be awarded from the moment when the three conditions for Member States' liability are met. Thus, Member States' liability is not limited to damages sustained after the delivery of a judgment of the European Court of Justice.

11.7.A.2 LIABILITY OF THE EUROPEAN UNION AND JOINT LIABILITY OF THE EUROPEAN UNION AND THE MEMBER STATES

Joined Cases 5/66, 7/66 and 13–24/66, 14 July 1967[106] **11.45 (EU)**

Firma E Kampffmeyer and others v Commission

JOINT LIABILITY OF THE EU AND THE MEMBER STATES

Kampffmeyer

The EU can be held liable if it authorises wrongful actions by the Member States, but national courts should be seized first, with EU liability having only a residual role.

Facts: The case concerns import levies imposed on cereal imports into Germany under Regulation No 19 of the Council on the gradual establishment of a common organization of the market in cereals. The rate of levy was to be fixed by the importing Member State. In the present case, the rate could be fixed in advance by the German authorities for the import of maize from France, and the applicable rate was the rate applicable on the day on which the request had been received. Relying on a publication of the German authorities of 1 October 1963, fixing the levy at zero, the claimants requested import licences for maize from France on that day. Some also purchased maize in France in anticipation of the grant of the licences requested. On the same day, the German authorities introduced protective measures raising the import levy. This measure was based on a Commission decision which was later annulled by the Court of Justice. The claimants had incurred losses because of having to pay the import levies or cancelling purchasing contracts. The Commission refused the claimants' request for damages. Thereupon the claimants brought actions for damages before both the EU and the competent German courts, arguing that Germany and the Community were to be held jointly responsible.

Held: The claims were dismissed.

Judgment: As is clear, moreover, from the judgment of the Court of 1 July 1965, this decision constituted an improper application of Article 22 of Regulation No 19, in particular in that it likened the undeniable difficulties caused by the decision of 27 September to serious disturbances which might endanger the objectives laid down in Article 39 of the Treaty. On 3 October 1963 the Commission applied Article 22 (2) of Regulation No 19 in circumstances which did not justify protective measures in order to restore the situation resulting from the fixing by it of a zero levy.

As it was aware of the existence of applications for licences, it caused damage to the interests of importers who had acted in reliance on the information provided in

[106] ECLI:EU:C:1967:31.

accordance with Community rules. The Commission's conduct constituted a wrongful act or omission capable of giving rise to liability on the part of the Community. ...

However, with regard to any injury suffered by the applicants belonging to the first and second categories above-mentioned, those applicants have informed the Court that the injury alleged is the subject of two actions for damages, one against the Federal Republic of Germany before a German court and the other against the Community before the Court of Justice. It is necessary to avoid the applicants' being insufficiently or excessively compensated for the same damage by the different assessment of two different courts applying different rules of law. Before determining the damage for which the Community should be held liable, it is necessary for the national court to have the opportunity to give judgment on any liability on the part of the Federal Republic of Germany. This being the case, final judgment cannot be given before the applicants have produced the decision of the national court on this matter, which may be done independently of the evidence asked of the applicant in the first category to the effect that they have exhausted all possible methods of recovery of the amounts improperly paid by way of levy.

Notes

(1) Because EU law is mostly implemented by national authorities, it is likely that, when damage is caused to an individual, this will not result exclusively from an EU act, but rather from a joint action of the EU and national authorities. Joint liability can arise in a number of different situations, such as in cases where the Commission unlawfully authorises a Member State to take a certain course of action,[107] gives wrongful instructions to a Member State authority[108] or fails to supervise Member States adequately.[109] Other situations which may give rise to the joint liability of EU and Member States are cases where Member States transpose[110] or apply unlawful EU legislation (ie they require payments on the basis of an unlawful EU measure).[111] In such cases, the claimant must first bring a claim before the competent national court, which will refer a preliminary question of validity to the Court of Justice under Article 267 TFEU. If the Court of Justice finds the EU measure unlawful, it will annul it. Subsequently, the national court will assess the liability of the Member State and award damages corresponding to the damage caused by the national authorities. Only after this step, can the claimant commence proceedings before the EU courts for the compensation of the damage caused by the EU authorities.[112]

(2) The *Kampffmeyer* approach, based on the principle of exhaustion of national remedies, has raised much criticism in legal doctrine, especially because it is said to lead to unequal legal protection due to various national rules on damages. In the view of the critics, the *Kampffmeyer* approach hindered effective judicial protection.

[107] *Kampffmeyer* (n 70 above).
[108] Case 175/84 *Krohn v Commission* ECLI:EU:C:1986:85.
[109] Case 4/69 *Lütticke v Commission* ECLI:EU:C:1971:40.
[110] Case C-63/89 *Assurances de Credit v Council and Commission* ECLI:EU:C:1991:152.
[111] Case 96/71 *Haegeman v Commission* ECLI:EU:C:1972:88.
[112] For further on this, see W Wils, 'Concurrent Liability of the Community and a Member State' (1992) 17 *European Law Review* 191; P Oliver, 'Joint Liability of the Community and the Member States' in T Heukel and A McDonnell (eds), *The Action for Damages in Community Law* (Deventer, Kluwer, 1997) 285–310, 300.

In 1984, the Court of Justice changed its approach and developed the principle of exhaustion of *effective* national remedies. In *Unifrex*, the Court ruled that action for damages brought against the EU may not be declared inadmissible on the grounds that the claimant has not made use of the legal remedies available in national law when it is not disputed that these remedies were not capable of guaranteeing him effective protection.[113] The *Unifrex* ruling, because of its vagueness, has generated a lot of case law, attempting to establish the circumstances under which a claimant will have to first bring a national claim before being able to directly challenge the actions of the EU.

11.7.B INTEGRATION OF EUROPEAN REQUIREMENTS IN THE DOMESTIC LIABILITY SYSTEM IN THE NETHERLANDS

Hoge Raad, 18 September 2015[114] **11.46 (NL)**

The State v Habing

PUBLIC LIABILITY FOR BREACHES OF EU LAW BY AN ACT OF PARLIAMENT

Habing

The state is liable for Acts of Parliament which infringe international or EU law and has to compensate all resulting losses, irrespective of whether the committed breach of supranational law is sufficiently serious.

Facts: According to the former Article 7:636 (4) BW, the holiday entitlement of employees who were unable to work due to illness was limited to the period of the last six months in which the work was not performed. This limitation was inconsistent with Article 7 of Directive 93/104/EC concerning certain aspects of the organisation of working time, as interpreted by the CJEU in *Bectu*.[115] As a result of the incorrect implementation of the Directive in the Burgerlijk Wetboek (Civil Code), Habing and other employees, who had been ill for quite a long time, were not granted the amount of holidays to which they were entitled under the Directive. In 2011, Habing filed a claim against the State of the Netherlands, stating that the state was liable for the damage he had sustained as a result of the incorrect implementation of the Directive by the legislator. In first instance, the district court of The Hague applied the strict *Brasserie du Pêcheur* criterion of a 'sufficiently serious breach' (see section 11.7.A.1 above), but nevertheless ruled in favour of Habing, because it considered the incorrect implementation by the legislator to be 'sufficiently serious'. On appeal, the Court of Appeal of The Hague upheld the judgment in substance, but, differently from the district court, was of the opinion that under Dutch tort law the state is already liable for the mere infringement of Union law and that the strict EU condition of the 'sufficiently serious breach' should not have been applied. In cassation before the Supreme Court, the main question concerned the conditions to be applied to a public liability claim for infringements of EU law by the legislature: the strict EU condition of a 'sufficiently serious breach' or the more generous Dutch condition of mere infringement of EU law.

Held: The state was held liable.

113 Case 281/82 *Unifrex v Council and Commission* ECLI:EU:C:1984:165, para 11.
114 ECLI:NL:HR:2015:2722.
115 Case C-173/99 *The Queen v Secretary of State for Trade and Industry, ex parte BECTU* ECLI:EU:C:2001:356.

Judgment: According to Article 94 of the Constitution, formal legislation (Acts of Parliament) should be tested for conformity with directly effective provisions of international treaties and of decisions of international institutions. If formal legislation is inconsistent with such provisions, this results not only in the disapplication of the law concerned, but also implies that the enactment and enforcement of it is unlawful and therefore that the state is, under Article 6:162 of the Civil Code, obliged to pay damages, provided that the other requirements for liability for unlawful action are also met.

In such cases, liability for unlawful action is consistent with the basic idea of Articles 93 and 94 of the Constitution, according to which the international law provisions concerned should be applied insofar as is possible in the national legal order, and according to which it is not necessary that the legislator should provide for such an application. It is thereby ensured that the application of the law in the Netherlands is consistent with these provisions, a result to which the state has committed itself by binding itself to the international treaties and decisions, as meant in both provisions of the constitution. The obligation to compensate damages is an effective and adequate remedy *par excellence* in case of non-observance of these provisions by the state. …

Differently from what has been stated by the state, the former [obligation] also applies in case of directly effective Union law, which, on the basis of the TFEU, applies of its own accord in the Member States. There is no reason to make an exception for Union law. To the contrary, the Union principle of equivalence resists to such exception. …

In the case of *State/Van Gelder* it has been decided that, if a public body commits an unlawful act by enacting a general rule which is inconsistent with superior law, and acting on the basis of this general rule, this unlawfulness is in principle attributable to the body. There is no reason for not applying this rule to formal legislation which is inconsistent with direct applicable international law or with the obligation to transpose an EU directive. After all, the legislator is responsible for ensuring that its legislation is consistent therewith.

Notes

(1) The Dutch liability regime, based on general tort law, is in general more lenient than the minimum liability conditions prescribed by EU law in, for example, *Brasserie du Pêcheur*.[116] Even in respect of formal legislation (ie Acts of Parliament), the state is liable for the 'mere infringement' of EU law. In addition, this infringement is in principle attributable to the state. The same regime applies to legislative violations of direct effective provisions of international law. To that extent, the strict EU criterion of a 'sufficiently serious breach' is not applied. Moreover, as the EU public liability dogmatics is thus fully realised in the Dutch system, the courts do not refer to CJEU judgments such as *Francovich* or *Brasserie du Pêcheur*.

[116] See, eg RJGM Widdershoven, 'Twee bevoegdheidssystemen, twee aansprakelijkheidsregimes? Tussen objectum litis en Francovich' in Schlössels et al (n 96 above) 705–26; J Polak, 'De klassieke onrechtmatige daasvordering als instrument van effectieve uitvoering van EG-recht: de Europese dimensie van de vangnetfunctie van de burgerlijke rechter' in T Barkhuysen et al (eds), *Europees recht effectueren* (Deventer, Kluwer, 2007) 257; HD Van Wijk, W Konijnenbelt and R Van Male, *Hoofdstukken van bestuursrecht*, 16th edn (Deventer, Kluwer, 2014) 767.

(2) The only exception to the foregoing is the '*Köbler* public liability' for judgments of courts of final instance infringing EU law, as was discussed above.[117] In this case, the Dutch courts do apply the EU conditions, as the Dutch conditions for imposing liability for unlawful decisions of the judiciary are more stringent than the EU conditions.

11.7.C SEPARATE LIABILITY CLAIM FOR EU LAW BREACHES IN ENGLAND AND WALES, GERMANY AND FRANCE

11.7.C.1 ENGLAND AND WALES

High Court, Queen's Bench Division (Divisional Court), 31 July 1997[118] **11.47 (EW)**

R v Secretary of State for Transport, ex parte Factortame Ltd

PUBLIC LIABILITY FOR BREACHES OF EU LAW

Factortame (No 5)

Damages for breaches of EU law are based on a sui generis public liability claim.

Facts: This case arose from the *Factortame* litigation, concerning a company of Spanish fishermen who claimed that the UK had breached EU law by requiring ships to have a majority of British owners if they were to be registered in the UK. The Court of Justice held that the requirement infringed EU law. The affected company claimed financial compensation for their losses and exemplary damages for the unlawful action.

Held: The UK government was held liable. However, no exemplary damages were granted.

Judgment: 173. In Community law, the liability of a state for a breach of Community law is described as non-contractual. … In our judgment it is best understood as a breach of statutory duty. The reasons which lead us to this conclusion are fully set out in the judgment of Mann J. in *Bourgoin v. MAFF.* 69. That case was concerned with the revocation of a licence to import frozen turkeys from France which the European Court of Justice had held to be a breach of Article 30 of the Treaty. He reviewed the authorities and followed what had been said by Lord Diplock in *Garden Cottage Foods v. Milk Marketing Board* at 70:

A breach of the duty imposed by Article 86 not to abuse a dominant position in the Common Market or a substantial part of it can thus be categorised in English law as a breach of statutory duty imposed … for the benefit of private individuals to whom loss is caused by a breach of that duty.

At p. 733, Mann J. said:

Accordingly, I hold that a contravention of Article 30 which causes damages to a person gives to that person an action for damages for breach of statutory duty, the duty being one composed by Article 30 (as interpreted by the European Court) and section 2(1) of the Act of 1972 when read in conjunction.

[117] See section 11.6.C above.

[118] [1998] 1 CMLR 1353 (QB).

This part of his reasoning was supported by the whole of the Court of Appeal. It is on the question of remedies that the decision of the majority of the Court of Appeal has been overtaken by later decisions, in particular the *Francovich* case …

174. Thus, whilst it can be said that the cause of action is sui generis, it is of the character of a breach of statutory duty. The United Kingdom and its organs and agencies have not performed a duty which they were statutorily required to perform.

Note

In the UK, liability arising from breaches of EU law is treated as a claim *sui generis*, which is different from the existing claims under the domestic public liability framework. The tort law system is generally more restrictive on public liability than the European Court of Justice.[119] Thus, a separate claim for EU law breaches was introduced, in order to maintain the existing legal regime for domestic law infringements.

11.7.C.2 GERMANY

Bundesgerichtshof, 24 October 1996[120] **11.48 (DE)**

PUBLIC LIABILITY FOR BREACHES OF EU LAW

German Reinheitsgebot

The legal prerequisites of state liability for loss or damage to an individual resulting from a breach of EU law may not differ without a special reason from the requirements that, in comparable circumstances, apply to the liability of the EU itself.

Facts: The claimant, a French brewery, exported beer into the Federal Republic of Germany until 1981. After 1981, the export was prevented, because the beer produced by the brewery concerned was rejected by the public authorities as being incompatible with the Beer Purity Law (Reinheitsgebot) of the German Beer Tax Law. The claimant initiated an infringement proceeding against the Federal Republic of Germany. The Court of Justice held that it was contrary to Article 30 of the EEC Treaty (now Article 28 TFEU) to apply the German Beer Purity Law to beer which had been legally produced and marketed in another Member State. Subsequently, the claimant demanded damages from the Federal Republic of Germany, amounting to instalments of DM1,800,000 for a part of the damages it had suffered as a result of the import restriction from 1981 to 1987.

Held: The appeal was dismissed, as the EU requirements of a state liability claim were not met.

Judgment: The direct deviation of a claim for damages from Community law is also highlighted by the fact that the legal prerequisites of state liability for loss or damage to an individual resulting from a breach of Community law may not differ without a special reason from the requirements that, in comparable circumstances, apply to the liability of the Community itself. For this purpose, the European Court of Justice has transferred the system which it, in accordance with Article 215(2) EC [Article 340 TFEU], has developed particularly to rule on the liability for legislative acts of the Community, to the liability of

[119] See section 11.3.B.1 above.
[120] (1997) NJW 123.

Member States at stake in such a way that the legal prerequisites for the liability of the Member States are congruent to the prerequisites of the liability of the Community itself. If therefore already on the basis of the general conditions of Community law it can be concluded that there is no liability in the case at hand, it is not necessary to fall back on domestic liability claims. The circumstances in the case at hand do not give the Senate any reason to reconsider its case law on state liability for legislative wrongdoings in as far as domestic German law is concerned. In particular, it does not need to be assessed whether the legal prerequisites of public liability for legislative wrongdoings would, if interpreted in accordance with Community law, need to be altered to such an extent that the condition establishing and limiting liability, namely that the violated official duty has to protect a third party would need to be questioned in the domestic public liability regime.

Notes

(1) In Germany, a liability claim *sui generis* has been introduced for breaches of EU law, because the domestic public liability framework was considered too restrictive. As examined in section 11.3.A.2 above, in Germany, the fault of the public authority or sacrificial or expropriatory encroachment suffered by the claimant must be shown. Furthermore, the domestic requirement of a 'protective duty'[121] is more restrictive than the EU concept.[122] Thus, a separate claim for EU law breaches was introduced, in order to maintain the existing legal regime for domestic law infringements.

(2) In the *German Reinheitsgebot* judgment of the Federal Court of Justice, the reluctance of German courts to establish a generally broader domestic public liability system is obvious. Here, the court clearly states that only where EU law so demands will liability claims be broadened. Otherwise, the Federal Court of Justice sees no reason to depart from the domestically developed criteria.

11.7.C.3 FRANCE

Conseil d'État, 28 February 1992[123] **11.49 (FR)**

Société Arizona Tobacco Products and Philipp Morris v The State

PUBLIC LIABILITY FOR BREACHES OF EU LAW BY LEGISLATION

Philip Morris

The EU standards for liability for breaches of EU law have led to a new claim of public liability based on illegality.

Facts: The law of 24 May 1976 stated that the prices of tobacco products were set for the whole territory. Thus, from 1 November 1982 to 31 December 1983, French authorities refused to determine different prices for the tobacco products sold by the claimants, two tobacco manufacturers, and adopted several administrative

[121] In German: *drittschützende Amtspflicht.*

[122] See also MPF Granger, 'National Applications of *Francovich* and the Construction of a European Administrative Ius Commune' (2007) 32 *European Law Review* 157, 175 ff.

[123] N° 87753.

measures against them. The claimants sought damages for the loss caused by these measures, arguing that they were incompatible with EU legislation.

Held: The state was held liable.

Judgment: Considering that Article 37 of the Treaty establishing the European Economic Community stipulates: 'Member States shall progressively adjust any state monopolies of a commercial character so as to ensure that when the transitional period has ended no discrimination regarding the conditions under which goods are procured and marketed exists between nationals of Member States'; considering that under Article 5-1 of Council Directive of the European Communities of 19 December 1972, adopted for the implementation, with respect to the tobacco manufactories, of this provision as well as of Article 30 of the Treaty containing the prohibition of quantitative restrictions on import and of all measures having equivalent effect: 'Manufacturers and importers shall be free to determine the maximum retail selling price for each of their products. This provision may not, however, hinder implementation of the national systems of legislation regarding the control of price levels or the observance of imposed prices'; considering also that as ruled by the Court of Justice of the European Communities in its rulings on infringement proceedings of 21 June 1983 and 13 July 1988, the only provisions authorised by Article 5-1 of the Directive are those of national legislation which have a general character, intended to block price increases; considering that the quoted provisions of Article 6 of the law of 24 May 1976 endow the government with a specific prerogative to fix the prices of tobacco imported from Member States of the European Communities, regardless of the application of national law on price control; that they thus allow the government to fix the prices for selling imported tobacco according to conditions which are not provided for under Article 5-1 of the Directive of 19 December 1972 and are incompatible with the objective set up by the Directive; considering that it follows that Article 10 of the aforementioned decree of 31 December 1976, adopted on the basis of Article 6 of the law of 24 May 1976, whose application is precluded, has no proper legal basis itself; considering that it results therefrom that, contrary to the ruling of the Administrative Court of First Instance of Paris, the ministerial decisions adopted in application of the decree of 31 December 1976 and refusing, for the period from 1 November 1982 to 31 December 1983, to fix the prices of the tobacco manufacturers as demanded by the applicant companies are illegal; considering that this illegality is of a nature to incur the liability of the state.

Conseil d'État, 8 February 2007[124] **11.50 (FR)**

Gardedieu v The State

PUBLIC LIABILITY FOR BREACHES OF INTERNATIONAL LAW BY LEGISLATION

Gardedieu

The breach of international law forms a new separate basis for public liability claims.

Facts: A decree concerning pension funds obliged the claimant to pay increased contributions, which he refused to do. He argued the decree was illegal, and this was later confirmed by the Conseil d'État. Subsequently,

[124] N° 279522.

the French Parliament adopted a statute that confirmed the provisions of the decree retroactively. The appellant sought damages, arguing that the retroactive law breached Article 6 ECHR.

Held: The state was held liable for the breach of international law.

Judgment: Considering that state liability for legislative wrongdoings may be triggered on the one hand on the basis of the *égalité devant les charges publiques*, in order to ensure the redress of damages stemming from passing an act, provided that this act was not intended to exclude any compensation and that the loss for which redress is requested, being of a serious and special nature, cannot, therefore, be considered as a disadvantage normally incumbent on the interested parties, and on the other hand due to its obligations to ensure the respect of international conventions by the public authorities, in order to compensate the damages resulting from the application of a law passed in violation of France's international commitments.

Notes

(1) In France, the EU standards for liability for breaches of EU law have led to a new claim of public liability which is based on illegality rather than fault. Public liability for legislative breaches of EU law has thereby been introduced into the system, without broadening the domestic claim in general. As EU law also grants public liability in cases of legislative wrongdoing, the French domestic public liability system was considered too restrictive. According to the French system, which is based on fault, the legislator could not, in principle, be liable as there was a doctrine that the Parliament – representing the French people – could do no wrong. In order to adapt to the European public liability requirements, the Council of State in the *Philip Morris* case introduced a new liability claim based on illegality to the effect that legislative wrongdoing is also covered. The conditions to be met under this new liability regime are that there has to be a violation of EU law, that certain damage has to be caused and that there is a causal link between the violation of EU law and the damage suffered.

(2) In the *Gardedieu* case, the Council of State accepted the violation of international law as a second basis for public liability for legislative acts.

11.8 LIABILITY FOR BREACHES OF ARTICLE 6 ECHR (REASONABLE TIME)

According to Article 6(1) ECHR, everyone is entitled to a fair hearing within a reasonable time. In order to ensure the effectiveness of this right, all analysed legal systems provide for public liability for breaches of Article 6(1) ECHR.

European Convention on Human Rights **11.51 (EU)**

Article 6 (1) In the determination of his civil rights and obligations or of any criminal charge against him, everyone is entitled to a fair and public hearing within a reasonable time by an independent and impartial tribunal established by law. Judgment shall be pronounced publicly but the press and public may be excluded from all or part of the trial in the interests of morals, public order or national security in a democratic society, where the interests of juveniles or the protection of the private life of the parties so require, or to the extent strictly necessary in the opinion of the court in special circumstances where publicity would prejudice the interests of justice.

11.8.A THE EUROPEAN UNION

Case C-385/07 P, 16 June 2009[125] **11.52 (EU)**

Der Grüne Punkt – Duales System Deutschland GmbH v Commission

EXCESSIVE LENGTH OF COURT PROCEEDINGS

Der Grüne Punkt

The failure on the part of the Court of First Instance to adjudicate within a reasonable time can give rise to a claim for damages but does not lead to the reopening of the proceedings if the failure had no effect on the outcome of the dispute.

Facts: Der Grüne Punkt – Duales System Deutschland GmbH (DSD) had brought an action for the annulment of a Commission Decision with which the Commission had declared DSD in breach of Article 82 of the EC Treaty. The Court of First Instance had rejected this claim. DSD appealed the judgment before the Court of Justice, alleging, inter alia, that the Court of First Instance had committed a procedural irregularity and adversely affected its interests by failing to have regard to the fundamental right to have a case dealt with within a reasonable time.

Held: The Court of Justice dismissed the appeal.

Judgment: 178. As a general principle of Community law, such a right [ie to a fair and public hearing within a reasonable time by an independent and impartial tribunal established by law] is applicable in the context of proceedings brought against a Commission decision …

181. It must also be borne in mind that the reasonableness of the period for delivering a judgment is to be appraised in the light of the circumstances specific to each case, such as the complexity of the case and the conduct of the parties (see, to that effect, *Sumitomo Metal Industries and Nippon Steel v Commission*, paragraph 116 and the case-law cited, and order of 26 March 2009 in Case C-146/08 P *Efkon v Parliament and Council*, paragraph 54).

182. The Court has held in that regard that the list of relevant criteria is not exhaustive and that the assessment of the reasonableness of a period does not require a systematic examination of the circumstances of the case in the light of each of them, where the duration of the proceedings appears justified in the light of one of them. Thus, the complexity of the case or the dilatory conduct of the applicant may be deemed to justify a duration which is prima facie too long (Joined Cases C-238/99 P, C-244/99 P, C-245/99 P, C-247/99 P, C-250/99 P to C-252/99 P and C-254/99 P *Limburgse Vinyl Maatschappij and Others v Commission* [2002] ECR I-8375, paragraph 188, and *Thyssen Stahl v Commission*, paragraph 156).

[125] ECLI:EU:C:2009:456.

183. In the present case, it must be stated that the length of the proceedings before the Court of First Instance, which amounted to approximately 5 years and 10 months, cannot be justified by any of the particular circumstances of the case. ...

188. In the light of the above, it must be held that there was a failure, in the proceedings before the Court of First Instance, to have regard to the requirement that the case be dealt with within a reasonable time.

189. As regards the consequences that arise where proceedings before the Court of First Instance fail to be completed within a reasonable time, DSD invokes the rule laid down in the first paragraph of Article 61 of the Statute of the Court of Justice that where an appeal is well founded the Court is to quash the decision of the Court of First Instance. Since the present plea alleges that judgment was not delivered within a reasonable time and that the failure to do so constitutes a breach of procedure which adversely affects the interests of the appellant within the meaning of Article 58 of the Statute, a finding that such a breach occurred must necessarily lead, in DSD'S view, to the setting aside of the judgment under appeal, irrespective of whether that breach of procedure had an effect on the outcome of the dispute. Were the judgment not to be set aside, the Court of Justice would not be acting in compliance with Article 61 of the Statute. ...

192. It nonetheless remains the case that the first paragraph of Article 61 of the Statute of the Court of Justice should be interpreted and applied purposively.

193. In so far as there is nothing to suggest that the failure to adjudicate within a reasonable time may have had an effect on the outcome of the dispute, the setting aside of the judgment under appeal would not remedy the infringement of the principle of effective legal protection committed by the Court of First Instance.

194. In addition, as the Advocate General stated at points 305 and 306 of his Opinion, having regard to the need to ensure that Community competition law is complied with, the Court of Justice cannot allow an appellant to reopen the question of the existence of an infringement, on the sole ground that there was a failure to adjudicate within a reasonable time, where all of its pleas directed against the findings made by the Court of First Instance concerning that infringement and the administrative procedure relating to it have been rejected as unfounded.

195. Conversely, as the Advocate General stated at point 307 et seq. of his Opinion, the failure on the part of the Court of First Instance to adjudicate within a reasonable time can give rise to a claim for damages brought against the Community under Article 235 EC and the second paragraph of Article 288 EC.

196. Consequently, DSD's argument that, where a reasonable period is exceeded, that fact must, in order for that procedural irregularity to be remedied, lead to the judgment under appeal being set aside, is unfounded.

Note

The Court of Justice acknowledged in this case that Article 6(1) ECHR is applicable to court proceedings on the EU level. As regards the consequences of a finding that the reasonable time requirement has been violated, the Court established that such a finding cannot lead to the setting aside of the judgment which was delivered in breach of this requirement or to the annulment of the measure which was at stake in the judgment. Instead, a violation of Article 6 ECHR can only lead to action for damages under Article 340 TFEU, with the violation constituting a 'sufficiently serious breach' for the purposes of that action.[126]

11.8.B THE NETHERLANDS

Raad van State, 29 January 2014[127] **11.53 (NL)**

A, B, C, D v the State

LIABILITY FOR BREACHES OF ARTICLE 6 ECHR

Uniform Fair Periods

The state is liable if the process of judicial review of administrative action, including the intra-administrative objection procedure, exceeds four years in total.

Facts: On 16 December 2005, the claimant applied for a residence permit. On 30 January 2006, the Secretary of State declared the request inadmissible. With the decision of 12 March 2010, the Secretary of State decided again on the intra-administrative objection of the claimant. By its decision of 31 January 2011, it declared the objection of the claimant unfounded. The claimant brought a claim against this decision and asked for compensation of the damage caused by undue delay of the decision. The district court of Oost-Brabant rejected this claim by its decision of 1 February 2013. The claimant then sought compensation for the undue delay of the procedure.

Held: The state was held liable.

Judgment: 4.3 Considering the societal relevance of speedy resolution of conflicts and the relevance of legal unity, the Judicial Division of the Council of State feels compelled to align its case law to that of the Central Appellate Court and the Supreme Court with regard to the question of what handling periods can be regarded as fair in non-punitive cases. By doing so, the periods are also aligned with those in punitive cases and with the periods used by criminal courts. As other courts, the Judicial Division of the Council of State also now rules that, as a point of departure, a court case in first instance is not solved within a reasonable time if it is not decided within two years after it has been started. The time for an objection procedure within the meaning of chapter 7 AWB, if applied, is included in this period. A judgment in appeal has to be issued, as a point of departure, within two years after the appeal is lodged. If the objection procedure and the lawsuit altogether took so long that the case was not solved within a reasonable time, it has to be considered, as a point of departure, with regard to the question of whether the administrative authority or the judge is responsible for the undue delay, that the objection procedure took too long if it lasted more than half a year and that the procedure before the court of first instance took too long if it lasted more than one and a half years.

4.3.1 When the periods mentioned above are applied, the existing case law of the Judicial Division considers that the complexity of the case, the way in which the administrative authority and the judge handle the case and the conduct of the claimant during the procedure may allow an exceedance of the periods mentioned above. …

[126] Case C-58/12 P *Groupe Gascogne v Commission* ECLI:EU:C:2013:770, paras 72–96.
[127] ECLI:NL:RVS:2014:188.

5. Based on a rate of €500 for each half year that the reasonable time period was exceeded, taking into account that the total sum of the awards for each period is rounded up, the Judicial Division will convict the Secretary of State of Security and Justice to pay an amount of €2,000 to each of the claimants.

Note

In administrative law cases (other than in criminal law cases), an intra-administrative objection procedure may last no longer than half a year, and judicial review in the first instance no longer than one and a half years and in the second instance no longer than two years. Hence, if an objection is required and two instances are used, the procedure of judicial review may last no longer than four years altogether. If the period is exceeded, the appellant is compensated with €500 for each half year that the period is exceeded by.[128]

11.8.C FRANCE

Conseil d'État, 28 June 2002[129] **11.54 (FR)**

Minister of Justice v Magiera

LIABILITY FOR BREACHES OF ARTICLE 6 ECHR

Magiera

The excessive length of judicial proceedings leads to public liability.

Facts: The state was ordered to pay a compensation of 30,000 francs to the defendant by the Administrative Court of Appeal of Paris for the injury caused by the excessive delay in ruling on a previous dispute. That dispute took over seven years to be solved, even though the case presented no particular difficulty. The Minister of Justice appealed to the Council of State against the judgment of the Administrative Court of Appeal of Paris granting compensation to the defendant.

Held: The appeal was dismissed; thus the state was held liable.

Judgment: ... Considering that, by the challenged judgment, the Administrative Court of Appeal of Paris, after having observed that the proceedings that Mr X had previously taken against the state ... had been excessively long with regard to the requirements of Article 6, paragraph 1 of the European Convention for the Protection of Human Rights and Fundamental Freedoms, ordered the state to pay Mr X a compensation of 30,000 francs in damages for the disturbances of all kinds suffered by him because of the length of the proceedings;

... Considering that, pursuant to the terms of Article 6 paragraph 1 of the European Convention for the Protection of Human Rights and Fundamental Freedoms: 'In the determination of his civil rights and obligations, everyone is entitled to a fair and public hearing

[128] ECLI:NL:RVS:2010:BM0213.
[129] N° 239575.

within a reasonable time by a tribunal; considering that, under the terms of Article 13 of the same convention: 'Everyone whose rights and freedoms as set forth in this Convention are violated shall have an effective remedy before a national authority notwithstanding that the violation has been committed by persons acting in an official capacity';

Considering that it follows from these provisions, when the dispute falls within their scope of application, as well as, in all cases, from the general principles which govern the operation of the administrative courts, that litigants have the right to have a ruling made on their applications within a reasonable time;

Considering that, although the breach of this obligation has no impact on the validity of the judicial decision taken at the end of the proceedings, the litigants shall nevertheless be able to ensure its observance; considering that, therefore, where the violation of the right to a reasonable length of proceedings has caused them damages, they may obtain remedy for the harm thus caused by the negligent operation of the public service of justice [which constitutes fault];

Considering that, after having stated that the length of the proceedings was excessive, the Administrative Court of Appeal concluded that the liability of the state was grounded in respect to Mr A; considering that, by so doing so, far from violating the texts and the principles mentioned above, it applied them in an exact manner; …

Considering that an action for damages initiated by a citizen whose application has not been decided within a reasonable time shall allow the reparation of all the damage both material and immaterial, direct and certain, which has been caused to him and whose reparation is not guaranteed by the decision adopted in the main dispute; considering that therefore, in particular, the damage caused by the loss of a benefit or an opportunity or the belated recognition of a right may be repaired. Considering that reparation may also be made for the inconvenience caused by excessively long proceedings when this is real and goes beyond the concerns usually caused by a trial, taking in particular the personal situation of the individual concerned into account; considering that the Administrative Court of Appeal of Paris considered, by a discretionary assessment, that Mr A had suffered, due to the length of the proceedings, 'worry and disturbances in his living conditions' for which it quantified the sum intended to compensate him as 30,000 francs; considering that it follows from what has been said above that, contrary to what the Minister maintains, the Administrative Court of Appeal of Paris did not commit an error of law.

Note

As seen above, in France, breaches of the judiciary are as a rule only compensable in the case of *faute lourde*.[130] However, with regard to Article 6(1) ECHR, a simple breach of the right to a hearing within a reasonable time is sufficient to cause public liability.[131]

[130] See section 11.6.C above.

[131] For more information on the reforms taken to avoid excessive delays of judicial review in France, see J Massot 'The Powers and Duties of the French Administrative Judge' in S Rose-Ackerman and PL Lindseth (eds), *Comparative Administrative Law* (Cheltenham, Edward Elgar, 2010) 415, 422.

11.8.D GERMANY

Gerichtsverfassungsgesetz **11.55 (DE)**

§198 (1) Whoever as the result of the unreasonable length of a set of court proceedings experiences a disadvantage as a participant in those proceedings shall be given reasonable compensation. The reasonableness of the length of proceedings shall be assessed in the light of the circumstances of the particular case concerned, in particular the complexity thereof, the importance of what was at stake in the case, and the conduct of the participants and of third persons therein.

(2) A disadvantage not constituting a pecuniary disadvantage shall be presumed to have occurred in a case where a set of court proceedings has been of unreasonably long duration. Compensation can be claimed therefore only insofar as reparation by other means, having regard to the circumstances of the particular case, is not sufficient in accordance with section 4. Compensation pursuant to the second sentence shall amount to €1,200 for every year of the delay. Where, having regard to the circumstances of the particular case, the sum pursuant to the third sentence is inequitable, the court can assess a higher or lower sum.

(3) A participant in proceedings shall obtain compensation only if he has complained about the length of the proceedings to the court seized of the case (censure of delay). A censure of delay can be filed only if there is cause to fear that the case will not be concluded within a reasonable time; a censure of delay can be reiterated at the earliest after six months, but not in a case where a shorter duration is necessary by way of exception. … Where the proceedings are further delayed before another court, it shall be necessary to file a new censure of delay.

(4) Reparation by other means shall be possible in particular where the court of compensation makes a finding that the length of the proceedings was unreasonable. Such finding shall not require the making of a prior application. In serious cases, the finding can be made in addition to compensation; it can also be made where one, or more than one, precondition under section 3 has not been fulfilled.

(5) A court action to enforce a claim under section 1 can be brought at the earliest six months after the filing of the censure of delay. The court action must be brought no later than six months following entry into final and binding force of the decision ending the proceedings, or following another manner of disposal of the proceedings. The claim shall not be transferable until a final and binding decision has been given in the court action.

(6) Within the meaning of this provision

1. a set of court proceedings shall mean every set of proceedings from their introduction until their conclusion with final binding force, including proceedings for granting provisional court relief and for granting legal aid …

Note

In Germany, the compensation for overly lengthy proceedings is regulated in depth by statute. Compensation usually amounts to €1,200 for every year of delay according to §198(2) and (3) of the Gerichtsverfassungsgesetz (Courts Constitution Act).

11.8.E ENGLAND AND WALES

On the whole, excessive duration of court proceedings is not an issue that has arisen in judicial review proceedings in England and Wales. Disposal of initial hearings is generally reasonably rapid. There are a small number of cases which have dealt with the lack of speed of the procedure in the Parole Board under Article 5(4) ECHR,[132] but very few Article 6 ECHR cases, most of which have arisen in private law proceedings.

11.9 COMPARATIVE OVERVIEW

The legal landscape in public liability law is quite diverse. Nonetheless, all the legal systems analysed acknowledge public liability for unlawful acts if the action leading to loss or injury can be attributed to a public authority, if a causal link can be established between the public action and the suffered loss, and if specific domestic limiting requirements, such as fault or 'scope of the norm' standards, are met.

Some legal systems, such as England and Wales and the Netherlands, integrate public liability in their general tort law system, adding some limitations or modifying some criteria in order to protect the state budget funds against excessive claims. Apart from that, the English public liability regime is very restrictive. In particular, the English system is the only one of the analysed national legal regimes (excluding the EU legal system) that does not grant liability for abnormal damages resulting from lawful public action. Only *ex gratia* payments may be offered by the administrative authorities in these cases. Dutch law, in contrast, provides a whole set of statutory rules and general principles concerning public liability for lawful administrative action, which are relatively broad. Abnormal, special damages resulting from legal administrative action are compensated. With regard to unlawful administrative action, the general rules of tort law are applied, which also results in a quite broad liability. As a consequence, Dutch law did not require further adjustments after the *Francovich* judgment.

France established an autonomous public liability regime which is based on fault. As is the case in the Netherlands, France also acknowledges public liability for lawful actions on the basis of public law principles if certain special conditions are met. The German public liability system lies somewhere in between. Even though public liability is rooted in tort law principles to a certain extent, the judiciary has developed an autonomous legal regime for public liability, which also provides for compensation of lawful state action under special circumstances. Furthermore, the public liability system in Germany is supplemented by the sacrificial and expropriatory encroachment claims which are rooted in the protection of fundamental rights and are thus fully independent from tort law claims.

In spite of all the differences between the analysed legal systems, supranational law has had some harmonising effects on public liability law throughout Europe.[133] First, the CJEU's case law concerning public liability for breaches of EU law has led to new

[132] See *R (Sturnham) v Parole Board* [2013] UKSC 23, [2013] 2 AC 254.

[133] See also W van Gerven, in S Moreira de Sousa and W Heusel (eds), *Enforcing EU Law from* Francovich *to* Köbler*: Twelve Years of the State Liability Principle* Cologne, Bundesanzeiger, 2004) 225, 239 ff; Granger (n 122 above) 192 ('unity in diversity').

liability claims in Germany and England and Wales, as well as sectorial modifications of the French public liability law with regard to EU law breaches. *Francovich* and *Brasserie du Pêcheur* thus serve as a minimum standard in European public liability law.[134] Secondly, the *Köbler* case of the Court of Justice has had a broadening effect on public liability for judicial wrongdoing at least within the scope of EU law in most countries. Thirdly, Article 6 ECHR has led to compensatory measures for unreasonably long court proceedings in the EU, the Netherlands, France and Germany. As a result, supranational law has a broadening effect on domestic public liability law.[135]

FURTHER READING

Bell, J and Bradley, AW (eds), *Governmental Liability: A Comparative Study* (Glasgow, UK Comparative Law Series, 1991).

Dari-Mattiacci, G, Garoupa, N and Gómez-Pomar, PF, 'State Liability' (2010) 18 *European Review of Private Law* 773.

Dörr, O (ed), *Staatshaftung in Europa. Nationales und Unionsrecht* (Berlin, de Gruyter, 2014).

Fairgrieve, D, *State Liability in Tort. A Comparative Law Study* (Oxford, Oxford University Press, 2003).

Fairgrieve, D, Andenas, M and Bell, J, *Tort Liability of Public Authorities in Comparative Perspective* (London, BIICL, 2002).

Granger, M-PF, 'National Applications of Francovich and the Construction of a European Administrative Jus Commune' (2007) 31 *European Law Review* 157.

Gutman, K, 'Liability for Breach of EU Law by the Union, Member States and Individuals: Damages, Enforcement and Effective Judicial Protection' in S Blockmans and A Łazowski (eds), *Research Handbook on EU Institutional Law* (Cheltenham, Edward Elgar, 2016).

Hartmann, BJ, 'Alignment of National Government Liability Law in Europe after Francovich' (2012) 12 *ERA Forum* 613.

Moreira de Sousa, S and Heusel, W (eds), *Enforcing Community Law from Francovich to Köbler: Twelve Years of the State Liability Principle* (Cologne, Bundesanzeiger Verlagsges.mbH, 2004).

Ortlep, R and Widdershoven, RJGM, 'Schendingen van EG-recht door rechters' (2004) 2 *Overheid & Aansprakelijkheid* 34.

Oliphant, K (ed), *The Liability of Public Authorities in Comparative Perspective* (Cambridge, Intersentia, 2016).

Scherr, KM, 'Comparative Aspects of the Application of the Principle of State Liability for Judicial Breaches' (2012) 12 *ERA Forum* 565.

Tjepkema, MKG, 'Between Equity and Efficiency: the European's Union's No-Fault Liability' (2013) 6 *Review of European Administrative Law* 7.

Varga, Z, 'In Search of a "Manifest Infringement of the Applicable Law" in the Terms Set Out in *Köbler*' (2016) 9 *Review of European Administrative Law* 5.

Varga, Z, 'National Remedies in the Case of Violation of EU Law by Member State Courts' (2017) 54 *Common Market Law Review* 51.

Widdershoven, RJGM, 'Twee bevoegdheidssystemen, twee aansprakelijkheidsregimes? Tussen objectum litis en Francovich' in RJN Schlössels et al (eds), *De burgerlijke rechter in het publiekrecht* (Deventer, Kluwer, 2015) 705–26.

[134] Granger (n 122 above) 161.

[135] KM Scherr, 'Public Liability for Administrative Acts under French Law' (2012) 12 *ERA Forum* 213, 214.

INDEX